ANNUAL REVIEW OF SOCIOLOGY

ANNUAL REVIEW
OF SOCIOLOGY

VOLUME 26, 2000

KAREN S. COOK, *Co-Editor*
Duke University

JOHN HAGAN, *Co-Editor*
University of Toronto

www.AnnualReviews.org   science@AnnualReviews.org   650-493-4400

ANNUAL REVIEWS
4139 El Camino Way • P.O. Box 10139 • Palo Alto, California 94303-0139

$\underline{\text{A\hspace-0.3em R}}$

ANNUAL REVIEWS
Palo Alto, California, USA

International Standard Serial Number: 0360-0572
International Standard Book Number: 0-8243-2226-6
Library of Congress Catalog Card Number: 75-648500

Annual Review and publication titles are registered trademarks of Annual Reviews.
⊗ The paper used in this publication meets the minimum requirements of American National Standards for Information Sciences—Permanence of Paper for Printed Library Materials, ANSI Z39.48-1992.

Annual Reviews and the Editors of its publications assume no responsibility for the statements expressed by the contributors to this *Annual Review*.

Typeset by Techbooks, Fairfax, VA
Printed and Bound in the United States of America

PREFACE

For the millennial volume of the *Annual Review of Sociology* we invited sociologists from different specialties to write about what they wished they knew but did not know at the dawn of the next century. Most of those invited agreed to submit brief essays. Since not all authors invited did accept, some fields of specialization are not represented in this collection of essays. Michael Burawoy, Michael Hechter, Doug Massey, Sara McLanahan, Barbara Reskin, Rob Sampson, Emanuel Schegloff, and Charles Tilly all provide very interesting comments on the state of knowledge in sociology in the year 2000.

Burawoy wants a revolutionary sociology that reconfigures what we already know in order to cultivate a critical imagination for feasible alternatives to the existing world order. Commenting on the pessimism of postsocialist and postcolonial thought, he challenges sociology to provide new road maps for what he calls the "second great transformation." Michael Hechter wants us to find out more about what motivates individuals. Where do their values come from and how do they influence behavior? How do they produce social outcomes such as revolutions and other forms of collective action? A critical step in the production of this knowledge will be the development of better instruments to measure individual values.

The role of biological determinants of behavior is the topic Doug Massey would most like sociology to address in the future. In an autobiographical essay he spells out how he came to this conclusion. As a demographer he wants us to develop a better understanding of how humans will adapt to life in cities as the world's population shifts finally and decisively to urban centers. For him the central question is how a species adapted to life in small groups will fare in this "new environment."

At the dawn of the twenty-first century there is an increase in nonmarital childbearing and a restructuring of the welfare state. Sara McLanahan challenges sociology to come to terms with these major changes and to assess their consequences for the family, child wellbeing and the state. A major component of this project will be to understand how welfare and child support policies actually affect the relationships between parents and ultimately the wellbeing of their children.

Reskin reminds us that sociology does not yet have a complete understanding of the causes of sex and race inequality in the world of work. Despite decades of documentation of the existence of such inequality singular explanations no longer ring true. What is needed is a more complex theory of how jobs are filled in the first place. So one challenge of the twenty-first century is to formulate empirically the nature of this process across a range of organizations and to study it at the level of the social processes involved. This will entail more nuanced and detailed ethnographic work. Ultimately her essay, like most of those included in this volume, calls for a deeper understanding of the micro level processes that result in the macro level outcomes sociologists have documented in the twentieth century.

Sampson strikes a similar note in his essay on the future of criminology in the 21st century. Recognizing the empirical fact that background variables are poor prognostic devices for projecting involvement of crime over the life course, Sampson argues that sociologists who study crime should look more closely at the underlying social processes that explain crime rates in modern communities. What really lies behind "neighborhood effects," and the influence of community context?

Schegloff shifts our attention to the micro-context of conversation, arguing that a more complete understanding of "granularity" will produce new insights into interaction and social events. He demonstrates this by analyzing a few lines abstracted from a conversation between actors. Knowing more in this case will provide not only new insights into substance, but also a methodological advance. Sociology does not get more micro than the detailed linguistic analysis of the text of two people in conversation!

Known for his interest in more macro level events, Tilly offers a surprise. He argues that we have no good answers to the questions surrounding the ways in which history represents and impinges on particular relevant social relations. His focus is on relations among social locations—not just persons, but also jobs, organizations, networks and other such sites. What Tilly seeks in the next century is better answers to the questions he poses. For him "good" answers have yet to be discovered to the central questions that lie at the crossroads of history and sociology. Like Massey, he calls for a rapprochement with genetic, evolutionary and neurophysiological theories, and here is the surprise.

Eclectic and provocative, these essays point to a future in which sociologists will expand their horizons beyond the limits of the social sciences to produce more profound and compelling explanations of the social world, one that is changing ever more rapidly at the dawn of the twenty-first century.

Karen S. Cook, Co-Editor

Annual Review of Sociology
Volume 26 (2000)

CONTENTS

INDIVIDUAL AND SOCIETY

DEMOGRAPHY

POLICY

SPECIAL SUPPLEMENT: REFLECTIONS ON SOCIOLOGY IN THE 21ST CENTURY

INDEXES

RELATED ARTICLES

Annu. Rev. Sociol. 2000. 26:1–20

COHABITATION IN THE UNITED STATES: An Appraisal of Research Themes, Findings, and Implications

Pamela J. Smock

Department of Sociology and Population Studies Center, University of Michigan, Ann Arbor, Michigan 48106-1248; e-mail: pjsmock@umich.edu

Key Words   family, marriage, union formation, children, gender, social change

■ **Abstract**   Cohabitation has risen dramatically in the United States in a very short time. So, too, has the amount of sociological research devoted to the topic. In the span of a bit more than a decade, family sociologists and demographers have produced a large and rich body of research, ranging from documentation of cohabitation to assessment of its various consequences and implications. I first review basic descriptive findings about cohabitation as well as common explanations for its striking increase over recent decades. I next identify the central questions motivating most of the extant research and provide an assessment of past research as a whole. Finally, I speculate about themes that will be central to future research on cohabitation and consider the implications of cohabitation for gender equality in the United States and social science research on families.

INTRODUCTION

Unmarried heterosexual cohabitation has increased sharply in recent years in the United States. It has in fact become so prevalent that the majority of marriages and remarriages now begin as cohabiting relationships, and most younger men and women cohabit at some point in their lives. It has become quite clear that understanding and incorporating cohabitation into sociological analyses and thinking is crucial for evaluating family patterns, the life course of individuals, children's well-being, and social change more broadly.

The number of sociological studies on cohabitation has also escalated in a very short time, with most researchers drawn from the closely allied subfields of family sociology and family demography. This article synthesizes and evaluates this relatively new but burgeoning literature. First, I set the context by briefly reviewing basic descriptive findings about cohabitation (i.e., patterns, trends, and differentials) and then presenting common explanations for cohabitation's dramatic

0360-0572/00/0815-0001$14.00

rise. Next I identify three analytic questions that have either explicitly or implicitly motivated much of the extant research, and I summarize the findings that bear on these questions. Third, I provide a critical assessment of past research as a whole and identify issues that have emerged as key themes in cohabitation research. Finally, I consider the implications of cohabitation for gender equality in the United States and for social scientific research on families.

Throughout the review I attempt to strike a balance between presentation of substantive findings and assessment of the state of research on cohabitation (see Seltzer 2000 for a related review). I give particular weight to identifying the main questions that have motivated research on cohabitation and to considering some of the most important implications of empirical findings. A word about coverage: I focus almost entirely on research on cohabitation in the United States and on studies published after the mid-1980s. The latter is not too restrictive because the vast majority of research on this topic has been published in the last 10 years or so. Additionally, I examine only heterosexual cohabitation. Although family sociologists and demographers are studying gay and lesbian families (e.g. Allen & Demo 1995, Fields & Clark 1999, Kurdek 1993, Patterson 2000, Stiers 1999, Tasker & Golombok 1997, Weston 1991), the topic is beyond the scope of this review.

Basic Facts About Cohabitation

Generalizable knowledge about cohabitation was sparse until the late 1980s (see Macklin 1980 for a review of early research). What was known was based on nonrepresentative samples such as college students or samples of restricted or undefined populations (Blumstein & Schwartz 1983, Clayton & Voss 1977, Macklin 1980, Tanfer 1987, Tanfer & Horn 1985). If one wanted to estimate the prevalence of cohabitation in the United States or assess very basic characteristics of cohabitors, one could use the Current Population Surveys (CPS) or the Decennial Census. But this, too, was problematic because these data sources did not directly measure cohabitation; it was necessary to infer cohabitation based on information on household composition (e.g., Glick & Spanier 1980). Direct measures did not become available in these data sources until the 1990s (see Casper & Cohen 2000 for a review of data issues involved in the study of cohabitation).

Representative surveys based on less restricted populations began to obtain detailed information about respondents' past and current cohabitation experiences around the mid-1980s. These included the National Survey of Families and Households (NSFH) (Sweet et al 1988), the Detroit Area Study (Thornton 1988), and the National Longitudinal Survey of the High School Class of 1972 (NLS-72). The National Survey of Family Growth (NSFG), primarily a fertility survey, ascertained limited information about cohabitation in the 1980s and included complete cohabitation histories in 1995 (e.g., Bachrach 1987).

The NSFH is particularly popular as a source of knowledge about cohabitation. It obtained complete cohabitation histories from a sample of women and men of all ages and thus is often used as a basis for representative estimates of cohabitation as well as estimates of cohort change in cohabitation. The other surveys focus on particular birth cohorts, have otherwise limited age ranges, include only women, or are based on restricted geographical areas. In addition, the first wave of the NSFH (1987–1988) is unique in oversampling *currently* cohabiting men and women as well as ascertaining a good deal of information about both members of the couple. A second wave of the survey, fielded in 1992–1993, allows researchers to evaluate the trajectories of these cohabitations.

Trends and Patterns

The most widely cited fact about cohabitation, a fact replicated with several different data sources, is that it has increased dramatically over the last two decades or so (Casper & Cohen 2000). It has gone from being a relatively uncommon experience to a commonplace one and has achieved this prominence quite quickly. A few sets of numbers convey both the change and its rapidity. First, the percentage of marriages preceded by cohabitation rose from about 10% for those marrying between 1965 and 1974 to over 50% for those marrying between 1990 and 1994 (Bumpass & Lu 1999, Bumpass & Sweet 1989); the percentage is even higher for remarriages. Second, the percentage of women in their late 30s who report having cohabited at least once rose from 30% in 1987 to 48% in 1995. Given a mere eight-year time window, this is a striking increase. Finally, the proportion of all first unions (including both marriages and cohabitations) that begin as cohabitations rose from 46% for unions formed between 1980 and 1984 to almost 60% for those formed between 1990 and 1994 (Bumpass & Lu 1999).

A second widely cited fact is that, for most couples, cohabitation is a rather short-lived experience with most ending it either by terminating the relationship or by marrying within a few years. The most recent estimates suggest that about 55% of cohabiting couples marry and 40% end the relationship within five years of the beginning of the cohabitation (Bumpass & Lu 1999, see also Thornton 1988 for similar estimates using a different data source and Wu & Balakrishnan 1995 for similar estimates for Canada). Only about one sixth of cohabitations last at least three years and only a tenth last five years or more (Bumpass & Lu 1999).

Finally, contrary to popular image, cohabitation is not a childless state. About one half of previously married cohabitors and 35% of never-married cohabitors have children in the household. In most cases (70%), these are the children of only one partner, making the arrangement somewhat akin to step-families, and the rest of the children involved are the biological offspring of the couple (Bumpass et al 1991). And contrary to much of the discourse on single motherhood, a very substantial proportion of births conventionally labeled as "nonmarital" are actually occurring in cohabiting families—almost 40% overall, and roughly 50% among white and latino women and a quarter among black women (Bumpass & Lu 1999). Thus, a large share of children born to supposedly "single" mothers today are born into two-parent households. Moreover, the widely cited increase over recent years in nonmarital childbearing is largely due to cohabitation and not to births to women living without a partner (Bumpass & Lu 1999).

Differentials

Although researchers have found statistically significant differences between co-habitors and others on a host of traits ranging from ideal fertility to the use of leisure time (Clarkberg et al 1995, Landale & Fennelly 1992, Nock 1995, Rindfuss & VandenHeuvel 1990), there are two overarching factors that consistently emerge as a basis of differentiation. First, cohabitation tends to be selective of people of slightly lower socioeconomic status, usually measured in terms of educational attainment or income (Bumpass & Lu 1999, Nock 1995, Thornton et al 1995). For example, recent data show that the percentage of 19- to 44-year-old women who have cohabited at some point is almost 60% among high school dropouts versus 37% among college graduates (Bumpass & Lu 1999). The other factor can generally be understood in terms of a "traditional" versus "liberal" distinction. Cohabitation tends to be selective of people who are slightly more liberal, less re-ligious, and more supportive of egalitarian gender roles and nontraditional family roles (Clarkberg et al 1995, Lye & Waldron 1997, Thornton et al 1992).

Notably, there are few apparent race-ethnic differences in the likelihood of cohabitation, at least among the groups for which there is adequate representation in surveys. Recent data show that 45% of white and black and 40% of latino women ages 19–44 have cohabited (Bumpass & Lu 1999). This is contrary to the case for marriage; blacks are less likely to marry than whites, and a fairly large sociological literature has emerged examining the possible causes of this disparity (e.g., Lichter et al 1992, Mare & Winship 1991, Raley 1996).

All in all, cohabitation is common in all subgroups, making it important to un-derscore that any existing differentials are only tendencies. In fact, one could make the case that we ought to invert the framing of past research on group differentials; instead of asking "who cohabits?" we might ask "who does not cohabit?"

WHY HAS COHABITATION BECOME SO COMMON?

In general, the same explanations that have been posed to understand changes in family patterns overall are also used to explain the trend in cohabitation; cohab-itation is taken to be just one component, albeit a recent one, of a constellation of longer-term changes occurring in the United States and in Europe (Cherlin & Furstenberg 1988; Kiernan 1988, 1999). Declining fertility levels, increasing age at marriage, rising marital disruption rates, and a growing proportion of children being born outside of marriage are other manifestations of this broader shift. While some trends, including cohabitation in the United States, began in earnest in the 1960s or 1970s, divorce has been gradually rising for over a century, and there is wide consensus that even the most recent trends have quite long-term historical roots (Bumpass 1990, Popenoe 1993).

Scholars emphasize various aspects of long-term social change to explain cohabitation's rise in both the United States and other Western industrialized countries. Some aspects may be labeled cultural. Rising individualism and secularism figure prominently in this category (Lesthaeghe 1983, Lesthaeghe & Surkyn 1988, Rindfuss & VandenHeuvel 1990, Thornton 1989). The former refers to the increasing importance of individual goal attainment over the past few centuries, and the latter to the decline in religious adherence and involvement. A second set of factors is generally labeled economic. This set ranges from broad conceptualizations of the massive social changes wrought by industrialization (Goode 1963) to narrower ones focusing on women's changing roles in the labor market and concomitant shifts in values and attitudes about gender roles (Cherlin & Furstenberg 1988). More proximate and direct sources of cohabitation's rise are also recognized, an important one being the "sexual revolution." As Bumpass (1990) notes, this revolution eroded the main grounds for earlier disapproval of cohabitation (i.e., that unmarried persons were having sexual relations). Once this stigma was removed, cohabitation was free to escalate.

There has also been some speculation about contemporary causal *processes.* One idea is that "feedback loops" are particularly important for understanding recent trends in family patterns (e.g., Bumpass 1990, Rindfuss & VandenHeuvel 1990). The idea is straightforward: The various trends are mutually reinforcing, with changes in one domain of family life maintaining and perhaps accelerating those in other domains. As one example, high aggregate levels of marital disruption can increase the likelihood that people will cohabit as they learn either through observation or experience that marriage may not be permanent. Empirical tests of feedback loops conceptualized in this way would require information on aggregate characteristics (the prevalence of cohabitation or marital disruption in one's community, for example) in addition to information on individuals, and such tests have not yet been done (JA Seltzer, unpublished observations). A series of papers by Thornton and colleagues, however, illustrates possible ways a feedback process could operate at the individual level. Using data that follow a cohort of children and their mothers over time, the authors find that children whose parents divorced and whose mothers expressed more approval of cohabitation were relatively more likely to cohabit as young adults (Axinn & Thornton 1993, Thornton 1991, Thornton et al 1992). Intragenerational processes may also be important, with the experience of cohabitation changing young people in ways (e.g., attitudes toward divorce) that are likely to increase their chances of eventual divorce (Axinn & Thornton 1992, Thornton et al 1992, but see Clarkberg 1999b).

MAJOR RESEARCH QUESTIONS
ABOUT COHABITATION

Research on cohabitation has gone well beyond basic documentation, as important as the latter has been and will continue to be to track evolving patterns. Most of the remaining research can be organized around the following three questions: "How does cohabitation affect marital stability?" "Where does cohabitation fit in the US family system?" And "How does cohabitation affect children?" The first and the third questions are more straightforward than the second; I argue below that three types of studies offer important, albeit indirect, clues about the second question.

How Does Cohabitation Affect Marital Stability?

Common sense suggests that premarital cohabitation should provide an opportunity for couples to learn about each other, strengthen their bonds, and increase their chances for a successful marriage. In fact, this notion is echoed in the sentiments of cohabitors themselves: Data from the NSFH indicate that over 50% of cohabitors view cohabitation as a way for couples to ensure they are compatible (Bumpass et al 1991). Thus, one would predict that those cohabiting prior to marriage ought to have higher-quality and more stable marriages.

The evidence, however, suggests just the opposite. Premarital cohabitation tends to be associated with lower marital quality and to increase the risk of divorce, even after taking account of variables known to be associated with divorce (e.g., education, age at marriage). Given wide variation in data, samples, measures of marital instability, and independent variables, the degree of consensus about this central finding is impressive (Axinn & Thornton 1992, Schoen 1992, Teachman et al 1991, Thomson & Colella 1992).[1] This pattern characterizes other countries such as Canada and Sweden as well (e.g., Bennett et al 1988, Hall & Zhao 1995, Rao & Trussell 1989).

Most of the research on this issue has been aimed at explanation and not simply documentation (Axinn & Thornton 1992, Booth & Johnson 1988, DeMaris & MacDonald 1993, DeMaris & Rao 1992, Lillard et al 1995, Teachman & Polonko 1990, Thomson & Colella 1992). Two main explanations have been posed to explain the association, and both have received empirical support. The first is what is termed the selection explanation. This refers to the idea that people who cohabit before marriage differ in important ways from those who do not, and these ways increase the likelihood of marital instability. In other words, the characteristics that select people into cohabitation in the first place, such as nontraditional values and attitudes or poor relationship skills, are also those that increase the risk of marital instability. The second explanation is that there is something about cohabitation itself, i.e., the *experience* of cohabitation, that increases the likelihood of marital disruption above and beyond one's characteristics at the start of the cohabitation. Through cohabitation people learn about and come to accept the temporary nature

---

[1] A disagreement about this association is whether the effect is due to multiple cohabitation experiences. Two studies suggest that cohabitation negatively affects marital stability only if an individual engaged in more than one cohabiting relationship prior to marriage (DeMaris & MacDonald 1993, Teachman & Polonko 1990). Two studies fail to support this finding (Bennett et al 1988, DeMaris & Rao 1992, p. 187), and the majority do not examine the issue.

of relationships, and in particular that there are alternatives to marriage. Note that the two explanations are not mutually exclusive, the first focusing on the characteristics that select people initially into cohabitation and the second positing that the experience of cohabitation alters these characteristics to make people even more divorce-prone.

There is a reasonable amount of empirical support for the selection argument (e.g., Axinn & Thornton 1992, Booth & Johnson 1988, also see DeMaris & MacDonald 1993), and at least two studies have suggested that selectivity entirely explains the association between premarital cohabitation and marital instability (Lillard et al 1995, Thomson & Colella 1992). Of course, the studies vary in their ability to precisely test the selectivity argument, often due to data limitations at the time of the research (e.g., having only cross-sectional information or only measures of perceived marital instability rather than actual separation or divorce). Still, the consensus is impressive especially because selectivity has been conceptualized and operationalized in quite different ways. For example, Axinn & Thornton (1992) conceptualize selectivity in terms of attitudes towards divorce and marriage. One attitude item they use is the following: "Divorce is usually the best solution when a couple can't seem to work out their problems" (Axinn & Thornton 1992, p. 363). Booth & Johnson (1988) conceptualize selectivity as also including certain personal characteristics that would make one less than an ideal partner (e.g., alcohol abuse, personality problems, and fiscal irresponsibility). Thomson & Colella (1992) elaborate on several different kinds of selectivity, one of which is that cohabitors tend to define marriage in more individualistic rather than couple terms (pp. 260–61).

The second explanation has received less attention: that the experience of cohabiting further increases the risk of marital instability by changing people's characteristics. This is probably because data requirements are somewhat steep. One needs comparable data on attitudes and other factors both prior to and following cohabitation. One exception is the work of Axinn & Thornton (1992), who examine whether the experience of cohabitation between the ages of 18 and 23 significantly alters young men's and women's attitudes toward marriage and divorce. They find that it does, with cohabitation changing people's attitudes in ways that make them more prone to divorce (see also Axinn & Barber 1997, Clarkberg 1999b).

Where Does Cohabitation Fit Into the US Family System?

There has been an effort to determine "where" cohabitation fits into the family system in the United States. What is the *meaning* or significance of cohabitation in the United States? This is a complex and rather ambiguous question; cohabitation researchers have thus attempted to frame it in more tractable terms. Two main possibilities have been posed: Cohabitation is either a stage in the marriage process (i.e., a form of engagement that culminates in marriage) or a substitute for marriage. According to the first view, marriage as an institution is not threatened by cohabitation. As part of the process leading to marriage, cohabitation plays much the same role as engagement. The large proportions of cohabitors that subsequently marry or have plans to marry generally support this notion (Brown & Booth 1996, Bumpass 1990). The second view—that cohabitation is an alternative to marriage—implies that marriage as an institution is threatened and losing its centrality in the United States. A third and less common view, advanced by Rindfuss & VandenHeuvel (1990), is that cohabitation is more appropriately viewed as an alternative to singlehood than to marriage. The authors argue that cohabitation represents an extension of dating and sexual relationships and that its ideology does not include permanence.

Three types of studies are relevant to this issue, all of them being comparisons of one kind or another. The first are those that compare various characteristics of individuals or couples in different statuses (i.e., married, cohabiting, or single). In this case, research is often explicitly motivated by the question of the meaning of cohabitation. The second type includes studies of mate selection. These studies evaluate partner similarity in marriages and cohabitations. Assuming that partner homogamy tells us something about the nature of marriage, the reasoning goes, then one can learn about the meaning of cohabitation by comparing patterns across union type. The third type includes studies on childbearing and how it varies among cohabiting, single, and married women. While this research has often been primarily motivated by a demographic interest in fertility, many authors use findings to speculate about the meaning of cohabitation.

General Comparisons   There appear to be differences on a range of characteristics between cohabitors and both married and single people. Rindfuss & VandenHeuvel (1990) compared childbearing intentions, schooling, home ownership, employment, and other characteristics between the three groups and found that cohabitors are more similar to single than married people in virtually all of the comparisons. For example, 33% of single and cohabiting males were homeowners compared to 80% for married men, the bivariate relationship remaining statistically significant when a number of background factors were controlled (p. 716). These comparisons lead the authors to conclude that cohabitation is not an alternative to marriage, but an alternative to conventional singlehood.

Other studies of this type emphasize *relationships* rather than individual traits (Brines & Joyner 1999, Brown & Booth 1996, Nock 1995). Nock (1995), for example, argues that cohabitation and marriage differ not necessarily because of the type of people drawn into each, but because cohabitation is less institutionalized than marriage. As Nock states, "Cohabitation is an incomplete institution. No matter how widespread the practice, nonmarital unions are not yet governed by strong consensual norms or formal laws" (p. 74). The weak institutionalization of cohabitation, Nock argues, has several implications. For example, there are fewer obstacles to ending a cohabiting relationship than a marriage, cohabitors are less likely to be integrated into important social support networks, and there is much more ambiguity about what it means to be a cohabiting partner than to be a spouse. Consistent with this conceptualization, Nock finds that cohabitors report lower levels of commitment and lower levels of relationship happiness than do married people (see also Thomson & Colella 1992). Brines & Joyner (1999) examine the factors that promote stability in the two types of couples, finding that egalitarian gender roles (based on similarity in employment and earnings of the two partners) reduce the risk of break-up among cohabiting but not married couples. Their findings suggest that the two types of relationships may operate on different principles, with cohabiting unions operating on a principle of equality.

At the same time, a study by Brown & Booth (1996) suggests instead that there may essentially be two types of cohabiting couples: those who have plans to marry and those who do not. They show that the former are quite similar to married couples in terms of several dimensions of relationship quality (e.g., happiness, conflict management); it is only cohabiting couples without plans to marry who report significantly lower-quality relationships. These findings lead the authors to speculate that cohabitation is similar to marriage for the majority of cohabitors; about three quarters of cohabitors in their NSFH sample report plans to marry their partners. It is important to note that this study relied on one partner's report of marriage intentions and relationship quality even though agreement between partners on these topics is by no means universal (Brown forthcoming, Sanchez et al 1998). For example, one partner expects marriage while the other does not in about one fifth of cohabiting couples (Bumpass et al 1991). However, Brown & Booth find that taking partner disagreement about marriage plans into account does not substantially alter their results

Mate Selection Studies   Assortative mating, or the propensity of people to marry those like themselves, is a well-established area of sociological research (Kalmijn 1998, Mare 1991). Studies most commonly investigate similarity between spouses in terms of race-ethnicity, educational attainment, religion, and age. Recently a few researchers expanded the scope of this literature by examining similarity between cohabiting partners and comparing it to that of spouses (Blackwell & Lichter forthcoming, Qian 1998, Qian & Preston 1993, Schoen & Weinick 1993). The underlying idea is that difference (or similarity) in mate selection patterns between the two kinds of couples ought to tell us something about whether cohabitation resembles marriage. Schoen & Weinick (1993) clearly state this reasoning: "Patterns of partner choice can provide insight into how cohabitations are similar to, or different from, marriages" (p. 412).

Overall, married couples appear to be somewhat more homogamous in age, religion, and race-ethnicity, although findings are mixed regarding education (Blackwell & Lichter forthcoming, Schoen & Weinick 1993). Schoen & Weinick's (1993) study suggests that cohabiting couples are more homogamous with respect to education than married couples, whereas Blackwell & Lichter's findings (forthcoming) suggest the opposite; this discrepancy is likely due to some very substantial differences between studies in data, samples, methodological approach, and even the coding of education.

At the same time, however, homogamy tends to characterize couples in both cohabiting and marital unions. As Blackwell & Lichter take care to emphasize, any differences are mainly a matter of degree. It is illustrative in this regard to consider the implications of Qian's (1998) study. He examined trends over time in mate selection patterns in the two types of relationships. Focusing on the period between 1970 and 1990, Qian's findings indicate that by 1990 partner choice patterns were similar in cohabiting and marital unions. The vantage point of time thus reinforces the interpretation that differences are a matter of degree.

Childbearing Studies   If we assume that a main purpose of marriage is, or at least has been, reproduction, then examining the fertility behavior of cohabitors and comparing it to that of married or single women can offer clues about the meaning of cohabitation. That is, if cohabitation is increasingly the arena for reproduction, then one might conclude that cohabitation is not merely a step in the process leading to marriage but perhaps an alternative to it.

An example of a relevant fertility study is Manning (1993). She evaluates the likelihood that an unmarried, pregnant woman will marry before the birth of her child, a topic traditionally called "legitimation" in fertility research. Her main empirical question is: Do cohabiting and noncohabiting single women have *equal* tendencies to marry before childbirth? While oversimplifying here, the answer varies for black and white women, even after controlling for socioeconomic status, and this variation suggests possible differences in the meaning of cohabitation. Essentially, she finds that for white women in their twenties cohabitation (relative to living alone) increases the likelihood of marriage before childbirth. Presumably, if the cohabiting women considered cohabitation an acceptable context for childbearing, there would be no differential and cohabiting women would remain cohabiting in response to a pregnancy. Manning thus concludes that, for white women, cohabitation is a stage in the marriage process.

The main conclusion emerging from studies of this type is that there are race-ethnic differences in the relationship between pregnancy, cohabitation, and marriage and thus possibly race-ethnic differences in the meaning of cohabitation. The overall interpretation of most of the authors is that cohabitation is more an alternative to marriage (at least in terms of childbearing) among black and mainland Puerto Rican women[2] and more a precursor to marriage among non-latino white women (Landale & Fennelly 1992, Landale & Forste 1991, Loomis & Landale 1994, Manning 1993, 1995, 1999, Manning & Landale 1996, Manning & Smock 1995, Oropesa 1996, Raley 1999).

At the same time, it is important to keep these findings and interpretations of them in perspective. The majority of women in the United States overall do not at this time conceive or give birth during cohabitation. Only about 11% of all children are born into cohabiting households, and about 40% of nonmarital births occur in

---

[2]There is often an insufficient number of cases in surveys to examine this issue for other race-ethnic groups.

cohabiting unions (Bumpass & Lu 1999). The key point is that patterns vary by race-ethnicity. Astone et al's (1999) study of a cohort of black men in Baltimore attests to the fact that a good deal of fatherhood among black men is occurring in the context of cohabitation. Assigning these men the label of "unwed fathers" based on marital status obscures that they are, in fact, co-resident parents.

How Does Cohabitation Affect Children?

Simply because a child isn't born to cohabiting parents does not mean he or she will not experience a parent's cohabitation at some point during childhood. This latter happens when a child has been living with one parent, typically the mother, and that parent enters a cohabiting relationship.

Just how pervasive is parental cohabitation in children's lives? Cross-sectional statistics indicate that only a small proportion of children live in cohabiting households at any one point in time. Data from the 1990 Public Use Microsample of the Census show that about 13% of children in single-parent families were actually living with cohabiting parents, which translates into just 3.5% of all children (Manning & Lichter 1996). However, the proportion of children who will *ever* live in a cohabiting household during childhood is estimated to be a substantial 40%, underscoring the importance of understanding the effects of parental cohabitation on children (Bumpass & Lu 1999). As Bumpass & Lu write, ". . . now that about two-fifths of all children spend some time living with their mother and a cohabiting partner . . . we simply cannot address the changing family experiences of children while ignoring cohabitation" (1999, p. 21).

Past studies have identified two important issues regarding children's experience of parental cohabitation. The first is that children already disadvantaged in terms of parental income and education are relatively more likely to experience this family form (Bumpass & Lu 1999, Graefe & Lichter 1999). This finding is consistent with other research showing that, on average, cohabiting households tend to be less well-off financially than married-couple households (e.g., Manning & Lichter 1996) and that good economic circumstances increase the likelihood of marriage among both cohabiting and noncohabiting individuals (e.g., Clarkberg 1999a, Lichter et al 1992, Smock & Manning 1997).

Second, children experiencing parental cohabitation are also more likely to undergo further transitions in family structure. Graefe & Lichter (1999) estimate that most children who are born or ever live in a cohabiting family will experience a change in family structure within a few years. These findings do not bode well for children's well-being. A large body of literature has established that family structure has important effects on children, with deleterious ones for children who grow up without both biological parents (McLanahan & Sandefur 1994, Seltzer 1994). While some of this effect is due to income and other factors, there is evidence that the *number* of changes in family structure is particularly important. The fewer the changes, the better for children (Wu & Martinson 1993, Wu 1996). While children in cohabiting households may in fact be living with two biological parents, although more typically one parent and a "step-parent," they are quite likely to experience future family transitions.

To date, however, we have very little direct knowledge about the possible effects of cohabitation on various aspects of children's well-being relative to other family structures. A study by Thomson and colleagues (1998) is an important exception (see also Thomson et al 1994). Using the two waves of the NSFH, they examine the impact of a single mother's entrance into either a cohabitation or a remarriage on mothering behaviors. They generally find few differences in the effects of the two union types. The authors note, however, that small sample size precludes conclusive interpretation (p. 16). It appears that not even the oversample of cohabitors in the NSFH provides a sufficient number of cases with which to fully examine the relationship between parental cohabitation and children's well-being (Bumpass & Lu 1999).

ASSESSMENT OF PAST RESEARCH AND FUTURE DIRECTIONS

A first observation is simply that an enormous amount has been accomplished in a very short time. Just 15 years ago very little was known about cohabitation. Since then family sociologists and demographers have rapidly created a solid base of generalizable knowledge about cohabitation in the United States. We know a good deal not only about overall trends, differentials, and patterns but also about the effect of cohabitation on marital stability, the nature of differences between cohabitation and marriage, and the role of cohabitation in nonmarital childbearing. Often in the guise of the latter two issues, researchers are also developing an understanding of the significance or meaning of cohabitation. Notably, too, appreciation of the importance of cohabitation has seeped into other strands of sociological research; witness Brines & Joyner's (1999) paper on couple cohesion and recent studies of assortative mating (Blackwell & Lichter forthcoming, Qian & Preston 1993, Qian 1998).

A second observation concerns comparisons between cohabitation and marriage, and in particular, the attempt to gauge the meaning of cohabitation by comparing it to marriage (i.e., some comparison studies and mate selection studies). What is sometimes omitted from studies of this ilk is full acknowledgment that the meaning of *marriage* is dynamic and undergoing radical change. In the last few decades, for example, women have been playing increasingly important roles as income providers (Bianchi 1995). The underlying issue is whether we can gauge what cohabitation means if we are using a standard that is also changing. To say that cohabitation is like or unlike marriage is useful only to the extent that we have adequate knowledge of what marriage is indeed "like."

A related issue is the emphasis in some past research on differences between those who cohabit and those who do not. It is probably time for most research on cohabitation to begin from a premise that the majority of men and women will cohabit, prior to marriage or afterwards, and that the cohabiting couples studied today are the married couples of tomorrow. Certainly, many researchers are already well aware of this issue (e.g., Blackwell & Lichter forthcoming, Clarkberg et al 1995, Nock 1995, 1998).

A third issue is that there are strong indications that *cohabitation* is changing in significant ways, even over the last few years. Consider these examples. First, there is evidence that the inverse relationship between premarital cohabitation and marital stability is diminishing. The effect, if any, is trivial for recent birth cohorts (Schoen 1992). Second, between 1987 and 1995 there has been significant change in cohabiting couples' trajectories: lower proportions are marrying and more are breaking up (Bumpass & Lu 1999). Third, Raley (1999) shows that there has been a significant shift in the relationship between fertility and cohabitation between the early 1980s and 1990s. Pregnant women are increasingly likely to cohabit or remain cohabiting rather than to marry in response to a premarital pregnancy, suggesting perhaps that cohabitation is becoming more a substitute for marriage as time goes on. Finally, the proportion of cohabitations with children present increased from 40% to 50% between 1987 and 1995 (Bumpass & Lu 1999).

Whatever the substantive implications, this assortment of facts illustrates the point that cohabitation is changing in substantial ways over very short spans of time. A continuing task for researchers will thus be simply to keep pace with developments; as new data become available new descriptive studies will be needed.

Future work on cohabitation is likely to elaborate on at least two existing themes in the literature. The first is the effect of cohabitation on children's well-being. This question follows a long line of research on the effects of family structure on children and engages an ongoing concern of policymakers and funding agencies. Given that currently available data are inadequate for discerning the effects of cohabitation versus other family structures (Bumpass & Lu 1999), there will likely be new data collection efforts as well as new content on existing surveys.

It is also probable that future research will pay relatively more attention to diversity than in the past, consistent with the fact that cohabitation has just about become a majority phenomenon; this will complement research that focuses on central tendencies. In particular, there will be a continuing effort to understand whether and how cohabitation's "meaning" may vary across subgroups given that past studies imply that there are at least race-ethnic differences in this meaning (e.g., Manning 1993). Raley's (1999) findings suggest the importance of ongoing temporal change in the meaning of cohabitation as well.

Finally, virtually all sociological knowledge about cohabitation in the United States has been based on quantitative analysis of survey or census data. Certainly, this approach has taught us a great deal about cohabitation in a very short time. Yet the broader question of the meaning of cohabitation remains difficult to address. To begin to answer it and similar questions, it would be useful additionally to be able to draw on qualitative data that ask people what cohabitation means to them. This approach could increase our understanding of possible diversity in the meaning of cohabitation by gender, social class, or race-ethnicity. More generally, it would provide the sort of in-depth data important for nuanced assessments of recent and possible future changes in family patterns. A practical payoff is that it would provide a basis for new survey content.

IMPLICATIONS OF COHABITATION

Below I briefly consider the implications of cohabitation for gender equality and for research on families. Although cohabitation of course bears on many issues, I've selected these two due to their centrality for broader sociological concerns.

Gender Equality

Blumstein & Schwartz's book *American Couples* (1983), pioneering in its inclusion of nontraditional couples, provided suggestive evidence that cohabiting couples were substantially more gender-egalitarian than their married counterparts. This was not true in all respects, but certainly in many, and particularly in cohabiting couples' tendency to eschew the traditional male breadwinner role. While Blumstein & Schwartz made no claim to having representative data, their findings were widely cited and probably formed part of the basis for many family scholars' expectation that cohabitation might provide the setting for enactment of less differentiated gender roles.

Are cohabiting couples indeed at the forefront of a revolution in gender roles? Blumstein & Schwartz conducted their research in the mid- to late 1970s, even more reason to suspect that the answer might be "yes."

Only a handful of studies are directly relevant to this question, and all in all, the evidence is quite mixed. On the one hand, cohabitors profess somewhat more liberal gender-role attitudes than do married people. Clarkberg et al (1995) found that young people with liberal gender-role attitudes are more likely to select cohabitation rather than marriage as their first union (see also Shelton & John 1993). There also may be somewhat different factors promoting cohesion in cohabiting versus married couples. Cohabiting couples are more likely to stay together when the two partners have similar income provision roles; this factor is unimportant for married couples (Brines & Joyner 1999).

On the other hand, cohabitors do not differ substantially from married couples in terms of their division of household labor. Cross-sectional data show little difference in the average number of housework hours men and women perform in the two unions, particularly for men (Shelton & John 1993, South & Spitze 1994). South & Spitze (1994), for example, report that cohabiting men do about as much housework as married men (19 and 18 hours per week for cohabiting and married men, respectively) while cohabiting women do 31 hours of housework per week compared to 37 for married women. Thus, women perform the vast majority of housework in both contexts.

Additional evidence emerges from one study that uses longitudinal data and analysis. Drawing on data from the two waves of the NSFH, Gupta (1999) tracks changes in men's and women's housework hours over roughly a five-year period.

His focus is on the impact of entering and exiting unions (either marriage or cohabitation) on changes in housework hours. Gupta's key finding is that men substantially reduce both their housework time overall and time doing "female-type" tasks specifically (e.g., preparing meals, house cleaning, washing dishes) when they enter *either* marriage or cohabitation. Women increase theirs under the same circumstances, and the magnitude of these gender-specific effects is about the same for the two unions.

As Gupta states, "... the results show that entry into cohabitation induces changes in housework behavior that are no less gender-typical than does entry into marriage ... the fact of entry into a coresidential union is of greater consequence for housework time than the form of that union" (p. 710). Moreover, given evidence that cohabiting couples are less likely to pool income than married couples (Blumstein & Schwartz 1983), the findings of these housework studies imply that cohabiting women are—in a very important sense—worse off than married women (LJ Waite, unpublished observations).

Finally, two studies show that the enactment of traditional gender roles increases the likelihood that a cohabiting couple will marry (Sanchez et al 1998, Smock & Manning 1997). One of these studies found that only the male partner's income, education, and employment status significantly affect the likelihood of marriage, implying asymmetry in the importance assigned to men's and women's economic characteristics (Smock & Manning 1997). The other study found that the amount of time the female, but not the male, partner spends doing housework is positively associated with the odds of marriage (Sanchez et al 1998). That these findings emerge even among cohabitors, a subgroup less traditional in terms of attitudes toward gender roles, suggests the intractability of a division of labor that assigns breadwinning to men and homemaking to women.

Research on Families

The literature on cohabitation challenges at least two aspects of sociological research on families. The first pertains to categories used by researchers and the second to prominent substantive issues in sociology.

Until recently much sociological research ignored the complexity of living arrangements; this was true even when studying the causes and consequences of family structure (Manning & Smock 1997). The literature tended to use simpler measures of family structure mostly framed by *marital* status. Thus, for example, a "two-parent" family included married couples but ignored cohabiting couples with biological children. In addition, the term "single parent" was generally applied not only when a mother was living with a cohabiting partner but even when the partner was the biological father of the child. These practices were in part due to lack of available data, given the lag between rapid social change and data collection geared to understand the change.

Bumpass and colleagues clearly demonstrate how continued reliance on simpler measures can distort our understanding of family structure in the United States. Almost one fifth of the estimated time that children spend in supposedly "single-parent" families is actually spent with a parent and her cohabiting partner (Bumpass & Raley 1995). And if one includes cohabitation in the definition of step-family, then almost *one half* of all step-families are cases of a biological parent and his, or, more typically, her cohabiting partner (Bumpass et al 1995).

The literature on cohabitation also transforms our understanding of some prominent sociological research questions. For example, there is a large literature focusing on the retreat from marriage in the United States, and particularly why that retreat has been more dramatic for blacks than for whites (e.g., Lichter et al 1992, Mare & Winship 1991, Wilson 1987). For the most part, cohabitation has been neglected in this literature. But Raley (1996) shows its potential importance. She finds that the black-white gap in union formation, tapped by estimates of the average age at entry into any coresidential union, is only about half that of the gap in marriage. Given the prevalence of cohabitation, that blacks and whites are about equally likely to cohabit, and that large proportions of cohabitors go on to marry their partners, it is clearly important to examine the factors that predict marriage among cohabiting couples to attempt to explain racial differences in marriage (Manning & Smock 1995). Interestingly, Brown (forthcoming) finds that while black and white cohabiting couples are about equally likely to *expect* to marry, blacks are substantially less likely to actually do so.

CONCLUDING THOUGHTS

In just a decade or so the amount of research on cohabitation in the United States has skyrocketed. Cohabitation has not only been the central focus of a relatively large and growing body of literature but has also been incorporated into various other strands of sociological research. These include assortative mating (Blackwell & Lichter forthcoming, Qian & Preston 1993, Schoen & Weinick 1993), theories of couple cohesion (Brines & Joyner 1999), and the division of domestic labor (Blair & Lichter 1991, Gupta 1999, Shelton & John 1993, South & Spitze 1994). Ten years ago in his address as president of the Population Association of America, Bumpass (1990) said that the remarkable rise in cohabitation ought to result in drastic changes in how scholars think about and measure family events. This review suggests that it has and will continue to do so.

Overall, cohabitation indicates how family life in the United States is being transformed, some argue radically, with legal marriage losing its primacy as the manifest center of family ties. While this review has highlighted several important research questions about cohabitation, the issue motivating all of these questions, and the researchers asking them, is the larger one of social change and how family patterns both express and contribute to such change.

ACKNOWLEDGMENTS

This research was supported by a grant from the National Institute of Child Health and Human Development (R01-34391). I am foremost grateful to

Wendy D. Manning for our ongoing intellectual exchange and collaboration and to our many teachers at the University of Wisconsin-Madison for demonstrating the value of such an exchange. Thanks go to Sanjiv Gupta and Mary Noonan for helping to carry on this tradition and providing me with another forum for lively discussions about families, gender, and social change. I also thank Judith A. Seltzer and Linda J. Waite for their (as usual) insightful comments and Mari Ellis of the Population Studies Center for her assistance in preparation of this manuscript. All errors and omissions are my own.

Visit the Annual Reviews home page at www.AnnualReviews.org

LITERATURE CITED

Allen KR, Demo DH. 1995. The families of lesbian and gay men: a new frontier in family research. *J. Marr. Fam.* 57:111–27

Astone NM, Schoen R, Ensminger M, Rothert K. 1999. *The family life course of African American men.* Presented at Annu. Meet. Pop. Assoc. Am., New York

Axinn WG, Barber JS. 1997. Living arrangements and family formation attitudes in early adulthood. *J. Marr. Fam.* 59:595–611

Axinn WG, Thornton A. 1992. The relationship between cohabitation and divorce: selectivity or causal influence? *Demography* 29:357–74

Axinn WG, Thornton A. 1993. Mothers, children, and cohabitation: the intergenerational effects of attitudes and behavior. *Am. Sociol. Rev.* 58:233–46

Bachrach CA. 1987. Cohabitation and reproductive behavior in the U.S. *Demography* 24:623–37

Bennett NG, Blanc AK, Bloom DE. 1988. Commitment and the modern union: assessing the link between premarital cohabitation and subsequent marital stability. *Am. Sociol. Rev.* 53:127–38

Bianchi S. 1995. The changing economic roles of women and men. In *State of the Union: American in the 1990s*, ed. R. Farley, 1:107–54. New York: Russell Sage. 375 pp.

Blackwell DL, Lichter DT. 2000. Mate selection among married and cohabiting couples. *J. Fam. Issues.*

Blair SL, Lichter DT. 1991. Measuring the household division: gender segregation of housework among American couples. *J. Fam. Issues* 12:91–113

Blumstein P, Schwartz P. 1983. *American Couples: Money Work Sex.* New York: William Morrow

Booth A, Johnson D. 1988. Premarital cohabitation and marital success. *J. Fam. Issues* 9:255–72

Brines J, Joyner K. 1999. The ties that bind: commitment and stability in the modern union. *Am. Sociol. Rev.* 64:333–56

Brown SL. Forthcoming. Union transitions among cohabitors: the significance of relationship assessments and expectations. *J. Marr. Fam.*

Brown SL, Booth A. 1996. Cohabitation versus marriage: a comparison of relationship quality. *J. Marr. Fam.* 58:668–78

Bumpass LL. 1990. What's happening to the family? Interaction between demographic and institutional change. *Demography* 27:483–98

Bumpass LL, Lu H. 1999. *Trends in cohabitation and implications for children's family contexts in the U.S. CDE Work. Pap. No. 98-15.* Cent. Demography Ecol., Univ. Wisc.-Madison

Bumpass LL, Raley RK. 1995. Redefining single-parent families: cohabitation and changing family reality. *Demography* 32:97–109

Bumpass LL, Raley RK, Sweet JA. 1995. The

changing character of stepfamilies: implications of cohabitation and nonmarital childbearing. *Demography* 32:425–36

Bumpass LL, Sweet JA. 1989. National estimates of cohabitation. *Demography* 26:615–25

Bumpass LL, Sweet JA, Cherlin A. 1991. The role of cohabitation in declining rates of marriage. *Demography* 53:913–27

Casper LM, Cohen PN. 2000. How does POSSLQ measure up? Historical estimates of cohabitation. *Demography.* In press

Cherlin A, Furstenberg FF. 1988. The changing European family: lessons for the American reader. *J. Fam. Issues* 9:291–7

Clarkberg ME. 1999a. The price of partnering: the role of economic well-being in young adults' first union experiences. *Soc. Forces* 77:945–68

Clarkberg ME. 1999b. *The cohabitation experience and changing values: the effects of premarital cohabitation on the orientation towards marriage, career and community. BLCC Work. Pap. No. 99-15.* Cornell Employment and Fam. Careers Inst., Cornell

Clarkberg ME, Stolzenberg RM, Waite LJ. 1995. Attitudes, values, and entrance into cohabitational versus marital unions. *Soc. Forces* 74:609–34

Clayton RR, Voss HL. 1977. Shacking up: cohabitation in the 1970s. *J. Marr. Fam.* 39:273–83

DeMaris A, MacDonald W. 1993. Premarital cohabitation and marital instability: a test of the unconventionality hypothesis. *J. Marr. Fam.* 55:399–7

DeMaris A, Rao VK. 1992. Premarital cohabitation and subsequent marital stability in the United States: a reassessment. *J. Marr. Fam.* 54:178–90

Fields JM, Clark CL. 1999. *Unbinding the ties: edit effects of marital status on same gender couples.* Presented at Annu. Meet. Pop. Assoc. Am., New York

Glick PC, Spanier GB. 1980. Married and unmarried cohabitation in the United States. *J. Marr. Fam.* 42:19–30

Goode WJ. 1963. *World Revolution and Family Patterns.* New York: Free

Graefe DR, Lichter DT. 1999. Life course transitions of American children: parental cohabitation, marriage and single motherhood. *Demography* 36:205–17

Gupta S. 1999. The effects of marital status transitions on men's housework performance. *J. Marr. Fam.* 61:700–11

Hall DR, Zhao JZ. 1995. Cohabitation and divorce in Canada: testing the selectivity hypothesis. *J. Marr. Fam.* 57:421–7

Kalmijn M. 1998. Intermarriage and homogamy: causes, patterns, trends. *Annu. Rev. Sociol.* 24:395–421

Kiernan K. 1988. The British family: contemporary trends and issues. *J. Marr. Fam.* 298–316

Kiernan K. 1999. Cohabitation in Western Europe. *Pop. Trends* 96:25–32

Kurdek L. 1993. The allocation of household labor in gay, lesbian, and heterosexual married couples. *J. Soc. Issues* 49:127–39

Landale NS, Fennelly K. 1992. Informal unions among mainland Puerto Ricans: cohabitation or an alternative to legal marriage? *J. Marr. Fam.* 54:269–80

Landale NS, Forste R. 1991. Patterns of entry into cohabitation and marriage among mainland Puerto Rican women. *Demography* 28:587–607

Lesthaeghe R. 1983. A century of demographic and cultural change in Western Europe: an exploration of underlying dimensions. *Pop. Dev. Rev.* 9:411–35

Lesthaeghe R, Surkyn J. 1988. Cultural dynamics and economic theories of fertility change. *Pop. Dev. Rev.* 14:1–45

Lichter DT, McLaughlin D, LeClere F, Kephart G, Landry D. 1992. Race and the retreat from marriage: a shortage of marriageable men? *Am. Sociol. Rev.* 57:781–99

Lillard LL, Brien MJ, Waite LJ. 1995. Premarital cohabitation and subsequent marital dissolution: a matter of self-selection? *Demography* 32:437–57

Loomis LS, Landale NS. 1994. Nonmarital

cohabitation and childbearing among black and white American women. *J. Marr. Fam.* 56:949–62

Lye D, Waldron I. 1997. Attitudes toward cohabitation, family, and gender roles: relationships to values and political ideology. *Sociol. Perspect.* 40:199–25

Macklin ED. 1980. Nontraditional family forms: a decade of research. *J. Marr. Fam.* 42:905–22

Manning WD. 1993. Marriage and cohabitation following premarital conception. *J. Marr. Fam.* 55:839–50

Manning WD. 1995. Cohabitation, marriage, and entry into motherhood. *J. Marr. Fam.* 57:191–200

Manning WD. 1999. *Childbearing in cohabiting unions: racial and ethnic differences.* Presented at Annu. Meet. Pop. Assoc. Am., New York

Manning WD, Landale NS. 1996. Racial and ethnic differences in the role of cohabitation in premarital childbearing. *J. Marr. Fam.* 58:63–77

Manning WD, Lichter DT. 1996. Parental cohabitation and children's economic well-being. *J. Marr. Fam.* 58:998–1010

Manning WD, Smock PJ. 1995. Why marry? Race and the transition to marriage among cohabitors. *Demography* 32:509–20

Manning WD, Smock PJ. 1997. Children's living arrangements in unmarried-mother families. *J. Fam. Issues* 18:526–44

Mare RD. 1991. Five decades of educational assortative mating. *Am. Sociol. Rev.* 56:15–32

Mare RD, Winship C. 1991. Socioeconomic change and the decline of marriage for blacks and whites. In *The Urban Underclass*, ed. C Jencks, PE Peterson, pp. 175–202. Washington DC: Urban. 490 pp.

McLanahan SS, Sandefur G. 1994. *Growing Up With a Single Parent: What Helps, What Hurts.* Cambridge, MA: Harvard Univ. Press. 196 pp.

Nock SL. 1995. A comparison of marriages and cohabiting relationships. *J. Fam. Issues* 16:53–76

Nock SL. 1998. *Marriage in Men's Lives.* Oxford, UK: Oxford Univ. Press. 165 pp.

Oropesa RS. 1996. Normative beliefs about marriage and cohabitation: a comparison of non-Latino whites, Mexican Americans, and Puerto Ricans. *J. Marr. Fam.* 58:49–62

Patterson CJ. 2000. The families of lesbian and gay men. *J. Marr. Fam.* 67: In press

Popenoe D. 1993. American family decline: a review and appraisal. *J. Marr. Fam.* 55:527–42

Qian Z. 1998. Changes in assortative mating: the impact of age and education, 1970–1990. *Demography* 35:279–92

Qian Z. Preston SH. 1993. Changes in American marriage, 1972–1987. *Am. Sociol. Rev.* 58:482–95

Raley RK. 1996. A shortage of marriageable men? A note on the role of cohabitation in black-white differences in marriage rates. *Am. Sociol. Rev.* 61:973–83

Raley RK. 1999. *Then comes marriage? Recent changes in women's response to a nonmarital pregnancy.* Presented at Annu. Meet. Pop. Assoc. Am., NY

Rao RK, Trussell J. 1989. Premarital cohabitation and marital stability: a reassessment of the Canadian evidence: feedback. *J. Marr. Fam.* 51:535–40

Rindfuss RR, VandenHeuvel A. 1990. Cohabitation: a precursor to marriage or an alternative to being single? *Pop. Dev. Rev.* 16:703–26

Sanchez LS, Manning WD, Smock PJ. 1998. Sex-specialized or collaborative mate selection? Union transitions among cohabitors *Soc. Sci. Res.* 27:280–304

Schoen R. 1992. First unions and the stability of first marriages. *J. Marr. Fam.* 54:281–84

Schoen R, Weinick RM. 1993. Partner choice in marriages and cohabitations. *J. Marr. Fam.* 55:408–14

Seltzer JA. 1994. Consequences of marital dissolution for children. *Annu. Rev. Sociol.* 20:235–66

Seltzer JA. 2000. Families formed outside of marriage. *J. Marr. Fam.* 62: In press

Shelton BA, John D. 1993. Does marital status make a difference? Housework among married and cohabiting men and women. *J. Fam. Issues* 14:401–20

Smock PJ, Manning WD. 1997. Cohabiting partners' economic circumstances and marriage. *Demography* 34:331–41

South SJ, Spitze G. 1994. Housework in marital and nonmarital households. *Am. Sociol. Rev.* 59:327–47

Stiers GA. 1999. *From This Day Forward: Commitment, Marriage, and Family In Lesbian and Gay Relationships.* New York: St. Martin's. 236 pp.

Sweet JA, Bumpass LL, Call V. 1988. *The design and content of the National Survey of Families and Households. NSFH Work. Pap. No. 1.* Cent. Demography Ecol., Univ. Wisc.-Madison

Tanfer K. 1987. Patterns of premarital cohabitation among never-married women in the United States. *J. Marr. Fam.* 49:483–97

Tanfer K, Horn MC. 1985. Contraceptive use, pregnancy, and fertility patterns among single American women in their 20s. *Fam. Planning Persp.* 17:10–19

Tasker FL, Golombok S. 1997. *Growing Up in A Lesbian Family: Effects on Child Development.* New York: Guilford. 194 pp.

Teachman JD, Polonko KA. 1990. Cohabitation and marital stability in the United States. *Soc. Forces* 69:207–20

Teachman JD, Thomas J, Paasch K. 1991. Legal status and stability of coresidential unions. *Demography* 28:571–86

Thomson E, Colella U. 1992. Cohabitation and marital stability: quality or commitment? *J. Marr. Fam.* 54:259–67

Thomson E, Hanson TL, McLanahan SS. 1994. Family structure and child well-being: economic resources vs. parental behaviors. *Soc. Forces* 73:221–42

Thomson E, Mosley J, Hanson TL, McLanahan SS. 1998. *Remarriage, cohabitation, and changes in mothering. NSFH Work. Pap. No. 80.* Cent. Demography Ecol., Univ. Wisc.-Madison

Thornton A. 1988. Cohabitation and marriage in the 80s. *Demography* 25:497–508

Thornton A. 1989. Changing attitudes toward family issues in the United States. *J. Marr. Fam.* 51:873–93

Thornton A. 1991. Influence of the marital history of parents on the marital and cohabitation experiences of children. *Am. J. Sociol.* 96:868–94

Thornton A, Axinn WG, Hill DH. 1992. Reciprocal effects of religiosity, cohabitation, and marriage. *Am. J. Sociol.* 98:628–51

Thornton A, Axinn WG, Teachman JD. 1995. The influence of school enrollment and accumulation on cohabitation and marriage in early adulthood. *Am. Sociol. Rev.* 60:762–74

Weston K. 1991. *Families We Choose: Lesbians, Gays, Kinship.* New York: Columbia Univ. Press. 261 pp.

Wilson WJ. 1987. *The Truly Disadvantaged.* Chicago: Univ. Chicago Press. 254 pp.

Wu LL. 1996. Effects of family instability, income, and income instability on the risk of premarital birth. *Am. Sociol. Rev.* 386–406

Wu LL, Martinson BC. 1993. Family structure and the risk of a premarital birth. *Am. Sociol. Rev.* 58:210–32

Wu Z, Balakrishnan TR. 1995. Dissolution of premarital cohabitation in Canada. *Demography* 32:521–32

Annu. Rev. Sociol. 2000. 26:21–42

DOUBLE STANDARDS FOR COMPETENCE: Theory and Research

Martha Foschi

Department of Anthropology and Sociology, University of British Columbia, Vancouver,
British Columbia, Canada V6T 1Z1; e-mail: mfoschi@interchange.ubc.ca

Key Words   ability inference, competence requirements, performance evaluation, status characteristics, experimental research

■ **Abstract**   This article reviews theory and research on double standards, namely, the use of different requirements for the inference of possession of an attribute, depending on the individuals being assessed. The article focuses on double standards for competence in task groups and begins by examining how status characteristics (e.g. gender, ethnicity, socioeconomic class) become a basis for stricter standards for the lower status person. I also discuss other bases for this practice (e.g. personality characteristics, allocated rewards, sentiments of either like or dislike). Next, I describe double standards in the inference of other types of valued attributes (e.g. beauty, morality, mental health) and examine the relationship between these practices and competence double standards. The article concludes with a discussion of "reverse" double standards for competence, namely, the practice of applying more lenient ability standards to lower status individuals.

INTRODUCTION

Most social interactions involve comparisons across participants, their attributes and their actions. As a result, the large majority of the assessments we make of ourselves and others in those settings have a relative character. For example, we compare test results from a university course we are taking in order to learn how our performance measures up to the performances of other individuals who wrote the same test, and we compare the immediately noticeable physical features of a person we have just met against our ideal of physical beauty. These comparisons are not always made explicitly. Without them, however, the vast number of items of information we receive daily in our social interactions would be very difficult—if not impossible—to interpret.

Some of those comparisons result only in a rank ordering (e.g. "my test results are better than yours"), whereas others involve the inference of an attribute (e.g. "this person is beautiful, in terms of my idea of physical beauty"). Here I focus on this second type of comparisons, namely, those made against a standard. Standards are norms defining requirements for the inference of an attribute, such as the level of performance considered necessary to conclude that a person is competent, or the type of behavior required to assign morality.

My interest in this article is in those situations where individuals are treated with differing standards depending on who they are—even though all of these individuals provide the same evidence regarding the attribute being assessed. The practice of using double (and sometimes even multiple) standards may be based on a variety of characteristics of the persons involved (e.g. gender, ethnicity, nationality, socioeconomic background, personality traits) and may be used to infer a wide range of attributes (e.g. competence, morality, mental health, criminality, citizenship suitability). For example, in many countries it is common to apply different standards in decisions granting refugee status, depending on the nationality of the applicants and in spite of their comparable qualifications. The core process in the use of double standards can be described as follows. There is a characteristic *differentiating* individuals into two categories, one viewed as carrying more value than the other. On the other hand, the available evidence indicates that particular individuals from both categories possess a given attribute to *similar* extents. This evidence reflects objective (i.e. unbiased) evaluations. Double standards are the practice of using different requirements to interpret that evidence. My focus here is on those situations where stricter requirements are applied to members of devalued groups and, as a result, inferences about the attribute are aligned with category membership. This article reviews theory and research on a variety of double standards and the conditions under which they occur, with special attention to their use in inferences of competence. I examine contributions from various traditions, identify areas where further research is needed, and make specific suggestions for that work.

STANDARDS, EVALUATIONS, AND THE INFERENCE OF COMPETENCE

This section provides theoretical background on the role of standards in the inference of competence. I define competence broadly to refer to the ability to do well on a task judged to be valuable. Thus, competence may range from the ability necessary to solve geometrical puzzles to the set of skills required to hold a professional position. The assessment of task competence is of central importance in person perception: It often anchors and defines how other judgments about individuals are made and has significant long-term consequences for their interactions, such as the distribution of opportunities to perform and the allocation of rewards. It is because of this centrality that the inference of competence is also the focus of the present article.

The process of competence inference can be seen in sharper relief if one considers individuals who (*a*) begin their interaction without any previous acquaintance with each other and (*b*) have to work as a group toward the completion of a task. Such groups are common in a wide variety of contexts. Examples are: a jury;

students selected at random from a course list and assigned to work as a team on a project; faculty members from various departments appointed to constitute a new committee. In those situations, a key decision that group members have to make is how much competence they have relative to each other to solve the problem that they face together. It is common to use the limited information received at the beginning of the interaction to form general ideas about competence.

Expectation states theory (Berger et al 1977, 1985b, Webster & Foschi 1988b, Wagner & Berger 1993) provides a solid, comprehensive account of how people assign levels of competence to each other in such task groups. The theory has a long-standing tradition, and empirical tests provide strong support for its predictions. In this article I formulate and develop ideas within the context of this theory while also making linkages with other literatures. Two core concepts are those of "status characteristic" and "performance expectations." The former is defined as any valued attribute implying task competence. Such characteristics contain at least two levels or states (e.g. either high or low level of mechanical ability), one of which is seen as worthier than the other. Status characteristics also range from specific to diffuse, depending on their perceived applicability. A specific characteristic is defined as associated with performance expectations in a limited area; a diffuse characteristic carries, in addition, expectations about performance on a wide, indeterminate set of tasks. In many societies, gender, ethnicity, physical beauty, and socioeconomic class, for example, have that "diffuseness" for large numbers of people.

"Performance expectations" are beliefs about the likely quality of the group members' task performances and reflect levels of perceived competence. The theory specifies how and under what conditions such characteristics will be used and corresponding expectations formed. Expectation states are said to develop for "self" (the focal actor) relative to each other person in the group. Expectations may be based on either status characteristics or actual task performances, or on both. The assumed relationship between status and the task at hand is also a factor (e.g. the task may be perceived to be "masculine," or "feminine," or not linked to gender). The theory includes scope conditions to specify the boundaries within which its hypotheses are proposed, and it focuses on the expectations formed under the following such conditions: group members value the task and are motivated both to do it well (i.e. are "task-oriented") and to take each other's ideas into account toward that end (i.e. are "collectively oriented"). Performance expectations, in turn, have a strong effect on the interaction that takes place: They affect the granting of action opportunities, the rate at which these are accepted, the type of evaluations made, and the amount of influence exerted. These four factors, comprising what is known as the power and prestige order of the group, contribute, in turn, to the self-maintenance of the initial expectations.

It is useful to view the theory as consisting of two main branches, each investigating a different basis for the formation of expectations. One branch ("evaluations and expectations") is concerned with the role of performance evaluations, while the other ("status characteristics") focuses on the role of status attributes. Of particular interest here is the work, formulated within the first of these branches, that examines the expectations developed on the basis of the evaluations received from a source outside the group. A "source" is defined as a person (or persons) who is (are) accepted by a group member as more capable of evaluating performances than is that group member himself or herself. Research within this branch has examined properties of the source, the group members, and the evaluations, and has tested for the effects of these variables on expectations. For example, the evaluations may be positive, negative, or neutral; they may be many or few; or they may be either consistent or inconsistent with each other (Webster & Sobieszek 1974, Crundall & Foddy 1981).

Working within this branch and focusing on the evaluations received, I have proposed that the standards for ability and lack of ability used by the source (and accepted as legitimate by the group members) constitute another important factor in the formation of expectations. For example, a score of 14 correct answers out of 20 is sufficient demonstration of ability if the standard is 12 or more correct responses, but the same score becomes unconvincing evidence if that standard is set at 17 or more. Thus, standards act as filters mediating the relationship between evaluations and expectations (Foschi & Foschi 1979). Standards may be classified as either strict or lenient, depending on the level and type of requirements imposed. A strict standard for ability requires more evidence of competence than does a lenient standard.

Conversely, a strict standard for lack of ability tolerates less evidence of incompetence than does a lenient standard. When evaluations meet a given standard, "strong" or conclusive expectations are formed. On the other hand, when evaluations fall outside that standard, expectations are "weak" or inconclusive (Foschi et al 1985, Foschi & Foddy 1988). The strength of the expectations, in turn, is reflected in the power and prestige order that the group develops. Several hypotheses on evaluations, standards, expectations, and influence have been tested empirically, with results showing clear support (Foschi et al 1985, Foschi & Freeman 1991, Foddy & Smithson 1999). For example, Foschi et al (1985) investigated the effects of scores and standards on influence in two-person groups. In two of the experimental conditions, subjects received the same set of scores indicating that they had outperformed the partner. Standards, however, differed in the two cases and created either strong or weak expectations of superior ability over the partner. As predicted, rejection of influence was higher in the first of these conditions. (There is also work formulated outside the expectation states program and investigating related ideas; see Miller & Prentice 1996 for a recent review).

DOUBLE STANDARDS FOR COMPETENCE: The Role of Status

Theoretical Formulations

Standards for either competence or lack of competence do not always originate in a source outside the group; there are also situations where they are generated by group members themselves. Those are the situations of interest in this article. Foschi & Foddy (1988) have proposed that, under some conditions, group members use status differences as the basis for double standards that disadvantage those in the devalued category. This idea is further elaborated in two theories (Foddy & Smithson 1989, Foschi 1989). Both combine elements from the two main branches of the expectation states program and constitute refinements and extensions of aspects of that program; my own theory also incorporates ideas from attribution research on the causal interpretation of success and failure by performers from different social categories. Although the two theories use different formalizations, they make compatible predictions.

The following is the core of the ideas I propose in Foschi (1989). The theory is formulated for a situation where two persons, self and other, work on a joint task—the same unit of analysis that is investigated in most expectation states research. The propositions are stated from self's point of view and apply to any attribute—specific or diffuse, individually or in combination with other(s)—that self treats as a status characteristic. In other words, levels of the attribute are considered to have informational value regarding competence. Other scope conditions include valuing the task, being motivated to do it well, and having a collective orientation. The situation of central interest is one in which the two persons differ with respect to status but perform at the same level (either equally well or equally poorly). The performance evaluations are made by a source outside the group and are accepted by self to be objective. The source, however, does not provide standards by which to infer either ability or lack of ability from the evaluations. Thus, apart from the information on status and the performance evaluations, self has no other grounds on which to form ideas about the two persons' relative competence.

Under such conditions, are the performances sufficient to equalize the two actors in perceived ability, or does the status difference still have an effect on these perceptions? In Foschi (1989) I have proposed that the latter will be the case—a result of the activation and application of different, status-based standards to the two persons. That is, those who are considered to be of lower status will have their successful performances scrutinized (since these are inconsistent with status) and then assessed by a stricter standard than similar performances by higher status actors. Conversely, when these other actors fail, they will be given the benefit of the doubt and treated with a more lenient standard than their lower status counterparts. I have also proposed a similar situation for the inference of lack of ability—in that case, the higher the status, the more convincing the demonstration of *incompetence* will have to be.

In addition, Foschi (1989) extends these ideas in several respects, as follows:

1. The attribute in question may have more than two states, e.g. three levels of socioeconomic class or four levels of ethnic background. In each of these cases, if a different standard is activated for each level of the characteristic, the standard is then a "multiple" one. (Although throughout this article I present ideas that apply equally to double and multiple standards, my

examples are about dichotomized attributes. Therefore, I mostly use the expression "double standards".)[1]

2. The theory also incorporates relevance between status and the task at hand as an additional variable with four levels. Thus, the task may be seen as either (*a*) masculine, (*b*) feminine, (*c*) explicitly dissociated from gender, or (*d*) not explicitly defined in relation to gender. More lenient standards for the male performer than for his female counterpart are predicted for (*a*). This is also the prediction for (*d*), where gender and task become related through status generalization—a process by which a status attribute becomes relevant to the task at hand unless there is specific information to the contrary. In such a case, the double standard will be less pronounced than when the task is masculine but will manifest itself nevertheless. No double standards benefiting the male performer are predicted for either (*b*) or (*c*).

3. Another extension includes situations where self is not engaged in a joint task with a partner but is instead a nonperforming evaluator of two or more performers—on the assumption that status effects are accentuated by the collaborative context but do not require it to manifest themselves. This implies recasting the scope condition of "collective orientation" in more general terms: thus, self does not have to take a partner's ideas into account in attempting to solve a joint task, but he or she still has to be motivated to arrive at accurate assessments of the performers' competence. This extension significantly enlarges the types of decisions to which the formulation applies—such as adjudicating competitions or making hiring recommendations.

Once a double standard is activated and used, it affects the extent to which ability is inferred—in much the same way as when standards are provided by an outside source. The application of a more lenient standard to the higher status person ensures that more ability is assigned to him or her than to the lower status person with the same record. Thus, double standards are both a consequence of status and a factor contributing to the initial, status-based assignment of competence.

It should be emphasized that the application of a double standard is different from the use of biased evaluations. The latter occur in situations where there are no objective means of evaluating performances and one or more characteristics of the actor become the evaluation criterion(a). This process is illustrated

---

[1]Note also that I use the singular form "double standard" to refer to either (i) the different requirements used by one person when assessing two specific actors or (ii) the average requirement applied to two actors by several assessors. However, I use the plural "double standards" if I wish to emphasize that a double standard of a *different magnitude* is being used in each case, either by each of several assessors or by the same assessor across various circumstances and/or actors.

in Goldberg's well-known study (1968) in which, regarding various professional fields, respondents made different evaluations of the same essay depending on whether they believed the author to be a man or woman. Double standards, on the other hand, occur when evaluations have already been made and are accepted to be objective (i.e. exempt from evaluation bias). The use of double standards is thus a subtle exclusionary practice, as it involves neither devaluing nor over-valuing a performance in a direct manner. It is also not necessarily conscious, as an actor does not have to formulate such standards explicitly in order to use them. Because even those who are aware of applying double standards often con-sider them to be of dubious legitimacy, the practice is seldom openly communi-cated to the performers. Moreover, double standards may take on many forms—from different requirements related to the ability in question (e.g. the standard may be set at a minimum of 70% correct responses for one group but at 80% such responses for another) to different requirements regarding qualities not di-rectly related or even unrelated to the task (Foschi & Foddy 1988). For example, Ridgeway (1982) found that women in mixed-sex task groups were more influ-ential when they exhibited a cooperative style than when they were perceived to be self-oriented; men, on the other hand, were equally influential in both cases. Carli (1990) reports similar findings regarding gender, portrayed confidence, and influence. Sometimes the practice assumes the form of applying a universalis-tic standard to one group and a particularistic standard to another (Long & Fox 1995). By including special circumstances, the latter is more lenient than the for-mer. Lorber (1984: Chapter 1) presents an insightful description of situations in which women are held to universalistic standards while exceptions are allowed for men.

Foschi (1989) is an elaboration of the graph-theoretic formulation of status characteristics theory (Berger et al 1977), which utilizes graphs and paths of rele-vance as its key concepts. Foddy & Smithson (1989), on the other hand, propose an alternative account of double standards that is formalized through fuzzy sets. The use of different formalizations is the major difference between these two models. Both treat double standards as an order-preserving mechanism whereby it is more difficult for the lower status person to be assigned ability (and easier to be assigned lack of ability). Outside the expectation states framework, the research by Biernat and associates on stereotypes and "shifting standards" is clearly of interest here (see Biernat 1995, Biernat et al 1998 for reviews). The core idea in their work is also that standards change as a function of who is being evaluated. Although eval-uatees are described in terms of social categories rather than status characteristics, these authors treat the two concepts as having considerable overlap, and they use, for the most part, examples of social categories that coincide with the examples of status characteristics used in expectation states research. However, Biernat and colleagues also propose that different conditions result in either a more lenient or a stricter standard for devalued groups, and they discuss attributes other than competence. For these reasons, their work is relevant to more than one section of this article and is therefore discussed at various places below.

Experimental Evidence

Double standards for competence that benefit the higher status actor are common in a variety of task settings—from informal discussion groups to the formal evaluation of performance at work and in educational organizations. Several authors have offered evidence of this practice, and although the expression "double standards" is not always explicitly used, it is clear that they are referring to the application of different criteria for competence to actors of different status. In most cases, the status characteristic discussed is gender, with women reported as having to try harder and being allowed fewer mistakes than men for the attribution of the same level of ability. The evidence on double standards ranges from accounts and descriptions to results from surveys, quasi-experiments, and experiments. Since the latter two types of designs provide the strongest inferences about a relationship between variables, in this article I focus on them. (For reviews of non-experimental evidence, see Foschi 1992, 1997, 1998.)

Several experiments test hypotheses derived from the two expectation states theories. A study reported in Foddy & Graham (1987) employed a variant of the research setting commonly used to study expectations and influence rejection (Webster & Sobieszek 1974, Appendix 1). Subjects participated in either same-sex or opposite-sex dyads and performed a visual perception task said to involve a valuable ability that was either masculine, feminine, or neutral. Next they received prearranged scores indicating that self was either superior or inferior to the partner; following this, standards for both ability and lack of ability were elicited. The results on ability standards set for oneself in the opposite-sex groups are of particular interest. As predicted, the authors found that for the masculine task, women set a stricter standard for themselves than did men; this effect was larger when self (regardless of sex) had a lower score than the partner. Compared to men, women also set a stricter standard for themselves in the neutral task, although here the effects were stronger when self (of either sex) had outperformed the partner. Also as predicted, no double standard was evident for the *feminine* task.

The two experiments I report in Foschi (1996) also used a variant of the expectation states setting described above. Subjects participated in opposite-sex dyads and were assigned at random to either control or experimental conditions. The perceptual task was defined as one on which men usually do better than women. In the first experiment, the focus was on standards for ability set for either self or the partner. In the experimental conditions, prearranged scores showed ordinary performances by both persons; in half of these conditions, self's scores were slightly better than the partner's, while the scores were reversed in the other half. (I chose an ordinary level of performance on the assumption that double standards would be more likely to occur when outcomes do not provide a clear indication of ability). Subjects then set ability standards for the performer with the higher score—either self or other. As predicted, the female performer was, overall, held to a higher standard than her male counterpart. The gap between standards was wider when the target person was the partner rather than self.

The second experiment examined the effects of accountability. This variable is defined as the extent to which an actor expects to have to justify his or her assessments of group members, including, in this case, the standards set for them. As anticipated, there was a significant difference between the standards set for male and for female partners when accountability was low, but this difference was no longer significant when accountability was increased to a medium level. The results suggest that, for these subjects, the legitimacy of using gender as an indication of competence was somewhat limited. This is not surprising, given the major changes in the status value of gender that have occurred in many parts of the world in recent years, particularly in the United States and Canada. It is also worth noting that, as proposed in these three experiments (Foddy & Graham 1987, Foschi 1996), measures of competence in self and other were consistent with measures of standards.

Another expectation states experiment in this area is the one reported in Foschi et al (1994). The study tests hypotheses about the use of double standards when self is a nonperforming assessor of two performers. This new design involves the examination of files of applicants for professional jobs and recreates several features of a hiring decision. Subjects were male and female undergraduates who believed they were members of a university-wide committee making recommendations on the selection of applicants for engineering positions. The critical choice to be made by each person was between a man and a woman with equally average but slightly different academic records (the difference was included to avoid suspicion). It is assumed that these records are accepted as objective evaluations of past performances. Both applicants were said to be semifinalists in the competition. The design also assumes a direct link between beliefs and decisions: The higher the level of ability an applicant is perceived to have, the higher his or her chances of being recommended. Thus, subjects were not asked directly about their standards but instead revealed them through their recommendations. In one experimental condition the man held the slightly better record; in the other, the situation was reversed. Results from male subjects indicate that when the male candidate was the better performer, he was chosen more often and considered more competent and more suitable for the job than when the female candidate was in that position. Female subjects, on the other hand, did not exhibit such a double standard. This corresponds with the authors' hypothesis that men and women would differ in the extent to which they treated gender as a cue to competence and thus activated different standards.

A variant of this design was employed by Foschi et al (1995) to explore conditions of activation of double standards for competence as well as rewards. In this study each subject made decisions about one candidate at a time (rather than about a pair). The candidate, again said to be a semifinalist for a professional position, was either a man or a woman with qualifications that were either average or outstanding. As anticipated, no double standards were found when decisions about competence had to be made in the absence of a direct comparison involving two or more persons. Instead, double standards emerged when subjects were likely to activate comparisons between the candidate and other performers, namely, when subjects had to make reward allocations (i.e. suggest a salary figure). Furthermore, the double standard favored the male applicant when level of performance was average but was reversed to benefit the female applicant when that level was outstanding. As proposed in that article, the woman with the outstanding qualifications may have been seen as better than, rather than equal to, the comparable male candidate. It is also possible that subjects felt it was legitimate to attempt to redress past gender inequalities as long as the female candidate was exceptional. I discuss some of these issues later in this article.

The topic investigated by Biernat and associates in their shifting standards model is similar to the one addressed by the expectation states work on double standards, namely, whether variations in requirements occur when assessing individuals from different social groups. The models from the two traditions, however, differ in several respects. One important contribution of the work on shifting standards is to ask whether the variation depends on the type of scale used (i.e. either objective or subjective). Biernat and colleagues propose that stereotypes would affect the standards applied if respondents were asked to set them on subjective scales, but not if the scales were objective. The reason for this is that subjective scales would enable different values to be assessed as indicating the same level of an attribute (e.g. a man measuring 6 feet 2 inches and a woman measuring 5 feet 9 inches could both be considered to be tall), but objective scales (e.g. a scale defining "tallness" as a specific range of values expressed in feet and inches) would not. Because they invite the use of different standards, subjective appraisals do not reveal evidence of stereotyping (e.g. that men are often judged to be taller than women) as much as objective appraisals do. Biernat & Manis (1994) examine inferences of academic and athletic abilities on the basis of either gender or skin color; Kobrynowicz & Biernat (1997) investigate mathematical skills and ethnicity. In all cases the predictions about stereotypes, type of scale, and shifting standards were supported. (See also Biernat et al 1991 and Kobrynowicz & Biernat 1997, both discussed later in this article, for double standards in the inference of other attributes.)

More recently, Biernat & Kobrynowicz (1997) have compared the shifting standards and the expectation states models, and have proposed that they apply to inferences about *different levels* of ability. Thus, these authors argue, if two clearly different questions are asked, one about conclusive demonstration of competence and the other about minimum ability, the two expectation states models address the former whereas the shifting standards model applies to the latter. Biernat & Kobrynowicz (1997) propose that, for the inference of minimum ability, decisions are made separately for lower and higher status groups, and standards are set to merely reflect the expectations held for each. Since these are of a lower level of performance for devalued groups, the standard is more lenient for them. This is exemplified by statements such as "the performance is good—for a woman." The expectation states models, on the other hand, concern decisions about clearly documenting ability and involve comparisons across (rather than within) groups. The same successful performance has different informational value depending on the performer's status, as the probability of the event is seen as varying with that factor. Standards for ability reflect these differences and are therefore set to be stricter for the lower status performer.

Biernat & Kobrynowicz (1997) report two studies designed to assess these ideas; both involve an applicant-evaluation context where evaluatees differ in either sex or skin color. In line with predictions, minimum entry requirements were found to be lower for women than for men, and for blacks than for whites. For each of these social categories, however, the reverse occurred when inferences about ability had to be made, also as predicted. It is worth noting that in the expectation states studies where questions about standards were explicitly asked (Foddy & Graham 1987, Foschi 1996), these questions were indeed phrased in terms of requirements to conclude that a person "definitely has (or does not have) ability." Furthermore, the competitive evaluation context created in Foschi et al (1994, 1995) entailed that subjects made inferences about the applicants' competence that went beyond minimum levels of ability.

Assessment

The experimental research reviewed above shows substantial support for the prediction that, when an inference about definite possession of ability is to be made, lower status individuals will be held to a stricter standard than their higher status counterparts. The research also identifies several conditions for the occurrence of this practice, notably a low level of accountability and a salient status difference between the performers. Moreover, the work shows that self need not be one of the performers for double standards to occur. The work originates in studies using different types of research settings and including both direct and indirect measures of standards, and this variety strengthens the findings. In my view, the results also suggest three areas for future research, as listed below. All three concern the scope condition that the attribute in question have status value (i.e. imply task competence), a condition that all the models incorporate either explicitly (expectation states) or implicitly (shifting standards).

1. Although the models use the closely related, abstract concepts of "status characteristic" and "social category" in this scope condition, most of the evidence gathered so far involves gender (a few studies investigate skin color and ethnicity). For a wider empirical basis, it would be useful to operationalize those concepts differently in future studies. This would help to establish that the process is not specific to any particular attribute.

2. It is important to distinguish between (*a*) an attribute having status value *in a social system* and (*b*) the attribute having that value *for an individual* in that system. Thus, gender may be a status characteristic in a given society but not for a particular individual in it, or gender may be such a characteristic for an individual but not for the society to which he or she belongs. I consider both conditions to be required for the activation of

double standards. This, in turn, has several research implications. For example, one must take into account that individuals usually belong to more than one social system at the same time and that, if they accept that a given characteristic has status value, they may do so with different levels of conviction. This conviction may, in turn, be affected by the consensus they perceive to exist in the social system in question. Furthermore, the levels of some characteristics imply a clearer contrast in status value than do others. I propose that both differences in degree of conviction and differences in status value affect the magnitude of the double standard.

3. Both Foddy & Smithson (1989) and Foschi (1989) include relevance between status and task as a variable in their models. Relevance refers to the strength of the perceived association between status level and either success or failure at the task (e.g. the extent to which a task is seen as "masculine"). This strength may also depend on the characteristic under consideration, a topic that needs further empirical examination. Thus, gender is more often seen as directly relevant to the task at hand than is physical attractiveness. Moreover, relevance between status and task may change over time in a society, as some of the research discussed above suggests regarding gender (Foschi et al 1994, Foschi 1996). (Note that, since the double standards hypotheses are formulated in both abstract and conditional terms, their validity is independent of the particular attributes that constitute status characteristics in any given case; on this point, see Foschi 1998, footnote 6).

These three research areas, in turn, relate to the creation and spread of status beliefs, and to the role of legitimation processes in the formation of performance expectations (for recent work on these topics, see Berger et al 1998, Ridgeway et al 1998, Webster & Hysom 1998). Developing theoretical links between this work and the activation of double standards promises to yield fruitful results.

DOUBLE STANDARDS FOR COMPETENCE: The Role of Other Factors

A growing literature, both within and outside expectation states theory, shows that factors other than status have an effect on inferences of competence. Three extensions of the theory that investigate those factors are of special interest here, namely, those extensions concerning (*a*) the allocation of rewards, (*b*) the assignment of personality and moral characteristics, and (*c*) the development of affective linkages among group members. Let us consider each of these factors with reference to the use of double standards for competence.

(*a*) The relationships between status, performances, and the allocation of rewards have been examined by expectation states researchers from the earlier formulations of the theory (Berger et al 1972, 1985a). Several experiments provide empirical evidence of these relationships. For example, Cook (1975) studied how consistent and inconsistent combinations of perceived ability and assigned rewards affected performance expectations, and Parcel & Cook (1977) tested hypotheses on how status influenced reward allocation. The reverse process has also been examined, i.e. the effects of assigned rewards on inferred ability and corresponding performance expectations. Thus, Harrod (1980) and Stewart & Moore (1992) investigated whether such expectations resulted from knowledge of the pay allocated to self and other by a third party. In both studies, the two actors were paid either the same or different amounts, and support was found for the hypothesis that rewards would generate congruent performance expectations.

One could then ask if rewards would also generate different standards for competence. This is precisely the question posed by Freeman (1995) in developing an extension of Foschi (1989). To explore that question, Freeman designed an experiment in which differences in rewards received by self and partner were either consistent or inconsistent with differences in their performance scores. Subjects were subsequently asked to set standards for themselves for both ability and lack of ability. Results indicate that rewards were indeed used as a basis for ability standards: Those subjects who had been underrewarded relative to the partner set stricter standards for themselves than those who had been overrewarded, and this occurred regardless of level of performance. Freeman also found that rewards had a stronger effect on those standards than did performance scores. On the other hand, these scores—but not rewards—showed a significant effect on standards for lack of ability. There was also a significant interaction, as follows: The strictest standard for lack of ability was set by those receiving lower scores but higher rewards; the most lenient, by those in the higher scores–lower rewards condition. It would be worthwhile to further investigate this asymmetry between standards for ability and lack of ability.

(*b*) Other extensions of the core ideas of expectation states theory include the introduction of the concepts of personality characteristics and moral characteristics, and the development of hypotheses about their effects in task groups (Driskell 1982, Berger 1988, Johnston 1988). Instances of the former type of characteristic are qualities such as "friendly," "shy," and "hostile," while the latter are exemplified by traits such as "honest," "trustworthy," and "devious." Both types entail broadly defined attributions of what is perceived to be a person's true character, but moral traits also include judgments of what is right and what is wrong in ethical terms. States of neither characteristic imply, by themselves, levels of competence. Nevertheless, in situations where an inference about competence must be made and no other information is available, those states can be used for such purpose. Hypotheses about this relationship and the conditions under which it occurs have been proposed for personality characteristics, in Driskell (1982) and for moral characteristics, in Webster (1982). Driskell (1982) also reports supporting experimental evidence. To my knowledge, no tests have yet been conducted on the effects of moral characteristics on performance expectations. If personality and moral attributes result in inferences of competence, the next logical step would be to study whether they activate different standards for competence as well.

(c) Considerable evidence now also exists on the role that interpersonal affect processes play in the formation of performance expectations. Under the term affect I include both emotions and sentiments; this research area is also often referred to as "socioemotional" behavior, in contrast to the more "task-related" aspects of interaction. Expectation states work carried out so far on affect includes a rich variety of topics. Examples are the role of status in the expression of socioemotional behavior (Ridgeway & Johnson 1990), the mechanisms through which affect creates performance expectations (Shelly 1993), and the relative effects of status and emotions on those expectations (Berger 1988, Johnston 1988, Lovaglia & Houser 1996, Driskell & Webster 1997, Shelly & Webster 1997).

Since affect processes have been found to play an important part in the formation of performance expectations, I have proposed that they also have such an effect on competence standards. In Foschi (1997) I present an extension of Foschi (1989) and compare status-based to affect-based double standards, with a focus on the role of sentiments of like and dislike in the emergence of the latter. As with personality and moral attributes, sentiments by themselves imply neither competence nor incompetence. However, in task settings where sentiments have been activated, participants are subjected to the often conflicting pressures of using those sentiments as well as objective performance evaluations in judging the competence of others. I propose that an assessor will base those judgements on sentiments of like and dislike if (i) these differentiate between two actors, (ii) no other bases for judging competence are available, and (iii) unbiased evaluations show that the actors have performed at similar levels.

As discussed earlier, the use of double standards involves neither devaluing nor overvaluing a performance in an explicit way. The performance, instead, can simply be deemed either to be "not good enough" or to surpass standards. For this reason, it may be the case not only that double standards can be activated by affect states but even that this practice is a *common* exclusionary procedure when assessors have clear affective linkages to the performers. That is, the use of different standards may be preferred over the direct expression of bias in favor of liked actors and against disliked ones, since such biases would not be appropriate in task settings.

The studies discussed in this section identify a variety of additional factors as bases for competence double standards and map out a promising research area. As in the case of status, the magnitude of the double standard should reflect the level of differentiation that these factors provide (e.g. either a wide or a narrow gap between the states of "friendly" and "unfriendly"). It would be important to investigate the relative effects of these various factors as well as to examine how each of them interacts with status in activating double standards. Work in this area has only just begun.

DOUBLE STANDARDS IN THE INFERENCE
OF OTHER ATTRIBUTES

Although the focus of this article is on double standards for competence, it is important to note that the practice is not limited to that domain but, in fact, often occurs with respect to a variety of other attributes. Two examples would be (*a*) the situation where the same evidence of criminal behavior results in a verdict of either guilt or innocence, depending on the accused person's skin color, and (*b*) the case where individuals with similar qualifications but differing in country of origin receive contrasting assessments on their suitability as immigrants. In general terms, a double (or multiple) standard is the practice of applying different requirements to various categories of people for the inference of a specified level of an attribute. The use of double standards for this wider set of attributes is similar to their use in the inference of competence. Thus, double standards are more likely to be used when only limited information is available about the performers. Also here, the greater the difference between levels of the category on which the double standard is based, the larger its magnitude should be. There are numerous accounts and descriptions of this larger family of double standards, as well as considerable research evidence on several of them. Contributions originate in various theoretical traditions. In this article I provide a brief overview of experimental and quasi-experimental work in this area. (For references to other types of evidence of this practice, see Foschi 1998).

The most commonly discussed and researched double standard is the one consisting of different codes of sexual behavior for the inference of marriage desirability, sexual morality, and personality traits in men and women. The two codes allow for a wider range and frequency of sexual experience for men than for women (e.g. Sprecher et al 1987, Oliver & Sedikides 1992, Hynie & Lydon 1995). It should be noted, however, that there is also some evidence (e.g. Jacoby & Williams 1985, O'Sullivan 1995) that this double standard is no longer accepted by many in the United States and Canada—a development in line with the changing attitudes regarding gender discussed earlier in this article.

Other frequently observed double standards that have been investigated through either experimental or quasi-experimental designs include: (*a*) the physical signs of aging in men and women and the resulting different inferences about a person's attractiveness and overall worth (Berman et al 1981, Deutsch et al 1986); (*b*) the assessment of the same behavior by both sexes through different definitions of mental health (Maslin & Davis 1975); (*c*) skin color and the extent to which a person is deemed to deserve financial assistance from the state (Sniderman et al 1991); (*d*) gender, qualifications, and variations in decisions about either just earnings (Jasso & Webster 1997) or recommended salary (Foschi et al 1995); (*e*) gender, quality, and role appropriateness of behavior, and whether causal attributions are personal or situational (Galper & Luck 1980); and (*f*) gender and different judgments of height, weight, age, income, and parenting skills (Biernat et al 1991, Kobrynowicz & Biernat 1997).

Even a brief review such as the one presented here shows that the basis for these other types of double standards is frequently a diffuse status characteristic (most often gender), as was the case for competence double standards. Here again, the standard imposed is stricter for the lower status person.

Given the focus of this article, it is also interesting to note that the qualities inferred are often closely related to competence: personal worth, mental health, income, just earnings, recommended salary. This suggests a variety of questions worth exploring, as follows. How do double standards operate when there is such a close connection between attributes? Does the practice simply extend from one domain to the other? If so, how much does the spread depend on the factor activating the initial double standard and the degree of differentiation the factor provides? For example, the work conducted so far identifies gender as a factor particularly apt to activate a multiplicity of double standards. Thus, it could be that treating men and women with different requirements for personal worth facilitates the use of a double standard for competence. A similar process may also operate in the other direction and link, for instance, double standards for competence with those for rewards. In addition, it would be worthwhile to explore such extensions when the association between the attributes is not as close (as, for example, between morality and competence). Addressing these questions would be a significant step toward increasing our knowledge of this practice.

"REVERSE" DOUBLE STANDARDS FOR COMPETENCE

The reviews presented in the previous sections reveal double standards to be a key mechanism through which actors, depending on their ranking on socially valued attributes, either benefit or are hindered in the assignment of other such attributes. The practice is subtle and not necessarily conscious, but nevertheless effective in contributing to the maintenance of the status quo in a variety of social interaction contexts. It is not surprising then that "reverse" double standards have been advocated by some as an instrument for change—both as an individual response and as policy. This has been the case particularly regarding inferences of competence on the basis of gender and skin color in the United States and Canada over the last two decades.

The reverse practice, however, can seldom escape having a patronizing component, that is, an implication that the lower status person cannot meet universalistic standards and therefore has to be judged by different, more lenient rules (for descriptions of this practice, see e.g. Epstein 1970, 1991, Blalock 1979, Biernat & Kobrynowicz 1997). In turn, applying a more lenient standard to the lower status person often results in the inference of a lower level of ability (see the procedural studies reviewed below). This contributes to *maintaining* rather than changing the status quo.

In other words, the lower status person is held back in one way or the other, most often through the application of stricter standards, although sometimes through more lenient standards. The occurrence of both practices is in line with the status-based argument presented earlier, namely that a successful performance by this person is an inconsistent occurrence and would tend to be scrutinized. The situation is accurately described as "loss-loss" by Reskin (1998:58), who also notes that higher status individuals who have been assessed with a lenient standard are seldom stigmatized as a result of this treatment (on this point, see also Lorber 1984: Chapter 1, Garcia et al 1981).

Several experiments investigate the inferences made about an applicant's competence as a function of strictness of selection procedure (either meritorious or preferential). Findings show negative consequences for the person chosen on a preferential basis, particularly when there is ambiguous evidence of his or her qualifications. Thus, authors report lower self-evaluation for this person (e.g. Heilman et al 1987, 1990, Turner et al 1991, Turner & Pratkanis 1993) as well as the assignment of a lower level of competence by others (e.g. Garcia et al 1981, Heilman et al 1992).[2] The affirmative action and employment equity programs implemented in the United States and Canada have varied widely in the measures they advocate regarding what standards to use in hiring procedures. The better designed programs avoid policies of reverse discrimination, including the lowering of standards for one group, as well as the *perception* that any of these reverse practices have occurred.

Of more direct relevance to this review is whether, and under what conditions, individuals use reverse double standards without having been instructed to do so—that is, generate such double standards themselves. Some of the research described above provides useful leads in this respect. Thus, the following conditions, identified by that work as required for the activation of stricter standards for the lower status actor, also contribute to the understanding of the reverse practice: (i) the assessor is motivated to arrive at accurate assessments of the performers' competence; (ii) the performers differ with respect to a status characteristic, and this difference is salient to the assessor; (iii) the characteristic carries status value for the assessor; (iv) the performances are of the same level but provide inconclusive evidence of either ability or lack of ability (that is, are neither outstanding nor extremely poor); and (v) the assessor anticipates a low level of accountability for his or her appraisals.

If any of these conditions is not met, one would expect the double standard to lessen or even disappear. This is, for example, exactly what I found (see Foschi 1996) when level of accountability was increased—as discussed earlier in this article. Similarly, if motivation to make accurate assessments of competence were

---

[2]It should be noted, however, that the consequences of not being chosen for a position due to the application of strict standards are usually more negative than the consequences of being chosen under the cloud of lenient standards. In the latter case, the person has at least the opportunity of proving himself or herself and eventually changing the negative perceptions; strict standards, on the other hand, often result in blocked access (see Major et al 1994, Reskin 1998 on this point).

no longer present, there would also be no need to rely on status as a source of information in this regard. But what about *reversing* the double standard? There are many indications that in both the United States and Canada, the number of people for whom gender is a cue to competence—although still substantial—has now decreased. This is also the case for skin color, although the decrease may not have been as pronounced. In other words, fewer assessors in these societies would now meet the third condition listed above if the characteristic in question is either gender or skin color. These assessors would tend to judge both performers by the same standard, and some may even use reverse double standards without implying lesser ability. They may do so because of their own motivation to make up for past discrimination, because of pressures to be "politically correct," or because they are mandated to meet quotas. It is also possible that assessors may think that equal but outstanding performances by, for instance, a man and a woman, are not really equal but in fact demonstrate the woman's superiority—given the obstacles that she likely had to overcome to produce such a performance. In other words, the assessors would be compensating for those difficulties. Results from Foschi et al (1995) indicate that an outstanding performance may be required for such a reversal (in that case, in standards for rewards) to occur.

Another condition for reverse double standards has been proposed by Biernat & Kobrynowicz (1997). As I discuss earlier, these authors argue that the nature of the decision affects the direction of the double standard—stricter for devalued groups if the issue is to infer definite ability, but more lenient for those groups if only minimal ability is to be appraised. More generally, the work by these authors suggests two factors that would be worth investigating for their effects on standards, namely, the importance of the decision to be made and the costs to the assessor for being wrong.

Finally, it is worth noting that the plight of the lower status person is often accentuated by the fact that he or she *does not know* whether the competence standards to be applied to him or her will be stricter or more lenient. Double standards of either type are, of course, seldom made explicit. However, the higher status person frequently has resources that include information about which standard will be applied. This additional predicament of the lower status person has been identified by several authors (e.g. Epstein 1970:978, Chacko 1982, Banks 1984, Taylor 1993) who describe the ambiguity and resulting stress experienced under those circumstances.

SUMMARY AND CONCLUSIONS

Double standards are an important exclusionary practice. As filters allowing for different interpretations of the same outcome, they effectively contribute to the maintenance of the status quo regarding a variety of attributes and in a wide array of social interaction domains—e.g. the evaluation of participants in informal task groups, formal hiring decisions, salary reviews, hearings on granting refugee status, and dating choices. In this article I focus on theory and research on the practice of applying standards of different strictness for the inference of competence, depending on who the performers are. Most of this work concerns status differences as the basis for the practice. Thus, experimental research provides clear evidence of stricter standards for women than for men when both perform at the same level and performance evaluations are objective—but can nevertheless be interpreted as either conclusive or inconclusive evidence of competence. Double standards provide the mechanism for those differences in interpretation. Several other conditions under which this practice occurs have been identified (such as a salient status difference between two or more performers, and an assessor who anticipates low accountability for his or her decisions), and considerable knowledge has now accumulated in this area.

I also discuss extensions of these ideas that include other, nonstatus bases for double standards. For example, I propose that personality characteristics, allocated rewards, and sentiments of like and dislike can similarly activate different standards for ability and lack of ability. Further, I examine how the use of double standards is not limited to the inference of competence, as I discuss evidence of their operation and consequences regarding other attributes, such as beauty, morality, and overall personal worth. Finally, I also identify some of the conditions under which reverse double standards occur, namely, the practice of using a more lenient standard to judge the lower status person. For all types of double standards, research evidence is reviewed and areas for further investigation are suggested.

ACKNOWLEDGMENTS

Preparation of this article was supported by Research Grant #410-97-0101 from the Social Sciences and Humanities Research Council of Canada. I gratefully acknowledge this support. I also thank Keiko Koizumi for expert assistance with library research, and Sandra Enns and Vanessa Lapointe for helpful comments on an earlier version.

Visit the Annual Reviews home page at www.AnnualReviews.org

LITERATURE CITED

Banks WM. 1984. Afro-American scholars in the university: roles and conflicts. *Am. Behav. Sci.* 27:325–38

Berger J. 1988. Directions in expectation states research. See Webster & Foschi 1988a, pp. 450–74, 522–28

Berger J, Fisek MH, Norman RZ, Wagner DG. 1985a. Formation of reward expectations in status situations. See Berger & Zelditch 1985, pp. 215–61

Berger J, Fisek MH, Norman RZ, Zelditch M Jr. 1977. *Status Characteristics and Social Interaction: An Expectation States Approach.* New York: Elsevier

Berger J, Ridgeway CL, Fisek MH, Norman RZ. 1998. The legitimation and delegitimation of power and prestige orders. *Am. Sociol. Rev.* 63:370–405

Berger J, Wagner DG, Zelditch M Jr. 1985b. Introduction: expectation states theory—review and assessment. See Berger & Zelditch 1985, pp. 1–72

Berger J, Zelditch M Jr, eds. 1985. *Status, Rewards and Influence: How Expectations Organize Behavior.* San Francisco, CA: Jossey-Bass

Berger J, Zelditch M Jr, Anderson B, eds. 1989. *Sociological Theories in Progress: New Formulations.* Newbury Park, CA: Sage

Berger J, Zelditch M Jr, Anderson B, Cohen BP. 1972. Structural aspects of distributive justice: a status-value formulation. In *Sociological Theories in Progress*, ed. J Berger, M Zelditch Jr, B Anderson, 2:119–46. Boston, MA: Houghton Mifflin

Berman PW, O' Nan BA, Floyd W. 1981. The double standard of aging and the social situation: judgments of attractiveness of the middle-aged woman. *Sex Roles* 7:87–96

Biernat M. 1995. The shifting standards model: implications of stereotype accuracy for social judgment. In *Stereotype Accuracy: Toward Appreciating Group Differences*, ed. Y Lee, LJ Jussim, CR McCauley, pp. 87–114. Washington, DC: Am. Psychol. Assoc.

Biernat M, Kobrynowicz D. 1997. Gender- and race-based standards for competence: lower minimum standards but higher ability standards for devalued groups. *J. Pers. Soc. Psychol.* 72:544–57

Biernat M, Manis M. 1994. Shifting standards and stereotype-based judgments. *J. Pers. Soc. Psychol.* 66:5–20

Biernat M, Manis M, Nelson TE. 1991. Stereotypes and standards of judgment. *J. Pers. Soc. Psychol.* 60:485–99

Biernat M, Vescio TK, Manis M. 1998. Judging and behaving towards members of stereotyped groups. In *Intergroup Cognition and Intergroup Behavior*, ed. C Sedikides, J Schopler, CA Insko, pp. 151–75. Mahwah, NJ: Erlbaum

Blalock HM. 1979. *Black-White Relations in the 1980's: Toward a Long–Term Policy.* New York: Praeger

Carli LL. 1990. Gender, language, and influence. *J. Pers. Soc. Psychol.* 59:941–51

Chacko TI. 1982. Women and equal employment opportunity: some unintended effects. *J. Appl. Psychol.* 67:119–23

Cook KS. 1975. Expectations, evaluations and equity. *Am. Sociol. Rev.* 40:372–88

Crundall I, Foddy M. 1981. Vicarious exposure to a task as a basis of evaluative competence. *Soc. Psychol. Q.* 44:331–38

Deutsch FM, Zalenski CM, Clark ME. 1986. Is there a double standard of aging? *J. Appl. Soc. Psychol.* 16:771–85

Driskell JE Jr. 1982. Personal characteristics and performance expectations. *Soc. Psychol. Q.* 45:229–37

Driskell JE Jr, Webster M Jr. 1997. Status and sentiment in task groups. In *Status, Network, and Structure: Theory Development in Group Processes*, ed. J Szmatka, J Skvoretz, J Berger, pp. 179–200. Stanford, CA: Stanford Univ. Press

Epstein CF. 1970. Encountering the male establishment: sex-status limits on women's careers in the professions. *Am. J. Sociol.* 75:965–82

Epstein CF. 1991. Constraints on excellence: structural and cultural barriers to the recognition and demonstration of achievement. In *The Outer Circle: Women in the Scientific Community*, ed. H Zuckerman, JR Cole, JT Bruer, pp. 239–58, 317–18, 336–37. New York: Norton

Foddy M, Graham H. 1987. *Sex and double standards in the inference of ability.* Presented at Annu. Meet. Can. Psychol. Assoc., Vancouver, B.C.

Foddy M, Smithson M. 1989. Fuzzy sets and double standards: modeling the process of ability inference. See Berger et al 1989, pp. 73–99

Foddy M, Smithson M. 1999. Can gender inequalities be eliminated? *Soc. Psychol. Q.* 62:307–24

Foschi M. 1989. Status characteristics, standards, and attributions. See Berger et al 1989, pp. 58–72

Foschi M. 1992. Gender and double standards for competence. In *Gender, Interaction, and*

Inequality, ed. CL Ridgeway, pp. 181–207. New York: Springer-Verlag

Foschi M. 1996. Double standards in the evaluation of men and women. *Soc. Psychol. Q.* 59:237–54

Foschi M. 1997. Status, affect, and multiple standards for competence. In *Status, Network, and Structure: Theory Development in Group Processes*, ed. J Szmatka, J Skvoretz, J Berger, pp. 201–21. Stanford, CA: Stanford Univ. Press

Foschi M. 1998. Double standards: types, conditions, and consequences. *Adv. Group Process.* 15:59–80

Foschi M, Foddy M. 1988. Standards, performances, and the formation of self-other expectations. See Webster & Foschi 1988a, pp. 248–60, 501–3

Foschi M, Foschi R. 1979. A Bayesian model for performance expectations: extension and simulation. *Soc. Psychol. Q.* 2:232–41

Foschi M, Freeman SK. 1991. Inferior performance, standards, and influence in same-sex dyads. *Can. J. Behav. Sci.* 23:99–113

Foschi M, Lai L, Sigerson K. 1994. Gender and double standards in the assessment of job applicants. *Soc. Psychol. Q.* 57:326–39

Foschi M, Sigerson K, Lembesis M. 1995. Assessing job applicants: the relative effects of gender, academic record, and decision type. *Small Group Res.* 26:328–52

Foschi M, Warriner GK, Hart SD. 1985. Standards, expectations, and interpersonal influence. *Soc. Psychol. Q.* 48:108–17

Freeman SK. 1995. *Double standards and pay: the relationship between standards for performance and rewards*. PhD Diss. Dep. Sociol., Stanford Univ., Stanford, CA. 103 pp.

Galper RE, Luck D. 1980. Gender, evaluation, and causal attribution: the double standard is alive and well. *Sex Roles* 6:273–83

Garcia LT, Erskine NE, Hawn K, Casmay SR. 1981. The effect of affirmative action on attributions about minority group members. *J. Pers.* 49:427–37

Goldberg P. 1968. Are women prejudiced against women? *Transaction* 5:28–30

Harrod WJ. 1980. Expectations from unequal rewards. *Soc. Psychol. Q.* 43:126–30

Heilman ME, Block CJ, Lucas JA. 1992. Presumed incompetent? Stigmatization and affirmative action efforts. *J. Appl. Psychol.* 77:536–44

Heilman ME, Lucas JA, Kaplow SR. 1990. Self-derogating consequences of sex-based preferential selection: the moderating role of initial self-confidence. *Organ. Behav. Hum. Decis. Process.* 46:202–16

Heilman ME, Simon MC, Repper DP. 1987. Intentionally favored, unintentionally harmed? Impact of sex-based preferential selection on self-perceptions and self-evaluations. *J. Appl. Psychol.* 72:62–68

Hynie M, Lydon JE. 1995. Women's perceptions of female contraceptive behavior: experimental evidence of the sexual double standard. *Psychol. Women Q.* 19:563–81

Jacoby AP, Williams JD. 1985. Effects of premarital sexual standards and behavior on dating and marriage desirability. *J. Marriage Fam.* 47:1059–65

Jasso G, Webster M Jr. 1997. Double standards in just earnings for male and female workers. *Soc. Psychol. Q.* 60:66–78

Johnston JR. 1988. The structure of ex-spousal relations: an exercise in theoretical integration and application. See Webster & Foschi 1988a, pp. 309–26, 509–10

Kobrynowicz D, Biernat M. 1997. Decoding subjective evaluations: how stereotypes provide shifting standards. *J. Exp. Soc. Psychol.* 33:579–601

Long JS, Fox MF. 1995. Scientific careers: universalism and particularism. *Annu. Rev. Sociol.* 21:45–71

Lorber J. 1984. *Women Physicians: Career, Status, and Power*. New York: Tavistock

Lovaglia MJ, Houser JA. 1996. Emotional reactions and status in groups. *Am. Sociol. Rev.* 61:867–83

Major B, Feinstein J, Crocker J. 1994. Attributional ambiguity of affirmative action. *Basic Appl. Soc. Psychol.* 15:113–41

Maslin A, Davis JL. 1975. Sex-role stereotyping as a factor in mental health standards among counselors-in-training. *J. Couns. Psychol.* 22:87–91

Miller DT, Prentice DA. 1996. The construction of social norms and standards. In *Social Psychology: Handbook of Basic Principles*, ed. ET Higgins, AW Kruglanski, pp. 799–829. New York: Guilford

Oliver MB, Sedikides C. 1992. Effects of sexual permissiveness on desirability of partner as a function of low and high commitment to relationship. *Soc. Psychol. Q.* 55:321–33

O'Sullivan LF. 1995. Less is more: the effects of sexual experience on judgments of men's and women's personality characteristics and relationship desirability. *Sex Roles* 33:159–81

Parcel TL, Cook KS. 1977. Status characteristics, reward allocation, and equity. *Sociometry* 40:311–24

Reskin BF. 1998. *The Realities of Affirmative Action in Employment*. Washington, DC: Am. Sociol. Assoc.

Ridgeway CL. 1982. Status in groups: the importance of motivation. *Am. Sociol. Rev.* 47:76–88

Ridgeway CL, Boyle EH, Kuipers KJ, Robinson DT. 1998. How do status beliefs develop? The role of resources and interactional experience. *Am. Sociol. Rev.* 63:331–50

Ridgeway CL, Johnson C. 1990. What is the relationship between socioemotional behavior and status in task groups? *Am. J. Sociol.* 95:1189–212

Shelly RK. 1993. How sentiments organize interaction. *Adv. Group Process.* 10:113–32

Shelly RK, Webster M Jr. 1997. How formal status, liking, and ability status structure interaction: three theoretical principles and a test. *Sociol. Perspect.* 40:81–107

Sniderman PM, Piazza T, Tetlock PE, Kendrick A. 1991. The new racism. *Am. J. Polit. Sci.* 35:423–47

Sprecher S, McKinney K, Orbuch TL. 1987. Has the double standard disappeared? An experimental test. *Soc. Psychol. Q.* 50:24–31

Stewart PA, Moore JC Jr. 1992. Wage disparities and performance expectations. *Soc. Psychol. Q.* 55:78–85

Taylor MC. 1993. Expectancies and the perpetuation of racial inequality. In *Interpersonal Expectations: Theory, Research, and Applications*, ed. PD Blanck, pp. 88–124. Cambridge, UK: Cambridge Univ. Press

Turner ME, Pratkanis AR. 1993. Effects of preferential and meritorious selection on performance: an examination of intuitive and self-handicapping perspectives. *Pers. Soc. Psychol. Bull.* 19:47–58

Turner ME, Pratkanis AR, Hardaway TJ. 1991. Sex differences in reactions to preferential selection: towards a model of preferential selection as help. *J. Soc. Behav. Pers.* 6:797–814

Wagner DG, Berger J. 1993. Status characteristics theory: the growth of a program. In *Theoretical Research Programs: Studies in the Growth of Theory*, ed. J Berger, M Zelditch Jr, pp. 23–63, 454–63. Stanford, CA: Stanford Univ. Press

Webster M Jr. 1982. *Moral characteristics and status generalization*. Research proposal funded by the Natl. Sci. Found.

Webster M Jr, Foschi M, eds. 1988a. *Status Generalization: New Theory and Research*. Stanford, CA: Stanford Univ. Press

Webster M Jr, Foschi M. 1988b. Overview of status generalization. See Webster & Foschi 1988a, pp. 1–20, 477–78

Webster M Jr, Hysom SJ. 1998. Creating status characteristics. *Am. Sociol. Rev.* 63:351–78

Webster M Jr, Sobieszek B. 1974. *Sources of Self–Evaluation: A Formal Theory of Significant Others and Social Influence*. New York: Wiley

Annu. Rev. Sociol. 2000. 26:43–61

THE CHANGING NATURE OF DEATH PENALTY DEBATES

Michael L. Radelet and Marian J. Borg

*Department of Sociology, University of Florida, Gainesville, Florida 32611-7330;
e-mail: radelet@soc.ufl.edu; mborg@soc.ufl.edu*

Key Words capital punishment, public opinion, deterrence, retribution,
social science research

■ **Abstract** Focusing on the last 25 years of debate, this paper examines the changing nature of death penalty arguments in six specific areas: deterrence, incapacitation, caprice and bias, cost, innocence, and retribution. After reviewing recent changes in public opinion regarding the death penalty, we review the findings of social science research pertinent to each of these issues. Our analysis suggests that social science scholarship is changing the way Americans debate the death penalty. Particularly when viewed within a historical and world-wide context, these changes suggest a gradual movement toward the eventual abolition of capital punishment in America.

INTRODUCTION

In a monumental 1972 decision by the US Supreme Court, all but a few death penalty statutes in the United States were declared unconstitutional (*Furman v. Georgia*, 408 US 238). Consequentially, each of the 630 or so inmates then on America's death rows was resentenced to life imprisonment. The nine opinions in the case, decided by a 5–4 vote, remain the longest ever written by the Supreme Court. Four years later, defying predictions that the United States would never again witness executions (Meltsner 1973:290–92), the Supreme Court reversed its course toward abolition by approving several newly enacted capital statutes (*Gregg v. Georgia*, 428 US 153). By mid-1999 there were some 3500 men and 50 women (including 65 juveniles whose capital offenses predated their eighteenth birthdays) on death rows in 38 states and two federal jurisdictions (NAACP Legal Defense Fund 1999). Another 550 death row inmates had been executed in the two preceding decades (Death Penalty Information Center 1999).

The goal of this paper is to review recent social science research that has examined various dimensions of capital punishment. We organize this review by examining how the public debate on the death penalty in the United States has changed over the past quarter century. We attempt to show that arguments supporting the

0732-0582/00/0815-0043$14.00

death penalty today, compared to 25 years ago, rely less on such issues as deterrence, cost, and religious principles, and more on grounds of retribution. In addition, those who support the death penalty are more likely today than in years past to acknowledge the inevitability of racial and class bias in death sentencing, as well as the inevitability of executing the innocent. We suggest that many of these arguments have changed because of social science research and that the changing nature of the death penalty debate in this country is part of a worldwide historical trend toward abolition of capital punishment.

Public opinion on the death penalty in America over the past 50 years has vacillated. Support decreased through the 1950s and until 1966, when only 47% of the American public voiced support; since 1982 about three quarters of the population has favored capital punishment (Ellsworth & Gross 1994). While it remains accurate to say that the vast majority of the American public supports the death penalty, at least under some circumstances, it is also true that support for the death penalty is highly conditional. The best data on public support for the death penalty come from Gallup Polls, and since the early 1980s these surveys have regularly found that approximately three quarters of the American population supports the death penalty. In 1991, Gallup found that 76% of Americans favored the death penalty; in 1994 support had reached 80% (Gallup & Newport 1991:44, Gillespie 1999).

More recent data indicate that public approval for the death penalty has peaked, and even decreased a bit in recent years. By 1999, support for capital punishment had dropped to 71% (Gillespie 1999). State polls in California, Texas, and Florida—the states with the highest number of prisoners on their death rows—further suggest that death penalty support has peaked. In California, a 1997 Field Poll found that support for the death penalty had dropped to 74% from a 1985 peak of 83% (Kroll 1997). In Texas, a 1998 Scripps Howard Poll found that support for the death penalty stood at 68%, down 18 points since 1994 (Walt 1998). A 1998 Florida poll conducted by the New York Times Regional Newspapers also found that 68% favored the death penalty (Judd 1998); a second 1998 Florida poll done by Mason/Dixon registered support at 63% (Griffin 1998).

What accounts for these patterns? To further probe fluctuations in public opinion on the death penalty and changes in the ways that people discuss the issue, we would like to turn the clock back 25 years and examine a handful of arguments that supporters of the death penalty were making at the time.

DETERRENCE

In the early 1970s, the top argument in favor of the death penalty was general deterrence. This argument or hypothesis suggests that we must punish offenders to discourage others from committing similar offenses; we punish past offenders to send a message to potential offenders. In a broad sense, the deterrent effect of punishment is thought to be a function of three main elements: certainty, celerity, and severity. First, people do not violate laws if they are certain that they will be caught and punished. Second, celerity refers to the elapsed time between the commission of an offense and the administration of punishment. In theory, the more quickly a punishment is carried out, the greater its deterrent effect. Third, the deterrent effect of a punishment is a function of its severity. However, over the last two decades more and more scholars and citizens have realized that the deterrent effect of a punishment is not a consistent direct effect of its severity—after a while, increases in the severity of a punishment no longer add to its deterrent benefits. In fact, increases in a punishment's severity have decreasing incremental deterrent effects, so that eventually any increase in severity will no longer matter. If one wishes to deter another from leaning on a stove, medium heat works just as well as high heat.

Writing in a special issue of the *Annals of the American Academy of Political and Social Science* devoted to the death penalty in 1952, criminologist Robert Caldwell asserted, "The most frequently advanced and widely accepted argument in favor of the death penalty is that the threat of its infliction deters people from committing capital offenses" (Caldwell 1952:50–51). Scores of researchers, including such eminent criminologists as Edward Sutherland (1925) and Thorsten Sellin (1959), have examined the possibility that the death penalty has a greater deterrent effect on homicide rates than long-term imprisonment (see reviews in Bailey & Peterson 1997, Bohm 1999, Hood 1996:180–212, Paternoster 1991:217–45, Peterson & Bailey 1998, Zimring & Hawkins 1986:176–86). While some econometric studies have claimed to find deterrent effects (e.g., Ehrlich 1975), these studies have been sharply criticized (e.g., Klein et al 1978). Overall, the vast majority of deterrence studies have failed to support the hypothesis that the death penalty is a more effective deterrent to criminal homicides than long imprisonment. As two of this country's most experienced deterrence researchers conclude after their review of recent scholarship, "The available evidence remains 'clear and abundant' that, as practiced in the United States, capital punishment is not more effective than imprisonment in deterring murder" (Bailey & Peterson 1997:155).

There is widespread agreement among both criminologists and law enforcement officials that capital punishment has little curbing effect on homicide rates that is superior to long-term imprisonment. In a recent survey of 70 current and former presidents of three professional associations of criminologists (the American Society of Criminology, the Academy of Criminal Justice Sciences, and the Law and Society Association), 85% of the experts agreed that the empirical research on deterrence has shown that the death penalty never has been, is not, and never could be superior to long prison sentences as a deterrent to criminal violence (Radelet & Akers 1996). Similarly, a 1995 survey of nearly 400 randomly selected police chiefs and county sheriffs from throughout the United States found that two thirds did not believe that the death penalty significantly lowered the number of murders (Radelet & Akers 1996).

Opinion polls show that the general public is gradually learning the results of this body of research. According to a 1991 Gallup Poll, only 51% of Americans believed the death penalty had deterrent effects, a drop of 11% from 1985 (Gallup & Newport 1991). By 1997 this had fallen to 45% (Gross 1998:1454). In short, a remarkable change in the way the death penalty is justified is occurring. What was once the public's most widely cited justification for the death penalty is today rapidly losing its appeal.

INCAPACITATION

A second change in death penalty arguments involves the incapacitation hypothesis, which suggests that we need to execute the most heinous killers in order to prevent them from killing again. According to this view, we need the death penalty to protect the public from recidivist murders. On its face it is a simple and attractive position: No executed prisoner has ever killed again, and some convicted murderers will undoubtedly kill again if, instead of being executed, they are sentenced to prison terms.

Research addressing this issue has focused on calculating precise risks of prison homicides and recidivist murder. This work has found that the odds of repeat murder are low, and that people convicted of homicide tend to make better adjustments to prison (and, if released, exhibit lower rates of recidivism) than do other convicted felons (Bedau 1982a, 1997b, Stanton 1969, Wolfson 1982). The best research on this issue has been done by James Marquart and Jonathan Sorensen, sociologists at Sam Houston State University, who tracked down 558 of the 630 people on death row when all death sentences in the United States were invalidated by the Supreme Court in 1972. Contrary to the predictions of those who advocate the death penalty on the grounds of incapacitation, Marquart and Sorensen found that among those whose death sentences were commuted in 1972, only about one percent went on to kill again. This figure is almost identical with the number of death row prisoners later found to be innocent (Marquart & Sorensen 1989). Interpreted another way, these figures suggest that 100 prisoners would have to be executed to incapacitate the one person who statistically might be expected to repeat. Arguably, today's more sophisticated prisons and the virtual elimination of parole have reduced the risks of repeat homicide even further.

While the incapacitation argument might have made sense in an era when there were no prisons available for long-term confinement, the empirical evidence suggests that today's prisons and the widespread availability of long prison terms are just as effective as capital punishment in preventing murderers from repeating their crimes. Still, in papers first coauthored in 1994 (Ellsworth & Gross 1994) and updated in 1998, Gross (1998) concludes that next to retribution, incapacitation is the second most popular reason for favoring the death penalty. In a 1991 national poll, for example, 19% of death penalty supporters cited incapacitation as a reason for favoring the death penalty (Gross 1998:1454). But in the last two decades it has become clear that if citizens are convinced that convicted murderers will never be released from prison, support for the death penalty drops dramatically.

The public opinion polls presented at the beginning of this paper measure support for the death penalty in the abstract, not support for the death penalty as it is actually applied. A key factor that has changed in sentencing for capital crimes since the *Furman* decision in 1972 has been the increased availability of "life without parole" as an alternative to the death penalty. Today, at least 32 states offer this option (Wright 1990), although it is clear that most citizens and jurors do not realize this and vastly underestimate the amount of time that those convicted of capital murders will spend in prison (Fox et al 1990–1991:511–15, Gross 1998:1460–62). Another segment of the population realizes that life without parole is an alternative to the death penalty, but in spite of this, believe that future political leaders or judges will find ways to release life-sentenced inmates. It is a paradoxical position: Such citizens support giving the government the ultimate power to take the lives of its citizens but do so because of distrust of these same governments and/or the perception of governmental incompetency.[1]

Nonetheless, when asked about support for the death penalty given an alternative punishment of life without parole, public support for the death penalty plummets. In Florida, for example, where those convicted of first-degree murder must be sentenced either to life without parole or to the death penalty, only 50% of the public polled in 1998 expressed support for the death penalty given the former alternative, and 44% of the respondents supported the idea of entirely banning the death penalty given the life without parole option (Griffin 1998). Nationally, the 1999 Gallup Poll found that 56% of the respondents supported the death penalty given the alternative of life without parole—a vast difference from the "overwhelming support" that many erroneously believe the death penalty enjoys. As more and more Americans learn that, absent the death penalty, those convicted of capital crimes will never be released from prison, further withering of death penalty support seems likely.

CAPRICE AND BIAS

As new death penalty laws were being passed in the 1970s to replace those invalidated by the *Furman* decision, many thought that the death penalty could be applied in a way that would avoid the arbitrariness and racial and class bias that had been condemned in *Furman* (Bedau 1982b, Black 1981). However, research conducted in the years since has all but unanimously concluded that the new laws have failed to achieve this goal.

Most of these analyses conclude that for crimes that are comparable, the death penalty is between three and four times more likely to be imposed in cases in which the victim is white rather than black (Baldus & Woodworth 1998, Baldus et al 1990, Bowers et al 1984, Gross & Mauro 1989, Radelet & Pierce 1991). In a 1990 review of 28 studies that had examined the correlation between race

---

[1]We are indebted to Professor Samuel Gross for this point.

and death sentencing in the United States post-1972, the US General Accounting Agency (1990:6) concluded:

> the synthesis [of the 28 studies reviewed] supports a strong race of victim influence. The race of offender influence is not as clear cut and varies across a number of dimensions. Although there are limitations to the studies' methodologies, they are of sufficient quality to support the syntheses' findings.

The problem continues to be documented in research published in the 1990s. Again, race-of-victim effects are regularly found (e.g., Keil & Vito 1995), although some research, such as an extensive study just completed by David Baldus and his colleagues in Philadelphia (Baldus et al 1998), also finds race-of-defendant effects. In the most recent overview of the problem of racial bias in the administration of the death penalty, Amnesty International concluded that it was "undeniable" that the death penalty in the United States "is applied disproportionately on the basis of race, ethnicity, and social status" (Amnesty International 1999a:2).

By any measure, the most comprehensive research ever produced on sentencing disparities in American criminal courts is the work of David Baldus and his colleagues conducted in Georgia in the 1970s and 1980s (Baldus et al 1990). After statistically controlling for some 230 variables, these researchers concluded that the odds of a death sentence for those who kill whites in Georgia are 4.3 times higher than the odds of a death sentence for those who kill blacks. Attorneys representing Georgia death row inmate Warren McCleskey took these data to the Supreme Court in 1987, claiming unfair racial bias in the administration of the death penalty in Georgia. But the Court rejected the argument, as well as the idea that a statistical pattern of bias could prove any bias in McCleskey's individual case (*McCleskey v. Kemp*, 481 U.S. 279 (1987).

The vote in the McCleskey case was 5 to 4. Interestingly, the decision was written and the deciding vote cast by Justice Lewis Powell, who was then serving his last year on the Court. Four years later, Powell's biographer asked the retired justice if he wished he could change his vote in any single case. Powell replied, "Yes, *McCleskey v. Kemp.*" Powell, who voted in dissent in *Furman* and in his years on the Court remained among the justices who regularly voted to sustain death sentences, had changed his mind. "I have come to think that capital punishment should be abolished ... [because] it serves no useful purpose" (Jeffries 1994:451–52). Had Powell had this realization a few years earlier, it is quite likely that, as in 1972, the death penalty would have been abolished, at least temporarily.

In effect, the *McCleskey* decision requires that defendants who raise a race claim must prove that race was a factor in their individual cases, and that as far as the courts are concerned, the statistical patterns indicating racial bias are basically irrelevant. In later years, the "Racial Justice Act," which would have required courts to hold hearings to examine statistical patterns of disparities in capital cases, failed to gain congressional approval (Bright 1995:465–66).

Two ways in which possible bias and arbitrariness in the death penalty can be reduced are through the provision of effective counsel to the poor and the careful use of executive clemency powers. Again, social science research addressing these issues has identified problems.

Research on the quality of attorneys provided to indigent defendants charged with capital offenses has relied on case-study methodology and examination of statutory law or customary procedures used to attract and compensate counsel. Stephen Bright has documented dozens of cases in which death sentences were given despite the fact that the defense attorneys were drunk, using drugs, racist against their own clients, unprepared or outright unqualified to practice criminal law, or otherwise incompetent (Bright 1997a,b). In several cases, the defense attorney slept during the trial—giving a new meaning to the term "dream team" (Bright 1997b:790, 830). State governments are increasingly appointing attorneys in capital cases who submit the lowest bids; typically, attorneys are compensated at less than the minimum wage (Bright 1997b:816–21). As a result, those sentenced to death are often distinguishable from other defendants convicted of murder not on the basis of the heinousness of the crime, but instead on the basis of the quality of their defense attorneys.

A possible remedy for these failures at trial is executive clemency. Executive clemency can be used not only to remove bias and arbitrariness, but also to correct mistakes (e.g., when doubts exist about the prisoner's guilt, or when previously unknown or underweighted mitigation—such as evidence of mental illness or retardation—emerges), or to reward rehabilitation. Again, social science research in this area suggests the ineffectiveness of executive clemency in achieving these goals. Compared to the years before the 1972 *Furman* decision, clemency today is rarely granted (Bedau 1990–1991). Between 1972 and the end of 1992, only 41 death sentences in American jurisdictions were commuted to prison terms through power of executive clemency (Radelet & Zsembik 1993), and an average of just over one per year has been granted since. Of the 51 commutations granted through mid-1999, only six were granted on grounds of "equity."

Public opinion on the death penalty shows that while most Americans recognize the problems of race and class bias, they do not view such discrimination as a reason to oppose the death penalty. In the 1999 Gallup Poll, for example, 65% of the respondents agreed that a poor person is more likely than a person of average to above-average income to receive the death penalty for the same crime (Gillespie 1999). Half the respondents believed that black defendants are more likely than whites to receive a death sentence for the same crime. Despite recognizing these inequities, 71% of those polled favored the death penalty.

COST

A fourth way in which death penalty arguments have changed in the past 25 years involves the issue of its fiscal costs. Two decades ago, some citizens and political leaders supported the death penalty as a way of avoiding the financial burdens of housing inmates for life or long prison terms. As recently as 1983, one of this century's most skilled proponents of the death penalty, Ernest van den Haag, was able to assert, "it is not cheaper to keep a criminal confined for all or most of his life than to execute him. He will appeal just as much [as a death-sentenced prisoner]" (van den Haag & Conrad 1983:34). A 1985 Gallup Poll found that 11% of those supporting the death penalty cited the high fiscal costs of imprisonment as a reason for their positions (Gallup Report 1985).

Since then, however, research has firmly established that a modern death penalty system costs several times more than an alternative system in which the maximum criminal punishment is life imprisonment without parole. This research has been conducted in different states with different data sets by newspapers, courts and legislatures, and academics (see reviews in Bohm 1998, Dieter 1997, Spangenberg & Walsh 1989). Estimates by the *Miami Herald* are typical: $3.2 million for every electrocution versus $600,000 for life imprisonment (von Drehle 1988). These cost figures for capital punishment include expenses for not only those cases that end in execution, but also the many more cases in which the death penalty is sought that never end with a death sentence, and cases in which a death sentence is pronounced but never carried out. They also include the costs both for trials and for the lengthy appeals that are necessary before an execution can be authorized. Consequently, the cost issue today has become an anti–death penalty argument, albeit of debatable strength. Absent the death penalty, its critics argue, states would have more resources to devote to the ends the death penalty is allegedly designed to pursue, such as reducing high rates of criminal violence or rendering effective aid to families of homicide victims. Those in favor of capital punishment, however, would argue that its retributive benefits are worth the costs.

MISCARRIAGES OF JUSTICE

Death penalty arguments are changing in a fifth way: Death penalty retentionists now admit that as long as we use the death penalty, innocent defendants will occasionally be executed. Until a decade ago, the pro–death penalty literature took the position that such blunders were historical oddities and could never be committed in modern times. Today the argument is not over the existence or even the inevitability of such errors, but whether the alleged benefits of the death penalty outweigh these uncontested liabilities. Several studies conducted over the last two decades have documented the problem of erroneous convictions in homicide cases (Givelber 1997, Gross 1996, Huff et al 1996, Leo & Ofshe 1998, Radelet et al 1992). Since 1970 there have been 80 people released from death rows in the United States because of innocence (Death Penalty Information Center 1999; for a description of 68 of these cases, see Bedau & Radelet 1987, Radelet et al 1996).

The cases of those wrongly sentenced to death and who were totally unin-volved in the crime constitute only one type of miscarriage of justice. Another (and more frequent) blunder arises in the cases of the condemned who, with a more perfect justice system, would have been convicted of second-degree murder or manslaughter, making them innocent of first degree murder. For example, consider the case of Ernest Dobbert, executed in Florida in 1984 for killing his daughter. The key witness at trial was Dobbert's 13-year-old son, who testified that he saw his father kick the victim (this testimony was later recanted). In a dissent from the Supreme Court's denial of certiorari written just hours before Dobbert's execution, Justice Thurgood Marshall argued that while there was no question that Dobbert abused his children, there was substantial doubt about the existence of sufficient premeditation to sustain the conviction for first-degree murder. "That may well make Dobbert guilty of second-degree murder in Florida, but it cannot make him guilty of first-degree murder there. Nor can it subject him to the death penalty in that State" (*Dobbert v. Wainwright*, 468 U.S. 1231, 1246 (1984)). If Justice Marshall's assessment was correct, then Dobbert was not guilty of a capital offense, and—in this qualified sense—Florida executed an innocent man.

In other cases, death row inmates have indeed killed someone, but, again, a more perfect system for deciding who should be convicted and who should die would have found these defendants not guilty because of insanity or self-defense, or because the killing was, in reality, an accident. Examined in this way, the class of "wrongful convictions" extends far beyond the group of those convicted who were legally and factually innocent of the crime.

Citing research by social scientists on racial disparities in death sentencing and on the inevitability of wrongful convictions, Supreme Court Justice Harry Blackmun, who until then counted himself as a supporter of the death penalty, wrote in 1994:

> From this day forward, I no longer shall tinker with the machinery of death. For more than 20 years I have endeavored . . . along with the majority of this Court, to develop procedural and substantive rules that would lend more than the mere appearance of fairness to the death penalty endeavor. Rather than continue to coddle the Court's delusion that the desired level of fairness has been achieved . . . I feel morally and intellectually obligated to concede that the death penalty experiment has failed (*Callins v. Collins*, 510 U.S. 1141, 1145 (1994)).

Clearly, concern about the execution of the innocent is an issue that, at the very least, gives pause to some of those who at first glance might count themselves as favoring the death penalty.

This conclusion is further supported by data from the Capital Jury Project, an on-going study under the direction of William Bowers and sponsored by the National Science Foundation. The research is attempting to discover how jurors in capital cases spread over 15 states have decided whether or not to impose or recommend death sentences (Bowers 1995). In a 1998 analysis, Bowers et al (1998:1533) provide clear evidence that lingering doubt over the defendant's guilt is the most significant factor in "fostering a pro-life commitment during the guilt phase of [a capital] trial." Among respondents who identified lingering doubt as a mitigator in their cases, 63% described it as "very important" in their punishment decisions. And 69% said that lingering doubt made them less likely to vote for death (Bowers et al 1998:1534). In comparison, the second most significant mitigator identified by the respondents was evidence that the defendant was mentally retarded. Forty-four percent cited this as "very important," and 55% considered it a factor in decreasing their likelihood of casting a death vote.

The results of the Capital Jury Project are consistent with findings from previous studies examining the significance of lingering doubt in jurors' final punishment decisions. In South Carolina, for example, lingering doubt about the defendant's guilt was identified as the single most important reason why jurors select prison sentences over death sentences (Garvey 1998:1559, 1562–64). And a study of capital jurors in Florida reported similar patterns (Bowers et al 1998:1536). In sum, "these data make it clear that lingering doubt, when it is present, is an integral element in forming a reasoned moral judgment about punishment. Indisputably, lingering doubt plays a central role in jurors' thinking about what punishment the defendant deserves" (Bowers et al 1998:1536).

THE GROWING FOCUS ON RETRIBUTION

Thus far we have argued that in the last two dozen years, debates over deterrence, incapacitation, cost, fairness, and the inevitability of executing the innocent have all been either neutralized or won by those who stand opposed to the death penalty. But while death penalty advocates increasingly acknowledge that these traditional justifications are growing less persuasive, in their place we have witnessed the ascendancy of what has become the most important contemporary pro–death penalty argument: retribution. Here one argues that justice requires the death penalty. Those who commit the most premeditated or heinous murders should be executed simply on the grounds that they deserve it (Berns 1979, van den Haag 1997, 1998). Life without parole, according to this view, is simply insufficient punishment for those who commit the most heinous and premeditated murders.

Retributive arguments are often made in the name of families of homicide victims, who are depicted as "needing" or otherwise benefitting from the retributive satisfaction that the death penalty promises. Perhaps the question most frequently posed to death penalty opponents during debates is "How would you feel if your closest loved one was brutally murdered?" For example, one of the most memorable and damaging questions of the 1988 presidential campaign was raised by Cable News Network (CNN) correspondent Bernard Shaw during the second debate between candidates George Bush and Michael Dukakis, when Shaw asked Dukakis whether his opposition to the death penalty would be swayed if someone raped and murdered his wife (Germond & Wircover 1989:5).

Those who oppose capital punishment can reasonably respond by pointing out that the death penalty offers much less to families of homicide victims than it first appears. For example, by diverting vast resources into death penalty cases—a small proportion of all homicide cases—the state has fewer resources for families of noncapital homicide victims and for more effective assistance for families of all homicide victims. Or, one could argue that the death penalty hurts families of homicide victims in cases in which the killer is *not* sentenced to death, since the prison sentence risks making them feel as if their loved one's death was not "worth" the life of the killer. Or, one could argue that the death penalty serves to keep the case open for many years before the execution actually occurs, often through resentences or retrials, continuously preventing the wounds of the family of the victim from healing. Motivated by a desire to express these arguments, an organization of families that oppose the death penalty, Murder Victims Families for Reconciliation (now located in Cambridge, MA) was formed in 1976. They and other groups of "homicide survivors" have regularly pointed out that the scholarly community has devoted very little attention to families of homicide victims (for an exception, see Vandiver 1998). Indeed, we are aware of no research specifically studying the short-term and long-term effects of the execution of a killer on the family of the homicide victim, or on the family of the executed inmate. On the other hand, the scholarship of Robert Johnson (1981, 1998a, 1998b) and others (e.g., Cabana 1996) gives readers some insights into what prison life in general, and life on death row in particular, is like. The conclusions of these researchers lend credence to those who argue that in some respects, life imprisonment without parole can be even worse than execution.

Finally, in one of the last papers published before his death, criminologist Marvin Wolfgang (1996) reminds us that even if someone might "deserve" to die in the abstract, that does not mean that death is a punishment required by any consistent philosophy of punishment. Given well-documented injustices in the application of the death penalty, Wolfgang raises the issue of whether such a penalty can be applied in the name of "justice." For Wolfgang, the question becomes not "Who deserves to die?," but instead, "Who deserves to kill?"

Unlike the arguments reviewed above, retribution is a non-empirical justification and thus all but impossible to test with empirical data. After all, there are no mathematical formulae available or on the horizon that can tell us precisely (or even roughly) how much of a given punishment a murderer—or any other offender—"deserves." In the end, the calculation of how much punishment a criminal "deserves" becomes more a moral and less a criminological issue.

To the extent that the death penalty is justified on moral (retributive) grounds, it is paradoxical that much of what can be called the "moral leadership" in the United States is already opposed to the death penalty. Leaders of Catholic, most Protestant, and Jewish denominations are strongly opposed to the death penalty, and most formal religious organizations in the United States have endorsed statements in favor of abolition (American Friends Service Committee 1998). In the words of Father Robert Drinan, a Jesuit priest and former member of Congress, "The amazing convergence of opinion on the death penalty among America's religious organizations is probably stronger, deeper, and broader than the consensus on any other topic in the religious community in America" (Drinan 1991:107).

Consequently, no longer are Old Testament religious arguments in favor of the death penalty widely used or heard. In the late 1990s the Catholic Church and its leader, Pope John Paul II, are increasingly speaking out against the death penalty. This activity likely has been fostered in part by the success of the book and movie *Dead Man Walking*, which presents the autobiographical "journey" of a Catholic nun who ministers to inmates on Louisiana's death row, as well as to the families of some of their victims (Prejean 1993). Prejean's account has become the most popular death penalty book of the century.

There is also evidence that the general public recognizes some limits to retributive punishments. In 1991, the Gallup Poll asked respondents which method of execution they preferred. After all, if one were *really* retributive, and if people like Oklahoma City bomber Timothy McVeigh *really* got what they "deserved," the preferred method might be slow boiling or public crucifixion. Yet, 66% of the respondents favored lethal injection, an increase of ten points from six years earlier (Gallup & Newport 1991:42). This preference likely reflects, at least in part, the belief that inmates might suffer too much in electric chairs and gas chambers. In contrast, lethal injection offers an ostensibly less painful death. In fact, death penalty opponents often argue against the use of lethal injection on the grounds that this method makes executions more palatable to the public by creating the appearance that the inmate is simply being put to sleep (Schwarzschild 1982).

A similar pattern in public opinion regarding execution methods is found in Florida, where one inmate burst into flames while sitting in the electric chair in 1990, and another did the same in 1997 (Borg & Radelet 1999, Denno 1997). Again, an ardent retributivist would shrug her shoulders at such painful botches and argue that while indeed these may be unfortunate, botched executions are not especially troubling. But contrary to the retributive hypothesis, half of the respondents polled in Florida in 1998 favored lethal injection, and only 22% the electric chair (10% chose "either" and 16% favored "neither") (Judd 1998). And in 1998, 77% of Floridians expressed support for the idea of allowing the condemned to choose between electrocution and lethal injection (Griffin 1998). Historically, these tendencies are not unique. The search for more "humane" methods of execution dates back at least to the eighteenth century when the guillotine was adopted because of botched beheadings (Laurence 1960), and to the nineteenth century when the electric chair was introduced as a "humane" remedy for botched hangings (Bernstein 1973). Nonetheless, the concern to reduce the prisoner's suffering is inconsistent with the idea that we need the death penalty on the grounds of retributive justice.

TRENDS TOWARD ABOLITION

The above changes in death penalty debates come at a time when there is a relatively rapid worldwide movement away from the death penalty. In 1998, five countries combined for over 80% of the world's executions–China, the Democratic Republic of the Congo, Iran, Iraq, and the United States (Amnesty International 1999b:15). These first four are countries with whom, normally, the United States does not share domestic policies.

Hugo Adam Bedau, the dean of American death penalty scholars, has argued that the history of the death penalty in the United States over the past two centuries is a history of its gradual retraction. Among specific changes that mark the path toward the decline of the death penalty have been:

> The end of public executions and of mandatory capital sentencing, introduction of the concept of degrees of murder, development of appellate review in capital cases, decline in annual executions, reduction in the variety of capital statutes, experiments with complete abolition, even the search for more humane ways to inflict death as a punishment . . . (Bedau 1982a:3–4).

With over 3500 men and women currently sentenced to death in the United States, it is quite easy for those who oppose the death penalty to preach doom and gloom. However, Bedau's observations invite students of the death penalty to take a long-term historical view. With such a lens, the outlook for abolition is more optimistic.

A century ago, only three countries had abolished the death penalty for all crimes; by the time of *Furman* in 1972 the number had risen to nineteen. But since then the number of abolitionist countries has tripled. By the end of 1998, 67 countries had abolished the death penalty for all offenses, fourteen more retained it only for "exceptional" crimes (i.e., during wartime), and 24 others had not had an execution in at least ten years. All fifteen members of the European Union have abolished the death penalty, and the Council of Europe, with 41 members, has made the abolition of the death penalty a condition of membership. In the first decision ever made by the newly constituted South African Constitutional Court in 1995— that country's Supreme Court—the death penalty was abolished as "cruel, inhuman and degrading" (Sonn 1996). Russia, a country that was among the world's leaders in executions in the early 1990s, announced in 1999 that it, too, was abolishing the death penalty (Amnesty International 1999b:16). In June 1999 President Boris Yeltsin commuted over 700 death sentences to terms of imprisonment. Clearly, in a comparatively short historical time span, more than half of the countries in the world have abolished the death penalty, and the momentum is unquestionably in the direction of total worldwide abolition.

The above is not meant to suggest the absence of countries that continue to swim against the tide of worldwide abolition. Internationally, the death penalty is slowly expanding in a few countries, such as the Philippines, Taiwan, Yemen, and the English-speaking Caribbean (Amnesty International 1999b). In the United

States, both Congress and the Supreme Court are increasingly restricting access to federal courts by inmates contesting their death sentences (Freedman 1998, Yackle 1998). Few would disagree with the prediction that the next few years will be busy ones for America's executioners.

On the other hand, as the 1990s draw to a close, more and more countries are signing international treaties that abolish or restrict the death penalty (Schabas 1997). For the third year in 1999, the UN Commission on Human Rights, headquartered in Geneva, passed a resolution calling for a moratorium on death sentencing. The resolution was cosponsored by 72 states (compared to 47 in 1997) (Amnesty International 1999b:16). Although the total abolition of the death penalty is its ultimate goal, the resolution encourages a strategy of "progressively restricting the offenses for which the death penalty can be imposed" (*New York Times* 1999a:A4). Toward this end, the 1999 resolution reaffirms an international ban on executions of those under 18, those who are pregnant, and those who are suffering from mental illness. The resolution also calls for non–death penalty nations to refuse to extradite suspects to countries that continue to use executions as a form of punishment.

Other calls for moratoriums on death sentencing are also being made. In May 1999, the Nebraska legislature passed a resolution calling for a two-year moratorium on executions because of questions of equity in the administration of its state's death penalty. This resolution was vetoed by the governor, but later the legislature unanimously overrode the governor's veto of that part of the legislation that allocated some $165,000 to study the issue (Tysyer 1999). In March 1999, the Illinois House of Representatives passed a similar resolution calling for a moratorium on executions; authorities in that state have acknowledged that 12 prisoners have been sent to death row in the past two decades who turned out to be innocent (*New York Times* 1999b). Finally, in February 1997, on behalf of its 400,000 members, the normally conservative House of Delegates of the American Bar Association called for a moratorium on the death penalty. The House of Delegates cited four principal reasons: the lack of adequate defense counsel, the erosion of state postconviction and federal habeas corpus review, the continuing problem of racial bias in the administration of the death penalty, and the refusal of states and the courts to take action to prevent the execution of juveniles and the mentally retarded (for an elaboration of this resolution and the reasons behind it, see the series of papers published in a special issue of *Law and Contemporary Problems*, Autumn 1998). Although the resolution cannot be seen as a statement of opposition to the death penalty per se, it is an attempt by the House of Delegates to bring these serious problems to the attention of legislators and the American public. What effect this resolution will have, of course, remains unknown.

CONCLUSION

The goal of this paper has been to present a brief overview of recent scholarship on the death penalty. We organized this discussion by examining six issues that have traditionally framed death penalty debates, paying particular attention to the social scientific literature that has evaluated each one. Our discussion suggests that changes in the discourse of capital punishment have evolved partly in response to the findings of this research. We conclude with three observations derived from the foregoing discussion.

First, the past two dozen years have witnessed significant changes in the nature of death penalty debates. Those who support the death penalty are less likely, and indeed less able, to claim that the death penalty has a deterrent effect greater than that of long imprisonment, or that the death penalty is cheaper than long imprisonment, or that it gives significant incapacitative benefits not offered by long imprisonment. Fewer and fewer religious leaders adopt a pro–death penalty position, and advocates of capital punishment have been forced to admit that the death penalty continues to be applied with unacceptable arbitrariness, as well as racial and class bias. A fair assessment of the data also leads to the conclusion that as long as the executioner is in the state's employ, innocent people will occasionally be executed. Increasingly, the best (and arguably the sole) justification for the death penalty rests on retributive grounds.

Second, at the same time as American discourse on the death penalty is changing, there is an accelerating worldwide decline in the acceptance of capital punishment. Indeed, the trend toward the worldwide abolition of the death penalty is inexorable. To be sure, the immediate future will continue to bring high numbers of executions in American jurisdictions. In all probability, these will increase over the numbers witnessed today. Nonetheless, taking a long-term historical view, the trend toward the abolition of the death penalty, which has now lasted for more than two centuries, will continue. Things could change quickly; the final thrust might come from conservative politicians who turn against the death penalty in the name of fiscal austerity, religious principles (e.g., a consistent "pro-life" stand), responsible crime-fighting, or genuine concern for a "smaller" government. Public support for the death penalty might also drop if there emerged absolute incontrovertible proof that an innocent prisoner had been executed. For those who oppose the death penalty, the long-term forecast should fuel optimism.

Finally, our review sends a positive message to criminologists and other social scientists who often feel as if their research is ignored by the public and by policy makers. As our review suggests, changes in the nature of death penalty debates are a direct consequence of social scientists' close and careful examination of the various dimensions of these arguments. Scholars have examined questions of deterrence, race, cost, methods of execution, innocence, juror decision-making, and the political and social environments in which death penalty legislation has emerged (Mello 1999, Tabak 1999). Clearly, this is one area of public policy where social science research is making a slow but perceptible impact.

ACKNOWLEDGMENTS

We would like to thank Hugo Adam Bedau and Samuel R. Gross for their insightful comments on earlier drafts.

Visit the Annual Reviews home page at www.AnnualReviews.org

LITERATURE CITED

Acker JR, Bohm RM, Lanier CS, ed. 1998. *America's Experiment With Capital Punishment.* Durham, NC: Carolina Acad. Press

American Friends Service Committee. 1998. *The Death Penalty: The Religious Community Calls for Abolition.* Philadelphia: Am. Friends Service Com.

Amnesty International. 1999a. Killing with prejudice: race and the death penalty. *Amnesty Int. Pub. No. AMR 51/52/99.* London: Amnesty Int. Publ.

Amnesty International. 1999b. *Amnesty International Report 1999.* London: Amnesty Int. Publ.

Bailey WC, Peterson RD. 1997. Murder, capital punishment, and deterrence: a review of the literature. See Bedau 1997a, pp. 135–61

Baldus DC, Woodworth G. 1998. Race discrimination and the death penalty: an empirical and legal overview. See Acker et al 1998, pp. 385–415

Baldus DC, Woodworth G, Pulaski CA Jr. 1990. *Equal Justice and the Death Penalty: A Legal and Empirical Analysis.* Boston: Northeastern Univ. Press

Baldus DC, Woodworth G, Zuckerman D, Weiner NA, Broffitt B. 1998. Racial discrimination and the death penalty in the post-*Furman* era: an empirical and legal overview, with recent findings from Philadelphia. *Cornell L. Rev.* 83:1638–770

Bedau HA. 1982a. *The Death Penalty in America.* New York: Oxford Univ. Press. 3rd ed.

Bedau HA. 1982b. Deterrence: problems, doctrines, and evidence. See Bedau 1982a, pp. 95–103.

Bedau HA. 1982c. Is the death penalty "cruel and unusual" punishment? See Bedau 1982a, pp. 247–53

Bedau HA. 1990–1991. The decline of executive clemency in capital cases. *NY Univ. Rev. Law & Soc. Change* 18:255–72

Bedau HA. 1997a. *The Death Penalty in America:* Current Controversies. New York: Oxford Univ. Press

Bedau HA. 1997b. Prison homicides, recidivist murder, and life imprisonment. See Bedau 1997a, pp. 176–82

Bedau HA, Radelet ML. 1987. Miscarriages of justice in potentially capital cases. *Stanford Law Rev.* 40:21–179

Berns W. 1979. *For Capital Punishment: Crime and the Morality of the Death Penalty.* New York: Basic Books

Bernstein T. 1973. 'A grand success': The first legal electrocution was fraught with controversy which flared between Edison and Westinghouse. *IEEE Spectrum* 10:54–58

Black CL. 1981. *Capital Punishment: The Inevitability of Caprice and Mistake.* New York: WW Norton. 2nd ed.

Bohm RM. 1998. The economic costs of capital punishment: Past, present, and future. See Acker et al 1998, pp. 437–58

Bohm RM. 1999. *Deathquest: An Introduction to the Theory and Practice of Capital Punishment in the United States.* Cincinnati, OH: Anderson

Borg MJ, Radelet ML. 1999. On botched executions. In *Routes to Abolition: The Law and Practice of the Death Penalty*, ed. P Hodgkinson, W Schabas. In press

Bowers WJ. 1995. The capital jury project: rationale, design, and preview of early findings. *Ind. Law J.* 70:1043–102

Bowers WJ, Pierce GL, McDevitt JF. 1984. *Legal Homicide: Death As Punishment in America, 1864–1982.* Boston: Northeastern Univ. Press

Bowers WJ, Sandys M, Steiner BD. 1998. Foreclosed impartiality in capital sentencing: jurors' predispositions, guilt-trial experience, and premature decision making. *Cornell Law Rev.* 83:1476–1556

Bright SB. 1995. Discrimination, death and denial: the tolerance of racial discrimination in infliction of the death penalty. *Santa Clara Law Rev.* 35:433–83

Bright SB. 1997a. Counsel for the poor: the death sentence not for the worst crime but for the worst lawyer. See Bedau 1997a, pp. 275–309

Bright SB. 1997b. Neither equal nor just: the rationing and denial of legal services to the poor when life and liberty are at stake. *Annu. Survey Am. Law* 1997:783–836

Cabana DA. 1996. *Death At Midnight: The Confession of an Executioner.* Boston: Northeastern Univ. Press

Caldwell RG. 1952. Why is the death penalty retained? *Annu. Rev. Am. Acad. Polit. Soc. Sci.* 284:45–53

Death Penalty Information Center. 1999. http://www.essential.org/dpic/

Denno D. 1997. Getting to death: Are executions constitutional? *Iowa Law Rev.* 82:319–464

Dieter RC. 1997. Millions misspent: What politicians don't say about the high costs of the death penalty. See Bedau 1997a, pp. 401–10

Drinan R. 1991. *The Fractured Dream: America's Divisive Moral Choices.* New York: Crossroad

Ehrlich I. 1975. The deterrent effect of capital punishment: a question of life and death. *Am. Econ. Rev.* 65:397–417

Ellsworth PC, Gross SR. 1994. Hardening of the attitudes: Americans' views on the death penalty. *J. Soc. Issues* 50:19–52

Fox JA, Radelet ML, Bonsteel JL. 1990–1991. Death penalty opinion in the post-*Furman* years. *NY Univ. Rev. Law & Soc. Change* 18:499–528

Freedman E. 1998. Federal habeas corpus in capital cases. See Acker et al 1998, pp. 417–36

Gallup Report. 1985. Support for death penalty highest in half-century. *Gallup Report* Nos. 232 & 233:3–13

Gallup A, Newport F. 1991. Death penalty support remains strong. *Gallup Poll Monthly,* June: No. 309:40–45

Garvey SP. 1998. Aggravation and mitigation in capital cases: What do jurors think? *Columbia Law Rev.* 98:1538–76

Germond J, Witcover J. 1989. *Whose Broad Stripes and Bright Stars? The Trivial Pursuit of the Presidency, 1988.* New York: Warner

Gillespie M. 1999. Public Opinion supports death penalty. http://www.gallup.com/POLL ARCHIVES/990219b.htm

Givelber D. 1997. Meaningless acquittals, meaningful convictions: Do we reliably acquit the innocent? *Rutgers Law Rev.* 49:1317–96

Griffin, M. 1998. Voters approve of death penalty: the support would be weaker if Florida voters were certain that killers would be locked up forever, a poll found. *Orlando Sentinel,* Apr. 23, p. D1

Gross SR. 1996. The risks of death: Why erroneous convictions are common in capital cases. *Buffalo Law Rev.* 44:469–500

Gross SR. 1998. Update: American public opinion on the death penalty–it's getting personal. *Cornell Law Rev.* 83:1448–75

Gross S, Mauro R. 1989. *Death & Discrimination: Racial Disparities in Capital Sentencing.* Boston: Northeastern Univ. Press

Hood R. 1996. *The Death Penalty: A World Wide Perspective.* Oxford: Oxford Univ. Press. Rev. ed.

Huff CR, Rattner A, Sagarin E. 1996. *Convicted But Innocent: Wrongful Conviction and Public Policy.* Thousand Oaks, CA: Sage

Jeffries JC Jr. 1994. *Justice Lewis F. Powell, Jr.: A Biography.* New York: Charles Scribner's Sons

Johnson R. 1981. *Condemned to Die: Life Under Sentence of Death.* New York: Elsevier

Johnson R. 1998a. *Death Work: A Study of the Modern Execution Process.* Belmont, CA: West/Wadsworth. 2nd ed.

Johnson R. 1998b. Life under sentence of death: historical and contemporary perspectives. See Acker et al 1998, pp. 507–25

Judd A. 1998. Poll: most favor new execution method. *Gainesville Sun,* Feb. 18

Keil TJ, Vito GF. 1995. Race and the death penalty in Kentucky murder trials: 1976–1991. *Am. J. Crim. Justice* 20:17–36

Klein LR, Forst B, Filatov V. 1978. The deterrent effect of capital punishment: an assessment of the estimates. In *Deterrence and Incapacitation: Estimating the Effects of Criminal Sanctions on Crime Rates*, ed. A Blumstein, J Cohen, D Nagin, pp. 336–60. Washington, DC: Natl. Acad. Sci.

Kroll M. 1997. Death penalty monolith begins to crack. *El Hispano*, Aug. 27

Laurence J. 1960. *The History of Capital Punishment.* Secaucus, NJ: Citadel Press

Leo RA, Ofshe RJ. 1998. The consequences of false confession: deprivations of liberty and miscarriages of justice in the age of psychological interrogation. *J. Crim. Law Criminol.* 88:429–96

Marquart JW, Sorensen JR. 1989. A national study of the *Furman*-commuted inmates: assessing the threat to society from capital offenders. *Loyola of Los Angeles Law Rev.* 23:101–20

Mello M. 1999. The real capital punishment: the (shotgun) marriage between social science and litigation, and the inviting footnote in *Brown v. Texas. Crim. Law Bull.* 35:107–26

Meltsner M. 1973. *Cruel and Unusual: The Supreme Court and Capital Punishment.* New York: Random House

NAACP Legal Defense Fund. 1999. *Death Row, USA* (Spring). New York: NAACP Legal Defense Fund

New York Times. 1999a. U.N. panel votes for ban on death penalty. *NY Times*, Apr. 29

New York Times. 1999b. *Innocents on Death Row* (editorial). *NY Times*, May 23.

Paternoster R. 1991. *Capital Punishment in America.* New York: Lexington Books

Peterson RD, Bailey WC. 1998. Is capital punishment an effective deterrent for murder? An examination of social science research. See Acker et al 1998, pp. 157–82

Prejean, H. 1993. *Dead Man Walking.* New York: Random House

Radelet ML, Akers RL. 1996. Deterrence and the death penalty: the views of the experts. *J. Crim. Law Criminol.* 87:1–16

Radelet ML, Bedau HA, Putnam CE. 1992. *In Spite of Innocence.* Boston: Northeastern Univ. Press

Radelet ML, Lofquist WS, Bedau HA. 1996. Prisoners released from death rows since 1970 because of doubts about their guilt. *Cooley Law Rev.* 13:907–66

Radelet ML, Pierce GL. 1991. Choosing those who will die: race and the death penalty in Florida. *Florida Law Rev.* 43:1–34

Radelet ML, Zsembik BA. 1993. Executive clemency in post-*Furman* capital cases. *Univ. Richmond Law Rev.* 27:289–314

Schabas WA. 1997. *The Abolition of the Death Penalty in International Law.* Cambridge, UK: Cambridge Univ. Press

Schwarzschild H. 1982. Homicide by injection. *NY Times*, Dec. 23

Sellin T. 1959. *The Death Penalty.* Philadelphia: Am. Law Inst.

Sonn FA. 1996. Keynote address: The ideals of a democracy. *Cooley Law Rev.* 13:853–61

Spangenberg RL, Walsh ER. 1989. Capital punishment or life imprisonment: some cost considerations. *Loyola of Los Angeles Law Rev.* 23:45–58

Stanton JM. 1969. Murderers on parole. *Crime Delinq.* 15:149–55

Sutherland EH. 1925. Murder and the death penalty. *J. Crim. Law Criminol.* 15:522–36

Tabak R. 1999. How empirical studies can affect positively the politics of the death penalty. *Cornell Law Rev.* 83:1431–47

Tysyer R. 1999. Death penalty study OK'd. *Omaha World Herald*, May 28

US General Accounting Agency. 1990. *Death Penalty Sentencing: Research Indicates Pattern of Racial Disparities* (GGD-90-57). Washington, DC: General Accounting Agency

van den Haag E. 1997. The death penalty once more. See Bedau 1997a, p. 445–56 van den Haag E. 1998. Justice, deterrence, and the death penalty. See Acker et al 1998, pp. 139–56

van den Haag E, Conrad JP. 1983. *The Death Penalty: A Debate.* New York: Plenum

Vandiver M. 1998. The impact of the death penalty on the families of homicide victims and of condemned prisoners. See Acker et al 1997, pp. 477–505

von Drehle D. 1988. Capital punishment in paralysis. *Miami Herald*, Jul. 10, p. 1

Walt K. 1998. Death penalty's support plunges to 30-year low. *Houston Chron.*, Mar. 13

Wolfgang ME. 1996. We do not deserve to kill. *Cooley Law. Rev.* 13:977–90

Wolfson W. 1982. The deterrent effect of the death penalty upon prison murder. See Bedau 1981a, pp. 159–80

Wright JH Jr. 1990. Life-without-parole: an alternative to death or not much of a life at all? *Vanderbilt Law Rev.* 43:529–68

Yackle LW. 1998. The American Bar Association and federal habeas corpus. *Law Contemp. Problems* 61:171–92

Zimring FE, Hawkins G. 1986. *Capital Punishment and the American Agenda.* Cambridge, UK: Cambridge Univ. Press

Annu. Rev. Sociol. 2000. 26:63–81

Wealth Inequality in the United States

Lisa A. Keister[1] and Stephanie Moller[2]

[1]*Department of Sociology, The Ohio State University, Columbus, Ohio 43210-1353;*
e-mail: Keister.7@osu.edu
[2]*Department of Sociology, University of North Carolina at Chapel Hill, Chapel Hill,*
North Carolina 27599-3210; e-mail: moller@email.unc.edu

Key Words   wealth distribution, wealth accumulation, social stratification, social mobility, economic sociology

■ **Abstract**   Wealth ownership in the United States has long been concentrated in the hands of a small minority of the population, yet researchers have paid relatively little attention to the causes and consequences of this inequality. In this essay, we review the literature that does exist on wealth accumulation and distribution. We begin with an examination of the reasons that wealth inequality has received little empirical attention. We then discuss methods of creating empirical estimates of wealth accumulation and distribution, and we present some estimates of recent trends in wealth inequality. We explore a diverse collection of research that explains these trends, covering treatments of aggregate influences and individual and household factors. We conclude the chapter with a review of research on intergenerational processes and wealth mobility.

INTRODUCTION

Wealth ownership in the United States has long been concentrated in the hands of a small minority of the population. Since the early 1920s, the top 1% of wealth holders has consistently owned an average of 30% of total household sector wealth. During economic downturns, the distribution of wealth has appeared more equal. However, studies of wealth mobility suggest that upward movement is rare and that eras of relative equality reflect deflated asset prices more than they do improvements in the financial well-being of the majority of the population. Recent trends in wealth inequality have been particularly startling. The top 1% of wealth owners owned nearly 40% of net worth and nearly 50% of financial assets in the late 1980s and 1990s. During this same period, the top 1% enjoyed two thirds of all increases in household financial wealth, and movement into the top segments of the distribution was nearly nonexistent. Moreover, while inequalities of wealth were consistently more extreme throughout Europe for many decades, by the early 1990s, the United States had surpassed all industrial societies in the extent of inequality of family wealth.

Despite extreme inequalities in wealth ownership, however, researchers have paid relatively little attention to wealth inequality and its causes. There are important exceptions, but wealth has largely been ignored in studies of inequality. Sociologists typically focus on income, or the flow of money received by an individual or household, as an indicator of financial well-being. In contrast, wealth, or net worth, is the value of assets owned by the household. More precisely, net worth is the difference between total assets (including real assets such as houses, real estate, and vehicles; and financial assets such as checking and savings accounts, stocks, and bonds) and total liabilities or debt (such as mortgages, car loans, student loans, and credit card debt). Researchers have documented that income inequality is extreme (Danziger & Gottschalk 1993), but recent evidence suggests that inequality is much worse if wealth is taken into account as there are advantages associated with wealth ownership that income alone cannot provide. Wealth provides for both short- and long-term financial security, bestows social prestige, contributes to political power, and can be used to produce more wealth (Domhoff 1970, 1990, Henretta & Campbell 1978, Oliver & Shapiro 1995). Moreover, the correlation between income and wealth ownership is relatively weak, suggesting that income tells only part of the financial story.

In this chapter, we review recent literature that describes trends in wealth ownership and the distribution of wealth among households. We also examine research that proposes explanations of wealth inequality. We begin with an examination of the reasons that wealth inequality has received little empirical attention from sociologists, including difficulties that arise in the collection of data on wealth ownership. We then discuss methods of creating empirical estimates of wealth accumulation and distribution, and we present some estimates of trends in wealth inequality in the United States. We review empirical research and literature that explains trends in wealth inequality, including both treatments of aggregate influences, such as stock market and real estate market fluctuations, and individual- and household-level factors, such as race, age, and divorce. We conclude the chapter with a review of research on intergenerational processes and wealth mobility. Much of the literature we review is from economics and policy studies as these are the disciplines most active in wealth research. Sociologists have relatively recently begun to study wealth (Jackman & Jackman 1980, Keister 2000b, Parcel 1982). However, we believe that sociological studies of inequality would benefit from a more thorough examination of wealth. We also believe that the study of wealth could be improved by the application of sociological theory and methods, particularly in the study of mobility and related processes.

MEASURES OF INEQUALITY: Wealth Versus Income

Because accurate data on wages and salaries are widely available, income is perhaps the most commonly studied indicator of financial well-being. The advent of the income tax, increasingly comprehensive census data, and advances in survey data collection have made accurate, longitudinal data on income widely available

(Winnick 1989). Using income alone to indicate the financial well-being of families would be adequate if income and wealth were highly correlated. In reality, however, the correlation between the two indicators is relatively low. Estimates from survey data during the 1980s suggested that the correlation between income and wealth was about 0.50, and that much of this already-weak correlation was attributable to the inclusion of asset income (income generated by wealth) in the definition of total income. When asset income was removed from total income, the correlation between income and net worth dropped to 0.26 (Lerman & Mikesell 1988:779). Family wealth is a critical component of well-being. Omitting wealth from studies of inequality leaves an important part of the stratification story untold.

There are several reasons that wealth and income are not more highly correlated. Many of the truly wealthy have rather low earnings because they are able to support current consumption with income derived from assets (Wolff 1995a). In addition, retired persons often have low incomes but substantial net worth because their wealth continues to accumulate after retirement when earnings cease (Radner 1989b). Racial differences in savings and asset accumulation also account for some of the weak correlation between wealth and income (Brimmer 1988). In fact, many families, particularly nonwhite families, have zero or negative net worth regardless of income (Radner 1989a, Winnick 1989). For these reasons, many families who are below the poverty line based solely on current income may be living quite comfortably on assets acquired during more prosperous years. Likewise, those with incomes above the poverty line may, in reality, have considerable debt and few assets, making them vulnerable if current income were to be reduced or to cease entirely. Hence, current income may be a poor indicator of true financial stability (Wolff 1990).

Moreover, wealth is even more unequally distributed than income. According to Wolff (1995b), in 1989 the top 1% of wealth owners held 38.9% of total household wealth, while the top 1% of income earners received 16.4% of total household income. The top quintile of wealth holders owned almost 85% of total household wealth, and the top quintile of income recipients received just over 50% of total family income. Another report (based on the Survey of Consumer Finances) found that wealth is more highly concentrated than income (Avery et al 1984). This report demonstrated that 28% of total wealth was owned by the top 2% of wealth owners in 1983, and 57% of wealth was owned by the top 10%. In contrast, in the same year, 14% of total income was received by families with the highest incomes and 33% by those in the top 10%. Moreover, the Gini coefficient for wealth increased from 0.80 in 1983 to 0.84 in 1989 (Wolff 1994). In contrast, the Gini coefficient for income in 1989 was 0.52.

EMPIRICAL ESTIMATES OF WEALTH INEQUALITY

Past estimates of wealth ownership and distribution have generally come from three sources: survey data, estate tax data, and the government's aggregate estimates of household wealth ownership. Both the Survey of Income and Program Participation

(SIPP) and the Panel Study of Income Dynamics (PSID) contain information on wealth holdings, but the most widely used source of survey information on household wealth holdings is the Survey of Consumer Finances (SCF) (Curtin et al 1989, Kennickell et al 1997). The SCF includes panel estimates, contains the greatest detail on the components of wealth such as the home and stocks, and oversamples high-income households in order to include more top wealth holders (Avery et al 1988). Accurate representation of top wealth holders is particularly important because the distribution of wealth is highly skewed. For this reason, researchers have also drawn on estate tax records to estimate the wealth of this group. These records of the taxes paid by survivors of the wealthy at the time of death are not perfect; there are loopholes that allow some to avoid paying estate taxes, and estate tax estimates do not include the wealthy who are still living. But methods designed to compensate for these shortcomings have allowed researchers to produce highly accurate estimates of the wealth of the rich (Johnson & Woodburn 1994). Finally, aggregate data on household wealth have been used to estimate trends in levels of wealth and to adjust survey estimates of wealth distribution (Antoniewicz 1996, Federal Reserve System 1993).

Two problems plague researchers who use these data to estimate the distribution of wealth. First, surveys underestimate the wealth of the rich. Because wealth is highly concentrated, estimates of wealth ownership must include an ample number of top wealth holders. This is difficult because surveys often sample too few wealthy families as they are a small slice of the population. Moreover, wealthy families generally do not welcome queries about the extent of their wealth holdings, and even if they were willing to answer questions openly, they may not be well informed about the details of their portfolios. Oversampling high-income families and using estate tax data reduce this problem but do not eliminate it (Avery et al 1984, Avery et al 1986a, Avery et al 1986b). Second, empirically estimating trends in household wealth distribution requires adequate longitudinal data. There are several cross-sectional surveys of wealth holdings, and occasionally these are conducted as panel surveys. However, neither provides long-term coverage of the same individuals that is ideal for addressing long-term trends in accumulation, distribution, mobility, or other intergenerational processes.

In addition to using basic data sources, researchers have developed methods of synthesizing data from multiple sources to compensate for the weaknesses and take advantage of the strengths of the various data sources. The goal of such methods is to combine two or more basic data sources to create a joint estimate of wealth ownership. Wolff (1980, 1983) statistically matched census data and tax returns and used income capitalization to estimate values of assets. Similarly, Greenwood (1983, 1987) matched income tax records with data from the Current Population Survey and used income capitalization to obtain asset values. In a more complex matching process, Keister (2000b) used microsimulation modeling to match estimates from Census data, the 1962 Survey of the Financial Characteristics of Consumers (SFCC), SCF panels and cross-sections, estate tax records, aggregate data, and other sources to build synthetic longitudinal estimates of wealth distribution, accumulation, and mobility. Although synthetic methods are resource-intensive and require assumptions that can quickly become prohibitive, they allow researchers to estimate inequality and explore accumulation processes that are evasive in basic data sources.

TRENDS IN WEALTH INEQUALITY

While their methods may vary, researchers agree that wealth ownership in the United States is extremely unequal and that inequality has worsened in recent decades. Table 1 summarizes some of what is known about the amount of wealth that Americans have owned. This table illustrates that both mean and median net worth increased from 1962 through 1989 and then began to decline. The table also highlights the gap between mean and median wealth, alluding to the disproportionate control of net worth by wealthy households. Mean net worth increased by more than 50% between 1962 and 1995. In 1962, mean net worth was just over $115,000. By 1983 it had increased to more than $170,000, and the mean was nearly $200,000 by the end of the 1980s. In the early 1990s, however, mean net worth began to decline. By 1992, the mean was just under $190,000, and it fell to about $175,000 by 1995. The trend in median values mirrored trends in mean values but at a much lower level. This table also demonstrates that there was a relatively steady increase in the percentage of households with zero or negative net worth between 1962 and 1995.

But how has wealth been distributed? Historical evidence indicates that while levels of inequality in the distribution of household wealth varied dramatically during the first part of the twentieth century, inequality in wealth ownership was consistently severe. Lampman (1962) was one of the first researchers to point to inequalities in wealth distribution as a source of social problems. Using estate tax data and the estate multiplier method (Johnson & Woodburn 1994), Lampman investigated trends in wealth ownership and inequality in the decades between 1920 and 1960. His findings indicated that between 1922 and 1953, the top 1% of wealth holders owned an average of 30% of total household sector wealth. While inequalities varied with macroeconomic trends during the decades Lampman studied, he

TABLE 1 Mean and median net worth, 1962–1995 (1990 dollars)

	1962	1983	1989	1992	1995
Mean	115,995	170,550	195,382	189,948	175,485
Median	30,996	43,801	46,881	39,995	39,146
Percent with no wealth[a]	11	16	18	18	19

Data are from the Survey of the Financial Characteristics of Consumers for 1962 and the Survey of Consumer Finances for other years.

[a]Households with zero or negative net worth.

provided convincing evidence that inequality was consistently extreme throughout that period.

Other historical estimates have produced similar evidence of inequality during the early twentieth century. Wolff & Marley (1989) used various data sources to study wealth inequality over the entire 1920–1990 period. For the early part of the century, their results were consistent with Lampman's findings. They demonstrated that the top 1% of wealth owners owned an average of 30% of total net worth between 1922 and the early 1950s. Between 1922 and the 1929 stock market crash, the share of wealth owned by the top 1% increased from about 29% to about 32%. During the 1930s and 1940s, the concentration of wealth declined, so that the top 1% owned less than 30% by the late 1940s. During the 1950s, economic prosperity brought with it increased wealth inequality, and by the late 1950s, estimates suggest that the top 1% of households owned nearly 35% of total wealth.

Wealth data, and the corresponding estimates of wealth distribution, began to improve in the 1960s. In 1962, the Federal Reserve Board's SFCC became the first comprehensive survey of wealth holdings in the United States. Table 2 contains estimates of wealth distribution from the SFCC and SCF panels for the 1980s and 1990s. These estimates demonstrate that a very small portion of households have consistently owned the vast majority of household wealth. In 1962, the top 1% of wealth owners held 33.5% of total net worth, and the top quintile held more than 80% of total net worth. Wealth inequality remained unequally distributed but relatively constant between 1962 and the mid-1970s due to an extended stock market slump and the growth of welfare programs such as AFDC and Social Security (Smith 1987). Using estate tax data, Smith found evidence that after 1973 wealth inequality began to drop once again. Others using similar methods have found that between 1972 and 1976, the share of total wealth owned by the top 1% of wealth owners declined from 29% to about 19% of total wealth (Smith 1987, Wolff 1992).

Wealth inequality began to rise considerably after 1979, a trend that continued throughout the 1980s. By 1983, wealth inequality had returned to, and indeed on

TABLE 2   Percent of total net worth held by position in the wealth distribution, 1962–1995

	Gini coefficient	Top 1%	Top 20%	2nd 20%	3rd 20%	Bottom 40%
1962	0.80	33.5	81.2	13.5	5.0	0.3
1983	0.80	33.8	81.3	12.6	5.2	0.9
1989	0.85	37.4	83.6	12.3	4.8	−0.7
1992	0.85	37.2	83.9	11.4	4.5	0.2
1995	0.87	38.5	83.9	11.4	4.5	0.2

Data are from the Survey of the Financial Characteristics of Consumers for 1962 and the Survey of Consumer Finances for other years.

some measures had surpassed, 1962 levels. The estimates in Table 2 indicate that the share of wealth owned by the top 1% of wealth holders was 33.8% in 1983 and 37.4% by 1989. Real mean wealth grew at 3.4% annually during this six-year period, a rate nearly double that of wealth growth between 1962 and 1983. Others have found similar trends (Danziger et al 1989, Wolff 1993). Wolff (1993) found that mean family wealth increased 23% in real terms but that median wealth grew by only 8% over that period. His research also suggested that the share of the top 0.5% of wealth owners rose 5% during this period, from 26.2% of total household sector wealth in 1983 to 31.4% in 1989. The wealth of the next half percent remained relatively constant at about 7.5% of total household wealth, but the share of the next 9% decreased from 34.4% in 1983 to 33.4% in 1989.

Most striking is evidence of the decline in the wealth of the poorest 80% of households. The wealth of this group decreased by more than 2 percentage points, from 18.7% of total wealth in 1983 to 16.4% in 1989. Moreover, nearly all growth in real wealth between 1983 and 1989 was accumulated by the top 20% of wealth holders, who gained 2.3 percentage points in their total wealth holdings, from 81.3% to 83.6%. The second 20% lost 0.3 percentage points, the middle 20% lost 0.4 points, and the bottom 40% lost 1.6 percentage points (from 0.9% to negative 0.7%). Wolff (1995b) found similar results in his examination of trends in wealth inequality. Past research has also suggested that in the 1980s, wealth inequality in the United States became severe relative to that found in European nations. Studies of wealth in the 1920s suggested that wealth in the United States was much more equally distributed than in Western European nations. By the late 1980s, however, research suggests that household sector wealth in the United States was considerably more concentrated than in Western Europe (Wolff 1995b).

While mean and median household net worth declined during the 1990s, the distribution of wealth continued to worsen. The wealth of the top 1% of wealth holders increased from 37.4% of total wealth in 1989 to 38.5% in 1995. The Gini coefficient, an indicator of the degree of inequality comparable to the Gini coefficient used to measure income inequality, increased from 0.85 in 1989 and 1992 to 0.87 in 1995. The Gini coefficient ranges from 0 to 1, with 0 indicating perfect equality and 1 indicating perfect inequality. Conceptually, if a single household were to own all wealth, the Gini coefficient would equal unity (Weicher 1995, 1997). The estimates of the wealth Gini in Table 2 indicate that wealth inequality is extremely severe, and that it worsened considerably between 1962 and 1995.

EXPLANATIONS OF WEALTH INEQUALITY

Explanations of wealth inequality typically fall into two camps: those that focus on aggregate-, or macro-, level influences, and those that focus on processes at the level of individuals and families. It is nearly impossible to discuss the wealth accumulation of individuals and families without speculating about the implications that this has on inequalities in the macrolevel distribution of wealth. Likewise, it is difficult to discuss the aggregate-level distribution of wealth among families without speculating about how the behavior of members of the society affects this distribution. Although most would agree that processes at both levels of aggregation are important, researchers seldom integrate the two levels. In this section, we review literature that takes each approach, and we conclude with a discussion of efforts to integrate macro and micro approaches.

Aggregate Processes

The impact of market fluctuations, particularly stock and real estate markets, has dominated discussions of the influence of aggregate processes on the distribution of wealth. When the value of a particular asset increases, those who own the asset have more wealth, net of any change in their behavior or other circumstances. Because the wealthy have generally been more likely than the nonwealthy to own stocks (Smith 1987, Winnick 1989), when the stock market booms, the concentration of wealth intensifies (Smith 1987, Wolff 1987, 1992). The concentration of wealth, therefore, tends to follow trends in the stock market. Similarly, when real estate values increase, those who own houses or other real estate enjoy an increase in their net worth. Because the ownership of other assets, such as housing, is more equally distributed, the impact of the ownership of other assets on wealth inequality is less pronounced.

Changes in portfolio behavior, that is, the combination of assets families own, thus has important implications for their wealth holdings. Table 3 documents trends

TABLE 3   Percentage of gross household assets held in various wealth categories, 1962–1995

	1962	1983	1989	1995
Primary residence	26	30	29	30
Other real estate	6	15	13	11
Business assets	15	19	16	18
Cash accounts	17	15	14	7
Stocks & mutual funds	20	9	12	12
Bonds	8	4	6	4
Whole life insurance	1	2	2	3
Pension assets	2	2	3	9
Personal trusts	4	3	3	3
Other assets	1	1	2	3
Total assets	100	100	100	100

Data are from the Survey of the Financial Characteristics of Consumers for 1962 and from the Surveys of Consumer Finances for other years.

in the percentage of gross household assets accounted for by various types of wealth. Until the 1980s in the United States, the single largest component of total wealth for most families was the primary residence (Holloway 1991, Levy & Michel 1991). In the 1990s, an increasing number of Americans began putting their savings into stocks and stock-based mutual funds (including Individual Retirement Accounts and pension plans), hoping to reap some of the benefits of a stock market that experienced record increases in the eight consecutive years between 1988 and 1995 (Kennickell & Starr-McCluer 1997, Kennickell et al 1997). While the stock market spiraled upward, the housing market topped out, making real estate investments less appealing and stock investments more appealing. Because increased numbers of households across the wealth distribution were investing in stocks, stock market booms in the 1990s had a less dramatic effect on inequality than they had in the past.

Ownership of other assets has fluctuated less. As stocks gained importance between 1983 and 1995, cash accounts declined in their relative share of the household wealth portfolio. Like housing, cash accounts tended to be owned primarily by the nonwealthy. More specifically, following housing ownership, checking accounts, savings accounts, and other demand deposits tend to dominate the portfolios of the middle and lower middle classes. The wealthy, of course, also own these assets, but their value tends to be overshadowed by more substantial investments in stocks, bonds, business assets, and real estate (Kennickell & Starr-McCluer 1997).

Life insurance ownership has had relatively little impact on wealth inequality, and ownership of this asset remained relatively constant between 1962 and 1995 as the estimates in Table 3 indicate. Yet life insurance ownership has attracted the attention of scholars because there are relatively pronounced differences in propensities to buy life insurance. Life insurance tends to comprise a smaller portion of the wealth portfolios of the wealthy than of the middle class and poor. These differences are largely thought to be a function of the size of net worth and of demographics such as family size (Fischer 1973, Lewis 1989, Pissarides 1980, Yaari 1965). There is also some evidence, however, that minorities, households headed by women, and poor families are more likely than others to use life insurance as savings plans (Kennickell & Shack-Marquez 1992, Kennickell et al 1997). As with other types of portfolio behavior, it is difficult to ascertain reasons for these differences given available data, but social pressure, unscrupulous insurance salesmen, and poorly regulated financial markets may contribute to the differences.

Individual and Family Processes

Individual- and family-level characteristics also influence wealth accumulation. Family income generally has a positive effect on saving and wealth (Atkinson 1980, Bomberger 1993, Greenwood 1987, Radner & Vaughan 1987), and research has shown that other attributes such as age, race, and family structure influence wealth ownership, net of income.

The effect of age on wealth ownership has attracted perhaps more attention than any other single process, particularly among economists working from a life cycle model. Keynesian economics, the predominant approach to economic behavior in the 1930s and 1940s, emphasized the role that individual saving played in the larger economy and held that current income was the sole determinant of saving (Modigliani & Brumberg 1952 (unpublished), 1954). Responding to the simplicity of this approach, Modigliani & Brumberg argued that saving is a function not of the absolute income of a family but instead of the family's income relative to both mean income across families and permanent income (the present value of lifetime labor earnings and bequests). They developed the life cycle hypothesis of saving and wealth accumulation, positing that households will accumulate assets in working years and use these assets to support consumption in old age (Modigliani 1992). According to the life cycle hypothesis, net worth should increase until retirement and then fall sharply (Ando & Modigliani 1963).

While the life cycle hypothesis is conceptually appealing, empirical support of the idea was limited from the beginning. Some researchers provided empirical evidence that supported the predictions of the hypothesis by showing that wealth increases until about age 60 or 65 and then declines at a relatively constant and sharp rate (Fisher 1952, King & Dicks-Mireaux 1982, Straw 1956). Yet other empirical studies directly contradicted the life cycle hypothesis by demonstrating that saving continued well after retirement (Bernheim 1987, Danziger et al 1982, David & Menchik 1988, Menchick & David 1983, Torrey 1988, Torrey & Taeuber 1986). After considerable debate, a relatively strong consensus developed around the idea that while the elderly do dissave after retirement, they do so at a rate much less than that predicted by the life cycle hypothesis (Darby 1979, Hurd 1987, 1990, Mirer 1979, 1980, Sheiner & Weil 1992, Shorrocks 1975, White 1978). An important reason for the lack of support of the dissaving hypothesis is that most people experience both a decline in income (minus saving) *and* a decline in expenditures at retirement. As a result, it is not surprising that the decline in postretirement income is less than predicted by the life cycle hypothesis. There is also evidence that when status attainment variables are controlled, the age at which net worth begins to decline is far beyond the normal retirement age (Land & Russell 1996).

There are two reasons that wealth decreases more slowly than predicted by the life cycle hypothesis. First, the timing of death is uncertain, and risk averse households appear to continue to save in preparation for the possibility of a relatively long life. Second, theories of inheritance have suggested that the elderly do not dissave because they are motivated to leave an inheritance to their offspring (Cheal 1983, Davies 1982, Hurd & Mundaca 1989, Osberg 1984). Modigliani's own research (1988a, 1988b) has found that transfers—both inter-vivos, made between living persons, and bequests, made after the death of the giver—account for only 20% of the net worth of US families. However, the bulk of research on inheritance has demonstrated that inter-vivos transfers and bequests account for at least 50% (Gale & Scholz 1994) and perhaps more than 80% of the net worth of US families (Kotlikoff & Summers 1981:706).

Research has also shown that race affects wealth ownership, net of income. Indeed, when wealth is included as an indicator of well-being, racial inequality is considerably more severe than other indicators suggest. Oliver & Shapiro documented that in the late 1980s, median income for blacks was about 60% of that of whites, while median net worth for blacks was only 8% of that of white families ($43,800 for white families versus $3,700 for black families). Similarly, while 25% of white families had zero or negative assets in 1992, more than 60% of black families were in such bleak financial straits in the late 1980s (Oliver & Shapiro 1989, 1990, 1995).

Various factors account for racial differences in wealth ownership. Status attainment theorists have argued that educational differences are central to explaining racial differences in wealth (Campbell & Henretta 1980, Henretta 1984, 1979, Henretta & Campbell 1978). Others have argued more generally that structural barriers and discrimination create these differences (Baer 1992, Blau & Graham 1990, Oliver & Shapiro 1995, Parcel 1982). Indeed, social scientists, particularly sociologists, generally agree that redlining in housing, dampened educational and occupational opportunities for minorities, and other structural constraints contribute to inequality (Barth et al 1980, Horton 1992, Jackman & Jackman 1980, Oliver & Shapiro 1989, Ong & Ill 1988, Williams 1975). Others, however, have focused on racial differences in portfolio behavior, that is, decisions about how to save, and have argued that there are systematic racial variations in asset ownership (Galenson 1972, Keister 2000a, Terrel 1971). The reasons that portfolio behavior varies racially, however, are less clear, although the dominant explanation suggests that differences in willingness to postpone consumption are important (Brimmer 1988, Lawrence 1991). Of course, social influences on current consumption (e.g., decisions about whether to save or buy a new car) are likely quite strong, but current data restrict empirical examination of such influences (Keister 2000b).

Family structure also plays an important role in creating and maintaining differences in wealth ownership. Some researchers have argued that a relatively small percentage of the increase in poverty in the 1970s through the 1990s was accounted for by changes in family structure (Gottschalk & Danziger 1984). Two separate studies contended that the "feminization of poverty" between 1960 and the mid-1980s was a result of changes in relative poverty rates for various household compositions rather than changes in family structure, particularly for blacks (Bane 1986, Danziger et al 1986). Yet evidence continues to mount that suggests some role for change in family structure. Few wealth researchers address issues of family structure, but both survey and simulated estimates suggest that gender and family structure affect both cross-sectional wealth ownership and longitudinal patterns of wealth mobility (Keister 2000b). These estimates suggest that at any given point in time, family structure is highly correlated with wealth ownership, net of income, education, and race. In particular, there is evidence that marriage and widowhood increase wealth ownership, while increased family size and family dissolution through divorce or separation have the opposite effect (Kennickell & Starr-McCluer 1994, Kennickell et al 1997). Researchers have also shown that family structure continues to affect poverty when it is defined in income terms (see McLanahan & Kelly 1999 for a review of the literature on the feminization of poverty).

Integrating Macro and Micro Approaches

Past research on wealth accumulation processes and wealth inequality has been concerned either with describing the distribution of wealth among families or with explaining how families acquire their wealth, usually with little regard for how processes at one level of aggregation affect outcomes or processes at other levels. One empirical approach to integrating macro and micro processes is that used by Steckel & Krishman (1992) to estimate changes in individuals' percentile positions in the wealth distribution based on demographic characteristics. Steckel & Krishman explained changes in individuals' positions in the wealth distribution (a macro measure) on characteristics of the individuals such as age and gender (micro measures). Angle (1986, 1993) suggested an alternative micro-macro link in his work which argued that the surplus theory of social stratification—the tendency for wealth to flow into the hands of those who already have wealth—could be used to explain wealth inequality. Large-scale modeling efforts that incorporate both aggregate processes and microlevel processes are also able to capture much of the interaction between levels of aggregation (Greenwood 1983, Keister 2000b, Wolff 1980). Ideally, however, these methods would be more clearly linked to theoretical approaches that incorporate both macro and micro processes.

INTERGENERATIONAL PROCESSES, MOBILITY, AND INHERITANCE

Intergenerational processes and mobility are vital to understanding how to relieve extreme wealth inequality. Literature on intergenerational processes has focused on generational comparisons in wealth ownership, with most of the focus on differences between the well-being of baby boomers and their parents. Relatively unfavorable labor market conditions (Berger 1985, 1989, Easterlin 1987, Easterlin et al 1993, Welch 1979) combined with changes in marriage and fertility patterns among baby boomers have raised suspicions that this may be one of the first generations to do worse than their parents financially (Campbell & O'Rand 1988, Levy & Michel 1986, 1991). Yet empirical estimates have demonstrated that the prospects for baby boomers are not as pessimistic as the simple demographic and economic trends indicate. A number of studies have documented that baby boomers, on average, have had higher incomes and have accumulated more wealth than other generations, including their parents' generation, at a comparable age (Easterlin et al 1990). One reason for achieving a higher living standards was, indeed, *because* the baby boomers had altered their demographic behavior from that of earlier generations. If remaining single is combined with child rearing, then parents are unlikely to be able to save for retirement. But it was not just single parenthood that increased among baby boomers. Baby boomers were also more likely than earlier generations to have fewer children or to remain childless, both choices that would *increase* rather than *decrease* ability to save for retirement. Others have documented similar patterns (Kingson 1992, Manchester 1993, Sabelhaus & Manchester 1995).

Perhaps more crucial to understanding the persistence of wealth inequality is understanding wealth mobility. Unfortunately, while the study of wealth distribution dates back to the writings of Smith, Mill, and Ricardo, discussions of wealth mobility are relatively rare. Early studies of mobility concluded that poverty, and thus wealth as well, was transmitted from parents to their children, typically via education (Blau & Duncan 1967). Other researchers extended Blau & Duncan's work and found similar patterns around that time (Corcoran 1995, Duncan et al 1972, Featherman & Hauser 1978, Jencks et al 1972, Sewell & Hauser 1975). Studies consistently found relatively weak, although statistically significant, correlations between parents' and children's income and concluded that mobility was, indeed, possible in the United States. These studies, however, relied on nonrandom, relatively homogenous samples of white, working men, and the studies typically used earnings or income estimates from a single year to generalize about lifetime earnings. None explicitly measured wealth, but most generalized their findings to wealth inequality as well as income inequality (Corcoran & Datcher 1981). By the late 1980s, new longitudinal data sets became available, and researchers began to uncover more evidence of status inheritance, but even these neglected wealth (Behrman & Taubman 1990, Zimmerman 1992).

Indeed, while some researchers attempted to incorporate wealth into their analyses, data limitations made this nearly impossible (Levy 1980). The researchers who have dominated the field of wealth distribution have occasionally used the panel Survey-of-Consumer-Finances data sets to estimate short-term trends in wealth ownership (see, for example, Wolff 1998). Short-term trends in mobility, however, tell us little about the intergenerational or life-course processes that lead to the persistence of either wealth or poverty. What is needed are longitudinal data on wealth ownership that would facilitate studies comparable to those conducted using the PSID's information on income.

Related to intergenerational processes is the inheritance of wealth. We know very little about how much wealth is actually inherited because data on inheritance is virtually nonexistent. Indeed, Menchik & Jianakoplos (1998) estimated that between the 1970s and 1990s, as little as 20% and as much as 80% of total wealth may have been inherited. Those who study inheritance typically refer to three forms of inheritance: inheritance at the death of a parent or other benefactor, inter-vivos transfers of money and other assets, and transfers of cultural capital (Miller & McNamee 1998:3). While we typically think of inheritance as occurring at the death of the benefactor, Kurz (1984) estimated that inter-vivos transfers account for nearly 90% of intergenerational wealth transfers. Miller & McNamee (1998:3) argue that cultural capital, transferred through formal education and informal experiences, is also a vital, inherited resource (Miller & McNamee 1998:3). Inheritance likely explains much of the persistence of wealth inequality. Racial differences in wealth ownership, for example, are bound to be exacerbated across generations if most wealth is inherited (Clignet 1998, Oliver & Shapiro 1995:152–156). Unfortunately, however, the majority of writing about inheritance processes addresses historical or legal issues because of data limitations (Chester 1998:23). Until such data are available, inheritance will likely remain a black box in most studies of wealth accumulation and distribution.

CONCLUSION

In this chapter, we reviewed recent literature that describes trends in wealth ownership and the distribution of wealth among households. We also examined research that proposes explanations of wealth inequality. We explored research that poses explanations for wealth inequality, including those that focus on aggregate explanations, those that concentrate on processes at the micro level, and those that attempt to integrate macro and micro explanations. We then discussed literature on intergenerational processes and mobility. We concluded that data limitations have made the study of wealth mobility nearly impossible, and we called for more comprehensive longitudinal data on asset ownership. Levels of wealth inequality are so extreme that most people register hardly any wealth at all, yet wealth is one of the most central indicators of financial well-being and security. To address this fundamental social problem, we must first acknowledge that it exists, and the first step in acknowledgment is acquiring adequate data to demonstrate the nature and causes of the problem. Only once we understand the problem better, can we decide what we are willing to do to alleviate it.

ACKNOWLEDGMENTS

We are grateful to Howard Aldrich, Judith Blau, Lori Campbell, and Rachel Rosenfeld for insightful comments, critiques, and suggestions.

Visit the Annual Reviews home page at www.AnnualReviews.org

LITERATURE CITED

Ando A, Modigliani F. 1963. The life-cycle hypothesis of saving: aggregate implications and tests. *Am. Econ. Rev.* 53:55–84

Angle J. 1986. The surplus theory of social stratification and the size distribution of personal wealth. *Soc. Forces* 65:293–326

Angle J. 1993. Deriving the size distribution of personal wealth from 'the rich get richer, the poor get poorer'. *J. Math. Sociol.* 18:27–46

Antoniewicz RL. 2000. A comparison of the household sector from the flow of funds accounts and the survey of consumer finances. *Board of Governors of Federal Reserve*

System, Finance and Economics, Discussion Ser. 96/26

Atkinson AT, ed. 1980. *Wealth, Income, and Inequality.* New York: Oxford Univ. Press. 2nd ed.

Avery RB, Elliehausen GE, Canner GB, Gustafson TA. 1984. Survey of consumer finances, 1983: a second report. *Fed. Reserve Bull.* Dec:857–68

Avery RB, Elliehausen GE, Canner GB, Gustafson TA. 1986a. Survey of consumer finances, 1983. *Fed. Reserve Bull.* March:163–77

Avery RB, Elliehausen GE, Canner GB, Gustafson TA, Springert J. 1986b. Financial characteristics of high-income families. *Fed. Reserve Bull.* 72:163–77

Avery RB, Elliehausen GE, Kennickell AB. 1988. Measuring wealth with survey data: an evaluation of the 1983 survey of consumer finances. *Rev. Income Wealth* 34:339–69

Baer W. 1992. *Race and the Shadow Market in Housing.* Los Angeles: Univ. South. Calif. Press

Bane MJ. 1986. Household composition and poverty. In *Fighting Poverty: What Works and What Doesn't,* ed. SH Danziger, DH Weinberg, pp. 209–31. Cambridge, MA: Harvard Univ. Press

Barth JR, Cordes JJ, Yezer AMJ. 1980. Redlining in housing markets. *J. Soc. Polit. Stud.* 5:221–42

Behrman JR, Taubman P. 1990. The intergenerational correlation between children's adult earnings and their parents' income. *Rev. Income Wealth* 36:115–27

Berger MC. 1985. The effect of cohort size on earnings growth: a reexamination of the evidence. *J. Polit. Econ.* 93:561–73

Berger MC. 1989. Demographic cycles, cohort size, and earnings. *Demography* 26:311–21

Bernheim R. 1987. Dissaving after retirement. In *Issues in Pension Economics,* ed. Z Bodie, JB Shoven, DA Wise, pp. 237–76. Chicago: Univ. Chicago Press

Blau FD, Graham JW. 1990. Black-white differences in wealth and asset composition. *Q. J. Econ.* May:321–39

Blau P, Duncan OD. 1967. *The American Occupational Structure.* New York: Wiley

Bomberger W. 1993. Income, wealth, and household demand for deposits. *Am. Econ. Rev.* 83:1034–44

Brimmer AF. 1988. Income, wealth, and investment behavior in the black community. *Am. Econ. Rev.* 78:151–55

Campbell R, Henretta J. 1980. Status claims and status attainment: the determinants of financial well-being. *Am. J. Sociol.* 86:618–29

Campbell RT, O'Rand AM. 1988. Settings and sequences: the heuristics of aging research. In *Emergent Theories of Aging,* ed. JE Birren, VL Bengston, pp. 58–79. New York: Springer

Cheal D. 1983. Intergenerational family transfers. *J. Marriage Fam.* 45:805–13

Chester R. 1998. Inheritance in American legal thought. In *Inheritance and Wealth in America,* ed. J Robert, K Miller, SJ McNamee, pp. 23–43. New York: Plenum

Clignet RP. 1998. Ethnicity and inheritance. In *Inheritance and Wealth in America,* ed. J Robert, K. Miller, SJ McNamee, pp. 119–38. New York: Plenum

Corcoran M. 1995. Rags to riches: poverty and mobility in the United States. *Annu. Rev. Sociol.* 21:237–67

Corcoran M, Datcher LP. 1981. Intergenerational status transmission and the process of individual attainment. In *Five Thousand American Families: Patterns of Economic Progress,* ed. MS Hill, DH Hill, JN Morgan. Ann Arbor, MI: Surv. Res. Cent.

Curtin R, Juster FT, Morgan J. 1989. Survey estimates of wealth: an assessment of quality. In *The Measurement of Saving, Investment, and Wealth,* ed. R Lipsey, HS Tice, pp. 473–551. Chicago: Univ. Chicago Press

Danziger S, DerGaag JV, Smolensky E, Taussig M. 1982. The life-cycle hypothesis and the consumption behavior of the elderly. *J. Post-Keynesian Econ.* 5:208–27

Danziger SH, Gottschalk P, Smolensky E. 1989.

How the rich fared, 1973-1987. *Am. Econ. Rev.* 79:310–14

Danziger SH, Gottschalk P, eds. 1993. *Uneven Tides: Rising Inequality in America.* New York: Russell Sage Found.

Danziger SH, Haveman RH, Plotnick RD. 1986. Antipoverty policy: effects on the poor and nonpoor. In *Fighting Poverty: What Works and What Doesn't*, ed. SH Danziger, DH Weinberg. Cambridge, MA: Harvard Univ. Press

Darby MR. 1979. *The Effects of Social Security on Income and the Capital Stock.* Washington, DC: Am. Enterprise Inst.

David M, Menchik P. 1988. Changes in cohort wealth over a generation. *Demography* 25:317–35

Davies JB. 1982. The relative impact of inheritance and other factors on economic inequality. *Q. J. Econ.* 97:471–98

Domhoff GW. 1970. *The Higher Circles.* New York: Random House

Domhoff GW. 1990. *The Power Elite and the State: How Policy is Made in America.* New York: Aldine de Gruyter

Duncan OD, Featherman DL, Duncan B. 1972. *Socioeconomic Background and Achievement.* New York: Seminar

Easterlin RA. 1987. *Birth and Fortune.* Chicago: Univ. Chicago Press. 2nd ed.

Easterlin RA, MacDonald C, Macunovich DJ. 1990. How have American baby boomers fared? Earnings and economic well-being of young adults, 1964–1987. *Popul. Econ.* 3:277–90

Easterlin RA, Schaeffer CM, Macunovich DJ. 1993. Will the baby boomers be less well off than their parents? Income, wealth, and family circumstances over the life cycle in the United States. *Popul. Dev. Rev.* 19:497–522

Featherman DL, Hauser RM. 1978. *Opportunity and Change.* New York: Academic

Fed. Reserve Syst. Board Gov. 1993. *Guide to the Flow of Funds Accounts.* Washington, DC: Board Gov. Fed. Reserve Syst.

Fischer S. 1973. A life cycle model of life insurance purchases. *Int. Econ. Rev.* 14:132–52

Fisher J. 1952. Income, spending and saving patterns of consumer units in different age groups. *Stud. Income Wealth* XV:89–122

Gale WG, Scholz JK. 1994. Intergenerational transfers and the accumulation of wealth. *J. Econ. Perspect.* 8:145–60

Galenson M. 1972. Do blacks save more? *Am. Econ. Rev.* 62:211–16

Gottschalk P, Danziger S. 1984. Macroeconomic conditions, income transfers and the trend in poverty. In *The Social Contract Revisited*, ed. DL Bawden. Washington, DC: Urban Inst. Press

Greenwood DT. 1983. An estimation of U.S. family wealth and its distribution from microdata, 1973. *Rev. Income Wealth* March:23–43

Greenwood DT. 1987. Age, income, and household size: their relation to wealth distribution in the United States. In *International Comparisons of the Distribution of Household Wealth*, ed. EN Wolff, pp. 121–40. New York: Oxford Univ. Press

Henretta JC. 1984. Parental status and child's homeownership. *Am. Sociol. Rev.* 49:131–40

Henretta JC. 1979. Race differences in middle class lifestyle: the role of home ownership. *Soc. Sci. Res.* 8:63–78

Henretta JC, Campbell R. 1978. Net worth as an aspect of status. *Am. J. Sociol.* 83:1024–1223

Holloway TM. 1991. The role of homeownership and home price appreciation in the accumulation and distribution of household sector wealth. *Bus. Econ.* 26:38–44

Horton HD. 1992. Race and wealth: a demographic analysis of black ownership. *Sociol. Inq.* 62:480–89

Hurd MD. 1987. Savings of the elderly and desired bequests. *Am. Econ. Rev.* 77:298–312

Hurd MD. 1990. Research on the elderly. *Am. Econ. Rev.* 77:298–312

Hurd MD, Mundaca G. 1989. The importance of gifts and inheritance among the affluent. In *The Measurement of Saving, Investment, and Wealth*, ed. RE Lipsey, HS Tice. Chicago: Univ. Chicago Press

Jackman MR, Jackman RW. 1980. Racial inequalities in home ownership. *Soc. Forces* 58:1221–33

Jencks C, Smith M, Acland H, Bane MJ, Cohen D, et al. 1972. *Inequality: A Reassessment of the Effect of Family and Schooling in America.* New York: Basic Books

Johnson BW, Woodburn L. 1994. The estate multiplier technique: recent improvements for 1989. In *Compendium of Federal Estate Tax and Personal Wealth Studies*, ed. IRS Dep. Treas. Washington, DC: IRS Stat. Income Div.

Keister LA. 2000a. Race and wealth inequality: the impact of racial differences in asset ownership on the distribution of household wealth. *Soc. Sci. Res.*

Keister LA. 2000b. *Wealth in America.* New York: Cambridge Univ. Press

Kennickell A, Shack-Marquez J. 1992. Changes in family finances from 1983 to 1989: evidence from the survey of consumer finances. *Fed. Reserve Bull.* 78:1–18

Kennickell AB, Starr-McCluer M. 1994. Changes in family finances from 1989 to 1992: evidence from the Survey of Consumer Finances. *Fed. Reserve Bull.* Oct:861–82

Kennickell AB, Starr-McCluer M. 1997. Household saving and portfolio change: evidence from the 1983–89 SCF Panel. *Rev. Income Wealth* Dec:381–99

Kennickell AB, Starr-McCluer M, Sunden AE. 1997. Family finances in the U.S.: recent evidence from the Survey of Consumer Finances. *Fed. Reserve Bull.* Jan:1–24

King MA, Dicks-Mireaux L-DL. 1982. Asset holdings and the life-cycle. *Econ. J.* 92:247–67

Kingson E. 1992. *The Diversity of the Baby Boom Generation: Implications for Their Retirement Years.* Washington, DC: Am. Assoc. Retired Persons

Kotlikoff LJ, Summers LH. 1981. The role of intergenerational transfers in aggregate capital accumulation. *J. Polit. Econ.* 89:706–32

Kurz M. 1984. Capital accumulation and the

characteristics of private intergenerational transfers. *Economica* 541:1–22

Lampman RJ. 1962. *The Share of Top Wealth-Holders in National Wealth, 1922–56.* Princeton, NJ: Princeton Univ. Press

Land KC, Russell ST. 1996. Wealth accumulation across the adult life course: stability and change in sociodemographic covariate structures of net worth data in the survey of income and program participation, 1984–1991. *Soc. Sci. Res.* 25:423–62

Lawrence EC. 1991. Poverty and the rate of time preference: evidence from panel data. *J. Polit. Econ.* 99:54–77

Lerman DL, Mikesell JJ. 1988. Rural and urban poverty: an income/net worth approach. *Policy Stud. Rev.* 7:765–81

Levy FS. 1980. *The Intergenerational Transfer of Poverty.* Washington, DC: Urban Inst.

Levy FS, Michel RC. 1986. An economic bust for the baby boom. *Challenge* 29:33–39

Levy FS, Michel RC. 1991. *The Economic Future of American Families: Income and Wealth Trends.* Washington, DC: Urban Inst.

Lewis FD. 1989. Dependents and the demand for life insurance. *Am. Econ. Rev.* 79:452–67

Manchester JM. 1993. *Baby Boomers in Retirement: An Early Perspective.* Washington, DC: Congr. US, Congr. Budget Off.

McLanahan S, Kelly E. 1999. Feminization of poverty: past and present. In *Handbook of Sociology of Gender*, ed. J Chafetz. New York: Plenum

Menchick P, David M. 1983. Income distribution, lifetime savings, and bequests. *Am. Econ. Rev.* 73:672–90

Menchik PL, Jiankoplos NA. 1998. Economics of inheritance. In *Inheritance and Wealth in America*, ed. J Robert, K Miller, SJ McNamee, pp. 45–59. New York: Plenum

Miller RK Jr, McNamee SJ, eds. 1998. *Inheritance and Wealth in America.* New York: Plenum

Mirer TW. 1979. The wealth-age relation among the aged. *Am. Econ. Rev.* 69:435–43

Mirer TW. 1980. The dissaving behavior of the retired aged. *South. Econ. J.* 46:1197–1205

Modigliani F. 1988a. Measuring the contribution of intergenerational transfers to total wealth: conceptual issues and empirical findings. In *Modelling the Accumulation and Distribution of Wealth*, ed. D Kessler, A Masson, pp. 21–52. New York: Oxford Univ. Press

Modigliani F. 1988b. The role of intergenerational transfers and life cycle saving in the accumulation of wealth. *J. Econ. Perspect.* 2:15–40

Modigliani F. 1992. Life cycle, individual thrift, and the wealth of nations. In *Nobel Lectures: Economic Sciences, 1981–1990*, ed. K-G Maler.

Modigliani F, Brumberg R. 1952. Utility analysis and aggregate consumption functions: an attempt at integration. Unpublished

Modigliani F, Brumberg R. 1954. Utility analysis and the consumption function: an interpretation of cross-sectional data. In *Post-Keynesian Economics*, ed. KK Kurihara. New Brunswick, NJ: Rutgers Univ. Press

Oliver ML, Shapiro TM. 1989. Race and wealth. *Rev. Black Polit. Econ.* 17:5–25

Oliver ML, Shapiro TM. 1990. Wealth of a nation: at least one-third of households are asset poor. *Am. J. Econ. Sociol.* 49:129–51

Oliver ML, Shapiro TM. 1995. *Black Wealth/White Wealth.* New York: Routledge

Ong P, Ill EG. 1988. Race and life cycle effects on home ownership in Los Angeles, 1970–1980. *Urban Aff. Q.* 23:601–15

Osberg L. 1984. *Economic Inequality in the United States.* New York: Sharpe

Parcel TL. 1982. Wealth accumulation of black and white men: the case of housing equity. *Soc. Probl.* 30:199–211

Pissarides CA. 1980. The wealth-age relation with life insurance. *Economica* 47:451–57

Radner DB. 1989a. Net worth and financial assets of age groups in 1984. *Soc. Secur. Bull.* 52:2–15

Radner DB. 1989b. The wealth of the aged and non-aged. In *The Measurement of Saving, Investment, and Wealth*, ed. R Lipsey, HS Tice, pp. 645–84. Chicago: Univ. Chicago Press

Radner DB, Vaughan DR. 1987. Wealth, income, and the economic status of aged households. In *International Comparisons of the Distribution of Household Wealth*, ed. EN Wolff, pp. 93–120. New York: Oxford Univ. Press

Sabelhaus J, Manchester J. 1995. Baby boomers and their parents: how does their economic well-being compare in middle age? *J. Hum. Resour.* 30:791–806

Sewell WH, Hauser RM. 1975. *Education, Occupation, and Earnings: Achievement in the Early Career.* New York: Academic

Sheiner L, Weil DN. 1992. The housing wealth of the aged. *Natl. Bur. Econ. Res. Work. Pap. No. 4115*

Shorrocks AF. 1975. The age-wealth relationship: a cross-section and cohort analysis. *Rev. Econ. Stat.* 57:158–63

Smith JD. 1987. Recent trends in the distribution of wealth in the U.S.: data, research problems, and prospects. In *International Comparisons of the Distribution of Household Wealth*, ed. EN Wolff, pp. 72–90. New York: Oxford Univ. Press

Steckel RH, Krishman J. 1992. Wealth mobility in America: a view from the national longitudinal survey. *Natl. Bur. Econ. Res. Work. Pap. Ser., Work. Pap. No. 4137.* Cambridge, MA

Straw KH. 1956. Consumer's net worth: the 1953 savings survey. *Bull. Oxf. Inst. Stat.* 18:1–60

Terrel HS. 1971. Wealth accumulation of black and white families: the empirical evidence. *J. Finance* 26:363–77

Torrey BB. 1988. Assets of the aged: clues and issues. *Popul. Dev. Rev.* 14:489–97

Torrey BB, Taeuber C. 1986. The importance of asset income among the elderly. *Rev. Income Wealth* 4:443–49

Weicher JC. 1995. Changes in the distribution of wealth: increasing inequality? *Fed. Reserve Bank St. Louis Rev.* 77:5–23

Weicher JC. 1997. Wealth and its distribution: 1983–1992: secular growth, cyclical stability. *Fed. Reserve Bank St. Louis Rev.* 79:3–23

Welch F. 1979. Effect of cohort size on earnings: the baby boom babies' financial bust. *J. Polit. Econ.* 87:S65–S97

White BB. 1978. Empirical tests of the life cycle hypothesis. *Am. Econ. Rev.* 68:547–60

Williams RM. 1975. Race and ethnic relations. *Annu. Rev. Sociol.* 1:125–64

Winnick A. 1989. *Toward Two Societies: The Changing Distributions of Income and Wealth in the U.S. Since 1960.* New York: Praeger

Wolff EN. 1980. Estimates of the 1969 size distribution of household wealth in the U.S. from a synthetic database. In *Modeling the Distribution and Intergenerational Transmission of Wealth*, ed. JD Smith, pp. 195–208. Chicago: Univ. Chicago Press

Wolff EN. 1983. The size distribution of household disposable wealth in the United States. *Rev. Income Wealth* 29:125–46

Wolff EN. 1987. Estimates of household wealth inequality in the U.S., 1962–1983. *Rev. Income Wealth* 33:231–56

Wolff EN. 1990. Wealth holdings and poverty status in the U.S. *Rev. Income Wealth* 36:143–65

Wolff EN. 1992. Changing inequality of wealth. *Am. Econ. Rev.* 82:552–58

Wolff EN. 1993. Trends in household wealth in the United States during the 1980s. *C.V. Starr Cent. Appl. Econ., New York Univ.*

Wolff EN. 1994. Trends in household wealth in the United States 1962–1983 and 1983–1994. *C.V. Starr Cent. Appl. Econ., New York Univ., #94-03*

Wolff EN. 1995a. The rich get increasingly richer: latest data on household wealth during the 1980s. In *Research in Politics and Society*, ed. RE Ratcliff, ML Oliver, TM Shapiro, 5:33–68. Greenwich, CT: JAI

Wolff EN. 1995b. *Top Heavy: A Study of the Increasing Inequality of Wealth in America.* New York: Twentieth Century Fund

Wolff EN, Marley M. 1989. Long term trends in U.S. wealth inequality: methodological issues and results. In *The Measurement of Saving, Investment, and Wealth*, ed. R Lipsey, HS Tice, pp. 765–839. Chicago: Univ. Chicago Press

Yaari ME. 1965. Uncertain lifetime, life insurance, and the theory of the consumer. *Rev. Econ. Stud.* 32:137–50

Zimmerman D. 1992. Regression towards mediocrity in economic stature. *Am. Econ. Rev.* 82:409–29

Annu. Rev. Sociol. 2000. 26:83–106

CRIME AND DEMOGRAPHY: Multiple Linkages, Reciprocal Relations

Scott J. South and Steven F. Messner

Department of Sociology, State University of New York at Albany, Albany, New York 12222; e-mail: s.south@albany.edu and s.messner@albany.edu

Key Words   deviance, family, life course, migration, race

■ **Abstract**   Individual demographic characteristics and aggregate population processes are central to many theoretical perspectives and empirical models of criminal behavior. Recent research underscores the importance of criminal and deviant behavior for understanding the demography of the life course and macrolevel population processes. We review research that explores the multiple linkages and reciprocal relations between criminal and demographic behavior at both microsocial and macrosocial levels. In reviewing research on how demography affects crime, we describe current debates over the impact of age, sex, and race on criminal behavior, and we distinguish between compositional and contextual effects of demographic structure on aggregate crime rates. Our review of how crime affects demography focuses on the intersection of criminal and demographic events in the life course, and the influence of criminal victimization and aggregate crime rates on residential mobility, migration, and population redistribution. Directions for future research on the many linkages between criminal and demographic behavior are discussed.

INTRODUCTION

Within sociology, the subfields of criminology and demography share several epistemological and scientific characteristics. Social statisticians of the eighteenth century, particularly Quetelet and Lexis (Stigler 1986), but also to some extent Durkheim (1897/1951), drew heavily on both criminological and demographic data. In the twentieth-century United States, the Chicago School emphasized the linkage between population dynamics and deviant behavior (Short 1971). Both criminology and demography have, to varying degrees and at various times, emphasized geographical variations and aggregate trends in their respective explananda, embraced biological explanations for these phenomena, and grounded their studies within a life-course perspective. From a methodological standpoint, both fields have traditionally favored quantitative over qualitative approaches.

The fields of criminology and demography also intersect in more substantive ways and at multiple levels. Our purpose here is to review and to some extent synthesize the extant research that explores the many interconnections between crime and demography. Although there is no single comprehensive theory that links criminal and demographic behavior, two related themes reverberate throughout our review. First, the study of crime and the study of demography intersect and interact in multiple arenas; some of these linkages are fairly obvious (though few are devoid of debate), but others are not. Second, while the effects of demographic characteristics and population structure on criminal and deviant behavior are widely acknowledged, the influence of crime and deviance on demographic behavior and population structure are, we believe, recognized less often and appreciated less well.

Our review is divided into two main sections. In the first section, we explore how demography, broadly construed, affects crime. The extensive amount of research on this topic necessitates a somewhat selective approach, and thus we focus on topics that have been at the center of theoretical and empirical debates. Our discussion addresses the question of how three main demographic statuses—age, sex, and race—influence criminal offending and victimization at both micro and macro levels.

The second main section reviews studies that, in some form, examine the effects of criminal and deviant behavior on the three primary demographic processes of mortality, fertility (and nuptiality), and migration (and residential mobility). We give particular attention to life-course studies of the impact of criminal events and behaviors on demographic outcomes, including marriage, divorce, and childbearing, and point to the indirect effects of crime on these behaviors. We also review both microlevel and macrolevel studies that explore the influence of criminal offending and victimization on the geographic redistribution of population.

HOW DEMOGRAPHY AFFECTS CRIME

Demographic phenomena are highly relevant to crime at both the individual and macro levels of analysis. Our discussion below begins with a review of three individual demographic correlates of crime: age, sex, and race. We identify the widely reported relationships between demographic characteristics and crime, and we review important debates concerning the interpretation of these relationships. Next, we explain the difference between "compositional" and "contextual" arguments over the effects of population structure on crime, and we illustrate these arguments with reference to the literature.

Individual Demographic Characteristics and Crime

The primary demographic characteristics of age, sex, and race are among the most powerful and robust individual-level risk factors for criminal offending and victimization. Evidence consistently indicates that young people, males, and members of disadvantaged minorities are at comparatively high risk of becoming offenders and victims, at least with respect to the common "street" crimes (for reviews, see Messner & Rosenfeld 1999, Sampson & Lauritsen 1994, 1996, Steffensmeier

& Allen 1996, Steffensmeier et al 1989). Indeed, it is hardly an exaggeration to claim that much of the sociological theorizing in criminology essentially represents an effort to account for the well-documented "demographic facts" about crime (cf. Braithwaite 1989, pp. 44–53).

Although the general patterns pertaining to these demographic characteristics and crime are well established, controversies about the specific nature of the patterns and their interpretation persist. One noteworthy debate surrounds the claim of "age invariance," advocated by Hirschi & Gottfredson (1983; see also Gottfredson & Hirschi 1990, pp. 123–144). Hirschi & Gottfredson do not challenge the inference that the young are disproportionately involved in crime. Rather, they propose that the age-crime relationship is invariant with respect to social characteristics (e.g., gender, race, income, marital status), and thus this relationship cannot be accounted for by the standard factors identified in sociological theories of criminality. They propose instead that the widely observed "desistance" from crime with age reflects nothing more than the simple aging of the human organism.

Hirschi & Gottfredson's claim of age invariance not only challenges sociological explanations for the age-crime relationship. It also calls into question the "criminal career" paradigm and undermines the rationale for longitudinal research designs (Blumstein et al 1988a,b). Presumably, all meaningful variation across individuals in offending should be reflected in a cross-sectional design if the age-crime relationship is in fact a constant.

Not surprisingly, the age-invariance hypothesis has been vigorously challenged. For example, using Uniform Crime Reports arrest data for two-year averages at three time points (1939–1940, 1960–1961, 1980–1981), Steffensmeier et al (1989) report that age-crime curves are not "invariant" strictly speaking; they vary for different offenses, and key features of these curves have changed over time (see also Greenberg 1985). More recent work has also challenged the view that the age-crime relationship in the aggregate adequately captures offending patterns for the entire population. A series of studies based on cohort data in different locales indicates that multiple groups or categories of offenders can be differentiated on the basis of their distinctive offending trajectories (D'Under et al 1998, Laub et al 1998, Nagin et al 1995, Nagin & Land 1993).

Another important debate related to age involves the persistence of antisocial behavior over the life span. A well-established finding in the literature is that misbehavior in childhood is one of the most powerful predictors of adult deviance and criminality (Krohn et al 1999, Sampson & Laub 1993). Two influential interpretations of this relationship have been advanced: the latent trait perspective and the life-course perspective (for general discussions, see Moffitt 1997, Simons et al 1998). The latent trait perspective maintains that the propensity to commit crime is developed at young ages, and that this propensity remains reasonably stable throughout life. Continuity in antisocial behavior thus reflects the stable differences in criminal propensities across individuals. In contrast, the life-course perspective emphasizes developmental processes. Misbehavior at a young age leads to responses, events, and transitions that tend to enhance and accentuate early behavioral tendencies, thereby generating behavioral stability. However, the life-course perspective views the correlation between early and later behavior as imperfect. Certain life transitions can alter and redirect behavioral trajectories.

Studies providing rigorous assessments of these approaches are just beginning to accumulate. Although some evidence supports aspects of the latent trait perspective (Paternoster & Brame 1998), the drift of the evidence seems to be in the direction of life-course theories (Bartusch et al 1997, Simons et al 1998). Of particular relevance to the present discussion is the role of the key demographic transition of marriage. Research suggests that marriage can alter offending trajectories and reduce the likelihood of adult crime. Identifying the mechanisms through which marriage exerts such a crime-preventive effect has emerged as in important issue in the literature (e.g., Horney et al 1995, Laub et al 1998, Warr 1998).[1]

The demographic characteristic of sex has also been at the center of much criminological inquiry. Similar to age, there is virtually universal agreement concerning the general pattern: Males are disproportionately involved in crime as both victims and offenders, especially for the more serious, violent offenses. Once again, however, controversies and unresolved issues about the nature and interpretation of gender differences in crime persist.

An on-going debate concerns stability or change in the gender gap in offending. For decades, criminologists have speculated about the implications of greater gender equality for the relative involvement of males and females in criminal behavior. One view that has received considerable media attention links higher female offending with more egalitarian gender roles, the so-called "dark side of female liberation" (Steffensmeier & Allan 1996, p. 468). Analyses of arrest rates by Steffensmeier & Allan (1996) question the extent to which the gender gap has actually decreased significantly over the recent decades during which gender roles have been changing (1960–1990). With the exception of minor property crimes, the percentage of females among arrestees has remained fairly stable.

At the same time, there is a strong theoretical rationale for anticipating a link between gender equality and a reduced gender gap. Consider the influential power-control theory of delinquency put forth by Hagan and colleagues (Hagan et al 1987, 1990). Power-control theory stipulates that greater equality in the workplace in authority relations for husbands and wives translates into more egalitarian (in contrast with patriarchal) relations in families. More egalitarian family relations, in turn, result in more similar socialization of sons and daughters, similar preferences for risk, and a smaller gender differential in delinquency.

Although power-control theory has been subjected to a number of empirical and theoretical critiques (Akers 1997, pp. 198–99), recent work by Grasmick and colleagues (Grasmick et al 1993, 1996) has offered renewed support for the approach. They report that gender differences in risk preferences are related to

---

[1] Research also indicates that marital status affects victimization, but that this effect varies by gender. Kposowa & Singh (1994) report that marriage reduces the risk of homicide victimization for males but increases the risk for females.

family relations in the manner predicted by the theory. At the same time, other scholars have argued for a prediction opposite to that implied by power-control theory: gender *inequality* should increase the likelihood of female crime because of the criminogenic consequences of disadvantage, as stipulated in most conventional theories of the causes of crime (Steffensmeier & Allan 1996, pp. 469–70). The effect of greater gender equality on the relative offending levels of males and females remains an open question.

Another key issue relevant to the relationship between sex and crime is the impact of gender inequality on female *victimization*. To illustrate, Bailey & Peterson (1995) hypothesize that female homicide victimization is inversely related to both the status of women in an absolute sense and the status of women relative to men. When the status of women is high, either relatively or absolutely, women are likely to be afforded greater legal protection, and men are less "free" to use violence against women. They assess these hypotheses with data for a sample of 138 US cities in 1980. They find no support for the hypothesis concerning absolute status, but they report that several measures of the status of women relative to men exhibit the expected effects on female homicide victimization. In contrast, research by Brewer & Smith (1995), also using data for US cities, indicates a meager impact of measures of gender inequality on female homicide victimization rates, net of the effects of standard structural determinants. At the societal level, Gartner et al (1990) have examined the influence of women's status on the differential between male and female homicide victimization. They find that greater status resources for women leads to a larger "gender gap" in victimization because female victimization decreases relative to male victimization.

One additional area of special interest in the study of gender and crime has been the adequacy of "gender-neutral" versus "gender-specific" explanations. The research suggests that, at least for minor forms of crime and delinquency, the predictors of criminal involvement are reasonably similar for males and females (Steffensmeier & Allan 1996, Mazerolle 1998; for contrary findings, see Simpson & Elis 1995). At the same time, criminologists recognize that the nature of involvement in crime tends to differ for women in comparison with men. For example, using data from the National Youth Survey, Triplett & Myers (1995) find that females offend in fewer settings and in a different manner than males. Moreover, the more serious the offense, the greater are the differences by gender. Similarly, in an analysis of active robbery offenders, Miller (1998) discovers that while the motives for robbery are similar for men and women, their enactment of the crime is quite different (see also Alarid et al 1996). Further inquiry into the distinct contexts surrounding male and female offending is clearly an important task for future research.

The characteristic of "race" is the most controversial demographic correlate of crime. Official arrest statistics have long suggested that African Americans are overrepresented as offenders for most types of serious crimes. Although some of the racial differences observed in official statistics can be attributed to differential responses by the criminal justice system, criminologists generally agree that there are real differences in behavior as well (Sampson & Lauritsen 1994, 1996). Race is thus almost always included in analyses of crime and delinquency as an individual-level control variable. However, as Sampson (1997, p. 58) observes, there has been a general reluctance "to speak openly about the race and crime connection," and thus the theoretical mechanisms underlying the race-crime connection are not well understood.

Traditionally, explanations of racial differences in crime have juxtaposed cultural arguments with social structural arguments. The cultural approaches have pointed to an alleged "subculture of violence" (Wolfgang & Ferracuti 1967) or a "violent contraculture" (Curtis 1975) among African Americans. The most influential structural approaches, in contrast, have identified economic strain and disadvantage rooted in race as the criminogenic forces underlying racial differences in crime (Blau & Blau 1982, Blau & Schwartz 1984). A good deal of research has been inspired by the culture/structure debate, the results of which are highly conflicting (for reviews, see Messner & Rosenfeld 1999, Parker et al 1999).

Recent work on the race-crime relationship entails several new points of departure. Sampson & Wilson (1995) have urged researchers to consider not only individual status characteristics when considering structural factors (e.g., poverty status, unemployment, family disruption) but also the larger community context. The evidence reveals clearly that the "ecological niches" occupied by whites and blacks tend to be quite disparate. Blacks are much more likely to confront concentrated disadvantage (Wilson 1987, 1996). For example, "racial differences in poverty and family disruption are so strong that the worst urban contexts in which whites reside are considerably better off than the average context of black communities" (Sampson 1997, pp. 61–62). This implies that racial differences in crime that persist with controls for individual status characteristics may reflect unmeasured features of the larger structural context.

To address this possibility, studies based on multilevel research designs have increasingly begun to appear in the criminological literature (Elliott et al 1996, Miethe & McDowall 1993, Rountree et al 1994, Sampson & Wooldredge 1987, Smith & Jarjoura 1988). These studies combine data on aggregate-level variables with individual characteristics, thereby permitting assessments of main effects of aggregate context along with the net effects of individual-level predictors once contextual factors have been statistically controlled. Research by Peeples & Loeber (1994) suggests that such multilevel analyses may help explain, at least to some extent, racial differences in crime. Using data for a sample of public school boys in Pittsburgh, they construct a measure of the underclass status of respondents' neighborhoods and examine the effects of race on delinquency controlling for neighborhood context. They report that race is related to several indicators of delinquency at the bivariate level, consistent with past research. They also observe that delinquent involvement of African American boys who reside outside of underclass neighborhoods is generally similar to that of white boys. Moreover, when they estimate a hierarchical regression equation with both individual-level factors and the neighborhood-level variable, race has no net effect on the delinquency measures, whereas residence in an underclass neighborhood has a significant positive effect.

Another distinguishing feature of recent efforts to explain the race-crime relationship is recognition of the interconnections between cultural and structural factors. Ethnographic studies have described how the distinctive structural contexts encountered by blacks foster cultural adaptations that are conducive to widespread crime and violence. For example, Anderson (1994) explains how the disadvantages and social dislocations in contemporary urban ghettoes lead to a "code of the streets" whose norms are at odds with conventional society's (see also Furstenberg 1993). Rose & McClain (1998) develop similar themes, arguing that the upsurge of black violence in the 1985–1993 period can be understood as the result of growing alienation from mainstream values and the emergence of an "oppositional culture" among young black males.

Finally, researchers have become increasingly sensitive to the need to go beyond the simple black/white dichotomy in the study of crime. Hawkins (1999) points out that homicide rates of African Americans have varied considerably across places and in comparison with other racial/ethnic groups historically. Similarly, Martinez & Lee (1999) document noteworthy differences in the rates of lethal violence between and within ethnic groups, focusing primarily on Latinos. Further inquiry into the diversity and complexity of racial/ethnic patterns of crime is likely in the years ahead.

Population Structure and Crime

In addition to efforts to document and explain individual demographic correlates of crime, researchers have devoted extensive attention to the effects of population structure on crime. The most straightforward implication of population structure for crime involves "compositional effects." If persons with differing demographic characteristics are at higher or lower risk of criminal involvement, then some of the variation in levels of crime across social collectivities will be due to differences in population composition, i.e., the relative size of the respective demographic groups. Accordingly, demographic factors are routinely controlled in aggregate studies of crime.

One technique to adjust for variation in demographic structure is the computation of "standardized" crime rates. The general logic of this approach is to use information on group-specific criminal involvement (e.g., age/sex-specific offending or victimization) and to estimate the rates that would be observed if all aggregate units exhibited the same, standard population structure. For example, Deane (1987) uses an indirect standardization technique to enhance cross-national comparisons of homicide rates.[2] He reports that the differences between homicide levels in the United States and other nations are reduced when variation in age and sex composition is taken into account (see also Phillips 1997).

---

[2]Given the lack of age/sex-specific data on homicide victimization for all nations, Deane is unable to employ direct standardization. In the indirect procedure, a standard country (in this case, the United States) provides the demographic-specific rates. The actual age/sex distributions and total numbers of incidents in various countries are then used to compute the indirectly standardized rates.

Researchers have also examined the extent to which crime trends can be attributed to changes in population composition, especially age composition, and have offered forecasts about future trends in crime based on projected demographic patterns. This research has underscored the contribution of the postwar baby boom in the United States to increasing crime rates in the 1960s and falling rates in the 1980s (Cohen & Land 1987, Fox 1978, Steffensmeier & Harer 1991, 1999; but see also Smith & Feiler 1995).

The most common procedure in the criminological literature to accommodate compositional effects is to include indicators of population structure on the right-hand side of a multiple regression equation. Features of population composition such as the sex ratio and the percentage of the population in specified age groups are standard control variables in aggregate studies of crime, at both the intra-national and the cross-national levels (for reviews, see LaFree 1999, Neopolitan 1997, Sampson & Lauritsen 1994). Interestingly, indicators of age/sex composition do not always relate to crime rates in the predicted manner, suggesting that the generalizability of individual-level relationships to the macro level is more complicated than expected (see, for example, Messner & Sampson 1991). Researchers also frequently include measures of racial composition in aggregate analyses of crime. The effects of these measures are rather unstable in multivariate models because of severe collinearity between racial composition and other structural factors (Land et al 1990).

In addition to the compositional effects associated with population distributions, demographic structure has been theorized as an important *causal* factor for crime. From this perspective, features of population structure alter the criminal motivations, the opportunities for crime, and the controls against crime for the population at large. In other words, these explanations emphasize the implications of population structure for the general context in which people act, and as such, they are often referred to as "contextual" explanations.

Perhaps the best-known causal explanation linking crime and population structure is social disorganization theory. Classical social disorganization theory identifies demographic processes and structures such as population growth, population turnover (migration and residential instability), and racial/ethnic heterogeneity as critical factors affecting a neighborhood's capacity to exert informal social control and to limit criminal activity (Bursik 1988). Social disorganization theory continues to provide a theoretical linkage between features of population structure and crime in contemporary macro level research (Parker et al 1999, Sampson et al 1997). Cross-national studies reveal a positive effect of indicators of population growth on homicide rates, although the evidence is somewhat mixed (LaFree 1999, Neopolitan 1997). At the community level, Sampson & Groves (1989) find that residential stability is associated with low rates of crime and victimization, an effect that occurs primarily through local friendship networks. Several studies based on metropolitan areas similarly report that migration exhibits positive effects on rates of both violent and property crime (Crutchfield et al 1982, Messner 1986, South 1987). Research by Tittle & Paternoster (1988) indicates that at the individual level residential mobility affects self-reported criminal behavior indirectly through reduced commitments to conventional norms, although this effect apparently varies by type of offense.

With respect to race, researchers typically anticipate a compositional effect and treat the relative size of the black (or nonwhite) population as a control variable (but recall the multicollinearity problem noted above). An exception is the work by Sampson (1985). Sampson argues that subculture-of-violence explanations of racial differences in crime imply a genuine contextual effect. Presumably, for subcultures to emerge, there must be a sufficient "critical mass" of persons. The logic of this argument implies not only a relationship between the relative size of the nonwhite population and the total crime rate (the compositional effect), but also a relationship between racial composition and the race-specific crime rate (i.e., the rate for nonwhites). Sampson finds no effect of racial composition on the nonwhite homicide rate in a sample of cities, contrary to the conventional subculture-of-violence hypothesis (see also Sampson 1987). Subsequent analyses also based on racially disaggregated data suggest that residential segregation, concentrated poverty, and social isolation from mainstream society are key determinants of black crime rates (Peterson & Krivo 1993, Shihadeh & Flynn 1996).

A somewhat different approach to the study of racial composition and crime shifts attention away from total crime rates to the racial patterning of crime. Drawing on Blau's (1977) macro-structural theory, South & Messner (1986, Messner & South 1986; see also South & Felson 1990) argue that racial composition and residential segregation affect the opportunities for social contacts between the races and, as a result, these structural characteristics should be related to levels of intra- and interracial crime. They find general support for their hypotheses in analyses of violent victimization using data from the National Crime Survey's Cities Sample. Applying a similar logic, O'Brien (1987) demonstrates that the apparent tendency for black offenders to seek out white victims in violent crimes is simply a function of relative group size. Violent crimes are actually far more *intra*-racial in nature than would be expected under models of statistical independence given the prevailing racial distributions of the population.

Turning to age, a highly influential contextual approach to crime is Easterlin's work on relative cohort size. Easterlin (1987) hypothesizes that members of relatively large birth cohorts are likely to experience less social control in childhood and adolescence because the size of the cohort strains the capacities of institutions of social control. Later in life, members of these large cohorts confront limited economic opportunities due to greater crowding in the labor market. Given the logic of conventional "strain" and "control" theories of crime, the prediction follows that relatively large birth cohorts will have high crime rates. A sustained tradition of research assessing the Easterlin thesis has developed, with rather mixed results (Maxim 1985, Pampel & Gartner 1995, O'Brien 1989, Savolainen 2000, Smith 1986, Steffensmeier et al 1992). Nevertheless, the theory continues to inspire inquiry on the criminogenic consequences of varying age distributions (e.g., Pampel & Gartner 1995).

Recently, O'Brien et al (1999) have expanded cohort theory to encompass an additional feature of age cohorts: the proportion of a cohort growing up in single-parent homes. This attribute of cohorts is expected to be related to criminogenic propensities through two general mechanisms. First, single-parent households are at high risk of poverty, which hinders their capacity to provide valuable resources to their children. Second, because children often have contacts with parents of friends, all children within cohorts characterized by large numbers of single-parent families (not simply those in single-parent families themselves) are likely to encounter less social control and adult supervision. In an age-period-cohort model using US data for 1960–1995, O'Brien et al (1999) find that the relative size of a cohort and its percentage of nonmarital births have significant positive effects on arrest rates for homicide. Moreover, these effects persist throughout the life span.

A final illustration of a theoretical explanation of crime that assigns primary importance to demographic structure is the research by South & Messner (1987) on the sex ratio and women's involvement in crime. Drawing on Guttentag & Secord's (1983) general theory relating societal-level sex ratios to women's life circumstances, South & Messner argue that the sex ratio affects the cultural valuation of women and the emphasis placed on traditional domestic roles for women. These values and roles are expected, in turn, to affect women's rate of victimization and offending, and their protection by the criminal justice system. The results of their analyses based on a sample of 60 countries offer some support for their hypotheses. A high sex ratio (i.e., a numerical abundance of men relative to women) decreases the rate of female property offending relative to men's and increases the percentage of rape cases solved by the police (an indicator of protection by the criminal justice system).

In sum, the research literature amply documents the myriad effects of demographic factors on crime and victimization at both the individual and macro levels of analysis. It is hardly an exaggeration to claim that demography broadly construed is indispensable to a sociological understanding of crime.

HOW CRIME AFFECTS DEMOGRAPHY

The bulk of the sociological literature addressing the linkages between crime and demography examines the impact of individual demographic statuses and aggregate population structure on criminal offending and deviant behavior. An emerging body of research has begun to explore how various dimensions of crime and deviance influence demographic outcomes. Research on this latter issue tends to be less cohesive and less organized around key theoretical debates than research examining the effects of demography on crime. However, by acknowledging the reciprocal effects of crime on demography, this developing literature provides a more nuanced and more complete characterization of the crime/demography nexus. Various studies have examined the impact of crime and deviance on the three major demographic processes of mortality, fertility, and migration, and here we review the research in each of these areas.

Homicide Mortality

Perhaps the most straightforward way in which crime influences demography is that homicide is, quite obviously, a cause of death. For some demographic groups, homicide is a particularly prominent cause of death and, accordingly, exerts a significant influence on life expectancy. In 1996, for the US population as a whole, there were 20,738 deaths from homicide and legal intervention, making this the fourteenth leading cause of death (Ventura et al 1997). But this ranking masks considerable variability among age, race, and sex groups (Anderson et al 1997). For example, in 1995, homicide and legal intervention was the second leading cause of death among persons age 15–24, and the third leading cause of death at ages 5–14. Homicide is the leading cause of death among both black males and black females ages 15–24. The homicide death rate for black males in this age group (132.0 per 100,000 population) is more than double the death rate from second leading killer, accidents (50.1 per 100,000 population).

Life-table analyses of cause-specific death rates show not only that homicide mortality exerts a substantial influence on life expectancy (Keith & Smith 1988), but also that race and sex differences in homicide rates account for a significant portion of race and sex differences in overall life expectancy. For example, among males, the higher homicide rates for blacks than for whites accounts for about 20% of the racial difference in life expectancy at birth (Keith & Smith 1988). Among blacks, the higher homicide rate among males than among females accounts for more than 15% of the sex difference in life expectancy (Keith & Smith 1988).

Crime, Deviance, and Family Demography

Just as criminological studies have explored the effects of demographic events and statuses on criminal involvement and deviant behavior, a small but developing literature has begun to examine the impact of criminal and deviant behaviors on the occurrence and timing of key demographic events in the life course. Given demography's traditional concern with the timing of such pivotal events as birth, marriage and divorce, death, and other "life" transitions, it is not surprising that this field was one of the first to embrace the life-course perspective (Elder 1975, Hogan 1978). Yet, demographers have generally not included criminal and deviant behaviors as explanatory variables in their empirical models of these events. And, despite calls for research examining the intersection and reciprocal influences of criminal and noncriminal events and behaviors (Hagan & Palloni 1988, Thornberry 1987), the field of criminology has been slow to adopt the life-course approach (Sampson & Laub 1990, 1992). Consequently, relatively few studies have examined the effects of criminal and deviant behavior on the timing of key demographic events in the life course.

In several papers drawing simultaneously on longitudinal life and drug histories, Yamaguchi & Kandel (1985a,b, 1987) examine the impact of marijuana and other illicit drug use on the timing of family-related events. They find that marijuana use during adolescence delays entry into marriage and parenthood, and increases the risk of marital dissolution (Yamaguchi & Kandel 1985b). Moreover, illicit drug use is associated with an increased probability of premarital cohabitation and increases the likelihood that a premarital cohabitation ends in separation rather than legal marriage (Yamaguchi & Kandel 1985a). Among women, the use of illicit drugs other than marijuana substantially raises the risk of a premarital pregnancy and, conditional upon becoming pregnant, drug use increases the likelihood of obtaining an abortion rather than having a live birth (Yamaguchi & Kandel 1987). Krohn et al (1997) find that alcohol and drug use during adolescence increases the risk of becoming pregnant (or, for males, impregnating a woman) and becoming a teenage parent. In turn, experiencing these life-course transitions prematurely raises the risk of alcohol and drug use in later life. Jessor et al (1991), however, suggest that problem behavior during adolescence is only weakly related to subsequent demographic transitions such as marriage, parenthood, and divorce.

Other forms of deviant behavior also appear to influence the timing of important demographic transitions in the life course. Gang membership, chronic drug use, and violent criminal offending, for example, all significantly increase the risk of becoming a teenage father, net of demographic and socioeconomic characteristics of young men and their families (Thornberry et al 1997). Having suicidal thoughts and running away from home are associated with early marriage and parenthood, perhaps reflecting a latent desire to exit from the role of adolescent (Hagan & Wheaton 1993).

An important but relatively unexplored issue in life-course studies linking criminal and deviant behaviors to demographic events is whether the former actually cause the latter or, alternatively, whether both types of events are attributable to common (but unmeasured) traits and predispositions. To the extent that deviant and criminal involvement creates peer pressure that socializes adolescents and young adults to engage in early sexual activity or to delay marriage, the observed associations between criminal and demographic events may indeed be causal in nature. A process of this type is broadly consistent with the developmental interpretation of the persistence of antisocial behavior over the life course described above. Conversely, deviant behaviors and non-normative or problematic demographic behaviors, such as early nonmarital childbearing, might share a common origin that accounts for their observed association, an interpretation consistent with the latent trait perspective. Because studies in this area usually control for a substantial battery of socioeconomic and sociodemographic characteristics, it is unlikely that the association between these types of behaviors can be attributed to social class or demographic background. But the associations may lie in shared psychosocial, or perhaps even biological, origins. It is perhaps worth noting in this regard that both demography and criminology have begun to explore biological determinants. For example, demographers have linked men's testosterone levels to delayed marriage and an increased likelihood of divorce (Booth & Dabbs 1993), and adolescents' hormonal development to early sexual behavior (Udry 1988, 1995, Udry et al 1985, 1986). Criminologists have attempted to link biological characteristics to aggression and other forms of deviant and criminal behavior (Fishbein 1990, Reiss et al 1994).

Both criminology and demography have also begun to emphasize neighborhood factors as primary determinants of behavior. Recent studies of sexual activity, marriage, and fertility—particularly nonmarital fertility—suggest that, independent of individual and family characteristics, neighborhood characteristics exert an important influence (Billy & Moore 1992, Billy et al 1994, Brewster 1994, Brewster et al 1993; Brooks-Gunn et al 1993, South & Crowder 1999). In general, these studies suggest that, compared to economically advantaged neighborhoods, the initiation of sexual activity occurs earlier (Billy et al 1994), and the risk of out-of-wedlock or teenage childbearing is greater (Brooks-Gunn et al 1993, Crane 1991, Hogan & Kitagawa 1985, Ku et al 1993), in economically disadvantaged communities. Criminology, of course, has long recognized local neighborhoods as primary settings for the genesis and transmission of criminal and deviant behavior (e.g., Shaw & McKay 1942), and, as noted above, the impact of neighborhood characteristics on criminal behavior has recently been approached with renewed vigor (Sampson et al 1997, Simons et al 1996). Given the parallel recognition by both demographers and criminologists of the importance of neighborhood effects, it may be worth exploring the possibility that the observed associations between criminal and demographic activities and events stem at least partly from shared neighborhood-level factors. Moreover, similar intervening mechanisms, including association with deviant peers, collective social control, and access to social capital, may link neighborhood characteristics to both deviant and demographic behaviors.

Crime and lethal violence may affect family-related demographic events through more subtle, macrosocial mechanisms as well. High rates of homicide and incarceration reduce the number of eligible males available to serve as sexual and marital partners for women, a situation that is especially acute for African Americans (Tucker & Mitchell-Kiernan 1995). In turn, this numerical deficit of males reduces women's marriage rates (Lichter et al 1991, 1992) and increases rates of out-of-wedlock childbearing and female-headed families (Fossett & Kiecolt 1993, Sampson 1995, South & Lloyd 1992a,b). To the extent that criminal offending and deviant behavior detract from the "desirability" of men in women's marriage markets, either directly or indirectly by diminishing men's economic status and employment stability, then these behaviors would also influence women's marriage and fertility patterns. However, it appears that few if any studies have attempted to quantify the impact of criminal and deviant behavior on the supply of potential and desirable mates available to women (or, for that matter, men).

Crime could conceivably influence fertility and nuptiality through more psychological mechanisms as well. For example, Wilson & Daly (1997) argue that high levels of homicide lead to steep future discounting among the urban poor. The low life expectancy among those with high homicide risks leads to a compressed time horizon and a consequent disinclination to defer major life transitions, including parenthood. Indirect evidence for this linkage is provided in the Wilson & Daly (1997) study of 77 Chicago community areas, where they observe age-specific birth rates through age 30 in neighborhoods with low life expectancies that are higher than in neighborhoods with high life expectancies. However, alternative interpretations for the earlier age at childbearing in distressed neighborhoods are also possible.

Crime, Migration, and Residential Mobility

Much of the research examining the impact of crime on demography focuses on effects of some aspect of criminal activity on residential mobility, migration, or overall population redistribution. Using survey data, several studies have examined the effect of an individual's or household's perceptions of neighborhood crime on the intention to move and on actual residential mobility. The evidence is somewhat mixed. In general, the belief that crime is an important neighborhood problem (Droettboom et al 1971) and satisfaction with neighborhood safety (Taub et al 1984) appear to be related to the intention or motivation to move, but perceptions of neighborhood crime do not appear to be a strong or consistent predictor of actual residential mobility (Droettboom et al 1971, Newman & Duncan 1979, South & Deane 1993). As Dugan (1999) suggests, one reason for this weak relationship is that a household's perceived seriousness of crime may be only weakly related to its actual risk of victimization. Skogan (1990) finds that, in a sample of 40 neighborhoods, a multi-item measure of neighborhood social disorder, which includes households' perceptions of neighborhood vandalism, drugs, and gangs, is strongly positively correlated with the percentage of neighborhood residents who intend to move within the next several years. Neighborhood social disorder directly affects plans to move and also indirectly affects mobility intentions by reducing neighborhood satisfaction. In perhaps the most direct evidence for this relationship, Dugan (1999) finds that households in which a member has been a victim of a crime are significantly more likely to move than households that are free from victimization. This relationship holds for both violent crimes and property crimes, and for both recent and more distal victimizations. Consistent with the idea that criminal victimization creates dissatisfaction with the neighborhood of residence, and through this, the desire to move, the impact of victimization on subsequent residential mobility is strongest for victimizations occurring in the respondents' immediate neighborhood. However, the effect of criminal victimization on residential mobility is weaker than conventional predictors of moving, such as age of the household head, home ownership, and duration of residence (Dugan 1999).

A more common strategy for examining the impact of crime on residential mobility is to link official crime rates at the neighborhood or city level to aggregate population flows. Early studies in this genre were concerned primarily with examining the effect of central-city social problems, including crime, on suburbanization and, in particular, white flight. Although the evidence here is also not entirely consistent, several studies reveal relatively small and often nonsignificant effects of city crime rates on city-to-suburb population flows and metropolitan deconcentration. Neither Guterbock (1976) nor Bradbury et al (1982) observes a significant effect of central-city crime rates on the spatial deconcentration of the total metropolitan population, while Frey (1979) and Marshall (1979) observe significant, but moderate, effects on the suburbanization of whites. Frey (1979) finds that high central city crime rates increase white city-to-suburb mobility largely by increasing the likelihood that movers will select a suburban rather than a central-city location, rather than by increasing the overall incidence of mobility. Marshall (1979) finds a modest but significant effect of the central-city crime rate on city-to-suburb mobility, but no impact of the crime rate on the rate of migration into central cities. Yet, Marshall & O'Flaherty (1987) find no effect of central-city crime rates on the probability that mobile white households without children will relocate to the suburbs rather than to a different central-city location. And South & Crowder (1997) find that, for black but not white families, high central-city violent crime rates relative to the suburban ring are positively associated with both the likelihood of leaving the central-city neighborhood and, conditional upon moving, the probability of selecting a suburban, rather than a different central-city, destination. South & Crowder (1997) find no effect of the ratio of central-city violent crime rates to suburban crime rates on the probability that suburban residents will move to the central city. In contrast, Katzman (1980), in a study of Dallas neighborhoods, finds little effect of the neighborhood property crime rate (as measured by official statistics) on out-mobility, but he also finds that neighborhood crime is inversely related to in-movement, especially for affluent families with children. Morenoff & Sampson (1997), in a study of Chicago census tracts between 1970 and 1990, report that high levels of homicide and increases in spatial proximity to neighborhoods with high homicide rates led to declines in the size of the neighborhood population during the subsequent decade. However, the effects of *increases* in neighborhood homicide rates and *increases* in the proximity to high-homicide neighborhoods varied by race. Both neighborhood characteristics were associated with white population loss and black population gain, suggesting that blacks are less able than whites to escape neighborhoods with increasing homicide rates and homicide potential.

Some observers suggest that high neighborhood crime rates and residential instability may be mutually reinforcing (Schuerman & Kobrin 1986). High rates of crime and violence drive out relatively affluent households, which leads to a weakened tax base, deteriorating institutional structure, and loss of civic leadership, which in turn lead to escalating crime rates (Wilson 1987). Crime and class-selective out-migration may thus intertwine in a downward spiral of neighborhood decay.

Supportive evidence for a link between crime and migration also comes from city-level studies. Sampson & Wooldredge (1986), in a study of the 55 largest US cities, find a significant negative effect of the 1970 crime rate both on overall population change between 1970 and 1980 and on the net migration rate over this period. The effects persist in the face of numerous controls and operate similarly for blacks and whites. Liska & Bellair (1995) extend this line of analysis by, among other things, examining the effect of city crime rates on decadal changes in the racial composition of US cities between 1950 and 1990. They find significant positive effects of the city robbery rate on changes in the percentage of the city population that is nonwhite and on growth in the size of the white population. From these effects they conclude that robbery rates play a substantial role in engendering white flight from central cities. Generally similar results are reported for a sample of US suburbs (Liska et al 1998). That African Americans are more likely than whites to live in high-crime neighborhoods, even after adjusting for racial differences in socioeconomic status (Alba et al 1994), also implies that blacks may be less able than whites to move out of high-crime areas.

Either implicitly or explicitly, most studies of the influence of crime on population movement focus on local or short-distance moves, e.g., out of the neighborhood, or from a central city to one of its suburbs. However, in some historical contexts, crime and violence may be important instigators of longer-distance migration. Tolnay & Beck (1990, 1992, 1995), for example, link racial violence against blacks in the American South between 1910 and 1930 to the migration of African Americans to the North during this period. In a study of ten Southern states, they find that counties where more lynchings of blacks had occurred witnessed significantly higher levels of black out-migration. They also find reciprocal effects: higher levels of black out-migration were associated with fewer lynchings in subsequent years.

Collectively, these studies suggest that exposure to crime and violence has an important influence on migration and residential mobility. To be sure, there are troubling inconsistencies across studies, and differences in research designs, methodological approaches, samples, measures, and control variables make it difficult to reconcile these discrepancies or to propose sweeping conclusions regarding this relationship. But several tentative generalizations can be advanced. First, actual victimization experience is a stronger predictor of mobility than are often vague perceptions of the level or seriousness of neighborhood crime. Second, at least at the aggregate level, violent crime may be more important than property crime in inducing out-mobility or deterring in-mobility. Third, African Americans are less able than whites to escape living in or near areas with high or increasing rates of crime. And fourth, at both the individual and ecological levels, victimization experience and aggregate crime rates are just two of many factors that shape population movements.

CONCLUSIONS

The fields of criminology and demography intersect and inform one another at multiple levels. Demographic variables, including age, sex, and race, are indispensable explanatory factors in many models of criminal and deviant behavior, and demographic methods, particularly standardization, are used frequently in criminological research. A growing body of research recognizes the potential for reciprocal effects of crime on demography, underscoring the importance of criminal and deviant behavior for life-course transitions and aggregate population processes.

Future research examining the impact of demography on crime might profit by further attempts to explain how and why the principal demographic attributes of age, sex, and race shape criminal behavior. The consistency and strength of these demographic determinants of crime and delinquency warrant continued efforts to develop theories that identify the causal mechanisms underlying these well-established associations. At the macro level, distinguishing between compositional and contextual effects of demographic structure on crime remains a fertile ground for research. Multilevel research designs and statistical models may have much to offer here.

Research exploring the influence of crime on demography, while still relatively inchoate, might benefit by focusing further on the implications of criminal and delinquent behavior for demographic and other life-course transitions. Determining whether the observed associations between criminal behavior and demographic events are truly causal, or whether both result from unmeasured latent traits or common environmental influences, may require richer—and especially longitudinal—data sets and more sophisticated statistical models than have been conventionally used to answer this question. And, although the weight of the evidence suggests that crime and victimization have important ramifications for individual residential mobility and aggregate migration patterns, future research in this area may serve to resolve troubling inconsistencies in empirical findings.

At a general level, we suggest that one of the main contributions of demography to criminology is to underscore the utility of a structural perspective in the study of crime and deviant behavior. Demography reminds us that characteristics such as age, sex, and race locate people in social space; these individual attributes give rise to systematic, patterned social relations with others. At the macro level, demography directs attention to the important ways in which population distributions yield the distinctive contexts in which individuals commit—or refrain from committing—criminal acts. The demographic emphasis on social structure thus constitutes an important counter-balance to the reductionist tendencies that periodically surface in criminology (Bursik 1988, Stark 1987).

With respect to the contribution of criminology to demography, criminologists alert demographers to behaviors that on the surface might not seem "demographic" but that are relevant to their inquiry. Engaging in, or being exposed to, criminal and deviant behaviors may exert an important influence on the timing and sequencing of key demographic events such as marriage, childbearing, and residential mobility. At the macro level, aggregate crime rates appear to be significant instigators of migration and population redistribution. Criminology, in other words, can help expand the scope of potential explanatory variables in models of demographic behavior (Hagan & Wheaton 1993).

Of course, criminal and demographic behaviors and statuses are linked in ways other than those addressed in this review. The influence of key demographic characteristics, particularly race and sex, on criminal justice processing, the impact of childhood family structure on delinquent and criminal behavior, and the effects of deviant (and criminal) behavior on nonhomicidal mortality are just a few of the other ways in which demography and crime influence one another. Research on these and other linkages will enhance our understanding of both criminal and demographic behavior and, consequently, contribute to the development of both disciplines.

ACKNOWLEDGMENTS

The authors contributed equally to this paper. Preparation of this paper was partially supported by a grant to the first author from the National Science Foundation (SBR-9729797). We thank Marv Krohn and Stewart Tolnay for helpful comments.

Visit the Annual Reviews home page at www.AnnualReviews.org

LITERATURE CITED

Akers RL. 1997. *Criminological Theories: Introduction and Evaluation.* Los Angeles, CA: Roxbury. 2nd ed.

Alarid LF, Marquart JW, Burton VS Jr, Cullen FT, Cuvelier SJ. 1996. Women's roles in serious offenses: a study of adult felons. *Justice Q.* 13:431–54

Alba RD, Logan JR, Bellair PE. 1994. Living with crime: the implications of racial/ethnic differences in suburban location. *Soc. Forc.* 73:395–434

Anderson E. 1994. The code of the streets. *Atlantic Monthly* 273:80–94

Anderson RN, Kochanek KD, Murphy SL. 1997. Report of final mortality statistics, 1995. *Monthly Vital Statist. Rep.* 45 (supplement 2):1–80

Bailey WC, Peterson RD. 1995. Gender inequality and violence against women. In *Crime and Inequality,* ed. J Hagan, RD Peterson, pp. 174–205. Stanford, CA: Stanford Univ. Press

Bartusch DRJ, Lynam DR, Moffitt TE, Silva PA. 1997. Is age important? Testing a general versus a developmental theory of antisocial behavior. *Criminology* 35:13–48

Billy JOG, Brewster KL, Grady WR. 1994. Contextual effects on the sexual behavior of adolescent women. *J. Marriage Fam.* 56:387–404

Billy JOG, Moore DE. 1992. A multilevel analysis of marital and nonmarital fertility in the United States. *Soc. Forc.* 70:977–1011

Blau PM. 1977. *Inequality and Heterogeneity: A Primitive Theory of Social Structure.* New York: Free Press

Blau JR, Blau PM. 1982. The cost of inequality: metropolitan structure and violent crime. *Am. Sociol. Rev.* 47:114–29

Blau PM, Schwartz JE. 1984. *Crosscutting Social Circles.* New York: Academic Press

Blumstein A, Cohen J, Farrington DP. 1988a. Criminal career research: its value for criminology. *Criminology* 26:1–35

Blumstein A, Cohen J, Farrington DP. 1988b. Longitudinal and criminal career research: further clarifications. *Criminology* 26:57–74

Booth A, Dabbs Jr JM. 1993. Testosterone and men's marriages. *Soc. Forc.* 72:463–77

Bradbury KL, Downs A, Small KA. 1982. *Urban Decline and the Future of American Cities.* Washington, DC: Brookings

Braithwaite J. 1989. *Crime, Shame, and Reintegration.* Cambridge: Cambridge Univ. Press

Brewer VE, Smith MD. 1995. Gender inequality and rates of female homicide victimization across U.S. cities. *J. Res. Crime Delinq.* 32:175–90

Brewster KL. 1994. Racial differences in sexual activity among adolescent women: the role of neighborhood characteristics. *Am. Sociol. Rev.* 59:408–24

Brewster KL, Billy JOG, Grady WR. 1993. Social context and adolescent behavior: the impact of community on the transition to sexual activity. *Soc. Forc.* 71:713–40

Brooks-Gunn J, Duncan GJ, Klebanov PK, Sealand N. 1993. Do neighborhoods influence child and adolescent development? *Am. J. Sociol.* 99:353–95

Bursik Jr. R. 1988. Social disorganization and theories of crime and delinquency: problems and prospects. *Criminology* 26:519–52

Cohen LE, Land KC. 1987. Age structure and crime: symmetry versus asymmetry and the projection of crime rates through the 1990s. *Am. Sociol. Rev.* 52:170–83

Crane J. 1991. The epidemic theory of ghettos and neighborhood effects on dropping out and teenage childbearing. *Am. J. Sociol.* 96:1226–59

Crutchfield RD, Geerken MR, Gove WR. 1982. Crime rate and social integration: the impact of metropolitan mobility. *Criminology* 20:467–78

Curtis LA. 1975. *Violence, Race, and Culture.* Lexington, MA: DC Heath

Deane GD. 1987. Cross-national comparison of homicide: age/sex-adjusted rates using the 1980 U.S. homicide experience as a standard. *J. Quant. Criminology* 3:215–27

Droettboom Jr T, McAllister RJ, Kaiser EJ, Butler EW. 1971. Urban violence and residential mobility. *Am. Inst. Plan.* 37:319–25

Dugan LJ. 1999. The effect of criminal victimization on a household's moving decision. *Criminology* 37:903–30

D'Under AV, Land KC, McCall P, Nagin DS. 1998. How many latent classes of delinquent/criminal careers? results from mixed Poisson regression analyses. *Am. J. Sociol.* 103:1593–630

Durkheim E. 1897/1951. *Suicide: a Study in Sociology.* Transl. JA Spaulding, G Simpson. New York: Free

Easterlin RA. 1987. *Birth and Fortune: The Impact of Numbers on Personal Welfare.* Chicago: Univ. Chicago Press. 2nd ed.

Elder GH Jr. 1975. Age differentiation and the life course. *Annu. Rev. Sociol.* 1:165–90

Elliott DS, Wilson WJ, Huizinga D, Sampson RJ, Elliott A, Ranjkin B. 1996. The effects of neighborhood disadvantage on adolescent development. *J. Res. Crime Delinq.* 33:389–426

Fishbein DH. 1990. Biological perspectives in criminology. *Criminology* 28:27–72

Fossett MA, Kiecolt KJ. 1993. Mate availability and family structure among African Americans in U.S. metropolitan areas. *J. Marriage Fam.* 55:288–301

Fox JA. 1978. *Forecasting Crime Data.* Lexington, MA: Lexington

Frey WH. 1979. Central city white flight: racial and nonracial causes. *Am. Sociol. Rev.* 44:425–48

Furstenburg F. 1993. How families manage risk and opportunity in dangerous neighborhoods. In *Sociology and the Public Agenda*, ed. WJ Wilson, pp. 231–58. Newbury Park, CA: Sage

Gartner R, Baker K, Pampel FC. 1990. Gender stratification and the gender gap in homicide victimization. *Soc. Prob.* 37:593–612

Grasmick HG, Blackwell BS, Bursik RJ Jr. 1993. Changes in the sex patterning of perceived threats of sanctions. *Law Soc. Rev.* 27:679–705

Grasmick HG, Hagan J, Blackwell BS, Arneklev BJ. 1996. Risk preferences and patriarchy: extending power-control theory. *Soc. Forc.* 75:177–99

Greenberg D. 1985. Age, crime, and social explanation. *Am. J. Sociol.* 91:1–21

Gottfredson MR, Hirschi T. 1990. *A General Theory of Crime.* Stanford, CA: Stanford Univ. Press

Guterbock TM. 1976. The push hypothesis: minority presence, crime, and urban deconcentration. In *The Changing Face of the Suburbs*, ed. B Schwartz. Chicago: Univ. Chicago Press

Guttentag M, Secord PF. 1983. *Too Many Women? The Sex Ratio Question*. Beverly Hills, CA: Sage

Hagan J, Gillis AR, Simpson J. 1987. Class in the household: a power-control theory of gender and delinquency. *Am. J. Sociol.* 92:788–816

Hagan J, Gillis AR, Simpson J. 1990. Clarifying and extending power-control theory. *Am. J. Sociol.* 95:1024–37

Hagan J, Palloni A. 1988. Crimes as social events in the life course: reconceiving a criminological controversy. *Criminology* 26:87–100

Hagan J, Wheaton B. 1993. The search for adolescent role exits and the transition to adulthood. *Soc. Forc.* 71:955–80

Hawkins DF. 1999. What can we learn from data disaggregation? The case of homicide and African Americans. In *Homicide: A Sourcebook of Social Research*, ed. MD Smith, MA Zahn, pp. 195–210. Thousand Oaks, CA: Sage

Hirschi T, Gottfredson M. 1983. Age and the explanation of crime. *Am. J. Sociol.* 89:552–84

Hogan DP. 1978. The variable order of events in the life course. *Am. Sociol. Rev.* 43:573–86

Hogan DP, Kitagawa EM. 1985. The impact of social status, family structure, and neighborhood on the fertility of black adolescents. *Am. J. Sociol.* 90:825–52

Horney J, Osgood DW, Marshall IH. 1995. Criminal careers in the short-term: intra-individual variability in crime and its relation to local life circumstances. *Am. Sociol. Rev.* 60:655–73

Jessor R, Donovan JE, Costa FM. 1991. *Beyond Adolescence: Problem Behavior and Young Adult Development*. Cambridge: Cambridge Univ. Press

Katzman MT. 1980. The contribution of crime to urban decline. *Urban Stud.* 17:277–86

Keith VM, Smith DP. 1988. The current differential in black and white life expectancy. *Demography* 25:625–32

Kposowa AJ, Singh GK. 1994. The effect of marriage on male and female homicides in the United States. *Sociol. Focus* 27:343–62

Krohn MD, Lizotte AJ, Perez CM. 1997. The interrelationship between substance use and precocious transitions to adult statuses. *J. Health Soc. Behav.* 38:87–103

Krohn MD, Thornberry TP, Rivera C. 1999. *Later careers of very young offenders*. Pap. prep. Off. of Juvenile Justice and Delinq. Prevent. Study Group on Very Young Offenders.

Ku L, Sonenstein FL, Pleck JH. 1993. Neighborhood, family, and work: influences on the premarital behaviors of adolescent males. *Soc. Forc.* 72:479–503

LaFree G. 1999. A summary and review of cross-national research of homicide. In *Homicide: A Sourcebook of Social Research*, ed. MD Smith, MA Zahn, pp. 125–45. Thousand Oaks, CA: Sage

Land KC, McCall PL, Cohen LE. 1990. Structural covariates of homicide: Are there any invariances across time and social space? *Am. J. Sociol.* 95:922–63

Laub JH, Nagin DS, Sampson SJ. 1998. Trajectories of change in criminal offending: good marriages and the desistance process. *Am. Sociol. Rev.* 63:225–38

Lichter DT, LeClere FB, McLaughlin DK. 1991. Local marriage market conditions and the marital behavior of black and white women. *Am. J. Sociol.* 96:843–67

Lichter DT, McLaughlin DK, Kephart G, Landry DJ. 1992. Race and the retreat from marriage: a shortage of marriageable men? *Am. Sociol. Rev.* 57:781–99

Liska AE, Bellair PE. 1995. Violent crime rates and racial composition: convergence over time. *Am. J. Sociol.* 101:578–610

Liska AE, Logan JR, Bellair PE. 1998. Race and violent crime in the suburbs. *Am. Sociol. Rev.* 63:27–38

Marshall H. 1979. White movement to the suburbs: a comparison of explanations. *Am. Sociol. Rev.* 44:975–94

Marshall H, O'Flaherty K. 1987. Suburbanization in the seventies: the "push-pull" hypothesis revisited. *J. Urban Affairs* 9:249–62

Martinez R Jr, Lee MT. 1999. Extending ethnicity in homicide research: the case of Latinos. In *Homicide: A Sourcebook of Social Research*, ed. MD Smith, MA Zahn, pp. 211–20. Thousand Oaks, CA: Sage

Maxim P. 1985. Cohort size and juvenile delinquency: a test of the Easterlin hypothesis. *Soc. Forc.* 63:661–79

Mazerolle P. 1998. Gender, general strain, and delinquency: an empirical examination. *Justice Q.* 15:65–91

Messner SF. 1986. Geographical mobility, governmental assistance to the poor, and rates of urban crime. *J. Crime Justice* 9:1–18

Messner SF, Rosenfeld R. 1999. Social structure and homicide: theory and research. In *Homicide: A Sourcebook of Social Research*, ed. MD Smith, MA Zahn, pp. 27–41. Thousand Oaks, CA: Sage

Messner SF, Sampson RJ. 1991. The sex ratio, family disruption, and rates of violent crime: the paradox of demographic structure. *Soc. Forc.* 69:693–713

Messner SF, South SJ. 1986. Economic deprivation, opportunity structure, and robbery victimization: intra- and interracial patterns. *Soc. Forc.* 64:975–91

Miethe TD, McDowall D. 1993. Contextual effects in models of criminal victimization. *Soc. Forc.* 71:741–59

Miller J. 1998. Up it up: gender and the accomplishment of street robbery. *Criminology* 36:37–66

Moffitt T. 1997. Adolescent-limited and life-course persistent offending: a complementary pair of developmental theories. In *Developmental Theories of Crime and Delinquency*, ed. TP Thornberry, pp. 11–54. New Brunswick, NJ: Transaction

Morenoff JD, Sampson RJ. 1997. Violent crime and the spatial dynamics of neighborhood transition: Chicago, 1970–1990. *Soc. Forc.* 76:31–64

Nagin DS, Farrington DP, Moffitt TE. 1995. Life-course trajectories of different types of offenders. *Criminology* 33:111–39

Nagin DS, Land KC. 1993. Age, criminal careers, and population heterogeneity: specification and estimation of a nonparametric, mixed Poisson model. *Criminology* 31:163–89

Neopolitan JL. 1997. *Cross-National Crime: A Research Review and Sourcebook.* Westport, CT: Greenwood

Newman SJ, Duncan GJ. 1979. Residential problems, dissatisfaction, and mobility. *J. Am. Planning Assoc.* 45:154–66

O'Brien RM. 1987. The interracial nature of violent crime: a reexamination. *Am. J. Sociol.* 92:817–35

O'Brien RM. 1989. Relative cohort size and age-specific crime rates: an age-period-relative cohort size model. *Criminology* 27:57–78

O'Brien RM, Stockard J, Isaacson L. 1999. The enduring effects of cohort characteristics on age-specific homicide rates, 1960–95. *Am. J. Sociol.* 104:1061–95

Pampel FC, Gartner R. 1995. Age structure, socio-political institutions, and national homicide rates. *Eur. Sociol. Rev.* 16:243–60

Parker KF, McCall PL, Land KC. 1999. Determining social-structural predictors of homicide: units of analysis and related methodological concerns. In *Homicide: A Sourcebook of Social Research*, ed. MD Smith, MA Zahn, pp. 107–124. Thousand Oaks, CA: Sage

Paternoster R, Brame R. 1998. The structural similarity of processes generating criminal and analogous behaviors. *Criminology* 36:633–69

Peeples F, Loeber R. 1994. Do individual factors and neighborhood context explain ethnic differences in juvenile delinquency? *J. Quant. Crim.* 10:141–57

Peterson RD, Krivo LJ. 1993. Racial segregation and Black urban homicide. *Soc. Forc.* 71:1001–26

Phillips JA. 1997. Variation in African-American homicide rates: an assessment of potential explanations. *Criminology* 35:527–59

Reiss AJ Jr, Miczek KA, Roth JA, eds. 1994. *Understanding and Preventing Violence, Volume 2: Biobehavioral Influences.* Washington, DC: Natl. Acad. Press

Rose HM, McClain PD. 1998. *Race, Place, and Risk* revisited: a perspective on the emergence of a new subcultural paradigm. *Homicide Stud.* 2:101–29

Rountree PW, Land K, Miethe TD. 1994. Macro-micro integration in the study of victimization: a hierarchical logistic model analysis across Seattle neighborhoods. *Criminology* 32:387–414

Sampson RJ. 1985. Race and criminal violence: a demographically disaggregated analysis of urban homicide. *Crime Delinq.* 31:47–82

Sampson RJ. 1987. Urban black violence: the effect of male joblessness and family disruption. *Am. J. Sociol.* 93:348–82

Sampson RJ. 1995. Unemployment and imbalanced sex ratios: race-specific consequences for family structure and crime. In *The Decline of Marriage among African Americans*, ed. MB Tucker, C Mitchell-Kiernan, pp. 229–54. New York: Russell Sage Found.

Sampson RJ. 1997. The embeddedness of child and adolescent development: a community-level perspective on urban violence. In *Violence and Childhood in the Inner City*, ed. J McCord, pp. 31–77. Cambridge: Cambridge Univ. Press

Sampson RJ, Groves WB. 1989. Community structure and crime: testing social-disorganization theory. *Am. J. Sociol.* 94:774–802

Sampson RJ, Laub JH. 1990. Crime and deviance over the life course: the salience of adult social bonds. *Am. Sociol. Rev.* 55:609–27

Sampson RJ, Laub JH. 1992. Crime and deviance in the life course. *Annu. Rev. Sociol.* 18:63–84

Sampson RJ, Laub JH. 1993. *Crime in the Making: Pathways and Turning Points Through Life.* Cambridge, MA: Harvard Univ. Press

Sampson RJ, Lauritsen JL. 1994. Violent victimization and offending: individual-, situational-, and community-level risk factors. *In Understanding and Preventing Violence*, ed. AJ Reiss, Jr, JA Roth, 3:1–114. Washington, DC: Natl. Acad. Press

Sampson RJ, Lauritsen JL. 1996. Racial and ethnic disparities in crime and criminal justice in the United States. In *Crime and Justice*, ed. M Tonry, 22:1–64. Chicago: Univ. Chicago Press

Sampson RJ, Raudenbush SW, Earls F. 1997. Neighborhoods and violent crime: a multilevel study of collective efficacy. *Science* 277:918–24

Sampson RJ, Wilson WJ. 1995. Toward a theory of race, crime, and urban inequality. In *Crime and Inequality*, ed. J Hagan, RD Peterson, pp. 37–56. Stanford, CA: Stanford Univ. Press

Sampson RJ, Wooldredge JD. 1986. Evidence that high crime rates encourage migration away from central cities. *Sociol. Soc. Res.* 70:310–14

Sampson RJ, Wooldredge JD. 1987. Linking the micro- and macro-level dimensions of lifestyle-routine activity and opportunity models of predatory victimization. *J. Quant. Criminol.* 3:371–93

Savolainen J. 2000. Relative cohort size and age-specific arrest rates: a conditional interpretation of the Easterlin effect. *Criminology.* In press

Schuerman L, Kobrin S. 1986. Community careers in crime. In *Communities and Crime*, ed. AJ Reiss, Jr, M Tonry, pp. 67–100. Chicago: Univ. Chicago Press

Shaw CR, McKay HD. 1942. *Juvenile Delinquency and Urban Areas.* Chicago: Univ. Chicago Press

Shihadeh ES, Flynn N. 1996. Segregation and crime: the effect of Black social isolation on the rates of Black urban violence. *Soc. Forc.* 74:1325–52

Short JF Jr. 1971. Introduction. In *The Social*

Fabric of the Metropolis: Contributions of the Chicago School to Urban Sociology, ed. JF Short, Jr, pp. xi–xlvi. Chicago: Univ. Chicago Press

Simons RL, Johnson C, Beaman J, Conger RD, Whitbeck LB. 1996. Parents and peer group as mediators of the effect of community structure on adolescent problem behavior. *Am. J. Comm. Psych.* 24:145–71

Simons RL, Johnson C, Conger RD, Elder G Jr. 1998. A test of latent trait versus life-course perspectives on the stability of adolescent antisocial behavior. *Criminology* 36:217–43

Simpson SS, Elis L. 1995. Doing gender: sorting out the caste and crime conundrum. *Criminology* 33:47–81

Skogan WG. 1990. *Disorder and Decline: Crime and the Spiral of Decay in American Neighborhoods*. Berkeley, CA: Univ. Calif. Press

Smith DR, Jarjoura GR. 1988. Social structure and criminal victimization. *J. Res. Crime Delinq.* 25:27–53

Smith MD. 1986. The era of increased violence in the United States: age, period, or cohort effect? *Sociol. Q.* 27:239–51

Smith MD, Feiler SM. 1995. Absolute and relative involvement in homicide offending: contemporary youth and the baby boom cohorts. *Violence Victims* 10:327–33

South SJ. 1987. Metropolitan migration and social problems. *Soc. Sci. Q.* 68:3–18

South SJ, Crowder KD. 1997. Residential mobility between cities and suburbs: race, suburbanization, and back-to-the-city moves. *Demography* 34:525–38

South SJ, Crowder KD. 1999. Neighborhood effects on family formation: concentrated poverty and beyond. *Am. Soc. Rev.* 64:113–32

South SJ, Deane GD. 1993. Race and residential mobility: individual determinants and structural constraints. *Soc. Forc.* 72:147–67

South SJ, Felson RB. 1990. The racial patterning of rape. *Soc. Forc.* 69:71–93

South SJ, Lloyd KM. 1992a. Marriage markets and nonmarital fertility in the United States. *Demography* 29:247–64

South SJ, Lloyd KM. 1992b. Marriage opportunities and family formation: further implications of imbalanced sex ratios. *J. Marriage Fam.* 54:440–51

South SJ, Messner SF. 1986. Structural determinants of intergroup association: interracial marriage and crime. *Am. J. Sociol.* 91:1409–30

South SJ, Messner SF. 1987. The sex ratio and women's involvement in crime: a cross-national analysis. *Sociol. Q.* 28:171–88

Stark R. 1987. Deviant places: a theory of the ecology of crime. *Criminology* 25:893–909

Steffensmeier D, Allan EA. 1996. Gender and crime: toward a gendered theory of female offending. *Annu. Rev. Sociol.* 22: 45–87

Steffensmeier D, Allan EA, Harer MD, Streifel C. 1989. Age and the distribution of crime. *Am. J. Sociol.* 94:803–31

Steffensemier D, Harer MD. 1991. Did crime rise or fall during the Reagan presidency? the effects of an "aging" U.S. population on the nation's crime rate. *J. Res. Crime Delinq.* 28:330–59

Steffensmeier D, Harer MD. 1999. Making sense of recent U.S. crime trends, 1980 to 1996/1998: age composition effects and other explanations. *J. Res. Crime. Delinq.* 36:235–74

Steffensmeier D, Streifel C, Shihadeh ES. 1992. Cohort size and arrest rates over the life course: the Easterlin hypothesis reconsidered. *Am. Sociol. Rev.* 57:306–14

Stigler SM. 1986. *The History of Statistics: the Measurement of Uncertainty before 1900*. Cambridge, MA: Harvard Univ. Press

Taub RP, Taylor DG, Dunham J. 1984. *Paths of Neighborhood Change: Race and Crime in Urban America*. Chicago: Univ. Chicago Press

Thornberry TP. 1987. Toward an interactional theory of delinquency. *Criminology* 25:863–91

Thornberry TP, Smith CA, Howard GJ. 1997. Risk factors for teenage fatherhood. *J. Marriage Fam.* 59:505–22

Tittle CR, Paternoster R. 1988. Geographic mobility and criminal behavior. *J. Res. Crime Delinq.* 25:301–43

Tolnay SE, Beck EM. 1990. Black flight: lethal violence and the great migration, 1900 to 1930. *Soc. Sci. Hist.* 14:347–70

Tolnay SE, Beck EM. 1992. Racial violence and black migration in the south, 1910 to 1930. *Am. Sociol. Rev.* 57:103–16

Tolnay SE, Beck EM. 1995. *A Festival of Violence: An Analysis of Southern Lynchings, 1882–1930.* Urbana and Chicago: Univ. Illinois Press

Triplett R, Myers LB. 1995. Evaluating contextual patterns of delinquency: gender-based differences. *Justice Q.* 12:59–84

Tucker MB, Mitchell-Kiernan C. 1995. African American marital trends in context: toward a synthesis. In *The Decline in Marriage among African Americans*, ed. MB Tucker, C Mitchell-Kiernan, pp. 345–61. New York: Russell Sage Found.

Udry JR. 1988. Biological predispositions and social control in adolescent sexual behavior. *Am. Sociol. Rev.* 53:709–22

Udry JR. 1995. Sociology and biology: What biology do sociologists need to know? *Soc. Forc.* 73:1267–78

Udry JR, Billy JOG, Morris NM, Groff TR, Raj MH. 1985. Serum androgenic hormones motivate sexual behavior in adolescent boys. *Fertility Sterility* 43:90–94

Udry JR, Talbert LM, Morris N. 1986. Biosocial foundations for adolescent female sexuality. *Demography* 23:217–30

Ventura SJ, Peters KD, Martin JA, Maurer JD. 1997. Births and deaths: United States, 1996. *Monthly Vital Statist. Rep.* 46 (supplement 2):1–41

Warr M. 1998. Life-course transitions and desistance from crime. *Criminology* 36:183–216

Wilson M, Daly M. 1997. Life expectancy, economic inequality, homicide, and reproductive timing in Chicago neighbourhoods. *Br. Med. J.* 314:1271–74

Wilson WJ. 1987. *The Truly Disadvantaged: The Inner City, the Underclass, and Public Policy.* Chicago: Univ. Chicago Press

Wilson WJ. 1996. *When Work Disappears: The World of the New Urban Poor.* New York: Knopf

Wolfgang ME, Ferracuti F. 1967. *The Subculture of Violence: Towards an Integrated Theory in Criminology.* London: Tavistock

Yamaguchi K, Kandel DB. 1985a. Dynamic relationships between premarital cohabitation and illicit drug use: an event-history analysis of role selection and role socialization. *Am. Sociol. Rev.* 50:530–46

Yamaguchi K, Kandel DB. 1985b. On the resolution of role incompatibility: a life event history analysis of family roles and marijuana use. *Am. J. Sociol.* 90:1284–1325

Yamaguchi K, Kandel DB. 1987. Drug use and other determinants of premarital pregnancy and its outcome: a dynamic analysis of competing life events. *J. Marriage Fam.* 49:257–70

Annu. Rev. Sociol. 2000. 26:107–33

ETHNICITY AND SEXUALITY

Joane Nagel

*Department of Sociology, University of Kansas, Lawrence, Kansas 66045;
e-mail: nagel@ukans.edu*

Key Words race, ethnicity, nationalism, sexuality, queer theory

■ **Abstract** This paper explores the connections between ethnicity and sexuality. Racial, ethnic, and national boundaries are also sexual boundaries. The borderlands dividing racial, ethnic, and national identities and communities constitute ethnosexual frontiers, erotic intersections that are heavily patrolled, policed, and protected, yet regularly are penetrated by individuals forging sexual links with ethnic "others." Normative heterosexuality is a central component of racial, ethnic, and nationalist ideologies; both adherence to and deviation from approved sexual identities and behaviors define and reinforce racial, ethnic, and nationalist regimes. To illustrate the ethnicity/sexuality nexus and to show the utility of revealing this intimate bond for understanding ethnic relations, I review constructionist models of ethnicity and sexuality in the social sciences and humanities, and I discuss ethnosexual boundary processes in several historical and contemporary settings: the sexual policing of nationalism, sexual aspects of US–American Indian relations, and the sexualization of the black-white color line.

INTRODUCTION

US Army photographers documented the liberation of France from German Nazi occupation by Allied forces in August 1944. The image captured in Figure 1 is a now-famous picture of two women who were accused of sexually collaborating with the Nazis in occupied France during the Second World War. In the photograph are visible the women's shaved heads, shoeless feet, stripped clothing, and swastikas tattooed on the women's foreheads. A young Frenchwoman, whose father was in the French resistance, described the fate of French women who were similarly identified as Nazi collaborators.

> The war was not finished, but in Paris it assumed another form—more perverse, more degrading ... The "shorn woman" of rue Petit-Musc ... walked along with her wedge-soled shoes tied around her neck, stiff like those undergoing a major initiation. Her face was frozen like a Buddha, her carriage tense and superb in the midst of a shouting, screeching mob of faces contorted by hatred, groping and opportunistic hands, eyes congested by excitement, festivity, sexuality, sadism (Weitz 1995:277).

0360-0572/00/0815-0107$14.00

Figure 1

This picture was published in a pictorial history of World War Two (Ambrose 1997:492). On the adjacent page of that volume is another photograph. It shows a man on his knees with a blindfold over his eyes; he is just about to be executed with a shot to the head. He is also a French collaborator, but the difference in the images and the treatment of the women and the man speak volumes about the sexualized and gendered nature of patriotism, treason, betrayal, and the relation and relative importance of men and women to the nation.

First, we can see that national and sexual boundaries are mutually reinforcing, since implicit in the meaning of national boundaries ("who are we?") are certain prescriptions and proscriptions for sexual crossings. In this case, "our" women should not be having sex with "their" (particularly "enemy") men. Second, is the ubiquitous double standard that applies to many sexual boundaries: "our" men can have consensual sex, rape, or even sexually enslave "their" women and not have their heads shaved, nor will they be tattooed and paraded around the town.[1]

Indeed, in times of war, "our" women might even want to do their patriotic duty by making themselves sexually available to "our" men while the sexual police look the other way—as long as internal racial or ethnic boundaries are not violated (see Enloe 1990, Saunders 1995, Smith 1988). Another lesson to be learned from this tale of punishing women sexual collaborators is that their rule breaking was seized as an opportunity to reinforce and reestablish sexual, gender, and nationalist hegemony. By disciplining women collaborators, proper sexual demeanor and approved ethnosexual partners were publicly proclaimed. The national sexual order was reinstated—a place for every man and woman and everyone in their place.

In this paper, I review the growing literature in the social sciences and the humanities that documents not only the sexual substructure of nationalist identities, boundaries, and processes, but also the sexualized nature of race and ethnicity—two common building blocks of nationalism. I discuss the interrelatedness of race, ethnicity, nationalism, and sexuality, outline contemporary constructionist models of ethnicity and sexuality, and review some of the more recent literature linking race, ethnicity, and nationalism with sexuality.

CONSTRUCTING ETHNICITY AND SEXUALITY

My analyses in the pages that follow rest upon social constructionist models of ethnicity and sexuality that stand in contrast to primordialist views of ethnicity and essentialist views of sexuality (Masters & Johnson 1966, Shaw & Wong 1989, van den Berghe 1978). This difference in language—"primordialist" versus "essentialist"—reflects, in part, the different intellectual sites where the theorizing has occurred. Social constructionist models of ethnicity emerged in the social sciences, primarily in the 1970s (Barth 1969, Horowitz 1975, Yancey et al 1976). Although the early work of Foucault (1978) shaped subsequent constructionist thinking about sexuality, currently influential models emerged mainly in the humanities—cultural studies, gender studies, queer theory—primarily in the 1980s and 1990s (Butler 1990, de Lauretis 1987, Grosz 1994, Haraway 1991, Sedgwick 1990; for an earlier sociological constructionist model of sexuality, see Gagnon & Simon 1973).

I have found more similarities than differences in constructionist thinking about ethnicity and sexuality in the social sciences and humanities, but there is little

---

[1] At least I have found no reports of this practice as retribution for male sexual misbehavior, and in fact, Japan has yet to make satisfactory restitution to Korean and Filipina "comfort women" who were sexually enslaved during the Second World War (see Hicks 1995, Howard 1995, Mydans 1996).

cross-referencing in the literatures. Disciplinary boundaries sometimes seem more impenetrable than the ethnic and sexual boundaries they describe. For instance, much queer theory fails to cite relevant sociological literature, and much sociological research on sexuality is uninformed by queer theory (for an exception, see Seidman 1996). Similarly, social science and humanities scholarship on racial, ethnic, and nationalist constructions seldom contains common bibliographies. Further hindering communication and shared discourse on ethnicity and sexuality between the social sciences and humanities are the significant differences in the vocabularies used by each, differences substantial enough to make interdisciplinary work a challenge. One goal of this essay is make humanities scholarship on both ethnic and sexual constructions more accessible to social scientists.

Constructing Ethnicity

Much current research on race, ethnicity, and nationalism in both the social sciences and humanities rests upon a model of ethnicity as a set of socially constructed boundaries in political, economic, cultural, social, and moral time and space (Cornell 1996, Leonard 1992, Nagel 1994, 1996, Waters 1990, 1994).[2]

While many studies focus only on race, ethnicity, or nationalism, the three concepts can be seen as intimately related—different facets of the same phenomenon—and are sometimes given a single name, such as cultural pluralism (Young 1976, 1993), multiculturalism or diversity (Modood & Werbner 1997), identity politics (Hasan 1994, 1998), or minorities (Yetman 1999). Some researchers privilege race as a core concept (Omi & Winant 1994), while others speak primarily in the language of ethnicity (Banks 1996). Which term is chosen often can be traced to the particular case or cases being studied. Research focusing on the United States, South and North Africa, or Great Britain often speak of race, while research on Canada, Europe, West and Central Africa, or the Indian subcontinent more often use the term ethnicity or variations on nationalism (ethnonationalism, subnationalism, ethnic nationalism).

I view ethnicity as the broader concept subsuming race—which generally refers to visible (often skin color) distinctions among populations (see Horowitz 1985). Ethnicity can be a signifier not only of somatic or physical (racial) differences, but also of differences in language, religion, region, or culture. Nationalism is commonly viewed as a particular kind of ethnically based social identity or mobilization generally involving claims to statehood or political autonomy, and most often rooted in assertions of cultural distinctiveness, a unique history, and ethnic or racial purity (Connor 1990, Hobsbawm 1990, Smith 1989, Weber 1978). Cornell & Hartmann (1998) acknowledge the interrelatedness of race and ethnicity, but distinguish them in terms of power and choice: Race is more likely to be an assigned attribute, and ethnicity is more likely to be volitional. Power differentials

---

[2]See Berger & Luckmann (1967) and Spector & Kitsuse (1977) for classical discussions of the social constructionist model; see Holstein & Miller (1993) for an assessment of the more current state of social constructionism.

are not restricted to racial boundaries, however, since much ethnic differentiation and conflict involve uneven power relations and often occur in the *absence* of racial (color) difference–e.g., recent conflicts in Rwanda, Northern Ireland, and the former Yugoslavia (see Denitch 1996, McGarry 1995, Smith 1998).[3]

Ethnicity is both *performed*—where individuals and groups engage in ethnic "presentations of self," and *performative*—where ethnic boundaries are constituted by day-to-day affirmations, reinforcements, and enactments of ethnic differences.[4]

Ethnicity is thus dramaturgical, situational, changeable, and emergent. An individual's ethnicity is presented and affirmed or not in various social settings; it is a transaction in which the individual and others exchange views about the true nature and meaning of an individual's ethnicity, where negotiations are often necessary to resolve disagreements, where adjustments in ethnic self-presentation and audience reaction may occur over time, and where ethnicity is a dialectical process that arises out of interactions between individuals and audiences.

Power is important in creating and regulating both racial and ethnic boundaries. The relative power of various actors in ethnic transactions can determine an individual's ethnic classification as well as the content and worth of the individual's ethnicity. This power to name ethnically can be formal, where, for instance, the state designates particular criteria for ethnic or racial classification, or informal, where audiences in social settings attribute ethnic meanings to an individual's social characteristics. Thus, my whiteness is an official fact in the US as reflected in documents like my birth certificate, driver's license, and eventually on my death certificate. Unofficially, while I might take my English native language for granted as an uncontroversial, nonethnic fact, a trip to Quebec or a meeting with Latino community organizers can quickly transform my assumed-to-be-neutral linguistic background into an assigned ethnic identity imbued with meanings over which I have no control and limited knowledge: Anglophone or Anglo.

In any society, we can identify boundaries dividing the population along ethnic lines. We can observe differences in language, religion, skin color or appearance, cultural practices or beliefs, or national origin. Sometimes these differences are benign and unimportant; at other times they can become the basis for segregation, conflict, and genocide. Thus, color, language, religion, or culture become *potential* bases for ethnic identity, community, or conflict, not inevitable or automatic bases

---

[3]It is important to acknowledge the prominence, some would say preeminence, of race in historical and contemporary US ethnic relations, in particular the volatility and controversy associated with the black/white ethnic boundary. But race should not be considered as the *most* or *only* volatile or violent basis of ethnic division. A quick review of the sites of ethnic conflict catalogued above–Northern Ireland, the Indian subcontinent, many African states, or the republics of the former Yugoslavia–reveals great conflict and bloodshed along nonracial ethnic divisions, although many of these differences get articulated and vilified in ways that have a familiar "racial" ring (see Eisenstein 1996).

[4]See my discussion of Butler (1990, 1993, 1997) below for further elaboration of the concept of performativity; see Jagose (1996:83–93) and Clough (1994:142–59) for translations of Butler.

for ethnic differentiation. As Duara (1996:168) notes, "Every cultural practice . . . is a potential boundary marking a community. These boundaries may be either soft or hard . . . . Groups with soft boundaries between each other are sometimes so unself-conscious about their differences that they do not view mutual boundary breach as a threat." As international and historical examples easily demonstrate, people are not always mobilizing or conflicting along ethnic lines, only sometimes . . . when boundaries harden. This leads to questions of when ethnic boundaries will become sites of conflict, movements, or revitalization.[5]

If we see ethnicity as a series of crisscrossing boundaries dividing populations into multiple groups differentiated by religion, color, language, culture, and if we note that these boundaries are changeable and permeable (with some boundaries weakening and other boundaries strengthening and with people crossing over from one group into another), then we can begin to move away from primordialist, essentialist understandings of ethnicity and race as biological or genetically inherited or as historically or culturally determined (Anderson 1983, Bhabha 1994, Hobsbawm & Ranger 1983). For instance, recent scholarship on the construction of whiteness as a basis for identity and group formation in the US and in a number of other national settings reminds us that white and black are not natural categories but are historically based and culturally constructed (see Allen 1994, Ignatiev 1995, Lipsitz 1998, Roediger 1991, Saxton 1990).

In the humanities the language of ethnic construction is often phrased in terms of borders, borderlands, and border studies (Anzaldua 1990, Darder & Torres 1998, Gutierrez-Jones 1995, Saldivar 1997). This scholarship is more likely to draw on literary sources to illustrate border processes and identities and to emphasize cultural aspects of and differences among ethnic individuals and communities. Scholars working in literary studies, cultural studies, gender studies, queer studies, ethnic studies, and area studies raise questions about the validity of "natural" essentialist racial and ethnic divisions (black/white, Anglophone/Francophone, American/non-American). They point out discontinuities, disputes, and disruptions within these bounded groups, and they explore such issues as challenges to individual or subgroup ethnic authenticity, historical changes in boundaries or meanings, diversity among ethnic group members, or disagreements over core notions of membership, group history, or cultural practices (Amit-Talai & Knowles 1996, Ginsberg 1996, Kawash 1997).

---

[5]Researchers suggest several conditions under which ethnic conflict or mobilization erupts on ethnic boundaries: during times of ethnic competition for land, resources, jobs, or access to political decisionmaking, during periods of international tension when diaspora populations become scapegoats or targets of hate crimes, during periods of high migration when large numbers of visibly or culturally distinct ethnic migrant populations appear to host residents as "invading" or "overrunning" host societies and changing the character of neighborhoods or communities, or during periods of political upheaval when opportunistic politicians "play the ethnic card" by targeting ethnic communities as a threat in order to consolidate and expand their constituencies (see Horowitz 1985, Young 1976, Banton 1983, Human Rights Watch 1995, Olzak 1996, 1998).

There are several sources of ethnic boundary stability and instability; arguably the greatest among them are gender, class, and sexuality. While ethnic boundaries and identities are built by self and others from such social materials as color, language, religion, and culture, they can be seen to rest on gendered and sexualized foundations, and they often are associated with differences in social class. The race/gender/class nexus has been the focus of a great deal of scholarly interest in recent years (see Anderson & Collins 1992, Chow et al 1996, Dines & Humez 1995, Horowitz 1991, Rothenberg 1992), and now sexuality has become the subject of conceptual and empirical attention as well, but mainly in the humanities (Arguelles 1998, Hodes 1999, Hurtado 1999, Parker et al 1991, Stavans 1998). The remainder of this paper reports on efforts to sexualize the sociological analysis of ethnicity by pointing out the intersections between ethnicity and sexuality, by outlining current constructionist models of sexuality and their relevance to theorizing and understanding ethnicity, and by reporting findings from some recent scholarship on ethnicity and sexuality.

Ethnosexual Frontiers

Ethnicity and sexuality are strained, but not strange, bedfellows. Ethnic boundaries are also sexual boundaries–erotic intersections where people make intimate connections across ethnic, racial, or national borders. The borderlands that lie at the intersections of ethnic boundaries are "ethnosexual frontiers" that are surveilled and supervised, patrolled and policed, regulated and restricted, but that are constantly penetrated by individuals forging sexual links with ethnic "others."

Of course, more than one kind of sexual boundary exists inside ethnic, racial, and national communities. It is the issue of multiple sexualities in ethnosexual contact that I think brings most clearly to light contradictory tensions in the relationship between ethnicity and sexuality. Across a wide variety of ethnic groups appropriate enactments of heterosexuality are perhaps the most regulated and enforced norms. In particular, correct heterosexual masculine and feminine behavior constitutes gender regimes that often lie at the core of ethnic cultures. Our women (often depicted as virgins, mothers, pure) v. their women (sluts, whores, soiled). Our men (virile, strong, brave) v. their men (degenerate, weak, cowardly). These heteronormative ethnosexual stereotypes are nearly universal depictions of self and other as one gazes inside and across virtually any ethnic boundary. Because of the common importance of proper gender role and sexual behavior to ethnic community honor and respectability, a great deal of attention is paid to the sexual demeanor of group members (by outsiders and insiders) in inspection and enforcement of both formal and informal rules of sexual conduct.

For instance, Rudrappa (1999) reports tensions experienced by young Indian-American women as they try to reconcile the two gender-sexual worlds in which they live: the more traditional expectations of their often-immigrant families against those of the larger US culture. White women who are depicted as weak or promiscuous are often foils against which ethnic group members in the United

States and abroad construct moral superiority (see Espiritu 1997, Harden 1997, Ortner 1996, Schein 1995). Even nonheterosexual or non-sexually-conservative groups and settings (e.g., lesbian, gay, transgendered, or desire communities) are marked by ethnosexual expectations for behavior, and insider critics point out the prevalence of ethnosexual stereotypes (e.g., the hypersexualization of black masculinity by white gay men; see Hemphill 1991) and the invisibility of non-heterosexuals in ethnic communities (e.g., the feelings of enforced silence by lesbian women of color; see Moraga 1983). Even in the face of great international diversity of sexual practice, where sexual expression does not follow Western models of heteronormativity, rules for sexual behavior often are found to be rigidly defined, strictly enforced, and ultimately used to uphold heteronormative family relations (e.g., Herdt's (1981, 1982) research on Papua New Guinean "Sambian" male homoeroticism, which underpins a misogynistic, patriarchal system of gender relations).

Researchers have also uncovered ethnosexuality underlying what would appear on the surface to be non-ethnic and/or non-sexual institutions and processes. For instance, recent scholarship on colonialism and postcolonialism is filled with discussions of the sexualization of exotic others by colonial authorities (Bulbeck 1998, McClintock 1995, Manderson & Jolly 1997, Ogden 1996, Stoler 1990, 1995, 1997), and researchers have documented sexualized aspects of citizenship (Bredbenner 1998, Evans 1993, Stychin 1998, Ward et al 1992), organizations (Hearn et al 1989), education (Barreca & Morse 1997), the US civil rights movement (Evans 1979, McAdam 1988, Rothschild 1982), the US white supremist movement (Daniels 1997, Ferber 1998), US foreign policy (Weber 1999), tourism (Ware 1997), photojournalism (Lutz & Collins 1997), the Peace Corps (Zimmerman 1999), and livestock (Nelson 1999).

Constructing Sexuality/Sexualities

Skin color, language, religion, or ancestry do not "automatically" serve as the basis for ethnic identities or groups, result in variations in cultural content, or generate interethnic conflict. The production of ethnic differences requires social and often political recognition, definition, and reinforcement as well as individual and collective assertion and acceptance to become socially real. Similarly, male and female bodies do not automatically result in socially meaningful "men" or "women." Rather the gender identities, meanings, cultures, and social divisions between men and women are social constructions, arising out of historical conditions, power relations, and ongoing social processes (Hartsock 1983, Ortner 1972, 1996, MacKinnon 1989, Scott 1988).

These same insights about the social construction of ethnicity and gender apply to sexuality. Male and female genitalia do not automatically result in predictable types of sexual men and women, in particular forms of sexual behavior or practices, or in specific kinds of sexual desire. The early work of anthropologists, with all of its admitted flaws, unveiled as many different sexual practices and sexualities as there were cultures to inspect.[6]

Despite Gagnon and Simon's (1973) pioneering work on sexual "scripting," sexual social constructionism did not become a dominant paradigm in sociology in subsequent decades, as did social constructionist conceptions of ethnicity. Much sociological work on sexuality has remained in the tradition of sexology (frequencies and types of sexual activity, see Kinsey et al 1948, 1953, Masters & Johnson 1966, 1970, Michael et al 1994, Laumann et al 1994).

Some of the most interesting contemporary work deconstructing and challenging assumptions about the nature and content of sexuality is by feminist and queer theorists (for a sampling of this literature, see edited works by Fuss 1991, Lancaster & di Leonardo 1997, Seidman 1996, Warner 1993). Perhaps most intriguing of all is queer theory's challenge to the essentialist sexual binary of male/female and its imbedded assumption of heteronormativity or "compulsory heterosexuality" (Rich 1980). In a section of her book, *Gender Trouble*, entitled, "'Women' as the Subject of Feminism," Butler (1990:1) wonders whether or not there really are "women," i.e., a gender category with a common meaning, position, interests:

> For the most part, feminist theory has assumed that there is some existing identity, understood through the category of women, who not only initiates feminist interests and goals within discourse, but constitutes the subject for whom political representation is pursued.

Butler and others ask what dangers might lie in assuming women's existence? They conclude that women bring men into being by their "otherness," and that women's abject (marginal, invisible) status affirms men's dominance and normalcy. The view of women as "not men" leads to a focus on women's lack of rights, women's troubles, women's marginality, and thus can be seen to be an affirmation, a reinforcement, and even a constitution of hegemonic manhood–men's dominance, men's privilege, men's centrality (Grosz 1994, Irigaray 1985; see also Hale 1996, Sedgwick 1990, 1993, Wittig 1992).

It is not only the existence of women that queer theorists question. What is so normal, they ask, about heterosexuality? What is so natural, predictable, assumable about women sexually desiring men or the reverse? In fact, what is so normal about women and men serving as the two basic building blocks of sexuality, sexual identity, or sexual desire? Ingraham (1996:169) refers to these assumptions about normal sex and sexuality as the "heterosexual imaginary"—and criticizes feminist theory for not questioning its own premises about the naturalness of the

---

[6]For the classical sexual inspection reports, see Malinowski (1927, 1929), Mead (1923, 1935), Evans-Pritchard (1940); for critical discussions of these and other anthropological "texts," see Crapanzano (1986), Fischer (1986), Clifford (1988); for a neoclassical approach that demonstrates both the strengths and weaknesses of anthropology's approach to sexualities, see the work of anthropologist Gilbert Herdt and his associate, psychoanalyst Robert J. Stoller (Herdt, 1981, 1982, 1994, 1997; Stoller & Herdt 1985; Herdt & Stoller, 1990).

categories "men" and "women" because such a dichotomy tends to affirm "in-stitutionalized heterosexuality . . . [as] the standard for legitimate and prescriptive sociosexual arrangements." Feminist critiques of patriarchy, since they arise out of this false essentialist assumption, Ingraham argues, inadvertently reinforce one important invisible structure of domination– phallocentric sexuality or heteronor-mativity (see also Jackson 1996).

Feminism is not the only target for criticism by queer theorists. Ironically and interestingly, so is the gay and lesbian rights movement and the sexual "identity" politics it has engendered. Critics argue that imbedded in a conception of gay rights as minority rights is a set of assumptions about another binary. Just as femi-nism's focus on women reifies the male/female binary, gay and lesbian identity and rights claims reify the heterosexual/homosexual binary. The fight for gay rights, like the fight for women's rights, has the unintended consequence of acknowledg-ing and "naturalizing" a system of heteronormativity (see Seidman 1997). The gender/sexual landscape painted by queer theory is a scenario of sexualities in social flux. Even queerness is in question. On the back cover of *PoMoSexuals: Challenging Assumptions about Gender and Sexuality* (Queen & Schimel 1997), transsexual Kate Bornstein writes:

> Ever wonder if you're the only one who doesn't quite fit into one of the sanctioned queer worlds? Like, are you really a lesbian? Are you really a gay man? Maybe you fall outside the "permitted" labels, and maybe you're the only one who knows you do, and so you feel a bit guilty? Well, I've got news for you. You're not guilty, you're simply postmodern.

In addition to framing and spreading the good news about decentered individual and collective notions of sexuality, queer theorists have shown themselves to be quite adept at deconstructing gender binaries, heterosexuality, and opposite-sex desire. They are less successful when it comes to providing systematic accountings of the ways these core social categories and regimes emerge as stable structures. Butler's (1990, 1993) notion of "performativity" is a step toward a general model of how hegemony (sexual and nonsexual) comes into being–through a series of iterations or repetitive acts that are largely unconscious, affirming, and constitutive. Butler's description of the performative construction of reality rests heavily on discursive acts, i.e., on the power of naming and speech to define reality:

> the policeman hails the passerby with "hey you there" and the one who recognizes himself and turns around (nearly everyone) to answer the call does not, strictly speaking, preexist the call . . . The passerby turns precisely to acquire a certain identity, one purchased, as it were, with the price of guilt. The act of recognition becomes an act of constitution: the address animates the subject into existence (Butler 1997:25).

A parallel example, more germane to the constitution of gender and sexuality, is Butler's birthing scenario where the doctor slaps the baby on the back and performatively proclaims, "It's a girl!" Extending this image to the arena of race, ethnicity, or nationalism, it is easy to envision such parallel performative constructions as "white," "black," "Cherokee," "Jewish," or "American"–similarly constituted through official and unofficial acts of discourse, classification, and registration, and to see these ethnic categories as equally unstable and volatile creations, subject to challenge, change, and controversy–Is he really an Indian, is she really black, are they really Jews (Pewewardy 1998, Williams 1998, Boyd 1997)?

The power of performative acts, verbal and otherwise, to constitute the social order lies not only the discursive pronouncements of authorities, but also in actions–theirs and others, insiders and outsiders, hegemonic and counterhegemonic. In these claims and counterclaims we can see revealed the power of boundaries, edges, and borders to define and expose the center. Butler (1990:31) points out the "'presence' of so-called heterosexual conventions within homosexual contexts," such as sociosexual roles of butch and femme and cross-dressing or drag. She argues that these replications of heterosexual conventions by nonheterosexuals reveal "the utterly constructed status of the so-called heterosexual original. Thus, gay is to straight *not* as copy is to original, but, rather, as copy is to copy." But do these homosexual enactments, even parodies of heterosexuality, really subvert the heteronormative order, or do these simulations simply reinforce it? A few years later, Butler (1993:125) expressed some doubts, suggesting that drag may both "denaturalize" as well as "reidealize" (reinforce) heterosexual gender norms.

We can see in the notion of the reidealization of heteronormativity an important clue about the utility of queer theory to instruct us about the construction of sexuality and sexual desire in general, not just in the queer case(s). Although queer theory's central project is devoted to challenging the naturalness of heterosexuality and to positing an equally genuine (natural?), more flexible and variable model of sexualit*ies*, theorists note the entrenched power of phallic-centered heteronormativity to stay on top (so to speak) and reproduce itself: "heterosexual privilege operates in many ways, and two ways in which it operates include naturalizing itself and rendering itself as the original and the norm" (Butler 1993:125–26). Not only is heterosexuality deeply socially imbedded and institutionalized (in the law, military, family, religion, education, notions of beauty, in everyday life), but it is a resilient system capable of absorbing and appropriating challenges on its edges in order to strengthen itself. Thus, sexual "deviance" from the heterosexual norm can provoke gender and sexual policing and panics that, in the end, strengthen and further naturalize particular forms of heterosexuality (see Steinberg et al 1997).

Indeed conventional heterosexuality seems to be an extremely elastic social fact, capable of enormous staying power even in the face of constant, widespread noncompliance. Take the norm and prevailing expectation of monogamy in marriage. While there is much variation and unreliability in sex surveys (see Ericksen 1999, Jones 1997), adultery appears to be a fairly common phenomenon in marriages and other monogamous relationships (e.g, 20% to 50% of respondents report extra-monogamous sexual activity; see Kinsey et al 1948, 1953, Michael et al 1994). In fact, high rates of marital dissolution and remarriage in the West often involve sex outside of marriage, and this reality can be seen as leading to a kind of institutionalized adultery in the form of "serial monogamy." Yet, despite widespread rulebreaking, monogamy persists as an almost sacred norm both in the law and in public opinion (if not actions; see Floris 1990:603). Although there is certainly historical change in sexual norms and actions (Rubin 1990), one can find similar discrepancies between ideology and behavior in other forms of contemporary US heteroconventionality, such as the appropriate age and general acceptability of premarital sex, number of acceptable serial or simultaneous sexual partners, types of sexual behavior, locations for sexual activity, nudity, and public attire (for provocative discussions of the norms governing sexual intimacy, see Berlant & Warner 1998, Kipnis 1998, Warner 1999, Weeks 1995). The race and ethnicity of sexual partners is another frequently transgressed, though often quite actively inspected, highly regulated, and potentially volatile sexual norm.

ETHNOSEXUAL INTERSECTIONS

Following the above analysis of heteronormativity, we can best expose the sexualized foundations of ethnicity by examining the ways in which the rule breaking, policing, and punishment of sexual deviants serves both to challenge and to reinforce racial, ethnic, and nationalist boundaries and hegemonies and to strengthen ethnosexual regimes. By returning to the discussion of the photograph at the beginning of this paper, we can see more clearly the usefulness of women sexual collaborators to French nationalists: by disciplining these sexual traitors, proper female sexual demeanor and approved ethnosexual partners were publicly proclaimed and local moral control over violated nationalist boundaries was reestablished. The US Army photographer who shot this photograph did *not* capture a rare image on film. The literatures on historical and contemporary sexualities are filled with examples of sexuality in the service of racial, ethnic, and nationalist agendas of various sorts: reproducing the nation or ethnic group, controlling women and men inside ethnic boundaries, reinforcing ethnic segregation, maintaining ethnic inequalities, intimidating and subjugating ethnic others under colonialism or imperialism and in times of war, extending and/or establishing sexual and ethnic regimes in postcolonial settings (see Anthias & Yuval-Davis 1992, Clark & Nagel 2000, Enloe 1990, Hansen 1996, Massad 1995, Nagel 1998, Sturdevant & Stoltzfus 1992). This list points to links between ethnicity and sexuality in many times and places. The following examples further illuminate the ethnicity/sexuality connection and illustrate the utility of examining this intimate bond to understand racial, ethnic, and nationalist identities, boundaries, conflicts, and movements.

Sexualities and Nationalisms

At least as familiar a picture from World War II as women sexual collaborators with shaved heads, is the pink triangle homosexuals were forced to wear in Germany and Nazi-occupied territories, and considerably more familiar than either image is the six-sided Star of David forced by the Nazis on Jews. Pink triangles and Stars of David served to distinguish publicly outcast non-Aryans from Aryans, and these symbols communicated potent and degenerate sexual stereotypes about their wearers. For instance, Mosse (1985:36) reminds us that early twentieth-century views of female sexuality (consistent with Freudian theory) depicted women's sexual passions as out of control (hysterical); thus sexual deviants were often feminized since their urges were seen as feminine failures of self-restraint. Mosse reports that while Jews were seldom accused of homosexuality in fascist and European racist discourse, they were considered "sexual 'degenerates'" and "inferior races." Sexualized racism, homophobia, and misogyny were all foils against which propagandists contrasted the superior morality and sexuality of fascist nationalists across Europe (Boyarin 1997, Spackman 1996). Depicting "others" as feminine is useful in other ways, to delegitimize or trivialize grievances or dissent (Brown 1996), to denigrate or dismiss opponents or colonized people (Ortner 1996, Petkov 1997, Sweet 1993), or as a critical discourse act against a dominant group (Mac An Ghaill 1994).

Nationalists' preoccupation with and fear of homosexuality were not confined to the Nazi targeting of homosexuals during the Second World War. The Cold War represented another period of homosexual panic (Sedgwick 1990:184–85) when many gay men working in Western governments, particularly in the British Foreign Office and US State Department, were fired or reassigned because they were considered to be security risks. In the United States, Senator Joseph McCarthy was not only interested in finding and flushing out communists in various arenas of American life, he was also interested in homosexuals, presumably because of their vulnerability to communist influence or blackmail (Epstein 1994, see also Corber 1997, Fried 1997, Patton 1997). The fact that one of his most vicious lieutenants, Roy Cohn, was a gay man, was the McCarthy era's best kept secret and most ironic breach of Republican security.

The issue of sexualities continues to complicate enactments and definitions of the nation–its boundaries and components. Davis (1995:297) recounts the queer saga of the struggle over the sexual meaning of Irish Americanness in Boston. In 1992 the Queer Nation/Boston formed the Irish-American Lesbian, Gay and Bisexual Pride Community (Later GLIB) and sought the right to participate in the annual St. Patrick's/Evacuation Day parade organized by the South Boston Allied War Veterans Council. The Veterans Council objected and the case ended up in the court. Boston City Councillor James Kelly, who represented the district in South Boston where the march was organized, opposed GLIB's inclusion in the march:

> GLIB, the gay, lesbian, and bisexual group of trouble makers who hate the Catholic Church and its teachings, are not welcome in South Boston's Evacuation Day Parade. If parading is so important to them, let them raise their own money, organize their own parade, and apply for a permit to march in downtown Boston to express their sexuality (Davis 1995:301).

Scholars studying the dispute argue that the resistance to the inclusion of GLIB in the march exposed an assumption about the heterosexuality of Irishness. Stychin (1998:41) characterized the subsequent court battle as a dispute that centered "directly on the *sexuality* of national identities and speaks to *both* the construction of the sexuality of an Irish American and to an American identity."[7]

The punishment of women for sexual contact with an enemy and suspicions about the patriotism of homosexuals reflect a particularly sexualized, indeed, heterosexualized, envisioning of masculinity and femininity and of men's and women's proper places in the gender, sexual, and national order (see Enloe 1990, Guttman 1996, Mosse 1996, Savran 1998, Stychin 1998).

Indian-White Ethnosexual Frontiers

US history offers many examples of racial and sexual intersections, sometimes in unexpected terrain. The settling of the US west was not only a saga of competitive positioning by colonial powers, conflicts with indigenous peoples, and spreading settler populations across the continent. The "conquest" of the west involved a series of sexualized encounters resulting in a confrontation of sexualities and sexual systems along various ethnosexual frontiers. Among the writings of the first European explorers were reports of native cannibalism, warlike behavior, and sexual excesses. Gutierrez (1991) reports that early accounts of Spanish soldiers and Franciscans were filled with commentary about Pueblo peoples' sexual practices. The Franciscans in particular were prolific in their documentation of what they saw as Pueblo "lewd" behavior and sexual promiscuity. The new printing press circulated these and other reports across Europe and, despite the offended tone of the text, the floodgates opened as mostly male Europeans eager to settle this sexually savage, brave new world swarmed across the Atlantic.[8]

Scholars question the biases and agendas of many of these and later reports because they served as justifications for colonial and later American policies of annihilation, pacification, and assimilation of native populations (see Berkhofer 1978, Brown 1996). For instance, the journals of Lewis and Clark, who set out on their westward explorations in 1804, are filled with references to encounters with native peoples along the way; many of these (both the encounters and the references) were of a sexual nature, and many emphasized trade:

---

[7]St. Patrick's Day is also known as "Evacuation Day" in commemoration of the ouster of British and loyalist troops from the city in 1737. While the Massachusetts state courts permitted GLIB to march in the parade in 1992 and subsequent years because of some public funding of the parade, in 1995 the US Supreme Court decided against GLIB (*Hurley and South Boston Allied War Veterans Council v. Irish-American Gay, Lesbian, and Bisexual Group of Boston*), ruling that the parade was a private function of the Veterans Council.

[8]For parallel discussions of European settlers' preoccupations with Australian indigenous sexuality and sexual liaisons with aboriginal Australians, see Povinelli (1994) and Bell (1980).

Thursday, November 21 1805: An old woman & Wife to a Cheif of the *Chunnooks* came and made a Camp near ours. She brought with her 6 young Squars I believe for the purpose of Gratifying the passions of the men of our party and receiving for those indulgiences Such Small [presents] as She (the old woman) thought proper to accept of. Those people appear to View Sensuality as a Necessary evel, and do not appear to abhor it as a Crime in the unmarried State (Bergon 1989:324).

Hurtado (1997, 1999) paints a less sanguine portrait of freely given Indian sexual favors. Acknowledging wide variation across indigenous communities, conditions, times, and places, Hurtado points out the relative powerlessness of many native women, and reports that sexual exchanges were often coerced, involving rape, forced prostitution, and slavery (see also Butler 1987:9ff, Godbeer 1999, Limerick 1987:50ff, Smith 1987, 1990).

Despite their frequent relative powerlessness, Indian women sometimes used whites' sexual desires against them. Brown (1996:67) recounts the story of George Cawson, a colonial man, who, in 1607, "met his death after [Powhatan] village women 'enticed [him]up from the barge into their howses' and delivered him to his executioners." She goes on to tell of the sexual trick of another Powhatan woman:

> Oppossunoquonuske, a clever werowansqua of another village, similarly led fourteen English men to their demise. Inviting the unwary men to come "up into her Towne, to feast and make merry," she persuaded them to "leave their Armes in their boat, because they said how their women would be afrayd ells of their pieces" . . . Her genius lay in persuading them to rely on other masculine "pieces" . . . [and] the men were easily killed. (Brown 1996:67)

Many negative reports about native life and sexuality were popularized in the form of Indian captivity narratives in which whites were the targets of native sexual aggression (*Garland Library* 1977). While most white women captives did not, for fear of public humiliation, report being sexually attacked themselves, they widely reported the sexual assault of other captives by native men. For instance, Mary Smith and her husband were allegedly captured by Kickapoos and Chickasaws in 1814. In her memoir, *An Affecting Narrative of the Captivity and Sufferings of Mrs. Mary Smith*, she reports that the Indians "ravished, rifled, murdered and mutilated the inhabitants without distinction of age or sex, without any other provocation or incitement than brutal lust and wantonness of barbarity!" (Derounian-Stodola & Levernier 1993:66). Not all captives escaped when they had the chance; in some cases they became members of tribes. So-called transculturated or white Indians married and chose to stay with their captors, some because of the shame of returning home as sexually damaged goods, others because of native generosity and sympathy for their plight (see Brooks 1997:107, Derounian-Stodola & Levernier 1993:73–85, Ebersole 1995, Kestler 1990). Namias (1993:109) describes an erotic ambivalence toward native men—an ethnosexual romantic longing that led captivity narratives to be popular reading among white women.

To what use were put these centuries of sexualized depictions of indigenous peoples? What were the social, political, economic, and policy consequences of these mainly uncomplimentary sexual descriptions of Indians—as wanton savages and brutal rapists? Certainly this portrayal of natives as sexually dangerous was a convenient justification for warfare against indigenous societies and for removing native communities from areas chosen by whites for settlement. Sexualized depictions of and beliefs about native peoples became part of the imagining of the US west, served as justifications for military, political, and economic policies, and ultimately, these images provided a rationale for seizing native resources to better manage and use them and to improve native individuals and cultures through programs of civilization and assimilation. Reports of Indian depredations and savagery also became a means of justifying white misbehavior and atrocities and provided opportunities for white self-aggrandizement. Smith (1990:68, 148) reports that massacres of indigenous women and children were defended by demonizing native women, and that frontier soldiers often described native men as skilled warriors, in part to explain a defeat or because "a successful campaign against a formidable foe rather than a weak one could enhance a soldier's reputation back home" as well as guarantee continued support for a frontier military presence. Such sexualized depictions were part of the ideological basis of US Indian policy, and their contribution to justifying and implementing policies that destroyed native cultures and expropriated indigenous land and resources cannot be underestimated, given the loaded, inflammatory power of sexual threats and discourses.

Black-White Ethnosexual Boundaries

No ethnic boundary is more sexualized, surveilled, and scrutinized in US society than the color line dividing blacks and whites. Looking back to the very earliest days of European settlement in North America, from the early sixteenth century when the first Africans arrived on the continent as indentured servants and later into the seventeenth century when these involuntary immigrants were formally enslaved, we can find frequent sexualized descriptions of Africans. Detailed early accounts of African sexuality echo those untamed, hypersexualized characteristics assigned to Native Americans, and such accounts were equally convenient justifications of enslavement and exploitation of Africans by Europeans and later Americans (Hartman 1997, Jordan 1968). What is particularly interesting about the African American case are the historical changes in the sexual depictions of Africans and scholars' tracing of the demonization of black male sexuality to the reconstruction period following the Civil War. Prior to the Civil War, during slavery, both black men and women were described as sexually promiscuous, but it was not until after the war, when freed blacks began to enter into commerce and politics, that black men were reconstructed as a sexual predators, as threats to white southern womanhood (Carby 1986, Fredrickson 1988, Gunning 1996:19–47, Williamson 1984). An 1872 US Senate inquiry into the conditions in the post–Civil War South and the activities of the Ku Klux Klan suggested that the bugaboo of white female vulnerability to black male sexual aggression served as a cover for white efforts to stop political competition between whites and blacks, and as an excuse for white men to reassert their control over black men (Ferber 1998, Hodes 1993, 1997).

In the twentieth century black sexuality remained a preoccupation of white America with lynchings and castrations of black men and the arrests of both black men and women for sexual misdeeds (e.g., for rape, "white slavery," prostitution), social controversies over entertainers and public figures who crossed the color line (e.g., boxer Jack Johnson—who defeated the "great white hope," Jim Jeffries— in the early 1900s, NAACP executive director Walter White in the 1950s, singer Sammy Davis, Jr. in the 1960s), and gendered and sexualized racial subtexts ("playing the race card") in electoral politics and policy discussions (e.g., the Republic focus on black felon, Willie Horton, during the 1988 US presidential campaign, the racialized image of welfare queens and teenage mothers during welfare reform policy debates in the 1990s) (see Bederman 1995, Cohen 1997, Davis et al 1989, Gabriel 1997, Giddings 1984:253, Gunning 1996:17–47, Hunt 1997, Luker 1996, Mumford 1997, Wiegman 1993). Although the black/white ethnosexual frontier is a somewhat less deadly zone today than it was a century ago, and despite increasing rates of black/white intermarriage, the color line is still a dangerous and controversial intersection, with vocal critics of miscegenation speaking out from both sides of the US racial divide (see di Leonardo 1997, Hodes 1999, Wallace 1990: 9–10) and where black male sexuality is still defined as dangerous (see Hutchinson 1997).

A final point about black-white ethnosexual boundaries in the US can be made by "queering" the heteronormative assumptions and focus of the preceding discussion. The above examples all involve heterosexual racial crossings and controversies, and these examples reinforce what many lesbians and gay men of color have noted with much irony and bitterness—that they are erased at best, stereotyped and demonized at worst, both inside and outside their ethnic communities. For instance, lesbian and gay African Americans report that a variation on the admonition not to mix race and sex often greets them in their home communities: don't mix race and sexualities (Beam 1986, Collins 1990, Hemphill 1991, Riggs 1991). One important feature of ethnic boundaries involves questions of membership–who *is* and who *is not* a bonifide member of the group; in the case of African Americans, who *is* and who *is not* black (see Davis 1991). In *Soul on Ice*, Eldridge Cleaver, articulated the meaning of black macho as exclusively heterosexual when he attacked James Baldwin's homosexuality as "somehow un-black" (Page 1996:101) and equated both heterosexual and homosexual black/white sexual crossings as reflecting a "racial death wish" (Cleaver 1968:102).

Nero (1991) finds support in the work of black scholars for Cleaver's assertions about the incompatibility of blackness and homosexuality, including Frantz Fanon's psychoanalytically based conclusion in *White Skin, Black Masks* that homosexuality was "an attribute of the white race" and did not exist in the Caribbean because blacks there don't experience the oedipal tensions that putatively give rise to same-sex desire (Fanon 1963:84; see also Asante 1980, Hare & Hare 1984, Pouissaint 1978). Similarly, Beam (1986:231) laments the exclusion of black homosexuals in their own communities in the United States:

> When I speak of home, I mean not only the familial constellation from which I grew, but the entire Black community; the Black press, the Black church, Black academicians, the Black literati, and the Black left. Where is my reflection? I am most often rendered invisible, perceived as a threat to the family, or I am tolerated if I am silent and inconspicuous.

Homophobia in the black community combines with the racism of gay whites to further isolate black homosexuals. Hemphill (1991:xviii) comments that "the contradictions of 'home' are amplified and become more complex when black gay men's relationships with the white gay community are also examined." Hemphill describes as a "colonial fantasy," white photographer, Robert Mapplethorpe's "Man in a Polyester Suit," which features a black male torso in a business suit, unzipped with his uncircumcised penis exposed. Hemphill wonders *who* is the man in the photo and *why* is his head missing? (see also Julien & Mercer 1986:6, Mercer 1991). The writings of black, Native Americans, Asian American, and Latino gay men resonate with those of African Americans reporting feelings of exclusion from home communities and from the white gay world. Lesbians of color have similar analyses of isolation and criticisms of white lesbians and feminists for insensitivity to the differing needs of lesbian and straight women of color:

> I think about all the white women I knew in San Francisco. Women with Master's degrees from Stanford University & cars that daddy bought, women with straight white teeth & clear skins from thousands of years of proper nutrition. They chose to be poor ... I no longer believe that feminism is a tool which can eliminate racism—or even promote better understanding between different races & kinds of women ... Perhaps white women are so rarely loyal because they do not have to be. There are thousands of them to pick up & discard (Chrystos 1981:68–70; see also Anzaldua 1990, Jacobs et al 1997, Leong 1996, Moraga & Anzaldua 1981, Ratti 1993, Plummer 1995).

CONCLUSION

The sexualization and sexual denigration of racial and ethnic others in the service of policy formulation and justification and racial ideological legitimation are not unique to the cases of western nationalism or US race relations. The sexualization of ethnicity is a ubiquitous, I would argue, universal feature of ethnic relations. And for good reason. It is the sexualized nature of things ethnic, racial, and national that heats up discourse on the values, attributes, and moral worth of "us" and "them," that arouses passions when there are violations of sexual contact rules, that raises doubts about loyalty and respectability when breaches of sexual demeanor occur, that stirs emotions when questions of sexual purity and propriety arise, and that sparks retaliations when threats to sexual boundaries are perceived or detected. I can think of no more potent an image to justify violence and subjugation than the "rape" of one's homeland or women, and no more convincing an argument for intervention to civilize or pacify than "other" sexual excesses or violence. Extending Foucault's (1977, 1985, 1986) observations about the sexual substructure of social life in general to the study of race, ethnicity, and nationalism holds the same promise to reveal ethnosexual regimes of discipline and punishment, of hegemony and domination, but also of revelation and reinvention.

ACKNOWLEDGMENTS

I wish to thank Omofolabo Ajayi-Soyinka for her comments on an earlier draft of this paper, Robert Antonio and Tony Tyeeme Clark for suggesting instances of and literature relevant to ethnosexual matters, and Barry Shank, my smart and generous guide into the worlds of queer theory and cultural studies.

Visit the Annual Reviews home page at www.AnnualReviews.org

LITERATURE CITED

Allen T. 1994. *The Invention of the White Race.* London: Verso

Ambrose S, Sulzberger CL, eds. 1997. *American Heritage New History of World War II.* New York: Viking. Rev. ed.

Amit-Talai V, Knowles C, eds. 1996. *Re-Situating Identities: The Politics of Race, Ethnicity, and Culture.* Orchard Park, NY: Broadview

Anderson B. 1983. *Imagined Communities.* London: Verso

Anderson ML, Collins PH, eds. 1992. *Race, Class, and Gender: An Anthology.* Belmont, CA: Wadsworth

Anthias F, Yuval-Davis N, eds. 1992. *Racial Boundaries: Race, Nation, Gender, Colour and Class and the Anti-Racist Struggle.* London: Routledge

Anzaldua G, ed. 1990. *Making Face, Making Soul: Creative and Critical Perspectives by Women of Color.* San Francisco: Aunt Lute Found

Arguelles L. 1998. Crazy wisdom: memories of a Cuban queer. See Darder & Torres 1998, pp. 206–10

Asante M. 1980. *Afrocentricity: A Theory of Social Change.* Buffalo, NY: Amulefi

Banks M. 1996. *Ethnicity: Anthropological Constructions.* New York: Routledge

Banton M. 1983. *Racial and Ethnic Competition.* Cambridge: Cambridge Univ. Press

Barreca R, Morse DD, eds. 1997. *The Erotics of Instruction.* Hanover, NH: Univ. Press of New England

Barth F. 1969. *Ethnic Groups and Boundaries.* Boston: Little, Brown

Beam J, ed. 1986. *Brother to Brother: Words from the Heart. In the Life: A Black Gay Anthology.* Boston: Alyson

Bederman G. 1995. *Manliness and Civilization: A Cultural History of Gender and Race in the United States, 1880–1917.* Chicago: Univ. Chicago Press

Bell D. 1980. Desert politics: choices in the "marriage market." In *Women and Colonization: Anthropological Perspectives,* ed. M Etienne, E Leacock, pp. 239–69. New York: Praeger

Berger PL, Luckmann T. 1967. *The Social Construction of Reality: A Treatise on the*

Sociology of Knowledge. Garden City, NJ: Anchor, 3rd ed.

Bergon F. 1989. *The Journals of Lewis and Clark.* New York: Penguin

Berkhofer RF. Jr. 1978. *The White Man's Indian: Images of the American Indian from Columbus to the Present.* New York: Knopf

Berlant L, Warner M. 1998. Sex in public. *Crit. Inquiry* 24 (Winter):547–66

Bhabha H. 1994. *The Location of Culture.* London: Routledge

Boyarin D. 1997. *Unheroic Conduct: The Rise of Heterosexuality and the Invention of the Jewish Man.* Berkeley: Univ. Calif. Press

Boyd T. 1997. *Am I Black Enough for You? Popular Culture from the 'Hood and Beyond.* Bloomington, IN: Indiana Univ. Press

Bredbenner CL. 1998. *A Nationality of Her Own: Women, Marriage, and the Law of Citizenship.* Berkeley: Univ. Calif. Press

Brooks JF. 1997. "This evil extends especially to the feminine sex": captivity and identity in New Mexico, 1700–1846. See Jameson & Armitage 1997, pp. 97–121

Brown KM. 1996. *Good Wives, Nasty Wenches, and Anxious Patriarchs: Gender, Race, and Power in Colonial Virginia.* Chapel Hill, NC: Univ. N. Carolina Press

Bulbeck C. 1998. *Re-Orienting Western Feminisms: Women's Diversity in a Postcolonial World.* New York: Cambridge Univ. Press

Butler AM. 1987. *Daughters of Joy, Sisters of Misery: Prostitutes in the American West, 1865–90.* Urbana, IL: Univ. Illinois Press

Butler J. 1990. *Gender Trouble.* New York: Routledge

Butler J. 1993. *Bodies that Matter.* New York: Routledge

Butler J. 1997. *Excitable Speech.* New York: Routledge

Carby H. 1986. "On the threshold of woman's era": lynching, empire, and sexuality in black feminist theory. In *"Race," Writing and Difference*, ed. HL Gates, Jr. Chicago: Univ. Chicago Press

Chow EN, Wilkinson D, Zinn MB, eds. 1996. *Race, Class, and Gender: Common Bonds, Different Voices.* Thousand Oaks, CA: Sage

Chrystos. 1981. I don't understand those who have turned away from me. See Moraga & Anzaldua 1981, pp. 68–70

Clark DAT, Nagel J. 2000. White men, red masks: appropriations of Indian manhood in imagined wests. In *Across the Great Divide: Cultures of Manhood in the American West*, ed. L McCall, M Basso, D Garceau. New York: Routledge

Cleaver E. 1968. *Soul on Ice.* New York: McGraw–Hill

Clifford J. 1988. *The Predicament of Culture: Twentieth Century Ethnography, Literature, and Art.* Cambridge, MA: Harvard Univ. Press

Clifford J, Marcus G, eds. 1986. *Writing Culture: The Poetics and Politics of Ethnography.* Berkeley: Univ. Calif. Press

Clough PT. 1994. *Feminist Thought: Desire, Power, and Academic Discourse.* Cambridge, MA: Blackwell

Cohen CJ. 1997. Punks, bulldaggers, and welfare queens: the radical potential of queer politics? *GLQ: J. Lesbian & Gay Stud.* 3:437–65

Collins PH. 1990. *Black Feminist Thought: Knowledges, Consciousness, and the Politics of Empowerment.* New York: Routledge

Connor W. 1990. When is a nation? *Ethnic Racial Stud.* 13(1):92–103

Corber RJ. 1997. *Homosexuality in Cold War America: Resistance and the Crisis of Masculinity.* Durham, NC: Duke Univ. Press

Cornell S. 1996. The variable ties that bind: content and circumstance in ethnic processes. *Ethnic Racial Stud.* 19:265–89

Cornell S, Hartmann D. 1998. *Ethnicity and Race: Making Identities in a Changing World.* Thousand Oaks, CA: Pine Forge

Crapanzano V. 1986. Hermes' dilemma: the masking of subversion in ethnographic description. See Clifford & Marcus 1986, pp. 51–76

Daniels J. 1997. *White Lies: Race, Class, Gender, and Sexuality in White Supremacist Discourse.* New York: Routledge

Darder A, Torres RD, eds. 1998. *The Latino Studies Reader: Culture, Economy, and Society.* Malden, MA: Blackwell

Davis JF. 1991. *Who Is Black? One Nation's Definition.* University Park, PA: Penn. State Univ. Press

Davis S Jr, Boyar J, Boyar B. 1989. *Why Me? The Sammy Davis, Jr. Story.* New York: Farrar, Straus, Giroux

Davis T. 1995. Diversity of queer politics and redefinition of sexual identity and community in urban spaces. In *Mapping Desire: Geographies of Sexualities,* ed. D Bell, G Valentine, pp. 285–303. New York: Routledge

de Lauretis T. 1987. *Technologies of Gender: Essays on Theory, Film, and Fiction.* Bloomington, IN: Indiana Univ. Press

Denitch B. 1996. *Ethnic Nationalism: The Tragic Death of Yugoslavia.* Minneapolis: Univ. Minn. Press. Rev. ed.

Derounian-Stodola KZ, Levernier JA. 1993. *The Indian Captivity Narrative, 1550–1900.* New York: Twayne

di Leonardo M. 1997. White lies, black myths: rape, race, and the black "underclass." See Lancaster & di Leonardo 1997, pp. 53–68

Dines G, Humez JM, eds. 1995. *Gender, Race, and Class in the Media.* Thousand Oaks, CA: Sage

Duara P. 1996. Historicizing national identity, or who imagines what and when. In *Becoming National,* ed. G Eley, RG Suny, pp. 151–77. New York: Oxford Univ. Press

Ebersole GL. 1995. *Captured by Texts: Puritan to Postmodern Images of Indian Captivity.* Charlottesville, VA: Univ. Press of Virginia

Eisenstein Z. 1996. *Hatreds: Racialized and Sexualized Conflicts in the 21st Century.* New York: Routledge

Enloe C. 1990. *Bananas Beaches, and Bases: Making Feminist Sense of International Politics.* Berkeley: Univ. Calif. Press

Epstein B. 1994. Anti-communism, homophobia, and the construction of masculinity in the postwar U.S. *Critical Sociol.* 20(3):21–38

Ericksen JA. 1999. *Kiss and Tell: Surveying Sex in the Twentieth Century.* Cambridge, MA: Harvard Univ. Press

Espiritu YE. 1997. *Asian American Women and Men: Labor, Laws, and Love.* Thousand Oaks, CA: Sage

Evans DT. 1993. *Sexual Citizenship: The Material Construction of Sexualities.* New York: Routledge

Evans S. 1979. *Personal Politics: The Roots of Women's Liberation in the Civil Rights Movement and the New Left.* New York: Vintage

Evans-Pritchard EE. 1940. *The Nuer.* Oxford, UK: Oxford Univ. Press

Fanon F. 1963. *White Skin, Black Masks.* New York: Grove

Ferber AL. 1998. *White Man Falling: Race, Gender, and White Supremacy.* New York: Rowman & Littlefield

Fischer MMJ. 1986. Ethnicity and the postmodern arts of memory. See Clifford & Marcus 1986, pp. 194–233

Floris JW, ed. 1990. *An American Profile— Opinions and Behavior, 1972-1989.* Detroit, MI: Gale Res.

Foucault M. 1977. *The History of Sexuality: An Introduction.* Vol. 1. New York: Random House

Foucault M. 1985. *The History of Sexuality: The Use of Pleasure.* Vol. 2. New York: Random House

Foucault M. 1986. *The History of Sexuality: The Care of the Self.* Vol. 3. New York: Random House

Fredrickson GM. 1988. *The Arrogance of Race: Historical Perspectives on Slavery, Racism, and Social Inequality.* Middletown, CT: Wesleyan Univ. Press

Fried A. 1997. *McCarthyism.* New York: Oxford Univ. Press

Fuss D. 1989. *Essentially Speaking: Feminism, Nature and Difference.* New York: Routledge

Fuss D. 1991. *Inside/Out: Lesbian Theories, Gay Theories.* New York: Routledge

Gabriel J. 1997. *Whitewash: Racialized Politics and the Media.* New York: Routledge

Gagnon JH, Simon W. 1973. *Sexual Conduct:*

The Social Sources of Human Sexuality. Chicago: Aldine

Garland Library of Narratives of North American Indian Captivities. 1977. Vols. 1–111. New York: Garland

Giddings P. 1984. *When and Where I Enter: The Impact of Black Women on Race and Sex in America.* New York: William Morrow

Ginsberg EK, ed. 1996. *Passing and the Fictions of Identity.* Durham, NC: Duke Univ. Press

Godbeer R. 1999. Eroticizing the middle ground: Anglo-Indian sexual relations along the eighteenth-century frontier. See Hodes 1999, pp. 91–111

Grosz E. 1994. *Volatile Bodies: Toward a Corporeal Feminism.* Bloomington, IN: Indiana Univ. Press

Gunning S. 1996. *Race, Rape, and Lynching: The Red Record of American Literature, 1890–1912.* New York: Oxford Univ. Press

Gutierrez RA. 1991. *When Jesus Came, the Corn Mothers Went Away: Marriage, Sexuality, and Power in New Mexico, 1500–1846.* Stanford, CA: Stanford Univ. Press

Gutierrez RA, Jones C. 1995. *Rethinking the Borderlands: Between Chicano Culture and Legal Discourse.* Berkeley: Univ. Calif. Press

Guttman MC. 1996. *The Meanings of Macho: Being a Man in Mexico City.* Berkeley: Univ. Calif. Press

Hale J. 1996. Are lesbians women? *Hypatia* 11(spring): 94–121

Hansen TB. 1996. Recuperating masculinity: Hindi nationalism, violence and the exorcism of the Muslim "other." *Critique Anthropol.* 16(2):137–72

Haraway DJ. 1991. *Simians, Cyborgs, and Women: The Reinvention of Nature.* London: Free Assoc.

Harden JD. 1997. The enterprise of empire: race, class, gender, and Japanese national identity. See Lancaster & di Leonardo 1997, pp. 487–501

Hare N, Hare J. 1984. *The Endangered Black Family: Coping with the Unisexualization and Coming Extinction of the Black Race.* San Francisco: Black Think Tank

Hartman SV. 1997. *Scenes of Subjection: Terror, Slavery, and Self-Making in Nineteenth-Century America.* New York: Oxford Univ. Press

Hartsock N. 1983. *Money, Sex, and Power: Toward a Feminist Historical Materialism.* New York: Longman

Hasan Z, ed. 1994. *Forging Identities: Gender, Communities and State in India.* Boulder, CO: Westview

Hasan Z. 1998. *Quest for Power: Oppositional Movements and Post-Congress Politics in Uttar Pradesh.* Delhi: Oxford Univ. Press

Hearn J, Sheppard DL, Tancred-Sheriff P, Burrell G, eds. 1989. *The Sexuality of Organization.* Newbury Park, CA: Sage

Hemphill E, ed. 1991. *Brother to Brother: New Writings by Gay Black Men.* Boston: Alyson

Herdt G. 1981. *Guardians of the Flutes.* New York: McGraw-Hill

Herdt G. 1982. *Rituals of Manhood.* Berkeley: Univ. Calif. Press

Herdt G. 1994. *Third Sex, Third Gender: Beyond Sexual Dimorphism in Culture and History.* New York: Zone

Herdt G. 1997. *Same Sex, Different Cultures: Gays and Lesbians Across Cultures.* Boulder, CO: Westview

Herdt G, Stoller RJ. 1990. *Intimate Communications: Erotics and the Study of Culture.* New York: Columbia Univ. Press

Hicks GL. 1995. *The Comfort Women: Japan's Brutal Regime of Enforced Prostitution in the Second World War.* New York: Norton

Hobsbawm EJ. 1990. *Nations and Nationalism since 1970.* Cambridge: Cambridge Univ. Press

Hobsbawm EJ, Ranger T, eds. 1983. *The Invention of Tradition.* Cambridge: Cambridge Univ. Press

Hodes M. 1993. The sexualization of reconstruction politics: white women and black men in the South after the Civil War. In *American Sexual Politics: Sex, Gender, and*

Race since the Civil War, ed. JC Fout, MS Tantillo, pp. 59–74. Chicago: Univ. Chicago Press

Hodes M. 1997. *White Women, Black Men: Illicit Sex in the Nineteenth-Century South.* New Haven, CT: Yale Univ. Press

Hodes M, ed. 1999. *Sex, Love, Race: Crossing Boundaries in North American History.* New York: New York Univ. Press

Holstein JA, Miller G, eds. 1993. *Perspectives on Social Problems: Reconsidering Social Constructionism,* Vol. 5. New York: Aldine

Horowitz D. 1975. Ethnic identity. In *Ethnicity: Theory and Experience*, ed. N Glazer, DP Moynihan, pp. 111–40. Cambridge: Harvard Univ. Press

Horowitz D. 1985. *Ethnic Groups in Conflict.* Berkeley: Univ. Calif. Press

Horowitz MC. 1991. *Race, Class, and Gender in Nineteenth Century Culture.* Rochester, NY: Rochester Univ. Press

Howard K. 1995. *Three Stories of the Korean Comfort Women.* London: Cassell

Human Rights Watch. 1995. *Slaughter among Neighbors: The Political Origins of Communal Violence.* New Haven, CT: Yale Univ. Press

Hunt DM. 1997. *Screening the Los Angeles "Riots:" Race, Seeing, and Resistance.* New York: Columbia Univ. Press

Hurtado AL. 1997. When strangers met: sex and gender on three frontiers. See Jameson & Armitage 1997, pp. 122–42

Hurtado AL. 1999. *Intimate Frontiers: Sex, Gender, and Culture in Old California.* Albuquerque, NM: Univ. New Mexico Press

Hutchinson EO. 1997 (1994). *The Assassination of the Black Male Image.* New York: Touchstone

Ignatiev N. 1995. *How the Irish Became White.* New York: Routledge

Ingraham C. 1996. The heterosexual imaginary: feminist sociology and theories of gender. See Seidman 1996, pp. 168–93

Irigaray L. 1985. *The Sex Which Is Not One.* Ithaca, NY: Cornell Univ. Press

Jackson S. 1996. Heterosexuality as a problem for feminist theory. In *Sexualizing the Social: Power and the Organization of Sexuality*, ed. L Adkins, V Merchant, pp. 15–34. New York: St. Martin's

Jacobs SE, Thomas W, Lang S, eds. 1997. *Two-Spirit People: Native American Gender Identity, Sexuality, and Spirituality.* Urbana, IL: Univ. Illinois Press

Jagose A. 1996. *Queer Theory: An Introduction.* New York: New York Univ. Press

Jameson E, Armitage S, eds. 1997. *Writing the Range: Race, Class, and Culture in the Women's West.* Norman, OK: Univ. Okla. Press

Jones JH. 1997. *Alfred C. Kinsey: A Public/Private Life.* New York: Norton

Jordan WD. 1968. *White over Black: American Attitudes Toward the Negro, 1550–1812.* Chapel Hill, NC: Univ. N. Carolina Press

Julien I, Mercer K. 1986. True confessions: a discourse on images of black male sexuality. *Ten–8 22*

Kawash S. 1997. *Dislocating the Color Line: Identity, Hybridity, and Singularity in African-American Narrative.* Stanford, CA: Stanford Univ. Press

Kestler FR. 1990. *The Indian Captivity Narrative: A Woman's View.* New York: Garland

Kinsey AC, Pomeroy WB, Martin CE. 1948. *Sexual Behavior in the Human Male.* Philadelphia: Saunders

Kinsey AC, Pomeroy WB, Martin CE. 1953. *Sexual Behavior in the Human Female.* Philadelphia: Saunders

Kipnis L. 1998. Adultery. *Crit. Inquiry* 24 (Winter) :289–327

Lancaster RN, di Leonardo M, eds. 1997. *The Gender/Sexuality Reader: Culture, History, Political Economy.* New York: Routledge

Laumann EO, Gagnon JH, Michael RT, Michaels S. 1994. *The Social Organization of Sexuality: Sexual Practices in the United States.* Chicago: Univ. Chicago Press

Leonard KI. 1992. *Making Ethnic Choices: California's Punjabi Mexican Americans.* Philadelphia, PA: Temple Univ. Press

Leong R, ed. 1996. *Asian American Sexualities:*

Dimensions of the Gay and Lesbian Experience. New York: Routledge

Limerick P. 1987. *The Legacy of Conquest: The Unbroken Past of the American West.* New York: Norton

Lipsitz G. 1998. *The Possessive Investment in Whiteness: How White People Profit from Identity Politics.* Philadelphia: Temple Univ. Press

Luker K. 1996. *Dubious Conceptions: The Politics of Teenage Pregnancy.* Cambridge: Harvard Univ. Press

Lutz CA, Collins JL. 1997. The color of sex: postwar photographic histories of race and gender in *National Geographic Magazine.* See Lancaster & di Leonardo 1997, pp. 291–306

Mac An Ghaill M. 1994. The making of black English masculinities. In *Theorizing Masculinities*, ed. H Brod, M Kaufman, pp. 183–99 Thousand Oaks, CA: Sage

MacKinnon C. 1989. *Toward a Feminist Theory of the State.* Cambridge, MA: Harvard Univ. Press

Malinowski B. 1927. *Sex and Repression in Savage Society.* New York: Harcourt, Brace

Malinowski B. 1929. *The Sexual Life of Savages in North-Western Melanesia.* New York: Horace Liveright

Manderson L, Jolly M, eds. 1997. *Sites of Desire, Economies of Pleasure: Sexualities in Asia and the Pacific.* Chicago: Univ. Chicago Press

Massad J. 1995. Conceiving the masculine: gender and Palestinian nationalism. *Middle East J.* 49:467–83

Masters WH, Johnson VE. 1966. *Human Sexual Response.* Boston: Little, Brown

Masters WH, Johnson VE. 1970. *Human Sexual Dysfunction.* Boston: Little, Brown

McAdam D. 1988. *Freedom Summer.* New York: Oxford Univ. Press

McClintock A. 1995. *Imperial Leather Race, Gender and Sexuality in the Colonial Contest.* London: Routledge

McGarry J, O'Leary B. 1995. *Explaining Northern Ireland: Broken Images.* Oxford: Blackwell

Mead M. 1923. *Coming of Age in Samoa.* New York: William Morrow

Mead M. 1935. *Sex and Temperament in Three Primitive Societies.* New York: William Morrow

Mercer K. 1991. Skin head sex thing: racial difference and the homoerotic imaginary. In *How Do I Look: Queer Film and Video*, ed. Bad Object-Choices, pp. 169–222. Seattle: Bay Press

Michael RT, Gagnon JH, Laumann EO, Kolata G. 1994. *Sex in America: A Definitive Survey.* Boston: Little, Brown

Modood T, Werbner P, eds. 1997. *The Politics of Multiculturalism in the New Europe: Racism, Identity and Community.* London: ZED

Moraga C. 1983. *Loving in the War Years.* Boston: South End Press

Moraga C, Anzaldua G, eds. 1981. *This Bridge Called My Back: Writings by Radical Women of Color.* Watertown, MA: Persephone

Mosse GL. 1985. *Nationalism and Sexuality: Middle-Class Morality and Sexual Norms in Modern Europe.* Madison, WI: Univ. Wisc. Press

Mosse GL. 1996. *The Image of Man: The Creation of Modern Masculinity.* New York: Oxford Univ. Press

Mumford KJ. 1997. *Interzones: Black/White Sex Districts in Chicago and New York in the Early Twentieth Century.* New York: Columbia Univ. Press

Mydans S. 1996. Inside a wartime brothel: the avenger's story. *New York Times* (11/12):A3

Nagel J. 1994. Constructing ethnicity: creating and recreating ethnic identity and culture. *Soc. Probl.* 41(1):152–76

Nagel J. 1996. *American Indian Ethnic Renewal: Red Power and the Resurgence of Identity and Culture.* New York: Oxford Univ. Press

Nagel J. 1998. Masculinity and nationalism: gender and sexuality in the making of nations. *Ethnic Racial Stud.* 21(2):242–69

Namias J. 1993. *White Captives: Gender and Ethnicity on the American Frontier.* Chapel Hill: Univ. No. Carolina

Nelson S. 1999. Livestock, boundaries, and public space in Spartanburg: African American men, elite white women, and the spectacle of conjugal relations. See Hodes 1999, pp. 313–27

Nero CI. 1991. Toward a black gay aesthetic: signifying in contemporary black gay literature. See E. Hemphill 1991, pp. 229–51

Ogden JA. 1996. "Producing" respect: the "proper woman" in postcolonial Kampala. In *Postcolonial Identities in Africa*, ed. R Werbner, T Ranger, pp. 165–92. London: ZED

Olzak S. 1998. Ethnic protest in core and periphery states. *Ethnic Racial Stud.* 21(2):187–217

Omi M, Winant H. 1994. *Racial Formation in the United States: From the 1960s to the 1980s.* New York: Routledge

Ortner SB. 1972. Is female to male as nature is to culture? *Feminist Stud.* 1(2):5–31

Ortner SB. 1996. *Making Gender: The Politics and Erotics of Culture.* Boston: Beacon

Page C. 1996. *Showing My Color: Impolite Essays on Race and Identity.* New York: Harper

Parker A, Russo M, Sommer D, Yaeger P, eds. 1991. *Nationalisms and Sexualities.* New York: Routledge

Patton C. 1997. To die for. In *Novel Gazing: Queer Readings in Fiction*, ed. E Sedgwick, pp. 330–52. Durham, NC: Duke Univ. Press

Petkov K. 1997. *Infidels, Turks, and Women: The South Slavs in the German Mind, circa 1400–1600.* New York: Peter Lang

Pewewardy C. 1998. Will the "real" Indians please stand up? *Multicult. Rev.* (June):36–42

Plummer K. 1995. *Telling Sexual Stories: Power, Change and Social Worlds.* New York: Routledge

Pouissaint A. 1978. What makes them tick. *Ebony* (October)

Povinelli EA. 1994. Sex acts and sovereignty: race and sexuality in the construction of the Australian nation. *Diacritics* 24(2–3):122–50

Queen C, Schimel L, eds. 1997. *PoMoSexuals: Challenging Assumptions about Gender and Sexuality.* San Francisco: Cleis

Ratti R, ed. 1993. *A Lotus of Another Color.* Boston: Alyson

Rich A. 1980. Compulsory heterosexuality and lesbian existence. *Signs* 5(4):631–60

Riggs M. 1991. Black macho revisited: reflections of a SNAP! queen, See E. Hemaphill 1991, pp. 253–57

Roediger DR. 1991. *The Wages of Whiteness: Race and the Making of the American Working Class.* London: Verso

Rothenberg PS. 1992. *Race, Class, and Gender in the United States: An Integrated Study.* New York: St. Martin's, 2nd ed.

Rothschild MA. 1982. *A Case of Black and White: Northern Volunteers and the Southern Freedom Summers, 1964–1965.* Westport, CT: Greenwood

Rubin LB. 1990. *Erotic Wars.* New York: Harper and Row

Rudrappa, Sharmila. 1999. Normative sexuality and the production of ethnicity: race and identity among (Asian) Indian immigrant families in the United States. Presented at Annu. Meet. Amer. Soc. Assoc., 94th, Chicago

Saldivar JD. 1997. *Border Matters: Remapping American Cultural Studies.* Berkeley: Univ. Calif. Press

Saunders K. 1995. In a cloud of lust: black GIs and sex in World War II. In *Gender and War: Australians at War in the Twentieth Century*, ed. J Damousi, M Lake, pp. 178–190. Cambridge: Cambridge Univ. Press

Savran D. 1998. *Taking It Like a Man: White Masculinity, Masochism, and Contemporary American Culture.* Princeton, NJ: Princeton Univ. Press

Saxton A. 1990. *The Rise and Fall of the White Republic.* New York: Verso

Schein L. 1995. The consumption of color and the politics of white skin in post-Mao China. *Social Text* 41:141–64

Scott JW. 1988. *Gender and the Politics of History.* New York: Columbia Univ, Press

Sedgwick EK. 1990. *The Epistemology of the Closet.* Berkeley: Univ. California Press

Sedgwick EK. 1993. Queer performativity: Henry James's *The Art of the Novel. GLQ: A Journal of Lesbian and Gay Studies* 1(1): 1–16

Seidman S, ed. 1996. Queer Theory/Sociology. New York: Blackwell

Seidman S. 1997. *Difference Troubles: Queering Social Theory and Sexual Politics.* Cambridge: Cambridge Univ. Press

Shaw RP, Wong Y. 1989. *Genetic Seeds of Warfare, Evolution, Nationalism, and Patriotism.* Boston: Unwin Hyman

Smith AD. 1989. The origins of nations. *Ethnic Racial Stud.* 12(3):340–67

Smith DN. 1998. The psychocultural roots of genocide: legitimacy and crisis in Rwanda. *The Am. Psychol.* 53(7):743–53

Smith G. 1988. *When Jim Crow Met John Bull: Black American Soldiers in World War II Britain.* New York: St. Martin's

Smith SL. 1987. Beyond princess and squaw: Army officers' perceptions of Indian women. In *The Women's West*, ed. S Armitage, E Jameson, pp. 63–75. Norman, OK: Univ. Oklahoma Press

Smith SL. 1990. *The View from Officers' Row: Army Perceptions of Western Indians.* Tucson, AZ: Univ. Arizona Press

Smits DD. 1991. "Squaw men," "half-breeds," and amalgamators: late nineteenth-century Anglo-American attitudes toward Indian-white race-mixing. *Am. Indian Cult. and Res. J.* 15(3):29–61

Spackman B. 1996. *Fascist Virilities: Rhetoric, Ideology, and Social Fantasy in Italy.* Minneapolis: Univ. Minn. Press

Spector M, Kitsuse JI. 1977. *Constructing Social Problems.* New York: Aldine

Stavans I. 1998. The Latin phallus. See Darder & Torres 1998, pp. 228–39

Steinberg DL, Epstein D, Johnson R, eds. 1997. *Border Patrols: Policing the Boundaries of Heterosexuality.* London: Cassell

Stoler AL. 1990. Making empire respectable: the politics of race and sexual morality in 20th-century colonial cultures. In *Imperial Monkey Business: Racial Supremacy in Social Darwinist Theory and Colonial Practice*, ed. J Breman, P de Rooy, A Stoler, WF Wertheim, pp. 35–70. Amsterdam: VU Univ. Press

Stoler AL. 1995. *Race and the Education of Desire.* Durham, NC: Duke Univ. Press

Stoler AL. 1997. Carnal knowledge and imperial power: gender, race, and morality in colonial Asia. See Lancaster & di Leonardo 1997, pp. 13–36

Stoller RJ, Herdt G. 1985. Theories of the origins of homosexuality. *Arch. Gen. Psychiatry* 42:399–404

Sturdevant SP, Stoltzfus B. 1992. *Let the Good Times Roll: Prostitution and the U.S. Military in Asia.* New York: New Press

Stychin CF. 1998. *A Nation by Rights: National Cultures, Sexual Identity Politics, and the Discourse of Rights.* Philadelphia, PA: Temple Univ. Press

Sweet T. 1993. Masculinity and self-performance in the *Life of Black Hawk. Am. Lit.* 65(3):475–99

van den Berghe P. 1978. Race and ethnicity: a sociobiological perspective. *Ethnic Racial Stud.* 1(1):401–11

Wallace M. (1978)1990. *Black Macho and the Myth of the Black Superwoman.* New York: Verso

Ward A, Gregory J, Yuval-Davis N, eds. 1992. *Women and Citizenship in Europe: Borders, Rights and Duties.* Stoke-on-Trent: Trentham Books and EFSF

Ware V. 1997. Purity and danger: race, gender and tales of sex tourism. In *Back to Reality? Social Experience and Cultural Studies*, ed. A McRobbie, pp. 133–51. Manchester: Manchester Univ. Press

Warner M, ed. 1993. *Fear of a Queer Planet.* Minneapolis: Univ. Minn. Press

Warner M. 1999. *The Trouble with Normal.* New York: Simon & Schuster

Waters MC. 1990. *Ethnic Options: Choosing*

Identities in America. Berkeley: Univ. Calif. Press

Waters MC. 1994. Ethnic and racial identities of second generation blacks in New York City. *Int. Migration Rev.* 28:795–820

Weber C. 1999. *Faking It: U.S. Hegemony in a "Post-Phallic" Era.* Minneapolis: Univ. Minn. Press

Weber M. 1978. *Economy and Society: An Outline of Interpretative Sociology*, ed. G Roth, C Wittich. Berkeley: Univ. California Press, vol. 1

Weeks J. 1995. *Invented Moralities: Sexual Values in an Age of Uncertainty.* New York: Columbia Univ. Press

Weitz MC. 1995. *Sisters in the Resistance: How Women Fought to Free France, 1940–45.* New York: Wiley

Wiegman R. 1993. The anatomy of lynching. In *American Sexual Politics: Sex, Gender, and Race since the Civil War*, ed. JC Fout, MS Tantillo, pp. 223–45. Chicago: Univ. Chicago Press

Williams D. 1998. *The "Soul Patrol": Gatekeepers of THE BLACK identity.* Presented at Annu. Meet. Midwest Soc. Soc 60th, Kansas City

Williamson J. 1984. *The Crucible of Race: Black-White Relations in the American South Since Emancipation.* New York: Oxford Univ. Press

Wittig M. 1992. *The Straight Mind and Other Essays.* Boston: Beacon

Yancey WL, Ericksen EP, Juliani R. 1976. Emergent ethnicity: a review and reformulation. *Am. Sociol. Rev.* 41:391–402

Yetman NR, ed. 1999. *Majority and Minority: The Dynamics of Race and Ethnicity in American Life.* Boston: Allyn & Bacon

Young C. 1976. *The Politics of Cultural Pluralism.* Madison, WI: Univ. Wisconsin Press

Young C. 1993. The dialectics of cultural pluralism: concept and reality. In *The Rising Tide of Cultural Pluralism: The Nation-State at Bay?* ed. C Young, pp. 3–35. Madison, WI: Univ. Wisc. Press

Zimmerman J. 1999. Crossing oceans, crossing colors: black Peace Corps volunteers and interracial love in Africa, 1961–1971. See Hodes 1999, pp. 514–29

Annu. Rev. Sociol. 2000. 26:135–68

PREJUDICE, POLITICS, AND PUBLIC OPINION: Understanding the Sources of Racial Policy Attitudes

Maria Krysan

Department of Sociology, University of Illinois at Chicago, Chicago, Illinois, 60607

Key Words   racial attitudes, African American attitudes, white attitudes, affirmative action, survey research

■ **Abstract**   This review examines the intersection of prejudice, politics, and public opinion. It focuses specifically on research that seeks to understand the sources of attitudes toward policies intended to benefit African Americans and other racial/ethnic minorities by ensuring equal treatment, providing opportunity enhancement, or striving for equal outcomes. After a review of the main patterns of white and African-American public opinion on this topic, three central theoretical interpretations of racial policy attitudes—new racism, politics and nonracial principles and values, and group conflict theories—are described and compared. The empirical evidence for each approach is assessed. Finally, directions of research that pursue a more complex view of racial policy attitudes are introduced. These include efforts to incorporate insights across theoretical domains as well as correcting an overemphasis on cognitive issues to the exclusion of affect. In addition, gaps in our understanding of "non-white" attitudes, nonprejudiced respondents, nonracial policies, and non-Americans are identified as potentially fertile ground for future research aimed at understanding the complexity of racial policy attitudes and what these can reveal about contemporary US race relations.

INTRODUCTION

Prejudice, Politics, Public Opinion. Separately, each of the three concepts constitutes a core interest for social scientists housed in one discipline or another—sociologists, social psychologists, political scientists. Researchers in these disciplines have developed theories of each concept and explored their connections, such as the extent to which public opinion comes into play in politics, or how prejudice plays out in politics more generally. This review does not examine the individual concepts, nor even pairs of them. Rather, the focus is on the intersection of all three. That is, how do we explain and understand public opinion on those political issues that are associated with race and are therefore potential factors in the influence of prejudice in politics?

0360-0572/00/0815-0135$14.00

The three-way connections across these concepts have generated a complex, controversial, and sometimes confusing body of research that seeks, in large part, to address the broader question of what racial policy attitudes reveal about the state of race and race relations in the contemporary United States. Clearly, racial policy attitudes are but one small piece of the complex picture that social scientists have assembled about racial attitudes—and an even smaller part of the fuller body of research on the issue of race more generally. Indeed, an interest in race and race relations spans many of the subareas within sociology—from efforts to describe and explain racial inequality in such areas as housing, income, wealth, education, and health (e.g., Farley 1996, Harrison & Bennett 1995, Williams & Collins 1995, Oliver & Shapiro 1995, Massey & Denton 1993, Farley et al 1994, Zubrinsky & Bobo 1996) to descriptions of the persistence of institutional and individual discrimination against African Americans in housing, employment, and everyday life (e.g., Yinger 1995, Feagin & Sikes 1994, Kirschenman & Neckerman 1991, Cose 1993, Turner et al 1991) to historical and theoretical discussions of race and racism (e.g., Bonilla-Silva 1997, Omi & Winant 1994, Steinberg 1995). By not covering these important areas of research, the scope of the present review may seem narrow. However, the theoretical and empirical work that seeks to understand the sources of racial policy attitudes is substantial—and the implications of this work extend beyond a narrow concern with public opinion on a currently contentious issue. Indeed, the theoretical developments in this area of research have broader significance for understanding the contemporary dynamics of racial prejudice and race relations more generally.

I begin with the basic patterns of public opinion on racial policies and then describe the main theoretical arguments that have emerged to explain them. The arguments fall into three categories: new racism approaches, politics and nonracial principles and values, and group conflict. Each perspective offers a different model of race in general, and racial attitudes in particular, and so draws our attention to the complexity of this issue—a complexity that regularly surfaces in studies of race and race relations. For example, research has identified the problems of high rates of African-American joblessness, the urban underclass, and huge disparities by race in wealth (Wilson 1987, Harrison & Bennett 1994, Oliver & Shapiro 1995), but these bleak findings are paralleled by an unprecedented growth of the black middle class (Jaynes & Williams 1989, Farley 1996). Similarly, while there are signs of a substantial increase in the suburbanization of African Americans (Frey 1995, Harrison & Bennett 1995) and modest declines in racial residential segregation, particularly in newer cities and the West (Farley & Frey 1994), the pervasive pattern is one of "hypersegregation" in most of our nation's largest metropolises (Massey & Denton 1993). The message from studies of racial attitudes—and racial policy attitudes in particular—is no less complex and paradoxical, as will be shown. These patterns invite and reinforce approaches that recognize this complexity, thus moving away from an either/or perspective that characterizes much of the literature (L Bobo, forthcoming$_a$).

In the second section of this review I identify several existing gaps and new research directions—both methodological and theoretical. These include increasing attention to the often neglected role of affect, and the importance of examining the impact of nonattitudinal (e.g., demographic and contextual) factors, and studying respondents who are "nonprejudiced," non-Americans, or "non-whites." Developing these areas will do much to clarify the interrelationships among prejudice, politics, and public opinion, which will add to our knowledge about each of these individual areas of social science inquiry, as well as provide further insight into the significance of race in the minds of the American people today.

PATTERNS OF PUBLIC OPINION ON RACIAL POLICIES

Racial policy attitudes are opinions about government policies that are concerned with African Americans and other minorities. Generally speaking, the survey questions[1] used to tap support or opposition for racial policies ask about programs that fall under one of the following categories:

1. Equal treatment policies to protect blacks from discriminatory treatment in a variety of settings;

2. Opportunity enhancement policies, including programs to "help blacks help themselves," which can consist of special college scholarships and tax breaks for businesses;

3. Equal outcome policies, which typically involve special preferences in hiring, promotion, or college admissions, as well as general questions about how much effort or money the government should expend on "programs that assist blacks."[2]

*A **Methodological Aside*** Before describing the results of survey data on these types of policy questions, a fundamental question warrants our consideration: How effective are surveys in revealing how Americans think and feel about issues of race? Critics of the survey approach generally raise three concerns:

1. Survey data report a remarkable liberalization over the past 5 decades—this change, it is argued, is inconsistent with nonattitudinal evidence about the persistence of prejudice, discrimination, and racial inequality;

---

[1]Most of the work on this topic analyzes survey data from one of three main sources: the General Social Survey, the National Election Studies, and the recent Race and Politics Survey. Many laboratory experiments and studies using college student samples have also contributed to the discussion. However, in light of concerns about the representativeness of such studies (Sears 1986), my emphasis is on research using nationally representative samples. Occasional mention will be made of important directions of research using convenience samples.

[2]During earlier periods in American history, anti-miscegenation and other Jim Crow laws were also legitimately seen as "racial policies," though the purpose of those laws was quite the contrary of racial policies that are debated today.

2. in the present racial climate in the United States, social desirability pressures operate to suppress self-reports of negative racial attitudes; and

3. survey data on racial attitudes have little relevance to behavior outside the survey context.

The first of these criticisms largely misreads the full survey record on racial attitudes. It is indeed the case that certain racial attitudes—particularly those pertaining to the principles of racial equality—have undergone dramatic changes since the 1940s, and today they are accepted by the vast majority of Americans. But the attitudinal record is far more complex than this; indeed, as we will shortly see, the survey results on the very topic of this review—racial policy attitudes—provide an important counterexample to the assertion that racial attitude surveys paint nothing but a rosy picture about racial attitudes.

The remaining two criticisms, which have both methodological and theoretical foundations, are more complicated issues. To be sure, self-reports of any socially sensitive topic, including race, are subject to social desirability pressures. To conclude, though, that survey data are therefore of little use is too extreme a position. On the one hand, we know from race-of-interviewer (e.g., Schuman & Converse 1971, Davis 1997) and mode of administration experiments (Krysan 1998) that the social context of the interview influences reports of racial attitudes. But we also know that not all racial attitude questions are equally influenced by such changes in the social context. Even more generally, it is also clear that different racial attitude questions yield very different patterns of responses. Respondents do not give uniformly liberal answers to all racial questions; nor do all questions show uniformly liberalizing trends. With respect to the former, for example, if social desirability concerns dominated responses, then it is difficult to explain why whites should find integration with "a few" blacks to be so much more acceptable than integration with "a majority" of blacks (Schuman et al 1997). Thus, on the one hand, the evidence for social desirability effects cautions against taking survey responses at face value; but it does not require us to dismiss their results altogether. Indeed, what are usually considered methodological flaws—such as race of interviewer or mode of administration effects—can be used instead as opportunities to observe interracial interactions and/or to identify racial issues that do and do not generate tension.

The third criticism—that attitudes have little bearing on behavior—calls for an equally nuanced perspective. LaPiere's (1934) classic study that compared innkeepers' responses to a survey about whether they would serve Chinese customers to their subsequent behavior, when LaPiere and his Chinese traveling companions arrived at their hotels or restaurants, questioned in dramatic fashion the connection between attitudes and behaviors. A detailed examination of this complex issue is beyond the scope of this review, but for useful discussions, see Schuman & Johnson 1976, Ajzen & Fishbein 1977, Eagly & Chaiken 1993, Schuman et al 1997. In general, the theoretical and empirical research on this topic suggests that it is unrealistic to expect a one-to-one correspondence between a respondent's report of their attitude in a survey and a subsequent behavioral act. Just as reports of attitudes vary depending on the context of the interview, so too does behavior in the real world vary depending on the social context. Thus, we should expect correlational consistency rather than literal consistency: Those who score higher on attitudinal reports of negative racial attitudes will behave, over a series of acts, in a manner more discriminatory or prejudicial than those who score lower (Schuman et al 1997).

Using this more complete perspective, there is evidence to support a connection between attitudes and behavior. In addition, the trend data argue for a general correspondence between attitudinal reports and actual behavior. For example, attitude survey data indicate that the principle of residential integration, white comfort levels with living with small numbers of African Americans, and approval for interracial marriage have all experienced quite considerable increases in support (Schuman et al 1997). Likewise, behavioral indicators, in the form of actual residential integration and racial intermarriage are consistent with this trend over time. Clearly, the survey data indicate much higher levels of support than the behaviors themselves (i.e., racial intermarriage continues to be rare, and residential segregation persists at high levels in many metropolitan areas); there is nevertheless change in the same direction within each behavior (Bobo forthcoming, Schuman et al 1997).

Finally, the specific attitudes that are our focus have political consequences in and of themselves. As Burstein (1985) demonstrated using the 1964 Civil Rights Act as an example, public opinion can play an important role in the passage of legislation. With regard to racial policy attitudes, public opinion has had an even more direct effect in recent years: Witness the cases in California and Washington where residents were asked to vote on ballot initiatives to eliminate affirmative action in their respective states; both iniatives were approved.

None of this is to argue that survey data are the only source of information about how people think and feel about race. Indeed, combinations of methodologies are the ideal approach to understanding social phenomenon. In addition to complementing survey research with other methods, such as in-depth interviewing, observational studies, and laboratory experiments, innovations within survey methods can also be exploited.

We turn now to the survey record itself. One clear message is that as the goal and type of policy vary, so too does the level of support among both African Americans and whites. Thus, to declare, as many do, that blacks are universally in support of progressive racial policies or that whites are equally emphatic in their opposition is to overlook the full body of survey data (Steeh & Krysan 1996). Indeed, sometimes within a single category of policies there is variation. For example, among policies intended to ensure equal treatment, white support for open housing laws climbed to 67% by the mid-1990s, while federal involvement to ensure school integration and fair treatment in jobs was supported by just over one quarter of whites (Schuman et al 1997).[3] Government efforts to improve the living standards of blacks are supported by about 1 of every 10 whites. At the same time, about one half view

---

[3] Recently, however, Krysan (1999) has argued that the questions used to tap fair treatment in employment and open housing may be uncertain in meaning.

the current level of spending by the government to be about right—and 20 to 25 percent would like to see it increased (Schuman et al 1997).

Specific programs to "help blacks help themselves," such as providing tax breaks to businesses that locate in black areas (42%), spending money on early education programs in predominantly black areas (67%), and awarding college scholarships to black students (69%) typically receive much higher levels of support (Kinder & Mendelberg 1995). Finally, white support for preferential treatment often varies as a function of the framing of the question.[4] For example, 41% of whites are in favor of preferences for blacks in cases where businesses were found to be guilty of racial discrimination (Stoker 1998). Outside of this context, support plummets to 12% for preferences in hiring and promotion and 26% for quotas in college admissions (Schuman et al 1997). Although time series data for questions on most racial policies are not available prior to the 1980s, the available data show little change over time (Steeh & Krysan 1996).

African Americans are substantially more supportive of racial policies than whites, but black public opinion is far from homogeneous (Schuman et al 1997, Kinder & Sanders 1996, Sigelman & Welch 1991, Tuch et al 1997). For example, in 1996, 84% of African Americans were in favor of open housing laws, but support for busing was just about 60% and support for the government's role in making sure that blacks received "fair treatment" in jobs was approved by 64% of African Americans (Schuman et al 1997). In the 1990s, African Americans are considerably more likely (between 70% and 84%) than whites to believe that government spending on programs to help blacks is too little. However, black support for general government efforts to help blacks has declined considerably since the 1970s, and in the mid-1990s, it fell below a majority, a pattern that has yet to be explained (Schuman et al 1997).

Preferences and quotas are more broadly supported by African Americans than by whites, though here, too, context is important. Quotas in college admissions are favored by more than three quarters of blacks; preferences in hiring and promotion are less popular, but still favored by a majority—59% in 1996 (Schuman et al 1997). However, when preferential treatment in jobs and college admissions are pitted directly against ability as determined by test scores, support in 1991 for preferences drops to barely one fifth (Steeh & Krysan 1996).

However, it is neither the variation in support by policy type nor by racial group that has sparked so much research attention. Instead, it is the lackluster support for policies as contrasted to the near-universal support for abstract principles of racial equality. For example, while 96% of whites and 99% of blacks in 1995 agreed that "blacks and whites should be allowed to go to the same schools," only about 25% and 57%, respectively, think the federal government should see to it that this happens (Schuman et al 1997). A flurry of research has emerged to address the problem posed by this pattern: In light of the gap between principle and policy,

---

[4]Framing effects are themselves the topic of considerable research. See, for example, Kinder & Sanders (1996), Nelson et al (1997), and Nelson & Kinder (1996).

what significance do we attach to the answers we get when we ask whites and blacks questions like the following:

> Some people say that the government in Washington should see to it that white and black children go to the same schools. Others claim that this is not the government's business. Have you been concerned enough about this question to favor one side or the other? Do you think the government in Washington should see to it that white and black children go to the same schools, or stay out of this area, as it is not its business? (National Election Studies)

> Some people think that African Americans have been discriminated against for so long that the government has a special obligation to help improve their living standards. Others believe that the government should not be giving special treatment to African Americans. Where would you place yourself on this (5 point) scale, or haven't you made up your mind on this? (General Social Survey).

> Here are several things that the government in Washington might do to deal with the problems of poverty and unemployment among black Americans. I would like you to tell me whether you favor or oppose them. Giving business and industry special tax breaks for locating in largely black areas? (General Social Survey)

> Some people say that because of past discrimination, blacks should be given preferences in hiring and promotion. Others say that such preferences in hiring and promotion of blacks is wrong because it gives blacks advantages they haven't earned. What about your opinions, are you for or against preferential hiring and promotion of blacks? (National Election Studies).

The pattern of results for racial policy attitudes like these—as compared to the patterns for other types of racial attitudes—serves as a reminder that the contentiousness surrounding questions of race has not disappeared. Survey data on racial attitudes do not, therefore, paint a universally optimistic picture; they paint a complex one, with different types of survey questions telling different stories about the degree to which racial prejudice has increased, decreased, or stayed the same. Indeed, this is at the core of the controversy about the meaning of racial policy attitudes—and about the meaning of race in this country today.

THEORETICAL INTERPRETATIONS OF RACIAL POLICY ATTITUDES

One way to organize the vast theoretical and empirical research aimed at understanding the positions people take on policy questions is to focus on what the questions are, at a basic level. Each item is intended to tap a respondent's attitude—that is, to assess whether the person evaluates a particular object (the attitude object) favorably or unfavorably (Ajzen 1988). In the case of all four examples, the attitude object is a racial policy, which is in fact an amalgamation of two objects: a racial group and a policy proposal.

The debate about the meaning of racial policy attitudes comes down to assertions about which combination of a number of attitudinal variables is responsible for generating support or opposition. Table 1 identifies, much as a taxonomist would, four general categories thought to explain a fifth category—opposition to racial policies: 1. nonracial, "higher order" values/principles and politics; 2. racial affect (how people feel about the group); 3. racial beliefs (how people understand the group); and 4. racial policy beliefs (how people understand the policy itself). Within each category on Table 1 is a list of the specific beliefs, affects, or values that have been investigated. A more satisfying presentation of this table would include arrows connecting the various boxes to each other. But where these arrows go, which boxes are connected, and even which boxes appear on the diagram, are precisely the topic of controversy.

My primary goal here is to provide a general sense of the three main theoretical interpretations of racial policy attitudes—what I refer to as the new racism approaches, the politics and nonracial principles and values, and the group conflict

TABLE 1   Summary of attitudinal predictors of white racial policy attitudes

Category 1: Nonracial values, principles, and politics
  –political ideology (liberal/conservative)
  –appropriate role of the government
  –individualism
  –equality
  –fairness & principles of justice (i.e. meritocracy, consistency)

Category 2: Racial affect (How people feel about the group)
  –anti-black affect
  –lack of sympathy/admiration for blacks
  –in-group affect

Category 3: Racial beliefs (How people understand the group)
  –beliefs about African Americans' current status, life experiences, and rightful expectations
  –beliefs attributing racial inequality to structural or individual causes
  –beliefs about the characteristics of African Americans
  –beliefs about the influence of African Americans and the threat that they pose

Category 4: Racial policy beliefs (How people understand the policy itself)
  –beliefs about the fairness of the policy
  –beliefs about the costs of the policy
  –beliefs about the benefits of the policy

Category 5: Racial policy attitudes
  –support or opposition for equal or treatment, opportunity enhancement, or equal
    outcome polices

perspectives. I draw on the taxonomy in Table 1 to highlight the similarities and differences across these theories by pointing out which categories are thought to be connected, which rise to prominence, and which fade to the background. The emphasis is on recent contributions rather than a complete history of each theory or a thorough accounting of all of the empirical evidence. Given the volume of research generated by this topic, such an attempt would try the patience of reader and writer alike.

Before turning to the three theories, it is important to note that research on racial policy attitudes has largely ignored the opinions of African Americans. The theoretical imbalance this has created has been highlighted recently (Bobo 2000, Dawson 2000, Jackman 1994). However, I am unfortunately bound to replicate this imbalance, since this is a review of the existing literature. Where available, results from analyses of blacks' racial policy attitudes is noted.

The New Racism Approaches

The theoretical interpretations I include under the rubric of the new racism approach are similar because they attempt to explain why whites show nearly universal support for the abstract principles of racial equality, while at the same time remaining stubbornly opposed to efforts to ensure that equality. Symbolic racism, defined as "a blend of antiblack affect and the kind of traditional American moral values embodied in the Protestant Ethic" (Kinder & Sears 1981, p. 416), was the first approach to emerge. Early work tested self-interest versus prejudice as explanations for whites' preferences in mixed-race political contests[5] and for their attitudes toward busing to achieve racial integration in schools (Sears & Kinder 1971, Sears et al 1979, 1980); subsequent work developed the symbolic racism perspective (Kinder & Sears 1981, Sears et al 1997). According to this perspective, white Americans' reactions to these issues were driven less by a rational calculus of the policy's impact on their own lives and interests, and more by a range of sentiments, including "the belief that racial discrimination is largely a thing of the past, that blacks should just work harder to overcome their disadvantages, and that blacks are making excessive demands for special treatment and get too much attention from elites, so their gains are often undeserved" (Sears et al 1997, p. 22).

---

[5]Mixed race political contests are an obvious arena in which prejudice, politics, and public opinion come together with great political significance. There is a substantial literature devoted to identifying how racial prejudice influences white voting patterns in mixed race elections (e.g., Pettigrew & Alston 1988, Citrin et al 1990, Sears et al 1979), as well as the degree to which candidates utilize campaign strategies designed to invoke racial fears and hostilities (Kinder & Sanders 1996, Mendelberg 1997, Metz & Tate 1995). Recent experimental work has shown subtle ways in which evaluations of black candidates are influenced by racial attitudes (Reeves 1997, Sigelman et al 1995, Terkildsen 1993). A detailed discussion of this research is beyond the scope of this review.

Since its introduction, symbolic racism has been joined by several other forms: modern racism, racial resentment, subtle prejudice, and laissez-faire racism. The focus of each is on the movement in the United States away from an old-fashioned racism based on beliefs about biological inferiority to new, more subtle forms. All of the new racism concepts are measured (wholly or in part) by some of the racial beliefs shown in Table 1, Category 3.

Despite this similarity, the new racism approaches vary in their theoretical foundations and emphases. Closest to symbolic racism is modern racism, which focuses on beliefs about the persistence of discrimination against blacks and emphasizes the methodological problem of measuring racial attitudes in an era when whites no longer see themselves as racist (McConahay 1986). Subtle prejudice (Pettigrew & Meertens 1995) is unique in that the theory and empirical tests of it have been developed in western Europe. In addition, subtle prejudice is measured only partly by racial beliefs (as reflected by perceptions of cultural differences). Affect, a second crucial component of subtle prejudice, is discussed in a later section. Kinder & Sanders (1996) recently proposed the term racial resentment to replace symbolic racism, defining it in much the same way as symbolic racism, but stating even more forcefully that individualism in particular combines with "racial anger and indignation" (p. 294) to create racial resentment.

Laissez-faire racism is theoretically very different from the other approaches in this category, but it is included here because of its use of racial beliefs similar to those used by the other new racism approaches. Laissez-faire racism explains historical patterns in racial attitudes by demonstrating how changes in political and social relations necessitated a change in racial ideology (Bobo et al 1997). At an individual level, laissez-faire racism is tapped in part by beliefs—stereotypes about blacks as a group, and a denial of societal level responsibility for racial inequality. Laissez-faire racism is distinctive in that these beliefs have their origin not in individual psychology but in group level conflict (Bobo et al 1997). Indeed, this form of new racism is rooted in Blumer's theory of prejudice as a sense of group position, and it is discussed in the section on group conflict theories.

The empirical evidence connecting the racial beliefs used to tap the different new racism approaches with racial policy attitudes is robust across different data sets, time periods, and cultures. The measures of new racism are a statistically significant—and often the strongest—predictor of white opposition to a variety of racial policies. Moreover, whereas the earliest research in this tradition—on symbolic racism—typically included only self-interest as a competing explanation, more recent work controls for numerous other attitudinal predictors derived from competing theoretical interpretations. In each of these, the specific racial beliefs identified with the new racism approaches prevail in importance. (Recent analyses include Alvarez & Brehm 1997, Kinder & Sanders 1996, Meertens & Pettigrew 1997, Sears et al 1997, Sears et al 2000, Hughes 1997, Bobo & Kluegel 1997.)

One might think the robustness of these findings would be irrefutable support for the new racism approaches. However, the ongoing dispute is about the significance—substantively—to assign to the statistical association, not its existence. In essence, the question is: Do racial beliefs emanate from individual-level psychological processes, group-level conflict, or nonracial principles such as political conservatism or individualism? The details of the latter perspectives are discussed shortly, but for now I highlight research that has responded to early criticisms, particularly of symbolic racism, since it has generated much of the debate.

In a 1988 description, Sears addressed measurement problems in early work on symbolic racism, such as the inclusion in symbolic racism scales of items tapping support for racial policies themselves or measures of group conflict (Sniderman & Tetlock 1986, Bobo 1983). The problem, in the case of the former, is that there is overlap in content between measures of the independent and dependent variables. This raises serious questions about whether it is the overlap that explains the statistical association, rather than the causal forces that are presumed and asserted by the theories. More recent analyses in the symbolic racism vein have responded by removing those items in the symbolic racism scale that refer to government actions (Sears et al 1997). However, Schuman (2000) presses the issue beyond initial objections to including items that refer to the government and instead points to a more subtle overlap between the independent and dependent variables. For example, he notes that the wording of one of the policy questions (used as a dependent variable) includes the statement that "blacks . . . should help themselves" as a reason to oppose the government in Washington "making every effort to improve the social and economic conditions of blacks." At the same time, one of the items routinely used to measure prejudice (including symbolic racism, racial resentment, etc) asks whether respondents agree that "if blacks would only try harder they could be just as well off as whites." As Schuman (2000: 305) concludes:

> These two questions are not identical . . . but they are so close in essential substance that they might conceivably be part of the same scale of racial attitudes. . . . More generally, the two types of items labeled "prejudice" and "racial policy"—are so close in implication that a strong association between them might be thought of as indicating somewhat different aspects of the same general construct, negative attitudes toward the need to help blacks, rather than as distinguishing cause from effect.

This is a thorny methodological and theoretical problem. One way to begin to tackle it is to address the fundamental question: What are the origins of the new racism beliefs—and are they consistent with the dynamics asserted by their respective theories? Recently, analysts have turned their attention to this important issue (Sears et al 1997, Sears et al 2000, Bobo & Kluegel 1997). For example, according to the symbolic racism theory, anti-black affect and individualism should be key predictors—thus, one would draw arrows from Categories 1 and 2 to Category 3. Although Sears et al (1997) conclude that racial affect predicts symbolic racism, they find scant support for the power of individualism. Instead, egalitarianism—which according to the theory should *not* be an important influence—is closely related to symbolic racism. Analyses like this, which test the theoretical underpinnings of the observed statistical associations between specific racial beliefs and policy attitudes, are an important next step in assessing a theory's utility.

Politics and Nonracial Principles and Values

The most vocal criticisms of the new racism approaches come from those who privilege nonracial politics, values, and principles over race and racial prejudice. For example, one set of scholars points to the different levels of support across policy types and concludes that the wide variation cannot be explained without moving beyond a racial framework. Policy support varies, it is argued, because of politics and because the policies are connected in different ways to key nonracial values and principles. Early work from this perspective downplayed the racial components of these attitudes (e.g., Rothbart 1976, Lipset & Schneider 1978, Feldman 1983). In Table 1, the principles approach connects Category 1 directly with racial policy attitudes (Category 5). Scholars have tested hypotheses about the influence of a long list of nonracial principles and values, including general political ideology and attitudes toward the appropriate role of the government, individualism, egalitarianism, stratification ideologies, and justice concerns.

Political Ideology and Attitudes Toward the Government   Partly in response to early criticisms, political ideology and attitudes toward the federal government have been incorporated more regularly into analyses of racial policy attitudes. Though mixed, the results generally confer some significance on political ideology and attitudes toward the government. People who prefer a limited government or identify their ideology as conservative tend to oppose equal treatment policies, government spending on blacks, and preferences in hiring and promotion (Kinder & Sanders 1996, Meertens & Pettigrew 1997, Sears et al 1997, Sniderman & Piazza 1993, Bobo 1991, Virtanen & Huddy 1998, Stoker 1998, Tuch & Hughes 1996). The question, though, is one of degree.

Sniderman & Carmines (1997) clearly privilege the role of politics: ". . . the contemporary debate over racial policy is driven primarily by conflict over what government should try to do, and only secondarily over what it should try to do *for blacks*" (p. 4). Sniderman and his colleagues (1993) trace the historical development of racial politics and argue that the oft-cited paradox between principle and policy disappears when politics are taken seriously. Indeed, only by taking politics into consideration, they argue, can variation in support across different policies be explained. Prejudice has a role—but it is limited and restricted to certain types of policies and people. For example, perceptions of the level of effort by blacks and discrimination against blacks[6] predict support for government spending on blacks, but such perceptions have little significance for equal treatment

---

[6]They interpret these perceptions, which are identical to those used by others to tap new racism, as reflecting "fairness" and "effort" principles.

policies (Sniderman & Piazza 1993). More recently, Sniderman et al (2000) conclude that racial prejudice "is a minor factor driving opposition to affirmative action—understood to entail either preferential treatment or racial quotas—while there is an accumulation of evidence that it is a more powerful force in fueling opposition to welfare" (p. 276). The work by Sniderman and colleagues has been the subject of considerable debate on both theoretical and methodological grounds (for critiques, see several chapters in the volume edited by Sears et al 2000).

Analyses controlling for a host of nonracial predictors draw a different conclusion about the relative importance of politics versus race. For example, Kinder & Sanders (1996) find that belief in a limited government reduces support for racial policies among both blacks and whites, but the effects are modest (small in comparison to racial resentment, for example), and they are consistent only for questions that mention the federal government explicitly. For the most part, when measures of ideology, views regarding the appropriate role of the government, and in a few cases, party identification are included, they are often statistically significant but rarely do they dwarf the effects of racial beliefs (see also Sears et al 1997).

Individualism   Kinder & Mendelberg (2000: 47) describe individualism's persistent hold on US society: "[I]n America today, idleness is still a moral defect; hard work, in and of itself, a moral virtue; dependence on others, a disreputable condition; economic success, still the American Dream". Lipset & Schneider (1978) were among the first to argue that these values are an important foundation for objections to racial policies, because certain policies are seen as violating the individualist's perception that people—including blacks—should "do it on their own." At the aggregate level, individualism provides a reasonably good interpretation of why, for example, support for equal treatment policies and compensatory programs is greater than support for preferential treatment. The latter more explicitly conflict with an individualist perspective (e.g. Lipset & Schneider 1978, Sniderman & Piazza 1993).

However, individualism comes up short in predicting individual-level variation: The most consistent finding is that those who value individualism more dearly do not oppose racial policies more strongly, a finding that holds for both blacks and whites (Alvarez & Brehm 1997, Kinder & Sanders 1996, Bobo & Kluegel 1993, Tuch & Hughes 1996, Bobo 1991, Bobo & Kluegel 1997, Hurwitz & Peffley 1992, Sears et al 1997, Hughes 1997, Kluegel & Smith 1983, Kluegel & Smith 1986). This lack of relation—which shows up in analyses of the predictors both of racial policy attitudes and of symbolic racism (Sears et al 1997, Sniderman et al 2000)—is particularly problematic for the symbolic racism and racial resentment perspectives, which rely heavily on individualism's force (Sidanius et al 1992). As Schuman (2000) notes, equally puzzling is that individualism does predict other kinds of policy attitudes, but not racial policies (Kinder & Mendelberg 2000).

Equality   Support for equality generally fares better than individualism in predicting racial policy attitudes; people who strongly endorse the principle of equality are generally more favorable toward progressive racial policies (Kinder & Sanders 1996, Sears et al 2000, Tuch & Hughes 1996, Alvarez & Brehm 1997, Bobo 1991, Kluegel & Smith 1983, Kluegel & Smith 1986, Sidanius et al 1992, Sidanius et al 1996). This holds for both blacks and whites, though Bobo (1991) finds that equality of a certain type—a belief in the collective responsibility of society to provide certain minimum guarantees to its citizens and thereby to reduce unfair social inequality—has a stronger effect for whites than blacks.

These findings, coupled with a lack of significance for individualism, pose a problem for symbolic racism theory, which presumes the opposite: that racial egalitarianism no longer plays a role in racism, while individualism is the dominant force. This puzzle leads Sears et al (2000) to dissect the frequently used National Election Studies scale of egalitarianism, which shows a strong effect on racial policy attitudes. They discovered that the scale taps belief in two very different kinds of equality. The first is a belief in the traditional notions of equal treatment. The second involves the perception that equality has not yet been achieved in our society, and beliefs about what has and should be done to ensure equality. Sears et al (2000) demonstrate that the first type of equality has little to do with either symbolic racism or racial policy attitudes. The second, with its individualistic overtones, is significantly related to both policy attitudes and symbolic racism, and is theoretically consistent with symbolic racism. An important message, also emphasized by Kinder & Sanders (1996), is that equality as a principle can take on many forms, and the Sears et al (2000) study confirms that adherence to different types of equality results in different views on racial policies.

Stratification Ideology   Kluegel & Smith (1983) directed attention to the importance of American beliefs about how the United States stratification system should and does operate. They argue that stratification ideology influences support for a variety of public policy issues, including racial policies, because often these policies involve interfering with this system. Kluegel & Smith (1983) tapped several different elements of stratification ideology, focusing on perceptions of how the system should work and how it does work. They found that people who believed that equality was just and beneficial were more likely to support programs to give preferences to blacks in college and business settings. Bobo & Kluegel (1993) also report that people who attribute poverty to structural causes are more supportive of the government's involvement in improving blacks' standard of living and increasing the amount of money the government should spend on assisting blacks. However, attributing poverty to individualistic causes generally does not influence support for progressive racial policies (Bobo & Kluegel 1993, Kluegel & Smith 1983).[7]

---

[7]In this work, individualism has a different meaning than described earlier. Individualism is treated here as attributing failure to individual traits; Kinder & Sanders (1996) were concerned instead with individualism in the sense of the Protestant work ethic. More generally, the concepts of both egalitarianism and individualism frequently suffer from a lack of conceptual and measurement clarity.

Racialized Stratification Ideology   Taking the importance of stratification ideology a step further, there is also a cognitively based body of research that focuses on stratification ideology as it applies specifically to blacks. This approach falls under Category 3 in Table 1 because it argues that racial policy attitudes are determined to a large degree by the beliefs people hold about why racial inequality exists in the first place (Apostle et al 1983, Sigelman & Welch 1991, Kluegel 1985). People who believe black inequality is due to a lack of motivation, willpower, or in-born ability to learn generally oppose progressive racial policies, while those who assign responsibility to discrimination or a lack of educational opportunities are more enthusiastic. This pattern holds for both blacks and whites (Tuch & Hughes 1996, Bobo & Kluegel 1993, Bobo & Kluegel 1997, Sniderman & Piazza 1993, Stoker 1998, Sigelman & Welch 1991, Kluegel 1990).

Fairness   The possibility that people object to racial policies because they hold strongly to certain principles of fairness has captured the attention of social psychologists in particular. Variation in level of support across different policies, for example, might be explained in terms of the extent to which the characteristics of a particular program violate norms of distributive or procedural justice. Bobocel et al (1998) have used laboratory experiments with Canadian college student convenience samples to show that those who hold more strongly to the general principles of meritocracy and consistency[8] are more strongly opposed to affirmative action programs—particularly those programs that violate these norms. People vary in the degree to which they value meritocracy and consistency; holding dearly to these beliefs translates into opposition to certain types of racial policies.

But the picture is more complicated than this. Concerns about fairness and justice also crop up indirectly and are reflected in another beliefs category in Table 1. So far the focus has been on beliefs about blacks as a group (Category 3); the question of fairness, however, draws attention to beliefs about the policies themselves (Category 4). In essence, if people view a policy as unfair or violating justice norms, they will be unlikely to support it. For example, Nosworthy et al (1995) observed that affirmative action programs involving preferential treatment were deemed less fair than those that expanded the racial diversity of the candidate pool. At an individual level, recent analyses have demonstrated that the beliefs a person holds about a policy—including the degree to which it is perceived as fair—is a strong predictor of whether or not they will support it (Sidanius et al 2000, Bobo 2000).

This observation leads naturally to the question: What influences the perception that a policy is unfair or that it violates certain principles? Are objections genuine, or are they mere rationalizations? Importantly, are such perceptions race-neutral? Evidence from survey research and laboratory experiments suggests that they are not. For example, Bobocel et al (1998) found that high-prejudice and low-prejudice subjects differed in the extent to which they evaluated an affirmative

---

[8] Specifically, the beliefs that rewards should be allocated based on merit, and that the rules should apply consistently to all people.

action program as violating meritocracy or consistency, even when the program was explicitly described as not violating either of these principles. Evidence from a study by Dovidio and colleagues offers one possible explanation for this: White subjects rated high-ability blacks as less competent than their equally high-ability white counterparts (Dovidio et al 1989, Dovidio & Gaertner 1996, Murrell et al 1994). Thus, with these biased perceptions as a foundation, it is not surprising that even affirmative action programs described as not violating meritocracy are nevertheless construed as such by some whites. Though this evidence comes largely from college student convenience samples, recent national surveys have included questions about racial policy beliefs and shown that racial animus or concerns about maintaining one's group dominance may color these beliefs (Bobo 2000, Sidanius et al 2000).

Summary   At times the exchange between the nonracial principles and new racism research agendas seems hopelessly mired in conflict and confusion. Nevertheless, out of this ongoing debate, our understanding of racial policy attitudes has grown. Methodologically, the criticisms of the new racism agenda have resulted in increased attention to measurement issues, as well as attempts to unravel the bases of new racism. The complexity of racial policy attitudes is further recognized by the now-routine inclusion of such nonracial principles as individualism, political party identification, ideology, and egalitarianism. The fundamental debate, of course, centers on the relative importance of these factors—and, in some cases, their presumed race-neutrality.

One observation, highlighted by the nonracial principles perspective, has not been satisfactorily addressed. Though there is a consensus that different racial policies are endorsed more and less enthusiastically by whites and blacks alike, the unanswered question is: Are the bases of support or opposition across different policy types fundamentally the same or different? The premise of the nonracial camp is that they are different; the premise of the new racism camp is that they are the same. On this point the empirical evidence is mixed. Some analysts report a smattering of differences across policy types but conclude that the correlates across different policies are fundamentally the same (e.g., Tuch & Hughes 1996, Sidanius et al 2000, Sears et al 1997). Others argue that policies from different domains have different bases of support, that racial prejudice has only narrow implications, and only for certain subgroups in the population such as liberals or those with less formal education (Sniderman & Piazza 1993, Sniderman & Carmines 1997). Finally, experimental social psychologists have also concluded that the predictors of racial policy attitudes differ importantly depending on the characteristics of the program (Bobocel et al 1998, Nosworthy et al 1995).

Neither side of the debate satisfactorily addresses the full body of evidence, however. From the new racism side, the question of why the levels of support vary so radically from policy to policy remains unanswered. Those arguing for the primary importance of nonracial principles, by contrast, have not reckoned with several empirical findings in which whites' level of support is sensitive to changes in the race of the interviewer, varies when the target of the policy is blacks versus other groups, and is consistently predicted by racial sentiments (Kinder & Sanders 1996, Bobo & Kluegel 1993, Murrell et al 1994, Sidanius et al 2000, Sears et al 1997).

Group Conflict

Sociologists have been responsible for bringing the issue of intergroup conflict and group interest to the discussion of racial policy attitudes. This approach reacts to the individual-level irrational pathology model of prejudice by reminding us that racial policies are about the allocation of resources, arguing that prejudice should be thought of as a sociological phenomenon growing out of unequal intergroup outcomes. There are three main variants of this approach, which are referred to here as the defense of dominant group interests, social dominance theory, and group interest.

Jackman (1994) argued that racial policy attitudes are not an outgrowth of personal prejudice, but a product of institutions and inequalities in our society—an ideology derived to defend the dominant group's interests. Drawing on conflict theory and Marxist assumptions, she argues that dominant groups creatively modify the important myths (dominant ideology) in society to justify and maintain existing inequalities (including race, class, and gender-based inequality). This ideology comes not from racial prejudice or negative affect but from the conflictual bases of group relations. From this macro-level perspective, the racial beliefs (Category 3) identified by the new racism scholars are merely "cognitive props" developed by the dominant group to effectively defend their dominance—not with force and hostility but with, as Jackman (1994) calls it, a "velvet glove." Specific racial beliefs emerge because they are politically self-serving (Jackman 1994). In this case, individualism reflects a legitimizing of the rights and requests of individuals while dismissing the rights and request of groups as illegitimate (Jackman & Muha 1984).[9]

Sidanius and his colleagues also operate from a conflict orientation but offer a psychological interpretation: The causal force behind group conflict (and by implication racial policy attitudes) is a human drive for group domination (Sidanius & Pratto 1993). Social dominance theory incorporates elements of symbolic racism, but symbolic racism is treated as simply one of the many legitimizing myths that serve to perpetuate the existing status hierarchy (Sidanius et al 1992). These myths are the link between a personality trait—social dominance orientation—and a specific racial policy attitude (Sidanius et al 1996).

Social dominance theory is in part a group-based interpretation of a characteristic that others have interpreted to be simply a principled objection rooted in strongly held American values: egalitarianism (or, more appropriately, according

---

[9]Again, the individualism central to Jackman's argument is therefore quite different from that previously discussed.

to Sidanius, inegalitarianism). After demonstrating a relationship between social dominance orientation and racial policy attitudes, more recent research has broadened to look more closely at individual differences in group dominance orientation by examining, for example, the influence of gender, work role, and ethnic identity (Pratto et al 1994). Sidanius and his colleagues have shown that social dominance orientation is discernible from other personality characteristics, such as interpersonal dominance and authoritarianism,[10] and is related to many of the legitimizing myths that contribute to social oppression (Pratto et al 1994). In contrast to other work, Sidanius and colleagues (2000) explicitly dismiss antiblack affect as an important predictor of racial prejudice and, by extension, racial policy attitudes.[11] However, dismissing affect does not discount race. For Sidanius and colleagues, what is important is one's attachment to the in-group, ethnocentrism, and a general ideology of group superiority (Levin et al 1998, Sidanius et al 2000).

The third group conflict-based theory is derived from Blumer's (1958) sociological interpretation of prejudice as a "sense of group position" and again shifts the focus from the individual to the group.[12]

Bobo and colleagues (Bobo et al 1997, Bobo 1999, Bobo 2000), in several recent publications, have been largely responsible for reinvigorating this theoretical approach and firmly placing Blumer's model of prejudice at a social psychological level, whereby attention is paid both to individual psychology and social structure. As Bobo (2000, pp. 142–43) argues:

> The core argument here is that racial politics unavoidably involves a nettlesome fusion of racial identities and attitudes with racial group interests. It suggests that many whites will oppose affirmative action not so much because they see a race-based policy as contravening their loftiest values or because they have learned a new, politically relevant set of resentments of blacks; but rather because they perceive blacks as competitive threats for valued social resources, statuses, and privileges.

---

[10]For further evidence of the difference between social dominance orientation and authoritarianism, see Altemeyer 1998.

[11]This assertion is based on the historical observation by van den Berghe (1967) that in the antebellum south, white attitudes toward blacks were a combination of neutral or even positive affect and beliefs in black inferiority; in the post-bellum period, affect turned more negative. Thus, affect cannot be conceived as the driving force behind racial prejudice. Jackman (1994) makes a similar argument.

[12]This perspective was initially applied to racial policy attitudes in direct response to symbolic racism, which ruled out the role of self-interest. Bobo (1983) argued it was a mistake to treat self-interest and group-interest as interchangeable. After pointing out that many of the measures of symbolic racism may belong more appropriately under perceptions of the threat posed by blacks, Bobo (1983) concluded that opposition to busing for racial integration reflects a defense of group interests, not a symbolic opposition rooted in non-rational and affective residues of socialization. See Sears & Kinder (1985) for a response to this critique.

Blumer (1958) identified four elements of group position that are central to prejudice: group identity, outgroup stereotyping,[13] preferred group status, and perceived threat. Of these, the last has received the most attention. Perceived threat is conceptualized not as a rational assessment of (group) interests, but as a subjective perception (Bobo 1988$_a$). For example, perceived group threat (whether one thinks the civil rights movement is moving too fast or too slow; or whether or not blacks are gaining too much influence in government) is derived from the realities of group conflict but is not necessarily an objective assessment of them; instead, perceived threat is connected to perceptions of incompatible interests and fraternal deprivation (Bobo 1988). As with several of the new racism approaches, the group interest perspective connects Category 3 with Category 5; the difference is in the theoretical basis for this connection. Some of the same beliefs that are used by symbolic racism researchers (e.g., that blacks are pushing too fast) are argued to be, instead, measures of group threat. In addition to these, however, are added beliefs such as: "[T]here is a high likelihood that a black person will get a job over an equally qualified white person" or "more jobs for blacks means less jobs for whites." Whites who endorse these beliefs are more opposed to the government ensuring equal opportunity (Tuch & Hughes 1996, Hughes 1997) and to special programs and preferential treatment for blacks (Virtanen & Huddy 1998, Hughes 1997, Kinder & Sanders 1990, Tuch & Hughes 1996).

Focusing on the group position and threat theory quite naturally raises the question of beliefs not just about blacks, but about the policy itself—Category 4. While earlier we discussed beliefs about the extent to which a policy violated norms of justice, here the emphasis is on beliefs about its costs and benefits. In an early study McClendon (1985) showed that respondents' beliefs about the costs of busing (such as whether children's safety would be jeopardized or the quality of

---

[13]As discussed earlier, Bobo, Kluegel & Smith's (1997) theory of laissez-faire racism, itself derived from Blumer's group position theory, is measured in part by outgroup stereotyping. Stereotypes are the subject of much study within psychology and social psychology, but they have played a less prominent role in analyses of racial policy attitudes. When included, they are sometimes labeled old-fashioned prejudice, and other times a new form of racism. Adding to the confusion, some indicators of individualistic attributions for racial inequality are difficult to distinguish from stereotypes: Compare a question asking whether blacks are disadvantaged because "they lack the motivation and willpower to work their way out of poverty" as against a question in which blacks are rated as either "lazy" or "hard-working." In general, it appears that racial stereotypes are not significant predictors of policies related to equal treatment, opportunity enhancement, or preferential treatment. However, general questions about government's efforts to improve the living conditions of blacks are related to stereotypes, though this appears to hold only for stereotypes about being hard-working, not about violence (Alvarez & Brehm 1997, Kinder & Mendelberg 1995, Sears et al 1997, Tuch & Hughes 1996, Bobo & Kluegel 1993, Virtanen & Huddy 1998, Sniderman & Piazza 1993, Hurwitz & Peffley 1992).

education would suffer) mediated the effects of both symbolic and old-fashioned racism on overall support or opposition toward busing. More recently, Bobo (2000) has shown that beliefs about the costs and benefits associated with affirmative action (that is, whether it is unfair to whites, forces employers to hire unqualified blacks, or gives an opportunity to qualified blacks who might not otherwise have had a chance) predict overall support for the policy. These racial policy beliefs are not purely political calculations; they correlate with measures of symbolic racism, ideology, perceived threat, and the race of the respondent (Bobo 2000).

To date, only the perceived costs and benefits of affirmative action–type policies have been closely examined. Exploring beliefs about the range of racial policies, including equal treatment policies, for example, may provide an alternative to the traditional grouping of racial policies based on their stated or implied goals—and their relationship to core principles and ideologies. The existing grouping is somewhat problematic because of the wide variation in support or opposition among policies with similar goals. The variation in support may be due in part to differences in perceived costs and benefits. Those policies perceived as not costing too much may be supported—regardless of racial prejudice, for example—simply because it does not hurt too much to do so. Thus, a more fruitful approach to conceptualizing different types of racial policies may be to focus on the degree to which policies differ in terms of their perceived costs and benefits.

WHAT ABOUT AFFECT?

Each of the theories discussed thus far turns largely on beliefs or values, with little attention to affect. This imbalance is consistent with—and probably in part attributable to—the dominance of the cognitive perspective in social psychology for the past several decades. Despite the importance of affect in early work on racial prejudice (Allport 1954), contemporary analyses of racial prejudice—and by extension, attitudes toward racial policies—give scant attention to it (Pettigrew 1997, Mackie & Hamilton 1993). The few studies that have included traditional measures of anti-black affect find that the extent to which a person feels cold toward blacks does influence support for government spending efforts or preferential hiring and promotion (Sears & Jessor 1996, Sears 1988, Sears et al 1997, McConahay 1982, Sears et al 2000, Hughes 1997, Jackman 1977). This is consistent with traditional conceptualizations of the role of anti-black affect in general, as well as the proposition that symbolic racism is a blend of anti-black affect and other traditional American values. But, as usually conceptualized, though statistically significant, the effects are comparatively weak.

Recent work has urged an expansion, both theoretically and methodologically, of the role of affect in racial prejudice. Dissatisfied with the adequacy of the cognitive approach, in particular because it fails to ask why expressions of prejudice appear to be context specific, Smith (1993) recently proposed a theory of prejudice that puts affect at center stage. Smith combines advances in the field of emotion research (appraisal theories of emotion) with the theory of self-categorization. Importantly, emotions are seen as reactions experienced by an individual as a member of a group, rather than merely as an individual. This observation, coupled with a recognition that emotions are comprised of more than just feeling warm or cold (e.g., they include anger, resentment, disgust, sympathy), provides a way to understand the context specificity of expressions of prejudice. It helps explain, for example, why people respond differently to eating in the same restaurant with a member of an outgroup as compared to working as a subordinate to an outgroup member. Though Smith does not say so, the model is also applicable to the persistent finding that different types of racial policies are supported at different levels. As Smith's model highlights, reactions to a policy are not dictated by the simple fact that a member of an outgroup is involved; instead, the specific characteristics of the situation (in this case, the details of the policy) are crucial. Affect, then, is not simply warmth or coldness toward an outgroup, but also feelings of threat, sympathy, resentment, or disgust.

Smith's (1993) theory converges with recent applications of Blumer's theory of prejudice. The emotions that are experienced are closely tied up with one's social identity—one's connection to a group—and the extent to which a particular action is threatening to that group. While prejudice is no longer viewed as an individual level pathology, at the same time, emotions do play an important role. This framework complements the cognitively oriented perceived group threat approach by overlaying group-based emotions. In this way, Smith (1993) provides an elaboration of group identity not yet fully developed within sociological discussions of Blumer's theory, though Bobo (1999) makes the more general point about affect and group position.

If empirical assessments are to match these theoretical advances, serious work on measurement is needed. Existing analyses that incorporate affect have relied almost exclusively on a single item: the thermometer ratings of how warm or cold a person feels toward different groups. This is clearly inadequate to the task of tapping the range of affect implied by Smith's model. Moreover, the item has rarely been subject to close scrutiny. Indeed, Schuman et al (1997) point out that since respondents are asked to rate several groups in succession (and the order of the groups has changed over time), there is a substantial potential for question order effects in the most frequently used dataset looking at affect and racial policy attitudes—the National Election Studies. In addition, this item is extremely sensitive to race-of-interviewer effects (Schuman et al 1997).

Pettigrew and his colleagues are an exception to the general lack of attention to affect. By definition, their variant of new racism—subtle prejudice—encompasses affect. Reflecting the move from blatant to subtle, affect is measured not by the presence of negative emotions but by the absence of positive ones. Using aversive racism (Dovidio et al 1989) as a theoretical justification, Pettigrew argues that what is important is how much admiration and sympathy one feels toward blacks or other racial/ethnic minorities, more than how much hostility or animosity (Pettigrew & Meertens 1995, Pettigrew 1997). These sentiments, in conjunction with perceptions of cultural differences, constitute the measure of subtle prejudice used by Pettigrew and his associates, and are a strong and significant predictor of attitudes toward immigration policy in Western Europe (Pettigrew et al 1998, Pettigrew & Meertens 1995). Sears et al (1997) recently included these sentiments as part of their symbolic racism scale. Unfortunately, neither analysis assesses the effect of these positive emotions when not embedded in a scale of symbolic racism or subtle prejudice.

In another, less explicit manner, emotions have begun to creep into discussions of racial policy attitudes, from Kinder & Sanders (1996), who name their version of new racism racial *resentment,* to Gilens et al (1998), Stoker (1998), and Kuklinski et al (1997), who tap white *anger* towards affirmative action. This corrective balance is a welcome one in a field that has recently been dominated by cognitive perspectives, but its incorporation requires explicit attention to both theoretical and methodological concerns.

PATHS OF COMPLEXITY IN THE PURSUIT OF CLARITY

The three main theories discussed already provide a complex treatment of racial policy attitudes; we now point to several areas of further complexity that may in the end help to clarify the important features of racial policy attitudes and shed light on aspects of race relations more generally. Each provides a somewhat different lens through which to view the intersection of prejudice, politics, and public opinion.

Nonattitudinal Predictors

Thus far the review has purposely avoided mention of nonattitudinal predictors and focused only on the attitudinal constructs found in Table 1. Opposing theories at times converged on which values or beliefs were connected to racial policy attitudes, but the crux of the matter is: What forces set these connections in motion? This question is crucial, since it is easy to become bogged down in the swirl of attitudinal forces. One way out of this maze is to incorporate nonattitudinal predictors.

Early research on racial policy attitudes involved determining whether attitudinal (symbolic racism) or nonattitudinal (self-interest) factors were the superior explanatory variables. Repeatedly, the former won out over the latter, and much of the recent emphasis has been on attitudinal predictors. Indeed, in some cases nonattitudinal predictors are entirely absent; or, if included as controls, their effects are rarely discussed. Sociologists in particular, however, ought to be engaging the question of nonattitudinal predictors, insofar as there is an interest in understanding how racial policy attitudes reflect and reinforce structural features of intergroup relations.[14] We now consider two such nonattitudinal predictors: size of the black population and level of education.[15]

Size of the Black Population It has long been argued that as the size of the black population increases, whites respond with increasingly negative racial attitudes (Blalock 1957, Pettigrew 1957). Fossett & Kiecolt (1989) refocused attention on this group-size threat hypothesis, and Taylor (1998, 2000) provides two recent tests. Grounding her work in group threat theory, Taylor uses proportion black as a measure of group threat[16] and concludes that white racial attitudes respond to the proportion of blacks in the local community.[17] Proportion black does not predict equally well across policy type: It is opportunity enhancing rather than equal or preferential treatment policies that respond most to local context. In addition, Taylor (2000) finds that many of the racial beliefs used to tap symbolic/modern racism and the perceptions of group threat are also influenced by the size of the local black population. Both of these findings pose a difficulty for those relying on a race-neutral interpretation of racial policies and other racial beliefs. In addition, as Taylor (1998) notes, the challenge that remains is to understand the mechanisms through which size of the black population influences racial policy attitudes because her analyses fail to show that actual economic or political threat accounts for these effects.

Education Education has always enjoyed a prominent place in discussions of racial attitudes in general, but it receives only sporadic attention in the context of racial policy attitudes. An early study (Jackman & Muha 1984) in part set the stage for this by noting that education mattered a great deal when looking at racial principles and old-fashioned racism, but very little when those principles were put to the test in racial policies. Jackman & Muha (1984) concluded that education simply made people more effective at defending their interests and not more racially liberal. That is, support for abstract principles among the well-educated was only superficial, since it did not translate into support for putting those principles into action.

---

[14]In addition, focusing on nonattitudinal predictors will help address whether the foundations of the three main theoretical explanations are viable. For example, if group interest underlies racial policy attitudes, then groups should differ; if early socialization matters, then early experiences should predict symbolic racism; if ideology underlies it all, then factors associated with holding a constrained ideology should predict this association.

[15]Other demographic characteristics, including age, gender, and region, are also important predictors of racial attitudes in general and in some cases for racial policy attitudes as well (Schuman et al 1997).

[16]This is in contrast with the earlier discussion of group threat, which favored subjective perceptions.

[17]Similar results are obtained using racial composition at the county and regional level (Glaser 1994, Quillian 1996).

More recently, analyses of policy attitudes routinely include education as a control variable, but rarely are its effects the focus of discussion. Existing analyses suggest a complex picture in which those with more and less education do, in fact, respond differently to racial policies. For example, the well-educated are more supportive of open housing laws, government spending to improve the living conditions of blacks, and opportunity-enhancing programs such as spending on early education and college scholarships (Schuman et al 1997, Bobo & Kluegel 1993, Bobo 1991, Glaser 1994, Tuch & Hughes 1996, Bobo & Kluegel 1997, Taylor 1998).[18]

By contrast, attitudes toward the federal government's involvement in ensuring that blacks are treated fairly in employment or go to the same schools as whites, and the specific issue of busing, do not vary by education (Bobo 1988, Tuch & Hughes 1996). Perhaps more puzzling than either of these findings is the relationship between education and preferential treatment policies: the well-educated are routinely *less* supportive of preferential treatment in hiring and promotion than those with fewer years of education (Schuman et al 1997, Hughes 1997, Stoker 1998, Tuch & Hughes 1996). This mixture of findings for education merits closer theoretical and methodological attention.

Though the main effects of education are not widely investigated, the possibility that attitudinal predictors operate differently for those with more and less education has captured the attention of a handful of scholars. Sniderman & Piazza (1993), for example, argue that political ideology and racial prejudice operate differently in people depending on their level of education. Ideology, they argue, pervades the views of the well-educated; prejudice, those of the less well-educated. However, several scholars (Sidanius et al 2000, Sears et al 1997, Pettigrew 2000, Bobo 2000) provide convincing empirical evidence to refute this conclusion, showing that racism predicts equally well, if not more so, the policy attitudes of those with higher levels of education. Nonadditive models like this, which explore how social groups might differ with respect to the important predictors of policy attitudes, will move the study of racial policy attitudes toward analysis consistent with sociologists' interest in connections between social structure and personality (House 1977).

"Non-White" Attitudes

A final nonattitudinal basis for differences in views on racial policy attitudes has been surprisingly understudied: racial group membership.[19] This inattention can be attributed to both theoretical and methodological reasons. As Jackman (1994) has observed, theoretically it was generally thought that it was white attitudes that

---

[18]In the case of tax breaks and preschool education programs for blacks, however, there is some evidence that these effects may be due in part to social desirability pressures among the well-educated (Krysan 1998).

[19]Recent important exceptions are provided by Sigelman & Welch (1991), Kinder & Sanders (1996), who examine black-white differences in the predictors of racial policy attitudes, and Dawson (1994), Tate (1994), and Gurin et al (1989), who examine black political opinion more generally.

needed to be explained. Methodologically, the necessary data have not been collected. A moment's reflection on how the policy attitudes of African Americans, Asians, and Latinos fit within the theories discussed makes obvious the serious limitation of any explanation that does not move beyond white racial policy attitudes. For example, those who take a nonracial perspective on policy attitudes might expect racial group differences to disappear once group differences in politics and principles are controlled.[20] Symbolic racism offers little guidance on this point; implicitly, the model would expect blacks to be almost universally in favor of progressive racial policies—a pattern that is not borne out by the data. Only the group conflict theories are explicit on issues of racial differences in policy attitudes.

The group conflict perspective highlights group identity as an important key to the intraracial heterogeneity of opinion, particularly among blacks. It should follow that the more connected black people feel to blacks as a group, the more supportive they will be of racial policies to assist their group. In much the same manner that self-interest has been eliminated from consideration as a driving force of white attitudes, so too has social class shown little effect on black racial policy attitudes. Instead, perceiving that one's own fate is closely connected with what happens to blacks as a group increases support for racial policies intended to reduce racial inequality (Dawson 1994, Gurin et al 1989, Tate 1994). A parallel analysis might be conducted for whites. That is, group conflict–based analyses of white racial policy attitudes have focused largely on the perceptions of threat posed by the subordinate group; equal attention might be paid to understanding the effects of group identity among whites. Some attempts have been made (Sears et al 1997, Kinder & Sanders 1990), but the measure of in-group identification is generally crude, consisting of a single thermometer rating item, though Sears & Jessor (1996) is an exception.

In sum, a serious theoretical imbalance has been created by ignoring black (and increasingly Asian and Latino) public opinion (Dawson 2000, Bobo & Hutchings 1996). It is inappropriate to assume homogeneity among blacks and other racial/ethnic groups on racial policy attitudes.[21]

The theories developed must be able to account for blacks and other minorities who do not support certain policies. Conversely, we would do well to grapple with

---

[20]Kinder & Sanders (1996) provide one of the most comprehensive assessments of black racial policy attitudes. They report similarity for blacks and whites in the predictive role of individualism, egalitarianism, and limited government. But they did not evaluate whether the racial gap in support for policies disappears after controlling for racial differences in these values. More recently, Bobo (2000) tested this implicit contention and found that controlling for group differences in background and political ideology did not eliminate the black-white gap in support for progressive racial policies.

[21]The Multi-City Study of Urban Inequality, a survey of residents of Atlanta, Boston, Detroit, and Los Angeles (with oversamples of African Americans in all cities, Latinos in Boston and Los Angeles, and Asians in Los Angeles), provides a rare glimpse into the policy attitudes of Asians and Latinos (Kluegel & Bobo forthcoming; Bobo, forthcoming).

the question of why there are whites who support policies to help blacks (Schuman 2000). This is an additional complexity to which we now turn.

Nonprejudiced Respondents

Sociologists are almost always more interested in those groups, individuals, and institutions that fail or that create some social problem. We study why families fail; but we rarely ask what makes them succeed. Similarly, we focus almost all our efforts on understanding conservative racial policy attitudes and rarely ask: Why do some whites support progressive racial policies? What makes some people sympathetic and admiring of blacks? What characterizes people who are not threatened by blacks as a group? What distinguishes those whites who believe that discrimination against blacks persists, as against those who do not?

Schuman & Harding (1963) called attention to this perspective in their analysis of what they labeled "sympathetic identification with the underdog." They concluded that feelings of sympathy toward a minority group were distinct from other measures of "prejudice," though one type of prejudice—in which a majority member is forced to choose between injuring a minority person and offending one or more majority members—was correlated with sympathetic identification. Schuman & Harding (1963, p. 238) conclude:

> To oppose discrimination in such circumstances may require more than a sense of abstract justice: the nondiscriminator may need the capacity to identify at least as strongly with the minority member in such situations as with fellow majority members.

This distinction may have an application in the case of race-based policies: White support of policies intended to help blacks—which in some cases may be construed as "hurting" whites—may require this kind of affect-based response to blacks and other minorities.

Nonracial Policies

This review has been restricted to explicitly racial policies—explicit by virtue of the fact that blacks are specifically named in the policy proposal. However, scholars have argued that other social policies—namely those relating to crime and welfare—though not explicitly racial are nevertheless racialized in the public's mind. Examination of the forces underlying these policy attitudes have found racial beliefs to be an important predictor—especially negative racial stereotypes (Gilens 1999, Peffley et al 1997). From a political standpoint, the results for welfare attitudes cast doubt on the feasibility of recent recommendations to move away from explicitly race-targeted programs to income-targeted programs. Economic-based policies that become associated in the public's mind with race will face many of the same obstacles from a public opinion standpoint as those that are explicitly racial (Gilens 1999).

Non-American Attitudes

Reaching beyond the borders of the United States is another path that increases complexity but has the potential to assist in clarifying the theoretical underpinnings of racial policy attitudes. The comparative perspective provided by Pettigrew and colleagues (Pettigrew & Meertens 1995, Pettigrew et al 1998, Pettigrew 2000) is illuminating: They have shown that subtle prejudice predicts in similar fashion the attitudes of citizens in Western Europe toward immigration policy. Sidanius and his colleagues also extend their work on social dominance theory to a number of cultures outside the United States (Sidanius et al 2000, Sidanius et al 1992). This complexity forces those who have developed their theories in an American context to take care not to rely too heavily on uniquely American values, principles, politics, and racial histories.

CONCLUSION

In order to make progress toward the goal of understanding the intersection of prejudice, politics, and public opinion, we would do well to continue to develop these paths of complexity. Throughout the review I have made explicit and implicit references to an obstacle to this progress: Theoretical advances must be met with methodological developments. We have been fortunate to have racial attitude items regularly included in nationally representative surveys like the General Social Survey and the National Election Studies; their value for understanding change over time in racial attitudes cannot be overstated. But the very same characteristic that makes these data an invaluable resource for time series analyses limits their contribution to the question at hand. The topics and questions asked in these surveys, by design, respond only slowly to changes in sociological thought and society more generally. The present review has highlighted, for example, the need to question taken-for-granted scales of egalitarianism and individualism; it has presented a case for more broadly construed measures of affect; and noted the importance of tapping beliefs about the fairness, costs, and benefits of different racial policies. Additionally, there have been constraints in the "dependent variable." The range of policy questions investigated has been relatively narrow (Steeh & Krysan 1996), the questions often do not reflect the kinds of trade-offs and complexities inherent in real-world policy choices, and the items are sometimes quite vague. What does it mean, after all, to spend money to "improve the conditions of blacks"?

The acquisition of new data and the asking of new types of survey questions must be balanced with attention to how the data will be collected. On the one hand, technological advances have allowed more complex experiments within surveys and nonverbal racial attitude measures, such as response time (Bassili & Fletcher 1991). But this zeal for technology should be balanced by fresh data collected using old-fashioned techniques, and the incorporation of less structured data collection methods such as open-ended follow-up probes to standard closed-ended survey questions (Schuman 1966) and depth interviews (Krysan 1999).

Prejudice, politics, and public opinion come together in ways subtle and not so subtle. In the academy as in the world of politics and public opinion, racial policies generate conflict and controversy. The scholarly controversy is productive as long as it results, as it has in many cases, in pushing forward the debate with new theoretical and empirical insights, or in some cases providing a fresh look at an old theory. Each serves to remind us of the complexity of the issue at hand. For example, while some racial attitude measures document tremendous progress, others, such as the topic of this review—racial policy attitudes—caution against painting an overly optimistic picture of contemporary race relations. Understanding the mix of social, psychological, and political forces underlying racial policy attitudes requires considerable attention to nuance and the integration of ideas and methods.

The move toward complexity that permeates this review is necessary to understand more fully what lies beneath racial policy attitudes. More importantly, however, such a move brings us closer to the larger goal of understanding what racial policy attitudes—as micro-level manifestations of inter-group relations— can reveal about the general state of contemporary race relations (Bobo 1999). Indeed, attitudinal expressions are but one sign of the persistent social and political significance of race. The challenge is to recognize that the complexity of the answers to the question of what underlies racial policy attitudes—and what underlies race relations in this country—is neither new, nor likely to diminish. Indeed, from both theoretical and methodological standpoints, we would do well to remember Gordon Allport's (1954, p. 208) perspective:

> Our own approach to the problem [of racial prejudice] is more eclectic. There seems to be value in all of the six main approaches, and some truth in virtually all of the resulting theories. It is not possible at the present time to reduce them to a single theory of human action. Nevertheless, as we proceed, we hope that the principal points of view will fall into a clear perspective. There is no master key. Rather, what we have at our disposal is a ring of keys, each of which opens one gate of understanding.

ACKNOWLEDGMENTS

The author thanks Lawrence Bobo, James Kluegel, Thomas Pettigrew, Howard Schuman, David O. Sears, Charlotte Steeh, and Marylee Taylor who read earlier drafts of this article and provided many valuable comments and suggestions. The author also gratefully acknowledges the Russell Sage Foundation because much of the work for the article was completed while the author was a Visiting Scholar there in 1998–1999.

LITERATURE CITED

Ajzen I, Fishbein M. 1977. Attitude-behavior relations: a theoretical analysis and review of empirical research. *Psychol. Bull.* 84:888–918

Ajzen I. 1988. *Attitudes, Personality, and Behavior.* Chicago, IL: Dorsey

Allport GW. 1954. *The Nature of Prejudice.* New York: Addison-Wesley

Altemeyer B. 1998. The other "authoritarian personality." *Adv. Exp. Soc. Psychol.* 30:47–92

Alvarez RM, Brehm J. 1997. Are Americans ambivalent towards racial policies? *Am. J. Polit. Sci.* 41(2):345–74

Apostle RA, Glock CY, Piazza T, Suelzle M. 1983. *The Anatomy of Racial Attitudes.* Berkeley: Univ. Calif. Press

Bassili JN, Fletcher JF. 1991. Response-time measurement in survey research: a method for CATI and a new look at nonattitudes. *Pub. Opin. Q.* 55:331–46

Blalock HM. 1957. Percent non-white and discrimination in the South. *Am. Sociol. Rev.* 22:667–82

Blumer H. 1958. Race prejudice as a sense of group position. *Pac. Sociol. Rev.* 1:3–7

Bobo L. 1983. Whites' opposition to busing: symbolic racism or realistic group conflict? *J. Pers. Soc. Psychol.* 45(6):1196–210

Bobo L. 1988a. Attitudes toward the black political movement: trends, meaning and effects on racial policy preferences. *Soc. Psychol. Q.* 51(4):287–302

Bobo L. 1988b. Group conflict, prejudice, and the paradox of contemporary racial attitudes. In *Eliminating Racism: Profiles in Controversy,* ed. PA Katz, DA Taylor, pp. 85–114. New York: Plenum

Bobo L. 1991. Social responsibility, individualism, and redistributive policies. *Soc. Forum* 6(1):71–92

Bobo L. 1999. Prejudice as group position: micro-foundations of a sociological approach to racism and race relations. *J. Soc. Issues* 55(3):445–72

Bobo L. 2000. Race and beliefs about affirmative action: assessing the effects of interests, group threat, ideology and racism. In *Racialized Politics: The Debate about Racism in America,* ed. DO Sears, J Sidanius, L Bobo, pp. 137–64. Chicago: Univ. Chicago Press

Bobo L. Forthcoming. Racial attitudes and relations at the close of the twentieth century. In *America Becoming: Racial Trends and Their Implications,* ed. N Smelser, WJ Wilson, F Mitchell. Washington, DC: Natl. Acad. Press

Bobo L, Hutchings VL. 1996. Perceptions of racial group competition: extending Blumer's theory of group position to a multiracial social context. *Am. Sociol. Rev.* 61: 951–72

Bobo L, Kluegel JR. 1993. Opposition to race-targeting: self interest, stratification ideology, or racial attitudes? *Am. Sociol. Rev.* 58:443–64

Bobo L, Kluegel JR. 1997. Status, ideology, and dimensions of whites' racial beliefs and attitudes: progress and stagnation. See Tuch & Martin 1997, pp. 93–120

Bobo L, Kluegel JR, Smith RA. 1997. Laissez-faire racism: the crystallization of a kinder, gentler, antiblack ideology. See Tuch & Martin 1997, pp. 15–42

Bobocel DR, Son Hing LS, Davey LM, Stanley DJ, Zanna MP. 1998. Justice-based opposition to social policies: Is it genuine? *J. Pers. Soc. Psychol.* 75(3):653–69

Bonilla-Silva E. 1997. Rethinking racism: toward a structural interpretation. *Am. Sociol. Rev.* 62:465–80

Burstein P. 1985. *Discrimination, Jobs, and Politics: The Struggle for Equal Employment Opportunity in the United States Since the New Deal.* Chicago: Univ. Chicago Press

Citrin JD, Green DP, Sears DO. 1990. White reactions to black candidates: When does race matter? *Pub. Opin. Q.* 54:74–96

Cose E. 1993. *The Rage of a Privileged Class.* New York: Modern Reader

Davis DW. 1997. Nonrandom measurement error and race of interviewer effects among African Americans. *Pub. Opin. Q.* 61:183–207

Dawson MC. 1994. *Behind the Mule: Race and Class in African-American Politics.* Princeton, NJ: Princeton Univ. Press

Dawson MC. 2000. Slowly coming to grips with the effects of the American racial order on American policy preferences. In *Racialized Politics: The Debate about Racism in America*, ed. DO Sears, J Sidanius, L Bobo, pp. 344–57. Chicago: Univ. Chicago Press.

Dovidio JF, Gaertner SL. 1996. Affirmative action, unintentional racial biases, and intergroup relations. *J. Soc. Issues* 52(4):51–75

Dovidio JF, Mann J, Gaertner SL. 1989. Resistance to affirmative action: the implications of aversive racism. In *Affirmative Action in Perspective*, ed. FA Blanchard, FJ Crosby, pp. 83–102. New York: Springer-Verlag

Eagly A, Chaiken S. 1993. *The Psychology of Attitudes.* New York: Harcourt Brace

Farley R, Frey WH. 1994. Changes in the segregation of whites from blacks during the 1980s: small steps toward a more integrated society. *Am. Sociol. Rev.* 59:23–45

Farley R, Steeh C, Krysan M, Jackson T, Reeves K. 1994. Stereotypes and segregation: neighborhoods in the Detroit area. *Am. J. Sociol.* 100:750–80

Farley R. 1996. *The New American Reality: Who We Are, How We Got There, Where We Are Going.* New York: Russell Sage Found.

Feagin JR, Sikes MP. 1994. *Living with Racism: The Black Middle-Class Experience.* Boston, MA: Beacon

Feldman S. 1983. Economic individualism and American public opinion. *Am. Polit. Q.* 11(1):3–29

Fossett MA, KJ Kiecolt. 1989. The relative size of minority populations and white racial attitudes. *Soc. Sci. Q.* 70:820–35

Frey WH. 1995. The new geography of population shifts. In *State of the Union: America in the 1990s*, Vol. 2, *Social Trends*, ed. R Farley, pp. 271–336. New York: Russell Sage Found.

Gilens M. 1999. *Why Americans Hate Welfare.* Chicago: Univ. Chicago Press

Gilens M, Sniderman PM, Kuklinski JH. 1998. Affirmative action and the politics of realignment. *Br. J. Polit. Sci.* 28:159–83

Glaser JM. 1994. Back to the Black Belt: racial environment and white racial attitudes in the South. *J. Polit.* 56(1):21–41

Gurin P, Hatchett S, Jackson JS. 1989. *Hope and Independence: Blacks' Response to Electoral and Party Politics.* New York: Russell Sage Found.

Harrison RJ, Bennett CE. 1995. Racial and ethnic diversity. In *State of the Union: America in the 1990s.* Vol. 2: *Social Trends*, ed. R Farley, pp. 141–210. New York: Russell Sage Found.

House JS. 1977. The three faces of social psychology. *Soc. Psychol. Q.* 40(2):161–77

Hughes M. 1997. Symbolic racism, old-fashioned racism, and whites' opposition to affirmative action. See Tuch & Martin 1997, pp. 45–75

Hurwitz J, Peffley M. 1992. Traditional versus social values as antecedents of racial stereotyping and policy conservatism. *Polit. Behav.* 14(4):395–421

Jackman MR. 1977. Prejudice, tolerance, and attitudes toward ethnic groups. *Soc. Sci. Res.* 6:145–69

Jackman MR. 1994. *The Velvet Glove: Paternalism and Conflict in Gender, Class and Race.* Berkeley: Univ. Calif. Press

Jackman MR, Muha MJ. 1984. Education and intergroup attitudes: moral enlightenment, superficial democratic commitment, or ideological refinement? *Am. Sociol. Rev.* 49: 751–69

Jaynes GD, Williams RM Jr. 1989. *A Common Destiny: Blacks and American Society.* Washington, DC: Natl. Acad. Press

Kinder DR, Mendelberg T. 1995. Cracks in American apartheid: the political impact of prejudice among desegregated whites. *J. Polit.* 57(2):402–24

Kinder DR, Mendelberg T. 2000. Individualism reconsidered: principles and prejudice in contemporary American opinion. In *Racialized Politics: The Debate about Racism in America*, ed. DO Sears, J Sidanius, L Bobo, pp. 44–74. Chicago: Univ. Chicago Press

Kinder DR, Sanders LM. 1990. Mimicking political debate with survey questions: the case of white opinion on affirmative action for blacks. *Soc. Cogn.* 8(1):73–103

Kinder DR, Sanders L. 1996. *Divided by Color: Racial Politics and Democratic Ideals.* Chicago: Univ. Chicago Press

Kinder DR, Sears DO. 1981. Prejudice and politics: symbolic racism versus racial threats to the good life. *J. Pers. Soc. Psychol.* 40:414–31

Kirschenman J, Neckerman KM. 1991. 'We'd love to hire them, but . . .': The meaning of race for employers. In *The Urban Underclass*, ed. C Jencks, PE Peterson, pp. 203–34. Washington, DC: Brookings Inst.

Kluegel J. 1985. If there isn't a problem, you don't need a solution: the bases of contemporary affirmative action attitudes. *Am. Behav. Sci.* 28(6):761–84

Kluegel J. 1990. Trends in whites' explanations of the black-white gap in socioeconomic status, 1977–1989. *Am. Sociol. Rev.* 55:512–25

Kluegel J, Bobo L. Forthcoming. Perceived group discrimination and policy attitudes: the sources and consequences of the race and gender gaps. In *Urban Inequality in the US: Evidence from Four Cities*, ed. A O'Connor, C Tilly, L Bobo. New York: Russell Sage Found. In press

Kluegel J, Smith ER. 1983. Affirmative action attitudes: effects of self-interest, racial affect, and stratification beliefs on whites' views. *Soc. Forces* 61(3):797–824

Kluegel J, Smith ER. 1986. *Beliefs about Inequality: Americans' Views of What Is and What Ought to Be.* New York: Aldine de Gruyter

Krysan M. 1998. Privacy and the expression of white racial attitudes: a comparison across three contexts. *Pub. Opin. Q.* 62:506–44

Krysan M. 1999. Qualifying a quantifying analysis on racial equality. *Soc. Psychol. Q.* 62(2):211–18

Kuklinski JH, Sniderman PM, Knight K, Piazza T, Tetlock PE, et al. 1997. Racial prejudice and attitudes toward affirmative action. *Am. J. Polit. Sci.* 41(2):402–19

LaPiere RT. 1934. Attitudes vs. actions. *Soc. Forces* 13:230–37

Levin S, Sidanius J, Rabinowitz JL, Federico C. 1998. Ethnic identity, legitimizing ideologies, and social status: a matter of ideological asymmetry. *Polit. Psychol.* 19(2):373–404

Lipset SM, Schneider W. 1978. The Bakke case: How would it be decided at the bar of public opinion? *Pub. Opin.* March/April:38–44

Mackie DM, Hamilton DL, eds. 1993. *Affect, Cognition, and Stereotyping: Interactive Processes in Group Perception.* New York: Academic

Massey DS, Denton NA. 1993. *American Apartheid: Segregation and the Making of the Underclass.* Cambridge, MA: Harvard Univ. Press

McClendon MJ. 1985. Racism, rational choice, and white opposition to racial changes: a case study of busing. *Pub. Opin. Q.* 49:214–33

McConahay JB. 1982. Self-interest versus racial attitudes as correlates of anti-busing attitudes in Louisville: Is it the buses or the blacks? *J. Polit.* 44:692–720

McConahay JB. 1986. Modern racism, ambivalence, and the modern racism scale. In *Prejudice, Discrimination, and Racism*, ed. JF Dovidio, S Gaertner, pp. 91–125. San Diego: Academic

Meertens RW, Pettigrew TF. 1997. Is subtle prejudice really prejudice? *Pub. Opin. Q.* 61(1):54–71

Mendelberg T. 1997. Executing Hortons: racial crime in the 1988 presidential campaign. *Public Opin. Q.* 61(1):134–57

Metz DH, Tate K. 1995. The color of urban campaigns. In *Classifying by Race*, ed. P Peterson, pp. 262-77. Princeton, NJ: Princeton Univ. Press

Murrell AJ, Dietz-Uhler BL, Dovidio JF, Gaertner SL, Drout C. 1994. Aversive racism and resistance to affirmative action: perceptions of justice are not necessarily color blind. *Basic Appl. Soc. Psychol.* 15(1&2): 71–86

Nelson TE, Kinder DR. 1996. Issues frames and group-centrism in American public opinion. *J. Polit.* 58(4):1055–78

Nelson TE, Oxley ZM, Clawson RA. 1997. Toward a psychology of framing effects. *Polit. Behav.* 19(3):221–46

Nosworthy GJ, Lea JA, Lindsay RCL. 1995. Opposition to affirmative action: racial affect and traditional value predictors across four programs. *J. Appl. Soc. Psychol.* 25(4):314–37

Oliver ML, Shapiro TM. 1995. *Black Wealth, White Wealth: A New Perspective on Racial Inequality.* New York: Routledge

Omi, M, Winant H. 1994. *Racial Formation in the United States: From 1960s to 1980s.* New York: Routledge. 2nd ed.

Peffley M, Hurwitz J, Sniderman PM. 1997. Racial stereotypes and whites' political views of blacks in the context of welfare and crime. *Am. J. Polit. Sci.* 41(1):30–60

Pettigrew TF. 1957. Demographic correlates of border-state desegregation. *Am. Sociol. Rev.* 22:683–89

Pettigrew TF. 1997. Generalized intergroup contact effects on prejudice. *Pers. Soc. Psychol. Bull.* 23(2):173–85

Pettigrew TF. 2000. Systematizing the predictors of prejudice. In *Racialized Politics: The Debate about Racism in America*, ed. DO Sears, J Sidanius, L Bobo, pp. 280–301. Chicago: Univ. Chicago Press

Pettigrew TF, Alston DA. 1988. *Tom Bradley's Campaigns for Governor: The Dilemma of Race and Political Strategies.* Washington, DC: Joint Ctr. Polit. Stud.

Pettigrew TF, Jackson JS, Brika JB, Lemain G, Meertens RW, et al. 1998. Outgroup prejudice in Western Europe. *Eur. Rev. Soc. Psychol.* 8:241–73

Pettigrew TF, Meertens RW. 1995. Subtle and blatant prejudice in Western Europe. *Eur. J. Soc. Psychol.* 25:57–75

Pratto F, Sidanius J, Stallworth LM, Malle BF. 1994. Social dominance orientation: a personality variable predicting social and political attitudes. *J. Pers. Soc. Psychol.* 67(4):741–63

Quillian L. 1996. Group threat and regional change in attitudes toward African Americans. *Am. J. Sociol.* 102:816–60

Reeves K. 1997. *Voting Hopes or Fears? White Voters, Blacks Candidates, and Racial Politics in America.* New York: Oxford Univ. Press

Rothbart M. 1976. Achieving racial equality: an analysis of resistance to social reform. In *Towards the Elimination of Racism*, ed. P Katz, pp. 341–75. New York: Pergamom

Schuman H. 1966. The random probe: a technique for evaluating the validity of closed questions. *Am. Sociol. Rev.* 31:218–22

Schuman H. 2000. The perils of correlation, the lure of labels, and the beauty of negative results. In *Racialized Politics: The Debate about Racism in America*, ed. DO Sears, J Sidanius, L Bobo, pp. 302–23. Chicago: Univ. Chicago Press

Schuman H, Converse J. 1971. The effects of black and white interviewers on black responses in 1968. *Pub. Opin. Q.* 35:46–68

Schuman H, Harding J. 1963. Sympathetic identification with the underdog. *Pub. Opin. Q.* 27:230–41

Schuman H, Johnson MP. 1976. Attitudes and behavior. *Annu. Rev. Sociol.* 2:161–207

Schuman H, Steeh C, Bobo L, Krysan M. 1997. *Racial Attitudes in America: Trends and Interpretations.* Cambridge, MA: Harvard Univ. Press. Rev. ed.

Sears DO. 1986. College sophomores in the lab: influences of a narrow database on social psychological views of human nature. *J. Pers. Soc. Psychol.* 51(3):515–30

Sears DO. 1988. Symbolic racism. In *Eliminating Racism: Profiles in Controversy*, ed. PA Katz, DA Taylor, pp. 53–84. New York: Plenum

Sears DO, Henry PJ, Kosterman R. 2000. Egalitarian values and contemporary racial politics. In *Racialized Politics: The Debate about Racism in America*, ed. DO Sears, J Sidanius, L Bobo, pp. 75–117. Chicago: Univ. Chicago Press

Sears DO, Hensler CP, Speer LK. 1979. Whites' opposition to 'busing': self-interest or symbolic politics? *Am. Polit. Sci. Rev.* 73:369–84

Sears DO, Jessor T. 1996. Whites' racial policy attitudes: the role of white racism. *Soc. Sci. Q.* 77(4):751–59

Sears DO, Kinder DR. 1971. Racial tensions and voting in Los Angeles. In *Los Angeles: Viability and Prospects for Metropolitan Leadership*, ed. WZ Hirsch, pp. 51–88. New York: Praeger

Sears DO, Kinder DR. 1985. Whites' opposition to busing: on conceptualizing and operationalizing group conflict. *J. Pers. Soc. Psychol.* 48:1148–61

Sears DO, Lau RR, Tyler TR, Allen HM Jr. 1980. Self interest vs. symbolic politics in policy attitudes and presidential voting. *Am. Polit. Sci. Rev.* 74:678–84

Sears DO, Sidanius J, Bobo LD, eds. 2000. *Racialized Politics: The Debate about Racism in America*. Chicago: Univ. Chicago Press

Sears DO, Van Laar C, Carrillo M, Kosterman R. 1997. Is it really racism? The origins of white Americans' opposition to race-targeted policies. *Pub. Opin. Q.* 61(1):16–53

Sidanius J, Devereux E, Pratto F. 1992. A comparison of symbolic racism theory and social dominance theory as explanations for racial policy attitudes. *J. Soc. Psychol.* 132(3):377–95

Sidanius J, Pratto F. 1993. The inevitability of oppression and the dynamics of social dominance. In *Prejudice, Politics, and the American Dilemma*, ed. PM Sniderman, PE Tetlock, EG Carmines, pp. 173–211. Stanford, CA: Stanford Univ. Press

Sidanius J, Pratto F, Bobo L. 1996. Racism, conservatism, affirmative action, and intellectual sophistication: a matter of principled conservatism or group dominance? *J. Pers. Soc. Psychol.* 70:476–90

Sidanius J, Singh P, Hetts JJ, Federico C. 2000. It's not affirmative action, it's the blacks: the continuing relevance of race in American politics. In *Racialized Politics: The Debate about Racism in America*, ed. DO Sears, J Sidanius, L Bobo, pp. 191–235. Chicago: Univ. Chicago Press

Sigelman CK, Sigelman L, Walkosz BJ, Nitz M. 1995. Black candidates, white voters: understanding racial bias in political perceptions. *Am. J. Polit. Sci.* 39:243–65

Sigelman L, Welch S. 1991. *Black Americans' Views of Racial Inequality: The Dream Deferred*. New York: Cambridge Univ. Press

Smith ER. 1993. Social identity and social emotions: toward new conceptualizations of prejudice. In *Affect, Cognition and Stereotyping: Interactive Processes in Group Perception*, ed. DM Mackie, DL Hamilton, pp. 297–315. New York: Academic

Sniderman PM, Carmines EG. 1997. *Reaching Beyond Race*. Cambridge, MA: Harvard Univ. Press

Sniderman PM, Crosby GC, Howell WG. 2000. The politics of race and political argument. In *Racialized Politics: The Debate about Racism in America*, ed. DO Sears, J Sidanius, L Bobo, pp. 236–79. Chicago: Univ. Chicago Press

Sniderman PM, Piazza T. 1993. *The Scar of Race*. Cambridge, MA: Harvard Univ. Press

Sniderman PM, Tetlock PE. 1986. Reflections on American racism. *J. Soc. Issues* 42:173–87

Sniderman PM, Tetlock PE, Carmines EG, Peterson RS. 1993. The politics of the American dilemma: issue pluralism. In *Prejudice, Politics, and the American Dilemma*, ed. PM Sniderman, PE Tetlock, EG Carmines, pp. 212–36. Stanford, CA: Stanford Univ. Press

Steeh C, Krysan M. 1996. Trends: affirmative action and the public, 1970–1995. *Pub. Opin. Q.* 60:128–58

Steinberg S. 1995. *Turning Back: The Retreat from Racial Justice in American Thought and Policy*. Boston, MA: Beacon

Stoker L. 1998. Understanding whites' resistance to affirmative action: the role of principled commitments and racial prejudice. In *Perception and Prejudice: Race and Politics in the United States*, ed. J Hurwitz, M Peffley, pp. 135–170. New Haven, CT: Yale Univ. Press

Tate K. 1994. *From Protest to Politics: The New Black Voters in American Elections*. New York: Russell Sage Found. and Cambridge, MA: Harvard Univ. Press

Taylor MC. 1998. How white attitudes vary with the racial composition of local populations: numbers count. *Am. Sociol. Rev.* 63:512–35

Taylor MC. 2000. The significance of racial context. In *Racialized Politics: The Debate about Racism in America*, ed. DO Sears, J Sidanius, L Bobo, pp. 118–36. Chicago: Univ. Chicago Press

Terkildsen N. 1993. When white voters evaluate black candidates: the processing implications of candidate skin color, prejudice, and self-monitoring. *Am. J. Polit. Sci.* 37:1032–53

Tuch SA, Hughes M. 1996. Whites' racial policy attitudes. *Soc. Sci. Q.* 77(4):723–45

Tuch SA, Sigelman L, Martin JK. 1997. Fifty years after Myrdal: blacks' racial policy attitudes in the 1990s. See Tuch & Martin 1997, pp. 226–37

Tuch SA, Martin JK. 1997. *Racial Attitudes in the 1990s: Continuity and Change*. Westport, CT: Praeger

Turner MA, Fix M, Struyk RJ. 1991. *Opportunities Denied, Opportunities Diminished: Racial Discrimination in Hiring*. Washington, DC: Urban Inst. Press

van den Berghe PL. 1967. *Race and Racism*. New York: Wiley

Virtanen SV, Huddy L. 1998. Old-fashioned racism and new forms of racial prejudice. *J. Polit.* 60(2):311–32

Williams DR, Collins C. 1995. US socioeconomic and racial differences in health: patterns and explanations. *Annu. Rev. Sociol.* 21:349–86

Wilson WJ. 1987. *The Truly Disadvantaged: The Inner-City, the Underclass, and Public Policy*. Chicago: Univ. Chicago Press

Yinger J. 1995. *Closed Doors, Opportunities Lost: The Continuing Costs of Housing Discrimination*. New York: Russell Sage Found.

Zubrinsky CL, Bobo L. 1996. Prismatic metropolis: race and residential segregation in the City of Angels. *Soc. Sci. Res.* 25:335–74

Annu. Rev. Sociol. 2000. 26:169–85

RACE AND RACE THEORY

Howard Winant

Department of Sociology, Temple University, Philadelphia, Pennsylvania 19104;
e-mail: hwinant@nimbus.temple.edu

Key Words   racism, racial formation, racial politics

■ **Abstract**   Race has always been a significant sociological theme, from the founding of the field and the formulation of classical theoretical statements to the present. Since the nineteenth century, sociological perspectives on race have developed and changed, always reflecting shifts in large-scale political processes. In the classical period, colonialism and biologistic racism held sway. As the twentieth century dawned, sociology came to be dominated by US-based figures. DuBois and the Chicago School presented the first notable challenges to the field's racist assumptions. In the aftermath of World War II, with the destruction of European colonialism, the rise of the civil rights movement, and the surge in migration on a world scale, the sociology of race became a central topic. The field moved toward a more critical, more egalitarian awareness of race, focused particularly on the overcoming of prejudice and discrimination. Although the recognition of these problems increased and political reforms made some headway in combatting them, racial injustice and inequality were not surmounted. As the global and domestic politics of race entered a new period of crisis and uncertainty, so too has the field of sociology. To tackle the themes of race and racism once again in the new millennium, sociology must develop more effective racial theory. Racial formation approaches can offer a starting point here. The key tasks will be the formulation of a more adequate comparative historical sociology of race, the development of a deeper understanding of the micro-macro linkages that shape racial issues, and the recognition of the pervasiveness of racial politics in contemporary society. This is a challenging but also exciting agenda. The field must not shrink from addressing it.

INTRODUCTION

As the world lurches forward into the twenty-first century, widespread confusion and anxiety exist about the political significance and even the meaning, of race. This uncertain situation extends into the field of sociology, which has since its founding devoted great attention to racial themes.

The extent of the literature on the race concept alone, not to mention the mountains of empirical studies that focus on racial issues, presents difficulties for any attempt at theoretical overview and synthesis. A wide range of concepts from both the classical and modern traditions can readily be applied to racial matters.

0360-0572/00/0815-0169$14.00

Variations among national and cultural understandings of the meaning of race cry out for comparative appproaches. World history has, arguably, been racialized at least since the rise of the modern world system; racial hierarchy remains global even in the postcolonial present; and popular concepts of race, however variegated, remain in general everyday use almost everywhere. Thus, any effective sociological theory of race seems to require, at a minimum, comparative historical and political components, some sort of sociology of culture or knowledge, and an adequate microsociological account.

Over the past few decades, interest in racial matters, and the pace at which racial dynamics have been changing worldwide, have both increased dramatically. Controversy over the meaning and significance of race was greatly heightened after World War II. The war itself had significant racial dimensions and left a legacy of revulsion at racism and genocide. The social movements and revolutionary upsurges that succeeded the war and brought the colonial era to an end also raised the problematic of race to a new level of prominence. The civil rights movement in the United States and the anti-apartheid mobilization in South Africa are but the most prominent examples of this. As it gained its independence, the postcolonial world was quickly embroiled in the competition of the Cold War, a situation that placed not only the legacy of imperial rule but also the racial policies of the superpowers (especially those of the United States) under additional scrutiny. Another consequence of the war was enormous migratory flows from the world's rural South to its metropolitan North; in these demographic shifts the empire struck back, pluralizing the former mother countries (Centre for Contemporary Cultural Studies 1982). All these developments raised significant questions about the meaning of race.

SOCIOLOGY'S RACIAL ODYSSEY

In this article I survey the theoretical dimensions of race as the new century (and new millennium) commences. I begin with an account of the *origins of the race concept.* Here I consider how the theme of race, though prefigured in earlier ages, only took on its present range of meanings with the rise of modernity. The deep interconnection between the development of the modern world system—of capitalism, seaborne empire, and slavery—and the exfoliation of a worldwide process of racialization is not in doubt.

Next I examine how sociological theory has addressed the linkage between modernity and race. I argue that, not surprisingly, *the sociological study of race has been shaped by large-scale political processes.* The founding statements of sociological theory, the so-called classics, were above all concerned to explain the emergence of modernity in Europe. Whether they understood this to mean the dawn of capitalism, the advent of "disenchanted" forms of social organization, or the generation of complex dynamics of social integration and solidarity, they could hardly escape some reckoning with the problem of the Other, however s/he was defined: as plundered and exploited laborer, as "primitive" or "uncivilized," or as "traditional" or mechanically solidaristic.

After sociology's center of gravity migrated across the Atlantic, racial themes became more central. Dealing with social problems such as crime, poverty, and disease; addressing urbanization, stratification, and underdevelopment; and confronting social psychological issues as well, analysts again and again had recourse to racial themes.

Contemporary approaches to the race concept have by and large parted with the biologism of the past, although some vestigial viewpoints of this type can still be detected (such as those of *The Bell Curve* authors). The sociology of race was vastly stimulated by the political, cultural, and demographic shifts that took shape in the postwar decades.

But as we begin the twenty-first century, sociological theory is confronted with the obsolescence of the Big Political Processes, such as decolonization and civil rights, that drove the theoretical vehicle forward from the war's end. So now, racial theory finds itself in a new quandary. Empires have been ended and Jim Crow and *apartheid* abolished (at least officially). How then is continuing racial inequality and bias to be explained? Some would argue that since racial injustice is at least tendentially diminishing, the race concept is finally being obviated: In the globalized twenty-first century, world society and transnational culture will finally attain a state of colorblindness and racial (or better, ethnic) pluralism. Others note that this new situation—of multiculturalism or diversification—provides a much prettier fig leaf for policies of *laissez-faire* vis-a-vis continuing racial exclusion and inequality than any intransigent white supremacy could ever have offered. But whatever political disagreements underlie the ongoing difficulties of racial theory, there can be little doubt that these difficulties persist.

In the final section of this paper, I offer some *notes toward a new racial theory.* Any such account must take seriously the reformed present situation: postcolonial, postsegregationist (or at least post–official segregation), and racially heterogeneous (if not "integrated"). It must also note the continuing presence of racial signification and racial identity, as well as the ongoing social structural salience of race. Racial theory must now demonstrate comparative and historical capabilities, as well as addressing the formidable problem of the micro-macro linkage that inheres in racial dynamics. As this already suggests, such a theory would also incorporate elements (let us call them revisionist elements) of recent political sociology: process models of politics, new social movement theory, and constitution theories of society. Over the past two decades, racial formation theory has made the most serious attempt to fulfill this mission.

This is obviously no small assignment; only the contours of such a new theoretical approach to race can be outlined here. But I am confident that these notes, however elliptical, will facilitate access to a substantial body of work already underway, not only on race, but on the great multitude of issues, both substantive and conceptual, that it intersects. After all, the theme of race is situated where meaning meets social structure, where identity frames inequality.

ORIGINS OF THE RACE CONCEPT

Can any subject be more central or more controversial in sociological thought than that of race? The concept is essentially a modern one, although prefigured in various ways by ethnocentrism, and taking preliminary form in ancient concepts of civilization and barbarity (Snowden 1983), citizen (or *zoon politikon*) and outsider/slave (Hannaford 1996, Finley 1983). Yes, the Crusades and the Inquisition and the Mediterranean slave trade were important rehearsals for modern systems of racial differentiation, but in terms of scale and inexorability the race concept only began to attain its familiar meanings at the end of the middle ages.

At this point it would be useful to say what I mean by "race." At its most basic level, race can be defined as a *concept that signifies and symbolizes sociopolitical conflicts and interests in reference to different types of human bodies.* Although the concept of race appeals to biologically based human characteristics (phenotypes), selection of these particular human features for purposes of racial signification is always and necessarily a social and historical process. There is no biological basis for distinguishing human groups along the lines of race, and the sociohistorical categories employed to differentiate among these groups reveal themselves, upon serious examination, to be imprecise if not completely arbitrary (Omi & Winant 1994).

The idea of race began to take shape with the rise of a world political economy. The onset of global economic integration, the dawn of seaborne empire, the conquest of the Americas, and the rise of the Atlantic slave trade were all key elements in the genealogy of race. The concept emerged over time as a kind of world-historical *bricolage*, an accretive process that was in part theoretical,[1] but much more centrally practical. Though intimated throughout the world in innumerable ways, racial categorization of human beings was a European invention. It was an outcome of the same world-historical processes that created European nation-states and empires, built the dark satanic mills of Britain (and the even more dark and satanic sugar mills of the Brazilian Reconcavo and the Caribbean), and explained it all by means of Enlightenment rationality.

But this is not to say that the European attainment of imperial and world-encompassing power gave rise to race. Indeed it is just as easy to argue the opposite: that the modern concept of race gave rise to, or at least facilitated the creation of, an integrated sociopolitical world, a modern authoritarian state, the structures of an international economy, and the emergence over time of a global culture. We must recognize all these issues as deeply racialized matters.

---

[1]Religious, philosophical, literary/artistic, political, and scientific discourses all were directed in a never ending flood of ink and image to the themes of "the Other"; variations in human nature; and the corporeal, mental, spiritual, sexual, and "natural historical" differences among "men." To the extent that this discussion addressed itself to the problem of patterns of human difference/identity and human variability, it may be fairly characterized as about race. To cite some valuable texts among a virtual infinity: Hannaford 1996, Gossett 1965, Todorov 1985, 1993, Kiernan 1969, Montagu 1997 [1942], Banton 1987.

THE SOCIOLOGICAL STUDY OF RACE HAS BEEN SHAPED BY LARGE-SCALE POLITICAL PROCESSES

The "Classics"

When we look at the treatment of racial matters in sociological theory, we find the concept present from the beginning, though often in an inchoate, undertheorized, or taken-for-granted form. Herbert Spencer, the usual example cited as the *ur*-sociologist, reads as a biological determinist today, preoccupied as he is with human evolution and the ranking of groups according to their "natural" characteristics.[2]

Marx's orientation to themes we would now consider racial was complex. His denunciation in *Capital* of the depredation, despoliation, and plunder of the non-European world in pursuit of primitive accumulation,[3] and his ferocious opposition to slavery, both commend him. But his insistence that the colonized pre-capitalist societies would ultimately benefit from their enmeshment in the brutal clutches of the European powers hints to present-day readers that he was not entirely immune to the hierarchization of the world that characterized the imperial Europe of his day.

Weber's treatment of the concept of *ethnie* under the rubric of "status" (a relational category based on "honor") presages a social constructionist approach to race; but in Weber's voluminous output there is no serious consideration of the modern imperial phenomenon, there are numerous instances of European chauvinism,[4] and there is an occasional indulgence in—let us call it—racialist meditation.[5] Durkheim too ranks the world eurocentrically, distinguishing rather absolutely

---

[2] Early treatments of the race concept in Europe and the United States combined supposedly biologistic or natural history–based conceptions of race with a high degree of arbitrariness, if not outright incoherence, in their application. Numerous groups qualified as "races": national origin (the Irish) and religion (Jews) as well as the more familiar criteria of color were frequently invoked as signs of racial otherness. Although this fungibility has been somewhat reduced and regularized over recent decades, it still remains in effect and indeed can never be supplanted by "objective" criteria. See the discussion of racial formation below.

[3] "The discovery of gold and silver in America, the extirpation, enslavement, and entombment in mines of the aboriginal population, the beginning of the conquest and looting of the East Indies, the turning of Africa into a warren for the commercial hunting of blackskins, signalized the rosy dawn of the era of capitalist production. These idyllic proceedings are the chief momenta of primitive accumulation. On their heels treads the commercial war of the European nations with the globe for a theater. It begins with the revolt of the Netherlands from Spain, assumes giant dimensions in England's AntiJacobin War, and is still going on in the opium wars with China, etc." (Marx 1967:351).

[4] Especially during the World War I years, when Weber was seriously afflicted with German nationalism.

[5] In fairness, Weber also recognizes racism, notably anti-black racism in the United States. See his remarks on U.S. racial attitudes in Gerth & Mills 1958:405–6. Weber's sensitivity to U.S. racial matters may be attributed, at least in part, to the orientation provided him by Du Bois. See Lewis 1993:225, 277.

between "primitive" and "civilized" peoples based on the limited ethnology available to him; he also muses somewhat racialistically.[6]

It is not my purpose to chide these masters. Far from it: They acquit themselves well when compared to the rank-and-file pundits and even the *bien philosophes* who were their contemporaries. They can hardly be expected to have remained totally immune from the racial ideology of their times. But that is precisely the point: Sociological thought arose in an imperialist, eurocentric, and indeed racist era, both in Europe and in the United States. In its classical early statements, it was racially marked by the time and place of its birth.

Across the Atlantic

It was largely in the United States that the early sociology of race first forsook the library for the streets, partaking in the great empirical effloresence that marked the field's establishment in that country. There was an inescapable association between the discipline's development in this period (the early twentieth century), and the rise of pragmatism in US philosophy and progressivism in US politics during the same epoch. Nor is it hard to understand why race was promoted to a more central sociological concern as the discipline acquired its foothold—indeed its headquarters—in the United States. This was, after all, a country where African slavery was still an artifact of living memory, where the frontier had only recently been declared closed, where immigration was a flood stage, and where debates over the propriety of imperial activity (in the Phillipines, for example) were still current.

At the beginning of the twentieth century, a nearly comprehensive view of the race concept still located it at the biological level. On this account, races were "natural": their characteristics were essential and given, immutable. Over the centuries such approaches had accomplished a wide range of explanatory work. Both the defense of slavery and its critique (abolitionism) had appealed to "natural" criteria in support of their views. In a similar vein the holocaust visited upon indigenous peoples, as well as the absorption of large numbers of former Mexican, Spanish, and Asian subjects through war and coercive immigration policies, had been justified as "natural," inevitable forms of human progress.[7] Even after emancipation and the "closing of the frontier" in the United States, scientific arguments still summoned "natural causes" to the defense of hierarchical concepts of race. In the late nineteenth and early twentieth centuries the impact of social Darwinism was

---

[6]Racial categories are employed as "social types" in *Suicide*, for example. See Fenton 1980.
[7]The Chicago theorists, particularly Park, proposed a deterministic version of this argument in the form of a "race relations cycle" through which macrosocial encounters between "peoples" were argued to pass. The four stages of the "cycle" were held to succeed each other more or less inevitably: first contact, then conflict, succeeded by accommodation, and finally assimilation. Residues of the "natural history" logic of race can be detected here, to be sure, but there is also something of a social constructionism at work. For example, Park suggests that alternative power dynamics among racially defined groups are possible at each of the cycle's phases.

enormous (not merely on Herbert Spencer), and the arguments of eugenics also acquired great support.

But the world racial system underwent significant shifts in the early twentieth century. As labor demands grew more complex and the agenda of democratization gradually assumed greater importance, biologistic racial theories became increasingly obsolete. The resurgence of anticolonial movements in Africa and Asia (a century after the success of such movements in the Americas), the spreading of democratic demands to countries considered "backward" and "uncivilized," and the increased mobility (both geographic and economic) of ex-slaves and former peasants during and after World War I, all motivated the gradual but inexorable development of a more sophisticated social scientific approach to race.

The two early twentieth century examples of pathbreaking racial theorizing that require mention here are the pioneering study by W.E.B. Du Bois of black life in Philadelphia (Du Bois 1998 [1899]), and the extensive body of work on racial matters that formed a crucial component of the Chicago School of sociology. Both these pioneers were oriented by the pragmatism that was the most original, and remains the most important, contribution of North American sociological theory.

Du Bois's *The Philadelphia Negro*[8] sought both to make a significant advance over previous knowledge (overwhelmingly ignorant and stereotyped) about black life and US racial dynamics; and to build, upon a solid base of empirical data, a powerful and strategic argument for the democratization of race relations in turn-of-the-century America. Though slightly marred by concessions demanded of Du Bois by his patrons (or perhaps imagined necessary by him) the work still stands, an entire century later, as a magisterial survey of the unique racial dementia of the United States: the country's foundational involvement with African enslavement and the permanent consequences of that involvement. In addition to his pathbreaking approach to racial theory, particularly evident in his concept of "the veil" and his understanding of racial dualism (Du Bois 1989 [1903]), Du Bois's early work is notable for its relentless empirical commitments and independent application of pragmatist philosophy (West 1989) to the sociological enterprise, both theoretical and practical. As Elijah Anderson points out in his introduction to the centennial reissue of *The Philadelphia Negro* (1996 [1899]), the tendency

---

[8]One should cite much more of Du Bois's contributions to the foundations of US sociology, and indeed to democratic theory and practice in respect to race: the Atlanta studies, the historical sociology (most notably *Black Reconstruction in America* (1977 [1935]), and an astounding wealth of other work (see Lewis 1995 for a good selection of materials). While Du Bois was not entirely ignored by the "mainstream" of the field, he was hardly given his due recognition either. As noted, Du Bois was associated with Weber, whom he had come to know in Berlin. The complex set of influences shaping Du Bois's intellectual and political development has been much explored in recent scholarship: He combined a high German philosophical, historical, and social scientific training with solid roots in American pragmatism (notably his work with William James), and a deep engagement with the popular African-American traditions he first met as a college student in the South (see Du Bois 1989 [1903]), Du Bois 1991 [1940]), Lewis 1993, West 1989, Marable 1986).

to attribute these innovations to more "mainstream" sociologists for many years banished Du Bois from his rightful place in the disciplinary canon.

The large body of work on race produced by the researchers of the Chicago School also demonstrates the influence of pragmatism and progressivism. Oriented by a social problems approach and consciously viewing the city of Chicago as a sociological laboratory, the Chicago sociologists authored a group of studies focusing on crime, poverty, "slums," etc., all problems that were frequently seen racially. The approaches that developed in Chicago were notable for their attentiveness to their empirical subjects, and for their intrinsically democratic orientation. Moving from the preliminary work of Burgess, through the great creativity and comprehensiveness of Thomas & Znaniecki's massive study,[9] the Chicago engagement with the problematic of race culminated in the work of Robert E. Park on the macro-dimensions of race (Park 1950).[10] There was also an important micro-side of the Chicago tradition, which proceeded from Mead and deeply informed Blumer's work on the symbolic dimensions of race (Blumer 1958). Perhaps most important, the work of the Chicago sociologists broke definitively with the racial biologism that had characterized earlier treatments, asserting with increasing clarity the position that race was a socially constructed, not naturally given, phenomenon.[11] The influence of this view on crucial later treatments of race throughout the social sciences—for example, Myrdal's *An American Dilemma* (1944) or Drake & Cayton's magisterial work (Drake & Cayton 1993 [1945])—was enormous. The Myrdal study would not even have come into being, much less exercised the tremendous political influence it did (Southern 1987, Jackson 1990), without vast assistance from Chicago-trained scholars.

CONTEMPORARY APPROACHES TO THE RACE CONCEPT

The same dynamics that prompted the Americanization of sociology and sparked the shift from classical theorizing to empirical research were also at work in the development of contemporary approaches to race. Once again, pressing sociopolitical issues drove the theoretical vehicle forward.

Sociological argument could only properly challenge biologistic positions after the race concept had been fully reinterpreted sociohistorically. Given the onrushing

---

[9]*The Polish Peasant* prefigured the entire contemporary field of migration studies (Thomas & Znaniecki 1994 [1923]). Thomas & Znaniecki's book on what would now be considered a white ethnic group could easily be seen as a racial work at the time of its original appearance.

[10]For a good overview, see Bulmer 1984.

[11]In this developing analysis, Chicago sociology not only led the field, but established the beginning of an interdisciplinary social scientific consensus. In cultural anthropology, the early contributions of Franz Boas—whom Du Bois invited to speak in Atlanta in 1911— were crucial here as well.

European disaster of facism, the task of elaborating a democratic and inclusionist theory of race fell largely to US scholars from the 1930s onward.[12] Here the sociological work carried out by the Chicago scholars and their successors, and the continuously powerful voice of Du Bois, combined with the insights and research of a growing number of progressive racial observers. To name but a few other important influences: the Boasian shift in anthropology, which refocused that discipline from physical to cultural preoccupations and had widespread effects in popular culture, was certainly significant. The association of fascism with eugenics—a movement that had developed strong bases both in Britain and the United States as well as in Germany—forced choices upon democratically and progressively inclined publics, both intellectual and political. The "retreat of scientific racism" was the result of these unsavory connections (Barkan 1992). Marxist accounts of race became more prominent in function of the upsurge of communism (a leading, though not unproblematic, antiracist influence, especially in the 1930s and 1940s). The growth of important black movements, both political and cultural,[13] also strongly affected the racial public sphere in the interwar period. And the liberal democratic ethos, strongly invoked in the United States by the wartime work of Myrdal, exercised tremendous influence (Myrdal 1944).

The Post–World War II Challenge

In the post–World War II period, the concept of race was more comprehensively challenged than ever before in modern history. Decolonization spread through the world's South, sometimes achieving its emancipatory aims by peaceful, or at least largely political, means and sometimes requiring prolonged warfare to dislodge the occupying northern (aka "white") power. Migration and urbanization of previously impoverished ex-colonials and former peasants—largely people of color—landed millions of dark faces in the world's metropoles. These newly urbanized groups soon mobilized and pressed for their political and social rights, contesting entrenched customs and institutionalized patterns of white supremacy and racism in numerous countries. Especially in the United States, the hegemonic postwar nation, these racially based movements took the political center-stage.

These new demands for inclusion, in turn, induced serious crises in national political systems. As racial regimes steeped in discriminatory or exclusionist

---

[12]Not exclusively of course. Resistance to nazism also bred important works, as did anticolonial struggle and cultural anthropology. A few examples: the Jewish and homosexual activist Magnus Hirschfeld first used (as far as I can tell) the term "racism" in a book he published with that title in 1935, whose topic was (logically) antisemitism. The pan-Africanist movement, which owed a lot to Du Bois, was well underway by this time, generating important works by such scholar-activists (and marxists) as George Padmore, C.L.R. James, and others. Boas's students such as Gilberto Freyre and Ruth Benedict were producing important studies on race in Brazil, as was exiled anthropologist Claude Levi-Strauss.

[13]Notably the Garvey movement, the Harlem Renaissance, and the development of successful (though still effectively segregated) black media: music, film and theater, newspapers, etc.

traditions were pressured to innovate and reform, sociological approaches to race were also transformed. A great (although quite belated) interest in patterns of discrimination and prejudice developed.[14] Interest in patterns of racial inequality grew at the international level. Not only the mainstream sociology, but also the radical sociology of race advanced, spurred on by the new movements as well as by dissatisfaction with the pace and scope of reform (Blauner 1972; Ladner, ed. 1973).

While an obvious advance over earlier views, postwar racial theory was subject to numerous limitations, in both its moderate and its radical versions. Most problematic was the tendency toward *reductionism*: The three main theoretical tendencies all subordinated the race concept to some supposedly more objective or "real" social structure. *Ethnicity*-based theories were generally the most mainstream or moderate. They saw race as a culturally grounded framework of collective identity. *Class*-based theories understood race in terms of group-based stratification and economic competition. *Nation*-based theories perceived race in the geopolitical terms largely given by the decolonization process so prominent in the postwar era. They focused attention on issues of peoplehood and race unity, rootedness, citizenship, and irredentism.[15]

As the twentieth century (whose "problem is the color-line," as Du Bois had famously written) drew toward its end, these approaches to the race concept also neared their limits. They were informed by and oriented to the pressing sociopolitical problems of their time: notably racial prejudice and discrimination (especially state-sponsored discrimination). After these grievances had been forcefully raised in many countries by antiracist movements, they were generally at least ameliorated by democratic and inclusionist efforts at reform. Although hardly eliminated by shifts in state racial policy, racial injustice became less visible as a result of these reforms, and overt racism was generally stigmatized. In such a situation the racial theory that sought to explain such phenomena slowly became obsolete. Thus are we left at century's end with a range of unanticipated, or at least theoretically unresolved, racial dilemmas.

The Limits of Contemporary Racial Theory

The inadequacy of the range of theoretical approaches to race available in sociology at the turn of the twenty-first century is quite striking. Consistent with the argument presented in this essay, this theoretical crisis can be seen as reflecting the continuing sociopolitical crisis of race. In particular, the *persistence of racially based distinctions*, distinctions that state-based racial reforms were supposed to overcome, poses major problems for racial theories inherited from the earlier post–World War II years.

---

[14] A valuable survey of "mainstream" sociological approaches to race in the United States over the entire twentieth century is Pettigrew 1980. For a more critical perspective, see McKee 1993.

[15] For a more extensive critical review of the reductionism of 1960s racial theorizing in the United States, see Michael Omi & Howard Winant 1994).

Ethnicity-oriented theories of race had suggested that the suppression of prejudiced attitudes could be achieved through contact, integration, and assimilation; and that discrimination could be ended by laws and regulations that made jobs, education, housing, and so on equally accessible to all. But the endurance of obstacles to integration severely undermined ethnicity-based approaches to race,[16] while assimilation into white cultural norms was hardly desirable to most racially defined minorities. Faced with these impasses in the United States today, ethnicity theories of race have devolved into neoconservatism, which can do no better than reprove racially defined minorities for their continuing race-consciousness and supposed failure to take advantage of civil rights reforms (Thernstrom & Thernstrom 1997). In Western Europe, these theories take the form of differentialism, which repudiates the racist cultural hierarchies of the past, but affirms the exclusionist commitments of (French, German, British etc.) "national culture," thus upholding barriers to immigration and racial pluralism, not to mention integration (Taguieff 1988, Wieviorka 1995, Balibar & Wallerstein 1991).

Class-based theories of race had argued that racial conflict was the mode in which class conflict was lived out or expressed (Hall et al 1978). This suggested that racial stratification and intergroup competition were fairly well-defined in the postwar world (Bonacich 1972, 1976, Gordon et al 1982, Reich 1981). If the inequality among racially defined groups was to be overcome, then this would require not only interracial solidarity, but also race-conscious programs designed to remedy the *effects* of discrimination. Such programs, put into place in many countries and under various names, have come to be known under the rubric of "affirmative action." But two factors have undermined the plausibility of this account. First, a growing inequality *within* racially defined minority groups weakens group cohesion both politically and culturally; this undermines the case for affirmative action. Second, enduring white commitments to racial privilege—that is, persistent racism— largely trump interracial working-class solidarity, defeating whatever potential for economic redistribution such programs as affirmative action may have offered. Thus, class-based theories of race have in practice been vitiated by the failure of the socialist (or social democratic, or New Deal) vision in the present epoch.[17]

Nation-oriented accounts of race have been called into question by the combined weight of international and intra-national heterogeneity. In a postcolonial era

---

[16]At a deeper level, governments often enacted racial reforms that were more symbolic than substantive, and enforced those they had managed to enact indifferently if at all. See Lipsitz 1998, Massey & Denton 1993 for U.S. examples.

[17]Perhaps the greatest effort to argue for a class-based contemporary racial theory in sociology has been that of William Julius Wilson. For more than two decades now Wilson has sought to present racial progress as dependent on generalized full-employment policies and politics. In recent work he has striven to revive well-used left arguments about the indispensability of interracial solidarity (Wilson 1996). But for all that is valuable in this approach, his dismissal of the continuing effects of racism, and of the experience of racial distinctions, is crippling. The sociocultural and organizational obstacles to interracial solidarity remain far more formidable than Wilson acknowledges.

that has witnessed tremendous migration, that offers unprecedented ease of movement, and that boasts of communicative powers (mass media, particularly music and film, but also telephonic and computer-based resources) unimaginable even a few years ago, the nation-based dimensions of racial solidarity have atrophied. Trans- (or perhaps post-) national forms of racial correspondence persist, but now take the form of *diasporic* identities of various kinds (Kilson & Rotberg, eds., 1976, Appadurai 1996, Lemelle & Kelley, eds., 1994). At this point, however, transnational racial solidarity generally lacks the kind of political commitment and organization once displayed under the banners of pan-Africanism or the "non-aligned" movements. In this situation, nation-based theories of race have devolved into crude and retro forms of cultural nationalism, informed more by mysticism than by social analysis.[18]

NOTES TOWARD A NEW RACIAL THEORY

If the strength of earlier theoretical accounts has atrophied and a new approach is needed, what would be its outlines? As a new century begins, a convincing racial theory must address the persistence of racial classification and stratification in an era officially committed to racial equality and multiculturalism. The present moment is one of increasing globalization and postcoloniality. It is a time when most national societies, and the world as a whole, are acknowledged to be racially multipolar, and when hybridity is frequently recognized as a key feature of racial identity. Today, in marked distinction to the situation that obtained before World War II, most states and members of state elites claim to oppose discrimination, deny their continuing adherence to racialized views of their populations, and may even claim to be colorblind or differentialist. How and why do racial distinctions endure in such changed circumstances?

Any minimally adequate theoretical response to this question must include recognition of the *comparative/historical dimension of race*. The mere fact that we are discussing race here and now (in a post-civil rights, post-cold war, post-colonial

---

[18]"Cultural nationalism" as politics and racial theory in the United States, Brazil, or South Africa may have entered a *cul-de-sac*, but it is essentially benign. The same cannot be said of the devolutionist nationalisms of the Balkans, Rwanda, or parts of South Asia, which have reintroduced the quasi-racist program of ethnic cleansing in forlorn and bloody attempts to achieve the utopian congruence of state and nation. Quite apart from the resemblance of such policies to genocides ancient and recent, they testify once again to the near-total hybridity of the human population and the impossibility of achieving any societal homogeneity, especially in the present. Such policies also reveal the flexibility of racialization, which has time and again been applied to exacerbate human distinctions not easily recognized (at least from "outside") as corporeal or phenotypic. Consider in this regard not only Hutu v. Tutsi or Bosnian Serb v. Bosnian Muslim, but also such cases of racialized conflict as: German "Aryan" v. German Jew, Palestinian Arab v. Israeli Jew, or British v. Irish.

period) itself imposes significant theoretical constraints and opportunities. As I argued earlier, earlier racial theories too were products of their times and places. We remain in a similar situation today.

A second dimension in which any successful theory must operate is the ability to range over, and hopefully to link, *the micro- and macro-aspects of racial signification and racialized social structure.* Such a multileveled and interconnected account is a general obligation of social theory in the present.[19] It is an obligation incurred by any attempt to conceptualize the continuing significance of race. A notable and intriguing feature of race is its ubiquity, its presence in both the smallest and the largest features of social relationships, institutions, and identities.

A third theoretical dimension will involve recognition of the *newly pervasive forms of politics* in recent times. This may be alternatively regarded as a racially conscious conception of action or agency. In the United States, much of the impetus behind the reconceptualization of politics that has occurred in recent decades was derived from racially based and indeed anti-racist social movements. The democratizing challenge posed after World War II to normal systems of domination and power, accepted divisions of labor, and rational-legal means of legitimation, all had inescapable racial dimensions. Racially based movements, then, and the second wave feminism that followed and was inspired by them, problematized the public-private distinction basic to an older generation of political theory and political sociology.[20] This has been recognized in new approaches to political sociology, such as political process models (McAdam 1982, Morris & Mueller, eds., 1992), It also appears in the revival of interest in pragmatist sociology, in symbolic interactionism, in constitution theories of society (Joas 1996, Giddens 1984), and in the belated revival of interest in the work of W.E.B. Du Bois (West 1989, Lewis 1993, Winant 1997).

For the past few decades these themes have been developed in a body of theoretical work that goes under the general heading of *racial formation theory.* As one of the founders of this approach, I must stipulate from the beginning to the lack of consensus, as well as the overall incompleteness, of this theoretical current. Still, I submit that racial formation theory at least begins to meet the requirements for a sociological account of race, one capable of addressing the *fin-de-siecle* conditions adumbrated here.[21]

---

[19]See Huber 1991, Giddens 1984, Collins 1987, Alexander et al, eds., 1987.

[20]In non-U.S. settings, the new social movement phenomenon has not always been so clearly recognized as racially structured. This is particularly notable in Europe where its study was prompted by the vicissitudes of the new left, the resurgence of feminism, the rise of green politics, and the upsurge of terrorism in the 1970s (Melucci 1989). But in the third world the rethinking of political theory and political sociology in terms of issues of subjectivity and of identity often took on a racial dimension. Consider the legacy of Fanon for example.

[21]Numerous writers now employ racial formation perspectives, both within sociology and in other social scientific (as well as in cultural studies, legal studies, etc.). See for example Gilroy 1991, Crenshaw et al 1995, Davis and Lowe 1997, Almaguer 1994, Espiritu 1992).

To summarize the racial formation approach: (*a*) It views the meaning of race and the content of racial identities as unstable and politically contested; (*b*) It understands racial formation as the intersection/conflict of racial "projects" that combine representational/discursive elements with structural/institutional ones; (*c*) It sees these intersections as iterative sequences of interpretations (articulations) of the meaning of race that are open to many types of agency, from the individual to the organizational, from the local to the global.

If we are to understand the changing significance of race at the beginning of the twenty-first century, we must develop a more effective theory of race. The racial formation perspective at least suggests some directions in which such a theory should be pursued. As in the past, racial theory today is shaped by the large-scale sociopolitical processes it is called upon to explain. Employing a racial formation perspective, it is possible to glimpse a pattern in present global racial dynamics.

That pattern looks something like the following: In the period during and after World War II an enormous challenge was posed to established systems of rule by racially defined social movements around the world. Although these movement challenges achieved some great gains and precipitated important reforms in state racial policy, neither the movements nor the reforms could be consolidated. At the end of the century the world as a whole, and various national societies as well, are far from overcoming the tenacious legacies of colonial rule, apartheid, and segregation. All still experience continuing confusion, anxiety, and contention about race. Yet the legacies of epochal struggles for freedom, democracy, and human rights persist as well.

Despite the enormous vicissitudes that demarcate and distinguish national conditions, historical developments, roles in the international market, political tendencies, and cultural norms, racial differences often operate as they did in centuries past: as a way of restricting the political influence, not just of racially subordinated groups, but of all those at the bottom end of the system of social stratification. In the contemporary era, racial beliefs and practices have become far more contradictory and complex. The old world racial order has not disappeared, but it has been seriously disrupted and changed. The legacy of democratic, racially oriented movements[22] and anticolonialist initiatives throughout the world's South, remains a force to be reckoned with. But the incorporative (or if one prefers this term, hegemonic) effects of decades of reform-oriented state racial policies have had a profound effect as well: They have removed much of the motivation for sustained, anti-racist mobilization.

In this unresolved situation, it is unlikely that attempts to address worldwide dilemmas of race and racism by ignoring or transcending these themes, for example by adopting so-called colorblind or differentialist policies, will have much effect. In the past the centrality of race deeply determined the economic, political, and cultural configuration of the modern world. Although recent decades have seen a

---

[22]For example, the US civil rights movement, anti-apartheid struggles, *SOS-Racisme* in France, the *Movimento Negro Unificado* in Brazil.

tremendous efflorescence of movements for racial equality and justice, the legacies of centuries of racial oppression have not been overcome. Nor is a vision of racial justice fully worked out. Certainly the idea that such justice has already been largely achieved—as seen in the "colorblind" paradigm in the United States, the "nonracialist" rhetoric of the South African Freedom Charter, the Brazilian rhetoric of "racial democracy," or the emerging "racial differentialism" of the European Union—remains problematic.

Will race ever be transcended? Will the world ever get beyond race? Probably not. But the entire world still has a chance of overcoming the stratification, the hierarchy, the taken-for-granted injustice and inhumanity that so often accompanies the race concept. Like religion or language, race can be accepted as part of the spectrum of the human condition, while it is simultaneously and categorically resisted as a means of stratifying national or global societies. Nothing is more essential in the effort to reinforce democratic commitments, not to mention global survival and prosperity, as we enter a new millennium.

Visit the Annual Reviews home page at www.AnnualReviews.org

LITERATURE CITED

Alexander J, et al, eds. 1987. *The Micro-Macro Link.* Berkeley: Univ. Calif. Press

Almaguer T. 1994. *Racial Faultlines: The Historical Origins of White Supremacy in California* Berkeley: Univ. Calif. Press

Appadurai A. 1996. *Modernity at Large: Cultural Dimensions of Globalization.* Minneapolis: Univ. Minn. Press

Balibar E, Wallerstein I. 1991. *Race, Nation, Class: Ambiguous Identities.* London: Verso

Banton M. 1977. *The Idea of Race.* London: Tavistock

Barkan E. 1992. *The Retreat Of Scientific Racism: Changing Concepts Of Race In Britain And The United States Between The World Wars.* New York: Cambridge Univ. Press

Bastide R, Fernandes F. 1971. *Brancos e Negros em São Paulo; Ensaio Sociológico Sôbre Aspectos da Formação, Manifestações Atuais e Efeitos do Preconceito de Côr na Sociedade Paulistana.* São Paulo, Brazil: Companhia Ed. Nacional. 3rd ed.

Blauner RA. 1972. *Racial Oppression in America.* New York: Harper

Blumer H. 1958. Race prejudice as a sense of group position. *Pac. Sociol. Rev.* 1(1) Spring:3–7

Bonacich E. 1972. A theory of ethnic antagonism: the split labor market. *Am. Sociol. Rev.* 37:547–59

Bonacich E. 1976. Advanced capitalism and black/white relations in the United States: a split labor market interpretation. *Am. Sociol. Rev.* 41:34–51

Bulmer M. 1984. *The Chicago School of Sociology: Institutionalization, Diversity, and the Rise of Sociological Research.* Chicago: Univ. Chicago Press

Centre for Contemporary Cultural Studies. 1982. *The Empire Strikes Back: Race and Racism in 70s Britain.* London: Hutchinson

Collins R. 1987. Iterated ritual chains, power and property: the micro-macro connection as an empirically based theoretical problem. In *The Micro-Macro Link,* ed. J Alexander, et al, pp.193–206. Berkeley: Univ. Calif. Press

Cotler J. 1970. The mechanics of internal domination and social change in Peru. In *Masses in Latin America,* ed. IL Horowitz, pp. 407–44. New York: Oxford Univ. Press

Crenshaw K, et al, eds. 1995. *Critical Race Theory: The Key Writings That Formed the Movement.* New York: New Press

Davis A, Lowe L. Reflections on race, class, and gender in the U.S.A. In *The Politics of Culture in the Shadow of Capital,* ed. L Lowe, D Lloyd. Durham, NC: Duke Univ. Press

Drake St. C, Cayton H. 1993 [1945]. *Black Metropolis: A Study of Negro Life in a Northern City.* Chicago: Univ. Chicago Press

Du Bois WEB. 1977 [1935]. *Black Reconstruction in America: An Essay Toward a History of the Part Which Black Folk Played in the Attempt to Reconstruct Democracy in America, 1860–1880.* New York: Atheneum

Du Bois WEB. 1989 [1903]. *The Souls of Black Folk.* New York: Penguin

Du Bois WEB. 1991 [1940]. *Dusk of Dawn: An Essay Toward an Autobiography of a Race Concept.* New Brunswick, NJ: Transaction

Du Bois WEB. 1996 [1899]. *The Philadelphia Negro: A Social Study.* Philadelphia: Univ. Penn. Press

Espiritu YL. 1992. *Asian American Panethnicity: Bridging Institutions and Identities.* Philadelphia, PA: Temple Univ. Press

Fenton S. 1980. Race, class, and politics in the work of Emile Durkheim. In *Sociological Theories: Race and Colonialism.* Paris: UNESCO

Finley MI. 1983. *Politics in the Ancient World.* New York: Cambridge Univ. Press

Gerth H, Mills CW, eds. 1958. *From Max Weber: Essays in Sociology.* New York: Oxford Univ. Press

Giddens A. 1984. *The Constitution of Society.* Berkeley: Univ. Calif. Press

Gilroy P. 1991. *There Ain't No Black in the Union Jack: The Cultural Politics of Race and Nation.* Chicago: Univ. Chicago Press

Gordon D, Reich M, Edwards R. 1982. *Segmented Work, Divided Workers: The Historical Transformations of Labor in the United States.* New York: Cambridge Univ. Press

Gossett TF. 1965. *Race: The History of an Idea in America.* New York: Schocken

Hall S, et al. 1978. *Policing the Crisis: Mugging, the State, and Law and Order.* London: Macmillan

Hannaford I. 1996. *Race: The History of an Idea in the West.* Washington, DC: Woodrow Wilson Center Press; Baltimore: Johns Hopkins Univ. Press

Hechter M. 1975. *Internal Colonialism: The Celtic Fringe in British National Development.* Berkeley: Univ. Calif. Press

Huber J, ed. 1991. *Macro-Micro Linkages in Sociology.* Newbury Park, CA: Sage

Jackson W. 1990. *Gunnar Myrdal and America's Conscience.* Chapel Hill: Univ. North Carolina Press

Joas H. 1996. *The Creativity of Action.* (Transl. J Gaines, P Keast). Chicago: Univ. Chicago Press

Kiernan VG. 1969. *The Lords of Human Kind: European Attitudes to the Outside World in the Imperial Age.* London: Weidenfeld & Nicolson

Kilson MA, Rotberg RI, eds. 1976, *The African Diaspora: Interpretive Essays.* Cambridge, MA: Harvard Univ. Press

Ladner JA, ed. 1973. *The Death of White Sociology.* New York: Random House

Lemelle SJ, Kelley RDG. 1994. *Imagining Home: Class, Culture, and Nationalism in the African Diaspora.* New York: Verso

Lewis DL. 1993. *W.E.B. Du Bois: Biography of A Race.* New York: Henry Holt

Lewis DL, ed. 1995. *W.E.B. Du Bois: A Reader.* New York: Henry Holt

Lipsitz G. 1998. *The Possessive Investment in Whiteness: How White People Profit from Identity Politics.* Philadelphia: Temple Univ. Press

Marable M. 1986. *W.E.B. Du Bois: Black Radical Democrat.* Boston: GK Hall/Twayne

Marx K. 1967. *Capital,* Vol. 1. New York: Int. Publ.

Massey DS, Denton NA. 1993. *American Apartheid.* Cambridge, MA: Harvard Univ. Press

McAdam D. 1982. *Political Process and the Development of Black Insurgency, 1930–1970.* Chicago: Univ. Chicago Press

McKee JB. 1993. *Sociology and the Race Problem: The Failure of a Perspective.* Urbana: Univ. Ill. Press

Montagu A. 1997 [1942]. *Man's Most Dangerous Myth: The Fallacy of Race,* Walnut Creek, CA. 6th ed.

Morris A, Mueller CM, eds. 1992. *Frontiers in Social Movement Theory.* New Haven: Yale Univ. Press

Myrdal G. 1944. *An American Dilemma: The Negro Problem and Modern Democracy.* New York: Harper

Omi M, Winant H. 1994. *Racial Formation in the United States: from the 1960s to the 1990s.* New York: Routledge. Rev. ed.

Park RE. 1950. *Race and Culture.* Glencoe, IL: Free Press

Pettigrew TF, ed. 1980. *The Sociology of Race Relations: Reflection and Reform.* New York: Free Press

Reich M. 1981. *Racial Inequality.* Princeton, NJ: Princeton Univ. Press

Snowden FM. 1983. *Before Color Prejudice: The Ancient View of Blacks.* Cambridge, MA: Harvard Univ. Press

Southern DW. 1987. *Gunnar Myrdal and Black-White Relations: The Use and Abuse of An American Dilemma.* Baton Rouge: Louisiana State Univ. Press

Taguieff P-A. 2000. *The Force of Prejudice: On Racism and Its Doubles.* (Transl. Hassan Melehy) Minneapolis: Univ. Minn. Press. Forthcoming

Tarrow SG. 1998. *Power in Movement: Social Movements and Contentious Politics.* New York: Cambridge Univ. Press. 2nd ed.

Thernstrom S, Thernstrom A, 1997. *America in Black And White: One Nation, Indivisible; Race in Modern America.* New York: Simon & Schuster

Thomas WI, Znaniecki F. 1994 [1923]. *The Polish Peasant in Europe and America.* Ed. and abridged by E Zaretsky. Urbana: Univ. Ill. Press

Todorov T. 1985. *The Conquest of America: The Question of the Other.* [Transl. R. Howard] New York: Harper & Row

Todorov T. 1993. *On Human Diversity: Nationalism, Racism, and Exoticism in French Thought.* (Transl. C Porter) Cambridge, MA: Harvard Univ. Press

UNESCO. 1966. *Research on Racial Relations.* Paris: UNESCO

UNESCO. 1980. *Sociological Theories: Race and Colonialism.* Paris: UNESCO

West C. 1989. *The American Evasion of Philosophy: A Genealogy of Pragmatism.* Madison: Univ. Wisc. Press

Wieviorka M. 1995. *The Arena of Racism.* (Transl. C Turner) Thousand Oaks, CA: Sage

Wilson WJ. 1996. *When Work Disappears: The World of the New Urban Poor.* New York: Knopf

Winant H. 1967. Racial dualism at century's end. In *The House That Race Built: Black Americans, U.S. Terrain,* ed. W Lubiano, pp. 87–115. New York: Pantheon

Wolpe H. 1975. The theory of internal colonialism: the South African case. In *Beyond The Sociology of Development,* ed. I Oxall, pp. 229–52. London: Routledge & Kegan Paul

Annu. Rev. Sociol. 2000. 26:187–213

States and Markets in An Era of Globalization

Seán Ó Riain

Department of Sociology, University of California, Davis, California 95616;
e-mail: sporiain@ucdavis.edu

Key Words   neoliberalism, welfare states, development, capitalism, socialism

■ **Abstract**   The paper considers how states and markets shape one another at the national and world-system levels and how globalization is transforming that relationship. This process is illustrated through a review of research on liberal, social rights, developmental, and socialist states in the postwar capitalist economy. These state models were reconciled with expanding international markets through a series of controls on trade and capital flows. Globalization has undermined many of these controls so that states must increasingly integrate themselves into local and global networks. States are experimenting with organizational and strategic changes nationally and internationally in order to respond to a networked economy and polity. Neoliberal institutions are the dominant force shaping the relation between states and markets in the contemporary era, but alternative state-society alliances are emerging to contest the hegemony of neoliberalism in shaping globalization.

PERSPECTIVES ON STATES AND MARKETS

Globalization is transforming the relationship between states and markets. Even as some authors predict the demise of the state in the face of increasingly global markets, others focus on the role states play in constructing markets themselves and making sustainable market interactions possible. As the times change so do our theories, generating new concepts that can be used to better understand the previous period. This essay undertakes such a project.

I argue that state, market, and society are embedded in each other and constructed by their interactions with one another.[1] This chapter briefly reviews

---

[1] Although the focus of the paper is on the relationship between states and markets, this inevitably leads us to a discussion of how these two modes of social organization intersect with the organization of society at large. 'Society' is of course a broad and ambiguous term. Here I use it in two senses. It refers to social groups that become actors relevant to the shaping of states and markets under particular circumstances, e.g., the role of the working class in mobilizing for welfare state expansion. However, I also use it to refer to

0360-0572/00/0815-0187$14.00

world-systems and comparative political economy analyses of the relation between states and markets. This analysis provides the framework for a discussion of the variety of models of state-market interaction in the postwar Golden Age of capitalism, an era when economic growth and rising living standards were sustained for the greater part of the industrialized countries' populations (Marglin & Schor 1990). Four dominant models of state-market interaction are considered: liberal states that promote market dominance of society, social rights states[2] that set social limits to market strategies, developmental states in which state and society coordinate market strategies, and socialist states where the state attempts to subsume market and societal action within its own structures. I review the challenges that globalization poses to these models and consider contemporary experiments with state-market relations built on the legacies of these models but operating within a transformed international order. Finally, the prospects for a transformation of the international institutions governing state-market relations are examined. Globalization does not consist of an inevitable march to a neoliberal order but is a politically contested process in which different state-market models of interaction come into conflict locally, nationally, and transnationally.

In the era after World War II a particular set of relations between state, society and market was institutionalized internationally, creating a system of relatively stable national economies organized through an international order of "embedded liberalism" (Ruggie 1982). These economies were tied together through a negotiated regime of multilateral trade but buffered from the full effects of these international markets by institutions limiting trade and capital flows. A diversity of national models of state-market interaction co-existed uneasily within these institutions, even as international markets gradually expanded in scope. Although embedded liberalism only extended to the industrialized capitalist countries, its institutions also shaped the relations between those countries and peripheral states and partly defined the terrain upon which industrializing countries could pursue their development strategies.

The globalization of the economy has consisted in large part of the weakening and even destruction of these institutional buffers between national economies and global markets. States find themselves trying to respond to pressures from local societies and global markets simultaneously without the breathing room previously offered by controls on transnational trade, finance, and production. These

---

the pattern of social interaction beyond the realm of the administrative efforts of the state (and corporate hierarchies) and the exchange relations of the market—that is in the more Polanyian sense of the associational life of society. An attention to society is demanded by recent trends within economic sociology that focus on the social basis of market activity and within political sociology toward the analysis of states-in-society.

[2]"Social rights states" refers to the states that are typically labeled welfare states. I follow Block's (1994) term due to its identification of the critical feature of those states—the extension and broadening of social rights in the market—rather than directing attention to just one, albeit crucial, part of this process—the expansion of the welfare state.

developments pose significant challenges to our current understanding of the re-lation between states and markets.

Within the tradition of comparative political economy, research on states and markets has focused on variations between different configurations of states and markets (Evans & Stephens 1988, Berger & Dore 1996, Boyer & Drache 1996). The *old paradigm* of research in political economy analyzed states and markets as self-contained separate entities battling in a zero-sum game for their share of a finite economic space (Block 1994). State administration, the associational life of society, and market exchange were seen as relatively distinct forms of social relations that compete as the dominant forms of social action. Where the territorial dimension of state-market relations was considered at all, the assumption was that they operated largely within a defined national economic space. The question became one of *how much* state intervention in the national economy was advisable. While research in this tradition provided a great deal of insight into the sources of diversity in national models of capitalism, it was weaker in analyzing how states and markets shaped each other, both within the national economy and internationally.

World-systems theory explicitly addresses these weaknesses as it emphasizes the ways in which states and markets shape one another at the level of the world-system. States and markets are inextricably intertwined at the level of the world-system in three distinct but related ways. Firstly, states are integrated into markets through the hierarchical structure of international trade and production (Wallerstein 1974, 1989). Secondly, states compete with one another to attract mobile capital, and core states struggle over the power to organize the global economy (Arrighi 1994). Furthermore, state and market expand in a symbiotic relationship: "Each bout of corporate and state expansion seems to have followed the same general course. A wave of technological change enabled an expansion in corporate size and control, stimulating popular demands for compensatory regula-tion on a corresponding governmental scale . . . Each round has led to an expanded state chasing after an expanding corporate size" (Chase-Dunn & Grimes 1995, p. 402).

A quite contradictory approach within world-systems theory suggests a third relationship between states and markets. This world society perspective suggests that a process of largely consensual adoption of common cultural and institutional forms (e.g., state-market relations) is occurring in a world of nations that is in-creasingly under the influence of a world society of stateless organizations and professionals (Meyer et al 1997). Models of state-market interaction may diffuse through the world-system through the interaction of states and particularly through the influence of transnational organizational actors. In particular, this perspective argues that a Western liberal democratic model of the organization of the liberal state and the free market are diffused across the nations of the world (Meyer 1980, Meyer et al 1997). Furthermore, Meyer et al argue that "globalization certainly poses new problems for states, but it also strengthens the world-cultural principle that nation-states are the primary actors charged with identifying and managing those problems on behalf of their societies" (1997, p. 157).

World-systems theories provide an analysis of some of the elements lacking in comparative political economy studies. However, while world-systems theory is valuable in orienting research toward system level processes, the theory is much weaker in explaining the mechanisms at work within subunits of the system. Within this broader structure of state-market relations at the world-system level, there are a variety of possible domestic arrangements, arrangements that themselves play a critical role in shaping the world-system. Consequently the theory also tends to be over deterministic and weak in identifying openings for political mobilization or alternative economic strategies.

Research in world-systems and comparative political economy appears to provide complementary insights into how states and markets construct the international economic order and into the diversity of national models of state-market interaction within that international order. However, until recently, relatively little dialogue has occurred between exponents of each tradition. This lack of dialogue led Evans and Stephens to call for an "interactive vision" in political economy, which aims "to explicate the political and social structural factors that enable individual countries to transform [international] ties to their benefit, while simultaneously analyzing the way in which the changing structures at the international level facilitate or limit possibilities for transformation" (Evans & Stephens 1988, p. 757).

This "interactive vision," combining national and world-system factors, was well suited to the era of embedded liberalism when domestic and international arenas interacted but were buffered from one another. However, as those institutional buffers have been weakened by globalization, we need a new integrative vision. This vision will see local, national, and global processes as shaped by each other but also as intertwined on a continuous basis. State-market interactions and regimes will be built not *between* the local and global but *out of* the local and the global. The boundaries between the spheres of state, society, and market are porous, and each sphere is intricately tied into the structures of the others. An integrative vision is attentive to both these connections between the different spheres and to the spaces created for social and political action within and between these connections.

Under embedded liberalism, states could maintain a janus-faced posture, dealing relatively separately with negotiating international markets with other states and with balancing domestic social and political pressures. Now that the buffering institutions of embedded liberalism have been weakened, states are increasingly faced with the integration of domestic and international policy (Ruggie 1995) and with negotiating the multiple connections of local society to transnational markets. The interactive vision was sustainable during an era of embedded liberalism, although it was blind to some of the connections that developed across institutional and territorial boundaries. Globalization, however, requires an integrative vision, a vision applied here to a reanalysis of the four most significant state-market models in the era of embedded liberalism and to their transformation within the process of globalization.

Contemporary approaches in political economy emphasize not the relative weight of state, market, and society, but the ways in which they shape each other (Block 1994, Evans 1997). New research in economic sociology has emphasized the associational foundations of economic action and its embeddedness in ongoing social relations (Smelser & Swedberg 1994). Political sociology and political economy have increasingly moved toward an analysis of states-in-society and the associational networks that blur the boundaries between the public and the private (Evans 1995, Stark & Bruszt 1998). Building on this research, I argue that the spheres of state, market, and society are shaped by each other and cannot exist in isolation from the others. Each sphere is *multiply embedded* within the others. Their boundaries cannot be clearly drawn, as each is intertwined with the others. Furthermore, the relations among them are inevitably tense, due to the inherent dilemmas of reconciling market, society, and state in a capitalist economy. Paths of economic development are determined by the variety of ways in which these tensions are reconciled through combinations of state, market, and society. The way in which these three spheres shape one another historically and form institutionalized sets of connections with one another becomes the central determinant of an economy's fate under globalization. This is a dynamic and path-dependent process, calling for detailed historical analysis of the mutual shaping of market, state, and society at the local, national, and transnational levels.

The integrative vision of political economy also approaches the analysis of social structure in a fundamentally different manner than either comparative or world systems approaches. The analysis of globalization raises difficult issues for sociology of how to pursue analysis across multiple levels of social structure. The dominant approaches to this point have been compositionist, treating high levels of social structure as the aggregate of lower levels, and hierarchical, treating lower levels of social structure as the effects of higher levels (Kontopoulos 1993). Comparative political economy analyses are for the most part compositionist, while world systems approaches are largely based on a hierarchical conception of the relations between levels of social structures. In contrast, the integrative vision treats social structures as heterarchical, with different levels integrating in different ways in a strucured but uneven manner (Kontopoulos 1993). We can identify particular critical structures at varying levels of analysis but must be attentive to the particular ways in which these structures integrate with one another in specific places and times. Neither can we a priori identify a dominant level of analysis.

This emphasis on path dependence, contingency, and political possibilities marks this perspective off from the more totalizing narratives of world-systems theory. However, its attention to the integration of local, national, and global processes goes beyond the classic states-and-markets studies. State-building, market reconstruction, and the constitution of society are interdependent social processes, therefore, which occur simultaneously at the local, national, and transnational level. An understanding of the concrete organization of the world-system at any historical juncture requires an understanding not only of world-system processes, but also of the specific ways in which state-market models interact at each of these levels. The rest of this paper provides a broad outline of the way in which this occurred in the post–World War II Golden Age of capitalism and of how that particular compromise is currently being reorganized.

STATES AND MARKETS UNDER EMBEDDED LIBERALISM

States play a critical role in constructing markets by guaranteeing their rules of operation but also by creating new market actors and shaping their strategies. However, they must balance this activity with the need to maintain support from the society that they claim to represent, placing the state at the heart of the process of managing the tensions between market and society. Society too is caught between supporting state efforts to promote growth and living standards through the market while simultaneously turning to the state for protection against the market (Polanyi 1944). Marxist theorists suggested in the 1970s that these tensions were insurmountable (Offe 1984, Habermas 1976). However, the tensions have been reconciled historically in a variety of institutionalized national and international models of capitalism, underpinned by different state-society alliances (Scharpf 1999, Evans et al 1985).

The historical compromise of embedded liberalism was one such institutional compromise. It was sustained by a number of buffering mechanisms that ensured that states could effectively use national economic policy to promote domestic stability, in the process sustaining support for an expanding global liberal order. In the area of trade, multilateral negotiations focused on the issue of discrimination in tariffs while retaining support for the concept of tariffs themselves. In the area of monetary policy, governments were permitted to maintain capital controls, and the focus of multilateral negotiations was maintaining balance-of-payments equilibrium in conjunction with full employment (Ruggie 1982). To these buffers in the areas of trade and finance, we might add the relatively national organization of industrial capital and the relatively limited labor migration during this period. In the critical areas of trade, finance, production, and labor supply, there were significant institutional buffers between the global expansion of markets and capital and the instruments available to governments to intervene domestically. The liberal international order was embedded in national economies that sustained support for it by mediating its effects.

Four distinct models of state-market interaction have dominated the history of this postwar world-system: the *liberal states* of the Anglo-American spheres of influence, the *social rights states* of parts of the industrialized west, the *developmental states* of East Asia, and the *socialist states* of Eastern Europe and China in particular. The fact that these models are embedded within an international liberal order is reflected in the market orientation of each, with the exception of the socialist states. In liberal regimes, states promote the domination of markets over society. In social rights states, state and society form an alliance to limit the range of market strategies to "high road" (high skill, high wage, extensive social protection) strategies. In developmental states, which seek to stake a place for themselves in the international liberal order, the state aggressively mobilizes society to participate in the market, and state and society coordinate market strategies. Socialist regimes differ in their position outside the embedded liberalism compromise and in their ability and desire to subsume market and society within the operations of the state. I examine each one in turn in order to examine the range of state-market interactions within this particular institutionalized organization of the world-system. In each case are outlined the key features of each model, its international and domestic conditions, and the critical dilemmas it faces.

It should be noted that each of these states avoids the potentially disastrous predatory relationship between the state and the market or society (Evans 1995). In these cases, individuals and agencies within the state treat their state power as a resource to be used to plunder resources generated by the market or within society. Whereas each of the models of state-market interaction examined here favors certain market strategies and social actors over others, none is based on this use of state power to extract resources from nonstate actors almost solely for the personal consumption of those within the state.

Liberal States and Hegemonic Power

The project of the liberal state is state promotion of markets into every sphere of society and even ultimately into the state itself. The irony is that the state is required to secure the conditions of reproduction of the market—laissez faire is inevitably and continuously planned (Polanyi 1944, Block 1996). In a world order where a hegemon exists, such as in the case of Britain in the late nineteenth century or the United States after World War II, then an international economic regime based around free trade is likely to emerge, as a liberal world order is consistent with the interests of the hegemonic power (Arrighi 1994, Ruggie 1982). The liberal welfare states of the industrialized west consist of the United Kingdom, the United States, and the countries to which the model has diffused through colonization, investment, and cultural connections (including Australia, New Zealand, Canada, and Ireland).

Hegemonic states are characterized by external strength and domestic weakness. The US state's central domestic economic strategy in the postwar era was to maintain its position of international pre-eminence through the promotion of a liberal economic order and the buildup of military power and influence. These twin pillars of US international power are reflected in the character of US domestic policy, which is more active than is typically supposed. Military spending has functioned for many years as closet industrial policy in the United States (Markusen & Yudken 1992, Hart 1992, Weiss & Hobson 1995) and has been central to the emergence, not only of such industries as aerospace and electronics (Markusen & Yudken 1992), but also software (Langlois & Mowery 1996) and the Internet (Newman 1998). Furthermore, social support for the state is sustained domestically in large part by the prosperity and status secured by international dominance.

The US working class has been tied to capital in part through its support for the international expansion of US firms (Herod 1997) and a social identity based on its role as the industrial backbone of US international economic might (Dudley 1994).

Even the state's relatively minimalist role in defining property rights and antitrust law has been central to the creation and destruction of particular market actors—witness the breakup of AT&T and the potential transformation of Microsoft (Campbell & Lindberg 1990). Fligstein (1990) argues that the US Federal government legitimated certain managerial world views, so that US postwar antitrust enforcement came to play a central role in reinforcing financial approaches to the large corporation. Nonetheless, the state in the United States has a much less direct influence over its major firms and over the macroeconomy. The economic malaise in the United States in the 1970s and 1980s led many authors to compare the US state unfavorably to the more interventionist European and Japanese strategies for managing stagflation (Scharpf 1999) and promoting competitiveness (Tyson & Zysman 1983, Hart 1992, Magaziner & Reich 1983, Campbell 1988). Britain, even more dramatically, was caught in a "low-skill equilibrium" and declined rapidly (Soskice 1990).

Furthermore, while the liberal strategy may be well-suited to the hegemonic power, it is less successful in economies that do not share the advantage of a dominant international position. Economies that have proved the most unwilling or least able to shape the actions of market participants (often due to a heavy reliance on transnational capital) are typically those with the closest relations to the most recent hegemonic powers—Britain and the United States. These states are typically ex-colonies of either country or have high concentrations of their transnational capital within them. Although states in Africa and Latin America may have expanded in the process of connecting with the global economy, they have proven to be restricted in their ability to reconstruct markets around developmental coalitions and outcomes, as illustrated by research in the dependency tradition (see for example Evans 1979, Gereffi & Wyman 1990). Relations of unequal exchange in primary commodity trade and a heavy reliance on foreign investment have been shown to be poor development strategies, whereas structural adjustment programs associated with foreign debt repayment have wreaked havoc on many economies (see Crowly et al 1998 for a review of the cross-national quantitative research on these topics).

The impact of foreign direct investment and dependence on foreign capital on economic growth has also been a controversial issue. A recent debate, focused on data from the period 1967–1973, has centered on the meaning and relative effects of, on the one hand, flows of foreign investments into a national economy and, on the other, the extent of a nation's dependence on foreign capital (Dixon & Boswell 1997a,b, Firebaugh 1992, 1997). Although controversies remain, some of the effects of foreign investment during this period have been clarified. Inflows of foreign capital boost economic growth in the short run, although significantly less so than does domestic investment. However, dependence on foreign investment (above a relatively low level of dependence) reduces growth. Furthermore, dependence on foreign investment also appears to inhibit domestic investment through negative externalities associated with dependence (Dixon & Boswell 1996a,b), although what these externalities are and how they operate is not made clear. A controversial summary of the results might be that both foreign and domestic investment promote short-run growth, that they operate according to different logics, that they appear to conflict under certain (poorly understood) circumstances, and that a long-run dependence on foreign capital is likely to be damaging to national economic growth. In related research Van Rossem (1997) finds that world system position and core-periphery relations only partially explain differential growth rates and are better thought of as the, often very powerful, context of development rather than as determining forces.

Social Rights States

Social rights states are based on limiting the range of feasible market strategies by strengthening society and setting social limits to market action—in the workplace through codetermination and union strength, in the labor market through welfare state expansion and decommodification and in the macroeconomy through corporatist bargaining. Social rights states are more therefore than a bundle of social policies; they are states that have institutionalized certain significant guarantees regarding the social, and occasionally the economic, rights of their citizens (Marshall 1950, Esping-Andersen 1994).

These institutions promote economic openness and adjustment to the global economy along with equality. In fact, the two aspects are related. The expansion of social rights sets a floor to cost competition and makes the low road option to development less feasible. This weakens industries that rely on low cost competition and forces firms to move into higher value-added sectors (Pontusson 1992) or to pursue higher quality, skill, and productivity strategies within those industries (Senghaas 1985, Streeck 1992). Decommodification through welfare state universalism and egalitarianism is a central plank of the strategy for pushing firms into these new, more dynamic sectors and activities. This process is supplemented by active labor market policies (Pontusson 1992) and by industrial policies (Katzenstein 1984). Corporatism improves economic performance as bargaining among the key actors in the economy can facilitate adjustment to change in the global economy (Katzenstein 1985, Scharpf 1999, Weiss 1998). Hicks & Kenworthy (1998) find that between 1950 and 1990 corporatist institutions at the national level in OECD countries were strongly associated with income redistribution, while cooperative relations at the firm level are strongly associated with improved economic performance.

There are of course a variety of social rights states (Castles 1993, Esping-Andersen 1990, 1996, 1999). The two most significant are the social democratic and the conservative models (along with the liberal model, which we have already discussed). The social democratic model was most fully developed in Scandinavia and is based on a state-society alliance where the power of the working class was combined with social democratic control of parliament and the state bureaucracy, making possible a deep institutionalization of the social democratic model. This institutionalization then served to reinforce the position of the key actors such as unions (Western 1997). The conservative model developed in countries such as Germany and France where the legacy of the authoritarian state shaped the state's constitution of the market, favoring state elites in order to assure loyalty and installing paternalist and familialist policies that incorporated the working class into the nation-building project without guaranteeing universalism and egalitarianism.

The mobilization of society is a critical factor explaining social rights states, although authors differ regarding the relative importance of the working class (Korpi 1983, Stephens 1979), risk-classes (Baldwin 1990, Esping-Andersen 1999), and sectoral coalitions (Gourevitch 1986). Gender ideologies and family structures are also increasingly recognized as central to the shaping of contemporary welfare states (Lewis 1993, Orloff 1993, Esping-Andersen 1999). Hicks et al (1995) combine working class strength with the mediating effect of existing political institutions in their explanation of early welfare state development. Others have argued that political institutions, and particularly the role of state elites and structures, is critical to explaining differences among social rights states (Weir & Skocpol 1985).

Regardless of the variety of social-rights states in question, the underlying logic is the same: An alliance between state and society sets limits to the ways in which markets can be organized. The strengthening of society reconciles the demands of market and society by promoting the high road of economic development within the wealthier industrialized economies. The problems that have plagued social rights states in recent years have consisted, not simply of the market dominating state and society, but of the fracturing of these state-society alliances under the strain of a variety of changes. These include the internationalization of business and finance, the fragmentation and dualism of the workforce under Post-Fordism, and the transformation of gender relations and family structures (Notermans 1997, Pontusson 1992, Esping-Andersen 1999, Huber & Stephens 1998, Kitschelt 1994, 1999, Garrett & Lange 1995).

Developmental States

The most vigorous efforts by the state to shape the market are found outside the core industrialized nations, in the developmental and socialist states. Perhaps the archetypal category of a statist alternative to the liberal model is the developmental states of East Asia. These states have promoted development and attempted to stake out a place for themselves within the institutions of embedded liberalism by aggressively mobilizing society to compete in international markets, while retaining a high degree of ongoing coordination of market strategy through state-society ties.

Developmental states achieve their goals in the contemporary era not by taking on the tasks of development themselves but by shaping the capabilities of society and the market to do so. In particular the state pokes and prods domestic firms to compete in the global economy and to constantly upgrade their organizational and technical capabilities to that end. The state assists in the birth and growth of domestic national firms. The East Asian developmental states forged an alliance with domestic capital in order to improve its ability to compete globally. Through policies such as selective and strategic use of protectionism, the provision of industrial subsidies and programs tied to performance, and the creation of close ties between financial capital, industrial capital, and the state, economies such as Japan, Korea, and Taiwan were able to industrialize rapidly based on improved productivity in manufacturing and "industrialization by learning" (Johnson 1982, Amsden 1989, Wade 1990, Evans 1995, Haggard 1990, Woo-Cumings 1999, Applebaum & Henderson 1992). Although the East Asian economies lay for the most part outside the institutions of embedded liberalism, they benefitted from some of its provisions, such as the right to impose relatively high tariffs.

The state cannot achieve these ends in isolation but in fact depends on its relation to society for its success. Close ties between business and the state can help to generate industrial transformation by improving information flows, generating a reciprocal exchange of subsidies for performance, and over the longer term, establishing credibility and trust on both sides (Maxfield & Schneider 1997). Of course significant differences exist among the Asian Tiger economies. The Korean model has the most authoritarian state and corporate structures, Japan combines corporatism without labor with enterprise unionism, while Taiwan displays a much less hierarchical political and corporate structure (Orru et al 1997).

The crucial institutional feature of developmental states is that they are characterized by embedded autonomy (Evans 1995). Such states are embedded in local capital through the close social ties between state bureaucrats and domestic business owners and managers. However, these states avoid being captured by local capital by retaining their autonomy. For Evans, this autonomy is safeguarded by the presence of a classic Weberian bureaucracy—based on meritocratic recruitment and promotion and norms of objective, procedural rationality (Evans 1995, Evans & Rauch 1999, Maxfield & Schneider 1997). Of course, coherent Weberian bureaucracies are relatively rare. However, some research suggests that, under certain conditions, encompassing business associations and associations that can monitor and sanction their members can promote a long-term developmentalist orientation to the market, even in the absence of a state able to enforce such an orientation (Maxfield & Schneider 1997: 25). Where labor is included in relations between business and the state in developing countries, it makes relations more formalized; but it is also likely to put pressure on state and business to engage in long-term collaborative planning (Schneider 1997). The situation of labor is typically less benign in developmental states, however, as trust between business and the state is often consolidated by the repression of labor (Deyo 1989).

Evans (1995) cautions that even the most successful and bureaucratically endowed states may run into problems. The developmental state promotes local firms and encourages them to compete globally. In becoming global firms, however, their alliances with the state are undermined as the firms become more and more closely aligned with the interests of their international partners. The Asian development project's basis in the domestic alliance between state and capital was undermined as Asian firms internationalized, became more integrated into international financial markets, and ran into the massive debt crisis of the 1990s; Asian and US capitalist institutions clashed, undermining the high debt financing of the Asian corporations (Wade 1998a,b,c,d, Wade & Veneroso1998, Biggart 1998). The delicate balance of state-society synergy in the East Asian developmental states is under threat from the disengagement of society from the state to form new, and potentially disastrous, alliances with international market actors.

Socialist States

Clearly the most ambitious attempt on the part of a state apparatus to shape market and society was the efforts of the socialist states of Eastern Europe and some parts of Asia to build an alternative model of socioeconomic development, both nationally and contesting with the liberal order at the level of the world-system. Where the theory of socialism had predicted that revolutionary attempts to overthrow capitalism would emerge in the developed nations, famously this has not been the case. Although the avowed goal of socialism was the dominion of society over state and market, in practice the socialist project turned into the effort of the state to subsume society and the market within itself. The mobilization of society by the state apparatus, controlled by the new class of experts (Konrad & Szelenyi 1979), has been the basis of economic development.

While ostensibly incompatible with the capitalist multilateralism of embedded liberalism, state socialism ultimately made its peace with this world order. As the Cold war became institutionalized and the US and USSR carved out their own spheres of influence, the spectre of communism became a legitimating element of the embedded liberalism compromise. Furthermore, the socialist states themselves used market-like mechanisms to coordinate their international relations, increasing their exports to the world market and their imports from capitalist countries and making deals to host transnational investment (Chase-Dunn 1982, 1989, p. 85).

How state socialist economies actually worked was a mystery to sociologists and other western social scientists for many years. This, despite the fact that until the 1970s the socialist economies had growth rates comparable to other countries at their level of development and much superior levels of literacy, infant mortality, and other measures of social welfare (Szelenyi 1994, Kornai 1989). It was only in the 1980s that studies began to go beyond the totalitarianism and modernization perspectives (Stark & Nee 1989). Kornai's (1980, 1990) major contribution in developing his theory of the economic logic of the plan was to analyze the logic of state socialism as an institutional formation in its own right. He argued that a plan-driven system ran into chronic problems of shortage, while a market driven system was threatened by problems of demand. Burawoy & Lukacs, in their study of firms in Hungary, developed this insight by showing that significant elements of market and social coordination existed within the planning system. In contrast to capitalism, where large firms sought to control uncertainty in the market economy by developing significant elements of corporate planning, socialist firms were subject to the plan externally but relied heavily on market-like mechanisms to deal flexibly with the chronic problems of shortages and make the necessary work process adjustments (Burawoy & Lukacs 1992).

Indeed, more generally, socialism was the mirror image of capitalism (Stark 1986). Where society turned to the state to ameliorate the inequalities of the market under capitalism, it turned to the market to compensate for the inequalities associated with the socialist redistributive state (Szelenyi 1978). Similar to capitalism, however, is the importance of social networks and personal ties in mobilizing and allocating resources, ties which may be so important that some authors have suggested a transition in postsocialist economies not so much from plan to market but from plans to clans (Stark & Bruszt 1998).

Socialist states vary a great deal in how these alternative forms of coordination have been combined with planning (Szelenyi 1994). Nonetheless, it was not until after the crises of 1989 that market and society were able to challenge and displace the state as the central organizing principle of the now postsocialist economies. The state system collapsed under the weight of its own inability to deal with the informational complexities of intensive growth in the information age (Castells 1997) and the growing gap between ideology and reality (Burawoy & Lukacs 1992). Authors disagree profoundly, however, on the legacy of socialism and its implications for transitions from socialism. Burawoy argues that in Russia the collapse of the socialist state has resulted in the involution of society with the destruction of the existing infrastructure of social cooperation and flight from production and accumulation into a degenerate merchant capitalism and usury (Burawoy 1997, Burawoy & Krotov 1992). Others are more optimistic, arguing that the socialist legacy leaves resources for the transition as well as obstacles, resources primarily located in the social relations of the populations of these economies themselves (Stark & Bruszt 1998).

Eyal et al (1998) argue that the cultural bourgeoisie of Eastern European post-socialist countries are promoting a capitalism without capitalists, creating market spaces before the capitalists are created to fill those spaces. Stark & Bruszt's research suggests that these capitalists are in the process of being created economically around new recombinant forms of property (Stark 1996) and politically through new deliberative associations (Stark & Bruszt 1998). New actors and institutional arenas are being formed that blur the boundaries between public and private and are deeply embedded in associational networks. Society is to provide the solution to the problems of market transition. Others, however, argue that the involution of society makes this impossible and that a strong state role is required to create a market that does not decimate the society but results in accumulation.

Burawoy (1997) points to China as the example of a coherent party-state that has promoted successful industrial transformation while retaining central political control, in contrast to the collapse of the Russian state and the rise of crime and usury to fill the vacuum. Oi (1999) argues that the state in China has not been undermined by its creation of an entrepreneurial class, as theorists of market transition suggest (Nee 1989). To a certain extent, the differences between these authors relate to their choice of cases, Russia and China having controlled society much more closely historically, while the Central European nations were left with a more vigorous associational life upon the collapse of socialism. Nonetheless, there are critical theoretical differences, reflected in Amsden et al's (1994) vigorous argument for a developmental state strategy for Eastern Europe. These differences might be fruitfully addressed through an increased attention to the conditions for state-society synergy (Evans 1997b) in contexts where *both* state and society are weak.

STATES, MARKETS AND GLOBALIZATION

In each model of state-market interaction, we see that a particular alliance between state and society shaped participation in markets in a different way. Social rights states strengthened society to promote a high road of economic development within the market. Developmental states mobilize society to participate in the market but are threatened by the increased strength of society. Socialist states veer between state and society as alternative roads to the market, or they face a bleak future if they cannot take either path (as in Russia). These dilemmas are themselves intensified by the crisis of embedded liberalism itself in recent years. The institutional buffers that shielded these state-society alliances from the international liberal order are being eroded, creating a new and uncertain terrain upon which new alliances are being tentatively forged.

World trade has expanded rapidly as a proportion of world income since at least the 1970s. More significantly, since the 1980s the value of world trade has been surpassed by the value of internal transnational corporate transactions as transnational industrial capital has become increasingly globalized (Ruggie 1995). Both of these are dwarfed by the enormous volume of international financial transactions, affecting both government's ability to control their own fiscal and monetary policy and making much more significant the market for corporate governance. Finally, migration has once again become a significant feature of advanced industrial economies, creating significant political problems for many states (for a review of these empirical trends and some of their implications, see Held et al 1999). While this period of globalization may be similar in quantitative terms to the late 1800s (Bairoch 1996, Hirst & Thompson 1996), it is qualitatively different in a number of ways. The connections between nations and localities are deeper and more instantaneous. The world-system itself has developed in quite a different manner in the intervening century, so that the current period of internationalization is occurring upon a very different institutional terrain. Furthermore, all of these intensified patterns of globalization occur alongside transformations in social structure (particularly around gender relations and family structures) and in social organization (the decentralization of bureaucratic organizations and the application of the new information technologies). It has also brought with it a rapid increase in within- and between-country inequality (Korzeniewicz & Moran 1997).

Globalization after Embedded Liberalism

Neither is this process of globalization an external, natural force undermining embedded liberalism from without. Rather, it is an outcome of the latent tensions within the postwar compromise, which were hidden under an apparently stable order for thirty to forty years. For some, these trends are manifested in the *market*, through weakening capital accumulation and dwindling profitability; such authors tend to be skeptical of the sustainability of US corporate profitability in the 1990s (R. Brenner 1998). Some argue that this is a result of the increased strength of labor and the welfare state, which eroded corporate profits—here the social rights state runs into its inherent limits (Boyer 1990). For others, however, the alleged crisis of profitability is a function of the global overcompetition between the leading exemplars of each state model above—the liberal state of the United States, the social rights state of Germany, and the developmental state of Japan (R. Brenner 1998).

Others are less concerned with a crisis within the market itself and in fact see markets as increasingly hegemonic over states and society due to their increasingly global organization. Global competition and trade pressurizes societies and states. Rodrik (1997), reviewing the economics literature, finds that unskilled workers are likely to experience increased labor market insecurity in the face of free trade, that national systems of social security are indeed threatened by trade liberalization, and that nations may have legitimate reasons to limit trade. While much commentary has focused on competition from the developmental states, Rodrik points out that there is also increased low cost competition from among the industrialized economies (Sassen 1988). Increasing global mobility of capital gave corporations increased power to demand concessions from states and societies (Harrison & Bluestone 1988). Gereffi & Korzeniewicz (1994) and Harrison (1994) combined these analyses to argue that market processes were increasingly organized on a transnational basis, with trade, production, labor, and finance organized through global commodity chains within an increasingly integrated global economy. Market, state, and society are in a hierarchical relationship with markets organized transnationally, while states remain stuck at the national level and society remains relatively fixed at the local level. The crisis is not of the market but of *society and the state* (and social rights states in particular).

For world-systems theorists, a crisis of the *liberal hegemonic state* lies behind these outward manifestations. They see the inability of the hegemon to organize capital accumulation on a world scale as a typical and recurrent feature of hegemonic cycles. The current crisis is brought on by interstate and interenterprise competition and by social conflicts associated with the emergence of new configurations of power. Ultimately they expect to see a new hegemonic power emerge to regulate a more deeply globalized economy (Arrighi & Silver 1999:29). Although these are broad generalizations, the world-systems theorists do point us toward a recognition of the crisis of the institutions reconciling international and domestic economies and social orders.

The current era of globalization is one in which the relationship between state, market, and society—and potentially a new institutionalized compromise between them—is being intensely contested. The structural changes outlined above pose a formidable set of challenges for states hoping to successfully remake state-society alliances and to reconstruct market actors, strategies, and environments. This is of course likely to be a period of transition and relative chaos to be followed by a newly institutionalized, increasingly globalized international economic order. However, it is the politics of this transition that will determine in large part some of the key elements of that new order. States are increasingly, sometimes desperately, experimenting with new ways of stimulating industrial transformation and economic growth. These experiments are built on the legacies of the state models of the era of embedded liberalism but must contend with a new economic and institutional terrain.

State Experimentalism

Some authors have argued that these changes have diminished the role of the state, weakening it to the point where it is essentially bypassed by the formation of a global system and transnational social structure (Sklair 1991, Robinson 1998, Mittelman 1997). Others rightly argue that the intensification of global processes has actually made the role of the state more important as an effective state becomes critical to promoting competitiveness within a global economy. However, this increased state role is limited to promoting economic competition and accumulation—even as the state becomes an increasingly critical enterprise association, its role as a civil association diminishes (Cerny 1995). Cerny argues that all states are now faced with the imperatives of global competition, causing a convergence around the model of the competition state (Cerny 1995). Certainly this resonates with aspects of the experience of recent years as states, both within and across national boundaries, compete to offer the greatest incentives and concessions to attract mobile investment.

However, this goes too far. Both the structure of the global economy and the space for local and national diversity are more varied and offer more opportunities than the concept of the competition state allows. There remain a variety of ways of connecting to the global economy, with significantly different implications for local and national populations (Gereffi 1994). It may be increasingly difficult to operate outside the reach of the market economy or in isolation from transnational capital, but we are also beginning to better understand the huge variety of ways in which such market activities can be organized—up to and including market socialism (Roemer 1991).

Clearly the specificity of national models of the economy is threatened by the challenges to the buffers that supported those models. However, there remain specific assets, which are of necessity tied to local places and can be a basis for persistent diversity in the global economy. These include the importance of local cultural differences in shaping economic systems (Biggart & Guillen 1999, Orru et al 1997). They also include the specific social relations of trust and effective communication, which are developed through proximate social relations (Piore & Sabel 1984, Storper 1997). Even the most diasporic or virtual community develops its own rules, resources, and boundaries (Wellman et al 1996).

Nonetheless, the governance of the economy has been transformed, and states are scrambling to learn the lessons of the new environment. Economic life and political governance has been rescaled as the national level has become destabilized, both from above by globalization and below by the increasing salience of regional economies. In this situation, the "glocal" state aims to promote capital accumulation by linking the local to the global and creating a location ideal for accumulation within a global set of connections (N. Brenner 1998, 1999). The organizational structure and strategy of these glocal states are only now beginning to be explored. The state that connects a wide range of local networks to a diverse set of global actors and networks must itself be more decentralized and flexible than states that presided over a centrally negotiated national development coalition (Ó Riain 2000).

Although it is transformed to deal with the new circumstances, the national state still plays a critical role in shaping markets by mediating these connections between the local and the global and by influencing how local specific assets are mobilized within the range of opportunities available in the global economy. Castells (1997) argues that the state is increasingly moving toward a position as a network state, embedded in a variety of levels and types of governance institution. Ansell's research on regional development in Europe "suggests that the 'network state' can operate as a liaison or broker in creating networks and empowering non-state actors, especially when state actors occupy a central role in these networks" (1999, p. 35). Network centrality is critical to this new state—isolation from the local or the global spells disaster. However, there remain a variety of ways of organizing these networks. The models of state-market-society interaction under embedded liberalism remain useful as conceptual organizing frameworks in considering the possibilities for the future. What might each of these models look like in such a networked economy and polity?

The *liberal* state is of course likely to prosper as an institutional form under neoliberal globalization. Jessop's (1993) concept of the "Schumpeterian workfare state" describes a state that combines the promotion of flexibility and innovation, oriented towards global markets, with punitive measures, such as workfare, directed toward those groups in society who fail to stake out a place in these markets. Although Jessop suggests that this state may prove to be the universal mode of regulation for a Post-Fordist economy (with variations across different systems), it seems to be most advanced in the liberal states of the United States and Britain, in particular the Thatcherite regime for which the analysis has been most comprehensively developed (Jessop 1994, Peck 1996). Liberal regimes have clearly moved in this direction, combining an intensified state promotion of markets with a more punitive relation between state and society. However, the Schumpeterian workfare state may run into its own problems as the workfare component proves insufficient to reproduce the labor force necessary for Schumpeterian innovation (Peck 1996, pp. 206-229). US computer industry success has for example been based heavily on immigrant technical labor (Saxenian 1999), even as technical graduates from US universities decline in number. The success of the industry, based on innovative regional economies combined with the United States' dominant international cultural position, is therefore threatened by its own liberalism.

Certainly, this intensified liberal model is no more likely than its predecessor to be successful for any industrializing economies to which it might be diffused (O'Hearn 1998). Liberal states are highly likely to encourage "smokestack chasing" behavior with the development of the kind of "competition state" that Cerny (1995) fears. However, some space remains for fruitful interaction between state and society, even in the United States, where some local governments have attempted to make themselves more responsive not only to capital but to their local communities (Sabel 1992, Harrison 1994).

Although the prototypical *social rights* states of Scandinavia have run into difficulties recently, they possess certain critical components of a reconstructed state-society alliance—including already vibrant local community institutions within the context of a cohesive state apparatus and an orientation to the global economy. The social rights state that has, perhaps surprisingly, attracted the most attention has been Italy. A perennial straggler among the leading European economies, with less well developed social protection, parts of Italy's economy have prospered based on developing strong local economies around networks of small firms. The strength of these local economies has been built on strong craft and civic traditions (Piore & Sabel 1984, Putnam 1993). However, state policies that supported small business (Weiss 1988) and that substituted microcorporatism for macrocorporatism (Regini 1995) have also been crucial. Combined, these state-society alliances supported highly effective and relatively egalitarian "polyarchic local orders" (Locke 1995). These local orders are an empirical example of the potential for generating a new social democratic compromise based on exchanging local flexibility and labor force reproduction for industrial upgrading and local solidarity (Sabel 1995, Amin & Thrift 1994). There are also suggestions in the recent experience of the Netherlands that neo-corporatist institutions can still potentially combine the flexibility of the new statist experiments with the coherence and communalism of the national models of embedded liberalism (Visser & Hemmerijck 1997). While each of the models of state-market relations we have discussed faces serious challenges, these states have not yet given up on their role in the economy, and state experimentalism suggests that the future remains relatively open.

The inability of the liberal regimes to provide sustainable innovation and the economic difficulties of the social rights states direct attention to the *developmental* states, which have focused precisely on molding society for effective market performance. Surprising examples have emerged of successful, if remade, developmental states in the 1990s. The Republic of Ireland and Israel have both developed innovative indigenous high technology industries such as software and telecommunications and have improved their economic growth and employment performance (Ó Riain 1999). This transformation has been stimulated by a flexible developmental state that promotes development by connecting local and global networks of innovation. It is able to mobilize this networked society to compete effectively in the market due to its own flexible, decentralized and networked, organizational structure (Ó Riain 2000). The East Asian developmental states also contain examples of this more flexible, multidimensional state structure. In contrast to the hierarchical, centralized Korean state, the Taiwanese state has always had a more decentralized internal structure with more diffuse and less well-understood ties to society (Wade 1990). These ties are well suited to its industrial structure, which is based on small and medium-sized enterprises that are closely integrated into international business networks. It is all the more interesting therefore that the Taiwanese economy has escaped the worst of the Asian debt and development crisis by resisting the temptation to dismantle critical elements of its developmental state apparatus (as Korea did), but rather making the state more densely tied into both the local and the global.

Although states remain central to development, efforts to subsume society and the market within the state are increasingly difficult to sustain as markets spread internationally. Thus, we see the wholesale privatization of state-owned enterprises in the capitalist nations and the collapse of many of the *socialist* economies. China remains the most significant exception. The Chinese economy is integrated into international networks through the increasingly important Chinese business networks (Hamilton 1996, Arrighi & Silver 1999), transnational communities (Portes 1996, Saxenian 1999), and even foreign investment in China. Furthermore, it relies heavily on dense local networks of cooperation (Oi 1998). Nonetheless, it succeeds in demanding that these network relationships be channeled through the state. The strength of the central state apparatus paradoxically allows it to provide autonomy to the local state while retaining control of shape and direction of economic activity (Burawoy 1997), a control reinforced by political and military power. The huge Chinese population and economy and the significance of China in shaping the new international order make it a profoundly important exception to the market hegemony rule.

Remaking the World Polity

There are signs therefore that states are adapting, whether out of necessity or desire, to the changed circumstances in the transition out of embedded liberalism. States themselves have been instrumental in shaping the current globalization project, often in conjunction with their own national bourgeois classes (McMichael 1996, Sassen 1999). Domestic and international policy can be separated only with great difficulty—the US legal innovations after World War II that promoted the 'financial conception of the firm' (Fligstein 1990: 192) are now playing out internationally through the global diffusion of Anglo-American corporate and trade law (Sassen 1998, Wade 1998a). It is states that have, for example, created a particular kind of market within the European Union and marginalized other rules for structuring the market (Fligstein & Mara-Drita 1996, Scharpf 1999). States may indeed be threatened by globalization, but they are also among the primary actors that will continue to shape the process itself.

Globalization is as much a political question as an economic one, and the politics of globalization are particularly crucial given their implications for local political possibilities. The shape of the global order will be critical in determining whether space exists in which alternative state-society alliances can emerge to challenge the politically dominant Anglo-American neoliberal model (Evans 1997a). Currently, the alliance that dominates globally is that between liberal states and transnational capital, imposing a set of market regulations that secure the privileges of capital against the rights of society and the capacities of the state (Wade 1998a). Even in Europe, where transnational governmental institutions are most developed, negative integration through eliminating barriers to trade has dominated over positive integration through the creation of new market-regulating institutions at the transnational level (Scharpf 1999). This is clear, for example, in how transnational pluralism in European Union industrial relations law undermines national corporatist institutions (Streeck & Schmitter 1992).

Any efforts to remake the role of the state in the economy also face an increasingly complex institutional field of market governance. Castells (1997) argues that globalization produces a pooling of economic sovereignty between institutions and across levels of governance. Of course, this may not mean the end of the state but simply its reconfiguration in a new relation to the local and the global. This networked polity consists of the "intermeshing of overlapping [policy] networks operating simultaneously in multiple functional areas and at multiple geographical scales" (Ansell 1999, p. 35). Ansell points to the possibilities this presents for local interests to empower themselves by bypassing the national state and appealing to the transnational bodies. Sassen (1997, 1998), on the other hand, points to the privatization of economic governance as there has been a rapid growth in bodies such as private commercial arbitrators that compete with public corporate regulation.

This polity generates new lines of social conflict, from which a new embedded liberalism may emerge. If so, it will be one characterized much less by the creation of buffers around national economies than by the provision of rules governing the ways in which the local and global are connected through the national. Limits to trade and controls on capital flows may be necessary and desirable (Block 1996, Rodrik 1997, Wade 1998a), but policy debates will increasingly focus on issues such as attaching labor and environmental standards to free trade agreements.

The future shape of the world-system and the potential for new local and national economic models will depend on which state-society alliances emerge transnationally to challenge the alliance between liberal states and transnational capital. Currently, supranational political institutions and transnational social movements suggest the potential of such alternative alliances. Supranational governance, although dominated by neoliberal approaches, may still be steered in alternative directions, and the European Union in particular may yet reflect the social democratic aspirations of many of its member states (Scharpf 1999). Indeed, Scharpf suggests that the strengthening of the European Union state bureaucracy's hand in promoting positive integration is the most likely strategy for successfully creating such a regulatory system. The recent debt-and-development crisis in Asia may prompt Japan to play a more active regional role and contest the dominance of US financial institutions and regulations (Wade 1998a,d).

The second development that offers interesting new political strategies is the increasing prevalence of transnational political activism—in particular advocacy networks around human rights, women's rights and environmentalism (among other issues); consumer/labor networks organizing boycott oriented campaigns such as those against NIKE; and, transnational labor organizing (Evans 2000).These transnational political networks have emerged from society as a Polanyian protection against the ravages of global markets and face huge odds. However, they may come to effectively catalyze local, national, and transnational political action in constructing an alternative to the neoliberal version of globalization (Evans 2000). Even more speculative at this point is how these social movements might connect to states to create new state-society alliances out of the local and the global.

A sociological approach to states and markets must be sensitive to the structuring of their relationships in the world-system but must also retain the tools for analyzing the variability of those relations within the system. Without the tools to analyze this variability, sociology's contribution to strategic and political consideration of developing and potential combinations of state, market, and society will be weakened. This paper has briefly drawn together research in sociology that is increasingly adopting an integrative vision of the international political economy. Such an integrative vision holds out the promise of making sense of the transnationally networked economy, polity, and society being built on the institutional legacies of embedded liberalism. It may also prove to be a tool combating the extreme pessimism and optimism that characterize debates on globalization by helping to identify the political possibilities within the current era. Globalization is a political process without an inevitable end point. Sociology requires a new vision to capture its complexity and the potentials within it.

ACKNOWLEDGMENTS

Special thanks to Peter Evans for extensive discussions in the early stages of this paper's development and for very helpful comments. Thanks also to Fred Block, Becky King and Steve Lopez for very helpful comments.

Visit the Annual Reviews home page at www.AnnualReviews.org

LITERATURE CITED

Amin A, Thrift N, eds. 1994. *Globalization, Institutions and Regional Development in Europe.* Oxford, UK: Oxford Univ. Press

Amsden AH. 1989. *Asia's Next Giant: South Korea and Late Industrialization.* Oxford, UK: Oxford Univ. Press

Amsden AH, Kochanowicz J, Taylor L. 1994. *The Market Meets Its Match: Restructuring the Economies of Eastern Europe.* Cambridge, MA: Harvard Univ. Press

Ansell C. 1999. The networked polity: regional development in Western Europe. Mimeo, Dept. Polit. Sci., Univ. Calif., Berkeley

Applebaum R, Henderson J, eds. 1992. *States and Development in the Asian Pacific Rim.* London: Sage

Arrighi G. 1994. *The Long Twentieth Century.* London: Verso

Arrighi G, Silver B. 1999. *Chaos and Governance in the Modern World System.* Minneapolis: Univ. Minn. Press

Bairoch P. 1996. Globalization, myths and realities: one century of external trade and foreign investment. See Boyer & Drache 1996, pp. 173–93

Baldwin P. 1990. *The Politics of Social Solidarity: Class Bases of the European Welfare States.* Cambridge, UK: Cambridge Univ. Press

Berger S, Dore R, eds. 1996. *National Diversity and Global Capitalism.* Ithaca, NY: Cornell Univ. Press

Biggart N. 1998. Deep finance—the organizational bases of South Korea's financial collapse. *J. Mgmt. Inq.* 7:311–20

Biggart N, Guillen M. 1999. Developing difference: social organization and the rise of the auto industries of South Korea, Taiwan, Spain, and Argentina. *Am. Sociol. Rev.* 64:722–47

Block F. 1994. The roles of the state in the economy. See Smelser & Swedberg 1994, pp. 691–710

Block F. 1996. *The Vampire State: And Other Myths and Fallacies about the US Economy.* New York: New Press

Boyer R. 1990. *The Regulation School: A Critical Introduction.* Trans. C Charney. New York: Columbia Univ. Press

Boyer R, Drache D, eds. 1996. *States Against Markets: The Limits of Globalization.* London: Routledge

Brenner N. 1998. Global cities, glocal states: global city formation and state territorial restructuring in contemporary Europe. *Rev. Int. Polit. Econ.* 5:1–37

Brenner N. 1999. Beyond state-centrism? Space, territoriality and geographical scale in globalization studies. *Theory Soc.* 28:39–78

Brenner R. 1998. The economics of global turbulence. *New Left Rev.* 229:1–264

Burawoy M. 1997. The state and economic involution: Russia through a China lens. See Evans 1997, pp. 150–77

Burawoy M, Krotov P. 1992. The Soviet transition from socialism to capitalism: worker control and economic bargaining in the wood industry. *Am. Sociol. Rev.* 57:16–38

Burawoy M, Lukacs J. 1992. *The Radiant Past: Ideology and Reality in Hungary's Road to Capitalism.* Chicago: Univ. Chicago Press

Campbell J. 1988. *Collapse of an Industry: Nuclear Power and the Contradictions of U.S. Policy.* Ithaca, NY: Cornell Univ. Press

Campbell J, Lindberg LN. 1990. Property rights and the organization of economic activity by the state. *Am. Sociol. Rev.* 55:634–47

Castells M. 1997. *The Information Age.* 3 vols. Oxford, UK: Blackwell

Castles F, ed. 1993. *Families of Nations: Patterns of Public Policy in Western Democracies.* Aldershot: Elgar

Cerny P. 1995. Globalization and the changing logic of collective action. *Int. Organ.* 49:595–625

Chase-Dunn C, ed. 1982. *Socialist States in the World-System.* Beverly Hills: Sage

Chase-Dunn C. 1989. *Global Formation: Structures of the World Economy.* New York: Blackwell

Chase-Dunn C, Grimes P. 1995. World systems analysis. *Annu. Rev. Sociol.* 21:387–417

Crowly AM, Rauch J, Seagrove S, Smith DA. 1998. Quantitative cross-national studies of economic development: a comparison of the economics and sociology literatures. *Stud. Compar. Int. Dev.* 33:30–57

Deyo FC. 1989. *Beneath the Miracle: Labor Subordination in the New Asian Industrialism.* Berkeley: Univ. Calif. Press

Dixon WJ, Boswell T. 1996a. Dependency, disarticulation and denominator effects: another look at foreign capital penetration. *Am. J. Sociol.* 102:543–62

Dixon WJ, Boswell T. 1996b. Differential productivity, negative externalities, and foreign capital dependency: reply to Firebaugh. *Am. J. Sociol.* 102:576–84

Dudley KM. 1994. *The End of the Line.* Chicago: Univ. Chicago Press

Esping-Andersen G. 1990. *The Three Worlds of Welfare Capitalism.* Princeton, NJ: Princeton Univ. Press

Esping-Andersen G. 1994. Welfare states and the economy. In Smelser & Swedberg 1994, pp. 711–32

Esping-Andersen G, ed. 1996. *Welfare States in Transition: National Adaptations in Global Economies.* Thousand Oaks, CA: Sage

Esping-Andersen G. 1999. *Social Foundations of Post-Industrial Economies.* Oxford, UK: Oxford Univ. Press

Evans PB. 1979. *Dependent Development: The Alliance of Multinational, State and Local Capital in Brazil.* Princeton, NJ: Princeton Univ. Press

Evans PB. 1995. *Embedded Autonomy.* Princeton, NJ: Princeton Univ. Press

Evans PB. 1997a. The eclipse of the state? Reflections on stateness in an era of globalization. *World Polit.* 50:62–87

Evans PB, ed. 1997b. *State-Society Synergy: Government and Social Capital in Development.* Berkeley: Int. Area Studies, Univ. Calif., Berkeley

Evans PB. 2000. Counter-hegemonic globalization: transnational networks as political tools for fighting marginalization. *Contemp. Sociol.* Forthcoming

Evans PB, Rauch J. 1999. Bureaucracy and growth: a cross-national analysis of the effects of 'Weberian' states structures on economic growth. *Am. Sociol. Rev.* 64:748–65

Evans PB, Rueschmeyer D, Skocpol T. 1985. *Bringing the State Back In.* Cambridge: Cambridge Univ. Press

Evans PB, Stephens JD. 1988. Development and the world economy. In *Handbook of Sociology*, ed. N Smelser, pp. 739–73. New York: Sage

Eyal G, Szelenyi I, Townsley E. 1998. *Making Capitalism Without Capitalists.* London: Verso

Firebaugh G. 1992. Growth effects of foreign and domestic investment. *Am. J. Sociol.* 98:105–30

Firebaugh G. 1996. Does foreign capital harm poor nations? New estimates based on Dixon & Boswell's measures of capital penetration. *Am. J. Sociol.* 102:563–75

Fligstein N. 1990. *The Transformation of Corporate Control.* Cambridge, MA: Harvard Univ. Press

Fligstein N, Mara-Drita I. 1996. How to make a market: reflections on the attempt to create a single market in the European Union. *Am. J. Sociol.* 102:1–33

Garrett G, Lange P. 1995. Internationalization, institutions and political change. *Int. Organ.* 49:627

Gereffi G. 1994. The international economy. See Smelser & Swedberg 1994, pp. 206–33

Gereffi G, Korzeniewicz M. 1994. *Commodity Chains and Global Capitalism.* Westport, CT: Greenwood

Gereffi G, Wyman D, eds. 1990. *Manufacturing Miracles: Paths of Industrialization in Latin America and East Asia.* Princeton, NJ: Princeton Univ. Press

Gourevitch PA. 1986. *Politics in Hard Times: Comparative Responses to International Economic Crises.* Ithaca, NY: Cornell Univ. Press

Habermas J. 1976. *Legitimation Crisis.* London: Heinemann

Haggard S. 1990. *Pathways from the Periphery: The Politics of Growth in the Newly Industrializing Countries.* Ithaca, NY: Cornell Univ. Press

Hamilton G, ed. 1996. *Asian Business Networks.* New York: de Gruyter

Harrison B. 1994. *Lean and Mean.* New York: Basic Books

Harrison B, Bluestone B. 1988. *The Great U-Turn.* New York: Basic Books. 2nd ed.

Hart JA. 1992. *Rival Capitalists:International Competitiveness in the United States, Japan and Western Europe.* Ithaca, NY: Cornell Univ. Press

Held D, McGrew A, Goldblatt D, Perraton J. 1999. *Global Transformations: Politics, Economics and Culture.* Stanford, CA: Stanford Univ. Press

Herod A. 1997. Labor as an agent of globalization and as a global agent. In *Spaces of Globalization*, ed. K Cox, pp. 167–200. London: Guilford

Hicks A, Kenworthy L. 1998. Cooperation and political economic performance in affluent democratic capitalism. *Am. J. Sociol.* 103:1631–72

Hicks A, Misra J, Ng TN. 1995. The programmatic emergence of the social security state. *Am. Sociol. Rev.* 60:329–49

Hirst P, Thompson G. 1996. *Globalization in Question.* Cambridge: Blackwell

Huber E, Stephens J. 1998. Internationalization and the social democratic model: crisis and future prospects. *Compar. Polit. Stud.* 31:353–97

Jessop B. 1993. Towards a Schumpeterian workfare state? Preliminary remarks on Post-Fordist political economy. *Stud. Polit. Econ.* 40:7–39

Jessop B. 1994. Post-Fordism and the state. In *Post-Fordism: A Reader*, ed. A Amin, pp.

251–79. Oxford: Blackwell

Johnson C. 1982. *MITI and the Japanese Miracle.* Stanford, CA: Stanford Univ. Press

Katzenstein P. 1984. *Small States in World Markets.* Ithaca, NY: Cornell Univ. Press

Katzenstein P. 1985. *Corporatism and Change.* Ithaca, NY: Cornell Univ. Press

Kitschelt H. 1994. *The Transformation of European Social Democracy.* Cambridge: Cambridge Univ. Press

Kitschelt H, ed. 1999. *Continuity and Change in Contemporary Capitalism.* Cambridge: Cambridge Univ. Press

Konrad G, Szelenyi I. 1979. *Intellectuals on the Road to Class Power.* New York: Harcourt Brace Jovanovich

Kontopoulos KM. 1993. *The Logics of Social Structure.* Cambridge, New York: Cambridge Univ. Press

Kornai J. 1980. *The Economics of Shortage.* Amsterdam: North-Holland

Kornai J. 1989. The Hungarian reform process. See Stark & Nee 1989, pp. 32–94

Kornai J. 1990. *The Road to a Free Economy.* New York: Norton

Korpi W. 1983. *The Democratic Class Struggle.* London: Routledge & Kegan Paul

Korzeniewicz RP, Moran TP. 1997. World-economic trends in the distribution of income, 1965–1992. *Am. J. Sociol.* 102:1000–39

Langlois RN, Mowery D. 1996. The Federal government role in the development of the U.S. software industry. In *The International Computer Software Industry: A Comparative Study of Industry Evolution and Structure*, ed. D Mowery, pp. 53–85. Oxford, UK: Oxford Univ. Press

Lewis J. 1993. *Women and Social Policies in Europe.* Aldershot: Edward Elgar

Locke R. 1995. *Remaking the Italian Economy.* Ithaca, NY: Cornell Univ. Press

Magaziner I, Reich RB. 1983. *Minding America's Business.* New York: Vintage Books

Marglin SA, Schor JB, eds. 1990. *The Golden Age of Capitalism: Reinterpreting the Postwar Experience.* Oxford: Clarendon

Markusen A, Yudken J. 1992. *Dismantling the Cold War Economy.* New York: Basic Books

Marshall TH. 1950. *'Citizenship and Social Class' and Other Essays.* Cambridge: Cambridge Univ. Press

Maxfield S, Schneider B, eds. 1997. *Business and the State in Developing Countries.* Ithaca, NY: Cornell Univ. Press

McMichael P. 1996. *Development and Social Change: A Global Perspective.* Thousand Oaks, CA: Pine Forge

Meyer JW. 1980. The world polity and the authority of the welfare state. In *Studies of the Modern World-System*, ed. A Bergesen. New York: Academic

Meyer JW, Boli J, Thomas GM, Ramirez FO. 1997. World society and the nation-state. *Am. J. Sociol.* 103:144–181

Mittleman J, ed. 1997. *Globalization: Critical Reflections.* Boulder, CO: Lynne Rienner

Nee V. 1989. A theory of market transition: from redistribution to markets in state socialism. *Am. Sociol. Rev.* 54:663–72

Newman NS. 1998. *Net loss: government, technology and the political economy of community in the age of the Internet.* PhD diss., Dep. Sociology, Univ. Calif., Berkeley

Notermans T. 1997. Social democracy and external constraints. In *Spaces of Globalization*, ed. K Cox, pp. 201–39. London: Guilford

Offe C. 1984. *Contradictions of the Welfare State.* London: Hutchinson

O'Hearn D. 1998. *Inside the Celtic Tiger: The Irish Economy and the Asian Model.* London: Pluto

Oi J. 1999. *Rural China Takes Off.* Berkeley: Univ. Calif. Press

Ó Riain S. 1999. *Remaking the Developmental State: The Irish Software Industry in the Global Economy.* PhD diss., Dep. Sociology, Univ. Calif., Berkeley

Ó Riain S. 2000, The flexible developmental state: globalization, information technology and the 'Celtic Tiger.' *Politics Soc.* Forthcoming

Orloff A. 1993. Gender and the social rights of citizenship. *Am. Sociol. Rev.* 58:303–28

Orrú M, Biggart N, Hamilton G. 1997. *The Economic Organization of East Asian Capitalism.* Thousand Oaks, CA: Sage

Peck J. 1994. *Work-Place.* London: Guilford.

Piore M, Sabel C. 1984. *The Second Industrial Divide.* New York: Basic Books

Polanyi K. 1944[1957]. *The Great Transformation.* Boston: Beacon

Pontusson J. 1992. *The Limits of Social Democracy: Investment Politics in Sweden.* Ithaca, NY: Cornell Univ. Press

Portes A. 1996. Global villagers: the rise of transnational communities. *Am. Prospect.* March-April, pp. 74–77

Putnam R. 1993. *Making Democracy Work: Civic Traditions in Modern Italy.* Princeton, NJ: Princeton Univ. Press

Regini M. 1995. *Uncertain Boundaries: The Social and Political Construction of European Economies.* Cambridge: Cambridge Univ. Press

Robinson WI. 1998. Beyond nation-state paradigms: globalization, sociology, and the challenge of transnational studies. *Sociol. Forum* 13:561–94

Rodrik D. 1997. *Has Globalization Gone Too Far?* Washington, DC: Inst. for Int. Econ.

Roemer J. 1991. Market socialism: a blueprint. *Dissent* 37:562–69

Ruggie JG. 1982. International regimes, transactions and change: embedded liberalism in the postwar economic order. *Int. Org.* 36:379–415

Ruggie JG. 1995. At home abroad, abroad at home: international liberalisation and domestic stability in the new world economy. *Millenium: J. Int. Stud.* 24:507–26

Sabel C. 1992. Studied trust: building new forms of co-operation in a volatile economy. In *Industrial Districts and Local Economic Regeneration*, ed. F Pyke, W Sengenberger, pp. 215–51. Geneva: Int. Inst. for Labour Stud.

Sabel C. 1995. Bootstrapping reform: rebuilding firms, the welfare state and unions. *Polit. Soc.* 23:5–48

Sassen S. 1988. *The Mobility of Labour and Capital.* Cambridge: Cambridge Univ. Press

Sassen S. 1996. *Losing Control? Sovereignty in an Age of Globalization.* New York: Columbia Univ. Press

Sassen S. 1998. *Globalization and its Discontents.* New York: New Press

Sassen S. 1999. Cracked casings: notes towards an analytics for studying transnational processes. Unpubl. ms., Dep. Sociol., Univ. Chicago

Saxenian AL. 1999. *Silicon Valley's New Immigrant Entrepreneurs.* San Francisco Public Policy Inst. Calif.

Scharpf F. 1999. *Governing in Europe.* Oxford, UK: Oxford Univ. Press

Schneider BR. 1997. Big business and the politics of economic reform: confidence and concertation in Brazil and Mexico. See Maxfield & Schneider 1997, pp. 191–215

Senghaas D. 1985. *The European Experience: A Historical Critique of Development Theory.* Dover, NH: Berg

Sklair L. 1991. *Sociology of the Global System.* Hemel Hempstead, UK: Harvester Wheatsheaf

Smelser N, Swedberg R, eds. 1994. *The Handbook of Economic Sociology.* Princeton, NJ: Princeton Univ. Press/ Russell Sage Found.

Soskice D. 1990. Wage determination: the changing role of institutions in advanced industrial countries. *Oxford Rev. Econ. Policy* 6:36–61

Stark D. 1986. Rethinking internal labor markets: new insights from a comparative perspective. *Am. Sociol. Rev.* 51:492–504

Stark D. 1996. Recombinant property in East European capitalism. *Am. J. Sociol.* 101:993–1027

Stark D, Bruszt L. 1998. *Postsocialist Pathways: Transforming Politics and Property in East Central Europe.* Cambridge: Cambridge Univ. Press

Stark D, Nee V. 1989. *Remaking the Economic Institutions of Socialism.* Stanford, CA: Stanford Univ. Press

Stephens J. 1979. *The Transition from Capitalism to Socialism.* London: Macmillan

Storper M. 1997. *The Regional World: Territorial Development in a Global Economy.* London: Guilford

Streeck W. 1992. *Social Institutions and Economic Performance.* London: Sage

Streeck W, Schmitter P. 1991. From national corporatism to transnational pluralism: organized interests in the single European market. *Polit. Soc.* 19:133– 64

Szelenyi I. 1978. Social inequalities under state redistributive economies. *Int. J. Compar. Soc.* 1:61–87

Szelenyi I, Beckett K, King LP. 1994. The socialist economic system. In *The Handbook of Economic Sociology*, ed. N Smelser, R Swedborg, pp. 234–51. Princeton, NJ: Princeton Univ. Press/Russell Sage

Tyson L, Zysman J, eds. 1983. *American Industry in International Competition: Government Policies and Corporate Strategies.* Ithaca, NY: Cornell Univ. Press

Van Rossem R. 1996. The world system paradigm as general theory of development—a cross-national test. *Am. Sociol. Rev.* 61:508–27

Visser J, Hemerijck A. 1997. *A Dutch Miracle.* Amsterdam: Amsterdam Univ. Press

Wade R. 1990. *Governing the Market.* Princeton, NJ: Princeton Univ. Press

Wade R. 1998a. The coming fight over capital flows. *Foreign Policy* 113:41–54

Wade R. 1998b. The Asian debt-and-development crisis of 1997–?: causes and consequences. *World Dev.* 26:1535–53

Wade R. 1998c. From 'miracle' to 'cronyism': explaining the great Asian slump. *Cambridge J. Econ.* 22:693–706

Wade R. 1998d. The Asian crisis and the global economy: causes, consequences, and cure. *Curr. Hist.* 97:361–73

Wade R, Veneroso F. 1998. The Asian crisis: the high debt model versus the Wall Street-Treasury-IMF complex. *New Left Rev.* 228:3–24

Wallerstein I. 1974. *The Modern World-System*

I: Capitalist Agriculture and the Origins of the European World Economy. New York: Academic

Wallerstein I. 1989. *The Modern World-System, III: The Second Era of Great Expansion of the Capitalist World Economy, 1730's-1840's.* New York: Academic

Weir M, Skocpol T. 1985. State structures and the possibilities for 'Keynesian' responses to the Great Depression in Sweden, Britain and the United States. See Evans et al 1985, pp. 107–67

Weiss L. 1988. *Creating Capitalism.* Oxford: Blackwell

Weiss L. 1998. *The Myth of the Powerless State.* Ithaca, NY: Cornell Univ. Press

Weiss L, Hobson J. 1995. *States and Economic Development.* Cambridge, UK: Polity

Wellman B, Salaff J, Dimitrova D, Garton L, Gulia M, Haythornthwaite C. 1996. Computer networks as social networks. *Annu. Rev. Sociol.* 22:213–38

Western B. 1997. *Between Class and Market: Postwar Unionization in the Capitalist Democracies.* Princeton, NJ: Princeton Univ. Press

Woo-Cumings M, ed. 1999. *The Developmental State.* Ithaca, NY: Cornell Univ. Press.

Annu. Rev. Sociol. 2000. 26:215–40

VOLUNTEERING

John Wilson

Department of Sociology, Duke University, Durham, North Carolina 27708;
e-mail: JWils@soc.duke.edu

Key Words   Volunteers, activism, motives, human capital, social capital, commitment

■ **Abstract**   Volunteering is any activity in which time is given freely to benefit another person, group or cause. Volunteering is part of a cluster of helping behaviors, entailing more commitment than spontaneous assistance but narrower in scope than the care provided to family and friends. Although developed somewhat independently, the study of volunteerism and of social activism have much in common. Since data gathering on volunteering from national samples began about a quarter of a century ago, the rate for the United States has been stable or, according to some studies, rising slightly. Theories that explain volunteering by pointing to individual attributes can be grouped into those that emphasize motives or self-understandings on the one hand and those that emphasize rational action and cost-benefit analysis on the other. Other theories seek to complement this focus on individual level factors by pointing to the role of social resources, specifically social ties and organizational activity, as explanations for volunteering. Support is found for all theories, although many issues remained unresolved. Age, gender and race differences in volunteering can be accounted for, in large part, by pointing to differences in self-understandings, human capital, and social resources. Less attention has been paid to contextual effects on volunteering and, while evidence is mixed, the impact of organizational, community, and regional characteristics on individual decisions to volunteer remains a fruitful field for exploration. Studies of the experience of volunteering have only just begun to plot and explain spells of volunteering over the life course and to examine the causes of volunteer turnover. Examining the premise that volunteering is beneficial for the helper as well as the helped, a number of studies have looked at the impact of volunteering on subjective and objective well-being. Positive effects are found for life-satisfaction, self-esteem, self-rated health, and for educational and occupational achievement, functional ability, and mortality. Studies of youth also suggest that volunteering reduces the likelihood of engaging in problem behaviors such as school truancy and drug abuse.

INTRODUCTION

Volunteering means any activity in which time is given freely to benefit another person, group, or organization. This definition does not preclude volunteers from benefiting from their work. Whether these benefits can include material rewards is open to debate. Some scholars believe that work is not truly volunteered if it is remunerated (J Smith 1991:115), whereas others believe that people who have elected to work in poorly paid jobs because they wish to do good should at least be considered "quasi-volunteers" (Smith 1982:25). Whether or not the definition of volunteering should include some reference to intentions is also subject to debate. Some think the desire to help others is constitutive of volunteering. Others subscribe to the view that volunteering means acting to produce a "public" good: No reference to motive is necessary. The recent emphasis on volunteering as a productive activity is compatible with this behavioral approach because volunteering is simply defined as an activity that produces goods and services at below market rate; no reference is made to the reasons for activity.

Volunteering is part of a general cluster of helping activities. Unlike the spontaneous help given to the victim of an assault, where it is necessary to decide rapidly whether or not to take action and the encounter is brief and often chaotic, volunteerism is typically proactive rather than reactive and entails some commitment of time and effort. Whether or not it should include behavior conventionally described as caring is currently under debate. In everyday usage, caring is associated with person-to-person emotional labor on behalf of family and friends; volunteering is thought of as being more formalized and public (Snyder & Omoto 1992:218). There are some obvious differences between these activities: There is a level of obligation implied by the care relationship that is not found in volunteering, and much of the social activism rightly labeled volunteering is caring only in a loose sense of the term. However, it would be wise not to make too much of this distinction. Volunteering can be seen as an extension of private behavior into the public sphere (Brudney 1990:3)—this is how many emergency squad volunteers see their work (Gora & Nemerowicz 1985:29)—and there is little question that volunteering should include informal helping behaviors, such as driving one's elderly neighbor for a medical check-up (Cnaan & Amrofell 1994:343).

Sociological convention distinguishes being an active participant in a voluntary association from volunteering (Cutler & Danigelis 1993:150, Gallagher 1994b:20, Payne & Bull 1985:253). There is something to be said for separating these roles. The first consumes the collective goods the organization provides, while the second helps produce those goods. Allowing this distinction, there is still some question as to whether people who help maintain the association they belong to should be counted as volunteers because the public good created is restricted to fellow members. But there seems to be no convincing reason to rule out such activities, although it might be useful to separate associational volunteers, who are members working for their organization, from program volunteers, who are members working on behalf of their organization (Smith 1997:20; see also Barkan et al 1995:116).

The relation between volunteering and activism also needs to be addressed. Conventional wisdom holds that social activists are oriented to social change while volunteers focus more on the amelioration of individual problems (Markham & Bonjean 1995:1556). There is some merit to distinguishing these roles: They might well attract different kinds of people (Caputo 1997). But it should not be forgotten that the roles of activist and volunteer are social constructions; the volunteers Eliasoph (1998:12) studied wanted to "care about people," not about politics, and were thus quick to deny they were activists. When the government was slow to respond to the AIDS crisis volunteers had to double up as activists to help mobilize resources to deal with the problem (Chambre 1991:273). Social circumstances thus help determine the meaning of these two roles and their relation to each other. There is no good sociological reason to study them separately (Marwell & Oliver 1993).

RATES

In the past twenty years, quite a large number of social surveys have asked respondents about their volunteer work, including the 1998 *General Social Survey*. The most accurate count is probably that provided by the biennial surveys conducted by the Gallup Organization on behalf of the Independent Sector. The 1998 survey reported 56% of the United States population as having volunteered at some point during the past year. Social surveys report higher rates when they focus explicitly on volunteer activities, define volunteer work broadly to include informal assistance, and use lists of volunteer activities to jog respondents' memories.

Practitioners have always been worried about maintaining a supply of volunteer labor, but this topic has received fresh scrutiny in recent years as a result of the debate over the possibility that civic life is declining in modern societies, making them less democratic. In fact, volunteering rates in the United States are either stable (Hodgkinson & Weitzman 1996:2) or rising (Ladd 1999:64). Neither an increase in the labor force participation of women nor a decline in club and union memberships has lowered the volunteer rate (Segal 1993:87–93). Many new grassroots community organizations have arisen to replace the older clubs and associations; women have simply changed what they volunteer for as they take up paid employment; and a "third age" population of healthy elderly is volunteering at higher rates than ever before.

THEORIES OF VOLUNTEERING

This overview of theories of volunteering follows the outline used by House (1981) in his survey of research on social support, of which volunteering is one instance. He identifies three sets of factors associated with the provision of social support: characteristics of the individual, the properties of the relationships in which that individual is involved, and the community context. The overview is largely restricted to material published during the last decade. An overview of earlier material is provided by Smith (1994). Space considerations dictate that this review be confined mainly to work conducted in the United States.

At the level of the individual, two perspectives on volunteering predominate. One assumes a complexity in the constitution of the person while treating the context as background; the other treats the human actor as driven by fairly simple mechanisms while treating the context in which those mechanisms work as complex. The first perspective is associated with more subjectivist approaches to sociological explanation, the second with more behaviorist. The first is dominated by the search for the motives behind volunteering; the second assumes that actors are rational and that the decision to volunteer is based largely on a weighing of costs and benefits in the context of varying amounts of individual and social resources.

Motives, Values and Beliefs

Many sociologists are skeptical of the existence of any identifiable drives, needs, or impulses that might inspire volunteerism. They dismiss the idea of motivation altogether from sociological discourse on this topic. This is a mistake because talk about motives is a key organizing feature of everyday life. Humans impute motives—to themselves and to others—and thereby validate or challenge identities, strengthen or weaken commitments (Broadbridge & Horne 1996:259). Motives play an important role in public thinking about volunteerism: Activities that seem to be truly selfless are the most esteemed (Cnaan et al 1996:375).

Social psychologists have devoted considerable effort to compiling an inventory of motives for volunteering (Clary et al 1996, Okun et al 1998, Snyder et al 1999, Sokolowski 1996). Much can be learned from this research about how people think about their volunteer work. However, most sociologists would not regard these motives as predispositions. Rather, they would treat motives as constitutive of action, part of a discourse giving meaning to and helping to shape behavior (Fischer & Schaffer 1993, Midlarsky & Kahana 1994, Smith 1982:28). Thus, one reason why teenagers are more likely to volunteer if their parents volunteer (Rosenthal et al 1998:490, Segal 1993:105, Sundeen & Raskoff 1994:392) is that their parents have taught them a positive way to think about volunteer work. They have learned motivational attributions as part of a larger set of cultural understandings passed on to them by their parents (Wuthnow 1995:105). Parents teach their children volunteer motivations when they teach them about social responsibility, reciprocity, and justice (Flanagan et al 1998:462, Fogelman 1997:150). For their teaching to be effective, they must practice what they preach, and they must actively manage their children's volunteer work to ensure it is neither too trivial nor too demanding (Pancer & Pratt 1999:43). Parents can even encourage pro-social attitudes in their children by *how* they raise them. Strong support (e.g. affection, praise, encouragement) is associated with a variety of positive outcomes among children and adolescents, including "the exhibition of considerate and altruistic behavior" (Amato & Booth 1997:17; see also Franz & McClelland 1994). There is little evidence, however, that motive talk learned in early childhood has a *direct* effect on adult volunteerism (Rosenthal et al 1998:491).

Besides their parents, young people learn how to think about volunteer work through schools. Children who volunteer during their high school years develop more pro-social attitudes and are more likely to volunteer in college and later in their adult life (Astin 1993, Damico et al 1998). Learning to think of citizenship as carrying responsibilities as well as rights encourages teenagers to volunteer when they become adults regardless of whether they volunteered when young (Janoski et al 1998).

If motive talk is learned as part of a larger set of cultural understandings, it makes sense to expect these frameworks of consciousness to influence the decision to volunteer directly (Schervish & Havens 1997:241, Straub 1997). Volunteers do indeed rate working to improve their communities, aiding the less fortunate, and doing something for their country (Flanagan et al 1999:149) higher than nonvolunteers. They also rank the life-goals of personal charity and helping others higher than nonvolunteers (Sundeen 1992). But overall, the relation between values and volunteering is weak and inconsistent (religious and civic values do little to encourage volunteering) (Greeley 1999, Hoge et al 1998, Ladd 1999:72, Smith 1998:39, Wilson & Janoski 1995).

There are a number of reasons why values fail to predict volunteering reliably. Volunteering takes many forms, each inspired by a different set of values. Highly generalized value questions fail to capture this variation. Another reason is that different groups in the population attach different values to the same volunteer work (Serow & Dreyden 1990:560, Sundeen & Raskoff 1995). For example, some religious beliefs encourage helping AIDS victims while other religious beliefs discourage it (Omoto & Snyder 1993). A third reason is that values tend to be ineffectual outside support communities where norm enforcement is possible (Wuthnow 1991:156). In general, then, values are less important in helping decide who volunteers than in helping decide what volunteering means to the people who do: Members of conservative religious denominations in the United States think of volunteer work in terms of sacrifice; liberals think of it in terms of self-improvement.

Human Capital

Individual-level theories of volunteering founded on behaviorist assumptions argue that the decision to volunteer is based on a rational weighing of its costs and benefits. Ability to work is determined by resources. Earlier theories tended to associate volunteering with status differentiation. Doing good works was believed to be part of an ensemble of characteristics giving a person prestige and respect (Smith 1994:247). From the rational choice perspective, individual attributes such as level of education assume a different significance. They become inputs that make it easier to face the demands of volunteering. From this perspective, volunteering is a productive activity—its meaning to the volunteer is not particularly relevant (Herzog et al 1989:S129).

Education   Level of education is the most consistent predictor of volunteering (McPherson & Rotolo 1996:181, Sundeen & Raskoff 1994:392). Education boosts volunteering because it heightens awareness of problems, increases empathy, and builds self-confidence (Brady et al 1995:285, Rosenthal et al 1998:480). Educated people are also more likely to be asked to volunteer (Brady et al 1999), which is partly a function of the fact they belong to more organizations (Herzog & Morgan 1993:137), where they develop more civic skills, such as the ability to run a meeting (Brady et al 1995:285). Nevertheless, the importance of education varies by type of volunteer work. For example, it is positively related to political volunteering and to AIDS-related volunteering but not related at all to informal community work (Omoto & Snyder 1993). The salience of education also increases if the task assigned requires literacy skills as opposed to social skills (Okun & Eisenberg 1992). In some instances, education has a curvilinear relation to volunteering: Volunteer firefighters are more likely than other members of their community to have graduated from high school but less likely to have a college degree (Thompson 1993a).

Human capital theory offers an explanation for why children inherit their parents' volunteering habits different from that found in motivation studies. Rather than modeling ideals, parents supply resources. And indeed, children of high-status parents are more likely to volunteer (Sundeen & Raskoff 1994:392). However, the scope of conditions of human capital theory are not clear. Janoski & Wilson (1995) show that offsprings' volunteering for groups concerned with community problems is predicted by parents' volunteering and by their own marital and parent status at the time, while neither parents' nor volunteers' socioeconomic status has much effect. Conversely, volunteering for more self-oriented organizations, such as unions and professional associations, is predicted by parents' and the volunteers' own socioeconomic status but is negatively related to the volunteers' family status. Parents role model the first but provide the resources for the second.

Work   It was long supposed that the volunteer labor force consisted mainly of women with time on their hands, the implication being that paid employment and volunteering were incompatible. A competing hypothesis is that work is a form of social integration and a means of building civic skills, both of which increase the chances of volunteering.

Free Time.   Role overload theory (Markham & Bonjean 1996) predicts a negative relation between paid work hours and volunteer hours. Time constraints do seem to operate *among the employed,* because part-time workers volunteer more than full-time workers. However, the relation between paid work and volunteer work is complicated by two other facts. The lowest rates of volunteering are found among those not in the labor force at all—unemployed people and homemakers (Stubbings & Humble 1984:27). This suggests that work is a form of social integration, which encourages volunteering. Getting a paid job can also boost self-confidence and teach organizational skills (Brady et al 1995, Schoenberg 1980:S264). It is worth noting in this context that the positive effect of employment on volunteering is stronger for women than men (Gerstel & Gallagher 1994:526). The other fact complicating the relation between work and volunteering is that, among full-time workers, there is a slight *upward* curve in volunteering as paid work hours increase (Segal 1993:84, Wuthnow 1998:76). Perhaps working hours are measuring not only the time demands of the job but also its importance—and people with higher-prestige jobs tend to volunteer more.

Further insight into the connection between work hours and volunteering awaits the exploration of a number of other issues. First, rather than hours worked, what might be important is the individual's control over those hours: The self-employed and people with flexible work schedules are the most likely to volunteer (Freeman 1997:S156, Thompson 1993a,b). Second, rather than counting how many hours people work for pay, it might be more important to learn *why* they are working those hours. Part-time workers for whom reduced hours are a matter of choice are the most likely to volunteer. Third, other demands on free time need to be considered simultaneously. When people say they are "too busy" to volunteer they are as likely to be referring to other caring responsibilities as they are to the demands of their job (Brady et al 1995:274, Gallagher 1994a:575).

Jobs.   Rather than counting how many hours people spend at work it might be more important to ask what they do when they get there. As occupational status increases so does the likelihood of volunteering (Smith 1994, Stubbings & Humble 1984:12, Wilson & Musick 1997b). Status generalization suggests that managerial and professional level people are more likely to be asked to volunteer. It is also probable that such people get more intrinsic rewards from their work, building up an attachment to work and work-like activities that easily translates into volunteerism (Herzog & Morgan 1993:140). Although it is possible that some people find in their volunteer work compensation for what is denied them in paid employment, rational choice theory predicts that volunteer work replicates paid work because the volunteer is using skills developed in the workplace. People who have self-directed jobs, those that score high on autonomy, decision-making, complexity and variety, volunteer for a wider range of activities than other workers (Wilson & Musick 1997b).

Income   Rational choice theorists assume that volunteer hours are inversely re-lated to wages because opportunity costs rise as pay rises (Wolff et al 1993:25). The evidence is mixed. Looking at hours volunteered among those who volun-teer, Freeman (1997:S152) finds a negative relation between wage income and volunteering. Menchik & Weisbrod (1987) find that hours of volunteering work are positively related to income from all sources, but at a decreasing rate (their data excludes married women). Segal (1993:47) finds that, among single adults (18–54), volunteer hours are positively related to wages and negatively related to wealth, but only among men. Among the elderly, income has a positive effect on the number of groups to which people belong, but has no effect on the number of hours volunteered overall (Gallagher 1994a:36). Raskoff & Sundeen (1995) find that income is positively associated only with health-related and education-related volunteering and has no impact on religious or informal volunteering. Although the balance of these studies denies the contention that an increase in income will depress volunteering hours, the net effect of income on volunteering varies by how income is measured, how volunteering is measured, and which other variables are included in the model.

Exchange Theory

Labeling human capital a resource does little more than predict that people with more human capital are more likely to volunteer. It does not provide a mechanism to explain why they do so. The rational choice assumption is that actors will not contribute goods and services to others unless they profit from the exchange (Smith 1982:39). There is reason to believe this might help explain some of the variation in volunteering. First, actors clearly do weigh costs and benefits when considering volunteer work. For example, the stigma attached to some kinds of volunteering makes it harder to recruit people (Snyder et al 1999). Second, many volunteers clearly have a stake in their volunteer work: Parents are more likely to join the PTA when their children enter school. Third, many people volunteer because they anticipate needing help themselves or have already received help and want to give something back (Banks 1997, Broadbridge & Horne 1996, Freeman 1997:S164, Kincade et al 1996). Fourth, volunteers explicitly acknowledge the benefits they receive from their work, as when homosexuals deal with their own fears and apprehensions by volunteering to help AIDS victims [Omoto & Snyder 1993:167, Chambre 1995:123; see Field & Johnson (1993:1627) for hospice workers]. Fifth, volunteers are not indifferent to rewards—principally recognition for their efforts—and are more likely to drop out if they fail to receive them (Field & Johnson 1993:1629). Sixth, volunteering often provides solidary benefits, the pleasure of socializing with staff, other volunteers, and clients to whom emotional attachments may be formed (Wuthnow 1998:149)—although these benefits will be most appealing to those who volunteer in order to make friends (Leighley 1996). Finally, some volunteers are quite explicit about seeking compensation for deprivations they experience in their paid employment or work as homemakers (Gora & Nemerowicz 1985:40).

A number of criticisms can be made of the explanation of volunteering in terms of exchange. First, in an attempt to apply their utilitarian calculus, exchange theorists focus too much on easily quantified costs, such as time spent and income lost, and not enough on the other resources demanded by volunteer work, such as civic skills—the ability to speak or write well, or organize and participate in meetings (Brady et al 1995)—that might be more important but are more difficult to quantify. Second, while volunteer work might provide psychic benefits, they are not necessarily the reason why people volunteer. A volunteer might feel good about doing the right thing, but she does not do it because it makes her feel good; rather it makes her feel good because she thinks she ought to have done it. Third, when volunteers say how much they benefit from serving others, they could simply be engaging in reciprocity talk in which they articulate their need to complete the transaction by indicating how much they enjoy the work so that a balance is restored to the relationship (Wuthnow 1991:95). Fourth, exchange theory assumes that people must act in a self-interested manner in order for social equilibrium to be achieved, placing their own interests before those of others, but a competing theory argues that people's identity is important and that many people think of themselves as the kind of person who helps others regardless of whether their actions receive praise (Hart et al 1996, Schervish & Havens 1997:240). This theory, better than exchange theory, might explain why it is often easier to get people to sign up for risky, challenging, demanding work than for mundane, trivial, and routine tasks: "they want to be challenged by what they're doing, and they don't hesitate to do something that's going to be hard" (Chambre 1991:276). A final criticism of exchange theory introduces the topic of the next section. Exchange theory assumes individuals make their volunteer decisions in isolation when, in reality, people assess their environments and decide on courses of action in the context of formal and informal networks that are expressive of feelings of group solidarity (Rochon 1998:97). What makes a resource like education capital is determined by the larger social context in which it is embedded.

Social Resources

Social Networks   Extensive social networks, multiple organizational memberships, and prior volunteer experience all increase the chances of volunteering (Jackson et al 1995:75, Marwell & Oliver 1993, McPherson et al 1992:157, Smith 1994:255, Walsh 1988:125, Wilson & Musick 1997a). Few volunteers learn about opportunities through the mass media, and face-to-face invitations are much more effective than impersonal appeals (Midlarsky & Kahana 1994:219), especially if they come from a volunteer who knows something about the work (McAdam & Paulsen 1993:644). Social resources play a crucial role when volunteering means activism to bring about social change or when collective goods, such as safer streets, are the goal. In this case, anything that promotes social solidarity among members of a community, such as frequent interaction, increases the rate of volunteering (Rochon 1998:102).

Social resources help explain why people of higher socioeconomic status volunteer more: They join more organizations and are more likely to be active in them (Wilson & Musick 1997a). Social networks help explain why extroverted people are more likely to volunteer, because there is nothing in extroversion as such that would predict helping others. Extroverts get to know more people and join more clubs and associations, and this in turn increases the chances they will volunteer (Herzog & Morgan 1993:136). Social networks help explain the higher rate of volunteering among married people and parents. Social networks also help explain why religious people volunteer more: They attend church more frequently (National Association of Secretaries of State 1999:35; Wilson & Janoski 1995). Social resources also work *in combination with* human capital. The effect of social resources on volunteering is stronger among higher-status people (Wilson & Musick 1998).

The mechanisms that link social resources to volunteering are only now being investigated. Social ties generate trust, and trust makes it easier for us to step forward and donate our time (Brady et al 1999:162, Wood 1997:601). Social ties also encourage manifold relations that can be used as "side payments" to overcome the free rider problem; we do not want to let our friends down. Social ties to organizations also help define the volunteer role and thus make it easier to perform (Wuthnow 1991:201). Organizations help spread the word about the need for volunteers and reduce uncertainty about who else will volunteer (Walsh 1988). They also share the work, reduce the risk, and defray the expense. This is one reason why recruiting appeals are more effective in smaller organizations (Murnighan et al 1993, Schaubroeck & Ganster 1991). Finally, social ties increase the chances of being asked to volunteer (Brady et al 1999:158), which helps explain why people with lots of human capital are more likely to volunteer—they have more social ties to expose them to being asked (Freeman 1997:162).

Integrating the idea of social resources into a theory of volunteering undoubtedly enriches it. A number of problems remain to be dealt with. First, whether social ties are positive or negative for volunteering depends on the nature of the volunteer work. Conventional activities, such as Meals on Wheels, might be supported by service clubs or church organizations, but less conventional activities, such as picketing, might be shunned (Anderson 1996). Family ties might encourage volunteering at a hospice but discourage taking part in dangerous civil rights campaigns (McAdam & Paulsen 1993, Wiltfang & McAdam 1991:995) or helping AIDS patients (Snyder et al 1999). Second, social ties can be relatively insignificant, depending on the nature of the volunteer work. Neither AIDS volunteers nor animal rights activists were recruited through network ties but were more likely to be responding to something they had seen in the mass media (Jaspers 1997:175, Omoto & Snyder 1993:167). Third, it is frequently difficult to decide in advance what will constitute a social resource, and the determination can be made only after the volunteering occurs. Not only does this mean that the term social capital varies in meaning from one study to another, but it also makes the theory difficult to disprove—something that must have functioned as social capital can always be found. For example, church attendance is often cited as an example of social capital, but it has no effect on the volunteer rate of moderate Protestants (Wilson & Janoski 1995). Does this disprove the theory or simply mean that church attendance is not a social resource for this group? Similarly, McAdam & Paulsen (1993) found that the sheer number of social ties did not encourage participation in civil rights campaigns. Only those ties with meaning and significance in light of the civil rights work for which these people were being recruited produced this result.

A fourth problem with the social resources theory is that one of its key elements, trust, does not predict volunteering consistently. The 1995 *Independent Sector Survey of Giving and Volunteering* shows that volunteers are more trusting than nonvolunteers, but another major study finds no relationship between volunteering and either institutional or interpersonal trust once a person's age, education and income are taken into account (Kohut 1998:6). Indeed, for African-Americans, the less they trust government the more likely are they to volunteer (Kohut 1998:44). Institutional trust is unlikely to increase volunteering when people are using their volunteer time to protest the government or work in some way to ameliorate the conditions created by a government they do not trust (Deckker et al 1997:230). Similar questions can be raised about interpersonal trust. It is a lack of trust in others to do what is right that spurs people to take action (Oliver 1984).

Family Relations   Although studies of charitable donations usually treat the household as the unit of analysis, this is rarely done in the study of volunteering. This is an error because much volunteer work is organized by and around family relations.

Marital Status.   Married people are more likely to volunteer than single people, although single people without children volunteer the most hours (Sundeen 1990:497). If one spouse volunteers, the chances are the other does also (Freeman 1997:S148, Thompson 1993b). If only one spouse volunteers, it is most likely to be the wife (Wuthnow 1995:272). A wife's volunteering *complements* her husband's—as his volunteer hours increase, hers also increase; but a husband's volunteering is a *substitute* for his wife's—as her hours increase, his decrease (Segal 1993:100).

The effect of marital status on volunteering is contingent on a number of other factors. It depends on where the volunteer work is being performed; studies of political volunteering find no marital status effect at all (Damico et al 1998, Schlozman et al 1994). The effect of marital status probably also varies by life course stage. If other studies of the social activities of retired persons are to be believed, it is likely when a couple reaches retirement age that the marriage becomes a constraint rather than a springboard to volunteering. However, the data on this topic are scarce and results confusing. Szinovacz (1992:243) finds that elderly married women volunteer more than single, but Gallagher (1994b:123) fails to replicate this finding.

Parental Status.   Children in the household are both a constraint and an opportunity when it comes to volunteering, depending on the number of children, the children's ages, the parents' ages, marital status and employment status, and the nature of the volunteer work. The effect of children on volunteering can also be indirect: Parents, particularly women, can choose to work only part time in order to rear their young children and for this reason have more time for volunteering.

Parents are more likely to volunteer if they have children at home (Wuthnow 1998:76), but parents with young children volunteer fewer hours than parents with older children (Damico et al 1998:20, Menchik & Weisbrod 1987:177, Schlozman et al 1994). School-age children forge social links to schools, sports organizations, and other youth-oriented nonprofits. It is also likely that when children enter school, parents have more free time (Gora & Nemerowicz 1985:17).

A number of moderating effects are suggested by the research literature. Unemployed women are more affected by having school-age children, possibly because they are using their children as a medium of social integration (Gallagher 1994b:131). Having school-age children in the household has a positive effect on the volunteer rate of married but not single people (Segal 1993:181, Sundeen 1990). Finally, the impact of children varies by the nature of the volunteer task: When the volunteer work is helping community-oriented groups, children are a plus; when it is helping professional associations or unions, they are a minus (Janoski & Wilson 1995, Woodard 1987).

DEMOGRAPHIC CORRELATES OF VOLUNTEERING

The theories outlined in the previous section can be used to explain some of the age, gender, and race variations in volunteering, although in all three cases residual and unexplained differences remain that might be attributable to prejudice and discrimination.

Age   As people age, their stock of human capital changes, and thus the likelihood they will volunteer. Aging also reconfigures social roles, creating fresh opportunities and imposing new constraints. Finally, people of different ages and generations have different outlooks on life, which may change their attitude toward volunteering.

The rate of volunteering tends to fall during the transition from adolescence to young adulthood, when the structure of school-related activities gives way to the social freedoms of the single and childless life. Volunteering rises to its peak in middle age (Herzog et al 1989:S134, Menchik & Weisbrod 1987, National Association of Secretaries of State 1999:23, Schoenberg 1980). The exception to this pattern is high-risk volunteering, which attracts mainly younger people, and this, coupled with a high burnout rate, skews its age profile toward youth (Thompson 1993a, Wiltfang & McAdam 1991:1005). Rational choice theory predicts an increase in volunteering at retirement because more free time becomes available. Exchange theory assumes that retirees seek volunteer work to replace psychic and social benefits formerly derived from paid employment (Fischer et al 1991:262, Midlarsky & Kahana 1994:53). On the other hand, all things being equal, social resource theory would predict a decline in volunteering to the extent that withdrawing from the labor force weakens social integration. Numerous studies have shown that retirement does not, in fact, draw people into the volunteering labor force, although it does increase the number of hours worked among those already volunteering (Caro & Bass 1995:74, Caro & Bass 1997, Gallagher 1994b:30, Herzog et al 1989). Only when infirmity or extreme old age sets in does the volunteer rate begin to fall (Glass et al 1995:S70, Kincade et al 1996, Wilson & Musick 1997a). Among the retired, those most likely to be volunteering are actually working in a part-time job, enjoying both the social contacts of the job and the leisure provided by the part-time employment (Caro & Bass 1997, Okun 1994, Stephan 1991:232).

As people move from young adulthood to middle age, they move out of self- and career-oriented activism into more community-oriented work (Janoski & Wilson 1995). As they make the subsequent transition from middle to old age, they turn away from youth-related, political and ethnic groups and toward service organizations, recreational clubs and agencies to help the elderly (Gallagher 1994b:33, Romero 1987). To some extent, these shifts are quite compatible with exchange theory because people are taking up work from which they might one day benefit. However, changing values over the life course offer a better explanation of why volunteering in a religious context becomes more popular as people age and why religiosity becomes a more powerful influence on volunteering (Caro & Bass 1995:75).

Gender   In North America, females are slightly more likely to volunteer than males, but in Europe there is no overall gender difference because females volunteer less than males in some countries and more than males in others (Gaskin & Smith 1997:29, Hodgkinson & Weitzman 1996:D148, Hall et al 1998). It is not clear why these patterns vary from one country to another. Among volunteers, men and women contribute the same number of hours (Hodgkinson & Weitzman 1996:D148). The effect of gender varies by life cycle stage. Among younger people, females tend to volunteer more hours than males (Wuthnow 1995:152), but among older people the pattern is reversed (Gallagher 1994b:74).

Human capital, motivations and beliefs, and social resources all help explain gender differences in volunteering. Females score higher on measures of altruism and empathy, attach more value to helping others (Wilson & Musick 1997a), feel more guilty when they have not been compassionate (Flanagan et al 1998:44), and believe they are expected to care for the personal and emotional needs of others (Daniels 1988). Many women see their volunteer work as an extension of their roles as wives and mothers (Negrey 1993:93). The reason these expectations do not produce much higher volunteer rates for women is that men have more human capital and free time. Women would volunteer even more if they had the same amount of human capital as men (Gallagher 1994b:74, Kendall & Knapp 1991:255, Rosenthal et al 1998:485). Men are also more likely than women, net of education, to hold the kinds of jobs that provide the civic skills on which much volunteering depends (Schlozman et al 1994:977). Resources also work better for men than women; for example, education has a stronger effect on the volunteering of men than women, at least in the political sphere (Schlozman et al 1994:969). There is some evidence, however, that women compensate for their lack of human capital by having more social resources, which brings their volunteer rate closer to that of men (Wilson & Musick 1997a).

Gender makes a difference not only to how much people volunteer but also to what kind of work they do. Women volunteers gravitate, or are steered, toward "women's work," more of the caring, person-to-person tasks and fewer of the public, political activities, and they are less likely to be found in leadership positions (Cable 1992:38, Cnaan & Goldberg-Glen 1991, Menchik & Weisbrod 1987, Perkins 1990, Schlozman et al 1994:970, Thompson 1993a, 1995:55). This pattern does not vary by country (Gaskin & Smith 1997:35), race (Woodard 1987) or age group (Fischer et al 1991, Sundeen & Raskoff 1994, Wuthnow 1995:163).

Gender ideologies help explain why volunteering fits into the social lives of men and women differently. Men are more likely to regard their volunteer work as complementary to their real work; there is much more heterogeneity among women with regard to how they relate these two spheres (Little 1997). The same could be said for the relation between social resources and volunteering. Young females are more likely to volunteer in the company of friends, to see volunteering as a way to have a social life, and to seek the approval of their peers by volunteering (Wuthnow 1995:163). Young males are more likely than females to seek out volunteer opportunities on their own (Sundeen & Raskoff 1995). Similar gender differences are found among the elderly. Women link their involvement as volunteers to their existing friendships with other women, while men volunteer in order to make friends (Gallagher 1994b:84).

Race   Data from a 1995 US national sample show 51.9% of whites and 35.3% of blacks having volunteered in the past month (Hodgkinson & Weitzman 1996:D148). Human capital theory explains this racial difference by pointing to lower levels of education, income, and occupational status among blacks. Several studies support this theory, finding that racial differences in volunteering disappear after controls for education, income, occupational status, and neighborhood conditions (Clary et al 1996, Cutler & Danigelis 1993:155, Latting 1990:122, Romero 1987, Woodard 1987:286, Wuthnow 1998:114, 236). Other studies conclude that the lack of human capital is even more detrimental to blacks' chances of volunteering than it appears because some of the effect of human capital is suppressed by the compensating social resources (mainly ties to their church) that blacks possess (Sundeen 1992, Wilson & Musick 1997a). Despite these social resources blacks are less likely to be asked to volunteer (Ferree et al 1998:64, Hodgkinson 1995:44).

Like age and gender, race makes a difference to what kind of volunteer work people do. Black volunteers focus on needs more pressing in the black community—efforts to deal with crime, provide human services, and organize for local political initiatives (Ferree et al 1998:17, Portney & Berry 1997:639, Sundeen 1992).

Race differences in the explanation of volunteering have not received much attention. One clear pattern is that blacks are more influenced by their church than are whites [Ferree et al 1998:76, Musick et al 2000; but see Calhoun-Brown (1996), who finds no relation between black political volunteering and church attendance]. One study of Mobile, Alabama, residents found that trust had a stronger positive effect on black volunteering than white volunteering (Emig et al 1996), but a study of Philadelphia residents found trust to be unrelated to volunteering for either race (Kohut 1998).

As far as cultural understandings are concerned, there is little solid evidence of racial differences in values regarding altruism. Wilson & Musick (1997a) show that blacks are less likely than whites to believe that helping others is important to living a good life, but this value does not account for any racial differences in volunteering. It is possible that blacks and whites volunteer for different reasons, but the evidence is mixed. From a small sample, Latting (1990) shows that blacks are more likely than whites to indicate altruistic norms and motives for volunteering, but data from a more representative national survey show no difference (Clary et al 1996).

CONTEXTUAL EFFECTS

By context is meant ecological factors ranging from units as small as households, residential blocks, workplaces, and schools to those as large as cities, regions, and countries. The impact of context on individual volunteering is one of the least understood issues in the field (Smith 1994:246, Wuthnow 1998:112).

Since schooling is believed to encourage volunteering, it is natural to examine the school as context. Sundeen & Raskoff (1994:393) find that, net of individual differences, the chances a student will volunteer increase if he or she attends a school that requires or encourages community service. Serow & Dreyden (1990) find that students attending private colleges with a strong religious orientation participate in community service more frequently than students at private colleges with less emphasis on religion or at public universities. Other than these studies of schools, the impact of organizational context on volunteering has hardly been explored. Wilson & Musick (1997b) show that people who work in the public sector—government workers—are more likely to volunteer than people who work in the private sector or work for themselves. It is not clear whether this is a function of self-selection or a result of a "corporate culture" of service fostered by government agencies.

More attention has been directed at the impact of neighborhood conditions on volunteering: "membership in civic and other voluntary organizations is significantly lower in low-income, central city areas than elsewhere, and this difference persists when most characteristics of individual respondents are taken into account" (Wuthnow 1998:113). Residents regard these neighborhoods as unsafe, and neighboring relations are weaker—fewer people know other people on the block (Chavis & Wandersman 1990). Nevertheless, research has failed to find consistent neighborhood effects on volunteering. In a study of community volunteering in three US cities, Perkins et al (1996) found that volunteers were more likely to engage in informal neighboring but no consistent neighborhood effects were found. In some instances healthy neighborhoods seemed to encourage activism, but in others the deteriorating condition of the neighborhood seemed to spur activism. Portney & Berry (1997) examined the impact of the racial composition of the neighborhood on volunteering: Predominantly black neighborhoods boosted involvement in neighborhood associations and crime-watch organizations at every socioeconomic level; predominantly white neighborhoods boosted involvement in issue-based organizations and social and service organizations. Each race seemed to be able to set its own agenda.

At a higher level of abstraction, context means urban-rural differences. Cities are thought to be less congenial to volunteering (Smith 1994:245), but data from a national sample fail to confirm this (Hodgkinson & Weitzman 1996:D153). Rather than determining whether people will volunteer, place of residence might influence their reasons for volunteering. Those who live in small towns emphasize solidarity benefits and norms of reciprocity while suburbanites emphasize self-development (Wuthnow 1998:136).

COMMITMENT

Practitioners' interest in holding onto the volunteers they recruit is one reason why sociologists have studied commitment to the volunteer role. Commitment can be thought of in two ways: as attachment to the volunteer role over time, and as commitment to a particular organization or task.

Little is known about the frequency and duration of involvement in the volunteer labor force. Segal (1993:79) found that, while 20% of the women in the National Longitudinal Survey were volunteering at any given time, only 9% volunteered for all five waves of the 15-year study. Robison et al (1995), following married women over a 30-year span, found that the average woman had volunteered for 12 years during that period, the most common pattern being one of intermittent involvement. Another panel study found that the strongest attachment was shown by volunteers who were white and highly educated, had children in the household and interacted frequently with their friends and neighbors (Wilson & Musick 1999).

Volunteer burnout is a serious problem for administrators, particularly where the work is costly or risky. This is one of several reasons why volunteer organizations have quite high turnover rates. Lack of resources can help explain some of the drop-out rate. The same set of variables that predict the decision to volunteer also predict commitment (Barkan (1995:131, McPherson 1981). For example, highly educated people are not only more likely to volunteer but also less likely to drop out. Motives also play a role. Snyder & Omoto (1992:231) were surprised to find that AIDS volunteers who espoused personal development reasons for their work were most likely to have stayed, while those who espoused values as reasons for volunteering were more likely to drop out. Any disjunction between the volunteer's motives for volunteering and the actual work assigned is likely to weaken commitment (Holden 1997, Snyder & Omoto 1992:229). Social resources also help explain commitment. AIDS volunteers are more highly committed if friends and family support them in their work (Snyder et al 1999:1180).

The peculiar moral economy of volunteering means that the normal predictions about the impact of job satisfaction on commitment do not apply. Level of satisfaction with current volunteering seems to have little to do with commitment (Penner & Finkelstein 1998:534, Wilson & Musick 1999), and people who stop volunteering rarely say they did so because of low job satisfaction. They are more likely to say their efforts went unrecognized (Gora & Nemerowicz 1985:31), their skills and interests were not properly matched with the assignments they were given, or they were not given enough autonomy or freedom to help those they wished to serve (Harris 1996, Holden 1997:132, Perkins 1987, Wharton 1991).

CONSEQUENCES

Surveys show that most people believe that helping others is good for the donor as well as the recipient (Wuthnow 1991:87). This section reviews some recent research on the consequences of volunteering in four areas: citizenship, antisocial behavior, health and socioeconomic achievement.

Citizenship

Volunteers tend to be more politically active than non-volunteers. Suggested reasons for this relationship include the sharing of information (Knoke 1990), the opportunity to develop "civic skills" such as the ability to organize a meeting (Verba et al 1995) and the fostering of generalized trust (Stolle 1998). Volunteering seems to play some role in political socialization: Adolescent volunteers express stronger support for society's responsibility to care for the needy (Hamilton & Fenzel 1988) and attach more importance to serving the public interest as a personal life goal (Flanagan et al 1998). High school students who volunteer are more likely to be also engaged in a variety of conventional political behaviors such as working on a political campaign (Youniss et al 1999).

Antisocial Behavior

It is part of folk wisdom that volunteering helps "keep kids out of trouble." Sociological research lends quite strong support for this notion, whether it be cross-sectional analysis (Hart & Atkins 1998), a pre-test/post-test design (Allen et al 1994:627), or panel study (Eccles & Bonner 1999:15, Uggen & Janikula 1999). Despite the use of longitudinal data, skeptics might still be concerned that these results are distorted by selection bias caused by conforming children self-selecting into volunteer work. A number of other issues remain unresolved. It is not clear *why* being a volunteer keeps young people out of trouble. Social control theory would argue that volunteering exposes young people to informal social controls and supervision. Differential association theory would argue that volunteering inhibits contact with law violators.

Physical Health

Because volunteering is an additional social role, it can be expected to produce the beneficial health effects associated with more social ties. Additionally, "the altruistic features of volunteerism might reduce destructive levels of self-absorption" (Oman et al 1999:303). A number of recent studies, all using longitudinal data, show that volunteers subsequently enjoy better physical health in old age (Stephan 1991), score higher on measures of functional ability (Moen et al 1992:1628) and, most striking of all, are at lower risk of mortality (Musick et al 1999, Oman et al 1999, Rogers 1996, Sabin 1993). Most of the health benefits accrue to those who volunteer in moderation and who volunteer in connection with a church. The panel design of these studies deals with some of the problems of causal attribution in this area, although possible problems of selection bias remain. However, causal effects and selection effects can be mutually reinforcing as well as mutually exclusive. Volunteering improves health, but it is also most likely that healthier people are more likely to volunteer. Good health is preserved by volunteering; it keeps healthy volunteers healthy.

Mental Health

Volunteering is a way for people to become integrated into their community, and it is well-established that social integration yields positive mental health effects (House et al 1988:302). Quite apart from its integrative role, volunteering is a way of providing help to others, which can be a self-validating experience (Krause et al 1992:P300). It can also convince people they can make a difference in the world, and this feeling is known to buffer people from depression (Mirowsky & Ross 1989). The data confirm that volunteering boosts self-esteem and self-confidence and increases overall life satisfaction (Harlow & Cantor 1996:1241). Volunteering assumes an especially important role among the elderly because it can "inoculate, or protect, [them] . . . from hazards of retirement, physical decline and inactivity" (Fischer & Schaffer 1993:9). In a meta-analysis by Wheeler et al (1998) of thirty-seven studies of the effects of volunteering on elderly populations, a significant positive relation between volunteering and life satisfaction was found, even after adjustments for socioeconomic status and physical health. Because most of the studies reviewed were cross-sectional, they cannot answer the question whether volunteering increases well-being over time. There is also some suggestion that the mental health consequences of volunteering are moderated by race, gender, and the nature of the volunteer work (McIntosh & Danigelis 1995).

Socioeconomic Achievement

Nearly a quarter of the volunteers in the 1995 *Independent Sector Survey of Giving and Volunteering* mentioned they were volunteering to "make new contacts that might help my business or career" (Hodgkinson & Weitzman 1996:4–112). However, reliable social science evidence to support the idea that volunteering actually helps people find jobs, or improves the quality of those jobs, is scarce.

One pathway from volunteering to occupational achievement is through education. Adolescents who volunteer have higher educational aspirations, higher grade point averages, higher academic self-esteem, and a stronger intrinsic motivation toward school work (Johnson et al 1998). Undergraduates who volunteer are more likely to earn postgraduate degrees (Astin et al 1998). College students who choose to participate in service learning projects are more likely to see an improvement in their grade point average; and, although all college students tend to lower their expectations about pursuing an advanced degree over the course of their college career, the decline is less steep for volunteers (Sax & Astin 1997).

Statham & Rhoton's (1986) unpublished paper provides one of the few analyses of the effects of volunteering on occupational achievement. Using data from the Mature Women's Module of the *National Longitudinal Survey,* they find that, among women who were working for pay in 1981, those who had reported volunteering in 1974 had higher occupational prestige, net of occupational prestige in 1974. It is not clear why volunteering should have these positive effects. Since it is known that volunteers have more social contacts, e.g. with neighbors and local government officials (Wuthnow 1998:235), they could be using these social ties to get better jobs.

CONCLUSION

The last quarter century has seen tremendous advances in the study of volunteering, prompted by more determined efforts to assess all forms of productive inputs to the public household, whether paid or not, by growing concern about how to provide social services in a time of government retrenchment, and by the debate over the future of the public sphere in an age of increasing materialism and individualism. In using sociological methods to address these concerns, social scientists, prodded and encouraged by an active and vocal community of practitioners in the nonprofit sector who are anxious to apply the insights of social science to advance their work, are able to draw on a deep bedrock of disciplinary interest in the explanation of altruistic behavior and collective action.

Much more is now known about the distribution and social correlates of volunteering, the variations in amounts and types of volunteering between major demographic groups, the pathways that lead to volunteer work, and the reasons why people detach themselves from it. We also now know much more about the mechanisms that link factors such as education, occupation, income, and group memberships to volunteer work. In the process, we have learned more about the difficulties of measuring volunteer work, the complexities of gathering accurate data in this area, and the importance of supplementing survey data with richer ethnographic understandings of the volunteer.

Despite these and other advances much work remains. One problem is that the generic term "volunteering" embraces a vast array of quite disparate activities. It is probably not fruitful to try to explain all activities with the same theory nor to treat all activities as if they were the same with respect to consequences. The taxonomies of volunteering that are used to disaggregate volunteer work are folk categories (e.g. school-related, helping the elderly), and there is little reason to believe these categorizations are sociologically useful. Second, panel data are only now beginning to make possible longitudinal analysis of volunteering. Until more such data are available, many of the associations between volunteering and background factors remain just that, correlations, and we are in no position to make causal statements. Nor is it possible to form a picture of the "career" of the volunteer as he or she moves in and out of the volunteer labor force. Third, much of the survey data analysis of volunteering ignores the household as the unit of analysis, thus underplaying the role of family interactions—and the interplay of these interactions with extra-family constraints such as work. Fourth, while much has been achieved in gaining a clearer understanding of the role of social resources in facilitating volunteer work, the concept is poorly developed and usually badly measured. It tends to be ego-centered, providing some information on the individual's social ties, but no information on the ties that might exist among his or her social contacts, or whether or not those contacts are also volunteers. Nor has the problem been solved of deciding in advance what is to count as a social resource. Fifth, the study of the consequences of volunteering has only just begun. Recently, a body of research has begun to accumulate findings on the contribution of volunteering to citizenship in a number of countries. The problem with this research is its rather narrow definition of citizenship, which is largely supportive of the status quo. It fails to consider the role of community organizations, for example in fostering new ideas of democratic politics and citizenship. The research on the consequences of volunteering for subjective well-being is full of promise, but it has largely been confined to the elderly population, among whom, it might be surmised, this kind of activity has most salience. More studies are needed for younger age groups, and more attention needs to be paid to how beneficial effects are contingent on such factors as freedom of choice of task and working hours.

Visit the Annual Reviews home page at www.AnnualReviews.org

LITERATURE CITED

Allen JP, Kuperminc G, Philliber S, Herre K. 1994. Programmatic prevention of adolescent behavior problems: the role of autonomy, relatedness, and volunteer service in Teen Outreach programs. *Am. J. Community Psychol.* 22:617–38

Amato P, Booth A. 1997. *A Generation at Risk: Growing up in an Era of Family Upheaval.* Cambridge, MA: Harvard Univ. Press

Anderson C. 1996. Political action and social integration. *Am. Polit. Q.* 24:105–25

Ascoli U, Cnaan R. 1997. Volunteers for human service provisions: lessons from Italy and the USA. *Soc. Ind. Res.* 40:299–327

Astin A. 1993. *What Matters in College?* San Francisco: Jossey-Bass

Astin A, Sax L, Avalos J. 1998. Long-term effects of volunteerism during the undergraduate years. *Rev. Higher Educ.* 22:187–202

Banks E. 1997. The social capital of self-help mutual aid groups. *Soc. Policy* 28:30–39

Barkan S, Cohn S, Whitaker W. 1995. Beyond recruitment: predictors of differential participation in a national anti-hunger organization. *Sociol. Forum* 10:113–34

Brady H, Verba S, Schlozman KL. 1995.

Beyond SES: a resource model of political participation. *Am. Polit. Sci. Rev.* 89:269–95

Brady H, Schlozman KL, Verba S. 1999. Prospecting for participants: rational expectations and the recruitment of political activists. *Am. Polit. Sci. Rev.* 93:153–69

Broadbridge A, Horne S. 1996. Volunteers in charity retailing: recruitment and training. *Nonprofit Manage. Leadership* 6:255–70

Brudney J. 1990. *Fostering Volunteer Programs in the Public Sector.* San Francisco: Jossey-Bass

Cable S. 1992. Women's social movement involvement: the role of structural availability in recruitment and participation processes. *Sociol. Q.* 33:35–51

Calhoun-Brown A. 1996. African-American churches and political mobilization. *J. Polit.* 58:935–54

Caputo R. 1997. Women as volunteers. *Nonprofit Volun. Sector Q.* 26:156–74

Caro F, Bass S. 1995. Increasing volunteering among older people. In *Older and Active: How Americans Over 55 Are Contributing to Society,* ed. S Bass, pp. 71–96. New Haven, CT: Yale Univ. Press

Caro F, Bass S. 1997. Receptivity to volunteering in the immediate post-retirement period. *J. Appl. Gerontol.* 16:427–42

Chambre S. 1987. *Good Deeds in Old Age.* Lexington, MA: DC Heath

Chambre S. 1991. The volunteer response to the AIDS epidemic in New York City: implications for research on voluntarism. *Nonprofit Volun. Sector Q.* 20:267–87

Chambre S. 1993. Volunteerism by elders: past trends and future prospects. *Gerontologist* 33:221–28

Chambre S. 1995. Being needful: family, love, and prayer among AIDS volunteers. *Res. Sociol. Health Care* 12:113–39

Chavis D, Wandersman A. 1990. Sense of community in the urban environment. *Am. J. Commun. Psychol.* 8:55–82

Clary E, Snyder M, Stukas A. 1996. Volunteers' motivations: findings from a national survey. *Nonprofit Volun. Sector Q.* 25:485–505

Cnaan R, Amrofell L. 1994. Mapping volunteer activity. *Nonprofit Volun. Sector Q.* 23:335–54

Cnaan R, Goldberg-Glen R. 1991. Measuring motivation to volunteer in human services. *J. Appl. Behav. Sci.* 27:269–285

Cnaan R, Kasternakis A, Wineburg R. 1993. Religious people, religious congregations, and volunteerism in human services: is there a link? *Nonprofit Volun. Sector Q.* 22:33–52

Cnaan R, Handy F, Wadsworth M. 1996. Defining who is a volunteer: conceptual and empirical considerations. *Nonprofit Volun. Sector Q.* 25:364–83

Conway M, Damico S, Damico J. 1996. Democratic socialization in the schools. In *Democracy, Socialization and Conflicting Loyalties in East and West,* ed. R Farnen, H Dekker, R Meyenberg, D German, pp. 421–42. New York: St Martin's

Cutler S, Danigelis N. 1993. Organizational contexts of activity. In *Activity and Aging,* ed. J Kelly, pp. 146–63. Newbury Park, CA: Sage

Damico A, Damico S, Conway M. 1998. The democratic education of women: high school and beyond. *Women Polit.* 19:1–31

Daniels A. 1988. *Invisible Careers: Women Civic Leaders from the Volunteer World.* Chicago: Univ. Chicago Press

Deckker P, Koopmans R, van den Broek A. 1997. Voluntary associations, social movements and individual political behavior in Western Europe. In *Private Groups and Public Life,* ed. J van Deth, pp. 220–39. London: Routledge

Eliasoph N. 1998. *Avoiding Politics.* Cambridge: Cambridge Univ. Press

Ferree G, Barry J, Manno B. 1998. *The National Survey of Philanthropy and Civic Renewal.* Washington, DC: Natl. Comm. Philanthropy and Civic Renewal

Field D, Johnson I. 1993. Satisfaction and change: a survey of volunteers in hospice organization. *Soc. Sci. Med.* 36:1625–34

Fischer K, Rapkin B, Rappaport J. 1991. Gender and work history in the placement and perception of elder community volunteers. *Psychol. Women Q.* 15:261–279

Fischer L, Schaffer K. 1993. *Older Volunteers.* Newbury Park, CA: Sage

Flanagan C, Bowes J, Jonsson B, Csapo B, Sheblanova E. 1998. Ties that bind: correlates of adolescents' civic commitments in seven countries. *J. Soc. Issues* 54:457–75

Flanagan C, Jonsson B, Botcheva B, Csapo B, Bowes J, Macek P, Averina I, Sheblanova E. 1999. Adolescents and the Social Contract: developmental roots of citizenship in seven countries. In *Roots of Civic Identity: International Perspectives on Community Service and Activism in Youth,* eds. M. Yates J. Youniss, pp. 135–55. Cambridge: Cambridge Univ. Press

Fogelman E. 1997. What motivates the rescuers? In *Resisters, Rescuers and Refugees,* ed. J. Michalczyk, pp. 147–54. Kansas City: Sheed & Ward

Franz C, McClelland D. 1994. Lives of women and men active in the social protests of the 1960s: a longitudinal study. *J. Pers. Soc. Psychol.* 66:196–205

Freeman R. 1997. Working for nothing: the supply of volunteer labor. *J. Labor Econ.* 15:140–67

Gallagher S. 1994a. Doing their share: comparing patterns of help given by older and younger adults. *J. Marriage Fam.* 56:567–78

Gallagher S. 1994b. *Older People Giving Care: Helping People and Community.* Westport, CT: Auburn House

Gaskin K, Smith J. 1997. *A New Civic Europe? A Study of the Extent and Role of Volunteering.* London: Natl. Cent. for Volun.

Gerstel N, Gallagher S. 1994 Caring for kith and kin: gender, employment, and the privatization of care. *Soc. Probl.* 41:519–39

Glass T, Seeman T, Herzog A, Kahn R, Berkman L. 1995. Change in productive activities in late adulthood. *J. Gerontol* 50B:S565–S76

Gora J, Nemerowicz G. 1985. *Emergency Squad Volunteers: Professionalism in Unpaid Work.* New York: Praeger

Greeley A. 1999. Who are the traditional Catholics? *Natl. Catholic Rep.* 35:20–21

Hall M, Knighton T, Reed P, Bussiere P, Macrae D, Bowen P. 1998. *Caring Canadians, Involved Canadians.* Ottawa: Statist. Canada

Hamilton S, Fenzel M. 1988. The Impact of volunteer experience on adolescent social development: evidence of program effects. *J. Adolescent Res.* 3:65–80

Harlow R, Cantor N. 1996. Still participating after all these years. *J. Pers. Soc. Psychol.* 71:1235–49

Harris M. 1996. An inner group of willing people: volunteers in a religious context. *Soc. Policy Admin.* 30:54–68

Hart D, Atkins R, Ford D. 1996. Urban America as a context for the development of moral identity in adolescence. *J. Soc. Issues* 54:513–530

Herzog A, Kahn R, Morgan J. 1989. Age differences in productive activity. *J. Gerontol.* 4:S129–S138.

Herzog A, Morgan J. 1993. Formal volunteer work among older Americans. In *Achieving a Productive Aging Society,* ed. S. Bass, F. Caro, Y. Chen, pp. 119–142. Westport CT: Auburn House

Hodgkinson V. 1995. Key factors influencing caring, involvement, and community. In *Care and Community in Modern Society,* eds. P. Schervish, V. Hodgkinson, M. Gates, pp. 21–50. San Francisco: Jossey-Bass

Hodgkinson V, Weitzman M. 1996. *Giving and Volunteering in the United States.* Washington, D.C: Independent Sector

Hoge D. Zech C, McNamara P, Donahue M. 1998. The value of volunteers as resources for congregations. *J. Sci. Stud. Relig.* 37:470–81

Holden D. 1997. "On equal ground": sustaining virtue among volunteers in a homeless shelter. *J. Contemp. Ethnogr.* 26:117–45 [n]

House J. 1981. *Work Stress and Social Support.* Reading, Mass.: Addison-Wesley

House J, Landis K, Umberson D. 1988 Social Relationships and Health. *Science* 241:540–45

Jackson E. Bachmeier M, Wood J, Craft E. 1995. Volunteering and charitable giving: do religious and associational ties promote helping behavior? *Nonprofit Volun. Sector Q.* 24:59–78

Janoski T, Wilson J. 1995. Pathways to voluntarism. *Soc. Forces.* 74:271–92

Janoski T. Musick M, Wilson J. 1998. Being volunteered?: The impact of social participation and pro-social attitudes on volunteering. *Sociol. Forum* 13:495–520

Jaspers J. 1997 *The Art of Moral Protest.* Chicago: Univ. Chicago Press

Jirovec R, Hyduk C. 1999. Type of volunteer experience and health among older volunteers. *J. Gerontol. Soc. Work* 30:29–42

Johnson M, Beebe T, Mortimer J, Snyder M. 1998. Volunteerism in adolescence: a process perspective. *Journal of Research on Adolescence.* 8:301–332

Kincade J, Rabiner D, Shulamit B, Woomert A. 1996. Older adults as a community resource: results from the National Survey of Self-Care and Aging. *Gerontologist* 36:474–82

Knoke D. 1990. Networks of political action: toward theory construction. *Soc. Forces* 68:1041–65

Kohut A. 1998. *Trust and Citizen Engagement in Metropolitan Philadelphia.* Washington, DC: Pew Res. Center

Krause N, Herzog A, Baker E. 1992. Providing support for others and well-being in later life. *J. Gerontol.* 47:P300–P311

Ladd E. 1999. *The Ladd Report.* New York: Free Press

Latting J. 1990. Motivational differences between Black and White volunteers. *Nonprofit Volunt. Sector Q.* 19:121–36

Leighley J. 1996. Group membership and the mobilization of political participation. *J. Polit.* 58:447–64

Little J. 1997. Constructions of rural women's voluntary work. *Gender, Place Culture.* 4:197–209

Lynn P, Smith J. 1991. *National Survey of Voluntary Activity in the UK.* Berkhampsted, UK: Volunteer Cent. UK.

Markham W, Bonjean C. 1995. Community orientations of higher-status women volunteers. *Soc. Forces* 73:1553–72

Markham W, Bonjean C. 1996. Employment status and the attitudes and behavior of higher status women volunteers, 1975 and 1992. *Sex Roles* 34:695–717

Marwell G, Oliver P. 1993. *The Critical Mass in Collective Action.* Cambridge: Cambridge Univ. Press

McAdam D, Paulsen R. 1993. Specifying the relationship between social ties and activism. *Am. J. Sociol.* 99:640–67

McIntosh B, Danigelis N. 1995. Race, gender and the relevance of productive activities for elders' affect. *J. Gerontol.* 50:229–40

McPherson J. 1981. A dynamic model of voluntary affiliation. *Soc. Forces* 59:705–23

McPherson J, Poplielarz P, Drobnic S. 1992. Social networks and organizational dynamics. *Am. Sociol. Rev.* 57:153–70

McPherson J, Rotolo T. 1996. Diversity and change in voluntary groups. *Am. Sociol. Rev.* 61:179–202

Menchik P, Weisbrod B. 1987. Volunteer labor supply. *J. Publ. Econ.* 32:159–83

Midlarsky E, Kahana E. 1994. *Altruism in Later Life.* Thousand Oaks, CA: Sage

Mirowsky J, Ross C. 1989. *Social Causes of Psychological Distress.* New York: Aldine de Gruyter

Moen P, Dempster-McClain D, Williams R. 1992. Successful aging: a life course perspective on women's multiple roles and health. *Am. J. Sociol.* 97:1612–38

Murnighan J, Kim J, Metzger A. 1993. The volunteer dilemma. *Admin. Sci. Q.* 38:515–39

Musick M, Herzog A, House J. 1999. Volunteering and mortality among older adults: findings from a national sample. *J. Gerontol.* 54B:S173–S180

Musick, M, Wilson, J Bynum W. 2000. Race and formal volunteering: the differential effects of class and religion. *Soc. Forces.* In press

National Association of Secretaries of State. 1999. *New Millenium Project—Phase 1: a*

Nationwide Study of 15–24 Year Old Youth. Washington, DC: Natl. Assoc. Secretaries of State

Negrey C. 1993. *Gender, Time and Reduced Work.* Albany: State Univ. NY Press

Okun M. 1994. Predictors of volunteer status in a retirement community. *Int. J. Aging Hum. Devel.* 36:57–74

Okun M, Eisenberg N. 1992. A comparison of office and adult day-care center older volunteers. *Int. J. Aging Hum. Devel.* 35:219–33

Okun M, Barr A, Herzog A. 1998. Motivation to volunteer by older adults: a test of competing measurement models. *Psychol. Aging* 13:608–17

Oliver P. 1984. If you don't do it, nobody else will: active and token contributors to local collective action. *Am. Sociol. Rev.* 49:601–10

Oman D, Thoreson C, McMahon K. 1999. Volunteerism and mortality among community-dwelling elderly. *J. Health Psychol.* 4:301–16

Omoto A, Snyder M. 1993. Volunteers and their motivations: theoretical issues and practical concerns. *Nonprofit Mgmt. Leadership* 4:157–76

Omoto A, Snyder M. 1995. Sustained helping without obligation: motivation, longevity of service and perceived attitude change among AIDS volunteers. *J. Personal Soc. Psychol.* 68:671–86

Pancer S, Pratt M. 1999. Social and family determinants of community service involvement in Canadian youth. In *Roots of Civic Identity: International Perspectives on Community Service and Activism in Youth,* ed. M. Yates, J. Youniss, pp. 32–55. Cambridge: Cambridge Univ. Press

Payne B, Bull C. 1985. The older volunteer: the case for interdependence. In *Social Bonds in Later Life: Aging and Interdependence*, ed. W. Peterson, J. Quadagno, pp. 251–72. Newbury Park, CA: Sage

Penner L, Finkelstein M. 1998. Dispositional and structural determinants of volunteerism. *J. Pers. Soc. Psychol.* 74:525–537

Perkins D, Brown B, Taylor R. 1996. The ecology of empowerment: predicting participation in community. *J. Soc. Issues* 52:85–111

Perkins K. 1987. Volunteer fire departments: community integration, autonomy and survival. *Hum. Org.* 46:342–48

Perkins K. 1990. Volunteer fire and rescue departments: structure, process and survival. *Nonprofit Volunt. Sector Q.* 19:359–70

Portney K, Berry J. 1997. Mobilizing minority communities: social capital and participation in urban neighborhoods. *Am. Behav. Sci.* 40:632–44

Raskoff S, Sundeen R. 1995. *Trends in volunteering: an analysis of a decade.* Paper presented at the annu. meet. Assoc. Res. on Nonprofit Organizations and Voluntary Assoc., Cleveland, Ohio

Robison J, Moen P, Dempster-McClain D. 1995. Women's caregiving: changing profiles and pathways. *J. Gerontol.* B50:S362–73

Rochon T. 1998. *Culture Moves: Ideas, Activism and Changing Values.* Princeton, NJ: Princeton Univ. Press

Rogers R. 1996. The effects of family composition, health, and social support linkages on mortality. *J. Health Soc. Behav.* 37:326–38

Romero C. 1987. Retirement and older Americans' participation in volunteer activities. In *The Problem Isn't Age: Work and Older Americans,* ed. S Sandell, pp. 218–27. New York: Praeger

Rosenthal S, Feiring C, Lewis M. 1998. Political volunteering from late adolescence to young adulthood: patterns and predictions. *J. Soc. Issues* 54:471–493

Sabin EP. 1993 Social relationships and mortality among the elderly. *J. Appl. Gerontol.* 12:44–60

Sax LJ, Astin A. 1997 The benefits of service: evidence from undergraduates. *Educ. Record* 78:25–32

Schaubroeck J, Ganster D. 1991. Beyond the call of duty. *Hum. Relat.* 44:13:569–82

Schervish P, Havens J. 1997. Social

participation and charitable giving: a multivariate analysis. *Voluntas* 8:235–60

Schlozman K, Burns N, Verba S. 1994. Gender and the pathways to participation: the role of resources. *J. Polit.* 56:963–90

Schoenberg S. 1980. Some trends in the community participation of women in their neighborhoods. *Signs* 5:S261–68

Segal L. 1993. *Four essays on the supply of volunteer labor and econometrics.* Unpublished doc. diss. Northwestern Univ., Evanston, Ill.

Serow R, Dreyden J. 1990. Community service among college and university students: individual and institutional relationships. *Adolescence* 25:553–66

Smith C. 1998. *American Evangelicalism: Embattled and Thriving.* Chicago: Univ. Chicago Press

Smith D. 1982. Altruism, volunteers, and volunteerism. In *Volunteerism in the Eighties,* ed. J Harman, pp. 23–44. Washington, DC: Univ. Press Am.

Smith D. 1994. Determinants of voluntary association participation and volunteering. *Nonprofit Volunt. Sect. Q.* 23:243–63

Smith D. 1997. The rest of the nonprofit sector. *Nonprofit Volunt. Sect. Q.* 26:114–31

Snyder M, Omoto A. 1992. Who helps and why? The psychology of AIDS volunteerism. In *Helping and Being Helped,* ed. S Spacapan, S Oskamp, pp. 213–39. Newbury Park, CA: Sage

Snyder M, Omoto A, Crain L. 1999. Punished for their good deeds: stigmatization of AIDS volunteers. *Am. Behav. Sci.* 42:1175–

Sokolowski S. 1996. Show me the way to the next worthy deed. *Voluntas* 7:259–76

Statham A, Rhoton P. 1986. *Mature and Young Women's Volunteer Work, 1974–1981.* Columbus: Cent. Hum. Resour. Res., The Ohio State Univ.

Stephan P. 1991. Relationships among market work, work aspirations and volunteering: the case of retired women. *Nonprofit Volunt. Sect. Q.* 20:225–36

Stolle D. 1998. Bowling together, bowling alone: the development of generalized trust in voluntary associations. *Polit. Psychol.* 19:497–525

Straub E. 1997. The psychology of rescue: perpetrators, bystanders and heroic helpers. In *Resisters Rescuers and Refugees,* ed. J Michalczyk pp. 137–46. Kansas City: Sheed & Ward

Stubbings P, Humble S. 1984. Voluntary work, unemployment and the labour market in Britain. In *Voluntary Work and Unemployment Study in the Countries of the European Communities,* pp. 1–63. London: Policy Stud. Inst.

Sundeen R. 1990. Family life course status and volunteer behavior: implications for the single parent. *Sociol. Perspect.* 33:483–500

Sundeen R. 1992. Differences in personal goals and attitudes among volunteers. *Nonprofit Volun. Sect. Q.* 21:271–91

Sundeen R, Raskoff S. 1994. Volunteering among teenagers in the United States. *Nonprofit Volun. Sect. Q.* 23:383–403

Sundeen R, Raskoff S. 1995. Teenage volunteers and their values. *Nonprofit Volun. Sect. Q.* 24:337–57

Szinovacz M. 1992. Social activities and retirement adaptation. In *Families and Retirement,* ed. M Szinovacz, D Ekerdt, B Vinick, pp. 236–53. Newbury Park, CA: Sage

Thompson A. 1993a. Volunteers and their communities: a comparative analysis of firefighters. *Nonprofit Volun. Sect. Q.* 22:155–66

Thompson A. 1993b. Rural emergency volunteers and their communities: a demographic comparison. *J. Community Health* 18:379–93

Thompson A. 1995. The sexual division of leadership in volunteer emergency medical service squads. *Nonprofit Manage. Leadersh.* 6:55–66

Uggen C, Janikula J. 1999. Volunteerism and arrest in the transition to adulthood. *Soc. Forces* 78:331–62

Verba S, Schlozman K, Brady H. 1995. *Voice and Equality: Civic Voluntarism in American Politics.* Cambridge: Harvard Univ. Press

Walsh E. 1988. *Democracy in the Shadows:*

Citizen Mobilization in the Wake of the Accident at Three Mile Island. New York: Greenwood

Wharton C. 1991. "Why can't we be friends?" Expectations versus experience in the volunteer role. *J. Contemp. Ethnogr.* 20:79–107

Wheeler J, Gorey K, Greenblatt B. 1998. The beneficial effects of volunteering for older adults and the people they serve. *Int. J. Aging Hum. Dev.* 47:69–80

Wilson J, Janoski T. 1995. The contribution of religion to volunteer work. *Sociol. Relig.* 56:137–52

Wilson J, Musick M. 1997a. Who cares? Toward an integrated theory of volunteer work. *Am. Sociol. Rev.* 62:694–713

Wilson J, Musick M. 1997b. Work and volunteering: the long arm of the job. *Soc. Forces* 76:251–72

Wilson J, Musick M. 1998. The contribution of social resources to volunteering. *Soc. Sci. Q.* 79:799–814

Wilson J, Musick M. 1999. Attachment to volunteering. *Sociol. Forum* 14:243–72

Wiltfang G, McAdam D. 1991. The costs and risks of social activism: a study of sanctuary movement activists. *Soc. Forces* 69:987–1011

Wolff N, Weisbrod B, Bird E. 1993. The supply of volunteer labor: the case of hospitals. *Nonprofit Manage. Leadersh.* 4:23–45

Wood R. 1997. Social capital and political culture: God meets politics in the inner city. *Am. Behav. Sci.* 40:595–606

Woodard M. 1987. Voluntary association membership among Black Americans. *Sociol. Q.* 28:285–301

Wuthnow R. 1991. *Acts of Compassion.* Princeton: Princeton Univ. Press

Wuthnow R. 1995. *Learning to Care.* New York: Oxford Univ. Press

Wuthnow R. 1998. *Loose Connections: Joining Together in America's Fragmented Communities.* Cambridge: Harvard Univ. Press

Annu. Rev. Sociol. 2000. 26:241–69

HOW WELFARE REFORM IS AFFECTING WOMEN'S WORK

Mary Corcoran,[1] Sandra K. Danziger,[2] Ariel Kalil,[3] and Kristin S. Seefeldt[2]

[1]School of Public Policy, University of Michigan, Ann Arbor, Michigan 48109; e-mail: marycor@umich.edu
[2]School of Social Work, University of Michigan, Ann Arbor, Michigan 48104; e-mail: sandrakd@umich.edu, kseef@umich.edu
[3]Harris School of Public Policy, University of Chicago, Chicago, Illinois 60637; e-mail: a-kalil@uchicago.edu

Key Words   poverty, TANF, gender, employment, self-sufficiency

■ **Abstract**   The new welfare system mandates participation in work activity. We review the evolution of the 1996 legislation and how states implement welfare reform. We examine evidence on recipients' employment, well-being, and future earnings potential to assess the role of welfare in women's work. Policies rewarding work and penalizing nonwork, such as sanctions, time limits, diversion, and earnings "disregards," vary across states. While caseloads fell and employment rose, most women who left welfare work in low-wage jobs without benefits. Large minorities report material hardships and face barriers to work including depression, low skills, or no transportation. And disposable income decreased among the poorest female-headed families. Among the important challenges for future research is to differentiate between the effects of welfare reform, the economy, and other policies on women's work, and to assess how variations in state welfare programs affect caseloads and employment outcomes of recipients.

INTRODUCTION

In August 1996, after years of partisan debate, President Clinton signed the Personal Responsibility and Work Opportunity Reconciliation Act (PRWORA) into law. PRWORA (P.L. 104–193) dramatically overhauled the system of cash assistance, abolishing Aid to Families with Dependent Children (AFDC), the program through which eligible families were entitled to cash assistance, and replacing it with Temporary Assistance to Needy Families (TANF), a time-limited, block grant program. TANF is a work-based program that requires recipients to participate in work or work-based activities in order to receive cash assistance. AFDC, legislated in the 1930s as an income maintenance program for widows and children, and evolved over 60 years into a program that primarily served families headed by divorced, separated, or never-married mothers. In part, PRWORA responded to concerns that AFDC encouraged joblessness (Mead 1992) and out-of-wedlock childbearing (Murray 1993); however, the driving force behind the legislation was the notion that cash assistance should be a temporary stop on the road toward employment (Bane & Ellwood 1994).

In this paper, we review how welfare reform has affected the work options of single mothers. Section one summarizes how PRWORA has changed the welfare system and how states now structure work incentives, work requirements, and employment services for welfare recipients. PRWORA, in addition to other federal policy changes (e.g. the Earned Income Tax Credit) and the booming economy of the 1990s, has greatly changed the employment context for single mothers. Two key assumptions underlying PRWORA are (1) that almost all recipients can get and keep jobs, and (2) that regular work will eventually lead to a living wage and self-sufficiency. The second and third sections of this paper review research concerning these assumptions. We conclude with a discussion of policy and research implications of the evidence to date.

WELFARE POLICY AND WORK EXPECTATIONS FOR SINGLE MOTHERS

Program History

AFDC, originally entitled Aid to Dependent Children, was modeled on mothers' state pension programs. The 1935 legislation was designed to provide cash relief to destitute widowed mothers so that they could raise their children in their own homes (Garfinkel & McLanahan 1986, Katz 1986, Ellwood 1988). At the time, it was expected the program would phase out as Social Security matured. However, legislation, court rulings, and socioeconomic and demographic changes led to a rapid expansion of AFDC in the 1960s and 1970s. The monthly number of AFDC recipients rose from under 4 million in the early 1960s to 8.4 million in 1970 (US Department of Health and Human Services, Administration for Children and Families 1999). The caseload grew rapidly in the early 1970s, rising to 11.39 million by 1976.

While both presidents Nixon and Carter attempted to revamp the welfare program, neither Nixon's Family Assistance Plan nor Carter's Program for Better Jobs and Income came to pass. But, in the late 1960s the Work Incentive (WIN) program provided voluntary work and training options for welfare recipients, and marked the beginning of the trend to tie benefit receipt to work. The number of recipients remained constant for most of the 1970s and was still at about 11 million in 1981, when President Reagan sought to reduce the size and cost of the program. The Omnibus Budget Reconciliation Act (OBRA) of 1981 lowered the income levels for eligibility and the amount a recipient could earn before her benefits were terminated. These changes reduced the caseload to 10.4 million in 1982 (US Department of Health and Human Services, Administration for Children and Families 1999).

The Family Support Act (FSA) of 1988, designed by Senator Moynihan, passed with bipartisan support. Its centerpiece was the Job Opportunities and Basic Skills (JOBS) program, which required certain categories of recipients to move to self-sufficiency through participation in education, training, and job search activities.[1] This emphasis evolved from randomized research demonstrations that showed increased future earnings and decreased reliance on public benefits for mandatory participants (Gueron & Pauly 1991). However, the change also reflected ideological concerns that without mandate, clients would view participation as "unrewarding" (Mead 1986) and employment and training programs would engage in "creaming" practices, whereby only the most employable of recipients would be served (Riccio & Hasenfeld 1996).

Participation in JOBS remained low during the 1990s, with states achieving at best only 15% participation rates (Bane & Ellwood 1994). Some states were dissatisfied with the many participation exemptions allowed under JOBS and requested waivers from federal rules to require greater participation. Under JOBS, caretakers of children under age 6 were exempted unless child care was guaranteed, while caretakers of children less than 3 years of age (or under age 1, at state option) were always exempt. Pregnancy was another exemption category, as was living in a remote area. From 1992 on, waivers allowing states to modify various aspects of JOBS and the AFDC program took on increasing importance. Some states began to experiment with measures to reduce out-of-wedlock childbearing and interstate migration as well as to increase work (Wiseman 1993). Over time, states showed more interest in time-limiting benefits as a way to promote work (Greenberg & Savner 1995) and stem rising welfare caseloads, which reached a historic peak of 14.2 million people in 1994 (US Department of Health and Human Services, Administration for Children and Families 1999).

President Clinton supported states' increasing use of welfare waivers and in the 1992 election went further by pledging to "end welfare as we know it." The original election campaign proposal also included a set of supports to "make work pay," modeled after the writings of David Ellwood (1988). In *Poor Support*, Ellwood proposed that with a floor of expanded health insurance, an expanded Earned Income Tax Credit (EITC), and broader child care access and affordability, welfare laws could be modified to reduce long, term reliance and to help single parents to move faster and become more stably engaged in the labor force. However, since the mid-1980s, conservatives had been mounting an assault on welfare dependency itself as the root cause of many of the problems of the poor. From

---

[1]Child support enforcement requirements were also increased in FSA to put more pressure on absent parents to contribute to the financial support of children, thus reducing welfare costs.

crime, to illegitimacy and child morbidity, to joblessness in the inner cities, welfare dependency was blamed as a source of moral and socioeconomic pathology (Novak et al 1987).

In the end, the conservative critique was the most important force shaping the 1996 welfare reform. After the Republicans gained control of the House of Representatives, the primary focus of welfare reform became "ending welfare," which translated into reducing caseloads, with little regard for whether or not single mothers could earn enough to support their families.

Theories of Welfare Reform

Many old themes resurfaced in the 1996 law. Welfare has always been politically vulnerable, unpopular, and subject to attack. Feminist analysts such as Mimi Abramovitz (1988) claim this is because the program offers women an option and protection against accepting untenable wages and/or remaining in or entering into marriages that may offer neither security nor safety. According to this theory, it is politically infeasible to have an income support program be too generous so as to allow too many women a viable alternative to work or marriage.

Other analysts who accept the need for providing cash assistance argue that means-tested programs have an inherent design flaw (Blank 1997a), because they must provide (a) benefit levels that are neither so low as to be damaging to families (b) nor so high as to artificially boost take-up rates and encourage "excess" participation, by virtue of creating (c) work and marriage disincentives. In other words, any means-tested system has inherent conflicts in providing a safety net that can meet needs without attracting the non-needy.

Conservatives have contended that the public's hostility to welfare has been fueled by its permissiveness. Mead (1997) argues that PRWORA reflects a turn toward paternalism, by demanding more from recipients in return for (or as a condition of) receipt of benefits. Enforcing the work obligation will, according to Mead and others, eventually alleviate more poverty and suffering as the reforms place greater pressure on government to provide services to help get people into the labor market. Progressive analysts consider this view of a more responsive system as naive and symbolic and doubt whether the new reform will have these beneficial effects (Handler & Hasenfeld 1997).

These theories lead to different assumptions about how PRWORA is likely to affect women's transitions from welfare to work. Conservatives assume that more employment will result from the increased behavioral requirements and that this will lead to greater self-sufficiency. Liberals also expect the reform to push more recipients into the labor market, but they expect that labor market outcomes will be primarily influenced by other factors, such as the state of the economy and public policies external to cash welfare (i.e. tax credits, health coverage, minimum wage, and unemployment policies). They worry that many recipients will be forced off of welfare and left without adequate income replacement. Regardless of theory, the effects of PRWORA will depend on what happens in welfare offices and how the program changes affect the work behavior of welfare recipients. We now describe the new welfare policies and programatic variation across states and how reform has been implemented since 1996.

Temporary Assistance to Needy Families (TANF)

Although welfare reform changed a number of social programs (child support, Food Stamps, Supplemental Security Income, child protection, child care, and child nutrition programs), only those concerning the Temporary Assistance to Needy Families program are considered here. TANF differs from AFDC in four important ways (Greenberg & Savner 1996).

Funding   AFDC was an open-ended matching grant program. Expenditures were shared between the states and the federal government based on a formula taking into account state per capita income. If states spent more (because of caseload increases, for example), the federal government contributed more. Under PRWORA, states receive a block grant of fixed size, the amount of which is based on spending in prior years.[2]

Individual Entitlement   As long as a family met eligibility requirements, it was entitled to AFDC benefits. No such guarantee exists under TANF. States may choose any eligibility criteria as long as all applicants receive "fair and equitable treatment" and as long as all geographic areas of the state are served.

Time Limits   Federal funds may not be used to provide assistance after a family has been on the rolls for 60 months (cumulative) or less, at state option. AFDC had no time limits. States may exempt up to 20% of families from the time limit because of hardships including domestic violence.

Work Requirements   While JOBS regulations exempted many individuals from participation in work and training activities, nearly all recipients must now be engaged in "work activities" within 2 years of receiving assistance. Furthermore, states must meet work participation requirements—each year, an increasingly larger share of the caseload must be working. Work can include subsidized or unsubsidized employment, community service, on-the-job training, participation in job search or job search readiness activities (limited to 6 weeks in a year and no more than 4 weeks consecutively per participant), or participation in short-term vocational training programs, although no more than 20% of the caseload can participate in the latter and count toward the participation rate.

---

[2]For any state, the block grant is the higher of FY 1994, FY 1995, or the average of FY 1992–1994 combined federal spending on AFDC benefit and administration costs, JOBS, and Emergency Assistance.

States also have considerably more discretion in designing their TANF programs than they did under AFDC. Supporters of the law praised this increased flexibility; others were alarmed, speculating that states might engage in a "race-to-the-bottom" by cutting benefit levels or dropping nonworking recipients off the rolls in order to meet work requirements (Edelman 1997), leading to an increase in poverty rates (Lehman & Danziger 1997, Super et al 1996). While a variety of other factors, most notably economic conditions and client characteristics, play a large role in determining the success or failure of welfare reform, state policy choices will play a key role.

State Variations in TANF Policies

States have unprecedented flexibility to design their programs, but they are constrained by federal work requirements and by bureaucratic inertia (Blank 1997b). For example, even though most states had waivers under AFDC, by the mid-1990s, most had not implemented radical reforms.[3] Many states did adopt a "Work First" approach as their primary strategy (Holcomb et al 1998). Work First programs use a labor force attachment model that assumes that finding a job and developing work skills through direct experience—rather than participating in education and training—is the best way to move recipients off the rolls.

Five aspects of TANF could increase the work effort of recipients: work requirements, time limits, sanctions, diversion, and earnings "disregards." In addition, some states provide transitional support services and/or counseling for recipients to increase movement into the work force. Here we discuss the choices states are making.

Work Requirements   Recipients must engage in work activities within 24 months of receiving assistance or at the time they are deemed "work ready" (Brown & Golonka 1998). States can set a shorter time period, and more than half have taken this option, with many requiring immediate engagement in work or a work-related activity.

Time Limits   Nearly two fifths of states have chosen to follow the federal lifetime limit of 60 months of receipt of cash assistance (Gallagher et al 1998, Brown & Golonka 1998). Another 10 states also terminate benefits at this point, but other state provisions limit assistance before the 5-year mark. For example, while Illinois maintains a 5-year cap of receipt of benefits, it also terminates benefits after 24 months of receipt, not allowing families to reapply for assistance until another 24 months have passed. The adult portion of an Arizona family's grant is eliminated after 24 months, then the entire grant is stopped after 60 months. Another group

---

[3]Most states operated their waivers in a few selected geographic areas of the state. Additionally, with a few exceptions, most of these waivers made fairly limited changes to programs.

of 21 states set time limits shorter than 60 months, ranging from 21 months in Connecticut to 48 months in Delaware, Florida, and Georgia. Three states have not established strict lifetime limits, and some states have variable time limits for recipients based on their characteristics (such as education level) or the region of the state in which they reside.

Sanctions   Like JOBS, PRWORA stipulates that states must sanction recipients who fail to comply with program requirements (Gallagher et al 1998). Many states have increased the severity of these sanctions: 36 states terminate benefits entirely, either at the initial point of noncompliance or after a period of noncompliance. Seven of these use "lifetime" sanctions against recipients who are in continued noncompliance—in effect, such sanctions function no differently from the time limit, but recipients may face them much sooner and they may end up affecting more families than time limits.

Diversion   Some states have intensified efforts to divert applicants from receiving cash welfare in the first place (Maloy et al 1998). This practice, called diversion, may be accomplished through: (1) providing one-time financial assistance, (2) requiring mandatory job search as a condition of eligibility, and/or (3) linking applicants to other services or resources. Three fifths of states use diversion activities, with lump sum payments and/or mandatory upfront job search being the most common. If an applicant accepts a lump sum payment, she faces a subsequent period of ineligibility. Mandatory job search prior to eligibility seeks to divert more job-ready applicants directly into the labor market. Referring applicants to other services in lieu of cash benefits is driven by beliefs that cash assistance should be a last resort and that services provide a better way of promoting work. According to Besharov (1999), the use of diversion in New York City's "Jobs Centers" reduced enrollment rates of welfare applicants from about 50% to 30%.

Earned Income Disregards   Prior to PROWRA, only a small portion of recipients' earnings were not counted, or "disregarded," when calculating benefits. After 4 months of work, recipients could expect a nearly dollar-for-dollar reduction in benefits for every dollar earned. To promote work, a number of states expanded this "earned income disregard," allowing recipients to keep more of their earnings without it affecting their grant amounts. PRWORA allows states to set their own policy in this area. A few have maintained the old policy, but most have implemented more generous policies. For example, Oregon and Pennsylvania disregard 50% of all earnings, and Connecticut disregards earnings below the poverty level (Gallagher et al 1998).

Service Delivery   Welfare reform has changed how services are delivered, the role of the welfare office, and the functions of welfare office staff. This transformation has been labeled as "culture change," as the function of welfare offices shifts from eligibility determination to employment preparation (Brodkin 1995, Corbett 1995, Kane & Bane 1994, Lurie 1996, Sandfort 1997).

The flexibility offered in PRWORA and a trend toward reinventing government by contracting out for services (Osborne & Gaebler 1992) have led a number of states to increasingly privatize parts of the welfare system. Some states would increase the involvement of private agencies, even in the welfare applications process[4] and other activities traditionally performed by state employees (Pindus et al 1998).

Implementation

Most states have enumerated situations that would exempt families from or grant families extensions to time limits. Under some extension/exemption policies, women who show a "good faith" effort to find work or are ill receive an exemption or extension. Caseworkers now have greater discretion than prior to 1996. Early evidence indicates that many clients have been granted extensions to time limits (Walters 1999). Despite this, caseloads are falling rapidly—by 38% since PRWORA was passed. While in many localities caseloads began to decline in 1994, much of the post-reform decline could result from strict enforcement of sanctions. In Delaware, for example, over two fifths of the caseload had received at least one sanction, and most of the sanctioned group either had their case closed because of continued noncompliance or left the rolls for some other reason. The probability of being sanctioned even within the state, however, varied significantly by local office (Fein & Wang 1999).

How any diversion policy is carried out will be important to know, since clients may be discouraged, rather than diverted, from applying for assistance. In states with upfront job search requirements, little or no assistance during that search may result in clients' giving up during the application process. Research on the former (Kane 1990, Hagen 1994, Hasenfeld & Weaver 1996, Meyers et al 1998) and current (Seefeldt et al 1998, Seefeldt et al 1999) system indicates that not all welfare staff are able to take on these functions since they were trained primarily to perform eligibility determination and income maintenance work. Finally, the involvement of private agencies in the new welfare system could have far-reaching consequences for clients; for example, because different contractors provide employment-related services in different areas of a state, clients could receive dissimilar services based solely on where they live (Nightingale & Pindus 1997).

Other Policy Changes and Economy

PRWORA was implemented under nearly ideal conditions. A long economic recovery has been underway, and the unemployment rate fell to a 30-year low. Policy changes, most notably the 1993 expansion of the Earned Income Tax Credit (EITC),

---

[4] This action was deemed unallowable, though, since PRWORA does not give states the authority to contract out Food Stamp and Medicaid eligibility functions.

have increased the relative attractiveness of work versus nonwork for low-wage single mothers. Some changes in health care such as the Child Health Insurance Program (CHIP) have made health coverage more affordable to some families, thus making jobs that do not provide this coverage more attractive. And because the federal block grant is tied to 1994 funding levels, and welfare enrollments in virtually all states have sharply declined since 1994, states have ample funds to encourage and support recipients as they move from welfare to work. Ellwood (1999) argues that these broader policy changes have decreased the work disincentives that welfare mothers have faced in the past, beyond the change in the penalties within the program. Consider, for instance, the situation of a single mother earning $10,000 (1996 dollars) per year. In 1986, her expected disposable income (after adjusting for taxes, Food Stamps, and work expenses) would have been $10,188, and she might not have had health insurance for her children; in 1996, her expected disposable income would be $14,523 and her children would be eligible for federally subsidized health insurance (Ellwood 1999, pp. 45–46).

CAN WELFARE RECIPIENTS GET AND KEEP JOBS?

If these welfare reforms are to both reduce welfare caseloads and improve recipient well-being, then two goals must be met. First, recipients must get jobs and maintain stable employment. Second, recipients eventually need to earn a "living wage." In this section, we examine what past research tells us about the likelihood that the first goal will be met. We review research on the job stability and economic situations of recipients pre-PRWORA. Then we examine research on recipients' employment and economic situations post-PRWORA. We also review results from surveys that ask employers about their hiring practices and willingness to hire welfare mothers.

Job Stability and Economic Well-Being of Recipients Pre-PRWORA

Work and Poverty   There is considerable volatility in recipients' work trajectories, but most can find a job. National longitudinal data show that about half of all AFDC mothers worked at some point while receiving welfare, with work accounting for about one half to two thirds of all welfare exits (Harris 1993, 1996, Pavetti 1993, Cancian et al 1999). Evaluations of welfare demonstrations typically find that most participants get jobs (Hershey & Pavetti 1997, Kalil et al 1998).

Keeping a job and staying off welfare are more problematic. Harris (1996) reports that 25–40% of women leaving AFDC via work returned within a year, and up to 70% returned to the rolls within 5 years. In most welfare demonstration programs, a large proportion of recipients who found jobs lost them within a year (Berg et al 1991, Fraker & Prindle 1996, Friedlander & Burtless 1995, Gueron & Pauly 1991, Hershey & Pavetti 1997, Nightingale et al 1990, Parker 1994, Pavetti & Duke 1995, Quint et al 1994, Riccio & Freedman 1995, Rangarajan et al 1992,

Thornton & Hershey 1990). This volatility means that only a minority of recipients establish long-term full-time work patterns. Cancian et al (1999) found that only 13% of women who left AFDC after taking a job worked full-time year-round in first year following their exit, and only 25% worked full-time year-round in year 5. Many of these former recipients remained poor: 55% of those who left were poor in the first year following an exit, and 42% were poor 5 years later.

Barriers to Stable Employment   For PRWORA to do more than reduce caseloads, the job stability of former welfare recipients must improve. Unfortunately, national surveys provide limited information about the causes of job instability for low-income women. Women with prior work experience, more than 12 years of schooling, and fewer than three children are more likely to remain employed and less likely to return to welfare, but these factors leave much of the instability in recipients' work patterns unexplained (Harris 1996, Cancian et al 1999).

There is some evidence that job instability is due to physical and mental health problems, substance abuse, family stresses, employer discrimination, violence by a partner, and inappropriate workplace behaviors. Riccio & Freedman (1995) conclude that serious health and personal problems made continuous employment impossible for a substantial minority of participants in a California program: almost 30% had been deferred at some point for a medically verified illness, and 27% had been deferred for a severe family crisis. Health problems accounted for 9–13% of all job losses in programs in New Jersey and Massachusetts (Hershey & Pavetti 1997).

Mothers reporting high levels of parental stresses were less likely to complete training programs (Orthner & Neenan 1996). Raphael (1996) reports that among participants in an employment training program in Chicago, those who dropped out before meeting their educational or employment goals experienced more domestic violence than participants who met their goals.

Berg et al (1991) report that a primary reason participants in a Chicago program lost jobs was that many failed to understand the importance of punctuality and the seriousness of absenteeism, and resented or misunderstood the lines of authority and responsibility in the workplace. They noted that several supervisors seemed to treat workers unfairly and to be impatient or prejudiced. Some supervisors also reported that they suspected workers were abusing drugs or alcohol. Employers may thus discriminate and/or perceive former recipients' workplace behaviors as inappropriate, and this could increase the risk of job loss among former recipients.

The evidence on these potential barriers from evaluation studies is mainly indirect, and most is based on small, localized studies. To provide more generalized estimates of their prevalence, Olson & Pavetti (1996) analyzed data from the 1991 National Longitudinal Survey of Youth (NLSY) and found that 30% of welfare recipients had one or more of the following problems: mothers' and children's poor health, alcohol and drug problems, depression, and low basic skills.

Work Expenses   Edin & Lein's (1997) pre-reform qualitative study of current and former AFDC recipients emphasizes that the costs associated with going to work outweight their benefits for many recipients. Most of their respondents could get jobs (83% had some formal work experience), but many had a hard time making ends meet because of increased costs in child care, medical care, transportation, housing, and work clothing. The wages they earned were not sufficient to cover these costs. The women who worked steadily tended to benefit from special circumstances, including co-residence with relatives or boyfriends, free child care provided by relatives or friends, receipt of regular and substantial child support, and access to transportation.

How Much More Can They Work?   Welfare mothers in the post-reform era face a radically different set of incentives and penalties for working than did AFDC mothers. One way to predict recipients' future work effort under TANF is to examine the work effort of women with similar characteristics (race and ethnicity, education, basic skills, family characteristics) who did not receive welfare (Pavetti 1999). Using the NLSY, Pavetti (1999) tracked employment paths of comparable women as they age from 18 to 27 years old and found that "women on welfare would work 30% more if their employment paths matched those of similar women who did not receive welfare." Although this increase is substantial, many recipients would still experience considerable joblessness; Pavetti predicts that only 61% would be steadily employed by age 27. This estimate could even be too high, as welfare mothers tend to have unmeasured barriers to work. The estimate, however, could be too low, as economic changes and policy changes (e.g. EITC) increased the availability of work and attractiveness of work since the mid-1990s.

Welfare, Work, and Economic Well-Being Post-PRWORA

Studies of welfare mothers' work behaviors after August 1996 provide initial evidence on the consequences of welfare reform. Researchers have analyzed several kinds of data: caseload data, the Current Population Surveys (CPS), state leavers studies, state time-limit studies, and surveys of TANF recipients.

Caseload Data and CPS Analyses   On two criteria, PRWORA is a success to date across the states. Caseloads are down, and employment of welfare mothers is up. Prior to 1996, more than half of the states had instituted work requirements for some portion of the welfare caseload under the JOBS program, and 31 states had received waivers to experiment with time limits. Between FY 1994 and FY 1996, the average AFDC caseload dropped by 14%. After PRWORA was passed, between August 1996 and June 1998, caseloads declined by 35%. As stated above, by March of 1999, there were only 7.3 million recipients in the program (US Department of Health and Human Services, Administration for Children and Families 1999).

Using Current Population Survey data (CPS), Rolston (1999) examined employment rates of recipients pre- and post-PRWORA. Thirty-four percent of women who had received welfare in 1996 were employed in 1997. Only 20% of women who had received welfare in 1992 were employed in 1993. O'Neill (1999), using CPS data, found that employment rates of unmarried single mothers increased from 58.5% in March 1994 to 69.2% in 1998.

But how much is the policy change versus the economic boom responsible for these caseload reductions and employment increases? Analysts who have used annual administrative data to assess the impact of economic conditions on caseload reductions between 1994 to 1996 typically find that declines in unemployment rates accounted for about one third to one half of the caseload reductions (Blank 1997c, Council of Economic Advisors 1997, Figlio & Ziliak 1999, Levine & Whitmore 1998, Wallace & Blank 1999, Ziliak et al 1997). But when Wallace & Blank (1999) used different model specifications and examined monthly caseload reductions over a longer period, 1994 to 1998, they found that declines in unemployment rates accounted for 8–12% of caseload reductions.

Evidence on changes in income and well-being following welfare reform is also mixed. On the positive side, CPS data indicate that the number of people in female-headed families whose pre-welfare incomes were below the poverty line fell by 5.4% (0.8 million people) between 1995 and 1997 (Primus 1999). On the negative side, caseload declines over this period far exceeded declines in poverty: the number of people receiving TANF/AFDC benefits dropped by 22.6% (3.0 million people). According to Primus et al (1999), the average disposable income of the poorest 20% of single mothers fell by 7.6%, and the average disposable income of the poorest 10% fell by 15.2%.

While it is tempting to attribute much of the employment and earnings growth to welfare reform, the research indicates that the booming economy and other policy reforms have also changed the work context of welfare mothers. Future studies need to assess the independent effects of each of these factors on recipients' employment. If the strong economy played the largest role in promoting the observed increases in employment, then employment rates of recipients may decline during the next recession (Danziger 1999).

Results from State-Based Leavers Studies   Most states have begun studies of "leavers," i.e. families who have left welfare or who have been sanctioned post-PRWORA. These studies provide preliminary evidence about employment and well-being that are consistent across studies and with the CPS data (Brauner & Loprest 1999). Combining sanctioned and nonsanctioned leavers, point-in-time employment rates range from 51% to 69%. "Durational estimates" (i.e. the percentage of leavers who worked at any time during a given period following a welfare exit) yield employment rates of 68–88% during the year after an exit. According to Tweedie et al (1999), the work rate is 5–10% higher than for recipients who left welfare for jobs under AFDC.

State TANF studies, like earlier AFDC studies, indicate that most recipients can find a job. Why someone leaves welfare, however, is strongly associated with subsequent employment status. Sanctioned recipients were not as likely to be employed as were other leavers: their rates of employment ranged from 20% to 50%.

Several states gathered data on leavers' hours of work, occupations, and economic circumstances. Over half of employed leavers worked 30 or more hours per week, but most were not earning enough to lift their families out of poverty (Brauner & Loprest 1999). Leavers were disproportionately employed in service and sales occupations and in occupations with low median wages. Leavers' economic well-being varied substantially across the states, reflecting in part state benefit levels and earnings disregards. Former recipients' average annual income increased after leaving TANF in states with generous benefits and disregards, but did not change in states with low benefits and standard disregards (Rolston 1999).

A few studies examined economic strain, but many of these studies suffer from poor response rates and may have missed families in the worst shape. In Wisconsin and South Carolina, over 50% of leavers claim to be "just getting by" (Brauner & Loprest 1999). In three states, over a third of leavers reported problems providing enough food for their families, and three out of five studies reported that a third or more of respondents had problems paying rent or utility bills (Brauner & Loprest 1999). In one study, former recipients were significantly more likely to report falling behind in house payments and not having enough money to buy food or pay for child care than when they received cash assistance. A concern has been raised that some families who are leaving or being diverted from welfare may also not be receiving Food Stamps and Medicaid even though they continue to be eligible (Primus et al 1999).

Results from Time-Limit Studies   State "leaver" studies primarily describe recipients who left the welfare rolls prior to time limits' taking effect, including both sanctioned recipients and those who left for income or other reasons. However, they provide little or no information about the work and economic situations of recipients who reach time limits. Several states obtained waivers from the federal government to institute and evaluate time-limited welfare programs prior to 1996, and early data on families who reach time limits are now available. These policies and practices differ widely across states and make comparisons difficult. For example, in Escambia County, Florida, nearly everyone who reached the time limit has had her or his grant entirely canceled, whereas one half of those who reached Connecticut's time limit have received at least one 6-month extension (Bloom 1999).

One goal of time limits was to spur recipients toward self-sufficiency early on so that many would leave welfare before time limits took effect. Employment rates (relative to a control group) increased, and welfare receipt decreased in most time-limit waiver programs before recipients had reached the time limits, but it is not clear whether time limits caused these impacts (Bloom 1999). The Connecticut and Florida evaluations surveyed the well-being of families who reached the time limits and had their benefits canceled. There is both good news and bad news in these data. First, employment status pre- and post-time limits was comparable: those who were employed (or unemployed) in the last month before the time limit were generally employed (unemployed) 6-months later (Bloom 1999). In addition, for the most part, material hardship did not increase when benefits ended, and most respondents did not report severe deprivation either before or after benefits ended (Bloom 1999).

However, 6 months after the time limit, about 21% of respondents reported that in the prior month, they had often "relied on low-cost food to feed the children because I was running out of money." In contrast, only about 14% said that this had often been true during their last month on welfare. A number of people stopped receiving Food Stamps after the time limit even though they were not employed, perhaps because they incorrectly believed that the time limit applied to their Food Stamp benefits. Future studies will need to monitor over longer time periods the material well-being of families who reach time limits and the strategies they employ to make ends meet.

Surveys of TANF Recipients   Many of the studies just reviewed have little or no data on potential barriers to employment such as poor health, psychological dysfunction, substance dependence, and domestic violence. Several new surveys collect data on a wider range of recipient characteristics. These include the National Survey of American Families (NSAF) of The Urban Institute, the Women's Employment Survey (WES) of the University of Michigan, The Impact Study of the Manpower Demonstration Research Corporation's Urban Change Project; and the survey component of the Welfare, Children, and Families' Multi Cities Project of Johns Hopkins University. Preliminary findings are available from the first waves of the NSAF and the WES.[5]

In both studies, the descriptions of recipients' employment and economic situations are consistent with results from the leavers studies. In the NSAF, 61% of women who left welfare between 1995 and 1997 were employed. In WES, 58% of women who were on the welfare rolls in February 1997 were employed 20 or more hours per week by Fall 1997 and 62% by Fall 1998. In both samples, a majority of employed recipients worked full-time; disproportionate proportions of recipients worked in service or sales occupations; and a majority of employed recipients

---

[5]The Urban Institute's NSAF conducted telephone interviews with a nationally representative sample of 40,000 families in 1997 (Loprest 1999). Their response rate was 70%. A new sample be interviewed in 1999. The NSAF collected detailed information on the health, economic, and social characteristics of respondents. The University of Michigan WES surveyed 753 women who represent a random sample of single mothers who received welfare in an urban Michigan county in February 1997. Women were interviewed in Fall 1997, Fall 1998, and Winter 2000. Response rates were 86% for wave 1, 92% for wave 2, and 91% for wave 3.

did not receive employer-provided health insurance (Loprest 1999, Danziger et al 2000a, Danziger et al 2000b). In WES, one third of respondents interviewed in Fall 1998 reported experiencing one or more of the following hardships in the past year: not enough food, eviction, homelessness, and utility cutoff (Danziger et al. 2000b).

Danziger et al (2000a) examined a much wider range of potential barriers to work than have previous researchers. They report that recipients have unusually high levels of physical and mental health problems, domestic violence, and lack of transportation, but relatively low levels of barriers such as drug or alcohol dependence and lack of understanding of work norms; that most recipients have multiple barriers; and that the number of barriers is strongly and negatively associated with employment status. In a multiple regression model that included 14 potential barriers to work, plus a set of demographics, the following variables were negatively associated with employment: residence in a nonurban census tract, age less than 25 years, presence of a child aged 2 or less, no high school diploma, low work experience, knowing fewer than four job skills, perceiving discrimination at work in the past, lack of transportation, meeting the diagnostic criteria for major depression and drug dependence, and having a health problem. These results suggest that low skills are only part of the reason recipients find it difficult to get and keep jobs.

Will Employers Hire and Keep Welfare Recipients?

Another way to assess recipients' economic prospects is to examine the demand-side of the labor market—i.e. to ask employers what qualities they require of new hires, and to assess how well TANF recipients' skills and credentials match up with employers' demands. Several surveys have interviewed employers about these issues.

Skills   Holzer (1996) surveyed 3200 urban employers about entry-level jobs available to workers without a college degree. The typical job required workers to perform several of the following tasks on a daily basis: reading paragraphs, writing paragraphs, arithmetic, dealing with customers, and using a computer. About 75% of entry-level jobs required high school diploma, general experience, and references; 65% required specific experience; 40% required training; and over 50% required applicants to pass a test.

There is a large gap between the skills that employers demand and those welfare recipients can offer. Seventy percent of long-term welfare recipients score in the bottom quartile of the Armed Forces Qualification Test (AFQT) (Burtless 1995). Many recipients have low literacy levels. Welfare recipients aged 17–21 read, on average, at the sixth-grade level (Barton & Jenkins 1995). The National Adult Literacy Survey (NALS) categorizes individuals into one of five literacy levels. Individuals at level 1 are able to do very simple tasks, such as totaling a bank deposit slip, but are unable to do level 2 tasks such as locating an intersection on a street map. Individuals at level 2 are unable to perform higher order tasks such as using a bus schedule or using a calculator to determine a 10% discount. About 76% of recipients score at levels 1 or 2. In contrast, more than two thirds of workers score at levels 3 or above (Levenson et al 1999). Many welfare mothers also lack the credentials required by employers. About half of welfare recipients lack a high school diploma or a GED, 10–30% have only a grade school education, and few report recent work experience (Harris 1993, 1996, Olson & Pavetti 1996).

Location   Skills mismatch is not the only problem recipients face in looking for work. Spatial mismatch is also an issue; Holzer (1996) estimates that about 60% of jobs potentially available to recipients are located in the suburbs, but the majority of recipients live in cities. Holzer & Danziger (1998) conducted simulations that matched workers to jobs on the basis of skill, location, and racial characteristics. They found that the lack of job availability for welfare recipients was nearly three times that of women in general. Levenson et al (1999) compared recipients' basic skills to occupational skill requirements and concluded that the economy would have to create 6% more jobs with very low basic skills to fully employ all welfare mothers. Cities with large TANF caseloads (e.g. Los Angeles, Washington, DC, Newark) will have to increase the number of jobs with very low basic skills by more than 20%.

Despite the skills and spatial mismatch, many employers, when asked directly, state they would be willing to hire welfare recipients. Regenstein et al (1998) report that most employers in a national survey express a willingness to hire TANF recipients. Holzer (1999a), reporting on surveys with 900 employers in three Michigan metropolitan areas, found that employers claim they are willing to fill 3% of their jobs right away with unskilled TANF recipients and up to 9% over the course of the next year. This is more than the number of household heads expected to be pushed into the labor force under welfare reform. However, Holzer cautions that whether recipients actually get these jobs will depend upon the skills and qualifications of competing applicants, whether jobs are accessible, and whether the current favorable economic conditions hold. Holzer (1999b) also shows that the employment of low-skill workers is very sensitive to economic conditions.

Finally, poor job quality characterizes the labor market that welfare recipients face. Many of the entry-level jobs available to them are low paid, offer few benefits, and involve part-time and unstable work. Two thirds of employers in a national survey report their entry-level employees earn an average of $6.00 or less per hour (Regenstein et al 1998). Although nearly half of employers offer health benefits, most do so after a lengthy waiting period, and 25% offer no benefits (health, paid sick leave, or paid vacation). Almost half of jobs provide only part-time work and, on average, entry-level employees leave their jobs within a year.

DO WAGES GROW ENOUGH TO ACHIEVE SELF-SUFFICIENCY?

Work has increased among recipients since welfare reform, but most women who leave welfare take low-wage, unstable jobs that offer few benefits; a large minority of leavers work part-time; and many have low incomes and experience material hardships. The hope is that if recipients work regularly, they will eventually move on to higher earnings. According to Bonilla (1995), "[A] job, most any job, has shown itself capable of generating the earnings growth which will make welfare reform a reality." Holcomb et al (1998, p. 13) sum up this reasoning as follows: "the underlying philosophy of these TANF programs begins with the expectation that most recipients are capable of finding work and assume the best way to succeed in the labor market is to join it. It is believed that job advancement and higher wages will come from the experience of working .... Hence, employment is both the goal and the expectation even if the only jobs that can be obtained pay low wages and lack benefits."

Many argue that this perspective is overly optimistic, that many recipients have very low skills and have access only to low-wage, dead-end jobs that offer few promotion opportunities and do not provide the training and work experience necessary to secure better paid jobs. According to Burtless (1995, p. 100): "The earnings capacity of most women who receive welfare is extremely low, and it rises only slowly with age."

These conflicting views about the future economic prospects of welfare re-cipients have different implications for the design of welfare programs. If recipients' wages grow as they acquire work experience, then time limits and short-term transitional support services will be sufficient to enable recipients to escape poverty. If recipients remain stuck in low-wage, dead-end jobs, then, when the mandated time limits are reached, many ex-recipients and their children will remain poor. Long-term supportive policies and/or policies to upgrade recipients' skills (wage subsidies, child care, guaranteed health care, training and education programs) may be required to enable ex-recipients and their children to become self-sufficient.

There are several reasons to believe that wages will grow for recipients under the new welfare regime. The costs of not working are now much higher given sanctions and time limits. And many states are providing more supports for TANF recipients who work, including reimbursement for some work-related expenses, such as child care expenses and transportation and transitional health insurance. These sanctions and supports should increase work incentives, and as recipients work more over time, they should acquire work experience and enhanced skills and should learn about appropriate workplace behaviors. Work may also improve psychological functioning (e.g. less depression, increased self-efficacy), may reduce stresses, may enable women to leave abusive partners, and may motivate women to seek additional schooling. These changes, in turn, could lead to better jobs and higher wages.

There are also reasons to expect that wages of welfare mothers will be flat over time. As we discussed earlier, many recipients are high school dropouts, lack basic skills, and have little or no work experience. In the 1980s, the wages and benefits associated with entry-level, low-skill jobs declined, and it became increasingly difficult for low-skilled workers to earn enough to support a family at or above the poverty line (Blank 1995, 1997, Danziger & Gottschalk 1995, Wilson 1987, 1996, Holzer 1996). Blank (1995, p. 63) speculates that "changes in the U.S. labor market are not leading to the elimination of jobs for low skilled workers but to the reconfiguration of those jobs into lower-paid positions that provide fewer opportunities for advancement."

A number of researchers have examined how quickly wages grow with work experience and/or age for women in the general population. They consistently find that (a) wages grow with work experience; (b) prolonged periods of joblessness lower women's wages; and (c) wage growth is lower when women work part-time (Altonji & Blank 1999, Mincer & Polachek 1974, Blau & Kahn 1997, Corcoran & Duncan 1979, England 1982, Corcoran et al 1983, England et al 1988, 1999, Gronau 1988, Jung & Magrabi 1991, Light & Ureta 1995, Loprest 1992, Stratton 1995, Wellington 1993).

If TANF recipients' wage growth follows the pattern of the typical woman, and if welfare reform leads recipients to acquire more work experience, especially full-time experience, and to have fewer and shorter periods of nonwork, then the expectation that "job advancement and higher wages will come from the experience of working" may be fulfilled.

But there are some theoretical reasons to suspect that welfare recipients have very different patterns of wage growth compared with the average woman. Recipients have lower skills, and may be less able to benefit from on-the-job training, and more likely to be relegated to jobs that provide little or no training, than the average worker. The experimental evaluation literature suggests that some recipients are not "work-ready," i.e. do not know appropriate workplace behaviors; this may interfere with investments in on-the-job training. And, as we noted earlier, many TANF recipients have health and mental health problems that may make it difficult for them to keep jobs and to benefit from on-the-job training. Finally, employers may stigmatize recipients, i.e. may label them as "irresponsible" and "shiftless," and may assign them to jobs that provide few training opportunities (Browne & Kennelly 1999). In the WES study, about 20% of welfare recipients reported having experienced prior employment discrimination because of their welfare status (M Corcoran, CM Heflin, J Levine, unpublished observations).

Below we review studies on the potential wage and earnings trajectories of TANF recipients as they move from welfare to work. We first review earlier studies that track how AFDC recipients' wages and earnings grew *with age*. These provide estimates of how much TANF recipients' wages might be expected to grow if they worked at the same rate and in the same kinds of jobs that AFDC recipients did in the past (Connolly & Gottschalk 1999). These studies likely underestimate expected wage growth with age for TANF recipients given the new sanctions and welfare rules. If welfare reform increases work effort among recipients, then their wages may grow faster over time than did those of AFDC recipients. We next review analyses of how much wages grow per year of work experience for AFDC recipients and low-skilled workers.

Rates of Wage Growth with Age

Moffitt & Rangarajan (1989) were among the first to track how AFDC recipients' wages grew over time. They drew a sample of women who were single mothers in at least 1 year between 1968 to 1983 from the Panel Study of Income Dynamics (PSID). Although recent AFDC participation was associated with lower wages, AFDC recipients and nonrecipients had relatively similar rates of wage growth with age (Table 6.4, p. 130). Moffitt and Rangarajan reported that single mothers' wages grew slowly with age, at an average rate of about 2% per year (Connolly & Gottschalk 1999). This is not surprising since many single mothers did not work every year, and many who did worked part-time when they did work. Thus, the rate at which single mothers' wages grew with age likely understates the extent to which their wages would grow with continuous, full-time work experience.

Burtless (1995) used the National Longitudinal Survey of Youth (NLSY) to compare wage growth with age for women who received AFDC (recipients) and those not receiving AFDC (nonrecipients) between 1979 and 1981. Wage growth with age averaged about 4.8% per year in subsequent years for nonrecipients and less than 1% per year for recipients. Burtless also focused on women with skills similar to those of recipients—high school dropouts and women with low cognitive test scores; they, like recipients, also experienced minimal wage growth. This suggests that many welfare mothers may never earn their way out of poverty.

Harris (1996) reports that earnings remained in the $5 to $7 an hour range for most women in the first years after leaving AFDC. Pavetti & Acs (1997) report that only 13% of women who ever received AFDC between the ages 18 of 27 were working full-time at a job that paid a "living wage" (at least $8 per hour) by age 27. Cancian et al (1999) report that median wages for women leaving AFDC grew from $6.36 in the first year to $6.73 in the fifth year.

None of these studies actually calculated how much recipients' wages grew per year of work experience. Burtless (1995) and Cancian et al (1999) estimated median wage growth in each year *only* for women employed in that year. Moffitt & Rangarajan (1989) regressed log earnings on age and age-squared, not on experience. But AFDC recipients were less likely to be employed in any given year than were nonrecipients. According to Burtless (1995), the vast majority of nonrecipients (80–90%), but only 45–65% of the recipients, worked in any given year. Cancian et al (1999) reported that only 5% of AFDC leavers worked full-time, full-year during all the 5 years after leaving AFDC. Because recipients worked in fewer years, their lower rate of wage growth with age could mean either that (a) recipients acquired less experience and spent more time out of the labor force than nonrecipients, or (b) recipients' wages grew slowly, if at all, with work experience.

Wage Growth with Work Experience

Several analysts have directly estimated the extent to which wages grow with work experience for welfare recipients. Acs (1990) used the NLSY to estimate change models of wage growth with work experience between 1979 and 1986 for women aged 17 to 22 years in 1979. Average rates of wage growth per year of full-time work experience were virtually identical for women who never received AFDC between 1979 to 1986 and welfare recipients—about 3.3% per year. But wages of recipients grew much less overall between 1979 and 1986 (5% versus 16%), largely because recipients acquired only half as much experience as did nonrecipients. This suggests that the low rates of wage growth with age for recipients reported by Burtless were due to spending fewer years working and not to lower wage returns to work experience.

Lin (1999) estimated wage change models over a 19-year period, using PSID samples of women between the ages of 18 and 37 in 1973 who were single mothers during at least 1 year between 1973 and 1992. Like Acs (1990), she found little difference in rates of wage growth per year of full-time work experience between recipients and nonrecipients. Rates of wage growth ranged from 4% to 5% for the first observed year of full-time work experience; wages grew more slowly when experience was part-time, and wages dropped by about 4% per year of nonwork (Lin 1999). Rates of wage growth per year of part-time work experience were lower for recipients than for nonrecipients, but this difference was not significant.

Loeb & Corcoran (1999) used the 1979 to 1993 waves of the NLSY to examine wage growth after age 18 years for recipients and nonrecipients using three different specifications: a pooled cross-section, a first-difference analysis, and a between analysis, in which the outcome measure was the average wage change for each individual. They report that wage growth averaged about 6% per year of work for nonrecipients, recipients, short-term recipients, and long-term recipients and that wage growth was slower when work experience was part-time. Average wage growth per year worked was also large for low-skilled workers—6% per year for high school dropouts and high school graduates and 5% per year for women with low cognitive test scores (one standard deviation below the mean on the Armed Forces Qualifying Test, AFQT).

Gladden & Taber (1998) used the NLSY to estimate models of wage growth in the first 12 years after school completion for men and women with 12 or fewer completed years of schooling. They reported that returns to a year of work experience ranged from 3.6% to 6.8% for women and did not vary significantly by number of years of school completed. They further reported that welfare recipients appeared to have higher returns-to-work experience than did other women.

Connolly & Gottschalk (1999) used the data from the Survey of Income and Program Participation (SIPP) to estimate separate wage growth models for women by levels of schooling. Relative to other education groups, white high school dropouts have below-average wage growth, but nonwhite high school dropouts have above-average wage growth, largely because of wage gains associated with job changes.

With the exception of Connolly & Gottschalk (1999), there is consistency across these studies.[6] Average rates of wage growth per year of work for recipients ranged from 3% to 7%, and average rates of returns per full-time year of work ranged from 3% to 8% per year. There is little evidence that returns to work experience differ for women who have received AFDC and for women who have not. Returns to work experience were also substantial for women with low skills—high school dropouts and women with low test scores. Welfare recipients' low rates of wage growth with age appear to be due to their meager work experience and not to lower returns to work experience.

There are several caveats here. One is that workers who spent more time working might have had higher wages regardless of experience. This could lead analysts to overestimate wage returns to experience. Acs (1990), Lin (1999), and Loeb & Corcoran (1999) deal with this by estimating difference (wage change) equations. Gladden & Taber (1998) and Connolly & Gottschalk (1999) deal with this by instrumenting experience.

Another problem concerns the endogeneity of the work experience in the wage change regressions. Women are likely to work more if they know that this work will lead to wage growth, and are likely to work less if they expect little wage growth. This within-individual variation in expected wage growth could inflate estimates of how much wages will grow with experience. Loeb & Corcoran (1999) dealt with this by estimating a between-analysis in which the dependent variable was the average wage change for individuals with 5 or fewer years of work experience.

The most serious issue is selection bias. Most of these studies use wage-change models and require that recipients have worked during at least 2 years. It is plausible that recipients who either did not work at all or worked only 1 year would have had the lowest wages and wage growth had they been working. Most of the authors reviewed here adjust for selection bias using the Heckman (1979) procedure, but selection bias may still pose a problem if the instruments used are weak ones.

These studies suggest that work experience will pay off for TANF recipients and ex-recipients *if* they are able to sustain full-time year-round work. Evidence on the extent of work among recipients is less encouraging because both the national longitudinal analyses of welfare-to-work transitions and evaluations of the welfare-to-work demonstrations suggested that many recipients had sporadic work patterns in the years after leaving AFDC and that few recipients worked full-time year-round on a long-term basis. Cancian et al (1999), for instance, report

---

[6]Connolly & Gottschalk's (1999) results could differ for a variety of reasons. They used SIPP data; they examined wage growth over a shorter period than did other authors; their model specifications differed.

that only 25 percent of recipients were working full-time year-round 5 years after they left AFDC. According to employer surveys, about half of the jobs available to recipients offer only part-time work. Advocates of the new welfare-to-work programs assume that part-time work will enable recipients to make the transition from not working to full-time employment. But when Blank (1998) used the PSID to analyze women's transitions between part-time work, nonemployment, and full-time work, she concluded that part-time work "is only infrequently used as a steppingstone to full-time work by women who are out of labor market."

Since PRWORA, welfare reform provides both carrots and sticks to encourage greater work effort. Time limits and sanctions are the sticks, while earned income disregards, transitional services, and work supports (subsidies for child-care and transportation costs, transitional health insurance, counseling and support services, EITCs) are the carrots. Pavetti (1999) predicts that if the new incentives lead recipients to work as much as did women with similar schooling, test scores, and family circumstances who never received welfare, then as many as 61% of recipients may be working regularly by age 27. This prediction is probably too optimistic, as recipients face a number of potential barriers to employment that Pavetti's prediction did not consider—health problems, mental health problems, substance abuse, perceived discrimination, few work skills, poor work norms, and other barriers (Danziger et al 2000a). Prospects for eventually earning a living wage surely differ across recipients. Those with few barriers to work may do very well, whereas those who face multiple barriers to work are unlikely to work steadily.

SUMMARY, CONCLUSIONS, AND POLICY IMPLICATIONS

Welfare reform has changed the employment context facing welfare applicants. First, recipients are required to work or to participate in work activities as a condition of receiving assistance. This focus on work will increase over time both because a larger proportion of cases will bump up against time limits and because the federally mandated work participation requirements increase with each year. Second, because states have considerable leeway in designing their TANF programs, there is great diversity across states in work requirements, time limits, sanctions, diversions, and earned income disregard policies. As a result, work incentives, the "hassles" associated with enrolling in welfare, and penalties for nonwork vary considerably by state. Implementation practices also differ within and across states leading to even more variation in the work-related "carrots" and "sticks."

In addition, a strong economy and expansion of federal assistance for the working poor affect the work choices of welfare mothers. It is easier for low-skilled workers to get jobs when unemployment rates are low. Expansion of the EITC, child care subsidies, and the availability of Medicaid have increased the payoffs to work versus nonwork for low-skilled workers.

It is not surprising, given all these changes, that welfare caseloads have fallen dramatically and that employment rates of single mothers have increased since the mid-1990s. Studies of welfare leavers show that the majority are employed, and that most employed leavers work full-time. Leavers' employment status varies significantly by their reason for leaving—sanctioned recipients are much less likely to be employed than are other leavers.

When welfare reform was passed, critics warned that child poverty, homelessness, and child neglect could rise precipitously. This has not yet happened—though it is unclear how welfare reform will affect child poverty when the economy goes through a downturn or when the "hard core" welfare cases bump up against time limits. There are also some disturbing patterns. Primus et al (1999) show that the disposable income of the very poorest female-headed families decreased between 1995 and 1997.

Almost all partisans in the welfare debate predicted that recipients would initially work at low-skilled, poorly paid jobs. This seems correct. About two thirds of the jobs available to recipients pay $6.00 or less per hour, many do not provide health benefits, and about half involve part-time work. The average wages of welfare leavers tend to be low, and many do not yet have employer-sponsored health care benefits.

The current research leaves much unanswered because it has only been 3 years since PRWORA became law. One set of questions concerns the causes of decreased caseloads and increased employment and earnings of welfare recipients and single mothers. How much of these improvements are due to welfare reform, to an improved economy, or to federal policies designed to "make work pay" (e.g. EITC, expansion of Medicaid)? What will happen when there is an economic downturn?

Another set of questions focuses on state policies. How much do welfare recipients' work and economic outcomes vary across states? How much of this variation is due to differences in state policies or implementation practices? What proportion of applicants are diverted from enrolling on welfare, and how are these diverted applicants faring? Are work requirements, anticipation of time limits, or sanctions the primary reason state welfare rolls are falling and single mothers' employment is up?

A third set of questions focuses on potential barriers to employment. Many welfare recipients have very low skills and low levels of literacy—even relative to women with the same levels of schooling who do not receive welfare. Danziger et al (2000a) report that recipients have high levels of other barriers to work, such as poor physical health, mental health problems, children with health problems, lack of transportation, and domestic violence problems. In addition, a majority of recipients possess multiple barriers, and the number of barriers is strongly associated with employment. Considerably more research is needed to identify the long-term possibly reciprocal relationships between work and well-being, especially in such domains as maternal and child physical and mental health, and domestic abuse.

The most important unanswered questions have to do with the long-term impacts of welfare reform. We have seen that more recipients are getting jobs when the national unemployment rate is below 5%. Will this persist when the economy falls into a recession? Even in a favorable economy, will recipients be able to sustain steady employment and move out of poorly paid jobs and into better paying jobs? Answers await further study and experience under PRWORA.

On the positive side, several studies show that when AFDC recipients, high school dropouts, and women with low test scores work full-time on a steady basis, their average wages grow with experience. This suggests that if recipients have the supports they need to maintain steady employment, their wages might grow over time and foster self-sufficiency. Future studies will need to take into account the effect of the wide variation in welfare programs and services that women are exposed to in this post-reform era.

Visit the Annual Reviews home page at www.AnnualReviews.org

LITERATURE CITED

Abramovitz M. 1988. *Regulating the Lives of Women.* Boston: South End Press

Acs G. 1990. *Welfare, Work, and Dependence: Analyzing the Potential Effects of Work-Related Welfare Reform.* PhD thesis. Univ. Michigan, Ann Arbor

Altonji JG, Blank RM. 1999. Race and gender in the labor market. In *Handbook of Labor Economics,* ed. O Ashenfelder, D Card. Amsterdam: North-Holland

Bane MJ, Ellwood DT. 1994. *Welfare Realities: From Rhetoric to Reform.* Cambridge, MA: Harvard Univ. Press

Barton PE, Jenkins L. 1995. *Literacy and Dependency: The Literacy Skills of Welfare Recipients in the United States.* Princeton, NJ: Educational Testing Service

Berg L, Olson L, Conrad A. 1991. Causes and implications of rapid job loss among participants in a welfare-to-work program. Presented at Ann. Res. Conf. Assoc. Public Policy Manage., Bethesda, MD

Besharov DJ. 1999. *Hearing on the Effects of Welfare Reform.* Testimony Before the Subcommittee on Human Resources of the House Committee on Ways and Means. http://www.house.gov/ways_means/humres/106cong/5-27-99/5-27besh.htm

Blank RM. 1995. Outlook for the US labor market and prospects for low-wage entry jobs. See Nightingale & Haveman 1995, pp. 33–69

Blank RM. 1997a. *It Takes a Nation.* New York: Russell Sage Foundation

Blank RM. 1997b. The 1996 welfare reform. *J. Econ. Perspect.* 11(1):169–77

Blank RM. 1997c. What Causes Public Assistance Caseloads to Grow? National Bureau of Economic Research Working Paper 6343. Cambridge, MA: NBER

Blank RM. 1998. Labor economics and part-time work. In *Research in Labor Economics,* ed. S Polachek, 11:137–58. Stamford, CT: JAI Press

Blau F, Kahn L. 1997. Swimming upstream: trends in the gender wage differential in the 1980s. *J. Labor Econ.* 15(1):1–42

Bloom D. 1999. *Welfare Time Limits: An Interim Report Card.* New York: Manpower Demonstration Research Corp.

Bonilla C. 1995. *Hearing on Welfare Reform.* Testimony before the US House Committee on Economic and Educational Opportunities. Washington, DC: Federal Document Clearing House, Inc.

Brauner S, Loprest P. 1999. *Where Are They*

Now? What States' Studies of People Who Left Welfare Tell Us. The Urban Institute, Washington, DC

Brodkin E. 1995. Administrative capacity and welfare reform. In *Looking Before We Leap: Social Science and Welfare Reform*, ed. RK Weaver, W Dickens, pp. 75–90. Washington, DC: Brookings Institution

Browne I, ed. 1999. *Latinas and African American Women at Work.* New York: Russell Sage

Browne I, Kennelly I. 1999. Stereotypes and realities: images of Black women in the labor market. See Browne 1999, pp. 302–26

Brown R, Golonka S. 1998. *Round Two Summary of Selected Elements of State Programs for Temporary Assistance for Needy Families.* National Governors' Association, Washington, DC

Burtless G. 1995. The employment prospects of welfare recipients. See Nightingale & Haveman 1995, pp. 71–106

Cancian M, Haveman R, Kaplan T, Meyer D, Wolfe B. 1999. Work, earnings, and well-being, after welfare: what do we know? See Danziger 1999

Connolly H, Gottschalk P. 1999. Early labor market experience—dead-end jobs or stepping stones for less-skilled workers? Boston College, unpublished manuscript

Corbett T. 1995. Changing the culture of welfare. *Focus* 16(2):12–22

Corcoran M, Duncan GJ. 1979. Work experience, labor force attachment and earnings differences between the races and sexes. *J. Hum. Resourc.* 14(1):3–20

Corcoran M, Duncan GJ, Ponza M. 1983. A longitudinal analysis of white women's wages. *J. Hum. Resourc.* 18:437–520

Council of Economic Advisors. 1997. *Technical Report: Explaining the Decline in Welfare Receipt, 1993–1996.* Council of Economic Advisors, Washington, DC

Danziger S, ed. 1999. *Economic Conditions and Welfare Reform: What Are the Early Lessons?* Kalamazoo, MI: Upjohn Institute.

Danziger S, Gottschalk P. 1995. *America Unequal.* New York: Russell Sage

Danziger SK, Corcoran M, Danziger S, Heflin C, Kalil A, et al. 2000a. Barriers to the employment of welfare recipients. In *The Impact of Tight Labor Markets on Black Employment Problems*, ed. R Cherry, W Rodgers. New York: Russell Sage, pp. 239–272.

Danziger SK, Corcoran M, Danziger S, Heflin C, 2000b. Work, income and material hardship after welfare reform. *Journal of Consumer Affairs* 34(1)

Edelman P. 1997. The worst thing Bill Clinton has done. *The Atlantic Monthly* 279 (3):43–46

Edin K, Lein L. 1997. *Making Ends Meet: How Single Mothers Survive Welfare and Low-Wage Work.* New York: Russell Sage Foundation

Ellwood DT. 1988. *Poor Support.* New York: Basic Books

Ellwood DT. 1999. Anti-poverty policy for families in the next century: from welfare to work—and worries. Harvard Univ., Boston, unpublished manuscript

England P. 1982. The failure of human capital theory to explain occupational sex segregation. *J. Hum. Resourc.* 17:358–70

England P, Christopher K, Reid L. 1999. Gender, race, ethnicity, and wages. See Browne 1999, pp 139–82

England P, Farkas G, Killbourne BS, Dow T. 1988. Explaining occupational segregation and wages: findings from a model with fixed effects. *Am. Sociol. Rev.* 53:544–58

Fein D, Wang L. 1999. *Carrying and Using the Stick: Financial Sanctions in Delaware's A Better Chance Program.* Abt Associates Inc., Boston, MA

Figlio DN, Ziliak JP. 1999. Welfare reform, the business cycle, and the decline in AFDC caseloads. See Danziger 1999

Fraker T, Prindle C. 1996. *Findings from the Evaluation of Iowa's Limited Benefit Plan.* Presented at the Annual Research Conference of the Assoc. Public Policy Manage., Pittsburgh, PA

Friedlander D, Burtless G. 1995. *Five Years*

After: The Long-term Effects of Welfare-to-Work Programs. New York: Russell Sage Foundation

Gallagher J, Gallagher M, Perese K, Schreiber S, Watson K. 1998. *One Year After Federal Welfare Reform: A Description of State Temporary Assistance for Needy Families (TANF) Decisions as of October 1997.* Assessing the New Federalism occasional paper no. 6. The Urban Institute, Washington, DC

Garfinkel I, McLanahan SS. 1986. *Single Mothers and Their Children.* Washington, DC: The Urban Institute Press

Gladden T, Taber C. 1998. Wage progression among less skilled workers. Northwestern Univ., Chicago, unpublished manuscript

Greenberg M, Savner S. 1996. *A Brief Summary of Key Provisions of the Temporary Assistance for Needy Families Block Grant of H. R. 3734, The Personal Responsibility and Work Opportunity Reconciliation Act of 1996.* Center for Law and Social Policy, Washington, DC

Greenberg M, Savner S. 1995. *The CLASP Guide to Welfare Waivers: 1992–1995,* Center for Law and Social Policy, Washington, DC

Gronau R. 1988. Sex-related wage differentials and women's interrupted labor careers—the chicken or the egg. *J. Labor Econ.* 6:277–301

Gueron J, Pauly E. 1991. *From Welfare to Work.* New York: Russell Sage Foundation

Hagen J. 1994. JOBS and case management: developments in 10 states. *Soc. Work* 39 (2):197–205

Handler JF, Hasenfeld Y. 1997. *We the People: Work, Poverty and Welfare.* New Haven: Yale Univ. Press

Harris KM. 1993. Work and welfare among single mothers in poverty. *Am. J. Sociol.* 99:317–52

Harris KM. 1996. Life after welfare: women, work, and repeat dependency. *Am. Sociol. Rev.* 61:407–26

Hasenfeld Y, Weaver D. 1996. Enforcement, compliance, and disputes in welfare-to-work

programs. *Soc. Serv. Rev.* 70(2):235–55

Heckman J. 1979. Sample selection as a specification error. *Econometrica* 47:1251–71

Hershey AM, Pavetti L. 1997. Turning job finders into job keepers: the challenge of sustaining employment. *The Future of Children* 7 (1):74–86

Holcomb P, Pavetti L, Ratcliffe C, Reidinger S. 1998. *Building an Employment Focused Welfare System: Work First and Other Work-Oriented Strategies in Five States.* The Urban Institute, Washington, DC

Holzer H. 1996. *What Employers Want: Job Prospects for Less-Educated Workers.* New York: Russell Sage

Holzer H. 1999a. Will employers hire welfare recipients? Recent survey evidence from Michigan. *J. Policy Anal. Manage.* 18 (3):449–72

Holzer H. 1999b. Will employers hire welfare recipients? *Focus* 20(2):26–30

Holzer H, Danziger S. 1998. *Are Jobs Available for Disadvantaged Workers in Urban Areas?* Institute for Research on Poverty Discussion Paper No. 1157:98. Univ. Wisconsin–Madison

Jung J, Magrabi FM. 1991. Work experience, specific human capital, and earnings. *Q. Rev. Econ. Business.* pp. 15–27

Kalil A, Corcoran M, Danziger SK, Tolman R, Seefeldt K, et al. 1998. *Getting Jobs, Keeping Jobs, and Earning a Living Wage: Can Welfare Reform Work?* Institute for Research on Poverty Discussion Paper No. 1170-98. Univ. Wisconsin-Madison

Kane T. 1990. *The Caseworker-Client Relationship and Welfare Reform.* Paper #H-90-9, Malcolm Wiener Center for Social Policy, John F. Kennedy School of Government, Harvard Univ., Boston

Kane T, Bane MJ. 1994. The context for welfare reform. See Bane & Ellwood 1994, pp. 1–24

Katz MB. 1986. *In the Shadow of the Poorhouse.* New York: Basic Books

Lehman J, Danziger S. 1997. Turning our backs

on the New Deal: the end of welfare in 1996. Univ. Michigan, Ann Arbor, unpublished manuscript

Levenson AR, Reardon E, Schmidt SR. 1999. *Welfare, Jobs, and Basic Skills: The Employment Prospects of Welfare Recipients in the Most Populous US Counties,* National Center for the Study of Adult Learning and Literacy, Washington, DC

Levine PB, Whitmore DM. 1998. The impact of welfare reform on the AFDC caseload. *Natl. Tax J. Proceedings of the National Tax Association's Nineteeth (1997) Annual Conference,* Washington, DC: National Tax Association, pp. 24–30

Light A, Ureta M. 1995. Early career interruptions and gender wage differentials. *J. Labor Econ.* 80:293–98

Lin LY. 1999. Welfare benefits, employment and unemployment spells. Univ. Connecticut, Storrs, unpublished manuscript

Loeb S, Corcoran M. 1999. Welfare, work experience, and economic self-sufficiency. Stanford Univ., Stanford, CA, unpublished manuscript

Loprest P. 1992. Gender differences in wage growth and job mobility. *Am. Econ. Rev.* 82:526–32

Loprest P. 1999. *Families Who Left Welfare: Who Are They And How Are They Doing?* The Urban Institute, Washington, DC

Lurie I. 1996. A lesson from the JOBS program: Reforming welfare must be both dazzling and dull. *J. Public Policy Manage.* 15(4):572–86

Maloy K, Pavetti L, Shin P, Darnell J, Scarpulla-Nolan L. 1998. *Description and Assessment of State Approaches to Diversion Programs and Activities Under Welfare Reform: An Interim Report of the Findings of the First Phase of the Research.* Assistant Secretary for Planning and Evaluation, Administration for Children and Families, US. Department of Health and Human Services

Mead LM. 1986. *Beyond Entitlement.* New York: Free Press

Mead LM. 1992. *The New Politics of Poverty.* New York: Basic Books

Mead LM. 1997. *The New Paternalism: Supervisory Approaches to Poverty.* Washington, DC: Brookings Institution Press

Meyers M, Glaser B, MacDonald K. 1998. On the front lines of welfare delivery: Are workers implementing policy reforms? *J. Policy Anal. Manage.* 17(1):1–22

Mincer J, Polachek S. 1974. Family investments in human capital: earnings of women. *J. Hum. Resourc.* 13:118–34

Moffitt R, Rangarajan A. 1989. The effect of transfer programs in work effort and human capital formation: evidence from the US. In *The Economics of Social Security,* ed. A Dilmot, I Walker, pp. 116–36. Oxford Univ. Press

Murray C. 1993. Welfare and the family: the US experience. *J. Labor Econ.* 11(1):S224–S262

Nightingale D, Haveman R, ed. 1995. *The Work Alternative: Welfare Reform and the Realities of the Job Market.* Washington, DC: The Urban Institute Press. 234 pp.

Nightingale D, Pindus N. 1997. *Privatization of public social services: a background paper.* The Urban Institute, Washington, DC

Nightingale DS, Wissoker D, Burbridge LC, Bawden DL, Jeffries N. 1990. *Evaluation of the Massachusetts Employment and Training Program.* Report 94-1. The Urban Institute, Washington, D.C.

Novak M, Cogan J, Bernstein B, Besharov DJ, Blum B, et al. 1987. *The New Consensus on Family and Welfare.* Washington, DC: American Enterprise Institute

Olson K, Pavetti L. 1996. *Personal and Family Challenges to the Successful Transition from Welfare to Work.* The Urban Institute, Washington, DC

O'Neill J. 1999. *Hearing on the Effects of Welfare Reform.* Testimony Before the Subcommittee on Human Resources of the House Committee on Ways and Means. http://www.house.gov/ways_means/humres/106cong/5-27-99/5-27 onei.htm

Orthner D, Neenan P. 1996. Children's impact on stress and employability of mothers in poverty. *J. Fam. Issues* 17:667–87

Osborne D, Gaebler T. 1992. *Reinventing Government: How the Entrepreneurial Spirit is Transforming the Public Sector.* New York: Plume Books

Parker L. 1994. The role of workplace support in facilitating self-sufficiency among single mothers on welfare. *Fam. Relations* 43:168–73

Pavetti L. 1993. *The Dynamics of Welfare and Work: Exploring the Process by Which Women Work Their Way off Welfare.* PhD dissertation, Harvard University

Pavetti L. 1999. How much more can they work? *Focus* 20(2):16–19

Pavetti L, Duke AE. 1995. *Increasing Participation in Work and Work-Related Activities: Lessons from Five State Welfare Reform Demonstration Projects.* The Urban Institute, Washington, DC

Pavetti L, Acs G. 1997 *Moving Up, Moving Out, or Going Nowhere? A study of the Employment Patterns of Young Women and the Implications for Welfare Reform.* The Urban Institute, Washington, DC

Pindus N, Capps R, Gallagher J, Giannerelli L, Saunders M, Smith R. 1998. *Income Support and Social Services for Low-Income People in Texas, Assessing the New Federalism State Reports.* The Urban Institute, Washington, DC

Primus W. 1999. *Hearing on the Effects of Welfare Reform.* Testimony Before the Subcommittee on Human Resources of the House Committee on Ways and Means. http://www.house.gov/ways_means/humres/106cong/5-27-99/5-27prim.htm

Primus W, Rawlings L, Larin K, Porter K. 1999. *The Initial Impact of Welfare Reform on the Incomes of Single-Mother Families.* Center for Budget and Policy Priorities, Washington, DC

Quint J, Musick J, Ladner J. 1994. *Lives of Promise, Lives of Pain: Young Mothers After New Chance.* Manpower Demonstration Research Corp. New York

Rangarajan A, Burghardt J, Gordon A. 1992. *Evaluation of the Minority Female Single Parent Demonstration: Technical Supplement to the Analysis of Economic Impacts, vol. II.* Mathematica Policy Research, Princeton, NJ

Rapheal J. 1996. *Domestic Violence: Telling the Untold Welfare-to-Work Story.* Taylor Institute, Chicago

Regenstein M, Meyer JA, Hicks JD. 1998. *Job Prospects for Welfare Recipients: Employers Speak Out.* The Urban Institute, Washington, DC

Riccio J, Freedman S. 1995. *Can They All Work? A Study of the Employment Potential of Welfare Recipients in a Welfare-to-Work Program, working paper.* Manpower Demonstration Research Corp., New York

Riccio J, Hasenfeld Y. 1996. Enforcing a participation mandate in a welfare-to-work program. *Soc. Serv. Rev.* 70(4):517–42

Rolston H. 1999. *Hearing on the Effects of Welfare Reform.* Testimony Before the Subcommittee on Human Resources of the House Committee on Ways and Means. http://www.house.gov/ways_means/humres/106cong/5-27-99/5-27rols.htm

Sandford J. 1997. *Peering into the "Black Box": A Study of Front-Line Organizations Implementing Welfare Policy in Michigan.* PhD thesis. Univ. Michigan, Ann Arbor

Seefeldt KS, Sandfort J, Danziger SK. 1998. *Moving Toward a Vision of Family Independence: Local Managers' Views of Michigan's Welfare Reforms.* Program on Poverty and Social Welfare Policy, Univ. Michigan, Ann Arbor

Seefeldt KS, Danziger SK, Anderson N. 1999. *What FIA Directors Have to Say About Welfare Reform.* Program on Poverty and Social Welfare Policy, Univ. Michigan, Ann Arbor

Stratton LS. 1995. The effect interruptions in work experience have on wages. *South. Econ. J.* 61:955–70

Super D, Parrott S, Steinmetz S, Mann C. 1996. *The New Welfare Law.* Center on Budget and Policy Priorities, Washington, DC

Thornton C, Hershey A. 1990. *After REACH: Experience of AFDC Recipients Who Leave Welfare with a Job.* Mathematica Policy Research, Princeton, NJ

Tweedie J, Reichert D, O'Conner M. 1999. *Tracking Recipients After They Leave Welfare.* National Conference of State Legislatures, Denver

US Department of Health and Human Services, Administration for Children and Families. 1999. Temporary assistance for needy families (TANF) 1936–1999. *US Welfare Caseload Data.* http://www.acf.dhhs.gov/news/tables.htm

Wallace G, Blank RM. 1999. What goes up must come down? Explaining recent changes in public assistance caseloads. See Danziger 1999

Walters J. 1999. Beyond the welfare clock. *Governing* 12(7):20–26

Wellington A. 1993. Changes in the male/female wage gap, 1976–85. *J. Hum. Resourc.* 28:383–411

Wilson WJ. 1996. *When Work Disappears.* New York: Knopf

Wilson WJ. 1987. *The Truly Disadvantaged: The Underclass, the Inner City, and Public Policy.* Chicago: Univ. Chicago Press

Wiseman M. 1993. Welfare reform in the states: the Bush legacy. *Focus* 15 (1):18–36

Ziliak JP, Figlio DN, Davis EE, Connolly LS. 1997. *Accounting for the Decline in AFDC Caseloads: Welfare Reform or Economic Growth?* Institute for Research on Poverty Discussion Paper No. 1151-97, Univ. Wisconsin–Madison

Annu. Rev. Sociol. 2000. 26:271–96

FERTILITY AND WOMEN'S EMPLOYMENT IN INDUSTRIALIZED NATIONS

Karin L. Brewster
Department of Sociology and Center for the Study of Population, Florida State University, Tallahassee, Florida 32306-2270; e-mail: Brewster@coss.fsu.edu

Ronald R. Rindfuss
Department of Sociology and Carolina Population Center, CB 8120, University of North Carolina, Chapel Hill, North Carolina 27510-3997; e-mail: Ron_Rindfuss@unc.edu

Key Words   fertility, female labor force participation, industrialized nations, work-family issues, public policy

■ **Abstract**

INTRODUCTION

Thirty years ago, Bumpass & Westoff (1970:95) asked, "Do women limit their fertility in order to have time to pursue their nonfamily-oriented interests, or do women work if their fertility permits them to do so?" In the ensuing decades, sociologists, demographers, and economists have learned much about the relationship between fertility and women's employment, and yet the answer to this fundamental question remains elusive. Even so, women's labor force behavior lies at the heart of most explanations of fertility and fertility change, and many nations, both industrialized and developing, have formulated policies based on the inverse association between these two central aspects of women's lives.

The association between fertility and women's labor force activity reflects the incompatibility between caring for children and participating in economically productive work that typifies industrialized societies (Weller 1977). Prior to industrialization, work and child rearing tasks could be performed more or less simultaneously. In historical and contemporary preindustrial societies, nonmechanized agricultural tasks and piecework could be combined with child supervision with relatively little danger to the child or marked loss of economic productivity (Degler 1980, Roos 1985, Stycos & Weller 1967). As industrialization proceeded, however, childcare and economically productive work became increasingly incompatible. Today, work sites are usually some distance from home, and work schedules, set by employers, lack the flexibility required by children. The presence of children at the work site, whether an office or factory, would jeopardize productivity; moreover, mechanical and electronic equipment may pose considerable danger to young children. Thus, women—and it is women who typically care for children—who wish to participate in the labor force must either limit their fertility or make alternative arrangements for the care of their children.

Increasingly, women in advanced industrialized societies are choosing both strategies. As a result, fertility rates in most countries are below the level needed for population replacement, and a rising proportion of children are in nonmaternal care while their mothers work. Concern with endemic low fertility and rising rates of nonmaternal care has stimulated considerable interest among researchers and policy makers in the relationship between childbearing and women's employment, and in the impact that paid childcare and various policy measures have on this relationship. This essay is a synthesis of recent European and American research on the linkages between fertility and female labor force participation in the countries of the European Union, the United States, Canada, Australia, and Japan. Research on the newly industrialized countries of Asia falls into a somewhat different literature and is not reviewed here.

Because the terminology used in this body of literature can be ambiguous, varying across articles and data sources, our review begins by fixing terms. We then summarize recent trends in fertility and in female labor force participation. The core of the essay comprises a discussion of the research concerning, first, the relationship between fertility and labor force activity at the individual level, and, second, the structural underpinnings of role incompatibility. We close by commenting on the implications of recent research for theoretical models of fertility.

TERMINOLOGY

Fertility is the least ambiguous of the major concepts we discuss. It refers simply to giving birth (a live birth as opposed to a stillbirth) and is biologically limited to females between menarche and menopause. Note that we use the terms fertility and childbearing interchangeably. The primary measure of fertility referred to in this essay is the *total fertility rate (TFR)*, an estimate of the number of children a woman would bear, if she survives to the end of her reproductive years and if the schedule of age-specific birth rates remains constant over her reproductive lifetime (Palmore & Gardner 1983). Although theories of fertility and fertility change are typically formulated in terms of the combined effects of period and cohort influences (Hirschman 1994), the TFR is typically calculated from period data, in part because they are more easily and immediately accessed than cohort data (Andersson 1999, Ní Bhrólchain 1992). A key concept is *replacement level fertility*, the level of births needed to ensure the replacement of the biological mother and father in the next generation. A replacement level TFR is just over two, to offset those children who do not survive to reproduce.

It is not childbearing per se but child rearing, the process of caring for and raising a child from birth to adulthood, that leads to the negative relationship between fertility and labor force participation (Bernhardt 1993). The time and attention demands of child rearing are highest during infancy and the preschool years, when children require constant supervision. We use the terms *child rearing* and *caretaking* interchangeably to refer to the supervisory aspects of raising a child. This usage is not intended to imply that child rearing involves only or even primarily supervision; rather, supervision, not the other aspects of parenting, is central to much of the research reviewed here. Child rearing is sometimes referred to as the "mother role" because, historically, mothers have assumed responsibility for raising children. Nevertheless, the supervisory aspects of the "mother role" can be—and increasingly are—performed by others.

By *work*, we refer to market work, that is, work for pay. As used here, then, work does not include the unpaid domestic labor, usually performed by women (Spain & Bianchi 1996: Table 7.4; see also Gershuny & Robinson 1988), which keeps most households functioning. Work is typically indexed at the individual level as *hours worked*, whether part-time (fewer than 35 hours per week) or full-time (more than 35 hours per week), although some studies assess work plans or the time elapsed between birth and return to the labor force. In the aggregate, women's work behavior is usually measured as the *female labor force participation rate*, the proportion of the female population between the ages of approximately 16 and 65 who are either working for pay or seeking paid employment. Finally, *career* refers to a sequence of jobs or positions that entail increasing responsibility along with rising income; such jobs typically have specific educational requirements. Noncareer type jobs, in contrast, require relatively little training, have a flatter age-earnings profile, and offer fewer prospects for mobility.

TRENDS

In describing trends in fertility and female labor force participation, we focus on the years since 1965. Comparable data on both variables are available for most industrialized nations at multiple time points throughout this period. Further, by 1965, the European and Japanese economies had largely recovered from World War II, and the unusually high fertility that characterized the United States, Canada, Australia, and various European countries after World War II had come to an end.

Fertility

Table 1 shows the trends in the TFR for Japan, Australia, Canada, the United States, and selected European countries. In 1965, the fertility of all of these countries was above replacement level; by 1998, all had below-replacement fertility levels. The period between 1998 and 1965 shows considerable variation across countries, indicating the different routes to below-replacement fertility. Of the

TABLE 1   Trends in total fertility rates for selected countries, 1965–1998

Country	1965	1970	1975	1980	1985	1990	1996	1998
Canada	3.1	2.3	1.8	1.9	1.8	1.7	1.7	1.6
United States	2.9	2.5	1.8	1.8	1.8	2.0	2.1	2.0
Australia	3.0	2.9	2.2	2.1	1.9	1.8	1.8	1.8
Japan	2.1	2.1	1.9	1.8	1.7	1.6	1.4	1.4
Austria	2.7	2.3	1.8	1.6	1.7	1.4	1.4	1.4
Belgium	2.6	2.3	1.7	1.7	1.6	1.6	1.5	1.6
Denmark	2.5	2.0	1.9	1.7	1.4	1.8	1.8	1.8
Finland	2.4	1.8	1.7	1.7	1.6	1.6	1.8	1.7
France	2.8	2.5	1.9	1.9	1.9	1.8	1.7	1.7
Germany						1.3	1.4	1.3
East	2.5	2.2	1.5	1.8	1.7	1.7	—	—
West	2.5	2.0	1.5	1.4	1.3	1.4	—	—
Greece	2.2	2.4	2.4	2.3	2.1	1.5	1.3	1.3
Iceland	3.7	2.8	2.6	2.3	2.2	2.3	2.2	2.0
Ireland	4.0	3.9	3.4	3.4	3.0	2.2	1.9	1.9
Italy	2.5	2.4	2.2	1.9	1.6	1.3	1.2	1.2
Luxembourg	2.3	2.0	1.6	1.5	1.6	1.4	1.8	1.8
Netherlands	3.0	2.6	1.7	1.6	1.5	1.5	1.5	1.5
Norway	2.9	2.5	2.0	1.8	1.7	1.8	1.9	1.8
Spain	2.9	2.9	2.8	2.6	2.0	1.5	1.2	1.2
Sweden	2.4	1.9	1.8	1.7	1.6	2.0	1.6	1.6
Switzerland	2.6	2.1	1.6	1.5	1.6	1.6	1.5	1.5
United Kingdom	2.7	2.4	1.8	1.7	1.8	1.8	1.8	1.8

Source: 1965–1975 figures from World Bank, 1984. 1980–1998 figures from Population Reference Bureau *World Data Sheet*, selected years.

21 countries listed in Table 1, only eight moved steadily toward lower fertility. Of these eight, two—Ireland and Iceland—did not reach below-replacement rates until 1996 and 1998, respectively. Notably, Greece, Italy, and Spain, which had above-replacement rates through the late 1980s, have sustained since 1995 the lowest levels of fertility recorded in any western country. Germany, too, has very low fertility; however, its current TFR reflects a continuation of the below-replacement levels characterizing the former Federal Republic of Germany and the dramatically lower fertility rates (less than one child per woman) in the former German Democratic Republic that followed reunification (Hooper 1999, Monnier & de Guibert-Lantoine 1993, Witte and Wagner 1995).

Cross-national differences in the demographic behaviors that determine fertility, including trends in first birth timing, birth spacing, and nuptiality (i.e., marriage patterns), underlie the aggregate variation in fertility levels and trends. A closer look at a few countries reveals the importance of each of these factors. In Japan, for example, where nonmarital births account for about 1% of all births, the substantial drop in fertility since 1975 is related to the avoidance or postponement of marriage among Japanese women (Tsuya & Mason 1995). Decreasing fertility in Ireland, Italy, and Spain also reflects marriage patterns (Pinnelli 1995), although the remarkable drop in Irish fertility over the past several decades and the exceedingly low fertility rates of the Mediterranean countries are due as well to a decrease in the number of children married women bear (Bettio & Villa 1998, Sporton 1993).

In much of western and northern Europe, where nonmarital fertility rates have risen substantially over the past three decades (Kuïjsten 1996, van de Kaa 1987), nuptiality is less strongly related to fertility levels. Even with the increases in nonmarital fertility, however, the total fertility rate has remained low, reflecting declining birth rates among women in their twenties (Lesthaeghe & Willems 1999, Sporton 1993). Spacing, the time between births, also has had a significant impact on fertility in the Nordic countries and in the United States. In Sweden, for example, period fertility rates received a boost in the early 1990s from the more rapid pacing of second births (Hoem 1996, Hoem & Hoem 1997), while in the United States, the lower fertility rates of the past several decades reflect a dramatic slowing in the transition to second and third births (Morgan 1996). Researchers have linked all of these factors—birth timing and spacing, nonmarital childbearing, and nuptiality—to women's labor force activities.

Female Labor Force Participation

Table 2 shows trends in female labor force participation rates in the 21 countries from 1965 through 1996, the most recent year for which data are available. Participation rates in all 21 countries were higher, sometimes substantially, in 1996 than in 1965. By 1996, only four countries had rates lower than 50%, whereas in 1965, 12 of the 14 countries for which data are available had rates less than 50%.

As with fertility, national trend lines vary substantially. Only 10 countries experienced steady increases between 1965 and 1990; of these, six continued to show rising rates of participation through 1996 while four experienced decreases. Three countries—Ireland, Spain, and Greece—had rather stagnant participation rates prior to 1980, followed by a 16-year period of sustained increase. In Italy, participation rates have fluctuated at a moderately low level, perhaps a reflection in part of continuing economic uncertainties (Chesnais 1996).

In describing the evolution in women's labor force activity in the post-World War II period in the industrialized world, Jensen (1995) relies on a metaphor of three "waves." During the 1950s—the first wave—the roles of mother and paid worker were separate for most women. The second wave, during the 1960s and 1970s, saw an increasing proportion of women integrating the mother and worker

TABLE 2   Trends in female labor force participation rates for selected countries, 1965–1996

Country	1965	1970	1975	1980	1985	1990	1996
Canada	39.6[a]	43.2	50.0	57.2	62.6	68.1	64.9
United States	44.3	48.9	53.1	59.7	63.9	68.2	71.0
Australia	39.8	45.1	49.3	52.7	54.1	62.1	64.9
Japan	55.8	55.3	51.7	54.9	57.2	60.4	62.2
Austria	—	49.2	47.6	48.7	51.0	55.4	62.1
Belgium	38.0	40.0	43.9	48.2	50.5	52.4	56.1
Denmark	49.3	58.0	63.5	69.9	74.5	78.4	74.1
Finland	62.6	62.5	65.6	70.1	73.5	72.9	70.5
France	—	48.2	50.5	54.3	55.0	56.6	59.9
Germany							61.0
East	—	—	—	—	—	—	
West	49.0	48.1	49.6	50.0	50.4	55.8[b]	—
Greece	—	32.1	30.8	33.0	41.8	43.5[c]	45.9
Iceland	—	44.7	45.1	—	—	—	80.0[d]
Ireland	35.2[a]	34.3	34.5	36.3	36.6	38.9	49.4
Italy	34.6	29.6	30.7	39.6	40.8	44.5	43.2
Luxembourg	—	33.8	38.3	39.9	43.2	47.2[c]	57.5
Netherlands	—	30.3	32.0	35.4	41.2	53.0	58.3
Norway	36.9	38.8	53.3	63.2	68.3	71.2	66.0
Spain	—	29.2	32.4	31.9	33.6	40.9	46.2
Sweden	54.1	59.4	67.6	74.1	78.2	81.1	73.7
Switzerland	51.7	51.4	51.7	54.1	53.2	59.2	67.1
United Kingdom	49.0	50.5	55.3	58.3	60.1	65.1	66.4

Source: All figures from OECD Labour Force Statistics, volumes from 1965 through 1997. Note that these rates are computed as the ratio of the female labor force of all ages to the female population aged 15–64. The numerator includes full- and part-time workers as well as those seeking employment. Endnotes: (a) 1966 (b) 1989 (c) 1988 (d) 1994

roles, albeit on a part-time basis or sequentially. The third wave, which began in the 1980s, comprises an increase in full-time, continuous labor force participation, even among mothers with preschool age children. As Jensen (1995:224) notes: "In the course of one generation, women's employment has gradually expanded . . . from quitting a job when marrying, to quitting when having a first child, and finally to today's expectation that women will take their share in providing for the economic needs of the family by interrupting employment only during maternity leaves." These changes reflect numerous factors, including the rising demand for female labor; an increasing preference among women for nondomestic roles; the rising opportunity costs of homemaking as women's real wages rose; falling real wages for men, particularly those in the lower middle and working classes; and rising consumption aspirations (Chafetz 1995, England & Farkas 1986, Hoem & Hoem 1989, Reskin & Padavic 1994).

This pattern describes reasonably well trends in western and northern Europe (Jensen 1995) and the United States (Spain & Bianchi 1996). There are exceptions, however. In Japan, where female labor force participation rates have long exceeded 50%, marriage continues to mark the start of a lengthy time-out from paid work for most women (White 1996). In 1995, a graph of women's age-specific participation rates reveals an M-shaped pattern, with peaks in the early 20s and the late 40s, and a deep trough between, during the peak childbearing and child-rearing years (Ogasawara 1998: Figure 2). This pattern, typical of countries in Jensen's second wave, characterizes Ireland, too, although here the M is lopsided as relatively few women reenter the paid labor force after childbearing (Pyle 1990).

The age-participation profiles of Ireland and Japan suggest that, in these countries, the roles of paid worker and mother are performed sequentially rather than simultaneously. This situation likely reflects longstanding and highly ingrained norms about the family and women's roles. It is possible that the strong hold of these norms may continue into the foreseeable future. Indeed, the stability of the age-participation profile in Japan, despite more than three decades of relatively high labor force participation rates and a constitutional guarantee of equal rights for women, suggests a continuation of this pattern. But it is also possible that the lack of role integration women now experience in some countries will succumb to exogenous pressures for change. In their examination of Japan, for example, Tsuya & Mason (1995) suggest that sustained below-replacement fertility levels and the prospect of eventual population decline may stimulate policy changes that allow women to fill simultaneously the mother and worker roles.

The Relationship Between Fertility Trends and Trends in Female Labor Force Participation

Translating the maternal role incompatibility hypothesis (Stycos & Weller 1967) into a hypothesis about trends over time would suggest that fertility levels will fall as female labor force participation rates rise because of the difficulties of accommodating the demands of child rearing to the requisites of employment. While this may once have been the case, there is now evidence that the relationship between these variables may be more complicated than this hypothesis predicts (Bernhardt 1993, Bettio & Villa 1998, Rindfuss et al 2000, Rindfuss & Brewster 1996, Sundström & Stafford 1991). Even a cursory comparison of Tables 1 and 2 indicates that the countries that now have the lowest levels of fertility are those with relatively low levels of female labor force participation and that countries with higher fertility levels tend to have relatively high labor force participation rates.

A positive association between fertility levels and female labor force participation rates has been suggested by several authors (Bernhardt 1993, Pinnelli 1995, Rindfuss & Brewster 1996). Subsequent work has shown that this positive association is a recent development; just two decades ago, the country-level correlation between fertility and female labor force participation rates was negative (Bettio & Villa 1998, Rindfuss et al 2000). Figure 1 illustrates this change for the 21 countries shown in Tables 1 and 2. Panel *a* graphs the relationship between total fertility rates

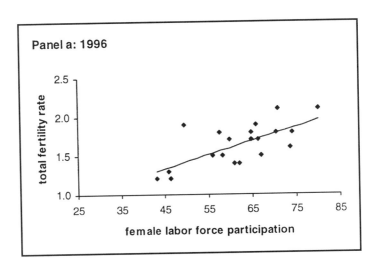

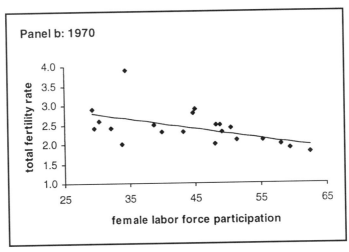

Figure 1 Relationship between female labor force participation rates and total fertility rates: 1995 and 1970.

and rates of female labor force participation in 1996. The regression line shows a strong positive relationship (r = .714, p < .001) between fertility and women's labor force activity; fertility rates tend to be higher in those countries with high rates of female labor force participation. Prior to the transition of most countries to the "third wave," however, the aggregate-level relationship was consistent with the maternal role incompatibility hypothesis, as shown in Panel *b*, which illustrates the fertility-employment relationship for the same set of countries in 1970. Then, the relationship was negative (r = −.517, p < .001); fertility rates were highest in those countries with the lowest fertility levels and vice versa.

What accounts for this reversal? Note that the relative positions of most countries have changed little. Sweden, Finland, Denmark, and the United States, for example, are clustered at the right-hand side of both panels, while Italy, Spain, and Greece are grouped at the left-hand side. Fertility in the former group barely changed from one time point to the next, even though the proportion of women in the labor force increased by an average of 15%. In contrast, fertility in the latter group declined by more than 1 child per woman, in the face of increases in participation rates similar in magnitude to those in the United States and northern Europe. This comparison suggests that, in some countries during the past quarter century, women have found ways to combine work and child rearing, and in other countries they have not. Where they have not, as in the Mediterranean countries, fertility has declined substantially. Thus, a viable explanation of the fertility-employment relationship must consider the social, economic, and policy contexts within which women make their work and fertility decisions. We return to this point below, after reviewing recent research bearing on the current relationship between fertility and female labor force participation.

ISSUES OF CAUSALITY AT THE INDIVIDUAL LEVEL

There is no question that, at the individual level, a negative association characterizes the relationship between fertility and female labor force participation. Women who work for pay have fewer children, on average, than women who do not, and mothers spend less time in paid employment, on average, than childless women. Four possible explanations for this association are: Women's fertility influences their labor force behavior; women's labor force behavior influences their fertility; a reciprocal relationship exists between the two variables; and the negative association is spurious, reflecting other factors (Cramer 1980, Weller 1977). Much evidence supports the first three models; the fourth model, advocated more often by economists (e.g. Macunovich 1996) than sociologists, has proven more difficult to support. Because the evidence has been reviewed previously by sociologists, demographers, and economists in the United States and elsewhere (Bernhardt 1993, Lehrer & Nerlove 1986, Macunovich 1996, Reskin & Padavic 1994, Spitze 1988), we focus here on recent findings, with any eye toward cross-national comparisons.

The Effects of Fertility on Labor Force Participation

The presence of children and their ages influence whether women participate in the paid labor force and, if they do, the nature of this participation. Indeed, women's work patterns are strongly tied to changes in their family status (Ellingsæter & Rønsen 1996, Rindfuss et al 1999, Rosenfeld 1996). Most employed women leave paid work for some period of time around a birth. The duration of nonworking periods varies among women and across countries, depending on leave policies, fiscal incentives, and childcare availability.

In Japan and Ireland, where norms dictate intensive maternal involvement in children's care and education, new mothers typically leave the labor force for prolonged periods, averaging a decade or more (Ogasawara 1998, Pyle 1990). German women also tend to leave the labor force for extended periods following a birth, encouraged by fiscal incentives, a serious shortage of childcare, and school-day schedules that vary by the age of the child (Huinink & Mayer 1995, Ondrich & Spiess 1998, Schiersman 1991).

In contrast, in the United States and the Scandinavian countries, where childcare is more readily available, the labor force participation rates of new mothers and the mothers of preschoolers are quite high, although most women in these countries take some leave (Desai & Waite 1991, Ellingsæter & Rønsen 1996, Jensen 1995, Klerman & Leibowitz 1994, 1999). In the Scandinavian countries, where employers must offer paid leave to new mothers (and new fathers), leave typically lasts from four months to about one year (Ellingsæter & Rønsen 1996, Bernhardt 1986). In the United States, maternal leaves average about twenty weeks and are typically unpaid (Waldfogel 1998); moreover, the rate of return is quite rapid: 40% of women are back at work within three months and 86% are back within a year (Desai & Waite 1991).

There are, of course, differences both within and between countries with respect to who leaves paid work, who returns, and when. Marital status and the presence of another adult in the household, whether a spouse, a partner, or someone else, are significant factors. In Sweden, unmarried mothers are less likely than married mothers to stay at home in the year following a birth; if they do take time off, they return to work at a faster rate (Bernhardt 1986). In the United States, it is married women and women who have another adult in the household who exit more slowly and return more quickly (Wenk & Garrett 1992); unmarried women are more likely to leave paid employment early in pregnancy and are less likely to return to work in the first three months following a birth (Desai & Waite 1991). Likewise, in Japan, young mothers living in three-generation households have shorter labor force exits, presumably because the grandmother is providing childcare (Morgan & Hiroshima 1983, Choe et al 1999).

The age and presence of other children also appear to influence leave patterns. In the United States, the presence of other preschool children has no effect on the rate at which new mothers return to work (Wenk & Garrett 1992). In Sweden, however, where parental leave and fiscal benefits are tied to the spacing of births, new mothers who have children younger than three years of age have delayed returns to paid employment (Oláh 1999). Similarly, in Norway, having two or more preschoolers inhibits women's return to the paid labor force (Ellingsæter & Rønsen 1996).

Educational background is another determinant of leave and labor force exit patterns. In most countries, women who are well-educated or who hold jobs that require lengthy training periods are less likely to leave paid work; if they do, they return to work more quickly (Bernhardt 1986, Desai & Waite 1991, Ellingsæter & Rønsen 1996, Klerman & Leibowitz 1999, Wenk & Garrett 1992). This finding, which is robust across data sets and time periods, likely reflects the strong link between education and career orientation.

When mothers return to work after paid leave or after a labor force exit, they often do so on a part-time basis, in an attempt to ease the work-parenting conflict. Although part-time employment may be more compatible with child rearing responsibilities, in some countries the costs of part-time employment are considerable. In the United States, for example, mothers who return to work on a part-time basis lose pay, seniority, and, often, benefits and job security (Corcoran et al 1984). In contrast, in Sweden and Norway, part-time workers enjoy the same employment rights and benefits as full-time workers, and part-time positions are available not only in marginal jobs but also in professional positions (Ellingsæter & Rønsen 1996, Hoem 1995, Sundström 1991). It is not surprising, then, that the likelihood of part-time employment among the mothers of preschoolers varies markedly across countries. In Norway, Sweden, and Denmark—all countries with high levels of labor market regulation—between 40% and 50% of the mothers of preschoolers work on a part-time basis (Hoem 1995, Jensen 1995, Stier et al 1998). Where part-time workers are marginalized, however, as in the United States, Canada, and Britain, levels of part-time employment among new mothers are roughly half those found in the Scandinavian countries (Rosenfeld & Birkelund 1995, Stier et al 1998).

A final factor that may mediate the impact of fertility on employment is the specific characteristics of the actual job. While job characteristics have yet to be linked to fertility per se, they are related to the timing of work exits and re-entry (Desai & Waite 1991). Moreover, jobs vary substantially in the extent to which they are compatible with caring for a child (Glass & Camarigg 1992). A few jobs allow paid work and childcare to be performed simultaneously. Jobs in the childcare industry presumably enable mothers to care for their own children while also supervising other children (Connelly 1992). Piecework and other work that can be performed in the home are additional examples. Shift work and jobs with flexible schedules can make it easier to coordinate childcare responsibilities with the father, grandparent, or some other relative (Presser 1989).

The Effects of Labor Force Participation on Fertility

In many industrialized countries, the impact of childbearing on labor force behavior tends to be relatively short-term, ending when the youngest child reaches school age, if not sooner. Over the long run, however, the causal relationship between fertility and labor force participation may be stronger in the opposite direction, with labor force participation and participation plans inhibiting fertility (Waite & Stolzenberg 1976, Hout 1978, Smith-Lovin & Tickameyer 1978). Although the nonrecursive models on which this finding is based have been criticized for their statistical shortcomings (Cramer 1980),[1] the negative impact of labor force activity on fertility is theoretically well grounded. Labor force participation raises the costs of childbearing in terms of foregone wages; further, time spent in market work reduces the time and energy available for child rearing (Becker 1981, Willis 1973), as well as for leisure. In addition, for women who are pursuing careers, time spent out of the labor force, especially when it occurs early in a career track, negatively affects occupational advancement (Bielby 1992, Rindfuss et al 1999, Rosenfeld 1992, Rosenfeld & Spenner 1992). Not surprisingly, then, women in the paid labor force have fertility levels roughly one-half to one child lower than women who are not labor force participants (Spain & Bianchi 1996, United Nations 1976).

Despite the potential importance of this relationship for our understanding of the likely direction of fertility trends (Rosenfeld 1996), few studies describe the specific mechanisms by which labor force participation lowers fertility. The age at which women first become parents is related to their cumulative fertility, although this relationship appears to be weakening, at least in the United States (Morgan & Rindfuss 1999). Thus, one possible mechanism by which labor force participation may depress fertility is by delaying the transition to parenthood. In Japan, for example, higher educational attainment and labor force participation, in conjunction with women's rejection of traditional domestic roles, appears to be leading to a postponement of parenthood (Tsuya & Mason 1995). Similarly, in the United States, married women who work for pay are more likely than married women who do not to postpone the first birth (Blau & Robins 1988). Such delays may reflect deliberate decisions that take into account the higher opportunity costs of childbearing among women with greater human capital (Rindfuss et al 1996), or simply the cumulative effects of time spent in activities that compete with childbearing, such as education or training, the job search process, and establishing oneself with an employer (Hoem 1996).

Other studies suggest that the negative impact of labor force participation on fertility is more pronounced following the first birth, once women have experienced juggling the demands of work and child rearing. This mechanism was first suggested by Stolzenberg & Waite (1977), who proposed that women become more aware of the conflict between work and child rearing as they get older and gain experience with work or children. Consistent with this "learning hypothesis,"

---

[1] In his review of problems in determining the causal relationship between fertility and female employment, Cramer (1980) observes that weak instrumental variables and the multicollinearity that result from inadequate instruments led to unstable, imprecise estimates in prior studies. More recent observers note the on-going dissatisfaction with simultaneous equation models and the failure of analysts to resolve these issues and, accordingly, questions about causal direction (Lehrer & Nerlove 1986, Spain & Bianchi 1996, Spitze 1988).

White & Kim (1987) reported that women in the United States do not view work as competing with child rearing until *after* they become mothers. It is not surprising, then, that Hoem & Hoem (1989) found that, for Swedish women, second- and third-order birth risk is significantly lower among labor force participants than housewives (Hoem & Hoem 1989). They also reported that the difference in third birth risk between labor force participants and nonparticipants is narrower for more recent cohorts of women, a finding they attribute to the deteriorating economic situation of single-earner families. Their interpretation points to the potentially dynamic nature of the employment-fertility relationship within countries across time, and, in particular, the likelihood that the relationship is mediated by the larger economic and social context—the issue we address in the next section.

INSTITUTIONAL DETERMINANTS OF ROLE INCOMPATIBILITY

Although the relationship between female labor force participation and fertility is negative at the individual level, as we saw above, it is now positive at the national level. Thus, while women in all countries experience difficulty balancing their work and family responsibilities, it is easier to coordinate these responsibilities in some countries than in others (Bernhardt 1993, Ellingsæter & Rønsen 1996, Rindfuss & Brewster 1996). Rindfuss & Brewster (1996:262) argue that role incompatibility mediates the relationship between female labor force participation and fertility, and further, that "the negative association between fertility and labor force participation can be expected to diminish as the conflict between work and family responsibilities is reduced—whether by a change in the nature of work life, shifts in the social organization of childcare, or a combination of the two." Such change can be mandated by the state, or it can occur in the absence of government regulation, as employers respond to evolving labor market conditions. In this section, we review the literature on the structural underpinnings of role incompatibility.

Family Policies and Cash Benefits

In reviewing the family policy literature, it quickly becomes apparent that there are nearly as many ways of classifying family policies as there are authors. Research on family-relevant policies has distinguished explicit from implicit policies; redistributive from pronatalist policies; and universal policies from those that consider financial means, child's age, or family size (Gauthier 1996, Hantrais 1997, Hecht & Leridon 1993). Thus, family policies have wide-ranging goals, from ensuring that household income differences do not translate into markedly inequitable living standards to encouraging larger family sizes. Regardless of intent, all state mandates falling under the rubric of family policy aim to regulate social and economic relations within families as well as between families and other social institutions (Wennemo 1993).

Although all advanced industrial nations make some type of provision for working families, states' orientations toward families and family policies differ markedly (Chesnais 1996, Gauthier 1996, Hantrais 1997, Wennemo 1993). In describing these differences, Chesnais (1996) distinguishes between "nations of families," in which the extended family has primacy in all important life decisions (e.g., marriage and childbearing) and in which family networks typically provide services ranging from childcare to banking, and "nations of individuals," which espouse a strong philosophy of individualism and social equality. This dichotomy provides a convenient summary of national orientations towards the resolution of work-family conflict. Chesnais (1996) observes that policies in "nations of families" take two forms: either they are strongly supportive of families comprising a breadwinner-father, homemaker-mother and their dependent children, as in Germany, or they do little that could be construed as challenging or interfering with the prerogatives of such families, as in Italy. Policies in "nations of individuals," such as Sweden and the United Kingdom, tend to be both supportive of women's rights and concerned with children's living standards; moreover, policies in these countries often recognize a diversity of family forms, not just the breadwinner-homemaker model.

Hantrais (1997) maps such differences in national policy environments onto demographic trends using detailed data on ten aspects of national family policies and Eurobarometer survey results for 15 European Union member states. She finds (1997:373–74) that the European Union countries can be categorized into five combinations of family policy and demographic outcomes. Four of these combinations correspond neatly to Chesnais' (1996) distinction between "nations of families" and "nations of individuals," while illustrating the diversity that is possible within these two groups. There is just one anomaly, Ireland, whose unique combination of demographic characteristics—high birth rates, low marriage rates and no divorce (prior to 1998)—distinguish it from all other European Union members.

The first of Hantrais' combinations, exemplified by the Nordic countries, comprises high rates of female labor force participation, relatively high fertility levels, and policies that are "family friendly" while discouraging the institutionalization of any particular family form. Indeed, Hantrais (1997:363–64) notes that the Nordic states have moved away from policies aimed at the family as a social institution and toward policies that target individuals in families. Such policies are characteristic of Chesnais' "nations of individuals." France and the United Kingdom provide a somewhat weaker illustration of "nations of individuals." Their policies, while grounded in strong traditions of individual rights, continue to institutionalize the family, although they recognize an increasing diversity of family forms. Demographically, France and the United Kingdom have fertility levels and female labor force participation rates that are slightly lower than those of the Nordic countries, but still above the European average. Hantrais (1997:361) describes these countries as "drifting" toward the Nordic model, with respect to both policy and demographic outcomes.

The two remaining combinations represent Chesnais' "nations of families." Austria, Belgium, Germany, the Netherlands, and Luxembourg share a strong commitment toward families, backed by monetary allowances for housing, child benefit packages, and well-paid maternal leave. As Hantrais (1997:373) observes, however, such "family friendly policies have not been matched by high rates of female economic activity among women of childbearing age [nor] . . . high birth rates." This is likely because these policies, which are intended to reify the breadwinner-homemaker family, cannot entirely compensate families for the income lost when mothers leave the labor force. Further, such policies do not accommodate women who wish to both pursue a career and raise children.

The final combination is illustrated by the Mediterranean states, which view the family as a private domain in which the government should not intervene and where consistently low rates of female labor force activity are accompanied by extremely low fertility. The lack of state services, in conjunction with pronounced gender inequality and difficult economic conditions, has created a situation in which women bear the burden of ensuring the welfare of extended family members, precluding labor force participation and limiting the time available for child rearing (Bettio & Villa 1998).

Hantrais' (1997) work suggests the potential importance of family benefits in regulating fertility and female labor force particiaption. Multivariate analyses, however, provide mixed evidence. Higher cash benefits are related to higher fertility, although the effects of such benefits, including housing allowances, tax relief, and child benefits are modest (Blanchet 1987, Ékert-Jaffe 1986, Gauthier 1991, Gauthier & Hatzius 1997, Zhang et al 1994). For example, one recent study, using data from 22 countries over a 20-year time span, estimates that, in the short run, a 25% increase in overall benefit levels would raise fertility by only 0.6%; over the long run, the same increase would raise fertility by just 4% (Gauthier & Hatzius 1997). Whether parental leave—which would seem more closely tied to role incompatibility than cash benefits—enhances either fertility or labor force activity is less clear. Gauthier (1991) reports a positive effect of leave that is particularly pronounced in countries with generous cash benefits and ample childcare facilities. More recently, however, she failed to observe effects of either leave duration or pay rate, once male and female wages, unemployment rates, and cash benefits were controlled (Gauthier & Hatzius 1997).

These findings may say more about the ability of broadly drawn, cross-national indicators to capture the effects of policy differences than they do about the relationship between role incompatibility, fertility, and women's labor force activity, especially given the very small number of countries included in the analyses. Policies with multiple dimensions that cannot be captured by easily constructed measures, such as duration or pay rate, are ill-suited for cross-national analysis. Such analyses are unable to consider the finer details of leave policies or relevant aspects of the larger social context. The implications of this shortcoming are apparent upon a closer look at Germany's leave policy. Germany's maternal leave policy mandates 14 weeks of paid leave at a generous 100% of pre-leave pay (Sundström & Stafford 1991). Leave length and pay rate are easily included in cross-national analyses; less easily incorporated are those aspects of German family policy that encourage new mothers to remain at home for a longer period. For example, mothers who do not return to paid work receive a tax-free childcare allowance for eighteen months. Mothers who return to work sacrifice this benefit unless they agree to work fewer than 19 hours a week; however, employers are under no obligation to provide part-time employment nor must they guarantee mothers returning from maternity leave the same or a comparable job (Schiersman 1991). Further, as we discuss below, Germany has a substantial shortage of child-care, particularly for children ages three and under (Schiersman 1991, Ondrich & Speiss 1998). Such factors, left uncontrolled in statistical analyses, likely obscure the impact on fertility or labor force activity of leave duration and pay rate.

Another approach is country-specific analysis of time-series data. Unfortunately, there are relatively few countries in which the influence of family benefits on fertility and labor supply have been examined in a multivariate framework. Sweden has received the most attention. Sweden mandates 52 weeks of paid leave at 90% of pre-leave pay and an additional 13 weeks at a flat pay rate, explicitly encourages paid employment among women, and encourages a gender-equitable division of household labor and childcare (Hoem 1990). Several multivariate studies indicate that the rise in Swedish period fertility during the late 1980s and early 1990s reflected, at least in part, changes in birth timing and spacing that appear to have been stimulated by newly enacted leave and wage compensation policies (Andersson 1999, Hoem 1993, Oláh 1999, Walker 1994). Likewise, the rising female labor force participation rates, which peaked in the early 1990s, have been attributed to policy provisions, particularly those related to parental leave (Sundström 1991). Although it is too early to tell, it is possible that the recent decline in Sweden's TFR is related to scaling back of its maternity benefits.

The United States provides an instructive counterpoint to Sweden. Fertility and labor force participation rates in the United States have been high over the past two decades relative to other industrialized nations. This is not the result of policies intended to reduce role incompatibility; indeed the United States had no family policy until 1993, when the Family and Medical Leave Act (FMLA) took effect. Prior to the FMLA, most new mothers relied on accumulated sick leave and vacation time or took unpaid leave (Klerman & Leibowitz 1994). Now, women who work for businesses with 50 or more workers are entitled to 12 weeks of job-protected, unpaid leave following the birth or adoption of a child. Although the proportion of the female labor force that is eligible for maternity leave jumped dramatically following the FMLA's enactment (Waldfogel 1999), fewer than half of all private-sector workers are covered. The FMLA has increased both the likelihood of leave among some women not already covered by employer or state policies and leave length among those already covered (Waldfogel 1999). It has not, however, substantially altered postnatal employment rates (Ross 1998), at least in the short term, nor is it likely to have much impact on the work patterns of new mothers over the long run (Klerman & Leibowitz 1999). Thus, while policies may help ease role conflict, as in Sweden, the experiences of the United States indicate that policy interventions are not necessary for relatively high fertility rates to occur along with high rates of female labor force participation.

Childcare Arrangements

Perhaps the most widely used strategy women adopt to assist them in accomodating their family duties to the demands of paid employment is to relinquish responsibility for childcare during the hours they are engaged in market work. Women in economically developed nations rely on a wide range of childcare providers, including fathers and other family members, paid providers, preschools, and, as children age, schools and after-school activities. The degree to which such alternatives influence the association between female labor force participation and fertility depends on norms about child supervision and the availability of providers of acceptable quality at a cost that seems affordable to parents—factors that vary substantially across countries and, within countries, across population subgroups and geographic regions (Rindfuss & Brewster 1996:270–71).

Childcare norms: Norms and attitudes about childcare lie at the heart of the concept of role incompatibility. The incompatibility between women's roles as workers and mothers varies with beliefs about appropriate caregivers and the ages at which children need intensive supervision. In short, the more maternal supervision that norms prescribe, the greater the role incompatibility and, hence, the stronger the negative association between fertility and female labor force activity (Rindfuss & Brewster 1996).

Despite their implications for role incompatibility, norms about child supervision represent an aspect of childcare left unaddressed in most research on the relationship between fertility and women's labor force activity. Consequently, we have no direct information on how childcare norms vary across national contexts or across population subgroups, or the relationship of these norms to fertility or women's labor force participation.[2] Studies of public attitudes toward working mothers provide some insight into child supervision norms, insofar as they indicate the acceptability of nonmaternal care. Available data suggest substantial cross-national differences. For example, Hantrais (1997: Tables 12a, 12b) observes considerable variation in levels of public support for working mothers in the European Union. Further, while her data are incomplete, they suggest a positive correlation between public attitudes on the one hand and both state subsidies for preschool care and female economic activity on the other. Recent studies also indicate that public acceptance of working mothers has increased. In the United States and in the Netherlands, public attitudes toward working mothers have become more positive in recent decades; while rates of change vary across population

---

[2]One problem, of course, is disentangling the relationship between norms and behaviors. While greater reliance on nonmaternal providers may be indicative of norms that are more accepting of nonmaternal care, use-levels also likely reflect the availability and affordability of nonmaternal providers (Rindfuss & Brewster 1996).

subgroups, the trend is universal (Brewster & Padavic 2000, Néve 1995, Rindfuss et al 1996). To the extent that such change is associated with reduced role conflict, it may help explain the concurrence of high rates of fertility and female labor force participation in some countries (Rindfuss et al 1996).

Childcare availability: Reliable and consistent data on childcare availability are difficult to find. International data cover child enrollment in centers receiving at least some state-funded support. While these data are admittedly limited in coverage, they suggest wide cross-national differences in (state supported) child care. In France and Belgium, for example, in 1988, more than 95% of children ages 3 to school age were enrolled in publicly funded daycare institutions, including creches, family daycare centers, and preschools; Italy, Germany, Denmark, and Sweden all reported figures of 80% or higher (Gauthier 1996: Table 10.6, Ondrich & Speiss 1998: Table 1). In contrast, in Japan and Canada, fewer than 20% of children in this age range were enrolled in institutions receiving public support (Gauthier 1996: Table 10.6).

As in the rest of the industrialized world, availability in the United States appears to be better for older preschoolers than for those under age three, although evaluation is complicated by the lack of a centralized registration system and by cross-state differences in care legislation. Survey data indicate that among children of employed mothers, 14% of infants are in child care centers. This figure rises to 21% and 37% for children aged 1–2 and 3–4 respectively (Hofferth 1996). Such a pattern reflects both availability of suitable childcare centers and the preferences of parents.

Related to the availability of care providers is the cost of care. While cross-national comparisons are difficult, it is clear that care is more affordable in some countries than in others. In most European countries, care is publicly funded, at least in part, for children aged three and older. In Sweden and Finland, for example, childcare is state-subsidized; parents pay a nominal fee, depending on income, for care in state-licensed centers or family daycare homes (Mikkola 1991, Sundström 1991). In France, the childcare system is a complex combination of private and public providers, all of which are partly state-subsidized; parents pay from approximately 28% to 90% of the cost of care, depending on provider type (David & Starzec 1991). In none of the English-speaking countries, however, is care subsidized for the majority of parents. In Canada, for example, the federal government withdrew its support for the development of universal childcare services in 1988, after nearly two decades of study and debate (Gauthier 1996). In Australia, Britain, and Ireland, the state encourages employer-sponsored facilities, and provides subsidies only for the poor and near-poor. In the United States, the Family Support Act of 1988 was intended to facilitate employment for mothers of young children by increasing their wages and reducing their childcare costs; however, only the poor are eligible.

While most research on childcare provisions focuses on preschoolers, the structure of the educational system also has implications for role incompatibility; the age at which children start school and the amount of time they spend there can affect the extent of work-family conflict experienced by employed mothers. By way of illustration, we contrast the educational systems of France and Germany. In France, children are in school or school-supervised programs from early morning through mid- to late afternoon on weekdays and Saturday mornings (Rindfuss & Brewster 1996). In Germany, where children can start kindergarten as early as age three, there has been a severe shortage of kindergarten slots; however, the German Parliament has recently passed legislation entitling all children to a slot by 1999 (Ondrich & Spiess 1998). Primary schools run on irregular hours and are in session, by and large, for only half the day; this situation is exacerbated by the paucity of daycare centers that run outside of school hours (Schiersman 1991). The German educational system, like the German family leave and benefits package, serves as an obstacle to women who wish to combine work and child rearing. The French educational system would appear far more friendly to mothers who engage in market work, consistent with the philosophy underlying its family policies.

Research results: While a substantial body of descriptive work on childcare availability and cost exists, there is a paucity of research addressing the impact of childcare constraints on either fertility or female labor force participation. No studies that we know of assess the extent to which such constraints account for variation in fertility and female labor force participation rates, although these factors appear to be correlated. Some individual-level studies suggest that childcare costs and availability influence women's fertility decisions, at least in the United States. Mason & Kuhlthau (1992) report, for example, that 8% of their sample of Detroit-area mothers indicated that problems with childcare costs, availability, or quality led them to have fewer children than they would have had otherwise, and nearly 4% indicated that they had postponed a birth because of childcare problems. For reasons outlined elsewhere (Rindfuss & Brewster 1996), these are likely to be underestimates of the actual effects. Employed women who rely on relatives for care are more likely to intend another birth (Lehrer & Kawasaki 1985), while those who have an additional adult in the household (other than the spouse) have a birth probability about 36% higher than those who do not (Blau & Robins 1989). While these findings suggest that childcare plays a role in individual decisions about work and fertility, the role of child care in explaining the aggregate-level relationship has yet to be demonstrated.

TOWARDS A CONCEPTUAL FRAMEWORK

Underlying the central question of this essay is the assumption that women either limit their fertility to accommodate their labor force activity, or they adjust their labor force behavior to their fertility. The evidence suggests that women do both. A substantial body of individual-level research describes the various strategies by which women in industrialized settings accommodate their employment patterns to their fertility and their fertility to their labor force participation. The evidence also suggests that these strategies vary across national settings and that the ability to combine labor force participation and motherhood varies across countries. In short, demographers, sociologists, and economists have amassed a great deal of data on the fertility-employment relationship. What has been lacking is a unifying conceptual framework that ties together the findings from different contexts and levels of analysis.

To account for the many, sometimes discrepant, findings, such a framework must have at least three features: it must be dynamic; it must recognize the multidimensionality of both labor force participation and fertility; and it must be multilevel, incorporating the institutional and normative arrangements that influence individual fertility and labor force behavior. We consider each of these aspects in turn.

A Dynamic Model

Both labor force participation and fertility are more accurately conceived as processes that unfold over time rather than as static phenomena (Bernhardt 1993, Rindfuss et al. 1999). Labor force participation, for men as well as women, is fluid; individuals may enter, exit, and re-enter the paid labor force at any point in time, voluntarily or involuntarily (Gerson 1985, Koenigsberg et al 1994, Rexroat 1992). Moreover, the nature of labor force activity is variable; time commitments may range from minor to great and may shift repeatedly over the life course (Spain & Bianchi 1996, Stier et al 1998). Even the hours of the day and the days of the week that women and men work can vary (Presser 1999), and this has changed over time. The dynamic nature of fertility may be somewhat less obvious since childbearing itself is irreversible; nevertheless, fertility proceeds one child at a time, and decisions about future births—both number and timing—can be re-evaluated at any point as relevant circumstances change (Udry 1983, Namboodiri 1983).

Because both phenomena are processual, each may influence and be influenced by the other at any one time point or at multiple points. Moreover, the nature of this influence may differ from one point to the next, as women gain experience with or knowledge of the degree to which paid work and parenting conflict (Stolzenberg & Waite 1977, White & Kim 1987). It is easy to imagine, for example, changes in work or schooling plans following the first birth or a revision of fertility plans in response to changes in labor force participation. Bernhardt (1993:35) refers to the complex interplay among behavior, intentions, and experience as "circular cumulative causality," suggesting that current states build, in cumulative fashion, on past experiences. Framing the relationship in this way focuses attention on the complexity of the transitions from one state to the next and the pathways women follow through the life course. Open for research are questions about the interaction of individual characteristics and circumstance in shaping women's life strategies.

Multidimensionality

Related to the dynamic nature of both labor force participation and fertility—and further complicating the conceptualization of their relationship—is their multidimensionality. Labor force activity encompasses far more than can be captured by simple binary measures of participation (Bernhardt 1993). Indeed, that an increasing proportion of women in advanced industrial societies engage in paid work throughout their lives suggests that the critical variables in studies of work-family conflict may no longer be work participation/nonparticipation, but the *organization* of work time. Thus, our thinking about role incompatibility and the fertility-employment relationship needs to move beyond the part-time versus full-time distinctions (or even hours worked per week) to consider when women work and the compatibility of their work schedules with the schedules of potential childcare providers, as well as the distinction between careers and jobs (Bettio & Villa 1998, Presser 1989, 1995).

Fertility, like labor force participation, encompasses multiple dimensions. Investigators have focused on the decision to have children or not and the number of children, but additional aspects of fertility are likely to be relevant. Birth timing and spacing, for example, may comprise key components of strategies to balance work and family responsibilities. As Bettio & Villa (1998:166) observe, where completed fertility tends to be two or fewer children, "the burden of making motherhood more compatible with working life falls mainly on the timing of births." This, of course, brings us back to the dynamics of the fertility-employment relationship and the importance of incorporating time into conceptual as well as statistical models.

Incorporating Institutional Influences

Inherent in the concept of role incompatibility is the assumption that participation in economically productive work is difficult, if not impossible, for individuals who are responsible for child-rearing tasks, particularly when the children are of preschool age. But, as we have seen, considerable evidence suggests that the degree of conflict between work and fertility varies across advanced industrialized countries. Family benefits, maternal or parental leave policies, and childcare availability also differ from one country to the next, as well as over time. These aggregate characteristics, however, are not particularly good predictors of national fertility levels. As we observed above, this is likely, at least in part, a measurement problem, yet it points to the need for a more comprehensive conceptualization of the structural and institutional aspects of role incompatibility.

Numerous aspects of the social context likely deserve consideration; we suggest two here. First, the work we have reviewed suggests the overriding importance of the state's philosophical orientation toward family policy and families. Policy effects are best interpreted in light of announced policy goals and the state's philosophy concerning families and individuals. Policies in states seeking to promote gender equality, for example, are likely to have very different effects from superficially similar policies aiming to encourage traditional family relations. Second, macrolevel economic conditions are likely to be important. Individuals may be less willing to bear children when the economy is uncertain, even where family policies and childcare availability reduce work-family conflict and encourage gender equity. In Sweden, for example, both female labor force participation and fertility have fallen in recent years as inflation and unemployment rates have risen (Andersson 1999).

While investigators have considered such factors, their true incorporation into our thinking about the fertility-employment relationship will require conceptual models that encompass individual and aggregate-level variables. The effects of institutional factors on rates of labor force participation and fertility are manifested through their influence on individual behavior. Thus, we cannot adequately assess the effects of structural factors, such as family benefits, without specifying the mechanisms by which these variables influence individual behaviors. Likewise, individuals act within contexts, and we run the risk of misleading ourselves about the association between individuals' work and family behaviors if we ignore the effects of contextual characteristics. In short, the incompatibility between work and fertility is a *variable*, and variation in this incompatibility is influenced by social, economic, and institutional forces.

ACKNOWLEDGMENTS

The authors would like to thank Larry Bumpass, Paula England, and Irene Padavic for their insightful comments on an earlier draft of this paper.

Visit the Annual Reviews home page at www.AnnualReviews.org

LITERATURE CITED

Andersson G. 1999. Trends in childbearing and nuptiality in Sweden, 1961–1997. Pap. presented at Annu. Meet. Pop. Assoc. Am., New York

Becker GS. 1981. *A Treatise on the Family.* Cambridge: Harvard Univ. Press

Bernhardt EM. 1993. Fertility and employment. *Eur. Sociol. Rev.* 9(1):25–42

Bernhardt EM. 1986. Women's home attachment at first birth: the case of Sweden. *Eur. J. Pop.* 2(1):5–29

Bettio F, Villa P. 1998. A Mediterranean perspective on the breakdown of the relationship between participation and fertility. *Cambridge J. Econ.* 22:137–71

Bielby D. 1992. Commitment to work and family. *Annu. Rev. Sociol.* 18:281–302

Blanchet D. 1987. Les éffets demographiques des differentes mésures de politique familiale: Un essai d'evaluation. *Population* 42(1):99–127

Blau DM, Robins PK. 1988. Child care costs and family labor supply. *Rev. Econ. Stat.* 70:374–438

Blau DM, Robins PK. 1989. Fertility, employment, and child care costs. *Demography* 26(2):287–99

Brewster KL, Padavic I. 2000. Change in gender ideology, 1977–1996: The contributions of intracohort change and population turnover. *J. Marr. Fam.* 62(2): In press

Bumpass LL, Westoff CF. 1970. *The Later Years of Childbearing.* Princeton: Princeton Univ Press

Chafetz JS. 1995. Chicken or egg? A theory of the relationship between feminist movements and family change. In *Gender and Fertility Change in Industrialized Countries*, ed. KO Mason, AM Jensen, pp. 63–81. Oxford: Clarendon

Chesnais JC. 1996. Fertility, family, and social

policy in contemporary western Europe. *Pop. Dev. Rev.* 22(4):729–39

Choe MK, Bumpass LL, Tsuya NO. 1999. *Employment hours, preferences, and their perceived impact on family life in Japan, South Korea, and the United States.* East-West Center: manuscript

Connelly R. 1992. Self–employment and providing childcare. *Demography* 29:17–29

Corcoran M, Duncan GJ, Ponza M. 1984. Work experience, job segregation, and wages. In *Sex Segregation in the Workplace: Trends, Explanations, Remedies,* ed. B Reskin, pp. 171–91. Washington, DC: Natl. Acad. Sci.

Cramer JC. 1980. Fertility and female employment: problems of causal direction. *Am. Sociol. Rev.* 45(2):167–901980

David MG, Starzec C. 1991. France: A diversity of policy options. See Kamerman & Kahn, pp 81–113

Degler C. 1980. *At Odds: Women and the Family in America from the Revolution to the Present.* New York: Oxford Univ. Press

Desai S, Waite LJ. 1991. Women's employment during pregnancy and after the first birth: occupational characteristics and work commitment. *Am. Sociol. Rev.* 56(4):551–66

Ékert-Jaffe O. 1986. Effets et limites des aides financières aux familles: Une expérience et une modèle. *Population* 41(2):327–48

Ellingsæter AL, Ronsen M. 1996. The dual strategy: motherhood and the work contract in Scandinavia. *Eur. J. Pop.* 12:239–60

England P, Farkas G. 1986. *Households, Employment, and Gender: A Social, Economic, and Demographic View.* Hawthorne, NY: Aldine

Gauthier AH. 1991. *Subsidizing parents: Does it make children more attractive?* Paper presented at Wksp. on Compar. Stud. of Welfare State Dev., Helsinki

Gauthier AH. 1996. *The State and the Family: A Comparative Analysis of Family Policies in Industrialized Countries.* Oxford: Clarendon

Gauthier AH, Hatzius J. 1997. Family benefits and fertility: an econometric analysis. *Pop. Stud.* 51:295–306

Gershuny J, Robinson JP. 1988. Historical change in the household division of labor. *Demography* 25:537–52

Gerson K. 1985. *Hard Choices: How Women Decide about Work, Career and Motherhood.* Berkeley: Univ. Calif. Press

Glass J, Camarigg V. 1992. Gender, parenthood, and job–family compatibility. *Am. J. Sociol.* 98:131–51

Hantrais L. 1997. Exploring relationships between social policy and changing family forms within the European Union. *Eur. J. Pop.* 13:339–79

Hecht J, Leridon H. 1993. Fertility policies: a limited influence? In *The Changing Population of Europe,* ed. D Noin, R Woods, pp 61–75. Oxford, UK: Blackwell's

Hirschman C. 1994. Why fertility changes. *Annu. Rev. Sociol.* 20:203–33

Hoem B. 1995. The way to the gender–segregated Swedish labor market. See Mason & Jensen 1995, pp. 279–29

Hoem B. 1996. *Some features of recent demographic trends in Sweden.* Pap. presented at Arbeitstagung der Deutchen Gesellschaft fur Bevolkerungswissenschaft, 30th, Walferdange, Luxembourg

Hoem B, Hoem J. 1989. The impact of women's employment on second and third births in Sweden. *Pop. Stud.* 43(1):47–67

Hoem B, Hoem J. 1997. *Fertility trends in Sweden up to 1996.* Pap. presented to the Expert Group Mtg. on Below–Replacement Fertility, UN Pop. Div., New York

Hoem J. 1990. Social policy and recent fertility change in Sweden. *Pop. Dev. Rev.* 16:735–48

Hoem J. 1993. Public policy as the fuel of fertility: effects of a policy reform on the pace of childbearing in Sweden. *Acta Sociol.* 36(1):19–31

Hofferth SL. 1996. Child care in the United States today. *The Future of Children* 6:41–61

Hooper LM. 1999. *Fertility trends in the German Democratic Republic and the Federal Republic of Germany: 1960–1994.* Paper presented at the Annu. Meet. Pop. Assoc. Am., New York

Hout M. 1978. The determinants of marital fertility in the United States, 1968–1970: inferences from a dynamic model. *Demography* 15:139–59

Huinink J, Mayer KU. 1995. Gender, social inequality, and family formation in West Germany. In *Gender and Fertility Change in Industrialized Countries*, ed. KO Mason and A-M Jensen, pp. 168–99. Oxford: Clarendon

Jensen A-M. 1995. Gender gaps in relations with children: closing or widening? See Mason & Jensen, pp. 223–42

Kamerman S, Kahn A, eds. 1991. *Child Care, Parental Leave, and the Under–3's*. New York: Auburn House

Kirshman N. 1983. Sequential fertility decision making and the life course. In *Determinants of Fertility in Developing Countries*, ed. R. Bulatao, R. Lee, vol. 2, pp. 444–72. New York: Academic

Klerman JA, Leibowitz A. 1994. The work–employment distinction among new mothers. *J. Hum. Resourc.* 29(2):277–303

Klerman JA, Leibowitz A. 1999. Job continuity among new mothers. *Demography* 36(2):145–55

Koenigsberg J, Garet MS, Rosenbaum JE. 1994. The effect of family on the job exits of young adults: a competing risk model. *Work Occup.* 21:33–63

Kuïjsten AC. 1996. Changing family patterns in Europe: a case of divergence? *Eur. J. Pop.* 12:115–43

Lehrer E, Kawasaki S. 1985. Child care arrangements and fertility: an analysis of two-earner households. *Demography* 22:499–513

Lehrer E, Nerlove M. 1986. Female labor force behavior and fertility in the United States. *Annu. Rev. Sociol.* 12:181–204

Lesthaeghe R. 1995. The second demographic transition in Western countries: an interpretation. In *Gender and Fertility Change in Industrialized Countries*, ed. KO Mason, A-M Jensen, pp. 17–62. Oxford: Clarendon

Lesthaeghe R, Willems P. 1999. Is low fertility a temporary phenomenon in the European Union? *Pop. Dev. Rev.* 25(2):211–28

Macunovich DJ. 1996. A review of recent developments in the economics of fertility. In *Household and Family Economics*, ed. P Menchik, pp. 91–158. Dordrecht: Kluwer Academic

Mason KO, Jensen AM, eds. 1995. *Gender and Fertility Change in Industrialized Countries*. Oxford, UK: Clarendon

Mason KO, Kuhlthau K. 1992. The perceived impact of child care costs on women's labor supply and fertility. *Demography* 29:523–44

Mikkola M. 1991. Finland: supporting parental choice. See Kamerman & Kahn 1991, pp 145–70

Monnier A. de Guibert–Lantoine C. 1993. The demographic situation of Europe and the developed countries overseas: an annual report. *Population: An English Selection* 5:249–72

Morgan SP. 1996. Characteristic features of modern American fertility. *Pop. Dev. Rev.* 22 (suppl):19–63

Morgan SP, Hirosima K. 1983. The persistence of extended family residence in Japan: anachronism or alternative strategy? *Am. Sociol. Rev.* 48:269–81

Morgan SP, Rindfuss RR. 1999. Re-examining the link of early childbearing to marriage and subsequent fertility. *Demography* 36:59–75

Néve R. 1995. Changes in attitudes towards women's emancipation in the Netherlands over two decades: unraveling a trend. *Soc. Sci. Res.* 24:167–87

Ní Bhrölchain M. 1992. Period paramount? A critique of the cohort approach to fertility. *Pop. Dev. Rev.* 18:599–629

Ogasawara Y. 1998. *Office Ladies and Salaried Men: Power, Gender, and Work in Japanese Companies*. Berkeley: Univ. Calif. Press

Olóh L Sz. 1999. Do public policies influence fertility? Evidence from Sweden and Hungary from a gender perspective. *Stockholm Res. Rep. in Demography, no. 130* Demogr. Unit, Stockholm Univ., Stockholm, Sweden

Ondrich J, Spiess CK. 1998. Care of children in a low fertility setting: transitions between home and market care for pre–school children in Germany. *Pop. Stud.* 52(1):35–48

Organisation for Economic Co–operation and Development. 1997. *Labour Force Statistics, 1976–1996.* Paris: OECD

Organisation for Economic Co–operation and Development. 1990. *OECD Employment Outlook.* Paris: OECD

Organisation for Economic Co–operation and Development. 1986. *Labour Force Statistics, 1965–1985.* Paris: OECD

Palmore JA, Gardner RW. 1983. *Measuring Mortality, Fertility, and Natural Increase: A Self–Teaching Guide.* Honolulu: East-West Center

Pinnelli A. 1995. Women's condition, low fertility, and emerging union patterns in Europe. See Mason & Jensen 1995, pp. 82–101

Population Reference Bureau. 1980–1999. *World Data Sheets.* Washington, DC: US-GPO

Presser H. 1989. Can we make time for the children? The economy, work, and child care. *Demography* 26(4):523–43

Presser H. 1995. Are the interests of women inherently at odds with the interests of children or the family? A viewpoint. See Mason & Jensen 1995, pp. 296–313

Presser H. 1999. Toward a 24–hour economy. *Science* 284:1778–79

Pyle JL. 1990. Female employment and export–led development in Ireland: Labour market impact of state–reinforced gender inequality in the household. In *Women, Employment and the Family in the International Division of Labour,* ed. S Stichter & J Parpart, pp. 137–160. Philadelphia, PA: Temple Univ. Press

Reskin B, Padavic I. 1994. *Women and Men at Work.* Thousand Oaks, CA: Pine Forge Press

Rexroat C. 1992. Changes in the employment continuity of succeeding cohorts of young women. *Work & Occup.* 19:18–34

Rindfuss RR. 1991. The young adult years: diversity, structural change, and fertility. *Demography* 28:493–512

Rindfuss RR, Benjamin K, Morgan SP. 2000. *How do marriage and female labor force participation affect fertility in low–fertility coun-* *tries?* Pap. to be presented at Annu. Meet. Pop. Assoc. Am., Los Angeles

Rindfuss RR, Brewster KL. 1996. Childrearing and fertility. *Pop. Dev. Rev.* 22 (suppl):258–89

Rindfuss RR, Cooksey EC, Sutterlin RL. 1999. Young adult occupational achievement: early expectations versus behavioral reality. *Work & Occup.* 26:220–63

Rindfuss RR, Morgan SP, Offutt K. 1996. Education and the changing age pattern of fertility. *Demography* 33:277–90

Roos PA. 1985. *Gender and Work: A Comparative Analysis of Industrial Societies.* Albany: State Univ. New York Press

Rosenfeld RA. 1992. Job mobility and career processes. *Annu. Rev. Sociol.* 18:39–61

Rosenfeld RA. 1996. Women's work histories. *Pop. Dev. Rev.* 22 (suppl):199–222

Rosenfeld RA, Birkelund G. 1995. Women's part-time work: A cross-national comparison. *Eur. Sociol. Rev.* 11(2):111–34

Rosenfeld RA, Spenner KI. 1992. Occupational sex segregation and Women's early career job shifts. *Work & Occup.* 19:424–29

Ross K. 1998. Labor pains: the effect of the Family and Medical Leave Act on the return to work after childbirth. *Focus* 20(1):34–36

Schiersmann C. 1991. Germany: recognizing the value of child rearing. See Kamerman & Kahn 1991, pp. 171–99

Smith–Lovin L, Tickemeyer AR. 1978. Nonrecursive models of labor force participation, fertility behavior, and sex role attitudes. *Am. Sociol. Rev.* 43:541–57

Spain D, Bianchi SM. 1996. *Balancing Act: Motherhood, Marriage, and Employment among American Women.* New York: Russell Sage Found.

Spitze G. 1988. Women's employment and family relations: a review. *J. Marr. Fam.* 50:595–618

Sporton D. 1993. Fertility: the lowest level in the world. In *The Changing Population of Europe,* ed. D Noin, R Woods, pp. 49–60. Oxford, UK: Blackwell's Publishers

Stier H, Lewin-Epstein N, Braun M. 1998. *The*

institutional context of women's employment consequences: evidence from eight industrialized countries. Pap. presented at the Annu. Meet. Am. Soc. Assoc. Am., San Francisco

Stolzenberg RM, Waite LJ. 1977. Age and the relationships between young women's plans for childbearing and employment. *Am. Sociol. Rev.* 42:769–83

Stycos JM, Weller RH. 1967. Female working roles and fertility. *Demography* 4:210–17

Sundström M. 1991. Sweden: supporting work, family, and gender equality. See Kammerman & Kahn 1991, pp 171–200

Sundström M, Stafford F. 1991. Female labor force participation, fertility, and public policy. *Stockhom Res. Rep. in Demogr.* No. 63, Stockholm Univ.

Tsuya NO, Mason KO. 1995. Changing gender roles and below–replacement fertility in Japan. See Mason & Jensen 1995, pp. 139–67

Udry JR. 1983. Do couples make fertility plans one birth at a time? *Demography* 20:117–28

United Nations. 1976. *Fertility and Family Planning in Europe around 1970.* New York: United Nations

van de Kaa DJ. 1987. Europe's second demographic transition. *Pop. Bull.* 42(1):1–57

Waite LJ, Stolzenberg RM. 1976. Intended childbearing and labor force participation of young women: insights from non–recursive models. *Am. Sociol. Rev.* 41:235–52

Waldfogel J. 1998. The family gap for young women in the United States and Britain: Can maternity leave make a difference? *J. Lab. Econ.* 16(3):505–45

Waldfogel J. 1999. The impact of the Family and Medical Leave Act. *J. Policy Anal. Mgmt.* 18(2):281–302

Walker JR. 1994. *The effect of public policies on recent Swedish fertility behavior.* Univ. Wisc.-Madison: Cent. for Demogr. Ecol. Work. Pap.

Weller RH. 1977. Wife's employment and cumulative family size in the United States, 1970 and 1960. *Demography* 14(1):43–65

Wenk D, Garrett P. 1992. Having a baby: some predictors of maternal employment around childbirth. *Gender & Soc.* 6(1):49–65

Wennemo I. 1993. *Motives and institutions in the formation of family policy: a comparative study of 18 OECD countries.* Pap. presented at the Conf. on Compar. Res. on Welfare States in Transition, Int. Sociol. Assoc., Res. Com. 19

White L, Kim H. 1987. The family building process: childbearing choices by parity. *J. Marr. Fam.* 49:271–79

White M. 1996. Contemporary Japanese women: family, education, and workplace. In *Women and Work: A Reader,* ed. P Dubeck, K Borman, pp. 464–66. New Brunswick, NJ: Rutgers Univ. Press

Willis RJ. 1973. A new approach to the economic theory of fertility behavior. *J. Polit. Econ.* 81:S14–S69

Witte J, Wagner G. 1995. Declining fertility in East Germany after unification: a demographic response to socioeconomic change. *Pop. Dev. Rev.* 21:387–97

World Bank. 1984. *World Tables.* Vol II. Baltimore: Johns Hopkins Univ. Press. 3rd ed.

Zhang J, Quan J, van Meerbergen P. 1994. The effect of tax–transfer policies on fertility in Canada, 1921–88. *J. Hum. Resourc.* 29(1):181–201

Annu. Rev. Sociol. 2000. 26:297–322

POLITICAL SOCIOLOGICAL MODELS
OF THE U.S. NEW DEAL

Jeff Manza

Department of Sociology, Northwestern University, 1810 Chicago Avenue, Evanston, Illinois 60208-1330; e-mail: manza@nwu.edu

Key Words   political sociology, political change, New Deal

■ **Abstract**   The U.S. New Deal raises issues of class, race, gender, region, social movements, and institutional constraint in the context of a societal-wide economic and political crisis, and has not surprisingly generated a considerable body of work by political sociologists over the past twenty years. In particular, the New Deal has served as a major empirical context for developing, testing, or applying broader theoretical models of political change in the United States. In this sense, it is a paradigmatic example of the "historical turn" in the social sciences. This paper examines the theoretical and empirical controversies that have persisted between four competing theoretical models of New Deal political change: (*a*) those emphasizing the importance of social movements from below in generating momentum for political reform, (*b*) those highlighting the centrality of business influence on successful New Deal reform initiatives, (*c*) feminist models, and (*d*) historical institutional models. I then turn to a survey of more recent work on some of the topics that have been the most widely debated in more recent scholarship and pose some questions for future research.

INTRODUCTION

Few historical conjunctures have excited as many sociological imaginations as the United States in the 1930s. The New Deal vortex raises issues of class, race, gender, region, social movements, and institutional constraint in the context of a societal-wide economic and political crisis. The cumulative body of work by political sociologists on the New Deal over the past twenty years is by now substantial. The New Deal has served as a major empirical context for developing, testing, or applying broader theoretical models of political change in the United States. In this sense, it is a paradigmatic example of the "historical turn" in the social sciences (McDonald 1996).

The purpose of this paper is to dissect the animated debates among political sociologists over the causes and consequences of political change during the New Deal era (bounded roughly by the years 1933 and 1940). I start with a brief overview

0360-0572/00/0815-0297$14.00

of some of the main contours of political development during the period, and I outline the subjects that have been studied by political sociologists writing about the New Deal. In reviewing what has been written over the past two decades, it is striking how much attention has been paid to issues of labor market regulation and (to a lesser extent) social movements, and how little attention has been paid to other New Deal policy arenas. Part two of the paper examines the theoretical and empirical controversies that have persisted between four competing theoretical models of New Deal political change: (*a*) those emphasizing the importance of social movements from below in generating momentum for political reform, (*b*) those highlighting the centrality of business influence on successful New Deal reform initiatives, (*c*) feminist models, and (*d*) historical institutional models. I also identify recent work that synthesizes insights from several theoretical traditions to develop more comprehensive accounts. Part three surveys in more detail some of the topics that have been the most widely debated in more recent scholarship and poses some questions for future research.

THE NEW DEAL AND POLITICAL SOCIOLOGY

The political reforms and policy innovations of the New Deal developed in response to an economic crisis of unprecedented magnitude (Kennedy 1999). Between 1929 and 1933, US GNP fell by 46%, and unemployment rose from less than 4% of the labor force to over 25% by 1933. The impact of economic decline was felt by virtually every sector of the economy, although there was variation in timing and severity of the downturn (for overviews of the economic crisis, see Bernstein 1987; Bordo et al 1998). The crisis spawned several social movements, including those among unemployed workers, old age movements, and the industrial labor movement (for an overview, see Amenta 1998). The Democratic Party swept the elections of 1932, picking up 97 new seats in the House of Representatives (after a gain of 53 seats in 1930), and Democrat Franklin Roosevelt was elected President, taking office in March 1933.

The reformist phase of the New Deal, directed by the Roosevelt Administration—frequently at the prodding of an activist Congress—lasted from 1933 to 1938. The infamous first "Hundred Days" of March-June 1933 was marked by an incredible array of legislative initiatives aimed at stimulating recovery. Among the most important of these were: the National Industrial Recovery Act [promoting the development of industrywide "codes of fair competition" to regulate production practices in each industry, to be jointly administered by management and labor under the supervision of a new National Recovery Administration (NRA)]; the Agricultural Adjustment Act (production controls and government subsidies for farmers); the Banking Act of 1933 (creating the Federal Deposit Insurance Corporation); the Tennessee Valley Authority Act (rural development, created the Tennessee Valley Authority); and banking and finance reform (including taking the United States off the gold standard). In the next 18 months, a series of emergency relief and work relief programs were adopted, including the Works Progress Administration, as well as the National Housing Act of 1934 (providing low-interest loans and creating the Federal Savings and Loan Insurance Corporation), and the Securities and Exchange Act.

Recovery was slow and uneven, but the Democrats made further (and unprecedented) gains in the midterm elections of 1934 (picking up 9 House and 10 Senate seats). In the summer of 1935, a second bout of reform legislation (sometimes referred to as the "Second New Deal") was adopted. These included, most importantly, the Social Security Act (establishing unemployment insurance, old age insurance, old age assistance, and Aid to Dependent Children), the National Labor Relations (Wagner) Act (pro-union legislation barring unfair employer labor practices and establishing a National Labor Relations Board to administer compliance), a wealth tax, the Banking Act (centralizing the Federal Reserve), and the Public Utilities Holding Company Act (regulating utility companies). The final major reform of the New Deal era was the adoption of the Fair Labor Standards Act of 1938 (setting minimum wages and maximum working hours across most industries).

Even the briefest of overviews of the political struggles and policy reforms of the New Deal era, such as that above, demonstrates that the political reforms launched during the New Deal proceeded on many fronts. Yet, as the rest of this paper demonstrates, almost all of the work of sociologists (and other social scientists) has addressed only a handful of topics: political struggles in policy fields relating to labor market regulation and social provision (especially the various provisions of the Social Security Act, the Wagner Act, and agricultural reform), and the social and political impact of the various social movements of the period. Other than the NRA, key New Deal business and financial regulations have gone largely unexplored by sociologists, perhaps because the focus has been on highly contested innovations that were not expected in the context of business dominance and limited-government ideology of the 1920s.

THEORETICAL CONTROVERSIES OVER THE NEW DEAL

Sociologists wrote about and, to some extent, participated in New Deal political struggles and policy contests in the 1930s and 1940s. Yet it was not until the generation of scholars who came of age in the 1960s sought to reassess the limits and possibilities of political change in the United States that the New Deal began to receive sustained attention from sociologists. Among the most influential early works of this generation were those of Domhoff (1970:ch. 6), Block (1977), Piven & Cloward (1977), and Skocpol (1980). Each sketched out early versions of theoretical standpoints that would much influence later debates. Domhoff (1970) first applied his version of a business-centered model of reform to the New Deal. Block (1977) advanced a class struggle model of the New Deal (and other reformist episodes in US political history), highlighting the dual roles of business confidence and pressures from below in creating (or denying) the possibility of reform. Piven

& Cloward (1977:41–180) emphasized the causal importance of social struggles from below, arguing that the Social Security Act and the Wagner Act resulted directly from the pressures brought to bear on state managers by New Deal era social movements. Skocpol (1980) argued that previous analysts had ignored the causal significance of the unique structure of American political institutions in shaping New Deal outcomes, and advanced an early "state-centered" theoretical model.

Following from these early works, three global explanations of New Deal political change developed and have persisted over the past two decades: political struggles models, business-centered models, and institutional models; these have been joined more recently by feminist models. Because each of these explanatory models remains a central pole in the debate over the New Deal, it is worth describing in some detail the main arguments and evidence their proponents have offered. At the same time, however, it is important to keep in mind that virtually no individual analyst is wedded solely to one theoretical model. Most have found it useful, especially in more recent contributions, to incorporate insights from more than one stance in the debate.

Political Struggle Models

The first model can be characterized as the political struggle approach. It argues that domestic state-building reforms often result from episodes of intense labor conflict or struggles by social movements of subordinate groups, forcing concessions by political elites from above. The larger theoretical proposition underlying such models is that capitalist states seek to maintain social equilibrium and will act against the wishes of dominant classes in cases where pressures from below cause the costs of not acting to exceed the costs of reform (cf. Poulantzas 1978, Therborn 1978). The New Deal can be viewed as a prototypical example of such dynamics in the context of American political history. The class struggles and social movements during the 1930s included the industrial labor movement, the unemployed councils movement, the Long, Townsend, and Coughlin movements, and local or regional third party movements. The cumulative political impact of these movements are viewed by political struggle analysts as having forced political elites to consider reforms that would have been otherwise inconceivable (e.g. Brenner 1985). The distinctive feature of the political struggle model in analyzing the New Deal is an emphasis on the key roles played by radicals in fomenting struggle from below.

The most systematic applications of political struggle models to the New Deal have focused on the Wagner Act (e.g. Piven & Cloward 1977:ch. 3, Milton 1982, Davis 1986, pp. 52–74, Levine 1988:ch. 6, Goldfield 1989, 1991) and the Social Security Act (e.g. Piven & Cloward 1977:ch. 2, Jenkins & Brents 1989, Casebeer 1994, L. Gordon 1994:ch. 8). These policies represented dramatic extensions of the previous commitments of New Deal politicians (including President Franklin Roosevelt) prior to 1933, and all emerged in the face of diffuse social movement pressures from below.

An uncompromising version of the political struggle thesis is advanced by Goldfield (1989, 1990) in an examination of the origins of the Wagner Act.

Goldfield argues that "the most reasonable hypothesis to account for the passage of the National Labor Relations Act is that labor militancy, catapulted into national prominence by the 1934 strikes and the political response to this movement, paved the way for the passage of the act" (1989, p. 1273). His account rests on two central claims. First, he argues there were important linkages between the industrial labor movement between 1933 and 1937, and the broader social movements of the period (1989, pp. 1269–70). Second, left-wing political forces, especially but not exclusively those associated with the Communist Party, were important for coordinating struggles and building the industrial labor movement (cf. Zeitlin & Stepin-Norris 1989). Reviewing the Congressional debates over the Wagner bill, Goldfield argues that the *combination* of New Deal social movements and the growing radicalization of the labor movement created a pervasive sense among members of Congress that events were spinning out of control and something had to be done to bring the growing radicalism to a heel. A desire to protect the forces of moderation within the labor movement, particularly the AFL unions, was a prime motivation for many liberal politicians to support the Wagner Act (1989:1274–75; see also Levine 1988:3).

These claims are not uncontroversial. Finegold & Skocpol (1984:177–78, Skocpol & Finegold 1990:1301–3) argue that it was changes in state policy (in particular, the adoption of the labor organizing provisions of the NIRA) that set in motion the labor insurgency (cf. Brody 1993:120–28; Piven & Cloward 1977:116ff.) or allowed it to succeed (cf. Amenta 1998:109–10). Further, Skocpol & Finegold (1990:1304–5) reason that if class struggles alone could produce prolabor reforms such as the Wagner Act, why didn't the equally extensive labor mobilizations of 1919–1920 and 1945–1946 produce favorable policy outcomes? Systematic work on such questions is still in its infancy. Amenta and his colleagues (Amenta 1998, Amenta et al 1992, Amenta et al 1994, Cauthen & Amenta 1996, Amenta & Poulsen 1996) use state-level variation in New Deal era social spending programs as a lens through which to systematically examine how and when social movements actually impact government priorities. Amenta (1998) concludes that social movement strength alone cannot explain state-level New Deal outcomes. Social movements making demands for social spending programs had their biggest impact in those states with democratic political systems and reform-oriented governments in place, but weaker impacts in patronage-oriented states, in those "undemocratic" states where large numbers of voters were disenfranchised (especially in the South), or in states without reform-oriented administrations in power. The emphasis in political struggle accounts on the roles of radicals in the development of insurgency is probably also overstated (see below for further discussion).

Business and the New Deal

A second set of models of the New Deal (and American political development more generally) explain reform outcomes as the result of the activities of key business groups and/or corporate leaders, sometimes viewed in the context of pressures for reform bubbling up from below. Among advocates of these business-centered models, there are important differences of opinion over *which* segment of the capitalist class may take on a progressive role, and the reasons *why*. Nevertheless, all business-centered models share two basic assumptions about the political change in the United States: (*a*) One or more segments of the capitalist class became influential in supporting and shaping the development of new policy initiatives; and (*b*) the dynamics of intraclass struggle among segments of the corporate community played crucial roles in shaping policy outcomes.

One version of the model was developed by Berkowitz & McQuaid (1992 [1980]). They argued the emergence of the American welfare state involved the gradual adoption of organizational innovations first developed in the private sector, especially the various forms of private social insurance, into the public sector (see also Jacoby 1993, Richards 1994, Sass 1997). Berkowitz & McQuaid argue that the underdevelopment of state administrative structures in the United States has often led government bureaucrats to look to the private sector for ideas and organizational forms [cf. Brand (1988) and Finegold & Skocpol (1995) on the case of National Recovery Administration]. In the case of the New Deal, reformers did not create new bureaucratic forms de novo, but rather built upon existing innovations in large-scale business enterprises and government/business cooperation in the 1920s and earlier (see also Jacoby 1993). The handful of welfare capitalists involved in the inner circle of the New Deal, including those on advisory panels such as the Business Advisory Council of the Department of Commerce or to the Committee on Economic Security, had disproportionate influence not because they represented a large faction of business, but by virtue of their leadership in private reform initiatives (Berkowitz & McQuaid 1992:chs. 5–6).

Quadagno's (1988a) analysis of the origins of old age pensions and Colin Gordon's (1994) analysis of New Deal labor and social insurance reforms go further to analyze the logic of business support for experimental public programs (see also Levine 1988, Ferguson 1984, 1995, Swenson 1996, n.d., Klein 1998). Employers had a number of incentives for maintaining private, or company, welfare programs: to promote employee loyalty, to reduce turnover, prevent unions, and to encourage the retirement of older, less-productive workers. But these initiatives also imposed costs on employers, costs that tended to rise over time. This was especially true of pensions, which increased as the proportion of superannuated workers in a plan increased (i.e. until the plan reached maturity). Quadagno (1988) and C. Gordon (1994) argue that these costs came to be viewed by the late 1920s as exceeding the benefits of the programs, especially in fragmented and competitive industries. Employer support among this group of employers for the Social Security Act was based on the advantages of a public program that would socialize such costs by imposing them on recalcitrant competitors.

Although most of the work on the logic of business support for the New Deal has focused on the Social Security Act or business and financial regulation, C. Gordon (1994) and Swenson (1996, n.d.) have developed a similar model with respect to New Deal labor reform (see also Domhoff 1990:ch. 4). They argue that some employers, especially those in highly fragmented industries such as coal, clothing, construction, textiles, and light manufacturing, experimented with regulatory unionism as a way of achieving industrywide cost standardization. The problem faced by employers in such industries was similar to the problems of welfare capitalist firms: Free-riding employers who refused to follow a union standard could gain competitive advantages (cf. Rogers 1990). This caused some employers to support section 7(a) of the National Industrial Recovery Act (which required industrywide codes to permit labor organization) and, ultimately, the Wagner Act after the NIRA was held unconstitutional in May 1935.

One of the crucial questions raised by all business-centered models is precisely how economic power gets translated into political power. C. Gordon (1994) unearths direct evidence of business support, whereas Swenson (n.d.:chs. 7–8) emphasizes the signals given off by some employers to New Deal elites as crucial to shaping the emerging legislation. In Swenson's model, these signals were of crucial importance, because they suggested what was, and was not, likely to generate long-run business support and create the possibilities for class compromise. These perceptions, in turn, shaped the choices made among competing reform proposals by New Deal elites.

Domhoff's (1970, 1990, 1996, 1998) work emphasizes the importance of corporate influence on policy ideas in shaping the responses to the emerging crisis. Domhoff argues that elite policy organizations and policy networks heavily influenced by business interests formulate the ideas and programs that state managers (who are themselves typically recruited from the same networks) are most likely to draw upon during periods of reform. He has applied this model to the New Deal in analyses of the AAA, the NRA, the Social Security Act, and the Wagner Act. For example, Domhoff's analysis of the formation of the Social Security Act posits a crucial role for the groups of policy experts and political reformers aligned with Rockefeller interests. Many key experts involved in drafting the Act were drawn from the Rockefeller-financed Industrial Relations Counsellors, Inc., a business consulting firm whose board of directors included the vice-president of US Steel and and the chairmen of General Electric and International Harvester. Experts working on the unemployment insurance provisions, and two of the three key experts working on old-age pensions, for example, were drawn from the ranks of the IRC. His most recent work (e.g. Domhoff 1996:ch. 5) shows the close links between this group and its corporate sponsors, including John D. Rockefeller Jr. himself, and provides evidence that they systematically drew upon years of providing advice to welfare capitalist firms in drawing up the social security legislation. This evidence is developed by Domhoff in the context of an overall model that also emphasizes the importance of the political constraints imposed by Southern Democrats on the New Deal.

Critics of business-centered models have argued that they overstate business involvement in the drafting and development of New Deal social legislation, and understate the depth of business opposition to political reform (Skocpol 1980, Skocpol & Amenta 1985, Amenta & Parikh 1991, Amenta 1998:117–19). The controversy has been sharpest over the Social Security Act. The more recent and direct evidence of corporate influence on the shaping of old-age insurance and unemployment insurance programs (e.g. C. Gordon 1994, Domhoff 1996, Swenson 1996, n.d., Klein 1998), however, has not to date been systematically considered or addressed by institutional critics of business-centered models.

Feminist Analyses of the New Deal

In the recent debates within political sociology, particularly with respect to the origins and development of the welfare state, gender-centered approaches have gained influence (Orloff 1993b, 1996). Traditional approaches to the origins and development of the welfare state in the United States often ignored the ways in which gendered social relations and ideological categories structure both political debates and policy outcomes (L. Gordon 1994, Mettler 1999). Two distinct contributions of feminist social scientists to understanding the New Deal can be identified. First, much has been written about the impact of women's organizations on the Progressive era, when an emergent maternalist form of social provision seemed to offer an alternative path to a modern welfare state in the United States (e.g. Fitzpatrick 1990, Muncy 1991, Skocpol 1992, Sklar 1993, L. Gordon 1994, Mink 1995). These maternalist programs included wage and hour legislation (which was often applied initially only to women workers), mothers' pensions, and the Shepard-Towner Act of 1921 (providing health benefits for mothers and children). They were developed and promoted by a group of women social scientists and reformers grouped around the Children's Bureau of the Department of Labor since the Progressive Era. Yet during the New Deal era itself, maternalist social programs were submerged by the development of the broader social insurance programs embodied in the Social Security Act, and the women's network lost influence in the social insurance policy field (cf. Muncy 1991, L. Gordon 1994). Indeed, the New Deal is the one period of welfare statebuilding that was directed primarily at men, or families with male breadwinners (Orloff & Monson n.d.).

The second point of departure for feminist contributions to the New Deal has centered on the basic insight that welfare state programs distinguish core programs that provide relatively generous benefits distributed in the form of *entitlements* and are directed at (primarily male) wage-earners from those (peripheral) programs providing means-tested, relatively stingy, and stigmatizing benefits that are available to nonwage earners (primarily women and children) (Orloff 1993b, Mettler 1999). Similar analyses have been developed concerning race (see below). Feminists have argued that during the New Deal, programmatic distinctions between social insurance and welfare first became entrenched in national public policy (Mink 1995, Mettler 1999). New Deal reformers assumed that men were, and should be, the primary breadwinners for their families, and thus social insurance programs were to be targeted first at men (thereby protecting married women and children as well). For example, the old age insurance provisions of the Social Security Act were offered primarily to the full-time workforce (disproportionately made up of men). By contrast, a majority of women workers were in occupations that were not covered by the old age insurance and unemployment provisions of the Act. For these recipients, meager state-run social assistance programs were the primary source of social support (Mink 1995, Mettler 1999).

Historical Institutional Models

Finally, there are approaches to explaining the New Deal that grant causal primacy to institutional factors. The appearance of a "new" institutionalism in the social sciences has occasioned considerable interest and debate in recent years. In comparative political sociology and political science, "scholars ... writing on subjects as diverse as the political economy of advanced capitalism and policy-making during China's Great Leap Forward have all focused on the significance of institutional variables for explaining outcomes in their respective fields" (Thelen & Steinmo 1992:1). The variant of institutionalist scholarship most influential in recent political sociology, generally referred to as historical institutionalism, emphasizes the ways in which institutions shape the perceptions of interests and the behaviors of individuals and groups, promoting some possible policy and/or political outcomes while discouraging others (Immergut 1998).

The general problem of American exceptionalism—why the United States is different on a number of political dimensions from comparable capitalist democracies—has been a frequent starting point for historical institutional analyses of American politics (e.g. Skocpol 1992, 1995, Steinmo 1993a, 1993b, Orloff 1993a). Political sociologists are in fairly widespread agreement that institutional factors have powerfully contributed to the making of American exceptionalism. The Constitution creates a set of governing institutions designed to pit factions against one another by explicitly protecting minority interests, for example, thereby creating a fragmented patchwork of decision-making nodes (Neustadt 1990). This institutional fragmentation is manifested in a variety of ways: (*a*) federalism: many important policy decisions are controlled by state governments, and policies hence varied, occasionally widely, across the states (Beer 1994, C. Gordon 1994, Moss 1996); (*b*) the unique power of federal and state courts to either bottle up legislation or, in some cases, to resolve legislative deadlocks (Weaver & Rockman 1993:31, Hattam 1992); (*c*) the decentralization of power in Congress, and the power of committee chairs to bottle up legislation they do not favor (Shepsle & Weingast 1987), an especially important source of Southern influence during the New Deal (e.g. Domhoff 1990:97–98, Skocpol 1995, pp. 29–30); (*d*) the requirement of legislative supermajorities: for example, presidents can sustain vetos with only one third plus one voting member of either chamber of Congress; and (*e*) the weakness of the federal bureaucracy, in particular its permeability at all levels and the dependence of bureaucratic officials on Congress for support, which weakens their allegiance to the President who appoints them (Heclo 1977, Skowronek 1982). One crucial consequence of the institutional and political fragmentation of the

American polity is to create multiple veto points (Immergut 1992) for groups contesting political reform proposals.

Institutional factors also contributed to the weakness of working class political forces. The early extension of the franchise (albeit only to white men) meant that struggles for voting rights were not linked to union organization or agitation for socialism or social insurance, as in many parts of Europe. The political defeats suffered by broad-based unions in the late nineteenth century at the hands of hostile employers, the courts, and in many cases from federal or state government intervention, precluded the emergence of class-wide organization until the 1930s (Hattam 1993, Voss 1994, but cf. Dubofsky 1994). At no time were American workers able to build stable ties to a labor-based political party comparable to those of Western Europe (Shefter 1994: ch. 4).

In their work on the New Deal, historical institutionalists have emphasized, in addition to the basic institutional constraints identified above, the importance of institutional and political legacies in constraining the possibilities for political reform in the 1930s. These legacies are often viewed as concentrated especially in the party system and national governmental capacity. Probably the most well-known applications to the New Deal can be found in the work of Skocpol (1980, 1995) and her collaborators (e.g. Skocpol & Ikenberry 1983, Weir & Skocpol 1985, Weir, Orloff, & Skocpol 1988, Finegold & Skocpol 1995). Finegold & Skocpol (1995) provide a recent and systematic application to the New Deal in a comparative study of the success of the Agricultural Adjustment Act, and the failure of the National Industrial Recovery Act. They argue that these reform outcomes in the two policy domains varied because of (*a*) crucial differences in the types of pre-existing state capacities in the two cases; and (*b*) the changing shape of the Democratic and Republican Party coalitions during the 1930s. In agriculture, unusual statebuilding successes prior to the New Deal made possible successful implementation of production control policies previously resisted by virtually all farm interests. In the case of the NIRA, however, the absence of previous state capacity made implementation of economy-wide measures deeply problematic, and the abandonment of the Democratic Party by powerful business interests after 1934 crippled intra-party incentives to fix the initial design (Finegold & Skocpol 1995).

Any assessment of the explanatory and analytical power of historical institutional models as applied to the New Deal must begin by distinguishing between weak and strong versions of the theory. In the weak version, political institutions are viewed as shaping actor strategies and beliefs on the one hand, and political outcomes on the other, by favoring some types of action and hindering others. The strong version asserts that state institutions and/or state managers have the potential capacity to become autonomous from other social forces and to carry out reforms reflecting their own interests or goals (e.g. Skocpol 1985, Hooks 1990).

The strong version has rarely been applied to the New Deal, with the exception of some early work by Skocpol and her collaborators that has been abandoned in more recent work. The comparative logic of the weak version of historical institutionalism, by contrast, has influenced many accounts. There is widespread agreement that institutional features of the American political system have shaped political strategies and policy outcomes and, in particular, placed considerable obstacles in the way of the kinds of social spending programs favored by many New Deal leaders. One major challenge to the weak version of the institutional model, however, has come from those analysts who have sought to identify the racial bases of state formation in the United States (Quadagno 1994, Goldfield 1997). The argument asserts that in the causal ordering of political change, institutional arrangements were themselves the result of race-based political dynamics and hence can be no more than mediating variables. Constitutional compromises such as divided government and states' rights stemmed from the demands of Southern elites to maintain slavery as an economic system (cf. Fredrickson 1981). The compromise of 1877 ended Reconstruction on terms favorable to the Southern planter elite, creating the conditions for the reconstruction of racial domination and eventually the one-party Southern political order that persisted into the 1930s (cf. Foner 1988). In other words, the very political institutions that hindered New Deal reform initiatives must themselves be traced to a system of racial domination in combination with the unique political economy of the South (Alston & Ferrie 1989, 1999, Quadagno 1994, Domhoff 1990, 1996, Goldfield 1997, Piven & Cloward 1997).

SOCIAL FORCES, POLITICAL CHANGE, AND THE NEW DEAL

The New Deal has excited sociological imaginations in part because of the diversity of social forces and political processes that it set in motion. Much of the recent (and likely future) work by political sociologists on the New Deal focuses more narrowly on particular aspects of the period. Comparative work has been fairly limited to date, but it is also likely that future investigations will examine the more broadly comparative aspects of the New Deal. In this section, I briefly highlight some of the recent scholarship on race and geography, labor, intellectuals, electoral realignment, and comparative perspectives.

Race and the New Deal

New Deal reforms were constructed in the face of racial division and conflict, and analysts have paid considerable attention to the ways in which racial politics undermined the prospects for certain types of reforms. There has also been considerable research on the racial impact of the New Deal. Finally, there has been extensive work on the logic of race and the political economy of the South in shaping both New Deal programmatic initiatives and their implementation.

African Americans and the New Deal   At the onset of the Depression, no group faced greater hardship than African Americans. Yet, across a range of New Deal programs, most programmatic initiatives either neglected the needs of African Americans or were implemented in ways that systematically favored whites over blacks (Quadagno 1988, 1994, Valocchi 1994, Brown 1999). There was, to be sure, variation across policy domains, and especially over time (cf. Amenta 1998:ch. 4 on New Deal work relief; Lieberman 1998:ch. 3 on old age insurance), but the general pattern has now been well documented (see Wolters 1970, Valocchi 1994: 352–55, Goldfield 1997:ch 6, and Hamilton & Hamilton 1997:ch. 1 for overviews).

For African Americans, the most important policy reforms of the early New Deal were those concerning agriculture. On the eve of the New Deal, over half of all blacks lived in rural areas, and nearly half were employed in agriculture (Valocchi 1994:352). By promoting production controls as the centerpiece of reform, however, the New Deal not only failed to help rural African Americans, they often made conditions worse. Farm owners often took land previously leased to African American tenant farmers out of production, usually without proper compensation (Wolters 1970, Hamilton & Hamilton 1997:13–14).

African Americans fared little better in other New Deal policy domains. The keystone labor market regulation measures of the Second New Deal—the old age insurance program of the Social Security Act, the Wagner Act, and the Fair Labor Standards Act—excluded most African-American workers from coverage by excluding all agricultural workers and domestic workers. In some cases it would be decades before full coverage would be granted (Lieberman 1998). The old-age assistance program did cover African Americans, but local administration of program benefits meant that Southern states could actively discriminate in the distribution of benefits (Quadagno 1988b, Brown 1999). Union-centered reforms such as the Wagner Act hardly inspired much confidence among African Americans, who had generally been excluded from AFL unions in the past (Hamilton & Hamilton 1997:33–36). The rise of industrial unions organized by the CIO, and in particular those unions in Communist Party orbit, did change this picture somewhat (Zieger 1995:83–85). But even many of the new CIO unions maintained segregated locals or failed to organize African-American workers (Goldfield 1993). The Roosevelt Administration and the Congress also did little to promote civil rights of African Americans in the 1930s, most notably failing to push through anti-lynching legislation opposed by Southern Democrats. The one partial exception to the otherwise bleak picture were the work relief programs of the Works Progress Administration (Hamilton & Hamilton 1997:24–26, Amenta 1998:ch. 4). Despite local administration, Amenta (1998:157–58) suggests that explicit anti-race discrimination provisions sometimes led to the over representation of African Americans on the WPA rolls (even in parts of the South).

New Deal housing programs are a key set of reforms that contributed in important ways to the future reproduction of racial inequality, though they have not been systematically studied by political sociologists to the same extent as other programs. The Housing Act of 1934 and the creation of the Federal Housing Administration influenced the development of metropolitan housing patterns, frequently in ways that had a powerful impact on racial segregation. In particular, by promoting (or overlooking) the use of racial covenants, or by refusing to insure mortgages in African-American neighborhoods, FHA programs from the 1930s contributed to both segregated housing patterns and the underdevelopment of urban black neighborhoods (cf. Gelfand 1975, Jackson 1985, Massey & Denton 1993). Federal housing officials frequently appointed local realtors in administrative capacities who had little interest in applying nondiscrimination policies (e.g. Goldfield 1997:206), and indeed, some early underwriting manuals explicitly called for segregation (Valocchi 1994:353–54).

Race and Political Geography   The unique political geography of the United States [see Bensel (1984) for a historical overview] had a powerful impact on the New Deal. The disfranchisement of African-American and many poor white voters in the late nineteenth and early twentieth centuries in most Southern states produced a shriveled, conservative electorate in most of those states and discouraged political action by social or labor movements from below. Uncompetitive elections in most parts of the South meant that Southern political elites had few incentives to respond to whatever popular pressures did emerge, especially once the populist movement was defeated in the 1890s. The labor-intensive, largely agrarian Southern economy encouraged Southern politicians to oppose most types of social spending that might reduce the supply of low-wage labor, and virulent racism further discouraged support for programs that would benefit African Americans (Quadagno 1988b, 1994, Alston & Ferrie 1999, Brown 1999).

Analysts from diverse intellectual traditions have focused on the importance of the South, recognizing both the role of class relations in the Southern political economy and institutional factors (especially Congressional seniority rules) that shaped the behavior of Southern members of Congress and enabled them to exercise disproportionate influence (cf. Domhoff 1970, 1990, C. Gordon 1994, Piven & Cloward 1997, Amenta 1998, Lieberman 1998). The consequences of Southern power have also been widely acknowledged. Two merit special mention. First, Southern members of Congress were able to use their leverage to ensure that New Deal social programs did not provide sufficient benefits for African Americans to disrupt the Southern agrarian economy (e.g. Quadagno 1988a, 1994, Linder 1992: ch. 4, Alston & Ferrie 1999). The overall impact of New Deal relief programs were thereby blunted upon implementation. Southern power also precluded nationalization of the most potentially intrusive labor market regulations (Alston & Ferrie 1999, Brown 1999). Thus, most African-American workers were not covered by the national provisions of the Social Security Act, the National Labor Relations Act, or the Fair Labor Standards Act (1938) but instead were limited to programs that were administered locally and frequently in arbitrary ways (Lieberman 1998). Because women were more likely to work in labor force locations that were excluded from full benefits under the Social Security Act, Southern influence also had a disparate gender impact (Mettler 1999). Although arguments about states' rights or limitations of administrative capacity were frequently invoked to support these exclusions (see e.g. Davies & Derthick 1997), both contemporary observers and most later analysts understood that the Southern racial order lay behind the rhetoric (see e.g. Lieberman 1998:51–56).

Second, the power and influence of Southern politicians was a crucial factor in shaping the Democratic Party. These politicians thus put a brake on the capacity of the party to develop into a labor-oriented social democratic party (see e.g. Domhoff 1990:ch. 9, Plotke 1996, Piven & Cloward 1997) and barred the development of a civil rights agenda (Weiss 1983, Hamilton & Hamilton 1997). The policy positions of Southern politicians were not, in general, hostile to social spending programs; in fact, Southern politicians aggressively embraced programs that combined federal resources with local control (Katznelson et al 1993, Lieberman 1998:37, Brown 1999). But anything that involved federal control that would interfere with the Southern political economy was strongly opposed by Southern politicians. It was only after the emergence of widespread mechanization following World War II, and the corresponding black migration to the North, that these pressures began to erode (Piven & Cloward 1997, Alston & Ferrie 1999).

Labor

The 1930s were a remarkable period of transition for the American labor movement, in particular with the creation of viable unions in many previously unorganized industries (even if it would take the economic boom produced by World War II and the postwar years before peak union density would be achieved). The impact of New Deal labor legislation on union growth and development has also been subjected to considerable discussion and analysis.

There has been controversy over the extent and nature of labor radicalism in the 1930s. Verba & Scholzman (1977) examined the limited survey data available from the late 1930s and concluded that there was little evidence of growing class consciousness among even unemployed working class citizens. Finegold & Skocpol (1984, 1995, Skocpol & Finegold 1990) argue that it was the New Deal labor reforms, first under the NIRA and then with the passage of the Wagner Act in 1935, that fundamentally spurred union organizing efforts (see also Brody 1993:120–28). Other analysts have focused on the deradicalizing impact of union bureucratization, noting that many of the CIO unions organized during the 1930s quickly developed organizational routines and hierarchies that blunted shop-floor militance (Mills 1948, Piven & Cloward 1977:ch. 3, Lichtenstein 1989), although such tendencies were less pronounced in those unions led by Communist or other left political forces (Kimmeldorf 1988, Zeitlin & Stepan-Norris 1989, 1992).

The bulk of the research on the labor movement in the 1930s, however, has concluded that labor radicalism was important for building industrial unions (Rubin, Griffin & Wallace 1983). The New Deal years were the high point of left influence in the labor movement, and left-wing labor organizers did a disproportionate share of the "boring of hard boards" during this period (Milton 1982, Fantasia 1988:ch. 2, Zeitlin & Stepan-Norris 1989, Goldfield 1989, Zieger 1995:253–61). Strike activity during the 1933–1934 and 1936–1937 periods was both extensive and unusual. It included several dramatic general strikes in 1934, and a wave of militant sit-down strikes in 1937. Further, a much higher proportion of strikes during this period than either before or since raised demands relating to union representation or workplace organization (Wallace 1989:13), though this would decline after the passage of the Wagner Act (McCammon 1993, 1994). New Deal labor legislation prior to 1937 is viewed by proponents of the labor militancy thesis as having had little enforcement power; hence it was only through the successful organizing drives that unions could began to be built (e.g. Cohen 1993:301ff.)

What was the impact of the organized labor on New Deal policy reforms? Frances Perkins, Roosevelt's choice to be Secretary of Labor, was opposed by union leaders. AFL unions in 1933 aggressively supported a 30-hour bill sponsored by Alabama Senator Hugo Black, and they were never significant factors in the debate over the Administration's alternative to the Black bill, the more sweeping National Industrial Relations Act of 1933 (e.g. Brand 1988). Unions consistently opposed the minimum wage provisions of the Fair Labor Standards Act of 1938, which the Roosevelt Administration nonetheless pushed through Congress (Hart 1989). Even if the labor insurgency of 1933–1935 (and the frequently hostile employer responses) contributed to the passage of the Wagner Act, few labor leaders were actively consulted during the drafting of the Act. AFL leaders were unsuccessful in attempting to amend the legislation during Congressional hearings, and when early rulings under the Act favored CIO unions over longstanding AFL organizing strategies, the AFL sought (unsuccessfully) to undermine the Act (Gross 1981, Tomlins 1985:161–95). For its part, CIO unions were unable to prevent the conservative counterattack against the Act beginning in the late 1930s. On other social legislation, notably the drafting and implementation of the Social Security Act, AFL and CIO officials were used in purely advisory roles by Administration officials, but they gained little influence over substantive decision-making processes on any aspect of the SSA (Derthick 1979, Tynes 1996). Both AFL and CIO unions did not begin pushing for national health insurance until 1938, after reform momentum had been lost (Derickson 1994). In short, although some labor leaders such as Sidney Hillman were regularly consulted by the Roosevelt Administration (Fraser 1992), the conclusion that organized labor's impact on New Deal policymaking was limited and indirect at best is probably inescapable.

Policy Experts, Political Intellectuals, and the New Deal

In the debates over the New Deal, the policy and political consequences of the activities of experts and intellectuals have received attention (Manza 1995:chs. 1–2 provides an overview). While some analysts dismiss the actions of experts and intellectuals as mere epiphenomena (e.g. Goldfield 1989, C. Gordon 1994), others have viewed their roles as more decisive. One set of approaches argues that the impetus for reform came from middle-class professionals, who patiently built support for pension reform during a long process of coalition building and reform advocacy dating to the Progressive era (Skocpol 1992, Moss 1996), including pressing the social question into arenas where it had not previously been pressed, frequently in alliance with labor or other social movements from below (Plotke 1996, Fink 1997). At the center of the efforts of these reformers were advocacy organizations such as the American Association for Labor Legislation and the American Association for Old Age Security. Such organizations provided intellectual and political leadership for early pension reform campaigns, and eventually, at the national level during the New Deal. In the case of agriculture, academic social scientists working on rural issues and the relatively large group of experts employed by the Department of Agriculture in the 1920s provided the intellectual foundation for a diverse array of policy ideas about farm planning and management (Finegold & Skocpol 1995, Gilbert & Howe 1991, Gilbert 1997). In these accounts, reform-oriented experts gained influence during the New Deal and were able to implement long promoted agendas.

In the types of analyses discussed in the previous paragraph, the ideas and strategic alliances of experts are seen as having direct causal influence. A more skeptical interpretation of the role of policy experts, but one that nonetheless takes seriously the role of policy ideas in the policymaking process, is developed in Domhoff's (1990:ch. 3–4, 1996:ch. 3, 5) work on New Deal reforms in agriculture, labor, and social security. Domhoff argues that the experts with influence were those who were directly or indirectly sponsored by a segment of the power elite. In the case of social insurance, he makes two arguments. First, key organizations of experts such as the American Association for Labor Legislation were not independent of the power elite, but rather received significant funding from it. Second, experts with more direct links to the power elite, especially through the Rockefeller-financed Industrial Relations Counsellors, Inc., had the greatest impact on the drafting of the Social Security Act.

Stryker (1989, 1990a,b), Shamir (1995), and Manza (1995, n.d.) have developed positions somewhere between these two standpoints. Stryker's work develops a "class-centered functionalist" account to explain the influence of particular types of expertise, and she argues that the advance of technical knowledge is constrained by power relations. In a case study of the elimination of the Division of Economic Research in the National Labor Relations Board, Stryker (1989) demonstrates that although the economists working for the NLRB provided a wide range of technical guidance for the lawyers running the Board, their input came to be perceived as too pro-union to be politically viable. Elsewhere, in comparative analyses of the NLRB and the Social Security Board (Stryker 1990a) and the NLRB and the Federal Trade Commission (Stryker 1990b), she argues that economic knowledge that is either neutral or beneficial for capitalist interests will not meet the same fate.

Shamir (1995) and Manza (1995, n.d.) emphasize the importance of political opportunity and strategic behavior on the part of groups of experts in determining when and how they gain influence. Shamir (1995:ch.6) argues that the promotion of administrative law and social scientific adjudication by a group of legal intellectuals known as the legal realists gave them wide influence inside the New Deal, whereas elite lawyers lost influence for their opposition to New Deal regulatory initiatives. Manza (n.d.) advances a model of strategic action to account for the political alignments of a coherent group of New Deal policy experts active in labor, pension, and health fields. In the labor case, the breakdown of the NIRA framework and the emergence of a revived labor movement from below promoted a set of alliances between experts and the labor movement (reversing the alliances of the 1920s with moderate corporate interests). In the case of pensions, the development of corporate support for some types of contributory pensions encouraged reforms to shift away from their previous support noncontributory pensions in the 1920s.

The Social Bases of the New Deal

Who supported the New Deal? A classical question of political sociology concerns the social bases of political movements, and the New Deal is no exception. Two aspects of the sources of support of the New Deal have received special attention: the electoral dimensions of the New Deal coalition, and campaign finance during the 1930s.

Electoral Realignment?   Roosevelt's (and the Democratic Party's) electoral sweeps from 1932 to 1936 were of unprecedented magnitude, inaugurating an era of Democratic dominance of national politics that would last through the late 1960s (and, with a couple of short interruptions, until 1980 at the Congressional level). Scholarly interest in the nature of the realignment toward the Democratic Party has focused most extensively on two questions: (*a*) To what extent was the New Deal electoral realignment driven by class divisions? (*b*) Did the Democratic vote come from the mobilization of new voters, or did it reflect the conversion of previously Republican voters?

Most scholarly assessments of the social bases of the New Deal coalition from the 1930s through the late 1940s have claimed to find unprecedented levels of class polarization, with urban working class, immigrant, and African-American voters swinging to the Democrats to a much greater extent than (white) middle class voters. Although the study of individual-level political behavior was very much in its infancy, contemporary research supported such class-based conclusions about the Democratic realignment (e.g. Lazarsfeld, Berelson, & Gaudet 1948). Postwar scholarship has generally confirmed the impression of class polarization at the ballot box during the New Deal (see e.g. Lawrence 1996:ch. 3). A number of arguments and pieces of evidence have been assembled. The spectacular failure of the *Literary Digest* poll in 1936 to predict Roosevelt's landslide victory has been construed by several analysts as indicating that class differences had increased (hence the significance of the unrepresentative character of the *Literary Digest* readership) (e.g. Burnham 1970:56, Sundquist 1983:215, Lawrence 1996:35). Early survey data confirm large class gaps in voter alignments (e.g. Ladd & Hadley 1978, Weakliem & Heath 1999). Later analysts have generally concluded that class divisions receded after World War II, although different assessments of the timing of this decline has been advanced (cf. Sundquist 1983, Weakliem & Heath 1999, Manza & Brooks 1999:ch. 3).

The debate over the sources of the enlarged Democratic vote beginning in 1932—whether from the mobilization of new voters or the conversion of previously Republican voters—has been investigated as well, though it is difficult to resolve in the absence of individual-level data. In the classical accounts of Key (1955) and Burnham (1970), the New Deal elections were viewed as a key instance of critical realignment of major blocs of voters. At the aggregate level, such conclusions are inarguable, but at the level of group alignments, the picture is more complicated. There is no doubt that in the North, African-American voters swung decisively from Republican to Democratic alignment during the 1930s (Weiss 1983). Studies of white ethnic voters have presented a more complicated picture of realignment. Andersen (1979) combined analyses of retrospective survey data with aggregate, ward-level data from Chicago, concluding that new voters (i.e. those voting for the first time) provided the decisive shift to Roosevelt and the Democrats. Gamm's (1986) analysis of the New Deal realignment in Boston isolated smaller, precinct-level units to permit more rigorous assessment of changes in group alignments. His analyses suggest that only among Jews and, to a lesser extent, African Americans does the group realignment model hold. Italians increased their turnout rates significantly, but not their alignment, while Yankees and the Irish maintained both similar turnout levels and patterns of alignment. Further work on these issues, especially where adequate precinct-level data has survived, is certainly warranted. King's (1997) recent methodological innovations for ecological studies may provide the foundation for a systematic reconsideration of the issues.

Campaign Finance   Research on campaign finance, in particular the sources of financial support for the Democratic Party during the 1930s, provides an important empirical context for assessing the question of whether there was an identifiable segment of business support for the New Deal. The Federal Corrupt Practices Act of 1925 required the parties to systematically report all contributions of $100 or more. All analysts recognize that most large contributors to the 1936 presidential campaign backed Republican candidate Alf Landon [Allen (1991) estimates 80% of "inner circle" business elites contributed to the Republicans, while Webber (2000:ch. 1, Webber & Domhoff (1996) estimates 83% of business executives from large companies). Even if the relative amounts they received were modest, understanding where Roosevelt and the Democrats did gain support from capitalist sources has been the subject of much interest. Two concrete hypotheses about the nature of business support for the New Deal were advanced in the 1980s. On the one hand, Fraser (1989) and Friedlander (1987) argue that consumption-oriented industries provided disproportionate Democratic support, on the grounds that policies that would promote income growth among the working class would generate enhanced business. Ferguson's (1995) "investment theory of party competition," by contrast, asserted that internationally oriented and capital-intensive firms were the most likely to support the Democrats. Because of their lower labor costs, Ferguson argues that such firms were willing to acquiesce to reform in exchange for an internationalist, free-trade regime. For these firms, the New Deal provided an attractive set of alliances, and that they (and their executives) provided crucial financial support in return.

Webber & Domhoff (1996) and Webber (2000) offer the most systematic reassessment of these claims, using the crucial 1936 election as a test case. Drawing from official campaign contribution data from records compiled in response to the 1925 Act, they find no evidence that any particular industrial sector—including either the mass consumption industries or capital-intensive, internationally oriented industries—was disproportionately supportive of the New Deal in comparison with the average of all large industries. The only groups of business executives who were disproportionately likely to fund the Democratic Party were Southerners and Jews (see also Allen 1991). In general, however, the ovewhelming majority of business leaders throughout this period were (or remained) Republican (cf. Allen 1991, Almond 1998).

Comparative Perspectives on the New Deal

Finally, it is worth commenting on scholarly efforts to place the New Deal in cross-national context. The economic depression that gripped the United States in the early 1930s was of global proportions, and the political consequences of this crisis of capitalism were felt everywhere. The impact was especially dramatic in the United States, which move from a laggard to a world leader in social spending. This suggests that comparative investigations of New Deal politics are warranted, yet relatively few works have sought to develop systematic comparative analyses.

Historical institutionalists have focused the greatest attention on comparative dimensions of the New Deal. Weir & Skocpol (1985) analyzed the factors that influenced the prospects for a "proto-Keynesian" response to the Great Depression in the United States, Great Britain, and Sweden during the 1930s. The puzzle is to account for why Sweden and the United States moved in the direction of Keynesianism, while Keynes' own Britain (which had high levels of unemployment in the 1920s) did not. Weir & Skocpol argue that the legacies of the early adoption of unemployment insurance and Treasury Policy in Britain shifted the terrain of debate away from macroeconomic measures designed to restore full employment, whereas in Sweden the absence of such programs made possible a more wide-ranging debate. In the United States, the difficulties of successful state-building in other arenas, the accumulation of policy-relevant knowledge, and rising class pressures in the late 1930s made a "proto-Keynesian" solution viable (cf. Weir 1992:ch.2). Dobbin (1993) develops an intriguing analysis of the ideological roots of industrial policy in the United States, Britain, and France in the 1930s. Each country responded to the Depression by reversing previous economic course; in the United States, this meant that a corporatist model gained influence, even to the point that it was embraced by many antimonopoly New Deal Democrats. Orloff

(1993a) examines how geopolitical factors combined with institutional structures and previous policy legacies to influence the substance and timing of the adoption of old-age pensions in Canada, Britain, and the United States. Other examples of comparative research on the New Deal by historical institutionalists would include the research of Amenta (1998:ch. 9) on social spending programs in the United States and Britain, Carruthers (1994) on British and American treasury policy, Hobson (1993) on social policy and women's right to work in the United States and Sweden, and Echeverri-Gent (1993) on rural antipoverty programs in the United States during the New Deal and in contemporary India.

Analysts from other theoretical traditions have, to date, been less concerned with developing comparative research. Richards (1994) examines the factors that led New Zealand to move in the direction of welfare state universalism in the 1930s and contrasts this case to the lingering parochialism in the US New Deal model. Swenson's (n.d.) forthcoming work examines how reformers interested in cross-class alliances in Sweden and the United States acted in cautious response to perceptions of employer interests that were radically different from each other in the two countries. He finds that such strategic behavior affected the different timing and shape welfare state development in the two countries in profound ways.

In general, however, cross-national comparative investigations of the New Deal have been much more limited than either comparative work on other periods of American political development (notably the late nineteenth century and the Progressive eras). Given the long-standing influence of comparative research in the field of political sociology—for example, in the work of Marx, Weber, Moore, and Lipset—it is all the more surprising that greater attention to comparative questions has not been developed. This is likely to be one growth area of New Deal studies in the future, and indeed such research promises to shed new light on the exceptional features of this period.

CONCLUSION

This paper has examined some of the myriad ways in which political sociologists have analyzed dimensions of political change during the New Deal. Early theoretical controversies developed among analysts arguing that the primary causal factors in accounting for New Deal political and policy outcomes lay in political struggles from below, business influence from above, gender relations, or the institutional contexts within which political actors struggled. Political sociologists have also begun to examine more refined empirical questions, including investigations of race, political geography, the social bases of New Deal political alignments, the role of intellectuals, and comparative issues. Perhaps more than any other single historical period, the New Deal has highlighted the rich potential for empirical and theoretical work made possible by the historic turn in contemporary social science.

ACKNOWLEDGMENTS

I would like to thank Peter Swenson, Ann Orloff, and especially Bill Domhoff for their helpful suggestions on an earlier draft of this paper, and Jerome Karabel and Michael Rogin for guidance with a much earlier discussion of these issues.

Visit the Annual Reviews home page at www.AnnualReviews.org

LITERATURE CITED

Almond GA. 1998. *Plutocracy and Politics in New York City.* Boulder, CO: Westview

Allen MP. 1991. Capitalist Response to State Intervention: Theories of the State and Political Finance in the New Deal. *Am. Sociol. Rev.* 56:679–89

Alston L, Ferree J. 1989. Social control and labor relations in the American South before the mechanizatrion of the cotton harvest in the 1950s. 145:133–57

Alston L, Ferree J. 1999. *Southern Paternalism and the American Welfare State.* New York: Cambridge Univ. Press

Amenta E. 1998. *Bold Relief: Institutional Politics and the Origins of Modern American Social Policy.* Princeton, NJ: Princeton Univ. Press

Amenta E, Carruthers BG, Zylan Y. 1992. A Hero for the Aged? The Townsend Movement and Social Security, 1934–1950. *Am. J. Sociol.* 98:308–39

Amenta E, Dunleavy K, Bernstein M. 1994. Stolen Thunder? Huey Long's 'Share Our Wealth,' Political Mediation, and the Second New Deal. *Am. Sociol. Rev.* 59:678–702

Amenta E, Parikh S. 1991. Capitalists Did Not Want The Social Security Act: A Critique of the 'Capitalist Dominance' Thesis. *Am. Sociol. Rev.* 56:124–29

Amenta E, Poulsen J. 1996. Social Politics in Context: The Institutional-Politics Theory and State-Level Social Spending at the End of the New Deal. *Soc. Forces* 75:33–60

Andersen K. 1979. *The Creation of a Democratic Majority.* Chicago: Univ. Chicago Press

Beer SH. 1994. *To Make a Nation: The Rediscovery of American Federalism.* Cambridge, MA: Harvard Univ. Press

Bensel RF. 1984. *Sectionalism and American Political Development: 1880–1980.* Madison, WI: Univ. Wisc. Press

Berkowitz E, McQuaid K. 1992. *Creating the Welfare State: The Political Economy of 20th Century Reform.* Rev. ed. Lawrence, KS: Univ. Presses of Kansas

Bernstein MA. 1987. *The Great Depression: Delayed Recovery and Economic Change in America, 1929–1939.* New York: Cambridge Univ. Press

Block F. 1977. The Ruling Class Does Not Rule: Notes on the Marxist Theory of the State. *Socialist Rev.* 33:6–27

Bordo MD, Goldin C, White EN, eds. 1998. *The Defining Moment: The Great Depression and the American Economy in the Twentieth Century.* Chicago: Univ. Chicago Press

Brand D. 1988. *Corporatism and Rule of Law.* Ithaca, NY: Cornell Univ. Press

Brenner R. 1985. The Paradox of Social Democracy: The American Case. In *The Year Left,* Vol 1, ed. M Davis, F Pfeil, M Sprinkler, pp. 32–86. London: Verso

Brody D. 1993. *Workers in Industrial America.* New York: Oxford Univ. Press. 2nd ed.

Brown M. 1999. *Race, Money, and the American Welfare State.* Ithaca, NY: Cornell Univ. Press

Burnham WD. 1970. *Critical Elections and the Mainsprings of American Politics.* New York: Norton

Carruthers BG. 1994. When Is the State Autonomous? Culture, Organization Theory, and the Political Sociology of the State. *Soc. Theory* 12:19–44

Casebeer K. 1994. Unemployment Insurance: American Social Wage, Labor Organization, and Legal Ideology. *Boston Coll. Law Rev.* 35:259–348

Cauthen NK, Amenta E. 1996. The Formative Years of Aid to Dependent Children. *Am. Sociol. Rev.* 61:427–48

Cohen L. 1993. *Making a New Deal: Industrial Workers in Chicago, 1919–1939.* New York: Cambridge Univ. Press

Davies G, Derthick M. 1997. Race and Social Welfare Policy: The Social Security Act of 1935. *Polit. Sci. Q.* 112:217–35

Davis M. 1986. *Prisoners of the American Dream.* London: Verso

Derickson A. 1994. Health Security for All? Social Unionism and Universal Health Insurance, 1935–1958. *J. Am. Hist.* 80:1333–56

Derthick M. 1979. *Policymaking for Social Security.* Washington DC: Brookings Inst.

Dobbin FR. 1993. The Social Construction of the Great Depression: Industrial Policy During the 1930s in the United States, Britain, and France. *Theory Soc.* 22:1–56

Domhoff GW. 1970. *The Higher Circles.* New York: Random House

Domhoff GW. 1990. *The Power Elite and the State.* New York: Aldine

Domhoff GW. 1996. *State Autonomy or Class Dominance?* New York: Aldine

Domhoff GW. 1998. *Who Rules America: Power and Politics in the Year 2000.* Menlo Park, CA: Mayfield

Dubofsky M. 1994. *The State and Labor in Modern America.* Chapel Hill, NC: Univ. N. Carolina Press

Echeverri-Gent J. 1993. *The State and the Poor.* Berkeley: Univ. Calif. Press

Fantasia R. 1988. *Cultures of Solidarity.* Berkeley: Univ. Calif. Press

Ferguson T. 1995. *Golden Rule: The Investment Theory of Party Competition and the Logic of Money-Driven Political Systems.* Chicago: Univ. Chicago Press

Finegold K, Skocpol T. 1984. State, Party and Industry: From Business Recovery to the Wagner Act in America's New Deal. In *Statemaking and Social Movements,* ed. C Bright, S Harding, pp. 159–92. Ann Arbor, MI: Univ. Mich. Press

Finegold K, Skocpol T. 1995. *State and Party in America's New Deal.* Madison WI: Univ. Wisc. Press

Fink L. 1997. *Progressive Intellectuals and the Dilemmas of Democratic Commitment.* Cambridge, MA: Harvard Univ. Press

Fitzpatrick E. 1990. *Endless Crusade: Women Social Scientists and Progressive Reform.* New York: Oxford Univ. Press

Foner E. 1988. *Reconstruction: America's Unfinished Revolution, 1863–1877.* New York: Harper

Fraser S. 1989. The 'Labor Question.' In *The Rise and Fall of the New Deal Order,* ed. S Fraser, G Gerstle, pp. 55–84. Princeton, NJ: Princeton Univ. Press

Fraser S. 1992. *Labor Will Rule: Sidney Hillman and the Rise of American Labor.* New York: Free Press

Fredrickson G. 1981. *White Supremacy: A Comparative Study of American and South African History.* New York: Oxford Univ. Press

Friedlander P. 1987. *The Origins of the Welfare State: The Keynesian Elite and the Second New Deal.* Unpub. ms., Dept. Hist., Wayne State Univ. Detroit, MI

Gamm GH. 1986. *The Making of the New Deal Democrats: Voting Behavior and Realignment in Boston, 1920–1940.* Chicago: Univ. Chicago Press

Gelfand M. 1975. *A Nation of Cities: The Federal Government and Urban America.* New York: Oxford Univ. Press

Gilbert J. 1997. *Organic Intellectuals in the State: A Collective Biography of Midwestern Social Scientists in the New Deal Department of Agriculture.* Presented at Annu. Meet. Soc. Sci. Hist. Assoc., Washington DC

Gilbert J, Howe C. 1991. Beyond 'State' vs. 'Society': Theories of the State and New

Deal Agricultural Policies. *Am. Sociol. Rev.* 56:204–20

Goldfield M. 1989. Worker Insurgency, Radical Organization, and New Deal Labor Legislation. *Am. Polit. Sci. Rev.* 83:1257–82

Goldfield M. 1990. Reply to Skocpol and Finegold. *Am. Polit. Sci. Rev.* 84:1304–15

Goldfield M. 1993. Race and the CIO: The Possibilities for Racial Egalitarianism During the 1930s and 1940s. *Int. Labor Working Class Hist.* 44:1–32

Goldfield M. 1997. *The Color of Politics.* New York: New Press

Gordon C. 1994. *New Deals: Business, Labor and Politics in America, 1920–1935.* New York: Cambridge Univ. Press

Gordon L. 1994. *Pitied But Not Entitled: Single Mothers and the History of Welfare.* New York: Free Press

Gross JA. 1981. *The Reshaping of the National Labor Relations Board.* Albany, NY: State Univ. NY Press

Hamilton DC, Hamilton CV. 1997. *The Dual Agenda: Race and Social Welfare Policies of Civil Rights Organizations.* New York: Columbia Univ. Press

Hart V. 1989. Minimum-Wage Policy and Constitutional Inequality: The Paradox of the Fair Labor Standards Act of 1938. *J. Policy Hist.* 1:319–43

Hattam V. 1993. *Labor Visions and State Power: The Origins of Business Unionism in the United States.* Princeton, NJ: Princeton Univ Press.

Heclo H. 1977. *A Government of Strangers: Executive Politics in Washington.* Washington DC: Brookings Inst.

Hobson B. 1993. Feminist Strategies and Gendered Discourses in Welfare States: Married Women's Right to Work in the United States and Sweden. In *Mothers of a New World,* ed. S Koven, S Michel, pp. 396–430. New York: Routledge

Hooks G. 1990. From an Autonomous to a Captured State Agency: The Decline of the New Deal in Agriculture. *Am. Sociol. Rev.* 55:29–43

Immergut E. 1992. *Health Politics: Interests and Institutions in Western Europe.* New York: Cambridge Univ. Press

Immergut E. 1998. The Theoretical Core of the New Insitutionalism. *Polit. Soc.* 26:5–34

Jackson KT. 1985. *Crabgrass Frontier: The Suburbanization of the United States.* New York: Oxford Univ. Press

Jacoby S. 1993. Employers and the Welfare State: The Role of Marion B. Folsom. *J. Am. Hist.* 47:525–56

Jenkins JC, Brents B. 1989. Social Protest, Hegemonic Competition, and Social Reform: A Political Struggle Interpretation of the Origins of the American Welfare State. *Am. Sociol. Rev.* 54:891–909

Katznelson I. 1981. *City Trenches.* Chicago: Univ. Chicago Press

Katznelson I, Geiger K, Krystof D. 1993. Limiting Liberalism: The Southern Veto in Congress, 1933–1950. *Polit. Sci. Q.* 108:283–306

Kennedy D. 1999. *Freedom From Fear: The American People in Depression and War, 1929–1945.* New York: Oxford Univ. Press.

Key VO. 1955. A Theory of Critical Elections. *J. Polit.* 17:3–18

King G. 1997. *A Solution to the Ecological Inference Problem.* Princeton, NJ: Princeton Univ. Press

Kimmeldorf H. 1988. *Reds or Rackets? The Making of Radical and Conservative Unions on the Waterfront.* Berkeley: Univ. Calif. Press

Klein J. 1998. *Welfare Capitalism in the Era of the Welfare State: Insurers, Employers, and the Politics of Security, 1933–39.* Presented at Annu. Meet. Soc. Sci. Hist. Assoc., Chicago, Nov 19

Ladd EC, Hadley C. 1978. *Transformations of the American Party System.* New York: Norton. 2nd ed.

Lazarsfeld PF, Berelson BR, Gaudet H. 1948. *The People's Choice.* New York: Columbia Univ. Press

Lawrence DG. 1996. *The Collapse of the*

Democratic Presidential Majority. Boulder, CO: Westview. Rev. ed.

Levine RF. 1988. *Class Struggle and the New Deal.* Lawrence, KS: Univ. Presses Kansas

Lieberman RC. 1998. *Shifting the Color Line: Race and the American Welfare State.* Cambridge, MA: Harvard Univ. Press

Linder M. 1992. *Migrant Workers and Minimum Wages.* Boulder, CO: Westview

Manza J. 1995. *Policy Experts and Political Change During the New Deal.* PhD diss, Dep. Sociol., Univ. Calif., Berkeley

Manza J. n.d. *The Rationality of Intellectuals: Policy Experts and Political Reform During the New Deal.* Unpubl. ms., Dep. Sociol., Northwestern Univ. Chicago, IL

Manza J, Brooks C. 1999. *Social Cleavages and Political Change: Voter Alignments and Party Coalitions in the United States.* New York: Oxford Univ. Press

Massey DS, Denton NA. 1993. *American Apartheid: Segregation and the Making of the Underclass.* Cambridge, MA: Harvard Univ. Press

McCammon HJ. 1993. From Repressive Intervention to Integrative Prevention: The U.S. State's Legal Management of Labor Militancy, 1881–1978. *Soc. Forces* 71:569–601

McCammon HJ. 1994. Disorganizing and Reorganizing Conflict: Outcomes of the State's Legal Regulation of the Strike Since the Wagner Act. *Soc. Forces* 72:1011–49

McDonald TJ, ed. 1996. *The Historic Turn in the Human Sciences.* Ann Arbor, MI: Univ. Mich. Press

Mettler S. 1999. *Dividing Citizens: Gender and Federalism in New Deal Public Policy.* Ithaca, NY: Cornell Univ. Press

Mills CW. 1948. *The New Men of Power.* New York: Harcourt, Brace

Milton D. 1982. *The Politics of U.S. Labor.* New York: Monthly Rev. Press

Mink G. 1995. *The Wages of Motherhood: Inequality in the Welfare State, 1917–1942.* Ithaca, NY: Cornell Univ. Press

Moss DA. 1996. *Socializing Security: Progressive-Era Economists and the Origins of* *American Social Policy.* Cambridge, MA: Harvard Univ. Press

Muncy R. 1991. *Creating a Female Dominion in American Reform 1890–1935.* New York: Oxford Univ. Press

Neustadt R. 1990. *Presidential Power and the Modern Presidents: The Politics of Leadership From Roosevelt to Reagan.* New York: Free Press

Orloff AS. 1993a. *The Politics of Pensions.* Madison: Univ. Wisc. Press

Orloff AS. 1993b. Gender and the Social Rights of Citizenship: The Comparative Analysis of Gender Relations and Welfare States. *Am. Sociol. Rev.* 58:303–28

Orloff AS. 1996. Gender in the Welfare State. *Annu. Rev. Sociol.* 22:51–78

Orloff AS, Monson RA. n.d. Citizens, workers, or fathers? Men in the history of US social policy. In *Making Fathers Out of Men? Fathers and the State,* ed. B. Hobson, unpubl. ms.

Piven FF, Cloward RA. 1977. *Poor People's Movements.* New York: Vintage

Piven FF, Cloward RA. 1988. *Why Americans Don't Vote.* New York: Pantheon

Piven FF, Cloward RA. 1997. *The Breaking of the American Social Compact.* New York: New Press

Plotke D. 1996. *Building a Democratic Political Order.* New York: Cambridge Univ. Press

Poulantzas N. 1978. *State, Power, Socialism.* London: Verso

Quadagno J. 1988a. *The Transformation of Old Age Security.* Chicago: Univ. Chicago Press

Quadagno J. 1988b. From Old Age Assistance to Supplemental Security Income: The Political Economy of Relief in the South, 1935–1972. In *The Politics of Social Policy in the United States,* ed. M Weir, et al., pp. 235–64. Princeton, NJ: Princeton Univ. Press

Quadagno J. 1994. *The Color of Welfare.* New York: Oxford Univ. Press

Richards R. 1994. *Closing the Door to Destitution.* University Park, PA: Penn. St. Univ. Press

Rogers Joel. 1990. Divide and Conquer: Further

'Reflctions on the Distinctive Character of American Labor Law.' *Univ. Wisc. Law Rev.* 1990:1–147

Rubin BA, Griffin LJ, Wallace M. 1983. 'Provided Only That Their Voice Was Strong': Insurgency and Organization of American Labor From NRA to Taft-Hartley. *Work Occup.* 10:325–47

Rueschemeyer D, Stephens E, Stephens J. 1992. *Capitalist Development and Democracy.* Chicago: Univ. Chicago Press

Sass SA. 1997. *The Promise of Private Pensions: The First Hundred Years.* Cambridge, MA: Harvard Univ. Press

Shamir R. 1995. *Managing Legal Uncertainty: Elite Lawyers in the New Deal.* Durham, NC: Duke Univ. Press

Shefter M. 1994. *Political Parties and the State: The American Historical Experience.* Princeton, NJ: Princeton Univ. Press

Shepsle KA, Weingast B. 1987. The Institutional Foundations of Committee Power. *Am. Polit. Sci. Rev.* 81:85–104

Sklar KK. 1993. The Historical Foundations of Women's Power in the Creation of the American Welfare State, 1830–1930. In *Mothers of a New World,* ed. S Koven, S Michel, pp. 43–93. New York: Routledge

Skocpol T. 1980. Political Response to Capitalist Crisis: Neo-Marxist Theories of the State and the Case of the New Deal. *Polit. Soc.* 10:155–201

Skocpol T. 1992. *Protecting Soldiers and Mothers.* Cambridge, MA: Harvard Univ. Press

Skocpol T. 1995. *Social Policy in the United States.* Princeton, NJ: Princeton Univ. Press

Skocpol T, Amenta E. 1985. Did Capitalists Shape Social Security? *Am. Sociol. Rev.* 50:572–75

Skocpol T, Finegold K. 1990. Explaining New Deal Labor Policy. *Am. Polit. Sci. Rev.* 84:1297–1304

Skocpol T, Ikenberry GJ. 1983. The Political Formation of the American Welfare State in Historical and Comparative Perspective. *Compar. Soc. Res.* 6:87–147

Skowronek S. 1982. *Building a New American State: The Expansion of National Administrative Capacities, 1877–1920.* New York: Cambridge Univ. Press

Steinmo S. 1993a. *Taxation and Democracy: Swedish, British, and American Approaches to Financing the Modern State.* New Haven, CT: Yale Univ. Press

Steinmo S. 1993b. Rethinking American Exceptionalism: Culture or Institutions? In *Dynamics of American Politics: Approaches and Interpretations,* ed. L Dodd, C Jillson, pp. 106–31. Boulder, CO: Westview

Stryker R. 1989. Limits on the Technocratization of the Law: The Elimination of the National Labor Relations Board's Division of Economic Research. *Am. Sociol. Rev.* 54:341–58

Stryker R. 1990a. Science, Class, and the Welfare State: A Class-Centered Functional Account. *Am. J. Sociol.* 96:684–726

Stryker R. 1990b. A Tale of Two Agencies: Class, Political-Institutional, and Organizational Factors Affecting State Reliance on Social Science. *Polit. Soc.* 18:101–40

Sundquist JL. 1983. *Dynamics of the Party System.* Washington DC: Brookings Inst. Rev. ed.

Swenson P. 1996. Arranged Alliance: Business Interests in the New Deal. *Polit. Soc.* 25:66–116

Swenson P. n.d. *Labor Markets and Welfare States: Employers in the Making of the American and Swedish Systems.* Unpub. ms., Dept. Polit. Sci., Northwestern Univ., Chicago, IL

Thelen K, Steinmo S. 1992. Historical Institutionalism in Comparative Politics. In *Structuring Politics: Historical Institutionalism in Comparative Analysis,* ed. S Steinmo, K Thelen, F Longstreth, pp. 1–33. New York: Cambridge Univ. Press

Therborn G. 1978. *What Does the Ruling Class Do When It Rules?* London: Verso

Tomlins C. 1985. *The State and the Unions.* New York: Cambridge Univ. Press

Tynes SR. 1996. *Turning Points in Social Security: From 'Cruel Hoax' to 'Sacred Entitlement.'* Stanford, CA: Stanford Univ. Press

Valocchi S. 1994. The Racial Bases of Capitalism and the State, and the Impact of the New Deal on African Americans. *Soc. Prob.* 41:347–62

Verba S, Scholzman KL. 1977. Unemployment, Class Consciousness, and Radical Politics: What Didn't Happen in the Thirties. *J. Polit.* 39:291–323

Voss K. 1994. *The Making of American Exceptionalism: The Knights of Labor and Class Formation in the Nineteenth Century.* Ithaca, NY: Cornell Univ. Press

Wallace M. 1989. Aggressive Economism, Defensive Control: Contours of American Labor Militancy, 1947–1981. *Econ. Ind. Democ.* 10:7–34

Weakliem DL, Heath AF. 1999. The Secret Life of Class Voting: Britain, France, and the United States Since the 1930s. In *The End of Class Politics?*, ed. G Evans, pp. 97–136. New York: Oxford Univ. Press

Weaver RK, Rockman BA. 1993. Assessing the Effects of Institutions. In *Do Institutions Matter?*, ed. RK Weaver, BA Rockman, pp. 1–41. Washington DC: Brookings Inst. Press

Webber MJ. 2000. *New Deal Fat Cats: Business, Labor and Campaign Finance in the 1936 Presidential Election.* New York: Fordham Univ. Press

Webber MJ, Domhoff GW. 1996. Myth and Reality in Business Support for Democrats and Republicans in the 1936 Presidential Election. *Am. Polit. Sci. Rev.* 90:824–33

Weir M, Orloff AS, Skocpol T, eds. 1988. *The Politics of Social Policy in the United States.* Princeton, NJ: Princeton Univ. Press

Weir M, Skocpol T. 1985. State Structures and the Possibilities for 'Keynesian' Responses to the Great Depression in Sweden, Britain, and the United States. In *Bringing the State Back In,* ed. PB Evans, T Skocpol, D Rueschemeyer, pp. 107–63. New York: Cambridge Univ. Press

Weiss N. 1983. *Farewell to the Party of Lincoln.* Princeton, NJ: Princeton Univ. Press

Wolters R. 1970. *Negroes and the Great Depression.* Westport, CT: Greenwood

Zeitlin M, Stepan-Norris J. 1989. 'Who Gets the Bird?' Or, How the Communists Won Power and Trust in America's Unions: The Relative Autonomy of Intraclass Political Struggles. *Am. Sociol. Rev.* 54:503–23

Zeitlin M, Stepan-Norris J. 1992. The Insurgent Origins of Union Democracy. In *Reexamining Democracy,* ed. G Marks, L Diamond, pp. 250–73. Newbury Park, CA: Sage Pub

Zieger RH. 1995. *The CIO, 1935–1955.* Chapel Hill: Univ. N. Carolina Press

Annu. Rev. Sociol. 2000. 26:323–39

THE TREND IN BETWEEN-NATION INCOME INEQUALITY

Glenn Firebaugh

Department of Sociology, Pennsylvania State University, 211 Oswald Tower, University Park, Pennsylvania 16803; e-mail: firebaug@pop.psu.edu

Key Words   income inequality, convergence theory, cross-national, income growth

■ **Abstract**   About seventy percent of the world's total income inequality is between-nation inequality as opposed to within-nation inequality. Between-nation inequality is the bigger component because average incomes in the richest nations are roughly 30 times greater than average incomes in the poorest nations. This highly uneven distribution of income across nations likely reflects the long-run divergence of national incomes over the course of the Industrial Revolution. Empirical investigations suggest, however, that between-nation income inequality has stabilized in recent decades. Because between-nation inequality has stabilized, the direction of the current trend in total world income inequality depends on the direction of the change in income inequality in the average nation.

THE BIG PICTURE: Incomes and Income Inequality Since 1800

To place the current trend in between-nation income inequality in historical context, the chapter begins with an overview of the twin income legacies of the Industrial Revolution: the increase in national incomes and the increase in income disparity between nations. The chapter then describes two conflicting narratives—a convergence story and a polarization story—that are both commonplace in the social science literature. Although cross-nation polarization apparently has been the order of the day over the past two centuries, recent empirical investigations observe a leveling-off of the trend in between-nation income inequality. The chapter reviews that evidence and then concludes with suggestions for strategic research to further understanding of how the world's income is distributed both across and within nations.

Rise in National Incomes

At the dawn of the Industrial Revolution, Thomas Malthus (1798) and other classical economists feared that humans might be doomed to near-subsistence levels

0360-0572/00/0815-0323$14.00

of living. The fear was based on a population-trap model positing that economic growth is unlikely to outpace population growth over the long run. In this model, economic gains are short-lived as the geometric growth of population inevitably catches up with linear economic gains. Unless there are preventive checks on population growth, then, income *per capita* will inevitably return to a low equilibrium level. A new round of economic expansion will upset that equilibrium in the short run, but in the long run income per capita will track back down to its pre-expansion level. In other words, economic growth will serve to increase the size of the human population, but it will not boost living standards over the long run.

The pace of population growth and economic growth over the last two centuries has proven the classical economists right about the expansion of the human population but wrong about the population trap. The productivity gains of the Industrial Revolution were accompanied by an era of unprecedented population growth. In 1820 the world's population was about 1.1 billion (Maddison 1995, Table 1-1a). Today the world's population is over six billion.

Has the quintupling of the world's population resulted in the stagnation of *per capita* incomes? No. Economic growth outpaced population growth over the period, so per capita incomes increased. The increase was substantial. According to recent estimates, per capita income for the world as a whole increased eight-fold over the past 170 years, from about $650 per capita in 1820 to about $5150 in 1992, in constant dollars (Maddison 1995, Table 1-1a). During a period of unprecedented population growth, then, the world's total income shot up even more rapidly.

With respect to the trend in the world's per capita income, the news has been encouraging over the past two centuries. Despite an unprecedented increase in the world's population over the period, the world's annual income stands at very roughly $5000 per person.

Although the rise in world incomes does not appear to be accompanied by rising human happiness or contentment (Easterlin 1998), at the least it can be said that at this juncture in history there is greater *potential* than there was in earlier eras for meeting the essential human needs for food, shelter, clothing, and medical attention. The central economic issue for our era is not whether there is enough to go around—there is more to go around now than ever before—but how evenly the world's income is distributed. The news in that regard is less heartening.

Rise in the Income Disparity Between Nations During the Industrial Revolution

The Industrial Revolution produced a sharp increase in the income disparity between the richest and poorest regions of the world. In 1820 per capita income in Western Europe (the world's richest region at the time) was roughly three times greater than per capita income in Africa. Today per capita income is almost 14 times greater in Western Europe than it is in Africa (Maddison 1995, Table 1-2). The gap is even larger for individual nations. Average incomes in the richest and the poorest nations now differ by a factor of about 30 (Summers, Heston, Aten and Nuxoll 1994). Apparently, then, *national* incomes have diverged over the long run, from the early nineteenth century through much of the twentieth.

So there are two big stories about world income trends over the past two centuries. The first story is that the world's average income has risen substantially, and the second story is that income appears to have become more unevenly distributed across nations. Both stories contradict important theoretical models. The sharp rise in per capita income flies in the face of the population-trap model of classical economics. The rise in income inequality across nations flies in the face of the convergence prediction of some income growth models.

Few dispute these stories. Average incomes have increased and regional and national incomes apparently have diverged over the course of the Industrial Revolution. The more vexing issue is whether the trends are continuing. In particular, has the cross-national divergence in incomes continued in the last half of the twentieth century as industrialization has spread to all regions of the world?

This article focuses on the question of recent cross-national divergence. I begin by describing two rival theses: the convergence thesis of income growth theory in economics and the polarization thesis of world system/dependency theory in sociology. Then I review the key studies that address that issue. Because those studies appear to present a mishmash of contradictory results, I try to make sense of the findings. Weighting by national population is the key. When nations are weighted equally—so small nations such as Luxembourg are given as much weight as large ones such as China—the distribution of income across nations has become more unequal in recent decades. But when nations are weighted by population size, the distribution of income across nations has remained relatively stable in recent decades. I argue that the latter fact is the one of more relevance to sociologists because change in the level of inequality for the world overall is a function of change in *population-weighted* between-nation inequality (plus change in population-weighted within-nation income inequality). I conclude by discussing the implications of these results for convergence, dependency, and population theories of national income growth.

CONVERGENCE THEORY VERSUS POLARIZATION THEORY*

Convergence Theory in Economics

The issue of whether national economies tend to converge or diverge over time has been a central concern in economics over the past decade. Economists are keenly interested in the convergence issue because of recent debates over the nature of economic growth. One popular view, often associated with neoclassical growth theory (Solow 1956), is that national economies tend to converge because of the

*Here and in a few other places in this chapter I draw on material from Firebaugh (1999).

principle of diminishing returns to capital and labor. As rich industrial nations experience diminishing returns, poorer nations (who are farther from the point of diminishing returns) will tend to catch up as they industrialize. DeLong (1988, p. 1138) summarizes the convergence argument this way in the *American Economic Review*: "Economists have always expected the 'convergence' of national productivity levels. The theoretical logic behind this belief is powerful. The per capita income edge of the West is based on its application of the storehouse of industrial and administrative technology of the Industrial Revolution .... The benefits of tapping this storehouse are great, so nations will strain every nerve to assimilate modern technology and their incomes will converge to those of industrial nations."

The convergence thesis has been challenged by the predictions of endogenous growth theory (Romer 1986, Lucas 1988). Endogenous growth theory argues that in today's world the principle of diminishing returns can be overcome by specialized inputs made possible by research. Thus, there is no inherent tendency toward long-run income convergence across nations. Because of their research advantages, it is possible for richer nations to maintain long-run rates of income growth that exceed those of poorer nations, implying cross-national divergence, not convergence.

By questioning some key elements of neoclassical growth theory, endogenous growth theory has reopened the debate about convergence and prompted a new generation of cross-nation growth studies in economics. However, many of the studies do not weight nations by their population size, so (as I argue below) the findings have limited relevance for sociologists interested in the trend in overall world inequality.

Despite the limited relevance of the findings of many of the endogenous growth studies, endogenous growth theory itself is relevant to sociology because it presents an important alternative explanation for income polarization across nations. If national incomes are diverging, the source of the divergence could be specialized research inputs in the richer nations. That explanation for divergence is quite different from the explanation offered by world system and dependency theories, as I now elaborate.

The Polarization Thesis in Sociology

Sociologists have no theory of between-nation income inequality that matches the level of formalization that one encounters in the economic literature on neoclassical growth theory and endogenous growth theory. Nevertheless, there is a rich empirical literature in sociology on the determinants of national economic growth, and much of this literature argues or assumes that rich nations are enriching themselves at the expense of poorer nations. Indeed, national divergence is a dominant theme in comparative sociology.

Dependency-Induced Divergence   The divergence theme in sociology most often is based on a world system or dependency perspective on national development.

The ready acceptance of the divergence thesis by world system theorists is not surprising because world system theory emphasizes the division of the world economy into identifiable economic strata. That said, nothing inherent in a strictly world system perspective would rule out convergence stories because one can imagine conditions under which the strata would converge.

What dependency theory adds are arguments for why the strata tend to diverge. Dependency theory is a theory of world stratification—of why some nations are so rich and others are so poor. Dependency theory rests on the premise that the development of core nations and the underdevelopment of peripheral nations are complementary processes in that core nations enrich themselves *at the expense of poor nations*. In other words, the development of rich core nations and the "underdevelopment" of poor peripheral nations are two aspects of the same process. This state of affairs comes about because core nations differentially benefit from core-periphery economic exchange.

Thus, in dependency theory the law of differential benefits from exchange (Mandel 1975)—not the law of diminishing returns—is the mainspring for trends in intercountry inequality. The law of differential benefits from exchange implies a "growing gap between core and periphery" in the world economy as a whole (Chase-Dunn 1975, p. 720). "A picture of unequal development emerges in which the core becomes progressively more developed while peripheral development is hindered as a result of its relationship to the core" (Peacock et al 1988, p. 839). In effect, then, dependency theory argues that Marx's law of uneven development applies to the world economy as a whole rather than to classes within individual industrial nations (Chase-Dunn 1975).

Population-Induced Divergence   Quite apart from differential benefits from exchange, there are other reasons why national incomes might diverge. One reason—noted earlier—is endogenous growth, as richer nations can use their advantages in research and development to offset the effects of diminishing returns to capital and labor. A second possibility is population-induced income divergence. National income is income *per capita*, so change in national income is determined by rate of population growth as well as by rate of economic expansion. Suppose two national economies expand at the same rate—say 6% in a given year. Do their national incomes converge or diverge? The answer depends on their respective population growth rates. The nation with the slower population growth rate will exhibit the more rapid growth in income per capita. So there is divergence if the richer nation has the slower rate of population growth and convergence if the poorer nation has the slower rate of population growth. This line of argument implies income divergence across nations because in recent decades population has tended to grow more rapidly in poorer nations than it has in richer nations. If income *per capita* has grown more slowly in poorer nations in recent decades, that slower growth may be due to the swelling of the young (nonworking) population in poor nations quite apart from any effects of international economic exchange. In analyses of trends in between-nation income inequality, then, it is important to distinguish this *population-induced* income divergence from *dependency-induced* divergence.

The argument for population-induced income divergence is reminiscent of the view of classical economists such as Malthus (1798), John Stuart Mill (1848), Ricardo (1817), and Smith (1776) that economic growth is a "race between increases in the population and capital stock" (Dorfman 1991, p. 577). If this is true, then at this point in history poor nations—with their more rapid rates of population growth—are inherently disadvantaged. The argument here is that rapid population growth *slows* income growth. This argument is not the population trap argument because I am not suggesting that slower growth means a *negative* growth rate. (The population-trap model requires periods of negative growth rates, as per capita income returns to its pre-expansion level. That is, following periods of economic expansion, per capita income tracks back down to its equilibrium point as population growth outpaces economic expansion—so there is a period of declining average income.)

WITHIN-NATION VERSUS BETWEEN-NATION INEQUALITY

The total income inequality in the world is the sum of within-nation inequality and between-nation inequality. In sociology, the vast majority of cross-national studies of inequality examine within-nation inequality. In a typical study of this sort, regression analysis is used to estimate the effects of various national characteristics (e.g., income level, type of political system) on a nation's level of income inequality (examples include Cutright 1967, Weede & Tiefenbach 1981, Bollen & Jackman 1985, Hoover 1989, Nielsen & Alderson 1997). Such studies have been a staple of social science research at least since the 1960s, when economists and other social scientists began to assemble data to test Kuznets's (1955) inverted-U thesis that a nation's income inequality tends to increase with the onset of industrialization and then decline at more advanced levels of industrialization. In sociology, cross-national research on inequality was especially fashionable during the heyday of world system and dependency theory in the 1970s and 1980s.

While cross-national studies of within-nation inequality are commonplace in sociology, studies of between-nation income inequality are rare. There are three apparent reasons for the neglect of between-nation inequality in favor of within-nation inequality. First, within-nation inequality can be studied with cross-sectional data, whereas the study of between-nation inequality requires longitudinal data. Second, within-nation inequality is more policy-relevant in that national income distribution can be compressed by state policies. There are no international organizations with the muscle to compress the distribution of income across nations. Third, it can be argued that psychic costs of inequality are greater for within-nation inequality, since feelings of relative deprivation derive largely from local comparisons.

Whatever the reasons, the relative neglect of between-nation income inequality is unfortunate since *the majority of the world's total income inequality is between-nation inequality, not within-nation inequality* (Korzeniewicz & Moran 1997). Total income inequality for the world is based on the variance of the world's income distribution: For a given mean income, the greater the variance, the greater the inequality. To measure inequality, one wants an index that is scale-invariant (Allison 1978), that is, an index that gives the same results regardless of the currency used (dollars or pesos or yen or whatever). One way to obtain scale invariance is to divide the standard deviation of the income distribution by the mean. This measure is called the coefficient of variation. A second way to obtain scale invariance is to log the income before taking the variance. This measure is called the variance of the logarithm or VarLog. The coefficient of variation and VarLog are both commonly used as indexes of inequality.

Importantly, because inequality can be measured as scale-invariant variance, inequality can be decomposed into a within-group and a between-group component. Suppose we knew the income of every person (or every household) in the world. Then we could calculate the variance of the income distribution for the whole world *and* we could decompose that total variance into its within-nation and between-nation components using the familiar ANOVA decomposition:

$$\sum_j \sum_i (X_{ij} - \mu)^2 / N \equiv \sum_j n_j (\mu_j - \mu)^2 / N + \sum_j \sum_i (X_{ij} - \mu_j)^2 / N \quad (1)$$

where j indexes nation, i indexes individual, and μ denotes mean. Equation 1 applies to VarLog because VarLog is a variance. But VarLog is also a measure of inequality. It follows that it is possible to separate the within-nation and between-nation components of total world inequality by applying Equation 1 to VarLog. Several other inequality indexes decompose in a similar manner (see Allison 1978).

The important point here is that, with income data for everyone, one could determine how much of the world's total income inequality is due to within-nation inequality, and how much is due to the disparity in incomes across nations. In the absence of complete income data, several studies have tried to estimate the relative magnitudes of the within- and between-nation components (Theil 1979, Ram 1979, Berry et al 1983b, Korzeniewicz & Moran 1997). Although the studies differ in the data they use and the years they examine, they all agree with Berry et al (1983b, p. 217) that "it is clear that the level of world inequality is ... primarily due to differences in average incomes across countries rather than to intra-country inequality."

Between-nation inequality is the larger component not because within-nation inequality is so small but because between-nation differences are so large. As noted earlier, the divergence of national incomes apparently has been part of the legacy of the Industrial Revolution, so average income in the richest nations and poorest nations now differs by a factor of about 30.

EVIDENCE ON RECENT TRENDS IN
BETWEEN-NATION INEQUALITY

Until recent years sociologists have largely ignored the issue of trends in between-nation income inequality. The recent publication of two articles in the *American Journal of Sociology* (Korzeniewicz & Moran 1997, Firebaugh 1999) might signal change in that state of affairs. Both articles argue that the study of between-nation inequality is important to sociologists for two reasons. First, the huge disparity in average incomes across nations is the major component of total income inequality for the world. Second, between-nation inequality is a significant issue for sociologists because of the centrality of the polarization thesis in the world system and dependency literatures on development.

But the articles arrive at different conclusions concerning the recent trend in between-nation income inequality. Korzeniewicz & Moran (1997) conclude that between-nation income inequality continued to rise during the 1960s, 1970s, and 1980s, with an especially sharp rise during the 1980s. Firebaugh (1999) concludes that between-nation inequality was no greater in 1989 than it was in 1960.

Before comparing the two studies to determine why their conclusions differ, it is useful first to review a few earlier studies in economics and political science (most of the key studies are by economists or political scientists). Studies that weight nations by their population reach conclusions that differ from studies that do not weight. I begin with the studies that do not weight nations by their population.

Unweighted Studies

Quantitative cross-national analyses most often are unweighted in sociology. In a typical sociological study, data are collected for a sample of nations, and regression analysis is used to estimate the effects of some set of variables on the dependent variable of interest. In some instances a statistical consideration (e.g. heteroskedastic disturbances) might be invoked as a rationale for weighting nations differently, but for the most part cross-national studies in sociology assume that a nation is a nation, so India and Norway are given equal weight. The implicit logic is that India and Norway represent equally valid realizations of the underlying causal process. Hence in a study of, say, the effects of political stability on a nation's rate of economic growth, one assumes that the experiences of small nations are as telling as the experiences of larger nations (otherwise one would weight them differently). As I explain subsequently, that logic does not hold when one is interested in between-nation inequality as a component of total world inequality.

One of the earliest reliable unweighted studies of cross-national convergence is Jackman's (1982) study of the relative income growth rates of 98 nations from 1960 to 1978. Jackman found an inverted-U pattern for the relationship between initial income and income growth rate—a pattern that was subsequently replicated in studies using different income measures and longer time periods (Summers & Heston 1991, Table IV; Sheehey 1996). Despite this faster growth in the middle of the distribution, there is *overall* divergence because growth rates tend to be higher for the richest nations than for the poorest nations. Subsequent research has replicated the divergence finding as well (Barro & Martin 1992, Table 3 and Figure 4; Sheehey 1996, Table 2; Jones 1997, Tables 2 and 3).

So when each national economy is given the same weight one finds (for recent decades) an inverted-U pattern in which nations in the upper middle of the distribution tend to exhibit the fastest rates of income growth and those at the lower end of the distribution tend to exhibit the slowest rates of growth. The upshot is that *national economies* are diverging for the world as a whole even though there are convergence "clubs" (for example, there is evidence of income convergence among Western European nations: Abramovitz 1986, Baumol 1986, Jones 1997).

Weighted Studies

The findings about between-nation inequality based on unweighted studies might not apply to weighted between-nation inequality since nations vary so much in population size. Large nations such as China and India greatly affect the weighted measure but have little effect on the unweighted measure, and the reverse is true for small rich nations such as Luxembourg and Norway. So it is important to determine how the two types of studies differ in the sorts of questions they are asking.

The evidence that national economies are diverging (unweighted studies, above) is generally of more interest to economists than it is to sociologists. Sociologists and economists are interested in international convergence/divergence for different reasons. The interest in economics is theoretical, to test theories of macroeconomic growth. Most often for economists, then, each nation represents one unit (one economy) and, in typical analyses, economic trends in Luxembourg count just as much as economic trends in China, even though China has nearly 3000 times more people. By contrast, sociologists generally study between-nation income inequality because of what it can reveal about income inequality for the world as a whole (Korzeniewicz & Moran 1997, Firebaugh 1999). In short, sociologists are interested in whether there is intercountry convergence in the case where *individuals, not nations,* are given equal weight. Thus sociologists are more interested in the results of *population-weighted* studies.

To verify that the contribution of between-nation income inequality to total world income inequality is calculated by weighting nations by their population size, consider Equation 1 (above), the ANOVA formula for within- and between-group variance. Observe that the between-group component, $\sum_j n_j (\mu_j - \mu)^2 / N$, is *weighted by group size* (n_j), so group effects in ANOVA are effects based on the *equal weighting of individuals.* The same principle governs the partitioning of world inequality into its between-nation and within-nation components, since inequality is a type of variance.

Despite the fact that it is *weighted* national convergence that bears most directly on total world inequality, most convergence studies are unweighted. ("Convergence studies" refers to research on the issue of whether national incomes are moving together or moving apart, so the term "convergence" as used here is shorthand for both convergence and divergence.) In contrast to the large and growing literature on unweighted convergence, the empirical literature on weighted convergence is rather sparse.

An early study by Berry et al (1983a) remains one of the best of the weighted studies. Based on a large sample of nations containing most of the world's population, Berry et al (1983a) conclude, first, that economic growth in China was the most potent force equalizing world incomes from 1950 to 1977 and, second, that there was no clearcut trend in intercountry income inequality from 1950 to 1977.

Peacock et al (1988, Figs. 1 and 2) replicate the Berry et al finding of relative stability in between-nation income inequality. The Peacock et al study is based on income data for 53 nations from 1950 to 1980. Although they find no evidence of an overall trend, Peacock et al do find evidence for convergence within world system strata and divergence between the strata. These patterns are offsetting, so overall there is stability in between-nation inequality.

In contrast to Berry et al (1983a) and Peacock et al (1988), Ram (1989, Table 1) finds that national incomes diverged from 1960 to 1980. The difference between Ram's findings and the findings of the prior two studies cannot be attributed to differences in the way inequality is measured, since all three studies use the Theil index. The apparent reason is that—unlike the other two studies—Ram's study excludes China. Both Berry et al (1983a) and Firebaugh (1999) stress the importance of China to the recent trend in between-nation income inequality. Between-nation income inequality declines as nations' incomes move toward the world mean and increases as nations' incomes move away from the world mean. Because China's per capita income is well below the world mean, China's faster-than-world-average income growth has reduced between-nation income inequality. Because China contains a large share of the world's population, the effect of China's income growth on (weighted) between-nation income inequality has been notable (Berry et al 1983a, Firebaugh 1999).

Based on income data for 120 nations containing almost all the world's population, Schultz (1998) finds that between-nation income inequality changed very little from 1960 to 1989. This finding holds whether inequality is measured using the Gini coefficient or the Theil index or VarLog (Schultz 1998, Table 1). All three measures *increase* over time, however, when conversion of local currencies to US dollars is based on official exchange rates instead of the actual purchasing power parities (PPPs) of the currencies (Schultz 1998, Table 1).

Firebaugh's (1999) results support Schultz's. Based on 120 nations representing 92% of the world's population, between-nation income inequality was about the same in 1989 as it was three decades earlier. Comparing 1960 inequality with 1989 inequality, the squared coefficient of variation declined by 1.5%, Gini increased by less than 1%, VarLog increased by 5.5%, and the Theil increased by 1.7% (Firebaugh 1999, Table 4). The trend appears to be relatively flat or even slightly downward since 1970, because all four measures of inequality indicate that between-nation income inequality was slightly lower in 1989 than it was in 1970 (Firebaugh 1999, Table 4).

Recall that Peacock et al (1988) found an offsetting pattern of convergence and divergence. If some regions of the income distribution are converging and other regions are diverging, then one's conclusions about overall inequality might be sensitive to the weight given to different regions of the income distribution. To test that possibility, Firebaugh (1999) used a measure of inequality—Atkinson's (1970) index—that allows researchers to assign different weights to different parts of the income distribution. The change in between-nation inequality was small regardless of the reweighting used (Firebaugh 1999, Table 6).

In sum: When China is included, weighted studies of between-nation income inequality generally find that national incomes (*per capita incomes*) have neither diverged nor converged in recent decades. That conclusion holds regardless of the inequality index used.

There is one notable exception, however. As Schultz (1998) shows, weighted national incomes diverge when income is based on foreign exchange (FX) rates rather than on PPP. The results of Korzeniewicz & Moran (1997) are instructive in this regard. By using an income series that is based on foreign exchange rates, Korzeniewicz & Moran conclude that, from 1965 to 1990, between-nation inequality increased by 12% as measured by the Gini and by 38% as measured by Theil's index (Korzeniewicz & Moran 1997, Table 3). These results resemble those of Schultz, who reports a 12% increase for the Gini and a 47% increase for the Theil from 1965 to 1989 *when national incomes are estimated using official foreign exchange rates* (Schultz 1998, Table 1). However, when incomes are estimated using purchasing power parity, both the Gini and the Theil *decline* slightly over that period (Schultz 1998, Table 1).

Hence Korzeniewicz & Moran's deviant finding is based on their use of exchange rate data. Economists who work closely with national income data warn that "it really makes a difference if exchange rates are used rather than PPPs" (Summers & Heston 1991, p. 355). Although early studies in economics used official exchange rates to convert local currencies to dollars, PPP-based estimation is now the industry standard. It is widely recognized that official exchange rates are badly flawed calibrators of currencies. Many goods and services are not traded on the international market, so exchange rates are based on a restricted bundle of goods and services (Grosh & Nafziger 1986, p. 351). The failure to capture economic activity is especially acute for nonmonetized exchange in nonindustrial nations, so income estimates based on exchange rates tend to miss significant economic activity in poorer nations. In addition, foreign exchange markets are not totally free but are routinely distorted by government policy and speculative capital movement.[1]

Because of such problems, convergence studies in economics now routinely use PPP-based income series (in addition to the studies summarized above, examples include Barro 1991; Mankiw et al 1992, Levine & Renelt 1992, Quah 1996). For the PPP-based income series, the trend in between-nation income inequality in recent decades has been (i) upward if one weights each nation equally and (ii) flat if one weights nations by their populations.

NEW DIRECTIONS FOR RESEARCH

The Schultz-Firebaugh Finding

Working independently, Schultz (1998) and Firebaugh (1999) found that population-weighted between-nation income inequality has been relatively stable over recent decades. This finding is important, first, because of what it indicates about total world income inequality. Because between-nation income inequality is the major component of total world income inequality, stable between-nation income inequality implies that total world income inequality is not likely to be changing very rapidly.

The Schultz-Firebaugh finding is important, second, because it suggests the following hypothesis: *Population-weighted between-nation income inequality has stabilized in recent decades.* Observe that the hypothesis assumes that between-nation income inequality had not been stable earlier. The premise is that the Industrial Revolution ushered in an epoch of diverging national incomes. This is not to say that national incomes diverged monotonically over the nineteenth and early twentieth centuries—there may well have been periods of divergence followed by periods of compression. But it is to say that between-nation income inequality was greater in the middle of the twentieth century that it had been at the outset of the Industrial Revolution.

Social scientists need to test further the Schultz-Firebaugh hypothesis that between-nation income inequality has stabilized in recent decades. Although Schultz and Firebaugh demonstrate that population-weighted between-nation income inequality changed little over the 1960s, 1970s, and 1980s, their data end in 1989, with the breakup of the USSR. So one does not know if the flat trend they observed has continued into the 1990s.

---

[1]To appreciate the severity of the problem with using foreign exchange rates to study the convergence issue, consider income estimates for China. The remarkable economic growth of China since 1978 (Nee 1991, Fig. 1; Mastel 1997) is reflected in the PPP income series, where China's income ratio jumps roughly 40% from 1975 to 1989. The foreign-exchange-rate-based World Bank income series used by Korzeniewicz & Moran fails to capture that growth but instead indicates that China's growth rate lagged so far behind the rest of the world that the FX income ratio for China declined by a whopping one-third from 1970 to 1989 (from .139 to .090).

Researchers need to go back in time as well, to determine more precisely the magnitude and timing of the apparent rise in population-weighted between-nation income inequality over the course of the Industrial Revolution. One recent study concludes that "Economic growth was extraordinarily fast from 1820–1992. World population increased five-fold, per capita product eight-fold, world GDP forty-fold .... The rise in per capita income differed widely between countries and regions, so intercountry and interregional spreads became very much wider" (Maddison 1995, p. 19). The trends in the income means for regions and nations in the Maddison data in fact point to intercountry and interregional income divergence. But these intercountry income trends have not been converted into population-weighted *inequality measures* along the lines of the Schultz and Firebaugh studies. What is lacking, then, is a direct comparison of the 1960–1989 trend in population-weighted between-nation income inequality with earlier trends in population-weighted between-nation income inequality. So studies that conclude that the trend in between-nation inequality has leveled off in recent decades are unable to specify very precisely how much the between-nation trend has leveled off.

The Trend in *Total* World Income Inequality

In addition to the need for more historical research on the trend in between-nation inequality, there is need for research on current trends in *total* world inequality. Reviewing briefly: Income inequality for the whole world is the sum of within-nation and between-nation income inequality. Empirical investigations conclude that the between-nation component is larger than the within-nation component. Schultz (1998) and Firebaugh (1999) find that the between-nation component has changed relatively little over recent decades.

Two implications follow. First, the *direction* of the current trend in total world income inequality depends on the direction of the change in within-nation income inequality. Because between-nation inequality is basically steady, then world income inequality is rising if the within-nation component is increasing and it is falling if within-nation income inequality is declining. Second, the *magnitude* of the change in world income inequality depends on (i) the magnitude of the change in within-nation income inequality *and* (ii) the *relative sizes* of the within-nation and between-nation contributions to the total. If Korzeniewicz & Moran (1997, Table 2 Gini coefficients) are correct in their conclusion that within-nation income inequality comprises less than 10% of the total world income inequality, then even a substantial increase or decline in within-nation inequality would have at most a modest effect on the trend in world income inequality.

To determine the direction and magnitude of recent change in total world income inequality, then, one needs to answer two questions. First, is within-nation income inequality increasing in the average nation (where nations are weighted by population)? Second, what proportion of total income inequality is between-nation as opposed to within-nation income inequality? I begin with the second question.

What Proportion of Total World Income Inequality Is Between-Nation Income Inequality? Although empirical investigations agree that between-nation inequality is the larger of the two components, estimates vary regarding their relative sizes. Theil himself (1979) estimated that between-nation income inequality accounted for roughly two thirds (65%) of the total inequality in 1970 (Theil index). Ram's (1979) re-estimation of Theil's study with more complete data yields the same result. Berry et al (1983b, Table 9) estimate that between-nation inequality accounted for 70% of the total in 1970 (Theil index).

By contrast, Korzeniewicz & Moran (1997, Table 2) estimated that between-nation income inequality accounted for 86% of the total income inequality in 1992 (Theil index). If within-nation inequality comprised about 30% of the total in 1970, then the Korzeniewicz-Moran estimates for 1992 imply that the within-nation contribution to total inequality was cut in half during the 1970s and 1980s. This result is highly unlikely. Because between-nation inequality did not increase over the period, the within-nation contribution could be halved only if income inequality in the average nation were also cut in half. Re-estimates based on inequality data for 59 nations (Theil index) comprising 82% of the world's population indicate that between-nation income inequality accounted for about 73% of the total in 1989 (B. Goesling, unpublished analysis).

In short, there is substantial evidence that most of the world's total income inequality is between-nation inequality, not within-nation inequality. Most studies find that between-nation income inequality accounts for very roughly two-thirds to three-fourths of the total. So even if income inequalities were completely eliminated within nations, the distribution of the world's income would remain highly uneven.

Estimating the Within-Nation Component   One important implication of the stable between-nation trend is that the trend in world income inequality depends on the trend in within-nation income inequality. Hence in this chapter on between-nation inequality some brief comments about within-nation inequality are appropriate.

The major hurdle for empirical studies of within-nation income inequality is the lack of reliable and comparable inequality data for nations. The study of between-nation and within-nation income inequality presents researchers with different types of data problems. In the case of between-nation inequality, knowledge is required only of nations' mean incomes, but those mean incomes must be converted to a common currency. So appropriate calibration is a major concern in the case of between-nation inequality. Nations' currencies must be calibrated before national incomes can be compared.

The calibration of currencies typically is of slight consequence for within-nation inequality, since nations generally have a common currency within their borders. But the information required to estimate the variance of an income distribution is greater than the information required to estimate the mean of an income distribution, so in that sense the data for estimating within-nation income inequality are harder to obtain and are more suspect than the data used for between-nation estimation. Because of the greater information required, the within-nation inequality data are spottier. Whereas reasonably reliable estimates of national per capita income are available for most of the world, there are large gaps in the coverage for within-nation income inequality.

Within-nation inequality data are improving, however, and it is not premature for researchers to think about how best to estimate total world inequality with data soon to be available. One helpful way to conceptualize the issue of estimating world inequality is to think of the data as being packaged in chunks called nations. If one had income data for everyone—that is, if the data were not aggregated into nation chunks—then total world income inequality could be estimated using any of the standard inequality indexes. But the agglomeration of the data into nations rules out indexes that are not easily decomposable into within-group and between-group components. For example, the between-nation Gini and the average within-nation Gini do not sum to the total Gini.

The Theil, the squared coefficient of variation, the variance of logged income (VarLog), and the mean logarithm deviation (that is, the log of the arithmetic mean minus the log of the geometric mean: Bourguignon 1979; see Jasso 1982 for related discussion) are inequality indexes that can be used for combining within- and between-nation inequality to estimate total inequality. Bourguignon (1979) argues that the Theil and the mean logarithm deviation have the most desirable decomposition properties. The variance of logged income can be decomposed into within and between components along the lines of Allison (1978) and Equation 1 above, even if it is not decomposable in the sense of Bourguignon (1979). The squared coefficient of variation is decomposable, but it is often avoided in cross-nation research because of its extreme sensitivity to values at the upper end of the distribution. The other three indexes all use the logarithm of income in one form or another, so they reflect the welfare principle that income increases at the lower end of the income distribution produce greater welfare benefit than do income increases at the upper end of the income distribution.

Allison (1978) gives decomposition formulas for the Theil, the squared coefficient of variation, and VarLog. As Allison demonstrates, the Theil weights the within-nation component part by nations' *income shares* whereas VarLog weights the within-nation component by nations' *population shares*. Firebaugh (1998, 1999) shows that inequality indexes can be expressed in a common form, as functions of the average distance of income ratios from 1.0 (the point of equality). Inequality indexes differ because they employ different distance functions. Recognition of the common form of inequality indexes enables researchers to more readily compare results of the different inequality indexes.

CONCLUSION

When Adam Smith published *The Wealth of Nations* in 1776, he could scarcely have foreseen the profound changes that would occur in nations' incomes over the remaining 225 years in the millennium. National incomes today are dramatically larger, on average, and apparently more unequal as well. Because income inequality across regions is greater today than it was in Smith's day, it appears that national incomes have diverged over the course of the Industrial Revolution.

Empirical investigations suggest, however, that the trend in between-nation inequality has stabilized in recent decades. These findings challenge the conventional sociological wisdom that the world is polarizing. The immediate task for researchers is threefold: To determine if the flat trend has continued into the 1990s; to determine more precisely the timing of the stabilization; and to combine the between-nation trend with careful studies of trend data for within-nation income inequality in order to determine the direction and pace of change in the world's total income inequality.

ACKNOWLEDGMENTS

This article is based on research supported by NSF grants SBR-9515153 and SBR-980870.

Visit the Annual Reviews home page at www.AnnualReviews.org

LITERATURE CITED

Abramovitz M. 1986. Catching up, forging ahead, and falling behind. *J. Econ. Hist.* 46:385–406

Allison P. 1978. Measures of inequality. *Am. Sociol. Rev.* 43:865–80

Atkinson AB. 1970. On the measurement of inequality. *J. Econ. Theory* 2:244–63

Barro RJ. 1991. Economic growth in a cross-section of countries. *Q. J. Econ.* 106:407–43

Barro RJ, Sala-i-Martin X. 1992. Convergence. *J. Polit. Econ.* 100:223–51

Baumol WJ. 1986. Productivity growth, convergence, and welfare: What the long-run data show. *Am. Econ. Rev.* 76:1072–85

Berry A, Bourguignon F, Morrisson C. 1983a. Changes in the world distribution of income between 1950 and 1977. *Econ. J.* 93:331–50

Berry A, Bourguignon F, Morrisson C. 1983b. The level of world inequality: How much can one say? *Rev. Income Wealth* 29:217–41

Bollen KA, Jackman RW. 1985. Political democracy and the size distribution of income. *Am. Sociol. Rev.* 50:438–57

Bourguignon F. 1979. Decomposable income inequality measures. *Econometrica* 47:901–20

Chase-Dunn C. 1975. The effects of international economic dependence on development and inequality: A cross-national study. *Am. Sociol. Rev.* 40:720–38

Cutright P. 1967. Inequality: a cross-national study. *Am. Sociol. Rev.* 32:562–78

De Long JB. 1988. Productivity growth, convergence, and welfare: comment. *Am. Econ. Rev.* 78:1138–54

Dorfman R. 1991. Economic development from the beginning to Rostow. *J. Econ. Lit.* 24:573–91

Easterlin RA. 1998. *Growth Triumphant.* Ann Arbor: Univ. Mich. Press

Firebaugh G. 1998. *Measuring inequality: a convenient unifying framework.* Pres. Annu. Meet. Pop. Assoc. Am., Chicago (April)

Firebaugh G. 1999. Empirics of world income inequality. *Am. J. Sociol.* 104:1597–1630

Grosh ME, Nafziger EW. 1986. The computation of world income distribution. *Econ. Dev. Cult. Change* 34:347–59

Hoover GA. 1989. Intranational inequality: a cross-national dataset. *Soc. Forc.* 67:1008–26

Jackman RW. 1982. Dependence on foreign investment and economic growth in the Third World. *World Polit.* 34:175–96

Jasso G. 1982. Measuring inequality: using the geometric mean/arithmetic mean ratio. *Sociol. Meth. Res.* 10:303–26

Jones CI. 1997. Convergence revisited. *J. Econ. Growth* 2:131–53

Korzeniewicz RP, Moran TP. 1997. World-economic trends in the distribution of income, 1965–1992. *Am. J. Sociol.* 102:1000–39

Kuznets S. 1955. Economic growth and income inequality. *Am. Econ. Rev* 45:1–28

Levine R, Renelt D. 1992. A sensitivity analysis of cross-country growth regressions. *Am. Econ. Rev.* 82:942–63

Lucas RE Jr. 1988. On the mechanics of economic development. *J. Monetary Econ.* 22:3–42

Maddison A. 1995. *Monitoring the World Economy 1820–1992.* Paris: OECD

Malthus TR. 1798 [1960]. *On Population.* New York: Modern Library

Mandel E. 1975. *Late Capitalism.* New York: Monthly Rev.

Mankiw NG, Romer D, Weil DN. 1992. A contribution to the empirics of economic growth. *Q. J. Econ.* 107:407–37

Mastel G. 1997. *The Rise of the Chinese Economy.* London: Sharpe

Mill JS. 1848 [1923]. *Principles of Political Economy with Some of Their Applications to Social Philosophy.* London: Longmans, Green

Nee V. 1991. Social inequalities in reforming state socialism: between redistribution and markets in China. *Am. Sociol. Rev.* 56:267–82

Nielsen F, Alderson AS. 1997. The Kuznets curve and the great U–turn: income inequality in U.S. counties, 1970 to 1990. *Am. Sociol. Rev.* 62:12–33

Peacock WG, Hoover GA, Killian CD. 1988.

Divergence and convergence in international development: a decomposition analysis of inequality in the world system. *Am. Sociol. Rev.* 53:838–52

Quah DT. 1996. Convergence empirics across economies with (some) capital mobility. *J. Econ. Growth* 1:95–124

Ram R. 1979. International income inequality: 1970 and 1978. *Econ. Lett.* 4:187–90

Ram R. 1989. Level of development and income inequality: an extension of Kuznets–hypothesis to the world economy. *Kyklos* 42:73–88

Ricardo D. 1817 [1962]. *Works and Correspondence, Volume I: On the Principles of Political Economy and Taxation,* ed. P. Sraffa. Cambridge: Cambridge Univ. Press

Romer P. 1986. Increasing returns and long-run growth. *J. Polit. Econ.* 94:1002–37

Schultz TP. 1998. Inequality in the distribution of personal income in the world: How it is changing and why. *J. Pop. Econ.* 11:307–44

Sheehey EJ. 1996. The growing gap between rich and poor countries: a proposed explanation. *World Dev.* 24:1379–84

Smith A. 1776. *An Inquiry into the Nature and Causes of the Wealth of Nations.* London

Solow RM. 1956. A contribution to the theory of economic growth. *Q. J. Econ.* 70:65–94

Summers R, Kravis IB, Heston A. 1980. International comparisons of real product and its composition, 1950–77. *Rev. Income Wealth* 26:19–66

Summers R, Heston A. 1991. The Penn World Table (Mark 5): an expanded set of international comparisons, 1950–1988. *Q. J. Econ.* 106:327–68

Summers R, Heston A, Aten B, Nuxoll D. 1994. *Penn World Table (PWT) Mark 5.6a Data* [MRDF].Cent. Int. Comparisons, Univ. Penn. Philadelphia, PA: Dep. Econ.

Theil H. 1979. World income inequality and its components. *Econ. Lett.* 2:99–102

Weede E, Tiefenbach H. 1981. Some recent explanations of income inequality: an evaluation and critique. *Int. Stud. Q.* 25:255–82

Annu. Rev. Sociol. 2000. 26:341–65

NONSTANDARD EMPLOYMENT RELATIONS:
Part-time, Temporary and Contract Work

Arne L. Kalleberg

Department of Sociology, University of North Carolina at Chapel Hill, Chapel Hill, North Carolina 27599-3210; e-mail: Arne_Kalleberg@unc.edu

Key Words   contingent work, part-time work, temporary work, contract work

■ **Abstract**   Nonstandard employment relations—such as part-time work, temporary help agency and contract company employment, short-term and contingent work, and independent contracting—have become increasingly prominent ways of organizing work in recent years. Our understanding of these nonstandard work arrangements has been hampered by inconsistent definitions, often inadequate measures, and the paucity of comparative research. This chapter reviews the emerging research on these nonstandard work arrangements. The review emphasizes the multidisciplinary nature of contributions to this field, including research by a variety of sociologists, economists, and psychologists. It also focuses on cross-national research, which is needed to investigate how macroeconomic, political, and institutional factors affect the nature of employment relations. Areas for future research are suggested.

INTRODUCTION

Nonstandard work arrangements—such as part-time work, temporary employment and contract work—have become an important topic in research and writing on work and employment relations. Nonstandard employment relations (Goldthorpe 1984, Casey 1991, Green et al 1993, Kalleberg et al 2000) have also been referred to as alternative work arrangements (Polivka 1996a, Sherer 1996), market-mediated arrangements (Abraham 1990), nontraditional employment relations (Ferber & Waldfogel 1998), flexible staffing arrangements (Abraham 1988, Houseman 1997), flexible working practices (Brewster et al 1997), atypical employment (Córdova 1986, Delsen 1995, De Grip et al 1997), vagrant or peripheral employment (Summers 1997), vulnerable work (Tregaskis et al 1998), precarious employment (Treu 1992), disposable work (Gordon 1996), new forms of employment (Bronstein 1991), and contingent work (see Polivka & Nardone 1989, Belous 1989).

These labels have in common their identification of employment relations that depart from standard work arrangements in which it was generally expected that work was done full-time, would continue indefinitely, and was performed at the employer's place of business under the employer's direction. Standard work arrangements were the norm in many industrial nations for much of the twentieth century and were the basis of the framework within which labor law, collective bargaining, and social security systems developed.

Changes beginning in the mid-1970s created conditions that led countries, organizations, and workers to search for greater flexibility in employment. Consequently, the standard employment relationship began to unravel (Rubin 1995, Cappelli et al 1997, Cappelli 1999). Global economic changes increased competition and uncertainty among firms and put greater pressure on them to push for greater profits and to be more flexible in contracting with their employees and responding to consumers. Sluggish economic growth triggered high unemployment that made it clear, especially in Europe, that economies were incapable of generating enough jobs to provide full-time wage employment for all workers (Córdova 1986). The adoption of nonstandard work was facilitated by technological improvements in communication and information systems that made it easier for organizations to specialize their production, assemble temporary workers quickly for projects, and rely more on outside suppliers. Labor laws designed to protect permanent employees also fueled the growth in nonstandard work by encouraging employers to avoid the mandates and costs associated with these laws (Lee 1996, Cappelli et al 1997). So too did demographic changes in the composition of the labor force, such as the increase in married women workers and older workers, who often preferred the flexibility available through nonstandard work arrangements (Pfeffer & Baron 1988).

Nonstandard employment relations are not new. There have always been work arrangements that did not fit the model of full-time work, and history is replete with examples of peripheral labor forces and flexible labor markets in which work is unstable and temporary (Morse 1969, Peck 1996, Summers 1997). For instance, in the inside contracting system that existed in the United States in the nineteenth century, management provided machinery and space in the factory, supplied raw material and capital, and arranged for the sale of the product while contractors were responsible for production and hired the workers and paid and supervised them (Butrick 1952). Employers have a choice between organizing work in markets or hierarchies (Williamson 1980). The efficiencies associated with organizing work in standard, hierarchical employment relations and internal labor markets in the post–World War II period may have been more of an historical irregularity than is the use of nonstandard employment relations.

This review surveys recent theory and research on the major kinds of nonstandard work arrangements: part-time work, temporary agency and contract company employment, short-term employment, contingent work, and independent contracting. The literature on these topics is multidisciplinary and includes research by sociologists of work, organizations, occupations, labor markets and social stratification, as well as by economists and psychologists. This review does not cover nonstandard work arrangements such as home working or telecommuting; employee ownership of companies; flexible scheduling such as flextime, job-sharing, home-based work, and compressed workweeks; or clandestine activities such as undeclared, illegal, or family work. An effort has also been made not to cover the material on nonstandard work previously reviewed by Smith (1997).

PART-TIME WORK

Definitions, Incidence, Trends

Part-time work is usually defined as regular wage employment in which the hours of work are less than "normal" (Thurman & Trah 1990). In the United States, part-time work is generally defined as less than 35 hours a week. This definition varies across countries. Canada and the United Kingdom normally use 30 hours as the cutoff for part-time (Kahne 1992). In France, part-time is defined as at least 20% below the statutory level of working hours (which became 35 hours on January 1, 2000), while in Germany it is less than 36 hours of work per week (Houseman 1995). By contrast, part-time employment in Japan is explicitly related to status within the firm and not to hours worked; indeed, recent Japanese surveys indicate that 20–30% of those classified by their employers as "part-time" actually work as many hours as "full-time" workers (Houseman & Osawa 1998).

Nearly one in five workers in the United States currently works part-time, making it by far the most widely used form of nonstandard work. [Part-time work also overlaps with other forms of nonstandard work, such as temporary work. Casey (1991) found that 54% of temporary workers in his British sample worked part-time.] The proportion of part-timers in the United States increased gradually from 13% in 1957 to 19% in 1993, with most of the growth coming before 1980 (Tilly 1996). This percentage has decreased slightly since the mid-1990s, though changes in the measurement of part-time work by the Current Population Survey (CPS) in 1994 have hampered assessments of trends since then (Nardone 1995). Part-time work has historically increased during economic recessions and decreased during economic expansions as those desiring full-time work are better able to obtain it (Sightler & Adams 1999).

The incidence of part-time work in Europe is slightly lower than in the United States, with an average of about 16% of the European Union's total labor force working part-time in 1996 (Fagan 1999). There is, however, wide variation among countries (Bosch et al 1993). In the Netherlands, about 38% of the labor force, and 69% of women, work part-time, leading Freeman (1998:2) to characterize it as the "only part-time economy of the world, with a finger in the dike of unemployment." Part-time employment is also relatively common in Scandinavia (with the exception of Finland), with over 20% of the labor force working part-time. By contrast, part-time work constitutes relatively small proportions of the labor force in Greece, Spain, Portugal (DeGrip et al 1997, Tregaskis et al 1998), and Italy (5% overall, 3.5% of women) (Thurman & Trah 1990). Unlike in the United States, part-time employment is increasing relatively rapidly in Europe, where it has been used as a way to alleviate unemployment and is the major source of employment growth since the 1980s (Brewster et al 1997). Again, there is wide variation among countries: Part-time employment has increased particularly rapidly in the Netherlands and Austria (increases of about 65% and 114%, respectively, since 1985) (Fagan 1999).

In all industrial countries, most part-time workers are women (Blossfeld & Hakim 1997, Fagan & O'Reilly 1998). This reflects in part women's greater responsibilities for housework and raising children. Women's share of part-time employment in the United States (about 65%) is much lower than in Germany and France (about 90%) and in the United Kingdom and Japan (about 80%). The lower proportion of women part-timers in the United States may reflect the greater incidence of part-time work among students, both male and female.

Demand for Part-time Jobs

Most of the increase in part-time work before 1970 in the United States was due to the growth of voluntary part-time work, mainly among women and young people who wanted to work part-time. Since 1970, virtually all of the increase has occurred among those who would prefer full-time work (i.e., "involuntary" part-timers), who currently make up about one quarter of part-timers (Tilly 1996). The overall incidence of voluntary part-time employment has not changed since the early 1970s, though the composition has changed (e.g., women aged 22–54 are less likely to be voluntary part-timers, while workers aged 16–24 and men over 55 are more likely to work part-time voluntarily) (Nardone 1995). Stratton (1996) found substantial evidence that those classified as involuntary part-time do indeed work part-time involuntarily.

Part-time work in the United States and other countries (such as Japan—see Houseman & Osawa 1998) in recent years has thus changed from an activity that mainly accommodates the needs of the workforce for shorter hours to one that meets employers' needs and preferences for such things as lower costs and more flexible staffing. This makes it important to study the demand for part-time work, by examining industry and organizational differences in the use of part-timers (Tilly 1996, Houseman 1997).

Employers have been motivated by cost-containment to use part-timers, since typically they cost less in wages and particularly in fringe benefits (though see Larson & Ong 1994). A substantial fraction of the recent increase in involuntary part-time workers is the result of legislation (such as the Federal Family and Medical Leave Act of 1993), which increases the cost to employers of full-time relative to part-time workers (Stratton 1996). Differences among industries in compensation, particularly health care provision, have a significant effect on the distribution of part-timers across industries (Pitts 1998). Montgomery's (1988) analysis of over 4500 US establishments found that larger establishments had lower proportions of part-timers, which he attributes to part-timers constituting higher quasi-fixed labor costs (e.g., recruiting and training costs) in larger establishments.

Employers also use part-timers to meet staffing needs (Thurman & Trah 1990). Part-time employment is flexible since it can be relatively easily decreased or increased and can be moved to a different time during the day. The health care industry, for example, has long used part-timers among both lower-level and professional jobs (nurses) as a way of staffing hospitals twenty-four hours a day, seven days a week (Sightler & Adams 1999). Zeytinoglu (1992) found that unionized organizations in Canada used part-timers primarily because of the flexibility they provided (for both employers and workers), rather than to save wages and benefits.

The growth in part-time work in the United States since 1979 appears to have been due to the expansion of industries that typically employ many part-timers (services, retail trade, finance, insurance, real estate) rather than to the substitution of part-time for full-time workers within industries that occurred mainly in the 1970s (Appelbaum 1992, Nardone 1995). The growth of part-time employment has similarly accompanied the expansion of the service sector in other industrial countries (Houseman 1995).

Good vs. Bad Part-time Jobs

Most studies have shown that part-timers in the United States usually earn less per hour than full-timers, even after controlling for education, experience, and other relevant factors (Tilly 1996, Ferber & Waldfogel 1998). Part-timers also obtain lower wage returns relative to experience (Corcoran et al 1984) and seniority (England et al 1999) than do full-timers. An exception is Blank's (1990) analysis, which found that part-time women earned more than equivalent full-time women, after controlling for selection into the labor market and part-time work. Part-timers in the United States also receive fewer fringe benefits than full-time workers do. Despite differences in wages and fringe benefits, part-timers are often as likely as full-timers to regard work as a "central life activity" and are equally committed to their organizations (Kalleberg 1995).

Part-time jobs and workers are heterogeneous (Feldman 1990, Tilly 1996). This heterogeneity has been characterized by some writers as the dualism of part-time work. Kahne (1992), for example, argued that part-time work is both "a hope and a peril," encompassing both good jobs ("new concept" part-time jobs that are often used to retain valued professional employees such as librarians, teachers, editors, and nurses) and bad ones that have low wages and few benefits. Similarly, Tilly (1996) applied dual labor market theory to the analysis of part-time work, distinguishing between retention and secondary part-time jobs.

Part-time work in Europe is often associated with marginal employment in low-paid, low status jobs (such as sales, catering, and cleaning). There is, however, also some growth of higher-level part-time jobs in some countries. There are also country differences in whether the use of part-timers represents a marginalization strategy that provides employers with a source of cheap labor or an integration strategy used to retain valued workers. One source of difference among countries is related to labor law and employment regulations such as job security entitlements. In some countries (Sweden, France, Belgium, The Netherlands, Spain), labor law enforces equal treatment between full-time and part-time workers (Thurman &

Trah 1990), preventing the use of part-time workers as a cheap labor source. By contrast, in the United Kingdom, Germany, and Japan, part-time employees' hours or income generally fall below thresholds that exclude them from coverage under certain laws (Houseman 1995, Fagan & O'Reilly 1998).

EMPLOYMENT INTERMEDIARIES

Some nonstandard employment relations involve the externalization of administrative control and responsibility (Pfeffer & Baron 1988). This creates "detached" workers (Summers 1997) or "triangular" employment relations where a worker establishes connections with several employers (Córdova 1986, Bronstein 1991, Vosko 1997). Examples of such nonstandard work arrangements include temporary help agency, leased, and contract company employment.

Temporary Help Agencies

Temporary help agencies employ workers and send them out to customers to work on an hourly basis at the client's premises and direction. These agencies recruit and screen employees, sometimes provide training, and are responsible for hiring and firing, issuing paychecks, withholding payroll taxes, and making required employer contributions to unemployment insurance and Social Security (Carey & Hazelbaker 1986).

The temporary help industry in the United States originated in Chicago during the late 1920s, with the first agencies supplying calculating-machine operators on a temporary basis. By 1956 there were still only about 20,000 employees in the temporary help industry (Gannon 1984). Since 1972, employment in the temporary help services industry has experienced explosive growth, increasing at an annual rate of over 11%, and its share of total US employment has risen from under 0.3% in 1972 to nearly 2.5% in 1998. By contrast, total nonfarm employment grew at an annual rate of 2% during this period (Segal & Sullivan 1997a, Laird & Williams 1996). Changes in temporary work exhibit much greater variance than do other forms of employment and are very sensitive to the business cycle, rising and falling with the state of the economy (Gannon 1974, Golden & Appelbaum 1992, Segal 1996).

Temporary help agencies are also growing rapidly in Europe (Bronstein 1991), though there is considerable variation among countries. Some nations feel that they are useful as employment intermediaries, while others object to them for reasons such as the principle that job placement should be done by public, not profit-making agencies. In the mid-1980s, temporary help agencies were authorized (subject to some restrictions) in Argentina, Belgium, Brazil, Denmark, France, Germany, Ireland, Japan, the Netherlands, Norway, Portugal, and Switzerland, among other countries. They were banned in Algeria, Costa Rica, Gabon, Greece, Italy, the Libyan Arab Jamahiriya, Madagascar, Mauritania, Senegal, Spain, Sweden, and Zaire (Córdova 1986: 657, note 16).

Demand for Temporary Help Agencies   The growth of temporary help agency employment in both the United States and Europe has been generally driven by employers' needs (De Grip et al 1997), as well as by the entrepreneurial efforts of temporary help agencies themselves (Ofstead 1999). Golden & Appelbaum (1992) found that the two-and-a-half times increase in the level of temporary help employment between 1982 and 1988 was due mainly to demand-side forces and employers' needs rather than the supply of labor. Golden (1996) found this as well for 1982–1992, a period when employment in the temporary help industry in the United States more than tripled. Laird & Williams (1996) found that supply (increase in married women workers) as well as demand variables contributed to the observed growth in the temporary help service industry between 1982 and 1992. [Golden (1996) also found that the proportion of married women in the labor force was positively related to temporary help agency employment levels, but its impact was dwarfed by the effects of demand-side variables.] However, Segal & Sullivan (1997a) point out that the rise in women's labor force participation is probably not a driving force behind the growth in temporary agency employment because much of this has come from increased male participation in temporary work. Moreover, studies of the preferences of temporary workers have found that most (e.g., 60%—Cohany 1998) work in temporary jobs involuntarily.

Temporary help agencies constitute a modern-day "reserve labor army" that helps employers to solve problems associated with understaffing as well as over-staffing positions with expensive full-time, permanent workers who may not be utilized. By using temporaries, employers can staff minimally and then add temporary employees on an as-needed basis. In support of this hypothesis, Houseman (1997) found that the seasonality of employment demand was positively related to both the incidence and intensity of organizations' use of temporary help agencies (see also Abraham 1990). While companies have always used temporaries to help out with special projects or at busy times, temporaries tended to be peripheral to the company's main business. What appears to be new is that the use of tempo-raries has become an integral feature of firms' personnel strategy (Nollen 1996, von Hippel et al 1997) that enables them to respond to the business cycle and makes their workforce problems more manageable and less costly (Gannon 1974).

Organizations also use temporary help agencies to lower recruitment and screen-ing costs, by hiring employees who perform well: Houseman (1997) found that 21% of the establishments in her sample said this was a reason for their use of temporary help agencies (see also von Hippel et al 1997). Organizations may also be able to reduce training costs through the use of temporary help agency workers, as is suggested by Krueger (1993), who reports the results of a survey that found that 62% of temporary help agencies trained clerical temps in the use of office software.

Major temporary help agencies are increasingly entering into long-term con-tracts with firms, suggesting further that the use of temporary workers has be-come a permanent strategy for them (Carnoy et al 1997). In many of these cases, the temporary help agency is really an extension of the client firm's human resources department. Peck & Theodore's (1998) study of temporary help agencies in Chicago underscored the polarization that is occurring within the increasingly heterogeneous temporary help industry: Some agencies restructure down into the lowest-paid and lowest-skill parts of the labor markets, while others restructure up to establish long-term relations with clients that involve insourcing and on-site management deals. In the latter cases, the temporary help agency often takes over supervisory and performance monitoring functions for its employees at the client's site, helping the client to "manage hassle" and providing its employees with more secure employment.

Using temporary help agencies is not always a low-cost strategy, despite the average low wages and fringe benefits that employees of these agencies receive (see below). The total hourly cost to customers may be more for temporaries than for permanent employees (Carey & Hazelbaker 1986); in 1995, client firms paid, on average, 40% more for temporary workers' time (the temp agency's "billing rate") than these workers received as wages (Segal & Sullivan 1997a). Temporary help agencies may lower firms' costs, though, by providing them with a convenient way of creating a two-tier wage structure. Firms may wish to pay some, but not all, workers efficiency wages (wages above their market wage) and pay different kinds of fringe benefits to different kinds of workers. It may be illegal for firms to institute such differential compensation schemes with their regular full-time workers, but they can do so with their regular full-time vs. temporary workers (Segal & Sullivan 1997a). In support of this hypothesis, Moore (1965) found that high-wage firms were most likely to use temporary help agencies; Mangum et al (1985) found that the use of agency temporaries (who do not receive benefits) was greater in firms that had a higher fringe benefit cost structure; and Houseman (1997) found that establishments that provided more fringe benefits to their regular employees were significantly more likely to use temporary help agencies.

Control of Temporary Workers   The defining characteristic of the temporary help industry is the triangular employment relationship (Córdova 1986, Moberly 1987, Gonos 1997, Vosko 1997), in which the temporary agency is the legal employer, while the client organization supervises the employee. This raises complex legal issues as to which organization is responsible for complying with governmental regulations and especially as to who is liable for accidents and other aspects of the employment relationship. These debates are often framed around principles of "joint employer" or "co-employment" (e.g., Axelrod 1987, Tansky & Veglahn 1995). One of the key factors that determine whether or not an organization is a worker's employer is the extent to which it supervises the worker's activity (Carnevale et al 1998). In order to avoid being considered a joint employer (and thus being liable for some employer responsibility), clients employing temporary help agencies (and contract companies) often use buffers to differentiate the way they treat contractors and regular employees (Jarmon et al 1998). The most severe buffer is time, specifying that the temp must leave after a fixed time period (Smith 2000).

The problem of control over temporary help agency workers is rooted in the need to manage individual workers dispersed over multiple job sites, since temporary workers have multiple bosses and are separated from their co-workers. This control problem differs from those explained by theories that assume that wage work takes place at the employer's place of business (e.g., industrial models of bureaucratic control—Collinson 1987). Gottfried (1991) found that temporary help agencies developed a dualistic form of control characterized by both centralization and decentralization. This dualistic control process involved a process of selection and transmission of information, employee recognition programs, and maintenance of uncertainty to retain the temp agency's control between assignments. It also included a fragmented labor process at the client site that isolated temps from regular workers to prevent temps from internalizing norms of output restriction. Cohen & Haberfeld (1993) found that temporary help agencies could not monitor their workers directly. Hence, they relied either on professional credentials for occupations where performance can be assessed (bookkeepers) or steep wage progressions (albeit from a very low base) as incentives in cases where performance could not be assessed very accurately (clerks). Peck & Theodore (1998) showed how temporary help agencies may take over supervision and performance monitoring at the high end of the temporary help industry.

These problems of control make it difficult for unions to organize temporary help agency employees. Unless the client and temporary help agency (or contract company) are considered "joint employers," the client can fire employees of the temporary help agency (or contractor) for joining a union. In addition, the capacities for collective opposition against an employment system characterized by temporary jobs are limited by structural divisions within the ranks of temps that are created by the systems used to control them (Smith 1998).

Careers of Temporary Workers   For many workers, working as a temporary is often temporary. However, the extent to which temporary workers are able to obtain permanent jobs is an unresolved issue. Segal & Sullivan's (1997b) analysis of administrative data from the unemployment insurance system of Washington State showed that about 58% of agency temps found permanent jobs by the end of six quarters; the remaining 42% either became unemployed, dropped out of the labor force, or remained with the agency. Using Current Population Surveys (CPS) data, Houseman & Polivka (2000) found that approximately 52% of agency temps had changed employers one year later; this is an upper-bound estimate of those finding permanent employment, since they might have switched to another temp agency (see also Segal 1996).

One reason why temps may obtain permanent jobs, either directly with a client (a "temp-to-perm" conversion—Carey & Hazelbaker 1986) or indirectly, is because they acquire skills (e.g., computer training) and experience with a variety of potential employers. Indeed, the primary motivation of temporary workers is often the opportunity to acquire skills and experience (von Hippel et al 1997). On the other hand, Nollen (1996) argues that most temporaries work in jobs that are low-skill and without career potential, and that temporary employment is adverse to human capital development by either the staffing company or client (see also Dale &

Bamford 1988). In any event, having temporary work is often better than not having a job at all (Lenz 1996, Segal & Sullivan 1997a).

Hiring temporary workers may affect the mobility of permanent workers, as is suggested by Barnett & Miner's (1992) analysis of career interdependence between core and temporary workers in a large US utility company. They found that the presence of temporary help agency employees slowed mobility among permanent workers in lower ranks and increased it among advanced workers.

Quality of Temporary Jobs   Temporary workers earn, on average, lower wages than regular workers (Segal & Sullivan 1997a), roughly one third less overall in the United States in 1994 (Nollen 1996). However, there is considerable heterogeneity in the wages that temporary workers receive (Williams 1989), as well as in the characteristics of temporary work more generally (Feldman et al 1995, Gallie et al 1998). Salaries of temporaries vary considerably by occupation and are sometimes higher than those of regular employees (Gannon 1974). Thus, temporary clerical workers are generally employed at lower wage rates than their permanent counterparts, and temporary industrial workers often receive much lower pay. On the other hand, engineers and technicians who are temporaries often earn more than their counterparts in regular jobs (Carey & Hazelbaker 1986). Cohen & Haberfeld (1993) found that some temporaries (bookkeepers) were similar to regular full-time workers with regard to wages and their determination, while temporary clerks resembled more those in secondary market jobs.

Temporaries usually receive fewer fringe benefits than do regular workers (Gannon 1974, Segal & Sullivan 1997a, Kalleberg et al 2000). Temporary workers' fringe benefits are very limited, even in occupations where they may earn more than regular workers such as engineers and technicians (Carey & Hazelbaker 1986).

Contract Work

Contract companies, in contrast to temporary help agencies, supervise their employees' work, though, as our discussion above of co-employment suggests, the degree of control exercised by the client may not always be clear-cut. Employees of contract companies may work either at the client's site or offsite (the latter is often called subcontracting) (Purcell & Purcell 1998). Until recently, subcontractors were independent businesses that provided a product or service; since the mid-1980s, subcontractors increasingly provide employees as well (Axelrod 1987). Contracting arrangements are used for various reasons: to meet increased demand, to provide skills that are not available in-house, and to reduce costs (Holmes 1986); these reasons may overlap, as shown by Harrison & Kelley's (1993) study of subcontracting in the metalworking industry.

Incidence and Trends   While contract work has always existed in some industries, such as construction, there has been an increase in the purchase of services (especially business services and engineering and management services) by US firms since the 1970s (Clinton 1997). As firms began to contract out services that were previously done in-house, they gained a greater appreciation of the variety of services that could be contracted and realized that business service organizations could often supply these services more cheaply and efficiently (Abraham & Taylor 1996). Consequently, it is likely that the trend toward contract companies to supply business services (advertising, consumer credit reporting and collection, mailing and stenography, maintenance and cleaning, personnel supply, computer and data processing, protection, research and development) will continue. Large-scale companies will continue to subcontract part of their production to smaller concerns. New organizational forms—such as network organizations, joint ventures, and strategic alliances—will also increase organizations' opportunities to contract out work.

The trend toward greater subcontracting also characterizes all major west European countries (Brewster et al 1997, Tregaskis et al 1998). France and Italy are two countries with strong traditions of small-scale enterprise, and in which there are abundant opportunities for subcontracting (Goldthorpe 1984). In the United Kingdom, outsourcing has grown substantially in the 1990s after agencies in the public sector were required in the 1980s to go through a process of competitive tendering for catering, laundering, and domestic services (Rees & Fielder 1992). Some employees who were transferred to subcontractors found that it enhanced their careers by providing them with opportunities to improve their skills. Indeed, clients increasingly expect in-house contractors to provide training for their employees (Purcell & Purcell 1998).

Rees & Fielder (1992) studied the process of subcontracting in two service industries in the United Kingdom—contract cleaning and catering—and found that organizations in these industries reorganized their work differently. In cleaning, improved service quality was sought through a labor intensification strategy involving more intense supervision and changes in organization of recruitment. People were selected from the external labor market based solely on their social characteristics. In catering, service quality improvements were sought through developing and retaining a high-quality staff by means of training and development within internal labor markets.

Benson & Ieronimo (1996) compared the outsourcing of maintenance work of Australian-owned firms to Japanese manufacturing firms operating in Australia. The Australian-owned firms sought to improve their flexibility via externalization (subcontracting), while Japanese firms sought to enhance flexibility via internalization strategies. Industrial relations issues such as labor rigidity, restrictive work practices, and demarcation disputes were central to outsourcing decisions.

Abraham & Taylor (1996) found that contracting saved costs especially when used for activities done by an organization's noncore workforce. They reasoned that there is little reason to pay high wages to workers who are easily monitored and replaced, or who perform work (such as janitorial services) that is peripheral to an organization's main activity. Gramm & Schnell (1998) found that organizations that had a low-cost producer strategy and whose core employees had a high relative wage (measured by the ratio of core employees' wages to average wages of production employees in the industry) were more likely to use subcontractors in core occupations.

Control of Contract Work   Contract employment also raises questions about who controls the employee, gives orders, directs work, hires and fires. A dramatic illustration of the dilemma of control was provided in the petrochemical industry, in which contract workers are a significant component of the workforce, being used to deal with fluctuations in demand for turnaround, renovation, and maintenance work (Rebitzer 1995). A major accident in this industry spurred investigations of contract work (Kochan et al 1994), which found that managers of petrochemical companies were advised by their lawyers not to train contract workers or to supervise them closely, in order to avoid co-employment liabilities. This created a fragmented system of managerial responsibility for training, supervising, and overseeing direct-hire vs. contract workers. To avoid co-employment, clients simply specified what they wanted done, not how to do it. Clients assumed that the contract companies trained their employees. This was often a dubious assumption that resulted in more accidents involving contract workers (Rebitzer 1995). These studies highlight some of the negative aspects of using contract workers, such as lack of training, low trust, and low commitment. There were also tensions between direct-hire and contract workers, and between management and labor, as unions charged that contract workers were used to reduce unions' presence in firms and to provide cheaper (at least in the short term) and less trained workers (Kochan et al 1994).

Rousseau & Libuser (1997) discuss the issue of contingent workers in high-risk environments more generally, suggesting that risk is highest when using temporaries and contractors because they are external ("outside") employees who are with the organization for only a short time. They suggest that the higher risks associated with the use of contingent workers are rooted in characteristics of the workers themselves (contingent workers tend to be younger, less experienced, and less well-trained) and in the failure of management to adopt appropriate structures for reducing risk. Managers can reduce risk by using structures characteristic of high-reliability organizations (air traffic control, naval aviation) and strategies such as developing quality relations with only a limited number of contractors.

Pearce (1993) found that the presence of contractors in a large US aerospace company was associated with less employee trust in the organization. While contractors (aerospace engineers) earned more than regular employees, they had less job security and often had to move to different geographical locations in order to keep working throughout the year. However, she found no difference between contractors and regular employees with regard to behaviors such as willingness to help with extra tasks and organizational commitment, which she interpreted as due to contractors taking on the norms of the teams in which they worked. Jarmon et al (1998) found that "contractors" (actually, employees of temporary help agencies) in high-technology settings in the United States performed overall as well as regular comparable employees and that managers' perceived overall contractor performance seemed unaffected by amount of buffering maintained by the organization.

SHORT-TERM EMPLOYMENT

Types, Incidence, Trends

Employers may hire some workers directly on a temporary basis, either for a short time on fixed-term contracts (which have a fixed ending point, determined by completion of task or date) or an on-call basis (e.g., substitute teachers). While the doctrine of employment at will in the United States implies that almost all employment is in principle temporary (Summers 1997), the employment relation is generally assumed to be permanent or at least nontemporary for an indefinite period unless it is explicitly designated as fixed-term or temporary.

In the United States, there is a lack of good data on the incidence and trends of short-term employment. A rough estimate is that 3.3 million workers (3.1% of the employed) were direct-hire temporaries in 1995 (Polivka 1996b). Polivka speculates that much of the growth of temporary help agencies (see above) may reflect a shift from firms hiring their own temporary workers directly to relying on outside agencies for them. If this is true, then the growth of the temporary help services industry overstates the increase in temporary work. This explanation would also help to reconcile data on the explosion in temporary help agency employment with the finding that aggregate job retention rates remained fairly stable in the United States since the 1970s (though there have been relative declines in job stability for some groups, such as high school dropouts, high school graduates relative to college graduates, and blacks relative to whites—Diebold et al 1997).

In Europe, temporary employment is usually equated with fixed-term contract employment. The number of people on temporary contracts has increased in the European Union by some 25% in the past decade, though this still represents only 11.5% of employees and there is significant country variation in this (De Grip et al 1997, Reilly 1998, Schömann et al 1998). Fixed-term contracts have been particularly important in countries where employers have difficulty terminating contracts of indefinite duration. This suggests that labor market rigidities can lead to the greater use of temporary workers. For example, the proportion of fixed-term contracts more than doubled between 1985 and 1996 in Spain and France (which had 34% and 13% fixed-term contracts in 1996, respectively), two countries that have strong restrictions on dismissals of regular workers (Fagan 1999). Spain also has severe limits on the use of temporary help agencies. On the other hand, there was no increase in fixed-term employment in the United Kingdom and Germany between 1985 and 1996 (which remained at about 7% and 11%, respectively), and some countries (e.g., Belgium, Greece, Luxembourg, and Portugal) experienced a decrease in fixed-term employment during this period (Fagan 1999).

Temporary work in Europe has generally grown less than part-time work and plays a lesser role in the overall labor market. There are also smaller inter-country differences in temporary than in part-time employment. Moreover, unlike part-time work, temporary employment does not seem to mitigate unemployment, being rather an indicator of weak worker labor market position (especially among youth) in periods of high unemployment (De Grip et al 1997).

Organizations' Use of Short-Term Temporaries

About 38% of US establishments use short-term hires (Houseman 1997). Employers appear to use short-term hires mainly to deal with seasonal demands, as well as to provide staffing for special projects and unexpected increases in demand, and to fill in for regular employees who are absent (Houseman 1997, Davis-Blake & Uzzi 1993). Organizations with a low-cost producer strategy are also more likely to use direct-hire temporaries in core occupations (Gramm & Schnell 1998). Uzzi & Barsness (1998) found that older organizations were less likely to use fixed-term temporaries in Britain.

Using temporary workers is not always beneficial for organizations (Delsen 1995). Geary (1992) found that the use of temporary workers by three US firms operating in Ireland led to considerable conflict between permanent and temporary workers as well as between management and labor. Nollen (1996, Nollen & Axel 1996) found that temporary work is not always cost-effective, since the productivity of temporaries may be lower than that of regular workers. Using temporaries could also result in a waste of training from the organization's point of view.

Employers in different countries may use temporaries for different reasons, as Casey et al (1989) showed in their study of temporary workers in Britain and the (then) Federal Republic of Germany. British employers were more likely to use temporaries to obtain numerical flexibility, in order to increase or decrease their workforce size. German employers sought instead to obtain functional flexibility (the ability of employees to do a variety of tasks) by giving temporaries permanent contracts once they acquired the needed skills.

CONTINGENT WORK

The notion of contingent work is related to short-term, unstable employment. The label of contingent work was first coined at a 1985 conference on employment security by economist Audrey Freedman, who used it to refer to work arrangements that were conditional on employers' needs for labor and thus lacked an attachment between employer and worker (Freedman 1996). Unfortunately, the term has often been equated with nonstandard employment relations more generally (e.g., Belous 1989, Blank 1998), which is often misleading since nonstandard work arrangements may differ considerably in their degree of employment security.

Contingent work may be defined as "any job in which an individual does not have an explicit or implicit contract for long-term employment or one in which the minimum hours worked can vary in a nonsystematic manner" (Polivka & Nardone 1989:11). This influential definition was the basis of an important program of data collection undertaken by the Bureau of Labor Statistics (BLS) in their Contingent

Work Supplements to the February Current Population Surveys (CPS) in 1995, 1997, and 1999. (BLS plans to repeat this supplement every two years.) Based on data from the first of these surveys, Polivka (1996a) estimated the number of contingent workers in the United States as being between 2.2% (2.7 million workers) and 4.9% (6 million) of the labor force. These estimates are considerably lower than those of the proportions of workers in nonstandard jobs, which is consistent with the view that many workers in alternative arrangements do not really have contingent jobs (see Kalleberg et al 1997). A comparison of the 1995 and 1997 surveys suggests that the number and proportion of contingent workers has declined, perhaps due to the expansion of the economy and tightening of the US labor market in the late 1990s (Hipple 1998).

Contingent work may affect workers' psychological experiences, though the nature of this relationship has not yet been well established. Beard & Edwards' (1995) literature review suggests that contingent workers are more likely to experience job insecurity and unpredictability, to have low control over their work and transactional psychological contracts, and to perceive themselves as disadvantaged relative to noncontingent workers. Other studies have found few differences between contingent and noncontingent workers in their organizational commitment (Pearce 1998). Van Dyne & Ang (1998) speculate that this may reflect the involuntary nature of contingent employment in the United States, where contingent workers may display positive work attitudes in the hopes of obtaining regular jobs. Accordingly, their comparison of work attitudes between contingent (temporary or on-call) and regular employees in Singapore—a country with labor shortages where contingent status is voluntary—found that contingent workers engaged in fewer organizational citizenship behaviors such as helping coworkers.

Contingent work may benefit organizations by helping to import valuable knowledge into the firm, such as public knowledge about industry best practices. It can also act as a catalyst to generate new private knowledge. (On the negative side, it can also help to leak private knowledge into the public domain.) Firms in dynamic environments characterized by extreme competition are most likely to benefit from using contingent workers, while organizations in environments that are stable and characterized by mild competitive pressures are least apt to benefit from contingent workers (Matusik & Hill 1998).

INDEPENDENT CONTRACTORS

Independent contractors are self-employed; they have neither an employer nor a wage contract and are responsible for their own tax arrangements. However, not all self-employed persons consider themselves to be independent contractors. For example, small shopkeepers who work at a fixed location are not likely to call themselves independent contractors. Moreover, many independent contractors are not capable of appropriating surplus value produced by labor but represent instead a form of disguised wage labor whose only capital is their tools, materials, and special expertise (Rainbird 1991).

Independent contractors are not employees. Unlike employees, whose work is usually defined in terms of labor expended, independent contractors are generally given specifications for the final product or result and they decide how best to accomplish it (Rebitzer 1995, Summers 1997). Indeed, controlling one's own work, along with bearing the economic risk of their employment, are key criteria for establishing whether someone is legally an independent contractor rather than an employee. Despite these conceptual distinctions, it is often difficult to distinguish between a "contract for service" (self-employed) and a "contract of service" (employed) (Purcell & Purcell 1998).

A client obtains several important advantages from hiring an independent contractor rather than an employee. Clients are not "vicariously liable" for the actions of independent contractors in the same way as they are for their own employees (Rebitzer 1995). In addition, clients are not required to provide independent contractors with fringe benefits or to pay them unemployment compensation, Social Security, or workman's compensation taxes. These advantages have often led to abuses: the US Internal Revenue Service (IRS) estimates that as many as 38% of employers misclassify their employees as independent contractors to avoid paying payroll taxes, despite the fact that many of these "independent contractors" have only one "client" who is their real employer (duRivage 1992). A landmark case related to the classification of contractors was *Vizcaino v. Microsoft*, in which the US Court of Appeals for the Ninth Circuit used a common-law definition of "employee" to require Microsoft to treat a group of "independent contractors" (who worked on projects often exceeding two years) as employees for tax purposes (Monthly Labor Review 1997).

Incidence and Trends

Relatively few hard data exist on the incidence of independent contractors within the US labor force. Perhaps the best estimates come from the February 1995 and 1997 Supplements to the CPS: nearly 7% of the US labor force identified themselves as independent contractors in each year (Cohany 1998). Unfortunately, these estimates are based on self-identification rather than on objective criteria such as those used by the IRS or other agencies. An additional 5% to 6% of CPS respondents identified themselves as self-employed but not independent contractors in these two years, suggesting that there is not a perfect correspondence between people's understanding of these two work arrangements. Nevertheless, the best time-series data related to independent contractors are probably those on self-employment. These data suggest relatively little change in the proportion of the US labor force that is self-employed since 1970 (Bregger 1996). Self-employment growth also correlates only modestly with aggregate employment growth (Segal 1996).

Despite the absence of direct information on trends in independent contractors, it is likely that this category of nonstandard work has increased in the past several decades. Changes in tax laws in particular have generated growth in this category of nonstandard work. The "safe harbor" provision of the 1978 Revenue Act helped to ensure the status of real estate brokers and members of other occupations as independent contractors. In addition, the 1982 Tax Equity and Fiscal Responsibility Act required many brokers who had formerly been employees to become independent contractors (Thomas & Reskin 1990, Carré & Joshi 1999).

Russell & Hanneman (1997) found that the use of independent contractors in Russia is similar to patterns observed in the west (Davis-Blake & Uzzi 1993): larger firms in Russia are less likely to use a high proportion of independent contractors. To the extent that private businesses make greater use of independent contractors than do state-owned businesses in Russia, then, it is because private firms are smaller.

Careers

Independent contractors tend to prefer this work arrangement to traditional employment (Cohany 1998). Many independent contractors earned higher wages than workers in traditional arrangements but were less likely to receive health insurance and pensions (Kalleberg et al 1997, Kalleberg et al 2000, Hipple & Stewart 1996). Kahn (1998) suggests that increased competitiveness in occupations with substantial numbers of independent contractors or self-employed persons may have contributed toward decreasing inter-industry wage differentials in the 1990s, though she notes that there were too few of these nonstandard work arrangements to explain the large drop in inter-industry wage differentials.

Some independent contractors conform to the image of "portfolio workers" (Handy 1990) who move from one firm to the next. Hakim (1994) describes this phenomenon as reflecting the fact that "we are all self-employed" both inside and outside organizations. DiTomaso (2001) describes the structural arrangements in which many of these workers work as loosely coupled systems, also called webs, networks, alliances, spin-offs, and new ventures. This phenomenon is illustrated by the case of Silicon Valley, where many highly skilled employees prefer working as independent contractors, since this status enables them to benefit from their ability to move among firms. Carnoy et al 1997 (see also Kunda et al 1999) describe the individualized, flexible employment defined by human capital portfolios of these workers, as opposed to stable, permanent jobs. Tight labor markets help independent contractors to move between workplaces filling particular positions on demand or providing labor services as needed.

FUTURE DIRECTIONS FOR RESEARCH ON NONSTANDARD EMPLOYMENT RELATIONS

Measuring Nonstandard Work Arrangements

Progress in understanding the nature and consequences of nonstandard work requires more valid and reliable measures of these work arrangements. For instance, indicators of whether a person is an independent contractor need to go beyond mere self-identification, yet be more amenable to survey research than the Internal Revenue Service's 20-factor test. Such measures should help to refine the distinctions between independent contracting and self-employment more generally, as well as to differentiate independent contractors from employees.

In addition, we need better measures of fixed-term temporary contracts and of the nature of the psychological contracts that encompass employees' and employers' understandings of the employment relation. More sophisticated indicators of workers' relationships to temporary help agencies and contract companies are also necessary to appreciate better the content and complexity of these relations. Further, we need to understand better the heterogeneous nature of part-time work.

The Quality of Nonstandard Jobs

Much of the controversy and concern about the rise in nonstandard work arrangements is due to the assumption that they are associated with bad jobs. Most analyses have shown that nonstandard work arrangements vary in their wages: Some nonstandard jobs (such as contract work) often pay better than standard work, while other kinds of nonstandard work (especially part-time and temporary work) pay relatively poorly (see Kalleberg et al 2000, Ferber & Waldfogel 1998; but see Blank 1998). There is substantial agreement, though, that nonstandard work arrangements are associated with the lack of health insurance, pensions, and other fringe benefits. This is particularly problematic in the United States since employment is the main source of these benefits. Further research is needed on the heterogeneity within nonstandard work arrangements in wages and fringe benefits.

Additional research is also needed on the relations between working in nonstandard arrangements and careers. How common, for example, are "temp-to-perm" contracts? Nonstandard working arrangements may be beneficial for workers if such employment enhances their skills and enables them to adapt to the rapid changes occurring in labor markets. Studies are also needed of the role of employment intermediaries in helping people make transitions from welfare to work.

Triangular Employment Relations

The emergence of triangular employment relations constitutes a major challenge to labor law, unionization, and other aspects of industrial relations systems. Theories of control systems also need to be revised to take into account the opportunities and challenges posed by co-employment and joint employer arrangements. Issues of who should provide training to workers emerge as critical public policy questions as well as matters of concern to employers and their employees. The effects of triangular employment relations on collective bargaining and unionization are particularly potentially devastating: The detachment of employees from their employers makes it difficult for unions to organize, and the existence of multiple employers provides them with leverage against unions.

Research also needs to understand better the inter-organizational networks that underlie triangular employment relations. Linkages between temporary help agencies and contract companies, on the one hand, and client organizations, on the other, are just beginning to be studied systematically. The interrelations among employment intermediaries themselves also deserve careful scrutiny.

Organizations' Staffing Practices

Nonstandard work arrangements reflect organizations' attempts to achieve flexibility by externalizing some of their activities (Pfeffer & Baron 1988). The focus on externalization contrasts with the dominant concern of organizational analysts during the post–World War II period, which was with how employers internalize their workforces to develop their skills and protect them from competition in external labor markets. We need to know more about the conditions under which organizations externalize their workforces. We also should explore the interrelations among the various types of nonstandard work arrangements, such as the extent to which these are complements or substitutes for one another.

However, the focus on externalization does not mean that processes of internalization can be neglected. Research is particularly needed on the bundles of practices that employers use to accomplish their human resource goals. The core-periphery model suggested by Atkinson (1985) and debated and refined by others offers a useful hypothesis for assessing systematically organizations' human resource strategies.

The growth of interest in nonstandard work arrangements in recent years serves to highlight the complexity of the relations between employers and their employees. The employment relation is potentially a very fruitful conceptual meeting place for research that seeks to merge macro and micro levels from a variety of disciplines, including economic, sociological, and psychological research on work, labor markets, organizations, and the linkages between these structures and individuals. In the coming decades, social science research on these topics will increasingly come to appreciate the utility of a focus on employment relations for understanding work-related issues.

ACKNOWLEDGMENTS

I thank Eileen Appelbaum, Lonnie Golden, Susan Houseman, Barbara Reskin, and Vicki Smith for their comments on earlier versions.

Visit the Annual Reviews home page at www.AnnualReviews.org

LITERATURE CITED

Abraham KG. 1988. Flexible staffing arrangements and employers' short-term adjustment strategies. In *Employment, Unemployment and Labor Utilization*, ed. RA Hart, pp. 288–311. Boston: Unwin Hyman

Abraham KG. 1990. Restructuring the employment relationship: the growth of market-mediated work arrangements. In *New Developments in the Labor Market: Toward a New Institutional Paradigm*, ed. KG Abraham,

RB McKersie, pp. 85–119. Cambridge, MA: MIT Press

Abraham KG, Taylor SK. 1996. Firms' use of outside contractors: theory and evidence. *J. Labor Econ.* 14(3):394–424

Appelbaum E. 1992. Structural change and the growth of part-time and temporary employment. In *New Policies for the Part-time and Contingent Workforce*, ed. VL duRivage, pp. 1–14. Armonk, NY: Sharpe

Atkinson J. 1985. The changing corporation. In *New Patterns of Work*, ed. D Clutterbuck, pp. 13–34. Aldershot, UK: Gower

Axelrod JG. 1987. Who's the boss? Employer leasing and the joint employer relationship. *Lab. Lawyer* 2:853–72

Barnett WP, Miner AS. 1992. Standing on the shoulders of others: career interdependence in job mobility. *Admin. Sci. Q.* 37 (2):262–81

Beard KM, Edwards JR. 1995. Employees at risk: contingent work and the psychological experience of contingent workers. In *Trends in Organizational Behavior*, ed. CL Cooper, DM Rousseau, 2:109–26. Chichester, UK: Wiley

Belous RS. 1989. *The Contingent Economy: The Growth of the Temporary, Part-Time and Subcontracted Workforce*. Washington, DC: Natl. Planning Assoc.

Benson J, Ieronimo N. 1996. Outsourcing decisions: evidence from Australian enterprises. *Int. Labour Rev.* 135(1):59–73

Blank RM. 1990. Are part-time jobs bad jobs? In *A Future of Lousy Jobs?*, ed. G Burtless, pp. 123–64. Washington, DC: Brookings Inst.

Blank RM. 1998 Contingent work in a changing labor market. In *Generating Jobs: How to Increase Demand for Less-Skilled Workers*, ed. RB Freeman, P Gottschalk, pp. 258–94. New York: Russell Sage Found.

Blossfeld H-P, Hakim C, eds. 1997. *Between Equalization and Marginalization: Women Working Part-Time in Europe and the United States of America*. New York: Oxford Univ. Press

Bosch G, Dawkins P, Michon F. 1993. Work-

ing time in 14 industrialised countries: an overview. In *Times are Changing: Working Time in 14 Industrialised Countries*, ed. G Bosch, P Dawkins, F Michon, pp. 1–47. Geneva: Int. Inst. for Lab. Stud.

Bregger JE. 1996. Measuring self-employment in the United States. *Monthly Labor Rev.* 119 (1–2):3–9

Brewster C, Mayne L, Tregaskis O. 1997. Flexible staffing in Europe. *J. World Bus.* 32 (2):133–51

Bronstein AS. 1991. Temporary work in Western Europe: threat or complement to permanent employment? *Int. Labour Rev.* 130 (3): 291–310

Buttrick J. 1952. The inside contracting system. *J. Econ. Hist.* 12(3):205–21

Cappelli P. 1999. *The New Deal at Work: Managing the Market-Driven Workforce*. Boston: Harvard Bus. Sch. Press

Cappelli P, Bassi L, Katz H, Knoke D, Osterman P, Useem M. 1997. *Change at Work*. New York: Oxford Univ. Press

Carey ML, Hazelbaker KL. 1986. Employment growth in the temporary help industry. *Monthly Labor Rev.* 109(4):37–44

Carnevale AP, Jennings LA, Eisenmann JM. 1998. Contingent workers and employment law. In *Contingent Work: American Employment Relations in Transition*, ed. K Barker, K Christensen, pp. 281–305. Ithaca, NY: Cornell Univ. Press

Carnoy M, Castells M, Brenner C. 1997. Labor markets and employment practices in the age of flexibility: a case study of Silicon Valley. *Int. Labour Rev.* 136(1):27–48

Carré FJ, Joshi P. 1999. *Looking for leverage in a fluid world: innovative responses to temporary and contracted work*. Presented at Annu. Meet. Midwest Econ. Assoc., Nashville, TN

Casey B. 1991. Survey evidence on trends in 'non-standard' employment. In *Farewell to Flexibility?*, ed. A Pollert, pp. 179–99. Oxford: Blackwell

Casey B, Dragendorf R, Heering W, Gunnar J. 1989. Temporary employment in Great Britain and the Federal Republic of Germany.

Int. Labour Rev. 128(4):449–66

Clinton A. 1997. Flexible labor: restructuring the American work force. *Monthly Labor Rev.* 120(8):3–17

Cohany SR. 1998. Workers in alternative employment arrangements: a second look. *Monthly Labor Rev.* 121(11):3–21

Cohen Y, Haberfeld Y. 1993. Temporary help service workers: employment characteristics and wage determination. *Indust. Relat.* 32(2):272–87

Collinson D. 1987. 'Picking women': the recruitment of temporary workers in the mail order industry. *Work, Employ. Soc.* 1(3):371–87

Corcoran M, Duncan G, Ponza M. 1984. Work experience, job segregation, and wages. In *Sex Segregation in the Workplace: Trends, Explanations, Remedies*, ed. BF Reskin, pp. 171–91. Washington, DC: Natl. Acad. Press

Córdova E. 1986. From full-time employment to atypical employment: a major shift in the evolution of labour relations? *Int. Labour Rev.* 125(6):641–57

Dale A, Bamford C. 1988. Temporary workers: cause for concern or complacency? *Work, Employ. Soc.* 2(2):191–209

Davis-Blake A, Uzzi B. 1993. Determinants of employment externalization: a study of temporary workers and independent contractors. *Admin. Sci. Q.* 38(2):195–223

De Grip A, Hoevenberg J, Willems E. 1997. Atypical employment in the European Union. *Int. Labour Rev.* 136(1):49–71

Delsen L. 1995. *Atypical Employment: An International Perspective—Causes, Consequences, and Policy.* Groningen: Wolters-Noordhoff

Diebold FX, Neumark D, Polsky D. 1997. Job stability in the United States. *J. Labor Econ.* 15(2):206–33

DiTomaso N. 2001. The loose coupling of jobs: the subcontracting of everyone? In *Sourcebook on Labor Markets: Evolving Structures and Policies*, ed. I Berg, AL Kalleberg. New York: Kluwer/Plenum. In press

duRivage V. 1992. Flexibility trap: the prolifer-ation of marginal jobs. *Am. Prospect.* 9:84–93

England P, Christopher K, Reid L. 1999. How do intersections of race-ethnicity and gender affect pay among young cohorts of African Americans, European Americans, and Latinos/as? In *Race, Gender, and Economic Inequality: African Americans and Latinas in the Labor Market*, ed. I Browne, pp. 139–82. New York: Russell Sage Found.

Fagan C. 1999. *Non-standard work arrangements: the UK in European perspective.* Presented at Conf. on the Growth and Implications of Non-standard Work Arrangements: The U.S., Japan and Europe in Comparative Perspective, Japan Women's Univ., Tokyo, July 2–3

Fagan C, O'Reilly J. 1998. Conceptualizing part-time work: the value of an integrated comparative perspective. In *Part-Time Prospects: An International Comparison of Part-Time Work in Europe, North America and the Pacific Rim*, ed. J O'Reilly, C Fagan, pp. 1–31. New York: Routledge

Feldman DC. 1990. Reconceptualizing the nature and consequences of part-time work. *Acad. Mgmt. Rev.* 15(1):103–12

Feldman DC, Doerpinghaus HI, Turnley WH. 1995. Employee reactions to temporary jobs. *J. Managerial Iss.* 7(2):127–41

Ferber M, Waldfogel J. 1998. The long-term consequences of nontraditional employment. *Monthly Labor Rev.* 121(5):3–12

Freedman A. 1996. Contingent work and the role of labor market intermediaries. In *Of Heart and Mind: Social Policy Essays in Honor of Sar A. Levitan*, ed. G Mangum, S Mangum, pp. 177–99. Kalamazoo, MI: Upjohn Instit. Employ. Res.

Freeman R. 1998. War of the models: Which labor market institutions for the 21st century? *Labour Econ.* 5(1):1–24

Gallie D, White M, Cheng Y, Tomlinson M. 1998. *Restructuring the Employment Relationship.* Oxford: Oxford Univ. Press

Gannon MJ. 1974. A profile of the temporary

help industry and its workers. *Monthly Labor Rev.* 97(5):44–49

Gannon MJ. 1984. Preferences of temporary workers: time, variety and flexibility. *Monthly Labor Rev.* 107(8):26–28

Geary JF. 1992. Employment flexibility and human resource management: the case of three American electronics plants. *Work, Employ. Soc.* 6(2):251–70

Golden L. 1996. The expansion of temporary help employment in the U.S., 1982–1992: an empirical test of alternative models. *Appl. Econ.* 28(9):1127–42

Golden L, Appelbuam E. 1992. What was driving the 1982–88 boom in temporary employment? Preference of workers or decisions and power of employers. *Am. J. Econ. Sociol.* 51(4):473–93

Goldthorpe JH. 1984. The end of convergence: corporatist and dualist tendencies in modern western societies. In *Order and Conflict in Contemporary Capitalism: Studies in the Political Economy of Western European Nations*, ed. JH Goldthorpe, pp. 315–43. Oxford: Oxford Univ. Press

Gonos G. 1997. The contest over 'employer' status in the postWar United States: the case of temporary help firms. *Law Soc. Rev.* 31(1):81–110

Gordon DM. 1996. *Fat and Mean: The Corporate Squeeze of Working Americans and the Myth of Managerial 'Downsizing'*. New York: Kessler Books/Free Press

Gottfried H. 1991. Mechanisms of control in the temporary help service industry. *Sociol. Forum* 6(4):699–713

Gramm CL, Schnell JF. 1998. *The use of flexible employment arrangements in core production jobs*. Presented at Sixth Bargaining Group Conf., Urbana-Champaign, IL

Green F, Krahn H, Sung J. 1993. Non-standard work in Canada and the United Kingdom. *Int. J. Manpower* 14(5):70–86

Hakim C. 1994. *We are All Self–Employed: The New Social Contract for Working in a Changed World*. San Francisco: Berrett-Koehler

Handy C. 1990. *The Age of Unreason*. Boston, MA: Harvard Bus. Sch. Press

Harrison B, Kelley MR. 1993. Outsourcing and the search for 'flexibility'. *Work, Employ. Soc.* 7(2):213–35

Hipple S. 1998. Contingent work: results from the second survey. *Monthly Labor Rev.* 121 (11):22–35

Hipple S, Stewart J. 1996. Earnings and benefits of workers in alternative work arrangements. *Monthly Labor Rev.* 119(10):46–54

Holmes J. 1986. The organization and locational structure of production subcontracting. In *Production, Work, Territory: The Geographical Anatomy of Industrial Capitalism*, ed. M Storper, AJ Scott, pp. 80–106. Boston: Allen and Unwin

Houseman SN. 1995. Part-time employment in Europe and Japan. *J. Labor Res.* 16(3):249–62

Houseman SN. 1997. *Temporary, part-time, and contract employment in the United States: new evidence from an employer survey*. Manuscript, WE Upjohn Inst. Employ. Res., Kalamazoo, MI

Houseman SN, Osawa M. 1998. What is the nature of part-time work in the United States and Japan? In *Part-Time Prospects: An International Comparison of Part-Time Work in Europe, North America and the Pacific Rim*, ed. J O'Reilly, C Fagan, pp. 232–51. New York: Routledge

Houseman SN, Polivka AE. 2000. The implications of flexible staffing arrangements for job stability. In *On the Job: Is Long-Term Employment a Thing of the Past?*, ed. D Neumark. New York: Russell Sage Found. In press

Jarmon R, Paulson AS, Rebne D. 1998. Contractor performance: how good are contingent workers at the professional level? *IEEE Trans. Eng. Mgmt.* 45(1):11–19

Kahn S. 1998. Falling interindustry wage differentials: has contingent work had an impact? *Proc. 50th Annu. Meet. Indust. Relat. Res. Assoc.*, ed. PB Voos, 1:259–67. Madison, WI: IRRA

Kahne H. 1992. Part-time work: a hope and a peril. In *Working Part-time: Risks and Opportunities*, ed. BD Warme, KP Lundy, LA Lundy, pp. 295–309. New York: Praeger

Kalleberg AL. 1995. Part-time work and workers in the United States: correlates and policy issues. *Washington & Lee Law Rev.* 52(3):771–98

Kalleberg AL, Rasell E, Cassirer N, Reskin BF, Hudson K, et al. 1997. *Nonstandard Work, Substandard Jobs: Flexible Work Arrangements in the U.S.* Washington, DC: Econ. Policy Inst.

Kalleberg AL, Reskin BF, Hudson K. 2000. Bad jobs in America: standard and nonstandard employment relations and job quality in the United States. *Am. Sociol. Rev.* 65(2): In press

Kochan TA, Smith M, Wells JC, Rebitzer JB. 1994. Human resource strategies and contingent workers: the case of safety and health in the petrochemical industry. *Hum. Resource Mgmt.* 33(1):55–77

Krueger AB. 1993. How computers have changed the wage structure: evidence from microdata, 1984–1989. *Q. J. Econ.* 108 (1):33–60

Kunda G, Barley SR, Evans J. 1999. *Why do contractors contract? The theory and reality of high end contingent labor.* Manuscript, Cent. for Work, Technol. Org., Stanford Univ.

Laird K, Williams N. 1996. Employment growth in the temporary help supply industry. *J. Labor Res.* 17(4):663–81

Larson T, Ong PM. 1994. Imbalance in part-time employment. *J. Econ. Issues* 28(1):187–96

Lee DR. 1996. Why is flexible employment increasing? *J. Labor Res.* 17(4):543–53

Lenz EA. 1996. Flexible employment: positive work strategies for the 21st century. *J. Labor Res.* 17(4):555–66

Mangum G, Mayall D, Nelson K. 1985. The temporary help industry: a response to the dual internal labor market. *Indust. Labor Relat. Rev.* 38(4):599–611

Matusik SF, Hill CWL. 1998. The utilization of contingent work, knowledge creation, and

competitive advantage. *Acad. Mgmt. Rev.* 23(4):680–97

Moberly RB. 1987. Temporary, part-time, and other atypical employment relationships in the United States. *Labor Law J.* 38:689–96

Montgomery M. 1988. On the determinants of employer demand for part-time workers. *Rev. Econ. Stat.* 70:112–17

Monthly Labor Rev. 1997. The law at work: contractors as employees. 120(10):34–35

Moore MA. 1965. The temporary help service industry: historical development, operation and scope. *Indust. Labor Relat. Rev.* 18:554–69

Morse D. 1969. *The Peripheral Worker.* New York: Columbia Univ. Press

Nardone T. 1995. Part-time employment: reasons, demographics, and trends. *J. Labor Res.* 16(3):275–92

Nollen S. 1996. Negative aspects of temporary employment. *J. Labor Res.* 17(4):562–82

Nollen SD, Axel HA. 1996. *Managing Contingent Workers: How to Reap the Benefits and Reduce the Risks.* New York: Am. Mgmt. Assoc.

Ofstead CM. 1999. Temporary help firms as entrepreneurial actors. *Sociol. Forum* 14(2): 273–94

Pearce JL. 1993. Toward an organizational behavior of contract laborers: their psychological involvement and effects on employee coworkers. *Acad. Mgmt. J.* 36(5):1082–96

Pearce JL. 1998. Job security is important, but not for the reasons you might think: the example of contingent workers. In *Trends in Organizational Behavior*, ed. CL Cooper, DM Rousseau, 5:31–46. Chichester, UK: Wiley

Peck J. 1996. *Work-Place: The Social Regulation of Labor Markets.* New York: Guilford

Peck J, Theodore N. 1998. The business of contingent work: growth and restructuring in Chicago's temporary employment industry. *Work, Employ. Soc.* 12(4):655–74

Pfeffer J, Baron JN. 1988. Taking the workers back out: recent trends in the structuring of employment. *Res. Org. Behav.* 10:257–303

Pitts MK. 1998. Demand for part-time workers

in the U.S. economy: Why is the distribution across industries uneven? *Soc. Sci. Res.* 27(2):87–108

Polivka AE. 1996a. Contingent and alternative work arrangements, defined. *Monthly Labor Rev.* 119(10):3–9

Polivka AE. 1996b. *Are temporary help agency workers substitutes for direct hire temps? Searching for an alternative explanation of growth in the temporary help industry.* Presented at Soc. Labor Econ. Conf., May 3–4, Chicago

Polivka AE, Nardone T. 1989. On the definition of 'contingent work.' *Monthly Labor Rev.* 112(12):9–16

Purcell K, Purcell J. 1998. In-sourcing, outsourcing, and the growth of contingent labor as evidence of flexible employment strategies. *Eur. J. Work Org. Psychol.* 7(1):39–59

Rainbird H. 1991. The self-employed: small entrepreneurs or disguised wage labourers? In *Farewell to Flexibility?*, ed. A Pollert, pp. 200–14. Oxford: Blackwell

Rebitzer JB. 1995. Job safety and contract workers in the petrochemical industry. *Indust. Relat.* 34(1):40–57

Rees G, Fielder S. 1992. The services economy, subcontracting and the new employment relations: contract catering and cleaning. *Work, Employ. Soc.* 6(3):347–68

Reilly P. 1998. Balancing flexibility—meeting the interests of employer and employee. *Eur. J. Work Org. Psychol.* 7(1):7–22

Rousseau DM, Libuser C. 1997. Contingent workers in high risk environments. *Calif. Mgmt. Rev.* 39(2):103–23

Rubin BA. 1995. Flexible accumulation, the decline of contract, and social transformation. *Res. Soc. Strat. Mob.* 14:297–323

Russell R, Hanneman R. 1997. *The use of part-time employees and independent contractors by small enterprises in Russia.* Presented at Annu. Meet. Am. Sociol. Assoc., Toronto

Schömann K, Rogowski R, Kruppe T. 1998. *Labour Market Efficiency in the European Union: Employment Protection and Fixed-Term Contracts.* New York: Routledge

Segal LM. 1996. Flexible employment: composition and trends. *J. Labor Res.* 17(4):525–42

Segal LM, Sullivan DG. 1997a. The growth of temporary services work. *J. Econ. Perspect.* 11(2):117–36

Segal LM, Sullivan DG. 1997b. *Temporary services employment durations: evidence from state UI data.* Work. Pap. WP-97-23, Federal Reserve Bank of Chicago

Sherer PS. 1996. Toward an understanding of the variety in work arrangements: the organization and labor relationship framework. In *Trends in Organizational Behavior*, ed. CL Cooper, DM Rousseau, 3:99–122. Chichester, UK: Wiley

Sightler KW, Adams JS. 1999. Differences between stayers and leavers among part-time workers. *J. Managerial Issues* 11(1):110–25

Smith V. 1997. New forms of work organization. *Annu. Rev. Sociol.* 23:315–39

Smith V. 1998. The fractured world of the temporary worker: power, participation, and fragmentation in the contemporary workplace. *Soc. Prob.* 45(4):411–30

Smith V. 2000. *Teamwork vs. tempwork: managers and the dualisms of workplace restructuring.* Manuscript, Univ. Calif., Davis

Stratton LS. 1996. Are "involuntary" part-time workers indeed involuntary? *Ind. Labor Relat. Rev.* 49(3):522–36

Summers CW. 1997. Contingent employment in the United States. *Compar. Labor Law J.* 18(4):503–22

Tansky JW, Veglahn PA. 1995. Legal issues in co-employment. *Labor Law J.* 46(5):293–300

Thomas BJ, Reskin BF. 1990. A woman's place is selling homes: occupational change and the feminization of real estate sales. In *Job Queues, Gender Queues: Explaining Women's Inroads into Male Occupations*, by BF Reskin, PA Roos, pp. 205–23. Philadelphia: Temple Univ. Press

Thurman JE, Trah G. 1990. Part-time work in international perspective. *Int. Labour Rev.* 129(1):23–40

Tilly C. 1996. *Half a Job: Bad and Good*

Part-Time Jobs in a Changing Labor Market. Philadelphia: Temple Univ. Press

Tregaskis O, Brewster C, Mayne L, Hegewisch A. 1998. Flexible working in Europe: the evidence and its implications. *Eur. J. Work Org. Psychol.* 7(1):61–78

Treu T. 1992. Labour flexibility in Europe. *Int. Labour Rev.* 131(4–5):497–512

Uzzi B, Barsness ZI. 1998. Contingent employment in British establishments: organizational determinants of the use of fixed-term hires and part-time workers. *Soc. Forces* 76(3):967–1007

Van Dyne L, Ang S. 1998. Organizational citizenship behavior of contingent workers in Singapore. *Acad. Mgmt. J.* 41(6):692–703

Von Hippel C, Mangum SL, Greenberger DB,

Heneman RL, Skoglind JD. 1997. Temporary employment: Can organizations and employees both win? *Acad. Mgmt. Executive* 11(1):93–104

Vosko LF. 1997. Legitimizing the triangular employment relationship: emerging international labour standards from a comparative perspective. *Comp. Labor Law J.* 19(1):43–78

Williams HB. 1989. What temporary workers earn: findings from new BLS survey. *Monthly Labor Rev.* 112(3):3–6

Williamson OE. 1980. The organization of work: a comparative institutional assessment. *J. Econ. Behav. Org.* 1:5–38

Zeytinoglu IU. 1992. Reasons for hiring part-time workers. *Indust. Relat.* 31(3):489–99

Annu. Rev. Sociol. 2000. 26:367–93

SOCIAL PSYCHOLOGY OF IDENTITIES

Judith A. Howard

Department of Sociology, University of Washington, Seattle, Washington 98195;
e-mail: jhoward@u.washington.edu

Key Words social construction of identity, language, intersections of identities, social cognition, symbolic interaction

■ **Abstract** In this chapter I review the social psychological underpinnings of identity, emphasizing social cognitive and symbolic interactionist perspectives and research, and I turn then to key themes of current work on identity—social psychological, sociological, and interdisciplinary. I emphasize the social bases of identity, particularly identities based on ethnicity, race, sexuality, gender, class, age, and (dis)ability, both separately and as they intersect. I also take up identities based on space, both geographic and virtual. I discuss struggles over identities, organized by social inequalities, nationalisms, and social movements. I conclude by discussing postmodernist conceptions of identities as fluid, multidimensional, personalized social constructions that reflect sociohistorical contexts, approaches remarkably consistent with recent empirical social psychological research, and I argue explicitly for a politicized social psychology of identities that brings together the structures of everyday lives and the sociocultural realities in which those lives are lived.

> "Identity ... is a concept that neither imprisons (as does much in sociology) nor detaches (as does much in philosophy and psychology) persons from their social and symbolic universes, [so] it has over the years retained a generic force that few concepts in our field have."
>
> (Davis 1991:105)
>
> "[I]dentity is never a priori, nor a finished product; it is only ever the problematic process of access to an image of totality."
>
> (Bhabha 1994:51)

INTRODUCTION

"Identity" is a keyword of contemporary society and a central focus of social psychological theorizing and research. At earlier historical moments, identity was not so much an issue; when societies were more stable, identity was to a great extent assigned, rather than selected or adopted. In current times, however, the concept of identity carries the full weight of the need for a sense of who one is, together with an often overwhelming pace of change in surrounding social contexts—changes in the groups and networks in which people and their identities are embedded and in the societal structures and practices in which those networks are themselves embedded.

Social cognition and symbolic interaction, two of the prevailing perspectives in sociological social psychology, provide the theoretical underpinnings of traditional understandings of identity. In the past several decades, the concept of identity has been taken up more broadly, both within sociology and in other disciplines. In this essay, I review key questions and recent research on identity in social cognition and symbolic interaction, then take up key themes of current social psychological work on identity: identity and social inequalities particularly as expressed in race and ethnicity, gender, sexuality, and other systems of social stratification; research on how these multiple identities intersect; identities based on locational indicators such as geography, place, cyberspace; questions of the (in)stability of identities; and the politicization of identities.

SOCIAL COGNITION

Social cognition is a theory of how we store and process information (Fiske & Taylor 1991, Augoustinos & Walker 1995). Social cognition has close roots to psychology and a reliance on experimental laboratory methodologies. Several central assumptions underlie social cognitive theories of identity: that human cognitive capacities are limited; that, therefore, we process information as cognitive misers, streamlining information to manage the demands of everyday interaction; that, following from this need for cognitive efficiency, we categorize information about people, objects, and situations before we engage memory or inferential processes.

Cognitive Structures

Cognitive schemas, abstract and organized packages of information, are the cognitive version of identities. Self-schemas include organized knowledge about one's self, the cognitive response to the question of identity: Who am I? These include the characteristics, preferences, goals, and behavior patterns we associate with ourselves. Group schemas (analogous to stereotypes) include organized information about social positions and stratification statuses, such as gender, race, age, or class. Because the social positions we occupy have immediate consequences for our sense of self, group schemas play a major part in processes of identification. Self and group schemas illustrate both advantages and disadvantages of categorization systems. They allow us to summarize and reduce information to key elements; thus, they also entail losing potentially valuable information. And, categorizations are almost always accompanied by systems of evaluation of some categories as better or worse. Schemas are not just perceptual phenomenona; they can serve as explanatory devices and justifications of social relationships (Tajfel 1981). Thus, social identities are embedded in sociopolitical contexts.

Social identity theory focuses on the extent to which individuals identify themselves in terms of group memberships (Tajfel & Turner 1986). The central tenet of social identity theory is that individuals define their identities along two dimensions: social, defined by membership in various social groups; and personal, the idiosyncratic attributes that distinguish an individual from others. Social and personal identities are thought to lie at opposite ends of a continuum, becoming more or less salient depending on the context. Deaux (1993), however, argues for an interplay between the two, suggesting they are not easily separable. Social identities provide status and enhance (or not) self-esteem. Because people are motivated to evaluate themselves positively, they tend to evaluate positively those groups to which they belong and to discriminate against groups they perceive to pose a threat to their social identity.

Empirical support has relied heavily on studies using the minimal group paradigm (Tajfel 1970), whereby people are classified into distinct groups on the basis of an arbitrary and trivial criterion under conditions free from other factors usually associated with group memberships. Under these minimal conditions, people do discriminate in favor of in-groups in allocation of various rewards. The most sociologically relevant recent studies have extended this tradition to socially meaningful groups and situations. Simon et al (1997), for example, demonstrate that being in a numerical minority (a predictor of identification in this tradition) does not lead to identification unless the in-group–out-group categorization is situationally meaningful.

The more positive, and more personally important, aspects of the self are likely to be bases on which a person locates her- or himself in terms of collective categories (Simon & Hastedt 1999), demonstrating the relationship between categorization and evaluation. This points toward more successful attainment of a positive social identity for those in dominant social groups. This process is a challenge for members of stigmatized, negatively valued groups, who may attempt to dissociate themselves, to evaluate the distinguishing dimensions of in-groups as less negative, to rate their in-group as more favorable on other dimensions, or to compete directly with the out-group to produce changes in the status of the groups. Much of this research accords considerable agency, both cognitive and material, to social actors.

One relevant line of research explores the psychological consequences of identifications with ethnic in- and out-groups. Fordham & Ogbu (1986), for example, suggest that academic failure among African-American students represents a desire to maintain their racial identity and solidarity with their own culture. High-achieving African-American children develop a "raceless" persona, but at the cost of interpersonal conflict and ambivalence; adoption of "raceless" behaviors and attitudes do have negative psychological consequences for African-American students (Arroyo & Zigler 1995). Direct impression management strategies intended to counter negative evaluations of their in-group also increase, one of many indicators of the interdependence of cognition and interaction. The focus on psychological consequences of identification speaks also to the interconnectedness of cognition and emotion. Thus, for example, individuals' prejudices may shape not only their own identifications but also their categorizations of others. Racially prejudiced individuals do appear to be more motivated to make accurate racial categorizations, both in-group and out-group, than do nonprejudiced individuals (Blascovich et al 1997); accurate categorizations maintain clear boundaries between groups.

Strong identification with a group need not, in principle, be correlated with out-group hostility. Only under conditions of intergroup threat and competition are in-group identification and out-group discrimination correlated (Branscombe & Wann 1994, Grant & Brown 1995). Social identity theory maintains that it is in-group identification that causes out-group bias. Realistic conflict theory (LeVine & Campbell 1972), on the other hand, maintains that out-group threat and hostility lead to in-group identification. In a study of Black South Africans' ethnic identifications before and after South Africa's transitional election in 1994, Black African identification was related only to attitudes toward Afrikaans Whites, not whites in general or English Whites (Duckitt & Mphuthing 1998). Longitudinal analyses suggest that attitudes affected identifications, more consistent with realistic conflict than social identity theory, a useful caution to overly cognitive approaches to identification.

Cognitive Processes

Cognitive processes are also implicated in the construction, maintenance, and change of identities. Attribution processes, that is, judgments of blame, causality, or responsibility, are particularly relevant. One key question is whether attributional patterns are biased in accord with intergroup identifications and allegiances. Many studies show a pattern of in-group favoritism such that positive behaviors of in-group members are attributed to internal factors and negative behaviors to external factors; some, but fewer, studies show out-group discrimination, that is, the opposite patterns of attributions about the behavior of out-group members (Islam & Hewstone 1993, and see Howard 1995). Consistent with social identity theory, when social categorizations are salient, these attributional patterns intensify (Islam & Hewstone 1993).

Cognitive structures and processes come together in Moscovici's (1981) theory of social representations. According to this perspective, knowledge structures are collectively shared, originating and developing via social interaction and communication (Augoustinos & Innes 1990). This approach reframes the concept of schemas, which have generally been seen as conservative and resistant to change. Given an increasing emphasis on social processes, one may expect to see continuing recasting of social schemas as more flexible and more grounded in social interaction.

Although the experimental tradition has been central to establishing the tenets of these theories, validation of these principles in sociologically meaningful contexts is crucial. Various of the studies cited here have been conducted in situations of real group memberships and real conflicts, underscoring the Spears et al (1997a,b) assertion that cognitive perception is meaningfully structured by groups and group life. One emphasis of this review is that cognitive and interactional processes are intimately intertwined; identity management strategies are often used to manipulate group comparisons for purposes of social identifications (Doosje & Ellemers 1997).

INTERACTIONISM

The basic premise of symbolic interaction is that people attach symbolic meaning to objects, behaviors, themselves, and other people, and they develop and transmit these meanings through interaction. People behave toward objects on the basis not of their concrete properties, but of the meanings these objects have for them. Because meanings develop through interaction, language plays a central part (see discussion below). Identities locate a person in social space by virtue of the relationships that these identities imply, and are, themselves, symbols whose meanings vary across actors and situations.

Interactionist approaches to identity vary in their emphasis on the structure of identity, on the one hand, and the processes and interactions through which identities are constructed, on the other. The more structural approach relies on the concept of role identities, the characters a person develops as an occupant of particular social positions, explicitly linking social structures to persons (Stryker 1980). Role identities are organized hierarchically, on the basis of their salience to the self and the degree to which we are committed to them, which in turn depends on the extent to which these identities are premised on our ties to particular other people. The second approach emphasizes the processes of identity construction and negotiation. Negotiations about who people are are fundamental to developing mutual definitions of situations; these negotiations entail self-presentation or impression management (Goffman 1959, McCall & Simmons 1978). Identities are thus strategic social constructions created through interaction, with social and material consequences.

This tradition articulates specific interactive mechanisms through which identities are produced (Cahill 1998). These processes are also always shaped by social hierarchies, as detailed in Goffman's ideas about how externally relevant status hierarchies are geared to "interactional cogs," for example, in his concept of hierarchical observation, the varying degrees to which people can control information others have about them. Members of total institutions are subject to compulsory visibility, and to "normalizing judgments," contrasting them to an ideal of a mentally healthy person, a law-abiding citizen, and so forth. Although these processes are most evident in total institutions, Goffman conceives these as more general, occurring in all institutional settings, even in informal interactions.

Identity and Language

How is identity "done"? The interactionist literature on identity articulates the construction, negotiation, and communication of identity through language, both directly in interaction, and discursively, through various forms of media (McAdams 1995). At the most basic level, the point is simply that people actively produce identity through their talk. Many studies (generally ethnographic) analyze identity work through everyday interaction. Identity talk is organized around two sets of norms, one concerning respect for situated identities and a commitment to basic moral precepts, and the second concerning ways in which people deal with failure to endorse these basic moral precepts, through denials of responsibility and other attributional tactics (Hunt et al 1994). Identity work is a micro-level performance of social (dis)order. Hunt & Miller (1997), for example, examine identity construction through interviews with sorority women, focusing on their talk about personal appearance. Their data reveal normative orders associated with dress and appearance; these women communicate, maintain, and repair identities through a "rhetoric of review" that provides ground rules for critical assessments of appearance. (For other examples, see MacPherson & Fine 1995, Freitas et al 1997.)

Many such studies focus on populations experiencing identity struggles, especially managing the stigma of social inequalities (see Goffman 1963, O'Brien & Howard 1998). Anderson et al (1994), for example, identify two distinct types of strategies used by homeless people to avoid stigmatization, many of which rely on language. In-group techniques used among street peers include drinking, cheap entertainment, hanging out, and positive identity talk. Out-group techniques, which reduce the impact of the stigma on public interactions with domiciled others, include passing (presenting an appearance that masks their homelessness), covering (minimizing the impact of their stigmatized status), defiance, and, sometimes, collective action, as in recent homelessness movements. Cherry's (1995) and Tewksbury's (1994) studies of people with AIDS also show how their respondents use language and identity performances to control and guide the social consequences of this discredited status.

In contrast to this emphasis on normative order, identity can be viewed as a more flexible resource in verbal interaction. Using conversational analysis, Antaki et al (1996) show how identities change as interaction proceeds, that is, how contextual variations shift identity claims. Their examples (drawn from tapes of natural English conversation between friends over drinks) show speakers not only avowing contradictory identities but also invoking both group distinctiveness and similarity. They argue strongly for working from participants' own orientations to identity, rather than analytically derived social categories. Verkuyten's (1997) study of how ethnic minority identity is presented in natural talk, based on focus groups of Turks living in the Netherlands, suggests the fruitfulness of this approach. Critiquing social identity theory, Verkuyten shows that people construct and cross borders of various categories in defining themselves; respondents did not use fixed categories, and differentiations were not always oppositional.

Language thus links the cognitive and interactive traditions. Hermans (1996) proposes development of a voiced conception of identity that integrates these traditions, a conception that points to collective voices (social dialects, professional jargons, languages of generations and age groups) and facilitates greater recognition of the dynamics of dominance and social power. Rapley (1998) aptly illustrates this last point in his analysis of Australian MP Pauline Hanson's first speech to the Australian Parliament (in 1996). Rapley addresses three questions: how speakers construct themselves as representative of the audience they wish to influence, how the appearance of truth/fact is constructed in political rhetoric, and how Hanson constructed her case as representative of and credible for her audience. Rapley shows how Hanson treats identities as discursive resources in her strategic manipulation of identity claims to membership category entitlement, claims that contributed to the mobilization necessary to her election. Rapley makes the intriguing point that identity work and facticity work are mutually supporting, and often inseparable, components of successful mobilization discourse.

Other scholars in this tradition extend the terrain to other forms of discourse, especially visual media. Epstein & Steinberg (1995) analyze the feminist potential of the Oprah Winfrey show through deconstructions of the show in relation to two themes, a presumption of heterosexuality, and the use of a therapy discourse. They note the show's emphasis on individual pathology (rather than social processes). Hollander's (1998) analysis of a dating game show, "Studs," shows how both verbal and nonverbal gestures do the identity work of gender, most obviously, but also of heterosexuality, race (in the show's homogeneity), and class. In one of the few empirical studies of discourse about social class, Bettie (1995) analyzes the class dynamics of sitcoms. Bettie suggests that a pattern of recent shows, in which working class women are cast as lead characters and men are either absent or buffoons, reflects demographic shifts toward more women in poverty. Analyses of media portrayals acknowledge how language works together with nonverbal expressions and interactional contexts as part of the interactive construction of identities.

Identities Across Time

With their emphasis on conservation of cognitive energy, theories of social cognition have underemphasized how identities shift over time. Interactionist approaches address this question more adequately. One model (Cote 1996) links identity shifts to historical cultural configurations, arguing that certain character types are encouraged by cultures through differential socialization practices. Helson et al (1995) address a more limited temporal range, contrasting identities of women raised in the 1950s with those raised in the 1960s. They report different identity types, which show differing degrees of stability over time. Another approach to the mutability of identities entails studying identity shifts during life transitions, periods of liminality. Karp et al (1998) report a great deal of interpretive effort by high school seniors preparing to leave home for college, as they anticipate affirmation of some identities, creation of new identities, and discovery of unanticipated identities. The authors also report racial similarities in concerns about identity and independence, but marked differences by social class, especially in the meaning of independence from family.

Another provocative approach to the instability of identities is to focus on what identities we distance ourselves from. Freitas et al (1997) examine who we say we are not, and whether such negative identities are merely an antithesis of identity or point to more complex identity ambivalences. They find complex patterns of identities that cut across dimensions such as age, temporality, gender, sexuality, and ethnicity, raising questions about the primacy of so-called master statuses. Identity instability may also signify multiple, and contradictory, identity goals. Miles et al (1998) focus on consumerism as a process through which young people attempt to fit in their peer groups, but also to maintain individuality, buying some goods in order to "stick out." (The methodology of this study is exemplary, combining focus group interviews, individual questionnaires, and participant observations over a sustained time.)

SOCIAL BASES OF IDENTITY

Much of the work on identity has emphasized single dimensions of social identities. In the sections that follow, I discuss the literatures on these separate dimensions, emphasizing the particularly nuanced work on racial and ethnic identity, and then I address the literature on intersections among identities.

Ethnic Identities

Phinney (1990) reviews more than 70 studies of ethnic identity. The great majority of these articles assume that identity development is particularly complicated for those belonging to ethnic and racial minority groups, owing to negative societal stereotypes and discrimination. Phinney considers the major theoretical frameworks of ethnic identity formation (social identity, acculturation, and developmental theories), key components of ethnic identity (ethnic self-identification, a sense of belonging, attitudes toward one's own ethnic group, social participation and cultural practices), and empirical findings on self-esteem, self-concept, psychological adjustment, ethnic identity in relation to the majority culture, changes related to generation of immigration, ethnic identity and gender, and contextual factors. She argues for construction of reliable and valid measures of ethnic identity, for more work on the impact of ethnic identity on attitudes toward both one's own and other groups and on the role of contextual factors such as family, community, and social structures. Phinney also notes the lack of attention to mixed ethnic backgrounds; the decade after her review has seen markedly more attention to multiethnic and mixed-race backgrounds (see below).

Other reviews emphasize developmental processes and socialization into ethnic identity (Spencer & Markstrom-Adams 1990). Knight et al (1993) detail specific socialization practices, including mothers' teaching about the ethnic culture, parental generation of migration, mothers' cultural knowledge and orientation, language spoken, and demographic characteristics such as parents' education and degree of community urbanization. In bringing together social interactions, cognitive beliefs and attitudes, and ecological and structural characteristics, this model exemplifies contemporary multilevel analyses of social identities.

One key question concerns the implications of ethnic identity for psychological adjustment. In another review article, Phinney (1991) explores the relationship between ethnic identity and self-esteem. Although findings do not add up to a clear picture, Phinney asserts that a strong ethnic identity, when accompanied by some adaptation to the mainstream, is related to high self-esteem. A related approach points to the importance of possible selves, the future-oriented components of self-schemas. Oyserman et al (1995) find markedly different racial patterns in what factors promote the construction of achievement-related possible selves: collectivism predicts these possible selves for African-American students, whereas for whites, individualism predicts the construction of such possible selves.

Another issue concerns the breadth of boundaries of ethnic in- and out-groups. Recent debates about inclusion of the category "Hispanic" as an ethnic group on the US Census, for example, assume this is a single, discrete category. Huddy & Virtanen (1995) show that Latinos differentiate their own subgroups from others but are no more likely than Anglos to differentiate among Latino subgroups to which they do not belong (here, Cuban Americans, Mexican Americans, and Puerto Ricans). Subgroup identification may be more pervasive than the development of loyalties to the in-group as a whole.

Consistent with this critique, many contemporary studies of ethnic identity cast ethnicity as fluid and ethnic boundaries as continually changing (though not without constraints). In her study of American Indian identifications, Nagel (1996) stresses ethnic identification as situational, volitional. Nagel characterizes ethnic identity as a dialectic between internal identification and external ascription, or, as Bhavnani & Phoenix (1994: 6) put it, "[identity] is the site where structure and agency collide." Nagel casts identity also as multilayered, with different identities activated at different times (e.g., for Native Americans—subtribal, tribal, supratribal-regional, or supratribal-national identities). Similarly, Espiritu's (1994) nuanced analysis asserts the construction of multiple and overlapping identities among Filipina/o Americans, as they rework dominant ideologies about their place in contemporary US society. She maintains that ethnic identification is a dynamic, more complex process than either assimilationist or pluralist models suggest.

Population shifts, especially immigrations, are a major instigator of changes in ethnic identities. One exemplary study examines the effects of relocation to the mainland US on Hawaiian students. Illustrating situational ethnicity, Ichiyama et al (1996) show shifts in ethnic identity with the shift in social context from majority to minority group status. Students who moved to the mainland showed a steady decline in identification with being Hawaiian; still, their affiliative behavior with other Hawaiians was not affected. Although ethnic identity may decline in intensity through exposure to stigmatized contexts, the need to participate in affirming social situations becomes a way of combatting these negative effects.

Waters (1994) addresses generational differences in pressures toward assimilation among black Caribbean immigrants to the United States. She finds three distinct patterns of identification: as Americans (presumably without ethnicity?), as ethnic Americans with some distancing from black Americans, or as immigrants unconnected to American racial and ethnic categories. Factors such as parents' class backgrounds, parents' social networks, type of school attended, and family structure influence these identifications. Waters contributes to the growing literature on intersections among identities in attending also to simultaneous class and ethnic identities and to gendered correlates of these patterns, noting that girls seem to live with greater restrictions and parental control than boys, but that girls have more leeway about choosing a racial identity than do boys. Anthias (1998) argues for more attention to history and context than such studies offer, maintaining that concepts of race and ethnicity are overly deterritorialized. For Anthias, "diaspora" is a more useful conceptualization of the identity implications of transnational migration.

Most of these studies assume individuals belong to a single racial or ethnic category. In contrast, recent work has begun to address a rapidly growing population in the United States: people with multiracial backgrounds. The number of biracial births in the 1990s is increasing at a rate faster than the number of monoracial births, and the "other" racial category on the 1990 US Census grew more than any other category. Root (1992, 1996; and see Zack 1995) has done a great deal of work exploring the complex racial and ethnic identities of those with mixed backgrounds. The debate over how to represent multiracial individuals on the census itself attests to Root's assertion that US history repeatedly shows ambivalence about recognizing multiracial people. Root articulates several patterns of identity negotiations: some actively identify with both (or more) groups, experiencing multiple perspectives simultaneously; others border-cross actively by shifting among different identities as they move among different social contexts; and yet others locate themselves on a border, experiencing "mestiza" consciousness (see discussion below).

All of the above models focus on racial and ethnic minorities. In the past several years scholars have begun to pay explicit attention to the racial and ethnic identity of whites. Rowe et al (1994) point out both that many whites do not have a racial identity and that white identity development may not fit a developmental stage model (a model used with many racial minority groups). Rowe et al focus on types of white racial consciousness, ranging from an unexamined racial identity to four types of achieved racial consciousness, moving from strong ethnocentrism to an integrative, morally responsible stance. Frankenberg (1993) proposes one of the most widely adopted models of white racial consciousness, beginning with "essentialist racism," emphasizing race difference as essential, biologically derived, and hierarchical; a discourse of essential sameness, or color-blindness (which she links with power evasiveness); and race cognizance, in which difference signals autonomy of culture and values. From this last perspective, social structures, not ascribed characteristics, generate racial inequalities (and see Helms 1994). In these models, increasing maturity signifies increasing awareness of the conditions of oppression associated with race; these are thus explicitly politicized models of racial and ethnic identity, a marked shift from earlier social psychological approaches to this question.

Sexual Identities

As Epstein (1987) observes, in a historical juncture in which group identity in general has assumed much importance, and where sexuality has become a central dimension of identity formation, it is not unlikely that gay and lesbian identities would arise. Sexual identity differs from racial identity in that awareness of one's self as a sexual being, and especially awareness of one's possible deviation from sexual norms, typically occurs later in one's life than awareness of one's race or ethnicity. Although implications of this difference have not been explored directly, most models of sexual identity are similar to those of racial identity. Cass (1983–1984) proposes a six-stage model, beginning with identity confusion, moving to comparison (with nonhomosexual others), to tolerance, and eventually to synthesis, including positive relationships with nonhomosexuals.

Kitzinger & Wilkinson (1995) propose a social constructionist model of lesbian identity, suggesting that the process is not one of coming to recognize what one always was, but rather one of recognizing, negotiating, and interpreting one's experiences. This model is framed in terms of discursive strategies and accounting mechanisms through which an identity change is accomplished and sustained, attesting to the central role of language and discursive processes in identity formation and maintenance. D'Augelli (1994) also proposes a social constructionist account but frames his model in a more explicitly sociopolitical context, referring to the social and legal penalties for overt expression of this sexuality. D'Augelli also emphasizes that people develop and change over the course of their life spans, and thus that sexual identity may be fluid at some points, more crystallized at others. Epstein's (1987) model of gay and lesbian identity is also explicitly sociopolitical, in keeping with his emphasis on gay social activism. Because a considerable stigma remains associated with this identity, Epstein observes, the attempts to assert its legitimacy and to claim that this is not grounds for social exclusion have the ironic effect of intensifying this identity. (For a general review of models of sexual identity, see Gonsiorek & Rudolph 1991.)

Cain (1991) emphasizes the complexities of the sociopolitical environment of sexual identities, analyzing how queer cultures respond to the behavior of passing, of hiding stigmatized sexual identities. Cain notes that in recent years, openness about one's sexuality has come in both professional literatures and subcultural communities to be seen as evidence of a healthy gay identity, and thus passing can be seen as problematic. He critiques the failure of such approaches to recognize the constraints of social factors, implying in his analysis that people manage information about their sexual identity, just as they manage information about other identities.

Analogous to the recent "discovery" of whiteness as an identity, heterosexuality has also begun to receive attention. In 1980 Adrienne Rich published an essay (later to become a classic) challenging the taken-for-grantedness of heterosexuality. More than a decade later, Wilkinson & Kitzinger (1993) solicited short reflections from a number of well-known feminists, many of them academic psychologists, about their heterosexuality. The responses indicated that "heterosexual" is not a popular label, and these respondents did not claim this as an identity. Most saw heterosexual and lesbian as points on a continuum, rather than recognizing their political asymmetry: as Wilkinson & Kitzinger (1993) assert, lesbian is an intrinsically politicized identity and heterosexuality is not. Jackson (1995) too notes that heterosexuality is rarely thought of in terms of identity or self-definition (and see Richardson 1996a,b). At the same time, many identities that are widely embraced are based in heterosexuality: wife, girlfriend, daughter, mother. Jackson points out the conundrum: to name oneself as heterosexual (as a woman) is to problematize heterosexuality and challenge its privileges, but for women, being heterosexual is not a situation of unproblematic privilege because the institution entails a hierarchical relation beween women and men. Although these discussions do not address the heterosexual identities of men, for whom heterosexuality does bring privilege, there is a considerable recent literature in this arena (see Robinson 1996 for a helpful overview).

Herek (1995) connects heterosexual identities with an accompanying ideology, heterosexism, which denigrates and stigmatizes nonheterosexual forms of behavior, identity, relationship, or community. In his analysis of antigay violence, Herek maintains that heterosexist practices allow people to express values central to their self-concepts, in this case norms based on the institutions of gender and sexuality. Consistent with principles of social identity theory, Herek suggests that antigay violence may help heterosexist people feel more positive about being heterosexual. And, antigay assaults also provide a means for young men (by far the most common type of perpetrator) to affirm their own heterosexuality or masculinity, serving an ego-defensive function.

Gender Identities

Gender identities have been explored more extensively than other social identities; thus I give less attention to this topic here and refer the reader to other reviews (Frable 1997, Howard & Alamilla 2001, Howard & Hollander 1997). Gender identities have been conceived either as gender self-schemas (Markus et al 1982), in the cognitive tradition, or as constructed achievements (West & Zimmerman 1987), in the interactionist tradition. In either case, gender identities, in the sense of organizing a sense of self around the perception one is female or male, and internalizing pre- and proscriptions of behaviors deemed culturally appropriate to these self-perceptions, are thought to be learned through early socialization and enacted and reinforced throughout the life span. Common to both perspectives is the assertion that gender is a social category and thus gender identity is about more than personality. Ashmore (1990) details components of gender identity, and Gurin & Townsend (1986) explore the relationship of gender identity to gender-related ideologies. Most studies find few differences in the existence of gender identity. In terms of content, a quasi meta-analysis by Kroger (1997) finds gender differences in identity structure, content, developmental process, and context. In an empirical follow-up, Kroger reports that the domains of sexuality and family are somewhat more salient for women than men, but more generally, there are few differences in identity content (this may be due to reliance on a highly educated upper and upper-middle class sample). Much recent work emphasizes contextual influences on the relative salience of gender identities (Ely 1995, Thorne 1993).

Class Identities

In a recent review Frable (1997: 154) reports: "With few exceptions, class as a meaningful identity is simply absent from the psychological literature." To the extent class identities have been considered in the social psychological literature, the emphasis tends to be on class identities in interaction with other identities (see below), and on contextual effects on the salience of class identities. Students from working-class (and ethnic minority) backgrounds negotiate their marginal status at elite academic institutions (Lopez & Hasso 1998, Stewart & Ostrove 1993), and later-generation immigrants are more likely than first-generation immigrants to have class identities similar to those prevalent in the U.S. (Hurtado et al 1994). Shockey's (1998) interviews with sex workers show a disjuncture between the subjective experience of class and these sex workers' occupational experiences and outcomes. Given the lack of attention to class in any regard, it is not surprising that there is virtually no research on class identities of those in privileged socioeconomic circumstances. Suggestive of the kind of approach that would be useful is Eichstedt's (1998) analysis of the relationships between white and ethnic minority artists in a local art community, as they negotiated issues of authenticity in the production of ethnic art and assimilation and cultural integrity in the production and recognition of art.

Identities of (Dis)ability

Relatively recently, scholars have begun to direct attention to identities based on physical and mental disabilities. Low (1996), for example, explores the experiences of college students with disabilities. Her interviews show these students' enduring dilemma, the desire to be perceived as "normal" while at the same time having to negotiate a disabled identity to deal with the various barriers to academic achievement. Many of the tactics they use to accomplish one goal conflict with accomplishment of the other.

Charmaz (1995) explores identity struggles imposed by severe illness and shows, in contrast, how people adapt their identity goals to respond effectively to their physical circumstances. Processes of bodily assessments and subsequent identity tradeoffs sum to a surrendering to an identity as ill. Although Charmaz characterizes this as relinquishing control to the illness, at least one theoretical model suggests this is a way to exert secondary control, ceasing a fight to achieve an unachievable identity (Rothbaum et al 1982). Consistent with an increasing emphasis on identities as mutable and contextually sensitive is Charmaz' observation that these identity struggles are rarely a single journey; rather these individuals experience many iterations of these identity struggles.

Only within the past decade has there been explicit recognition of a "disability culture" (Scheer 1994). Scheer usefully outlines features that distinguish people with disabilities from other minorities; they do not often grow up in families with other members of this group, and they usually become a group member well into their lives, often in isolation, features they share with lesbians and gay men. These factors can motivate a search for a disability culture, with its attendant identity implications. Scheer notes that it is not clear whether other divisive social characteristics, such as race, gender, and class, have been muted by a common identification in disability culture. Gerschick (1998) speaks directly to this issue, in an analysis of the gendered dynamics of some forms of physical disability. Gerschick maintains that men with physical disabilities struggle with an hegemonic gender order defined by the masculinities of those who are able-bodied. Although many of his interviewees struggle for acceptance within these standards, some reject hegemonic masculinity and attempt to construct alternative identities.

Age Identities

Being aged is unique as a social category; essentially everyone moves from not being in this group to being in it. Yet identities based on age have received little explicit attention from social psychologists. In one exception, Gatz & Cotton (1994) speak to the identity dynamics of aging: Age identities are both ascribed and achieved; the boundaries of group membership are permeable, but defined developmentally; and an influx of new members into the aged category is certain, with numbers increasing much more rapidly than those of other minority groups with permeable boundaries. The definition of "aged" is itself flexible, both culturally and personally.

The ubiquitous pattern is that the older people are, the less closely their subjective age identity matches their chronological age. The proportion of people who say they feel younger than their chronological age increased from 54% when they were in their forties, for example, to 86% when in their eighties (Goldsmith & Heiens 1992). Similarly, as people grow older, their definition of when old age begins becomes older and older (Logan et al 1992). Older adults even engage in greater stereotyping of all age groups than do younger people (Rothbaum 1983). One might conclude that greater self-esteem is associated with feeling younger; data suggest that life satisfaction is lower and stress is higher for those who see themselves as old (Logan et al 1992), but congruency between subjective and actual age leads to greater life satisfaction for older women (Montepare & Lachman

1989). Evolving more positive conceptions of aging should lead more older people to identify as old and to have more positive self-evaluations.

INTERSECTING IDENTITIES

Analyses of identities based on single social positions, such as gender, race, ethnicity, class, sexuality, or age, have given way to a chorus of calls for analyses of how identities intersect (see O'Brien & Howard 1998). Most of the empirical studies focus on two co-existing, typically both subordinated, identities. (Most of these essays elide the question of whether models of two identities can be extended unproblematically to multiple intersections.) Most are ethnographic, qualitative studies. Many of these articles focus on race-ethnicity and gender (Reid & Comas-Diaz 1990). Shorter-Gooden & Washington (1996), for example, explore identities of adolescent African-American women, assessing the salience of various identity domains—race, gender, sexuality, relationships, career, religion, political beliefs. Racial identities were markedly strongly than other identities. Further, these women's racial identities were quite positive, one of many indicators that the societal context of racism does not necessarily translate into negative racial identities. Relationships, primarily with other women, were also a strong part of their identities. Woollett et al (1994) reveal fluid conceptions of ethnic identities operating across gender, among young mothers of Asian origin or descent, and speak also to developmental changes in these identities, associated with motherhood.

Takagi (1994) explores intersections between sexual and ethnic identities, here lesbian and gay Asian Americans. She offers a theoretical context for thinking about these intersections as, for example, in her analysis of how silence operates in both Asian American and queer history and experiences. Greene's (1998) parallel analysis of lesbian and gay African Americans points to cultural contradictions and the negotiations enactment of these identities entails; she stresses themes of family and ethnic group loyalty, the importance of parenting, a cultural history of sexual objectifications, the importance of community, and a cultural legacy of homophobia. Rust (1996) also addresses intersections between sexual and ethnic identities, focusing on bisexuality. She cautions that while developing an identity as bisexual might be positive for some racial or ethnic backgrounds, it may not be so for others, and she focuses on how bisexuals in marginalized racial and ethnic groups manage these interacting oppressions.

Beckwith (1998) also addresses conflicts between two identities, here between class and gender as experienced by working class women striking against a coal firm in Virginia. In this case, the collective identity of women was subsumed in the context of a wider working-class collective identity. Except for an initial all-women strike, no other all-women events were organized, owing to the UWMA's control of strike activity, a reminder of structural constraints on identity enactment. Beckwith moves toward theorization of how multiple identifications might intersect, and she argues that collective identity generally emerges in response to specific social contexts and struggles.

Indeed, several different theories of intersectionality suggest that politically motivated identity work generates attention to intersecting identities. Crenshaw (1997) too argues that political investments and commitments motivate analyses of intersectionality. She sees intersectionality as oriented toward recognition of political coalitions among groups, explicit attempts to resist all forms of subordination, rather than relying on particular positions of advantage to resist only the subordination that directly affects a particular group. This emphasis on political realities underscores a prominent theme, that analyses of intersectionality must take into account structural inequalities and the recognition of multiple (dis)advantages. At the same time, and in tension with an emphasis on structural inequalities, much of the emerging theory of intersectionalities shows the influence of a weak form of postmodernism, in its recognition of multiple, fluid identities (see discussion below). The study by Freitas et al (1997) of negative identities, for example, problematizes the notion of a unified, rational self and argues for the need to negotiate border spaces, to conceptualize identities and identity work as tenuous, fragile, elastic, rather than as fixed and dichotomous. The empirical work points to a lack of closure between one master status and another, between previous and future identities.

IDENTITIES AND SPACE

Space, both geographic and virtual, is another recent basis of identities, a direction that attests to the interdisciplinary character of recent research on identities. Some studies focus on literal space; Cuba & Hummon (1993a, 1993b) consider "place identities," that is, identities based on a sense of being at home. Key questions concern the effects of mobility on place affiliation and intersections between place identities and transitions in the life course. Their empirical study of immigrants' place identities points to generational differences in people's relationships to place. Lindstrom (1997) adds a structural element, considering intersections of place stratification and place identity. One's home address, he argues, is a marker of values and socioeconomic position. Espin (1995) connects questions of spatial identity and spatial dislocations to intersections with national, gender, and sexual identities, exploring how struggles about acculturation center on immigrant women's sexual behaviors and gender performances. She suggests that the crossing of borders through migrations may provide women the space to cross other boundaries, here boundaries of sexuality and gender. These essays address those who have some degree of choice about where they live. Although presumably those who have less choice, or those who do not have homes, undoubtedly have a place identity, how these dynamics differ when this identity is chosen or not remains to be explained.

Moving to a less literal conception of space, Ruddick's (1996) analysis of reactions to a public crime suggests that public space is not simply a passive arena for predetermined social behaviors but rather an active medium for the construction of objective and subjective identities. McCorkel (1998) analyzes a markedly less literal conception, "critical space." Analyzing women's responses to the intense social control of a drug treatment program for women in prison, McCorkel points to the construction of critical space, resident-initiated subversions of formal structure, based centrally in interactions among residents. McCorkel suggests that most people construct critical spaces in their lives in order to distance themselves from the constraints some identities pose for their personal sense of self.

Cyberspace is another spatial arena in which questions of identity arise. Explorations of these issues in cyberspace ask whether people play with identities, adopting virtual, online identities different from their offline identities, when interacting in virtual, therefore invisible, space. That is, do people try to "pass" in new identities when they cannot be monitored? Kendall (1998a,b, and see O'Brien 1999) suggests the answer is no. In two years of participant observation in a multi-user domain, Kendall shows that people persist in seeking essentialized groundings for the selves they encounter and the selves they offer. Where passing does occur, it is most prominent with gender, but even "gender-switchers" distance themselves from their online experiences of differently gendered identities.

McKenna & Bargh (1998) take an opposite tack but come up with a similar answer. While Kendall's informants are mostly young white men, McKenna & Bargh ask whether Internet participation offers opportunities for those with culturally stigmatized identities, here people with marginalized sexual and ideological orientations. Internet newsgroups allow these people to interact anonymously with similar others; membership in these newsgroups becomes an important part of identity. Those who participate most frequently experience greater self-acceptance and are more likely to come out about their identity to family and friends. Both studies attest to a close correspondence between online and offline identities and to a persistent preference for stable identities.

IDENTITY STRUGGLES

Nationalisms

Recent years have seen increasing attention to struggles over national and ethnic identities, mirroring the real world identity-based ethnic conflicts that have had a resurgence in the 1990s. Comas-Diaz et al (1998) offer a comparative analysis of ethnic identity and conflict in three Latin American nations, Guatemala, Peru, and Puerto Rico. Arguing that ethnic conflicts are intimately related to ethnic identities, they link an explicit social psychology of liberation to indigenous social psychologies. Rouhana & Bar-Tal (1998) ask why some ethnonational conflicts are more entrenched than others, using the Israeli-Palestinian conflict to argue that societies in particularly intractable conflicts form societal beliefs that help them cope with, but also perpetuate, these conflicts. They also speak to ways in which social psychological work on social identities can change such beliefs, thus contributing to immediate societal concerns.

The influence of sociopolitical forces is central to national and ethnic identity struggles. Perera & Pugliese (1998) chronicle the active attempts by the Australian Government and majority culture to impose particular ethnic definitions on the Aboriginal population, and Aboriginal responses, claiming their own conceptions of their ethnic identities. These have been both cultural and material campaigns, the latter primarily battles over land ownership. The authors argue persuasively that Australia's stated policy of multiculturalism is intelligible only within a mono-cultural framework that imposes the democratic Constitutional government and a national language. These struggles, of course, are analogous to those between American Indians and the US Government (Nagel 1996).

Not all debates about national and ethnic identities have been as conflicted as the Australian-Aboriginal or Israeli-Palestinian cases. The formation of the European Community provides a real-world context in which to study identities and social change. Breakwell & Lyons' (1996) edited collection addresses processes and expressions of national identifications, and their significance for understanding sociopolitical actions in various European contexts. These articles range from explorations of current trends in Spanish nationalism within the context of the historical connection between Spain and its American colonies (Torregrosa 1996), to analysis of how the Scottish National Party has attempted to make the concept of Scottishness relevant to Scots while undermining the relevance of Britishness (successfully, witness the establishment of a national Scottish Parliament) (Hopkins & Reicher 1996), to Ruzza's (1996) discussion of the attempts of the Lega Lombarda movement to promote cultural, economic, and political self-determination among Northern Italians. The tendency to adopt a European identity varies with the prior power of the nation: British respondents perceive European integration as a threat and show almost no evidence of a sense of European identity, whereas Italian respondents show a stronger European identity than an Italian identity (Cinnirella 1997).

Social Movements

Identity struggles may also generate explicit social movements. One influential theory of social movements hypothesizes a collective identity that motivates group action (Taylor & Whittier 1992). This identity requires a perception of membership in a bounded group, consciousness about that group's ideologies, and direct opposition to a dominant order. Simon et al (1998) used an identity approach in studying a movement of the elderly in Germany and the gay movement in the United States. Both showed two different pathways to willingness to participate in collective action, one based on cost-benefit calculations, the other on collective identification as an activist. Bernstein (1997) reveals a strategic dimension to the use of identities in collective action, in her analysis of when and how identities that celebrate or suppress difference from the mainstream are used in strategic collective action about gay rights.

Epstein (1987) also explores identity issues in gay activism; he equates his model of gay and lesbian identity (discussed above) with an ethnic identity. Both combine affective ties to a group with the pursuit of sociopolitical goals; both groups direct activity toward the terrain of the state; both are progressive, with a goal of advancing the group position; lacking structural power, both groups press demands by appealing to and manipulating hegemonic ideologies; and both groups tend toward a local character organized around a specific geographic space or community. This is an excellent summary of the parameters of contemporary identity more generally, especially in intersection with society.

POLITICIZING A SOCIAL PSYCHOLOGY OF IDENTITIES

Several recent articles have made significant theoretical contributions to an explicitly politicized social psychology of identity and provided analysis of how identity processes intersect with the (re)production of social inequalities (see Bhavnani & Phoenix 1994). Langman (1998) analyzes how identity constructions serve hegemonic ends; legitimating ideologies construct identities that obscure an awareness of injustice. She asserts, accurately, that relatively little scholarship has been devoted to understanding the ideological constitution of the self, the social production of identities, and the legitimation of inequalities. Langman identifies key moments of child development as sites of colonization, a more politicized understanding of socialization. She identifies particular desires as key forces in shaping identity: to seek attachments to others; the pursuit of recognition and dignity; feelings of agency and empowerment; avoiding fear and anxiety. While each of these motivations has been an important locus of social psychological research, Langman theorizes how each is harnessed through socialization to ensure dependable citizens. At the same time, she is careful not to portray individuals as passive robots.

Collective identities generally do provide social and emotional compensations for subordinate statuses that sustain systems of inequality. Wolf (1994) explores this theme, theorizing that people in subordinate social positions attempt in a sort of reality-construction process to translate coercive relationships into dependency relationships, through maneuvering their oppressors into accepting obligations toward them. Her empirical analyses of responses of Japanese Americans during the Relocation, African- American slaves, and nineteenth century European-American women, show that the more successful they are, ironically, the more entrenched they become in these dependent relationships.

DECONSTRUCTING IDENTITIES

Much of the literature discussed above makes several key assumptions: Identities have an intrinsic, essential content, defined by a common origin or a common structure of experience, and often, both. When identity struggles arise, they generally take the form of redefining negative images as positive, or of deciphering the "authentic" identity. An alternative approach emphasizes the impossibility of authentic identities based on a universally shared experience or origin (Grossberg 1996); identities are relational, defined by their difference from something, processual, and multiple.

Hall (1996, Hall & Du Gay 1996) notes that this deconstructive critique does not supplant inadequate concepts with "truer" ones, and thus that there is no way to avoid thinking about the former concepts. He argues that identity is such a concept—something that cannot be thought about in the "old way" but without which certain key questions cannot be thought about at all. For Hall, identity moves away from signaling a stable core of self, to becoming a strategic, positional concept: "identities are points of temporary attachments to the subject positions which discursive practices construct for us" (Hall 1996: 6).

Key principles underlying this approach stand in marked contrast to much of the traditional literature. Fragmentation emphasizes the multiplicity of identities and of positions within any identity. Hybridity is also key, evoking images of liminality and border-crossings in which a subaltern identity is defined as different from either of several competing identities. Disapora is another key idea, resonant with the discussion above of geography and identity. Diaspora emphasizes not just transnationality and movement, but also political struggles to "define the local . . . as a distinctive community, in historical contexts of displacement" (Clifford 1994: 308).

Anzaldúa's (1987) early discussion of these ideas in *Borderlands/La Frontera* has been especially influential; she emphasizes the construction of a mestiza consciousness, a destabilization of a unified identity, espressed in the language of fluidity, migration, postcolonialism, and displacement. Bauman (1996) connects this conception of identity directly to the conditions of postmodernity. Bauman paints a dismal picture, asking what chance of morality or of engaged citizenship, such a world allows. Hall, Bauman, and Grossberg all seek ways to articulate a notion of democratic citizenship that can be effective in a postmodern world. They focus on questions of agency and possibilities for action, and they argue for a conception of identity based in people's existence in specific communities and contexts. Identities become the problem of citizenship.

As an example of what sorts of questions this more explicitly policitized approach might point toward, one consistent critique of social cognition takes issue with the seemingly natural character of categorization and with the seeming obviousness of which dimensions become bases for categorization. Asserting that a category "race" would not exist without racist ideology, Hopkins et al (1997) argue that racialized categories are socially constructed, and they argue for a social psychology that focuses on the social processes through which categories are constructed, including the power relationships and social practices that affect who is able to act on the basis of their category constructions, make them heard, and impose them on others. As empirical support, they analyze the speech of a police officer accused of expressing racist views in a public school, using this linguistic analysis to reveal the social construction of racialized categories.

Regardless of where one aligns one's self in terms of these models of identity, there is no question that contemporary research reveals and analyzes various crises of confidence. One response to these crises is an increased interest in authenticity, as a commitment to self-values. Erickson (1995) argues that authenticity has captured both cultural and sociological imaginations, partly due to the power of images and mass media. Maintaining that postmodernism does not do away with selves and identities but rather directs attention to how they are constructed, Erickson emphasizes meanings—what it means, for example, to be white, female, or gay—and the challenge of achieving authenticity and meaning when most human actors experience simultaneously a multiplicity of relationships and identities. She also argues that members of oppressed groups are more likely to confront "problems" of authenticity, being more often faced with dilemmas that require them to choose between acting in accord with their self values or in accord with the expectations of powerful others. Erickson argues for a conception of self that is both multidimensional and unified, both emotional and cognitive, both individual and social—a notion not so far afield from traditional conceptions of identity. The postmodern element is that authenticity is no longer a question of being true to self for all time, but rather of being true to self in context or self in relationship.

IDENTITIES TO COME

Attempting to derive an overall picture from these many and diverse approaches to understanding identities is impossible. These are several strong traditions of theory and research on identities, traditions that co-exist but rarely come together. The more traditional social psychological literature reflects a modernist approach to identities, casting them as specifiable, measurable, ordered, and, in some sense, rational. Whether from a cognitive or an interactionist perspective, or perhaps most fruitfully, from some synthesis of the two, this approach sees identities as generally stable, although sensitive to social context, as relevant both for individuals and for social groups, as having both cognitive and affective components, as cognitive structures but also resources available for interactional negotiations, and as motivators for social action.

The deconstructionist literature reflects a postmodernist approach to identities, casting them as multiple, processual, relational, unstable, possibly political. Although this identity is elusive, Hall's (1996) comment that certain questions cannot be thought about without the concept of identity is well taken. What those questions address is the possibility of agency and social action, questions that have not been central in social psychology. In anticipating future directions, it is difficult not to argue for some degree of interchange among these seemingly unconnected literatures. There is room, indeed need, for studies of social identities that are both theoretically and methodologically rigorous, in touch with the contemporary world, and directed toward advancing both theory and progressive social action. Frable (1997) concludes her review of research on social identities with a call for "seeing people as whole," referring to the need to address gender, racial, ethnic, sexual, and class identities as multiple identities of whole people. In the same vein, seeing people as whole means recognizing that both our everyday lives and the larger cultures in which we operate shape our senses of who we are and what we could become. For most social actors, the details of our everyday lives are relatively predictable and orderly. The details of our larger cultural environments may be markedly more unsettled and shifting. Both contexts are part of our experiences of identities. In anticipating the next century's approaches to identities, then, we might look to analyses that bring together both the structures of everyday lives and the sociocultural and sociopolitical realities in which those lives are lived, but without imposing a false coherence on that synthesis.

ACKNOWLEDGMENTS

I want to express deep gratitude to Ramira Alamilla for her invaluable assistance in procuring, summarizing, and being so enthusiastic about hundreds of references on identity, only some of which are represented in this review, as well as for her insightful comments on this essay. Many thanks as well to Jodi O'Brien for her ever-incisive comments, and to Carolyn Allen for always reminding me that social psychologists don't corner the market on the concept of identity.

Visit the Annual Reviews home page at www.AnnualReviews.org

LITERATURE CITED

Anderson L, Snow DA, Cress D. 1994. Negotiating the public realm: stigma management and collective action among the homeless. *Res. Commun. Soc.* (Supp.) 1:121–43

Antaki C, Condor S, Levine M. 1996. Social identities in talk: speakers' own orientations. *Br. J. Soc. Psychol.* 35:473–92

Anthias F. 1998. Evaluating "diaspora": beyond ethnicity? *Sociology* 32:557–80

Anzaldúa G. 1987. *Borderland = La Frontera: The New Mestiza.* San Francisco: Aunt Lute Books

Arroyo C, Zigler E. 1995. Racial identity, academic achievement, and the psychological well-being of economically disadvantaged adolescents. *J. Pers. Soc. Psychol.* 69:903–14

Ashmore R, 1990. Sex, gender, and the individual. In *Handbook of Personality: Theory and Research*, ed. L. Pervin, pp. 486–526. New York: Guilford

Augoustinos M, Innes JM. 1990. Towards an integration of social representations and social schema theory. *Br. J. Soc. Psychol.* 29:213–31

Augoustinos M, Walker I. 1995. *Social Cognition: An Integrated Introduction.* London: Sage

Bauman Z. 1996. From pilgrim to tourist–or a short history of identity. See Hall & Du Gay 1996, pp. 18–36

Beckwith K. 1998. Collective identities of class and gender: working-class women in the Pittston Coal Strike. *Polit. Psychol.* 19:147–67

Bernstein M. 1997. Celebration and suppression: the strategic uses of identity by the lesbian and gay movement. *Am. J. Sociol.* 103:531–65

Bettie J. 1995. Class dismissed? Roseanne and the changing face of working-class iconography. *Soc. Text* 45(14):125–49

Bhabha H. 1994. *The Location of Culture.* London, UK: Routledge

Bhavnani K, Phoenix A. 1994. *Shifting Identities Shifting Racisms.* London: Sage

Blascovich J, Wyer N, Swart L, Kibler J. 1997. Racism and racial categorization. *J. Pers. Soc. Psychol.* 72:1364–72

Branscombe N, Wann D. 1994. Collective self-esteem consequences of outgroup derogation when a valued social identity is on trial. *Eur. J. Soc. Psychol.* 24:641–57

Breakwell GM, Lyons E. 1996. *Changing European Identities: Social Psychological Analyses of Social Change.* Oxford, UK: Butterworth–Heineman

Cahill S. 1998. Toward a sociology of the person. *Sociol. Theory* 16:131–48

Cain R. 1991. Stigma management and gay identity development. *Soc. Work* 36:67–73

Cass V. 1983–1984. Homosexual identity: a concept in need of definition. *J. Homosex.* 9:105–26

Charmaz K. 1995. The body, identity, and self: adapting to impairment. *Sociol. Q.* 36:657–80

Cherry K. 1995. The best years of their lives: a portrait of a residential home for people with AIDS. *Symb. Interact.* 18:463–86

Cinnirella M. 1997. Towards a European identity? Interactions between the national and European social identities manifested by university students in Britain and Italy. *Br. J. Soc. Psychol.* 36:19–31

Clifford J. 1994. Diasporas. *Cult. Anthropol.* 9:302–38

Comas-Diaz L, Lykes M, Alarcon R. 1998. Ethnic conflict and the psychology of liberation in Guatemala, Peru, and Puerto Rico. *Am. Psychol.* 53:778–92

Cote J. 1996. Sociological perspectives on identity formation: the culture-identity link and identity capital. *J. Adolesc.* 19:417–28

Crenshaw C. 1997. Women in the Gulf War: toward an intersectional feminist rhetorical

criticism. *Howard J. Commun.* 8:219–35

Cuba L, Hummon D. 1993a. Constructing a sense of home: place affiliation and migration across the life cycle. *Sociol. Forum* 8:547–72

Cuba L, Hummon D. 1993b. A place to call home: identification with dwelling, community, and region. *Sociol. Q.* 34:111–31

D'Augelli AR. 1994. Identity development and sexual orientation: toward a model of lesbian, gay, and bisexual development. See Trickett, Watts & Birman 1994, pp. 312–33

Davis F. 1991. Identity ambivalence in clothing: the dialectic of the erotic and the chaste. In *Social Organization and Social Processes: Essays in Honor of Anselm Strauss,* ed. D Maines, pp. 105–16. New York: Aldine de Gruyter

Deaux K. 1993. Reconstructing social identity. *Pers. Soc. Psychol. Bull.* 19:4–12

Doosje B, Ellemers N. 1997. Stereotyping under threat: the role of group identification. See Spears, Oakes, Ellemers & Haslam 1997a, pp. 257–72

Duckitt J, Mphuthing T. 1998. Group identification and intergroup attitudes: a longitudinal analysis in South Africa. *J. Pers. Soc. Psychol.* 74:80–85

Eichstedt JL. 1998. Reproducing racial and class inequality: multiculturalism in the arts. See O'Brien & Howard 1998, pp. 309–35

Ely R. 1995. The power of demography: women's social constructions of gender identity at work. *Acad. Mgmt. J.* 38:589–634

Epstein D, Steinberg D. 1995. Twelve steps to heterosexuality? Common-sensibilities on the Oprah Winfrey Show. *Fem. Psychol.* 5:275–80

Epstein S. 1987. Gay politics, ethnic identity: the limits of social constructionism. *Social. Rev.* 17:9–54

Erickson RJ. 1995. The importance of authenticity for self and society. *Symb. Interact.* 18:121–44

Espin O. 1995. "Race," racism, and sexuality in the life narratives of immigrant women. *Fem. Psychol.* 5:222–38

Espiritu YL. 1994. The intersection of race,

ethnicity, and class: the multiple identities of second-generation Filipinos. *Identities* 1:249–73

Fiske ST, Taylor SE. 1991. *Social Cognition.* New York: McGraw-Hill. 2nd ed.

Fordham S, Ogbu JU. 1986. Black students' school success: "Coping with the burden of 'acting white.'" *Urban Rev.* 18:176–206

Frable DES. 1997. Gender, racial, ethnic, sexual, and class identities. *Annu. Rev. Psychol.* 48:139–62

Frankenberg R. 1993. *The Social Construction of Whiteness: White Women, Race Matters.* Minneapolis: Univ. Minn. Press

Freitas A, Kaiser S, Chandler J, Hall C, Kim J-W, Hammidi T. 1997. Appearance management as border construction: least favorite clothing, group distancing, and identity—not! *Soc. Inq.* 67:323–35

Gatz M, Cotton B. 1994. Age as a dimension of diversity: the experience of being old. See Trickett, Watts & Birman 1994. pp. 334–58

Gerschick TJ. 1998. Sisyphus in a wheelchair: Men with physical disabilities confront gender domination. See O'Brien & Howard 1998, pp. 189–211

Goffman E. 1959. *The Presentation of Self in Everyday Life.* New York: Doubleday

Goffman E. 1963. *Stigma: Notes on the Management of Spoiled Identity.* Englewood Cliffs, New Jersey: Prentice Hall

Goldsmith RE, Heiens RA. 1992. Subjective age: a test of five hypotheses. *Gerontologist* 32:312–17

Gonsiorek J, Rudolph J. 1991. Homosexual identity: Coming out and other developmental events. In *Homosexuality: Research Implications for Public Policy*, ed. J Gonsiorek, J. Weinrich, pp. 161–76. Newbury Park, CA: Sage

Grant P, Brown R. 1995. From ethnocentrism to collective protest: Responses to relative deprivation and threats to social identity. *Soc. Psychol. Q.* 58:195–211

Greene B. 1998. Family, ethnic identity, and sexual orientation: African-American lesbians and gay men. In *Lesbian, Gay, and Bisexual Identities in Families: Psychological Perspectives*, ed. CJ Patterson, AR D'Augelli, pp. 40–52. New York: Oxford Univ. Press

Grossberg L. 1996. Identity and cultural studies—Is that all there is? See Hall & Du Gay 1996, pp. 87–107

Gurin P, Townsend A. 1986. Properties of gender identity and their implications for gender consciousness. *Br. J. Soc. Psychol.* 25:139–48

Hall S. 1996. Who needs 'identity'? See Hall & Du Gay 1996, pp. 1–17

Hall S, Du Gay P, eds. 1996. *Questions of Cultural Identity.* London: Sage

Helms J. 1994. The conceptualization of racial identity and other "racial" constructs. See Trickett, Watts & Birman 1994, pp. 285–311

Helson R, Stewart A, Ostrove J. 1995. Identity in three cohorts of midlife women. *J. Pers. Soc. Psychol.* 69:544–57

Herek G. 1995. Psychological heterosexism in the United States. In *Lesbian, Gay, and Bisexual Identities over the Lifespan*, ed. AR D'Augelli, CJ Patterson, pp. 321–46. New York: Oxford Univ. Press

Hermans H. 1996. Voicing the self: from information processing to dialogical interchange. *Psychol. Bull.* 119:31–50

Hollander JA. 1998. Doing Studs: The performance of gender and sexuality on late-night television. See O'Brien & Howard 1998, pp. 43–71

Hopkins N, Reicher S. 1996. The construction of social categories and processes of social change: Arguing about national identities. See Breakwell & Lyons 1996, pp. 69–93

Hopkins N, Reicher S, Levine M. 1997. On the parallels between social cognition and the 'new racism'. *Br. J. Soc. Psychol.* 36:305–29

Howard JA. 1995. Social cognition. In *Sociological Perspectives on Social Psychology*, ed. KS Cook, GA Fine, JS House, pp. 90–117. Needham Heights, MA: Allyn & Bacon

Howard JA, Alamilla R. 2001. Gender identity. In *Gender Mosaics: Social Perspectives*, ed.

D Vannoy. Los Angeles: Roxbury. In Press

Howard JA, Hollander JA. 1997. *Gendered Situations, Gendered Selves: A Gender Lens on Social Psychology.* Thousand Oaks, CA: Sage

Huddy L, Virtanen S. 1995. Subgroup differentiation and subgroup bias among Latinos as a function of familiarity and positive distinctiveness. *J. Pers. Soc. Psychol.* 68:97–108

Hunt S, Benford RD, Snow DA. 1994. Identity talk in the peace and justice movement. *Contemp. Ethnogr.* 22:488–517

Hunt S, Miller K. 1997. The discourse of dress and appearance: identity talk and a rhetoric of review. *Symb. Interact.* 20:69–82

Hurtado A, Gurin P, Peng T. 1994. Social identities: A framework for studying the adaptations of immigrants and ethnics: the adaptations of Mexicans in the United States. *Soc. Probl.* 41:129–51

Ichiyama M, McQuarrie E, Ching K. 1996. Contextual influences on ethnic identity among Hawaiian students in the mainland United States. *J. Cross-Cult. Psychol.* 27:458–75

Islam MR, Hewstone M. 1993. Intergroup attributions and affective consequences in majority and minority groups. *J. Pers. Soc. Psychol.* 64:936–50

Jackson S. 1995. Gender and heterosexuality: a materialist feminist analysis. In *(Hetero)sexual Politics*, ed. M Maynard, J Purvis, pp. 11–25. London: Taylor & Francis

Karp D, Holmstrom LL, Gray P. 1998. Leaving home for college: expectations for selective reconstruction of self. *Symb. Interact.* 21:253–76

Kendall L. 1998a. Meaning and identity in "cyberspace": the performance of gender, class, and race online. *Symb. Interact.* 21:129–53

Kendall L. 1998b. "Are you male or female?" Gender performances on MUDS. See O'Brien & Howard 1998, pp. 131–53

Kitzinger C, Wilkinson S. 1995. Transitions from heterosexuality to lesbianism: the discursive production of lesbian identities. *Dev. Psychol.* 31:95–104

Knight G, Bernal M, Garza C, Cota M, Ocampo K. 1993. Family socialization and the ethnic identity of Mexican-American children. *J. Cross-Cult. Psychol.* 24:99–114

Kroger J. 1997. Gender and identity: the intersection of structure, content, and context. *Sex Roles* 36:747–70

Langman L. 1998. Identity, hegemony, and social reproduction. Curr. *Perspect. Soc. Theory* 18:185–226

LeVine R, Campbell D. 1972. *Ethnocentrism, Theories of Conflict, Ethnic Attitudes, and Group Behavior.* New York: Wiley

Lindstrom B. 1997. A sense of place: housing selection on Chicago's North Shore. *Sociol. Q.* 38:19–39

Logan JR, Ward R, Spitze G. 1992. As old as you feel: Age identity in middle and later life. *Soc. Forces* 71:451–67

Lopez LM, Hasso FS. 1998. Frontlines and borders: identity thresholds for Latinas and Arab American women. See O'Brien & Howard 1998, pp. 253–80

Low J. 1996. Negotiating identities, negotiating environments: an interpretation of the experiences of students with disabilities. *Disability & Soc.* 11:235–48

MacPherson P, Fine M. 1995. Hungry for an us: adolescent girls and adult women negotiating territories of race, gender, class and difference. *Fem. Psychol.* 5:181–200

Markus H, Crane M, Bernstein S, Siladi M. 1982. Self-schemas and gender. *J. Pers. Soc. Psychol.* 42:38–50

McAdams D. 1995. What do we know when we know a person? *J. Pers.* 63:365–96

McCall GJ, Simmons JL. 1978. *Identities and Interactions: An Examination of Human Associations in Everyday Life.* New York: Free Press

McCorkel J. 1998. Going to the crackhouse: critical space as a form of resistance in total institutions and everyday life. *Symb. Interact.* 21:227–52

McKenna K, Bargh J. 1998. Coming out in the age of the internet: identity "demarginalization" through virtual group participation. *J.*

Pers. Soc. Psychol. 75:681–94

Miles S, Cliff D, Burr V. 1998. 'Fitting in and sticking out': consumption, consumer meanings and the construction of young people' identities. *J. Youth Stud.* 1:81–96

Montepare JM, Lachman ME. 1989. "You're only as old as you feel": Self-perceptions of age, fears of aging, and life satisfaction from adolescence to old age. *Psychol. Aging* 4:73–78

Moscovici S. 1981. On social representations. In *Social Cognition: Perspectives on Everyday Understanding*, ed. JP Forgas, pp. 115–50. The Hague: Nijhoff

Nagel J. 1996. *American Indian Ethnic Renewal: Red Power and the Resurgence of Identity and Culture.* New York: Oxford Univ. Press

O'Brien J. 1999. Writing in the body: gender (re)production in online interaction. In *Communities in Cyberspace*, ed. MA Smith, P Kollock, pp. 76–104. New York: Routledge

O'Brien J, Howard JA, eds. 1998. *Everyday Inequalities: Critical Inquiries.* Malden, MA: Blackwell

Oyserman D, Gant L, Ager J. 1995. A socially contextualized model of African American identity: possible selves and school persistence. *J. Pers. Soc. Psychol.* 69:1216–32

Perera S, Pugliese J. 1998. Wogface, anglo-drag, contested aboriginalities' making and unmaking identities in Australia. *Soc. Identities* 4:39–72

Phinney J. 1990. Ethnic identity in adolescents and adults: Review of research. *Psychol. Bull.* 108:499–514

Phinney J. 1991. Ethnic identity and self-esteem: a review and integration. *Hisp. J. Behav. Sci.* 13:193–208

Rapley M. 1998. 'Just an ordinary Australian': self-categorization and the discursive construction of facticity in 'new racist' political rhetoric. *Br. J. Soc. Psychol.* 37:325–44

Reid P, Comas–Diaz L. 1990. Gender and ethnicity: perspectives on dual status. *Sex Roles* 22:397–408

Rich A. 1980. Compulsory heterosexuality and

lesbian existence. *Signs* 5:631–60

Richardson D, ed. 1996a. *Theorising Heterosexuality.* Buckingham, UK: Open Univ. Press

Richardson D. 1996b. Heterosexuality and social theory. See Richardson 1996, pp. 1–20

Robinson V. 1996. Heterosexuality and masculinity: theorising male power or the male wounded psyche? See Richardson 1996a, pp. 109–24

Root MPP, ed. 1992. *Racially Mixed People in America.* Newbury Park, CA: Sage

Root MPP, ed. 1996. *The Multiracial Experience: Racial Borders as the New Frontier.* Thousand Oaks, CA: Sage

Rothbaum F. 1983. Aging and age stereotypes. *Soc. Cogn.* 2:171–84

Rothbaum F, Weisz JR, Snyder SS. 1982. Changing the world and changing the self: a two–process model of perceived control. *J. Pers. Soc. Psychol.* 42:5–37

Rouhana N, Bar–Tal D 1998. Psychological dynamics of intractable ethnonational conflicts: the Israeli–Palestinian case. *Am. Psychol.* 53:761–70

Rowe W, Bennett S, Atkinson D. 1994. White racial identity models: a critique and alternative proposal. *Couns. Psychol.* 22:129–46

Ruddick S. 1996. Constructing difference in public spaces: race, class, and gender as interlocking systems. *Urban Geog.* 17:132–51

Rust PC. 1996. Managing multiple identities: diversity among bisexual women and men. In *Bisexuality: The Psychology and Politics of an Invisible Minority*, ed. B A Firestein, pp. 53–83. Thousand Oaks, CA: Sage

Ruzza CE. 1996. Regional identity formation and community integration in the Lega Lombarda. See Breakwell & Lyons 1996, pp. 195–207

Scheer J. 1994. Culture and disability: an anthropological point of view. See Trickett, Watts & Birman 1994, pp. 244–60

Shockey ML. 1998. Class dismissed? Quad City women doing the life. See O'Brien & Howard 1998, pp. 213–36

Shorter-Gooden K, Washington NC. 1996.

Young, black, and female: the challenge of weaving an identity. *J. Adolesc.* 19:465–75

Simon B, Hastedt C. 1999. Self-aspects as social categories: the role of personal importance and valence. *Eur. J. Soc. Psychol.* 29:479–87

Simon B, Hastedt C, Aufderheide B. 1997. When self–categorization makes sense: the role of meaningful social categorization in minority and majority members' self–perception. *J. Pers. Soc. Psychol.* 73:310–20

Simon B, Loewy M, Sturmer S, Ulrike W, Freytag P, et al. 1998. Collective identification and social movement participation. *J. Person. Soc. Psychol.* 74:646–58

Spears R, Oakes P, Ellemers N, Haslam SA, eds. 1997a. *The Social Psychology of Stereotyping and Group Life.* Cambridge: Blackwell

Spears R, Oakes P, Ellemers N, Haslam SA. 1997b. The social psychology of stereotyping and group life. See Spears et al 1997a, pp. 1–19

Spencer MB, Markstrom-Adams C. 1990. Identity processes among racial and ethnic minority children in America. *Child Dev.* 61:290–310

Stewart A, Ostrove J. 1993. Social class, social change, and gender: working-class women at Radcliffe and after. *Psychol. Women Q.* 17:475–97

Stryker S. 1980. *Symbolic Interactionism: A Social Structural Version.* Menlo Park, CA: Benjamin–Cummings

Takagi D. 1994. Maiden voyage: excursion into sexuality and identity politics in Asian America. *Amerasia J.* 20:1–17

Tajfel H. 1970. Experiments in intergroup discrimination. *Sci. Am.* 23:96–102

Tajfel H. 1981. Social stereotypes and social groups. In *Intergroup Behaviour*, ed. JC Turner, H Giles. Oxford: Blackwell

Tajfel H, Turner J. 1986. The social identity theory of intergroup behaviour. In *Psychol-ogy of Intergroup Relations*, ed. S Worchel, WG Austin, pp. 7–24. Chicago: Nelson

Taylor V, Whittier NE. 1992. Collective identity in social movement communities: Lesbian feminist mobilization. In *Frontiers in Social Movement Theory*, ed. AD Morris, CM Mueller, pp. 104–29. New Haven: Yale Univ. Press

Tewksbury R. 1994. "Speaking of someone with AIDS. . .": identity constructions of persons with HIV disease. *Dev. Behav.* 15:337–55

Thorne B. 1993. *Gender Play: Girls and Boys in School.* New Brunswick NJ: Rutgers Univ. Press

Torregrosa JR. 1996. Spanish international orientations: Between Europe and Iberoamerica. See Breakwell & Lyons 1996, pp. 111–21

Trickett E, Watts R, Birman D, eds. 1994. *Human Diversity: Perspectives on People in Context.* San Francisco: Jossey–Bass

Verkuyten M. 1997. Discourses of ethnic minority identity. *Br. J. Soc. Psychol.* 35:565–86

Waters M. 1994. Ethnic and racial identities of second–generation Black immigrants in New York City. *Int. Migr. Rev.* 28:795–820

West C, Zimmerman DH. 1987. Doing gender. *Gender Soc.* 1:125–51

Wilkinson S, Kitzinger C, eds. 1993. *Heterosexuality: A Feminism & Psychology Reader.* London: Sage

Wolf C. 1994. Dependency-bond as construct. *Symb. Interact.* 17:367–93

Woollett A, Marshall H, Nicolson P, Dosanjh N. 1994. Asian women's ethnic identity: the impact of gender and context in the accounts of women bringing up children in East London. *Fem. Psychol.* 4:119–21

Zack N, ed. 1995. *American Mixed Race: The Culture of Microdiversity.* Lanham, MD: Rowman & Littlefield

Annu. Rev. Sociol. 2000. 26:395–418

SCHOOLS AND COMMUNITIES: Ecological and Institutional Dimensions

Richard Arum

Department of Sociology, University of Arizona, Tucson, Arizona 85721-0027;
e-mail: arum@u.arizona.edu

Key Words neighborhood effects, racial segregation, educational resources, school-to-work transitions, school discipline

■ **Abstract** Research on the relationship between schools and communities has reemerged as a principal focus of the sociology of education. Current research, however, rejects earlier conceptualizations of school communities as being organized locally and identifiable by reference to demographic and neighborhood characteristics. Neoinstitutional research on schools has focused examination instead on school communities defined as *organizational fields*. From this perspective, state regulation, professional associations, and market competition are institutional forces that combine with local neighborhood characteristics to shape school-level practices. The historical development of this theoretical approach is first discussed; current research on neighborhood effects is then critiqued for ignoring how schools vary in response to institutional environments; finally, examples of the utility of a broader institutional conceptualization of community are suggested in five current areas of educational research: racial segregation, resource inequality, curriculum variation, school-to-work transitions, and school discipline.

INTRODUCTION

The relationship between the school and the community has reemerged as a principal focus of sociological research on schooling. While this renewed interest in explicating the multifaceted and reciprocally formative connections between schools and communities continues a long history of sociological investigation of the topic, recent research has attempted to respecify and redefine what is meant by a school community. This redefinition has emphasized political, institutional, and network dimensions of community-school relationships. Critical in this reformulation has been neoinstitutional research in the sociology of organizations. Neoinstitutionalists argue that schools are embedded not simply in local ecological communities, but more importantly in larger organizational communities. Organizational communities are what neoinstitutionalists refer to as *organizational fields*, and these comprise the set of institutions that are either directly

0360-0572/00/0815-0395$14.00

connected to a school (e.g., a regulating agency, a union association, a professional school) or share a structurally equivalent position (e.g., public schools—and to a lesser extent private schools—in the same state).[1] Neoinstitutionalists place particular focus on state regulation and how organizations are embedded in these larger, nonlocal environments. From this perspective, educational practices are more a reflection of a school's institutional community (e.g., state regulatory agencies, professional associations, training organizations, and market competition) than of a school's neighborhood demographic community (Meyer 1994, Scott 1994, DiMaggio & Powell 1983, 1991). Neoinstitutional educational research, therefore, offers an explicit challenge to traditional ecological educational research, which has conceptualized schools as being embedded primarily in localized community settings (see e.g., Bronfenbrenner 1979). Schools are organizations, and as such their communities are by definition largely institutional in character.

Reformulation of conceptualizations of community-school relationships has occurred in the context of renewed interest in the study of the role of neighborhoods in reproducing social inequality and generating crime. Current research on the role of communities in generating poverty, inequality, deviance, and crime, however, has largely relied on a sociological conceptualization of neighborhood ecological effects that was developed in the first half of the twentieth century (Park 1916, Shaw & McKay 1942). This research has focused on demographic and social organization within neighborhoods but has largely ignored variation in the structure of schooling and the organizational environment of schools that has produced institutional variation. The emergence of renewed but reformulated analyses of schools and communities is evident in many areas, including investigations of racial segregation, resource inequality, curriculum variation, school-to-work transitions, and school disciplinary climates. The changing conceptualization of school-community relationships is not just the result of abstract theoretical developments; it also reflects the changing ways communities and schools are organized and constituted.

---

[1]Neoinstitutionalists have argued that organizational fields "identify communities of organizations that participate in the same meaning systems, are defined by similar symbolic processes, and are subject to common regulatory processes" (Scott 1994:71). In population ecology research, Hannan and Freeman (1989) have referred to the "community ecology of organizations." They note: "A community of organizations is a set of interacting populations. Some analysts refer to such communities as organizational fields (Warren 1967) or as societal sectors (Meyer and Scott 1983). A typical community of organizations in industrial settings is composed of populations of firms, populations of labor unions, and populations of regulatory agencies" (pp. 14–15). Research in the sociology of education on schools as organizations has been influenced more directly by neoinstitutional theory than population ecology. When an ecological perspective emerges in sociology of education research, it is generally focused on local demographically defined and organized communities, rather than on institutions as defined by population ecology as understood in the sociology of organizations.

SCHOOLS AND COMMUNITIES: Prior Conceptualizations

Public schools in the United States emerged in many respects at the local level; well into the twentieth century they were also largely controlled and funded by local government. Discussions of schooling, therefore, could not avoid incorporating explicit reference to school community. Educational philosophers such as John Dewey and Horrace Mann saw school practices as emerging from the democratic nature of American communities; schools were likewise considered necessary to develop the enlightened and rational citizenry that communities in a democracy depended upon. "The realization of a form of social life in which interests are mutually interpenetrating, and where progress, or readjustment, is an important consideration," Dewey (1916) wrote, "makes a democratic community more interested than other communities have cause to be in deliberate and systematic education" (p. 87).

Early American sociological examination of schooling explored issues related to the inherent tension between community influence and the effective organization of educational practice. Willard Waller (1937), for example, described how communities often imposed antiquated sets of moral standards constraining both the personal and institutional behaviors of school personnel. Pitrim Sorokin (1927) identified limitations and contradictions inherent in democratic demands for schooling to facilitate increased social mobility. Sociological research on education prior to World War II, however, generally assumed that communities influenced school practices primarily through formal democratic processes or through the informal pressures of public opinion and participatory involvement.

In the 1950s and 1960s, functionalist accounts of schooling emerged that served to sever sociological appreciation of the relationship between schools and communities. Functionalist interpretations of education argued that school practices mirrored the needs of a *larger* society. In sociology, this perspective had roots in Emile Durkheim's classic interpretation of how school organization changed to reflect existing and emerging economic conditions (see e.g., Durkheim 1977). Social scientists from a variety of political perspectives came to see American schools as having a generally uniform character that was divorced from conditions in local communities and responded instead to the needs of a larger social system, economic structure, or—given certain political preconceptions—capitalist ruling class (see e.g., Parsons 1959, Blau & Duncan 1967, Carnoy & Levin 1985, Bowles & Gintis 1976). If schools were shaped by macrolevel functional imperatives, local communities were implicitly assumed to be inconsequential—not only in continental settings such as France, with a strongly centralized education system, but also in the United States.

The nadir of social scientific appreciation for the relationship between schools and community occurred in the 1970s. Functional accounts of schooling largely convinced many researchers that schools did not significantly vary as a result of community setting; institutionalists further argued that schools had their own organizational culture and were "encapsulated" by, or only "loosely coupled" to, other organizations in their environment (Meyer & Rowan 1977, Sarason 1971, Weick 1976). In addition, a number of prominent social scientists began to assert that even if variation in school practices existed, this variation had few if any significant effects on student outcomes. Many researchers had interpreted the Coleman Report as evidence for the absence of traditional school effects, and the influential study of Jencks et al (1972) further contributed to a profound level of academic skepticism and disinterest in the further exploration of systematic community-based school variation (see Karabel & Halsey 1977: pp. 19–26).[2] By the end of the 1970s, it is not much of an exaggeration to summarize the conventional wisdom within sociology as a belief that public school variation within the United States was small, insignificant, and largely inconsequential.[3]

SCHOOLS AND COMMUNITIES: Recent Reformulations

While I have just described how research in the 1960s and 1970s contributed to the demise of an appreciation for the relationship between schools and communities, ironically some of these same scholars (particularly James Coleman and John Meyer) had begun to sow the intellectual seeds of a reconceptualization of the nature of school community. Two sociological theoretical developments—the elaboration of the concept of social capital and the neoinstitutional articulation and definition of organizational environment—allowed for a redefinition of what was meant by a school's community.

Coleman's work on social capital identified both a clearer focus on the structural organization of individual relationships within communities and a mechanism whereby communities could therefore affect educational processes. While Coleman had long been interested in how peer relationships affected student orientations and academic performance (Coleman 1960, Coleman et al 1966), his development of the concept of social capital extended his focus on student network ties to incorporate intergenerational linkages amongst youth and adults in a larger community. Specifically, Coleman (1988) argued that when greater interpersonal and intergenerational closure exists amongst individuals within schools and the surrounding community, student behavior and actions were more aligned with socially productive conventional adult norms. When schools were in communities that were socially disintegrated in terms of the amount of adult contact with other adults or their children, the monitoring and constraining of youth misbehavior was more difficult. When intergenerational closure in school communities was weak, youth

---

[2]Robert Hauser's (1970) astute and influential methodological critique of some common errors in contextutal school research also possibly discouraged work in this area.

[3]There were, of course, notable exceptions to this. James Coleman, for example, never failed to appreciate the importance of recognizing school-level differences; Charles Bidwell has long argued for the importance of comparative research on schools as organizations (see e.g., Bidwell 1965 and 1999). On the other hand, others have remained largely skeptical of significant school effects (see e.g., Jencks and Mayer 1990, Hanushek 1989).

had opportunities to develop their own autonomous peer cultures with distinctive sets of values and norms often divorced from or antagonistic to conventional adult behavior.[4]

During roughly the same time period, neoinstitutionalists began arguing that schools were located in specific organizational environments or fields. John Meyer's early work on education served as a catalyst for the development of many aspects of this approach (Meyer & Rowan 1977). Coercive, normative, and mimetic pressures were argued to exist within organizational environments, which worked to produce a common but distinct set of organizational forms (DiMaggio & Powell 1983). Neoinstitutionalists focus particular attention on the role of state authority in structuring organizational practices. While initial neoinstitutional research on education often adopted existing social scientific assumptions about the lack of variation in public schools within the United States (see e.g., Scott & Meyer 1988), a framework had been generated that could serve to structure renewed investigation of school community in terms of *organizational field*. Neoinstitutionalists who examined schools began to focus not just on the earlier examined demographic and cultural characteristics of local communities, but on legal climates, regulatory contexts, and political institutions as well as other relevant organizations (see e.g., Wirt & Kirst 1997, Meyer et al 1988, Meyer et al 1987, Chubb & Moe 1990). From this perspective, a school community was defined not simply by the residents who lived in areas surrounding a school, but rather by a school's organizational environment (Barr et al 1983, Bidwell & Kasarda 1985, Gamoran & Dreeben 1986). If one adopted assumptions of little meaningful school variation, public schools across the United States could be argued to share a common organizational field; if one rejected assumptions of the absence of school variation, the effects of context-specific institutional features of the organizational environment could be examined.

While theoretical developments around neoinstitutional theory and the concept of social capital created an intellectual justification for a redefinition of school community, society itself had changed over the past century in ways that provided a material basis for this redefinition. Specifically, technology, individual mobility, increased female labor market participation, and the spatial organization of metropolitan areas had in many ways undermined traditional forms of neighborhood organization. Putnam (1995), for example, has argued that over the past few decades not only has voter participation in elections and membership in unions declined, but so too has citizen participation in many local voluntary organizations (such as church-related groups, parent-teacher associations, civic organizations, and fraternal organizations). While some of the specific declines that Putnam mentions have been vigorously debated (see e.g., Chaves 1990, Hout & Greeley 1990),

---

[4]Recent ecological research on schools has focused on how school-community relationships are defined primarily by interconnectedness at this interpersonal level (Epstein 1995; Steinberg, Brown and Dornbusch 1996).

it is likely that many traditional forms of civic community and involvement are in decline. It is also likely, however, that they are simultaneously being replaced by new forms of community organization, activity, and influence (Skocpol 1997). In particular, new communities have organized around shared identities and have often pressed their demands in legal and other (political and professional) *institutional* settings (Schudson 1998). In many areas of educational practice, courts—not parent-teacher associations or local school boards—have become the primary mechanism whereby communities can affect school organization. In other areas of educational practice, educational communities are organized around professional schools, teacher and administrator professional associations, and state departments of education. In short, defining school communities in ecological terms at the neighborhood-level misses the extent to which school practices are shaped by larger sets of institutional forces. Today more than ever, a school's relevant community is not just a neighborhood demographic environment, but equally an institutional environment. Changes in the actual character of community involvement and participation partially underlay this social scientific redefinition of school community.

Renewed interest and redefinition of school community that encompasses a school's institutional environment is apparent in many areas of research on education. To give a sense of the character of these changes, I describe developments in a handful of key research areas involving the sociology of education. While in some areas an appreciation for the institutional significance of the organizational environment around schools is fully developed, in other areas research incorporating these new definitions of community are still somewhat embryonic and fragmentary. Before illustrating the redefined sociological understanding of what is meant by school community through a very broad and general review of recent research on racial segregation, resource inequality, curriculum variation, school-to-work transitions, and school discipline, I first digress to discuss the contributions and limitations of renewed research on neighborhood effects as it relates specifically to an appreciation of the relationship between schools and communities.

NEIGHBORHOOD EFFECTS

Since the turn of the twentieth century, social scientists and reformers such as W.E.B. DuBois used social surveys to document how neighborhood communities varied in terms of race, poverty, and socioeconomic characteristics such as educational attainment. Scholars at the University of Chicago, however, developed a distinct focus on how isolation of ethnic neighborhoods produced less social integration and increased rates of social disorder, delinquency, and crime (Bulmer 1991, Bulmer et al 1991, Bulmer 1984).

Much of the contemporary research on neighborhood effects has applied this focus, relying on demographic and social integration to explore neighborhood influences that produce variation in educational outcomes (for a review of this research, see Gephart 1997). For example, Brooks-Gunn et al (1993) used the Panel Study of Income Dynamics to demonstrate an association between the likelihood of dropping out of school and income levels, occupational category, and marital status of neighborhood residents. Clark (1992) and Crane (1991) identified similar relationships using Census data, debating, however, whether there were nonlinearities in the effects of concentrated neighborhood poverty. Educational attainment in terms of years of schooling has also been explained by reference to its association with demographic factors present in zip-code or census tract– defined neighborhoods (Ensminger et al 1996, Duncan 1994, Datcher 1982). It is quite remarkable, however, that these studies usually model neighborhood effects on individual educational outcomes without incorporating consideration of variation in the structure of schooling across neighborhoods: i.e., ignoring the most important probable source of institutional variation affecting educational achievement within neighborhoods. Models of neighborhood effects on educational outcomes that fail to incorporate measures of school characteristics thus implicitly assume that either schools vary solely as a function of demographic and organizational characteristics of neighborhood settings (usually defined by census tracts) or that variation in schooling is inconsequential and insignificant. If schools, however, vary as a result of (unmeasured) political and institutional factors, and variation in the structure of schooling affects student achievement, then much of the research on how neighborhoods affect educational outcomes has been characterized by significant omitted-variable bias.

While research on neighborhood effects as a whole has failed to consider adequately the role of schooling, researchers applying a similar emphasis on the demographic characteristics of social environments have for several decades explored the effects of school composition on individual-level attainment and attitudes (see Jencks & Mayer 1990 for a skeptical and pessimistic evaluation of school compositional effects identified in this research tradition). Researchers, for example, have identified the effects, net of individual family background, of attending schools with socially disadvantaged students on test scores (Bryk & Raudenbush 1992) and the increased risk of poverty (Fischer et al 1996). Buchmann & Dalton (1999), however, have recently argued that the effects of peer influences vary across countries as a result of institutional context. Buchmann & Dalton demonstrate that a school's institutional context—in terms of educational stratification—structures the parameters whereby peers can have either more or less influence on educational aspirations. In addition, the social and cultural competencies of neighborhood parents structure variation in both how parents interact with schools and how educational institutions respond to community pressures (e.g., Wells & Crain 1997, Lareau 1987).

Criminological investigations of school effects—perhaps due to the field's intellectual debts to the Chicago School of Sociology—have also recognized and incorporated school community setting in the analysis of the determinants of delinquency and crime. Variation in peer climates, which are partially the result of a school's neighborhood setting, affect youth behavior, as does the disruption of social capital produced by family migration (Hagan et al 1996). School settings that fail to produce meaningful adolescent attachment to conventional activities are characterized by higher rates of delinquency (Sampson & Laub 1993). Students that go to schools in settings of more concentrated poverty have higher rates of adolescent delinquency (Rutter et al 1979) and during later points in their life course suffer higher rates of adult incarceration (Arum & Beattie 1999).

Prominent researchers at the University of Chicago have reinvigorated this research tradition through their work on social capital (Coleman 1988), social control (Sampson & Laub 1993), and the urban underclass (Wilson 1987). Coleman, Wilson, and Sampson have all appreciated the role of community forces in shaping educational processes and the critical role of schooling in determining life course outcomes. Coleman's work on social capital and educational attainment, for example, elaborated on the theme of social integration and closure. Coleman theorized that different degrees of closure in social networks of private compared to public school communities created variation in student educational achievement (e.g., Coleman & Hoffer 1987). William Julius Wilson (1987) also argued that youth from racially segregated neighborhoods suffered the effects of concentrated poverty: In particular they developed nonconventional peer cultures due to insufficient numbers of middle-class role models and limited interpersonal and institutional connections to the larger community. In recent work, Wilson (1996) has emphasized the critical role of schools in the design of effective policy interventions to address the problems of concentrated poverty. In addition, Robert Sampson has worked to elaborate social control theories within criminology (e.g., Sampson & Morenoff 1997, Sampson & Laub 1993, Sampson & Groves 1989). Sampson extended Hirschi's (1969) concept of social control by emphasizing social capital and the critical role of schools in the life course; his emphasis on the role of the education system in social control is consistent with the earlier work of Durkheim (1925) and Park & Burgess (1921).

While Coleman, Sampson, and Wilson's research continues the Chicago tradition of conceptualizing community largely in terms of demographic composition and social organization (see e.g., Park 1916, Shaw & McKay 1942), the work provides a new emphasis on the identification of the importance of specific social relationships and network ties. Rather than assuming that neighborhood-level social organization affects all residents of a community through a diffuse process relying on broad models of social contagion, the research tradition suggests instead that an individual's community is actually both created and defined by an individual's specific social relationships. It is also worth emphasizing that these researchers are theorizing and modeling effects of school variation not simply on small changes in test scores, but more often through exploring how schooling affects more dramatic life course outcomes (such as the likelihood of dropping out of high school, unemployment, poverty, and criminality).

Recent research on schools located in immigrant comunities has particularly benefited from attention to the role of social capital and intergenerational closure in the educational process (see e.g., Zhou & Bankston 1998, Portes & Rumbaut 1996). Schools located in neighborhoods with high concentrations of middle-class ethnic immigrants are exceptional, however, in the extent to which families in these neighborhoods still form coherent locally constituted demographic communities and orient social activities toward fellow residents of the ethnic enclaves where they reside.

RACIAL SEGREGATION

The limitations inherent in assuming that school communities are defined solely by local neighborhood demographic and social organizations are apparent in research on school segregation. Sociologists have long recognized: that schools were situated in local neighborhoods that in the United States were often characterized by racial, ethnic, and class segregation, and that the concentration of minorities in certain public schools reduced educational achievement in those settings (Coleman et al 1966, Rivkin 1994, Bankston & Caldas 1996). Educational research, however, has demonstrated that political factors also independently affect racial school enrollment patterns (e.g., Werum 1999, James 1988) and that it is thus possible to generate variation in educational outcomes by creating distinct school communities not solely based on residential neighborhood enrollment (Orfield & Eaton 1996). Courts have mandated desegregation plans in many US school districts over the last four decades. This court intervention highlights how the relevant school community currently is defined as much by institutional as neighborhood demographic context. Research on school segregation demonstrates that student composition, school neighborhood setting, and court interventions interact to affect the structure of schooling and educational achievement. Wells & Crain (1997) have recently published a descriptive case study of how these multiple factors affect the structure of schooling in the St. Louis public schools.

While some researchers have remained skeptical of the effects of racial school segregation (see e.g., Jencks & Mayer 1990, Hanushek 1997), social scientists have repeatedly demonstrated the effects of racial segregation on individual-level outcomes. Research on summer setback, for example, has extended Heyns' (1978) earlier work by demonstrating that youth have distinct patterns of in-school and out-of-school learning associated with school and neighborhood composition (Entwisle & Alexander 1994, 1992). African-American students in integrated schools show larger than expected gains in mathematics (Entwisle & Alexander 1992, Prager et al 1986, Wortman & Bryant 1985). Entwisle & Alexander (1994), however, have also demonstrated a more complex pattern of segregation on elementary reading test scores. Since reading test scores are more sensitive to informal nonschool learning of language, summer family and neighborhood context account for a larger role in annual cognitive gains in that area. Researchers have also demonstrated that integrated schools (net of individual background) lead African-American students to have greater likelihood of college attendance and higher occupational prestige (Kaufman & Rosenbaum 1992, Rosenbaum 1991, Braddock 1980).

School composition also has been argued to affect long-term patterns of individual racial interactions. Wells & Crain (1994), for example, have used perpetuation theory to account for the long-term effects of racial segregation on individual-level attitudes and behavior. Following McPartland & Braddock (1981), Wells & Crain argue that individuals who have experienced desegregated settings earlier in life are likely to have different life course trajectories and different institutional experiences as adults. African-Americans who have attended integrated high school settings are more likely to attend predominately white colleges (Dawkins 1983, Braddock 1980), to have social networks as adults that incorporate whites, and to work in settings with greater numbers of whites (Trent 1991, Crain & Strauss 1985).

While research on school desegregation effects is particularly sensitive to problems of selection bias—since both African-Americans and whites face selective pressures affecting their presence in desegregated neighborhoods and schools—it is worth noting that quasi-experimental studies have tended to yield similar sets of findings. For example, researchers have examined outcomes associated with the Gautreaux Assisted Housing Program and Project Concern. The Gautreaux Assisted Housing Program was established by court order in 1976 and led the Chicago Housing Authority to assign suburban integrated housing on the basis of availability, rather than preference (Kaufman & Rosenbaum 1992, Rosenbaum 1991). Project Concern assigned randomly selected students in Hartford to attend racially integrated schools (Crain & Strauss 1985). Research based on both of these quasi-experimental programs identifies the positive effects of integrated settings on minority educational and occupational outcomes.

RESOURCE INEQUALITY

While research on resource inequality in the sociology of education has been a prominent feature of the field since Coleman et al's (1966) report on the role of racial segregation in structuring access to educational opportunities, research over the last decade has changed many of the ways social scientists understand these issues. Social scientists have begun to explore systematically the institutional causes for variation in educational resource allocation. In addition, a general consensus has recently emerged on the relationship between educational resource investment and student achievement.

The Coleman Report's exploration of resource inequality was quite limited and focused only on determinants such as region, racial segregation, and rural school setting. Recent research has worked to identify much more concretely the institutional and political factors affecting educational resource allocations. Research has explored how demographic factors, such as the age structure of the population, affect per-student allocations. Chew (1992) identified both demographic and ideological factors that influence voters' support for public education in California. Poterba's (1997) examination of time series data on US state support for K-12 public education also found that increases in the fraction of the population that was elderly led to decreased school funding, particularly when students were of a different racial background than that of elderly voters. In addition, research on the allocation of educational resources has suggested that voter decisions are often made on the basis of fiscal illusions, with voters largely unaware of actual current levels of resources available per student (Romer & Rosenthal 1984). Poterba (1997) also demonstrated how state educational funding fails to closely reflect changes in school enrollment levels, with large cohorts negatively affected by corresponding reductions in per-student expenditures. In my own research, I found quite similar trends, with public school per-student expenditures being both higher and more nearly equal to private schools when private school enrollments significantly reduced the number of public school students (Arum 1996).

Research on educational funding has also demonstrated how state constitutional requirements and court actions have led to variation in local school funding. Differences in state constitutional statutes have led state courts to allow different degrees of disparities in local school funding. Courts in some states have allowed only very limited inequities in local funding of public schools; when state funding predominates, schools receive more equitable intrastate funding (Evans et al 1997, Murray et al 1998). Other institutional factors affect educational resources at the classroom level. Increased demands for greater bureaucracy and increased resource-intensive special education programs in urban public schools, for example, are internal organizational factors affecting resource-per-student levels in regular classrooms (Boozer & Rouse 1995). The unionization of teachers also increases the cost of instruction. Conservative economists have argued that teacher unionization has led to lower productivity (Hoxby 1996) and that schools should adopt anti-union employment policies, such as the imposition of two-tiered employment contracts, fewer tenure guarantees, and the use of computers to replace school personnel (Hanushek et al 1994).

In the past decade, social scientists have also come to appreciate the role of resource investment in affecting educational outcomes. Because of the political significance of this research area, debate on the topic continues. Erik Hanushek in 1996, for example, testified as an expert witness in favor of ending court-ordered remediation of St. Louis public school segregation; he insisted that differences in classroom size of 40 students to one teacher compared to 15 students to one teacher were inconsequential and not related to school performance (Hanushek 1997). While some politically conservative researchers thus still attempt to assert that public school inefficiencies are so great that increases in educational inputs are not significantly related to educational attainment (see also Hanushek 1989, Hanushek et al. 1994), a variety of sophisticated methodological studies have demonstrated a clear set of positive associations. Card & Krueger (1992), for example, examined individuals in post-World War II US census reports who had left their original home state. Individuals from states with fewer students per teacher had increased years of educational attainment and higher lifetime annual earnings. Randomized experiments in Tennessee demonstrated increased gains on elementary school cognitive tests when students are enrolled in smaller classes (Finn & Achilles 1990). Hedges et al (1994) have also countered Hanushek's assertions with the use of meta-analysis. In secondary school settings, I have shown that state-level investment in resources per vocational student leads to dramatically different student outcomes (Arum 1998). In spite of the overwhelming evidence that educational resources affect school performance and student outcomes, politically motivated challenges will likely continue.

CURRICULUM VARIATION

Recent research within the sociology of education has also expanded our understanding of the structure of curriculum variation between schools. While research prior to the past decade often applied the concept of academic tracking to nationally representative data sets without consideration of local variation, researchers have begun to specify how and why the organization of curricular tracks varies between schools. Critical in this developing research was Gamoran's (1992) work, which demonstrated that schools actually organized tracking systems in a variety of ways. Gamoran argued that the effects of tracking varied as a function of the structural dimensions of the tracking system, including selectivity, electivity, inclusiveness, and scope. In related work, I have demonstrated that the effects of vocational curriculum are dependent on resource investment: in states that invest high levels of resources per vocational student, students have increased likelihood of graduation relative to other nonvocational students in similar schools: in states that invest low levels of resources per student, the programs have harmful effects, decreasing the likelihood of graduation (Arum 1998).

Researchers have also attempted to specify how variation in the organizational environment produces variation in the structure of curriculum and curricular enrollments (Loveless 1999). Political, economic, and institutional factors have been identified in an effort to account for this variation. The expansion of community colleges and their vocational curricular emphasis, for example, have been explored from this perspective. While Brint & Karabel (1989) argued that developments in community colleges were largely the product of the organizational self-interest of community college administrators, more recent work has identified the role of local politically elected officials in this process (Dougherty 1994).

Dougherty's recognition of the role of local politics in shaping schools and their curricular offerings supports many social historical accounts of the development of educational policies and practices. While Dougherty emphasizes the role of local elected officials, others have provided evidence of the critical role of local unions, middle-class women's organizations, and ethnic associations (Kliebard 1999, Peterson 1985, Reese 1986; for an excellent review of how political factors structure urban school variation, see also Rury & Mirel 1997). Historical analyses have also identified patterns of how enrollment patterns reflect local labor market conditions (Walters & James 1992, Walters et al 1990) and local political mobilization (Werum 1999).

Interestingly, researchers analyzing contemporary associations between occupational curricular content and local labor market structure have argued that vocational programs have not been closely linked with local labor market needs. The responsiveness of vocational programs to economic and institutional forces was explored by Starr (1983), who examined 1979 and 1980 state vocational plans to determine the degree to which labor market needs affected program design. Starr noted that in the majority of states there was no clear relationships among program and enrollment goals, funding decisions, and employment needs, with only eight states mentioning skilled labor shortages as a factor influencing program design. Franchak (1983) interviewed 105 randomly chosen secondary and postsecondary occupational administrators to determine what factors influenced administrative decisions to add, terminate, or modify course offerings: institutional factors by far dominated economic factors in determining program decisions.

Research on school curricular reform efforts also illustrates the extent to which the relevant school community encompasses political and institutional aspects, rather than simply neighborhood demographic characteristics. Mickelson (1999) recently identified how access to technology-enriched curriculum can be the outcome of both corporate business sponsorship and local political contestation. Wilson & Rossman (1993) have examined how various layers of educational bureaucracy can combine to shape state curriculum reforms. Wilson & Rossman argue that the organizational environment affecting school curriculum includes not only school site personnel, but district administrators and state department of education staff.

SCHOOL-TO-WORK TRANSITIONS

Recent research on school-to-work transitions and status attainment processes has also suggested ways in which institutional and interpersonal aspects of school communities are of critical importance. A school's institutional relationships can shape curricular offerings (as identified above) as well as structure the process whereby students find initial employment. While certain forms of vocational curriculum can facilitate positive school-to-work transitions particularly for women (see Arum & Hout 1997, Arum & Shavit 1995), the specific character of vocational programs is often linked to a school's political and institutional relationships. In addition, the effects of vocational programs are often dependent on actual student attainment of desirable occupations for which they have been trained (Hotchkiss 1993, Bishop 1989). Difficulties in student transitions to the labor market are thus often related to the institutional environment surrounding schools (Kerckhoff 1995).

Sociologists have explicated how the process of finding a job can be structured by both interpersonal and institutional relationships. Both these types of relationships are related to how schools are embedded in specific demographically defined neighborhoods and institutional environments. Employers often rely on personal or institutional ties to reduce uncertainty in hiring new employees.

Employers will develop and utilize these types of ties more frequently when such relationships provide solutions to specific problems faced by firms. Firms will seek to lower transaction costs (Williamson 1975) and reduce risks of uncertainty (March & Olson 1980) when making hiring decisions. Network relationships, such as those implicit in most school-assisted job placement, "are particularly apt for circumstances in which there is a need for efficient reliable information" (Powell 1990:304). Research on job findings has demonstrated that employers use formal and informal network relationships in this manner. Granovetter (1974), for example, has stressed the role of informal, weak interpersonal ties; researchers such as Kirschenman & Neckerman (1991) have demonstrated the racial dimensions of these processes and how a school's reputation can affect hiring decisions. Italian research on school-to-work transitions also has focused on how social networks affect status attainment outcomes. Barbieri (1997), for example, has identified the importance of strong network ties to individuals with higher social standing as an important resource facilitating individual attainment of more desirable occupations. Barbieri's research demonstrates that in Italy, community-based interpersonal contacts are critical for individuals attempting to move into jobs with higher occupational status.

The role of institutional school-business relationships has also been explored. Researchers in the United States have identified the significance of school-business institutional ties in promoting new models of vocational education (Olson 1997, Bailey 1995). Federal, state, and local forces have encouraged many US public schools to create partnerships with local businesses (Frazier 1991). These partnerships have often taken the form of school academies with specific vocational focuses organized within a larger school setting. Maxwell & Rubin (1998) and Stern et al (1992) have described in detail how these programs are organized and can affect student outcomes. Poczik (1995) has examined how these partnerships have encouraged vocational student placement in the workplace.

In other countries, the significance of school-business ties has long been apparent. In Germany and Japan, for example, researchers have identified how school-assisted job placement can facilitate school-to-work transitions (Hamilton & Hurrelmann 1994, Rosenbaum & Kariya 1989). Vocational education is more effective in Germany than in the United States, not simply owing to higher levels of resource investment there, but because of the close relationship between schools and industry (Hamilton & Hurrelmann 1994, Rosenbaum et al 1990). School-business institutional ties are an integral part of the German apprenticeship system (Vickers 1995). In a comparative cross-national project, Mueller & Shavit (1997) recently also focused attention on how institutional characteristics of particular countries can affect school-to-work transitions. Mueller & Shavit demonstrate that national school systems with greater stratification, standardization, postsecondary opportunities and vocational specificity have more effective vocational programs.

In the United States, several recent studies have focused on how high school–assisted job placement can affect characteristics of first job. Rosenbaum & Binder (1997), for example, found that employers use high school linkages to screen applicants who otherwise are likely to present limited reliable information; they also found that employers have an interest in the information that school personnel possess. Approximately one third of the 51 employers Rosenbaum & Binder (1997) interviewed in the Chicago area had developed long-term close relationships with schools that utilized school-assisted job placement. In related work, I have found that employers are much more likely to utilize school-assisted job placement for filling clerical positions with female job candidates and that these placements can improve women's early labor market outcomes (Arum & Way 1998).

SCHOOL DISCIPLINE

The importance of considering both demographic and institutional characteristics of school environments can also be clearly demonstrated when one approaches the issue of variation in school disciplinary climates. School disciplinary climates emerge out of a complex interaction between the demographic characteristics of students and teachers and the social organization of school interpersonal communities as well as the institutional environment around schools (for a vivid description of the climate in urban public schools, see Devine 1996). In recent decades, courts and professional schools in particular have influenced school practices affecting the school's ability to control student disorder. Gerald Grant's (1988) history of an urban high school provides an exceptionally lucid account of how institutional factors can produce changing disciplinary practices and peer climates at the school-level.

Researchers, for example, have argued that over the past thirty years public schools in general have systematically weakened their disciplinary measures, lessening the constraints on acceptable student behavior (Toby 1995, Phillips 1993). Symbolic of this change at a national level was the 1975 Supreme Court *Goss v. Lopez* decision extending the right of *due process* to public school students. Public school administrators no longer could act on their own discretion and authority to expel unruly and misbehaving adolescents; students instead were given the right to both formal hearings and legal representation (Wise 1979). Although there has been a national decline in the severity of public school disciplinary practices, states have varied to the extent that they have constrained the latitude of local school authorities (Pressman 1990, Paquet 1982). While certain states severely restrict the prerogative of school personnel to punish students, other states have maintained strict disciplinary practices by giving school administrators broad powers through the school's assumption of *loco parentis* authority.

In exploring contemporary variation in school disciplinary practices, researchers have made descriptive use of US Department of Education Office of Civil Rights data to identify a pattern of prevalent and racially discriminatory school disciplinary practices (Hyman 1990, Hyman & Wise 1979). Analysis of OCR data has been supplemented by the use of independent school-level surveys. Rose (1988, 1984) documented the declining but continued use of corporal punishment in US schools in the 1980s by surveying school administrators. In the 1980s, schools located in the South reported the greatest use of the practice, but principals in all regions of the country with the exception of New England reported its use. In 1988, 58.1% of principals reported the use of corporal punishment down from 74.1% in 1984.

DiPrete et al (1981) provide the most systematic and comprehensive analysis of school disciplinary practices in their analysis of High School and Beyond student and school personnel survey responses. DiPrete et al (1981) measured a school's disciplinary climate in two ways. They calculated a ratio of sophomores who were disciplined to sophomores who misbehaved; and they created a measure of whether five specific rules of conduct were enforced (requirement of hall passes, requirement of dress codes, prohibition of vandalism, prohibition of smoking, and maintenance of a closed campus at lunchtime). Both these measures varied significantly across regions. Schools in western states punish relatively few students compared to the number who misbehave and have the weakest reports of rule enforcement; schools located in central states have the highest level of rule enforcement.

Sociologists recently have begun to focus increased attention on how school practices such as school discipline are influenced not just by demographic factors, but by legal pressures around schools. Critical work in this area emerged out of a Stanford-based conference that brought together sociologists, such as John Meyer, Ann Swiddler, and Aaron Benavot, with educational and legal researchers, including Robert Kagan, David Kirp, David Tyack, and Thomas James (see Kirp & Jensen 1986). Educational research from a law and society perspective highlighted the extent to which litigation and judicial action had hyperregulated public school operations (Tyack et al 1987, Kirp 1986, Kagan 1986). Legal researchers (Rebell & Hughes 1996, Bardach & Kagan 1982, Lieberman 1981) have argued that "adversarial legalism" has created organizational inefficiencies in both schools and society. After World War II, educational litigation increased dramatically (Zirkel 1997), giving state-level and Federal District-level judiciaries increasing opportunities to interpret laws regulating public school operations differently (Pressman 1990). From a demographic perspective, Grasmick et al (1992) have shown that individuals with higher levels of education, income, and occupational prestige are less likely to support the use of corporal punishment in schools.

Variation in school disciplinary policies has also been argued to have had significant effects on student achievement. For more than three decades, Coleman and his colleagues (e.g., Coleman & Hoffer 1987, Coleman et al 1966, Coleman 1960) have demonstrated that adolescent peer climates vary by school and are important determinants of educational achievement. School disciplinary policies provide the parameters in which student peer climates emerge. More recently, Coleman & Hoffer (1987) argued that private schools, partially because they are able more easily to expel unruly students, have less disruptive peer climates and higher educational achievement than public schools. DiPrete et al (1981) found that rates of misbehavior during the senior year are lower in schools that have higher rates of disciplining sophomore students. Misbehaving students also have lower levels of educational achievement as measured by change in grades and test scores (Myers et al 1987). Critics of traditional disciplinary measures, however, have countered that strict, authoritarian school regimes are counterproductive in that such settings stifle individual creativity, produce student resistance, and are therefore detrimental to educational achievement (e.g., Noguera 1992, Metz 1978). My own recent work has attempted to examine this issue in the context of both demographic and institutional factors.

CONCLUSION

In reviewing literature on such a broad topic as schools and communities, I have been forced to rely on illustrative examples from a variety of topics in the sociology of education to suggest the emergence of a shift in how researchers are defining school community. In recent years, school settings have reemerged as a renewed focus of analysis with researchers exploring demographic factors related to neighborhood setting and also exploring institutional aspects of a school's organizational environment. Communities have re-emerged as a principal focus of analysis, but sociologists now define these communities in much broader ways than in the past. Sociologists have come to recognize that although local neighborhood settings are often (but not always) the location where students reside, schools are also shaped by institutional aspects of organizational environments. School personnel often commute from neighborhoods that are geographically and socially distant from schools where they are employed. Regardless of the geographic neighborhood, teachers and administrators as professionals (Abbott 1988) likely define their communities in terms of common sets of professional—not neighborhood—norms and values. As organizational research reminds us (DiMaggio & Powell 1983), school practices are structured by coercive, normative, and mimetic institutional pressures.

Several theoretical and methodological obstacles exist, however, that threaten the successful realization of extending research in this direction. Theoretically, innovative and policy-relevant research on schools and communities must rely on concepts from more than one intellectual tradition (Lagemann 1999). Research on social organization and demographic aspects of school communities usually rely on the Chicago School of Sociology's ecological definition of neighborhoods. Research on political and institutional influences present in a school's organizational environment rely on concepts developed within political sociology or the sociology of organizations. Lastly, modeling of how variation in schooling affects individual-level student outcomes largely has its roots in research on social stratification and status attainment. There are several difficulties in attempting to bring these separate traditions together, including theoretical debate over the appropriate level of analysis. In the US federal system, the state level—as opposed to the local level—has become increasingly important as institutional variation in laws, regulations, and court opinions are often structured at that level.

Methodologically, researchers have attempted to deal with the problems inherent in multiple levels of analysis by increasingly relying on hierarchical linear modeling (Bryk & Raudenbush 1992). Although these techniques provide some advantages over ordinary least square regression—particularly in the estimation of standard errors—the models are far from a methodological panacea. The central problems in estimating the effects of demographic and institutional environments remain model misspecification and omitted variable bias.

ACKNOWLEDGMENTS

The author would like to thank the National Academy of Education Spencer Postdoctoral Fellowship Program for financial support during the time that this article was written.

Visit the Annual Reviews home page at www.AnnualReviews.org

LITERATURE CITED

Abbott A. 1988. *The System of Professions: An Essay in the Division of Expert Labor.* Chicago: Univ. Chicago Press

Arum R. 1996. Do private schools force public schools to compete? *Am. Sociol. Rev.* 96:29–46

Arum R. 1998. The effects of resources on vocational student educational outcomes: invested dollars or diverted dreams. *Sociol. Educ.* 71:130–51

Arum R, Beattie IR. 1999. High school educational experiences and the risk of incarceration. *Criminology* 37:515–39

Arum R, Hout M. 1997. The early returns: transitions from school to work in the United States. In *Educational Qualifications and Occupational Destinations*, ed. W Mueller, Y Shavit. Cambridge: Oxford Univ. Press

Arum R, Shavit Y. 1995. Secondary vocational education and the transition from school to work. *Sociol. Educ.* 68:187–204

Arum R, Way S. 1998. The significance of school-business institutional ties: effects of school assisted job placement on male and female early labor market outcomes. Presented at the Int. Sociol. Assoc. Meet., Montreal

Bailey T, ed. 1995. *Learning to Work: Employer Involvement in School-to-Work Transition Programs.* Washington, DC: Brookings

Bankston C, Caldas S. 1996. Majority African American schools and social injustice: the influence of de facto segregation on academic achievement. *Soc. Forc.* 75:535–55

Barbieri P. 1997. Non c'e rete senza nodi: il ruolo del capitale sociale nel mercato del lavoro *Stato e Mercato.* 49:67–110

Bardach E, Kagan R. 1982. *Going by the Book: The Problem of Regulatory Unreasonableness.* Philadelphia, PA: Temple Univ. Press

Barr R, Dreeben R, Wiratchai N. 1983. *How Schools Work.* Chicago: Univ. Chicago Press.

Bidwell CE. 1999. Sociology and the study of education: continuity, discontinuity, and the individualist turn? In *Issues in Educational Research: Problems and Possibilities*, ed. EC Lagemann, L Shulman, pp. 85–104. San Francisco:Jossey–Bass

Bidwell CE. 1965. The school as a formal organization. In *Handbook of Organizations*, ed. JG March, pp. 972–1022. Chicago: Rand McNally

Bidwell CE, Kasarda JD. 1985. *The Organization and its Ecosystem: A Theory of Structuring in Organizations.* Greenwich, CT: JAI

Bishop J. 1989. Occupational training in high school: when does it pay off? *Econ. Educ. Rev.* 8:1–15

Blau P, Duncan OD. 1967. *The American Occupational Structure.* New York: Free Press

Boozer M, Rouse C. 1995. *Intraschool variation in class size: patterns and implications. NBER Work. Pap. Ser. No. 5144*

Bowles S, Gintis H. 1976. *Schooling in Capitalist America.* New York: Basic Books

Braddock JH. 1980. The perpetuation of segregation across levels of education. *Sociol. Educ.* 53:178–186

Brint S, Karabel J. 1989. *The Diverted Dream: Community Colleges and the Promise of Vocational Education in America, 1900–1985.* New York: Oxford Univ. Press

Bronfenbrenner U. 1979. *The Ecology of Human Development: Experiments by Nature and Design.* Cambridge, MA: Harvard Univ. Press

Brooks-Gunn J, Duncan GJ, Klebanov PK, Sealand N. 1993. Do neighborhoods influence child and adolescent development? *Am. J. Sociol.* 99:353–95

Bryk A, Raudenbush S. 1992. *Hierarchical Linear Models: Applications and Data Analysis Methods.* Newbury Park, CA: Sage

Buchmann C, Dalton B. 1999. *Peer influences and educational aspirations in thirteen countries: the importance of institutional context.* Pres. at Summer Meet. Int. Sociol. Assoc. Res. Com. on Social Stratification and Mobility, RC28, Madison, WI

Bulmer M. 1984. *The Chicago School of Sociol.: Institutionalization, Diversity, and the Rise of Sociological Research.* Chicago: Univ. Chicago Press

Bulmer M. 1991. W.E.B. DuBois as a social investigator: the Philadelphia Negro 1899. In *The Social Survey in Historical Perspective 1880–1940*, ed. M. Bulmer, K Bales, KK Sklar, pp. 170–188. Cambridge: Cambridge Univ. Press

Bulmer M, Bales K, Sklar KK. 1991. The social survey in historical perspective. In *The Social Survey in Historical Perspective 1880–1940*, ed. M. Bulmer, K Bales, KK Sklar, pp. 1–48. Cambridge: Cambridge Univ. Press

Card D, Krueger A. 1992. Does school quality matter: returns to education and the characteristics of public schools in the United States. *J. Polit. Econ.* 100:1–40

Carnoy M, Levin H. 1985. *Schooling and Work in the Democratic State.* Stanford, CA: Stanford Univ. Press

Chaves M. 1990. Holding the cohort: reply to Hout and Greeley, *J. Sci. Stud. Relig.* 29:525–31

Chew K. 1992. The demographic erosion of political support for public education: a suburban case study. *Sociol. Educ.* 65:280–92

Chubb J, Moe T. 1990. *Politics, Markets and American Schools.* Washington, DC: Brookings Inst.

Clark RL. 1992. *Neighborhood effects on dropping out of school among teenage boys.* Washington, DC: Urban Inst.

Coleman J. 1960. *The Adolescent Society.* New York: Free Press

Coleman J. 1988. Social capital in the creation of human capital. *Am. J. Sociol.* 94:S95–121

Coleman J, Campbell E, Hobson C, McPartland J, Mood A, et al. 1966. *Equality of Educational Opportunity.* Washington, DC: Dep. Health, Educ., Welfare

Coleman J, Hoffer T. 1987. *Public and Private High Schools.* New York: Basic Books

Crain R, Strauss J. 1985. *School Desegregation and Black Occupational Attainments: Results from a Long–term Experiment.* Baltimore: Cent. Soc. Org. Schools

Crane J. 1991. The epidemic theory of ghettos and neighborhood effects on dropping out and teenage childbearing. *Am. J. Sociol.* 96:1226–59

Datcher L. 1982. Effects of community and family background on achievement. *Rev. Econ. Stat.* 64:32–41

Dawkins MP. 1983. Black students' occupational expectations: a national study of the impact of school desegregation. *Urban Educ.* 18:98–113

Devine J. 1996. *Maximum Security: The Culture of Violence in Inner-City Schools.* Chicago: Univ. Chicago Press

Dewey J. 1916. *Democracy and Education: An Introduction to the Philosophy of Education.* New York: Free Press

DiMaggio P, Powell W. 1983. The iron cage revisited: institutional isomorphism and collective rationality in organizational fields, *Am. Sociol. Rev.* 48:147–60

DiMaggio P, Powell W. 1991. Introduction. In *The New Institutionalism in Organizational Analysis,* pp. 1–40, ed. W Powell, P DiMaggio. Chicago: Univ. Chicago Press

DiPrete T, Muller C, Shaeffer N. 1981. *Discipline and Order in American High Schools.* USGPO: Natl. Cent. Educ. Statist.

Dougherty K. 1994. *The Contradictory College: The Conflicting Origins, Impacts and Future of the Community College.* New York: State Univ. New York Press

Duncan GJ. 1994. Families and neighbors as sources of disadvantage in the schooling decisions of black and white adolescents. *Am. J. Educ.* 103:20–53

Durkheim E. 1977. On education and society. In *Power and Ideology in Education,* ed, J Karabel, AH Halsey, pp. 92–105. New York: Oxford Univ. Press

Durkheim E. 1925 [1973]. *Moral Education: A Study in the Theory and Application of the Sociol. Educ.* New York: Free Press

Ensminger ME, Lamkin RP, Jacobson N. 1996. School leaving: a longitudinal perspective including neighborhood effects. *Child Dev.* 67:2400–16

Entwisle D, Alexander K. 1992. Summer setback: race, poverty, school composition and mathematics achievement. *Am. Sociol. Rev.* 57:72–84

Entwisle D, Alexander K. 1994. Winter setback: the racial composition of schools and learning to read. *Am. Sociol. Rev.* 59:446–60

Epstein J. 1990. School and family connections: theory, research, and implications for integrating sociologies of education and family.

In *Families in Community Settings: Interdisciplinary Perspectives,* ed. DG Unger, MB Sussman, pp. 99–126. New York: Haworth

Evans WN, Murray S, Schwab RM. 1997. Schoolhouses, courthouses, and statehouses after Serano. *J. Policy Anal. Manage.* 16:10–31

Finn J, Achilles C. 1990. Answers and questions about class size: a statewide experiment. *Am. Educ. Res. J.* 27:557–77

Fischer C, Hout M, Lucas S, Sanchez-Jankowski M, Swidler A, Voss K. 1996. *Inequality By Design: Cracks in the Bell Curve Myth.* Princeton, NJ: Princeton Univ. Press

Franchak SJ. 1983. Factors influencing vocational education program decisions. In *Responsiveness of Training Institutions to Changing Labor Market Demands,* ed. R Taylor, H Rosen, F Pratzner, pp. 267–95. Columbus, OH: Natl. Cent. Res. Voc. Educ.

Frazier F. 1991. *Transition from School to Work: Linking Education and Worksite Training.* Washington, DC: General Accounting Office; GAO/HRD-91-105

Gamoran A. 1992. The variable effect of high school tracking. *Am. Sociol. Rev.* 57:812–29

Gamoran A, Dreeben R. 1986. Coupling and control in educational organizations. *Admin. Sci. Q.* 31:612–32

Gephart MA. 1997. Neighborhoods and communities as contexts for development. In *Neighborhood Poverty: Context and Consequences for Children,* Vol. 1. ed. J Brooks-Gunn, GJ Duncan, JL Aber, pp. 1–43. New York: Russell Sage

Granovetter M. 1974. *Getting a Job.* Chicago: Univ. Chicago Press

Grant G. 1988. *The World We Created at Hamilton High.* Cambridge, MA: Harvard Univ. Press

Grasmick H, Morgan C, Kennedy M. 1992. Support for corporal punishment in the schools: a comparison of the effects of socioeconomic status and religion. *Soc. Sci. Q.* 73:177–87

Hagan J, MacMillan R, Wheaton B. 1996. New kid in town: social capital and the life course effects of family migration in children, *Am. Sociol. Rev.* 61:369–85

Hamilton S, Hurrelmann K. 1994. The school-to-career transition in Germany and the United States. *Teachers Coll. Rec.* 96:329–44

Hannan MT, Freeman J. 1989. *Organizational Ecology.* Cambridge, MA: Harvard Univ. Press

Hanushek E. 1989. The impact of differential expenditures on school performance. *Educ. Researcher* 18:45–65

Hanushek E et al. 1994. *Making Schools Work: Improving Performance and Controlling Costs.* Washington: Brookings Inst.

Hanushek E. 1996. Measuring investment in education, *J. Econ. Perspect.* 10/4:9–30

Hanushek E. 1997. Are resources important? (Testimony of Eric Alan Hanushek, March 11, 1996), *J. Negro Educ.* 66:289–303

Hauser R. 1970. Context and consex: a cautionary tale. *Am. J. Sociol.* 75:645–64

Hedges L, Laine R, Greenwald R. 1994. Does money matter? a meta analysis of studies of the effects of differential school inputs on school outcomes. *Educ. Researcher* 23:5–14

Heyns BL. 1978. *Summer Learning and the Effects of Schooling.* New York: Academic Press

Hirschi T. 1969. *Causes of Delinquency.* Berkeley: Univ. Calif. Press

Hotchkiss L. 1993. Effects of training, occupation, and training–occupation match on wage. *J. Hum. Resourc.* 28:482–97

Hout M, Greeley A. 1990. The cohort doesn't hold: comment on Chaves (1989), *J. Sci. Stud. Relig.* 29:519–25

Hoxby CM. 1996. How teachers' unions affect education production. *Q. J. Econ.* 111:671–719

Hyman I. 1990. *Reading, Writing and the Hickory Stick.* Lexington, MA: Lexington

Hyman I, Wise J. 1979. *Corporal Punishment in American Education.* Philadelphia, PA: Temple Univ. Press

Imber M, Thompson G. 1991. Developing a typology of litigation in education and deter-mining the frequency of each category. *Educ. Admin. Q.* 27:225–44

James D. 1988. The transformation of the southern racial state: class and race determinants of local–state structures. *Am. Sociol. Rev.* 53:191–208

Jencks C, Mayer S. 1990. The social consequences of growing up in a poor neighborhood. In *Inner City Poverty in the United States*, ed. M Lynn, M McGeavy, pp. 111–86. New York: Natl. Acad. Press

Jencks C, Smith M, Achland H, Bane MJ, Cohen D, et al. 1972. *Inequality: A Reassessment of the Effect of Family and Schooling in America.* New York: Basic Books

Kagan R. 1986. Regulating business, regulating schools. See Kirp & Jensen 1986, pp. 64–90

Karabel J, Halsey AH. 1977. Educational research: a review and an interpretation. In *Power and Ideology in Education*, ed. J Karabel, AH Halsey, pp. 1–86. New York: Oxford Univ. Press

Kaufman J, Rosenbaum J. 1992. The education and employment of low income black youth in white suburbs. *Educ. Eval. Policy Anal.* 14:229–40

Kerckhoff A. 1995. Institutional arrangements and stratification processes in industrial societies. *Annu. Rev. Sociol.* 15:323–47

Kirp D, Jensen D, ed. 1986. School Days, Rule Days. Philadelphia, PA: Falmer

Kirp D. 1986. The fourth r: reading, writing, 'rithmetic–and rules. See Kirp & Jensen 1986, pp. 1–21

Kirschenman J, Neckerman K. 1991. 'We'd love to hire them, but . . .': the meaning of race for employers. In *The Urban Underclass*, ed. C Jencks, P Peterson, pp. 203–34. Washington, DC: Brookings Inst.

Kliebard H. 1999. *Schooled to Work: Vocationalism and the American Curriculum, 1876–1946.* New York: Teacher's Coll. Press

Lagemann EC. 1999. An auspicious moment for educational research? In *Issues in Educational Research: Problems and Possibilities*, ed. EC Lagemann, L Shulman, pp. 3–17. San Francisco: Jossey–Bass

Lareau A. 1987. Social class differences in family school relationships: the importance of cultural capital. *Sociol. Educ.* 60:73–85

Lieberman JK. 1981. *The Litigious Society.* New York: Basic Books

Loveless T. 1999. *The Tracking Wars: State Reform Meets School Policies.* Washington, DC: Brookings

March J, Olson J. 1980. *Ambiguity and Choice in Organizations.* New York: Oxford Univ. Press

Maxwell N, Rubin V. 1998. *Improving the Transition from School to Work: Assessing the Impact of Old and New Strategies.* Kalamazoo, MI: Upjohn Inst. Employment Res.

McPartland JM, Braddock JH. 1981. Going to college and getting a good job: the impact of desegregation. In *Effective School Desegregation: Equality, Quality and Feasibility,* ed. WD Hawley, pp. 141–54. London: Sage

Metz M. 1978. *Classrooms and Corridors: The Crisis of Authority in Desegregated Schools.* Berkeley, CA: Univ. Calif. Press

Meyer J. 1994. Rationalized environments. In *Institutional Environments and Organizations,* ed. WR Scott, J Meyer, pp. 55–80. Thousand Oaks, CA: Sage

Meyer J, Rowan B. 1977. Institutionalized organizations: formal structure as myth and ceremony. *Am. J. Sociol.* 83:340–63

Meyer J, Scott R, Strang D. 1987. Centralization, fragmentation, and school district complexity. *Admin. Sci. Q.* 32:186–201

Meyer J, Scott R, Strang D, Creighton A. 1988. Bureaucratization without centralization: changes in the organizational system of U.S. public education. In *Institutional Patterns and Organizations: Culture and Environment,* ed. L Zucker, pp. 139–68. Cambridge, MA: Ballinger

Mickelson RA. 1999. International business machinations: a case study of corporate involvement in local educational reform. *Teachers Coll. Rec.* 100:476–512

Mueller W, Shavit Y. 1997. The institutional embeddedness of the stratification process: a comparative study of qualifications and occupations in thirteen countries. *Educational Qualifications and Occupational Destinations,* ed. Y Shavit, W Mueller, pp. 1–29. Cambridge: Oxford Univ. Press

Murray SE, Evans WE, Schwab RM. 1998. Education–finance reform and the distribution of education resources. *Am. Econ. Rev.* 88:789–812

Myers D, Milne A, Baker K, Ginsburg A. 1987. Student discipline and high school performance. *Sociol. Educ.* 60:18–33

Noguera P. 1992. Preventing and producing violence: a critical analysis of responses to school violence. *Harvard Educ. Rev.* 189–212

Olson L. 1997. *The School-to-Work Revolution: How Employers and Educators are Joining Forces to Prepare Tomorrow's Skilled Workforce.* Reading, MA: Perseus

Orfield G, Eaton S. 1996. *Dismantling Desegregation: The Quiet Reversal of Brown v. Board of Education.* New York: New Press

Paquet R. 1982. *Judicial Rulings, State Statutes and State Administrative Regulations Dealing with the Use of Corporal Punishment in Public Schools.* Palo Alto, CA: R & E Research Assoc.

Park R. 1916. The city: suggestions for the investigations of human behavior in the urban environment. *Am. J. Sociol.* 20:577–612

Park R, Burgess E. 1921. *Introduction to the Science of Sociology.* Chicago: Univ. Chicago Press

Parsons T. 1959. The school class as a social system: some of its functions in American society. *Harvard Educ. Rev.* 29:297–318

Peterson P. 1985. *The Politics of School Reform, 1870–1940.* Chicago: Univ. Chicago Press

Phillips EL. 1993. *Permissiveness in Child Rearing and Education—A Failed Doctrine?* New York: Univ. Press

Poczik R. 1995. Work-based education and school reform. In *Learning to Work: Employer Involvement in School-to-Work Transition Programs,* ed. B Thomas. Washington, DC: Brookings Inst.

Portes A, Rumbaut RG. 1996. *Immigrant America: A Portrait.* Berkeley: Univ. Calif. Press

Poterba JM. 1997. Demographic structure and the political economy of public education. *J. Policy Anal. Manage.* 16:48–66

Powell W. 1990. Neither market nor hierarchy: network forms of organization. *Res. in Org. Behav.* 12:295–336

Prager J, Longshore D, Seeman M. 1986. *School Desegregation Research.* New York: Plenum

Pressman R. 1990. *State Law Challenges to School Discipline: An Outline of Claims and Case Summaries.* Cambridge, MA: Cent. Law Educ.

Putnam R. 1995. Bowling alone: America's declining social capital, *J. Democracy.* 6:65–78

Rebell M, Hughes R. 1996. Schools, communities, and the courts: a dialogic approach to education reform, *Yale Law Policy Rev.* 14:99–168

Reese W. 1986. *Power and the Promise of School Reform: Grassroots Movements during the Progressive Era.* Boston: Routledge Keegan Paul.

Rivkin S. 1994. Residential segregation and school integration. *Sociol. Educ.* 67:279–92

Romer T, Rosenthal H. 1984. *Dynamic Analysis of School Spending Referenda.* Washington, DC: Natl. Inst. Educ.

Rose T. 1988. *Corporal Punishment in American Public Schools: Five Years Later.* Washington, DC: Eric Doc.; 304–221

Rose T. 1984. Current uses of corporal punishment in American public schools. *J. Educ. Psychol.* 76:427–41

Rosenbaum J. 1991. Black pioneers: Do their moves to the suburbs increase economic opportunities for mothers and children? *Housing Policy Debate* 2:1179–1213

Rosenbaum J, Binder A. 1997. Do employers really need more educated youth? *Sociol. Educ.* 70:68–85

Rosenbaum J, Kariya T. 1989. From high school to work: market and institutional mechanisms in Japan. *Am. J. Sociol.* 94:1334–66

Rosenbaum J, Kariya T, Settersten R, Maier T.

1990. Market and network theories of the transition from high school to work. *Annu. Rev. Sociol.* 16:263–99

Rury J, Mirel J. 1997. The political economy of urban education. *Rev. Res. Educ.* 22:49–110

Rutter M, Maughan B, Mortimore P, Ouston J. 1979. *Fifteen Thousand Hours: Secondary Schools and their Effects on Children.* Cambridge, MA: Harvard Univ. Press

Sampson RJ, Groves WB. 1989. Community structure and crime: testing social disorganization theory. *Am. J. Sociol.* 94:774–802

Sampson RJ, Laub J. 1993. *Crime in the Making: Pathways and Turning Points through Life.* Cambridge, MA: Harvard Univ. Press

Sampson RJ, Morenoff JD. 1997. Ecological perspectives on the neighborhood context of urban poverty: past and present. In *Neighborhood Poverty: Policy Implications in Studying Neighborhoods,* ed. J Brooks–Gunn, GJ Duncan, JL Aber, pp. 1–22. New York: Russell Sage Found.

Sarason S. 1971 [1996]. *Revisiting the Culture of the School and the Problem of Change.* New York: Teachers Coll. Press

Schudson M. 1998. *The Good Citizen: A History of American Civic Life.* New York: Free Press

Shaw C, McKay H. 1942. *Juvenile Delinquency and Urban Areas.* Chicago: Univ. Chicago Press.

Scott WR. 1994. Institutions and organizations: toward a theoretical synthesis. In *Institutional Environments and Organizations,* ed. WR Scott , J Meyer, pp. 55–80. Thousand Oaks, CA: Sage

Scott R, J Meyer. 1988. Environmental linkages and organizational complexity. In *Comparing Public and Private Schools.* Vol. 1. *Institutions and Organizations,* ed. T James, H Levin, pp. 128–52. Philadelphia, PA: Falmer

Skocpol T. 1997. The Tocqueville problem. *Soc. Sci. Hist.* 21:455–79

Sorokin P. 1927. *Social and Cultural Mobility.* New York: Free Press

Starr H. 1983. Vocational education's response to skilled industrial worker's shortage. In

Responsiveness of Training Institutions to Changing Labor Market Demands, ed. R Taylor, H Rosen, F Pratzner, pp. 267–95. Columbus: Natl. Cent. Res. in Voc. Educ.

Steinberg L, Brown B, Dornbusch S. 1996. *Beyond the Classroom: Why School Reform has Failed and What Parents Need to Do.* New York: Simon & Schuster

Stern D, Raby M, Dayton C. 1992. *Career Academies: Partnerships for Restructuring American High Schools.* San Francisco: Jossey Bass

Toby J. 1995. The schools. In *Crime*, ed. JQ Wilson, J Petersilia, pp. 141–70. San Francisco, CA: Inst. Contemp. Stud.

Trent W. 1991. *Desegregation Analysis Report.* New York: Legal Defense & Educ. Fund

Tyack D, James T, Benavot A. 1987. *Law and the Shaping of Public Education, 1785–1954.* Madison, WI: Univ. Wisc. Press

Vickers M. 1995. Employer participation in school-to-work programs: the changing situation in Europe. In *Learning to Work: Employer Involvement in School-to-Work Transition Programs*, ed. T Bailey. Washington, DC: Brookings Inst.

Waller W. 1937. *The Sociology of Teaching.* New York: Wiley

Walters P, James D. 1992. Child labor, race, and school enrollment in the early 20th–century south. *Am. Sociol. Rev.* 57:635–50

Walters P, McCammon H, James D. 1990. Schooling or working? Public education, racial politics, and the organization of production in 1910. *Sociol. Educ.* 63:1–26

Weick KE. 1976. Educational organizations as loosely coupled systems. *Admin. Sci. Q.* 21:1–19

Wells AS, Crain R. 1997. *Stepping over the Color Line: African-American Students in White Southern Schools.* New Haven: Yale Univ. Press

Wells AS, Crain R. 1994. Perpetuation theory and the long-term effects of school desegregation. *Rev. Educ. Res.* 64:531–55

Werum R. 1999. Tug-of-war political mobilization and access to schooling in the southern racial state. *Sociol. Educ.* 72:89–110

Williamson O. 1975. *Markets and Hierarchies: Analysis and Antitrust Implications.* New York: Free Press

Wilson WJ. 1987. *The Truly Disadvantaged: The Inner City, the Underclass, and Public Policy.* Chicago: Univ. Chicago Press

Wilson WJ. 1996. *When Work Disappears: The World of the New Urban Poor.* New York: Knopf

Wilson B, Rossman G. 1993. *Mandating Academic Excellence: High School Responses to State Curriculum Reform.* New York: Teachers Coll. Press

Wirt F, Kirst M. 1997. *The Political Dynamics of American Education.* Berkeley, CA: McCutchan

Wise A. 1979. *Legislated Learning: The Bureaucratization of the American Classroom.* Berkeley, CA: Univ. Calif. Press

Wortman P, Bryant F. 1985. School desegregation and black achievement. *Sociol. Meth. Res.* 13:289–324

Zhou M, Bankston CL. 1998. *Growing Up American: How Vietnamese Children Adapt to Life in the United States.* New York: Russell Sage Found.

Zirkel P. 1997. The 'explosion' in education litigation: an update. *West's Educ. Law Rep.* 114:341–51

Annu. Rev. Sociol. 2000. 26:419–39

RACIAL AND ETHNIC VARIATIONS IN GENDER-RELATED ATTITUDES

Emily W. Kane

Department of Sociology, Bates College, Lewiston, Maine 04240;
e-mail: ekane@bates.edu

Key Words   gender role attitudes, beliefs about gender inequality, race, ethnicity

■ **Abstract**   Research on how gender-related attitudes vary across racial/ethnic groups has produced contradictory results, depending upon the type of attitudes addressed. In this chapter, I review the literature on racial and ethnic variations in three broadly defined types of gender attitudes: attitudes toward gender roles; beliefs about the origins and extent of gender inequality; and preferences for social action to reduce gender inequalities. I address three racial/ethnic groups in the United States: African Americans, whites, and Hispanic Americans. While research on attitudes toward gender roles has yielded mixed results, research addressing attitudes within the other two domains clearly indicates greater criticism of gender inequality among African Americans relative to whites; research on the various groups often combined under the label Hispanic is too limited to draw any clear conclusions. Along with addressing variations across these three types of gender-related attitudes, I also summarize several other patterns evident in the literature: convergence across groups over time; gender gaps in gender-related attitudes; and differential predictors of gender attitudes across racial/ethnic groups.

INTRODUCTION

As scholars of gender have increasingly recognized, gendered social arrangements vary substantially by race, ethnicity, and class in the United States. Thus, the analysis of gender-related phenomena requires recognition of the interconnections between gender inequality and racial/ethnic as well as class inequality. While public opinion regarding gender roles in the United States has received considerable attention in the social science literature over the last three decades, less attention has been focused on racial and ethnic variations in gender-role attitudes. And even less attention has been paid to variations by race and ethnicity in other types of gender-related attitudes. In this review, I address the literature on such variations across a broad array of beliefs about gender inequality, including gender-role attitudes, beliefs about the extent and origins of gender inequality, and preferences for social action in response to the unequal status of men and women. I argue that

0360-0572/00/0815-0419$14.00   **419** an accurate picture of racial/ethnic variations requires attention to such an array of beliefs, as patterns of racial difference vary by attitude domain.

Given the scope of the topic of racial and ethnic variations in gender-related attitudes, it is necessary to limit the literature covered in several ways. I limit my attention to the United States, and I emphasize studies based on sample surveys using national or regional probability samples of adults. Much excellent qualitative work has been conducted on gender relations and gender ideologies within various racial/ethnic groups, but a comprehensive review of that literature is beyond the scope of this chapter. Because the issue of racial variations in gender-related attitudes has not received extensive attention in the literature, I do refer to some studies using convenience samples of college students, but the general conclusions I draw rely most heavily on probability samples. In addition, I include here only literature that either (*a*) focuses on racial and ethnic differences in gender-related attitudes or (*b*) addresses the gender-related attitudes of people of color. In other words, I do not include an overview of the gender attitude literature as a whole, which is primarily focused on white Americans' attitudes. Rather, I focus on those studies that shed light on racial/ethnic variations specifically. Among the gender-related attitudes covered are gender-role attitudes and beliefs directly related to gender inequality, such as beliefs about social action in response to gender inequalities and beliefs about the origins of such inequalities. I do not include other attitude domains involving issues that are deeply gendered but more complex in terms of their links to gender inequality such as attitudes toward abortion, rape, and pornography.

A clear indication of the limited extent of large-scale, probability sample research on racial and ethnic variations in gender attitudes in the United States is provided by the paucity of studies addressing racial differences other than those between African Americans and white Americans. As a result, I focus mainly on the contrast between African Americans and whites. A small number of studies address the gender-role attitudes of Hispanic Americans, including a few probability samples and a larger number of convenience samples of college students, and I address these as well. Too little evidence is available regarding Asian American[1] or Native American gender attitudes to merit inclusion here, a limitation of the literature that should be addressed in future research. As I intend to document in the remainder of this review, the complex interconnections of race and gender demand attention to racial/ethnic variations in analyses of gender attitudes, and such attention needs to include all of the major ethnic groups represented in the US population. The patterns of variation evident in comparing African American and white gender attitudes suggest the rich possibilities that would be offered by such an extension of the existing literature.

---

[1] There are a small number of studies of Asian American gender-related attitudes available, based on college student samples. These generally suggest more traditional gender attitudes among Asian Americans (Jones & Jacklin 1988, Lottes & Kuriloff 1992, Mori et al 1995).

INTERSECTIONS OF RACE/ETHNICITY AND GENDER

Variations in gendered social arrangements by race/ethnicity compose the context in which racial differences in gender-related attitudes must be understood. Thus, I begin with a very brief overview of unique aspects of the history and contemporary patterns of gender relations within each of the three racial and ethnic groups addressed in this review: African Americans, Hispanic Americans, and white Americans.

Race, Gender, and Employment

Gendered patterns of labor force experience vary tremendously by class, but overall differences are evident by race/ethnicity as well. White women have a history of lower levels of labor force participation and higher levels of economic dependence on men than do African-American women (Almquist 1979, Farley & Allen 1987, Sorenson & McLanahan 1987). But along with high rates of labor force participation relative to white women's, African-American women also "suffer from higher unemployment rates (twice white women's), experience greater difficulty finding full-time work, and are much more likely to support families alone" (Amott & Matthaei 1991:189). Hill Collins (1991) argues that African Americans experience a distinct pattern of gender inequality in employment from that experienced by white Americans, with "higher paying yet less secure work for Black men as contrasted with lower-paying, more plentiful work for Black women" (p. 59). For Hispanic Americans, on the other hand, women's labor force participation rates have been somewhat lower than those for whites, although they are converging in recent years (Welch & Sigelman 1992). And Hispanic women are more likely than African-American women to be economically dependent on men, with a much higher proportion of Hispanic households headed by a married couple rather than by a woman (O'Hare et al 1991). But like African Americans, Hispanic Americans face racial/ethnic discrimination in the labor force. They are more likely than whites to occupy low-paying and/or seasonal jobs, and they experience high rates of unemployment and poverty; these labor market disadvantages are particularly marked for women, both Chicanas and Puerto Rican women (Amott & Matthaei 1991, Chilman 1993). In these ways and many others, gendered patterns of employment are different for whites, African Americans, and Hispanics in the United States; labor force experiences are shaped simultaneously by gender inequality and racial/ethnic inequality.

Race, Gender, and Family

Patterns of variation in family experiences by ethnicity have been documented and debated in the literature as well. African Americans are less likely than whites or Hispanics to live in households headed by a married couple (O'Hare et al 1991), and, as noted previously, African-American women are less likely than whites or Hispanics to be economically dependent on men. In addition, while white families in the United States have a long tradition of male dominance, scholars of the history of the African-American family have argued that the legacy of slavery has been one of greater equality in family decision making and division of household labor among African Americans (Gutman 1976, Hill 1971). As Wade (1993:58) asserts, African-American gender roles are more egalitarian than those found among whites. Along with the greater role equality noted in African-American households relative to white households, there has been a long tradition of assuming that male dominance is particularly prevalent among Hispanic Americans. Several critical literature reviews on the topic have noted that previous studies of Hispanic family life often claimed a highly patriarchal structure based on Mexican and Puerto Rican traditions. But these reviews argue that previous work offered little evidence supporting that claim, countering instead that male dominance is not substantially greater among Hispanic Americans than among whites (Baca Zinn 1980, Gonzalez 1982, Montoya 1996, Vazquez-Nuttall et al 1987, Ybarra 1982).

Thus, these scholars suggest either similarity or greater egalitarianism in gender relations within the family for Hispanics and African Americans relative to whites. But others have also argued that racial discrimination has sometimes encouraged a compensatory emphasis on masculine dominance among men of color. For example, in the form of traditional machismo among Hispanic men (Strong et al 1994), aggressive masculinity among young African-American men (Rowan et al 1996), or a reassertion of African-American masculinity as part of a move toward "Black Power" (Ransford & Miller 1983). Hunter & Davis (1992:472) have noted that African-American men face a tension in terms of gendered expectations, as they balance "family role expectations grounded in patriarchy and the comparatively egalitarian work and family roles in Afro-American families." In addition, feminist scholars have noted that family work often takes on particular meanings for women of color. For these women, the family is a site of resistance to racial/ethnic oppression rather than primarily a site of gendered inequalities as some feminists have argued it is for whites (Davis 1983, Garcia 1989, Hill Collins 1991). Thus, as for gendered patterns of employment, it is important to consider that gendered patterns of family structure and experience may vary by race and ethnicity. It is these variations, and many others beyond the scope of this brief review, that suggest the importance of considering how racial/ethnic group membership shapes gender-related attitudes.

RACE/ETHNICITY AND GENDER-RELATED ATTITUDES

The racial variations in employment and family patterns noted above have led some scholars to expect people of color to hold more traditional gender-related attitudes than do whites. A variety of factors are associated with this expectation. These include the assumed tradition of male dominance among Mexican Americans (Kranau et al 1982) and a tendency toward male dominance as compensation for racial disadvantage among African-American men (Ransford & Miller 1983). Other authors have argued that African-American women may view stay-at-home parenting as a luxury rather than a constraint because they have often participated in the paid labor force out of economic necessity (Gackenbach 1978, Gump 1975, Rosen 1978). In addition, some have speculated that the greater salience of racial inequality may lead African Americans to be less concerned about gender inequality (King 1975, Rosen 1978). A comprehensive review of the literature on racial/ethnic variations in gender-related attitudes indicates some variations in gender-role attitudes, some of which are consistent with the expectations noted but many of which are not. By expanding beyond emphasis on role-related attitudes alone, it becomes clear that there are consistent variations in other types of gender-related attitudes, with people of color in the United States more critical of gender inequality than white Americans.

While gender-role attitudes are the predominant measures evident in the literature on racial differences in gender-related attitudes, a variety of other beliefs about inequality are also addressed. Feminist scholars have offered compelling critiques of the analytic limits of relying on role theory as the predominant framework for understanding gender inequality. As Stacy & Thorne (1985:307) argue, exclusive emphasis on roles within the literature on gender "strip(s) experience from its historical and political context and neglect(s) questions of power and conflict." This kind of critique indicates the importance of expanding the analysis of gender-related attitudes beyond an emphasis on role-related attitudes to incorporate a broader array of attitudes. The importance of that expansion is further indicated, as I document below, by the appearance of variations by race/ethnicity that follow different patterns for attitude domains beyond the domain of gender-role attitudes. I have organized the array of attitude measures available into three distinct categories: attitudes toward gender roles (both in the family and in employment); beliefs about the extent and origins of gender inequality; and beliefs about whether social action should be taken to address gender inequality. My review of the literature is organized around these three categories. Following the presentation of patterns of racial variation documented in the literature within each of these three attitudinal domains, I summarize several other trends and patterns evident in the literature: racial/ethnic convergence over time in gender-related attitudes; racial variations in gender gaps in such attitudes; and other predictors of gender attitudes by race/ethnicity.

Attitudes Toward Gender Roles

Role-related attitudes have received by far the most attention in the literature reviewed here, and it is in this domain only that any substantial amount of evidence is available for Hispanic Americans. Thus, I begin my consideration of the literature on racial/ethnic variations in gender-related attitudes by addressing gender-role attitudes. This attitude domain is mainly composed of questions measuring normative preferences for men's and women's roles, in both home and family as well as in the more public sphere of employment and political leadership. For example, is maternal employment acceptable or harmful to children? Are women suited to participate as leaders in politics? Should men be actively involved in housework and child care? Is motherhood a woman's most important fulfillment?

The evidence available on Hispanic gender-role attitudes is very limited, but consistent in what it suggests. Some argue that variation among the main groups that comprise the category of Hispanic is too great to justify use of the category (Garcia 1996, Montoya 1996, Strong et al 1994, Williams 1988), while others find too little variation to merit disaggregating Cubans, Mexican-Americans, and Puerto Ricans (Harris & Firestone 1998). The available probability sample evidence that contrasts Hispanics as a single group with other racial/ethnic groups indicates less egalitarian gender-role attitudes among Hispanics than among whites or African Americans (Harris & Firestone 1998, Wilkie 1993). College student samples suggest the same pattern (Gonzalez 1982, Strong et al 1994). As a single group, then, what little evidence is available points toward more traditional gender-role attitudes among Hispanic Americans than among African Americans or whites. But I return to consideration of studies suggesting variation among groups commonly categorized under the label Hispanic, as well as predictors of gender-role attitudes among Hispanic groups, later in this review when I consider various predictors of gender-related attitudes across racial and ethnic groups.

Turning to the contrast between whites and African Americans, a greater array of evidence is available, but no consistent pattern arises regarding differences in gender-role attitudes. A number of probability sample studies comparing the two groups note no significant racial differences in role-related attitudes, whether among men only (Wilkie 1993), women only (Marshall 1990, Ransford & Miller 1983, Rinehart 1992, Wilcox 1989), or both men and women (Kane 1998, Kluegel & Smith 1986). A similar lack of racial difference is evident in some convenience sample studies as well, most of which focus on college students (Bailey et al 1990, Hershey 1978, Jones & Jacklin 1988, Lottes & Kuriloff 1992, Rao & Rao 1985). On the other hand, where racial differences do appear in African American/white comparisons of role-related attitudes, they often follow an intriguing pattern. Whites are more critical of maternal employment than African Americans, seeing paid employment as less compatible with the role of wife/mother and as more harmful to children, both in probability samples (Bielby & Bielby 1984, Blee & Tickamyer 1986, Blee & Tickamyer 1995, Cazenave 1983a, Dugger 1988, Rice & Coats 1995) and in college student samples (Crovitz & Steinmann 1980, Lyson 1986, Murrell et al 1991). In addition, in studies relying on indices that combine a variety of gender-role attitude items that refer to both home and employment, African Americans are sometimes more egalitarian than whites, as is indicated in several studies that include probability samples of women (Fulenwider 1980, Harris & Firestone 1998, Mason & Bumpass 1975). Greater egalitarianism is also evident among African Americans in one study using a single role-related item that addresses the gendered division of labor into a public sphere for men and a private sphere for women (French & Nock 1981). This theme of commitment to egalitarianism among African Americans is also asserted in several national probability sample studies focusing on African Americans only. Hatchett & Quick (1983), Hunter &

Sellers (1998), and Welch & Sigelman (1989) all argue that African Americans are largely egalitarian in their gender-roles attitudes. As Hunter & Sellers (1998:95) note regarding African Americans in their study, "both women and men endorsed egalitarian views of work and family roles."

But some analysts who have relied on multiple, separate attitude measures have concluded that it is only in the arena of women's participation in the paid labor force that African Americans are more egalitarian than whites in their gender-role attitudes. These authors have argued that on some other dimensions, especially some more closely tied to family life or to leadership, African Americans are more traditional than whites in their gender-role attitudes. In terms of probability samples, this claim has generally been made regarding African-American men only (Blee & Tickamyer 1995, Ransford & Miller 1983, Rice & Coats 1995). A similar claim is echoed in some convenience samples studies of women (Gackenbach 1978, Gump 1975) or both men and women (Lyson 1986).

Ransford & Miller's (1983) work has been particularly often cited in terms of this pattern among men. In their analysis of General Social Survey (GSS) data on gender-role attitudes, Ransford & Miller found no African-American/white differences among women. But among men, the only significant racial differences evident were ones in which African-American men were more traditional than their white counterparts. African-American and white men were similar in their endorsement of women working for pay outside the home, but African-American men were more traditional in terms of women assuming leadership positions in the community or being involved in politics.[2] Ransford & Miller's (1983:58) interpretation of this finding is as follows: "This pattern of sex-role traditionalism (work outside the home is acceptable but political leadership is not) matches the Black Power emphasis noted earlier: the assertion that black males need to occupy positions of power and leadership." Blee & Tickamyer (1995) report a similar pattern in their analysis of men's gender-role attitudes. African-American men are more supportive of maternal employment than white men, but less supportive than whites on another series of questions, including whether men should help with housework and whether women are happiest when home taking care of children. When a similar pattern has been documented in convenience samples of women, the interpretation has been offered that due to their economic disadvantage, African-American women may view stay-at-home parenting as a luxury rather than a constraint, as noted previously (Gackenbach 1978, Gump 1975, Rosen 1978).

Overall, this set of findings suggests no clear pattern. As noted, many studies find no significant difference between African Americans and whites in their gender-role attitudes, while others find African Americans more egalitarian and

---

[2]Ransford and Miller (1983) find no racial difference in men's attitudes toward a woman as President, although Sigelman and Welch (1984) find that African-American men are less likely than African-American women or whites of either gender to endorse a woman as President. In addition, Wilcox (1992) finds that African Americans are less supportive than whites of women occupying combat roles and other non-traditional roles in the military.

less traditional than whites in their beliefs about gender roles. But some have found African Americans, and especially African-American men, more traditional regarding certain issues related to women's leadership and the centrality of motherhood as the source of women's fulfillment. These competing findings have led some to conclude that African Americans are less concerned about gender inequality than whites, and/or that African-American men in particular may have an investment in gender inequality as providing some compensation for the disadvantage they suffer from racial inequality. A review of the literature on racial and ethnic variations in a broader array of beliefs about gender inequality, expanding beyond the role attitudes reviewed above, will indicate that neither of these conclusions is supported by the literature. Across attitude domains, the better supported argument is that the sensitization to inequality created by racial inequality and the legacy of more egalitarian family forms lead both African-American women and African-American men to greater criticism of gender inequality than tends to be evident among whites in the United States.

Beliefs About the Extent and Origins of Gender Inequality

While attitudes toward appropriate roles for women and men are an important part of the system of beliefs structuring gender relations, other attitude domains are important as well. As Therborn (1980) has noted regarding ideology and power, one of the key levels at which ideas can defend power is by defining what exists. Analysis of people's beliefs about the extent of gender inequality addresses this notion that ideas may play a role in structuring inequality by defining whether it even exists. To what extent do Americans perceive gender inequalities as existing? In addition, given the centrality of biological justifications in legitimating gender inequality, beliefs about the origins of gender inequality are crucial in structuring gender relations as well. Is gender inequality viewed as the outgrowth of natural differences between men and women, or as a function of social causes, including socialization into gender roles or structural barriers like discrimination? Within this attitude domain, evidence is, for the most part, available only for African Americans and whites. And that evidence, with a few exceptions, suggests that African Americans are more aware of the extent of gender inequality and more likely to attribute such inequality to structural origins.

In analyses of women, Wilcox (1989) indicates that African-American women express greater discontent than white women at the level of women's power and influence in society, while Dugger (1988) notes that African-American women are more aware, and more critical, of gender discrimination than are their white counterparts. Fulenwider (1980) finds nonwhite women (most of whom are African American) more feminist than white women on a scale that includes measures of beliefs about the extent and origins of gender inequality. Studies using probability samples that include both men and women point to a similar conclusion. French & Nock's (1981) analysis indicates that African-American and white women are similar in their beliefs about the extent of gender inequality, while African-American men are more aware of such inequality than are white men. In terms of origins, they find that African Americans are more likely than whites to attribute unequal outcomes by gender in the labor force to sex discrimination, rather than to natural differences. African-American women are particularly likely to do so, while white men are the group least likely to reject biological explanations. Kluegel & Smith (1986) indicate that nonwhites (again, most of whom are African American) are more likely than whites to perceive gender discrimination. According to previous work of mine (Kane 1992), African Americans, especially African-American women, are more critical regarding both the extent and the origins of gender inequalities in employment than are whites (with African-American men similar to white women in their beliefs, and white men least likely to perceive inequality and to attribute it to social origins). In analyses of African Americans only, Hunter & Sellers (1998) document substantial recognition of the extent of gender inequality among both African-American men and women, while Wilcox (1990) documents substantial recognition of gender discrimination among African-American women.

There are a few exceptions to this pattern of greater criticism of the extent and social origins of gender inequality among African Americans than among whites. In terms of the extent and origins of home-related inequality, I have found white women more critical than African Americans of either gender, with white men again the least likely to perceive gender inequality in the home and the least likely to attribute it to social origins (Kane 1992). This may reflect the more egalitarian patterns evident within many African-American households relative to white households. Kluegel & Smith (1986), though they find greater recognition of gender discrimination among non-whites than among whites, also find among non-whites a higher level of belief that good employment opportunities exist for women,[3] perhaps an indication of a lesser perception of the extent of gender inequality in the labor force.

These exceptions are outweighed, though, by the pattern more often noted: most probability sample studies of racial variations in beliefs about the extent and origins of gender inequality indicate greater recognition of such inequality and of its social origins among African-Americans than among whites. In addition, only one college student sample study addresses this attitude domain for Hispanics. In that study, which includes a sample of college women, Chicanas were more likely than Anglo women to attribute a woman's occupational failure to gender discrimination (Romero & Garza 1986). Taken together, these findings suggest that the experience of racial/ethnic discrimination is associated with greater awareness of the extent and the social origins of another form of social inequality, gender inequality. Counter to the conclusion suggested by some studies indicating more traditional attitudes about family and leadership roles for women, these studies

---

[3]It is also interesting to note that Cazenave has reported that many working and middle-class African-American men believe that African-American women have better employment opportunities than do African-American men (Cazenave 1983b, 1984, Cazenave and Smith 1990).

indicate not lesser awareness of gender inequality among people of color but greater awareness, as well as lesser acceptance of biological justifications for gender inequality.

Preferences for Social Action

The pattern of greater awareness and concern about gender inequality among African Americans suggested by findings regarding beliefs about the extent and origins of inequality is further supported within the final attitude domain reviewed here: preferences for social action. Attitudes included in this domain address policy preferences and beliefs about collective action. Policy preferences range from attitudes about whether the government should do more to ensure equal opportunities for women, to support for gender-based affirmative action and endorsement of the Equal Rights Amendment (ERA). Beliefs about collective action include support for the women's movement and preferences for whether women should organize collectively to seek change in the gendered status quo.

While policy preferences and beliefs about collective action have received considerable attention in the literature on racial attitudes, they are addressed in only a limited number of gender attitude studies. When such studies also explore racial/ethnic variations, they point clearly toward greater support for social action to address gender inequality among African Americans than whites. Analyses of attitudes toward the ERA consistently indicate greater support among African Americans, both in probability samples of women only (Dugger 1988, Marshall 1990, Wilcox 1989) and of women and men (Burris 1983, Kluegel & Smith 1986, Spitze & Huber 1982; although Huber et al 1978, in a probability sample of men and women in Illinois only, found non-white women more supportive of the ERA than white women but no racial difference for men). This pattern is evident for other measures of action orientation as well. In probability samples of women, Dugger (1988) finds African-American women significantly more supportive of "efforts to strengthen and change women's status in society." Wilcox (1989) documents that African-American women are more likely to endorse government intervention as well as collective action to reduce gender inequality, and Fulenwider (1980) reports higher levels of support for the women's movement among non-white women than among white women. Given the speculation some have offered about African-American men's stake in gender inequality as compensation for racial inequality, it is especially interesting to note that studies including men have indicated that African-American men are often more supportive of gender-related social action than are white women. I have reported (Kane 1992) that both African-American women and men score as more critical than whites on a four-item measure of preferences for social action that includes items on how much the government should do to reduce gender inequalities and whether women should organize collectively to seek change on gender-related issues. "The role-related items analyzed by Ransford and Miller (1983) indeed may suggest greater traditionalism among Black men than among white men, but survey questions addressing group-related social action clearly reveal Black men's criticism of gender inequality" (Kane 1992:317). Analyzing a series of items measuring concern about gender issues and inclinations to take action on such issues, Gooley (1989) concludes that African-American women express the greatest concern and action orientation, followed by African-American men, then white women; she finds the lowest level of concern/action orientation expressed by white men. My analyses of GSS data (Kane 1998) indicate much greater support for gender-based affirmative action among African Americans than among whites (with about 40% of African-American men and women both strongly in support, and only about 10–15% of white men and women expressing the same level of support). In work not directly focused on reporting public opinion data, both Goode (1992) and Cazenave (1983a) review poll data on men's beliefs indicating greater support for policies aimed at reducing gender inequality among African American men relative to white men. Goode (1992) notes that African-American men are more likely than white men to favor laws forbidding gender discrimination, and Cazenave (1983a) indicates that African-American men are somewhat more likely to favor efforts to strengthen women's status in society.

Two studies based on probability samples of African Americans point to similarly high levels of support for social action on gender-related issues, although without explicit comparison to whites. Hunter & Sellers (1998) offer evidence that African Americans of both genders are generally supportive of political organizing on gender issues. In addition, Wilcox (1990) reports that African-American women have a substantial degree of commitment to collective action by women (including commitment to movements that bring together African-American and white women). As he puts it, "... there is widespread feminist consciousness among Black women, and a strong consensus in favor of joining with White women in eradicating gender discrimination" (Wilcox 1990:79).

Overall, the findings within this attitude domain point clearly to the conclusion that African Americans are more supportive of social action to reduce gender inequalities than are whites. A conclusion I offered elsewhere is supported by all of the literature reviewed in this attitude domain: "Blacks are generally more critical (on gender-related issues) than Whites, especially on issues related to group-based social action; this finding suggests that criticism of racial inequality indeed may influence their orientation to gender inequality" (Kane 1992:316). Most analysts conclude that this greater support is a result of heightened awareness of inequality and greater support for government intervention as well as collective action in general, shaped by the experience of racial inequality and the successes of social action in addressing such inequality (Gooley 1989, Hunter & Sellers 1998, Kane 1992, Marshall 1990, Wilcox 1989, Wilcox 1990).

Convergence Over Time

Along with patterns of racial/ethnic variation within each of the three attitude domains identified, several other patterns emerged from my review of the public opinion literature on race and gender-related attitudes. The first of these is a tendency toward convergence in attitudes by race/ethnicity over time. While Blee

& Tickamyer's (1995) longitudinal work on men's gender-role attitudes revealed no change over time in the degree of difference between African-American and white men, most studies addressing change over time have concluded that racial/ethnic differences in gender-role attitudes are declining. As Harris & Firestone (1998:249) note in an analysis of the gender-role attitudes of African-American, white, and Hispanic women over the period from 1974 to 1994, ". . . independent of those factors that have been shown to influence gender role orientation, white, black, and Hispanic women are becoming more similar in their attitudes about appropriate roles for women." Blee & Tickamyer (1986) also report evidence of convergence between African-American and white women in their gender-role attitudes, finding that the size of the racial difference has decreased over time and that it is smaller for younger women than older ones. In a study of men's gender-role attitudes, Wilkie (1993) reaches a similar conclusion. She notes that differences between African-American, white, and Hispanic men in their role-related attitudes are decreasing, and she predicts that they will continue to do so: ". . . if Black, Hispanic, and white groups become more similar in education, marital status, and married women's employment rates, racial and ethnic differences in attitudes, already declining, will likely decline further" (Wilkie 1993:275). Vazquez-Nuttall et al (1987), in their review of the literature on gender-roles among Hispanic Americans, conclude that role preferences are changing in this group and are becoming increasingly similar to those of Anglo Americans. This indication of convergence is also echoed in Garcia's (1996:102) more general discussion of Latino social and political attitudes, which he argues "are much more like non-Latinos in the United States than had previously been realized."

These studies all address only one of the attitude domains noted here, gender-role attitudes. A small piece of evidence is available for the domain of social action, in Fulenwider's (1980) work on gender-related attitudes. She finds that while African-American women are more supportive of the women's movement than are white women, their support declined somewhat during the period between 1972 and 1976, resulting in a convergence between African-American and white women's views of the movement. She concludes that this may reflect growing disaffection among African-American women with the white, middle-class biases of the women's movement. Given that little work addresses convergence in beliefs about the extent and origins of gender inequality, or in preferences for social action, and given that Fulenwider's analysis covers only a brief time period, there is too little evidence to draw conclusions regarding whether convergence by race/ethnicity is taking place for other gender-related attitudes.

Gender Gaps by Race/Ethnicity

The intersections of race and gender noted previously suggest not only the importance of attending to racial and ethnic variations in gender-related attitudes, but also the importance of asking whether race and gender interact in predicting such attitudes. To address this question, it is helpful to look at what the literature suggests about whether gender differences in gender-related attitudes vary by race and ethnicity. Generally, the pattern evident is one of greater gender gaps in gender-related beliefs among whites than among African Americans, while too little evidence is available to draw conclusions about gender gaps among Hispanic Americans.

Early work on college student samples suggested that African-American men and women were more similar in their gender-role attitudes than were white men and women (Crovitz & Steinmann 1980, Gackenbach 1978, Hershey 1978). This variation was mainly due to African-American women's lesser endorsement of egalitarian family roles (Gackenbach 1978, Hershey 1978), a pattern noted previously as leading some authors to conclude that stay-at-home parenting was viewed as a luxury rather than a burden by some African-American women. Probability sample studies indicate the same pattern of lesser gender gaps among African Americans than whites, but not usually the same pattern of more traditional attitudes on the part of African-American women. Wilcox (1992), in his analysis of attitudes toward women in nontraditional roles in the military, finds a smaller gender gap for African Americans than whites, resulting from African-American women's lesser support for women in nontraditional military roles. But both Gooley (1989) and I (Kane 1992) find larger gender gaps among whites that are the result of African-American men's more critical and egalitarian gender-related attitudes. In other words, in both of these studies, African-American men are more similar to African-American women than white men are to white women. This greater similarity for African Americans stems from African-American men's much greater support for efforts to achieve gender equality, relative to white men's support. As I have noted previously (Kane 1992:317), "Being black is associated with greater criticism of the gendered status quo, especially among men; this attitude draws them closer to black women. Being a woman is also associated with greater criticism, especially among whites; this attitude draws white women farther from white men and leads to greater gender disagreement among whites."

Studies focusing only on African Americans suggest the same pattern of little gender difference in African Americans' gender-related attitudes. Welch & Sigelman (1989) find no gender gap among African Americans in their gender-role attitudes and also report no gender gap for other political attitudes for which gaps are evident among whites. Hatchett & Quick's (1983:2) analysis of African-Americans' gender-role attitudes also indicates little gender gap; their findings ". . . further document the existence of a great deal of support for egalitarianism among Black Americans—both men and women." And while Hunter & Sellers (1998) do document a gender gap among African Americans in their gender-role orientations, they find no gender gap for beliefs about the extent/origins of gender inequality nor for attitudes toward collective action. Both of these are domains in which I report significant gender gaps for whites but not African Americans (Kane 1992).

Very little evidence is available to address gender gaps in gender-related attitudes among Hispanic Americans. In the only probability sample survey work addressing this issue, Montoya (1996) argues that it is crucial to differentiate

Mexican-Americans, Puerto Ricans, and Cubans in such analyses. She finds limited evidence of gender gaps in gender-role attitudes in all three groups, but these gaps are notably smaller among Cubans, who offer the most traditional gender-role responses. Leaper & Valin (1996), in a convenience sample analysis of Mexican-American mothers and fathers, report no gender gap in gender-role attitudes.

Other Predictors of Gender Attitudes Within Racial/Ethnic Groups

Attention to gender gaps within racial/ethnic groups begins to point to the importance of recognizing heterogeneity within such groups. No single social identity such as race or ethnicity will exert an overriding influence on gender attitudes, and thus it is crucial to attend to variations within racial and ethnic groups as well as variation across them. As Hunter & Sellers (1998:87) have argued, "Most studies . . . typically look only at the effect of group membership (i.e., being Black or not) without explicit consideration of the context or content of those experiences that may make race a meaningful factor." This not only limits our understanding of that context or content but also tends to depict non-white racial/ethnic groups as homogeneous in their gender-related attitudes, while extensive research on the predictors of gender attitudes among largely white samples does not similarly universalize their experience.

While a number of studies have noted differential predictors, especially of the gender attitudes of African Americans and whites in the United States, only a handful of studies have directly addressed the question of what predicts such attitudes across racial/ethnic groups. I begin with the studies that most directly address this question for whites and African Americans. Ransford & Miller's (1983) widely cited analysis of gender-role attitudes is an excellent case in point, offering a nuanced exploration of how other factors interact with race to predict gender role orientations. They report several differential predictors that suggest the variation that exists within racial/ethnic groups, as well as the potentially divergent sources of attitudes within those groups. Gender-role traditionalism is positively associated with social class identity among African Americans but not among whites. For African-American men, their interpretation of this pattern suggests "It may be the case that 'middle class' has special meaning for black males. Those who call themselves 'middle class' may be saying more about their idea of 'respectability' and 'steady provider' than about their idea of objective standing" (Ransford & Miller 1983:58). They also report that having a mother who was employed outside the home during one's childhood has a negative effect on white men's gender-role traditionality but has no effect among African-American men. Blee & Tickamyer's (1995) analysis of African-American and white men's gender attitudes also reveals some factors that predict white men's gender-role attitudes but not African-American men's. They report that both education and income are positively associated with white men's level of egalitarianism but are unrelated to African-American men's. They suggest that the presence of such differential predictors may be partially the result of lesser variation in African-American men's role attitudes. But they also suggest it "may reflect a larger problem of the salience of these measures of gender role attitudes for African Americans compared with Whites" (Blee & Tickamyer 1995:29), an important possibility also raised in work reviewing measurement issues related to gender attitudes (Gibbons et al 1997, McHugh & Frieze 1997).

In terms of women's gender-related attitudes, Dugger (1988) offers a compelling exploration of differential predictors of African-American and white women's gender-related attitudes, in which she emphasizes how misleading it is to assume that gendered patterns are the same across racial groups. She argues for the importance of not "treating such phenomena as production and reproduction as though the meaning and impact they have on women's lives is independent of their race (and class) location" (Dugger 1988: 442). Reviewing racial differences in women's productive and reproductive experiences, she hypothesizes that such experiences may be differentially associated with African-American and white women's attitudes. Her analyses support that expectation, with employment outside the home having a greater impact on white women's gender-related attitudes than on African-American women's. She also finds education less consistently associated with African-American women's attitudes than with white women's. This finding is echoed in Ransford & Miller's (1983) analysis, in which they found education a better predictor of white women's role egalitarianism. I too report education as a more consistent predictor of gender-role attitudes among white women than among African-American (Kane 1998), but I find that education is positively associated with support for gender-based affirmative action among African-American women and negatively associated with such support among white men. Fulenwider (1980) addresses differential predictors of women's gender-related attitudes by race as well, concluding that being employed outside the home is positively associated with rejection of gender inequality among white women but has no effects among African-American women. She also finds that income is positively associated with such rejection for white women but negatively associated for African-American women.

Many of these differences in predictors of gender-related attitudes likely reflect differences in the meaning of employment, education, parenthood, marital status, and other social experiences for African Americans versus whites in the United States. Along with such differences in the meaning of gendered social experiences, gender-related attitudes are linked with more general beliefs about social inequality. These links often lead to greater criticism of gender inequality among African Americans, as noted previously. Thus a particularly key differential predictor of beliefs about gender inequality among whites versus African Americans is beliefs about racial inequality. I have discussed a variety of authors who conclude that increased sensitivity to inequality and a commitment to collective action, shaped by experiences of racial inequality, encourage more critical gender-related attitudes among African Americans (Gooley 1989, Hunter & Sellers 1998, Kane 1992, Marshall 1990, Wilcox 1989, Wilcox 1990). In a related finding, Wilcox &

Thomas (1992) document that religiosity, which has been reported as negatively associated with criticism of gender inequality among white women, has no association with various gender-related beliefs among African-American women. They conclude that this pattern flows from the varying meanings religiosity has had for women of different racial groups. For African-American women, a tradition of religiosity has been associated with a sense of racial solidarity and support for social action to reduce racial inequalities, while for white women religiosity has often been associated with more conservative political agendas.

This brief review of what the literature documents in terms of differential predictors of gender-related attitudes among African Americans and whites certainly raises more questions than it answers, and space limitations prevent me from exploring the potential meaning of these various patterns further. But this brief review clearly indicates the importance of recognizing that processes for arriving at particular beliefs about gender inequality vary across racial groups and that heterogeneity within groups should not be ignored.

Little research has addressed the notion of differential predictors of gender attitudes for Hispanic Americans versus African Americans or white Americans. However, in studies focusing only on Hispanics, rather than on inter-ethnic comparisons, some intriguing patterns emerge. These patterns suggest what kinds of predictors have received attention in research on Hispanics and suggest the importance of recognizing heterogeneity within this broadly defined ethnic group as well. First, as noted previously, while Harris & Firestone (1998) found no significant differences in the gender attitudes of Mexican Americans, Cuban Americans, and Puerto Ricans, others have found such variation. Montoya (1996) reports on gender-role attitudes separately for each of these three major subgroups that are often collapsed into the Hispanic label. She finds that Cuban Americans are substantially more traditional in such attitudes than are Mexican Americans or Puerto Ricans; as she puts it, her analyses of gender-related attitudes "... cast further doubt on the practice of analyzing Latinos as one group" (Montoya 1996:256). And in studies based on nonprobability samples, a number of authors have emphasized the importance of differentiating these various ethnic origin subgroups (Segura 1991, Strong et al 1994, Williams 1988).

The potential predictors that have garnered the most attention in literature on gender-related beliefs among Hispanic groups have been, as Vazquez-Nuttall et al (1987:411) note in their review of the literature, "(a) the acculturation process resulting from increased exposure to the host culture, in this case the U.S.; (b) increased levels of women's education; and (c) increased participation of Hispanic women in the labor force." A number of studies, mainly either qualitative or quantitative work based on nonprobability samples, have concluded that acculturation, as defined by measures such as number of years in the United States, number of generations in the United States, and/or language spoken at home, is associated with more egalitarian gender attitudes among various Hispanic subgroups (Kranau et al 1982, Leaper & Valin 1996, Vazquez-Nuttall et al 1987). On the other hand, some scholars of gender relations among Latino groups have argued strongly against acculturation approaches (Baca Zinn 1980, Baca Zinn 1982, Segura 1991, Ybarra 1982), noting that such approaches obscure structural factors as predictors of gender-related beliefs. Whether intentionally or not, critics have argued that emphasis on acculturation points to the misleading conclusion that Latino culture is problematic for women and characterized uniformly by male dominance and female passivity, conclusions that some analysts have countered in their more in-depth analyses of qualitative interview data (Baca Zinn 1980, Williams 1988). Wilkie (1993) also argues, in her analysis of white, African-American, and Hispanic men's gender-role attitudes, that structural locations rather than cultural differences explain the variation she finds. Such authors, and others, have noted that the best predictors of gender-related attitudes are not measures of acculturation but instead measures of women's employment status (Baca Zinn 1980, Segura 1991, Ybarra 1982), education (Leaper & Valin 1996), and social class location (Williams 1988). All of these variables suggest the importance of structural locations in shaping gender attitudes, as well as the importance of recognizing heterogeneity within the various subgroups categorized as Hispanic.

CONCLUSIONS

Literature on the gender-related attitudes of African Americans and whites in the United States documents that the intersection of race and gender translates into clear variations by race/ethnicity in such attitudes. This is especially evident in the domains of beliefs about the extent and origins of gender inequality and preferences for social action to achieve greater gender equality, domains in which African Americans clearly express greater criticism of gender inequality than do whites. Variations by race/ethnicity have several important implications for research on gender attitudes. First, analysts of gender-related attitudes need to take race and ethnicity into account, as the character of gender relations varies across racial/ethnic groups and that variation affects gender attitudes. No large-scale study of gender-related attitudes should fail to acknowledge the possibility of racial variations, and more studies should make such variations their central focus. Second, the unique patterns of gendered social arrangements across ethnic groups suggest the possibility that gender attitude questions in general, and perhaps role-related questions in particular, may be understood differently by members of different racial/ethnic groups. This possibility could be pursued more fully in focus group research and qualitative studies, as well as in pre-tests for large-scale surveys. Perhaps some of the conflicting findings in the domain of role-related attitudes reflect differential interpretations of the meaning of various items. Third, the fact that it is in domains other than gender-role attitudes that African-American/white differences in gender-related attitudes become most clear indicates the importance of expanding beyond the current literature's focus on role-related attitudes as the central indicators of gender attitudes. If such an expansion more clearly documents African-Americans' greater awareness and criticism of gender inequality, it may challenge other patterns within the gender-role attitude literature as well. Fourth, analyses of racial variations in gender-related attitudes need to attend to heterogeneity within racial/ethnic groups, exploring factors shaping attitudes within groups rather than only offering comparisons between groups.

Fifth, and finally, there is a serious need for research using probability samples to address the gender-related attitudes of racial/ethnic groups other than African Americans and whites. The literature on the various groups that comprise the Hispanic population of the United States is very limited, and almost no survey evidence is available regarding the gender-related beliefs of Asian Americans and Native Americans. The differences noted between African Americans and whites clearly demonstrate that much can be learned about the intersections of race and gender from analyses of racial variations in gender attitudes. Our understanding of gender relations, and of the gender-related attitudes that contribute to structuring and challenging gender inequality, is incomplete and even misleading without attention paid to all of the major ethnic groups in the United States today.

ACKNOWLEDGMENTS

I am grateful to Karen Bilodeau for bibliographic assistance and to Christine Tronnier for research assistance. This project was partially supported by Bates College, through funding from its Summer Research Apprenticeship Program and the Department of Sociology.

Visit the Annual Reviews home page at www.AnnualReviews.org

LITERATURE CITED

Almquist EM. 1979. Black women and the pursuit of equality. In *Women: A Feminist Perspective*, ed. J Freeman, pp. 430–50. Palo Alto, CA: Mayfield

Amott TL, Matthaei JA. 1991. *Race, Gender, and Work.* Boston: South End

Baca Zinn M. 1980. Employment and education of Mexican-American women: the interplay of modernity and ethnicity of eight families. *Harvard Educ. Rev.* 50:47–62

Baca Zinn M. 1982. Mexican-American women in the social sciences. *Signs: J. Women in Cult. Soc.* 8(2):259–72

Bailey WT, Silver NC, Oliver KA. 1990. Women's rights and roles: attitudes among black and white students. *Psychol. Rep.* 66:1143–6

Bielby DDV, Bielby WT. 1984. Work commitment, sex-role attitudes, and women's employment. *Am. Sociol. Rev.* 49(2):234–47

Blee KM, Tickamyer AR. 1986. Black-White differences in mother-to-daughter transmission of sex-role attitudes. *Sociol. Q.* 28(2):205–22

Blee K, Tickamyer A. 1995. Racial differences in men's attitudes about gender roles. *J. Marriage Fam.* 57:21–30

Burris V. 1983. Who opposed the ERA? An analysis of the social bases of antifeminism. *Soc. Sci. Q.* 64(2):305–17

Cazenave NC. 1983a. 'A woman's place': the attitudes of middle-class black men. *Phylon* 64(1)12–32

Cazenave NA. 1983b. Black male-black female relationships: the perceptions of 155 middle-class black men. *Fam. Relat.* 32(3):341–50

Cazenave NA. 1984. Race, socioeconomic status, and age: the social context of American masculinity. *Sex Roles* 11(7–8):639–56

Cazenave NA, Smith R. 1990. Gender differences in the perception of black male-female relationships and stereotypes. In *Black Families*, ed. HE Cheatham, JB Stewart, pp. 148–70. New Brunswick, NJ: Transaction

Chilman CS. 1993. Hispanic families in the United States. In *Family Ethnicity: Strength in Diversity*, ed. HP McAdoo, pp. 141–163. Newbury Park, CA: Sage

Crovitz E, Steinmann A. 1980. A decade later: black-white attitudes toward women's familial role. *Psychol. Women Q.* 5(2):170–76

Davis AY. 1983. *Women, Race, and Class.* New York: Vintage

Dugger K. 1988. Social location and gender-role attitudes: a comparison of black and white women. *Gender Soc.* 2(4):425–48

Farley R, Allen A. 1987. *The Color Line and the Quality of American Life.* New York: Russell Sage.

French SS, Nock SL. 1981. Social advantage and attitudes toward women's roles. *Sociol. Inq.* 51(1):55–60

Fulenwider CK. 1980. *Feminism in American Politics: A Study of Ideological Influence.* New York: Praeger

Gackenbach J. 1978. The effects of races Sex and career goal differences on sex-role attitudes at home and at work. *J. Vocat. Behav.* 12:93–101

Garcia AM. 1989. The development of Chicana feminist discourse, 1970–1980. *Gender Soc.* 3(2):217–38

Garcia FC. 1996. Ethnicity and politics. *Hisp. J. Behav. Sci.* 18(2):91–103

Gibbons JL, Hamby BA, Dennis WD. 1997. Researching gender-role ideologies internationally and cross-culturally. *Psychol. Women Q.* 21(1):151–70

Gonzalez A. 1982. Sex roles of the traditional Mexican family. *J. Cross-Cult. Psychol.* 13(3):330–9

Goode WJ. 1992. Why men resist? In *Rethinking the Family: Some Feminist Questions*, ed. B Thorne, M Yalom, pp. 287–310. Boston: Northeastern Univ. Press

Gooley R. 1989. The role of black women in social change. *West. J. Black Stud.* 13(4):165–72

Gump JP. 1975. Comparative analysis of black women's and white women's sex-role attitudes. *J. Consult. Clin. Psychol.* 43(6):858–63

Gutman HG. 1976. *The Black Family in Slavery and Freedom.* New York: Vintage

Harris RJ, Firestone JM. 1998. Changes in predictors of gender role ideologies among women: a multivariate analysis. *Sex Roles* 38(3–4):239–52

Hatchett S, Quick A. 1983. Correlates of sex role attitudes among black men and women: data from a national survey of black Americans. *Inst. Urban Aff. Res.* 9(2):1–11

Hershey M. 1978. Racial differences in sex-role identities and sex stereotyping: evidence against a common assumption. *Soc. Sci. Q.* 58(4):583–96

Hill RB. 1971. *The Strengths of Black Families.* New York: Emerson Hall

Hill Collins P. 1991. *Black Feminist Thought.* New York: Routledge

Huber J, Rexroat C, Spitze G. 1978. A crucible of opinion on women's status: ERA in Illinois. *Soc. Forces* 57(2):549–65

Hunter A, Davis J. 1992. Constructing gender: an exploration of Afro-American men's conceptualization of manhood. *Gender Soc.* 6(3):464–79

Hunter A, Sellers SL. 1998. Feminist attitudes among African American women and men. *Gender Soc.* 12(1):81–99

Jones JP, Jacklin CN. 1988. Changes in sexist attitudes toward women during introductory women's and men's studies courses. *Sex Roles* 28:611–22

Kane EW. 1992. Race, gender, and attitudes

toward gender stratification. *Soc. Psychol. Q.* 55(3):311–20

Kane EW. 1998. *Race, gender, education and beliefs about social inequality.* Presented at Annu. Meet. Am. Sociol. Assoc., 93rd, San Francisco

King MC. 1975. Oppression and power: the unique status of black women in the American political system. *Soc. Sci. Q.* 56:116–28

Kluegel JR, Smith ER. 1986. *Beliefs About Inequality: Americans' Views of What Is and What Ought to Be.* New York: Aldine

Kranau EJ, Green V, Weber GV. 1982. Acculturation and the Hispanic woman: attitudes toward women, sex-role attribution, sex-roles behavior, and demographics. *Hisp. J. Behav. Sci.* 4:21–40

Leaper C, Valin D. 1996. Predictors of Mexican American mothers' and fathers' attitudes toward gender equality. *Hisp. J. Behav. Sci.* 18(3):343–55

Lottes IL, Kuriloff PJ. 1992. The effects of gender, race, religion and political orientation on the sex role attitudes of college freshman. *Adolescence* 27:675–88

Lyson TA. 1986. Race and sex differences in sex role attitudes of southern college students. *Psychol. Women Q.* 10(4):421–7

Marshall SE. 1990. Equity issues and black-white differences in women's ERA support. *Soc. Sci. Q.* 71(2):299–314

Mason KO, Bumpass LL. 1975. U.S. women's sex-role ideology, 1970. *Am. J. Sociol.* 80(5):1212–19

McHugh MC, Frieze IH. 1997. The measurement of gender role attitudes: a review and commentary. *Psychol. Women Q.* 21(1):1–16

Montoya LJ. 1996. Latino gender difference in public opinion. *Hisp. J. Behav. Sci.* 18(2):255–76

Mori L, Bernat JA, Glenn PA, Selle LL, Zarate MG. 1995. Attitudes toward rape: gender and ethnic differences across Asian and caucasian college students. *Sex Roles* 32(7–8):457–67

Murrell AJ, Frieze IH, Frost JL. 1991. Aspiring to careers in male- and female-dominated professions: a study of black and white college women. *Psychol. Women Q.* 15(1):103–26

O'Hare WP, Pollard KM, Mann TL, Kent MM. 1991. African-Americans in the 1990s. *Pop. Bull.* 46(1)

Ransford HE, Miller J. 1983. Race, sex and feminist outlooks. *Am. Sociol. Rev.* 48(1):46–59

Rao VVP, Rao VN. 1985. Sex-role attitudes: a comparison of sex-race groups. *Sex Roles* 12(9–10):939–53

Rice TW, Coates DL. 1995. Gender role attitudes in the southern United States. *Gender Soc.* 9(6):744–56

Rinehart ST. 1992. *Gender Consciousness and Politics.* New York: Routledge

Romero GJ, Garza RT. 1986. Attributions for the occupational success/failure of ethnic minority and non–minority women. *Sex Roles* 14(7–8):445–52

Rosen R. 1978. Sex role attitudes of black and white women. *Int. J. Women's Stud.* 1(6):544–54

Rowan GT, Pernell EJ, Akers TA. 1996. Gender role socialization in African American men: a conceptual framework. *J. Afr. Am. Men* 1(4):3–22

Segura DA. 1991. Ambivalence or continuity?: motherhood and employment among Chicanas and Mexican immigrant women workers. *Aztlan* 20(1–2):119–50

Sigelman L, Welch S. 1984. Race, gender, and opinion toward black and female presidential candidates. *Public Opin. Q.* 48(2):467–75

Sorenson A, McLanahan S. 1987. Married women's economic dependency, 1940–1980. *Am. J. Sociol.* 93:659–87

Spitze G, Huber J. 1982. Effects of anticipated consequences on ERA opinion. *Soc. Sci. Q.* 63(2):323–31

Stacy J, Thorne B. 1985. The missing feminist revolution in sociology. *Soc. Probl.* 32:301–316

Strong WF, McQuillen JS, Hughey JD. 1994. En El Laberinto De Machismo. *The Howard J. Comun.* 5(1–2):18–35

Therborn G. 1980. *The Ideology of Power and the Power of Ideology*. London: Verso

Vasquez-Nuttall E, Romero-Garcia I, De Leon B. 1987. Sex roles and perceptions of femininity and masculinity of Hispanic women: a review of the literature. *Psychol. Women Q.* 11(4):409–25

Wade BH. 1993. The gender role and contraceptive attitudes of young men: implications for future African American families. *Urban League Rev.* 16(2):57–65

Welch S, Sigelman L. 1989. A black gender gap? *Soc. Sci. Q.* 70(1):120–33

Welch S, Sigelman L. 1992. A gender gap among Hispanics? A comparison with blacks and anglos. *West. Polit. Q.* 45:181–99

Wilcox C. 1989. Race, gender role attitudes and support for feminism. *West. Polit. Q.* 43: 113–21

Wilcox C. 1990. Black women and feminism. *Women & Polit.* 10(3):65–84.

Wilcox C. 1992. Race, gender, and support for women in the military. *Soc. Sci. Q.* 73(2):310–23

Wilcox C, Thomas S. 1992. Religion and feminist attitudes among African-American women: a view from the nation's Capitol. *Women & Polit.* 12(2):19–40

Wilkie J. 1993. Changes in U.S. men's attitudes toward the family provider role, 1972–1989. *Gender Soc.* 7(2):261–79

Williams N. 1988. Role making among married Mexican American women: issues of class and ethnicity. *J. Appl. Behav. Sci.* 24(2):203–17

Ybarra L. 1982. When wives work: the impact on the Chicano family. *J. Marriage Fam.* 44(1):169–78

Annu. Rev. Sociol. 2000. 26:441–62

MULTILEVEL MODELING FOR BINARY DATA

Guang Guo
Department of Sociology, University of North Carolina, Chapel Hill,
North Carolina 27599; e-mail: guang_guo@unc.edu

Hongxin Zhao
Center for Children and Families, Teachers College, Columbia University,
New York, NY 10027

Key Words   hierarchical models, contextual analysis, logistic regression, logit, generalized linear mixed models

■ **Abstract**   We review some of the work of the past ten years that applied the multi-level logit model. We attempt to provide a brief description of the hypothesis tested, the hierarchical data structure analyzed, and the multilevel data source for each piece of work we have reviewed. We have also reviewed the technical literature and worked out two examples on multilevel models for binary outcomes. The review and examples serve two purposes: First, they are designed to assist in all aspects of working with multilevel models for binary outcomes, including model conceptualization, model description for a research report, understanding of the structure of required multilevel data, estimation of the model via a generally available statistical package, and interpretation of the results. Second, our examples contribute to the evaluation of the approximation procedures for binary multilevel models that have been implemented for general public use.

INTRODUCTION

This article reviews multilevel models for binary outcome variables and their sociological applications. The emphasis of the review is on the practical usage of the models. The review of the applications draws from articles published in *American Sociological Review, American Journal of Sociology*, and *Social Forces* over the past ten years. See DiPrete & Forristal (1994) for an earlier review of multilevel analysis.

The interest in multilevel models for binary data is a natural development of two traditions in sociological analysis. First, sociologists, perhaps more than any other social scientists, are interested in explaining and predicting phenomena that can be characterized by a binary variable. Such phenomena may be the occurrence of discrete events such as dropping out of high school, getting a four-year college education, marrying, giving birth, divorcing, using narcotic drugs, having a business go bankrupt, adopting a new technology, on implementing a new public policy. Other examples include whether to vote for a Republican or Democratic candidate and whether to say yes or no to an opinion poll. We have counted 85 articles published in *Social Forces*, 61 in *American Sociological Review*, and 39 in *American Journal of Sociology* during 1990 and 1999, which employed standard binary regression techniques in their analysis. Regression models for binary data including logistic regression and probit regression have long been sociologists' standard analytical tools.

The second tradition that prompted an interest in multilevel models is the practice of examining hierarchical social structure. Multilevel models have a natural appeal to sociologists because social structure is often hierarchical. Examples for multilevel social structure are plentiful. In schools, students (level 1) are nested in classes (level 2), and classes are nested in schools (level 3). Individuals are nested in families, and families are nested in communities or neighborhoods. In for-profit and non-profit organizations, employees are the first level and the organization the second. Even prior to the development of the formal statistical methodology for multilevel models, sociologists were engaged in multilevel or contextual analysis. Blalock (1984) reviewed and discussed various theoretical and methodological issues in the literature on multilevel analysis before the statistical models were developed.

Mason et al (1983) were among the first to develop the concepts and methodology for analyzing multilevel data. Further methodological and substantive work by Bryk & Raudenbush (1992) and Goldstein (1987, 1995) has popularized the multilevel models for linear data. It is no surprise that sociologists of education were among the first to apply the methodology to the study of school effects. Using data from the High School and Beyond Study, Gamoran (1992) examined how the characteristics of high school tracking such as selectivity, electivity, inclusiveness, and scope affect students' educational achievement. Roscigno (1998) estimated linear multilevel models of math and reading achievement on race, family/peer influences, class characteristics, and racial composition of school by employing data from the restricted-use National Educational Longitudinal Survey (NELS) and the Common Core of Data. Another common design of multilevel analysis treats metropolitan areas in the United States defined by the Bureau of the Census as level-2 units and individuals as level-1 units. Combining data from the 1% and 5% 1990 Public Use Microdata Samples (PUMS) data from 261 metropolitan areas, Cotter et al (1997) investigated the impact of occupational integration by gender at the metropolitan level on gender earnings equality. Using the same data sources, Cohen (1998) estimated the effects of metropolitan-area black population proportions on earnings inequality between blacks and whites and between men and women. In their longitudinal Beginning School Study in Baltimore, Entwisle et al (1994) examined neighborhood environment as a possible cause of gender gap in math. Xie & Hannum (1996) studied the regional variation in earnings inequality in contemporary urban China, using data at household and city levels.

Considering individuals or some other observations as level-2 units and repeated measures of these level-2 units as level-1 units, we have another application of multilevel linear models: the growth curve model. This model has been used to examine the trajectory of self-reported crime over time among adolescents (Lauritsen 1998), the timing of the influences of poverty on children's cognitive ability and achievement (Guo 1998), the long-term effects of parental divorce on individuals' mental health from age 7 to age 33 (Cherlin et al 1998), and the Kuznets curve or the growth curve of income inequality as measured by the Gini coefficient among US counties from 1970 to 1990 (Nielsen & Alderson 1997).

Social scientists' interest in binary outcome variables and hierarchical social structure made the development of multilevel models for binary data a near certainty. Earlier methodological work on multilevel logit models includes Wong & Mason (1985), Anderson & Aitkin (1985), and Goldstein (1991). Using data from fifteen World Fertility Survey (WFS) countries, Entwisle et al (1986) studied contraceptive behavior of couples as a function of socioeconomic origins at the individual level, of the gross national product per capita (GNP), and of the family planning effort at the country level. Crane (1991) tested the epidemic theory of ghetto and neighborhood effects on dropping out and teenage childbearing, drawing data from the 1979 PUMS. Although Crane's analysis does not fall within formal multilevel modeling, his insights into the functional relationship between neighborhood quality and social problems are valuable to multilevel modelers working on the same topic.

More recent years saw an increased number of applications of multilevel models for binary data. Rountree & Land (1996) reported distinctive differences between a general perceived risk of crime and a burglary-specific fear. They based their analysis on a victimization survey collected in Seattle, Washington, in 1990. In the dataset, more than 5000 individuals are clustered into about 300 city-blocks, which are in turn clustered into about 100 census tracts. In an effort to explain the "southern migrant advantage" in family stability, which refers to more stability among black southern families that migrated to northern cities, Tolnay & Crowder (1999) estimated the effects of metropolitan-level distress on urban black family patterns and explored whether group differences in exposure to these contextual conditions can explain the greater stability of migrant families. Their data are from the 1970 Integrated Public Use Microdata Series and 1970 Summary Statistic File Fourth Count. Multilevel data have also been collected in other countries. Using data from Norway, Kalleberg & Mastekaasa (1998) documented and sought to explain the relationships between an organization's size and an individual's interorganizational mobility (i.e., quits and layoffs). Analyzing data collected by the Chinese Academy of Preventive Medicine at the household and village levels, Nee (1996) tested the hypothesis that the shift to a market economy in China caused a redistribution of economic gains among those with political power and those who produce.

WHY MULTILEVEL MODELS?

The multilevel models we review in this article are statistical multilevel models, which allow not only independent variables at any level of a hierarchical structure, but also at least one random effect above level one. In a particular analysis, multilevel modeling offers a number of the following advantages. Some influential sociological work was conceptualized as multilevel analysis but analyzed by traditional models (Hogan & Kitagawa 1985, Sampson 1991, Billy & Moore 1992, Brooks-Gunn et al 1993). Traditional linear or nonlinear models, however, do not enjoy all the advantages we describe.

First, a multilevel model provides a convenient framework for studying multilevel data. Such a framework encourages a systematic analysis of how covariates measured at various levels of a hierarchical structure affect the outcome variable and how the interactions among covariates measured at different levels affect the outcome variable. One of the frequently examined cross-level interaction effects is how the macro context affects the impact of a covariate at the micro level. For example, Entwisle et al (1986) tested the idea that the strength of the effect of maternal education on fertility depends on the characteristics of a country such as gross national product (GNP) and the intensity of family planning efforts.

Second, multilevel modeling corrects for the biases in parameter estimates resulting from clustering. In contrast to the popular belief, ignoring multilevel structure can result in biases in parameter estimates as well as biases in their standard errors. The more highly correlated the observations are within clusters, the more likely that ignoring clustering would result in biases in parameter estimates.

Third, multilevel modeling provides correct standard errors and thus correct confidence intervals and significance tests. When observations are clustered into higher-level units, the observations are no longer independent. Independence is one of the most basic assumptions underlying traditional linear and binary regression models. When the clustering structure in the data is ignored and the independence assumption is violated, the traditional linear and binary models tend to underestimate the standard errors. The following is an intuitive argument for this statement. The observations in the same cluster tend to be more similar in their outcome measures if clustering matters regarding the outcome measures. Similarity within a cluster implies that we can, to some extent, predict the outcome of an observation if we know the outcome of another observation in the same cluster. This suggests that not every observation provides an independent piece of information and that the total amount of information contained in a sample with clustering is less than that in a sample without clustering.

The estimation of standard errors is not merely a technical issue. The size of a standard error can uphold or overturn an important conclusion. Using linear regression techniques and ignoring the fact that the students are grouped into teachers and classes, Bennett (1976) showed that in Great Britain elementary school students benefitted more from a formal style of teaching. The results were widely known and became quite influential until Aitkin et al (1981) demonstrated that, once the grouping of the students is taken into consideration in a multilevel model, the results obtained by Bennett concerning teaching styles were no longer statistically significant.

When all variations at levels higher than one are captured by observed variables, multilevel data can be analyzed by traditional linear or nonlinear models. In such a case, conditional on the observed variables, the observations in the same cluster are no longer dependent, and the standard errors obtained by traditional models are correct.

Fourth, estimates of the variances and covariances of random effects at various levels enable investigators to decompose the total variance in the outcome variable into portions associated with each level. Using the 1987 National Survey of Maternal and Child Health in Guatemala, Pebley et al (1996) modeled a binary variable of whether the child has received a complete set of immunizations as a function of observed variables at the individual, family, and community levels and unobserved variables at the family and community levels. After controlling for observed variables, they showed that the variance due to families is about five times larger than that due to communities.

THE MULTILEVEL LINEAR MODEL

To provide a familiar starting point, we begin with a review of the multilevel linear model. Our review focuses on a few specific multilevel models that sociologists are likely to estimate. For a description of the multilevel linear model in its most general form, see Mason et al (1983), Goldstein (1987, 1995), and Bryk & Raudenbush (1992). We first consider a simple two-level model with a single explanatory variable,

$$y_{ij} = \beta_0 + \beta_1 x_{ij} + u_j + e_{ij}, \tag{1}$$

where y_{ij} is the outcome variable for the ith unit at level one and the jth unit at level two, β_0 is the intercept, x_{ij} is the explanatory variable, β_1 is its effect, u_j is a random effect accounting for the random variation at level two, and e_{ij} is the level-one random effect. The parameters for the random effects are $E[u_j] = E[e_{ij}] = 0$, $var(u_j) = \sigma_u^2$, $var(e_{ij}) = \sigma_e^2$, $cov(u_j, e_{ij}) = 0$, and $cov(u_j, u_{j'}) = 0$ for $j \neq j'$. The within-cluster or intraclass correlation after controlling for the explanatory variable can be obtained from $\rho = \sigma_u^2/(\sigma_u^2 + \sigma_e^2)$. Equation (1) can also be considered as a random effect model for panel data or a growth curve model. In both cases, i and j would index time points and individuals, respectively, and x_{ij} would be a time-varying covariate. A linear growth model requires that a linear term be added to Equation (1) and a quadratic growth model requires an additional quadratic term.

We next extend the simple two-level model to a three-level model with random coefficients,

$$y_{ijk} = \beta_0 + \beta_1 x_{ijk} + u_{1jk} x_{ijk} + v_{0k} + u_{0jk} + e_{0ijk}, \tag{2}$$

where k indexes level 3, v_{0k} and u_{0jk} are the random intercepts for level three and level two, respectively, x_{ijk} is an observed explanatory variable at level one, and u_{1jk} is x_{ijk}'s random effect at level two. Other parameters of the model include $E[v_{0k}] = E[u_{0jk}] = E[e_{0ijk}] = 0$, $var(v_{0k}) = \sigma_{v0}^2$, $var(u_{0jk}) = \sigma_{u0}^2$,

$var(u_{1jk}) = \sigma_{u1}^2$, $var(e_{0ijk}) = \sigma_{e0}^2$, and $cov(u_{0jk}, u_{1jk}) = \sigma_{u01}$. The model assumes again that the random effects across different levels and the random effects across different clusters in the same level are uncorrelated. More complex models can be constructed by adding more observed variables to Equation (2) and allowing cross-level interactions.

The multilevel models have not only the familiar regression parameters β_0 and β_1 but also the unknown random parameters u_{0jk}, u_{1jk}, and v_{0k}. Viewing the multilevel model as a special case of the mixed model, statisticians mostly estimate the model parameters via the generalized least squares (GLS), which minimizes $(y - X\beta)' V^{-1}(y - X\beta)$. Because of the unknown random parameters in V, however, either maximum likelihood or restricted maximum likelihood is generally used first to estimate the variances and covariances of u and e under the assumption that they are normally distributed (Thompson 1971, Harville 1977, Laird & Ware 1982). Mason et al (1983), Goldstein (1986), Raudenbush & Bryk (1986), and Longford (1987) have also studied the estimation of the multilevel linear models.

MULTILEVEL MODELS FOR BINARY DATA

We first consider a two-level model for binary outcomes with a single explanatory variable. Conceptually, this model is equivalent to model (1) except for the outcome variable. Suppose we have data consisting of students (level one) grouped into schools (level two). We observe y_{ij}, a binary response for student i in school j and x_{ij}, an explanatory variable at the student level. We define the probability of the response equal to one as $p_{ij} = Pr(y_{ij} = 1)$ and let p_{ij} be modeled using a logit link function. The standard assumption is that y_{ij} has a Bernoulli distribution. Then the two-level model can be written as

$$\log[p_{ij}/(1 - p_{ij})] = \beta_0 + \beta_1 x_{ij} + u_j \quad (combined\ model) \qquad (3)$$

where u_j is the random effect at level two. Without u_j, (3) would be a standard logistic regression model. Conditional on u_j, y_{ij}s are assumed to be independent. As in the case of multilevel linear models, u_j is assumed to be normally distributed, with the expected value 0 and the variance σ_u^2. Model (3) is often described alternatively in the literature on multilevel models by Equations (4)

$$\log[p_{ij}/(1 - p_{ij})] = \beta_{0j} + \beta_1 x_{ij} \quad (level\ 1\ model) \qquad (4)$$

and (5)

$$\beta_{0j} = \beta_0 + u_j \quad (level\ 2\ model). \qquad (5)$$

Relative to Equations (4) and (5), Equation (3) is the so-called combined model.

The multilevel model for binary outcomes can also be derived through a latent variable conceptualization. We assume that there exists a latent continuous variable y_{ij}^* underlying y_{ij}. We observe only our binary response variable y_{ij} directly, but not y_{ij}^*. We know, however, $y_{ij}^* > 0$ if $y_{ij} = 1$ and $y_{ij}^* \leq 0$ if $y_{ij} = 1$. A multilevel model for y_{ij}^* equivalent to (3) can be written as

$$y_{ij}^* = \beta_0 + \beta_1 x_{ij} + u_j + e_{ij}. \tag{6}$$

Conditional on the random effect u_j at level two, either a logit multilevel model such as (3) or a probit multilevel model can be derived from (6) depending on whether we assume that e_{ij} in (6) has a standard logistic distribution or a normal distribution. This conceptualization illustrates the close connections between the multilevel models for linear data and those for binary data. Later in this paper, we use this result to calculate intra-cluster correlations for binary data.

Conditional on u_j or assuming that u_j were observed, the conditional density function for cluster j for model (3) is identical to that for the logistic regression

$$f(\mathbf{y}_j \mid \mathbf{x}_j, u_j) = \prod_{i=1}^{n_j} \frac{\exp[y_{ij}(\beta_0 + \beta_1 x_{ij} + u_j)]}{1 + \exp(\beta_0 + \beta_1 x_{ij} + u_j)}, \tag{7}$$

where $\mathbf{y}_j$ and $\mathbf{x}_j$, respectively, denote the responses and the explanatory variables in cluster j. The standard strategy for estimating the model parameters in the literature is to assume that u_j, is normally distributed and to integrate out the unobserved random effect u_j,

$$f(\mathbf{y}_j \mid \mathbf{x}_j) = \int f(\mathbf{y}_j \mid \mathbf{x}_j, u_j) g(u_j) du_j, \tag{8}$$

where $g(.)$ represents the normal density function. The resulting unconditional density $f(\mathbf{y}_j \mid \mathbf{x}_j)$, however, does not have a closed expression. Maximum likelihood estimation has to resort to approximation procedures such as numerical integration. Anderson & Aitkin (1985) estimated a model similar to (3) via the EM algorithm, and the solution still requires numerical integration.

Model 3 is almost the simplest possible multilevel model for binary data. Greater challenges arise in the estimation of more general models with multiple random effects. Equation (9) describes a three-level model with a single explanatory variable that has both a fixed effect and a random effect,

$$\log[p_{ijk}/(1-p_{ijk})] = \beta_0 + \beta_1 x_{ijk} + u_{1jk} x_{ijk} + v_{0k} + u_{0jk} \quad (combined\ model), \tag{9}$$

where i, j, and k index, respectively, levels 1, 2, and 3, v_{0k} and u_{0jk} are the random intercepts for level 3 and level 2, respectively, and u_{1jk} is the random coefficient for the explanatory variable x_{ijk}. To fix the idea, we could let levels 1, 2, and 3 represent students, classes, and schools. Again, Equation (9) is the combined model.

Alternatively, model (9) can be described by the multiple equation system

$$
\begin{aligned}
\log[p_{ij}/(1 - p_{ij})] &= \beta_{0jk} + \beta_{1j}x_{ij} \quad \textit{(level 1 model)} \\
\beta_{0jk} &= \beta_{0k} + u_{0jk} \quad \textit{(level 2 model)} \\
\beta_{1j} &= \beta_1 + u_{1j} \quad \textit{(level 2 model)} \\
\beta_{0k} &= \beta_0 + v_{0k} \quad \textit{(level 3 model)}.
\end{aligned}
\tag{10}
$$

The conditional density for (9) is still identical to that for the logistic regression; but with three random effects in the model, the unconditional density is a high-dimensional integral. Numerical integration over the high-dimensional integral is the most straightforward solution. As computing gets less and less expensive, numerical integration has become feasible. Traditionally, however, software packages for multilevel models for binary data tend to use other approximate methods.

Social scientists usually do not need to be concerned with the estimation method of a statistical model because the estimation procedures of most of the statistical models (e.g., linear regression, logit models, and log-linear models) routinely used are well established. But this is not true for multilevel models for binary data. Marginal quasi-likelihood or MQL (Goldstein 1991, Goldstein & Rasbash 1996) and penalized quasi-likelihood or PQL (Breslow & Clayton 1993) are the two prevailing approximation procedures. Both MQL and PQL rely on the Taylor expansion to achieve the approximation. Rodriguez & Goldman (1997) compared four approximation estimation procedures (first-order MQL, second-order MQL, first-order PQL, and second-order PQL) with the maximum likelihood achieved through high-dimensional numerical integration and the method of Gibbs sampling. The second-order MQL and PQL are expected to yield more accurate estimates than the first-order ones because they use some of the second-order terms in the Taylor expansion. The maximum likelihood method based on numerical integration and Gibbs sampling are treated as standards.

Using a sample collected in Guatemala in 1987, Rodriguez & Goldman (1997) estimated a three-level model of complete immunization among children receiving any immunization. Their sample consists of 2159 children from 1595 families in 161 communities. They reported large differences among the estimates from different estimation methods. For instance, the estimated variances of the random effect at the family level are respectively .40, .52, .53, 3.06, 5.38, and 6.76 for MQL-1, MQL-2, PQL-1, PQL-2, ML, and Gibbs sampling. The differences among the estimated fixed effects are also large. The odds ratios of receiving a complete set of immunization among children whose fathers have had a primary education to those whose fathers have had no education are, respectively, 1.34, 1.32, 1.40, 1.26, 1.55, 1.72, and 1.80 for MQL-1, MQL-2, PQL-1, PQL-2, ML, and Gibbs sampling. The same article reported much larger differences across different estimation procedures from an analysis that examined the usage of modern prenatal care. The conclusion is that all approximation methods (MQL-1, MQL-2, PQL-1, and PQL-2) underestimate the random as well as fixed effects and that the underestimations of MQL-1, MQL-2, and PQL-1 are severe.

The evaluation clearly demonstrates that the parameters of the multilevel model for binary data can be severely downwardly biased. Social scientists who work with the models must be aware of the possibility that the estimates they are obtaining from the commercial packages such as HLM and MLn can be seriously inaccurate. Unfortunately, we usually do not know the extent of the biases or even whether the biases are substantively important in a particular analysis. For any particular analysis, the estimates from PQL-2 or even PQL-1 can be accurate enough. The huge differences across different estimation procedures reported by Rodriguez & Goldman are likely to be the exception rather than the rule in typical social science work. In their analysis on the use of prenatal care, the variance of the unobserved family effect estimated by PQL-2 (7.56) is about five time as large as that estimated by PQL-1 (1.56), and the same variance estimated by the Gibbs sampling (112.3) is about 72 times as large as that estimated by PQL-1. In the same analysis, the odds ratio by PQL-2 (6.89) of those whose mothers have had at least a secondary education to those whose mothers have had no education is about 2.6 times as large as that by PQL-1 (2.66) and the same odds ratio by the Gibbs sampling (424) is about 160 times as large as that by PQL-1.

The huge differences across different estimation methods in Rodriguez & Goldman's analysis could be related to two factors. First, the approximation procedures tend not to work well when the observations in a cluster are highly correlated. In the analysis on use of prenatal care, the intrafamily correlation estimated by the Gibbs sampling is 0.98 after controlling for observed variables. This is extremely high. Recall that the correlation between identical twins with respect to IQ is typically estimated to be between 0.65 and 0.75.

Second, in both analyses, a large proportion of family clusters contains one observation. The proportions of single-observation clusters in the two analyses are at least 24% and 32%, respectively. In both analyses, the sizes of family clusters are small, averaging 1.35 for one analysis and 1.60 for the other.

Another way of understanding Rodriguez & Goldman's work is to compare their results with those from previous work on random effects models for multivariate event history data (Guo & Rodriguez 1992, Guo & Grummer-Strawn 1993) and count data (Guo 1996). These random effects models are random-intercept-only or variance-component two-level multilevel models for event history data and count data; but unlike the multilevel models for binary data, the likelihood function for these models has a closed expression. Therefore, no approximation procedure is needed for estimating these models. The applications of these two models generally reported small-to-moderate variances of random effects and small-to-moderate changes between the fixed effects estimated by conventional models and those estimated by multilevel models. The size of the random effects and the changes in the fixed effects are considerably larger (but never approach the magnitudes reported by Rodriguez & Goldman) when the observations in a cluster are highly correlated (twins) than when the observations in a cluster are moderately correlated (siblings).

To further evaluate the approximate estimation procedures, we have estimated a number of two-level logit models using individual/community data from the National Longitudinal Study of Adolescent Health (called Add Health) (Bearman et al 1997) and the generally available estimation procedures. The results from PQL-1 differ very little from those from PQL-2.

THE EXAMPLES

The purpose of the examples is twofold: to illustrate the multilevel models for binary data and to compare a variety of estimation procedures that are generally available to the research community. Add Health is a school-based study of the health-related behaviors of adolescents in grades 7–12 in the United States. Our sample was drawn from the first wave of the in-home survey of the Add Health study. The interviews were carried out from April through December of 1995. Adolescents and block groups are level-1 and level-2 units, respectively. The block group is the smallest geographic area for which the Census Bureau publishes sample data. In 1990, block groups averaged 452 housing units or 1100 individuals. In comparison, the more familiar census tract usually contains between 2500 and 8000 individuals. The block group variables in Add Health have been created from the Census of Population and Housing, 1990.

In this article, we present two examples. The outcome variable for the first example is grade retention coded as 1 if the individual has ever repeated a grade and 0 otherwise. After excluding observations whose information is missing on any of the variables used in the analysis, the working sample consists of 13,900 adolescents. Of the 13,900 adolescents, 2,916 or 21% had ever repeated a grade by the time of the in-home survey in 1995. In the sample, each block group contains about 154 adolescents on average, with 89% of the block groups containing at least 45 adolescents and with no census block containing fewer than 2 adolescents. The basic input dataset for multilevel analysis looks almost identical to the standard input dataset. The only difference is that the multilevel dataset has an ID for block group. This is in addition to the individual ID. This block group ID tells the computer the community membership of each individual.

We first estimated an intercept-only model that predicts the probability of having ever repeated a grade. The multilevel model is described by Equation (11). Readers interested in a multiple-equation description of the model should refer to Equations (3), (4), and (5). The Appendix gives the SAS and MLn codes for the model. See Littell et al (1996: Ch. 11) for more examples on the SAS codes. The estimates of

$$\log[p_{ij}/(1 - p_{ij})] = \beta_0 + u_j \tag{11}$$

parameters and standard errors are presented in Table 1. The ML estimate from the standard logit model of the ratio of repeaters to nonrepeaters is $\exp(-1.326) = .265$, which is the same as the sample ratio of 2,916 repeaters to 10,984 nonrepeaters. In comparison, the same ratio is estimated to be $\exp(-1.476) = .228$ from the multilevel model by PQL-2. Failing to take into account the clustering within block groups, the standard logit model has overestimated the ratio by about 15%. The parameters under *random effect* in Table 1 are the estimated variances of the random intercepts. To understand the random effect, one can imagine a unique effect for each block group in addition to the fixed intercept of -1.476, which is the average of all block groups. The addition of the block-group specific effects makes

TABLE 1   Parameters and standard errors of an intercept-only logit model and an intercept-only multilevel model predicting the probability of ever repeating a grade: Add Health

	Logit		Multilevel models			
	SAS		**MLn**			
	Logit	**GLIM-MIX**	**MQL-1**	**MQL-2**	**PQL-1**	**PQL-2**
Fixed effect						
Intercept	-1.326	-1.457	-1.354	-1.471	-1.457	-1.476
	(.021)	(.076)	(.070)	(.075)	(.076)	(.077)
Random effect						
Intercept		.428	.359	.389	.426	.439
		(.078)	(.063)	(.073)	(.075)	(.077)
Intra-block correlation (ρ)		.11	.10	.11	.11	.12
Deviance		13430.6				
Extradispersion		.976				
$-2\log L$	14280.0					
N	13,900	13,900	13,900	13,900	13,900	13,900

the model more accurate than the fixed intercept only model. In a random effect model, the block-group specific effects are assumed to be distributed normally for the purpose of estimation. The estimate of the random effect does increase as we go from MQL-1 to MQL-2, to PQL-1, and to PQL-2; but the increases are much smaller than those Rodriguez & Goldman (1997) reported, and the increases between PQL-1 and PQL-2 are minuscule.

The estimate from the SAS' GLIMMIX macro is particularly close to, but not the same as, the estimate from MLn's PQL-1. The GLIMMIX macro is based on Wolfinger & O'Connell's (1993) pseudo-likelihood (PL), which is the same as Breslow & Clayton's (1993) PQL-1 except that PL explicitly estimates the extra-dispersion parameter ϕ. PQL-1 sets ϕ to one. In this sense, PL is a slight generalization of PQL-1. By adding an additional parameter ϕ in the conditional variance $\phi[\pi_{ij}(1 - \pi_{ij})]/n_{ij}$, the GLIMMIX macro or PL takes into consideration both underdispersion when ϕ is substantially smaller than 1, and overdispersion when ϕ is substantially greater than 1. Underdispersion or overdispersion can lead to unreliable estimates of standard errors. In Table 1, the extradispersion parameter is estimated to be 0.976, and we conclude that there is no evidence for extradispersion.

The intra-block-group correlations are estimated by $\rho = \sigma_u^2/(\sigma_u^2 + \sigma_e^2)$, where $\sigma_e^2 = \pi^2/3$ is the variance of the standard logistic distribution (Table 1). These correlations are computed on the logit scale, that is, the correlation is between y_{ij}^* and $y_{i'j}^*$, where $i \neq i'$ and y_{ij}^* and $y_{i'j}^*$ are the unobserved latent variables described earlier in the latent variable formation of the multilevel model for binary data. According to the estimate from PQL-2 in Table 1, the intra-block-group correlation in terms of the latent variable representing grade retention is 0.12.

Table 2 presents parameters and standard errors from a logit model predicting the probability of having repeated a grade and its equivalent multilevel model. We describe the multilevel model as follows:

$$\log[p_{ij}/(1 - p_{ij})] = \beta_0 + \beta_1\ age_{ij} + \beta_2 female_{ij} + \beta_3\ black_{ij}$$
$$+ \beta_4\ income_{ij} + \beta_5\ education_{ij} + \beta_6\ below15k_j$$
$$+ u_{1j}\ income_{ij} + u_{2j}below15k_j + u_{0j}. \qquad (12)$$

See Appendix for the SAS and MLn programs for the model. We have included six observed covariates in the model with five at the individual level and one at the block group level. The observed covariate, gender, is coded as 1 if the adolescent is female and 0 if the individual is male. Ethnicity is coded as 1 if the adolescent is African American and 0 otherwise. Mother's education is length of schooling in years. Family income is in thousands of US dollars. Proportion <$15,000 is the proportion of the households in a block group with an annual income of less than $15,000. Age is in years measured at the time of the survey.

The multilevel model has one random intercept and two random coefficients, with one for family income and the other for proportion below $15,000. We were unsuccessful in obtaining estimates through MLn's MQL-2 and PQL-2 for this model. Neither converged after more than 2,000 iterations. We came across the same problems when estimating a similar model using college plan as the outcome variable. The second-order approximation procedures seem to have difficulty converging when estimating multiple random coefficients.

The differences in parameter estimates between MQL-1 and PQL-1 appear rather small. The estimates from GLIMMIX are again very similar to those from MLn's PQL-1 except for the random coefficient for proportion <$15,000. The estimates from the standard logit model differ moderately from those from the multilevel models. The standard logit model has overestimated the effects of African American and proportion <$15,000 and underestimated the effect of age. The standard logit model has also underestimated the standard error of the effect of proportion <$15,000.

We now interpret the estimates from GLIMMIX. The results from GLIMMIX have been obtained after taking into account unobserved block-group specific random effects. The parameters of observed variables can be interpreted much the same way as those from the standard logit model. Thus, everything else being equal, female adolescents are about $100\% - \exp(-.661)*100 = 48.4\%$ less likely to have repeated a grade than male adolescents. Similarly, the likelihood of having repeated a grade for those adolescents with an annual family income of $50,000 is about $100\% - \exp[-.011(50 - 15)]*100 = 32\%$ lower than those with an annual family income of $15,000. This fixed effect of family income is the average effect of income across block groups. One can imagine a block-group-specific effect of

TABLE 2   Parameters and standard errors of a logit model and a multilevel model (with one random intercept and two random coefficients) predicting the probability of ever repeating a grade: Add Health

	Logit	Multilevel models		
		SAS		MLn
	Logit	GLIM-MIX	MQL-1	PQL-1
Fixed effect				
Intercept	−3.614	−4.000	−3.921	−4.000
	(.258)	(.268)	(.269)	(.272)
Female	−.647	−.661	−.638	−.661
	(.045)	(.045)	(.045)	(.046)
African-American	.433	.308	.301	.310
	(.052)	(.066)	(.066)	(.067)
Mother education	−.156	−.146	−.144	−.147
	(.009)	(.009)	(.009)	(.009)
Family income	−.009	−.011	−.009	−.011
	(.001)	(.001)	(.002)	(.001)
Age	.281	.305	.294	.305
	(.014)	(.014)	(.014)	(.014)
Proportion <$15,000	1.215	1.056	1.070	1.059
	(.146)	(.193)	(.190)	(.193)
Random effect				
Intercept		.224	.239	.222
		(.059)	(.060)	(.054)
Family income		.00005	.00006	.00005
		(.00002)	(.00005)	(.00002)
Proportion <$15,000		.083	.026	.046
		(.319)	(.217)	(.220)
Deviance		12054.2		
Extradispersion		.968		
−2logL	12656.0			
N	13,900	13,900	13,900	13,900

family income that serves as a correction for the fixed average slope of family income. The variance of the block-group specific effects is estimated to be .00005.

Many researchers prefer to interpret the model in terms of predicted probabilities rather than odds ratios. The predicted probability for adolescent i in block group j is

$$\hat{p}_{ij} = \exp(\boldsymbol{x}_{ij}\hat{\beta} + \hat{u}_{1j}\ income_{ij} + \hat{u}_{2j}\ below15k_j + \hat{u}_{0j})/$$
$$(1 + \exp(\boldsymbol{x}_{ij}\hat{\beta} + \hat{u}_{1j}\ income_{ij} + \hat{u}_{2j}\ below15k_j + \hat{u}_{0j})), \qquad (13)$$

TABLE 3 Parameters and standard errors of an intercept-only logit model and an intercept-only multilevel model predicting the probability of having a college plan: Add Health

	Logit		Multilevel models			
		SAS		MLn		
	Logit	GLIM-MIX	MQL-1	MQL-2	PQL-1	PQL-2
Fixed effect						
Intercept	.991	.952	.913	.956	.951	.960
	(.019)	(.057)	(.053)	(.054)	(.057)	(.057)
Random effect						
Intercept		.225	.193	.198	.224	.229
		(.045)	(.036)	(.037)	(.041)	(.042)
Intra-block		.06	.06	.06	.06	.07
correlation (ρ)						
Deviance		16184.7				
Extradispersion		.988				
−2logL	16750.9					
N	13,849	13,849	13,849	13,849	13,849	13,849

where

$$x_{ij}\hat{\beta} = \hat{\beta}_0 + \hat{\beta}_1\,age_{ij} + \hat{\beta}_2\,female_{ij} + \hat{\beta}_3\,black_{ij} + \hat{\beta}_4\,income_{ij}$$
$$+ \hat{\beta}_5\,education_{ij} + \hat{\beta}_6\,below15k_j.$$

An analyst can obtain $\hat{u}_{0j}$, $\hat{u}_{1j}$, and $\hat{u}_{2j}$ from GLIMMIX by adding the option "solution" in the line that specifies the random component of the model. Predicted probabilities can be calculated in a number of ways. For instance, for adolescents who are from block group 403($j = 403$), aged 15, white, with an annual family income of $30,000, with a mother having a high school education, and living in a community with 20% of the families having an income of less than $15,000, the predicted probability of having repeated a grade is estimated to be about 8% for females and 14% for males. The random effects $\hat{u}_{0j}$, $\hat{u}_{1j}$, and $\hat{u}_{2j}$ for block group 403 are −.505, .0014, and −.094, respectively. Another common practice is to simulate the predicted probabilities. Suppose we are again interested in gender differences. The first step in the simulation is to compute $\hat{p}_{ij}$ for all ijs. The computation is done twice. Both times, all individuals are allowed to retain their own characteristics except gender. The first time, gender is set to male and the second time female. The second step is to compute the average over $\hat{p}_{ij}$s. This is also done twice, once for males and once for females. The predicted probabilities for males and females can then be compared.

TABLE 4   Parameters and standard errors of a logit model and a multilevel model (with one random intercept and two random coefficients) predicting the probability of having a college plan: Add Health

	Logit	Multilevel models		
		SAS	MLn	
	Logit	GLIM-MIX	MQL-1	PQL-1
Fixed effect				
Intercept	.684	.898	.930	.896
	(.219)	(.227)	(.228)	(.229)
Female	.421	.423	.414	.423
	(.039)	(.039)	(.039)	(.039)
African-American	.286	.365	.364	.364
	(.049)	(.061)	(.061)	(.061)
Mother education	.132	.121	.118	.121
	(.008)	(.008)	(.008)	(.008)
Family income	.005	.005	.004	.005
	(.001)	(.001)	(.001)	(.001)
Age	−.121	−.122	−.119	−.121
	(.011)	(.012)	(.012)	(.012)
Proportion <\$15,000	−.277	−.600	−.628	−.601
	(.135)	(.189)	(.188)	(.189)
Random effect				
Intercept		.115	.119	.114
		(.031)	(.034)	(.031)
Family income		.00002	.00004	.00002
		(.00001)	(.00001)	(.00001)
Proportion <\$15,000		.264	.247	.251
		(.236)	(.234)	(.233)
Deviance		15473.8		
Extradispersion		.984		
−2logL	15940.5			
N	13,849	13,849	13,849	13,849

Assuming that the three random effects in (12) are uncorrelated, we can calculate the intra-block-group correlation using

$$\rho(income_{ij},\ lowinc_j) = \frac{\sigma_{u0}^2 + \sigma_{u1}^2\ income_{ij}^2 + \sigma_{u2}^2\ lowinc_j^2}{\sigma_{u0}^2 + \sigma_{e0}^2 + \sigma_{u1}^2\ income_{ij}^2 + \sigma_{u2}^2\ lowinc_j^2}, \qquad (14)$$

where lowinc is proportion <\$15,000. Now the intra-cluster correlation ρ is a function of family income and neighborhood poverty. For example, the intra-block-group correlation ρ is estimated to be .12 for adolescents who have an annual family income of \$70,000 and who live in a block group with 0% of families having an income below \$15,000. The ρ is estimated to be .08 for adolescents whose family income is \$15,000 and who live in a community with 75% of families having an income below \$15,000. We obtained all the parameter estimates necessary for the calculation from Table 2.

The deviance statistic D reported by the GLIMMIX macro can be used to carry out a likelihood ratio test for hypothesis testing. The deviance is defined as

$$D = 2(\ln f(y \mid \tilde{\theta}) - \ln f(y \mid \hat{\theta})), \qquad (15)$$

where $\ln f(y \mid \tilde{\theta})$ is the loglikelihood for the saturated model or the observed data and $\ln f(y \mid \hat{\theta})$ is the loglikelihood for the model of interest. Suppose we have two models of interest: model 1 with p_1 parameters and model 2 with p_2 parameters. The two models are nested with $p_2 > p_1$. To test if model 2 has improved the explanatory power of model 1 significantly, we use $D_1 - D_2$, the difference between the deviance for model 1 and that for model 2, as a likelihood ratio statistic, which has an approximate χ_2 distribution with $p_2 - p_1$ degrees of freedom. A likelihood ratio test of the model in Table 2 against the model in Table 1 $(13430.6 - 12054.2 = 1376.4$ with 8 degrees of freedom) shows that the addition of the six fixed effects and two random coefficients has significantly improved the fit of the model.

In Tables 3 and 4, we present the results from the second example that runs parallel to the first. Also based on Add Health, the second example uses having a college plan as the binary outcome variable. Having a college plan was constructed from the responses to the question "do you want to attend college?" "Yes" is coded as one and all the other responses are coded as 0. Our analysis sample consists of 13,849 adolescents, 9,792 or 71% of whom are coded as one. The comments we can make from the second example concerning different estimation methods are generally similar to those we made based on the first example, except that the coefficient of proportion <\$15,000 in the second example (Table 4) is seriously underestimated by the standard logit model.

SUMMARY, CONCLUSIONS, AND FINAL REMARKS

Many social scientists have applied multilevel models for binary data. We have reviewed some of the work published over the past ten years. We attempt to provide a brief description of the hypothesis tested, the hierarchical data structure analyzed, and the multilevel data source for each piece of work we have reviewed. We have also reviewed the technical literature and worked out two examples on multilevel models for binary outcomes. The review and examples serve two purposes. First, they are designed to assist in all aspects of working with multilevel models for binary outcomes, including model conceptualization, model description for a research report, understanding of the structure of required multilevel data, estimation of the model via a generally available statistical package, and interpretation of the results. Second, our examples contribute to the evaluation of the approximation procedures for binary multilevel models that have been implemented for general public use.

Our examples have further demonstrated the tendency for the standard logit model to seriously bias the parameter estimates of observed covariates when analyzing multilevel data. The differences in estimates across the different estimation procedures for the binary multilevel models, however, are much smaller in our examples than those reported by Rodriguez & Goldman (1995, 1997). The differences between PQL-1 and PQL-2 in our example are minimal (Tables 1 and 3). We have estimated other models than those presented in Tables 1 and 3, in which we included a number of observed covariates and a random intercept, and we succeeded in getting estimates from MQL-2 and PQL-2. The differences between PQL-1 and PQL-2 are always very small. This is consistent with Goldstein & Rasbash's (1996) observation that in the more common case where variances in a multilevel model for binary data do not exceed about 0.5, the first order PQL model can be expected to perform well. Our conclusion is that while an analyst should always be aware of the possibility that his or her estimates are seriously biased, MLn's PQL-1 and PQL-2 and SAS' GLIMMIX are likely to be adequate for most of the projects undertaken in social sciences. Additional work is needed to determine more precisely the relationship between bias size and factors such as level of within-cluster correlation, proportion of clusters that has a single observation, average size of clusters, number of clusters, and so on. Before an entirely reliable and practical estimation procedure is developed, such a systematic evaluation of the approximate procedures will yield more precise recommendations for researchers.

We have shown through the examples how the multilevel logit model can be interpreted in terms of odds ratios and predicted probabilities, how the intra-cluster correlation can be calculated for a simple two-level random-intercept model and a model with a random intercept as well as random coefficients, and how hypothesis testing can be carried out for nested models using deviance provided by SAS GLIMMIX. These results will remain useful even if an entirely new estimation procedure is to replace all the procedures currently used.

Finally, our review of sociological applications of multilevel analysis reveals a few inadequacies regarding the presentation of analysis results. First, it is essential that researchers get across the basic structure of the hierarchical data and model. State clearly and in a prominent place how many levels the data have, what they are, how many units there are at level 2 and level 3, how many observations each level-2 or level-3 unit has on average, and what is the proportion of level-2 units that has only one observation. Equations are very useful in conveying the structure of hierarchical data and the model if they are used correctly. Define the elements including the subscripts in the equations immediately before or after the equations. Equations convey much more substantive information about the analysis in multilevel analysis than, say, in analysis that uses the techniques of sample selection. Second, researchers need to pay special attention to the presentation of random effects. It is a good idea to always present random effects in the table in which the results are presented even if they are not statistically significant. Random effects are necessarily part of a multilevel model. In the table, label random effects clearly. Let the audience know which random effect(s) is a random intercept and the level at which it varies. Label which random effect(s) is a random coefficient and the level at which it varies. A more precise presentation of random effects is to use, in the table, the mathematical symbols that are used in the equations for the multilevel model. Third, researchers probably want to present the intra-cluster correlation to give a sense of how the observations are correlated within clusters. Fourth, because of the lack of entirely reliable estimation methods, researchers should report the specific estimation method used, not just the statistical package, so that the analysis can be replicated and compared if necessary.

ACKNOWLEDGMENTS

We acknowledge the support of the W. T. Grant Foundation to Guo through the Faculty Scholars Program and a postdoctoral fellow grant to Zhao from NICHD (HD08189). We are grateful to Jianmin Wang, Jeremy Reynolds, and Erin Leahey for helpful comments.

APPENDIX

(1) SAS codes for the intercepts-only model

```
%INCLUDE 'D:/DATA/GLM/GLMM612.SAS' /NOSOURCE;
%GLIMMIX(DATA=TEMP3, PROCOPT=COVTEST, STMTS=%STR(
  CLASS COMMID;
  MODEL REPEAT=/SOLUTION;
  RANDOM INTERCEPT/SUB=COMMID;),
  ERROR=BINOMIAL, LINK=LOGIT);
```

The intercepts-only multilevel model described in (10) is estimated by SAS' GLIMMIX macro contained in glmm612.sas. The first line shows the location of the SAS macro. The second line shows the location of the SAS data file. After the first two lines, the syntax of the SAS codes is the same as that in PROC MIXED. COMMID is block group ID and CLASS COMMID declares COMMID as a categorical variable. REPEAT is the binary outcome variable and SOLUTION is an option asking SAS to print out the estimates. INTERCEPT after RANDOM indicates that the model has a random intercept. SUB=COMMID tells SAS that the observations within the same block group are subject to the same random effect. The last line of the SAS codes indicates that we are estimating a multilevel model or generalized linear mixed model for a binary outcome using the logit transformation.

(2) MLn codes for the intercepts-only model

$$repeat_{ij} \sim Binomial(denom_{ij}, \pi_{ij})$$

$$repeat_{ij} = \pi_{ij} + e_{0ij} \, bcons*$$

$$logit(\pi_{ij}) = \beta_{1j} \, cons$$

$$\beta_{1j} = \beta_1 + u_{1j}$$

$$[u_{1j}] \sim N(0, \Omega_u) : \Omega_u = \left[\sigma_{u1}^2\right]$$

$$bcons* = \, bcons[\pi_{ij}(1 - \pi_{ij})/denom_{ij}]^{0.5}$$

$$[e_{0ij}] \sim (0, \Omega_e) : \Omega_e = [1]$$

The analyst does not need to create the whole program shown here. The window version of MLn provides the general setting and the analyst fills in the rest. Before "writing" the program, the analyst must create three columns of ones, name them "bcons", "cons", and "denom", and add them to the input dataset. The right-hand side of the third equation defines the model. The intercepts-only model has only one β, but this β changes by j because it has a random component u_{1j} as defined in line four. The parameter β_1 is the fixed intercept. In line five, the random effect u_{1j} is assumed to have a normal distribution with $E[u_{1j}] = 0$ and $var(u_{1j}) = \sigma_{u1}^2$.

(3) SAS codes for the multiple random effects model

```
%INCLUDE 'D:/DATA/GLM/GLMM612.SAS' /NOSOURCE;
%GLIMMIX(DATA =TEMP3, PROCOPT=COVTEST, STMTS=%STR(
CLASS COMMID;
MODEL REPEAT=FEMALE BLACK AGE MEDUC INCOME LOW-INC/
    SOLUTION;
RANDOM INTERCEPT INCOME LOWINC/SUB=COMMID;),
ERROR=BINOMIAL, LINK=LOGIT);
```

In line four, we have added the six observed covariates to the model. In line five, we have added two random coefficients, one for INCOME and the other LOWINC both varying by block groups.

(4) MLn codes for the multiple random effects model

$$repeat_{ij} \sim Binomial(denom_{ij}, \pi_{ij})$$

$$repeat_{ij} = \pi_{ij} + e_{0ij} \, bcons*$$

$$logit(\pi_{ij}) = \beta_{1j} \, cons + \beta_2 \, age_{ij} + \beta_{3j} \, lowinc_j + \beta_4 \, black_{ij}$$

$$+ \beta_{5j} \, income_{ij} + \beta_6 \, meduc_{ij} + \beta_7 \, male_{ij}$$

$$\beta_{1j} = \beta_1 + u_{1j}$$

$$\beta_{3j} = \beta_3 + u_{3j}$$

$$\beta_{5j} = \beta_5 + u_{5j}$$

$$\begin{bmatrix} u_{1j} \\ u_{3j} \\ u_{5j} \end{bmatrix} \sim N(0, \Omega_u) : \Omega_u = \begin{bmatrix} \sigma_{u1}^2 & & \\ 0 & \sigma_{u3}^2 & \\ 0 & 0 & \sigma_{u5}^2 \end{bmatrix}$$

$$bcons* = bcons[\pi_{ij}(1 - \pi_{ij})/denom_{ij}]^{0.5}$$

$$[e_{0ij}] \sim (0, \Omega_e) : \Omega_e = [1]$$

In line three, we have added six observed covariates and their coefficients, among which those for lowinc and income are allowed to vary by j. Lines four, five, and six are level-2 equations defining β_{1j}, β_{3j}, and β_{5j}. Line seven defines the random components of level-2 models. In this particular model, we set the covariances of the random effects (u_{1j}, u_{3j}, and u_{5j}) to zeros under the assumption that these random effects are uncorrelated.

Visit the Annual Reviews home page at www.AnnualReviews.org

LITERATURE CITED

Aitkin M, Anderson D, Hinde J. 1981. Statistical modeling in school effectiveness studies (with discussion). *J. R. Statis. Soc. A* 149:1–43

Anderson DA, Aitkin M. 1985. Variance component models with binary response: interviewer variability. *J. R. Statist. Soc. B* 47:203–10

Bearman PS, Jones J, Udry JR. 1997. *The National Longitudinal Study of Adolescent Health: Research Design* [WWW Document]. URL: *http://www.cpc.unc.edu/projects/addhealth/design.html*

Bennett N. 1976. *Teaching Styles and Pupil Progress.* London: Open Books

Billy JOG, Moore DE. 1992. A multilevel analysis of marital and nonmarital fertility in the U.S. *Soc. Forces* 70:977–1011

Blalock H. 1984. Contextual-effects models: theoretical and methodological issues. *Annu. Rev. Sociol.* 10:353–72

Breslow NE, Clayton DG. 1993. Approximate inference in generalized linear mixed models. *J. Am. Statist. Assoc.* 88:9–25

Brooks-Gunn J, Duncan GJ, Klebanov PK, Sealand N. 1993. Do neighborhoods influence child and adolescent development? *Am. J. Socio.* 99:353–95

Bryk AS, Raudenbush SW. 1992. *Hierarchical Linear Models: Applications and Data Analysis Methods.* Newbury Park, CA: Sage

Cherlin AJ, Chase-Lansdale PL, McRae C. 1998. Effects of parental divorce on mental health throughout the life course. *Am. Sociol. Rev.* 63:239–49

Cohen P. 1998. Black concentration effects on black-white and gender inequality: multi-level analysis for U.S. metropolitan areas. *Soc. Forces* 77:207–29

Cotter DA, JoAnn D, Hermsen JM, Kowalewski BM, Vanneman R. 1997. All women benefit: the macro-level effect of occupational integration on gender earnings equality. *Am. Sociol. Rev.* 62:714–34

Crane J. 1991. The epidemic theory of ghettos and neighborhood effects on dropping out and teenage childbearing. *Am. J. Sociol.* 96:1226–59

DiPrete TA, Forristal JD. 1994. Multilevel models: methods and substance. *Annu. Rev. Sociol.* 20:331–57

Entwisle B, Mason WM, Hermalin AL. 1986. The multilevel dependence of contraceptive use on socioeconomic development and family planning program strength. *Demography* 23:199–216

Entwisle DR, Alexander KL, Olson LS. 1994. The gender gap in math: its possible origins in neighborhood effects. *Am. Sociol. Rev.* 59:822–38

Gamoran A. 1992. The variable effects of high school tracking. *Am. Sociol. Rev.* 57:812–28

Goldstein H. 1987. *Multilevel Models in Educational and Social Research.* London: Griffin.

Goldstein H. 1991. Nonlinear multilevel models with an application to discrete response data. *Biometrika* 78:45–51

Goldstein H. 1995. *Multilevel Statistical Models.* London: Arnold; New York: Halstead. 2nd ed.

Goldstein H, Rasbash J. 1996. Improved approximations for multilevel models with binary responses. *J. Roy. Statist. Soc. A.* 159:505–13

Guo G. 1998. The timing of the influences of cumulative poverty on children's cognitive ability and achievement. *Soc. Forces* 77:257–88

Guo G. 1996. Negative multinomial regression models for clustered event counts. *Sociol. Methodol.* 26:113–32

Guo G, Rodríguez G. 1992. Estimating a multivariate proportional hazards model for clustered data using the em algorithm, with an application to child survival in Guatemala. *J. Am. Statist. Assoc.* 87:969–76

Guo G, Grummer-Strawn L. 1993. Child mortality among twins in developing countries. *Pop. Stud.* 47(3):1–16

Harvill DA. 1977. Maximum likelihood approaches to various component estimation and to related problems. *Journal of the American Statistical Association.* 72:320–38

Hogan DP, Kitagawa EM. 1985. The impact of social status, family structure, and neighborhood on the fertility of black adolescents. *Am. J. Sociol.* 90:825–55

Kalleberg A, Mastekaasa A. 1998. Organizational size, layoffs, and quits in Norway. *Soc. Forces* 76:1243–73

Laird NM, Ware JH. 1982. Random-effects models for longitudinal data. *Biometrics* 38:963–74

Lauritsen J. 1998. The age-crime debate: assessing the limits of longitudinal self-report data. *Soc. Forces* 77:127–55

Littell RC, Milliken GA, Stroup WW, Wolfinger RD. 1996. *SAS System for Mixed Models.* Cary, NC: SAS Inst.

Mason WM, Wong GM, Entwistle B. 1983. Contextual analysis through the multilevel linear model. *Sociol. Methodol.* 13:72–103

Nee V. 1996. The emergence of a market society: changing mechanisms of stratifcation in China. *Am. J. Sociol.* 101:908–49

Nielsen F, Alderson AS. 1997. The Kuznets curve and the great U-turn: income inequality in U.S. counties, 1970 to 1990. *Am. Sociol. Rev.* 62:12–33

Pebley AR, Goldman N, Rodriguez G. 1996. Prenatal and delivery care and childhood immunization in Guatemala: do family and community matter? *Demography* 33:231–47

Rodriguez G, Goldman N. 1995. An assessment of estimation procedures for multilevel models with binary response. *J. R. Statist. Soc. A.* 158:73–89

Rodriguez G, Goldman N. 1997. *Multilevel models with binary response: a comparison of estimation procedures.* Paper Pres. Pop. Assoc. Am. Annu. Meet. Washington, DC, March 27–29, 1997

Roscigno VJ. 1998. Race and the reproduction of educational disadvantages. *Soc. Forces* 76:1033–60

Rountree PW, Land KC. 1996. Perceived risk

versus fear of crime: empirical evidence of conceptually distinct reactions in survey data. *Soc. Forces* 74:1353–76

Sampson RJ. 1991. Linking the micro- and macrolevel dimensions of community social organization. *Soc. Forces* 70:43–64

Tolnay SE, Crowder KD. 1999. Regional origin and family stability in northern cities: the role of context. *Am. Sociol. Rev.* 64: 97–112

Wolfinger R, O'Connell M. 1993. Generalized liner models: a pseudo-likelihood approach. *J. Statist. Comput. Simul.* 48:233–43

Wong GY, Mason WM. 1985. The hierarchical logistic regression model for multilevel analysis. *J. Am. Statist. Assoc.* 80: 513–23

Xie Y, Hannum E. 1996. Regional variation in earnings inequality in reform-era urban China. *Am. J. Sociol.* 101:950–92

Annu. Rev. Sociol. 2000. 26:463–96

A SPACE FOR PLACE IN SOCIOLOGY

Thomas F. Gieryn

Department of Sociology, Indiana University, Bloomington, Indiana 47405;
e-mail: gieryn@indiana.edu

Key Words   place and space, built environment, architecture,
material culture, design

■ **Abstract**   Sociological studies sensitive to the issue of place are rarely labeled
thus, and at the same time there are far too many of them to fit in this review. It may be
a good thing that this research is seldom gathered up as a "sociology *of* place," for that
could ghettoize the subject as something of interest only to geographers, architects,
or environmental historians. The point of this review is to indicate that sociologists
have a stake in place no matter what they analyze, or how: The works cited below
emplace inequality, difference, power, politics, interaction, community, social movements, deviance, crime, life course, science, identity, memory, history. After a prologue
of definitions and methodological ruminations, I ask: How do places come to be the
way they are, and how do places matter for social practices and historical change?

INTRODUCTION

This may or may not be a propitious moment to review the sociological literatures
on place. We have been told about the "transcendence of place" (Coleman 1993),
the "placelessness of place" (Relph 1976), cities "without a place" (Sorkin 1992),
and how place becomes, with modernity, "phantasmagoric" (Giddens 1990). Technological revolutions in transportation and communication, it is said, have all but
eliminated the drag once imposed by location and distance on human interaction
and on the flow of goods, capital, or information. Social life now moves through
nodes in one or another network, through points of power or convergence or translation but not anchored at any place necessarily. The places we build appear as
clones of places elsewhere: suburban tracts, shopping malls, freeway interchanges,
office complexes, and gussied up old neighborhoods vary less and less. As places
lose their distinctiveness, place loses its reality and significance, some believe. The
uniqueness of New York, New York, gets packaged for reassembly in Las Vegas,
next to pyramids and the Eiffel Tower. Disneyland is in France.

Could it be that place just does not matter anymore? I think it does. In spite of
(and perhaps because of) the jet, the 'net, and the fast-food outlet, place persists
as a constituent element of social life and historical change (Friedland & Boden

1994). And that significance is measured by an enduring tradition of robust socio-logical studies of place that remains invisible only because it is rarely framed that way. Sociologists have given the appearance of not being interested in place—perhaps preferring to leave the matter to specialists from geography, or fearing that environmental determinism would rob social and cultural variables of their explanatory oomph, or worrying that the particularities of discrete places might compromise the generalizing and abstracting ambitions of the discipline (Agnew 1989, Entrekin 1991). My task is to reveal the riches of a place-sensitive sociology and propel it forward.

I begin with some definitional necessities and illustrate these with one soci-ological study that takes place for all that it is worth. Next I consider the so-ciology of how places come to be, and, after that, how place matters for social life. Rather than pursue an exhaustive review of work on place from collateral disciplines of geography (Gregory 1994, Soja 1989), architecture and planning, environmental psychology, anthropology (Lawrence & Low 1990, Low 1996), environmental history, and philosophy (Casey 1997), I have instead been cava-lier in choosing books and articles that inform themes and issues already some-where on the sociological agenda. Wherever available, I cite only the good trail-head to a path of inquiry—that is, something recently published with a long bibliography.

GROUND RULES

Some definition of place is needed if only to restrict the domain of work under review. But more: the definition offered here is designed to bring together sev-eral literatures now rarely connected. For present purposes, place will have three necessary and sufficient features:

(1) Geographic Location

A place is a unique spot in the universe. Place is the distinction between here and there, and it is what allows people to appreciate near and far. Places have finitude, but they nest logically because the boundaries are (analytically and phenomeno-logically) elastic. A place could be your favorite armchair, a room, building, neigh-borhood, district, village, city, county, metropolitan area, region (Entrikin 1989, 1991), state, province, nation, continent, planet–or a forest glade, the seaside, a mountaintop. This gradient of place is one reason why it is difficult to appreci-ate what sociologists in particular have written about place because the discipline chops up the phenomena into incommunicado bits: urban sociology, rural soci-ology, suburban sociology, home, the environment, neighborhood, workplaces, ecology. To pursue place itself is to ask what these places of varying scale have in common and how they differ.

(2) Material Form

Place has physicality. Whether built or just come upon, artificial or natural, streets and doors or rocks and trees, place is stuff. It is a compilation of things or objects at some particular spot in the universe. Places are worked by people: we make places and probably invest as much effort in making the supposedly pristine places of Nature as we do in cities or buildings (DuPuis & Vandergeest 1996, Schama 1995). Sociologists are again alive to the significance of material culture in social life. A thriving literature on technology (not just on its social effects but its physical guts) has generated concepts and theories for discussing places as assemblages of things (Bijker et al 1987, Latour 1996, MacKenzie 1990). Social processes (difference, power, inequality, collective action) happen *through* the material forms that we design, build, use, and protest (Habraken 1998).

(3) Investment with Meaning and Value

Without naming (on toponyms: Feld & Basso 1996), identification, or representation by ordinary people, a place is not a place. Places are doubly constructed: most are built or in some way physically carved out. They are also interpreted, narrated, perceived, felt, understood, and imagined (Soja 1996). A spot in the universe, with a gathering of physical stuff there, becomes a place only when it ensconces history or utopia, danger or security, identity or memory. In spite of its relatively enduring and imposing materiality, the meaning or value of the same place is labile—flexible in the hands of different people or cultures, malleable over time, and inevitably contested.

What Place is Not

To define place this way excludes several phenomena potentially of keen interest to sociologists. First, place is not space—which is more properly conceived as abstract geometries (distance, direction, size, shape, volume) detached from material form and cultural interpretation (Hillier & Hanson 1984). Space is what place becomes when the unique gathering of things, meanings, and values are sucked out (de Certeau 1984, Harvey 1996; for contrasting definitions: Lefebvre 1991). Put positively, place is space filled up by people, practices, objects, and representations. In particular, place should not be confused with the use of geographic or cartographic metaphors (boundaries, territories) that define conceptual or analytical spaces–as the title of this piece makes plain (also: Gieryn 1999). Neither is place to be found in cyberspace: virtual it is not, at least for purposes of this review. Websites on the internet are not places in the same way that the room, building, campus, and city that house and locate a certain server is a place (S Graham 1998, Purcell 1997). Still, it is fascinating to watch geography and architecture become the means through which cyberspace is reckoned by designers and users (Boyer 1996, Jones 1998, King 1998, Mitchell 1995).

Second, place is not just a setting, backdrop, stage, or context for something else that becomes the focus of sociological attention, nor is it a proxy for demographic, structural, economic, or behavior variables. Nothing of interest to sociologists is nowhere (Casey 1993): Everything that we study is emplaced; it happens somewhere and involves material stuff, which means that every published piece of sociology legitimately belongs in this review. No: in much research, pseudo-places are identified only as a means to bound the unit of analysis (as when a survey asks questions of respondents who happen to live in Kalamazoo or Kankakee, but nothing more is said about those cities). Place is equally irrelevant to studies that compare Kalamazoo and Kankakee in terms of behavior patterns, structural changes, or attitudes—if nothing more is hypothesized about the effects of the geographic location, material form, or attributed meanings of the two cities. A sensitivity to place must be more than using two "places" simply to get a comparative wedge. The strong form of the argument is this: place is not merely a setting or backdrop, but an agentic player in the game—a force with detectable and independent effects on social life (Werlen 1993).

In the same way, place must be more than (say) racial proportions of neighborhoods, unemployment rates in cities, birth rates in nation-states. Here, place becomes a stand-in for clusters of variables located in spaces chosen for their analytic utility but generally denuded of architecture, landscape, and actors' own narrations. Perhaps the classic example from sociology is the census tract, used so effectively in research on the persistence of poverty, violence, and residential segregation in urban neighborhoods (e.g. Bergeson & Harman 1998, Jargowsky 1997, South & Crowder 1999). If the census tract is simply a bundle of analytic variables used to distinguish one neighborhood from another in terms of its economic or demographic features, then it is not place. Such studies become place-sensitive as they feed in information about relative location of the census tract in a metropolitan area, the patterns of streets or significance of particular buildings like churches or markets, and the perceptions and understandings of the place by people who might live there or not.

Working Metatheoretical Premises

A sociology informed by place will be most effective, I think, if it is neither reductionist nor determinist. That is, the three defining features of place—location, material form, and meaningfulness—should remain bundled. They cannot be ranked into greater or lesser significance for social life, nor can one be reduced down to an expression of another. Place has a plenitude, a completeness, such that the phenomenon is analytically and substantively destroyed if the three become unraveled or one of them forgotten (Entrikin 1991, Sack 1997, Thrift 1996). This anti-reductionism precludes geographical fetishism and environmental determinism, just as it precludes an unbridled social constructivism. "If you build it, they will come" is good Hollywood (or Iowa), but bad social theory; equally bad is "If you perceive it so, it is thus." Place is, at once, the buildings, streets, monuments, and open spaces assembled at a certain geographic spot *and* actors' interpretations, representations, and identifications. Both domains (the material and the interpretive, the physical and the semiotic) work autonomously *and* in a mutually dependent way (Bourdieu 1990).

Antideterminism applies as well to the analytical relationship between place and the other ontological realms that sociologists routinely study: behavior, belief, institutions, change. Place saturates social life: it is one medium (along with historical time) through which social life happens. The analogy is to gender: to code a respondent male or female is not the same as grasping how social institutions (and places) are gendered. The task ahead is to see all social phenomena as emplaced, as being constituted in part through location, material form, and their imaginings (Appadurai 1996). Put more tractably, place stands in a recursive relation to other social and cultural entities: places are made through human practices and institutions even as they help to make those practices and institutions (Giddens 1984). Place mediates social life; it is something more than just another independent variable (Abu-Lughod 1968).

Exemplar

To bring this flighty prolegomena down to earth, consider *Childerley*. Bell's (1994) ethnographic study of a pseudonymous exurban English village in Hampshire (pop. 475) epitomizes a sociology sensitive to place. Its topics read like the table of contents from an intro text: values, morality, class, gender, deviance, power, change, culture, politics—but these are all emplaced, and we learn about them in and through Childerley. Almost every chapter starts out by situating the reader there: "Childerley . . . is best known for the Horse and Hound, a genuine sixteenth-century pub at the end of the village. Visitors come from miles away to take a pint of good ale in front of its huge fireplace, ten feet wide and five feet deep, and to soak in the ambiance of the head-bashingly-low timbered ceiling and rude board tables and benches" (Bell 1994:27). Incidental detail? Hardly. Pubs (along with council houses, tied cottages, manor houses—and how fireplaces or televisions are differently arranged therein) (Halle 1993) contribute to the reproduction of class distinctions in Childerley: the Horse and Hound is favored by the moneyed, the Fox (described as "a bit grotty") is favored by ordinary working-class folks. Even the concepts that Bell devises to analyze class in Childerley are place-terms: the moneyed are "front-door" people (formal, distanced, individualistic), the ordinary folks are "back-door" (local, informal, group-oriented, experiential).

But social class is distrusted among residents of Childerley, and it is rarely chosen by them as a legitimate source of identity and motivation or seen as a guarantee of morality and sincerity—too easily polluted by materialist self-interest, they might say. Bell finds instead that place itself—Childerley the village and even more the nature found in the surrounding pastoral countryside—becomes the interpretive frame through which people there measure their lives, evaluate others, take political positions, and just make sense. The countryside itself becomes a "moral rock" (1994:8) for Childerleyans, as they see themselves in and from this "good" place (where patient, sincere, and friendly people respect nature on a first-name basis), distant from the evil metropole. People are ranked and trusted by how authentically "country" they are, though not everyone agrees on its determinants. For ordinary folks, the country village that Childerley was imagined to be has been lost to gentrifying arrivistes from London who build huge new homes and want to clean the place up. Place is as vital for securing tradition as for manifesting class difference: "The stories we tell take place in places, and most ordinary Childerleyans live right in the setting of most of their lifetime's accumulated stories" (Bell 1994:170). Geographic location, material forms, Childerleyan's representations of their home—these are the means through which readers learn about inequality, morality, capitalism, and other squarely sociological matters.

A space for place in sociology is not to be found in a sociology *of* place, with its own ASA section and specialty journal. Rather, it will come from sociological studies of anything and everything that are informed by a sense of place—as with Childerley (which was chosen as exemplar not because the village evokes nostalgia or tradition but because it is one of many sites where battles over the authenticity and even existence of "the local" are waged). How do geographic locations, material forms, and the cultural conjurings of them intersect with social practices and structures, norms and values, power and inequality, difference and distinction? There are two ways to answer this question: the first is explore how places come into being, the second is to find out what places accomplish. In the Real World, the construction of places and their social achievements or consequences are tough to disentangle—so consider it an arbitrary distinction good only for immediate organizational ends.

PLACE-MAKING

The making of places—identifying, designating, designing, building, using, interpreting, remembering—has been examined in three sociological literatures, only sometimes brought together: upstream forces that drive the creation of place with power and wealth; professional practices of place-experts; perceptions and attributions by ordinary people who experience places (and act on those understandings).

Powers Behind Places

Most research has been done on how urban places come to look the way that they do, with less on the powers shaping rural areas (on rusticity: Ching & Creed 1997, Cloke & Little 1997, Summers 1986), small towns (Hummon 1990), individual buildings and lightly built landscapes (Bantjes 1997). An enduring debate over factors driving the location and built form of cities pits urban ecologists vs. political economists (Feagin 1998, Flanagan 1993, Frisbie & Kasarda 1988, Gottdeiner 1994, Gottdeiner & Feagin 1988, Hughes 1993, Walton 1993). Urban ecologists see cities as the result of a survival of the fittest, shaped by competitions for efficient locations among individuals and corporate actors of diverse means and powers to control the physical terrain in a self-interested way. "Natural" processes of competition and mobility lead to segregated niches of homogeneous activities or demographic characteristics. The spatial arrangement of these natural areas—central business district, residential, manufacturing, warehouses—have been described as a set of concentric zones, sectors that slice through the concentric zones and as a spatially distributed multiplicity of nuclei or centers (reviewed in Wilson 1984). More recent ecological perspectives (Hawley 1986) have explored patterns of ethnic segregation, changing population densities, decentralization and suburbanization, and sought to identify empirically socioeconomic and ethnic factors that underlie differences among residential niches (Berry & Kasarda 1977).

Political economic models of place-making find nothing "natural" about the architecture of urbanity: cities assume material forms (and cultural meanings) congruent with economic interests and political alignments in a resolutely capitalist world (for socialist alternatives: Blau 1999). The natural physical environment, technology, transportation, and the individual choices of self-interested actors are less consequential than the pursuit of profit (through production of goods and services, or—more immediately—investments in land) and political complicity with such enlargements of wealth (Lefebvre 1991). Capitalist industrial strategies are unavoidably territorial strategies, as geographic patterns in production and consumption create places of growth and decline (Clarke 1992, Storper & Walker 1989). Simultaneous decay in the urban core and sprawling suburbs (Baldassare 1992) is traced back, for example, to selective capital investments by banks and government (Harvey 1973) or to economic restructuring and the rise of high tech industries (Castells 1977) that find it more profitable to locate in (and spawn) "edge cities" (Garreau 1991), or to legal structures that set in motion economic competitions among fractured municipal sovereignties (Frug 1999). Theme parks represent a double commodification, as the place itself is consumed by tourists as they also consume schlock: "Sea World is a like a mall with fish" (Davis 1997:2; on themed places generally: Gottdiener 1997, Wright & Hutchison 1997). Globalization of economic activity (Cox 1997, Knox 1993) has not made place unimportant but rather has given rise to new kinds of places such as the "global city" (AD King 1996, Knox & Taylor 1995, Sassen 1991) and dependent cities in the "third world" (Smith 1996), or total makeovers of extant places like Times Square (Reichl 1999), or massive changes among existing cities such as the tilt toward the American Sunbelt (Scott 1988).

A kind of structural determinism haunts these ecological and political economic models, leading them both to overlook the play of agency and contingency in place-making. Metropolitan areas are not shaped by faceless forces of natural succession-and-competition or capitalist logics of accumulation: people and groups organized into coalitions actively accomplish places, and the process is never the same from here to there (Logan & Molotch 1987). "Growth machines" of place-entrepreneurs—local rentiers, politicians, media, and utilities—pursue ever more intensive land-use so that greater amounts of exchange-value may be extracted from commodified property (Rudel 1989). They sometimes face resistance from community organizers more concerned about the use-value of place, who oppose growth because of its detrimental consequences for neighborhood quality of life or environmental health. The struggle between those who produce places for profit and those who consume it in their daily rounds is played out against a global struggle *among* places for the wherewithal to grow. Cities compete nationally and globally for investors, jobs, spectacles, state-supported places like military bases (Hooks 1994), cultural treasures, shoppers and tourists by differentiating themselves from the rest. Artists drawn to Lower Manhattan by initially cheap digs in lofts soon found themselves in the midst of intense economic development, which has remade Soho into a tourist-and-shopping destination with astronomical rents (Zukin 1982). A century-old residential neighborhood in Brussels is transformed (not without opposition) into an administrative home for the European Community (Papadopolous 1996). On-the-ground case studies of Atlanta (Rutheiser 1996), Beijing (Sit 1995), Berlin (Ladd 1997, Strom 1996), Dallas (Fairbanks 1998), Los Angeles (Davis 1990, 1998, Dear et al 1996, Hayden 1995, Keil 1998, Scott & Soja 1996), Houston (Feagin 1988), Miami (Croucher 1997, Portes & Stepick 1993) Milwaukee (Orum 1995), and Minneapolis-St. Paul (Orfield 1997) put human faces on the winners and losers in these layered struggles over place-making.

Place-Professionals

From a different perspective, urban growth machines become *clients* for professions whose bailiwick is the design of built-places: architects (Blau 1984, Brain 1989, Cuff 1991, Gutman 1988, Sarfatti Larson 1993, Zeisel 1975); urban and regional planners (Boyer 1983, Cherry 1974, Forester 1989, Gans 1968, Hall 1988, Perin 1977, Sandercock 1998, Suttles 1990); landscape architects (Mukerji 1997); interior designers (Fehrenbacher-Zeiser 1996); cartographers (Buisseret 1998, G King 1996, Pickles 1995, Thrower 1996); surveyors, historic preservationists (Barthel 1996); even public relations specialists with expertise in promoting a place (Gold & Ward 1994). Design-experts mediate the relationship between political, economic, or mobilized powers and the built-places that they desire. Interests and agendas of diverse clients are filtered through a profession, a culture, and a "discipline" of design. The design of a place may involve planners, architects, policymakers, financial institutions, patrons, regulatory agencies, potential users, developers, engineers, and variously interested audiences. It is, at once, the making of a place *and* the negotiation, translation, and alignment of political and economic interests, technical skills and imperatives, aesthetic judgments and societal futures (Stieber 1998). The finished places that we see, inhabit, visit, and suffer are as much the consequence of decisions made by place-professionals as of the wishes of clients upon whom they depend for their livelihood.

The practice of architecture (for example) situates place-making within a profession that must defend its jurisdiction or market niche (Brain 1991), legitimate its cultural authority, socialize its members, standardize its procedures, and reward its heroes and (infrequently: Hughes 1996) heroines. Buildings take shape as individual draftpersons seek promotion to project architects and then partners, as design firms hustle clients by specializing in a particular building type or by promoting a signature style, and as the profession patrols its porous boundaries from encroachments by engineers, developers, amateurs, and U-design-it software. All of these struggles—melded with emergent constraints from clients' preferences and budget, local building codes, the terrain of the physical site—get materialized in the built-form of a place. For instance, suburban shopping malls (Crawford 1992, Gottdeiner 1995, 1997; Zukin 1991, 1995) have a certain sameness to them not only because capitalist logic demands that the same retail chains locate in almost every one of them, but also because developers buy architectural plans from a small number of bureaucratically organized firms who save considerable time and money by hiring draftpersons to crank out (routinized by computer-assisted design) an effective and low-risk one-size-fits-all mall.

This routinization, standardization, and rationalization of design practice that makes architecture firms efficiently profitable and professionally accountable also raises questions about what it is exactly that architects provide. Architects survive because there are innumerable ways to translate "function" (selling goods) into built "form" (a mall). The profession's marketability depends upon convincing clients that architects alone possess the creative skills and artistic judgments necessary for making this transit from idea or need to place. Architects sell "style," which—when built-in—becomes the look or feel that people associate with a place. Most everybody notices at some level that the big-box suburban mall landing like a spaceship in a sea of parking is not the same as the postmodern confection like Boston's Quincy Market or Baltimore's Harborplace that is contextualized into the surrounding urban fabric and decorated with appropriate historical referents. The stylistic turn from modernism to postmodernism [which has yielded vastly different places (R King 1996, Ley 1989)] is not just about changing tastes (or changing political economies: Harvey 1990); it is also about architects seeking to convince clients that they have hit upon a better way to move function to form amidst the changing political economy of urban areas (Ellin 1996). As the failed urban renewal programs of modernism gave way to gentrifying city neighborhoods (Ley 1997), postmodern emporiums became right not only for selling but for other social goals such as growing community or attracting capital.

A Sense of Place

Places are endlessly made, not just when the powerful pursue their ambition through brick and mortar, not just when design professional give form to function, but also when ordinary people extract from continuous and abstract space a bounded, identified, meaningful, named, and significant place (de Certeau 1984, Etlin 1997). A place is *remarkable*, and what makes it so is an unwindable spiral of material form and interpretative understandings or experiences.

Something in the built-form of a place encourages people to distinguish this building or that patch of ground from its overlookable backdrop. Urban environments are designed and built in ways that either enhance or prevent their "imageability" and "legibility" (Lynch 1960). The perceived contrast between a place and its surrounding unidentified spaces may be achieved through continuity (when the architectural homogeneity of buildings in a neighborhood lead people to see it as Beacon Hill or Seaside), or through uniqueness (when a landmark stands out as utterly unlike any other thing in town, like New York's Flatiron Building or the Vietnam Veterans Memorial in Washington) (Milgram et al 1972). Research on mental (or cognitive) mapping—how individuals identify and locate a place when asked to map it—suggests that places emerge along paths (linear streets) or nodes (transportation transfer points), and they are bounded by imposing physical edges (waterfront, building facades that wall an open space) (Downs & Stea 1973, Peponis et al 1990). When asked to describe their apartment, New Yorkers presented either a map (giving the location of adjacent rooms) or a tour (moving the respondent through space) (Linde & Labov 1975).

But mental maps drawn by naive geographers also measure what people bring to the material forms they inhabit (Tuan 1974, 1977). Foremost, perhaps, is pragmatic utility: people identify as places those spots that they go to for some particular purpose or function. The sequence of places along one's daily rounds (home, shopping, employment, entertainment) is often the core cartographic feature of subjective cityscapes—with identified districts and landmarks then grafted on as a means of orientation (Pred 1990). The egoistic particularity of mapped-out places (Jameson 1984:90) suggests that such representations will vary among individuals in terms of their biographical characteristics and experiences: research shows considerable racial and ethnic differences in how people choose places to put on their maps (Lewis 1996). Also, people recall more easily places that they associate with momentous events in their lives (literatures on cognitive mapping, and environmental psychology generally, are reviewed in Kitchin 1994, Sundstrom et al 1996).

A sense of place is not only the ability to locate things on a cognitive map, but also the attribution of meaning to a built-form or natural spot (Rotenberg & McDonogh 1993, Walter 1988). Places are made as people ascribe qualities to the material and social stuff gathered there: ours or theirs; safe or dangerous; public or private; unfamiliar or known; rich or poor; Black or White; beautiful or ugly; new or old; accessible or not. Rankings of city neighborhoods in terms of perceived desirability and quality of life are key variables in "place stratification" models used to explain patterns of residential dispersion of racial and ethnic groups in metropolitan areas (Alba & Logan 1993, Farley et al 1994, Harris 1999, Lindstrom 1997, South & Crowder 1998). Advantaged groups (and individuals) seek to put distance between themselves and the less advantaged. The very idea of "neighborhood" is not inherent in any arrangement of streets and houses, but is rather an ongoing practical and discursive production/imagining of a people. "Locality" is as much phenomenological as spatial, achieved against the ground of globalization or nationalization (Appadurai 1996, Crain 1997, Koptiuch 1997, Lippard 1997).

Meanings that individuals and groups assign to places are more or less embedded in historically contingent and shared cultural understandings of the terrain—sustained by diverse imageries through which we see and remember cities (Boyer 1994). Cultural geography (or metageography) studies the (often implicit) spatial representations and images through which people arrange their behavior and interpretations of the social world (Anderson & Gale 1992, Basso 1996, Norton 1989, Sopher 1973). To shift ground: the familiar seven-continent spatialization of the earth's prominent land masses has been described as a "myth" (Lewis & Wigen 1997) that gets reproduced, transmitted, learned, and assumed as fact—but not among all peoples at all times, and with heavy ideological freight. Is North America a "place," or Africa? Conventional demarcations among continents are not based on any consistently applied decision-rule: Europe and Asia are not completely divided by water; not all islands are continents–Madagascar isn't. Moreover, the homogeneities implied by gathering up social practices, demographic distributions, cultural beliefs, built-environments, and physical topography onto *one* continent are belied by obvious internal differentiation (what else does sub-Saharan Africa share with Mediterranean Africa—or Mexico with Canada and the United States—apart from sitting on the same continental land mass?)

These culturally reproduced images of places are thus arbitrary but real in their consequences—for what people *do* to the land, as they make (or destroy) places. Nomadic hunting and gathering lifestyles of Native Americans in New England did much less to reduce the diversity of flora and fauna of this place than the agricultural lifestyles of the colonists who carved up the land into parcels of privately owned property (Cronon 1983). Navaho beliefs that Arizona's Black Mesa is a sacred place did not prevent the Peabody Coal Company from strip mining it for coal starting in 1970 (Kelley & Francis 1994). Whether Native American understandings of places are consistently in tune with ecologically sound noninvasive practices is a matter of dispute (Krech 1999, Stea & Turan 1993). So much is at stake in these diverse images and experiences of a place, and it becomes a sociological truism to say that such symbolic constructions will be forever precarious and contested (Griswold 1992, Hiss 1990, Laclau 1990). The Bastille, for example, started out as a profane place, and became by turn, a sacred place, a liminal place, and finally a mundane place (Smith 1999).

WHAT PLACE DOES

If place matters for social life and historical change—how? Scattered literatures suggest that place: stabilizes and gives durability to social structural categories, differences and hierarchies; arranges patterns of face-to-face interaction that constitute network-formation and collective action; embodies and secures otherwise intangible cultural norms, identities, memories—and values like the American

Dream (Whitaker 1996). These consequences result uniquely (but incompletely) from material forms assembled at a particular spot, in part via the meanings that people invest in a place.

Emplacing Difference and Hierarchy

Fundamental social classifications take on an imposing and constraining force as they are built in to everyday material places. The kinship structure of simple societies is secured as it is spatialized in the geographic arrangement of villages and dwellings (Durkheim & Mauss 1963), and the interior allocation of spaces in the Kabyle house corresponds to basic dichotomies in the Berber cosmogony: male/female, wet/dry, high/low, light/dark (Bourdieu 1990). This structuralist tradition says little about agency and choice in the planning of places (Pearson & Richards 1997). Instead, seeking theoretical escape from artificial oppositions of the objective and subjective, Bourdieu suggests that the architectural and geographic form of places is generated (self-reproduced) by not-fully-conscious-or-strategic practices and symbolic logics that are (at the same time) embodied in and structured by the resulting material arrangements of buildings.

Place sustains difference and hierarchy both by routinizing daily rounds in ways that exclude and segregate categories of people, and by embodying in visible and tangible ways the cultural meanings variously ascribed to them. The spatial division of labor between home and work has profound consequences for women's identities and opportunities (Ahrentzen 1992, Hayden 1981, Hayden 1984, Nippert-Eng 1995, Wright 1981). What it is to be female is constructed in part through idealized qualities (domestic security, family stability) ascribed to the home (Benjamin 1995, Cieraad 1999)—which has been traditionally (and for many is still) a woman's place (Massey 1994). Gendered segregations via the geography and architecture of built-places contribute to the subordination and spatialized social control of women, either by denying access to knowledge and activities crucial for the reproduction of power and privilege or by limiting mobility more generally within places defined as unsafe, physically threatening, or inappropriate (McDowell 1999, Spain 1992, Weisman 1992, Wilson 1992; in Africa: Moore 1986, Prussin 1995). Racial, ethnic, and class segregations are achieved via restrictive land-use zoning that requires homes to be of a certain size or value, especially in suburbs (DeSena 1990, Haar 1996, Kirp et al 1995, Wilson 1998). Class differences and hierarchies are reproduced through segregated class-specific localities of residence and consumption, geographic patterns of relocation that differentially affect labor and capital, and place-shaped capacities for working-class mobilization or expression (Thrift & Williams 1987). Still, at the same time that ethnic enclaves segregate, they also provide conditions of ethnic solidarity, community, and economic advance (Zhou 1992).

Places reflect and reinforce hierarchy by extending or denying life-chances to groups located in salutary or detrimental spots. Most of the literature on ethnic enclaves has focussed on segregated urban neighborhoods whose physical, social, and cultural deterioration (whether due to the exodus of middle-class minorities or to racist real estate practices) has made it difficult for residents to better their conditions (Massey & Denton 1993, Oliver & Shapiro 1995, Wilson 1996). However, the point may be generalizable: being in the wrong place at the wrong time imposes costs on ethnic minority populations, as Clark (1998) has shown for several European minorities in the seventeenth century. The fate of these groups was a contingent matter of place: those located in regions strategically in between two international powers at war suffered greater persecution and violence. The situation is not all that different for long-time residents of supposedly declining urban neighborhoods, who are compelled by gentrification to relocate elsewhere when they are given offers that they cannot refuse (Zukin 1987).

Power-Vessels and Strongholds

Places have power sui generis, all apart from powerful people or organizations who occupy them: the capacity to dominate and control people or things comes through the geographic location, built-form, and symbolic meanings of a place. The array of building-types is, on this score, also a catalog of how places differently become terrains of powers (Markus 1993). Spatializations of normal/pathological, often accompanied by architectures of enclosure, display, segregation, surveillance, and classification, give an impersonal and autonomous power over docile subjects to hospitals, prisons, asylums, schools—the Panopticon (Foucault 1979). Power-spots vary in form and function: the co-location of exclusive clubs and corporate headquarters create local and comfortable places where interlocking directorates can assemble informally and plot moves (Davis & Greve 1997, Kono et al 1998). The "command of heights" has strategic advantage in ground warfare: places of high ground afford a wider view of adversaries' maneuvers, inhibit their uphill attack, and facilitate construction of powerful defensive strongholds (Clausewitz 1976). The aestheticization of politics means that Mussolini's fascist power is inscribed even on the sewer plates of Rome (Falasca-Zamponi 1997:98). Still, the hold of a place on power is never permanent or absolute: as markets and capital go global, rusted steel mills and ghostly impoverished towns stay behind (Pappas 1989, Zukin 1991).

Domination over nature is housed in buildings that become—for this reason—places of social power too. Scientific laboratories are places where wild creatures are tamed, enculturated by insertion into artificial territorial regimes that create purified and workable objects of inquiry (Knorr Cetina 1999). From their domination over nature, laboratories dominate society as they become "obligatory passage points" standing between desperate people and their panacea. For example, the vaccine for anthrax was uniquely emplaced at Pasteur's Parisian laboratory, which became a "center of calculation" with the power to move a healthier France toward enlarged and enthusiastic patronage of science (Latour 1988). The power of laboratories as "truth-spots" depends considerably upon sequestrations achieved architecturally, walls and doors that exclude or inhibit people, and pollutants that might challenge or compromise the cognitive authority of experimental science (Galison & Thompson 1999, Gieryn 1998, Gutman 1989, Shapin 1998).

The exercise of political power is also intimately connected with place: geography and built environments organize political behavior such as voting or activism (Sellers 1998), spaces become the focus of government development policies, and control of territory is one measure of effective state sovereignty (Agnew 1987). Place enables power to travel, to extend its reach over people and territory. This can result from standardizations of the land itself—gridding the countryside, village, and city in a "high modernist" way, or even just mapping it (Kain & Baigent 1992)—that facilitate state control over its people (Holston 1989, Price 1995, Rabinow 1989, Scott 1998, Sennett 1970). Or such power can merely be displayed in a kind of architectural chest-thumping: Louis XIV's straight-jacketed gardens at Versailles demonstrated for all to see the capacity of the French state for material domination over the land and, thus, its prowess to control people (Mukerji 1997). Imposing monuments or government buildings erected all over the colonies extended imperial power, in part by asserting with "superior" engineering or decor that indigenes simply lacked the civilization to do the same for themselves (Anderson 1983, Metcalf 1989, Vale 1992, Wright 1991, cf. Carter 1988, Robinson 1989). Such power can also be symbolized and reproduced through distinctive building-types or styles—the bungalow in India (King 1995)—that materialize colonization. In all these cases, the absolute (power) becomes local through its emplacement (Deleuze & Guattari 1986). These architectural and geographic power-moves sometimes meet resistance: recent construction of modern and globally typical factories for making silk in Hangzhou could not deter workers' subversive practices grounded in long-standing traditions (e.g., commandeering open spots on the shop-floor for long breaks) (Rofel 1997; cf. Baldry 1999).

Proximity, Interaction, Community

Places bring people together in bodily co-presence—but then what (Boden & Molotch 1994, Sennett 1994)? Put crudely, the possibilities are two—engagement or estrangement (Sennett 1990)—and debates over the conditions making for one or the other outcome constitute perhaps the most celebrated and enduring contribution of sociologists to the study of place (reviewed in Choldin 1978, Fischer 1975). Urban places have been described as the locus of diversity, tolerance, sophistication, sociation, public participation, cosmopolitanism, integration, specialization, personal network-formation (Fischer 1977, 1982), coping, frequent spontaneous interactions, freedom, creativity—i.e., community (as a coming together in local collective projects requiring civil negotiations of differences that are inevitable) (Young 1990). But urban places have also been described as the locus of anonymity, detachment, loneliness, calculating egoism, privatization, formalized social controls, segregations, individualism, withdrawal, detachment, parochialism, disconnections, isolation, fear, seclusion, mental illness (Halpern 1995)—i.e., the last place on earth one would expect to find community.

Whether or not community results from the gathering up of people into proximate face-to-face interactions depends–sociologists routinely say–on their number, their differentiations along lines of class, race, ethnicity, taste or lifestyle, and the cultural beliefs they share (Wellman 1979). But is there a "place effect" as well, in which the tight coupling of geography, built-form, and subjective topological understanding mediates the effects of size, demographic patterns, and values on the possibility or achievement of community? Enough studies suggest that the design and serial construction of places is at the same time the *execution* of community (in one or the other sense of that word) (Hummon 1990, Kunstler 1996, Suttles 1972).

Engagement can be built-in. At the scale of individual buildings, Allen (1977) found that the rate of innovation in high-tech R&D organizations could be enhanced by designing facilities to maximize chance interactions (e.g., by forcing everybody to use the same stairwell, open and inviting enough to encouraging lingering talk). In the same way, the built-form of cities may help to explain outbreaks of cultural effervescence and creativity (Hannerz 1992). Ordinary neighborhood residents may be brought together in unplanned interactions when individual dwellings are compactly–built rather than widely dispersed, or when front porches and stoops permit seamless moves from home to a pedestrian-friendly street (Festinger et al 1950, cf. Logan & Spitze 1994). Presence of perceivedly public places such as parks, plazas (Moore 1996), squares, libraries, agora—owned by no one (legally or informally), inviting and accessible to all—fosters mingling of diverse people who don't already know each other and provides a setting for spectacles and communal celebrations (Carr et al 1992, Lofland 1998, Rowe 1997, Sarkis 1997). If those public places are designed effectively—providing comfortable places to sit, movable chairs, water, street food, maybe something erotic (Young 1990)—more people will be drawn to them (Whyte 1980). Or perhaps the places most conducive to community are not "designed" at all (Cline 1997), but are disordered—and lose much when they are purified (Jacobs 1961, Sennett 1970). Places like neighborhood bars, restaurants (Ferguson 1998), corner stores, churches, and clubs provides spots for informal engagements and organizational meetings, often among people who already know each other (Oldenburg 1989). Giving residents a stake in the process of place-making—"New Urbanist" planners involve residents in "charrettes," where strategic design decisions are made collectively—leads to greater civic interest and participation in subsequent public policy deliberations (Brain 1997, Brain 1998, MacCannell 1999).

So, too, can estrangement be built-in. Residential development that sprawls further and further away from city centers creates the need for mobile pods of seclusion if they are connectable only by private car traveling at high speeds (de Boer 1986, Sorkin 1999). Conversion of once public places into private or semi-public ones—shopping malls replace Main Street and the town square (consider what Benjamin said of European urban arcades from a century ago: "At the exit . . . I breathe more easily; the street, freedom, the present!" Buck-Morss 1989:38), new neighborhoods are gated (Blakely & Snyder 1997), the grid of residential streets is selectively closed off—restrict the range and diversity of people with whom one is likely to interact on daily rounds (Lofland 1998). The borders among ethnic (or class) enclaves in the urban mosaic often become impassable (Massey 1985, Young 1990; but see Sigelman et al 1996). The spatial specialization of function—magnet places like stores, workplaces, office parks, or civic centers are distanced from residential neighborhoods, which are then differentiated by the property values of their homes—further segregates denizens along lines of race, class, ethnicity, age, and gender (Lofland 1973). These patterns are inspired by narrations of place that in effect legitimate the resulting homogeneous enclaves—for example, when suburbs are envisaged through imageries of romantic pastoralism or unique historical heritages (Bridger 1996, Dorst 1989), and thus as escapes from the risks, pollutions, and undesirables simultaneously planted in The City. When "community" does arise inside such enclaves—wealthy 'burb or gentrifying neighborhood—it tends to be defensive, exclusionary, and protectionist (Frug 1999), and works against a more inclusive public sphere.

Places Spawn Collective Action

Gould's rich studies of Parisian insurrections in 1848 and 1870–1871 epitomize a place-sensitive perspective on collective behavior (Gould 1995). Haussmann's rebuilding of central Paris between these two uprisings changed the identity-contours along which protest was organized. In 1848, most workers were residentially clustered by trade or craft in neighborhoods replete with cabarets and cafes where they mobilized and schemed: networks forged in the workplace and reinforced in neighborhood centers of sociability organized insurgency along class lines. By 1870, Haussmann's boulevards had fractured some of these neighborhoods and, more importantly, pushed many workers out to peripheral areas just annexed as part of Paris. In these outlying areas, workers from different trades along with others from different classes formed a new collective identity based on the neighborhood itself: they were drawn to local public meetings, where they organized their neighbors into active resistance against the French state. Neighborhood ties became the via media of recruitment and mobilization for the Paris Commune. In the twentieth century, the "red belt" of Paris moved even further out into suburbs such as Bobigny, where the combination of radical politics and neighborhood attachments is sustained (Stovall 1990).

Place was equally consequential in the 1989 Beijing student revolt. The fine structure of campus architecture and of surrounding streets shaped patterns of mobilization. Here, the built environment was not a source of collective identity but rather structured the spatial distribution and flow of activists (Zhao 1998). Community organization of racial groups in Los Angeles was affected by the spatial patterns of "tertiary" residential streets (Grannis 1998). In the case of Swedish trade unionists between 1890 and 1940, spatial proximity in itself inspired collective activism (Hedstrom 1994). On different occasions, place provided a site where numbers of participants could and would gather—Leipzig's Karl Marx Platz for

East German protests in 1989 (Opp & Gern 1993), Groveland Church for political rallies in a Chicago African-American community (Pattillo-McCoy 1998).

Place can become the *object* of collective action, as in NIMBY [not in my backyard] movements (Norton & Hannon 1997) or protests grounded in charges of environmental racism (Bullard 1990). Saving Owens Valley from thirsty Los Angeles (Walton 1992; for Arizona: Espeland 1998), saving "Black Corona" (a neighborhood in Queens, New York) from an intrusive elevated train line (Gregory 1998), saving the Cedar-Riverside neighborhood in Minneapolis from urban renewal (Stoecker 1994), and saving Manhattan's Lower East Side from gentrification (Abu-Lughod 1994) became rallying cries for protest movements.

Other studies call attention to the locations of places, in geographic space, as factors in collective action. In the seventeenth-century Ottoman Empire, villages that were neither too close to the center of political power nor too isolated were more prone to peasant uprisings (Barkey & Van Rossem 1997). In eighteenth century England, political autonomy and solidarity—leading eventually to emerging rights of citizenship—were more common in pastoral areas than in arable lands more tightly controlled by ruling elites (Somers 1993, cf. Brustein & Levi 1987). And, in a quite different way, place affects media coverage of collective action: public events are more likely to receive coverage if they occur on the customary beat of reporters (Oliver & Myers 1999).

If places spawn collective action, so too can they become its contraceptive. As public spaces in cities are privatized, stigmatized, avoided or destroyed, the effect is chilling on the possibility of mobilization and public protest. Streets and sidewalks, squares and markets, increasingly give way to pedways and skyways, malls and arenas that are constructed with material (locks), legal (armed guards and surveillance cameras), and semiotic (informal codes that announce appropriate users and uses) devices that discourage public displays of political activism (Boddy 1992, Davis 1990, Winner 1992). In a very different way, identities grounded in attachment to local communities or neighborhoods can *inhibit* an individual's commitment to collective action—as Bearman (1991) found for deserters from the Confederate Army who stopped thinking about themselves as generic Southerners.

Normative Landscapes (Resistance, Transgression, Control)

Place is imbricated in moral judgments and deviant practices as well. Conduct appropriate backstage is often not permissible out front (Goffman 1959). Tags of graffiti artists violate legal norms when sprayed on the sides of subway cars or public walls, but they become legitimate art when moved inside a gallery or museum (Lachmann 1988). Openly gay behavior may be expected and approved in Castro Valley, San Francisco (Castells 1983; for Stockholm, M Graham 1998; for lesbians in Northhampton, Massachusetts, Forsyth 1997), but not (it seems) in rural Wyoming. Whether a workers' strike is legal or not, and how police respond to it, depends much on its geography (Blomley 1994). Constructions of behavior, appearances, or even people as deviant depend upon where they happen—but as these three examples illustrate, to engage in "out of place" practices is also a form of resistance (de Certeau 1984, Pile & Keith 1997) against forces imposing a territorialized normative order (Cresswell 1996). Still, just as place is caught up in definitions of deviance, so deviance on occasion defines place: sites of mass murders, terrorist violence, atrocities, or natural tragedies are variously memorialized, erased, sanctified, stigmatized, or merely rectified (Foote 1997, Gregory & Lewis 1988).

Place also plays a role in shaping rates of behavior generally considered deviant or criminal no matter where they occur. Environmental criminologists suggest that the geographic location of various social activities and the architectural arrangements of spaces and building can promote or retard crime rates—mainly crime against property (Brantingham & Brantingham 1990). City blocks with bars or public schools have higher rates of burglaries than elsewhere, and a study in Vancouver found that the number of streets leading in to a block was directly proportional to the rate of property crime—convenient access and egress seems to enable some forms of street crime (Felson 1994). Likewise, property crime rates may be lowered if places are designed to avoid large unassigned public spaces (with nobody interested enough to watch over them), to separate schools from shopping malls, to remove walls and shrubbery that make good hiding places (Jeffery 1971; on "defended neighborhoods:" De Sena 1990, Green et al 1998). On some occasions, places are designed and constructed explicitly to clean up vice and other disorderly practices—as was the case with George Pullman's model village in Chicago, which nevertheless failed to avert the destructive strike of 1894 (Buder 1967, Smith 1995, cf. Littmann 1998; on company towns: Crawford 1995; on model villages and planned communities: Buder 1990). Debate rages on over whether environmental factors affect crime rates net of other social, demographic, or economic variables (Birkbeck & LaFree 1993, Ekblom 1995, McCarthy & Hagan 1992). Interestingly, however, places perceived by people as dangerous often do not match up with the geographic distribution of crime: in an ethnically mixed urban neighborhood, residents typically defined narrow and closed-off streets as more dangerous than open and busy spaces, even though only one quarter of the neighborhood's robberies happened there (Merry 1981). But even *perception* of one's neighborhood as dangerous increases the frequency of symptoms of depression, anxiety, oppositional defiant disorder among adolescents (Aneshensel & Sucoff 1996).

Social control is also territorialized, in both its formal and informal guises. Police squad cars in Los Angeles maintain order in part by patrolling boundaries and restricting access—they use place as a means to decide who and what properly belongs where (Herbert 1997). The same tactics are used by gang members seeking to establish and control their turf (Venkatesh 1997, White 1990). Public places provide the circumstances for the most degrading forms of informal social control: on-the-street harassment of women or racial minorities is surely one way to keep disadvantaged groups in their place (Duneier & Molotch 1999, Feagin 1991, Gardner 1995). Offices have become open, facilitating surveillance and bureaucratic control (Hatch 1990). What Venkatesh writes of gangs and their territories holds as well for formal policing, public harassment, and crime generally: "On the one hand, the formal qualities of a built environment exert a powerful effect on individuals by shaping the possibilities for their behaviors. On the other hand, individuals produce their space by investing their surroundings with qualitative attributes and specified meanings" (1997:90).

Place Attachment: Identity, Memory, Loss

The formation of emotional, sentimental bonds between people and a place brings together (in yet another way) the material formations on a geographic site and the meanings we invest in them (Altman & Low 1992, Gupta & Ferguson 1997). Place attachments result from accumulated biographical experiences: we associate places with the fulfilling, terrifying, traumatic, triumphant, secret events that happened to us personally there. The longer people have lived in a place, the more rooted they feel, and the greater their attachment to it (Elder et al 1996, Herting et al 1997). Other research shows that place attachment results from interactive and culturally shared processes of endowing rooms or buildings or neighborhoods with an emotional meaning. The good times shared by friends at a university coffee shop (Milligan 1998) or a Chicago cafeteria (Duneier 1992) formed the basis for tight bonds of group affiliation—then disrupted when the special place was shut down. Generally, involvement in local public activities (shopping, politics) increases attachment to one's neighborhood—i.e., community sentiment (Cuba & Hummon 1993, Hummon 1992). But the attachment to places also depends some on the geography and architecture of the places themselves. Residents of neighborhoods near prominent landmarks, or with easily defined edges, or with better quality housing stock, are more likely to have stronger emotional bonds to where they live. Because of these kinds of attachments, sociologists should perhaps add place to race, class, and gender as a wellspring of identity, drawn upon to decide just who we are in an always unsettled way (Keith & Pile 1993).

Place attachment facilitates a sense of security and well-being, defines group boundaries, and stabilizes memories (Halbwachs 1980) against the passage of time (generally: Logan & Molotch 1987; among children: Chawla 1992, Marcus 1992; among the elderly: Reed et al 1997, Rubinstein & Parmelee 1992). Perhaps for this reason, mnemonic places (Zerubavel 1997) are specifically designed and constructed to evoke memories, trigger identities, and embody histories. National monuments commemorating wars or centennials or atrocities (Barber 1972, Sarfatti Larson 1997, Spillman 1997, Wagner-Pacifici & Schwartz 1991) inspire patriotism, at least in theory (on place and contested national identities: Borneman 1997, Gupta 1997, Zelinsky 1988), just as sacred places become the destination of pilgrimages because of their mythic or symbolic connection to the transcendent (Barrie 1996, Friedlander & Seligman 1994, Hecht 1994). In these cases, built places give material form to the ineffable or invisible, providing a durable legible architectural aide-memoire (on national identities: Cerulo 1995, Radcliffe

& Westwood 1996). They might also be home to ghosts (Bell 1997) and—as with cemeteries (Sloane 1991)—we go to such places to visit those who are no longer.

The loss of place, it follows, must have devastating implications for individual and collective identity, memory, and history—and for psychological well-being (Fullilove 1996). To be without a place of one's own—persona non locata—is to be almost non-existent, as studies of the homeless imply (Dordick 1997, Rossi 1989, Snow & Anderson 1993, Wolch & Dear 1993, Wright 1997). Among the problems of those discharged from total institutions (mental hospitals, prisons) is the difficulty of reattaching to a place—finding a home, a neighborhood, a community, often amid local opposition to the deinstitutionalized (Dear & Wolch 1987, Taylor 1989). Effects of displacement vary (Brown & Perkins 1992) depending upon whether the dislocation is forced, as in natural disasters (Erikson 1967), urban renewal (Gans 1962) and political exile (Bisharat 1997, Malkki 1995, Portes & Stepick 1993); or voluntary, as in job relocations and tourism (MacCannell 1976)—and on whether the displacement is temporary or permanent (on migrant workers: Mitchell 1996; on immigrant ethnic communities: Kasinitz 1992). The immense literature on diasporas calls attention to idealizations of homelands that (sometimes) never were, as part of the affirmation of ethnic or tribal solidarity and continuity (Appadurai 1996, Cohen 1997, Naficy 1999, Safran 1991, Sorenson 1992). One can be displaced even without going anywhere: victims of residential burglaries report (for some time thereafter) a violation of their personal space and a loss of security (Brown & Perkins 1992), and the same loss of meaning is reported by those whose sacred places are desecrated (de Certeau 1984), by Native Americans whose homelands have been made invisible (Blu 1996) and by people in regions of the United States chronically marginalized, exploited, forgotten, and unforgettable like West Virginia coal country (Stewart 1996).

CONCLUSION

Review articles typically end by looking ahead to questions and problems most in need of research tomorrow. This is impossible, mainly because the books and articles reviewed here as exemplifying a place-sensitive sociology do not add up to a neat propositional inventory of empirical findings about the social causes and effects of place. It is difficult to spot the most vitally overlooked gaps when the domain of study is as unbounded as the one discussed here—place matters for politics and identity, history and futures, inequality and community. Is there anything sociological not touched by place? Probably not.

An alternative conclusion came to mind while spending a week in Maastricht, Holland, where I had been invited to give a series of lectures. It is a place not exactly like the place where I had earlier gathered up and studied the books and articles needed for what I have written so far. The difficulties in imagining just what a place-sensitive sociology might become next were obvious as I struggled to see how Maastricht differed from Bloomington, Indiana, or how they might be alike—and why those differences or similarities might matter for the thinking I was doing. As a sociologist, it was easy for me to start demographically: how many people lived in each place, and how are the two populations differentiated by age, race, gender, occupation, SES, religion, ethnicity? I could just as easily put into words historical tidbits about them: the treaty to create a European Union was signed at Maastricht in 1992, Hoagy Carmicheal composed "Stardust" at the Book Nook on Bloomington's Indiana Avenue in 1929. And it was no sweat to theorize Maastricht and Bloomington as instances of global capitalism or urban sprawl or liberal democratic regimes or town-gown relations. Still, neither numbers nor words nor abstract concepts seemed sufficient to capture the sociologically significant characteristics of Maastricht and Bloomington as places.

Maybe a place-sensitive sociology is not a set of empirical findings at all or even a distinctive kind of explanatory model, but rather a way to do sociology in a different key–a visual key.

Figure 1   Street in Maastricht.

I walked down this street in Maastricht a dozen times and forced myself to wonder how I knew that I was not back in Bloomington. Surely I could measure the width of the lane between buildings (noting that no street in Indiana is that narrow), or tell a story about the absence of front lawns, or theorize medieval vs. twentieth-century architectural styles. But so much is lost in this translation of street scene to measurement or narration or abstraction. What I lacked were tools to analyze place in its given two and three dimensions. I am a victim, perhaps, of trained incompetence in a discipline that cultivates statistics and words as means to grasp the social. Sociologists could become more adept with maps, floor plans, photographic images, bricks and mortar, landscapes and cityscapes, so that interpreting a street or forest becomes as routine and as informative as computing a chi-square. That visualizing (I think) is the next step.

ACKNOWLEDGMENTS

For helpful readings of earlier drafts, I thank Clem Brooks, Laurel Cornell, Roger Friedland, Mark Gottdeiner, Eric Graig, Christopher Henke, Steven K. Herbert, Jason Jimerson, Magali Sarfatti Larson, John R. Logan, Harvey Molotch, Martin Murray, Susan H. Roschke, Saskia Sassen, Sheldon Stryker, Indermohan Virk and Sharon Zukin.

LITERATURE CITED

Abu-Lughod J. 1968. The city is dead–Long live the city. In *Urbanism in World Perspective*, ed. SF Fava, pp. 154–65. New York: Crowell.

Abu-Lughod J, ed. 1994. *From Urban Village to East Village: The Battle for New York's Lower East Side*. Cambridge, MA: Blackwell.

Agnew JA. 1987. *Place and Politics: The Geographical Mediation of State and Society*. Boston: Allen & Unwin

Agnew JA. 1989. The devaluation of place in social science. In *The Power of Place: Bringing Together Geographical and Sociological Imaginations*, ed. JA Agnew, JS Duncan, pp. 9–29. Boston: Unwin Hyman

Agnew JA, Duncan JS. 1989. *The Power of Place: Bringing Together Geographical and Sociological Imaginations*. Boston: Unwin Hyman

Alba RD, Logan JR. 1993. Minority proximity to whites in suburbs: An individual-level analysis of segregation. *Am. J. Sociol.* 98:1388–1427

Allen T. 1977. *Managing the Flow of Technology*. Cambridge, MA: MIT Press

Altman I, Low SM, eds. 1992. *Place Attachment*. New York: Plenum

Anderson B. 1983. *Imagined Communities*. London: Verso

Anderson K, Gale F, eds. 1992. *Inventing Places: Studies in Cultural Geography*. New York: Wiley

Aneshensel CS, Sucoff CA. 1996. The neighborhood context of adolescent mental health. *J. Health Soc. Behav.* 37:293–310

Appadurai A. 1996. *Modernity at Large: Cultural Dimensions of Globalization*. Minneapolis: Univ. Minn. Press

Ahrentzen SB. 1992. Home as a workplace in the lives of women. See Altman & Low 1992, pp. 113–37

Baldassare M. 1992. Suburban communities. *Annu. Rev. Sociol.* 18:475–94

Baldry C. 1999. Space—The final frontier. *Sociology* 33:535–53

Bantjes R. 1997. Benthamism in the countryside: the architecture of rural space, 1900-1930. *J. Hist. Sociol.* 10:249–69

Barber B. 1972. Place, symbol and the utilitarian function in war memorials. In *People and Buildings*, ed. R Gutman, pp. 327–34. New York: Basic

Barkey K, Van Rossem R. 1997. Networks of contention: Villages and regional structure in the seventeenth-century Ottoman Empire. *Am. J. Sociol.* 102:1345–82

Barrie T. 1996. *Spiritual Path, Sacred Place: Myth, Ritual and Meaning in Architecture*. Boston: Shambhala

Barthel D. 1996. *Historic Preservation: Collective Memory and Historical Identity*. New Brunswick, NJ: Rutgers Univ. Press

Basso KH. 1996. *Wisdom Sits in Places: Landscape and Language Among the Western*

Apache. Albuquerque: Univ. New Mexico Press

Bearman PS. 1991. Desertion as localism: Army unit solidarity and group norms in the U.S. Civil War. *Soc. Forc.* 70:321–42

Bell MM. 1994. *Childerly: Nature and Morality in a Country Village.* Chicago: Univ. Chicago Press.

Bell MM. 1997. The ghosts of place. *Theory Soc.* 26:813–36

Benjamin DN, ed. 1995. *The Home: Words, Interpretations, Meanings, and Environments.* Aldershot: Avebury

Bergesen A, Harman M. 1998. Immigration, race and riot: The 1992 Los Angeles uprising. *Am. Sociol. Rev.* 63:39–54

Bijker WE, Hughes TP, Pinch T, eds. 1987. *The Social Construction of Technological Systems.* Cambridge, MA: MIT Press

Birkbeck C, LaFree G. 1993. The situational analysis of crime and deviance. *Annu. Rev. Sociol.* 19:113–37

Bisharat GE. 1997. Exile to compatriot: transformations in the social identity of Palestinian refugees in the West Bank. See Gupta & Ferguson 1997a, pp. 203–33

Blau E. 1999. *The Architecture of Red Vienna 1919–1934.* Cambridge: MIT Press

Blau JR. 1984. *Architects and Firms: A Sociological Perspective on Architectural Practice.* Cambridge, MA: MIT Press

Blakely EJ, Snyder MG. 1997. *Fortress America: Gated Communities in the United States.* Washington, DC: Brookings Inst.

Blomley NK. 1994. *Law, Space, and the Geographies of Power.* New York: Guilford

Blu K. 1996. "Where do you stay at?": Homeplace and community among the Lumbee. In *Senses of Place,* ed. S Feld, KH Basso, pp. 197–227. Sante Fe: Sch. Am. Res. Press

Boden D, Molotch HL. 1994. The compulsion of proximity. In *NoWhere: Space, Time and Modernity,* ed. R Friedland, D Boden, 257–86. Berkeley: Univ. Calif. Press

Boddy T. 1992. Underground and overhead: Building the analogous city. In *Variations on a Theme Park: The New American Theme*

Park and the End of Public Space, ed. M Sorkin, 123–53. New York: Hill & Wang.

Borneman J. 1997. State, territory and national identity formation in the two Berlins, 1945–1995. See Gupta & Ferguson 1997, pp. 93–117

Bourdieu P. 1990. *The Logic of Practice.* Stanford, CA: Stanford Univ. Press.

Boyer MC. 1983. *Dreaming the Rational City: The Myth of American City Planning.* Cambridge, MA: MIT Press

Boyer MC. 1994. *The City of Collective Memory: Its Historical Imagery and Architectural Entertainments.* Cambridge: MIT Press

Boyer MC. 1996. *CyberCities.* Princeton, NJ: Princeton Architectural Press

Brain D. 1989. Discipline and style: the Ecole des Beaux-Arts and the social production of an American architecture. *Theory Soc.* 18:807–68

Brain D. 1991. Practical knowledge and occupational control: the professionalization of architecture in the United States. *Sociol. Forum* 6:239–68

Brain D. 1997. From public housing to private communities: the discipline of design and the materialization of the public/private distinction in the built environment. In *Public and Private in Thought and Practice,* ed. J Weintraub, K Kumar, pp. 237–67. Chicago: Univ. Chicago Press.

Brain D. 1998. *The 'New Urbanism' as a way of life: Neotraditional design, technologies of place, and the architecture of community.* Pres. Annu. Meet. Am. Sociol. Assoc., 93rd, San Francisco

Brantingham PJ, Brantingham PL, eds. 1990. *Environmental Criminology.* Prospect Heights, IL: Waveland.

Bridger JC. 1996. Community imagery and the built environment. *Sociol. Q.* 3:353–74

Brown BB, Perkins DD. 1992. Disruptions in place attachment. See Altman & Low 1992, pp. 279–304

Brustein W, Levi M. 1987. The geography of rebellion: rulers, rebels and regions, 1500 to 1700. *Theory Soc.* 16:467–95

Buck-Morss S. 1989. *The Dialectics of Seeing: Walter Benjamin and the Arcades Project.* Cambridge: MIT Press

Buder S. 1967. *Pullman: An Experiment in Social Order and Community Planning, 1880–1930.* New York: Oxford Univ. Press

Buder S. 1990. *Visionaries and Planners: The Garden City Movement and the Modern Community.* New York: Oxford Univ. Press

Buisseret D, ed. 1998. *Envisioning the City.* Chicago: Univ. Chicago Press

Bullard RD. 1990. *Dumping in Dixie: Race, Class and Environmental Quality.* Boulder, CO: Westview.

Carr S, Francis M, Rivlin LG, Stone AM. 1992. *Public Space.* Cambridge: Cambridge Univ. Press.

Carter PA. 1988. *The Road to Botany Bay: An Exploration of Landscape and History.* New York: Knopf

Casey ES. 1993. *Getting Back into Place: Toward a Renewed Understanding of the Place-World.* Bloomington: Indiana Univ. Press

Casey ES. 1997. *The Fate of Place: A Philosophical History.* Berkeley: Univ. Calif. Press

Castells M. 1977. *The Urban Question: A Marxist Approach.* Cambridge, MA: MIT Press

Castells M. 1983. *The City and the Grassroots.* Berkeley: Univ. Calif. Press

Cerulo KA. 1995. *Identity Designs: The Sights and Sounds of a Nation.* New Brunswick, NJ: Rutgers Univ. Press

Chawla L. 1992. Childhood place attachments. See Altman & Low 1992, pp. 63–86

Cherry GE. 1974. *The Evolution of British Town Planning.* New York: Wiley

Ching B, Creed GW, eds. 1997. *Knowing Your Place: Rural Identity and Cultural Hierarchy.* New York: Routledge

Choldin HM. 1978. Urban density and pathology. *Annu. Rev. Sociol.* 4:91–113

Cieraad I, ed. 1999. *At Home: An Anthropology of Domestic Space.* Syracuse, NY: Syracuse Univ. Press

Clark S. 1998. International competition and the treatment of minorities: seventeenth-century cases and general propositions. *Am. J. Sociol.* 103:1267–1308

Clarke L. 1992. *Building Capitalism: Historical Change and the Labor Process in the Production of the Built Environment.* London: Routledge

Clausewitz C. 1976. *On War.* Princeton, NJ: Princeton Univ. Press

Cline A. 1997. *A Hut of One's Own: Life Outside the Circle of Architecture.* Cambridge, MA: MIT Press

Cloke P, Little J, eds. 1997. *Contested Countryside Cultures: Otherness, Marginalization, and Rurality.* London: Routledge

Cohen R. 1997. *Global Diasporas: An Introduction.* Seattle: Univ. Wash. Press

Coleman JS. 1993. The rational reconstruction of society. *Am. Sociol. Rev.* 58:1–15

Cox KR, ed. 1997. *Spaces of Globalization: Reasserting the Power of the Local.* New York: Guilford

Crain MM. 1997. The remaking of an Andalusian pilgrimage tradition: debates regarding visual (re)presentation and the meanings of "locality" in a global era. See Gupta & Ferguson 1997a, pp. 291–311

Crawford M. 1992. The world in a shopping mall. In *Variations on a Theme Park: The New American Theme Park and the End of Public Space*, ed. M Sorkin, pp. 3–30. New York: Hill & Wang

Crawford M. 1995. *Building the Workingman's Paradise: The Design of American Company Towns.* London: Verso

Cresswell T. 1996. *In Place/Out of Place: Geography, Ideology, and Trangression.* Minneapolis: Univ. Minnesota Press.

Cronon W. 1983. *Changes in the Land: Indians, Colonists, and the Ecology of New England.* New York: Hill & Wang.

Croucher SL. 1997. *Imagining Miami: Ethnic Politics in a Postmodern World.* Charlottesville: Univ. Press of Virginia

Cuba L, Hummon DM. 1993. A place to call home: identification with dwelling, community, and region. *Sociol. Q.* 34:111–31

Cuff D. 1991. *Architecture: The Story of*

Practice. Cambridge, MA: MIT Press

Davis GF, Greve HR. 1997. Corporate elite networks and governance changes in the 1980s. *Am. J. Sociol.* 103:1–37

Davis SG. 1997. *Spectacular Nature: Corporate Culture and the Sea World Experience*. Berkeley/Los Angeles: Univ. Calif. Press

Davis M. 1990. *City of Quartz*. New York: Vintage

Davis M. 1998. *Ecology of Fear*. New York: Vintage

Dear MJ, Wolch JR, eds. 1987. *Landscapes of Despair: From Deinstitutionalization to Homelessness*. Princeton, NJ: Princeton Univ. Press

Dear MJ, Schockman HE, Hise G, eds. 1996. *Rethinking Los Angeles*. Thousand Oaks, CA: Sage

de Boer E, ed. 1986. *Transport Sociology: Social Aspects of Transport Planning*. Oxford: Pergamon

de Certeau M. 1984. *The Practice of Evveryday Life*. Berkeley: Univ. Calif. Press

De Sena JN. 1990. *Protecting One's Turf: Social Strategies for Maintaining Urban Neighborhoods*. Lanham, MD: Univ. Press Am.

Deleuze G, Guattari F. 1986. *Nomadology: The War Machine*. New York: Semiotext(e)

Dordick GA. 1997. *Something Left to Lose: Personal Relations and Survival Among New York's Homeless*. Philadelphia, PA: Temple Univ. Press

Dorst JD. 1989. *The Written Suburb: An American Site, an Ethnographic Dilemma*. Philadelphia: Univ. Penn. Press

Downs RM, Stea D, eds. 1973. *Image and Environment*. Chicago: Aldine

Duneier M. 1992. *Slim's Table: Race, Respectability and Masculinity*. Chicago: Univ. Chicago Press

Duneier M, Molotch H. 1999. Talking city trouble: Interactional vandalism, social inequality, and the 'urban interaction problem.' *Am. J. Sociol.* 104:1263–95

Dupuis EM, Vandergeest P, eds. 1996. *Creating the Countryside: The Politics of Rural and Environmental Discourse*. Philadelphia: Temple Univ. Press

Durkheim E, Mauss M. 1963 [1903]. *Primitive Classification*. Chicago: Univ. Chicago Press

Ekblom P. 1995. Less crime, by design. *Ann. AAPSS* 539:114–29

Elder GH, King V, Conger RD. 1996. Attachment to place and migration prospects: a developmental perspective. *J. Res. Adolesc.* 6:397–425

Ellin N. 1996. *Postmodern Urbanism*. Cambridge, MA: Blackwell

Entrikin JN. 1989. Place, region and modernity. See Agnew & Duncan 1989, pp. 30–43

Entrikin JN. 1991. *The Betweeness of Place: Towards a Geography of Modernity*. London: Macmillan

Erikson K. 1967. *Everything in its Path*. New York: Simon & Schuster

Espeland WN. 1998. *The Struggle for Water: Politics, Rationality, and Identity in the American Southwest*. Chicago: Univ. Chicago Press

Etlin RA. 1997. Space, stone, and spirit: the meaning of place. In *The Eight Technologies of Otherness*, ed. S Golding, pp. 306–19. London: Routledge

Fairbanks RB. 1998. *For the City as a Whole: Planning, Politics, and the Public Interest in Dallas, Texas, 1900–1965*. Columbus: Ohio State Univ. Press

Falasca-Zamponi S. 1997. *The Aesthetics of Power in Mussolini's Italy*. Berkeley, CA: Univ. Calif. Press

Farley R, Steeh C, Krysan M, Jackson T, Reeves K. 1994. Stereotypes and segregation: Neighborhoods in the Detroit area. *Am. J. Sociol.* 100:750–80

Feagin JR. 1988. *Free Enterprise City: Houston in Political-Economic Perspective*. New Brunswick, NJ: Rutgers Univ. Press

Feagin JR. 1991. The continuing significance of race: antiblack discrimination in public places. *Am. Sociol. Rev.* 56:101–16

Feagin JR. 1998. *The New Urban Paradigm: Critical Perspectives on the City*. Lanham, MD: Rowman & Littlefield

Fehrenbacher-Zeiser S. 1996. Interior architectural design: Conventions and innovations. *Curr. Res. Occup. Professions* 9:211–31

Feld S, Basso KH, eds. 1996. *Senses of Place.* Sante Fe, NM: Sch. Am. Res. Press

Felson M. 1994. *Crime and Everyday Life.* Thousand Oaks, CA: Pine Forge Press

Ferguson PP. 1998. A cultural field in the making: gastronomy in 19th-century France. *Am. J. Sociol.* 104:597–641

Festinger L, Schachter S, Back K. 1950. *Social Pressures in Informal Groups.* Stanford, CA: Stanford Univ. Press

Fischer CS. 1975. The study of urban community and personality. *Annu. Rev. Sociol.* 1:67–89

Fischer CS. 1977. *Networks and Places: Social Relations in the Urban Setting.* New York: Free Press

Fischer C. 1982. *To Dwell Among Friends.* Chicago: Univ. Chicago Press

Flanagan WG. 1993. *Contemporary Urban Sociology.* Cambridge, UK: Cambridge Univ. Press.

Foote KE. 1997. *Shadowed Ground: America's Landscapes of Violence and Tragedy.* Austin: Univ. Texas Press

Forester J. 1989. *Planning in the Face of Power.* Berkeley: Univ. Calif. Press

Forsyth A. 1997. "Out" in the valley. *Int. J. Urban Regional Res.* 21:38–62

Foucault M. 1979. *Discipline and Punish.* New York: Vintage

Friedland R, Boden D, eds. 1994. *NowHere: Space, Time and Modernity.* Berkeley: Univ. Calif. Press

Friedlander S, Seligman AB. 1994. The Isreali memory of the Shoah: on symbols, rituals, and ideological polarization. See Friedland & Boden 1994, pp. 356–71

Frisbie WP, Kasarda JD. 1988. Spatial processes. In *Handbook of Sociology,* ed. NJ Smelser, pp. 629–66. Beverly Hills, CA: Sage

Frug GE. 1999. *City Making: Building Communities Without Building Walls.* Princeton, NJ: Princeton Univ. Press

Fullilove MT. 1996. Psychiatric implications of displacement: contributions from the psychology of place. *Am. J. Psychiatry* 153:1516–23

Galison P, Thompson E, eds. 1999. *The Architecture of Science.* Cambridge, MA: MIT Press

Gans HJ. 1962. *Urban Villagers.* New York: Free Press

Gans HJ. 1968. *People and Plans: Essays on Urban Problems and Solutions.* New York: Basic

Gardner CB. 1995. *Passing By: Gender and Public Harassment.* Berkeley: Univ. Calif. Press

Garreau J. 1991. *Edge City.* New York: Doubleday

Giddens A. 1984. *The Constitution of Society.* Cambridge, MA: Polity Press

Giddens A. 1990. *Consequences of Modernity.* Stanford, CA: Stanford Univ. Press

Gieryn TF. 1998. Biotechnology's private parts (and some public ones). In *Private Science,* ed. A Thackray, pp. 219–53. Philadelphia: Univ. Penn. Press

Gieryn TF. 1999. *Cultural Boundaries of Science: Credibility On the Line.* Chicago: Univ. Chicago Press

Goffman E. 1959. *The Presentation of Self in Everyday Life.* Garden City, NY: Doubleday.

Gold JR, Ward SV, eds. 1994. *Place Promotion: The Use of Publicity and Marketing to Sell Towns and Regions.* New York: Wiley

Gottdiener M. 1994. *The Social Production of Urban Space.* Austin: Univ. Texas Press

Gottdiener M. 1995. *Postmodern Semiotics: Material Culture and the Forms of Postmodern Life.* Oxford: Blackwell

Gottdiener M. 1997. *The Theming of America: Dreams, Visons, and Commercial Spaces.* Boulder, CO: Westview

Gottdiener M, Feagin J. 1988. The paradigm shift in urban sociology. *Urban Affairs Q.* 24:163–87

Gould RV. 1995. *Insurgent Identities: Class, Community, and Protest in Paris from 1848 to the Commune.* Chicago: Univ. Chicago Press

Graham M. 1998. Identity, place and erotic community within gay leather culture in Stockholm. *J. Homosexuality* 5:163–83

Graham S. 1998. The end of geography or the explosion of place?: Conceptualizing space, place and information technology. *Progress in Hum. Geogr.* 22:165–85

Grannis R. 1998. The importance of trivial streets: residential streets and residential segregation. *Am. J. Sociol.* 103:1530–64

Green DP, Strolovitch DZ, Wong JS. 1998. Defended neighborhoods, integration and racially motivated crime. *Am. J. Sociol.* 104:372–403

Gregory D. 1994. *Geographical Imaginations.* Cambridge, MA: Blackwell

Gregory S. 1998. *Black Corona: Race and the Politics of Place in an Urban Community.* Princeton, NJ: Princeton Univ. Press

Gregory SW, Lewis JM. 1988. Symbols of collective memory: the social process of memorializing May 4, 1970 at Kent State Univ. *Symbolic Interact.* 11:213–33

Griswold W. 1992. The writing on the mud wall: Nigerian novels and the imaginary village. *Am. Sociol. Rev.* 57:709–24

Gupta A. 1997. The song of the nonaligned world: transnational identities and the reinscription of space in late capitalism. See Gupta & Ferguson 1997a, pp. 179–99

Gupta A, Ferguson J, eds. 1997a. *Culture, Power, Place.* Durham, NC: Duke Univ. Press

Gupta A, Ferguson J. 1997b. Beyond "culture": Space, identity, and the politics of difference. See Gupta & Ferguson 1997a, pp. 33–51

Gutman R. 1988. *Architectural Practice: A Critical View.* Princeton, NJ: Princeton Architect. Press

Gutman R. 1989. Human nature in architectural theory: the example of Louis Kahn. In *Architects' People*, ed. R Ellis, D Cuff, pp. 105–29. New York: Oxford Univ. Press

Haar CM. 1996. *Suburbs under Siege: Race, Space, and Audacious Judges.* Princeton, NJ: Princeton Univ. Press.

Habraken NJ. 1998. *The Structure of the Ordinary.* Cambridge, MA: MIT Press

Halbwachs M. 1980 [1950]. *The Collective Memory.* New York: Harper & Row

Hall PG. 1988. *Cities of Tomorrow: An Intellectual History of Urban Planning and Design in the Twentieth Century.* Oxford: Basil Blackwell

Halle D. 1993. *Inside Culture: Art and Class in the American Home.* Chicago: Univ. Chicago Press

Halpern D. 1995. *Mental Health and the Built Environment.* London: Taylor & Francis

Hannerz U. 1992. *Cultural Complexity: Studies in the Social Organization of Meaning.* New York: Columbia Univ. Press

Harris DR. 1999. 'Property values drop when blacks move in, because . . .': Racial and socioeconomic determinants of neighborhood productivity. *Am. Sociol. Rev.* 64:461–79

Harvey D. 1973. *Social Justice and the City.* Baltimore: Johns Hopkins Univ. Press

Harvey D. 1990. *The Condition of Postmodernity.* Cambridge, MA: Blackwell

Harvey D. 1996. *Justice, Nature and the Geography of Difference.* Cambridge, MA: Blackwell

Hatch MJ. 1990. The symbolics of office design: an empirical exploration. In *Symbols and Artifacts: Views of the Corporate Landscape*, ed. P Gagliardi, pp. 129–46. New York: Walter de Gruyter

Hawley AH. 1986. *Human Ecology.* Chicago: Univ. Chicago Press

Hayden D. 1981. *The Grand Domestic Revolution: A History of Feminist Designs for American Homes, Neighborhoods, and Cities.* Cambridge, MA: MIT Press

Hayden D. 1984. *Redesigning the American Dream.* New York: Norton

Hayden D. 1995. *The Power of Place.* Cambridge, MA: MIT Press.

Hecht RD. 1994. The construction and management of sacred time and space: Sabta Nur in the Church of the Holy Sepulcher. See Friedland & Boden 1994, pp. 181–235

Hedstrom P. 1994. Contagious collectivities:

On the spatial diffusion of Swedish trade unions, 1890–1940. *Am. J. Sociol.* 99:1157–79

Herbert S. 1997. *Policing Space: Territoriality and the Los Angeles Police Department.* Minneapolis: Univ. Minn. Press

Herting JR, Grusky DB, Van Rompaey SE. 1997. The social geography of interstate mobility and persistance. *Am. Sociol. Rev.* 62:267–87

Hillier B, Hanson J. 1984. *The Social Logic of Space.* Cambridge: Cambridge Univ. Press

Hiss T. 1990. *The Experience of Place.* New York: Knopf

Hooks G. 1994. Regional processes in the hegemonic nation: political, economic, and military influences on the use of geographic space. *Am. Sociol. Rev.* 59:746–72

Holston J. 1989. *The Modernist City: An Anthropological Critique of Brasilia.* Chicago: Univ. Chicago Press

Hughes F, ed. 1996. *The Architect: Reconstructing Her Practice.* Cambridge, MA: MIT Press

Hughes HL. 1993. Metropolitan structure and the suburban hierarchy. *Am. Sociol. Rev.* 58:417–33

Hummon DM. 1990. *Commonplaces: Community, Ideology and Identity in American Culture.* Albany: State Univ. New York Press

Hummon DM. 1992. Community attachment: local sentiment and sense of place. In *Place Attachment*, ed. I Altman, SM Low, pp. 253–78. New York: Plenum

Jacobs J. 1961. *The Death and Life of Great American Cities.* New York: Random House

Jameson F. 1984. Postmodernism, or the cultural logic of late capitalism. *New Left Rev.* 46:53–92

Jargowsky PA. 1997. *Poverty and Place: Ghettos, Barrios and the American City.* New York: Russell Sage

Jeffery CR. 1971. *Crime Prevention through Environmental Design.* Beverly Hills, CA: Sage

Jones SG, ed. 1998. *Cybersociety 2.0: Revisiting Computer-Mediated Communication and Community.* Thousand Oaks, CA: Sage

Kain RJP, Baigent E. 1992. *The Cadastral Map in the Service of the State: A History of Property Mapping.* Chicago: Univ. Chicago Press

Kasinitz P. 1992. *Caribbean New York: Black Immigrants and the Politics of Race.* Ithaca, NY: Cornell Univ. Press

Kelley KB, Francis H. 1994. *Navajo Sacred Places.* Bloomington: Indiana Univ. Press

Keil R. 1998. *Los Angeles: Globalization, Urbanization and Social Struggles.* New York: Wiley

Keith M, Pile S, eds. 1993. *Place and the Politics of Identity.* London: Routledge

King A. 1998. *Mapping the Unmappable: Visual Representations of the Internet as Social Constructions.* Presented at Annu. Meet. Am. Sociol. Assoc., 93rd, San Francisco

King AD. 1995. *The Bungalow: The Production of a Global Culture.* New York: Oxford Univ. Press

King AD, ed. 1996. *Re-Presenting the City: Ethnicity, Capital and Culture in the 21st-Century Metropolis.* New York: New York Univ. Press

King G. 1996. *Mapping Realities: An Exploration of Cultural Cartographies.* New York: St Martin's

King R. 1996. *Emancipating Space: Geography, Architecture, and Urban Design.* New York: Guilford

Kirp DL, Dwyer JP, Rosenthal LA. 1995. *Our Town: Race, Housing and the Soul of Suburbia.* New Brunswick, NJ: Rutgers Univ. Press

Kitchin RM. 1994. Cognitive maps: What are they and why study them? *J. Environ. Psychol.* 14:1–19

Knorr Cetina K. 1999. *Epistemic Cultures: How the Sciences Make Knowledge.* Cambridge, MA: Harvard Univ. Press

Knox PL, ed. 1993. *The Restless Urban Landscape.* Englewood Cliffs, NJ: Prentice-Hall

Knox PL, Taylor PJ, eds. 1995. *World Cities in a World-System.* Cambridge, UK: Cambridge Univ. Press

Kono C, Palmer D, Friedland R, Zafonte M. 1998. Lost in space: the geography of corporate interlocking directorates. *Am. J. Sociol.* 103:863–911

Koptiuch K. 1997. Third-worlding at home. See Gupta & Ferguson 1997a, pp. 234–48

Krech S. 1999. *The Ecological Indian: Myth and History.* New York: Norton

Kunstler JH. 1996. *Home from Nowhere.* New York: Simon & Schuster

Laclau E. 1990. *New Reflections on the Revolution of our Time.* London: Verso

Lachmann R. 1988. Graffiti as career and ideology. *Am. J. Sociol.* 94:229–50

Ladd B. 1997. *The Ghosts of Berlin: Confronting Urban History in the Urban Landscape.* Chicago: Univ. Chicago Press

Latour B. 1988. *The Pasteurization of France.* Cambridge, MA: Harvard Univ. Press

Latour B. 1996. *Aramis, or the Love of Technology.* Cambridge, MA: Harvard Univ. Press

Lawrence DL, Low SM. 1990. The built environment and spatial form. *Annu. Rev. Anthropol.* 19:453–505

Lefebvre H. 1991. *The Production of Space.* Oxford: Blackwell

Lewis E. 1996. Connecting memory, self, and the power of place in African American urban history. In *The New African American History,* ed. KW Goings, RA Mohl, pp. 116–41. Thousand Oaks, CA: Sage

Lewis MW, Wigen KF. 1997. *The Myth of Continents: A Critique of Metageography.* Berkeley: Univ. Calif. Press

Ley D. 1989. Modernism, postmodernism and the struggle for place. See Agnew & Duncan 1989, pp. 44–65

Ley D. 1997. *The New Middle Class and the Remaking of the Central City.* New York: Oxford Univ. Press

Linde C, Labov W. 1985. Spatial networks as a site for the study of language and thought. *Language* 51:924–39

Lindstrom B. 1997. A sense of place: housing selection on Chicago's North Shore. *Sociol. Q.* 38:19–39

Lippard LR. 1997. *The Lure of the Local: Senses of Place in a Multicentered Society.* New York: New Press

Littmann W. 1998. Designing obedience: The architecture and landscape of welfare capitalism, 1880–1930. *Int. Labor Working-Class Hist.* 53:88–114

Lofland LH. 1973. *A World of Strangers.* Prospect Heights, IL: Waveland

Lofland LH. 1998. *The Public Realm.* New York: Aldine de Gruyter

Logan JR, Molotch HL. 1987. *Urban Fortunes: The Political Economy of Place.* Berkeley, CA: Univ. Calif. Press

Logan JR, Spitze GD. 1994. Family neighbors. *Am. J. Sociol.* 100:453–76

Low SM. 1996. The anthropology of cities. *Annu. Rev. Anthropol.* 25:3830

Lynch K. 1960. *The Image of the City.* Cambridge, MA: MIT Press.

MacCannell D. 1976. *The Tourist: A New Theory of the Leisure Class.* New York: Schocken Books

MacCannell D. 1999. "New Urbanism" and its discontents. In *Giving Ground: The Politics of Propinquity,* ed. J Copjec, M Sorkin, pp. 106–28. New York: Verso

MacKenzie D. 1990. *Inventing Accuracy: A Historical Sociology of Nuclear Missile Guidance.* Cambridge, MA: MIT Press

Malkki LH. 1995. *Purity and Exile: Violence, Memory, and National Cosmology among Hutu Refugees in Tanzania.* Chicago: Univ. Chicago Press

Marcus CC. 1992. Environmental memories. See Altman & Low 1992, pp. 87–112

Markus TA. 1993. *Buildings and Power: Freedom and Control in the Origin of Modern Building Types.* London: Routledge

Massey D. 1994. *Space, Place, and Gender.* Minneapolis: Univ. Minn. Press

Massey DS. 1985. Ethnic residential segregation: a theoretical synthesis and empirical review. *Sociol. Soc. Res.* 69:315–50

Massey DS, Denton NA. 1993. *American Apartheid: Segregation and the Making of the Underclass.* Cambridge, MA: Harvard Univ. Press

McCarthy B, Hagan J. 1992. Mean streets: the theoretical significance of situational delinquency among homeless youths. *Am. J. Sociol.* 98:597–627

McDowell L. 1999. *Gender, Identity and Place.* Minneapolis: Univ. Minn. Press

Merry SE. 1981. *Urban Danger: Life in a Neighborhood of Strangers.* Philadelphia: Temple Univ. Press

Metcalf TR. 1989. *An Imperial Vision: Indian Architecture and Britain's Raj.* Berkeley: Univ. Calif. Press

Milgram S, Greenwald J, Kessler S, McKenna W, Waters J. 1972. A psychological map of New York. *Am. Scientist* 60:194–200

Milligan MJ. 1998. Interactional past and present: the social construction of place attachment. *Symbolic Interact.* 21:1–33

Mitchell D. 1996. *The Lie of the Land: Migrant Workers and the California Landscape.* Minneapolis: Univ. Minn. Press

Mitchell WJ. 1995. *City of Bits: Space, Place, and the Infobahn.* Cambridge, MA: MIT Press

Moore HL. 1986. *Space, Text and Gender: An Anthropological Study of the Marakwet of Kenya.* Cambridge, UK: Cambridge Univ. Press

Moore JD. 1996. The archaeology of plazas and the proxemics of ritual: Three Andean traditions. *Am. Anthropol.* 98:789–802

Mukerji C. 1997. *Territorial Ambitions and the Gardens of Versailles.* Cambridge, UK: Cambridge Univ. Press

Naficy H, ed. 1999. *Home, Exile, Homeland.* New York: Routledge

Nippert-Eng CE. 1995. *Home and Work.* Chicago: Univ. Chicago Press

Norton BG, Hannon B. 1997. Environmental values: a place-based theory. *Environ. Ethics* 19:227–45

Norton W. 1989. *Explorations in the Understanding of Landscape: A Cultural Geography.* New York: Greenwood

Oldenburg R. 1989. *The Great Good Place.* New York: Paragon House

Oliver ML, Shapiro TM. 1995. *Black Wealth/White Wealth.* New York: Routledge

Oliver PE, Myers DJ. 1999. How events enter the public sphere: Conflict, location, and sponsorship in local newspaper coverage of public events. *Am. J. Sociol.* 105:38–87

Opp K-D, Gern C. 1993. Dissident groups, networks, and spontaneous cooperation: the East German revolution of 1989. *Am. Sociol. Rev.* 58:659–80

Orfield M. 1997. *Metropolitics: A Regional Agenda for Community and Stability.* Washington, DC: Brookings Inst. Press

Orum AM. 1995. *City-Building in America.* Boulder, CO: Westview

Papadopoulos AG. 1996. *Urban Regimes and Strategies: Building Europe's Central Executive District in Brussels.* Chicago: Univ. Chicago Press

Pappas G. 1989. *The Magic City: Unemployment in a Working-Class Community.* Ithaca, NY: Cornell Univ. Press

Pattillo-McCoy M. 1998. Church culture as a strategy of action in the Black community. *Am. Sociol. Rev.* 63:767–84

Pearson MP, Richards C, eds. 1997. *Architecture and Order: Approaches to Social Space.* London: Routledge

Peponis J, Zimring C, Choi YK. 1990. Finding the building in wayfinding. *Environ. Behav.* 22:555–90

Perin C. 1977. *Everything in its Place: Social Order and Land Use in America.* Princeton, NJ: Princeton Univ. Press

Pickles J, ed. 1995. *Ground Truth: The Social Implications of Geographic Information Systems.* New York: Guilford

Pile S, Keith M, eds. 1997. *Geographies of Resistance.* New York: Routledge

Portes A, Stepick A. 1993. *City on the Edge: The Transformation of Miami.* Berkeley: Univ. Calif. Press

Pred A. 1990. *Making Histories and Constructing Human Geographies.* Boulder, CO: Westview

Price ET. 1995. *Dividing the Land: Early American Beginnings of our Private Property Mosaic.* Chicago: Univ. Chicago Press

Prussin L. 1995. *African Nomadic Architecture: Space, Place, and Gender.* Washington, DC: Smithsonian Inst. Press

Purcell K. 1997. Towards a communication dialectic: Embedded technology and the enhancement of place. *Sociol. Inquiry* 67:101–12

Rabinow P. 1989. *French Modern: Norms and Forms of the Social Environment.* Cambridge, MA: MIT Press

Radcliffe S, Westwood S. 1996. *Remaking the Nation: Place, Identity and Politics in Latin America.* London: Routledge

Reed J, Payton VR, Bond S. 1997. The importance of place for older people moving into care homes. *Soc. Sci. Med.* 46:859–67

Reichl AJ. 1999. *Reconstructing Times Square.* Lawrence: Univ. Press of Kansas

Relph E. 1976. *The Placelessness of Place.* London: Pion

Robinson DJ. 1989. The language and significance of place in Latin America. See Agnew & Duncan 1989, 157–184

Rofel L. 1997. Rethinking modernity: space and factory discipline in China. See Gupta & Ferguson 1997a, pp. 155–78

Rossi P. 1989. *Down and Out in America: The Origins of Homelessness.* Chicago: Univ. Chicago Press

Rotenberg R, McDonough G, eds. 1993. *The Cultural Meaning of Urban Space.* Westport, CT: Bergin & Garvey

Rowe PG. 1997. *Civic Realism.* Cambridge, MA: MIT Press

Rubinstein RL, Parmelee PA. 1992. Attachment to place and the representation of the life course by the elderly. See Altman & Low 1992, pp. 139–63

Rudel TK. 1989. *Situations and Strategies in American Land-Use Planning.* New York: Cambridge Univ. Press

Sack RD. 1997. *Homo Geographicus.* Baltimore: Johns Hopkins Univ. Press

Safran W. 1991. Diasporas in modern societies: myths of homeland and return. *Diaspora* 1:83–99

Sandercock L, ed. 1998. *Making the Invisible Visible: A Multicultural Planning History.* Berkeley: Univ. Calif. Press

Sarfatti Larson M. 1993. *Behind the Postmodern Facade.* Berkeley: Univ. Calif. Press

Sarfatti Larson M. 1997. Reading architecture in the Holocaust Memorial Museum. In *From Sociology to Cultural Studies*, ed. E Long, pp. 62–91. Oxford: Blackwell

Sarkis H. 1997. Space for recognition: on the design of public space in a multicultural society. *New Polit. Sci.* 38–39:153–70

Sassen S. 1991. *The Global City: New York, London, Tokyo.* Princeton, NJ: Princeton Univ. Press

Schama S. 1995. *Landscape and Memory.* New York: Vintage

Scott AJ. 1988. *Metropolis.* Berkeley: Univ. Calif. Press

Scott AJ, Soja EA, eds. 1996. *The City: Los Angeles and Urban Theory at the End of the Twentieth Century.* Berkeley, CA: Univ. Calif. Press

Scott JC. 1998. *Seeing Like a State.* New Haven, CT: Yale Univ. Press

Sellers JM. 1998. Place, post-industrial change, and the new left. *Eur. J. Polit. Res.* 33:187–217

Sennett R. 1970. *The Uses of Disorder: Personal Identity and City Life.* New York: Vintage

Sennett R. 1990. *The Conscience of the Eye: The Design and Social Life of Cities.* New York: Norton

Sennett R. 1994. *Flesh and Stone: The Body and the City in Western Civilization.* New York: Norton

Shapin S. 1998. Placing the view from nowhere: historical and sociological problems in the location of science. *Trans. Inst. Br. Geogr. NS* 23:5–12

Sigelman L, Bledsoe T, Welch S, Combs MW. 1996. Making contact? Black-white social interaction in an urban setting. *Am. J. Sociol.* 101:1306–32

Sit VFS. 1995. *Beijing: The Nature and Planning of a Chinese Capital City.* New York: Wiley

Sloane DC. 1991. *The Last Great Necessity: Cemeteries in American History*. Baltimore: Johns Hopkins Univ. Press

Smith C. 1995. *Urban Disorder and the Shape of Belief: The Great Chicago Fire, the Haymarket Bomb, and the Model Town of Pullman*. Chicago: Univ. Chicago Press

Smith DA. 1996. *Third World Cities in Global Perspective: The Political Economy of Uneven Urbanization*. Boulder, CO: Westview

Smith P. 1999. The elementary forms of place and their transformations: A Durkheimian model. *Qualit. Sociol.* 22:13–36

Snow D, Anderson L. 1993. *Down on Their Luck: A Study of Homeless Street People*. Berkeley: Univ. Calif. Press

Soja EW. 1989. *Postmodern Geographies: The Reassertion of Space in Critical Social Theory*. London: Verso

Soja EW. 1996. *Thirdspace: Journeys to Los Angeles and Other Real-and-Imagined Places*. Cambridge, MA: Blackwell

Somers MR. 1993. Citizenship and the place of the public sphere: Law, community, and political culture in the transition to democracy. *Am. Sociol. Rev.* 58:587–620

Sopher DE. 1973. Place and location: notes on the spatial patterning of culture. In *The Idea of Culture in the Social Sciences*, ed. L Schneider, C Bonjean, pp. 101–17. Cambridge, UK: Cambridge Univ. Press

Sorenson J. 1992. Essence and contingency in the construction of nationhood: Transformations of identity in Ethiopia and its disaporas. *Diaspora* 2:201–28

Sorkin M. 1999. Introduction: Traffic in Democracy. In *Giving Ground: The Politics of Propinquity*, ed. J Copjec, M Sorkin, pp. 1–15. New York: Verso

South SJ, Crowder KD. 1998. Leaving the 'hood: Residential mobility between black, white and integrated neighborhoods. *Am. Sociol. Rev.* 63:17–26

South SJ, Crowder KD. 1999. Neighborhood effects on family formation: concentrated poverty and beyond. *Am. Sociol. Rev.* 64:113–32

Spain D. 1992. *Gendered Spaces*. Chapel Hill: Univ. North Carolina Press

Spillman L. 1997. *Nation and Commemoration: Creating National Identities in the United States and Australia*. Cambridge, UK: Cambridge Univ. Press

Stea D, Turan M. 1993. *Placemaking: Production of Built Environment in Two Cultures*. Aldershot, UK: Avebury

Stewart K. 1996. *A Space on the Side of the Road: Cultural Poetics in an "Other" America*. Princeton, NJ: Princeton Univ. Press

Stieber N. 1998. *Housing Design and Society in Amsterdam: Reconfiguring Urban Order and Identity, 1900–1920*. Chicago: Univ. Chicago Press

Stoecker R. 1994. *Defending Community: The Struggle for Alternative Development in Cedar-Riverside*. Philadelphia: Temple Univ. Press

Storper M, Walker R. 1989. *The Capitalist Imperative: Territory, Technology, and Industrial Growth*. New York: Basil Blackwell

Stovall T. 1990. *The Rise of the Paris Red Belt*. Berkeley: Univ. Calif. Press

Strom E. 1996. In search of the growth coalition: American urban theories and the redevelopment of Berlin. *Urban Affairs Rev.* 31:455–81

Summers GF. 1986. Rural community development. *Annu. Rev. Sociol.* 12:347–71

Sundstrom E, Bell PA, Busby PL, Asmus C. 1996. Environmental psychology, 1989–1994. *Annu. Rev. Psychol.* 47:485–512

Suttles G. 1972. *The Social Construction of Communities*. Chicago: Univ. Chicago Press

Suttles G. 1990. *The Man-Made City: The Land-use Confidence Game in Chicago*. Chicago: Univ. Chicago Press

Taylor SM. 1989. Community exclusion of the mentally ill. In *The Power of Geography: How Territory Shapes Social Life*, ed. J Wolch, M Dear, pp. 316–30. Boston: Unwin Hyman

Thrift N. 1996. *Spatial Formations*. London: Sage

Thrift N, Williams P, eds. 1987. *Class and Space: The Making of Urban Society.* London: Routledge

Thrower NJW, ed. 1996. *Maps and Civilization.* Chicago: Univ. Chicago Press

Tuan Y-F. 1974. *Topophilia: A Study of Environmental Perception, Attitudes, and Values.* New York: Columbia Univ. Press

Tuan Y-F. 1977. *Space and Place: The Perspective of Experience.* Minneapolis: Univ. Minn. Press

Vale LJ. 1992. *Architecture, Power, and National Identity.* New Haven, CT: Yale Univ. Press

Venkatesh SA. 1997. The social organization of street gang activity in an urban ghetto. *Am. J. Sociol.* 103:82–111

Wagner-Pacifici R, Schwartz B. 1991. The Vietnam Veteran Memorial: Commemorating a difficult past. *Am. J. Sociol.* 97:376–420

Walter EV. 1988. *Placeways: A Theory of the Human Environment.* Chapel Hill: Univ. North Carolina Press

Walton J. 1992. *Western Times and Water Wars: State, Culture, and Rebellion in Calif.* Berkeley: Univ. Calif. Press

Walton J. 1993. Urban sociology: The contributions and limits of political economy. *Annu. Rev. Sociol.* 19:301–20

Weisman LK. 1992. *Discrimination by Design: A Feminist Critique of the ManMade Environment.* Urbana: Univ. Illinois Press

Wellman B. 1979. The community question: the intimate networks of East Yorkers. *Am. J. Sociol.* 84:1201–31

Werlen B. 1993. *Society, Action and Space: An Alternative Human Geography.* London: Routledge

Whitaker C. 1996. *Architecture and the American Dream.* New York: Clarkson N. Potter

White R. 1990. *No Space of Their Own: Young People and Social Control in Australia.* Cambridge, UK: Cambridge Univ. Press

Whyte WH. 1980. *The Social Life of Small Urban Spaces.* Washington, DC: Conservation Found.

Wilson E. 1992. *The Sphinx in the City: Urban Life, the Control of Disorder, and Women.* Berkeley: Univ. Calif. Press

Wilson FD. 1984. Urban ecology: urbanization and systems of cities. *Annu. Rev. Sociol.* 10:283–307

Wilson WH. 1998. *Hamilton Park: A Planned Black Community in Dallas.* Baltimore, MD: Johns Hopkins Univ. Press

Wilson WJ. 1996. *When Work Disappears: The World of the New Urban Poor.* New York: Knopf

Winner L. 1992. Silicon Valley mystery house. In *Variations on a Theme Park: The New American Theme Park and the End of Public Space*, ed. M Sorkin, pp. 31–60. New York: Hill & Wang.

Wolch J, Dear M. 1993. *Malign Neglect: Homelessness in an American City.* San Francisco: Jossey-Bass

Wright G. 1981. *Building the Dream: A Social History of Housing in America.* New York: Pantheon

Wright G. 1991. *The Politics of Design in French Colonial Urbanism.* Chicago: Univ. Chicago Press

Wright T. 1997. *Out of Place: Homeless Mobilizations, Subcities, and Contested Landscapes.* Albany: State Univ. New York Press

Wright T, Hutchison R. 1997. Socio-spatial reproduction, marketing culture, and the built environment. *Res. Urban Sociol.* 4:187–214

Young IM. 1990. *Justice and the Politics of Difference.* Princeton, NJ: Princeton Univ. Press

Zeisel J. 1975. *Sociology and Architectural Design.* New York: Russell Sage Found.

Zelinsky W. 1988. *Nation into State: The Shifting Symbolic Foundations of American Nationalism.* Chapel Hill, NC: Univ. North Carolina Press

Zerubavel E. 1997. *Social Mindscapes: An Invitation to Cognitive Sociology.* Cambridge, MA: Harvard Univ. Press

Zhao D. 1998. Ecologies of social movements: student mobilization during the 1989 prodemocracy movement in Beijing. *Am.*

J. Sociol. 103:1493–529

Zhou M. 1992. *Chinatown: The Socieconomic Potential of an Urban Enclave.* Philadelphia: Temple Univ. Press

Zukin S. 1982. *Loft Living.* Baltimore, MD: Johns Hopkins Univ. Press

Zukin S. 1987. Gentrification: culture and capital in the urban core. *Annu. Rev. Sociol.* 13:129–47

Zukin S. 1991. *Landscapes of Power: From Detroit to Disney World.* Berkeley: Univ. Calif. Press

Zukin S. 1995. *The Culture of Cities.* Cambridge, MA: Blackwell

Annu. Rev. Sociol. 2000. 26:497–524

WEALTH AND STRATIFICATION PROCESSES

Seymour Spilerman

Department of Sociology, Columbia University, New York, NY 10027;
e-mail: ss50@Columbia.edu

Key Words intergenerational transfers, inequality, living standards

■ **Abstract** This paper reviews current information on wealth trends, with particular attention to the role of household wealth in the stratification system. The first section considers the relevance of wealth for stratification processes and examines why an appreciation of household wealth has been slow to materialize in stratification research. Subsequent sections discuss aspects of the distribution of household wealth in the United States, the transmission of inequality across generations, and implications of a consideration of wealth for stratification theory and social policy. The concluding section conveys some observations about the need for developing models of consumption potential and living standards, akin to the socioeconomic attainment formulation, which incorporate measures of household wealth and the transmission of wealth.

INTRODUCTION

American stratification research has been characterized by an almost exclusive focus on labor market processes and rewards, to the neglect of a consideration of wealth and unearned income. This has meant adoption of the *individual* as the unit of analysis since the individual is the actor in the labor market, rather than the *family*, though most theoretical writings have emphasized the latter as the appropriate unit in a stratification system (Barber 1975, p. 75; Parkin 1971, pp. 14–15). In the socioeconomic attainment paradigm this discrepancy was often finessed by arguing that family status is derivative of head's occupational status and that family income can be approximated by head's labor market earnings (e.g. Jencks 1979, p. 9; Rosenfeld & Kalleberg 1990, pp. 80–82).

This focus on achievement has meant a preoccupation with the *production* of labor market rewards (occupational status and earnings). The influential socioeconomic attainment model (Blau & Duncan 1967; Jencks et al 1972), for example, can be thought of as specifying a transformation of education and other background variables into a status trajectory or an earnings stream. An alternative theoretical formulation, less developed in stratification research, would focus on *consumption potential*, essentially the capacity of a family to maintain a particular standard of living. Such a formulation would be better suited to examining questions of living standards, economic security, and poverty, which reflect a family's total resource base, not just its income from labor market activity.

Definitions of social class have also been firmly anchored in the sphere of production (Giddens 1973, p. 80; Blau & Duncan 1967, p. 5), to the extent that Saunders (1984) has objected to the use of the term "class" in connection with consumption processes, though he had earlier contributed to the development of this very literature (Saunders 1978).[1] It is also the case that Weber (1958, pp. 180–95), in his influential delineation of stratification systems, locates consumption on the *status* dimension of his typology. However, the referent in Weber's discussion is to "lifestyle"—i.e. consumption *pattern*—not to level of consumption or consumption potential. The latter themes, I suggest, are more rooted in economic calculations than in status concerns.

Why, then, this almost exclusive concentration on labor market processes and the neglect of wealth and unearned income in stratification research? In part, this proclivity can be attributed to the theoretical formulations that have guided empirical studies. A dismissal of private property (possessions) and inheritance is implicit in the functionalist theory of stratification, since the role of these factors is anomalous in a conceptual system that stresses the contributions of merit and skill to the social order (Davis & Moore 1945; Parkin 1978, p. 610). Also, in Marxian theory, it is one's position in the productive system that underlies life chances and living standards. Neo-Marxian authors have expanded the traditional Marxian formulation by considering the unique situations of different occupational groups, yet location in the productive order remains the essential explanatory dynamic (e.g. Wright & Perrone 1977; Wright 1985; Poulantzas 1975; see Parkin 1978, pp. 613–16 for a review).

There is also an empirical basis to the neglect of wealth in stratification research since occupational rewards are clearly the principal determinant of living standards in a modern industrial country. "Because property ownership is so heavily concentrated in the hands of so few, it does not figure as the primary source of reward for the mass of the population" (Parkin 1971, p. 24). Parkin continues by noting that the long-run tendency in Western countries has been for the share of family income deriving from property to diminish, relative to income from employment (p. 24). Calculations from Internal Revenue Service data of the proportion of family income that can be attributed to wages, salary, and entrepreneurial activity are

---

[1] Saunders (1978), along with others, formulated the concept of *housing class*, in recognition of the opportunity provided by home ownership for wealth accumulation as well as the particular economic interests generated by home ownership. In a subsequent paper, Saunders (1984) rejected the use of the term "class" in connection with housing or the consumption sector, while continuing to emphasize the importance of consumption cleavages as a fault line in Western society. In an earlier literature, Lipset & Zetterberg (1956, p. 158) did use the term *consumption class*, but in conformity with the Weberian specification of status group: "It is the way income is spent, rather than the total amount, that determines a man's consumption class." In contrast, in this essay, the term *consumption potential* is used to refer to the totality of a family's economic resources.

in the vicinity of 84% (Lenski 1984, p. 188), though there are variant estimates (e.g. Jencks et al 1972, p. 212; Rainwater et al 1986, p. 40; Slemrod 1991).

Yet, despite the centrality of labor market attainment to economic well-being, I argue in the next section that the presence of household wealth is much more consequential to a family's living standard than can be conveyed by a simple calculation of the share it contributes to family income. Moreover, there has been a substantial decline in wealth concentration in the American population, a trend that began early in the twentieth century. As a result of the consequent wealth dispersion, considerations of family asset holdings have become increasingly relevant to *general* stratification analysis, aside from their long-established salience in elite studies (e.g. Mills 1956, Kolko 1962).

From a stratification perspective, a derivative consideration to addressing the contributions of household wealth concerns the role played by family assets in the replication of inequality across generations. Empirical research has long taken as one of its central themes a clarification of the opportunity structure for young persons—essentially a determination of the prospects for upward mobility starting from father's location (e.g. Blau & Duncan 1967; Jencks et al 1972). To the extent that this question is framed in the context of labor market prospects, the principal policy issues relate to the effectiveness of educational institutions in facilitating occupational attainment. However, to the degree that stratification outcomes are framed in terms of *consumption potential*—living standards and economic well-being—the analysis must also encompass considerations of wealth and the means for acquiring wealth, whether through parental transfers or life-cycle accumulation.

In this review I examine the role of household wealth in the stratification system.[2] In the next section I discuss the relevance of wealth and convey some reasons why an appreciation of wealth processes has been slow to materialize in stratification research. Subsequent sections discuss aspects of the distribution of household wealth in the United States, the transmission of inequality across generations, and implications of a consideration of wealth for stratification theory and social policy. I conclude with some observations about the need for developing models of consumption potential and living standards—akin to the socioeconomic attainment formulation—which incorporate measures of wealth and the transmission of wealth.

THE IMPORTANCE OF HOUSEHOLD WEALTH

Attention has long been given to the privileges and life styles that derive from wealth (e.g. Baltzell 1958; Mills 1956; Kolko 1962); this body of work is a recognized specialty in sociology and economics—the field of "elite studies." As the

---

[2]A related issue concerns the impact of public transfer programs on living standards. Because these programs are diverse and targeted to particular qualifying populations (e.g. the poor, the elderly), I do not address governmental transfer programs in the present review.

name suggests, investigations into the sources and benefits of household wealth were traditionally limited to appraisals of the circumstance of very rich families. Indeed, until perhaps a decade ago, little consideration was given to how the possession of *modest* financial resources might influence economic well-being in the wider American population.

The lack of acknowledgment of wealth holdings in assessments of the living standard of the average family began to change in the 1980s. I would cite three factors as particularly responsible: (*a*) an emergent appreciation of the contributions of family wealth—even modest financial resources—to living standards; (*b*) the rapid equity buildup in the American population since World War II; and (*c*) the growing availability of wealth data at the level of the family or household unit.

Attractiveness of Wealth

By the term *wealth* I refer to a family's liquid financial assets (stocks, bonds, savings accounts) and its real property, such as a home. If income is depicted as a "flow" (with units of dollars/time), then wealth can be viewed as a "stock," a potential for an income flow. Following this imagery, one approach to establishing comparability between wealth and income is to view the former as a capitalized income stream. That is, an annuity can be purchased that will provide the asset holder with a certain lifetime income. By means of this transformation, wealth can be compared with the income flow generated by labor market activity.

However, wealth has several attractive features that are not shared by earnings (Sherraden 1991, chap. 8; Spilerman et al 1993, p. 169): (*a*) The income generated by wealth does not require a tradeoff between leisure and work—there is no cost in the form of foregone alternative use of time. (*b*) Unlike labor market earnings, the income flow generated by wealth does not decline with illness or unemployment. (*c*) Wealth can be enjoyed without being consumed, such as when held in the form of a fine painting or a dwelling. (*d*) Tax law treats wealth appreciation more favorably than labor market income. (Currently, the maximum tax rate for earned income is 39.6% versus 20% for capital gains.) (*e*) In time of economic crisis the wealth principal can be consumed—which is hardly the case with human capital.

The last point has particular relevance for low income families. Even modest levels of financial assets, which normally provide only a small addition to total income, can cushion a family from the economic shock of illness or job loss, enabling a home mortgage, car loan, and other bills to be paid for a number of months and thereby preventing a temporary loss of employment from snowballing into a wider crisis for the family. Households with few financial assets, especially African-American families (Oliver & Shapiro 1995; Conley 1999), are particularly vulnerable to such economic dislocations.

Whether a family's income derives principally from work effort or from asset holdings will influence its consumption behavior. Wealth reduces the need to accumulate savings, which an individual lacking financial assets must do in order to build a security cushion or in anticipation of retirement. Sizable household wealth obviates the need to purchase life insurance, freeing funds for other uses. Thus, with family income held constant, the extent to which the income flow stems from wealth, rather than from labor market activity, will affect the allocation between consumption and savings (Danziger et al 1991). Even the anticipation of future wealth, such as the expectation of an inheritance, may influence the allocation, in that the expected availability of assets would be factored into a family's calculation of its need to save (Weil 1994).

Buildup of Wealth in the American Population

The above comments provide a rationale for giving consideration to family wealth as a potentially significant factor in living standards. Yet, to the extent that household wealth remains concentrated in the hands of a few, the preceding argument would carry little import for general stratification processes, as distinct from elite studies.

It is therefore crucial to observe that in addition to the buildup in average family wealth, there has been a pronounced trend toward wealth dispersion in Western countries (Shorrocks 1987; Spant 1987); details are presented in a later section. While the average family may have accumulated only modest assets in an investment portfolio or in a savings account, home equity and pension equity have grown by substantial amounts (Wolff 1995; Ratcliff & Maurer 1995; see Shorrocks 1987 for similar findings for Great Britain). These forms of wealth holdings are more widely distributed in the population than are investment assets, and their growth is responsible for much of the noted decline in wealth concentration.

Availability of Data on Asset Holdings

I would suggest that the single most responsible factor for the growing attention to family wealth and to the impact of family assets on living standards is the recent availability, from several large surveys, of asset data at the household level. The first survey of a large representative sample that inquired about asset holdings was the 1962 Survey of Financial Characteristics of Consumers (Projector & Weiss 1966). While their findings concerning the composition and distribution of household wealth were quoted widely, no significant follow-up study of wealth holdings was conducted until 1983, at which point the Survey of Consumer Finances (SCF) and the Survey of Income and Program Participation (SIPP) entered the field with detailed sections on household assets. In the following year, the Panel Study of Income Dynamics (PSID), an ongoing survey since 1968 of the characteristics of American households, added a module on family wealth.

Because the 20-year hiatus in data collection was a period rich in social surveys on related topics, such as labor market behavior and family income, one can only surmise that household wealth information was not considered important enough to warrant an investment of time and money in its gathering.[3] I am not sure there was a triggering event which suddenly produced three quality surveys in 1983–1984. More likely, it was a confluence of the first two of the three considerations enumerated above; collectively, a realization that the contribution of household wealth to living standards could no longer be ignored. But whatever the instigating factor, the availability of micro-level data on asset holdings has, in turn, stimulated much activity aimed at discerning the particular ways by which financial resources contribute to well-being, prompting a concern with definitions of wealth and categorization of types of assets (e.g. Smith 1995; Wolff 1995; Sherraden 1991, chap. 6), as well as a new round of data collection, this time more focused on substantive themes such as wealth transfers and particular target populations, especially the elderly [e.g. Survey of Assets and Health Dynamics among the Oldest Old (AHEAD); The Health and Retirement Study (HRS)].

THE MEASUREMENT OF HOUSEHOLD WEALTH

Wealth is commonly identified with net worth and assessed by survey questions that measure the total value of family assets and the amount of debt, and that equate net worth with the difference between the two quantities. However, there are various categories of household assets, with different features, and if the wealth variable is to be used to explain individual or household behavior, it can be important to distinguish among the wealth components.

Wolff (1995; 1996, pp. 75–84) differentiates among marketable wealth, financial wealth, and augmented wealth. He equates *marketable* wealth with net worth, though his measure excludes some assets that are usually included in a net worth measure—consumer durables such as an automobile, television, and household appliances. This is done on the grounds that these items have less resale value than their consumption services to the household and, presumably, would not be marketed to free up funds. A criticism of the exclusion is that it distorts the net worth of poor households because consumption durables, especially an automobile, account for the bulk of asset holdings by these families (Current Population Reports 1986, Tables 1, 3).

Financial wealth is defined by Wolff as marketable wealth minus equity in owner-occupied housing. It is intended as a measure of "liquid" resources, since a home is difficult to convert into cash in the short term. Financial wealth therefore reflects the resources immediately available for consumption (Wolff 1995, p. 36). *Augmented wealth* adds to marketable wealth some items not customarily included

---

[3]Notwithstanding the absence of surveys, research on wealth issues continued during the 1960s and 1970s, often addressing macro-level questions and relying on estimates of the wealth distribution from filings of estate tax returns (e.g. Menchik 1979; Wolff 1980). Indeed, the main professional society on the subject of wealth, the International Association for Research on Income and Wealth, was founded more than 50 years ago, in 1947.

in a net worth measure—principally pension wealth and Social Security wealth, the latter calculated as the discounted present value of the Social Security retirement benefit.

Burkhauser & Weathers (2000) employ a similar but more detailed decomposition of household wealth, using the categories financial wealth, housing equity, Social Security wealth, and employer pension wealth. They examined the wealth holdings of a mature population, the age cohort 51–61. With this population divided into deciles of total wealth, they report that in the lowest deciles the principal asset is Social Security wealth, in the middle deciles housing wealth comprises a major proportion of total wealth, and in the highest deciles financial wealth is the dominant component.

Yet, in all but the very highest decile, Social Security wealth and pension wealth comprise at least 50% of total household wealth in this middle-aged cohort (Burkhauser & Weathers 2000). This raises a question of whether it is appropriate to include these asset types in the wealth measure, a determination that is especially consequential since they would dominate the wealth estimate. Calculations of household wealth or net worth typically exclude retirement assets (e.g. Oliver & Shapiro 1995, p. 58; Current Population Reports 1986, p. 1). A more general phrasing of the question would inquire how wealth should, in fact, be measured if the intent is to assess its impact on some behavioral outcome.

Three considerations would appear to be relevant: (*a*) the formulation of the household resource measure, (*b*) the features of different kinds of assets, and (*c*) the salience of the prospective wealth components to the behavioral outcome under investigation.

(*a*) The first issue relates to whether income and wealth are retained as distinct concepts or merged into a single resource variable. As an example of the latter, in a discussion of family vulnerability to a financial crisis, Wolff (1990) created a single measure of economic resources by annuitizing the wealth stock and adding the result to household income. When this approach is taken, it matters little whether a particular household asset is viewed as an income flow or as a wealth component.

If the distinction between income and wealth is maintained [e.g. Conley (1999) in an analysis of racial disparities; Conley & Spilerman (2000) concerning wealth effects on educational outcomes], the question of asset classification becomes relevant. For example, by capitalizing Social Security income and converting it into a wealth stock, this asset is moved from one resource category to the other. Clearly, the respective effects of income and wealth on a behavioral outcome will be sensitive to this manipulation.

(*b*) The second issue concerns the features of a resource item. As noted earlier, Wolff (1996) emphasized the dimension of *marketability* as a basis for differentiating among wealth components. An alternative categorization would stress the *degree of control over the asset* by its owner (Sherraden 1991, chap. 6). For example, the withdrawal of money from an IRA account is subject to IRS regulations. Access to pension funds held by an employer can be even more restricted, since these monies are intended for distribution as an income stream upon retirement. Thus, while we can formally proceed by adding pension assets to a household's net worth, access to the funds, especially to the pension principal, can be severely limited.

In discussing pension assets it is important to distinguish between a *defined contribution* and a *defined benefit* plan. In the case of the former, a wealth principal is present in the name of the asset holder; however, in a defined benefit plan—e.g. Social Security benefits—there is no underlying principal that can be withdrawn or inherited, only the promise of an income stream during the asset owner's lifetime. While one can capitalize the income flow and speak of "Social Security wealth," the same can be done with any income stream, including labor market income. In short, if the distinction between income and wealth is to be maintained, it does not seem appropriate to include the capitalized value of a defined benefit plan as a component of household wealth.

(*c*) The third issue is of a different sort, referring to the definition of the wealth variable in the context of the behavioral outcome under investigation. This sort of issue is not addressed when the resource variable is household income, because income is fungible and rarely carries use restrictions that relate to its source.[4] However, the features of a household's wealth components can differ in terms of marketability and control over the principal. As a consequence, one cannot assume that a measure of total household wealth is necessarily the appropriate wealth variable for use in examining a particular behavior. In a study of endstate bequests, for example, it would make little sense to include the capitalized value of Social Security income as a parental wealth component since this asset cannot be transferred.

On a similar note, if one seeks to explain parental financial assistance with a child's education, it is not evident that the value of the parental home should be included in the wealth measure, versus using a calculation of "liquid" wealth. In general, when it is unclear how to formulate the wealth variable, when it is not evident to which wealth components an individual would be responding, it is recommended that an analysis be made of the "sensitivity" of the behavioral outcome to alternative specifications of the wealth variable.

THE WEALTH HOLDINGS OF AMERICAN FAMILIES

Trends in Household Wealth

As noted, the first large scale survey of household wealth was carried out in 1962 (Projector & Weiss 1966). Nonetheless, estimates of wealth holdings have

---

[4]Food stamps issued to the poor provide an exception, since their use is restricted to certain kinds of purchases.

been available for many prior years, dating back to the early decades of the twentieth century. These early estimates are based on aggregate household balance sheet accounts (macro data) and on estate tax returns filed on behalf of the deceased.

Wolff (1989) presents four time series of wealth estimates which differ in their treatment of trust fund holdings and retirement assets. Using the narrowest definition of wealth—essentially a measure of net worth—Wolff reports an increase from $5,300 in 1921 to $13,400 in 1983 (1967 dollars); with retirement assets added, the change is from $5,400 to $23,220. These figures refer to mean per capita wealth (not to the more customary household estimates), and reveal a strong trend toward wealth accumulation in the American population over the referenced period. The growth in home equity and pension assets is responsible for much of the wealth increase: The former, as a proportion of total wealth holdings, rose from 10% to approximately 20% during this period; the latter expanded from 2% to 42% [calculated from Wolff (1989, pp. 20, 24)].

More recent computations cover the period 1962–1995 and report wealth estimates based on survey data. With the *household* as the unit of analysis, and excluding retirement assets, Mishel et al (1999, p. 264) find an increase in mean net worth from $143,000 to $215,000 (1997 dollars). Because the estimates are from micro data it is possible to also calculate medians, which are more informative about the living standard of the average household. These are much lower than the mean figures, ranging from $35,200 in 1962 to $45,600 in 1995 (1997 dollars). The enormous disparity between the median and mean figures attests to the considerable skewness in the wealth distribution.

Wealth Inequality   Calculations from estate tax returns indicate a substantial decline in wealth concentration during the twentieth century. According to the Lampman-Smith-Schwartz time series (Committee on Ways and Means 1992, p. 1564), the richest 1% of the population owned 36% of household net worth in 1929; by 1982 the figure had dropped to 20%. Wolff (1996, pp. 75–86) refined this time series, distinguishing between net worth and "augmented wealth": In the latter, pension and Social Security assets have been added to net worth. Not surprisingly, the decline in wealth concentration is more steep under the second measure, since retirement assets have grown rapidly and are more widely dispersed than other wealth components, especially investment assets. The spread of home ownership, which grew from 44% to 65% between 1940 and 1995, has also contributed to the reduction in wealth concentration (Wolff 1987, p. 241).

It appears, however, that since the early 1980s there has been a sharp reversal in the trend to lesser wealth inequality. Wolff (2000) reports a 2% decline in median wealth between 1983 and 1997, along with a 14% increase in mean wealth. The divergence of these two statistics suggests a growing polarization in wealth holdings and, consequently, greater inequality in 1997; this assessment is supported by calculations of the proportion of household net worth held by the richest 1% of the population, which grew from 34% to 40% in the noted 15-year interval (Wolff 2000).[5]

Another way to look at shifts in the distribution of household wealth is to examine the change for different wealth deciles. Compilations by Wolff (2000) reveal that between 1983 and 1995 the wealthiest 1% of households experienced a 17% growth in net worth, the next wealthiest 4% saw their net worth increase by 0.5%, and the remaining 95% of the population witnessed a decline in net worth, the loss being greater for the poorer households. Also telling, during this period the proportion of households with zero or negative net worth increased from 15.5% to 18.5% (Mishel et al 1999, p. 259). In summary, the evidence is compelling that after several decades of declining wealth inequality, there has been a renewed trend to wealth concentration and greater inequality.

Components of Wealth   A principal factor in the wealth buildup among the very rich is the concentration of their resources in business equity and investment assets—stocks, bonds, commercial real estate—which have appreciated rapidly in the past decade (Mishel et al 1999, pp. 266–74). Indeed, there is a striking difference in the composition of asset holdings among families at different net worth deciles. Thus, in 1995, a principal residence accounted for 73% of net worth in the 40% of families with lowest household wealth, but only 6% of net worth in the richest 1%. In contrast, the wealthiest 1% of households held 78% of their net worth in the form of business and investment assets (Wolff 2000).

Wolff does not provide details on asset holdings by wealth level for the poorer half of the population. However, some insight can be gleaned from earlier studies. In Current Population Reports (1986, pp. 9–15) calculations are presented for the incidence of asset ownership and for the mean value of an asset, conditional on ownership. With respect to a principal residence, the data indicate a low ownership rate among poor households[6] (10.5% versus a population mean of 64%), but in regard to an automobile, the rate of ownership by the poor is relatively high (64.5% versus a population mean of 86%). These data do not permit a simple calculation of the proportion of household wealth that is accounted for by particular asset types, but they do suggest that a large proportion of the resources of the poor is tied up in automobile equity.

The earlier survey by Projector & Weiss (1966, p. 110) permits a clearer assessment. Among middle wealth households (the 58% of families with net worth in the

---

[5]Wolff's time series of net worth concentration shows a turning point in 1976, whereas the Lampman-Smith-Schwartz series does not exhibit a termination to the decline in wealth inequality even as late as 1982, the final year of this series. According to Wolff (1996, pp. 78–79) the proportion of wealth owned by the richest 1% of households was 20% in 1976 and 31% in 1983. Wolff (2000), in his comparison with 1997 data, reports a concentration figure of 34% for 1983.

[6]Poor households are defined here as the approximately 25% of families with net worth below $5,000 in 1984.

range $1,000 to $25,000 in 1962), some 54% of total net worth was accounted for by home ownership and 9.5% was tied up in automobile equity; among the 24% of households with wealth holdings below $1,000, 10% of net worth was associated with home ownership and 48% was held in the form of an automobile.

The significance of this asset-holding pattern is that home residences, which account for the bulk of net worth among households in the middle wealth range, have tended to appreciate in value over time; moreover, mortgage interest payments and capital gains from the sale of a primary residence are treated favorably in tax law. In contrast, automobile equity—the form of asset holding most common among poor families—depreciates rapidly in value. This is not to suggest that poor persons make faulty decisions with regard to the selection of assets. An automobile can be critical for getting to a place of work and could even be a job requirement; moreover, the purchase of a home may necessitate a down payment, which might not be within the reach of a poor household. The point to be emphasized is that poor families are constrained in their asset allocation decisions, and there are strong imperatives for purchasing the sorts of assets that do not result in wealth appreciation.

Distributional Features of Wealth Holdings

Household wealth increases with education and age, and is much lower for African-American and Hispanic households than for white families (Committee on Ways and Means 1992, p. 1573). The education effect captures the greater opportunity for life-cycle accumulation by highly educated and therefore high income families, though it also taps the likelihood of coming from a parental home with some assets and receiving parental transfers, unless these factors have been controlled.

Regarding the *age effect*, cross-sectional data reveal a pattern of wealth accumulation through the mid-60s, followed by a subsequent decline in wealth holdings. While this pattern is consistent with the life-cycle explanation of household wealth (Osberg 1984, p. 196)—accumulation during the years of maximum earnings, followed by a spending down of assets—the decline is also consistent with a cohort explanation in which there is no spending down but a history of lower rates of accumulation by the earlier cohorts. Indeed, from studies based on longitudinal data, Shorrocks (1987) and Alessie et al (1997) concluded that a sizable fraction of households do not dissave in old age. This suggests that the age-wealth profiles from cross-sectional data should be interpreted descriptively and not used to infer life-cycle behavior.

There have also been troublesome changes in the age distribution of wealth holdings, essentially a decline in the wealth level of young cohorts, relative to the wealth base of older households. Levy & Mishel (1991, p. 53) documented this tendency for the period 1977–1983; Wolff (2000), reviewing recent data, finds a continuation of the trend during 1983–1995. These findings are probably responsible for a second trend—the decline in home ownership rates among young families. While the overall rate of home ownership grew between 1983 and 1995, reaching 64.7% in the latter year, the rate declined for families in their 40s or younger (Wolff

2000). Levy & Mishel (1991, pp. 68–69) reported similar findings for the earlier time period, and noted an especially pronounced fall in young households with low education. In summary, there is evidence of a growing liquidity constraint among young cohorts, compelling a delay in home purchase. This, in turn, will deprive young couples of several years' participation in the wealth buildup that frequently derives from home ownership.

The *racial disparity* in wealth holdings is immense. According to Current Population Reports (1986, p. 19), median net worth in 1984 was $39,135 for a white household and $3,397 for an African-American household. Results from a follow-up survey four years later reveal a slight improvement in the ratio of African-American to white net worth—a decline from the 10:1 ratio in 1984 to 8:1 in 1988 (Committee on Ways and Means 1992, p. 1577). More recent estimates by Wolff (2000) for 1995 show white median net worth at $61,000 versus $7,400 for African-American households, which maintains the 8:1 ratio. The disparity is only partially explained by racial differences in income or marital status, in that the wealth gap remains huge even within categories of these variables (Current Population Reports 1986, p. 5).

Further insight into the racial wealth gap emerges from an examination of how the gap varies by age, and from a consideration of alternative wealth measures. Wolff (1994, p. 166) reports the ratio of nonwhite to white mean net worth for different age cohorts, showing a decline from .58 to .14 as one moves to the older age groups. In short, white families are either more successful in saving from their incomes, accumulating assets over time, or, more likely, they receive larger inheritances from parents, an assessment supported by transfer data in Smith (1995, p. S175) based on the 1992 Health and Retirement Study. In the same paper, Smith shows that if the net worth measure of wealth is augmented by adding to it the capitalized value of Social Security benefits, the wealth gap between the races is much reduced since Social Security transfers are redistributive in character.

There have been two noteworthy attempts to tease out the implications of lower asset holdings by African-Americans. Oliver & Shapiro (1995) first document the impact on living standards and economic opportunity, such as depressed rates of home ownership and business entrepreneurship, since some resources are necessary for establishing credit-worthiness to secure a mortgage or a business loan. They then consider strategies to assist poor households. These involve programs to foster asset accumulation and promote what Sherraden (1991) has termed a "stakeholder's society." Essentially, private groups or government agencies would encourage the establishment of individual savings accounts that could be used only for targeted purposes—to further one's education or for investment in a business or a residence. The accounts would be subsidized for poor families, either through matching deposits or by a refundable tax credit. Conley (1999) makes similar policy recommendations, again emphasizing the importance of property ownership and wealth accumulation for the welfare of African-American families.

The Effects of Wealth

In contrast to the considerable literature documenting trends in asset holdings and inequality, few studies have attempted to formally assess the impact of household wealth, net of income, on aspects of living standards. Rather, the causal argument as to the importance of wealth is usually verbal, involving an appeal to common knowledge about the mechanisms underlying attainment in a particular institutional area, such as home ownership, sometimes coupled with the presentation of cross-sectional data showing an association between wealth and the attainment variable of interest. However, the direction of causality is often ambiguous in cross-sectional data—for example, are current homeowners more wealthy than renters because of an increase in home values, or were they able to purchase because of greater wealth at an earlier time point?

One area in which causality is not an issue concerns the effects of parental wealth on the living standards of adult children. This literature is reviewed in the next section. Here, I limit my comments to wealth effects on current asset holders. These have been documented in regard to labor market participation and expenditure behavior, especially for large-ticket items that cannot be readily financed from an income flow. Thus, Semyonov et al (1996), using Israeli data, find wealth effects on the standard of living as reflected in the ownership of household appliances. The impact is stronger for European-origin Israelis, who have greater net worth, than for Israelis from Asian or North African lands; possibly these effects occur only above some threshold level of wealth holdings. Wealth effects have also been reported for wife's labor force participation [a decline with net worth (Theeuwes 1981)], for self-employment prospects [enhanced by household wealth (Lindh & Ohlsson 1998)], and for the likelihood that an elderly homeowner will move to smaller quarters [lower for wealthier families (Feinstein & McFadden 1987)].

A different kind of wealth effect, one in which household net worth is viewed as a reserve, may be more consequential for assessing living standards and economic security. In particular, Wolff (2000) examines the protective effects provided by wealth, calculating the number of months that current consumption can be sustained by families in different income quintiles. On average, households in the top quintile have sufficient net worth for 16.5 months; in the next to lowest quintile the wealth holdings can sustain a family for 0.9 months, and in the lowest there is no wealth reserve, hence, great vulnerability to illness or loss of employment. Wolff's calculation is little more than an accounting device, a restandardization of the wealth values, yet the protections from economic dislocation conveyed by his figures are very real.

A Note on the Wealth Figures

Estimates of household wealth are much less consistent over representative surveys than is the case with income estimates. This is true even when household wealth is measured by putatively the same statistic, such as net worth. The differences among estimates arise from several factors: (*a*) the complexity of wealth surveys, which must assess an array of wealth components—stocks, bonds, savings accounts, a principal residence, other real estate, business equity, life insurance equity, and consumer durables; (*b*) the lack of standardization in questions used for inquiring about the wealth components; (*c*) the difficulty that respondents have in estimating the value of some components; and (*d*) the high rate of refusal in responding to asset items. The last has given rise to a small industry on strategies for imputing missing data; see Smith (1995) for a review of the various techniques.

There are, however, disparities in estimates. According to Wolff (2000), median net worth is uniformly higher in SCF estimates (Survey of Consumer Finances) than in either SIPP (Survey of Income and Program Participation) or in PSID (Panel Study of Income Dynamics). In 1988–1989, for example, median net worth was estimated as $46,100 in SIPP, $45,200 in PSID, but $62,400 in SCF. Mean net worth for the same years shows an even greater range: $118,500 in SIPP, $153,600 in PSID, and $237,700 in the SCF.[7] Trends in median net worth are also strikingly different in the various surveys: The extreme cases are the SIPP surveys, which document a 17.3% decline in median net worth between 1984 and 1993, and the PSID waves, which show an 8.3% *increase* between 1984 and 1994!

For the narrow purpose of estimating household wealth there is some consensus that SCF is the best of the surveys and that SIPP is the least reliable (Wolff 2000; Smith 1995, p. S165). The SCF is more detailed in regard to questions about asset holdings and it uses a stratified design, with an oversample of the rich. Since wealth holdings are highly concentrated, a stratified sample will provide better estimates of the holdings of the very wealthy than will a representative design, which is used in the SIPP. Most of the estimates presented in this section of the paper come from calculations by Edward Wolff and by Mishel and his colleagues, which are based on the SCF.

THE TRANSMISSION OF INEQUALITY

There is a long-standing interest in stratification research in regard to assessing the extent of replication of advantage across generations. Indeed, a defining feature of the status attainment model is the decomposition of the association between father's occupational status and son's status (Blau & Duncan 1967; Duncan et al 1972). The mechanisms underlying this linkage are presumed to be parental support for educational attainment, peer and family values regarding the importance of education, and, sometimes, parental assistance with occupational entrance, especially when craft union membership is involved. As such, in the attainment model,

---

[7]Some insight into the sources of the differences is provided by Radner (1988). For example, the SIPP survey includes automobile equity in the net worth estimate; SCF does not. SCF includes the cash value of life insurance and equity in an employer-sponsored profit-sharing savings plan, while SCF does not inquire about these matters.

the transmission of status focuses on opportunities made available by parents to their children. There is no presumption of a *direct* transfer of occupational position because occupations are not formally inherited in a market economy. Similarly, the empirical correlation between father's and son's earnings is not addressed in terms of a transfer of the parental earnings stream.

The situation is different with respect to parental wealth because most kinds of family assets (except for some pension assets) can be transmitted across generations. Because of the growing recognition of household wealth as a determinant of living standards and economic security, much research in recent years has been carried out on the particular role of parental transfers in the replication of advantage. A variety of component issues relate to this topic, concerning the importance of transfers in the buildup of household wealth, the pattern of intergenerational transmission (whether inter vivos gifts or bequests), the parental "motive" in transferring wealth, and the impact of transfers on the behavior of the recipients.

The Volume of Transfers

This is a surprisingly difficult matter to summarize because the relevant survey questions have been formulated in a variety of ways which have produced different estimates. With respect to *inter vivos transfers*, information about incidence and dollar amount is usually collected only for families that have exceeded some threshold value of gifts in a defined time interval. Clearly, an estimate of the amount transferred is sensitive to both the threshold value and the length of the time period about which respondents were queried. Estimates of received *inheritances* are even more sensitive to length of the time interval, since we are addressing here a relatively rare event.

Nevertheless, to cite some figures on the volume of transfers: McGarry & Schoeni (1995), examining 1992 Health and Retirement Study (HRS) data, report that 13.8% of adult children obtained parental assistance in excess of $500 in the preceding 12 months; the average transfer totaled $3,061. MacDonald (1989), analyzing 1987 data from the National Survey of Families and Households, found that 16.8% of respondents received gifts in the past 5 years, mainly from parents, with an average value of approximately $5,600. In the same study, a question about inheritances elicited information that 22.3% of households had received a bequest, with an average value of $28,000 for the sum of all inheritances received.

The Contribution of Transfers to Household Wealth

Estimates of the relative importance of transfers versus life-cycle accumulation range from 20% (Modigliani 1988) to 80% (Kotlikoff & Summers 1981, 1988). The enormity of the range is due to a variety of measurement problems, in part reflecting whether the estimate of the transfer value is calculated from household surveys, from probate records, or from other sources. Also relevant is whether the estimate reflects only bequests or includes inter vivos assistance as well [see Modigilani (1988) or Gale & Scholz (1994) for a review of the issues].

In addition, definitional problems have contributed to the wide range of estimates. Which assets should be credited to parental transfers and which to life-cycle accumulation? Receipt of a $100,000 gift is clearly a transfer. But suppose the gift was left in a bank account and, some 20 years later, has compounded to $200,000. The latter increment to household wealth is often credited to life-cycle accumulation, but it is the case that the addition is entirely a result of the original transfer (Gale & Scholtz 1994, p. 153). Related issues concern the distinction between parental consumption and intergenerational transfers. College expenditures for a child who lives with parents are usually treated as parental consumption; however, if the child has established a separate household, the same expenditure is considered a transfer (Modigliani 1988).

Clearly, how one categorizes these different expenditures will influence the amount of current household wealth that is attributed to transfers versus life-cycle accumulation. It also seems evident that this issue would be better served by considering explanatory models that provide for direct and indirect transfers—akin to direct and indirect effects in structural equation models—rather than by arguing over essentially arbitrary definitional distinctions. See Kessler & Masson (1989) for an excellent discussion of these matters.

The Pattern of Transfers

How much parental wealth is transmitted to children during parental lifetimes and how much is transferred as end-state bequests? Empirical estimates are few: Cox & Raines (1985) conclude that 60–67% of transfers are inter vivos; Gale & Scholz (1994) suggest a figure of 43%. Tax law affects the parental decision, especially the IRS provision that permits gifts of $10,000 per year, tax free, to each recipient, since these transfers can be made outside of a donor's $650,000 lifetime exemption from gift and estate taxes. There is also evidence that the material needs of children affect the allocation. In the State of Israel, for example, the absence of a rental housing market places pressure on parents to transfer a sizable portion of their assets at a relatively early point in the life course in order to assist newly married children with the purchase of housing (Spilerman 1999).

When there are several adult children, parents must make decisions about the allocation of inter vivos transfers as well as the timing of gifts. Studies consistently show that the incidence and amount of transfers received decline with the age and financial resources of the child and with number of siblings, and increase with parental income and wealth (Cox & Rank 1992; McGarry & Schoeni 1997). Net of these effects, there is evidence of larger transfers when grandchildren are present (Schoeni 1997) and reduced amounts when parents are divorced (Altonji et al 1996). Both Cox & Raines (1985) and Altonji et al (1996) conclude that financially more needy children are apt to receive larger transfers.

Parental Motives

Explanations of the transmittal pattern and, indeed, of why parents make transfers rather than consume all their assets have given rise to a small research industry. First, there is evidence that bequests are not simply a result of parental miscalculations of expected lifetimes (unintended transfers), but that parents deliberately accumulate savings in order to leave assets to their children (Gale & Scholz 1994; Bernheim 1991). Beyond this finding, a variety of presumed motives have been proposed to explain parental calculations, especially when allocations must be divided among several children. These broadly fall under the rubric of *altruistic* and *exchange* motives.

Altruism-based transfers presume that the utility function of the donor includes a term for the recipient's welfare, in short, that the well-being of the adult child matters to the parent (Becker 1974; Laitner 1997). A key implication of the altruism model is that the incidence and amount of transfer will be negatively correlated with the child's household income; indeed, a strict formulation asserts that a dollar decline in the child's income, coupled with a dollar increase in parental income, will result in an additional dollar being transferred to the child (Altonji et al 1997, p. 1121). If several offspring are present, the altruism argument suggests that there will be compensating behavior by parents—more resources given to less well off children.

In the exchange model, in contrast, intergenerational transfers serve as payment for services rendered to a parent, such as visits and telephone calls (Hotlz-Eakin & Smeeding 1994; Cox 1987). Stark & Falk (1998) argue that in exchange-based transfers the amount will be positively correlated with the child's income, i.e. parents must pay more for the child's time when his/her income is higher. Others (Cox 1987; McGarry & Schoeni 1997) point out that the parent could purchase fewer hours at the higher price and conclude that the exchange model is consistent with both a positive and a negative correlation.

Distinguishing between the parental motives has implications for the effectiveness of government redistribution policies (Rosenzweig & Wolpin 1994; Holtz-Eakin & Smeeding 1994; Laitner 1997). Altruistic motives could make governmental assistance less essential than it appears, since it would partially offset family aid. For example, the parents of an unemployed child might give less help if a generous government benefit is available to unemployed workers (McGarry & Schoeni 1995, p. S185). However, if private transfers are motivated by exchange considerations, they need not be crowded out by public assistance programs (Cox & Rank 1992).

The many studies of parental motives have not produced a consensus. The strict altruism model, in which an increase in the child's income of one dollar is offset by an identical reduction in the transfer amount, is invariably rejected in empirical investigations (e.g. Altonji et al 1996; Cox & Rank 1992). However, there is evidence for weaker formulations of altruism, in which transfers are seen as compensatory, directed to less well off family members, and intended to reduce the variance among them in living standards (McGarry & Schoeni 1997; Altonji et al 1996; Cox & Raines 1985). Nonetheless, Cox (1987) and Cox & Rank (1991) conclude that the transfer data are more consistent with exchange motives than with altruism.

This literature is further complicated by the recent introduction of variant models in an attempt to account for the often contradictory empirical findings. These include "warm glow" giving [parents derive satisfaction from the mere fact of assistance (Schoeni 1997)] and "preference shaping" giving [parents aid children with the intent of instilling guilt and, hopefully, repayment in later years in the form of services to the parents (Stark 1995, p. 50)]. Little consideration has been given in the "motive" literature to the possibility that one or the other model may more accurately characterize the behavior of a particular cultural group or a particular wealth category, as an alternative to a single motive being universally true.

The preceding observations refer to inter vivos transfers. Parental motives have also been investigated with regard to bequest decisions. The basic altruism model predicts that bequests will be allocated so as to compensate for income and asset differences among siblings. Tomes (1981) has argued that bequests do, indeed, function in this way, but more recent research (Bernheim et al 1985; Wilhelm 1996) suggests that the bequest data are more consistent with exchange motives. Yet all these assessments are made tenuous by the fact that the majority of estates are divided equally among children (Menchik 1980; Wilhelm 1996). Moreover, we know little about the extent of compensation by parents in their bequest decisions for prior inter vivos transfers.

The Impact of Transfers

Less work has been done on the behavioral consequences of transfers than on measurement of the sums transmitted or on inferences of parental motives. There is fairly consistent evidence of a correlation in the neighborhood of 0.4 between the *incomes* of fathers and sons (Solon 1992; Zimmerman 1992). Although these studies do not identify the mechanisms by which income status is transmitted, Holtz-Eakin & Smeeding (1994, pp. 132–33) suggest that inter vivos transfers for college study constitute one important factor. Consistent with this contention, Rumberger (1983), in an analysis of fathers and sons from the National Longitudinal Survey of Labor Market Experience, reported that parental wealth has an influence on educational attainment that is independent of other background variables.

Aside from parental wealth effects on the human capital of offspring, Holtz-Eakin et al (1993), in an analysis of the household supply of labor, reported a decline with size of inheritance received. In a study of wealth in Israel, Spilerman (1999) documented earlier home purchases and greater home equity when parental assistance was provided; Kennedy & Stokes (1982) reported similar findings with US data. Finally, there is evidence that even the *expectation* of a bequest can lower the savings rate of young families (Weil 1994).

Race and Intergenerational Transfers

African-Americans have a lower incidence of providing transfers and lesser amounts are involved when a transfer takes place (Smith 1995). An obvious reason is the smaller wealth holdings of African-American families. But it is also the case that, controlling for parental income (Cox & Rank 1992) and for income and wealth (McGarry 1997; McGarry & Schoeni 1995), the incidence of receipt of financial aid by African-Americans falls well below the white rate.[8] A possible explanation is that the funds available for transfer are nonlinearly related to parental resources (since there is little asset accumulation in poor households or even in ones moderately above the poverty line), and the usual linear regression misspecifies the relationship, overestimating the transfer volume by low-asset, disproportionately nonwhite parents. The negative coefficient for African-American or nonwhite would then partially offset the misspecification.

One implication of the lesser transfer volume by African-American parents relates to the potentially lower rate of future wealth buildup in this population group. At the beginning of the section it was noted that a sizable portion of current household wealth is attributable to intergenerational transfers, though the precise amount is in dispute. A low rate of asset transmission by African-American families might retard the process of narrowing the racial gap in wealth and living standards. Apropos this observation is the contention by Blau & Graham (1990) that even if policies intended to reduce racial differences in income and other human capital characteristics were successful, some three-quarters of the wealth gap would remain. They go on to suggest that much of the wealth disparity is attributable to racial differences in inter vivos transfers and in the value of inheritances.

Family Organization and Transfers

I conclude this section by noting that while I have emphasized stratification issues, the material on intergenerational transfers is equally relevant to an understanding of family structure and interfamily relations. This somewhat different take on the subject matter brings into the discussion a greater concern with exchanges of time, space, backward flows of assistance to elderly parents, and an assessment of how these transactions are played out in different cultures and family contexts. Insights into this perspective on intergenerational relations can be found in Soldo & Hill (1993), Rossi & Rossi (1990), Hogan & Spenser (1993), Attias-Donfut (1995), Attias-Donfut & Segalen (1998) and Kohli (1999). The last three provide

---

[8] Findings for socio-emotional and instrumental support (assistance with cleaning, shopping, repairs) are less clear with respect to a racial effect. Mutran (1985) reports that African-American parents give and receive more support than white parents. Silverstein & Waite (1993) conclude that the racial assistance patterns are complex and depend on the type of support and on the ages of the provider and recipient. Hogan et al (1993) find that African-Americans are consistently less likely than whites or Mexican-Americans to be involved in any sort of intergenerational assistance.

an excellent overview of many of the themes considered in this paper as they pertain to the French and German context.

SOCIAL POLICY AND STRATIFICATION THEORY

Policy Considerations

I wish to discuss two implications for social policy that derive from the preceding review of wealth and its correlates: (*a*) asset building strategies for low income households, and (*b*) the role of tax policy in mediating the replication of inequality across generations.

Asset-Building Strategies   I have outlined a number of benefits that derive from even modest levels of household wealth, especially as they pertain to economic security, prospects for home ownership, and the possibility of self-employment. Based on a similar appraisal of the contributions of household wealth, Michael Sherraden has drawn several implications for anti-poverty policy.

Sherraden (1991, 2000) first points out that the poor are not in a position to participate in the asset building programs available to middle class families, such as IRA accounts, 401(k)s, and home mortgage subsidies. The poor do not benefit because the advantages are provided through the tax structure, in the form of tax credits, and are available only to families that pay income tax. Moreover, anti-poverty policy is dominated by an income support philosophy that has the goal of maintaining a minimum consumption level in poor households. There are no incentives for asset building; indeed, most poverty programs are means tested and impose limits on asset ownership, often requiring a needy family to spend down its resources in order to qualify for welfare support.

As a consequence, current poverty policy discourages the buildup of savings by poor households, accentuating a family's vulnerability to economic dislocation were it to leave welfare. The prospects for capital accumulation are inhibited, along with the possibility of purchasing a residence or engaging in entrepreneurial activity—the very sorts of behavior that, ostensibly, we seek to encourage: family stability and investment in the community and in one's future, along with the values of thrift and economic betterment.

Extrapolating from this argument, Sherraden (1991, chap. 10; 2000), together with Oliver & Shapiro (1995), have outlined a strategy intended to institutionalize asset building by poor households for the targeted purposes of home purchase and income-generating investments. The vehicle would be a program of "individual development accounts" (IDAs)—savings accounts from which monies could be withdrawn only for the designated uses. Participation by the working poor would be encouraged through the provision of matching deposits. For the very poor, who are not able to save from their incomes, deposits would be provided by means of refundable tax credits, akin to the Earned Income Tax Credit. The key to all this is the term "refundable," which would entail government payments when household income falls below a threshold level, in contrast to the more standard tax credits, which have value only to higher income households.

This approach would represent a fundamental departure from existing poverty policy. It would supplement, or replace, current income maintenance programs with a new objective of *empowering* poor persons. They would now have to evaluate alternative expenditures for their monies and calculate the potential risk from different investments, and they would reap the benefits or loss from their decisions. The presumption is that such a program would encourage poor individuals to undertake better economic planning, adopt lengthier time horizons, and develop an increased civic involvement, if only to protect their investments in homes and small businesses (Sherraden 2000). Research to assess the effectiveness of an asset-building strategy is currently being undertaken by the Ford Foundation.

Inheritance and the Tax Code   There are many factors involved in the genera-tion of social inequality. Inheritance of wealth, however, invites particular atten-tion because, unlike labor market rewards, it is unrelated to a recipient's efforts or contributions (Britain 1977; Chester 1998; Thurow 1975, p. 197). Moreover, inheritance provides an individual with a clear and obvious lead in life's economic race. This has troubled some who have accumulated great fortunes, as well as several founders of this country. Both Andrew Carnegie[9] and Thomas Jefferson, for example, felt that society had an interest in regulating, and moderating, the transmission of advantage (Johnson & Eller 1998; Chester 1982).

The principal means for regulating estate transfers is through the tax code. Nominally, estate taxation is progressive, with marginal rates rising from 37% to 55% after an exclusion of $650,000 ($1.3 million for a married couple). In practice, there are a great many loopholes in estate taxation, with the effect that, as Thurow (1975, p. 197) has written, "for all practical purposes, gift and inheritance taxes do not exist in the United States," while Cooper (1979) has labeled these levies a "voluntary tax." Indeed, in 1985, wealth transfer taxes accounted for less than 1% of total IRS tax revenues (Wolff 1996, p. 36).

With the massive buildup of family wealth over the past 50 years, much of which is stored in the form of a primary residence and not spent down by the elderly, and with the growing volume of intergenerational transfers as the parental generation departs (Johnston 1999, p. C2), it is likely that the matter of gift and estate taxation will be revisited in public policy debates. Indeed, during the 1996 presidential campaign, Robert Dole proposed that estate taxes be abolished, and the Congressional Republicans' 1999 tax bill included a provision that would have

---

[9]In *The Gospel of Wealth* Carnegie remarked that "the thoughtful man" must say: "I would as soon leave to my son a curse as the almighty dollar" [Carnegie 1962 (originally 1889), p. 21]. Additionally, commenting on tax policy, he wrote: "The budget presented to the British Parliament the other day proposes to increase the death duties; and, most significant of all, the new tax is to be a graduated one. Of all forms of taxation this seems the wisest" (Carnegie 1962, pp. 21–22).

repealed the estate tax. The recent advocacy of such legislation is surely a result of the growing amount of wealth that is now at stake.

At the same time, reflecting a concern with the replication of wealth inequality across generations, there have been recommendations to revise the tax code and reduce the availability of tax avoidance strategies—e.g. legacy insurance plans, private annuity arrangements, trusts of various kinds—that can effectively reduce the estate tax burden for a wealthy household to near zero.[10] Spilerman (2000) has suggested that a parallel rate schedule be incorporated into the estate tax code, analogous to the Alternative Minimim Tax in income taxation. Thus, rather than eliminate the existing vehicles for wealth sheltering at the time of estate transfers, the second schedule, with firm minimum rates, would come into play once the sheltering provisions of current tax law are invoked.

Munnell (1988), in a comprehensive review of estate taxation, put forward a more radical plan. Arguing that estate and gift tax law is so deeply permeated with avoidance possibilities that it cannot be effectively repaired, he proposed that these transfer taxes be eliminated in favor of a different arrangement. In their place, Munnell would have the income tax code expanded to include the value of gifts and inheritances in "adjusted gross income" of the recipient in the annual filing of income returns. In short, instead of taxing a deceased's total estate and leaving the bequests received by inheritors untaxed—the current approach in transfer taxation—inheritances would be treated as taxable income in the year received, possibly subject to a lower levy than ordinary income, as is the case with capital gains.

Implications for Stratification Research

I conclude with some observations about household wealth and stratification processes. As noted in the introduction, a consideration of wealth becomes relevant once the agenda of the field is enlarged, from a focus narrowly on labor market success and its rewards to a concern with living standards and economic security—what I have termed *consumption potential*, i.e. the resource base for ensuring a particular living standard. Income from labor market activity can be then viewed as comprising but one component of this broader measure of economic well-being.

While a consumption perspective has not been at the forefront of theory development in stratification, it has not been entirely absent either. The writings of the British urban sociologists—Forrest & Murie (1989), Dunleavy (1979), and Saunders (1984; 1986)—are pertinent to this matter. Thus, Saunders (1984, p. 217) has argued that consumption sector cleavages, in regard to housing tenure (homeowner

---

[10] A different approach to reducing inequality would be to directly tax household wealth by means of an annual net worth tax. A number of European countries have such a provision in their tax code. However, there is no tradition of wealth taxation in this country and there appears to be little public interest in the possibility. For details on wealth taxation, see Wolff (1996) and Thurow (1987).

versus renter), access to quality schooling, and access to health care, are to a considerable degree replacing production-based divisions as the major fault line in social stratification, with implications for the pattern of future social conflict. These cleavages are seen by Saunders as not merely derivative of ones arising from the organization of production, but as cross-cutting the production-based (class) divisions.

Saunders' analysis, and that of the British urban school, remains rooted in the particular theme of housing tenure. He writes about home ownership generating a buildup of household wealth, about the financial security provided by home equity, and about the inheritance of home equity in amounts that often exceed what a working class family could hope to save from its employment earnings (Saunders 1986, pp. 322–24). However, the above assessment readily generalizes to the benefits of most kinds of household assets, and this is reflected in his concluding comments: "As this process unfolds, it will force social scientists to reconsider their nineteenth-century conceptions of class and inequality as simply phenomena of the organization of production" (Saunders 1986, p. 324).

It is not my intention here to discuss the constituents of a proper formulation of economic class and whether or not it should be defined solely on the basis of position in the productive order. This view, however, does appear to be the consensus; even Saunders (1984, p. 206) has repudiated the notion of housing classes, agreeing that "class relations are constituted only through the social organization of production." Rather, my intent is to emphasize the growing awareness of the need to extend stratification theory and analysis to encompass a consideration of a family's total resource base, not just the returns from labor market activity.

In his classic distinction between *acquisition classes* and *property classes*, Weber (1947) also gives greater weight to household wealth than applications of his formulation would suggest. The first of his class types has been the more influential in stratification research since it refers to the disposition of marketable skills and, hence, to occupational differentiation. Property classes have received less attention because, as Parkin (1978, p. 608) observed, "the entire weight of class analysis [at the current time] is borne by the consideration of those inequalities stemming from the division of labor." Yet, in Weber's formulation, property class is a more inclusive concept than the Marxian definition of class, in that it is not limited to considerations of ownership of capital goods, but encompasses other kinds of household wealth; indeed, Weber notes that "positively privileged property classes" might live on income from securities (Weber 1947, p. 425), in short, on wealth assets external to the labor market.

Weber's evocative concept of "life chances" is also based on a broader view of opportunity and economic well-being than is subsumed under occupational rewards. Although he defines life chances variously [see Dahrendorf (1979, pp. 62–74) for an account of Weber's use of this term], it consistently relates to the "chance for a supply of goods [and] external living conditions" (Weber 1958, p. 181), that is, to the fundamental aspects of a household's future possibilities. This formulation, clearly, concerns the totality of marketable resources available to a household.

There have been a few attempts to expand the formulation of economic status by incorporating considerations of net worth and transfers of wealth into an attainment model. Prominent among these are Henretta & Campbell (1978; 1980) and Rumberger (1983). Possibly these impressive papers from some 20 years ago failed to stimulate a new line of work because few data on household wealth were available at the time; possibly they were too far ahead of the established paradigms in stratification research to be appreciated. Whatever the reason, the result can be seen from this review: The great majority of the cited papers on wealth issues come from studies carried out by economists, not sociologists.

Yet recent trends should bring a consideration of wealth issues to the fore. These include the buildup of household wealth in the American population, the intergenerational transfer of sums that are substantial for an average family, and pronounced shifts in wealth inequality—trends that cannot be ignored in a discipline that places living standards and economic well-being at the core of its domain. The conceptual approach to incorporating wealth variables is not complex, though the proper formulation of the wealth measure, especially in assessments of its impact on some behavioral outcome, is not obvious. At a minimum, this will require a consideration of which components of a household's asset holdings to include, whether to combine income and wealth into a single resource measure, and how to incorporate parental resources which a respondent expects to receive in the future but which may influence his or her current behavior.

ACKNOWLEDGMENTS

The author wishes to thank Michael Sobel and Yuval Elmelech for their helpful comments.

Visit the Annual Reviews home page at www.AnnualReviews.org

LITERATURE CITED

Alessie R, Lusardi A, Aldershof T. 1997. Income and wealth over the life cycle: evidence from panel data. *Rev. Income Wealth* 43:1–32

Altonji JG, Hayashi F, Kotlikoff LJ. 1997. Parental altruism and inter vivos transfers: theory and evidence. *J. Polit. Econ.* 105:1121–66

Altonji JG, Hayashi F, Kotlikoff LJ. 1996. *The effects of income and wealth on time and money transfers between parents and children.* Natl. Bur. Econ. Res. Working paper 5522. Unpublished

Attias-Donfut C. 1995. *Les Solidarités Entre*

Generations: Vieillesse, Familles Etat. Paris: Nathan

Attias-Donfut C, Segalen M. 1998. *Grands-Parents: La Famille a Travers les Generations.* Paris: Odile Jacob

Baltzell ED. 1958. *Philadelphia Gentleman: The Making of a National Upper Class.* New York: Free Press

Barber B. 1975. *Social Stratification.* New York: Harcourt, Brace and World

Becker G. 1974. A theory of social interactions. *J. Polit. Econ.* 82:1045–76

Bernheim B, Douglas AS, Summers LH. 1985.

The strategic bequest motive. *J. Polit. Econ.* 93:1045–76

Bernheim D. 1991. How strong are bequest motives? Evidence based on estimates of the demand for life insurance and annuities. *J. Polit. Econ.* 99:899–927

Blau FD, Graham J. 1990. Black-white differences in wealth and asset compositon. *Q. J. Econ.* 105:321–40

Blau P, Duncan OD. 1967. *The American Occupational Structure.* New York: John Wiley

Brittain JA. 1977. *The Inheritance of Economic Status.* Washington, DC: Brookings Inst.

Burkhauser RV, Weathers R. 2000. Access to wealth among the new-old and how it is distributed: data from the health and retirement study. In *The Benefits and Mechanisms for Spreading Asset Ownership*, ed. T Shapiro, EN Wolff. New York: Russell Sage. In press

Carnegie A. 1962. The gospel of wealth. In *The Gospel of Wealth and other Timely Essays.* ed. EC Kirkland, pp. 14–49. Cambridge, MA: Harvard Univ. Press

Chester R. 1982. *Inheritance, Wealth and Society.* Bloomington: Univ. Indiana Press

Chester R. 1998. Inheritance in American legal thought. In *Inheritance and Wealth in America*, ed. RK Miller Jr, SJ McNamee, pp. 23–44. New York: Plenum Press

Committee on Ways and Means. 1992. *Overview of Entitlement Programs (1992 Green Book).* US House of Rep. Washington, DC: Gov. Print. Office

Conley D. 1999. *Being Black, Living in the Red: Race, Wealth, and Social Policy in America.* Berkeley: Univ. Calif. Press

Conley D, Spilerman S. 1999. *Capital for college: parental assets and educational attainment.* Dept. of Sociol., Yale Univ. Unpubl. paper

Cooper G. 1979. *A Voluntary Tax? New Perspectives on Sophisticated Tax Avoidance.* Washington, DC: Brookings Inst.

Cox D. 1987. Motives for private income transfers. *J. Polit. Econ.* 95:508–46

Cox D, Raines F. 1985. Interfamily transfers and income redistribution. In *Horizontal Eq-*

uity, Uncertainty, and Economic Well-Being, ed. M David, T Smeeding, pp. 393–425. Chicago: Univ. Chicago Press

Cox D, Rank MR. 1992. Inter-vivos transfers and intergenerational exchange. *Rev. Econ. and Stat.* 74:305–14

Current Population Reports. 1986. *Household Wealth and Asset Ownership.* Household Economic Studies P-70(7). US Dept. of Commerce. Washington, DC: Gov. Print. Office

Dahrendorf R. 1979. *Life Chances.* Chicago: Univ. Chicago Press

Danziger S, Haveman R, Plotnick R. 1991. How income tranfers affect work, savings, and the income distribution. *J. Econ. Literature* 19:975–1028

Davis K, Moore WE. 1945. Some principles of stratification. *Am. Sociol. Rev.* 10:242–49

Duncan OD, Featherman D, Duncan B. 1972. *Socioeconomic Background and Achievement.* New York: Seminar Press

Dunleavy P. 1979. The urban basis for political alignment: social class, domestic property ownership, and state intervention in consumption processes. *Br. J. Polit. Sci.* 9:409–43

Feinstein J, McFadden D. 1987. *The dynamics of housing demand by the elderly: wealth, cash flow, and demographic effects.* Natl. Bur. Econ. Res. Working paper 2471. Unpublished

Forrest R, Murie A. 1989. Differential accumulation: wealth, inheritance and housing policy reconsidered. *Policy Polit.* 17:25–39

Gale WG, Scholz JK. 1994. Intergenerational transfers and the accumulation of wealth. *J. Econ. Perspect.* 8:145–60

Giddens A. 1973. *The Class Strture of the Advanced Societies.* New York: Harper & Row

Henretta JC, Campbell RT. 1978. Net worth as an aspect of status. *Am. J. Sociol.* 83:1204–23

Henretta JC, Campbell RT. 1980. Status claims and status attainment: the determinants of financial well-being. *Am. J. Sociol.* 86:618–29

Hogan DP, Eggebeen DJ, Clogg CC. 1993. The structure of intergenerational exchanges in

American families. *Am. J. Sociol.* 98:1428–58

Hogan DP, Spenser LJ. 1993. Kin structure and assistance in aging societies. In *Annual Review of Gerontology and Geriatrics*, ed. GL Maddox, MP Lawton. New York: Springer

Holtz-Eakin D, Joulfaian D, Rosen HS. 1993. The Carnegie conjecture: some empirical evidence. *Q. J. Econ.* 63:413–36

Holtz-Eakin D, Smeeding TM. 1994. Income, wealth, and intergenerational economic relations of the aged. In *Demography of Aging*, ed. LG Martin, SH Preston. Washington, DC: National Academy Press

Jencks C. 1979. *Who Gets Ahead: The Determinants of Economic Success in America.* New York: Basic Books

Jencks C, Smith M, Acland H, Bane MJ, Cohen D, Gintis H, et al 1972. *Inequality.* New York: Basic Books

Johnson BW, Eller MB. 1998. Federal taxation of inheritance and wealth transfers. In *Inheritance and Wealth in America*, ed. RK Miller Jr, SJ McNamee, pp. 61–90. New York: Plenum Press

Johnston DC. 1999. A larger legacy may await generations X, Y, and Z. *New York Times*, Oct. 20:C2

Kennedy LW, Stokes DW. 1982. Extended family support and the high cost of housing. *J. Marriage Fam.* 44:311–18

Kessler D, Masson A. 1989. Bequest and wealth accumulation: Are some pieces of the puzzle missing? *J. Econ. Perspect.* 3:141–52

Kohli M. 1999. Private and public transfers between generations: linking the family and the state. *Eur. Soc.* 1:81–104

Kolko G. 1962. *Wealth and Power in America: An Analysis of Social Class and Income Distribution.* New York: Praeger

Kotlikoff LJ, Summers LH. 1981. The role of intergenerational transfers in aggregate capital accumulation. *J. Polit. Econ.* 89:706–32

Kotlikoff LJ, Summers LH. 1988. The contribution of intergenerational transfers to total wealth: a reply. In *Modelling the Accumulation and Distribution of Wealth*, ed.

D Kessler, A Masson, pp. 53–67. Oxford, UK: Clarendon Press

Laitner J. 1997. Intergenerational and inter-household economic links. In *Handbook of Population and Family Economics*, ed. M Rosenzweig, O Stark, pp. 190–237. New York: Elsevier

Lenski G. 1984. Income stratification in the United States: toward a revised model of the system. *Res. Soc. Stratification Mobility* 3:175–205

Levy F, Michel RC. 1991. *The Economic Future of American Families.* Washington, DC: Urban Inst. Press

Lindh T, Ohlsson H. 1998. Self-employment and wealth inequality. *Rev. Income Wealth* 44:25–42

Lipset SM, Zetterberg HL. 1956. A theory of social mobility. *Trans. 3rd World Congr. Sociol.* 5:155–77

MacDonald MM. 1989. *Family background, the life cycle and inter-household transfers.* NSFH working paper 13. Center for Demogr. Ecol. Univ. Wisconsin. Unpublished paper

McGarry K. 1997. *Intervivos transfers and intended bequests.* Natl. Bur. Econ. Res. Work. pap. 6345. Unpublished

McGarry K, Schoeni R. 1995. Transfer behavior in the health and retirement study. *J. Hum. Resourc.* (Supplement) 30:S184–225

McGarry K, Schoeni R. 1997. Transfer behavior within the family: results from the asset and health dynamics study. *J. Gerontol.* 52B:82–92

Menchik P. 1979. Intergenerational transmission of inequality: an empirical study of wealth mobility. *Economica* 46:349–62

Menchik P. 1980. Primogeniture, equal sharing, and the US distribution of wealth. *Q. J. Econ.* 94:299–316

Mills CW. 1956. *The Power Elite.* New York: Oxford Univ. Press

Mishel L, Bernstein J, Schmitt J. 1999. *The State of Working America.* Ithaca, NY: ILR Press

Modigliani F. 1988. Measuring the contribution of intergenerational transfers to total wealth.

In Modelling the Accumulation and Distribution of Wealth, ed. D Kessler, A Masson, pp. 21–52. Oxford: Clarendon Press

Munnell AH. 1988. Wealth transfer taxation: the relative role for estate and income taxes. *N. Engl. Econ. Rev.* (Nov./Dec.), pp. 3–28

Mutran E. 1985. Intergenerational family support among blacks and whites: response to culture or to socioeconomic differences. *J. Gerontol.* 40:382–89

Oliver ML, Shapiro TM. 1995. *Black Wealth/White Wealth.* New York: Routledge

Osberg L. 1984. *Economic Inequality in the United States.* Armonk, NY: Sharpe

Parkin F. 1971. *Class Inequality and Political Order.* New York: Praeger

Parkin F. 1978. Social stratification. In *A History of Sociological Analysis*, ed. T Bottomore, pp. 599–632. New York: Basic Books

Poulantzas N. 1975. *Classes in Contemporary Capitalism.* London: New Left Books

Projector D, Weiss GS. 1966. *Survey of financial characteristics of consumers. Federal Reserve Tech. Paper.* Washington, DC: Board of Governors of the Federal Reserve System

Radner DB. 1988. *The wealth of the aged and non-aged, 1984.* Bureau of the Census. Survey of Income and Program Participation, Paper 8807. Unpublished

Rainwater L, Rein M, Schwartz J. 1986. *Income Packaging in the Welfare State: A Comparative Study of Family Income.* Oxford: Clarendon Press

Ratcliff RE, Maurer S. 1995. Savings and investment among the wealthy: the uses of assets by high-income families in 1950 and 1983. In *Research in Politics and Society: The Politics of Wealth and Inequality* (5), ed. G Moore, JA Whitt, RE Ratcliff, ML Oliver, T Shapiro, pp. 99–125. Greenwich, CT: JAI Press

Rosenfeld RA, Kalleberg AL. 1990. A cross-national comparison of the gender gap in income. *Am. J. Sociol.* 96:69–106

Rosenzweig MR, Wolpin KI. 1994. Parental and public transfers to young women and their children. *Am. Econ. Rev.* 84:1195–212

Rossi AS, Rossi PH. 1990. *Of Human Bonding.* New York: Aldine

Rumberger RW. 1983. The influence of family background on education, earnings, and wealth. *Soc. Forces* 61:755–73

Saunders P. 1978. Domestic property and social class. *Int. J. Urban Regional Res.* 2:233–51

Saunders P. 1984. Beyond housing classes. *Int. J. Urban Regional Res.* 8:202–27

Saunders P. 1986. *Social Theory and the Urban Question.* London: Hutchinson

Schoeni RF. 1997. Private interhousehold transfers of money and time: new empirical evidence. *Rev. Income Wealth* 43:423–48

Semyonov M, Lewin-Epstein N, Spilerman S. 1996. The material possessions of Israeli ethnic groups. *Eur. Sociol. Rev.* 12:289–301

Sherraden M. 1991. *Assets and the Poor: A New American Welfare Policy.* Armonk, NY: Sharpe

Sherraden M. 2000. Asset building in community development and public policy. In *The Benefits and Mechanisms for Spreading Asset Ownership*, ed. T Shapiro, EN Wolff. In press

Shorrocks AF. 1987. UK wealth distribution: current evidence and future prospects. In *International Comparisons of the Distribution of Household Wealth*, ed. EN Wolff. Oxford: Clarendon Press

Silverstein M, Waite LJ. 1993. Are Blacks more likely than Whites to receive and provide support in middle and old age? Yes, No, and maybe so. *J. Gerontol.* 48:s212–22

Slemrod J. 1991. *Taxation and inequality: a time exposure perspective.* Presented at the NBER Conf. Tax Policy and the Economy, Nov. 19

Smith JP. 1995. Racial and ethnic differences in wealth in the health and retirement study. *J. Hum. Resourc.* 30 (Suppl.):S159–83

Soldo BJ, Hill MS. 1993. Intergenerational transfers: economic, demographic, and social pespectives. In *Annual Review of Gerontology and Geriatrics*, ed. GL Maddox, MP Lawton. New York: Springer

Solon GR. 1992. Intergenerational income mobility in the United States. *Am. Econ. Rev.* 82:393–408

Spant R. 1987. Wealth distribution in Sweden: 1920–1983. In *International Comparisons of the Distribution of Household Wealth*, ed. EN Wolff. Oxford: Clarendon Press

Spilerman S. 1999. *Home ownership, intergenerational assistance, and wealth inequality in Israel.* Dept. Sociol., Columbia Univ., New York. Unpublished

Spilerman S. 2000. Some observations on asset ownership, living standards, and poor families. In *The Benefits and Mechanisms for Spreading Asset Ownership*, ed. T Shapiro, EN Wolff. In press

Spilerman S, Lewin-Epstein N, Semyonov M. 1993. Wealth, intergenerational transfers, and life chances. In *Social Theory and Social Policy*, ed. A Sorensen, S Spilerman. New York: Praeger

Stark O. 1995. *Altruism and Beyond.* Cambridge, UK: Cambridge Univ. Press

Stark O, Falk I. 1998. Transfers, empathy formation, and reverse transfers. *AEA Papers Proc.* 88:271–76

Theeuwes J. 1981. Family labor force participation: multinomial logit estimates. *Appl. Econ.* 13:481–98

Thurow LC. 1975. *Generating Inequality.* New York: Basic Books

Thurow LC. 1987. Tax wealth, not income. In *Structured Social Inequality*, ed. CS Heller, pp. 145–50. New York: Macmillan

Tomes N. 1981. The family, inheritance, and the intergenerational transmission of inequality. *J. Polit. Econ.* 89:925–58

Weber M. 1947. Social stratification and class structure. In *Max Weber: The Theory of Social and Economic Organization*, ed. T Parsons. New York: Free Press

Weber M. 1958. Class, status, party. In *From Max Weber*, ed. HH Gerth, CW Mills. New York: Oxford Univ. Press

Weil DN. 1994. The savings of the the elderly in micro and macro data. *Q. J. Econ.* 109:55–81

Wilcox D. 1991. Household spending and saving: measurement, trends, and analysis. *Federal Reserve Bull.* (Jan.):

Wilhelm MO. 1996. Bequest behavior and the effect of heirs' earnings: testing the altruistic model of bequests. *Am. Econ. Rev.* 86:874–92

Wolff EN. 1980. Estimates of the 1969 size distribution of household wealth in the US from a synthetic data base. In *Modeling the Distribution and Intergenerational Transmission of Wealth*, ed. JD Smith. Chicago: Univ. Chicago Press

Wolff EN. 1987. Estimates of household wealth inequality in the US, 1962–83. *Rev. Income Wealth* 33:231–42

Wolff EN. 1989. Trends in aggregate household wealth in the US, 1900–83. *Rev. Income Wealth* 34:1–29

Wolff EN. 1990. Wealth holdings and poverty status in the US. *Rev. Income Wealth.* 36:143–65

Wolff EN. 1994. Trends in household wealth in the United States, 1962–83 and 1983–89. *Rev. Income Wealth* 40:143–74

Wolff EN. 1995. The rich get increasingly richer: latest data on household wealth during the 1980s. In *Research in Politics and Society: The Politics of Wealth and Inequality* (5), ed. G Moore, JA Whitt, RE Ratcliff, ML Oliver, T Shapiro. Greenwich, CT: JAI Press

Wolff EN. 1996. *Top Heavy.* New York: New Press

Wolff EN. 2000. Recent trends in wealth ownership. In *The Benefits and Mechanisms for Spreading Asset Ownership*, ed. T Shapiro, EN Wolff. In press

Wright EO. 1985. *Classes.* London: New Left Books

Wright EO, Perrone L. 1977. Marxist class categories and income inequality. *Am. Sociol. Rev.* 42:32–55

Zimmerman DJ. 1992. Regression toward mediocrity in economic stature. *Am. Econ. Rev.* 82:409–29

Annu. Rev. Sociol. 2000. 26:525–46

THE CHOICE-WITHIN-CONSTRAINTS NEW INSTITUTIONALISM AND IMPLICATIONS FOR SOCIOLOGY

Paul Ingram
Columbia Business School, Columbia University, New York, New York 10027-6902; e-mail: pi17@columbia.edu

Karen Clay
Heinz School of Public Policy, Carnegie Mellon University, Pittsburgh, Pennsylvania 15213; e-mail: kclay@andrew.cmu.edu

Key Words   economy, commitment, exchange, state, organization

■ **Abstract**   The variant of new institutionalism that is our focus is a pan-disciplinary theory that asserts that actors pursue their interests by making choices within institutional constraints. We organize our review of the theory around its behavioral assumptions, the operation of institutional forms, and processes of institutional change. At each stage, we give particular attention to the potential contributions of sociology to the theory. The behavioral assumptions of the theory amount to bounded rationality and imply transaction costs, which, in the absence of institutions, may frustrate collective ends. The principle weakness of these behavioral assumptions is a failure to treat preferences as endogenous. We categorize the institutions that arise in response to transaction costs as to whether they are public or private in their source and centralized or decentralized in their making. In detailing the resulting categories of institutional forms, we identify key interdependencies across the public/private and centralized/decentralized dimensions. The new institutionalism is in particular need of better theory about private decentralized institutions, and theorists could turn to embeddedness theory and cognitive new-institutional theory as a source of help on this topic. The dominant view of institutional change is that it is evolutionary, driven by organizational competition, and framed by individual beliefs and shared understandings. Sociology can refine the change theory by adding better explanations of the behavior of organizations, and of the processes by which institutional alternatives come to be viewed as acceptable or unacceptable.

INTRODUCTION

Ronald Coase (1998, p. 73) likens mainstream economics to studying "the circulation of the blood without a body." The new institutionalism that is the focus of this essay is about the body. Its fundamental assertion is that actors pursue their interests by making choices within constraints. This assertion can be expanded to identify three characteristic elements of the theory. First, it holds that actors are boundedly rational in the sense that they pursue a broad set of self interests, but with limited knowledge and cognitive capacity. Second, institutions are defined as the rules, combined with their enforcement mechanisms, that constrain the choices of actors. These rules include the laws of states, the policies of organizations, and the norms of social groups. Third, institutions ideally constrain actors such that their best choices are consistent with the collective good, enabling, for example, mutually profitable exchange between actors. However, there is no assumption that ideal institutions will exist, and globally inefficient institutions sometimes persist because they favor particular actors who have the power to defend them. The theory is pan-disciplinary, and major contributions have come from economics (Coase 1937, Williamson 1975, North 1990, Greif 1994), political science (North & Weingast 1989, Ostrom 1990), law (Ellickson 1991), sociology (Nee & Ingram 1998), and anthropology (Ensminger 1992).

This "choice-within-constraints" framework is only one of many theories to be called new institutional (Fligstein 1997). We do not attempt in this essay to give full treatment to all new institutional theories (for broader new institutional reviews, see Scott 1995, Stinchcombe 1997, Nee 1998). Instead, we try to give a more complete treatment of the accomplishments and shortcomings of the variant of new institutionalism that is our focus. However, other theories come into play as sources of solutions to the theoretical problems with which the choice-within-constraints framework is currently struggling. Particularly likely sources for intellectual exchange with the choice-within-constraints framework are the more cognitive version of new institutionalism, from sociology's organizational theory, and the related theory of embeddedness from economic sociology. Indeed, it is one of our main assertions that sociologists are well poised to make contributions to the new institutional theory that we elucidate.

This essay has three main parts. In each, we treat a core component of the theory, describing and critiquing its current state. We begin by detailing its behavioral assumptions. These assumptions amount to bounded rationality, and they imply the foundation problem of the new institutionalism, that exchange is associated with uncertainty and risk. Uncertainty and risk in exchange create transaction costs, which frustrate efforts to attain collective ends (from simple gains from trade to the fruit of complex collective action). A key weakness of these behavioral assumptions is their inattention to the origin of preferences. This is the missing link in all theories based on behavioral assumptions of rationality. On this topic the new institutionalism can use the findings of embeddedness theory (Granovetter 1985, Uzzi 1996) and cognitive institutionalism (Meyer & Rowan 1977, Powell & DiMaggio 1991).

We then denote the major classes of institutions and explain the mechanisms of their operation. Institutions can facilitate the attainment of collective ends that transaction costs might otherwise prevent. They do this by aligning individual incentives to be consistent with collective ends. We propose a classification system for institutions based on two dimensions—public or private and centralized or decentralized. Public or private refers to who makes the institutions, with public indicating the state and private indicating organizations or individuals. The centralized/decentralized distinction captures the degree to which institutions are codified and responsibility for enforcement is centralized with identifiable functionaries. These two dimensions define three classes of institutions, public-centralized, private-centralized, and private-decentralized (there are no institutions that are public and decentralized in the literature on which we focus). We describe in detail these three classes, and we consider the interdependence between them.

Finally, we consider the question of institutional creation and change. Currently, an evolutionary explanation of institutional change is most prominent. Processes of the selection of social systems (groups, organizations, states) and political competition over institutions push the institutional framework gently in the direction of transaction cost efficiency. "Gentle," however, is key to describing these evolutionary pressures, and consequently, new institutionalists are not surprised to observe inefficient institutions that persist for very long periods of time. Missing from current ideas on institutional change are realistic views of the role of organizations in the process and how beliefs and shared understandings affect change of other types of institutions.

BEHAVIORAL ASSUMPTIONS

To denote the behavioral assumptions of the new institutionalism, it is useful to break down a simple summary of the fundamental behavioral assertion of the theory: "actors pursue their interests by making choices within constraints." The significant classes of actors are individuals, organizations, and states. Individuals constitute the other classes of actors, and are the focus of our discussion of interests and choice. Organizations are defined broadly as groups of all types, whether they are social groups, coalitions, or corporations, structured to pursue some collective purpose. States are a special type of organization "... invested with the authority to make binding decisions for people and organizations juridically located in a particular territory and to implement these decisions using, if necessary, force" (Rueschemeyer & Evans 1985, pp. 46–47).

These three classes of actors each produce their own form of institutional constraint: individuals produce private-decentralized institutions, organizations produce private-centralized institutions, and states produce public-centralized institutions. In this sense, it can be said that actors lead a double life in the new institutionalism, pursuing their own interests within constraints, while producing constraints for other actors. The interplay between the actors can best be understood as a three-layered hierarchy, with states superordinate to organizations, which are superordinate to individuals (Nee & Ingram 1998). States constrain organizations and individuals that are their subjects, and organizations constrain the individuals that are their participants. There is also upward influence in the hierarchy, as actors try to affect the institutions that constrain them.

This hierarchy of actors is useful to illustrate some key differences between the choice-within-constraints framework and the cognitive institutionalism and embeddedness arguments that are prominent in sociology. Those latter two lines of new institutional argument recognize the same classes of actors that we do, although in both cases they see all of these actors as embedded in something outside (culture and networks of social relations, variously). This embedding adds other influences, beyond the immediate action frame, on the actors and their relationships. The choice-within-constraints new institutionalism that we focus on strips away those outside influences, and relies on the interplay among individuals, organizations, and states to explain institutions and behavior. One of our goals is to illustrate for sociologists the advantages of this narrowing, although we also recognize many limitations.

Moving from actors to interests and choice, the new institutionalism views individuals as rational in the basic sense of making choices that further their interests. The theory, however, interprets both interests and the rationality of choice much more broadly than neoclassic economics does. For example, the new institutionalism distinguishes itself from neoclassical assumptions of rationality by attending to "cognitive costs" of decision making. The pursuit of benefits is limited by individuals' capacity to retain and process information; in other words, individuals are boundedly rational (Coase 1937, Simon 1957). Furthermore, information is often costly (Barzel 1989). These two factors create transactions costs—the costs of writing and enforcing contracts—because individuals cannot foresee at the time of writing all of the contingencies that might be relevant, nor can they observe all of the actions of their partners. Also, transactions costs give rise to the possibility of opportunism (Williamson 1975).

The possibility of opportunism and its role in the new institutionalism deserve particular attention because opportunism has been the basis of criticism from sociologists and because it contrasts with the emphasis on trust in the network embeddedness approach to economic sociology (Granovetter 1985, Uzzi 1996). Often, the opportunism-trust debate takes place on rhetorical ground, with new institutionalists criticized for unwarranted cynicism (Ghoshal & Moran 1996) and responding with warnings that "there are real dangers in adopting the more benevolent construction" of human nature (Williamson 1994, p. 81). Such debate quickly reaches an impasse, and the gains from intellectual exchange would be greater if the starting point was a recognition that the new institutionalism does not rely on the assumption that individuals will engage in malfeasance, but rather on the assumption that they pursue their self interest. From the assumption of self interest, the interesting question becomes "Why shouldn't individuals engage in malfeasance?" As we explain, the new institutional answer is that sometimes institutions constrain individuals so as to remove the gains from malfeasance.

The problem of credible commitment emerges from the possibility of opportunism, and is at the core of the new institutionalism. It is illustrated by the dilemma faced by a kidnap victim whose kidnapper has a change of heart and decides to set her free (Schelling 1960). The victim gladly promises not to reveal the kidnapper to the authorities in exchange for her freedom. However, the kidnapper realizes that once the victim is free she will have no incentive to keep her promise and reluctantly decides the victim must be killed. More generally, the problem of credible commitment is faced by any party to an exchange who wants to promise in the present to do something in the future that may not be in his or her interest to do when the future actually arrives. The problem is endemic because in almost every exchange there is at least a moment when one of the parties has control over all or most of the goods and must decide whether to follow through on the agreed upon bargain or make a grab for more.

Although the costs of rational decision making have been thoroughly analyzed as the basis of transaction costs and the need for institutions, interests or preferences have been largely ignored. The new institutionalism applies a "thick" view of preferences, which often includes, in addition to material goods, ideology and social goods such as status. In practice, however, nonmaterial preferences have been given short shrift in the theory. This is illustrated by North's (1990, p. 22) characterization of the trade-off between ideological and material preferences: "... where the price to individuals of being able to express their own values and interests is low, they will loom large in the choices made; but where the price one pays for expressing one's own ideology, or norms, or preferences is extremely high, they will account much less for human behavior." This is too weak a concession to the role of ideology, particularly in the face of evidence such as that from Poole & Rosenthal's (1996) analyses of the whole history of US Congress roll-call voting, which indicated that ideology explained more of the variance in voting behavior than did economic interests.

Another limitation of the behavioral assumptions is that the new institutionalism, like most other theories based on rationality, suffers from the absence of an explanation for the origin of preferences. This is one of the areas in which sociology is poised to make a critical contribution to the theory. Economists have generally taken a complete set of well-ordered preferences as a starting assumption, although preferences are almost certainly endogenous. Thus the explanation of preferences has been left to others (DiMaggio 1990). Veblen (1899) explicitly recognized the relationship between preference and social structure, and more recently sociologists have argued that preferences are socially constructed (DiMaggio 1990, Friedland & Alford 1991). Certainly, the status and social identity implications of objects explain much of their appeal to consumers. Sociologists are also able to help with explanations of how actors form strategies to achieve their preferences. Strategy formulation is inhibited by bounded rationality, and it is clear that actors do not weigh the full set of means to achieve their preferred ends (Cyert & March 1963). Recent organizational sociology has explained, for example, how corporate diversification or mergers become accepted and popular strategies (Fligstein 1990, Dobbin & Dowd 1997).

OPERATION OF INSTITUTIONS

If the main problem derived from the new institutionalism's behavioral assumptions is transaction costs, institutions can be seen as a partial solution. Institutional rules and their enforcement mechanisms can structure the interactions of actors such that the costs of acquiring and processing information are less debilitating, and the opportunities for malfeasance are reduced. This proposition raises a number of questions. Who makes rules? How are the rules made? Who enforces the rules? And how are the rules enforced? In this section, we briefly discuss each of these questions and then examine the literature on three broad classes of institutions.

Institutions are typically categorized as formal or informal (North 1990, Nee & Ingram 1998). We use a more fine-grained categorization based on two dimensions, who makes the rules (the state or some other entity) and how are they made and enforced (in centralized or decentralized fashion). We use this two-dimensional categorization scheme because we think it is better than the formal/informal categorization for (*a*) differentiating the most relevant distinctions between institutional forms, (*b*) emphasizing the ways that different institutional forms are interdependent, and (*c*) relating the different institutional forms to the actors with which they are most closely associated.

States make rules in a centralized manner, but so do other entities. Many clubs and other organizations, like the American Medical Association, create rules in much the same way as a state does, through the actions of one or more appointed or elected members. Rules, however, may also arise in a decentralized way, through interaction and taking the form of norms. Norms may specify that neighboring ranchers look out for one another's cattle or that coworkers cover for one another in an illness. In what follows, we refer to institutions as being one of three types: public (effectively, public-centralized), private-centralized, or private-decentralized.

If institutions are constraints, it is not sufficient for rules to exist; they must also be enforced. Enforcement can be by the party who was harmed (second-party enforcement) or some other party (third-party enforcement). Public and private-centralized institutions typically have third-party enforcement. For instance, the US government punishes individuals who are convicted of federal crimes. Similarly, the California State Bar Association can vote to suspend a member's license to practice law. Except in rare cases, the breaking of the rule did not harm the federal government or the California Bar. In contrast, private-decentralized institutions can have either third-party or second-party enforcement. For instance, among medieval merchants, one merchant might refuse to interact in the future with a merchant who had cheated him, a form of second-party enforcement. If other merchants also refused to interact with the cheater because of this episode, then punishment would also be of the third-party type.

A related issue is how rules are enforced. Many institutions offer some form of dispute resolution to ensure that a rule has actually been broken before the sanctions are applied. The government maintains a court system for this purpose, trade groups maintain arbitration panels, and, even in decentralized institutions, the parties may at times turn to an impartial third party. Sanctions, if they are deemed necessary, can take a variety of forms, both economic and noneconomic. Economic sanctions can include fines, restitution, or penalties that impair future earnings, such as restrictions on economic activity. Noneconomic sanctions can include loss of certain rights, status, or interaction with certain groups. For example, social groups often punish indiscretion with ostracism.

Against this background on the nature and enforcement of institutions, we now examine in detail the three institutional forms we have identified. We emphasize the ways that each institutional form operates to affect the choices of actors. We also identify interdependencies among the forms.

Public Institutions

There are four major ways that the public institutions provided by the state can be understood to affect its choices and those of organizations and individuals. First, the state may smooth exchange between its subjects by providing institutions that allow them to make credible commitments. This can be achieved if the state provides a legal system to protect property rights, decrease transaction costs, and enforce contracts. Spicer (1997) illustrates the role of such a system by examining a case in which the state did not play this role, the mass privatization of financial markets in Russia from 1992 through 1996. During this period, regulation of organizations that had formed to attract consumer savings was weak to nonexistent. It was unclear who had regulatory authority in the market, and the contenders to supply regulation lacked the necessary resources. A number of well-publicized and unpunished scams by organizations in the industry reduced the willingness of Russians to transact with financial organizations. The institutional weakness was recognized by the executive of a US bank operating in Russia, who expressed a wish that the state would regulate his bank more heavily. Such a hope sounds unusual coming from an American banker, but it indicates how the state enables the credible commitments of subject organizations by constraining them.

There is quantitative evidence of the role of public institutions for enabling credible commitments. Some studies exploit changes in laws governing specific industries to show that increased legal constraint on organizations causes them to flourish. Studies of populations as diverse as US health maintenance organizations and telephone companies, Toronto day-care centers, Niagara Falls hotels, and Singapore banks have demonstrated that their failure is reduced by increasing government involvement in monitoring, certifying, authorizing, and endorsing their activities (Wholey et al 1992, Barnett & Carroll 1993, Baum & Oliver 1992, Ingram & Inman 1996, Carroll & Teo 1998). The effects of broader changes in public institutions are seen in Ingram & Simons' (2000) analysis of the effect of the formation of the Israeli State on the failure rates of workers' cooperatives in many industries. The transition from the weak British Mandate for Palestine to the strong Israeli State caused a radical improvement in the institutional support for credible commitment and a corresponding 60% decrease in organizational failure rates.

Stone et al (1996) use, to exciting effect, a comparative analysis of the institutions of Chile and Brazil as these institutions affect their countries' garment industries. Brazilian laws governing the economy are so complex and their enforcement so expensive that ". . . [public] institutions could not be relied on for dealing with day-to-day problems in regulation and business transactions" (100). By contrast, Chile is ". . . regarded as having a relatively well-defined property-rights system and a liberal economy" (102). The comparison between the two supports the claim that effective public institutions facilitate economic exchange, but also indicates that private institutions may often be a decent substitute. In some areas, Chile appeared to have lower transaction costs than Brazil. For example, customer orders were much more likely to be renegotiated before delivery in Brazil, and, as a result, Brazilian garment manufacturers were less likely to produce customized goods. In other areas, however, private institutions have arisen in Brazil to offset the inefficiency of public institutions. Starting a business in Brazil requires the negotiation of complex government rules, but specialized professionals handle the details in ~7 weeks, for an average cost to the founding firm of $640, comparable with the time and expense of starting a business via Chile's simpler process. And Brazilian garment manufacturers rely heavily on credit, despite the cumbersome and expensive contract enforcement procedures they face. Apparently, they substitute a reliance on reputation, facilitated by institutions of credit agencies and customer credit references. The emergent picture of an interdependence between public and private institutions presents a rich set of questions for the new institutionalism. This issue reasserts itself repeatedly as we discuss the various institutional forms.

The second key feature of public institutions is whether the state can credibly commit to not subsidize subject organizations when they struggle. The recent transitions from state socialism have demonstrated that, absent such a commitment, entrepreneurs will direct their energies towards "holding up" the state treasury rather than to producing economic value. As Stark & Bruszt (1998, p. 119) put it, when the state hears organizations' ". . . siren cry, 'Give me a hand, give me your hand,' it must be bound to respond not simply that it should not, or that it will not, but that it cannot." McFaul (1995) describes the problem of state subsidies to enterprises in Russia, which, by the spring of 1993, were estimated to be 22% of the gross domestic product. According to McFaul, state weakness was the cause of Russia's failure to make credible its commitments not to subsidize. Stark & Bruszt (1998) refine that position by emphasizing that state strength is relative to the strength of other actors. Their analysis of transformations in east-central Europe shows that efforts to credibly commit against subsidies were sometimes implemented not by strengthening the state, but by attempting to weaken subsidy-seeking groups by limiting the size and interconnectedness of organizations.

The third key feature of public institutions is an outgrowth of the first two. A state that is strong enough to guarantee the property rights of its subjects and to resist their calls for subsidies is also strong enough to appropriate their wealth (Weingast 1993). Unless the state can credibly commit itself against such appropriations, its subjects' incentives for productive economic activity will be greatly curtailed. This is aptly illustrated in North & Weingast's (1989) account of the Stuarts' impact on the economy of seventeenth century England. After coming to the Crown in 1612, the Stuarts exploited their subjects in numerous ways: they sold monopolies (at the expense of industry incumbents and potential entrants), they sold special dispensations from laws, and they even committed outright theft, as in 1640 when they seized £130,000 that private merchants had placed in the Tower of London for safekeeping. Evidence that citizens recognized the parasitic nature of their sovereign and incorporated it into their economic calculus comes from the Stuarts' inability to raise debt through normal means (they resorted to "forced loans," the payment terms of which they subsequently violated). These abuses [among other causes (Carruthers 1990)] led eventually to the Glorious Revolution of 1688, which resulted in numerous institutional changes to reduce the Crown's capacity to act independently of Parliament and the courts. This loss of Crown autonomy had, however, positive implications in that it enabled the Crown to make a credible commitment not to appropriate subjects' wealth. The value of this commitment can be seen in the dramatic increase in the Stuarts' capacity to borrow funds—government debt grew 17-fold in the 9 years after the revolution. North & Weingast argue that the improvements in Crown finance were mirrored by improvements in private financial markets.

Striking as this account is, to attribute the state's capacity to make credible commitments to a constitutional division of powers is to finesse the central issue. If a state is powerful enough to enforce property rights, why need it be constrained by the "parchment barrier" provided by a constitution? Why doesn't the state simply break the law? Weingast (1993) examines this question with a game-theoretic analysis. He considers a state that decides whether to transgress against each of two constituent groups, which in turn decide whether to acquiesce to or challenge the state. The repeated game has multiple equilibria, but the normal diversity of interests among constituents makes it more likely that the game will result in an equilibrium in which the state transgresses the rights of some constituents and retains the support of others. The "credible-commitment equilibrium," in which the constituents challenge the state for any transgressions, and the state therefore abstains from transgressing, can be expected only if there is substantial agreement among constituents about the appropriate role and limits of the state. "[T]he foundations for institutional restriction fundamentally rest on the attitudes of citizens." This recognition of the normative underpinnings of public order may sound to sociologists like a second Glorious Revolution. Certainly, it is sociology that is best positioned to explain how individuals come to share attitudes towards the state, and indeed this question has been the subject of recent sociological effort (Meyer et al 1997).

Fourth and finally, some institutions provided by the state are not to be understood as part of a grand effort to facilitate the credible commitments of actors, but rather in terms of the distributional battles over zero-sum interests (Knight 1992). These may be the battles between suppliers and consumers, as shown in Dobbin & Dowd's (1997) analysis of the effects of competition policy on railroad foundings in early Massachussetts. Or they may be the battles between rival organizational forms without apparent efficiency differences, as for thrift-savings organizations that fought as much in the legislative arena as in the market (Haveman & Rao 1997) or national coffee roasters in the United States, that derived a competitive advantage over regional roasters through an international treaty (Bates 1997).

Although our categorization of institutions as public/private and centralized/decentralized suggests two types of public institutions, centralized and decentralized, this discussion of public institutions has been exclusively about public-centralized institutions. In the choice-within-constraints framework, the public-decentralized cell is empty—there is no literature on state-level institutions that emerge without central authority. New institutional sociologists, however, have addressed that cell, describing the equivalent of national and international norms of state structure and behavior that emerge through cultural and associational processes (e.g. Fligstein & Mara-Drita 1996, Meyer et al 1997, Dobbin & Sutton 1998). The failure of the choice-within-constraints theory to account for the influence of national culture and world society is one of the costs of its reliance only on influences within the immediate action frame created by interacting individuals, organizations, and states.

Private-Centralized Institutions

Private-centralized institutions may be divided into two types based on the nature of their effects on actors: those that govern property rights, and those that enable transactions. The first type is illustrated in the American West of the nineteenth century, where individuals formed claims clubs, cattlemen's associations, and mining districts to protect their property rights in agricultural, ranch, and mineral-bearing land. In each case, they reaped or tried to reap the benefits from excluding others. Members of claims clubs in Iowa prevented speculators from buying up the land they had been squatting on (Bogue 1958). Ranchers in the American West who ran their cattle on federal land kept out later arrivals by excluding them from the roundup (Dennen 1976). Also, during the California Gold Rush, groups of miners established mining districts on federal land that allowed individuals to mine without interference from others (Umbeck 1981, Clay & Wright 1999). All of these groups had some type of written rules, although, as Clay & Wright show for mining districts, written rules were often augmented by norms or even supplanted by them. Enforcement was at least nominally centralized, with members of the claims club, cattlemen's association, or mining district using third-party enforcement to protect their property rights. This enforcement took different forms in each case: for claims clubs, it was physical force against speculators; for the cattlemen's association, it was exclusion of outsiders from the annual roundup, an economic penalty; and for mining districts, it was removal of interlopers by physical force. By enforcing rules against speculators buying their land, later entrants running cattle on federal land, or new miners seizing property held by others, members provided outsiders with incentives to respect their property rights.

The formation of private-centralized institutions to govern property rights is not just a historical phenomenon. Ostrom (1990) documents a variety of contemporary institutions that have arisen to manage property rights over resources that are common property (that is, resources that are held in common by many actors). Some or all of the individuals who hold the property in common make the rules, and enforcement is through third-party imposition of economic and social sanctions. One difference between these institutions and the ones in the previous paragraph is the types of incentives that the rules and enforcement create. In this case, rules and third-party enforcement of these rules create incentives for members not to overutilize the resource, rather than for outsiders to respect members' property rights. For example, in Torbel, Switzerland, alpine meadows are held in common by the 600 villagers. Grazing rights are allocated based on the number of cows that a citizen can support in the winter. During the summer, a group of herdsmen tend the village cattle in the communal meadow. Milk from the cows is used to produce cheese that is allocated to families based on the number of cattle that were grazed. Elected officials hire the herdsmen and impose fines on households who misuse the commons by sending too many cattle (Ostrom 1990, pp. 60–65).

Private-centralized institutions do not always arise to address common-property problems. Johnson & Libecap (1982) address the question of why these institutions do not arise, in a study of the shrimp industry in the Gulf of Mexico. In this industry, over-fishing is an ever-present problem. During the 1930s, 1940s, and 1950s, an industry association had managed shrimp stocks on the Gulf Coast by setting price floors that made it unprofitable to harvest small shrimp. Union members were given incentives to adhere to the price floors through fines, and the union pressured packers not to buy below union price or from nonunion shrimpers. In 1956, however, the Fifth Circuit Court of Appeals found the union to be in violation of the Sherman Act, making further efforts to limit entry or effort illegal. This illustrates the interdependence between institutional forms, because it was a public institution that defeated a private-centralized institution that was designed to solve the problem of over-fishing. In other cases, private-centralized institutions cannot solve common-property problems because of the difficulty of monitoring compliance with the institutions or because of holdout by actors with a stake in the common property (Wiggins & Libecap 1985).

Examples of the second role of private-centralized institutions, to govern trade, date at least from the rise of merchant guilds in the late-medieval period. Although some authors have interpreted these guilds as a vehicle for merchants to capture rents by limiting entry, Greif et al (1994) provide evidence indicating that their real purpose was ". . . to allow rulers of trade centers to commit to the security of alien merchants." The guilds created incentives for rulers to respect member merchants' rights by credibly committing to end trade if these rights were violated. Guilds had and enforced rules that required members to punish by ostracism any members found to be trading with rulers who had violated members' rights. Third-party enforcement by the guild of these rules through the imposition of fines or other sanctions created incentives for members not to trade with such rulers, thereby making a guild's commitment to end trade credible.

In the twentieth century, a private-centralized institution has arisen to facilitate trade in the diamond industry. Bernstein (1992) examines the rules that govern transactions and the reasons why diamond dealers have chosen to enforce these rules through a private-centralized institution and not through standard legal channels. As in the foregoing cases, members are governed by formal written rules that represent the codification of, and are supported by, industry norms. Bernstein finds that the use of arbitration panels and mandatory prearbitration conciliation is a response to members' need for speed, secrecy, and specialized knowledge of industry laws and norms. The industry enforces arbitration decisions with the threat of suspension of membership in the diamond bourse. In the case of non-compliance, a bourse faxes the individual's picture to all other diamond bourses worldwide. Informed of noncompliance, members then refuse to trade with the individual in question because of the risk that they will be cheated. Through this reputation mechanism, the institution creates incentives for members to adhere to industry rules and norms in their transactions with other members.

The most ubiquitous private-centralized institutions that govern trade are orga-nizations that internalize transactions. In his seminal 1937 paper, Coase took up the pivotal question of why organizations exist. His central insight was that the governance of exchange within organizations as opposed to markets depended on the cost of transacting in each type of institution. In more recent work, Williamson (1985) and others have systematically investigated the effect of information, op-portunism, and asset specificity on the governance of exchange, concluding that, in some transaction environments, exchange is more efficient within an organi-zation than the market. Furthermore, the prevailing public institutions influence the attractiveness of various governance arrangements (Nee 1992). Ficker (1999) illustrates the relationship between the environment of public institutions and other factors, and the market/organization trade-off in the evolution of the Mexican Cen-tral Railroad. The Mexican Central Railroad was founded in 1880 into "a country characterized by economic backwardness and an incipient and precarious insti-tutional framework." The company initially pursued a strategy of building main lines and depending on market transactions with railroads and other types of trans-portation organizations to supply them with freight. These market transactions did not materialize, however, owing to the weak Mexican infrastructure, and the difficulties of organizational and technological coordination. In response to this failing of the market, the Mexican Central Railroad switched to a strategy of inter-nalization, extending its trunk lines and building branch lines to supply itself with freight.

Private-Decentralized Institutions

Institutions of the third form—those consisting of private-decentralized rules such as norms—were widely ignored until recently, no doubt because they are much less visible than centralized institutions. An exception to the neglect of this category was the pioneering work by Macaulay (1963) on contract enforcement by executives. Macaulay showed that, when problems arose in a relationship, business norms dictated that the two parties attempt to resolve the problem informally rather than go to court. This was true even if going to court would have provided a higher payoff for the plaintiff. Plaintiffs had an incentive to agree to informal resolution, because developing a reputation for litigiousness would adversely affect future business dealings within the community.

Private-decentralized institutions have also been seen to support long-distance trade in the absence of a legal system. In long-distance trade, merchants can often profit from using other merchants as agents to sell goods, collect debts, and so forth. This agency relationship, however, raises the possibility that the agent will act opportunistically, keeping some or all of the monies owed. The Maghribi traders in the eleventh century western Mediterranean (Greif 1989, 1994) and American merchants on the nineteenth-century California coast (Clay 1997a, 1997b) overcame this problem by forming coalitions, which allowed exchange to flourish. In both cases, merchants in the coalition conditioned future use of other merchants as agents on those merchants' having acted in accordance with group norms in the past. For instance, when a Maghribi merchant was accused of cheating in 1041–1042, he found that "people became agitated and hostile and whoever owed [me money] conspired to keep it from me" (Greif 1994, p. 925). Merchants checked on agents' past behavior and verified trade-related information in letters to one another, creating an information network. By tying future economic gains to past behavior as an agent, merchants were able to ensure that the future gains to membership in the coalition were greater than the gains to cheating and being punished. Punishment was decentralized in that each merchant, having learned that an agent had violated group norms, then had an incentive not to interact with that merchant in the future because he expected the merchant to cheat him. The incentives created by this reputation mechanism enabled merchants to enter into and enforce contracts in the absence of a legal system.

The ability of private-decentralized institutions to support "order without law" goes beyond trade. For instance, Reid (1980) shows that, on the Overland Trail during the nineteenth century, individuals acted as if laws existed, carrying prevailing legal norms with them, even though there was no legal system to enforce them. The threat of social and economic ostracism on the trail created incentives for individuals to adhere to the norms that led to order. In addition, Ellickson (1991) documents Shasta County cattlemen's use of norms that dealt quickly and effectively with the ongoing problem of cattle that strayed and damaged neighbors' property. By tying the prompt return of stray cattle and other forms of cooperation to adherence to norms, the institution created incentives for cattlemen in the area to act in accordance with the norms. There were laws regarding stray cattle, but few cattlemen knew them, and fewer still relied on them.

Nee & Ingram (1998) argue that decentralized-private institutions, which exert the most immediate control on individuals, determine the effectiveness of institutions of the other two forms. Whether pubic- or private-centralized institutions have their intended effects will depend on whether private-decentralized institutions encourage individuals to accede to or oppose them. Heckathorn (1990) presents formal models to show that the coercive efforts of states may fail if affected populations develop "opposition norms," which supply social rewards for opposing state coercion. Homans' (1950) reanalysis of the Bank Wiring Room shows a similar result for the private-centralized institutions maintained by the Western Electric Company. There, norms in the work group influenced employees to engage in behavior that was the opposite of what the organization's pay system tried to encourage.

Embeddedness theory, from economic sociology, is also informative about the operation of private-decentralized institutions. Indeed, at the surface level of observed causes and effects, the two approaches are sometimes difficult to distinguish. For example Maurer & Haber's (1999) new institutional analysis and Uzzi's (1999) embeddedness analysis both find that organizations' access to bank loans is greater if they have social relationships with their bankers. There are differences, however, in the behavioral assumptions that these two theories use to arrive at predictions. New institutionalists believe that the significance of interpersonal relationships is in their capacity to create social sanctions, which give norms their teeth. Participants adhere to norms when to do so is justified by a comparison of current and future payoffs for adhering to or violating the norm (Ulman-Margalit 1977). In contrast, embeddedness theorists argue that social relationships have a logic of their own, which is sometimes divorced from the rational calculus of benefits (Granovetter 1985, Uzzi 1996). New institutionalists could gain by incorporating something of the embeddedness view of relationships, because even rational-choice theorists concede that interpersonal relationships rest on more than calculated self-interest and that norms are sometimes internalized (Coleman 1990).

It is also true that embeddedness theory could gain from the new institutionalism, because the latter theory has gone farther towards understanding the role of interpersonal relationships in the broader institutional framework. Greif's (1994) seminal study comparing the institutions that the Maghribi and the Genoese used to support long-distance trade in the Mediterranean during the late Medieval Period illustrates the limitations of private-decentralized institutions (embeddedness). We previously described the Maghribi coalition in which trade was embedded in a network of coethnics with close informational ties. In contrast, in the twelfth century, the Genoese used vertical agency relations under which merchants were almost never agents, agents could be of any ethnic background, and information was not shared. Merchants began to rely on a public institution—the legal system—to enforce contracts. Thus trade became more anonymous, allowing the Genoese to respond effectively to the geographic expansion of trade. In contrast, the Maghribi merchants' reliance on the information network and the need for merchants' to be of a specific ethnic background and to act as agents may have limited their ability to expand geographically. The lesson here is that there is a limitation to managing exchange through relationships, because relationships can only be stretched so far while maintaining the characteristics that make them effective. For some forms of exchange, particularly those over large spans of space and time, centralized institutions may be more effective than private-decentralized institutions or embedded relationships.

A final issue, both for the relationship between decentralized-private institutions and other institutional forms and for the relationship between the new institutionalism and other sociological theories, concerns the beliefs and shared understandings held by individuals. It is becoming increasingly apparent that these mental constructs affect the operation of both public- and private-centralized institutions. For instance, North (1993), comparing the performance of public institutions from Western economies to those making the transition from state socialism, attributes variance in performance to differences in the mental constructs of individuals in different societies. In addition, Williamson (1975) argues that the appropriate mode of governance in an organization will be conditioned on the prevailing "contractual atmosphere," by which he means the receptiveness of individuals to alternative governance modes. Despite the importance of beliefs and shared understandings, the new institutionalism that is our focus has little to say about how they are acquired. Organizational theory's cognitive new institutionalism, however, has made this one of its central questions (Meyer & Rowan 1977, Powell & DiMaggio 1991, Scott 1995). It contends that individuals come to beliefs and shared understandings through processes of social construction. It offers another institutional form, cognitive institutions, which act as interpretive lenses for social facts, including other institutions. Without downplaying the difficulties of combining ideas from theories with very different behavioral assumptions, the choice-within-constraints framework needs a concept like that of cognitive institutions.

INSTITUTIONAL CHANGE

New institutionalists need to account both for how institutions emerge and change and for the timing of emergence and change. Early work on institutions by Davis & North (1971), North (1981), Williamson (1975, 1985), and others asserted that efficient institutions would emerge and change as the need arose and that the timing of their emergence or change would be economically optimal. This view has now largely been discredited by economists and sociologists. In a now famous critique, Granavotter (1985) attacked Williamson's early accounts of institutional change as bad functionalism. What made Williamson's arguments bad functionalism was that they did not do a sufficient job of tying the function of institutional forms to the mechanisms by which they came to predominate. Even North's (1993, p. 12) view has changed; as he puts it, "there is ... little evidence to support the view ... that the necessary institutions will be the automatic outcome of getting the prices right."

The challenge for institutionalists is to create a richer theory of the origin and change of institutions. One of the biggest barriers to creating a richer theory is a lack of empirical work, particularly on private institutions. Ostrom's (1990) discussion of the emergence of institutions to govern water in the Los Angeles Basin, and Ingram & Inman's (1996) study of the emergence of an institution to promote tourism at Niagara Falls are some of the few accounts of the origin of private institutions. Yet, precisely how actors overcome the second-order collective action problem inherent in the creation of institutions is central to any theory of the origin of institutions. Empirical studies of change are equally scarce. Part of the problem is that most private institutions are not well documented, making it difficult to do careful, detailed empirical work. Ostrom's and Ingram & Inman's work suggests that studies can be done; more studies are badly needed.

The limited empirical work that has been done has focused on public institutions. North (1993) summarizes the current understandings, beginning with the emphasis on organizations as the primary source of institutional change: "... competition forces organizations to continually invest in skills and knowledge to survive. The kinds of skills and knowledge that individuals and their organizations acquire will shape evolving perceptions about opportunities and hence choices that will incrementally alter institutions" (p. 17). The organizational engine of change operates within the existing institutional framework, which affects efforts to change institutions because existing organizations have a stake in the status quo (North 1990). Particularly relevant parts of the existing institutional framework are the beliefs and shared understandings of individuals, which frame proposed institutional changes.

North's summary points to two key questions that must be answered for a theory of institutional change to advance. First, if organizations are the motor of institutional change, then the new institutionalism needs a theory of organizational action and change. Empirical work suggests that organizations are inertial, that they pursue noneconomic interests, and that they are only boundedly rational. Organizations are notoriously poor filters of changing interests because they are rife with inertia (Hannan & Freeman 1984), so much so that they tend to reflect the conditions of their founding, even decades later (Stinchcombe 1965). Having been founded to exploit a given institutional framework and with limited capacity to change, existing organizations are favored by stability of institutions. Rather than the source of pressure to change institutions, existing organizations are a source of resistance to institutional change. And although it is true that entrepreneurs are driven to develop new skills and knowledge, they tend to exploit these opportunities through new types of organizations (Ingram 1998).

Efforts to effect institutional change may be motivated by a variety of factors, of which economic interest is only one. Carruthers (1990) points to the role of noneconomic interests for institutional change in a criticism of North & Weingast's (1989) account of the Glorious Revolution. This instance of institutional change, among the most celebrated in terms of the gains in economic efficiency it created, was, according to Carruthers, largely the product of religious competition, determined by "popery, not property." The prominence of noneconomic interests does not decline when competing organizations are the engines of institutional change. Organizations, like individuals, pursue political ideologies, even at substantial material expense (Simons & Ingram 1997). Organizational efforts to change institutions often reflect a mix of economic and noneconomic interests. For example, hotel chain entrepreneurs in the United States of the 1920s changed institutions surrounding training by establishing university hotel schools, partly to generate the professional managers their organizations required, but also in the hope that university education would improve the social status of their occupation (Ingram 1998). In other instances, organizations seek to affect institutions for purely ideological purposes, but economic results occur as well, as when the Women's Christian Temperance

Union lobbied for prohibition legislation that forced breweries out of business in the jurisdictions in which it was passed (Wade et al 1998).

Finally, the bounded rationality that the new institutionalism attributes to individuals does not conveniently disappear when those individuals form organizations (Cyert & March 1963). As North (1993) notes, the complexity of the institutional framework presents a particular strain on actors that might manage to be more or less rational when making simple decisions. Consequently, even if inertial organizations pursue their varied interests by trying to change institutions, there is no reason to believe that they will always attempt the right changes. It is not uncommon to find that organizational efforts to change institutions in their favor backfire (Ingram & Inman 1996, Wade et al 1998).

The second key question that emerges from North's summary is, like the need for a better organizational theory, one that sociologists are already working to answer. It concerns the role of beliefs and shared understandings, which were also identified as relevant to the operation of institutions. Beliefs and shared understandings feature prominently in efforts of institutional change as they define the perceived legitimacy of institutional arrangements, forming the frames through which proposed changes can be related to broader societal interests (Fligstein 1997, Rao 1998). This framing may determine what institutional alternatives are accepted or rejected. This is seen in the efforts of South American coffee producers to present US acquiescence to the International Coffee Organization, a treaty-based cartel that raised prices to consumers, as necessary to fight communism (Bates 1997). It is also apparent in the efforts of hoteliers in Niagara Falls, Ontario, and Niagara Falls, New York, to frame laws that aimed to make the Falls more attractive for tourists, as acts of nationalism in a United States-Canadian rivalry (Ingram & Inman 1996). These examples make it clear that the process of institutional change goes far beyond the weighing of competing interests. Instead, it appears to be as much a comparison of rhetorical claims, the outcome of which depends on deep social values of the audience.

This argument contributes to a broader recognition that, in institutional change as in the operation of institutions, centralized actions often rely on decentralized ones. Knight (1992) offers a theory of institutional change that is notable in that it focuses on social norms as the foundation for change in other types of institutions and it focuses on the distributional consequences of institutions. Often, new institutionalists are sufficiently taken by the public-good nature of many institutions that they characterize them as cooperative arrangements that benefit all. In contrast, Knight emphasizes that institutional change always has distributional consequences and that bargaining between interested parties is the process that determines institutional outcomes. The role of such bargaining seems clear when we consider change in centralized institutions, like a law that would favor some financial organizations but disfavor others (Haveman & Rao 1997), but Knight argues that bargaining also occurs over decentralized institutions and that relative bargaining power determines which social norms arise and persist. Knight & Ensminger (1998) illustrate the argument with a case study of changing norms among the

Galole Orma of the Tana River District, Kenya. The norm of clan exogamy, for example, is declining among the Orma. This change occurred after a redistribution of bargaining power from those who the old norm favored—the clan elite who hope to build alliances through marriage ties—to those it harmed—young men and women who want more freedom to choose marriage partners.

Hopcroft (1998) also examines the role of institutional interdependence for institutional change, arguing that changes in state laws and ideologies flowed from local institutions in rural villages. In doing so, Hopcraft challenges the emphasis on public institutions to explain economic development in the Western world (North & Thomas 1973), observing that, in preindustrial England, there were local differences in economic action and performance, although regions shared the same umbrella of state institutions. Hopcraft attends particularly to the differences between the champion (regular open-field) system of central England and the nonchampion systems of eastern and southwestern England, arguing that the nonchampion systems, which provided for more individual property rights, resulted in lower transaction costs and higher productivity. Beyond that, these private-centralized institutions formed the groundwork for subsequent institutional change. Enclosure occurred early and easily in the nonchampion regions, whereas it was late and difficult in champion areas, often forced by an act of Parliament. The nonchampion regions adopted wage labor, while feudal rules persisted elsewhere. People from the nonchampion regions also spearheaded efforts to change state institutions, for example, campaigning against the granting of royal trading monopolies and supporting the parliamentary cause in the Civil War of the 1640s. Hopcroft goes as far as to attribute ideological change, in the form of a shift from a communitarian culture to one of puritanical, civic-minded individualism, to the advantages of the nonchampion system.

CONCLUSION

The potential of the choice-within-constraints new institutionalism is apparent in the scope of the preceding sections. This is a theory that can be applied to explain a substantial portion of the performance and change of all social systems, including states, organizations, and groups. This comprehensiveness is also what is most exciting about the empirical analyses conducted within the paradigm. The new institutionalism has been applied to explain the differential performance of economies throughout history, the structures of parliaments, the rise and fall of particular organizations and industries in the twentieth century, and even changes in marriage norms of African tribes. Impressively, these phenomena are tackled without falling back on a trivial theory of action—the behavioral assumptions of the new institutionalism recognize the constraints on human information-processing capability and the range of interests pursued by individuals, organizations, and states. Indeed, the recent trend is to give an increasing role to the influence of ideologies, beliefs, and shared understandings on behavior.

At the same time, there remain many weaknesses in the new institutionalism. Sociologists are particularly well positioned to address the key weaknesses in the theory. In the behavioral assumptions, there is a need for a theory of the origin of preferences. Preferences, no doubt, arise partly through processes of social interaction, which are deep within sociological territory.

Our categorization scheme for institutional forms allowed us to identify and describe three. This approach indicated that there were interdependencies among the forms across the dimensions of categorization: public institutions rely on private institutions, and centralized institutions rely on decentralized institutions. These interdependencies are also reciprocal. Sociological theory can be useful in unpacking the interdependencies. In particular, embeddedness theory and cognitive new institutionalism can contribute to understanding private-decentralized institutions, which are the foundation of the institutional framework.

Regarding the question of institutional change, the emerging answers emphasize the role of competing organizations as an engine for change and the importance of framing institutional alternatives for legitimacy. Sociology's organizational theory can provide the necessary underpinnings for a change theory that is driven by organizations. At the same time, cognitive new institutionalists in sociology have begun to analyze the processes of cultural entrepreneurship through which an institutional alternative comes to be accepted.

ACKNOWLEDGMENTS

Helpful comments on an earlier draft were provided by Frank Dobbin, Guy Holburn, Stan Li, Michael Lounsbury, John Meyer, Victor Nee, Peter Roberts, Jeff Robinson, Tim Rowley, Sampsa Samila, and Tal Simons.

Visit the Annual Reviews home page at www.AnnualReviews.org

LITERATURE CITED

Barnett WP, Carroll GR. 1993. How institutional constraints affected the organization of early American telephony. *J. Law. Econ. Organ.* 9:98–126

Barzel Y. 1989. *The Economic Analysis of Property Rights.* New York: Cambridge Univ. Press

Bates RH. 1997. *Open Economy Politics: The Political Economy of the World Coffee Trade.* Princeton, NJ: Princeton Univ. Press

Baum JAC, Oliver C. 1992. Institutional embeddedness and the dynamics of organizational populations. *Am. Sociol. Rev.* 57:540–59

Bernstein L. 1992. Opting out of the legal system: extralegal contractual relations in the diamond industry. *J. Leg. Stud.* 21:115–57

Bogue AG. 1958. The Iowa claims clubs: symbol and substance. *Mississippi Val. Hist. Rev.* 45:231–53

Carroll GR, Teo ACY. 1998. *How regulation and globalization affected organizational legitimation and competition among commercial banks in Singapore, 1840–1994.* Presented at Annu. Meet. Acad. Manage., 58th, San Diego

Carruthers BG. 1990. Politics, popery, and property: a comment on North and Weingast.

J. Econ. Hist. 50:693–98

Clay K. 1997a. Trade without law: private-order institutions in Mexican California. *J. Law Econ. Organ.* 13:202–31

Clay K. 1997b. Trade, institutions, and credit. *Explor. Econ. Hist.* 34:495–521

Clay K, Wright G. 1999. *Order without law: property rights during the California gold rush.* Dept. Econ., Stanford Univ. Unpublished paper

Coase RH. 1937. The nature of the firm. *Economica* 4:86–405

Coase RH. 1998. The new institutional economics. *Am. Econ. Rev.* 88:72–74

Coleman J. 1990. *Foundations of Social Theory.* Cambridge, MA: Harvard Univ. Press

Cyert RM, March JG. 1963. *A Behavioral Theory of the Firm.* Englewood Cliffs, NJ: Prentice Hall

Davis LE, North DC. 1971. *Institutional Change and American Economic Growth.* London: Cambridge Univ. Press

Dennen RT. 1976. Cattlemen's associations and property rights in land in the American west. *Explor. Econ. Hist.* 14:423–36

DiMaggio PJ. 1990. Cultural aspects of economic organization. In *Beyond the Market Place*, ed. R Friedland, A Robertson, pp.113–36. New York: Aldine de Gruyter

Dobbin F, Dowd TJ. 1997. How policy shapes competition: early railroad foundings in Massachusetts. *Admin. Sci. Q.* 42:501–29

Dobbin F, Sutton JR. 1998. The strength of a weak state: the rights revolution and the rise of human resource management divisions. *Am. J. Sociol.* 104:441–76

Ellickson RC. 1991. *Order Without Law.* Cambridge, MA: Harvard Univ. Press

Ensminger J. 1992. *Making a Market: The Institutional Transformation of an African Society.* New York: Cambridge Univ. Press

Ficker SK. 1999. *Institutional constraints and the strategy of the firm: an American railroad corporation in nineteenth-century Mexico.* Presented at Conf. Inst. Mark. Comp.-Hist. Perspect., Palo Alto, CA

Fligstein N. 1990. *The Transformation of Corporate Control.* Cambridge, MA: Harvard Univ. Press

Fligstein N. 1997. *Fields, power, and social skill: a critical analysis of the new institutionalisms.* Presented at Conf. Power Organ., Hamburg, Germany

Fligstein N, Mara-Drita I. 1996. How to make a market: reflections on the attempt to create a single market in the European Union. *Am. J. Sociol.* 102:1–33

Friedland R, Alford R. 1991. Bringing society back in: symbols, practices, and institutional contradictions. In *The New Institutionalism in Organizational Analysis*, ed. WW Powell, PJ DiMaggio, pp. 232–66. Chicago: Univ. Chicago Press

Ghoshal S, Moran P. 1996. Bad for practice: a critique of the transaction cost theory. *Acad. Manage. Rev.* 21:13–47

Granovetter MS. 1985. Economic action and social structure: the problem of embeddedness. *Am. J. Sociol.* 91:481–510

Greif A. 1989. Reputation and coalitions in medieval trade: evidence on the Maghribi traders. *J. Econ. Hist.* 49:857–82

Greif A. 1994. Cultural beliefs and the organization of society. *J. Polit. Econ.* 102:912–50

Greif A, Milgrom P, Weingast BR. 1994. Coordination, commitment, and enforcement: the case of the merchant guild. *J. Polit. Econ.* 102:715–76

Hannan MT, Freeman J. 1984. Structural inertia and organizational change. *Am. Sociol. Rev.* 49:149–64

Haveman HA, Rao H. 1997. Institutional and organizational coevolution in the thrift industry. *Am. J. Sociol.* 102:1606–51

Heckathorn DD. 1990. Collective sanctions and compliance norms: a formal theory of group-mediated social control. *Am. Sociol. Rev.* 55:366–84

Homans GC. 1950. *The Human Group.* New York: Harcourt Brace Jovanovich

Hopcroft RL. 1998. The importance of the local rural institutions and economic change in preindustrial England. In *The New Institutionalism in Sociology*, ed. MC Brinton, V Nee, pp. 277–304. New York: Russell Sage Found.

Ingram P. 1998. Changing the rules: interests, organizations, and institutional change in the U.S. hospitality industry. In *The New Institutionalism in Sociology*, ed. MC Brinton, V Nee, pp. 258–76. New York: Russell Sage Found.

Ingram P, Inman C. 1996. Institutions, intergroup rivalry, and the evolution of hotel populations around Niagara Falls. *Admin. Sci. Q.* 41:629–58

Ingram P, Simons T. 2000. State formation, ideological competition, and the ecology of Israeli workers' cooperatives, 1920–1992. *Admin. Sci. Q.* 45(1):25–53

Johnson RN, Libecap GD. 1982. Contracting problems and regulation: the case of the fishery. *Am. Econ. Rev.* 72:1005–22

Knight J. 1992. *Institutions and Social Conflict*. New York: Cambridge Univ. Press

Knight J, Ensminger J. 1998. Conflict over changing social norms: bargaining, ideology, and enforcement. In *The New Institutionalism in Sociology*, ed. MC Brinton, V Nee, pp. 105–26. New York: Russell Sage Found.

Macaulay S. 1963. Non-contractual relations in business: a preliminary study. *Am. Sociol. Rev.* 28:55–67

Maurer N, Haber S. 1999. *Institutional change and productivity growth: access to credit and liquidity constraints in the Mexican cotton textile manufacture, 1878–1913*. Presented at Conf. Inst. Mark. Compar.-Hist. Perspect., Palo Alto, CA

McFaul M. 1995. State power, institutional change, and the politics of privatization in Russia. *World Polit.* 47:210–43

Meyer JW, Boli J, Thomas GM, Ramirez FO. 1997. World society and the nation-state. *Am. J. Sociol.* 103:144–81

Meyer JW, Rowan B. 1977. Institutionalized organizations: formal structure as myth and ceremony. *Am. J. Sociol.* 83:340–63

Nee V. 1992. Organizational dynamics of market transitions: hybrid forms, property rights, and mixed economy in China. *Admin. Sci. Q.* 37:1–27

Nee V. 1998. Sources of the new institutionalism. In *The New Institutionalism in Sociology*, ed. MC Brinton, V Nee, pp. 1–16. New York: Russell Sage Found.

Nee V, Ingram P. 1998. Embeddedness and beyond: institutions, exchange, and social structure. In *The New Institutionalism in Sociology*, ed. MC Brinton, V Nee, pp. 19–45. New York: Russell Sage Found.

North DC. 1981. *Structure and Change in Economic History*. New York: Norton

North DC. 1990. *Institutions, Institutional Change and Economic Performance*. New York: Cambridge Univ. Press

North DC. 1993. Institutions and credible commitment. *J. Inst. Theor. Econ.* 149:11–23

North DC, Thomas RP. 1973. *The Rise of the Western World*. London: Cambridge Univ. Press

North DC, Weingast BR. 1989. Constitutions and credible commitments: the evolution of the institutions of public choice in 17th century England. *J. Econ. Hist.* 49:803–32

Ostrom E. 1990. *Governing the Commons*. New York: Cambridge Univ. Press

Poole KT, Rosenthal H. 1996. *Congress: A Political-Economic History of Roll Call Voting*. New York: Oxford Univ. Press

Powell WW, DiMaggio PJ, eds. 1991. *The New Institutionalism in Organizational Analysis*. Chicago: Univ. Chicago Press

Rao H. 1998. Caveat emptor: the constructions of nonprofit consumer watchdog organizations. *Am. J. Sociol.* 103:912–61

Reid JP. 1980. *Law for the Elephant*. San Marino, CA: Huntingt. Libr.

Rueschemeyer D, Evans PB. 1985. The state and economic transformation: toward an analysis of the conditions underlying effective intervention. In *Bringing the State Back In*, ed. PB Evans, D Rueschemeyer, T Skocpol, pp. 44–77. London: Cambridge Univ. Press

Schelling TC. 1960. *The Strategy of Conflict*.

Cambridge, MA: Harvard Univ. Press

Scott WR. 1995. *Institutions and Organizations*. Beverly Hills, CA: Sage

Simon HA. 1957. *Models of Man*. New York: Wiley & Sons

Simons T, Ingram P. 1997. Organization and ideology: kibbutzim and hired labor, 1951–1965. *Admin. Sci. Q.* 42:784–813

Spicer A. 1997. *Building markets from scratch: institutions and agency in the Russian mass privatization program*. Presented at Annu. Meet. Acad. Manage., 57th, Boston

Stark D, Bruszt L. 1998. *Postsocialist Pathways*. New York: Cambridge Univ. Press

Stinchcombe AL. 1965. Social structure and organizations. In *Handbook of Organizations*, ed. JG March, pp. 142–93. Chicago: Rand McNally

Stinchcombe AL. 1997. On the virtues of the old institutionalism. *Annu. Rev. Sociol.* 23:1–18

Stone A, Levy B, Paredes R. 1996. Public institutions and private transactions: a comparative analysis of the legal and regulatory environment for business transactions in Brazil and Chile. In *Empirical Studies in Institutional Change*, ed. LJ Alston, T Eggertsson, DC North, pp. 95–128. New York: Cambridge Univ. Press

Ullmann-Margalit E. 1977. *The Emergence of Norms*. Oxford, UK: Clarendon

Umbeck JR. 1981. *A Theory of Property Rights, with Application to the California Gold Rush*. Ames, IA: Iowa State Univ. Press

Uzzi B. 1996. The sources and consequences of embeddedness for the economic performance of organizations: the network effect. *Am. Sociol. Rev.* 61:674–98

Uzzi B. 1999. Embeddedness in the making of financial capital: how social relations and networks benefit firms seeking financing. *Am. Sociol. Rev.* 64:481–505

Veblen TB. 1899. *The Theory of the Leisure Class: An Economic Study of Institutions*. New York: Macmillan

Wade JB, Swaminathan A, Saxon MS. 1998. Normative and resource flow consequences of local regulations in the American brewing industry, 1845–1918. *Admin. Sci. Q.* 43:905–35

Weingast BR. 1993. Constitutions as governance structures: the political foundations of secure markets. *J. Inst. Theor. Econ.* 149:286–311

Wholey DR, Christianson JB, Sanchez SM. 1992. Organizational size and failure among health maintenance organizations. *Am. Sociol. Rev.* 57:829–42

Wiggins SN, Libecap GD. 1985. Oil field unitization: contractual failure in the presence of imperfect information. *Am. Econ. Rev.* 75:368–85

Williamson OE. 1975. *Markets and Hierarchies: Analysis and Antitrust Implications*. New York: Free Press

Williamson OE. 1985. *The Economic Institutions of Capitalism*. New York: Free Press.

Williamson OE. 1994. Transaction cost economics and organization theory. In *The Handbook of Economic Sociology*, ed. NJ Smelser, R Swedberg, pp. 77–107. Princeton, NJ: Princeton Univ. Press

Annu. Rev. Sociol. 2000. 26:547–62

Poverty Research and Policy for the Post-Welfare Era

Alice O'Connor

Department of History, University of California, Santa Barbara, California 93106;
e-mail: aoconnor@humanitas.ucsb.edu

Key Words   inequality, political economy, stratification, community

■ **Abstract**   The "end of welfare as we know it" constitutes an important challenge for poverty research, shifting the focus away from once-dominant themes of dependency and toward the reality of widespread "working poverty." The literature reviewed in this chapter points in the direction of a reformulated research agenda, built around issues of inequality, political economy, and stratification by gender, race, class, and place. It also calls into question the traditional distinction between welfare and working poor, as well as the notion of an isolated underclass existing apart from the social and economic mainstream. Finally, it points to the need to broaden a policy discourse that has been narrowly fixated on welfare and on changing the behavior of the poor. A real anti-poverty agenda would focus instead on the elements of mainstream political economy and culture that continue to produce widespread economic inequality.

INTRODUCTION

Three years after President Clinton signed the legislation bringing Aid to Families with Dependent Children (AFDC) to an end, poverty research remains fixated on welfare, the characteristics of people "on" (and soon to be "off") it as well as what it takes to rid welfare mothers of their "dependency." Having watched in all-too-predictable frustration as conservative politicians hijacked their own best-laid plans to replace "welfare as we know it" with temporary assistance, training, and work (Ellwood 1996), the country's leading poverty experts are now absorbed in a wide array of efforts to assess the aftermath of welfare repeal.[1] While politicians

---

[1] Among the many research and policy institutions engaged in formal evaluation of AFDC's replacement, the state-operated Temporary Assistance to Needy Families, or TANF, program, are the Urban Institute, the Institute for Research on Poverty at the University of Wisconsin, the Northwestern/University of Chicago Joint Center for Poverty Research, the Manpower Demonstration Research Corporation, and a consortium of prominent scholars from Johns Hopkins, Harvard University, University of Chicago, and Pennsylvania State University.

0360-0572/00/0815-0547$14.00   **547**

celebrate the vast reductions in the welfare rolls, these social scientific assessments offer a sobering and much-needed reminder that the zeal to reform welfare had little to do with reducing poverty. As recently reported in a study by the Washington-based Center on Budget and Policy Priorities (1999), welfare's end has left large numbers of poor families with children substantially worse off than before. This is despite the fact that these very families had earlier benefited from the overall economic recovery. The reality so far, much as predicted, is that the end of welfare has pushed many a dependent family into the already-swelled ranks of the working poor (Solow 1998, Parrott 1998).

The end of welfare also provides the occasion for reassessing what poverty research and policy have been—and should be—about. For despite widespread social scientific opposition to the legislation President Clinton signed, poverty research did little to undermine its central underlying premise: that dependency was the crux of the poverty problem and that the answer was to change poor people's behavior, whether by threatening to eliminate welfare entirely (Murray 1984), by enforcing a wide array of authoritarian and paternalistic sanctions against childbearing, school drop-out, and the like (Mead 1986, 1992), or, most of all, by putting welfare recipients to work (Kaus 1992, Gingrich et al 1994). Indeed, since the early 1980s no issues have loomed larger in poverty research than those clustered around welfare dependency—its extent and consequences, whether it is intergenerational, and its place in the culture of the underclass (summarized in Corcoran 1995). During the same two decades, a great deal of research and social experimentation was also devoted to moving people from welfare into the paid labor force (Gueron & Pauly 1991), in sharp contrast to the guaranteed income experiments of the 1970s (Watts & Rees 1977).[2] More generally, the vast store of social scientific knowledge built up since the War on Poverty has focused far more heavily on the behavior, culture, and demographic characteristics of poor people than on the characteristics of the broader social structure, political culture, and economy that foster such high rates of poverty (Katz 1993: Introduction; O'Connor 2000). The challenge for social scientists of poverty, then, is to break the hold of a still-prevalent welfare discourse—what Heclo (1994) calls the Welfare Fixation—that social science has helped to create (Katz 1989, Lynn 1993, Schram 1995).

There are practical reasons, too, why the end of welfare calls for shifting the prevailing focus of poverty research, and none more immediate than the sudden transformation of all those former welfare recipients into the working poor. Indeed, this alone has given added weight to an older critique of the official poverty line: not, as conservative analysts charge, that it fails to count social welfare benefits

---

[2] A more recent experiment, known as the New Hope Program and conducted in Milwaukee from 1994 to 1998, attempted to combine elements of both. The program required participants to work at least 30 hours per week (providing community service jobs for those who could not find private-sector work) and offered assistance with health insurance, child care, and a guaranteed above-poverty income (Bos et al 1999).

as income, but that it fails to take account of child care, transportation, and other work-related expenditures (Citro & Michael 1995). Equally important, the by-no-means-recent rise of working poverty calls into question two additional premises of the current post-welfare regime: one, that work in the paid labor force is *always* the better way to support non-disabled, non-elderly adults and their families; the other, that the private market will provide adequately, consistently, and beneficently for social needs. Now, the immediate problem for poverty research is not so much to explain dependency as it is to explain why so many working-class Americans do not earn enough to sustain even a minimalist standard of living in this extraordinarily prosperous economy.

Fortunately, social scientists will not be approaching this question in a vacuum. In focusing on the changing economy as well as on patterns of class, gender, and racial stratification, the work reviewed in this chapter points to an alternative framework for poverty research, beginning with the problem of rising inequality. The backdrop to much of this literature rests in the structural changes that have affected far more than those with incomes below the poverty line, and in particular the much-debated forces that brought the post–World War II era of growth, prosperity, and rising incomes to an end (Levy 1987, Bernstein & Adler 1994).

ECONOMIC RESTRUCTURING AND THE RISE OF INEQUALITY

While welfare reformers concentrated their energies on eliminating dependency, by far the more dramatic and consequential development of the past quarter century has been the combination of stagnating middle- and lower-class incomes and the sharp and sustained rise of economic inequality (Levy & Murnane 1992, Danziger & Gottschalk 1993, Mishel et al 1999). At first greeted with some skepticism in a field accustomed to distinguishing between poverty and inequality[3] (Sawhill 1988), by the early 1990s the growing disparity in wages and income had emerged as a leading explanation for the persistence, even during economic growth periods, of high rates of poverty (Blank 1993). Indeed, while often dated from the economic decline and wage stagnation of the 1970s, the fastest and most sustained rise in measured inequality took place during the post-1983 Reagan recovery, when those at the bottom actually lost income, while both wealth and income became far more concentrated among the top 5%, and especially the top 1% of the distribution (Krugman 1992, Wolff 1995). Wages for less educated, non-unionized and otherwise uncredentialed workers dropped precipitously, while college-educated

---

[3]Economists in particular maintain a conceptual distinction between poverty and inequality, distinguishing the former as a measure of absolute deprivation as opposed to the more relativistic measure of inequality. The distinction is also a political one, however, and as such was built into the official definition of poverty endorsed by the economists who took the lead in conceptualizing the War on Poverty (Ruggles 1990, O'Connor 1998).

(with the important, recent exception of young college graduates) and technologically highly-skilled workers earned more (Juhn et al 1993, Levy 1998). Clearly, most researchers agreed, something had changed in the economy to make faster growth—the sure-fire weapon in the War on Poverty—no guarantee of better times for the poor (Blank 1997).

The question of why remains subject to a great deal of debate among the economists who have tracked trends in inequality. While much of the literature points to a mismatch between the skills of less educated workers and the demands of better-paying, technology-driven jobs (Blank 1997, Levy 1998), others point to more structural, institutional, and political factors, including deindustrialization, globalization, the decline of unionization, and the deliberately low-wage, upwardly redistributive bias of economic policy (Bluestone & Harrison 1982, Harrison & Bluestone 1988, Howells 1994, Galbraith 1998). The larger point, from the perspective of poverty research and policy, is that the combination of rising inequality and declining prospects for workers reframes the poverty problem in at least three significant ways.

First, it has drawn attention to what economists refer to as the demand side of the problem: the quality and distribution of jobs (Burtless 1990, Kasarda 1995a), the practices and perspectives of employers (Holzer 1996, Moss & Tilly 1995, Henly 1999), and the persistence of discriminatory barriers for whole categories of workers, and in particular for minorities (Kirschenman & Neckerman 1991, Fix & Struck 1993). Along with this has come renewed social scientific interest in the possibility of direct labor market interventions to improve the job and income prospects for disadvantaged workers (Freeman & Gottschalk 1998)—albeit an interest not currently discernible in public policy debates.

Second, research on inequality and economic restructuring has helped to flesh out, refine, and in some instances to challenge the structural dimensions of William Julius Wilson's concept of the underclass, which linked the post-1970 growth of concentrated inner city poverty to a combination of urban deindustrialization, job dispersal to the suburbs, and the flight of black middle-class residents from ghetto neighborhoods (Wilson 1987, 1996). While still overshadowed by the heavily behavioral emphasis of popular (Auletta 1982) as well as scholarly (Ricketts & Sawhill 1988) writing on the underclass, a substantial body of empirical literature has confirmed the devastating impact of manufacturing losses on the economic prospects for low-skilled minority workers in general and for inner city residents in particular (Kasarda 1990, 1995b, Johnson & Oliver 1992, Bound & Holzer 1993). A related and especially prominent theme in the literature concentrates on the geographic restructuring of industrial space and job opportunities within the broader metropolitan area, much of it supporting at least some version of the long controversial notion that a spatial mismatch separates inner-city neighborhoods from suburban jobs (summarized in Holzer 1991, Kain 1992, Jargowsky 1997). And while much of it remains focused on Wilson's controversial emphasis on black middle-class out-migration (Massey & Denton 1993, Jargowsky 1997), research on urban demographic restructuring has begun to explore the significance of the new, post-1965 immigration on changing patterns of urban disadvantage and opportunity (Foner 1987, Kasinitz 1992, Moore & Pinderhughes 1993, Lamphere et al 1994, Waldinger & Bozorgmehr 1996). Particularly when viewed in historical perspective, these processes of industrial, geographic, and demographic restructuring challenge the tendency, exaggerated in the notion of an isolated underclass, to treat poverty as itself an isolated phenomenon existing apart from the day-to-day functioning of the social and economic mainstream. Historical research also challenges the tendency to treat structural change as a self-generating, inexorable force. The structural roots of contemporary poverty are very much the reflection of past and ongoing political choice (Katz 1993).

Third, research on inequality and economic restructuring has drawn attention to a growing, but as far as policy and public attention goes, virtually forgotten segment of people in poverty: the so-called working poor (Schwarz & Volgy 1992, Swartz & Weigart 1995). The terminology itself is problematic for several reasons, not in the least because it plays into an artificial and now largely outdated distinction between the employed ("deserving") and the welfare ("undeserving") poor. The reality, as a great deal of quantitative and qualitative research has shown, is that welfare recipients have always worked, whether or not as part of the officially recognized labor force. For most, welfare is a temporary stopgap, part of a broader income strategy that takes them between paid, low-wage, low-benefit employment and the welfare rolls, where at least they can gain access to insured medical care (Bane & Ellwood 1994, Harris 1993, Rank 1994). Very few recipients, however, can possibly survive on welfare benefits alone; instead they often turn to part-time, seasonal work or work in the underground economy to, as in the title of one study, "make ends meet" (Edin & Lein 1997). And in households or extended kin networks where employment opportunities are irregular, unstable, and poorly compensated, the welfare mother (or grandmother) often provides the essential work of child care that allows a sibling, cousin, son or daughter to hold down a paying job (Anderson 1995, Newman 1999). In these and other ways, the working/welfare poor distinction devalues work inside the home, a form of unpaid labor-force participation that falls heavily to women, whether they are formally employed or not (Mink 1998).

Nevertheless, the relatively small but now (by definition) growing literature on the working poor brings several familiar (to scholars) but largely unrecognized facts about poverty into full view. One is that the struggle to make ends meet on below-poverty or otherwise inadequate income is quite widespread. Certainly it is not confined to the isolated pockets famously described by John Kenneth Galbraith (1958) as backwaters of the Affluent Society and recently memorialized by President Clinton in his "poverty tour." A second is that economic growth and full employment, under current wage and labor market conditions, are not creating jobs that will move people out of poverty: Getting a job, even when combined with the Earned Income Tax Credit, is not enough (Burtless 1995, Blank 1997, Handler & Hasenfeld 1997). A third, evident in quantitative but especially in more detailed qualitative research, is that the kinds of entry-level, low-wage jobs that proliferate in the new economy do not carry much promise of upward mobility. They are concentrated at the bottom end of the domestic service, child care, food service, agricultural, textile, health and retail sectors, paying poverty wages to a heavily female labor force (Kasarda 1995a). They are economically as well as socially stigmatized, rarely attached to benefit plans let alone to unions, and often unstable as a source of regular hours or steady employment (Tilly 1996, Mishel et al 1999, Newman 1999). Nor, for people with low skills and few outside resources such as child care, transportation, and family support networks, are these "lousy jobs" necessarily easy to get and maintain (Burtless 1995, Holzer 1999, Newman 1999). Finally, these studies highlight the gaping and dangerous disjuncture between reality and policy rhetoric. The problem, ignored in the ongoing push to minimize public assistance and to get poor people into "work first," is not with the propensity of welfare to coddle dependency and bad behavior. It is with a political economy that has tolerated such high concentrations of wealth (to reverse the usual formulation) amidst steadily declining standards of living for the working class and much of the middle class (Mishel et al 1999).

GENDER, RACE, AND CLASS

While important as a starting point, the literature linking poverty, inequality, and economic restructuring has thus far been dominated by a limited range of principally economic theories, telling a story of skill and other human capital deficits while paying scant attention to the broader processes of gender, race, and class stratification that regulate access to education and skill training. Other research, some of it in direct response to the limitations of the prevailing framework, reveals the inadequacy of this explanation and begins to provide a fuller picture of the dimensions of inequality.

Up until recently, the inequality story was based almost entirely on the labor market experience of men, typically downplaying the consequences of deindustrialization and wage inequality among women as less severe (Levy & Murnane 1992). As recent research indicates, however, the reality is more complicated than that. While on the whole women have increased both employment and earnings since the 1970s (Blau 1998), not all women have shared equally—and some not at all—in the gains (Corcoran 1998, Bound & Dresser 1998). Thus, buried within the measured progress, which includes a reduction in the gender gap, are wide variations among women across race and ethnicity (Browne 1998). Moreover, for low-skilled women in general, closing the gender gap did not come from better wages and job opportunities, but from the deteriorating labor market position of men (Waldfogel & Mayer 1999). Nor do conventional measures adequately capture the impact of economic restructuring and wage decline—and now, the end of welfare—on the organization of child care, household labor, and related family arrangements, where women continue to assume primary responsibility (MacDonald 1995, Spain & Bianchi 1996). Indeed, when the issue of family structure has entered the poverty literature, it has been more often to draw attention to the absence of a male breadwinner and psychological role model than to the structural barriers between women and the family wage (Spalter-Roth et al 1994a). In contrast, research that focuses attention on the experience of women as mothers and wage earners emphasizes how unequal gender relations have been and continue to be structured into the economy, social norms, and social welfare policy (Gordon 1990, Gordon 1994, Spalter-Roth et al 1994b, Handler & White 1999).

Similarly, much of the research linking poverty to economic inequality and restructuring has been cast in a racially neutral tone, taking note of persistent racial gaps in earnings but often explaining these differences as part of such presumably color-blind processes as skill mismatch, or as a product of changing family structure (O'Neill 1990, Smith 1988). A growing body of literature since the early 1990s has challenged and complicated this view, however, arguing not only that race matters in limiting opportunity for low-income families, but that racial inequality is built in, reinforced, and perpetuated in the restructured economy in several ways.

One is through the mechanism of continued racial residential segregation, which concentrates the minority poor in economically declining, neglected neighborhoods that are often remote from job opportunities. Equally important, segregationist practices have limited access for minorities across the income spectrum to the mortgages and housing markets that represent a principal source of wealth, upward mobility, and, for the working class in particular, a modicum of economic stability amidst large-scale economic change (Massey & Denton 1993, Bobo & Zubrinsky 1996, Oliver & Shapiro 1995). A second is through employer attitudes and practices that shape labor market opportunities, including outright discrimination in hiring and wages (Kirshenman & Neckerman 1991, Fix & Struck 1993, Holzer 1996, Wilson 1996), a heavy reliance on network hiring (Newman 1999), decisions about plant location and relocation (Tilly & Moss 2000), and race and gender hierarchies in hiring, internal promotion, and supervisory practices (Browne et al 2000). Third is through a racially segmented structure of public support for social policies directed at poverty and racial inequality (Gilens 1996, Bobo & Smith 1994), a pattern that has long been both exploited and exacerbated by politicians seeking to demonize welfare and anti-poverty policy more generally (Edsall & Edsall 1992).

Finally, there is the historical and ongoing legacy of social policies designed to establish or maintain a hierarchical and racially segregated status quo. Perhaps best-documented among these are the post–World War II housing, land use, urban renewal, highway-building, and related development policies that literally paved the way for white middle and working-class suburbanization while simultaneously containing minorities in inner city ghettoes and barrios (Jackson 1985, Hirsch 1998). Other studies have looked further, to show how locally constructed education, social services, transportation, and employment policies maintained the color line in major cities (Bayor 1996, Sugrue 1996), and how racial inequality has been built into and sustained by the structure of the national welfare state (Quadagno 1994, Lieberman 1998). For all that has changed in US race relations over the course of the twentieth century, what comes through most notably in these studies is the persistence of historic patterns of racial stratification. More than a century after the publication of W.E.B. DuBois' *The Philadelphia Negro* (1899) and five decades after Myrdal's *An American Dilemma* (1944) and Drake & Cayton's *Black Metropolis* (1945), these classic works of sociology offer a still-trenchant and comprehensive analysis of the structural factors—residential segregation, labor market discrimination, racial attitudes, and social policy—that explain the disproportionately high rates of poverty among nonwhite minorities.

For all the emphasis on its rising significance, class analysis has been largely missing from recent poverty research, where class is more often conceptualized in terms of individualized family background, education, or skill variables than as a structured pattern of economic, social, and political relations. The underclass literature, despite the terminology, is premised on concepts of detachment, cultural and social isolation, and self-generating cycles of self-destructive behavior. Recent studies by Newman (1999), Fine & Weis (1998), and Duncan (1999) offer a more fluid, variegated rendering, in research that uses qualitative and ethnographic methods to explore the consequences of working-class destabilization and class polarization in communities with high rates of poverty.

Following a group of young adult fast-food workers in Harlem, Newman (1999) shows them negotiating the complicated, often conflicted class (and ethnic) relationships that structure their family, work, education, and neighborhood lives. Looking beyond the underclass label and beneath the statistics in Census reports, she finds family and personal networks that stretch across class lines—and that, particularly when viewed from an intergenerational perspective, tell a story—not of uninterrupted joblessness and welfare dependency—but of downward mobility brought about by the loss of job opportunities for the inner city working class. Similarly concentrating on the experiences of young adults in declining urban economies, Fine & Weis (1998) portray a generation struggling to establish a foothold in the no longer stable post-industrial working class. Like their counterparts in Harlem, they are very much aware that the unionized manufacturing, public sector, and civil service jobs that sustained an earlier generation have largely disappeared from view. These two studies bring texture and a sense of lived experience to what has been reported in statistical trends. On the one hand, they relate poverty to the declining fortunes of the middle- and working-class post baby-boom generations. On the other, they recognize that poverty is not a fixed status, but a constant threat to already disadvantaged workers trying to make a living in a precarious economy.

Situating her research in three different rural communities, Duncan (1999) takes a different angle on class and poverty, in a detailed analysis of the polarized class and caste relations that sustain poverty in the coal counties of Appalachia and in the primarily agricultural Mississippi Delta. A central theme of her study is the devastating social cost of maintaining a social structure in which a rich, white elite holds such enormous political and economic power, leaving the poor powerless, dependent, and with severely limited access to economic and educational opportunities, or even to the social welfare services that are firmly controlled by the upper class oligarchy. Isolated though they may be from one another, the haves and have-nots in Duncan's study are bound together by a kind of mutual dependence. The haves rely on a pool of cheap, subordinate, contingent labor; the have-nots on such opportunities to make a living that their rich neighbors are willing to dole out. What they lack is any sense of the shared civic culture that Duncan finds in a far less polarized, principally blue collar New England mill town which, despite its own experience of job loss and economic hard times, sees far less of the entrenched poverty that Duncan describes in Appalachia and the Delta.

In drawing explicit links between poverty, politics, and power, Duncan is raising themes that, with some notable exceptions (Piven & Cloward 1993, Gans 1995), have been neglected or remain in the backdrop of social scientific poverty research. Related to this is a larger absence of political analysis in the poverty and inequality literature, of how, for example, the decline of wages and opportunity is related to what analyst Kevin Phillips (1990) called the "politics of rich and poor" as well as to the frayed infrastructure of political representation for low-income groups (Imig 1996). Here again, the "working poor" designation is telling as a categorization that avoids reference to social class and, as such, to real or potential membership in a more broadly based political coalition based on common economic interest.

And yet, these studies in poverty and stratification also reveal the complications of categorization. If they point to any single conclusion, it is that the disadvantages of class, race, and gender do not operate as easily separable variables, let alone as alternative explanations for poverty or strategies for change. Indeed, this same complicated array of structural divisions is often reflected in the way poor and working class people analyze their own situations in ethnographic interviews, and particularly in their tendency to blame presumably competing racial and ethnic "others" for the loss of opportunity (Rubin 1994, Fine & Weis 1998, Newman 1999). This is hardly a new theme in social research. Progressive-era social investigators, revealing their own cultural biases, lamented the absence of working-class consciousness among immigrant newcomers willing to work for less than a living wage. But it does speak to the need for further investigation into how poor people do engage, politically and socially, in ways that are often overlooked in poverty research (Kelley 1993, Weir 1999).

POVERTY AND PLACE

Having been eclipsed by the turn to national-level statistical data in the 1970s and 1980s, the study of community and neighborhood has once again emerged as a central theme in poverty research. To some degree this renewed interest might be linked to broader cultural and ideological trends. Concerns about the decline of community and civic culture, after all, are not confined to or even primarily associated with the poor (Putnam 1995). And although prominently associated with arguments for welfare state retrenchment and privatization (Olasky 1992), a communitarian ethos has also been invoked in the name of a strengthened public sector as a countervailing force to market inequities (Kaus 1992, Kuttner 1997).

But the revival of social scientific interest in community and neighborhoods has also been stimulated by developments more specific to poverty research, in particular by Wilson's theory of the underclass, and by the related research finding that the extent of geographically concentrated poverty has grown enormously since 1970 (Wilson 1987, Jargowsky 1997). As a result, a great deal of this research has focused on investigating the existence and mechanisms of so-called neighborhood effects: the impact, that is, of levels of neighborhood poverty and other environmental factors on various aspects of individual development, especially among children and adolescents (Jencks & Mayer 1990, Brooks-Gunn et al 1997). Anchored in a combination of Chicago-school ecology, social capital, and psychological development theory, this inquiry has produced a substantial, if inconclusive, body of interdisciplinary research on the impact of growing up in neighborhoods that lack the economic, institutional, and, presumably, the social resources that make middle-class neighborhoods work.

In fact, the very notion of neighborhood effects remains controversial and contested. Despite efforts to integrate ethnographic with statistical analysis, the recent literature has not resolved the basic tension that has long characterized research on poor communities: Beneath indicators of what the Chicago school called social disorganization are what a host of ethnographers since the 1940s have characterized as coherent and resourceful forms of social organization replete with social capital (Whyte 1943, Liebow 1967, Stack 1974; 1996a). Nor does the neighborhood effects literature capture the powerful sources of elite resistance to neighborhood organizing, exercised in local politics as well as in social welfare institutions (Stack 1996b, Weir et al 1998). In the meantime, poverty researchers have paid far less attention to what is arguably the more important question of what determines the spatial distribution of wealth, poverty, and resources, particularly in this era of globalized economic restructuring. For that, research needs to look beyond the characteristics of poor people and places to the metropolitan (Jargowsky 1997), regional (Lyson & Falk 1993), and national levers of political and economic decision making.

POVERTY AND POLICY

Ever since the publication of Charles Murray's *Losing Ground* (1984), investigating the relationship between policy and poverty has never been quite the same. Having invested considerable energy in assessing the effectiveness—and documenting the flaws—of anti-poverty and especially welfare programs, liberal analysts found themselves having to justify the existence of any safety net at all. Nevertheless, over the past several years a number of sociologists and historians have built up a persuasive critique of the American welfare state, showing how its two-tiered, public/private, federal/local and what Patterson (1994: p. 56) calls "jerry-built" structure was grounded in a politics that relegated poor people to second-class citizenship, and left women and non-whites particularly vulnerable to poverty (Weir et al 1988, Gordon 1994, Katz 1996). More recently, scholars working in the "new institutionalist" tradition have developed the argument further, focusing on how the courts (Bussiere 1997), federal administrative agencies (Lieberman 1998), and political regimes at the subnational level (Amenta 1998) played a powerful role in shaping social relations and limiting the scope of anti-poverty policy.

An equally important project taken up in research on poverty and policy has been to imagine the alternatives, and in the process to expand the constricted boundaries, of a debate that has been driven by the politics of welfare backlash, deficit reduction, and anti-statism. While hardly constituting a social scientific consensus, recurrent themes in much of the literature point in precisely the opposite direction from what has actually come about in the United States: a preference for universalistic rather than narrowly targeted (and stigmatized) programs; a call for cross-class, cross-racial coalitions in social politics; and an expanded role for the federal government in battling social and economic inequality (Skocpol 1991, Wilson 1996).

CONCLUSION: Social Science and the Poor

Ultimately, the task of imagining a different future does not rest with social science alone. But it does require a different kind of knowledge than that we have known as poverty research. A starting point, as suggested by the ongoing trend toward greater inequality, is to shift the focus of research, away from the characteristics and failings of poor people, and toward those of a mainstream political economy and culture that relegates so many people to economic insecurity and social marginality. It is also to break the still-powerful hold of the Welfare Fixation by turning attention to the decline and changing nature of work opportunities in the post-industrial economy. And it is to rethink the categorizations that, however inadvertently, reinforce what close scrutiny reveals to be artificial distinctions among and between poor people and the rest of society.

The literature reviewed above points in the direction of a reformulated poverty research agenda; the realities of post-welfare poverty make it that much more of an imperative.

ACKNOWLEDGMENTS

Thanks to Melissa Davis and Colleen Egan for research and editorial assistance.

Visit the Annual Reviews home page at www.AnnualReviews.org

LITERATURE CITED

Amenta E. 1998. *Bold Relief: Institutional Politics and the Origins of Modern American Social Policy.* Princeton, NJ: Princeton Univ. Press

Anderson E. 1995. The black inner–city grand-

mother: transition of a heroic type? See Swartz & Weigart 1995, pp. 9–43

Auletta K. 1982. *The Underclass.* New York: Random House

Bane MJ, Ellwood DT. 1994. *Welfare Realities:*

From Rhetoric to Reform. Cambridge: Harvard Univ. Press

Bayor R. 1996. *Race and the Shaping of Twentieth Century Atlanta.* Chapel Hill: Univ. N. Carolina Press

Bernstein MA, Adler DE, eds. 1994. *Understanding American Economic Decline.* New York: Cambridge

Blank RM. 1993. Why were poverty rates so high in the 1980s? In *Poverty and Prosperity in the USA in the Late Twentieth Century,* ed. D Papadimitriou, E Wolff, pp. 21–55. London: Macmillan

Blank RM. 1997. *It Takes a Nation: A New Agenda for Fighting Poverty.* New York: Russell Sage/Princeton, NJ: Princeton Univ. Press

Blau FD. 1998. Trends in the well-being of American women, 1970–1995. *J. Econ. Lit.* 36:112–65

Bluestone B, Harrison B. 1982. *The Deindustrialization of America: Plant Closings Community Abandonment, and the Dismantling of Basic Industry.* New York: Basic

Bobo L, Smith R. 1994. Antipoverty policy, affirmative action, and racial attitudes. In *Confronting Poverty: Prescriptions for Change,* ed. SH Danziger, GD Sandefur, DH Weinberg, pp. 365–95. New York: Russell Sage/Cambridge: Harvard Univ. Press

Bobo L, Zubrinsky CL. 1996. Attitudes on residential integration: perceived status differences, mere in-group preferences, or racial prejudice? *Soc. Forces* 74:883–909

Bos J, Huston A, Granger R, Duncan G, Brock T, McLoyd V. 1999. *New Hope for People with Low Incomes: Two–Year Results of a Program to Reduce Poverty and Reform Welfare.* New York: MDRC

Bound J, Holzer H. 1993. Industrial shifts, skills levels, and the labor market for white and black men. *Rev. Econ. Statist.* 75:387–96

Bound J, Dresser P. 1998. Losing ground: the erosion of the relative earnings of African American women during the 1980s. See Browne 1998, pp. 61–104

Brooks-Gunn J, Duncan GJ, Aber JL, eds. 1997. *Neighborhood Poverty.* 2 vols. New York: Russell Sage

Browne I, ed. 1998. *Latinas and African American Women at Work: Race, Gender and Economic Inequality.* New York: Russell Sage

Browne I, Tigges L, Press J. 2000. Inequality through labor markets, firms and families: the intersection of gender and race in three cities. In *Urban Inequality in the United States: Evidence from Four Cities,* ed. A O'Connor, C Tilly, L Bobo. New York: Russell Sage. In press

Burtless G, ed. 1990. *A Future of Lousy Jobs? The Changing Structure of U.S. Wages.* Washington, DC: Brookings Inst.

Burtless G. 1995. Employment prospects of welfare recipients. In *The Work Alternative: Welfare Reform and the Realities of the Job Market,* ed. DS Nightingale, RH Haveman. Washington, DC: Urban Inst.

Bussiere E. 1997. *(Dis)Entitling the Poor: The Warren Court, Welfare Rights, and The American Political Tradition.* University Park: Penn. State Univ. Press

Center on Budget and Policy Priorities. 1999. The initial impacts of welfare reform on the economic well-being of single mother families. Washington, DC; USGPO

Citro C, Michael R. 1995. *Measuring Poverty: A New Approach.* Washington DC: National Acad. Sci.

Corcoran M. 1995. Rags to rags: poverty and mobility in the United States. *Annu. Rev. Sociol.* 21:237–67

Corcoran M. 1998. The economic progress of African American women. See Browne 1998, pp. 35–60

Danziger S, Gottschalk P, eds. 1993. *Uneven Tides: Rising Inequality in America.* New York: Russell Sage

Drake S, Cayton H. 1945. *Black Metropolis: A Study of Negro Life in a Northern City.* New York: Harcourt, Brace, Jovanovich

DuBois WEB. 1899. *The Philadelphia Negro.* Philadelphia: Univ. Penn. Press

Duncan CM. 1999. *Worlds Apart: Why Poverty*

Persists in Rural America. New Haven: Yale Univ. Press

Edin K, Lien L. 1997. *Making Ends Meet: How Single Mothers Survive Welfare and Low-Wage Work.* New York: Russell Sage

Edsall TB, Edsall MB. 1992. *Chain Reaction: The Impact of Race, Rights, and Taxes on American Politics.* New York: Norton

Ellwood D. 1996. Welfare reform as I knew it. *The American Prospect.* May-June: 22–29

Fine M, Weis L. 1998. *The Unknown City: Lives of Poor and Working Class Young Adults.* Boston: Beacon

Fix M, Struck R, eds. 1993. *Clear and Convincing Evidence: Measurement of Discrimination in America.* Washington DC: Urban Inst.

Foner N, ed. 1987. *New Immigrants in New York.* New York: Columbia Univ. Press

Freeman R, Gottschalk P, eds. 1998. *Generating Jobs: How to Increase Demand for Less-Skilled Workers.* New York: Russell Sage

Galbraith JK. 1958. *The Affluent Society.* Boston: Little, Brown

Galbraith JK. 1998. *Created Unequal: The Crisis in American Pay.* New York: Free Press

Gans HJ. 1995. *The War Against the Poor.* New York: Basic

Gilens M. 1996. "Race–coding" and white opposition to welfare. *Am. Polit. Sci. Rev.* 90:593–604

Gingrich N, Armey D, et al. 1994. *Contract With America.* New York: Random House

Gordon L, ed. 1990. *Women, the State, and Welfare.* Madison: Univ. Wisc. Press

Gordon L. 1994. *Pitied But Not Entitled: Single Mothers and the History of Welfare 1890–1935.* Cambridge: Harvard Univ. Press

Gueron JM, Pauly E. 1991. *From Welfare to Work.* New York: Russell Sage

Handler J, Hasenfeld Y. 1997. *We the Poor People: Work, Poverty, and Welfare.* New Haven, CT: Yale Univ. Press

Handler J, White L, eds. 1999. *Hard Labor: Women and Work in the Post-Welfare Era.* New York/London: Sharpe

Harris KM. 1993. Work and welfare among single mothers in poverty. *Am. J. Sociol.* 99:317–52

Harrison B, Bluestone B. 1988. *The Great U-Turn: Corporate Restructuring and the Polarizing of America.* New York: Basic

Heclo H. 1994. Poverty politics. In *Confronting Poverty: Prescriptions for Change,* ed. SH Danziger, GD Sandefur, DH Weinberg, pp. 396–437. New York: Russell Sage/Cambridge: Harvard Univ. Press

Henly JR. 1999. Barriers to finding and maintaining jobs: the perspectives of workers and employers in the low-wage labor market. See JF Handler, L White, 1999, pp. 48–75

Hirsch A. 1998 [1983]. *Making the Second Ghetto: Race and Housing in Chicago 1940–1960.* Chicago: Univ. Chicago Press. Rev. ed.

Holzer HJ. 1991. The spatial mismatch hypothesis: What has the evidence shown? *Urban Studies* 28:105–22

Holzer HJ. 1996. *What Employers Want: Job Prospects for Less-Educated Workers.* New York: Russell Sage

Holzer HJ. 1999. Employer demand for welfare recipients and the business cycle: evidence from recent employer surveys. Inst. Res. Poverty Discuss. Pap.

Howells DR. 1994. The skills myth. *Am. Prospect* Summer: 81–90

Imig DR. 1996. *Poverty and Power: The Political Representation of Poor Americans.* Lincoln: Univ. Neb. Press

Jackson KT. 1985. *Crabgrass Frontier: The Suburbanization of the United States.* New York: Oxford Univ. Press

Jargowsky PA. 1997. *Poverty and Place: Ghettos, Barrios and the American City.* New York: Russell Sage

Jencks C, Mayer SE. 1990. The social consequences of growing up in a poor neighborhood. In *Inner-City Poverty in the United States,* ed. LE Lynn, M McGeary. Washington, DC: Natl Acad. Sci.

Johnson JH, Oliver ML. 1992. Structural changes in the U.S. economy and black male joblessness: a reassessment. In *Urban Labor Markets and Job Opportunity*, ed. G Peterson, W Vroman, pp. 113–47. Washington, DC: Urban Inst.

Juhn C, Murphy KM, Pierce B. 1993. Wage inequality and the rise in returns to skill. *J. Polit. Econ.* 101:410–42

Kain JF. 1992. The spatial mismatch hypothesis: three decades later. *Housing Policy Debate* 3:371–460

Kasarda JD. 1990. Urban industrial transition and the underclass. *Annals Am. Acad. Polit. Soc. Sci.* 501:26–47

Kasarda JD. 1995a. America's working poor: 1980–1990. See Swartz & Weigart 1995, pp. 44–68

Kasarda JD. 1995b. Industrial restructuring and the changing location of jobs. In *State of the Union: America in the 1990s*, ed. R Farley, pp. 215–68. New York: Russell Sage

Kasinitz P. 1992. *Caribbean New York: Black Immigrants and Politics of Race.* Ithaca NY: Cornell Univ. Press

Katz MB. 1989. *The Undeserving Poor.* New York: Pantheon

Katz MB, ed. 1993. *The "Underclass" Debate: Views from History.* Princeton, NJ: Princeton Univ. Press

Katz MB. 1996. *In the Shadow of the Poorhouse: A Social History of Welfare in America.* New York: Basic. Rev. ed.

Kaus M. 1992. *The End of Equality.* New York: Basic

Kelley RDG. 1993. The black poor and the politics of opposition in a new south city, 1929–1970. In *The "Underclass" Debate: Views from History*, ed. MB Katz, pp. 293–333. Princeton, NJ: Princeton Univ. Press

Kirschenman J, Neckerman K. 1991. We'd love to hire them, but . . . : the meaning of race for employers. In *The Urban Underclass*, ed. C Jencks, PE Peterson, pp. 203–34. Washington, DC: Brookings Inst.

Krugman PR. 1992. The rich, the right and the facts: deconstructing the income distribution debate. *Am. Prospect.* Fall: 19–31

Kuttner R. 1997. *Everything for Sale: The Virtues and Limits of Markets.* New York: Knopf

Lamphere L, Stepick A, Grenier G, eds. 1994. *Newcomers in the Workplace: Immigrants and the Restructuring of the U.S. Economy.* Philadelphia: Temple Univ. Press

Levy F. 1987. *Dollars and Dreams: The Changing American Income Distribution.* New York: Russell Sage

Levy F. 1998. *The New Dollars and Dreams: American Incomes and Economic Change.* New York: Russell Sage

Levy F, Murnane RJ. 1992. U.S. earnings levels and earnings inequality: a review of recent trends and proposed explanations. *J. Econ. Lit.* 30:1333–81

Lieberman RC. 1998. *Shifting the Color Line: Race and the American Welfare State.* Cambridge: Harvard Univ. Press

Liebow E. 1967. *Tally's Corner.* Boston: Little, Brown

Lynn LE. 1993. Ending welfare reform as we know it. *Am. Prospect.* Fall: 83–92

Lyson TA, Falk WW, eds. 1993. *Forgotten Places: Uneven Development in Rural America.* Lawrence: Univ. Press Kans.

MacDonald M. 1995. The empirical challenges of feminist economics: the example of economic restructuring. In *Out of the Margin: Feminist Perspectives on Economics*, ed. E Kuiper, J Sap, pp. 175–97. London: Routledge

Massey DS, Denton NA. 1993. *American Apartheid: Segregation and the Making of the Underclass.* Cambridge: Harvard Univ. Press

Mead L. 1986. *Beyond Entitlement: The Social Obligations of Citizenship.* New York: Free Press

Mead L. 1992. *The New Politics of Poverty: The Non Working Poor in America.* New York: Basic

Mink G. 1998. *Welfare's End.* Ithaca NY: Cornell Univ. Press

Mishel L, Bernstein J, Schmitt J. 1999. *The State of Working America, 1998–99.* Ithaca NY: Cornell Univ. Press

Moore J, Pinderhughes R, eds. 1993. *In the Barrios: Latinos and the Underclass Debate.* New York: Russell Sage

Moss P, Tilly C. 1995. Raised hurdles for black men: evidence from employer interviews. Mimeo

Murray C. 1984. *Losing Ground: American Social Policy, 1950–1980.* New York: Basic

Myrdal G. 1944. *An American Dilemma: The Negro Problem and Modern Democracy.* New York: Harper & Brothers

Newman KS. 1999. *No Shame in My Game: The Working Poor in the Inner City.* New York: Knopf /Russell Sage

O'Connor A. 1998. Neither charity nor relief: the war on poverty and the effort to redefine the basis of social provision. In *With Us Always: A History of Private Charity and Public Welfare,* ed. DT Critchlow, CH Parker, pp. 191–210. Lanham MD: Rowman & Littlefield

O'Connor A. 2000. *Poverty Knowledge: Social Science, Social Policy and the Poor in Twentieth Century U.S. History.* Princeton, NJ: Princeton Univ. Press. In press

Olasky M. 1992. *The Tragedy of American Compassion.* Washington, DC: Regenery

Oliver ML, Shapiro TM. 1995. *Black Wealth/White Wealth: A New Perspective on Racial Inequality.* New York: Routledge

O'Neill J. 1990. The role of human capital in earnings differences between black and white men. J. Econ. Perspect. 4:25–45

Parrott S. 1998. *Welfare Recipients Who Find Jobs.* Washington, DC: Center on Budget & Policy Priorities

Patterson JT. 1994. *America's Struggle Against Poverty, 1900–1994.* Cambridge: Harvard Univ. Press. Rev. ed.

Phillips K. 1990. *The Politics of Rich and Poor: Wealth and the American Electorate in the Reagan Aftermath.* New York: Random House

Piven F, Cloward R. 1993. *Regulating the Poor: The Functions of Public Welfare.* New York: Random House. Rev. ed.

Putnam RD. 1995. Bowling alone: America's declining social capital. *J. Democracy* 6:65–78

Quadagno J. 1994. *The Color of Welfare: How Racism Undermined the War on Poverty.* New York: Oxford Univ. Press

Rank M. 1994. *Living on the Edge: The Realities of Welfare in America.* New York: Columbia Univ. Press

Ricketts ER, Sawhill IV. 1988. Defining and measuring the underclass. *J. Policy Anal. & Mgmt.* 7:316–25

Rubin LB. 1994. *Families on the Fault Line: America's Working Class Speaks about the Family, the Economy, Race, and Ethnicity.* New York: Harper Collins

Ruggles P. 1990. *Drawing the Line: Alternative Poverty Measures and Their Implications for Public Policy.* Washington, DC: Urban Inst.

Sawhill IV. 1988. Poverty in the United States: why is it so persistent? *J. Econ. Lit.* 26:1073–1119

Schram SF. 1995. *Words of Welfare: The Poverty of Social Science and the Social Science of Poverty.* Minneapolis: Univ. Minn. Press

Schwarz JE, Volgy TJ. 1992. *The Forgotten Americans.* New York: WW Norton

Skocpol T. 1991. Targeting within universalism: politically viable policies to combat poverty in the United States. In *The Urban Underclass,* ed. C Jencks, PE Peterson, pp. 411–436. Washington, DC: Brookings Inst.

Smith JP. 1988. Poverty and the family. In *Divided Opportunities: Minorities, Poverty, and Social Policy,* ed. GD Sandefur, M Tienda, pp. 141–72. New York: Plenum

Solow RM. 1998. *Work and Welfare.* Princeton, NJ: Princeton Univ. Press

Spain D, Bianchi SM. 1996. *Balancing Act: Motherhood, Marriage, and Employment Among American Women.* New York: Russell Sage

Spalter-Roth R, Hartmann H, Andrews L. 1994a. Mothers, children and low-wage work: the ability to earn a family wage. In *Sociology and the Public Agenda,* ed. WJ Wilson, pp. 316–38. Newbury Park, Calif: Sage

Spalter-Roth R, Hartmann H, Burr B. 1994b. *Income Security: The Failure of Unemployment Insurance to Reach Working Mothers.* Washington, DC: Inst. for Women's Policy Res.

Stack CB. 1974. *All Our Kin: Strategies for Survival in a Black Community.* New York: Harper & Row

Stack CB. 1996a. Holding hands: African Americans reclaim the rural south. *Dissent* Spring: 85–91

Stack CB, 1996b. *Call to Home: African Americans Reclaim the Rural South.* New York: Basic

Sugrue TJ. 1996. *The Origins of the Urban Crisis: Race and Inequality in Postwar Detroit.* Princeton, NJ: Princeton Univ. Press

Swartz TR, Weigart KM, eds. 1995. *America's Working Poor.* Notre Dame Ind.: Univ. Notre Dame Press

Tilly C. 1996. *Half a Job: Bad and Good Part—Time Jobs in a Changing Labor Market.* Philadelphia: Temple Univ. Press

Tilly C, Moss P. 2000. Space as a signal: how employers perceive neighborhoods in four metropolitan labor markets. In *Urban Inequality in the United States: Evidence from Four Cities,* ed. A O'Connor, C Tilly, L Bobo. New York: Russell Sage. In press

Waldfogel J, Mayer S. 1999. Differences between men and women in the low-wage labor market. *Inst. for Res. on Poverty Focus* Winter: 11–16

Waldinger R, Bozorgmehr M, eds. 1996. *Ethnic Los Angeles.* New York: Russell Sage

Watts HW, Rees A. 1977. *The New Jersey Income-Maintenance Experiment.* New York: Academic Press. 3 vols.

Weir M. 1999. Power, money, and politics in community development. In *Urban Problems and Community Development,* ed. RF Ferguson, WT Dickens, pp. 139–92. Washington, DC: Brookings Inst.

Weir M, Orloff AS, Skocpol T, eds. 1988. *The Politics of Social Policy in the United States.* Princeton, NJ: Princeton Univ. Press

Whyte WF. 1943. *Street Corner Society: The Social Structure of an Italian Slum.* Chicago: Univ. Chicago Press

Wilson WJ. 1987. *The Truly Disadvantaged: The Inner City, the Underclass, and Public Policy.* Chicago: Univ. Chicago Press

Wilson WJ. 1996. *When Work Disappears: The World of the New Urban Poor.* New York: Knopf

Wolff EN. 1995. *Top Heavy: A Study of the Increasing Inequality of Wealth in America.* New York: Twentieth Century Fund

Annu. Rev. Sociol. 2000. 26:563–84

CLOSING THE "GREAT DIVIDE": New Social Theory on Society and Nature

Michael Goldman and Rachel A. Schurman

Department of Sociology, University of Illinois, Urbana, Illinois 61801;
e-mail: mgoldman@uiuc.edu, ras2@uiuc.edu

Key Words   environmental sociology, ecological Marxism, political ecology, ecofeminism, science studies, social theory

■ **Abstract**   Twenty years ago, two environmental sociologists made a bold call for a paradigmatic shift in the discipline of sociology—namely, one that would bring nature into the center of sociological inquiry and recognize the inseparability of nature and society. In this essay, we review recent scholarship that seeks to meet this challenge. The respective strands of this literature come from the margins of environmental sociology and border on other arenas of social theory production, including neo-Marxism, political ecology, materialist feminism, and social studies of science. Bringing together scholars from sociology, anthropology, geography, and history, each of these strands offers what we consider the most innovative new work trying to move sociology beyond the nature/society divide.

INTRODUCTION

> Jorge Luis Borges once remarked that the absence of camels in the Koran reveals the book's authenticity. It has roots in a culture in which camels are taken for granted. By the same logic, the neglect of nature in contemporary Western social theory perhaps shows the extent to which the massive appropriation of natural resources upon which the modern world depends has come to be assumed as a fact of life. Yet if one instance of habituation expresses a millenarian dynamic between society and nature, the other reflects the abrupt rise of a short-term perspective that threatens the future of both nature and humanity.
>
> (Coronil 1997, p. 21)

Twenty years ago, a bold and prescient call for a paradigmatic shift in the discipline of sociology catapulted the field of environmental sociology onto the scene. Two early pioneers, Riley Dunlap and William Catton, emerged from Earth Day and other political demonstrations to argue that sociology, despite the appearance of a wide range of competing social theories, was actually composed of minor variants of a single paradigm, the "human exemptionalism paradigm" (Catton & Dunlap

1978, Dunlap 1997). From Marxism to symbolic interactionism, all were closely linked by the common trait of anthropocentrism. Social dynamics that produce environmental degradation and resource depletion would remain undertheorized, or worse, ignored, they argued, without a "new ecological paradigm" to displace the chauvinisms of the old. Moreover, the environment should not be introduced as just another new variable or theme, but as a radically new way of thinking about society. As the sun rose on the antinuclear, antitoxics, and limits-to-growth movements, Dunlap and Catton asked sociology to retool with a lens that brings nature into the center of sociological inquiry and recognizes the inseparability of nature and society.

Dunlap and Catton's call to sociology has turned out to represent an exceedingly difficult challenge. In part, this has to do with the history of the discipline. Because early theorists were trying to establish the need for a separate science of society, nature was not a major concern or concept for exploration in classical sociological theory. These classical sociologists sought to emphasize that which was outside the domain of the dominant physical and natural sciences to legitimate themselves and their discipline; the desire by some to distinguish their perspective from the dominant scientific perspective of biological determinism also contributed to this tendency. This was true of Marx and Engels, for example, who were in vigorous debate with Malthusianism. In emphasizing the social construction of natural limits, they underemphasized the importance of the biophysical world (Benton 1989) and the inextricability of nature and society.

A second reason nature has not been better integrated into sociological theory is related to the powerful influence that Enlightenment thought has had on the structure and production of sociological knowledge. Although the subdiscipline of environmental sociology has burgeoned in recent years, most of the literature treats nature as a discrete and external object of study, one that can be known through the application of an objective, dispassionate science. Yet as environmental historians, sociologists of science, and environmental philosophers have pointed out, the Enlightenment ontology of nature as primordial, autonomous, and mechanistic is highly problematic (Merchant 1980, 1989; Latour 1993; FitzSimmons & Goodman 1998). Not only is the idea of nature socially constructed, but the "natural" is deeply embedded in all social forms (cf Williams 1980).

Over the past decade, environmental sociology has focused on the study of "greening" as a new social trend that has worked its way into many of our major social institutions. Environmental sociologists have investigated attitudinal, behavioral, and consumer shifts, finding that the health of the biophysical world really does matter to people, that many are willing to make changes consistent with this, and that some social groups are particularly sensitive to environmental stewardship concerns (Mohai 1992, Scott & Willits 1994, Ozanne et al 1999). They have analyzed state regulatory regimes, industrial production practices, and waste disposal regimes (Schnaiberg & Gould 1994, Szasz 1994, Mol 1995, Sonnenfeld 1998), revealing the nexus among social protest, governmental regulatory activity, media coverage, and industrial receptivity, or "ecological modernization"

(Spaargaren & Mol 1992, Freudenburg & Gramling 1994). They have brought attention to the worst social inequities related to environmental pollution, degradation, and disasters, helping to establish that environmental racism/injustice—or the disproportionate displacement of waste and pollution on people of color and working-class communities—is prevalent throughout the United States and beyond (Bullard 1990, 1993; Bryant & Mohai 1992). In addition, they have tracked the rapid growth of environmental movements and collective behavior around environmental issues, finding new social movements that are vast, differentiated, and highly strategic (Gottlieb 1993, Bullard 1993, Hofrichter 1993, Gould et al 1996).

These contributions have been productive and useful and have begun to influence other areas of sociology (e.g. social movements, development studies) in important ways. Because others have successfully reviewed this literature (Buttel 1996, 1997; Pulido 1996; Dunlap 1997; Redclift & Woodgate 1997; Szasz & Meuser 1997; Mol & Spaargaren 2000) our focus in this review is on literature that grapples specifically with a retheorization of the nature/society divide. The respective strands of this literature come from the margins of environmental sociology and border on other arenas of social theory production. Bringing together scholars from sociology, anthropology, geography, and history, each of these strands—ecological Marxism, new political ecology, environmental feminism, and sociology of knowledge and science—offers what we consider the most innovative new work trying to make a paradigmatic shift away from nature/society dualisms.

At its best, we argue, this work brings into focus four critical insights: (*a*) not only must society be studied as constitutive of nature and vice versa, but nature must be understood as an actor with a conjoined materiality with society (Freudenburg et al 1995, Pickering 1996, Demeritt 1998); (*b*) sociology must become a reflexive science that understands knowledge (including ecological knowledge) as situated, partial, and internal to exercises of power, and people (as subjects and scientists of inquiry) in their organically embodied and ecologically embedded contexts; (*c*) studies of nature-society relations need to consider ecological processes, political-economic structures, and meanings, values, and agency as necessary and complementary components of analysis; and (*d*) the boundaries assumed by traditional units of analysis (e.g. nation, economy, biology, culture, or species) are inherently unstable and permeable (cf Buttel 1998). To the extent that environmental sociology can further develop these insights and incorporate them into its theoretical and empirical core, we suggest that it would not only advance the subdiscipline, but could greatly affect the discipline of sociology as a whole.

ECOLOGICAL MARXISM

Many have argued that the theoretical limit of the Marxist-socialist project has been its preoccupation with a productivist paradigm that endorses unlimited economic growth and ignores environmental degradation (Habermas 1984, Goldblatt 1996).

Yet a new wave of social theory seeks precisely to overcome these charges (see O'Connor 1988, 1998, and much of the work published in the journal *Capitalism, Nature, Socialism*; Toledo 1989; M O'Connor 1994; Benton 1989, 1993, 1996; Redclift & Benton 1994; Leff 1995; Harvey 1996; Foster 1999, 2000).

This theory is not rooted in nineteenth-century politics but in observations of current political and environmental trends—e.g. air, land, and water pollution, workplace and community-based movements against toxic poisoning and other threats to human health—with hardly a trace of the "normative presuppositions of unprincipled vanguardism" (Goldblatt 1996). It is neither stuck in an evolutionary model of progress, nor does it gloss over the contradictions of economic rationality. On the contrary, it explicitly theorizes these contradictions, recognizing the relations between nature and society as profoundly dialectical (Goldfrank et al 1999).

Over the past decade, Marxist political economy has taken a major step forward with James O'Connor's theoretical work on the current contradictions of capitalism (1988, 1994, 1998). O'Connor has revitalized the Marxist notion of contradiction by introducing nature alongside capital and labor as a fundamental category. In addition to the primary contradiction, which exists between capital and labor and reflects an overproduction or realization crisis, is a second contradiction that exists between capital and labor on the one hand, and nature on the other. Under certain circumstances, argues O'Connor, capitalism today undermines its own production conditions, namely, human nature (labor power), nonhuman nature (the external biophysical world), and the built environment (including public space and infrastructure). As ecosystems become heavily polluted and mined, workers and communities poisoned, and infrastructure destroyed, capitalists suffer a cost crisis due to the high costs (economic and noneconomic) of revitalizing degraded production conditions. To overcome these new barriers to expansion, capital must either restructure production conditions in productivity-enhancing ways, or seek more social forms of reproducing the conditions of production. O'Connor (1994) suggests that the latter does not seem likely to occur today because of the large measure of regulation and planning required, which is anathema to current ideological trends in most liberal democracies. More likely, individual capitals will seek to lower their production costs through technological innovation, e.g. through genetic engineering or by employing "toxic-eating" microorganisms to clean up toxic spills. As this happens, "we [will] enter a world in which capital does not merely appropriate nature, then turn it into commodities ... but rather a world in which *capital remakes nature* and its products biologically and physically (and politically and ideologically) in its own image." (O'Connor 1994, p. 158; emphasis ours).

Ted Benton is another sociologist actively pushing Marxist sociology in a more ecological direction (Benton 1989, 1993; Redclift & Benton 1994). His work can be seen as an important touchstone for scholars trying to retheorize nature-society relations through the prism of nature-based productive activities. Taking Marx's focus on the labor process as his starting point, Benton argues that different kinds of human activities have distinct "intentional structures" that go beyond the primary ideal type identified by Marx (productive-transformative intentional structures). By ignoring appropriative labor processes such as fishing or felling trees, and ecoregulatory activities such as agriculture, Benton contends that "Marx underrepresents the significance of non-manipulable natural conditions of labor processes and overrepresents the role of human intentional transformative powers vis-à-vis nature" (Benton 1989, p. 64).

For Benton, ecoregulatory practices are labor processes that aim to sustain, regulate, or reproduce rather than transform the conditions of agricultural production. Benton suggests that the work of transformation in seed and livestock production is actually carried out by organic and inorganic natural processes such as photosynthesis and metabolism, which are "relatively impervious to intentional manipulation." (Benton 1989, p. 68) There are strong parallels here with the work of Stephen Bunker (1985, 1989, 1992; also see Barham et al 1994), who has also attempted to theorize the difference between industrial or transformative activities and resource extraction, and was one of the first sociologists seeking to ecologize Marxism. Building on the work of both of these authors, a recent paper by Boyd et al (1999) develops the idea of nature as actor in nature-based industries (e.g. mining, agriculture, or silviculture), arguing that a direct reliance on the biophysical world introduces a unique source of surprise, opportunity, and risk into the capitalist production process.

Approaching the idea of nature in capitalist production from the field of semiotics, Martin O'Connor (1993) suggests that capital's response to ecological crisis has been to represent formerly noncapitalist realms—the biophysical world, non-industrialized economies, and the household—as reservoirs and stocks of "capital" and therefore no longer external to capitalism. Once particular conditions of production are colonized in this way, argues O'Connor, it becomes possible to justify their rational and ecological management by economic actors. That is, in the semiotic shift toward the capitalization of nature, environmental degradation and resource exhaustion are being diagnosed as management problems rather than as a crisis or breakdown; this management exercise then becomes a new source of dynamism for capitalism.

David Harvey, perhaps the most accomplished theorist of urban geography and a major contributor to the ecological reformation of Marxism, takes us in yet another direction (Harvey 1996). Instead of romanticizing the imagined world of nature, Harvey focuses on the built environment—arguably the most common environment today, especially to the working class and, in some countries, for minority ethnic groups. Harvey argues that nature is so mediated by capitalist structures and practices that there is no other way to think of nature as currently experienced except as a product of capital. In fact, Harvey's attention to the urban environment could be read as a corrective to the mainstream US environment movement's parochial interpretation of environmental issues (see also Di Chiro 1998).

Besides reconceptualizing the idea of nature vis-à-vis capitalism, ecological Marxists are also emphasizing how social movements and other agents of change respond to capital-driven ecological transformations. James O'Connor (1998) perceives many of today's social movements, from the public health movement to women's movements to movements of people of color, as a direct response to the ecological contradictions of capitalism. Harvey (1996) has a similar interpretation of the environmental justice movement as it unfolds in multiple local-to-global sites around the world. Harvey draws together Raymond Williams' idea of "militant particularism" with his own notion of "global ambition" as a practical way to overcome the pitfalls of "localist" politics. These politics often exclude people with whom there could be potential solidarity, such as people from different ethnic groups or nations but similar locations in relation to contemporary capitalism (see also Schaeffer 1997, Gille 2000). Daniel Faber's work on U.S. environmental movements makes a clear link between changes in U.S. capitalism, social movement politics, and state regulatory practices (Faber 1998). He shows that local-based environmental activists have stopped numerous planned municipal incinerators and forced many public and private employers to clean up neighborhoods and make workplaces safer. These successful actions have, in turn, fed into national and international political strategies for greater democratic participation in decision-making processes over the means of production and the circulation of toxic waste (see also Schaeffer 1999).

In all of these discussions, the social "production of nature" is central (Smith 1984, 1998). Significantly, when ecological Marxists use the concept of production, they do not relegate themselves only to the corridors of Fordist factories. Indeed, their scholarship reveals an understanding of production in the broadest terms—as social, economic, cultural, and ecological production, circulation, and consumption. Nature is, or natures are, internal to these transformations (LeFebvre 1991). This intellectual project—to comprehend both the social production of nature and the natural production of society—is enormous. Now we will turn to another literature that takes up this challenge from a different perspective.

NEW POLITICAL ECOLOGY

Refashioning traditional methodologies from geography and anthropology with new tools from cultural and postcolonial studies, the new political ecology is a flourishing terrain of scholarship that emphasizes locality-based studies of people interacting with their environments. Whereas once this field was largely a remake of cultural ecology with research on poverty and ecological stress in peasant production practices, recently it has taken remarkable strides to retheorize not only place-based analysis, but also social theory of nature in general. The formidable task of new political ecology has been to articulate the natural as constitutive of the social, and vice versa, unpacking these relations for a better understanding of the political, ecological, and cultural. The literature has taken three approaches in its latest inquiries: theorizing environmental struggles as both material and symbolic, discursive practices as embodying power relations, and, unconventionally, land use practices in the highly industrialized North.

Along the first of these lines, Rocheleau and Ross (1995) analyze the roles of trees as "tools and text." They show how different social groups in the Dominican Republic utilized the *Acacia* tree, as well as ideas about *Acacia* trees, in their efforts to establish claims to land and other productive resources. Similarly, Donald Moore's (1996) work on environmental struggles in Zimbabwe emphasizes the symbolic aspects of peasant land claims. Drawing on Antonio Gramsci and Raymond Williams, Moore contends that symbolic struggles effect material transformation, and that "cultural meanings are constitutive forces, that is, shapers of history, and not simply reflections of a material base" (Moore, p. 127). A number of scholars have interrogated the gendered nature of struggles over meaning (e.g. Carney 1996, Bassett 1999, Rocheleau & Ross 1995), showing, for instance, how men and women mobilize differing cultural understandings to justify their claims over particular resources.

The inspiration for many of these analyses of ideology, symbolism, and the cultural construction of meaning was Nancy Peluso's (1992) pioneering study of the struggle between the Indonesian State and forest dwellers over the Indonesian teak forests. Building on the works of E. P. Thompson and James Scott on cultures of resistance, Peluso shows how the Indonesian State sought to maintain control of the forests through a certain conception of property rights and an ideology of criminality, and how forest dwellers challenged those conceptions by engaging in "criminal behavior" and developing a counter-discourse on what is a fair, legal, and legitimate use of the forest.

The account by Michael Watts (1998) of the putatively environmental struggles over oil in southern Nigeria reveals an extraordinary social movement configuration that created a new politics based on a constructed hybrid identity. Although this "black gold" was found in the swamps where they lived, the Ogoni people accumulated no oil wealth; moreover, the exploitation of oil helped destroy the environment on which these people once thrived. Nonetheless, oil became more than a natural resource for which the Ogoni had a natural affinity or on which they built their natural/moral economy; it came to represent a discourse and artifact of transnational petrol capital and the brutal state apparatuses that allowed for constant oil spills and fires, and murdered Ken Saro-Wiwa and other Ogoni leaders. Watts' key contribution is his observation that this movement does not at all reflect the imagined alternative movement that most seem to find dotting the postcolonial map. The recent history of Ogoni oppositional politics reveals that a unified conception of "Ogoniness" had to be invented for this moment, bringing together the "locals" who otherwise did not have a common political identity, fighting for rights to a nature (oil) for which they had no love, history, or locally privileged knowledge.

Similarly, Fernando Coronil in *The Magical State* retells the modern history of Venezuela from a new perspective that emphasizes oil and oil-producing land as an autonomous force in the making of states and state-society relations. He argues that the oil in petrostates such as Venezuela (and Nigeria) has an enormously transformative effect on the body politic and the historical trajectory of a nation in terms of nationalism and state-building, wealth production and distribution, and the subaltern modernity of a semiperipheral nation in the world-system (Coronil 1997).

A second, closely related line of the new political ecology scholarship analyzes alternative discourses on nature, the environment, and environmental degradation, seeking to understand the power dynamics circulating through Western truth regimes related to North-South relations. Michael Dove (1993), for example, explores the way in which the Indonesian State, transnational nongovernmental organizations (NGOs), and Northern environmental movements frame the problem of deforestation in the Indonesian rainforest as one of forest dweller impoverishment, instead of as a reflection of the enormous inequalities characterizing Indonesian society, as well as its relationship with the rest of the world. In a similar vein, Lucy Jarosz (1996) analyzes colonial and postcolonial discourses on peasant land use in Madagascar, revealing the state's efforts to control the terms of the debate as to what counts as rational and irrational land use practices. Like Peluso, Jarosz stresses the way in which peasants' subaltern discourses are developed as powerful tools of resistance to state authority and as a basis for organizing against the state. All of these works artfully combine political-economic analysis with much needed attention to the discursive and ideological realms and reveal how perceptions and constructions of nature and politics actively shape material reality. They also respond directly to Watts' criticism that political ecology's understanding of politics needed to be broadened (Watts 1990, Peet & Watts 1996). Finally, discourse analysis has been used to explore and expose the power relations embodied in national and global conservation agendas, including those of seemingly progressive environmental groups (Peluso 1993, Schroeder 1995, Luke 1997, Goldman 1998).

A third approach in the new political ecology involves a shift to the North, where scholars challenge the notion that urbanized and industrialized environments are areas of no nature, with little effect on culture, politics, or identity. Studying the North allows political ecologists to reconsider their assumptions about North-South differences. For instance, in a study of two Chicano struggles in the southwestern United States (the pesticide campaign of the United Farm Workers and the Ganados del Valle Hispano grazing rights campaign), Laura Pulido concludes that struggles over environmental issues are simultaneously struggles over livelihood, an argument that has been made about many environmental struggles in the South (Hecht & Cockburn 1990, Friedmann & Rangan 1993).

In critical dialogue with scholars who analyze the role of race and ethnicity in environmental politics, Pulido suggests that the literature on environmental justice/racism is effective in documenting the landscape of race-based injustice, but does not capture the multifaceted dimensions of racism. When race becomes a variable in studies on pollution, it can be effective in demonstrating a type of racism in which race is statistically significant in the siting of toxic producers. But what about situations when it is not? Because racism is so deeply implicated in our institutions and material life, race-as-variable analyses often fail to capture many structural, insidious, and enduring forms of oppression. Moreover, the evidence presented by Pulido reveals an identity politics amongst oppressed minority and ethnic communities that does not fit the common portrayal of these communities as either closer to (e.g. Native Americans) or further from nature (e.g. African Americans). In actively creating a new Hispano-pastoral culture to challenge Anglo claims of superior environmental concerns, the Chicanos Pulido studies have effectively mobilized essentialist identities to their advantage (see also Di Chiro 1998). In other words, what counts as nature and what works as nature politics are two arenas that are being effectively remade by some environmental justice organizations and social movements as they confront their respective adversaries and obstacles (Alston 1990, Hofrichter 1993, Szasz 1994).

ENVIRONMENTAL FEMINISM

In social theory, feminist theorists have always played a central role in working through problematic ontological dualisms such as nature/culture, subject/object, human/nonhuman, and the resulting naturalized classifications of sex, race, species, and class (Soper 1995). There is common agreement amongst feminist theorists that these distinctions emanate from a masculinist ideal of what it means to be truly human, i.e. what characteristics do or do not qualify, which are attributed to nature and which to culture, which to the animal kingdom and which to the human. From there, however, agreement wavers; nowhere is it more true than with the wide range of feminists who could fall under the rubric of environmental feminism, which, for this essay, includes gender and feminist analyses of nature/social relations. A brief perusal of works by Merchant (1980, 1992), Mellor (1997), and Sturgeon (1997) shows that a diverse range of analytical frameworks exists on the question of feminism and ecology.

Some find the origins of universalized oppression of women and nature rooted in the Enlightenment and the (Western) scientization of society, with its consequent objectification of nature as the formal object of dispassionate [read: male, scientific] inquiry (Merchant 1980, 1992; Shiva 1989; Mies & Shiva 1993). Others are less convinced by this macrostructural rigidity, yet maintain a strong critique of dominant scientific practices and related oppressive effects for objects of science, such as nature, and for subjects excluded from the scientific professions, such as (until recently) women (Haraway 1991, 1997b; Martin 1994; Ginsburg & Rapp 1995; Downey & Dumit 1997). Nonetheless, the shared project of destabilizing common myths around what is nature, culture, and biology, is yielding some of the most fruitful scholarly work in social theory today. Two substantive areas stand out: gender and the environment, particularly in developing countries; and biotechnology and the politics of the body (human and nonhuman). These areas overlap and cross-pollinate intellectually, with scholars borrowing from and contributing to each other's work.

Through multiple lenses, feminists walk the tightrope of explicating what biological/ecological traits are meaningful for whom, and which are used as weapons.

For example, an assumed promise of late capitalism is that we humans all have the potential of transcending the biological limits of nature: to produce food without soil, prolong human life with techno-surrogate body parts, and consume more than the earth can sustain. Environmental feminists recognize that the promise of limitless consumption exists, but only for the most privileged, for whom "[the] limits are borne by others, including the earth itself" (Mellor 1997, p. 190). They contend that biology does matter and, moreover, that it is a contested zone in which constructed gender, race, class, nationality, and species differences have significant consequences. In contrast to the notion of transcendence, which underlies Enlightenment thought on society's relationship to nature, environmental feminists theorize social-natural relations in terms of ecological embeddedness and biological embodiment (Mellor 1997, Salleh 1997). This alternative perspective is associated with the idea of immanence, or a reflexive awareness of one's position in nature.

Gender and the Environment

An important strand of recent feminist inquiry consists of gender analyses that emphasize the materialist and semiotic dimensions of the relationships of people to each other and to nonhuman nature. The most sophisticated of this gender and the environment (hereafter referred to as G&E) literature eschews the essentialist and universalizing character of the early "ecofeminist" literature (cf Starhawk 1990, Shiva 1989) and the policy-oriented literature on women, environment, and development emanating from the World Bank, United Nations agencies, and some international NGOs. Explicitly rejecting the notion that "women are to nature as men are to culture," G&E scholars show how depictions of Third World women's sacred in their naturalized indigeneity and affinity to nature, say much more about "the gaze of western eyes" (Mohanty et al 1991) than they do about specific relationships that women may have to the environment (Jackson 1994, Leach et al 1995).

G&E scholars argue that society-nature relations are patterned by gender, and gender relations are fundamental to understanding resource access, use, and degradation around the world (Agarwal 1992, 1994; Leach 1991, 1994; Joekes et al 1995). Bina Agarwal (1994), for example, develops a gender analysis of land relations in India to show how gender (as well as class/caste) relations at a variety of levels (e.g. nation, village, household) mediate people's access to land and the effects of India's land reform laws on women. Leach & Fairhead (1995) examine gendered practices of gardening in Kuranko, Guinea, to illustrate how changing gender relations shaped, and were shaped by, local patterns of environmental change. They also show how different land use practices by women and men create gendered knowledges of agroecological systems, a theme also highlighted by Rocheleau (1995) and Mackenzie (1995).

Related to the notion that environmental knowledges are gendered is the point that the very definition of environmental degradation varies not only across different societies and cultures, but also by gender, class, and race within a particular society (Leach et al 1995, Joekes et al 1995, Shah & Shah 1995). Cecile Jackson

(1994, 1995) takes this idea a step further by challenging the notion, common among NGOs and multilateral development institutions, that the interests of women and environmentalism are coterminous. She notes that the presumed synergy between women's interests and environmental interests derives from the observation that "because of their daily tasks—growing food and gathering water, fuel and fodder—poor women are especially dependent upon the natural resources of the environment and the first to suffer when the environment becomes degraded" (Davidson et al 1992, cited by Jackson 1995). However, as her study of conjugal contracts in southern Zimbabwe shows, the well being of particular groups of women and of particular environments can also be at odds. More generally, she observes that the dominant, yet often incorrect, assumption of synergy can lead to development projects that place extra burdens on women, as they are expected to provide the labor to effect change (Jackson 1994).

The Politics of the Body

A second area of theorization is associated with recent work on the reinvention of the body, particularly in the contested terrain of reproduction. One strand of this literature focuses on the technologies of contraception and sterilization used, coercively or otherwise, whereas another emphasizes the latest medical technologies with which women interact in dealing with concerns about pregnancy and fertility. The former reflects on the twin-headed hydra in public discourse on the fate of the planet—overpopulation and environmental degradation—and how solutions are typically sought in "depoliticized" global instruments of reproductive control, namely, contraception and sterilization. The latter draws attention to the fluid divide between private and public, for example public discourses on what parts of a woman's body are hers and which are not and when public citizenship should be awarded to a developing fetus and when it should not.

Over the years, feminists have shown that the discourse on population control/family planning has been characterized by zenophobism as well as reductionism, which not only enables international and state agencies to manipulate the bodies and rights of women but seeks to stabilize certain notions of family, race, nation, and social order (Hartmann 1987, Mohanty et al 1991, Scheper-Hughes 1992, Ginsburg & Rapp 1995, Bandarage 1997). Although this critique of conventional reproduction politics is not new, it has served as the basis for investigating how other bodily interventions have proliferated in scope and scale (Franklin & Ragoné 1998). Both old and new studies help us rethink social theory in light of the contested terrain of human biology, nature, and technology.

Martin, Rapp, Ginsberg, Clarke, Cussins, and others have created a subfield of inquiry on the anthropology of the body with global topics of exploration such as AIDS (Booth 1998, Treichler 1999), viruses and immunities (Martin 1994), and the trade in bodies, body parts, and body fluids. Many of these studies find kinship networks that are effectively strewn across the planet, as far as a frozen embryo, tissue, or sperm can travel, blurring traditional distinctions among—and requiring new ontological definitions of—animal, human, race, and technology (Cussins 1998). Such analyses lead to questions about the directions in which "possessive individualist" capitalist culture is being taken, if parts of the person/body are being spread across time and space. As Martin (1998, p. 78) asks: "Who is the owner of these new bodies? How do these new techno-science incursions destabilize existing ownership structures of nature and personhood?"

Some suggest that the body itself has become an accumulation strategy. Indeed, capital accumulation now occurs within cell membranes functioning as microfactories within our bodies, giving new meaning to the idea of social (and natural) labor and blurring the line between production and reproduction. Emily Martin (1998) periodizes scientific and popular perceptions of the function of the human body in western capitalist societies into a Fordist accumulation strategy of mass production and distribution of commodified contraceptive and menstrual products, and a post-Fordist regime of individualization and deep intervention in the form of surgical interventions, fetal surveillance, and genetic testing. In the latter, the body and bodily practices are not just commodified, but nature is capitalized and remade (note the overlap with J O'Connor, cited above). Others studying global biodiversity and human genome projects—the collection of seemingly scarce global resources (human/nonhuman) for classifying, saving, and valorizing—reveal how emerging markets for gene information represent new arenas for capital accumulation as well as the reconstitution of meanings and structures of human and nonhuman natures (Hayden 1998; Flitner 1998; Heath 1997; Haraway 1997a, b; Rose 1998; Wilkie 1996). As Haraway (1997a) notes, some view the production and patenting of transgenic organisms as the last straw for upsetting the "natural *telos*, or self-defining purpose" of all life forms; whereas others (such as Haraway herself) see much more ambiguity, contention, and potential political transformation in these and other sociotechnological developments.

Feminist scholars of the body politic and biologic also inquire into the distributional implications of these interventions, asking questions such as: Which social groups have access to these new reproductive technologies, and which are providing the raw material for the cell, tissue, and body-parts trade? Could these scientific-corporate incursions into the bodies of indigenous peoples (the ambition of the alternative Human Genome Diversity Project) and ecosystems (the ambition of bioprospecting projects) find some salve to modern diseases while also deepening local and global structures of inequality? Are these new missions, endowed with rarefied technical expertise and new strategies for capitalizing nature, creating new forms of race- and class-based exploitation (Haraway 1997b, Flitner 1998, Hayden 1998)?

SCIENCE, KNOWLEDGE, AND POWER

As several scholars have astutely observed, environmentalism today (as scholarship, politics, and activism) depends heavily upon environmental science for its reasoning and observations (Yearley 1994, Beck 1992, Buttel & Taylor 1994). From global warming to bacterial water contamination, most modern environmental issues have become "knowable" only through particular scientific practices and with technologies with limited accessibility (e.g. super-capacity computers, satellites, or laboratory infrastructure). Even for those issues that first become public through detection by those who are not professional scientists (e.g. people living downwind from toxic incinerators), science has become a contested site for problem definition, problem framing, and risk adjudication, with tremendous legal, financial, and political ramifications (Irwin 1995, Agarwal & Narain 1991).

Recognizing that environmental science has been an undertheorized domain, a handful of sociologists have begun to critically examine the practice of environmental science and the production of scientific knowledge on nature and the environment. Among the first to try to fill this lacuna were Buttel and colleagues (Buttel et al 1990, Taylor & Buttel 1992, Buttel & Taylor 1994). In "How Do We Know We Have Global Environmental Problems?," Taylor & Buttel (1992) used The Limits to Growth study and the global climate change issue to show that "politics are woven into environmental science at its 'upstream' end" (Taylor & Buttel 1992, p. 406). They argued that global constructs of environmental issues involve a universalizing discourse that steers us away from the difficult politics of enduring structural inequalities and differentiated interests and toward technomanagerialist remedies, preferred (and constituted) by elite, Northern-based scientists and bureaucrats.

Although acknowledging the insights of Buttel and Taylor's "interest-based" analysis of science, Brian Wynne (1994) argues that it does not fully capture "the deeper sense in which scientific knowledge tacitly reflects and reproduces normative models of social relations, cultural and moral identities, as if these were natural" (Wynne 1994, p. 176). Wynne contends there is a need to interrogate science for its virtually invisible cultural constructions of the human subject (e.g. as a rational, utility-maximizing actor) and its connections to the cultural milieu of late modern society. The point of such an interrogation is not to debunk scientific knowledge, but rather to expose its unspoken social and moral commitments (Wynne 1994, p. 188). Such cultural analyses of science underscore the point that there is no one-to-one correspondence between nature and its representations, and that all human understandings of nature are crucially mediated by social and cultural practices, assumptions, and belief systems.

The "social studies of science" literature, of which Wynne is a part, has stimulated innovative conceptualizations of nature-society relations and agency. The most exciting of this work theorizes nature and society not as separate—or separable—entities, but in terms of their "conjoined materiality" (Demeritt 1998) or "conjoint constitution" (Freudenburg et al 1995). In these renderings of nature-society relations, nature and society are effectively coproduced through the reciprocal and symmetric interplay of the social and the physical (Pickering 1996).

Bruno Latour (1993), operating within the framework of actor-network theory, suggests that there is no such thing as pure nature or pure society, only nature-culture hybrids (for useful reviews of actor-network theory, see Hess 1997 and the forthcoming book by CT Cussins). Following Michel Serres, Latour suggests that nature-culture hybrids are "quasi-objects, quasi-subjects" which stand in between the two Modern poles of Nature and Society. In this "Middle Kingdom," humans and nonhumans produce "artifactual nature" through their collective associations, known as networks. Donna Haraway (1991) also develops the idea of nature as artifact, introducing the notion of the "cyborg" to suggest that we are all composed of the natural-technological-social. She uses the metaphor of kinship to acknowledge that humans and nonhumans are active partners in the enterprise of making nature, society, and what counts as reality. These and other authors working in this vein (Pickering 1995, 1996; FitzSimmons & Goodman 1998) advocate an understanding of agency that encompasses human as well as nonhuman actors, emphasizing the collective, rather than individual, character of natural-social agency (Latour 1993, Callon & Law 1995).

'Green' Knowledge/Power

Whereas some look at the production of scientific knowledge from the perspective of political interests (e.g. Taylor & Buttel 1992), others take a different approach by considering how particular cultural-social values become naturalized and diffused beyond the intentions of any particular interests (Mackenzie 1995; Escobar 1995; Luke 1997; Goldman 1998, 2000; Darier 1999). These scholars deploy a Foucauldian analysis of power/knowledge (Foucault 1980, Burchell et al 1991) for which exercises of power and the accumulation of (environmental) knowledge are co-constitutive, producing power relations and scientific discourses that are intentional yet nonsubjective. These power/knowledge relations are imbued with calculation, rationality, and a productive influence on global norms of ecological and social governance (i.e. what constitutes the eco-rational citizen or state). Hence, we find globalizing discourses of environmentalism, reproduced by nonstate international institutions—e.g. NGO, intergovernmental, and scientific networks—that energetically push to establish universalizing norms, behaviors, and procedures to regulate the security of the environment. These power/knowledge incursions elide heterogeneity and conflict and instead represent the world as rational, consensual, and easily molded for sustainability.

For example, tools such as environmental impact assessments and green cost-benefit analyses are now commonly used by public and private agencies around the world, and they are, in fact, often requirements for governments seeking international debt relief and financial support from institutions such as the World Bank and the International Monetary Fund. Yet despite their practice in vastly different settings (e.g. Laos, Lesotho, or Lithuania), environmental impact assessments and cost-benefit analyses rarely reflect localized cultural forms and norms, but, rather, newly contrived universal norms and models of sustainability, resource valuation, and degradation. The kinds of questions this knowledge/power literature asks include the following: What specific micro-technologies of power do these new methodologies and sciences engender? What perspectives, issues, and questions get disguised, buried, or eliminated (i.e. subjugated knowledges) in the production and circulation of these universal scientific tools and models (i.e. elite knowledge)?

Scholars working from this perspective have begun to theorize nature-society relations in Foucauldian terms of biopolitics and biopower (Dean 1994, Burchell et al 1991). For example, Arturo Escobar's (1995) analysis of development discourse deconstructs the concept of sustainable development as deployed in the South by Northern-based institutions. Playing with Carolyn Merchant's trenchant analysis of the Enlightenment, Escobar argues that these institutions have brought about the semiotic "death of nature" and replaced it with the "rise of the environment," a discursive strategy rooted in the destructive processes of post-World War II development and the proliferation of new governing strategies of nature. Everything in nature that is useful for increased industrial production falls under the rubric of the environment; all else disappears. Moreover, localized forms of knowledge become useful only in as much as they serve the new disciplinary mechanisms of local "participation" and global integration. The new scientific discourses of economism and ecologism coalesce under new regimes of power that, Escobar concludes, do more to undermine ecological-social balances around the world than to sustain them.

Studying the changing agrarian landscape in rural India, Akhil Gupta (1998) argues that new technological innovations in biotechnology, intellectual property rights, and bioengineered seeds and food products are factors in the respatialization of sovereignty, that is, who controls what farmers can grow on what land, and the reconfiguration of socio-ecological relations. Gupta contends that new global environmental regulations emanating from the 1992 Rio Earth Summit and other global accords have given birth to new technologies of government unhitched from the nation-state and found in the realm of transnationality (cf Ong 1999). In his work on the World Bank, Michael Goldman (2000) uses the term eco-governmentality to denote the rapid diffusion of power/knowledge technologies that simultaneously operate on the levels of the individual, society, and the state. These practices are at the center of new political battles over what counts as nature and environmental problems, and what constitutes an eco-rational citizen.

According to these scholars, this type of green knowledge production has become prolific, controversial, and hegemonic. Its "ways of seeing" have poured through the arteries of popular, political, and economic networks that have as their mission the accumulation of knowledge for the control of nature's value. It is a process that frames current discourses of sustainability, and disguises the engines of capitalist expansion as liberalizing and rational. In short, the production of green knowledge should be understood as internal to, and constitutive of, new and existing exercises of power.

CONCLUSION

In this essay, we have tried to show that recent theorizing on social-natural relations has been highly dynamic. From a multitude of perspectives, social theorists are grappling with the entrenched idea that nature and society are phenomenologically and scientifically distinct. In the process, new research agendas and methodological approaches are being crafted. Because ecological (and social) problems traverse conceptual, geographic, and species boundaries, human membranes as well as cultures, these scholars suggest that social analysis must follow them wherever they lead.

From this literature, we have also learned to recognize nature-culture hybrids—people, organisms, and things that are more complex than the distinctions between human and nonhuman suggest. This idea is useful for understanding the production and effects of new biotechnologies and commodities, which can lead to new political identities, tools, and strategies. However, it is not useful—and this is our biggest caveat—if the lens on this latest trend in commodity production sidetracks social theorists into digging up the spectacular at the cost of losing sight of the fundamental. Sociology remains at its best when it tries to understand how new and enduring structures, institutions, and practices exploit and dominate people and nature, as well as reveal new strategies for emancipatory politics. We believe that once scholars begin to rethink the framework of the society-nature divide, other cherished but flawed ideas will also reveal their weaknesses. We hope that from this process, a new sociological imagination will spring.

ACKNOWLEDGMENT

We thank Tuba Üstüner for her very helpful research assistance on this article.

Visit the Annual Reviews home page at www.AnnualReviews.org

LITERATURE CITED

Agarwal A, Narain S. 1991. *Global Warming in an Unequal World: a Case of Environmental Colonialism.* Centre for Sci. Environ. New Delhi, India. 88 pp.

Agarwal B. 1992. The gender and environment debate: lessons from India. *Fem. Stud.* 18:119–58

Agarwal B. 1994. *A Field of One's Own: Gender and Land Rights in South Asia.* New York: Cambridge Univ. Press

Alston D, ed. 1990. *We Speak for Ourselves:* *Social Justice, Race, and Environment.* Washington, DC: PANOS. 32 pp.

Bandarage A. 1997. *Women, Population and Global Crisis: A Political-Economic Analysis.* Atlantic Highlands, NJ: Zed Books. 397 pp.

Barham B, Bunker SG, O'Hearn D, eds. 1994. *States, Firms, and Raw Materials: The World Economy and Ecology of Aluminum.* Madison, WI: Univ. Wisc. Press. 341 pp.

Bassett TJ. 1999. *Contested cropping: peasant cotton and the spaces of gender politics in northern Cote d'Ivorie.* Presented at Conf. on Peasants Comp. Interdiscip. Perspect.: Landsc. Identity Nat. Power, Univ. Ill. Urbana-Champaign

Beck U. 1992. *Risk Society: Towards a New Modernity.* London: Sage. 260 pp.

Benton T. 1989. Marxism and natural limits: an ecological critique and reconstruction. *New Left Rev.* 178:51–86

Benton T. 1993. *Natural Relations: Ecology, Animal Rights, and Social Justice.* London: Verso

Benton T, ed. 1996. *The Greening of Marxism.* New York: Guilford. 310 pp.

Booth KM. 1998. National mother, global whore and transnational femocrats: the politics of AIDS and the construction of women at the World Health Organization. *Fem. Stud.* 24:115–39

Boyd W, Prudham W, Schurman R. 1999. *Industrial Dynamics and the Problem of Nature.* Energy and Resour. Group, Berkeley, Calif.

Bryant BI, Mohai P. 1992. *Race and the Incidence of Environmental Hazards: A Time For Discourse.* Boulder, CO: Westview. 251 pp.

Bullard RD. 1990. *Dumping in Dixie: Race, Class, and Environmental Quality.* Boulder, CO: Westview. 195 pp.

Bullard RD. 1993. *Confronting Environmental Racism: Voices from the Grassroots.* Boston, MA: South End Press. 259 pp.

Bunker SG. 1985. *Underdeveloping the Amazon: Extraction, Unequal Exchange, and the Failure of the Modern State.* Urbana, IL: Univ. Ill. Press. 279 pp.

Bunker SG. 1989. Staples, links, and poles in the construction of regional development theories. *Sociol. Forum* 4:589–610

Bunker SG. 1992. Natural resource extraction and power differentials in a global economy. In *Understanding Economic Process*, ed. S Ortiz, S Lees, pp. 61–84. Washington, DC: Univ. Press Am.

Burchell G, Gordon C, Miller P. 1991. *The Foucault Effect: Studies in Governmentality.* Chicago, IL: Univ. Chicago Press. 307 pp.

Buttel FH. 1996. Environmental and resource sociology: theoretical issues and opportunities for synthesis. *Rural Sociol.* 61:56–76

Buttel FH. 1997. Social institutions and environmental change. In *The International Handbook of Sociology*, ed. M Redclift, G Woodgate, pp. 40–53. Cheltenhaum, UK: Elgar.

Buttel FH. 1998. Some observations on states, world orders, and the politics of sustainability. *Organ. Environ.* 11:261–86

Buttel FH, Hawkins A, Power AG. 1990. From limits to growth to global change: contrasts and contradictions in the evolution of environmental science and ideology. *Glob. Environ. Chang.* 1:57–66

Buttel FH, Taylor P. 1994. Environmental sociology and global environmental change: a critical assessment. In *Social Theory and the Global Environment*, ed. M Redclift, T Benton, pp. 228–55. New York: Routledge. 271 pp.

Callon M, Law J. 1995. Agency and the hybrid collectif. *S. Atl. Q.* 94:481–507

Carney JA. 1996. Converting the wetlands, engendering the environment: the intersection of gender with agrarian change in Gambia. In *Liberation Ecologies: Environment, Development, Social Movements*, ed. R Peet, M Watts, pp. 165–87. New York: Routledge. 273 pp.

Catton WRJ, Dunlap RE. 1978. Environmental sociology: a new paradigm. *Am. Sociol.* 13:41–49

Coronil F. 1997. *The Magical State: Nature, Money, and Modernity in Venezuela.* Chicago, IL: Univ. Chicago Press. 447 pp.

Cussins CT. 1998. Producing reproduction: techniques of normalization and naturalization in infertility clinics. In *Reproducing Reproduction*, ed. S Franklin, H Ragoné, pp. 66–101. Philadelphia, PA: Univ. Pa. Press. 245 pp.

Cussins CT. 2000. *Primate Encounters: Models of Science, Gender, and Society.* Chicago, IL: Univ. Chicago Press. In press

Darier E, ed. 1999. *Discourses of the Environment.* Oxford, UK: Blackwell.

Davidson J, Myers D, Chakraborty M. 1992. *No Time to Waste Poverty and the Global Environment.* Oxford, England: Oxfam. 217 pp.

Dean M. 1994. *Critical and Effective Histories: Foucault's Methods and Historical Sociology.* London: Routledge. 237 pp.

Demeritt D. 1998. Science, social constructivism and nature. In *Remaking Reality: Nature at the Millennium,* ed. B Braun, N Castree, pp. 173–93. New York: Routledge. 295 pp.

Di Chiro G. 1998. Nature as community: the convergence of environment and social justice. In *Privatizing Nature: Political Struggles for the Global Commons,* ed. M Goldman, pp. 120–42. New Brunswick, NJ: Rutgers Univ. Press. 257 pp.

Dove MR. 1993. A revisionist view of tropical deforestation and development. *Environ. Conserv.* 20:17–56

Downey GL, Dumit J, eds. 1997. *Cyborgs and Citadels.* Santa Fe, NM: Sch. Am. Res. Press

Dunlap RH. 1997. The evolution of environmental sociology: a brief history and assessment of the American experience. In *The International Handbook of Environmental Sociology,* ed. M Redclift, G Woodgate, pp. 21–39. Cheltenhaum, UK: Elgar. 485 pp.

Escobar A. 1995. *Encountering Development: The Making and Unmaking of the Third World.* Princeton, NJ: Princeton Univ. Press. 290 pp.

Faber D, ed. 1998. *The Struggle for Ecological Democracy: Environmental Justice Movements in the United States.* New York: Guilford. 366 pp.

Ferguson J. 1990. *The Anti-Politics Machine: "Development," Depoliticization, Bureaucratic Power in Lesotho.* Minneapolis, MN: Univ. Minn. Press. 320 pp.

FitzSimmons M, Goodman D. 1998. Incorporating nature: environmental narratives and the reproduction of food. In *Remaking Reality: Nature at the Millennium,* ed. B Braun, N Castree. pp. 194–220. London: Routledge. 295 pp.

Flitner M. 1998. Biodiversity: of local commons and global commodities. In *Privatizing Nature: Political Struggles for the Global Commons,* ed. M Goldman, pp. 144–16. New Brunswick, NJ: Rutgers Univ. Press

Foster JB. 1999. Marx's theory of metabolic rift: classical foundations for environmental sociology. *Am J. Sociol.* 105:366–405

Foster JB. 2000. *Marx's Ecology: Materialism and Nature.* New York: Mon. Rev.

Foucault M. 1980. *Power/Knowledge: Selected Interviews and Other Writings, 1972–1977.* New York: Pantheon. 270 pp.

Foucault 1991

Franklin S, Ragoné H, eds. 1998. *Reproducing Reproduction.* Philadelphia, PA: Univ. Pa. Press. 245 pp.

Freudenburg WR, Frickel S, Gramling R. 1995. Beyond the nature/society divide: learning to think about a mountain. *Sociol. Forum* 10:361–92

Freudenburg WR, Gramling R. 1994. *Oil in Troubled Waters: Perceptions, Politics, and the Battle over Offshore Oil.* Albany, NY: State Univ. N. Y. Press. 179 pp.

Friedmann J, Rangan H, eds. 1993. *In Defense of Livelihood: Comparative Studies on Environmental Action.* West Hartford, CT: Kumarian Press. 219 pp.

Gille Z. 2000. Cognitive cartography in a European wasteland: multinationals and greens vie for village allegiance. In *Global Ethnography: Forces, Connections, and Imaginations in a Postmodern World,* ed. M Burawoy, JA Blum, S George, Z Gille, T Gowan, et al, pp. 345–78. Berkeley, CA: Univ. Calif. Press. 611 pp.

Ginsburg FD, Rapp R, eds. 1995. *Conceiving the New World Order: The Global Politics of Reproduction.* Berkeley, CA: Univ. Calif. Press. 450 pp.

Goldblatt D. 1996. *Social Theory and the Environment.* Boulder, CO: Westview. 247 pp.

Goldfrank WL, Goodman D, Szasz A, eds. 1999. *Ecology and the World-System*. London: Greenwood

Goldman M, ed. 1998. *Privatizing Nature: Political Struggles for the Global Commons*. New Brunswick, NJ: Rutgers Univ. Press. 252 pp.

Goldman M. 2000. *'Greening' the Globe: The New Politics and Science of the World Bank*. Soc. Dep., Univ. Ill. Urbana-Champaign

Gottlieb R. 1993. *The Transformation of the American Environmental Movement*. Washington, DC: Island Press. 413 pp.

Gould KA, Schnaiberg A, Weinberg AS, eds. 1996. *Local Environmental Struggles: Citizen Activism in the Treadmill of Production*. Cambridge, UK: Cambridge Univ. Press. 239 pp.

Gupta A. 1998. *Postcolonial Developments: Agriculture in the Making of Modern India*. Durham, NC: Duke Univ. Press. 409 pp.

Habermas J. 1984. *The Theory of Communicative Action*. Boston, MA: Beacon

Haraway DJ. 1991. *Simians, Cyborgs, and Women: The Reinvention of Nature*. New York: Routledge. 287 pp.

Haraway DJ. 1997a. Mice into wormholes: a comment on the nature of no nature. In *Citadels and Cyborgs: Anthropological Interventions in Emerging Sciences and Technologies*, ed. GL Downey, J Dumit, pp. 209–44. Santa Fe, NM: Sch. Am. Res. Press

Haraway DJ. 1997b. *Modest Witness at Second Millennium: FemaleMan Meets OncoMouse*. New York: Routledge. 287 pp.

Hartmann B. 1987. *Reproductive Rights and Wrongs: The Global Politics of Population Control and Contraceptive Choice*. New York: Harper & Row. 368 pp.

Harvey D. 1996. *Justice, Nature and the Geography of Difference*. Cambridge, MA: Blackwell. 468 pp.

Hayden CP. 1998. A biodiversity sampler for the millennium. In *Reproducing Reproduction*, ed. S Franklin, H Ragoné, pp. 173–206. Philadelphia, PA: Univ. Pa. Press

Heath D. 1997. Bodies, anti-bodies, and modest interventions. In *Citadels and Cyborgs: Anthropological Interventions in Emerging Sciences and Technologies*, ed. GL Downey, J Dumit, pp. 67–82. Santa Fe, NM: Sch. Am. Res. Press. 312 pp.

Hecht S, Cockburn A. 1990. *The Fate of the Forest: Developers, Destroyers and Defenders of the Amazon*. New York: HarperCollins. 357 pp.

Hess DJ. 1997. *Science Studies: An Advanced Introduction*. New York: N. Y. Univ. Press. 197 pp.

Hofrichter R, ed. 1993. *Toxic Struggles: The Theory and Practice of Environmental Justice*. Philadelphia, PA: New Society Publ. 260 pp.

Irwin A. 1995. *Citizen Science: A Study of People, Expertise, and Sustainable Development*. New York: Routledge. 198 pp.

Jackson C. 1994. Gender analysis and environmentalisms. In *Social Theory and the Global Environment*, ed. M Redclift, T Benton, pp. 113–49. New York: Routledge. 271 pp.

Jackson C. 1995. From conjugal contracts to environmental relations: some thoughts on labor and technology. *Inst. Dev. Stud. Bull.* 26:33–39

Jarosz L. 1996. Defining deforestation in Madagaskar. In *Liberation Ecologies: Environment, Development, Social Movements*, ed. R Peet, M Watts, pp. 148–64. New York: Routledge. 273 pp.

Joekes S, Leach M, Green C, eds. 1995. Gender relations and environmental change. *IDS Bull.* (Suppl.)26(1) 102 pp.

Latour B. 1993. *We Have Never Been Modern*. Cambridge, MA: Harvard Univ. Press. 157 pp.

Leach M. 1991. Engendering environments: understanding the West African forest zone. *IDS Bull.* 22:17–24

Leach M. 1994. *Rainforest Relations: Gender and Resource Use Among the Mende of Gola, Sierra Leone*. Washington, DC: Smithsonian Inst. Press. 272 pp.

Leach M, Fairhead J. 1995. Ruined settlements and new gardens: gender and soil ripening among Kuranko farmers in the forest-savanna transition zone. *IDS Bull.* 26:24–32

Leach M, Joekes S, Green C. 1995. Gender relations and environmental change. *IDS Bull.* 26:1–8

LeFebvre H. 1991. *The Production of Space.* Oxford, UK: Blackwell. 454 pp.

Leff E. 1995. *Green Production: Toward an Environmental Rationality.* New York: Guilford. 168 pp.

Luke TW. 1997. *Ecocritique: Contesting the Politics of Nature, Economy, and Culture.* Minneapolis, MN: Univ. Minn. Press. 253 pp.

Mackenzie F. 1995. Selective silence: a feminist encounter with the environmental discourse in colonial Africa. In *Power of Development,* ed. J Crush, pp. 100–12. New York: Routledge. 324 pp.

Martin E. 1994. *Flexible Bodies: Tracking Immunity in American Culture from the Days of Polio to the Age of AIDS.* Boston, MA: Beacon. 320 pp.

Martin E. 1998. Fluid bodies, managed nature. In *Remaking Reality: Nature at the Millenium,* ed. B Braun, N Castree, pp. 64–83. New York: Routledge. 295 pp.

Mellor M. 1997. *Feminism and Ecology.* New York: N. Y. Univ. Press. 221 pp.

Merchant C. 1980. *The Death of Nature: Women, Ecology, and the Scientific Revolution.* San Francisco: Harper & Row

Merchant C. 1989. *Ecological Revolutions: Nature, Gender and Science in New England.* Chapel Hill, NC: Univ. N. C. Press

Merchant C. 1992. *Radical Ecology.* London: Routledge. 276 pp.

Mies M, Shiva V. 1993. *Ecofeminism.* London: Zed Books. 328 pp.

Mohai P. 1992. Men, women, and the environment: an examination of the gender gap in environmental concern and activism. *Soc. Nat. Resour.* 5:1–19

Mohanty CT, Russo A, Torres L. 1991. *Third World Women and the Politics of Feminism,* Bloomington, IN: Ind. Univ. Press

Mol APJ. 1995. *The Refinement of Pro-* duction: Ecological Modernization Theory in the Chemical Industry. Utrecht, The Netherlands: Van Arkel. 452 pp.

Mol APJ, Spaargaren G. 2000. Ecological modernisation theory in debate: a review. *Environ. Polit.* 9: In press

Moore DS. 1996. Marxism, culture and political ecology: environmental struggles in Zimbabwe's Eastern Highlands. In *Liberation Ecologies,* ed. R Peet, M Watts, pp. 125–147. New York: Routledge. 273 pp.

O'Connor J. 1988. Capitalism, nature, socialism: a theoretical introduction. *Capital. Nat. Soc.* 1:11–38

O'Connor J. 1994. Is sustainable capitalism possible? In *Is Capitalism Sustainable? Political Economy and the Politics of Ecology,* ed. M O'Connor, 152–175. New York: Guilford

O'Connor J. 1998. *Natural Causes: Essays in Ecological Marxism.* New York: Guilford. 350 pp.

O'Connor M. 1993. On the misadventures of capitalist nature. *Capital. Nat. Soc.* 4:7–40

O'Connor M, ed. 1994. *Is Capitalism Sustainable? Political Economy and the Politics of Ecology.* New York: Guilford. 283 pp.

Ong A. 1999. *Flexible Citizenship: The Cultural Logics of Transnationality.* Durham, NC: Duke Univ. Press. 322 pp.

Ozanne LK, Humphrey CR, Smith PM. 1999. Gender, environmentalism, and interest in forest certification: Mohai's paradox revisited. *Soc. Nat. Resour.* 12:613–22

Peet R, Watts M, eds. 1996. *Liberation Ecologies: Environment, Development, Social Movements.* New York: Routledge. 273 pp.

Peluso NL. 1992. *Rich Forests, Poor People: Resource Control and Resistance in Java.* Berkeley, CA: Univ. Calif. Press. 321 pp.

Peluso NL. 1993. Coercing conservation? The politics of state resource control. *Glob. Environ. Chang.* 3:199–217

Pickering A. 1995. *The Mangle of Practice: Time, Agency and Science.* Chicago, IL: Univ. Chicago Press. 281 pp.

Pickering A. 1996. Further beyond the society/nature divide: a comment on Freudenburg, Frickel, and Gramling. *Sociol. Forum* 11:151–57

Pulido L. 1996. *Environmentalism and Economic Justice: Two Chicano Struggles in the Southwest.* Tucson, AZ: Univ. Ariz. Press. 282 pp.

Redclift M, Benton T, eds. 1994. *Social Theory and the Global Environment.* New York: Routledge. 271 pp.

Redclift M, Woodgate G, eds. 1997. *The International Handbook of Environmental Sociology.* Cheltenhaum, UK: Elgar. 485 pp.

Rocheleau D, Ross L. 1995. Trees as tools, trees as text: struggles over resources in Zamrana-Chacuey, Dominican Republic. *Antipode* 27:407–28

Rocheleau DE. 1995. Gender and biodiversity: a feminist political ecology perspective. *IDS Bull.* 26:9–16

Rose H. 1998. Moving on from both state and consumer eugenics. In *Remaking Reality: Nature at the Millennium,* ed. B Braun, N Castree, pp. 84–99. New York: Routledge. 295 pp.

Salleh A. 1997. *Ecofeminism as Politics: Nature, Marx and the Postmodern.* London: Zed Books. 208 pp.

Schaeffer RK. 1997. *Understanding Globalization: The Social Consequences of Political, Economic and Environmental Change.* Lanham, MD: Rowman & Littlefield. 360 pp.

Schaeffer RK. 1999. Success and impasse: the environmental movement in the United States and around the world. In *Ecology and the World-System,* ed. WL Goldfrank, D Goodman, A Szasz, pp. 189–211. London: Greenwood. 295 pp.

Scheper-Hughes N. 1992. *Death Without Weeping: The Violence of Everyday Life in Brazil.* Berkeley, CA: Univ. Calif. Press. 614 pp.

Schnaiberg A, Gould KA. 1994. *Environment and Society: The Enduring Conflict.* New York: St. Martin's. 255 pp.

Schroeder RA. 1995. Contradictions along the commodity road to environmental stabiliza-

tion: foresting Gambian gardens. *Antipode* 27:325–42

Scott D, Willits FK. 1994. Environmental attitudes and behavior. *Environ. Behav.* 26:239–60

Shah MK, Shah P. 1995. Gender, environment and livelihood security: an alternative viewpoint from India. *IDS Bull.* 26:75–82

Shiva V. 1989. *Staying Alive: Women, Ecology, and Development.* London: Zed Books. 224 pp.

Smith N. 1984. *Uneven Development: Nature, Capital and the Production of Space.* Oxford, UK: Blackwell. 295 pp.

Smith N. 1998. Nature at the millennium: production and re-enchantment. In *Remaking Reality: Nature at the Millennium,* ed. B Braun, N Castree, pp. 271–85. New York: Routledge. 295 pp.

Sonnenfeld DA, 1998. From brown to green? Late industrial, social conflict, and adoption of environmental technologies in Thailand's pulp industry. *Organ. Environ.* 11:59–87. 289 pp.

Soper K. 1995. *What is Nature? Culture, Politics and the Nonhuman.* Oxford, UK: Blackwell. 289 pp.

Spaargaren G, Mol APJ. 1992. Sociology, environment, and modernity: ecological modernization as a theory of social change. *Soc. Nat. Resour.* 5:323–44

Starhawk. 1990. Power, authority and mystery: ecofeminism and earth-based spirituality. In *Reweaving the World,* ed. I Diamond, GF Orenstein, pp. 73–86. San Francisco, CA: Sierra Club. 320 pp.

Sturgeon N. 1997. *Ecofeminist Natures: Race, Gender, Feminist Theory, and Political Action.* New York: Routledge. 260 pp.

Szasz A. 1994. *Ecopopulism: Toxic Waste and the Movement for Environmental Justice.* Minneapolis, MN: Univ. Minn. Press. 216 pp.

Szasz A, Meuser M. 1997. Environmental inequalities: literature review and proposals for new direction in research and theory. *Curr. Sociol.* 45:99–120

Taylor PJ, Buttel FH. 1992. How do we know we have global environmental problems? Science and the globalization of environmental discourse. *Geoforum* 23:405–16

Toledo V. 1989. The ecological crisis: a second contradiction of capitalism. *Capital. Nat. Soc.* 3:84–88

Treichler PA. 1999. *How to Have Theory in an Epidemic: Cultural Chronicles of AIDS.* Durham, NC: Duke Univ. Press. 477 pp.

Watts M. 1990. *Land Degredation and Society.* (Review) *Capitalism, Nat. Soc.* 3:123–31

Watts M. 1998. Nature as artifice and artifact. In *Remaking Reality: Nature at the Millennium*, ed. B Braun, N Castree, pp. 243–68. New York: Routledge. 295 pp.

Wilkie T. 1996. Genes 'R' Us. In *Future Natural: Nature/Science/Culture*, ed. G Robertson, M Mash, L Tickner, J Bard, B Curtis, et al., pp. 133–45. New York: Routledge. 310 pp.

Williams R. 1980. *Problems in Materialism and Culture: Selected Essays.* London: Verso. 277 pp.

Wynne B. 1994. Scientific knowledge and the global environment. In *Social Theory and the Global Environment*, ed. M Redclift, T Benton, pp. 169–89. New York: Routledge. 271 pp.

Yearley S. 1994. Social movements and environmental change. In *Social Theory and the Global Environment*, ed. M Redclift, T Benton, New York: Routledge. 271 pp.

Annu. Rev. Sociol. 2000. 26:585–609

SOCIALISM AND THE TRANSITION IN EAST AND CENTRAL EUROPE: The Homogeneity Paradigm, Class, and Economic Inefficiency

Linda Fuller

Department of Sociology, University of Oregon, Eugene, Oregon 97403-1291;
e-mail: lofuller@oregon.uoregon.edu

Key Words working class, intelligentsia, transition politics, epistemology, work

■ **Abstract** The homogeneity (mass-elite) paradigm exerts inordinate influence over social research on East and Central European socialism and its transition. I explore the epistemological and methodological underpinnings of this paradigm and argue that it has masked the importance of class relations for grasping the dynamics of these societies. I help retrieve class in general, and the working class in particular, from the analytic obscurity to which the homogeneity paradigm has relegated them by juxtaposing workers' and intellectuals' perceptions of economic inefficiency. Finally, I suggest ways that inattention to class under socialism has retarded understanding of the political struggles that have accompanied its demise.

INTRODUCTION

Much of the scholarship on East and Central Europe begins, whether explicitly or implicitly, from an assumption of social homogeneity. In saying this I mean to draw attention to the fact that, aside from a minuscule political elite who thoroughly monopolize all forms of power, these societies are understood to be composed of an amorphous and largely undifferentiated mass, a sociologically lifeless abstraction. Originally associated with totalitarian analyses of socialism (Ekiert 1999:300; Lane 1996:136, 139), this oversimplified view has survived periodic theoretical and empirical challenges and indeed seems to have been revived in their wake (Lane 1996:136–37; Crowley 1997:209, n. 14). The homogeneous paradigm continues to exert, if sometimes more subtly, a perceptible influence on the burgeoning number of studies of the wrenching post-socialist transitions in which countries of the region now find themselves. While the hegemony of the paradigm has never been total, its imprints on our social understanding of the area are deeper and more plentiful than is often acknowledged.

0360-0572/00/0815-0585$14.00

Although the perception of uniformity has always obscured many significant social fissures and complexities within East and Central Europe, I limit my focus to class. In the general spirit of Konrád & Szelényi's (1979) argument, I understand the fundamental class division plaguing socialism in these countries, which has not disappeared in successor formations, to run between workers and intellectuals. I define the intelligentsia as all those with college or university degrees *and* all those with top and mid-level decision-making and management posts in government, administrative, economic, educational, political, and mass organizations and units. For some years before socialism disintegrated, the overlap between these two groups was considerable throughout East and Central Europe. In the following section I examine how the homogeneous habit of thought is associated with a research approach that begins and ends with the epistemological and methodological standpoint of the region's intellectual class. A principal intent of this section is to suggest that the cause of sound social knowledge about East and Central Europe would be better served were researchers more modest in their use of the homogeneous paradigm and more cognizant of its influence on their scholarship.

The second and third sections draw on disparate strands in the literature on socialism and its transition to help retrieve class in general, and the working-class in particular, from the analytic obscurity to which the homogeneous paradigm has relegated them. These discussions center around economic inefficiency, a topic at the center of many debates about East and Central European socialism and its transition in the countries on which I concentrate: Bulgaria, Romania, and Hungary, as well as the Soviet Union, the German Democratic Republic, and Czechoslovakia, and their successors. These sections underscore how different from, and at times diametrically opposed to one another, the views of workers and intellectuals were on this subject. My larger purpose in highlighting this contrast is neither to adjudicate whose perceptions are closer to reality nor to minimize the many differences within each class, but rather to offer one clear illustration of the significance and persistence of the socialist class divide.

The final two sections suggest that the damage done by the reigning paradigm goes beyond mere inattention to and ignorance of class in East and Central European socialist societies. These deficiencies in our understanding of socialism have, in turn, hobbled analyses of one question sure to occupy scholars for some time: How and why did these social systems disintegrate? In concluding, I address working-class political involvement in the simultaneous processes of social, economic, and political collapse and reconfiguration in the region, one facet of this complex and multidimensional question.

HOMOGENEITY AND CLASS, EPISTEMOLOGY AND METHODOLOGY

That the homogeneous paradigm has been produced largely from the epistemological standpoint of intellectuals does not, in and of itself, distinguish it from most other knowledge about social life. Yet in light of the substantive content of this paradigm, it is inadvisable to dismiss the relationship between know-ledge producers and knowledge produced as unextraordinary and thus befitting no further comment. According to the homogeneous paradigm, East and Central European societies are best regarded as places where virtually everyone, save a tiny political elite, belongs to the same sociologically faceless and nondescript assem-blage. Considered another way—and this is the basis of my major epistemological worry—many East and Central European intellectuals who have created know-ledge about the area have generated a particular understanding that encourages us to think of knowledge producers themselves as largely indistinguishable from nearly everyone else. Many scholars from outside the area have joined the same paradigmatic chorus—indeed some must be counted among its founders—thereby reinforcing the flattened view of the region's social landscape.

The hegemony of the undifferentiated depiction of East and Central Europe is accomplished and reproduced in a variety of covert and overt, simple and more complicated ways. Often the notion of homogeneity is advanced through the juxta-position of undefined and unexamined descriptors, which serve as semantic stand-ins for this unvaried vision of society, and even scholars whose work otherwise casts some doubt on the utility of the homogeneous paradigm, sometimes revert to the use of labels that reinforce it (Lane 1996:124; Curry 1988:495; Bonnell 1989:311, 313, 314; Kennedy 1992:38, 39). "Elite" and "mass" are the most com-mon of these, though authors who focus on the socialist period on occasion opt for alternative terms, which nonetheless convey the same uniform meaning. "Ben-eficiaries" and "victims," "nomenclature" and "others," "party people" and "non-party people" belong on this list (Tökés 1996:11; Pano 1997:304; Curry 1988:490, 495; Cook 1993:3; Kostecki & Mrela 1984:138; Staniszkis 1979:182, 183, 187; Parrott 1997:13). The use of terminology connoting homogeneity did not end with socialism. Transition scholarship, however, demonstrates growing preference for "the public," "citizens," "public opinion", and, most recently, "the electorate" as referents that unite the overwhelming majority of the region's inhabitants into a single, sociologically undifferentiated group (Schöpflin 1991:235; Parrott 1997:2; Offe 1997:38, 73, 83; Kluegel & Mason 1999:41; Wolicki 1995:75; Jasiewicz 1995:149; Tökés 1997:380).

The cause of social homogeneity is advanced in other ways as well. Many studies of political culture, a concept in which Dawisha (1997:51) reports a resur-gence of interest, fall into this trap (McFalls 1995:Ch 4, Parrott 1997:21–22). This happens because political cultures are commonly perceived as conglomerates of politically relevant attitudes, value systems, and behaviors held more or less uni-versally within a particular unit. In terms of the ease with which it lumps nearly everyone into a single social heap, a concept like "East German political culture" is thus just as successful as the "East German masses." Institutionalists do not nec-essarily fare any better. Róna-Tas, for instance, despite his stated desire to move beyond a simplistic elite-mass analysis of Hungary, ends up perpetuating his own brand of homogeneous socialism by centering his inquiry around universal state employment, "the central fact of life for *almost all adults* under communist rule," which reduced "*the entire population*" to wage labor" (Róna-Tas 1997:4, 5; my italics). As with many analyses based on political culture, his glazes over a great deal of social difference with a frosting of homogeneity.

For a number of reasons civil society, "one of the more fashionable concepts in the context of Central and Eastern Europe" (Schöpflin 1991:240), bears a more complex and ambiguous relationship to the homogeneity paradigm. This is partly because, when it comes to the social identity of those who actually create and comprise civil society, a topic often avoided entirely, the literature displays a contradictory bifurcation. On the one hand, civil society is seen as the province of narrow bands, small pockets, and tiny circles of dissident intellectuals (Kennedy 1992:51, 54; Schöpflin 1991:224; Torpey 1995:186; Parrott 1997:13, 38, n. 99; Tismaneanu 1997:409; 427–43). On the other, authors use the term as another proxy for the monotonous social mass, of which the homogeneous paradigm understands nearly everyone in East and Central Europe to be a member. As examples, we find civil society considered to be the articulation of society's interests independent of the state and the representative of "a higher ethics and morality," rather than "any particular fraction, or class of society" (Schöpflin 1991:241; Szelényi et al 1997:207; Iankova 1998:240; Meininger & Radoeva 1996:47). Kennedy's (1990) discussion highlights the pitfalls likely to await any attempt to reconcile these two highly inconsistent conceptions of "civil society as virtually no one" and "civil society as virtually everyone." For Kennedy, civil society in Eastern Europe depends for its formation and democratic vitality on critical intellectuals. He further reinforces, though unintentionally, an exclusive conception of civil society by detailing how Polish physicians and peace activists, small minorities of the population, become critical intellectuals. But at the same time, in describing these new members of civil society as "ordinary individuals" and mere "people" (Kennedy 1990:281, 300), Kennedy reverts to the mass notion of East and Central European civil societies as comprised of a wide swatch of citizens of equal social prospect.

Given my discussion thus far, it should come as little surprise that many intellectuals who produce knowledge about East and Central Europe assume the right to speak for everyone in the region with far less hesitation than they might have, had the content of the elite-mass paradigm not encouraged them to view the lives, experiences, opinions, and interests of the region's intellectuals as analogous to those of almost everyone else. The logic here is unassailable. So long as nearly everyone is in the same social boat, what should it matter that it is only from the intelligentsia that we learn about the area, or that outside scholars dutifully reproduce these same voices as those of society in general? Because intellectuals are principal producers of academic social knowledge of all types, the danger of overexposure to their renditions of complex social formations is never completely absent. In other instances, however, the content of guiding paradigms can help temper this epistemological danger. But in the case of East and Central Europe, the thread of homogeneity weaving so prominently through our knowledge base magnifies this risk (Burawoy 1989:32, n. 40; Daskalov 1996:80; Burawoy 1996:97).

A number of troubling, even contradictory, practices accompany the paradigm-induced ease with which intellectuals assume the right to speak for everyone else in analyses of East and Central Europe. Sometimes, authors simply redefine inclusive terms like "people" to be synonymous with the much narrower social category of intellectuals. "Hungary's political transformation . . . was facilitated by people and their ideas for change. By 'people' I mean professional political, academic, and literary elites and unattached intellectuals" (Tökés 1996:167; Frentzel-Zagórska & Zagórski 1989:96). We hear scholars, under cover of the paradigm, over-eagerly delivering all manner of pronouncements on what "the masses" think, feel, do, want, need, and care about, which are at least debatable and at most challenged by some credible evidence (Schöpflin 1991:249; Kennedy 1992:65; Torpey 1995:10; Offe 1997:38; Judt 1988:207; Djilas 1998:301). Finally, we detect an air of superiority in some statements about intellectuals and a patronizing tone in many of those referring to everyone else. "That the introduction of property rights and market mechanisms," Offe (1997:38) informs us, "is in the interest of society as a whole is, however, typically not reliably recognized and appreciated by the empirical will of the majority of the population" (Kennedy 1990:287, 299; Kostecki & Mrela 1984:137, quoting Sztompka; Baylis 1998:299; Kurczewska 179, n. 11).

Of course, the political intelligentsia under socialism has long been criticized for speaking on behalf of the rest of society (Kennedy 1990:282; Djilas 1998:179, 296–297; Stark & Bruszt 1998:27, 40, 41). But, as the preceding reveals, many scholars who have published before and after the transition, who study different countries, and who harbor a variety of political persuasions, many critical of the socialist political elite of the region, have followed suit. Nor has this inclination to speak for everyone been limited to the socialist political intelligentsia and the heterogeneous group of scholars who write about the area. East Central European dissident intellectual activists often do the same. "What distinguishes all these [East German, Czech, and Slovak church leaders, scholars, lawyers, former communists, bankers, etc.]," according to Baylis (1998:298–99), "is their ability to speak for very different needs and feelings in their population" (Tökés 1996:306; Stark & Bruszt 1998:28, 40, 214, n. 41; Tismaneanu 1997:428; Meininger & Radovea 1996:60; Kennedy 1992:38, 51). And, insofar as opinion polls capture the thinking of additional intellectuals who have not necessarily produced written knowledge of or been politically active in the area, we encounter a similar proclivity. Thus, according to Kurczewska (1995:179, n. 11), 37% of a national sample of college-educated Poles "believed that intellectuals should act in behalf of society and offer values on society's behalf."

Although such epistemologial concerns are always intertwined with method-ological ones, it is worth focusing more specifically on the latter for a moment. Here my principal discomfort is the remarkably high proportion of scholarship on East and Central Europe that relies exclusively, or near exclusively, on primary evidence gathered from or about the minority of individuals I have defined as in-tellectuals. Goodwyn (1991:xxiv), at least, has detected an even more worrisome tendency to offer no substantiating evidence at all in some cases, since "in views from afar, supporting evidence is not presumed to be needed."

Explanations for the narrowness of the evidence vary. The most disconcerting revolve around the epistemological matters broached above. If intellectuals feel especially entitled by the substance of the paradigm to speak on behalf of everyone, why should the collection of data from beyond their own class circle be of pressing concern? In addition, it is usually easier and simpler for intellectuals to establish research contacts with other intellectuals, whether supporters or opponents of the powerful. In my experience in the GDR these people sought me out, indeed were sometimes difficult to shake, whereas workers were usually far less curious about who I was and what I was up to. Moreover, despite my determination to gather data from nonintellectual sources, I found that being among people with whom I shared the most was troublingly seductive. Unfortunately, while in other research situations, reigning knowledge paradigms can provide a strong antidote to such predilections, the homogenous paradigm serves to encourage them.

A more familiar explanation offered for the socially restrictive character of much data on socialist countries is that these societies were closed, heavily policed, and tightly censored (Siegelbaum & Walkowitz 1995:1; Crowley 1997:3; Goodwyn 1991:vii–xxx). Access to evidence from non-party, non-party–approved, and non-intellectual sources, when it could be had at all, was severely limited. Yet this difficulty, which I do not minimize, cannot explain why, once socialism collapsed and evidence from expanded sectors of the population became more accessible, so many analyses continue to be crafted from a scaffold of intellectual data. Thankfully, this seems to be changing; post-communist studies of workers and scholarship self-consciously based on information emanating from beyond the socially narrow confines of the intelligentsia are more common (Goodwyn 1991; Laba 1991; Crowley 1997; Błaszkiewicz et al 1999; Creed 1998; Burawoy & Lukács 1992). But the death throes of scholars' data-gathering and methodological habits have been prolonged. For example, two major works on Hungary by Tökés (1996) and Róna-Tas (1997) are based largely on transcripts of Central Committee and Politburo deliberations, party and ministerial archives, parliamentary minutes, interviews with policy makers, top party leaders, and private entrepreneurs, and, in the case of Tökés (1996:xiii, xiv), meetings with the "crème de la crème" of the reform intelligentsia and his work as a senior advisor to the foreign minister. Data for three important volumes on the GDR by Torpey (1995), Joppke (1995), and Maier (1997) come from socially analogous sources, and, even though McFalls' (1995:13–15, 191) work on the GDR utilizes data from over two hundred survey responses from "ordinary East Germans," nearly 60% of these people turn out to have college or university degrees, a sure sign of a sample heavily weighted toward the intelligentsia. Finally, so far as I can tell, a significant portion of the primary evidence undergirding Lane's (1996) study of the rise and fall of socialism relies on interviews with communist-era political intellectuals.

Objections may be raised that such research projects intend to produce knowledge about intellectuals or that they deal with topics about which intellectual sources simply have the most to tell us. Yet wherever scholars hint at broader foci, for example, through their titles [*The Rise and Fall of State Socialism (Lane 1996), The Dissolution: The Crisis of Communism and the End of East Germany* (Maier 1997)], this argument does not satisfy me. Whether intended or not, such titles based on such data advance, however implicitly, the cause of the uniformity paradigm and embolden knowledge producers to promote their own interpretations as those of everyone else, which is one of the paradigm's most discomforting by-products. All the while, the principal point is worth remembering: We can never produce credible scholarship on matters about which we have gathered no evidence.

Finally, as the following otherwise provocative piece of scholarship exemplifies, even when the research agenda has more to do with workers than intellectuals, and even when authors themselves are aware that information on worker-related topics is sorely lacking, evidence can still end up heavily skewed toward what Goodwyn (1991:xxvi) terms the "evidential desert" of intellectual sources. Thus Ost & Weinstein's (1999) article on governance changes in post-communist Polish workplaces is based largely on surveys of managers, workers elected or appointed to management bodies, and trade union officials. Rank-and-file workers are mostly ignored as a data source. Even in the one subsection that does focus on "Polish workers, in general, not union activists" (Ost & Weinstein 1999:7), the authors, despite the revelation that they had engaged in field research in over twenty enterprises, rely on information from two attitudinal surveys conducted by other people. In making such methodological choices, Ost & Weinstein pass up an all-too-rare opportunity to broaden our knowledge of East Central European societies, based on close-in and unmediated evidence from the working-class majority.

ECONOMIC INEFFICIENCY FROM THE STANDPOINT OF INTELLECTUALS

From the perspectives of a great many intellectuals, those hailing from East and Central Europe and those analyzing the area from the outside, those who have written about the region and those who have not, socialist economies were monstrously inefficient, and most detect vestiges of this inefficiency in the transition period. On this matter even partial dissenters are few (Burawoy & Lukács 1985; Szelényi & Szelényi 1994:218–21; Spenner et al 1988:604). Many times intellectuals convey this judgment haphazardly and without amplification by qualifying nouns like "economy" and "enterprise" with a string of uncomplimentary adjectives. Favorites include not only inefficient but also irrational, unsustainable, uncompetitive, submarginal, dismal, decaying, closed, corrupt, distorted, bloated, subsidy-dependent, crisis-ridden, self-suffocating, obsolete, and unsophisticated (Georgescu 1988:69, 75, 77; Judt 1988:201; Pantev 1996:18; Offe 1997:13; Gerber & Hout 1998:36; Clarke et al 1994:182; Staniszkis 1979:167, 170, 171, 186; Clarke & Donova 1999:214; Dawisha 1997:47; Pano 1997:297; Glasman 1994:69; Ekiert 1997:304).

Other times the meaning of inefficiency emerges in more thorough and systemic discussions. Some intellectuals, for instance, associate it with low productivity, outdated and inferior technology, unbalanced and declining growth, lack of innovation, high debt, waste, misallocation of resources, and poor quality. For others, inefficiency acquires more organizational meanings, such as lack of coordination between economic units and actors, undersupply of production inputs, centralization, bureaucratization, monopolization, and the inability to self-monitor. But beyond such understandings of socialist and post-socialist economic inefficiency, intellectuals often stress one other—bad workers. There is an obvious contradiction here. To associate bad workers with economic inefficiency is, on some level, to acknowledge the existence of class, something the homogenous paradigm disputes. The point I mean to emphasize here, however, is that, despite this contradiction, the connection intellectuals often draw between bad workers and economic inefficiency stands as strong testimony to the importance of the class divide, for, as we soon discover, it contrasts sharply with working-class perspectives on what efficiency means.

For some intellectuals, five Soviet factory workers come to typify the shortcomings of the socialist working class:

> Ivanov left without permission before work had finished; Grigor'ev followed Ivanov's example; Gretyukov came 10 minutes late twice in September; Piskunov, a fitter, goes walking around the shop during work hours. He does this on average 40 to 60 minutes a day. Pashkevich loves to stroll around the shop with 'his hands in his pockets'. This is putting it mildly: one of his strolls lasts 10 to 20 minutes. (Filtzer 1996:26 quoting a factory newspaper)

The intellectual-derived list of worker failings does not end here, however. Regularly, even viscerally, accounts refer to workers as dependent, dawdling, irresponsible, egoistic, unmotivated, undisciplined, insubordinate, and uncontrollable drunks and thieves. Intellectuals seem rarely to tire of portraying how workers likewise withhold effort, go shopping during the work day, lack regard for the quality of their work, and are quite prepared to take leisurely lunches when they show up for work at all (Kotkin 1996:6; Filtzer 1996:9, 10, 17, 18, 26, n. 12; Creed 1998:176, 198, 217, 257; Crowley 1997:15, 56, 64, 96, 164, 167, 168; Clarke et al 1994:197; Burawoy 1989:23; Róna-Tas 1997:55–57, 59, 154–55; Laba 1991:123). According to Filtzer (1996:20), a scholar particularly alert to workers' defects, "Negligence also took its toll." Given the prevalence of such characterizations of workers' attitudes and behaviors, one sometimes wonders how socialist economies ever produced or delivered any products or services at all, let alone inefficiently.

While there is no question that students of East and Central Europe have made immense contributions to our knowledge of the structural underpinnings of inefficiency in socialist and transition economies (Nove 1983; Kornal 1986, 1992), it should come as no surprise, given their readiness to associate economic inefficiency with bad workers, that many intellectuals also view workers as, to some degree, responsible for the problem. Certainly not a few have qualified this stance, perceiving the causal connection between bad workers and economic inefficiency as indirect, partial, or neither deliberate nor irrational on workers' part (Tökés 1996:109; Creed 1998:198; Crowley 1997:55; Pano 1997:304; Filtzer 1996:16, 26, quoting *Pravda*). Still, in the course of assigning workers some liability, intellectuals have expanded the previous list of ways worker behaviors and qualities might result in economic inefficiency. As examples, Spenner and his co-authors (1998:107), puzzled by their finding that layoffs have a negative impact on efficiency in some Bulgarian firms undergoing transition, suggest part of the reason may be workers' uncertainty about their future employment, which could lower their productivity. And the fact that workers exercised even a "limited" amount of control over their own labor under socialism becomes, for Filtzer (1996:12, 19), "a source of the myriad dysfunctions and disruptions which plagued production and distribution."

Intellectuals are far less eager to assign themselves any blame for economic inefficiency, and, when they do, their discussions are notable for their comparative lack of both elaboration and vehemence (Georgescu 1988;76; Burawoy 1996:86–87; Lane 1996:101; Róna-Tas 1997:33; Dimitrov 1996:107; Filtzer 1996:20). In other instances, intellectual culpability is chalked up to guilt by association. Thus, Tökés (1996:261) notes that some socialist economists view managers' negative effects on economic performance as attributable to their membership in an "unholy alliance" with workers and unionists. Rather than making a palpable contribution to economic inefficiency, as workers are often understood to do, intellectuals are more likely to apprehend themselves as the ones who struggle to keep the economy afloat.

Yet the sharpest disagreement between intellectuals and workers on the causes of economic inefficiency, both before and after the socialist era, revolves not around bad workers but around remunerative equality. Again, to posit remunerative equality as a cause of inefficiency reveals a contradiction, for in order to make such an argument, intellectuals must to some extent acknowledge class, thereby renouncing the homogeneity proposition. This contradiction notwithstanding, because intellectuals' and workers' views on this matter are so discordant, the intellectual stance on remunerative equality and economic inefficiency simultaneously suggests the depth of the class divide.

The intellectual argument regarding economic inefficiency and remunerative equality has several variants, but most begin from the premise that, under socialism, intellectuals were decidedly underpaid in comparison to workers. Some even complain they were underrewarded in absolute terms, and that, despite mounting claims to the contrary (Róna-Tas 1997:205; Clarke et al 1994:197, 201–6, 214 n. 36; Spenner et al 1998:605; Matějů 1999:18; Słomczyński & Shabad 1997:170), the "pauperization" of the intelligentsia has continued into the subsequent era (Frentzel-Zagórska & Zagórski 1989:94; Daskalov 1996:83). Intellectual complaints on this score are periodically punctuated with what, in their judgment, are humiliating examples of the absurdities to which remunerative equality leads– theoretical physicists earning less than gutter cleaners and research scientists forced into prostitution (Gerber & Hout 1998:37; Siegelbaum & Walkowitz 1995:164; Crowley 1997:246, n. 11).

As in other class societies, intellectuals often employ human capital reasoning to support their case for higher relative pay. They invest more in acquiring or they possess more skills, training, and education than workers, and they deserve a return commensurate with their trouble and accomplishments. In a less genteel version of the claim, intellectuals simply understand themselves to work harder, take more initiative, and be more critical than workers and therefore to be worthy of higher pay. The general director of a Russian chemical factory even attempted to justify widening wage differentials with a sort of perverted affirmative action logic. For years, he claimed, workers had earned much more than their supervisors, who had "suffered in silence." "Now it is your turn to suffer in silence," he told an undoubtedly skeptical work force (Clarke et al 1994:214, n. 38).

Some intellectuals reinforce their argument for a wider pay gap between classes by maintaining that their greater stock of human capital translates into greater productivity and hence greater economic efficiency (Ruble 1986:44). Vastly underresearched in the literature on socialist and transition economies, this linkage between human capital attributes, productivity, and efficiency requires intellectuals to embark upon a journey of faith on which few workers would accompany them. I would expect, however, that this last argument for the inegalitarian basis of economic efficiency undergirds the often vociferous intellectual support for actions that countered "dysfunctional" wage-levelling policies under socialism. Many intellectuals assume an analogous stance toward transition policies, supporting those that "accord priority to responding to the needs of the rich and successful" (Zloch-Christy 1996:153), and opposing inefficient "populist" policies associated with egalitarian moves such as income redistribution, collective ownership, and working-class wage increases (Zloch-Christy 1996:160; Crowley 1997:162; Clarke et al 1994:198, 201, 205; Lane 1996:161, 162, 168, 169; Comisso 1988:462–63; Fuller 1999:87–88; Słomczyński & Shabad 1997:186).

ECONOMIC INEFFICIENCY AS WORKERS SAW IT

Workers in East and Central Europe understood socialist economies to be inefficient in some of the same ways intellectuals did, and like intellectuals they have witnessed the persistence of many of these same inefficiencies into the transition period. In major ways, however, their perspectives on the relationship between economic inefficiency and effort, and of management, technology, discipline, remuneration systems, and other topics diverged notably from those of the intelligentsia, and recognition of the depth and breadth of these differences proves a good illustration of the social prominence of the class divide in the region.

We have seen how many intellectuals view bad workers both as an illustration and a cause of economic inefficiency. Yet neither the intellectual position that many workers judged it their "social right" not to work hard under socialism

(Connor 1991:147) nor the idea that workers are now daunted by the "grim prospect of competitive hard work" (Lasky 1991:22) jibes with workers' experiences or judgments. Both before and during the transition many workers have insisted, and observers with some knowledge of workers' lives have corroborated, that they work hard, sometimes very hard, at their paid jobs and that periods of idleness embarrass and anger rather than please them (Creed 1998:247; Szlajfer 1995:18–20; Clarke & Donova 1999; Burawoy and Lukács 1985:727, 734; Fuller 1999:42–44; Laba 1991:122–123; Ferguson 1998:460–61).

There are a number of reasons why workers often experienced their paid jobs as demanding under socialism. Not only had normal work weeks often been 20% longer than those in the West, but also overtime was commonly expected of many workers (Laba 1991:123; Fuller 1999:43; Róna-Tas 1997:59, 101, 154; Georgescu 1998:79; Jankowska 1995:317). Workers who were paid on a piece-rate system faced continuous norm increases. "Establish a record today, and it will be the norm tomorrow," a Ukrainian miner once told Siegelbaum & Walkowitz (1995:28). Not a few workers performed more than one job, whether at the same worksite, for example simultaneously tending multiple machines, or at a different work-site, sometimes in the second economy (Fuller 1999:190, n. 8; Burawoy 1996:81; Róna-Tas 1997:118, 154; Creed 1998:4, 104, 176; Tökés 1996:159). Shortages, the bane of the workday for many producers, were often implicated in these and many other experiences of hard work. They lay behind the uneven rhythm of labor, which workers found particularly tiring and stressful, and behind the phenomenon of "storming," which was the normal state of affairs for up to half the month in some workplaces, leaving workers in urgent need of "rest and repair" (Goodwyn 1991:56, 60; Filtzer 1996:126; Stark 1986:494). The absence of necessary and proper tools, machinery, materials, and labor made completing any job far more difficult. Electricians with insufficient wire, office workers without typewriter ribbons, sewage plant workers lacking proper protective clothing, steel workers forced to transport alloys by wheelbarrow because automatic chutes were inoperable, even farmworkers without enough produce crates, were commonplace situations throughout East and Central Europe (Fuller 1999:42; Creed 1998:87; Burawoy 1989:12). A GDR machinist explained it best: "Workers in the shops have always worked hard. On top of that, their work required much more energy than in the West, because they had to make gold out of shit" (Philipsen 1993:287).

More often than not, workers placed the blame for economic inefficiency not with themselves but with the intelligentsia. For workers, the critical link between the intellectuals and inefficiency, both during and especially before the transition, is the disorganization of the work process. From their perspectives, disorganization is the epitome of economic inefficiency, and they often judge bosses and bureaucrats, both at their worksites and above them, as responsible for this chaos. Especially under socialism, workers could see that the confusion at their workplaces sometimes stemmed as much from managerial powerlessness as managerial blunder. Nonetheless, workers regularly suggested, and at times adamantly insisted, otherwise.

We can infer this from their general comments on work and their superiors ("Many rank-and-file workers began to wonder whether we had idiots organizing our production. If we as workers understood [how badly things were organized], one would assume that someone who went to college should be able to grasp that as well" [Philipsen 1993:128]), and we know that such assessments have not automatically evaporated during the transition (Crowley 1997:233; Laba 1991:122–23; Siegelbaum & Walkowitz 1995:4; Clarke & Donova 1999:225; Clarke et al 1994:206; Curry 1988:501–503; Błaszkiewicz et al 1994:129). Workers also offered more specific formulations of the socialist link between the intelligentsia, disorganization, and economic inefficiency. For instance, they saw disorganization as a consequence of superiors who drew plans incorrectly or refused to schedule preventative equipment maintenance, who changed economic targets in mid-year, who hoarded labor, and who put little effort into marketing or design improvements. As a result of such management mistakes and miscalculations, workers witnessed production slow downs, job orders and projects abandoned or half completed, and the translation of their hard work into useful and desired products and services thwarted (Filtzer 1996:16, 21; Clarke & Donova 1999:237; Clarke et al 1994:199; Creed 1998:156, 181, 239). Workers also faulted the authoritarian and arbitrary management style of many bosses, which rarely solved production problems and often made them worse, for the turmoil at work (Burawoy 1989:18, 26; Curry 1988:503). While socialist management regularly shifted the blame for disorganization onto shortages, workers often did not buy this excuse. Bulgarian hay collectors instructed to show up to work with plum-picking buckets, GDR construction workers demolishing new construction because they received conflicting orders from multiple supervisors, Polish colonels telling plumbers how to fix broken pipes, party secretaries overwatering strawberries until they rotted, all these were examples of the maddening disorder that prevailed at their workplaces for which workers often judged their superiors, not shortages, responsible (Creed 1998:88, 103, 104; Laba 1991:122; Fuller 1999:46; Szlajfer 1995:21).

An additional example further illustrates how far apart workers and intellectuals were in their thinking on the causes of socialist economic inefficiency. Many intellectuals were unabashed technophiles. They associated the lack of up-to-date technology with inefficiency and regarded more advanced technology as one solution to socialist economic woes. Workers' outlook on this matter was more complicated. There were many instances in which they would like to have seen technological improvements at their workplaces. Yet, in many workers' judgment, management decisions about technology many times exacerbated, rather than alleviated, inefficiency. Workers often considered technologies ridiculously expensive, and, given the real-life workplace environments in which they knew they would operate, immensely impractical. High-tech cooling systems left rusting in the open air, robot technology, not estimated to pay for itself in 500 years, abandoned for lack of parts, steel mill technology requiring highly accurate, but impossible to attain, input calibrations in order to function properly, even a dough mixing machine that did not function correctly yet was inexplicably never returned, all seemed to workers foolhardy in the extreme (Fuller 1999:46; Filtzer 1996:27, n. 36; Burawoy 1996:86; Creed 1998:156–157; Burawoy 1989:17–18; Philipsen 1992:128). Such examples taught them that technology alone was too simple a prescription for reversing the spiral of inefficiency in which their economies were trapped.

Workers also understand disciplinary systems to contribute to economic inefficiency, and here too differences between their viewpoints and those of intellectuals are discernible. Many of the bad behaviors for which intellectuals have impugned workers, from the earliest decades of socialism through the transition, fall into the category of indiscipline (Róna-Tas 1997:56–57; Siegelbaum & Walkowitz 1995:100; Crowley 1997:96, 167, 168). From the perspectives of many intellectuals, socialist disciplinary systems were partially responsible for the widespread problem of indiscipline. Laws were full of loopholes; procedures were cumbersome; cases against workers were initiated too rarely, and when they were, penalties were lax and prosecutions few (Voskamp & Wittke 1991:359; Creed 1998:256, 257; Clarke et al 1994:180; Róna-Tas 1997:55–56, 101, 161; Crowley 1997:73, 164, 168, 169; Burawoy and Lukács 1985:732). Disciplinary systems needed drastic overhaul. The scope of offenses had to be broadened, and penalties had to be stiffened. Economic efficiency demanded it.

Workers, on the other hand, expressed a more nuanced view. As workers saw it, not only did most of them labor hard and well under far less than optimal circumstances but also many workers whom intellectuals labeled undisciplined had little choice about how they worked. How could they not be occasionally late to work when the only living quarters they could find were miles from their workplaces? Could playing cards at work really be considered indiscipline when there were either no orders to fill or necessary production inputs had not been delivered? How could they afford not to leave work early or take unauthorized mid-day breaks when shops were out of everything by the time work was over? (Filtzer 1996:18, 19; Crowley 1997:168; Fuller 1999:220, n. 31). More important, producers felt intellectuals did not acknowledge that workers themselves were extremely distressed by the few egregious violators who were a great burden and a danger to their co-workers but who were never fired. Drunks were merely reassigned to less desirable jobs; thieves only had their wages cut; even workers who were actually let go, something most everyone agreed was virtually impossible, usually found another job quickly, sometimes at the same factory, often for higher pay, and occasionally with compensation for unused vacation time (Crowley 1997:85, 168; Creed 1998:177; Philipsen 1992:291; Voskamp & Wittke 1991:359; Filtzer 1996:28, n. 48; Róna-Tas 1997:59). Individual workers undoubtedly disagreed over where to draw the line between indiscipline and indiscipline extreme enough to warrant termination. But to recognize no line at all, which is what many workers saw happening at their workplaces, was quite simply inefficient. The few outrageous, yet atypical, offenders wasted extraordinary amounts of their workmates' and their bosses' time and energy. Workers even complained that unions, when forced to devote so much time to defending total laggards, were unable to attend to the pressing needs of the remainder of workers, whose productivity suffered as a result.

Given these concerns, workers could not agree that indiscriminately tightening workplace disciplinary systems would do much to improve economic efficiency. Periodic attempts to do so during the socialist era, which have become more frequent and zealous during the transition, not only miss the point but also are counterproductive because they provoke worker resentment and resistance (Filtzer 1996:11, 26, n. 12; Lane 1996:101; Offe 1997:223, n. 33; Crowley 1997:164, 168, 169; Clarke et al 1994:186, 191, 198; Szlajfer 1995:20, 61–62, n. 22). Workers' lived experience of socialism had taught them that the cause of economic efficiency was far better served in any system by disciplinary procedures that differentiate between unavoidable and intentional indiscipline and that focus the spotlight on the few chronic and flagrant offenders who truly interfere with efficient production, rather than turning a floodlight on the majority of conscientious workers, upon whose best efforts and ongoing cooperation economic efficiency depends.

How pay differentials relate to socialist, and later post-socialist, economic efficiency is another topic on which the thinking of workers and intellectuals diverges. Workers did not concur with many intellectuals' human capital arguments linking wage equality to socialist economic inefficiency. In their view, such arguments obscured a more important issue. Workers were not primarily concerned about the damage to economic efficiency of remuneration systems that did not sufficiently reward people for prestigious job titles, higher education credentials, entrepreneurial traits, and so forth. Their principal apprehension was that socialist remuneration systems glossed over distinctions between *any* job well done and *any* job poorly done. Workers focused on how productively people actually used their labor, on the quantity and quality of the contributions they made at work, and for them economic efficiency was enhanced to the extent that those who contributed more were paid more.

Many workers, however, saw no straightforward correspondence between human capital attributes and how much and how well someone produced at work. Quite the contrary, they expressed deep reservations about the economic contributions of many intellectuals occupying managerial and professional positions, often describing them as ineffective, superfluous, and unproductive. Thus one Bulgarian claimed the agro-industrial complex in his village had over thirty officials, a "specialist for every type of agricultural activity," none of whom really did much (Creed 1998:77). Crowley (1997:44, 134) discovered Soviet coal miners to harbor a similar view that "bosses, after all produced nothing," while a part of each miner's labor went to support five to seven "parasites" in the managerial apparatus (Crowley 1997:135, 136; Burawoy 1996:86; Comisso 1988:464; Fuller 1999:29, 55; Bahro 1978:209; Siegelbaum & Walkowitz 1995:121–22). In other words, workers located an important source of inefficiency in remunerative systems that guaranteed the highest rewards to intellectuals who, though they had more formal education, higher status job descriptions, and so forth, did not appear to produce as much, or as much of value, as workers did. In workers' vision of economic efficiency, these things were no substitute for accomplishment as determinants of remuneration. This position helps explain workers' frequent criticism of socialist and post-socialist era schemes to promote income inequality, their repeated calls for reductions in the number and the remuneration levels of administrative and managerial staff during the transition, and perhaps even the empirical and anecdotal evidence from throughout the region that reveals widely held post-socialist preferences for reducing the gap between rich and poor (Crowley 1997:41, 57 243, n. 65; Clarke et al 1994:206; Laba 1991:40, 68, 162, 165; Fuller 1999:87–88, 200, n. 35; Siegelbaum & Walkowitz 1995:115; Szelényi et al 1996:472; Schöpflin 1991:247).

Perspectives on socialist economic functioning differed by class on one final count as well. Where many intellectuals were unlikely or unwilling to attribute any manner of efficiency to socialist economies, many workers' saw things differently. Along with incisive economic critiques, workers also spoke with pride about innovations at their workplaces, their ongoing acquisition of new skills, the quality of production, and high productivity levels at particular plants and on particular projects. They likewise praised a panoply of job-related benefits, for example paid sick and maternity leave, cheap meals, vacation spots, and emergency financial assistance, not to mention system-wide benefits such as high employment levels and the availability of affordable and varied public services (Siegelbaum & Walkowitz 1995:35–36; Fuller 1999:44, 60, 194–95, n. 7). For many workers these things constituted some evidence of socialist economic efficiency, even as intellectuals regularly argued such benefits and outcomes "coddled" and "controlled" workers, relegating them to a position of perpetual dependency on the state (Róna-Tas 1997:84; Glasman 1994; Fuller 1999:29). It was, in other words, socialism's most advantaged who were most inclined to dismiss socialist economies as unmitigated disasters, "disproven by history" (Offe 1997:189), and who are unable to conceive of changes wrought during the transition as "anything other than improvement" (Róna-Tas 1997:8; Schöpflin 1991:239). From workers' experience matters were not so clear cut. As suggested in Crowley's (1997:180) observation that socialism both "protected and enraged" them, many workers entertained more mixed, more complicated, and less narrow views of what economic efficiency was all about. Workers' equivocal reactions to developments during the transition are undoubtedly grounded in their ambivalent opinions of what their economies were like under socialism (Creed 1998:29, 73, 278; Fuller 1999:152–53; Słomczyński & Shabad 1997:188).

Workers detected efficiency in an economic system they otherwise understood as plagued by inefficiencies in one more important way. In contrast to some intellectuals, many workers perceived the amount of control they enjoyed over the socialist labor process, despite its limits and despite scholarly disagreements over its nature, as a cornerstone of efficiency, not inefficiency, in socialist economic systems (Filtzer 1996:17, 19; Burawoy 1989:18, 20; Clarke et al 1994:181, 182; Fuller 1999:123–26). On the one hand, workers' control meant that, for production to continue, producers were continuously required successfully to make, repair, and improve machinery and equipment without standard parts or preformulated plans, often acceptable products and services could not be produced or delivered at all unless resourceful workers, lacking sufficient or proper production inputs, could invent a way to do so. Exercise of this brand of workers' control varied by economic sector, gender, and skill level. Yet in the GDR at least, white-collar workers recounted "making everything from scratch" and "figuring out how to finish a report without the typewriter ribbon or the duplicating machine," just as blue-collar workers told of "making new things from old things or keeping old things going from new things" (Fuller 1999:123–24; Filtzer 1996:14, 21; Wierling 1996:54; Clarke & Donova 1999:228). In other words, day in and day out for decades, many workers had engaged in a number of the very same flexible, creative, enterprising, frugal, imaginative, and solution-oriented work practices that many intellectuals associate with economic efficiency.

A second brand of control socialist producers exercised was the self-management of their own labor. Workers' self-management meant that many producers continually made decisions about work and production that are routinely left to managers in capitalist settings. Thus we find references to socialist workers formulating their own job classifications, concocting their own division and integration of tasks, establishing and maintaining cooperative networks inside and outside the shop, overseeing discipline, determining production speeds and job assignments, deciding work and delivery schedules, arranging production sequences, determining the quality and mix of production, hiring co-workers, determining how pay should be divided, and even assuming some control over the amount of goods and services they produced and delivered. Surely it was in specialized work groups like the Hungarian VGMKs and in brigades, which elsewhere proliferated as socialism matured, that workers' self-management reached its apex (Creed 1998:153, 154, 180; Lane 1996:100; Róna-Tas 1997:149; Burawoy 1989:15). But self-management had long been part of the daily work experience of many who did not participate in such forms of work organization as well (Fuller 1999:125–26; Mitchell 1992:693; Filtzer 1996:14, 19, 23). Burawoy (1996:92) even maintains that workers' self-management has increased in some places during the transition, and others report forceful worker attempts to protect and increase self-management during the struggles that have everywhere accompanied the demise of socialism (Fuller 1999:114–20; Kennedy 1992:40). Soviet and Russian coal miners, some of whom expanded their conception of self-management to include workers' ownership and election of enterprise management, are a case in point (Crowley 1997).

From workers' perspectives, self-management was not just an obligatory response to an inefficient economy. It was also a noteworthy sign of system efficiency. Workers judged self-management economically rational and productive. They saw how it allowed for smooth, non-bureaucratized, and coordinated control and monitoring of work, and how it conserved time and resources and minimized conflict at the point of production. While many intellectuals defined precisely such outcomes as efficient, most never admitted any such connection between workers' self-management and socialist economic efficiency.

HOMOGENEITY AND WORKING-CLASS POLITICAL ACTIVISM

It is certainly a truism, though one of which it is good to remain mindful, that to comprehend the present social researchers must understand the past. Despite their different views on how the socialist past matters for understanding the present, this point has often been made with regard to East and Central Europe (Sørensen 1997:47; Stark & Bruszt 1998:5–7; Iankova 1998:257–58; Gerber & Hout 1998:37; Ekiert 1997:300, 337–38; Błaszkiewicz et al 1994:126–27). But the past can only help illuminate what succeeds it if we have gotten the past right, and, as I have argued, insofar as scholarship on East and Central Europe has been dominated by the homogenous view of socialism, we have not gotten the past right.

My particular concern has been how the attachment to homogeneity has concealed a deep social fissure between workers and intellectuals in socialist societies. The fact that this fundamental class fissure has been inadequately explored, indeed often ignored altogether, has meant serious misreadings and significant blind spots in our understanding of how and why East and Central European socialism unraveled. I fear the number of these to be potentially quite large, but in this and the following section I highlight only two. Both concern working-class politics, particularly in the earliest phases of socialism's collapse.

To begin with, compared to the voluminous analyses of what intellectuals were up to during this period, we know desperately little about any active political roles workers assumed. Too many scholars dismiss workers in a sentence or two as marginal to these historic struggles, mention their involvement in strikes, demonstrations, and so forth with little attempt to integrate working-class politics into their broader analyses, or seem willing to ascribe workers an influential role only by denying their class identity (Lane 1996:143; Dimitrov 1996:112; Georgescu 1988:93; Słomczyński & Shabad 1997:171; Tismaneanu 1997:414–15; Pantev 1996:21; Michnik 1995:234–35; Stark & Bruzst 1998:34). Even in the scholarship on Poland, the country where working-class activism is hardest to overlook, the homogenous paradigm encourages interpretations that de-emphasize working-class and highlight intellectual activism (Schöpflin 1991:244; Kennedy 1992:40). Insofar as scholars rely on versions of reality forwarded by dissident Polish intellectuals, this is understandable. Hence, Jacek Kuroń, one of the better known of this lot, has let it be known that he considers Solidarity his "brainchild" and that he was the one who "dreamed up" the Interfactory Strike Committee (Jankowska 1995:293, 296; Goodwyn 1991:324; Kennedy 1990:289).

The homogeneity paradigm interferes with the ability to uncover political activism among East and Central European workers in at least two ways. First, it deflects our research gaze away from the social nooks and crannies in which we would likely find it. If history is any guide, a major site of working-class politics during crisis periods is the workplace, where workers around the globe have taken advantage of power vacuums to refashion and expand their control over production and the economy. Such actions occurred as socialism disintegrated in

Poland, the GDR, and the Soviet Union (Fuller 1999:ch 6; Philipsen 1993:289; Crowley 1997), and it is probable that, were more researchers disposed to consider this obvious working-class space, we would know more than we do about workers' activism elsewhere in the region. Working-class families and neighborhoods may also prove fruitful spaces in which to unearth more information about the forms and dynamics of working-class political activism during this era (Siegelbaum & Walkowitz 1995).

We need also to broaden our vision beyond what counts as politics for intellectuals, if we are to comprehend how working people's actions affect processes of political change. In the case of political struggles surrounding the demise of socialism, workers' efforts to reform pre-existing unions might be one example, as might activities reminiscent of socialist-era "silent boycotts" in Hungary. So too might be many people's refusal to vote once elections became regularized (Siegelbaum & Walkowitz 1995:125; Szelényi & Szelényi 1994:228–29; Fuller 1999:101, 110–14; Szelényi et al 1996:466, 469, 473, 476; Szelényi & Szelényi 1991:128–29; Ferguson 1998:462). In sum, to come upon evidence of working-class political involvement researchers must be willing to scrutinize different social spaces and different activities than those commonly associated with the political activism of intellectuals.

HOMOGENEITY AND WORKING-CLASS POLITICAL DEMOBILIZATION

Some may object to what I have said above on the grounds that in most countries workers were simply not very involved in politics at the beginning of the transition. Researchers' emphasis on intellectual politics therefore reflects reality. While I remain skeptical of this argument, out of suspicion that it reveals as much about the substantive, epistemological, and methodological limits of the reigning paradigm as it does about workers' politics, it is clear that many workers were not active in these events. This, however, is not a reason for continued attachment to the homogeneity paradigm. Quite the contrary. The homogeneity paradigm, in blinding us to class relationships, bears much responsibility for how little effort has gone toward explaining the political demobilization of so many workers. There are a potentially large number of investigative paths we might pursue in searching for clues about how class relations under socialism are implicated in working-class political withdrawal during the transition. Below I mention three.

First, it is impossible to ignore the amount of tension and hostility between workers and intellectuals reported in the literature on East Central European socialism. The relationship between the two classes is frequently described as estranged, formal, and uneasy at best and as tense, deeply antagonistic, and sharply contradictory at worst (Djilas 1998:140; Connelly 1997:313; Judt 1988:188; Szelényi & Szelényi 1994:229; Filtzer 1996:11). While we might wonder that the overwhelmingly negative portrayal of this relationship did not raise more doubts about the utility of the homogeneous paradigm, when we review the opinions intellectuals and workers held of each other more closely, it is not surprising that their relationship would come to be described in such dismal terms.

Workers often considered intellectuals, both party-identified and not, as parasites and spongers, and as arrogant, authoritarian, manipulative, and genuinely dangerous bullies. Add to this list weak-kneed and obsequious in the face of authority, hypocritical, condescending, and even laughable, and the none-too-pretty impression many workers harbored of the intelligentsia is near complete (Crowley 1997:72, 119, 228, n. 15; Creed 1998:235, 244; Curry 1988:492, 501, 502, 506; Torpey 1995:161, 162, 164; Kennedy 1992:39; Fuller 1999:30; Błaszkiewicz et al 1994:129, 132; Clarke et al 1994:203; Siegelbaum & Walkowitz 1995:190, 194, 199). Thanks to the homogenous paradigm, we know much more about how intellectuals viewed workers, and their perceptions appear equally, if not more, unflattering. To many intellectuals workers seemed children in the most pejorative sense of the term. They were immature, irresponsible, easily duped, and not all that sharp either (Schöpflin 1991:238, 242, 249; Djilas 1998:117, 127; Szlajfer 1995:30–40, 33; Staniszkis 1979:178–79; Kostecki & Mrela 1984:138; Connelly 1997:327, 329; Wolicki 1995:78; Fuller 1999:30; Clarke et al 1994:204; Curry 1988:501; Tismaneanu 1997:44, n. 35; Creed 1998:219; Freed 1996:175; Torpey 1995:156, 163; Róna-Tas 1997:159). Although they sometimes saw workers as cowardly, timid, and politically ineffective, at other times intellectuals worried that workers were, at least potentially, too active and too influential. This appears Offe's (1997:45–46) fear as he counsels "patience," "discipline," and "civilized behaviour," especially among society's less fortunate, during the transition (Ost & Weinstein 1999:22; Kennedy 1992:65; Crowley 1997:13; Ekiert 1997:305, 311; Stark & Bruzst 1998:20–24; Freed 1996:172; Tőkés 1996:167).

A second matter that holds promise for the development of explanations for workers' political demobilization expands the theme of the second and third sections of this paper. There I argued that, in terms of their perceptions of economic inefficiency, workers and intellectuals were miles apart. Their divergent views stemmed from the fact that their lived experiences of socialism were so dissimilar, though the homogeneous paradigm succeeded in disguising the extent to which this was so.

There are numerous ways in which workers and intellectuals could be said to have inhabited separate socialist worlds, a number reminiscent of those familiar in other class societies (Konrád & Szelényi 1979:172–74; Andorka et al 1984:36, 40; Szelényi 1978:67; Schöpflin 1991:246–48; Tőkés 1996:122, 123, 414; Fuller 1999:19–20, 88–97; Connelly 1997; Ferguson 1998:466; Słomczyński & Shabad 1997:181, 183). But in terms of explaining the dearth of working-class involvement in the demise of socialism, one of the most important is that they had rarely done any sort of transformative politics together. They did not, in other words, share a joint oppositional history under socialism. In Romania, Czechoslovakia, the GDR, and Hungary, they engaged in very different kinds of activities, and neither offered support to nor solicited it from those on the other side of the class divide (Georgescu

1988:88, 89; Tismaneanu 1997:427; Offe 1997:141; Schöpflin 1991:244; Judt 1988:189; Torpey 1995:chs 1–3, 208; Joppke 1995:57–65; Tökés 1996:175, 188; Kennedy 1992:46–51). At certain times and places, they even publicly opposed the political undertakings of the other class. In the early days of Czechoslovak socialism, for example, workers and unions chastised student demonstrators, called for investigations of their activities, urged that no mercy be shown them, and attacked property in at least one university (Connelly 1997:313–15). In like fashion, during the workers' rebellion of 1953, the secretary of the GDR writers' union published a letter castigating workers, smugly warning them, "You will have to lay a great deal of brick and very well ... before you will be forgotten [for] this disgrace" (Torpey 1995:30). Even in the rare instances when workers and intellectuals undertook opposition politics together, Poland between 1976–1981 being the most notable example, their efforts were replete with difficult moments and proved impossible to sustain over the long run (Kostecki & Mrela 1984:138, 139; Jankowska 1995:306, 313, 322, 324; Kennedy 1992; Judt 1988:228; Iankova 1998: 248–49).

The homogeneous paradigm has obscured a final feature of the class relationship in East and Central European socialist societies that might also yield insights into the lack of political participation among workers during the struggles surrounding the end of socialism. Put simply, workers tended to perceive *all* intellectuals, whether party or government officials, bosses, engineers, artists, educators, or dissidents, as socially similar. From the bottom of the class ladder looking up, all these people shared a good deal. Whether we think workers accurate in their unvariegated assessment of the intelligentsia, it is worth reviewing some of the reasons they embraced such a view. Here I focus on the overlap between the socialist political intelligentsia and the rest of the intellectual stratum, which many adherents of the homogeneous paradigm consider of minor consequence.

To begin with, as socialism matured, intellectuals of all kinds came increasingly to dominate the membership and leadership of the communist parties in numbers far exceeding their proportion of the general population. While some intellectual party members were surely reluctant participants in party life and exercised little power within these organizations, such subtleties were easily lost on most workers, who were neither party members themselves nor privy to internal party processes (Kennedy 1991:264; Lane 1996:163, 164, 169; MatěJů 1999:31; Pravda 1979:233; Fuller 1999:25–26; Tökés 1996:134, 135). What was more obvious to many workers was how frequently representatives of the academic, technical, cultural, and even dissident intelligentsia lent open support to the political intelligentsia, often in moments of crisis (Offe 1997:2; Lane 1996:169; Torpey 1995:74–75; Tökés 1996:175; Kennedy 1992:49; see also Gerber & Hout 1998:9; Kornai 1992:325; Fuller 1999:26–27; Creed 1998:167). The conspicuous reluctance of many intellectuals ever to challenge or oppose the political intelligentsia less overtly in more ordinary times further reinforced workers' impression of proximity between the two subgroups of intellectuals (Fuller 1999:26; Torpey 1995:40, 51, 123, 143; Daskalov 1996:75–76; Tökés 1996:187).

The other side of the coin was that the political intelligentsia often coddled and rewarded, humored and courted their intellectual brethren. Whether best considered calculated moves at cooptation or reflections of a less conscious prejudice in favor of those for whom they felt a certain social affinity, the political intelligentsia afforded others of their stratum preferential treatment so often and so obviously that Daskalov (1996:74) declares it one-sided and incorrect "(t)o see the career of the intelligentsia under state socialism only or even predominantly in terms of 'oppression'." Rather than persecuting other intellectuals, the political intelligentsia was often as likely to grant them visas, cede them degrees of personal, professional, and organizational freedom unmatched elsewhere in society, shower them with prestigious public awards and positions, channel hefty public resources in their direction, and safeguard their ability to take disproportionate advantage of certain social opportunities, such as higher education and participation in the private sector of the economy (Ekiert 1997:314; Connelly 1997:309, 321, 323, 325, 332; Fuller 1999:27–28; Schöpflin 1991:246–47; Creed 1998:167; Róna-Tas 1997:131–32; Torpey 1995:17, 24; Szelényi & Szelényi 1994:226–27). Beyond this, in many countries the political intelligentsia treated workers who opposed them more harshly than they did other intellectuals who did so. While intellectual opponents of the regime were sometimes ignored, allowed to emigrate, granted concessions, drafted, or expelled from school, oppositional workers were more likely arrested and jailed, disappeared, beaten, wounded, and even killed (Georgescu 1988:89; Torpey 1995:38; Kennedy 1992:55–56; Kostecki & Mrela 1984:139, 140, n. 10; Ekiert 1997:310, 318, 320, 325).

When we assign these three features of the relationship between workers and intellectuals a prominent place in our sociological conception of what East and Central European socialism was like—a task never easily accomplished in the shadow of the homogeneous paradigm—working-class withdrawal from the political maelstrom accompanying the end of socialism seems less a mystery. Merely to pose the logical questions prompted by the recognition that the relationship between workers and intellectuals was marred by tension and antagonism, that the two had virtually no joint history of oppositional political engagement, and that workers tended to view all intellectuals as socially similar, is to suggest how we might begin to explain the political passivity of many East and Central European workers at this critical historical juncture.

Why would workers, who had hitherto not rushed to the support of opposition intellectuals, all of a sudden, historically speaking, have done so? Given their lack of a joint political history, not to mention other ways in which they could be said to live in separate social worlds, on what shared understandings and experiences could workers and intellectuals have built the trust essential for joint politics in risky times? Would not their low opinions of intellectuals have made it unlikely workers would have been attracted to, or taken the initiative to form, alliances with them? Equally important, given that workers' negative perceptions of intellectuals were reciprocated, why would activist intellectuals have gone out of their way to recruit workers to their political cause, be that supporting or challenging the socialist status quo? Wouldn't this have simply been too difficult and unrewarding a task, abandoned in favor of the easier one of reaching out to one's own kind? Might the few intellectuals who tried anyway not have floundered on clumsy and ineffective attempts to enter worlds and to reach people they did not know? Might it not have been more likely that intellectual activists did things and said things with an arrogance guaranteeing workers would rebuff their overtures? Viewing all intellectuals as close social kin, why would workers have been much interested in the struggles of the day? Why wouldn't they instead have seen them as none of their affair, as quarrels between members of a privileged family of which they were not a part, as socialist politics as usual? Why would the eventual elections, an outstanding feature of which has been the circulation of power between parties of the old political intelligentsia and those led by other segments of the intellectual stratum, have inspired working-class political activism? Would the issues raised by the all-intellectual protagonists in these struggles and electoral contests, the analyses they offered, and the solutions they proposed have found much resonance with the working class?

On occasion, researchers have suggested answers to such questions that clarify how socialist class relations are an important key to explaining working-class political demobilization in the transition period (Judt 1988:226; Clarke et al 1994:194; Baylis 1998:294; Szelényi et al 1996; Jankowska 1995:323; Fuller 1999:97–105; Crowley 1997:29, 190, 204, 218, n. 26 and 27; Stark & Bruszt 1998:ch 1; Kennedy 1992:51–52, 56; Schöpflin 1991:244–46; Ferguson 1998:459; Tökés 1996:394; Lane 1996:162, 185, 196; Goodwyn 1991:328; Róna-Tas 1997:197). But as a consequence of the continuing, if hopefully diminishing, adherence to the homogenous paradigm, this key has too seldom been noticed and more rarely turned. In my view, unlocking the many doors now closed through both unwitting and enthusiastic acceptance of homogeneity is precisely what is required to uncover new evidence, reopen long settled questions, and generally deepen and expand our knowledge of East and Central Europe's socialist past, in order that it better inform our analyses of what succeeds it.

Visit the Annual Reviews home page at www.AnnualReviews.org

LITERATURE CITED

Andorka R, Harcsa I, Gyenei M. 1984. First results of a survey of social stratification. In *Stratification and Inequalities*, ed. R Andorka, T Kolosi, pp. 1–15. Budapest: Inst. Soc. Sci.

Bahro R. 1978. *The Alternative in Eastern Europe*. London: Verso

Baylis TA. 1998. Elite change after communism: Eastern Germany, the Czech Republic, and Slovakia. *East Eur. Polit. Soc.* 12:265–99

Bernhard M, Szlajfer H, ed. 1995. *From the Polish Underground*. University Park, PA: Penn. State Univ. Press, 458 pp.

Błaszkiewicz A, Rykowski Z, Szwajcer P, Wertenstein-Żuławski. 1994. The Solidarność spring? *Com. Post-Com. Stud.* 27:125–34

Bonnell VE. 1989. Moscow: a view from below. *Dissent.* Summer: 311–17

Burawoy M. 1989. Reflections on the class consciousness of Hungarian steelworkers. *Polit. Soc.* 17:1–34

Burawoy M. 1996. From capitalism to capitalism via socialism: the odyssey of a Marxist ethnographer, 1975–1995. *Int. J. Labor Working-Class Hist.* 50:77–99

Burawoy M, Lukács J. 1985. Mythologies of work: a comparison of firms in state socialism and advanced capitalism. *Am. Soc. Rev.* 50:723–37

Burawoy M, Lukács J. 1992. *The Radiant Past.* Chicago/London: Univ. Chicago Press

Clarke S, Donova I. 1999. Internal mobility and labour market flexibility in Russia. *Eur.-Asia Stud.* 51:213–43

Clarke S, Fairbrother P, Borisov V, Bizyukov, P. 1994. The privatisation of industrial enterprises in Russia: four case-studies. *Eur.-Asia Stud.* 46:179–214

Comisso E. 1988. Market failures and market socialism: economic problems of the transition. *East. Eur. Polit. Soc.* 2:433–65

Connelly J. 1997. Students, workers, and social change: the limits of Czech Stalinism. *Slav. Rev.* 56:307–35

Connor WD. 1991. *The Accidental Proletariat.* Princeton, NJ: Princeton Univ. Press

Cook LJ. 1993. *The Soviet Social Contract and Why It Failed.* Cambridge, MA: Harvard Univ. Press

Creed GW. 1998. *Domesticating Revolution.* University Park, PA: Penn. State Univ. Press

Crowley S. 1997. *Hot Coal, Cold Steel.* Ann Arbor: Univ. Mich. Press

Curry JL. 1988. The psychological barriers to reform in Poland. *East Eur. Polit. Soc.* 2:484–509

Daskalov R. 1996. Transformations of the East European intelligentsia: reflections on the Bulgarian case. *East Eur. Polit. Soc.* 10:46–84

Dawisha K. 1997. Democratization and political participation: research concepts and methodologies. In *Politics, Power, and the Struggle for Democracy in South-East Europe,* ed. K Dawisha, B Parrott, pp. 40–65. Cambridge: Cambridge Univ. Press. 472 pp.

Dimitrov M. 1996. Privatization: its goals, progress to date and prospects. See Zloch-Christy, pp. 107–18

Djilas M. 1998. *Fall of the New Class.* New York: Knopf

Ekiert G. 1997. Rebellious Poles: political crises and popular protest under state socialism, 1945–89. *East Eur. Polit. Soc.* 11:299–338

Ferguson R. 1998. Will democracy strike back? Workers and politics in the Kuzbass. *Eur.-Asia Stud.* 50:445–68

Filtzer D. 1996. Labor discipline, the use of work time, and the decline of the Soviet system, 1928–1991. *Int. J. Labor Working-Class Hist.* 50:9–28

Freed R. 1996. Legal structure: its present status and challenges. See Zloch-Christy, pp. 165–76

Frentzel-Zagórska J, Zagórski K. 1989. East European intellectuals on the road of dissent: the old prophecy of a new class re-examined. *Polit. Soc.* 17:89–113

Fuller L. 1999. *Where Was the Working Class?* Urbana/Chicago: Univ. Ill. Press

Georgescu V. 1988. Romania in the 1980s: the legacy of dynastic socialism. *East Eur. Polit. Soc.* 2:69–93

Gerber TP, Hout M. 1998. More shock than therapy: market transition, employment, and income in Russia, 1991–1995. *Am. J. Soc.* 104:1–50

Glasman M. 1994. The great deformation: Polanyi, Poland and the terrors of planned spontaneity. *New Left Rev.* 205:59–86

Goodwyn L. 1991. *Breaking the Barrier.* New York/Oxford: Oxford Univ. Press

Iankova EA. 1998. The transformative corporativism of Eastern Europe. *East Eur. Polit. Soc.* 12:222–64

Jankowska J. 1995. In every situation I look for a way out: Janka Jankowska interviews Jacek Kuroń. See Bernhard & Szlajfer 1995, pp. 289–332

Jasiewicz K. 1995. The Polish voter—ten years after August 1980. See Bernhard & Szlajfer 1995, pp. 143–67

Joppke C. 1995. *East German Dissidents and the Revolution of 1989.* Washington Square, NY: New York Univ. Press

Judt T. 1988. The dilemmas of dissidence: the politics of opposition in East-Central Europe. *East Eur. Polit. Soc.* 2:185–240

Kennedy M. 1990. The constitution of critical intellectuals: Polish physicians, peace activists and democratic civil society. *Stud. Compar. Commun.* XXIII:218–303

Kennedy M. 1991. *Professionals, Power and Solidarity in Poland.* Cambridge: Cambridge Univ. Press

Kennedy M. 1992. The intelligentsia in the constitution of civil societies and post-communist regimes in Hungary and Poland. *Theory Soc.* 21:29–76

Kluegel JR, Mason DS. 1999. Political involvement in transition. *Int. J. Comp. Soc.* XL:41–60

Konrád G, Szelényi I. 1979. *The Intellectuals on the Road to Class Power.* New York: Harcourt Brace Jovanovich

Kornai J. 1986. *Contradictions and Dilemmas.* Cambridge, MA: MIT Press

Kornai J. 1992. *The Socialist System.* Princeton, NJ: Princeton University Press

Kostecki M, Mrela K. 1984. Collective solidarity in Poland's powdered society. *Insurgent Sociologist* 12:131–41

Kotkin S. 1996. Introduction: a future for labor under communism? *Int. J. Labor Working-Class Hist.* 50:1–8

Kurczewska J. 1995. The Polish intelligentsia: departure from the scene. See Bernhard & Szlajfer 1995, pp. 169–80

Laba R. 1991. *The Roots of Solidarity.* Princeton, NJ: Princeton Univ. Press

Lane D. 1996. *The Rise and Fall of State Socialism.* Cambridge: Polity

Lasky M. 1991. *Voices in a Revolution.* Southwick, UK: Grange

Maier CS. 1997. *Dissolution.* Princeton, NJ: Princeton Univ. Press

Matěj̊u P. 1999. Who votes left after the fall of communism? *Int. J. Comp. Soc.* XL:13–40

McFalls LH. 1995. *Communism's Collapse, Democracy's Demise?* Washington Square, NY: New York Univ. Press

Meininger TA, Radoeva D. 1996. Civil society: the current situation and problems. See Zloch-Christy, pp. 45–73

Michnik A. 1995. Three fundamentalisms. See Bernhard & Szlajfer, pp. 231–36

Mitchell K. 1992. Work authority in industry: the happy demise of the ideal type. *Compar. Stud. Soc. Hist.* 34:679–94

Nove A. 1983. *The Economics of Feasible Socialism.* London: Allen & Unwin

Offe C. 1997. *Varieties of Transition.* Cambridge, MA: MIT Press

Ost D, Weinstein M. 1999. Unionists against unions: toward hierarchical management in post-communist Poland. *East Eur. Polit. Soc.* 13:1–33

Pano N. 1997. The process of democratization in Albania. In *Politics, Power, and the Struggle for Democracy in South-East Europe,* ed. B Parrott, K Dawisha, pp. 285–352. Cambridge: Cambridge Univ. Press. 472 pp.

Pantev A. 1996. The historic road of the third Bulgarian state. See Zloch-Christy, pp. 7–22

Parrott B. 1997. Perspectives on postcommunist democratization. In *Politics, Power, and the Struggle for Democracy in South-East Europe,* ed. B Parrott, K Dawisha, pp. 1–39. Cambridge: Cambridge Univ. Press. 472 pp.

Philipsen D. 1992. *We Were the People.* Durham/London: Duke Univ. Press

Pravda A. 1979. Industrial workers: patterns of dissent, opposition and accommodation. In *Opposition in Eastern Europe,* ed. RL Tökés, pp. 209–62. Baltimore/London: Johns Hopkins Univ. Press. 306 pp.

Róna-Tas A. 1997. *The Great Surprise of the Small Transformation.* Ann Arbor, MI: Univ. Michigan Press

Ruble B. 1986. Industrial trade unions in the USSR. In *Trade Unions in Communist States,* ed. A Pravda, B Ruble, pp. 23–52. London: Allen & Unwin

Schöpflin G. 1991. Post-communism: constructing new democracies in Central Europe. *Int. Aff.* 67:235–50

Siegelbaum LH, Walkowitz DJ. 1995. *Workers of the Donbass Speak.* Albany, NY: State Univ. New York Press

Słomczyński KM, Shabad G. 1997. Systemic transformation and the salience of class structure in East Central Europe. *East Eur. Polit. Soc.* 11:155–89

Sørensen C. 1997. Social classes and democracy. In *Forward to the Past*, ed. LB Sørensen, LB Eliason, pp. 8–18. Aarhus, Denmark: Aarhus Univ. Press. 307 pp.

Spenner KI, Suhomlinova OO, Thore SA, Land KC, Jones DC. 1998. Strong legacies and weak markets: Bulgarian state-owned enterprises during early transition. *Am. Soc. Rev.* 63:599–617

Staniszkis J. 1979. On some contradictions of socialist society: The case of Poland. *Sov. Stud.* XXXI:167–87

Stark D. 1986. Rethinking internal labor markets: new insights from a comparative perspective. *Am. Soc. Rev.* 51:492–504

Stark D, Bruszt L. 1998. *Postsocialist Pathways.* Cambridge: Cambridge Univ. Press

Szelényi I. 1978. Social inequalities in state socialist redistribution economies. *Int. J. Compar. Soc.* 19:63–87

Szelényi I, Fodor É, Hanley E. 1997. Left turn in post-communist politics: bringing class back in? *East Eur. Polit. Soc.* 11:190–224

Szelényi I, Szelényi B. 1994. Why socialism failed: toward a theory of system breakdown—causes of disintegration of East European state socialism. *Theory Soc.* 23:211–31

Szelényi I, Szelényi S. 1991. The vacuum in Hungarian politics: classes and parties. *New Left Rev.* 187:121–37

Szelényi S, Szelényi I, Poster W. 1996. Interests and symbols in post-communist political culture: the case of Hungary. *Am. Sociol. Rev.* 61:466–77

Szlajfer H. 1995. Under the military dictatorship: between "freeze frame" and "restoration". See Bernhard & Szlajfer, pp. 1–67

Tismaneanu V. 1997. Romanian exceptionalism? democracy, ethnocracy, and uncertain pluralism in post-Ceauşescu Romania. In *Politics, Power, and the Struggle for Democracy in South-East Europe*, ed. K Dawisha, B Parrott, pp. 403–51. Cambridge: Cambridge Univ. Press. 472 pp.

Tökés RL. 1996. *Hungary's Negotiated Revolution.* Cambridge: Cambridge Univ. Press

Torpey JC. 1995. *Intellectuals, Socialism, and Dissent.* Minneapolis/London: Univ. Minn. Press

Voskamp U, Wittke V. 1991. Industrial restructuring in the former German Democratic Republic (GDR): barriers to adaptive reform become downward development spirals. *Polit. Society.* 19:341–71

Wierling D. 1996. Work, workers, and politics in the German Democratic Republic. *Int. J. Labor Working-Class Hist.* 50:44–63

Wolicki K. 1995. About the future. See Bernhard & Szlajfer, pp. 69–92

Zloch-Christy I. 1996. Problems, challenges and priorities of economic policy: costs of transition and some policy proposals. See Zloch-Christy 1996, pp. 145–63

Zloch-Christy I, ed. 1996. *Bulgaria in a Time of Change.* Aldershot, U.K. Avebury. 221 pp.

Annu. Rev. Sociol. 2000. 26:611–39

FRAMING PROCESSES AND SOCIAL MOVEMENTS:
An Overview and Assessment

Robert D. Benford

Department of Sociology, University of Nebraska, Lincoln, Nebraska 68588-0324;
e-mail: Rbenford1@unl.edu

David A. Snow

Department of Sociology, University of Arizona, Tucson, Arizona 85721;
e-mail: snowd@u.arizona.edu

Key Words   social movements, frame, collective action, reality
construction, culture

■ **Abstract**   The recent proliferation of scholarship on collective action frames and framing processes in relation to social movements indicates that framing processes have come to be regarded, alongside resource mobilization and political opportunity processes, as a central dynamic in understanding the character and course of social movements. This review examines the analytic utility of the framing literature for understanding social movement dynamics. We first review how collective action frames have been conceptualized, including their characteristic and variable features. We then examine the literature related to framing dynamics and processes. Next we review the literature regarding various contextual factors that constrain and facilitate framing processes. We conclude with an elaboration of the consequences of framing processes for other movement processes and outcomes. We seek throughout to provide clarification of the linkages between framing concepts/processes and other conceptual and theoretical formulations relevant to social movements, such as schemas and ideology.

INTRODUCTION

The concept of frame has considerable currency in the social sciences today. References to it, for both descriptive and analytic purposes, and to the more fluid conception of framing processes can be readily found in psychology, particularly cognitive psychology (Bateson 1972, Tversky & Kahneman 1981), linguistics and discourse analysis (Tannen 1993, Van Dijk 1977), communication and media studies (Pan & Kosicki 1993, Scheufele 1999), and political science and policy studies (Schon & Rein 1994, Triandafyllidou & Fotiou 1998). The frame concept and kindred processes have been applied analytically and explored empirically in sociology as well, probably more so than in other areas because of the influence of Goffman's (1974) book on the topic.

0360-0572/00/0815-0611$14.00

Within sociology, not only has the framing concept been applied most extensively to the substantive study of social movements and collective action, but interest in framing processes in relation to the operation of social movements has animated an increasing amount of conceptual and empirical scholarship. Evidence of this trend can be found (*a*) in recent edited volumes based on papers presented at social movement conferences (Johnston & Klandermans 1995, Laraña et al 1994, McAdam et al 1996, Morris & Mueller 1992); (*b*) in the almost meteoric increase in articles, chapters, and papers referring to the framing/movement link since the mid-1980s, from only one such reference in the *Sociological Abstracts* in 1986 to 43 in 1998, with almost two thirds of the nearly 250 references during this period occurring since 1994; (*c*) in the parallel pattern of citations in the three core conceptual articles on framing and social movements (Snow et al 1986, Snow & Benford 1988, 1992) beginning with seven citations in 1990 and increasing to 106 in 1998, with more than half of the over 500 citations appearing after 1995; and (*d*) in a variety of recent critiques focusing on specific conceptual dimensions of the movement framing literature (Benford 1997, Fisher 1997, Hart 1996, Jasper 1997, Oliver & Johnston 2000, Sherkat 1998, Steinberg 1998, Williams & Benford 2000) or on its relationship to other perspectives (Goodwin & Jasper 1999, Meyer 1999). Clearly there has been a pronounced proliferation of scholarship on collective action frames and framing processes in relation to social movements within the past decade and a half, so much so, in fact, that framing processes have come to be regarded, alongside resource mobilization and political opportunity processes, as a central dynamic in understanding the character and course of social movements.

The purpose of this review is to evaluate this burgeoning literature in terms of two general questions. First, does this literature congeal or hang together in a fashion suggestive of a coherent perspective, or can such a perspective be stitched together from various strands of the literature in a way that adds to a more refined and integrated understanding of the relationship between framing processes and the operation of social movements? And second, does this evolving perspective enhance our understanding of social movements, casting analytic light on areas and aspects of the dynamics of social movements that other conceptual schemes or perspectives have glossed over or ignored altogether? What, in short, can be concluded about the analytic utility of the framing literature for understanding the social movement processes it seeks to understand and illuminate, namely the generation, diffusion, and functionality of mobilizing and countermobilizing ideas and meanings? Our approach to addressing these questions is conceptually and theoretically developmental, and selective in terms of the literature we look at most closely. We proceed by organizing the review around four broad fundamental areas of concern that require both elaboration and synthesis if we are to address the above questions: (*a*) conceptualization of collective action frames and delineation of their characteristic features; (*b*) identification of framing processes relevant to the generation, elaboration, and diffusion of collective action frames; (*c*) specification of various socio-cultural contextual factors that constrain and facilitate framing processes; and (*d*) elaboration of the consequences or implications of framing processes for other movement processes and outcomes. At various points, we also seek to provide clarification of the linkages between framing concepts and processes and other conceptual and theoretical formulations relevant to social movements, such as ideology. We draw on and evaluate the literature in terms of how it informs one or more of these issues and, in the process, build our answers to the two general questions.

COLLECTIVE ACTION FRAMES

Social movement scholars interested in framing processes begin by taking as problematic what until the mid-1980s the literature largely ignored: meaning work—the struggle over the production of mobilizing and countermobilizing ideas and meanings.[1] From this perspective, social movements are not viewed merely as carriers of extant ideas and meanings that grow automatically out of structural arrangements, unanticipated events, or existing ideologies.[2] Rather, movement actors are viewed as signifying agents actively engaged in the production and maintenance of meaning for constituents, antagonists, and bystanders or observers (Snow & Benford 1988). They are deeply embroiled, along with the media, local governments, and the state, in what has been referred to as "the politics of signification" (Hall 1982).

---

[1] Although references to meanings, beliefs, values, and the more general notion of ideology have been prevalent historically in the social movement literature, the treatment of these concepts generally has been unsatisfactory because of two tendencies: either they were discussed descriptively and statically rather than analytically and dynamically, as in much of the work prior to the 1970s; or they were dismissed as being largely irrelevant to the development of social movements, as in the early resource mobilization literature (see Snow & Benford 1992:135–36).

[2] Recent investigations of the link between culture and social movements (Kane 1997, Williams 1995) and frames, ideology, and related concepts (Fisher 1997, Oliver & Johnston 2000, Zald 1996) have directly or indirectly called for clarification of the relationship of frames and ideology. Clearly they are not one and the same. Ideology is generally portrayed as a fairly broad, coherent, and relatively durable set of beliefs that affects one's orientation not only to politics but to everyday life more generally. This conception holds whether one subscribes to a more general and neutral view of ideology (e.g. Geertz 1973) or to a more critical view wherein ideology is seen as functioning to sustain existing class structures and relations of domination (e.g. Thompson 1984). In either case, the reference is to fairly pervasive and integrated set of beliefs and values that have considerable staying power. In contrast, collective action frames function as innovative amplifications and extensions of, or antidotes to, existing ideologies or components of them. Accordingly, ideology functions as both a constraint and resource in relation to framing processes and collective action frames, a relationship we touch upon at several points throughout the article. For an elaborated discussion of the relationship between ideology and framing, see Oliver & Johnston (2000), Snow & Benford (2000), and Snow (2000).

Framing as Meaning Construction

Social movement scholars conceptualize this signifying work or meaning construction by employing the verb "framing" (Gamson et al 1982, Snow et al 1986, Snow & Benford 1988). This denotes an active, processual phenomenon that implies agency and contention at the level of reality construction. It is active in the sense that something is being done, and processual in the sense of a dynamic, evolving process. It entails agency in the sense that what is evolving is the work of social movement organizations or movement activists. And it is contentious in the sense that it involves the generation of interpretive frames that not only differ from existing ones but that may also challenge them. The resultant products of this framing activity are referred to as "collective action frames."

Characteristic Features of Collective Action Frames

The concept of frame as used in the study of social movements is derived primarily from the work of Goffman (1974). For Goffman, frames denoted "schemata of interpretation" that enable individuals "to locate, perceive, identify, and label" occurrences within their life space and the world at large (p. 21). Frames help to render events or occurrences meaningful and thereby function to organize experience and guide action. Collective action frames also perform this interpretive function by simplifying and condensing aspects of the "world out there," but in ways that are "intended to mobilize potential adherents and constituents, to garner bystander support, and to demobilize antagonists" (Snow & Benford 1988:198). Thus, collective action frames are action-oriented sets of beliefs and meanings that inspire and legitimate the activities and campaigns of a social movement organization (SMO).

Some scholars (e.g. Johnston 1995, Klandermans 1997, Klandermans et al 1999, Sherkat & Ellison 1997) tend to treat collective action frames in a fashion that is more consistent with psychological concepts such as "schema," thereby overlooking the interactive, constructionist chatacter of movement framing processes. A crucial feature that distinguishes collective action frames from schema and other related cognitive constructs is that "[c]ollective action frames are not merely aggregations of individual attitudes and perceptions but also the outcome of negotiating shared meaning" (Gamson 1992a:111).[3]

---

[3]The implied distinction between schemas and frames can be stated more concretely by thinking of schemas as "participants' expectations about people, objects, events, and settings in the world, as distinguished from alignments being negotiated in particular interaction," which is what frames do (Tannen & Wallat 1993:60). Frames and schemas interact during the course of interaction between two or more individuals, with frames providing an interpretive "footing" that aligns schemas that participants to the interaction bring with them. Thus, frames and schemas are not different concepts for the same phenomena but are highly interactive, with frames constituting a broader, interpretive answer or definition to "what is going on" or "should be going on."

Collective action frames are constituted by two sets of characteristic features: one concerns their action-oriented function—an SMO's "core framing tasks" (Snow & Benford 1988); the second refers to the interactive, discursive processes that attend to these core framing tasks and thus are generative of collective action frames (Gamson 1992a, Snow & Benford 1992). We examine the discursive processes later in the review under the more general topic of framing processes and dynamics.

Core Framing Tasks   Collective action frames are constructed in part as movement adherents negotiate a shared understanding of some problematic condition or situation they define as in need of change, make attributions regarding who or what is to blame, articulate an alternative set of arrangements, and urge others to act in concert to affect change. Building on Wilson's (1973) decomposition of ideology into three component parts, Snow & Benford (1988) refer to these core framing tasks as "diagnostic framing" (problem identification and attributions), "prognostic framing," and "motivational framing." By pursuing these core framing tasks, movement actors attend to the interrelated problems of "consensus mobilization" and "action mobilization" (Klandermans 1984). Simply put, the former fosters or facilitates agreement whereas the latter fosters action, moving people from the balcony to the barricades.

To date, scholars have devoted considerable empirical attention to identifying and analyzing the various types of diagnostic, prognostic, and action mobilization framings specific movements and their SMOs have constructed and proffered (e.g. Benford 1993b, Gerhards & Rucht 1992, Johnson 1997, Marullo et al 1996, McCarthy 1994, Meyer 1995, Nepstad 1997, Weed 1997). Regarding diagnostic framing, several case studies focus on the development and articulation of what Gamson and colleagues (1982, 1992a,b) refer to as "injustice frames" (Anheier et al 1998, Cable & Shriver 1995, Čapek 1993, Carroll & Ratner 1996a,b, Klandermans & Goslinga 1996, Klandermans et al 1999). A plethora of studies call attention to the ways in which movements identify the "victims" of a given injustice and amplify their victimization (Benford & Hunt 1992, Best 1987, Čapek 1993, Hunt et al 1994, Jasper & Poulsen 1995, Jenness 1995, Weed 1997, White 1999). Taken together, these studies support Gamson et al's (1982) initial conceptualization of injustice frames as a mode of interpretation—prefatory to collective noncompliance, protest, and/or rebellion—generated and adopted by those who come to define the actions of an authority as unjust. While the empirical evidence reported in the foregoing studies clearly demonstrates that injustice frames are commonplace across a variety of types of social movements, there is little theoretical or empirical support for Gamson's more sweeping assertion that all "collective action frames are *injustice* frames" (1992b:68, original emphasis); nor is there support for the less ambitious assertion that all collective action frames contain an injustice component (Gamson 1992a). In the case of many religious, self-help, and identity movements, for example, it is questionable whether a well-elaborated collective action frame need include an injustice component. Nevertheless, injustice frames appear to be fairly ubiquitous across movements advocating some form of political and/or economic change.

Since social movements seek to remedy or alter some problematic situation or issue, it follows that directed action is contingent on identification of the source(s) of causality, blame, and/or culpable agents. This attributional component of diagnostic framing attends to this function by focusing blame or responsibility. However, consensus regarding the source of the problem does not follow automatically from agreement regarding the nature of the problem. Controversies regarding whom or what to blame frequently erupt between the various SMOs comprising a social movement as well as within movement organizations. In his study of the 1980s nuclear disarmament movement, Benford (1987, 1993a) reported that this attributional component of collective action frames was frequently the source of rancorous intramovement conflict, with peace groups divided over whether to attribute "*the* most salient cause of the nuclear threat" to a general decline in morality, runaway technology, the defense industry, capitalism, an anachronistic geopolitical structure, or the United States, the Soviet Union, or both (Benford 1987:67–74).

The import of such attributional processes to collective action had, of course, been noted by a number of scholars well before the emergence of the social movement framing perspective (Ferree & Miller 1985, Turner & Killian 1972, Zurcher & Snow 1981). More recently, movement theorists have called attention to the ways in which activists engage in "boundary framing" (Hunt et al 1994:194; also see Silver 1997) and "adversarial framing" (Gamson 1995)—related attributional processes that seek to delineate the boundaries between "good" and "evil" and construct movement protagonists and antagonists. That movement adversarial framings are not always effective is well illustrated by recent comparative research conducted by Klandermans et al (1999) on agrarian mobilizations in the Netherlands and Spain. They found that many farmers who had been the targets of mobilization were not sure whom to hold responsible for their adverse situation. Among Dutch farmers surveyed, there was a disparity between the cognitive and affective components of their adversarial frames. They blamed their adverse situation on the European Union, but directed their anger at the Dutch government or at politics in general.

Prognostic framing, the second core framing task, involves the articulation of a proposed solution to the problem, or at least a plan of attack, and the strategies for carrying out the plan. In short, it addresses the Leninesque question of what is to be done, as well as the problems of consensus and action mobilization. Although this remains an empirical question, some research suggests that there tends to be a correspondence between an SMO's diagnostic and prognostic framings (Benford 1987, Gerhards & Rucht 1992, Nepstad 1997). In other words, the identification of specific problems and causes tends to constrain the range of possible "reasonable" solutions and strategies advocated.

Studies have identified additional constraints on prognostic framings. As with other framing activities, it is important to keep in mind that prognostic framing takes place within a multi-organizational field (Evans 1997, Klandermans 1992; also see Curtis & Zurcher 1973) consisting of various SMOs constituting a movement industry, their opponents, targets of influence, media, and bystanders. Thus it is not surprising that an SMO's prognostic framing activity typically includes refutations of the logic or efficacy of solutions advocated by opponents as well as a rationale for its own remedies. The former has been referred to as "counterframing" (Benford 1987:75), a topic we discuss more fully below. The important point is that opposing framing activity can affect a movement's framings, on the one hand, by putting movement activists on the defensive, at least temporarily, and, on the other hand, by frequently forcing it to develop and elaborate prognoses more clearly than otherwise might have been the case. In the case of the Chinese democracy movement (in 1989), for example, students accurately anticipated the state counterframings of the student movement as "counterrevolutionary," "turmoil," and "upheaval." To deflect these counterframings, the students carefully fashioned and articulated reformist prognoses and employed a tactical repertoire that was consistent with traditional Chinese cultural narrations of community devotion and self-sacrifice (Zuo & Benford 1995).

Case studies reveal that the prognostic dimension is one of the primary ways in which a movement's SMOs differ from one another. In a study of the US anti-death penalty movement, Haines (1996) observed that the movement eventually evolved into two distinct wings: abolitionists and litigators, the former advocating abolishment of capital punishment and the latter focusing on "the more modest task of saving lives of their clients one by one rather than as a class" (p. 118). Although the factions still interact, recognizing one another's indispensability, they differ in terms of their prognostic framings and the techniques they advocate and employ.

Motivational framing, the final core framing task, provides a "call to arms" or rationale for engaging in ameliorative collective action, including the construction of appropriate vocabularies of motive. Attending to this framing task essentially entails the development of what Gamson (1995) refers to as the "agency" component of collective action frames. In a study of the US nuclear disarmament movement, Benford (1993b) addressed this agency issue by identifying four generic vocabularies of motive that emerged in the course of interaction among movement activists, rank-and-file supporters, recruits, and significant others: vocabularies of severity, urgency, efficacy, and propriety. These socially constructed vocabularies provided adherents with compelling accounts for engaging in collective action and for sustaining their participation. When adopted and espoused in particular combinations, and depending on their relative saliency for the participants, these four vocabularies of motive worked in a contradictory rather than complementary fashion. Ironically, activists' framings amplifying the severity and urgency of the nuclear threat contributed to a diminished sense of efficacy among the frame articulators. However, activists overcame this by constructing an elaborated vocabulary of propriety or duty. Further research needs to specify the conditions that affect the construction and adoption of various vocabularies of motive as well as assess their relative impact on social movement participation, collective identity processes, and other movement framing activities.

Variable Features of Collective Action Frames

In addition to focusing conceptual and empirical attention on the characteristic features of collective action frames, movement scholars have also identified and elaborated their variable features, including problem identification and direction or locus of attribution; flexibility and rigidity, inclusivity and exclusivity; interpretive scope and influence; and degree of resonance.

Problem Identification and Direction/Locus of Attribution   The most obvious way in which collective action frames vary is in terms of the problems or issues addressed and the corresponding direction of attribution. It appears that the bulk of research on the link between framing and movements has focused on this variable feature, yielding a long list of specific types of collective action frames (Benford 1997:414–15). Although we do not question the analytical utility of identifying and elaborating new types of collective action frames, this particular focus appears to have yielded diminishing returns in terms of contributing to the accumulation of knowledge regarding movement framing dynamics.

A few studies have attended comparatively to variations in problem identification and attributions across social movements, SMOs, and/or time (e.g. Benford & Valadez 1998, Berbrier 1998, Ellingson 1995, Evans 1997, Marullo et al 1996, Mooney & Hunt 1996, Taylor 1999). For instance, Gerhards & Rucht (1992) reported differences between two late-1980s West German mobilization campaigns with respect to the number of problems activists identified. They hypothesize that the "larger the range of problems covered by a frame, the larger the range of social groups that can be addressed with the frame and the greater the mobilization capacity of the frame" (p. 580). They qualify their hypothesis by suggesting that it would hold only to the extent that the various problems covered by a frame could be "plausibly connected to one another."

Flexibility and Rigidity, Inclusivity and Exclusivity   Collective action frames may vary in the degree to which they are relatively exclusive, rigid, inelastic, and restricted or relatively inclusive, open, elastic, and elaborated in terms of the number of themes or ideas they incorporate and articulate. Hypothetically, the more inclusive and flexible collective action frames are, the more likely they are to function as or evolve into "master frames" (discussed below).

Variation in Interpretive Scope and Influence   The scope of the collective action frames associated with most movements is limited to the interests of a particular group or to a set of related problems. However, some collective action frames are quite broad in terms of scope, functioning as a kind of master algorithm that colors and constrains the orientations and activities of other movements. We have referred to such generic frames as "master frames," in contrast to more common movement-specific collective action frames that may be derivative from master frames (Snow & Benford 1992). We also distinguish the foregoing conceptualization of master frames from another common usage of the term as an SMO's general, central, or primary frame (Gerhards & Rucht 1992, Johnston 1991, Meyer 1995, Voss 1996). This type of collective action frame would seem to be more aptly referred to as an "organizational frame" (Evans 1997:454) or a movement-specific frame. Just because a particular SMO develops a primary frame that contributes to successful mobilization does not mean that that frame would have similar utility for other movements or SMOs. Only a handful of collective action frames have been identified as being sufficiently broad in interpretive scope, inclusivity, flexibility, and cultural resonance to function as master frames, including rights frames (Valocchi 1996, Williams & Williams 1995), choice frames (Davies 1999), injustice frames (Carroll & Ratner 1996a,b, Gamson et al 1982), environmental justice frames (Cable & Shriver 1995, Čapek 1993), culturally pluralist frames (Berbier 1998, Davies 1999), sexual terrorism frames (Jenness & Broad 1994), oppositional frames (Blum-Kulka & Liebes 1993, Coy & Woehrle 1996), hegemonic frames (Blum-Kulka & Liebes 1993), and a "return to Democracy" frame (Noonan 1995). Noonan's study of the mobilization of women against the state in Chile illustrates the importance of both flexibility and inclusivity with respect to variation in the mobilizing potency of master frames and their relationship to specific social movements and their collective action frames. She found, for example, that while the leftist master frame of the 1950s and 1960s was not as robust as it might have been because it focused only on working class issues and did not accommodate feminism, its subsequent repression and the eventual emergence of the more elaborated and inclusive "return to democracy" master frame in the 1980s created space for a variety of movement-specific frames, including feminism. Such findings show that master frames may indeed vary in terms of how inclusive and flexible they are, and thus in their interpretive scope, and that this variability can affect the mobilization of some aggrieved groups in comparison to others. According to Swart (1995), frames that have been adopted by two or more distinctive movements, and thus function as master frames, exist not only because of the aforementioned qualities but also because they are "culturally resonant to their historical milieu" (p. 446).

Resonance   The fourth major way in which collective action frames can vary is in terms of the degree of resonance. The concept of resonance is relevant to the issue of the effectiveness or mobilizing potency of proffered framings, thereby attending to the question of why some framings seem to be effective or "resonate" while others do not (Snow & Benford 1988). Two sets of interacting factors account for variation in degree of frame resonance: credibility of the proffered frame and its relative salience.

The credibility of any framing is a function of three factors: frame consistency, empirical credibility, and credibility of the frame articulators or claimsmakers. A frame's consistency refers to the congruency between an SMO's articulated beliefs, claims, and actions. Thus, inconsistency can manifest itself in two ways: in terms of apparent contradictions among beliefs or claims; and in terms of perceived contradictions among framings and tactical actions (as between what the SMO says and what it does). Hypothetically, the greater and more transparent the apparent contradictions in either realm, the less resonant the proffered framing(s) and the more problematic the mobilization. To date, little research has been conducted on this frame resonance factor, although there are some hints of it in the literature. Zuo & Benford (1995) found that one factor that contributed to the rapid mass mobilization of ordinary Chinese citizens in 1989 was the perceived consistency between what the student activists asserted in their public framings and their behavior at Tiananmen Square compared with the apparent inconsistencies between what state elites claimed and their actual policies. In a study of Operation Rescue (an "antiabortion rights" organization), Johnson (1997) found that inconsistencies between the group's framings regarding nonviolent direct action and their tactical actions, which violate traditional tenets of nonviolent philosophy, have created inconsistencies that mute the prospect of broader support.

A second factor affecting frame resonance has to do with the empirical credibility of the collective action frame. This refers to the apparent fit between the framings and events in the world. The issue here is not whether diagnostic and prognostic claims are actually factual or valid, but whether their empirical referents lend themselves to being read as "real" indicators of the diagnostic claims (Snow & Benford 1988; but see Gamson 1992b). Can the claims be empirically verified? Is there something out there that can be pointed to as evidence of the claim embedded in the framing? Hypothetically, the more culturally believable the claimed evidence, and the greater the number of slices of such evidence, the more credible the framing and the broader its appeal. The important point is not that the claimed connection has to be generally believable, but that it must be believable to some segment of prospective or actual adherents. A prime example of this was illustrated in the case of the Heaven's Gate "cult," whose members committed mass suicide predicated on the belief that trailing behind a comet was a space craft in which they would ascend to heaven (Maniscalco 1997). In the case of the more broad-based Chinese democracy movement, student activists were able to point to the political reforms in the Soviet Union under Gorbachev as evidence that calls for similar reforms in the People's Republic were within the realm of possibility (Zuo & Benford 1995). While these examples suffice to lend support to Jasper & Poulsen's (1995:496) assertion that "empirical credibility is in the eyes of the beholder," it also is the case that the difficulties some movements experience in expanding their ranks is likely to be due in part to the empirical incredibility of their framings to more than a small cadre of people.

The final factor affecting the credibility of a collective action frame has to do with the perceived credibility of frame articulators. It is a well-established fact in the social psychology of communication that speakers who are regarded as more credible are generally more persuasive (Hovland & Weiss 1951, Aronson & Golden 1962). Variables such as status and knowledge about the issue in question have been found to be associated with persuasiveness (Hass 1981, McGuire 1985). Hypothetically, the greater the status and/or perceived expertise of the frame articulator and/or the organization they represent from the vantage point of potential adherents and constituents, the more plausible and resonant the framings or claims. In his study of the nuclear disarmament movement, Benford (1987) observed that peace groups would enlist former members of the defense establishment, such as Admiral Eugene Carroll, Daniel Ellsberg, and John Stockwell, to speak at rallies and press conferences so as to enhance the apparent credibility of the movement's claims. In a related vein, Coy & Woehrle (1996) report that during the Persian Gulf War, peace movement activists frequently engaged in a "credentialing process" whereby they would highlight the credentials of the organizations they represented.

In addition to issues of credibility, the resonance of a collective action frame is affected by its salience to targets of mobilization. Three dimensions of salience have been identified: centrality, experiential commensurability, and narrative fidelity (Snow & Benford 1988). Centrality has to do with how essential the beliefs, values, and ideas associated with movement frames are to the lives of the targets of mobilization. Research on values and beliefs indicates that they are typically arrayed in a hierarchy (Rokeach 1973, Williams 1970). Hypothetically, the more central or salient the espoused beliefs, ideas, and values of a movement to the targets of mobilization, the greater the probability of their mobilization. Sherkat & Ellison's (1997) examination of conservative Protestant's organized opposition to pornography provides indirect support for this proposition. And although the literature lacks a direct test of the relative importance of this variable to successful mobilization, a few studies appear to confirm it (e.g. Carroll & Ratner 1996a, Donovan 1995, Evans 1997).

Experiential commensurability constitutes a second factor contributing to a collective action frame's salience. Are movement framings congruent or resonant with the personal, everyday experiences of the targets of mobilization? Or are the framings too abstract and distant from the lives and experiences of the targets? Hypothetically, the more experientially commensurate the framings, the greater their salience, and the greater the probability of mobilization. This proposition has received support from both activists (e.g. Alinsky 1971) and researchers (Babb 1996, Erwin 1993, Zuo & Benford 1995). For instance, Czech women's experiences in the 1980s under state socialism appear to have undermined the resonance of feminist framings in post-Communist Czech Republic in the 1990s. Heitlinger (1996:83) explains:

> The conflict between the demands of home and work, the stress and exhaustion caused by excessive obligations, as well as the discrimination against women in the workplace, led many to reject the goal of women's equality itself. These attitudes were reinforced by the fact that women's

paid employment were chosen as goals not by women themselves but were imposed on them by the unpopular communist party-state.

Heitlinger's study is also methodologically instructive for movement framing researchers because it constitutes one of the few studies that examines the failure of framing attempts.

The last factor that appears to have significant impact on frame resonance is narrative fidelity. To what extent are the proffered framings culturally resonant? To what extent do they resonate with the targets' cultural narrations, or what Campbell (1988) would call its "myths," Gouldner (1970) its "domain assumptions," and Rudé (1980) "inherent ideology" in contrast to its "derived ideology"? When such correspondence exists, framings can be said to have what has been termed "narrative fidelity" (Fisher 1984). Hypothetically, the greater the narrative fidelity of the proffered framings, the greater their salience and the greater the prospect of mobilization.

The importance to mobilization of constructing collective action frames that have narrative fidelity—or "cultural resonance," the preferred term of several movement framing researchers—has been confirmed by a plethora of studies across a wide array of social movements, including the Central American refugee sanctuary movement (Park 1998), the contemporary white separatist movement (Berbrier 1998), the liturgical movement in the Vatican II Catholic church (McCallion & Maines 1999), a US antitoxics/incinerator movement (Kubal 1998), the eighteenth-century slavery abolitionist movement in Great Britain (D'Anjou & Van Male 1998), and the aforementioned women's movement in Chile (Noonan 1995) and democracy movement in China (Zuo & Benford 1995). By contrast, Valocchi (1996) found that the civil rights movement's "rights frame" and the associated integrationist ideology emerged from internal battles not over which of the competing frames engendered the greatest cultural resonance but rather from materialist and political considerations regarding "who controlled important sources of funding, which organization was able to court favor with political elites, and which organizations were actively repressed by those political elites" (p. 126). Taken together, the foregoing studies appear to address the frequently repeated criticism of movement framing research for its failure to take seriously the constraints that "culture out there" imposes on social movement framing activity (e.g. Hart 1996, Jasper 1997, Swidler 1995, Williams & Kubal 1999).

FRAMING PROCESSES AND DYNAMICS

We now turn to a selective review of the literature on framing processes and dynamics. We begin by examining the processes associated with the development, generation, and elaboration of collective action frames, and then we examine how frames are diffused across movements, cultures, and time.

Frame Development, Generation, and Elaboration

Hart (1996), among others (Fine 1995, Johnston 1995, Steinberg 1998), has correctly noted that, beyond examining how activists select "frame characteristics that will be appealing to potential participants," little is known about how "frames get made" (Hart 1996:95). The literature now appears to offer extensive insights into a number of the processes associated with frame development and innovation (e.g. Cable & Shriver 1995, Čapek 1993, Gamson 1992a, Gamson et al 1982, Johnston & Snow 1998, Kubal 1998, Neuman 1998, Triandafyllidou & Fotiou 1998, White 1999, Zdravomyslova 1996; DA Snow & J Miller, unpublished data). What this literature suggests is that frames are developed, generated, and elaborated on not only via attending to the three core framing tasks discussed above, but also by way of three sets of overlapping processes that can be conceptualized as discursive, strategic, and contested.

Discursive Processes   Discursive processes refer to the talk and conversations—the speech acts—and written communications of movement members that occur primarily in the context of, or in relation to, movement activities. Collective action frames are generated by two basic interactive, discursive processes: frame articulation and frame amplification or punctuation. Frame articulation involves the connection and alignment of events and experiences so that they hang together in a relatively unified and compelling fashion. Slices of observed, experienced, and/or recorded "reality" are assembled, collated, and packaged. What gives the resultant collective action frame its novelty is not so much the originality or newness of its ideational elements, but the manner in which they are spliced together and articulated, such that a new angle of vision, vantage point, and/or interpretation is provided.

The frame amplification process involves accenting and highlighting some issues, events, or beliefs as being more salient than others. These punctuated or accented elements may function in service of the articulation process by providing a conceptual handle or peg for linking together various events and issues. In operating in this fashion, these punctuated issues, beliefs, and events may function much like synecdoches, bringing into sharp relief and symbolizing the larger frame or movement of which it is a part. Movement slogans such as "Liberte, Fraternite, Egalilte," "Power to the People," "We Shall Overcome," and "Homeless, Not Helpless" illustrate this function.

There are few studies of these processes. One such exception is Gamson's study (1992a) of how ordinary people discuss and frame political ideas in the context of focus groups. Another is the ethnographic examination (DA Snow & J Miller, unpublished data) of how the discursive processes of frame articulation and amplification have contributed to the development, elaboration, and maintenance of a number of overlapping collective action frames within a radical, right-wing group in Arizona. This research indicates that collective action frames are continuously reconstituted during the course of interaction that occurs in the context of movement gatherings and campaigns, and that the key to understanding the evolution of frames resides in the articulation and amplification processes rather than in the topics or issues comprising the frames. The problem with such research is that it is highly labor intensive, requiring not only fieldwork over time but access to and retrieval of the discourse that is part and parcel of the framing process.

Strategic Processes   Much more empirical attention has been devoted to the strategic processes associated with social movement framing. By strategic processes, we refer to framing processes that are deliberative, utilitarian, and goal directed: Frames are developed and deployed to achieve a specific purpose—to recruit new members, to mobilize adherents, to acquire resources, and so forth. Strategic efforts by social movement organizations to link their interests and interpretive frames with those of prospective constituents and actual or prospective resource providers were initially conceptualized as "frame alignment processes" (Snow et al 1986). Four basic alignment processes have been identified and researched: frame bridging, frame amplification, frame extension, and frame transformation.

Frame bridging refers to the linking of two or more ideologically congruent but structurally unconnected frames regarding a particular issue or problem. Bridging can occur between a movement and individuals, through the linkage of a movement organization with an unmobilized sentiment pool or public opinion cluster, or across social movements. Although there has been little systematic focus on this frame alignment strategy, we suspect that this is among the most prevalent of framing strategies. McCallion & Maines (1999) report that the liturgical movement within the Catholic Church relied extensively on frame bridging by using the Catholic academic world to link sentiment pools of lay professionals and clergy to the liturgical renewal movement. Gerhards & Rucht (1992) found that West German activists mobilizing against the World Bank and the Internationcl Monetary Fund successfully bridged their frames with those of peace, ecology, women's, neighborhood, and labor movement groups.

Frame amplification involves the idealization, embellishment, clarification, or invigoration of existing values or beliefs. Given that one of the key factors affecting whether or not a proffered frame resonates with potential constituents has to do with the extent to which the frame taps into existing cultural values, beliefs, narratives, folk wisdom, and the like, it is not surprising to find that most movements seek to amplify extant beliefs and values (McCallion & Maines 1999, Park 1998, Reese 1996, Skillington 1997, Weed 1997, Williams 1995, Zuo & Benford 1995). And while frame amplification seems to be deemed necessary for most movement mobilizations, it appears to be particularly relevant to movements reliant on conscience constitutents who are strikingly different from the movement beneficiaries (Paulsen & Glumm 1995) and to movements that have been stigmatized because their beliefs and/or values contradict the dominant culture's core values (Berbrier 1998). In the case of the latter, Berbrier's (1998) analysis of "new racist" rhetoric revealed that contemporary white separatists employed a host of frame amplification tactics in an attempt to transform the stigma of white supremacy by deploying "ethnic affectations" such as "love," "pride," and "heritage preservation."

Frame extension entails depicting an SMO's interests and frame(s) as extending beyond its primary interests to include issues and concerns that are presumed to be of importance to potential adherents. Empirical examinations of frame extension indicate that although movements often employ this alignment strategy (Carroll & Ratner 1996b, Davies 1999), it is subject to various hazards and constraints. McCallion & Maines (1999) and Benford (1993a) report that frame extension activities spawned increases in intramural conflicts and disputes within movements regarding issues of ideological "purity," efficiency, and "turf." In their historical analysis of the American Federation of Labor (1881–1955), Cornfield & Fletcher (1998) conclude that the "actions of institutional actors in the market and polity seemed to constrain and compel the AFL to extend its frame among potential adherents" (p. 1317). Babb's (1996) study of the US labor movement (1866–1886) demonstrates how a movement's constituents can extend the movement's frame, which in turn "can lead to instability in the movement" when the extended frame turns out to be "unpalatable to movement leaders" (p. 1046). These studies serve to underscore the fact that movement framing processes are frequently contested and negotiated processes, not always under the tight control of movement elites, and that employing a particular alignment strategy does not always yield the desired results.

Frame transformation, the final strategic alignment process, refers to changing old understandings and meanings and/or generating new ones. Few movement studies deal explicitly with this form of frame alignment. One recent notable exception is White's (1999) participant observation study of a Black feminist collective's attempts to overturn various racist and sexist myths regarding rape, and to transform public understanding of the seriousness of rape, especially within an African American community. In addition to constructing a powerful and compelling counterdiagnosis of the problem of sexual assault, the collective "countered rape myths with FBI statistics and social science research in an attempt to lend 'empirical credibility' to [their] frame tranformation efforts" (p. 86).

Contested Processes   There is widespread agreement among movement framing researchers that the development, generation, and elaboration of collective action frames are contested processes. All actors within the collective action arena who engage in this reality construction work are embroiled in the politics of signification. This means that activists are not able to construct and impose on their intended targets any version of reality they would like; rather there are a variety of challenges confronting all those who engage in movement framing activities. Thus far the literature elaborates on three forms these challenges tend to take: counterframing by movement opponents, bystanders, and the media; frame disputes within movements; and the dialectic between frames and events.

The very existence of a social movement indicates differences within a society regarding the meaning of some aspect of reality (Benford 1993a). Those who oppose the changes advocated by a movement sometimes publicly challenge the movement's diagnostic and prognostic framings. Attempts "to rebut, undermine, or neutralize a person's or group's myths, versions of reality, or interpretive framework" have been referred to as counterframing (Benford 1987:75). Opponents' counterframes, in turn, often spawn reframing activity by the movement: attempts "to ward off, contain, limit, or reverse potential damage to the movement's previous claims or attributes" (Benford & Hunt 1994). Such square-offs between movements and their detractors have been referred to as "framing contests" (Ryan 1991).

Although the literature is replete with references to and descriptions of counterframing tactics (Benford & Hunt 1994, Freudenberg & Gramling 1994, Zuo & Benford 1995) and framing contests (Coles 1998, Davies 1999, Krogman 1996, Neuman 1998, Williams 1995), these studies fail to shed much light on the factors that tend to shape the outcomes of such contests, other than stating or implying the tautology that those who won employed the most resonant framings. One thing we do know, however, is that these framing contests occur within complex, multi-organizational—and sometimes multi-institutional—arenas (McAdam 1996, Meyer 1995), that movement actors often take this fact into account (Ellingson 1995, Evans 1997), and that social movement framing activity and the extent of its resonance are affected by the cultural and political environment, including the framings/counterframings of institutional elites (McAdam 1996).

Perhaps the most well-studied topic related to counterframing/framing contests is the subject of movements and media framing. Indeed, how the mass media framed movements of the 1960s was the first topic researched by scholars drawing on the framing concept (Gitlin 1977, 1980, Tuchman 1978). Since this topic has recently been the subject of extensive reviews (Gamson et al 1992, Gamson & Wolsfeld 1993, Ryan 1991, Scheufele 1999), we do not review that literature here. Suffice it to say, in the present context of contested meanings, that social movement activists rarely exercise much control over the "stories" media organizations choose to cover (Entman & Rojecki 1993, McCarthy et al 1996) or how the media represent the activists' claims (Baylor 1996, Gamson & Modigliani 1989, Klandermans & Goslinga 1996).

Framing contests not only take place between movements and their opponents, they can also occur internally. Following Goffman's (1974) use of the term, Benford (1993a) referred to intramovement disagreements regarding diagnoses and prognoses as "frame disputes." These are essentially disputes over reality (present or projected). A third type of dispute, referred to as "frame resonance disputes," entails disagreements regarding "how reality should be presented so as to maximize mobilization" (Benford 1993a:691). Analyzing disputes within the Austin (Texas) nuclear disarmament movement, Benford found that frame disputes were a pervasive aspect of the movement's dynamics, shaping the movement's structure, interorganizational relations, and collective identity construction. He concluded that the intramural conflicts were both detrimental and facilitative of movements and their SMOs. Other scholars have reported similar findings within the US anti-death penalty movement (Haines 1996), the 1920s Ku Klux Klan (Jessup 1997), a Black feminist collective (White 1999), and the US labor movement (Clemens 1996).

The final way in which movement framings can be contested, and thus modified or transformed, concerns the dialectic tension between collective action frames and collective action events. This dynamic was well illustrated by Ellingson's (1995) analysis of public discourse and riots about abolitionism in antebellum Cincinnati. He found that initial framings helped to legitimate and make possible some forms of action and, conversely, how collective action transformed the meaning and the structure of the discourse, thereby limiting subsequent opportunities for collective action. Thus the discourse affects the events which, in turn, "... may change the underlying ideas or beliefs that make up the discourses and frames used by movement actors, resignify which set of collective beliefs are salient, and alter the meaning of actors' interests—all of which affect the power of a particular discourse or frame" (Ellison 1995:136). Ellingson's analysis suggests the need to develop a more complex model of the relationship between collective action frames and collective action than has traditionally been assumed.

Frame Diffusion

Thus far we have examined the literature concerning the discursive, strategic, and contested processes associated with the development, generation, and elaboration of collective action frames. We now turn to the role of framing in diffusion processes. How do movement ideas, collective action frames, and practices spread from one movement to another, and from one culture to another? How do framing processes affect the diffusion of movement beliefs, objects, and practices? Extrapolating from recent theorizing on cross-national diffusion in the social movement arena (Snow & Benford 1999), framing activity is most relevant to social movement diffusion processes when only one party in the process—either the transmitter or the adopter—takes an active role in the process, or when the conditions of similarity or compatibility between transmitters and potential adopters are not given but are problematic and in need of construction. When these conditions are present, there are two ideal types of social movement diffusion processes in which the objects of diffusion—whether cultural ideas, items, or practices—are framed so as to enhance the prospect of their resonance with the host or target culture: strategic selection or adaptation and strategic fitting or accommodation. Strategic selection encompasses situations in which there is intentional cross-cultural borrowing, with the adopter or importer assuming the role of an active agent in the process, strategically selecting and adapting the borrowed item to the new host context or culture. Strategic fitting encompasses situations in which there is intentional cross-cultural promotion, with the transmitter actively engaged in tailoring and fitting the objects or practices of diffusion to the host culture.

To date, few movement framing scholars have considered diffusion issues. Jenness & Broad (1994) and Jenness (1995) examined how the gay/lesbian movement strategically selected and adapted collective action frames from the women's movement concerning "sexual terrorism" in order to define violence against gays/lesbians as a social problem. Borrowing the assertion from the women's movement that "*all* women are at risk at all times," the movement's "educational efforts and street patrols underscore the notion that gays and lesbians—as well as any one presumed to be gay or lesbian—are at risk at all times" (Jenness & Broad 1994:417).

CONTEXTUAL CONSTRAINTS AND FACILITATION

Taken together, research on the core framing processes indicates that collective action frames are not static, reified entities but are continuously being constituted, contested, reproduced, transformed, and/or replaced during the course of social movement activity. Hence, framing is a dynamic, ongoing process. But this process does not occur in a structural or cultural vacuum. Rather, framing processes are affected by a number of elements of the socio-cultural context in which they are embedded. Although hypothetically any number of such factors might affect framing processes and the character and continuity of the resultant frames, the literature points to three factors that are particularly important: political opportunity structure, cultural opportunities and constraints, and the targeted audiences.

Political Opportunity Structure

One of the major foci of social movement research and theory over the past 25 years has concerned the relationship between changes in the structure of political opportunities, especially changes in the institutional structure and/or informal relations of a political system, and movement mobilization (McAdam et al 1996). The movement framing literature has also attended to such macro factors by investigating how political opportunity structures constrain and facilitate collective action frames (Anheier et al 1998, Benford & Valadez 1998, Evans 1997, Flam 1996, Johnston & Snow 1998, Marullo et al 1996). In their historical analysis of agrarian mobilization in the United States, for example, Mooney & Hunt (1996) found that some agrarian master frames, such as "agrarian fundamentalism," contained logical structures and fidelity qualities that contributed to their sustained resonance, even during times of contracting political opportunities, in contrast to the "competitive capitalism" and "producer" master frames that were subject to declining resonance among farmers as the agrarian economy changed. Thus, for some frames, changes in material conditions led to changes in frame resonance, which in turn led to reframing; for other frames, they found continuity across several decades of agrarian mobilizations.

Cultural Opportunities and Constraints

Just as the political opportunity structure constrains and facilitates movement frames and framing activities, so too does the cultural context in which movement activity is embedded. This is a central thesis in the work of Jasper (1997) and Goodwin & Jasper (1999), among others. In their critique of political process theory, and particularly its emphasis on political opportunity structures, Goodwin & Jasper (1999:48) contend that the perspective's proponents have erred in incorporating and privileging "frame analysis as the preferred form, much less only form, of cultural inquiry for the study of social movements" because it reifies culture and ignores the ways in which culture shapes framing processes as well as political opportunities. Since we attended in part to this issue earlier when we discussed "narrative fidelity" and "cultural resonance," here we briefly clarify culture's role with respect to framing processes.

The cultural material most relevant to movement framing processes include the extant stock of meanings, beliefs, ideologies, practices, values, myths, narratives, and the like, all of which can be construed as part of Swidler's metaphorical "tool kit" (1986), and thus which constitute the cultural resource base from which new cultural elements are fashioned, such as innovative collective action frames, as well as the lens through which framings are interpreted and evaluated. From this perspective, movements are "both consumers of existing cultural meanings and producers of new meanings" (Tarrow 1992:189). As Tarrow (1998:118) elaborates:

> Then lessons of the civil rights movement is that the symbols of revolt are not drawn like musty costumes from a cultural closet and arrayed before the public. Nor are new meanings unrolled out of whole cloth. The costumes of revolt are woven from a blend of inherited and invented fibers into collective action fremes in confrontation with opponents and elites.

Several recent movement studies lend support to this conception of the recursive relationship between extant culture and movement frames (Berbrier 1998, d'Anjou 1998, Kubal 1998, Nepstad 1997, Platt & Fraser 1998, Taylor 1999). Davies (1999) analyzed a contemporary movement in Ontario that had been lobbying the provincial government to fund separate religious schools. In doing so, they drew on extant frames grounded in traditional cultural values and myths and fashioned new frames based on emerging values. Mindful of the changing political cultural supporting "multiculturalism," activists reframed religion as culture in need of protection. But also mindful of the value/myth of individual freedom to choose, they argued that parents should be allowed to choose whether or not their children attended secular or religious schools. Fusing "these two frames—multiculturalism and school choice—is doubly strategic because it allows one to assert the rights of collectivities (to have their cultures accommodated) and individuals (to demand particular schools)" (Davies 1999:9). The lessons drawn from these studies are that changing cultural resonances and collective action frames reciprocally influence one another and that framing processes typically reflect wider cultural continuities and changes.

Audience Effects

It has long been taken as a given in communication studies that the target of the message can affect the form and content of the message. In the social movement arena, activists and targeted audiences interact. Moreover, movements find it necessary to appeal to multiple audiences who vary in terms of their relative interests, values, beliefs, and knowledge, as well as with respect to which of the various movement or countermovement roles they can potentially play.

The movement framing literature suggests that the audience(s) targeted are one of the major contextual factors that help explain why movements seek, from time to time, to modify their collective action frames. Several researchers have observed how factors relevant to the targets of mobilization can precipitate frame transformations (Coy & Woehrle 1996, Ellingson 1995, Evans 1997). In his extensive investigation of the civil rights movement, McAdam (1996) noted how various "reference publics," including segregationists, the media, the public, and the federal government, affected movement framing activities. From their study of environmental controversies related to incinerator settings, Walsh et al (1993) concluded that "early framing of protest ideology to appeal to wider publics (e.g., recycling vs. NIMBY), may be more important factors in determining the outcome of grass-roots protests in environmental disputes" than various "static variables such as a host community's socioeconomic status, its degree of organization, its level of discontent ... and the proposed facility's size" (pp. 36–37). Following Goffman (1959), other movement scholars have pointed out how activists adjust frames depending on whether the audience targeted is in the back or the front region (Benford & Hunt 1992, Kubal 1998). Along similar lines, Jasper & Poulsen's (1995) research on the animal rights and anti-nuclear movements demonstrates how different mechanisms work to recruit strangers and friends. Such studies clearly indicate that the dynamic relationship between collective action frames and audiences warrants additional analytical attention from movement researchers.

FRAMING CONSEQUENCES FOR OTHER MOVEMENT PROCESSES AND OUTCOMES

Having considered how various contextual factors constrain and facilitate framing processes in the previous section, we now turn to a brief examination of the consequences or implications of framing processes. Our focus is not on the effects of framing processes with respect to micro- and meso-mobilization and differential recruitment and participation. These effects, which have been theorized and demonstrated empirically, constituted a central rationale for this review in the first place. Rather, we examine the effects or consequences of framing processes and their resultant collective action frames for other movement-related processes and outcomes. Although this connection could be explored with respect to almost any aspect of the operation and functioning of social movements, the literature, albeit somewhat sparse on this topic, mainly addresses three sets of implications:

one with respect to political opportunity, a second pertaining to individual and collective identity, and the third concerning movement-specific outcomes.

Framing and Political Opportunity

Although political opportunity structures can constrain or facilitate collective action framing processes, the degree or extent of political opportunity in any society is seldom, if ever, a clear and easily read structural entity. Rather, its existence and openness is subject to debate and interpretation and can thus be framed by movement actors as well as by others. In fact, Gamson & Meyer (1996) suggest that movement actors do this routinely, asserting that "the framing of political opportunity is . . . [a] central component of collective action frames" (p. 285). Indeed, to proffer a collective action frame is to suggest that an opportunity to affect social change exists, and that people are "potential agents of their own history" (Gamson & Meyer 1996:285). Moreover, if "movement activists interpret political space in ways that emphasize opportunity rather than constraint, they may stimulate actions that change opportunity, making their opportunity frame a self-fulfilling prophecy" (Gamson & Meyer 1996:287). Diani's (1996) research on Italy's Northern League lends support to Gamson & Meyer's proposition, as does Goodwin & Jasper's (1999) critique of the political opportunity perspective.

To argue that framing processes and political opportunity are linked interactively is not to suggest that political opportunities are purely socially constructed entities. It is to argue, however, that the extent to which they constrain or facilitate collective action is partly contingent on how they are framed by movement actors as well as others (Koopmans & Duyvendak 1995).

Framing and Individual and Collective Identity

One of the major themes permeating the movement literature in recent years is the contention that an understanding of identity processes, and particularly collective identity, is fundamental to understanding the dynamics of social movements (e.g. Jasper 1997, Melucci 1989, Snow & Oliver 1995, Taylor & Whittier 1992). This recent interest in the connection between identity and movements is stimulated in part not only by the rise of identity-based movements during the past several decades, but also by the very real, longstanding connection between identity and movement participation. As Gamson (1992b) has noted regarding this linkage, "[c]leansed of its assumptions about a spoiled or ersatz identity, there is a central insight that remains. Participation in social movements frequently involves enlargement of personal identity for participation and offers fulfillment and realization of the self" (p. 56).

While few would argue with Gamon's contention, the question of how participation precipitates the enlargement of personal identity, or the correspondence between individual and collective identities, has not been satisfactorily answered by scholars investigating this linkage. In exploring this issue, Snow & McAdam (2000) have suggested that collective action framing processes constitute a central mechanism facilitating this linkage. The reason for this is that identity constructions are an inherent feature of the framing process. As Hunt et al (1994) have noted, "not only do framing processes link individuals and groups ideologically but they proffer, buttress, and embellish identities that range from collaborative to conflictual" (p. 185). Framing processes do this in two ways: at a general level, "by situating or placing relevant sets of actors in time and space and by attributing characteristics to them that suggest specifiable relationships and lines of action" (Hunt et al 1994:185); and, at a more concrete level, during the course of identity talk among adherents and activists (Hunt & Benford 1994) and other movement activities, such as preparing press releases and making public pronouncements. Framing processes are not the only mechanism that accounts for the correspondence between personal and collective identities, of course, but it can be argued both theoretically and empirically that it is one of several mechanisms that facilitates this alignment and thus the enlargement of personal identity in movement contexts.

Framing and Specific-Movement Outcomes

Social movements presumably emerge in order to advance the interests of their adherents or beneficiaries by securing specifiable objectives typically conceptualized as outcomes. Research on this topic has identified several sets of factors (e.g. organization, tactical disruption, and political mediation) that appear to affect movements' outcome attainment efforts (see Giugni 1998 for a summary). Although a number of studies have suggested the importance of framing processes in relation to movement goal attainment (Čapek 1993, Diani 1996, Reese 1996, Walsh et al 1993, Zdravomyslova 1996, Zuo & Benford 1995), there have been few systematic studies of the actual contribution of framing processes. The one exception is Cress & Snow's (2000) investigation of how organizational, tactical, political, and framing variables interact and combine to account for differences in the outcomes attained by 15 homeless social movement organizations active in eight US cities. Of the four sets of independent variables, robust diagnostic and/or prognostic frames were found to be the most persistently present condition across the six pathways leading to the attainment of one or more of four different types of outcomes, with no other condition present in more than three of the pathways. While a single study such as this hardly demonstrates conclusively the importance of framing processes to outcome attainment for movements in general, it certainly suggests that for some movements, framing processes are critical to the attainment of desired outcomes. As well, it calls for further investigation of the relationship between framing processes and the goal attainment efforts of different varieties of movements.

CONCLUSION

At the outset we raised two orienting questions. Does the literature congeal or hang together in a fashion suggestive of a coherent, albeit still evolving, perspective that contributes to a more thoroughgoing and integrated understanding of the relationship between framing processes and the operation of social movements? And does this evolving perspective cast analytic light on aspects of movement dynamics that other perspectives have glossed over or failed to illuminate altogether? Based on our review and assessment of the burgeoning literature on social movement framing processes, we think the answer to each question is affirmative. To assert this is not to claim that there are not unresolved issues and questions, however. Thus, we conclude with an itemization of a number of the more glaring unresolved issues and concerns, each of which warrants further inquiry: the discursive and narrative processes generative of collective action frames (Fisher 1997, Polletta 1998, Steinberg 1998); the relationship between framing and emotions (Berbrier 1998, Jasper 1997); the relationship between framing processes and movement types (Jasper 1997, Snow et al 1998); the relationship between collective action frames and actual collective action (Ellingson 1995); and methodologies for investigating framing processes and conducting frame analysis (Johnston 1995, Gerhards 1995).

ACKNOWLEDGMENTS

We gratefully acknowledge the research assistance provided by Debra Bozell and Jason Miller, and the financial support provided by the Center for Advanced Study in the Behavioral Sciences, where D.A. Snow was a Fellow during a portion of the period in which this article was written.

Visit the Annual Reviews home page at www.AnnualReviews.org

LITERATURE CITED

Alinsky SD. 1971. *Rules for Radicals: A Pragmatic Primer for Realistic Radicals.* New York: Random House

Anheier HK, Neidhartdt F, Vortkamp W. 1998. Movement cycles and the Nazi Party: activities of the Munich NSDAP, 1925–1930. *Am. Behav. Sci.* 41:1262–81

Aronson E, Golden B. 1962. The effect of relevant and irrelevant aspects of communicator credibility on opinion change. *J. Perspect.* 30:325–42

Babb S. 1996. 'A true American system of finance': frame resonance in the U.S. labor movement, 1866 to 1886. *Am. Sociol. Rev.* 61:1033–52

Bateson G. 1972. *Steps to an Ecology of the Mind.* New York: Ballantine

Baylor T. 1996. Media framing of movement protest: the case of American Indian protest. *Soc. Sci. J.* 33:241–55

Benford RD. 1987. *Framing activity, meaning, and social movement participation: the nuclear disarmament movement.* PhD thesis. Univ. Texas, Austin, 297 pp.

Benford RD. 1993a. Frame disputes within the nuclear disarmament movement. *Soc. Forces* 71:677–701

Benford RD. 1993b. 'You could be the hundredth monkey': collective action frames and vocabularies of motive within the nuclear disarmament movement. *Sociol. Q.* 34:195–216

Benford RD. 1997. An insider's critique of the social movement framing perspective. *Sociol. Inq.* 67:409–30

Benford RD, Hunt SA. 1992. Dramaturgy and social movements: the social construction and communication of power. *Sociol. Inq.* 62:36–55

Benford RD, Hunt SA. 1994. *Social movement counterframing and reframing: repairing and sustaining collective identity claims.* Presented at Midwest Sociol. Soc. Conf., St. Louis

Benford RD, Valadez DL. 1998. *From blood on the grapes to poison on the grapes: strategic frame changes and resource mobilization in the farm workers' movement.* Presented at Am. Sociol. Assoc. Conf., San Francisco

Berbrier M. 1998. 'Half the battle': cultural resonance, framing processes, and ethnic affectations in contemporary white separatists rhetoric. *Soc. Probl.* 45:431–50

Best J. 1987. Rhetoric in claims-making: constructing the missing children problem. *Soc. Probl.* 34:101–21

Blum-Kulka S, Liebes T. 1993. Frame ambiguities: Intifada narrativization of the experience by Israeli soldiers. In *Framing the Intifada: People and Media*, ed. AA Cohen, G Wolsfeld, pp. 27–52. Norwood, NJ: Ablex

Cable S, Shriver T. 1995. Production and extrapolation of meaning in the environmental justice movement. *Soc. Spectr.* 15:419–42

Campbell J. 1988. *The Power of Myth.* New York: Doubleday

Čapek SM. 1993. The 'environmental justice' frame: a conceptual discussion and application. *Soc. Probl.* 40:5–24

Carroll WK, Ratner RS. 1996a. Master frames and counter-hegemony: political sensibilities in contemporary social movements. *Can. Rev. Sociol. Anthropol.* 33:407–35

Carroll WK, Ratner RS. 1996b. Master framing and cross-movement networking in contemporary social movements. *Sociol. Q.* 37:601–25

Clemens ES. 1996. Organizational form as frame: collective identity and political strategy in the American labor movement. See McAdam et al 1996, pp. 205–26

Coles RL. 1998. Peaceniks and warmongers' framing fracas on the home front: dominant

and opposition discourse interaction during the Persian Gulf crisis. *Sociol. Q.* 39:369–91

Cornfield DB, Fletcher B. 1998. Institutional constraints on social movement 'frame extension': shifts in the legislative agenda of the American Federation of Labor, 1881–1955. *Soc. Forces* 76:1305–21

Coy PG, Woehrle LM. 1996. Constructing identity and oppositional knowledge: the framing practices of peace movement organizations during the Persian Gulf War. *Sociol. Spectr.* 16:287–327

Cress DM, Snow DA. 2000. The outcomes of homeless mobilization: the influence of organization, disruption, political mediation, and framing. *Am. J. Sociol.* 105:1063–1104

Curtis RL, Zurcher LA. 1973. Stable resources of protest movements: the multi-organizational field. *Soc. Forces* 52:53–61

d'Anjou L, Van Male J. 1998. Between old and new: social movements and cultural change. *Mobilization* 3:207–26

Davies S. 1999. From moral duty to cultural rights: a case study of political framing in education. *Sociol. Educ.* 72:1–21

della Porta D, Kriesi H, Rucht D, eds. 1999. *Social Movements in a Globalizing World.* London: Macmillan

Diani M. 1996. Linking mobilization frames and political opportunities: insights from regional populism in Italy. *Am. Sociol. Rev.* 61:1053–69

Donovan BL. 1995. Framing and strategy: explaining differential longevity in the Woman's Christian Union and the Anti-Saloon League. *Sociol. Inq.* 65:143–55

Ellingson S. 1995. Understanding the dialectic of discourse and collective action: public debate and rioting in antebellum Cincinnati. *Am. J. Sociol.* 101:100–44

Entman RM, Rojecki A. 1993. Freezing out the public: elite and media freming of the U.S. anti-nuclear movement. *Polit. Commun.* 10:155–73

Erwin L. 1993. Neoconservatism and the Canadian pro-family movement. *Can. Rev. Sociol. Anthropol.* 30:401–20

Evans JH. 1997. Multi-organizational fields and social movement organization frame content: the religious pro-choice movement. *Sociol. Inq.* 67:451–69

Ferree MM, Miller FD. 1985. Mobilization and meaning: toward an integration of social psychological and resource mobilization perspectives on social movements. *Sociol. Inq.* 55:8–51

Fine GA. 1995. Public narration and group culture: discerning discourse in social movements. See Johnston & Klandermans 1995, pp. 127–43

Fisher K. 1998. Locating frames in the discursive universe. *Sociol. Res. Online* 2(3):<http://www.socresonline.org.uk/socresonline/2/3/4.html>

Fisher WR. 1984. Narration as a human communication paradigm: the case of public moral argument. *Commun. Monogr.* 51:1–23

Flam H. 1996. Anxiety and successful oppositional construction of societal reality: the case of KOR. *Mobilization* 1:103–21

Freudenberg WR, Gramling R. 1994. Midrange theory and cutting edge sociology: a call for cumulation. *Environ. Technol. Soc.* 76:3–6

Gamson WA. 1992a. *Talking Politics.* New York: Cambridge Univ. Press

Gamson WA. 1992b. The social psychology of collective action. See Morris & Mueller, pp. 53–76

Gamson WA. 1995. Constructing social protest. See Johnston & Klandermans 1995, pp. 85–106

Gamson WA, Croteau D, Hoynes W, Sasson T. 1992. Media images and the social construction of reality. *Annu. Rev. Sociol.* 18:373–93

Gamson WA, Fireman B, Rytina S. 1982. *Encounters with Unjust Authority.* Homewood, IL: Dorsey

Gamson WA, Meyer DS. 1996. The framing of political opportunity. See McAdam et al 1996, pp. 275–90

Gamson WA, Modigliani A. 1989. Media discourse and public opinion on nuclear power:

a constructionist approach. *Am. J. Soc.* 95:1–37

Gamson WA, Wolsfeld MA. 1993. Movements and media as interacting systems. *Ann. Am. Acad. Polit. Soc. Sci.* 528:114–25

Geertz C. 1973. *The Interpretation of Cultures.* New York: Basic Books

Gerhards J. 1995. Framing dimensions and framing strategies: contrasting ideal- and real-type frames. *Soc. Sci. Inf.* 34:225–48

Gerhards J, Rucht D. 1992. Mesomobilization: organizing and framing in two protest campaigns in West Germany. *Am. J. Sociol.* 98:555–95

Gitlin T. 1977. Spotlights and shadows: television and the culture of politics. *College English* 38:789–801

Gitlin T. 1980. *The Whole World Is Watching: Mass Media in the Making & Unmaking of the New Left.* Berkeley: Univ. Calif. Press

Giugni MG. 1998. Was it worth the effort? The outcomes and consequences of social movements. *Annu. Rev. Sociol.* 24:371–93

Goffman E. 1959. *The Presentation of Self in Everyday Life.* Garden City, NY: Anchor Books

Goffman E. 1974. *Frame Analysis: An Essay on the Organization of the Experience.* New York: Harper Colophon

Goodwin J, Jasper JM. 1999. Caught in a winding, snarling vine: the structural bias of political process theory. *Sociol. Forum* 14:27–54

Gouldner AW. 1970. *The Coming Crisis in Western Sociology.* New York: Basic Books

Haines HH. 1996. *Against Capital Punishment: The Anti-Death Penalty Movement in America, 1972–1994.* New York: Oxford Univ. Press

Hall S. 1982. The rediscovery of ideology: return to the repressed in media studies. In *Culture, Society and the Media*, ed. M Gurevitch, T Bennett, J Curon, J Woolacott, pp. 56–90. New York: Methuen

Hart S. 1996. The cultural dimension of social movements: a theoretical reassessment and literature review. *Sociol. Rel.* 57:87–100

Hass RG. 1981. Effects of source characteristics on cognitive responses and persuasion. In *Cognitive Responses in Persuasion*, ed. TM Ostrom, TC Brock, pp. 141–74. Hilsdale, NJ: Erlbaum

Heitlinger A. 1996. Framing feminism in post-communist Czech Republic. *Communist Post-Communist Stud.* 29:77–93

Hovland C, Weiss W. 1951. The influence of source credibility on communication effectiveness. *Public Opin. Q.* 15:635–50

Hunt SA, Benford RD. 1994. Identity talk in the peace and justice movement. *J. Contemp. Ethnog.* 22:488–517

Hunt SA, Benford RD, Snow DA. 1994. Identity fields: framing processes and the social construction of movement identities. See Laraña et al 1994, pp. 185–208

Jasper JM. 1997. *The Art of Moral Protest.* Chicago: Univ. Chicago Press

Jasper JM, Poulsen JD. 1995. Recruiting strangers and friends: moral shocks and social networks in animal rights and antinuclear protests. *Soc. Probl.* 42:493–512

Jenness V. 1995. Social movement growth, domain expansion, and framing processes: the gay/lesbian movement and violence against gays and lesbians as a social problem. *Soc. Probl.* 42:145–70

Jenness V, Broad KL. 1994. Antiviolence activism and the (in)visibility of gender in the gay/lesbian and women's movements. *Gend. Soc.* 8:402–23

Jessup MM. 1997. Legitimacy and the decline of the 1920s Ku Klux Klan. *Res. Soc. Mov. Confl. Chang.* 20:177–221

Johnson V. 1997. Operation rescue, vocabularies of motive, and tactical action: a study of movement framing in the practice of quasi-nonviolence. *Res. Soc. Mov. Confl. Chang.* 20:103–50

Johnston H. 1991. Antecedents of coalition: frame alignment and utilitarian unity in the Catalan anti-Francoist opposition. *Res. Soc. Mov. Confl. Chang.* 13:241–59

Johnston H. 1995. A methodology for frame analysis: from discourse to cognitive schemata. See Johnston & Klandermans 1995, pp. 217–46

Johnston H, Klandermans B, eds. 1995. *Social Movements and Culture.* Minneapolis: Univ. Minn. Press

Johnston H, Snow DA. 1998. Subcultures and the emergence of the Estonian nationalist opposition 1945–1990. *Sociol. Perspect.* 41:473–97

Kane AE. 1997. Theorizing meaning construction in social movements: symbolic structures and interpretations during the Irish land war, 1879–1882. *Soc. Theory* 15:249–76

Klandermans B. 1984. Mobilization and participation: social-psychological expansions of resource mobilization theory. *Am. Soc. Rev.* 49:583–600

Klandermans B. 1992. The social construction of protest and multiorganizational fields. See Morris & Mueller 1992, pp. 77–103

Klandermans B. 1997. *The Social Psychology of Protest.* Oxford, UK: Blackwell

Klandermans B, de Weerd M, Sabucedo JM, Costa M. 1999. Injustice and adversarial frames in a supranational political context: farmers' protest in the Netherlands and Spain. See della Porta et al 1999, pp. 134–47

Klandermans B, Goslinga S. 1996. Media discourse, movement publicity, and the generation of collective action frames: theoretical and empirical exercises in meaning construction. See McAdam et al 1996, pp. 312–37

Koopmans R, Dyvendak JW. 1995. The political construction of the nuclear energy issue and its impact on the mobilization of antinuclear movements in Western Europe. *Soc. Probl.* 42:235–51

Krogman NT. 1996. Frame disputes in environmental controversies: the case of wetland regulations in Louisiana. *Sociol. Spectr.* 16:371–400

Kubal TJ. 1998. The presentation of political self: cultural resonance and the construction of collective action frames. *Sociol. Q.* 39:539–54

Laraña E, Johnston H, Gusfield J, eds. 1994.

New Social Movements: From Ideology to Identity. Philadelphia: Temple Univ. Press

Maniscalco ML. 1997. Cult spirit and virtual vertigo: the collective suicide of heaven's gate. *Sociologia* 31:41–68

Marullo S, Pagnucco R, Smith J. 1996. Frame changes and social movement contraction: U.S. peace movement framing after the cold war. *Sociol. Inq.* 66:1–28

McAdam D. 1996. The framing function of movement tactics: strategic dramaturgy in the American civil rights movement. See McAdam et al 1996, pp. 338–55

McAdam D, McCarthy JD, Zald MN, eds.1996. *Comparative Perspectives on Social Movements Opportunities, Mobilizing Structures, and Framing.* Cambridge, UK: Cambridge Univ. Press

McCallion MJ, Maines DR. 1999. The liturgical social movement in the Vatican II Catholic Church. *Res. Soc. Mov. Confl. Chang.* 21:125–49

McCarthy JD. 1994. Activists, authorities, and media framing of drunk driving. See Laraña et al 1994, pp. 133–67

McCarthy JD, Smith J, Zald MN. 1996. Assessing public media, electoral, and governmental agendas. See McAdam et al 1996, pp. 291–311

McGuire WJ. 1985. Attitudes and attitude change. In *Handbook of Social Psychology*, ed. G Lindzey, E Aronson, pp. 233–346. New York: Random House. 3rd ed.

Melucci A. 1989. *Nomads of the Present.* Philadelphia: Temple Univ. Press.

Meyer DS. 1995. Framing national security: elite public discourse on nuclear weapons during the cold war. *Polit. Commun.* 12:173–92

Meyer DS. 1999. Tending the vineyard: cultivating political process research. *Sociol. Forum* 14:79–92

Mooney PH, Hunt SA. 1996. A repertoire of interpretations: master frames and ideological continuity in U.S. agrarian mobilization. *Sociol. Q.* 37:177–97

Morris AD, Mueller CM, eds. 1992. *Frontiers*

in Social Movement Theory. New Haven, CT: Yale Univ. Press

Nepstad SE. 1997. The process of cognitive liberation: cultural synapses, links, and frame contradictions in the U.S.-Central America peace movement. *Sociol. Inq.* 67:470–87

Neuman WL. 1998. Negotiated meanings and state transformation: the trust issue in the progressive era. *Soc. Probl.* 45:315–35

Noonan RK. 1995. Women against the state: political opportunities and collective action frames in Chile's transition to democracy. *Sociol. Forum* 10:81–111

Oliver P, Johnston H. 2000. *What a good idea! Frames and ideologies in social movement research. Mobilization* 5:In press

Pan Z, Kosicki GM. 1993. Framing analysis: an approach to news discourse. *Polit. Commun.* 10:55–75

Park K. 1998. The religious construction of sanctuary provision in two congregations. *Sociol. Spectr.* 18:393–421

Paulsen R, Glumm K. 1995. Resource mobilization and the importance of bridging beneficiary and conscience constitutencies. *Natal J. Sociol* 9:37–62

Platt GM, Fraser MR. 1998. Race and gender discourse strategies: creating solidarity and framing the civil rights movement. *Soc. Probl.* 45:160–79

Polletta F. 1998. 'It was like a fever . . . ': narrative and identity in social protest. *Soc. Probl.* 45:137–59

Reese E. 1996. Maternalism and political mobilization: how California's postwar child care campaign was won. *Gend. Soc.* 10:566–89

Rokeach M. 1973. *The Nature of Human Values.* New York: Free

Rudé G. 1980. *Ideology and Popular Protest.* New York: Knopf

Ryan C. 1991. *Prime Time Activism: Media Strategies for Grassroots Organizing.* Boston: South End

Scheufele DA. 1999. Framing as a theory of media effects. *J Commun.* 49:103–22

Schon DA, Rein M. 1994. *Frame Reflection: Toward the Resolution of Intractable Policy*

Controversies. New York: Basic Books

Sherkat DE. 1998. *What's in a frame? Toward an integrated social psychology of social movements.* Presented at Int. Sociol. Assoc. Conf., Montreal, Quebec

Sherkat DE, Ellison C. 1997. The cognitive structure of a moral crusade: conservative Protestantism and opposition to pornography. *Soc. Forces* 75:957–82

Silver I. 1997. Constructing 'social change' through philanthropy: boundary framing and the articulation of vocabularies of motives for social movement participation. *Sociol. Inq.* 67:488–503

Skillington T. 1997. Politics and the struggle to define: a discourse analysis of the framing strategies of competing actors in a 'new' participatory forum. *Br. J. Sociol.* 48:493–513

Snow DA. 2000. *Ideology, Framing processes, and Islamic movements.* Presented at Sociology of Islamic Social Movements Conf., New York

Snow DA, Benford RD. 1988. Ideology, frame resonance, and participant mobilization. *Int. Soc. Mov. Res.* 1:197–218

Snow DA, Benford RD. 1992. Master frames and cycles of protest. See Morris & Mueller 1992, pp. 133–55

Snow DA, Benford RD. 1999. Alternative types of cross-national diffusion in the social movement arena. See della Porta et al 1999, pp. 23–49

Snow DA, Benford RD. 2000. Clarifying the relationship between framing and ideology in the study of social movements: a comment on Oliver and Johnston. *Mobilization* 5: In press

Snow DA, Cress DM, Downey L, Jones A. 1998. Disrupting the 'quotidian': reconceptualizing the relationship between breakdown and the emergence of collective action. *Mobilization* 3:1–22

Snow DA, McAdam D. 2000. Identity work processes in the context of social movements: clarifying the identity/movement nexus. In *Self, Identity, and Social Movements,* ed.

S. Stryker, T Owens, R White. New York: Aldine de Gruyter. In press

Snow DA, Miller J. 1999. An empirical examination of frame articulation and amplification. Unpublished manuscript

Snow DA, Oliver PE. 1995. Social movements and collective behavior: social psychological dimensions and considerations. In *Sociological Perspectives on Social Psychology,* ed. KS Cook, GA Fine, JS House, pp. 571–99. Boston: Allyn & Bacon

Snow DA, Rochford EB, Worden SK, Benford RD. 1986. Frame alignment processes, micromobilzation, and movement participation. *Am. Sociol. Rev.* 51:464–81

Steinberg MW. 1998. Tilting the frame: consideration on collective action framing from a discursive turn. *Theory Soc.* 27:845–64

Swart WJ. 1995. The League of Nations and the Irish question: master frames, cycles of protest, and 'master frame alignment.' *Sociol. Q.* 36:465–81

Swidler A. 1986. Culture in action: symbols and strategies. *Am. Sociol. Rev.* 51:273–86

Swidler A. 1995. Cultural power and social movements. See Johnston & Klandermans 1995, pp. 25–40

Tannen D, ed. 1993. *Framing in Discourse.* New York: Oxford Univ. Press.

Tannen D, Wallat C. 1993. Interactive frames and knowledge schemas in interaction: examples from a medical examination/interview. See Tannen 1993, pp. 57–76

Tarrow S. 1992. Mentalities, political cultures, and collective action frames: constructing meaning through action. See Morris & Mueller 1992, pp. 174–202

Tarrow S. 1998. *Power in Movement.* New York: Cambridge Univ. Press. 2nd ed.

Taylor V. 1999. Gender and social movements: gender processes in women's self-help movements. *Gend. Soc.* 13:8–33

Taylor V, Whittier N. 1992. Collective identity in social movement communities: lesbian feminist mobilization. See Morris & Mueller 1992, pp. 104–29

Thompson JB. 1984. *Studies in the Theory of Ideology*. Cambridge, UK: Polity

Triandafyllidou A, Fotiou A. 1998. Sustainability and modernity in the European union: a frame theory approach to policymaking. *Sociol. Res. Online* 3(1):<http://www.socresonline.org.uk/socresonline/3/1/2.html>

Tuchman G. 1978. *Making News: A Study in the Construction of Reality*. New York: Free

Turner RH, Killian LM. 1972. *Collective Behavior*. Englewood Cliffs, NJ: Prentice-Hall. 2nd ed.

Tversky A, Kahneman D. 1981. The framing of decisions and the psychology of choice. *Science* 211:453–58

Valocchi S. 1996. The emergence of the integrationist ideology in the civil rights movement. *Soc. Probl.* 43:116–30

van Dijk TA. 1977. *Text and Context Exploration in the Semantics and Pragmatics of Discourse*. London: Longman

Voss K. 1996. The collapse of a social movement: the interplay of mobilizing structures, framing, and political opportunities in the Knights of Labor. See McAdam et al 1996, pp. 227–58

Walsh E, Warland R, Smith DC. 1993. Backyards, NIMBYs, and incinerator sitings: implications for social movement theory. *Soc. Probl.* 40:25–38

Weed FJ. 1997. The framing of political advocacy and service responses in the crime victim rights movement. *J. Sociol. Soc. Welf.* 24:43–61

White AM. 1999. Talking black: micromobilization processes in collective protest against rape. *Gend. Soc.* 13:77–100

Williams GI, Williams RH. 1995. 'All we want is equality': rhetorical framing in the fathers' rights movement. In *Images of Issues*, ed. J Best, pp. 191–212. New York: de Gruyter. 2nd ed.

Williams RH. 1995. Constructing the public good: social movements and cultural resources. *Soc. Probl.* 42:124–44

Williams RH, Benford RD. 2000. Two faces of collective frames: a theoretical consideration. *Curr. Perspect Soc. Theory* 20:127–51

Williams RH, Kubal TJ. 1999. Movement frames and the cultural environment: resonance, failure, and the boundaries of the legitimate. *Res. Soc. Mov. Confl. Chang.* 21:225–48

Williams RM. 1970. *American Society: A Sociological Interpretation*. New York: Knopf

Wilson J. 1973. *Introduction to Social Movements*. New York: Basic Books

Zald MN. 1996. Culture, ideology, and strategic framing. See McAdam et al 1996, pp. 261–74

Zdravomyslova E. 1996. Opportunities and framing in the transition to democracy: the case of Russia. See McAdam et al 1996, pp. 122–37

Zuo J, Benford RD. 1995. Mobilization processes and the 1989 Chinese democracy movement. *Sociol. Q.* 36:131–56

Zurcher LA, Snow DA. 1981. Collective behavior: social movements. In *Social Psychology: Sociological Perspectives*, ed. M Rosenberg, RH Turner, pp. 447–82. New York: Basic Books

Annu. Rev. Sociol. 2000. 26:641–66

FEMINIST STATE THEORY: Applications to Jurisprudence, Criminology, and the Welfare State

Lynne A. Haney

Department of Sociology, New York University, 269 Mercer St. 4th Floor, New York, NY; e-mail: Haney@mail.soc.nyu.edu

Key Words   gender, social policy, law, criminal justice

■ **Abstract**   This chapter discusses developments in feminist state theory through a comparison of feminist interventions into jurisprudence, criminology, and welfare state theory. Early feminist work on the state analyzed how women were subordinated by a centralized state. More recently, feminist scholars unearthed how states are differentiated entities, comprised of multiple gender arrangements. This discovery of state variation surfaced differently in these three branches of scholarship. Feminist legal theorists concentrated on multiple legal discourses, feminist criminologists on the diverse sites of case processing, and feminist welfare theorists on the varied dimensions of welfare stratification. Because of their different approaches to state gender regimes, these scholars have much to offer, and to gain from, one another. Thus, this chapter argues for the importance of an interdisciplinary feminist dialogue on the state. It also suggests ways to promote such a dialogue and to insert a sociological perspective into this new mode of theorizing.

INTRODUCTION

State theory is a relatively recent addition to feminist scholarship. Although many political sociologists spent the last decade bringing the state back into their field, many feminist social scientists used this period to conceptualize ways to bring the state into the study of gender. Initially, feminists drew the state into gender studies through analyses of the state's role in reproducing patriarchal social relations; they examined how women, as a homogenous group, were oppressed by a centralized state. More recently, feminists have eschewed such conspiratorial notions of state patriarchy to take up the more complicated task of illuminating the ways states shape, and are shaped by, gender relations. Through studies of state spheres—including welfare provisions, legal codes, and penal policies—feminist theorists uncovered how states are differentiated entities, composed of multiple gender arrangements. The result has been the proliferation and diversification of feminist analyses of the state. This chapter charts the trajectories of the new feminist scholarship on different state realms.

To a large extent, this new feminist scholarship is organized by the type of state apparatus. Some scholars focus on the dynamics of welfare redistribution and policy formulation (Skocpol 1992, Orloff 1993, Gordon 1994); others center on the assignment of political citizenship and legal rights (Pateman 1988, MacKinnon 1989, Rhode 1989). Still others are concerned with the formation of penal and disciplinary practices (Smart 1990, Daly 1994, Messerschmidt 1997). Existing reviews tend to echo these divisions by systematizing feminist analyses of a particular state apparatus and fleshing out their contributions to general scholarly debates (Smart 1991, Orloff 1996, Daly & Maher 1998). By dialoguing with nonfeminist scholars, feminists made inroads into "mainstream" social science and heightened the visibility of their work (Chavetz 1997). Although extraordinarily important, these external dialogues often deflected attention from internal feminist exchanges. Feminist welfare scholars rarely refer to the work of feminist legal theorists or criminologists; the reverse is also true. Thus, we lack an understanding of the theoretical developments and empirical findings of different branches of feminist state theory.

This chapter crosses the traditional borders of subfields to compare feminist interventions into jurisprudence, criminology, and welfare state theory. I chose these fields for three primary reasons. First, although not all of these scholars claim to study the state per se, they all analyze the gendered dynamics of state apparatuses. Second, feminist research in these areas has been the most extensive, thus allowing me to compare work of similar complexity. Third, feminist scholarship in these fields has the most relevance to a broad sociological audience; it addresses issues of concern to sociologists of law, criminologists, and political sociologists. This does not imply that I confine my analysis to texts written exclusively by sociologists. Although I place sociological work in the forefront, feminist state theory is too interdisciplinary to be limited to one field. At the same time, I do restrict my discussion in several ways. Most importantly, I address feminist analyses of the state's gender regime—or the "state of play of gender relations in a given institution" (Connell 1987, p. 120). I review works that illuminate the state processes and arrangements active in fashioning gender relations in the legal, criminal justice, and welfare systems. My interest is less in feminist discussions of how or why women and men reach state systems, and more in their theories of the gendered processes that subjects encounter once embedded in these systems.

Even within these conceptual parameters, it is exceedingly difficult to do justice to the vast literature on gender and the state. Thus, this chapter is necessarily schematic; it paints a portrait of feminist state scholarship in broad strokes. Nonetheless, the portrait has a frame. As I analyze developments in these three fields, I compare feminist work in two dimensions: their accounts of the state as "need interpreter" and as "need satisfier" (Fraser 1989). I explore the extent to which feminists in these fields view state gender regimes as operating through interpretive structures, redistributive structures, or some combination of the two.

How do feminists understand the state's role in interpreting the categories of gender? Do they see these acts of interpretation as key to the gender regimes of law, criminal justice, and welfare? Or do they conceptualize state regimes as primarily redistributive in nature, that is, as stratifying women and men through differential access to material goods, social rights, and punishment? Have feminists connected these dimensions to link state interpretation and stratification? In short, I investigate the trajectories of three branches of feminist scholarship through "cultural" and "structural" perspectives.

This two-dimensional framework will facilitate dialogue among feminist thinkers who too often seem to talk past each other. It also offers a way to disentangle the complex processes that make up state gender regimes, and it highlights the similarities and differences in feminist theoretical trajectories and empirical findings. In all of these fields, feminists have moved away from simply critiquing nonfeminist scholarship or imposing mainstream paradigms onto gender analyses. They have developed models that draw on and expand existing frameworks. Their models tend to share a critical, albeit tacit, understanding of the state as a multifaceted entity. In a similar manner, they expose the way state arenas are often fraught with conflicting and contradictory messages about gender. When taken together, this feminist work replaces the notion of a singular, centralized state structure with a conception of the diversity of state apparatuses.

This recognition of state variation has surfaced differently in these three fields of feminist studies. Feminist legal scholars have developed sophisticated theories of legal interpretation and textual representation, but remain less attentive to the law's stratifying dimensions. I discuss this development in the first section of this chapter. Feminist criminologists, on the other hand, have done extraordinary empirical work on the redistributive inequalities of the criminal justice system, but have yet to advance a full theorization of the politics of representation. I describe this trajectory in the second part of the chapter. Recent feminist welfare state theory has moved in two directions—one strand examining the politics of redistribution and the other examining the politics of recognition. It has also begun to link these state dimensions in provocative ways. These theoretical innovations have much to offer, and to gain from, feminist jurisprudence and criminology. I outline these lessons in the chapter's third section. In the concluding section, I argue for the importance of establishing a dialogical field that encompasses feminist analyses of the state. I also suggest ways to create such a field and to insert a sociological perspective into this new mode of theorizing.

REPRESENTATIONS OF EQUALITY AND DIFFERENCE: Feminist Jurisprudence

Feminist jurisprudence arose in the 1970s in response to political and intellectual developments in the field of law. From the onset, feminist legal scholars were closely tied to the second-wave women's movement (Weisberg 1993). As more women entered law school, they began to problematize issues of sexual discrimination; as many of them became practitioners, they confronted difficulties "doing law" as feminists (Kay 1985, Littleton 1987). Feminist jurisprudence also emerged along with critical legal studies, forming part of a larger critique of legal liberalism and the inherent logic of law (Menkel-Meadow 1988). Feminist jurisprudence also arose at a time when sociologists of law had largely moved away from structural approaches toward ideological and interpretive frameworks (Seron & Munger 1996). Thus, the timing of feminist jurisprudence's birth shaped its subsequent maturation. These broad intellectual currents surfaced in the development of feminist jurisprudence—in its view of the law as a sexist ideology, then as an interpretation of gender relations, and finally as a constitutive discourse.

Much of the early work in feminist jurisprudence chronicled the law as an institution of male dominance. Like many Marxist feminists, these scholars indicted the law as a tool and a symbol of male power. Echoing Hartmann (1976), they claimed that the law acted to secure private patriarchy—by excluding women from the public sphere and refusing to interfere in the domestic realm, the law ensured that women remained subordinate to men (Taub & Schneider 1982, Polan 1982). Moreover, echoing Rubin (1975), feminist legal theorists argued that law was constructed around the exchange and commodification of women (Rifkin 1980). The law distorted social reality in the interest of men and was thus integral to patriarchal culture (McIntosh 1978).

Such conspiratorial arguments were a sign of the times, reminiscent of early trends in feminist theory. Although provocative, these conspiracy theories soon proved to be limited. They were of little help to feminist practitioners in their struggles doing law. Nor did they offer particularly nuanced accounts of legal institutions. Like feminist theory in general, feminist jurisprudence began to shift focus to view the law as an interpretive structure that articulated powerful statements about gender differentiation. Throughout the 1980s, feminist scholars unearthed the legal system's gender regime and explicated the state of play of gender relations in legal doctrine. There was little consensus over the character of this regime: For some, the law's gender regime operated through its assumptions of gender difference, for others through its sameness standard, and for still others through its constitution of gendered subjects.

Gender Regimes of Difference and Sameness

The equality/difference debate within feminist jurisprudence is well documented in the literature (Fineman & Thomadsen 1991, Weisberg 1993, Smith 1993, Holland 1996). At the center of the debate were competing visions of the legal system's representation of gender. On one side were those scholars who viewed the law's insistence on gender difference as the core of its regime: by conceiving of women and men as fundamentally different, the law perpetuated discrimination against women. Commonly known as "equality feminists," these scholars analyzed the gendered assumptions of U.S. legal theory and practice. Like their feminist predecessors, they located the law's gender bias in women's exclusion from the rights granted to some men (Minow 1987). Their work documented the long history of such exclusion and linked it to classifications of "real" sex differences (Eisenstein 1988). In effect, they argued that the law reproduced gender inequality by adhering to an ideology of difference (Williams 1984). The solution was therefore clear: if the law's gender regime rested on sexual difference, it could be countered by accentuating sexual similarity. Equality feminists therefore pushed legal liberalism to its limits—claiming that the law should indeed become a neutral instrument and treat women as citizens not classified by sex (Minow 1987, Eisenstein 1988).

These arguments about gender sameness unquestionably led to a series of court victories. By appropriating notions of equality, feminists challenged long-standing legal biases, especially in the areas of employment and divorce (Smart 1986, Rhode 1989, Hoff 1991). Yet this approach had more troubling outcomes in other areas, particularly in reproductive law. For instance, the Pregnancy Discrimination Act of 1978 sparked a heated debate within feminist jurisprudence. The Act applied a disability standard to pregnancy and effectively compelled employers to treat it like all other disabilities (Kay 1985, Finley 1986). Some feminists found such reasoning entirely appropriate—to secure equality, pregnant workers should be treated like workers with temporary disabilities (Williams 1984). For others, the absurdity of viewing pregnancy as a disability exemplified the danger inherent in the application of a single standard and the overall poverty of equality feminism (Krieger & Cooney 1983, Scales 1986, Eisenstein 1988).

Equality feminism was not only challenged on practical grounds; legal scholars who advanced a deeper critique of law also subjected it to theoretical scrutiny. For these scholars, equality feminists accepted precisely what was most problematic about law—its myth of equal treatment and individualism. Often referred to as "difference" or "inequality" feminists, these scholars saw the law's gender regime as rooted in the tyranny of male objectivity and male norms (Weisberg 1993). They located the law's gender bias in its viewpoint, that is, in its objective, neutral, and distanced stance toward the social world. They argued that objectivity was male in both the cultural and the psychological sense: It not only reflected male interests, but it was integral to male socialization and the male psyche (Scales 1986). They also faulted legal liberalism's assumptions about human separation and distance—assumptions that failed to appreciate the connectedness fostered by women's child-rearing experiences (West 1988). As MacKinnon (1989, p. 162) put it, the law "sees and treats women as men see and treat women" and is thus the institutionalization of male subjectivity.

Other feminist scholars used a difference approach to analyze the masculine foundations of legal norms. They revealed how legal notions of reasonable behavior worked to dismiss the experiences of those who refused to conform—the structures of sexism, racism, and homophobia often conditioned people to act in ways that made them appear unreasonable and therefore not entitled to legal protection (Lahey 1991). Legal interpretations of suffering also failed to acknowledge the distinct quality of women's pain. According to West (1991), men and women experience pleasure and pain differently; men often find pleasure in those acts that cause women pain, such as sexual harassment on the street, the consumption of pornography, or domestic abuse. Here too the law adhered to a male standard by excluding women-specific forms of injury from legal redress (Dixon 1994). Moreover, legal constructions of relevancy insisted on a male mode of argumentation—by demanding that women frame arguments in legal or administrative categories and abandon a story-telling mode, the law systematically curtailed women's ability to speak or be heard (Finley 1986, Bumiller 1990).

Still other feminists exposed how the law's gender regime of sameness obscured social relations of domination. They problematized equality doctrine's promise of similar treatment for the similarly situated—pointing out that it masked those social processes that situated women and men differently (Minow 1987). As MacKinnon (1987) argued, the sameness standard removed power from the social world and negated women's economic dependency and sexual accessibility. It also failed to recognize the distinct nature of women's embodiment, that is, how women's bodies are used as an entrance point for the regulation of social norms (Eisenstein 1988, Smart 1993). In this way, the law's denial of structural inequality ended up reproducing male dominance and privilege.

Thus, the equality/difference debate encompassed competing perspectives on the law's gender regime: For some, the law was unjust in its unequal treatment of equals, whereas for others its injustice lay in its equal treatment of unequals. By the late 1980s, many legal scholars concluded that this debate had reached an impasse. They then proposed ways to link the insights offered by each side. These scholars advanced alternative conceptions of equality—equality as acceptance (Littleton 1987), equality as a strategy (Majury 1987), and equality as "episodic" (Kay 1985). They also redefined notions of difference by shifting focus from difference to disadvantage (Rhode 1989) and by emphasizing multiple axes of difference (Harris 1990, Crenshaw 1991). In addition, they attempted to break down the dichotomies inherent in the difference/equality debate to argue for a theory of equality based on a pluralized notion of difference, what Eisenstein (1988, p. 5) termed "radical egalitarianism."

All of these theorists provided powerful readings of the law's interpretive bias. Their theoretical sophistication is largely unparalleled in other areas of feminist state theory. However, their concentration on legal interpretation often deflected attention from full analyses of redistributive practices. By eschewing empirical work in favor of abstract theorizing, feminist jurisprudence left a series of issues underexplored. How have different legal interpretations been received in the courtroom? What practical and discursive resources have they accorded women as claimants? As practitioners? How have these interpretations been adjudicated? What were the outcomes?

The one case in which feminists have explored these practical outcomes was the infamous Sears Case—the 1979 case in which the Equal Employment Opportunity Commission accused Sears, Roebuck and Co. of sex discrimination in their assignment, training, and promotion of women (Milkman 1986, Scott 1988, Eisenstein 1988). The case exemplified what could happen when certain legal interpretations were put into action. Few feminists liked what they saw: The case pitted "difference" feminism, articulated by Rosalind Rosenberg, against "equality" feminism, articulated by Alice Kessler Harris. Even more troubling than the court's 1986 ruling in favor of Sears was its selective use of difference arguments to justify discrimination. Once they hit the courtroom, both feminist approaches were stripped of their complexity and nuance (Scott 1988). Although the ominous tale of the Sears case could have provoked a renewed interest in the relationship between legal theory and practice, it did not. Instead, feminist jurisprudence moved toward increasingly abstract conceptions of the law as a constitutive discourse.

Postmodern Legal Feminism

Feminists' disillusionment with the difference/equality debate coincided with the rise of postmodernism in critical legal studies. For many, postmodernism offered a way out of the impasse (Ashe 1987, Smart 1991). Instead of viewing law as a series of rules and doctrines, feminists defined it as a constitutive discourse (Frug 1992). The law, they argued, produces meaning and creates social categories (Smart 1992). Through representation and subjectivization, the law sets social boundaries. Like literature and the media, the law is a cultural product that defines knowledge and power (Heinzelman & Wiseman 1994, Fineman 1995, Fineman & McCluskey 1997). In the process of rethinking law, these scholars also reconceptualized gender. Unlike feminist scholars who worked with fixed gender categories, postmodern legal feminists saw gender as a classificatory scheme open to negotiation. The legal system's gender regime encompassed precisely this classificatory work—the discursive processes through which gender categories accrued significance (Cornell 1992). In Smart's (1992) terms, postmodern legal feminists analyze the "technology of gender": the law as a mechanism that fixes gender signifiers, subject positions, and differentiation (de Lauretis 1987).

Another key element of postmodern legal feminism is its recognition of the law's constitution of multiple categories of difference. Here too postmodern legal feminists found fault in the work of their predecessors. They argued that the equality/difference debate focused on a single axis of oppression; it was infused with essentialism and premised on unified gender interests (Crenshaw 1991, Dixon 1994). Such reductionism missed the complex ways the law subordinates citizens along the lines of race, class, and sexuality (Coombs 1996). According to Harris (1990), these classifications form "inexplicable webs" of oppression; the law sets down multiple boundaries of inclusion and exclusion. Thus, in Crenshaw's (1989) terms, legal theory and politics should begin to "demarginalize the intersections" by centering on the multiply disadvantaged.

Postmodernism thus marked a profound shift in feminist jurisprudence. For these theorists, the law became a framing discourse. Legal language became the site of power struggles (Frug 1992). Gender became a subject position that the law brings into being (Smart 1993). Cases like the Sears affair became texts to be unpacked for their levels of rhetorical signification (Scott 1988). When postmodern legal feminists veered away from abstract deconstruction, they turned to personal narratives of legal power and subversion (Williams 1991, White 1991). Like legal deconstruction, such narratives fostered an appreciation of juridical variability. They revealed that the law's regime does not operate through sameness or difference, but through interpretive processes that shape experience in complex ways. Although provocative, it is not clear whether such narratives led feminist scholars any closer to answering the questions posed earlier. How do legal discourses distribute resources, rights, and tools to those they target? As Seron & Munger (1996) ask of legal theory in general: what about the power of race, class, and gender that extends beyond individual experience, consciousness, or discursive signification? In short, what about a more sociologically inspired legal feminism?

PRACTICES OF BENEVOLENCE AND PUNISHMENT: Feminist Criminology

In contrast to the abstract theorizing of feminist jurisprudence, feminist criminology is quite empirically grounded. Feminist criminologists have been less influenced by the theoretical and epistemological shifts of postmodernism (Carrington 1994). They have also been less engaged in the conceptual debates of feminist theory (Simpson 1989). Until recently, their focus was primarily on the field of criminology. This dialogue with criminology left its mark on feminist analyses—surfacing in the kinds of questions they ask and the ways they answer them (Daly & Maher 1998). Feminist criminologists are arguably the least theoretical of the feminist scholars discussed in this essay, but they are also the most empirically sophisticated. They investigate precisely those issues that elude feminist legal theorists, that is, distributive patterns of punishment and stratification in the justice system.

Overall, analyses of the justice system's gender regime constitute only a small part of feminist criminology. As Daly & Chesney-Lind (1988) argue, feminist criminologists were more preoccupied with gender-ratio and generalizability problems. First, feminist criminologists conducted important research on the gender gap in crime rates. They found that women commit fewer crimes than men (Morris 1987, Triplett & Myers 1995); they discovered that women and men commit different kinds of crime (Heimer 1995), and they unearthed historical changes in patterns of female offending (Adler 1975, Simon 1975). Second, feminist criminologists challenged the misogyny underlying traditional explanations of female crime, such as theories of hormonal imbalances, mental illness, and sexual malfunction (Smart 1977, Naffine 1987). They also critiqued criminologists who imposed male models onto female experience—arguing that an "add women and stir" approach led to distorted explanations of female crime (Morris 1987, Gelsthorpe & Morris 1988). In response, feminist scholars proposed their own explanations for female criminality. They pointed to a series of explanatory factors, including structures of gender and racial inequality, levels of anomie, modes of informal/ formal social control, socialization patterns, gender norms, and opportunity structures (Steffensmeier & Allan 1996, Mann 1996, Messerschmidt 1997).

In addition to analyses of the nature and causes of female crime, feminist criminologists offered important insights into how the justice system genders its subjects. At one level, their accounts parallel those of feminist legal theorists; both groups are centrally concerned with questions of equality and difference. Yet feminist criminologists approach these questions differently; they are less interested in interpretive structures and more in patterns of tracking or labeling. In particular, feminist criminologists sought to understand how women and men are treated in the justice system, that is, whether women are subjected to more severe or more lenient treatment than men.

Gender Regimes of Severity and Leniency

Unlike feminist jurisprudence's debate about the law's gender regime of sameness or difference, feminist criminology began from the premise of difference. Empirical evidence collected since the 1970s clearly pointed to differential treatment of women in the justice system. Yet it was not entirely clear how to characterize this treatment. Sometimes referred to as the "evil woman thesis," a few early studies found that women were treated more harshly by the justice system (Temin 1973, Chesney-Lind 1977). This was particularly true for those who engaged in serious offenses; women who were thought to repudiate female norms had their "morality" called into question (Visher 1983). State officials were said to deal with these women retributively and to come down harder on those who did not conform to conventional female expectations (Parisi 1982).

This argument about the severe treatment of females was especially prominent in studies of the juvenile system. For example, Chesney-Lind & Sheldon (1997) documented the discrimination that girls experienced in the justice system. They argued that girls were drawn into the state's web for less serious offenses, such as sexual transgressions and status violations. They asserted that the justice system attempted to secure female obedience and compliance, particularly for those girls thought to be sexually active. Thus, the justice system's gender regime was said to operate through its harsh treatment and further victimization of girls.

Using large-scale statistical surveys, other feminist criminologists uncovered the opposite pattern: The justice system treated women more leniently than men (Steffensmeier et al 1993). Attention then turned to explaining this variation. On the one hand, some criminologists used these data to suggest that the justice system worked with stereotypical notions of gender (Eaton 1986). They claimed that the state took a chivalrous approach to women; justice officials did not believe women could commit crime and were unwilling to inflict harm on them (Webb 1984). State actors were also said to act paternalistically, assuming that women were childlike and not responsible for their actions (Anderson 1976). The outcome was lenient treatment designed to protect the vulnerable.

Feminist criminologists who supplemented statistical surveys with qualitative data discovered that state officials seemed less influenced by paternalist impulses and more affected by practical exigencies (Allen 1987, Ferraro 1989, Simpson 1991). Although they also saw the justice system's gender regime as one of leniency, they viewed its motives differently. For instance, in a study of >1000 probation cases, Kruttschnitt (1982) found that a defendant's level of economic dependency was the primary factor determining sentence severity. Instead of attributing this to state patriarchy, she revealed that probation officers saw dependent women as safer bets owing to the control exerted over them by their families. In a similar manner, Steffensmeier et al (1993) suggested that judges viewed female defendants as less culpable in part because of women's ties to and responsibilities in the community. They also discovered that judges weighted practical concerns quite heavily in sentencing decisions, factoring in whether women had child-care responsibilities and physical or emotional problems. Daly (1987, 1989) uncovered a similar reasoning at work in the court system. She claimed that the justice system was invested in policing traditional economic and familial roles—the court "familied" women not because they wanted to protect them, but because they sought to maintain conventional domestic arrangements and informal modes of social control.

Like the equality/difference debate, the severity/leniency debate preoccupied feminists for much of the 1980s. As in feminist jurisprudence, feminist criminologists eventually deemed this debate futile (Daly 1994). Instead of insisting on a dichotomous gender regime, some suggested that the regime operated through both severity and leniency. Perhaps the system did not function the same way at all points for all women; in arrest and imprisonment decisions, sex had a positive effect, but in sentencing decisions it exerted little influence; in all of these decisions, race and class exerted their own influence (Morris 1987, Simpson 1991, Mann 1996). Others suggested that the "evil woman" and "state paternalism" theses be seen as complementary (Crew 1991). Perhaps the system's gender regime was rooted in its enforcement of traditional sex roles, which sometimes bred more severe, and sometimes more lenient, treatment. Still others questioned the premise of the severity/leniency debate, arguing that it took men as the norm to analyze how women deviated from that norm (Daly 1994, Naffine 1996). The political implications of this troubled many feminists: In this case, applying a male standard to women could imply incarcerating more women under worse conditions for longer periods (Rafter 1990). Why not take women as the norm? In short, perhaps the justice system consisted of multiple regimes and diverse disciplinary practices.

Processing Gender, Race, and Class

Although many legal theorists transcended their equality/difference debate through postmodernism, few feminist criminologists took this route out of the severity/leniency impasse. Instead, in recent years they have broadened their empirical focus to illuminate the gendered dynamics of case processing. Rather than examine how gender affects sentencing outcomes, these criminologists elucidate the way gender constructs become embedded in case processing. With this new focus, feminist criminologists discovered variations in the justice system's messages, targets, and mode of operation. Hence, like feminist jurisprudence, feminist criminology has become more sensitive to the diversity of gender regimes. Yet they center on a different type of variation—exploring the diversity in the justice system's stratifying and labeling processes.

Daly's (1994) research on the New Haven court system is an excellent example of this approach. Daly uses multiple methods to capture the diverse contexts and dimensions of case processing. She reveals that the behavior of court officials was not motivated by patriarchy, but was guided by gendered presuppositions about criminality and justice. As cases made their way through the court, defendants were constructed in contrasting ways: notions of appropriate domestic arrangements, good mothering, familial responsibility, reformability, and victimization were deployed to label women and men. This labeling helped to shape gender differences in outcomes. Daly's analysis thus moves beyond the severity/leniency dichotomy to reject the idea of a singular gender regime. It also offers a compelling account of the many justifications used to explain female and male criminality. In short, Daly's work introduces one type of state variation—diversity in the processes through which the justice system genders its subjects.

Daly's work identifies another form of variation through an analysis of how the justice system constructs defendants along race, class, and gender lines. In doing so, Daly rejects the essentialism that plagued so much feminist work in criminology. As Simpson & Elis (1994) put it, early feminist criminology had privileged gender subordination. By ignoring the intersection of race, class, and gender, feminist criminologists had produced inaccurate analyses of the causes of female crime and the system's gender regime (Hill & Crawford 1990, Simpson 1991, Mann 1996). The justice system did not hold all women up to the same gender norms (Ferraro 1989, Carrington 1994). Nor did it label all women according to the same evaluative criteria (Arnold 1990, Naffine 1996). Thus, these scholars pointed to a second type of variation—differences in the social constructions and disciplinary practices applied to women themselves.

Reflecting these shifts, Messerschmidt's (1997) most recent work lays out an important framework for analyzing the construction of gender, race, class, and crime. Messerschmidt's framework combines Connell's (1987) structural theory of gender and West & Fenstermaker's (1995) theory of "doing difference." Like crime, Messerschmidt claims that gender, race, and class must be "done." They are situational accomplishments that can take on a multiplicity of forms. Their precise form depends largely on a social actor's structural location and context—positions that make available different constructive resources. To demonstrate this, Messerschmidt presents four case studies of gender, race, class, and crime in the making: He analyzes individual, institutional, and cultural stories to explicate how these categories were constructed and how crime became a resource for "doing" other identities. In acknowledging the constructive quality of these categories, Messerschmidt urges criminologists to unpack the diverse nature of gender, race, and class relations. Moreover, in illuminating these constructs' structural and situational aspects, he encourages criminologists to examine the ways social relationships are "made" in different institutions, including the state.

At one level, there are definite parallels between developments in feminist jurisprudence and feminist criminology. Both fields emerged with a critique of state patriarchy and evolved to recognize variations in the form and content of state gender regimes. However, their analyses of variations are of a different sort. Overall, feminist criminologists remain focused on how the justice system stratifies its subjects. Some examine how gender affects arrest and sentencing outcomes, thus offering compelling accounts of the system's structural tracking; others link these structural dynamics to the labeling of women and men, thus providing insights into the construction of gender relations. Feminist criminologists' empirical focus therefore enables them to capture precisely what is missing from feminist jurisprudence: a sociologically inspired legal feminism attentive to forms of juridical stratification and redistributive inequities.

Yet one could argue that the reverse is also true. Feminist criminologists have yet to develop the sophisticated interpretive analyses advanced by feminist legal theorists. Most feminist criminologists continue to study patterns of treatment by sex. However, the justice system also gives meaning to the categories of gender. Although some feminist criminologists have begun to illuminate how state actors draw on available gendered scripts, they tend to assume the existence of a stable symbolic order. That is, they take gendered meanings and scripts as being "out there," ready to be utilized by actors in different situations. However, as feminist legal theorists reveal, the legal and penal systems help to establish this gendered order: They produce key social categories, often in dichotomous terms, and imbue those categories with significance. State actors not only use the available repertoires to construct gender relations; they also help to constitute those repertoires. Thus, these two feminist fields have much to gain from each other. Together, they point to the importance of analyzing state structures of stratification and of interpretation in all of their nuance and complexity. It is here that feminist welfare scholars have much to offer, and to learn from, their colleagues in law and criminology.

POLICIES OF REDISTRIBUTION AND INTERPRETATION: Feminist Welfare State Scholarship

Although feminist welfare scholarship emerged at roughly the same time as feminist jurisprudence and criminology, it arose in response to different intellectual developments. As Gordon (1990) argued, feminist welfare scholars stood in dialogue with the broader state scholarship. Many feminists drew on the long tradition of theoretical work on welfare development. They confronted structural functionalist theories of the welfare state's usurpation of family functions, they grappled with Marxist theories of the welfare state as an instrument of capitalism, and they encountered state-centered theories that traced the welfare state to particular political configurations. These theoretical perspectives left their mark on feminist welfare scholarship. Of all the feminists scholars reviewed here, welfare scholars are most likely to define themselves as state theorists. They also tend to adhere to a more comparative and historical focus. From this perspective, feminist welfare scholars have begun to combine their approaches to produce innovative theories of state stratification and interpretation.

Yet these theoretical innovations took time to blossom. As in legal theory and criminology, feminist welfare scholars began by inserting women into existing frameworks. Unlike feminist jurisprudence, the welfare scholarship was not characterized by debates about equality and difference—the welfare state clearly enmeshed men and women in different programs. Thus, like feminist criminology, the welfare scholarship began from a premise of difference. For them, the key question was whether this differential treatment hurt or helped women. Early welfare scholars tended to view the state as accentuating sexual hierarchies and reproducing capitalism and patriarchy (Hartmann 1976). Through its support of the nuclear family, codification of a family ethic, and insistence on the family wage, the state was said to bolster "private" patriarchy, or female dependence on individual men (Abramovitz 1988). In addition, the state was indicted for creating a new form of "public" patriarchy, or female reliance on men as a collective embodied in the state (Brown 1981). By taking over men's familial power and stepping in to manage women's lives, feminists argued that the welfare state fostered female dependence on the state itself (Boris & Bardaglio 1983).

At the same time, other feminists advanced a more sanguine view of the welfare state. They argued that, whatever its limitations, welfare policy does help women. They pointed out that generous welfare states tend to be associated with lower levels of female poverty (Ruggie 1984, Kamerman 1984). Even when states do not eliminate female poverty, assistance programs can shield women from extreme deprivation and enhance their ability to survive materially (Piven 1990, Edin & Lein 1996). These scholars also claimed that welfare policies can foster female activism and heighten solidarity among the otherwise disconnected (Piven & Cloward 1977, Schneider 1990).

Both feminist approaches offered insights into the welfare system's effects on women. Nonetheless, as Orloff (1996) argued, these analyses failed to capture the complexity of welfare provision. They lacked an appreciation of how states actually operate; they were blind to national and historical variation in state structure. To correct for these omissions, recent feminist welfare scholarship branched off in two directions—some unpacked variation in systems of redistribution and others explored variations in interpretive structures (Haney 1998). Together, these scholars unearthed the stratifying and discursive practices of different welfare states as they develop over time.

Gender Regimes of Need Satisfaction and Interpretation

To transcend the good state/bad state divide, feminist scholars began to probe into the actual workings of the U.S. welfare state. They arrived at a critical discovery: the welfare state was bifurcated into masculine and feminine subsystems that operated in contrasting ways (Gordon 1990). The top tier, commonly known as the "social insurance" subsystem, positioned recipients as rights-bearing individuals entitled to assistance (Sapiro 1990). Policies like workmen's compensation, unemployment insurance, and Social Security bolstered recipients' provider roles and enabled them to support their families (Nelson 1990). The bottom tier, commonly known as the "social assistance" subsystem, positioned recipients as dependent clients who lacked a male breadwinner (Mink 1994). Policies like Mothers' Pensions, Aid to Dependent Children, and Aid to Families with Dependent Children accorded assistance based on a principle of care; they allocated benefits in a discretionary fashion that subjected recipients to means-tests and considerable regulation (Nelson 1990).

Although few feminist scholars disputed this characterization of the two-tiered welfare state, many found it to be incomplete. It relied on a narrow set of income-maintenance programs; the state's redistributive regime looked far more complex when a fuller range of state policies were considered (Gordon 1994). As Orloff (1996) points out, the two-tiered characterization also took the U.S. case as the norm—implicitly assuming that other states were similarly bifurcated. This assumption proved to be inaccurate. Drawing on Esping-Andersen's (1990) welfare regime typology, feminist scholars conducted comparative studies of the redistributive outputs of different welfare states. They began by adding women to Esping-Andersen's typology to ascertain whether liberal, conservative, and social-democratic regimes had different effects on women's material well being (Hobson 1994, Gustafsson 1994). They discovered that these regimes varied in several dimensions, including the organization of care work, rates of female employment, and reproductive policies. They also unearthed variations among countries of similar regime types—social-democratic regimes differed in their support for employed mothers, conservative regimes differed in their support for women's paid employment, and liberal regimes differed in their support for sole mothers (Leira 1992, Shaver 1993, Borchorst 1994, Orloff 1996). Perhaps there was not a single, uniform state gender regime; perhaps gender regimes varied by system type?

With this insight, feminist scholars probed further into the gendered dimensions of state redistribution. This resulted in a plethora of feminist welfare regime models that emphasized different dimensions and redistributive outcomes (Lewis 1992, O'Connor 1993, Sainsbury 1994). Of all these models, Orloff's work (1993, 1996) provides the most elaborate gender analysis of state welfare regimes. Her regime analysis began with an extension of Esping-Andersen's framework—she added gender differentiation to his stratification dimension, she expanded his notion of decommodification to account for care work, and she conceptualized a new dimension to capture women's ability to maintain autonomous households (Orloff

1993). More recently, O'Connor, Orloff & Shaver (1999) proposed the most comprehensive regime model to date: Their model assesses three policy arenas—labor markets, income support, and reproduction—to explicate gendered patterns of stratification, social/civil rights, income organization, and power relations. The result is a multidimensional analysis of the redistributive practices of several liberal welfare states.

As these regime analysts constructed new maps of the gendered dimensions of state redistribution, another strand of feminist scholarship explicated the interpretive bases of the welfare state. These scholars drew on and expanded the conception of the welfare state articulated by other political sociologists (Skocpol 1992, Quadagno 1994, Amenta 1998). For them, the welfare state was not only a redistributive arena; it was also a site of clashes over gendered meanings (Fraser & Gordon 1994). State gender regimes were reflections of these ideological and discursive battles. Welfare states embodied distinct claims-making modes and offered an array of rhetorical possibilities for framing needs (Peattie & Rein 1983). Like its distribution of material benefits, the allocation of discursive resources had profound political and strategic importance. The state's cultural dimensions were thus as critical as its stratifying dimensions; both dimensions fixed social relations and shaped social identities (Pringle & Watson 1992).

With this interpretive focus, feminist scholars produced a rich historiography of the formation of state conceptions of gender. Their discoveries were many. First, they complicated arguments about the state's masculine origins—revealing how female reformers appropriated a discourse of maternalism, and mixed it with a unique version of professionalism, to participate in the construction of Western welfare states (Bock & Thane 1991, Koven & Michel 1993). Exalting women's capacity to mother, female activists in the United States used a politics of difference to enter the policy sphere and fill the political vacuum occupied by working-class movements in other countries (Skocpol 1992, Sklar 1993). In doing so, they helped establish policies that emphasized women's child-rearing responsibilities and the desirability of female dependence (Muncy 1991, Goodwin 1997).

However, female reformers were not the only ones motivated by gender interests. Feminist historians also unearthed the gendered scripts adhered to by other social movements as they helped to construct the welfare state. Feminists recast the traditional battle between capital and labor, movements of militarism, and the politics of pronatalism to expose their gendered undercurrents (Klaus 1993). For example, Gordon's (1994) study of the US welfare state revealed that a variety of political forces worked with gendered agendas—from professional caseworkers to social security advocates to New Deal social movements. In her comparative study of the origins of the British and French welfare states, Pedersen (1993) provides a similarly nuanced account of the interests at stake in state formation. She shows the policy sphere to be a crowded arena occupied by unions, employers, feminists, and Catholic leaders, all with their own visions of social relationships. Ultimately, these conflicting discourses became embodied in the French parental state and the British male breadwinner model.

These two strands of welfare scholarship expose the dynamics of state stratification and interpretation. Their work adheres to a comparative and historical perspective unmatched in other areas of feminist state theory. The forms of state variation they uncover are thus of a different sort: Feminist welfare theory points to national variation among state gender regimes as they evolve. Yet there is another insight to be garnered from their scholarship—a way to link the redistributive and interpretive dimensions of state gender regimes.

Linking State Stratification and Interpretation

Feminist analyses of welfare stratification and interpretation did not develop in isolation from one another. Perhaps because of their comparative and interdisciplinary focus, these scholars forged links between their approaches. As Adams (1998) argues, feminists working in other areas of state theory might want to consider how welfare scholars have connected the state's structural and cultural dimensions.

Sainsbury (1996) offers one example of how welfare scholars made these linkages. Her work begins from a redistributive focus and expands to include the interpretive effects of welfare stratification. On the one hand, Sainsbury locates her comparative study of the U.S., U.K., Dutch, and Swedish welfare states in a traditional welfare regime framework. She then extends this framework by highlighting the bases of entitlement operative in each state, that is, how recipients are drawn into the state and on what terms. Sainsbury reveals that states provide a variety of modes of claims-making; they base entitlement claims on recipients' needs, employment, families, or citizenship. By including types of claims-making in her regime analysis, Sainsbury connects the insights of poststructuralist scholars like Pringle & Watson (1992) to those of regime analysts like Orloff (1993) and Lewis (1992). Her approach has empirical payoffs. She reveals why women fare better in regimes that base claims on citizenship (like Sweden) and fare worse in regimes that base claims on need and/or employment (like the United States).

As Sainsbury's work moves from the redistributive to the interpretive, Fraser's (1989, 1997) scholarship makes the reverse connection. Influenced by critical theory, Fraser's (1989) work explicates the "politics of need interpretation" by showing how needs leak out of the private sphere, are taken up in the social sphere, and become administered in the state sphere. In the process, needs are translated into juridical, administrative, or therapeutic issues. To investigate this translation of needs, Fraser grounds her discursive model in an analysis of the two-tiered welfare state: a state bifurcated between masculine and feminine subsystems that distribute resources differently. Fraser then links these redistributive patterns and interpretations of need. The masculine subsystem translates need into juridical and administrative issues as it constructs recipients as rights-bearing individuals; the feminine subsystem translates need into administrative and therapeutic issues as it frames recipients as dependent clients or troubled souls in need of therapeutic intervention. In Fraser's (1997) recent work, she suggests that this formulation be used as an evaluative standard. She puts out a critical call to feminist scholars—urging them to consider both redistribution and recognition when assessing state gender regimes.

THE LOOSE COORDINATION OF FEMINIST STATE SCHOLARSHIP

This review of developments in feminist jurisprudence, feminist criminology, and feminist welfare theory revealed parallels among these fields. They all arose with arguments about state patriarchy, moved on to track state conceptions of equality and/or difference, and reached a recognition of state diversity. Together, these scholars have come to reject the notion of a univocal state; they reveal that state systems speak many languages. Moreover, as their research evolved, these scholars confronted similar dilemmas. They encountered obstacles as they conceptualized the dimensions of state systems and analyzed their influence on gender relations. Yet feminists came at these issues quite differently. In their differences, they have much to offer one another.

One of the main strengths of feminist jurisprudence is its sophisticated account of the politics of representation. Feminist legal theorists provide ways to mine legal norms for their gendered meanings—frameworks that could help welfare scholars expand their focus on social policy to include a broader range of state projects and interventions. Feminist jurisprudence also offers powerful arguments about the limitations of opposing equality and difference—arguments that could help feminist criminologists transcend the severity/leniency dichotomy. At the same time, feminist jurisprudence has much to gain from feminist work in other fields. They could look to feminist criminology for clues on how to retain a structural analysis of juridical stratification. They could also appropriate welfare scholars' comparative focus to illuminate the modes of claims-making that women have utilized over time and in different national contexts to secure state resources.

Feminist criminologists also have important contributions to make to an interdisciplinary feminist dialogue on the state. One of their main strengths is their willingness to conduct both quantitative and qualitative analyses; these scholars are a model for how to mix research methods. Their work is also exemplary in its concrete description of state stratifying processes—from arrest rates to sentencing patterns to courtroom dynamics. From their concrete pictures, feminist criminologists reveal the practical effects of state gender regimes and how they vary by race and class. Thus, their empirical work provides a model of how to account for the intersections of gender, race, and class in the legal and welfare systems. However, feminist criminologists have much to take from these other fields. They could appropriate feminist jurisprudence's conception of law as an interpretive structure to capture the discursive dimensions of penal policies. Feminist welfare theorists also offer the tools to approach this issue historically. Their historical frameworks could enable feminist criminologists to explore how these discourses were inserted into the justice system and how they evolved. In fact, the few historical accounts of the justice system's gender practices have revealed unexpected findings with grave conceptual implications (Feeley & Little 1991).

In addition to offering a comparative approach to existing analyses of state stratification and interpretation, feminist welfare theory formulates ways to join these two state dimensions. This is perhaps their most important contribution to an interdisciplinary dialogue on the state. They not only recognize that state redistribution and interpretation are intricately linked, but they have constructed frameworks to capture these linkages. Their recent work explicates the stratifying effects of different modes of claims-making; it also exposes the interpretive underpinnings of different redistributive models. At the same time, welfare scholars have much to gain from increased dialogue with other fields. Feminist jurisprudence's conceptualization of gender as a process of signification could deepen welfare scholars' accounts of need interpretation and the constitution of gender identities. Welfare theorists could also draw on feminist criminologists' use of multiple methods to reveal the complex dynamics of welfare case processing.

In this way, the creation of a dialogical field that encompasses feminist scholars of law, criminology, and the welfare state could foster theoretical and empirical insights in all three areas. In this chapter, I established such a field through a two-dimensional framework of state stratification and interpretation. Using this frame, I uncovered the ways in which feminist analyses have become attentive to the diversity of state gender regimes—from the recognition of multiple legal discourses to the acknowledgment of multiple sites of case processing to the identification of multiple dimensions of welfare stratification. Yet this framework did little to explain these variations. Such an explanation would require the development of broader explanatory models or concepts, that is, a way to integrate feminists' arguments about state diversity and to assess their common features. One way to achieve this would be to begin to theorize the layered quality of state apparatuses (Haney 1996).

Hagan's (1998) formulation of the organizational dynamics of the criminal justice system provides a promising way to approach such theorizing. Hagan proposes a framework for explaining the seemingly random, and frequently inconsistent, operations of the criminal justice system. He argues that the system is composed of a series of loosely coupled subsystems: entities that are organizationally distinct but highly responsive to one another. His is an image of state layering, of state apparatuses with macro- and microlevel embodiments that are loosely coordinated and synchronized. This looseness is a key element of the framework. It opens up the possibility of disjuncture—of rules that go unimplemented, of mandates that go unobserved, and of precedents that go unfollowed in different state arenas.

Moreover, instead of viewing the criminal justice system as perpetually fractured and unpredictable, Hagan posits that its level of looseness can wax and wane over time. He roots such fluctuations in the presence of political power directed at crime-oriented goals. At historical junctures, when the political environment makes proactive demands on this state sphere, there is often a tightening of the links among subsystems. In a similar manner, in highly politicized settings where particular social groups are targeted, the system's boundaries tend to tighten in an attempt to maximize desired outcomes. Yet state systems not only act in accordance with larger political mandates, but can also tighten their systemic links to direct public attention to certain political goals. In Hagan's model, politics and political power are key determinants of the organization of state systems and their degree of looseness.

Although Hagan's model of the loosely coupled system was not designed with feminist state theory in mind, it may offer the kind of conceptual framework needed to better integrate this scholarship. On the one hand, the concept provides a way to make sense of the diversity of gender regimes within particular state apparatuses. If feminist scholars begin to think of state arenas as loosely coupled, it becomes understandable why they find different messages and agendas within a given state sphere (Horowitz 1995). It also becomes clear how state gender regimes can take on macro- and microlevel embodiments: At one level, welfare policy might position women as dependent mothers, whereas at another level welfare institutions might center on women as wage laborers. Rather than view these messages as competing or contradictory, they can be seen as rooted in the welfare system's loose coupling. This approach could also help explain why feminist criminologists' large-scale statistical findings often diverge from those of observational studies (Daly 1994). In short, it could clarify how feminists' arguments about the state depend on their unit of analysis and on the specific subsystem from which they theorize.

Conceptualizing state spheres as loosely coordinated not only explains the diversity in feminists' empirical findings—it also raises a series of new issues ripe for investigation. As Hagan (1998) notes, we know very little about the nature of the links within state subsystems; we need a far more detailed understanding of how macro- and microlevel subsystems remain organizationally distinct yet responsive to one another. Feminist scholars are in a unique position to theorize such linkages. They have collected extensive data on different state subsystems; they could use these data to probe into how gendered messages are relayed among state levels. For instance, although some scholars analyze abstract legal narratives, others research the concrete practices of court officials and state administrators. Drawing this work together would enable feminists to reflect on the macro- and microlevel translation of gendered messages and signifiers. Hence, the concept of the loosely coupled system raises common questions about state filtering processes—questions that could unite feminist scholars working in a variety of subfields.

This concept also raises new questions regarding historical variability in these macro- and microlinkages. Once the legal, criminal justice, and welfare systems are seen as loosely coupled, feminists can begin to explore potential shifts in their systemic tightness over time (Haney, forthcoming). Throughout this chapter, I have argued that feminist scholars in all three fields have moved away from the assertion of a singular, uniform gender regime to recognize the varied, and often inconsistent, nature of state gender regimes. Is this shift a reflection of organizational and institutional changes in these state systems—of a political environment that loosened the coupling of their respective subsystems? Or is it a reflection of the theoretical and empirical tools now used by feminist scholars? Recent work by welfare scholars indicates that the U.S. welfare system has always been characterized by diverse gender regimes: Their research on welfare policies and practices reveals that loose linkages have held this system together since its inception (Kunzel 1993, Gordon 1994, Goodwin 1997). Similar analyses of the evolution of macro- and microconnections in the legal and criminal justice systems could provide the basis for broader comparison and theorizing. Again, the goal is to use the concept of the loosely coupled system to tighten the links among feminist scholars working in different subfields.

In addition to illuminating and explaining diversity within a given state apparatus, the concept of the loosely coupled system can be extended to expose the connections among different state apparatuses. Such an extension would push the concept beyond Hagan's formulation: Although his concept was designed to explicate the organizational dynamics within one system, the state itself can be conceptualized as a composite of loosely coordinated systems that draw on and respond to one another. Such a conceptualization would then open up another level of dialogue among feminist scholars, enabling them to explore connections among the legal, criminal justice, and welfare systems. It would allow them to compare the macro- and microfiltering processes and translation work characteristic of different state apparatuses. For example, feminist legal scholars and criminologists have uncovered strikingly similar dichotomies: The equality/difference bifurcation embodied in law bears a close resemblance to the justice system's practices of severity/leniency. With increased dialogue, feminist scholars could theorize how the legal and justice systems, although organizationally distinct, remain responsive to similar doctrines and organizational routines.

Finally, not only would the development of a shared analytical framework be theoretically innovative, but it has also become increasingly politically imperative. In the last decade, tighter links seem to be forming among state apparatuses; transformations in one state sphere appear to feed off of and inform changes in other spheres. Evidence of this abounds. At the structural level, expansion in the criminal justice apparatus occurred along with retrenchment in the welfare system (Western & Beckett 1999). At the policy level, tougher sentencing laws were passed along with the legislation of time limits and work requirements for welfare recipients (Danner 1998). At the institutional level, new welfare agencies have set up shop in some legal aid centers and criminal justice offices. These linkages among state systems are certainly not new; they clearly existed at other historical junctures, most notably the Progressive Era (Clapp 1998). But these connections will make it difficult for feminist scholars to continue to limit their analyses to one state realm. The profound shifts underway in the U.S. legal, criminal justice, and welfare systems call for a more integrated feminist social science and politics.

Hence, I am not proposing that feminist scholars reunite around a grand theory of the centralized, tightly coordinated state. Nor am I suggesting that they move to the opposite extreme through a theory of uncoordinated, dispersed sites of state power. Rather, I would argue that feminist scholars make use of their collective finding of state diversity to theorize the dimensions of state layering, both within and among apparatuses. I would also maintain that an interdisciplinary feminist dialogue on the state is the best way to capture this layering. By loosely coordinating their scholarship, feminist social scientists could retain their focus on specific state spheres, while remaining responsive to theoretical and empirical developments in research on other state arenas.

ACKNOWLEDGMENTS

Many colleagues and students offered valuable feedback on different incarnations of the ideas presented in this chapter. For contributing to my understanding of feminist legal theory and criminology, I thank Liena Gurevich, Vanessa Barker, and Jo Dixon. For helping me to refine my general arguments about the welfare scholarship, I thank Julia Adams, Michael Burawoy, Nancy Cauthen, Ruth Horowitz, Sonya Michel, and graduate students in my 1998 seminar on gender and the welfare state at New York University.

Visit the Annual Reviews home page at www.AnnualReviews.org

LITERATURE CITED

Abramovitz M. 1988. *Regulating the Lives of Women: Social Welfare Policy from Colonial Times to the Present.* Boston, MA: South End

Adams J. 1998. Feminist theory as fifth columnist or discursive vanguard: some contested uses of gender analysis in historical sociology. *Soc. Polit.* 3:1–16

Adler F. 1975. *Sisters in Crime: The Rise of the New Female Criminal.* New York: McGraw-Hill

Allen H. 1987. Rendering them harmless: the professional portrayal of women charged with serious violent crimes. In *Gender, Crime, and Justice,* ed. P Carlen, A Worrall, pp. 81–94. Philadelphia, PA: Open Univ. Press

Amenta E. 1998. *Bold Relief: Institutional Politics and the Origins of Modern American Social Policy.* Princeton, NJ: Princeton Univ. Press

Anderson E. 1976. The 'chivalrous' treatment of the female offender in the arms of the criminal justice system. *Soc. Probl.* 23:49–57

Arnold R. 1990. Processes of victimization and criminalization of black women. *Soc. Justice* 17:153–66

Ashe M. 1987. Mind's opportunity: birthing a poststructuralist feminist jurisprudence. *Syracuse Law Rev.* 38:1129–65

Bock G, Thane P, eds. 1991. *Maternity and Gender Policies: Women and the Rise of the European Welfare States, 1880s–1950s.* New York: Routledge

Borchorst A. 1994. The Scandinavian welfare states: patriarchal, gender neutral or woman-friendly? *Int. J. Contemp. Sociol.* 31:1–23

Boris E, Bardaglio B. 1983. The transformation of patriarchy: the historic role of the state. In *Families, Politics, and Public Policy,* ed. I Diamond, pp. 70–93. New York: Longman

Brown C. 1981. Mothers, fathers, and children: from private to public patriarchy. In *Women and Revolution,* ed. L Sargent, pp. 239–68. Boston, MA: South End

Bumiller K. 1990. Fallen angels: the representation of violence against women in legal culture. *Int. J. Sociol. Law* 18:125–42

Carrington K. 1994. Postmodern and feminist
criminologies: disconnecting discourses?
Int. J. Sociol. Law 22:261–77

Chavetz JS. 1997. Feminist theory and sociology: underutilized contributions for mainstream theory. *Annu. Rev. Sociol.* 23:97–120

Chesney-Lind M. 1977. Judicial paternalism
and the female status offender: training
women to know their place. *Crime Delinq.*
23:121–30

Chesney-Lind M, Sheldon R. 1997. *Girls,
Delinquency, and Juvenile Justice.* Pacific
Grove, CA: Brooks & Cole

Clapp E. 1998. *Mothers of All Children: Women
Reformers and the Rise of Juvenile Courts in
Progressive Era America.* University Park,
PA: Pa. State Univ. Press

Connell RW. 1987. *Gender and Power.* Stanford, CA: Stanford Univ. Press

Coombs M. 1996. Interrogating identity. *Berkeley Women's Law J. Afr. Am. Law Policy Rep.
Jt. Issue* 11:222–49

Cornell D. 1992. *Beyond Accommodation.* London: Routledge

Crenshaw K. 1989. Demarginalizing the intersection of race and sex: a black feminist critique of antidiscrimination doctrine, feminist
theory, and antiracist politics. *Univ. Chicago
Legal Forum* 1989:139–67

Crenshaw K. 1991. Mapping the margins: intersectionality, identity politics, and violence
against women of color. *Stanford Law Rev.*
43:1241–99

Crew K. 1991. Sex differences in criminal sentencing: chivalry or patriarchy? *Justice Q.*
8:59–81

Daly K. 1987. Structure and practice in a criminal court. *Law Soc. Rev.* 21:267–90

Daly K. 1989. Rethinking judicial paternalism:
gender, work-family relations, and sentencing. *Gender Soc.* 3:9–36

Daly K. 1994. *Gender, Crime, and Punishment.*
New Haven, CT: Yale Univ. Press

Daly K, Chesney-Lind M. 1988. Feminism and
criminology. *Justice Q.* 5:497–538

Daly K, Maher L. 1998. Crossroads and in-
tersections: building from feminist critique.
In *Criminology at the Crossroads: Feminist
Readings in Crime and Justice*, ed. K Daly,
L Maher, pp. 1–20. New York: Oxford Univ.
Press

Danner M. 1998. Three strikes and it's women
who are out: the hidden implications for
women of criminal justice policy reforms.
In *Crime Control and Women: Feminist Implications of Criminal Justice Policy*, ed. S
Miller, pp. 1–14. London: Sage

de Lauretis T. 1987. *Technologies of Gender.*
Bloomington, IN: Indiana Univ. Press

Dixon J. 1994. The nexus of sex, spousal abuse,
and the state. *Law Soc. Rev.* 29:359–76

Eaton M. 1986. *Justice for Women?* Philadelphia, PA: Open Univ. Press

Edin K, Lein L. 1996. *Making Ends Meet:
How Single Mothers Survive Welfare and
Low-wage Work.* New York: Russell Sage
Found.

Eisenstein Z. 1988. *The Female Body and the
Law.* Berkeley, CA: Univ. Calif. Press

Esping-Andersen G. 1990. *The Three Worlds of
Welfare Capitalism.* Princeton, NJ: Princeton
Univ. Press

Feeley M, Little D. 1991. The vanishing female:
the decline of women in the criminal process,
1687–1912. *Law Soc. Rev.* 25:719–57

Ferraro K. 1989. Policing woman battering.
Soc. Probl. 36:61–74

Fineman M. 1995. *The Neutered Mother, the
Sexual Family, and Other Twentieth Century
Tragedies.* New York: Routledge

Fineman M, McClusky M, eds. 1997. *Feminism, Media, and the Law.* New York: Oxford
Univ. Press

Fineman M, Thomadsen N, eds. 1991. *At the
Boundaries of Law: Feminism and Legal
Theory.* New York: Routledge

Finley L. 1986. Transcending equality theory:
a way out of the maternity and workplace
debate. *Columbia Law Rev.* 86:1118–83

Fraser N. 1989. *Unruly Practices.* Minneapolis,
MN: Univ. Minn. Press

Fraser N. 1997. *Justice Interruptus: Critical Reflections on the 'Postsocialist' Condition.* New York: Routledge

Fraser N, Gordon L. 1994. Dependency demystified: inscriptions of power in a keyword of the welfare state. *Soc. Polit.* 1:14–31

Frug MJ. 1992. *Postmodern Legal Feminism.* New York: Routledge

Gelsthorpe L, Morris A. 1988. Feminism and criminology in Britain. *Br. J. Sociol.* 28:213–26

Goodwin J. 1997. *Gender and the Politics of Welfare Reform.* Chicago, IL: Univ. Chicago Press

Gordon L, ed. 1990. *Women, the State, and Welfare.* Madison, WI: Univ. Wisc. Press

Gordon L. 1994. *Pitied but Not Entitled: Single Mothers and the History of Welfare.* Cambridge, MA: Harv. Univ. Press

Gustafsson S. 1994. Childcare and types of welfare states. See Sainsbury 1994, pp. 45–61

Hagan J. 1998. The everyday and the not so exceptional in the social organization of criminal justice practices. In *Everyday Practices and Trouble Cases*, ed. A Sarat, M Constable, D Engel, V Hans, S Lawrence, pp. 109–25. Evanston IL: Northwest. Univ. Press

Haney L. 1996. Homeboys, babies, men in suits: the state and the reproduction of male dominance. *Am. Sociol. Rev.* 61:759–78

Haney L. 1998. Engendering the welfare state. *Comp. Stud. Soc. Hist.* 40:748–76

Haney L. *Inventing the Needy: The Gendered Transition from Socialist Welfare to Welfare Capitalism in Hungary.* Berkeley, CA: Univ. Calif. Press. Forthcoming.

Harris A. 1990. Race and essentialism in feminist legal theory. *Stanford Law Rev.* 42:581–616

Hartmann H. 1976. Capitalism, patriarchy, and job segregation by sex. *Signs* 3:137–69

Heimer K. 1995. Gender, race and the pathways to delinquency: an interactionist explanation. In *Crime and Inequality*, ed. J Hagan, R Peterson, pp. 140–73 Stanford, CA: Stanford Univ. Press

Heinzelman SS, Wiseman ZB. 1994. *Representing Women: Law, Literature, and Feminism.* Durham, NC: Duke Univ. Press

Hill G, Crawford E. 1990. Women, race, and crime. *Criminology* 28:601–23

Hobson B. 1994. Solo mothers, social policy regimes and the logics of gender. See Sainsbury 1994, pp. 170–87

Hoff J. 1991. *Law, Gender, and Justice: A Legal History of U.S. Women.* New York: NY Univ. Press

Holland FS. 1996. *Feminist Jurisprudence: Emerging from Plato's Cave.* London: Scarecrow

Horowitz R. 1995. *Teen Mothers: Citizens or Dependents?* Chicago, IL: Univ. Chicago Press

Kamerman S. 1984. Women, children, and poverty: public policies and female-headed households in industrialized countries. In *Women and Poverty*, ed. B Gelpi, N Hartsock, C Novak, M Strober, pp. 41–63. Chicago, IL: Univ. Chicago Press

Kay HH. 1985. Equality and difference: the case of pregnancy. *Berkeley Women's Law J.* 1:1–38

Klaus A. 1993. *Every Child a Lion: The Origins of Maternal and Infant Health Policy in the United States and France, 1890–1920.* Ithaca, NY: Cornell Univ. Press

Koven S, Michel S, eds. 1993. *Mothers of the New World: Maternalist Policies and the Origins of the Welfare State.* New York: Routledge

Krieger L, Cooney P. 1983. The Miller-Wohl controversy: equal treatment, positive action, and the meaning of women's equality. *Golden Gate Univ. Law Rev.* 13:513–72

Kruttschnitt C. 1982. Women, crime, and dependency. *Criminology.* 19:495–513

Kunzel R. 1993. *Fallen Women, Problem Girls: Unmarried Mothers and the Professionalization of Social Work, 1890–1945.* New Haven, CT: Yale Univ. Press

Lahey K. 1991. Reasonable women and the law. See Fineman and Thomadsen 1991, pp. 3–21

Leira A. 1992. *Welfare States and Working Mothers: The Scandinavian Experience.* New York: Cambridge Univ. Press

Lewis J. 1992. Gender and the development of welfare regimes. *J. Eur. Soc. Policy* 3:159–73

Littleton CA. 1987. Reconstructing sexual equality. *Calif. Law Rev.* 75:1279–337

MacKinnon C. 1987. *Feminism Unmodified.* Cambridge, MA: Harvard Univ. Press

MacKinnon C. 1989. *Toward a Feminist Theory of the State.* Cambridge, MA: Harv. Univ. Press

Majury D. 1987. Strategizing in equality. See Weisberg 1993, pp. 264–75

Mann CR. 1996. *When Women Kill.* Albany, NY: State Univ. NY Press

McIntosh M. 1978. The state and the oppression of women. In *Feminism and Materialism*, ed. A Kuhn, A Wolpe, pp. 254–89. London: Routledge

Menkel-Meadow C. 1988. Feminist legal theory, critical legal studies, and legal education or, "the fem crits go to law school." *J. Legal Educ.* 38:49–66

Messerschmidt J. 1997. *Crime as Structured Action: Gender, Race, Class, and Crime in the Making.* Thousand Oaks, CA: Sage

Milkman R. 1986. Women's history and the Sears case. *Fem. Stud.* 12:375–400

Mink G. 1994. *Wages of Motherhood: Inequality in the Welfare State, 1917–1942.* Ithaca, NY: Cornell Univ. Press

Minow M. 1987. The Supreme Court 1986 term, justice engendered. *Harv. Law Rev.* 101:10

Morris A. 1987. *Women, Crime, and Criminal Justice.* Oxford, UK: Basil Blackwell

Muncy R. 1991. *Creating a Female Dominion in American Reform, 1890–1935.* New York: Oxford Univ. Press

Naffine N. 1987. *Female Crime: The Construction of Women in Criminology.* Boston, MA: Allen & Unwin

Naffine N. 1996. *Feminism and Criminology.* Philadelphia, PA: Temple Univ. Press

Nelson B. 1990. The origins of the two-channel welfare state: workmen's compensation and mothers' aid. See Gordon 1990, pp. 123–51

O'Connor J. 1993. Gender, class, and citizenship in the comparative analysis of welfare state regimes: theoretical and methodological issues. *Br. J. Sociol.* 44:501–18

O'Connor J, Orloff A, Shaver S. 1999. *States, Markets, and Families: Gender, Liberalism and Social Policy in Australia, Canada, Great Britain, and the United States.* New York: Cambridge Univ. Press

Orloff A. 1993. Gender and the social rights of citizenship: the comparative analysis of gender relations and welfare states. *Am. Sociol. Rev.* 58:303–28

Orloff A. 1996. Gender and the welfare state. *Annu. Rev. Sociol.* 22:51–78

Parisi N. 1982. Are females treated differently? A review of theories and evidence on sentencing and parole decisions. In *Judges, Lawyers, Victims, Thieves: Women, Gender Roles, and Criminal Justice*, ed. NH Rafter, EA Stanko, pp. 205–20. Boston, MA: Northeast. Univ. Press

Pateman C. 1988. *The Sexual Contract.* Stanford, CA: Stanford Univ. Press

Peattie L, Rein M. 1983. *Women's Claims: A Study in Political Economy.* New York: Oxford Univ. Press

Pedersen S. 1993. *Family, Dependence, and the Origins of the Welfare State: Britain and France, 1914–1945.* New York: Cambridge Univ. Press

Piven FF. 1990. Ideology and the state: women, power and the welfare state. See Gordon 1990, pp. 250–64

Piven P, Cloward R. 1977. *Poor People's Movements: Why They Succeed, How They Fail.* New York: Vintage

Polan D. 1982. Toward a theory of law and patriarchy. In *The Politics of Law*, ed. D Kairys. New York: Pantheon. See Weisberg 1993, pp. 419–26

Pringle R, Watson S. 1992. Women's interests and the poststructuralist state. In *Destabilizing Theory*, ed. M Barret, A Phillips, pp. 53–73. Stanford, CA: Stanford Univ. Press

Quadagno J. 1994. *The Color of Welfare: How*

Racism Undermined the War on Poverty. New York: Oxford Univ. Press

Rafter NH. 1990. *Partial Justice: Women, Prisons, and Social Control.* New Brunswick, NJ: Transaction Books

Rhode DL. 1989. *Justice and Gender: Sex Discrimination and the Law.* Cambridge, MA: Harv. Univ. Press

Rifkin J. 1980. Toward a theory of law and patriarchy. *Harv. Women's Law J.* 3:83–95

Rubin G. 1975. The traffic in women: notes on the political economy of sex. In *Toward an Anthropology of Women*, ed. R Reiter, pp. 157–210. New York: Mon. Rev.

Ruggie M. 1984. *The State and Working Women.* Princeton, NJ: Princeton Univ. Press

Sainsbury D, ed. 1994. *Gendering Welfare States.* Thousand Oaks, CA: Sage

Sainsbury D. 1996. *Gender, Equality, and Welfare States.* New York: Cambridge Univ. Press

Sapiro V. 1990. The gender bias of American social policy. See Gordon 1990, pp. 36–54

Scales A. 1986. The emergence of feminist jurisprudence: an essay. *Yale Law J.* 95:1373–403

Schneider A. 1990. The dialectic of rights and politics: perspectives from the women's movement. See Gordon 1990, pp. 226–49

Scott J. 1988. *Gender and the Politics of History.* New York: Columbia Univ. Press

Seron C, Munger F. 1996. Law and inequality: race, gender . . . and, of course, class. *Annu. Rev. Sociol.* 26:187–212

Shaver S. 1993. Body rights, social rights, and the liberal welfare state. *Crit. Soc. Policy* 13:66–93

Simon R. 1975. *Women and Crime.* Boston, MA: Lexington Books

Simpson S. 1989. Feminist theory, crime, and justice. *Criminology* 27:605–31

Simpson S. 1991. Caste, class, and violent crime: explaining difference in female offending. *Criminology* 29:115–34

Simpson S, Elis L. 1994. Doing gender: sorting out the caste and crime conundrum. *Criminology* 33:47–79

Sklar KK. 1993. The historical foundations of women's power in the creation of the American welfare state. See Koven & Michel 1993, pp. 43–93

Skocpol T. 1992. *Protecting Soldiers and Mothers.* Cambridge, MA: Harv. Univ. Press

Smart C. 1977. Criminological theory: its ideology and implications concerning women. *Br. J. Sociol.* 28:89–100

Smart C. 1986. Feminism and law: analysis and strategy. *Int. J. Soc. Law* 14:109–23

Smart C. 1990. Feminist approaches to criminology, or postmodern woman meets atavistic man. In *Feminist Perspectives in Criminology*, ed. L Gelstorpe, A Morris, pp. 70–84. Philadelphia, PA: Open Univ. Press

Smart C. 1991. Feminist jurisprudence. In *Dangerous Supplements: Resistance and Renewal in Jurisprudence*, ed. P Fitzpatrick, pp. 133–58. New York: Pluto

Smart C. 1992. The women of legal discourse. *Soc. Legal Issues* 1:29–44

Smart C. 1993. Proscription, prescription and the desire for certainty? Feminist theory in the field of law. *Law Polit. Soc.* 13:37–54

Smith P, ed. 1993. *Feminist Jurisprudence.* New York: Oxford Univ. Press

Steffensmeier D, Allan E. 1996. Gender and crime: toward a gendered theory of female offending. *Annu. Rev. Sociol.* 22:459–87

Steffensmeier D, Kramer J, Streifel C. 1993. Gender and imprisonment decisions. *Criminology* 31:411–46

Taub N, Schneider E. 1982. Perspectives on women's subordination and the role of law. In *The Politics of Law*, ed. D Kairys, pp. 328–55. New York: Pantheon

Temin C. 1973. Discriminatory sentencing of female offenders: the argument for the ERA in a nutshell. *Am. Crim. Law Rev.* 11:355–72

Triplett R, Myers L. 1995. Evaluating contextual patterns of delinquency: gender-based differences. *Justice Q.* 12:59–79

Visher C. 1983. Gender, police arrest decisions, and notions of chivalry. *Criminology* 21:2–28

Webb D. 1984. More on gender and justice. *Sociology* 18:367–81

Weisberg DK, ed. 1993. *Feminist Legal Theory: Foundations.* Philadelphia, PA: Temple Univ. Press

West C, Fenstermaker S. 1995. Doing difference. *Gender Soc.* 9:8–37

West R. 1988. Jurisprudence and gender. *Univ. Chicago Law Rev.* 55:1–72

West R. 1991. The difference in women's hedonic lives: a phenomenological critique of feminist legal theory. See Fineman and Thomadsen 1991, pp. 115–34

Western B, Beckett K. 1999. How unregulated is the U.S. labor market? The penal system as a labor market institution. *Am. J. Sociol.* 104:1030–60

White L. 1991. Subordination, rhetorical survival skills, and Sunday shoes: notes on the hearing of Mrs. G. See Fineman and Thomadsen 1991, pp. 40–58

Williams P. 1991. *The Alchemy of Race and Rights: Diary of a Law Professor.* Cambridge, MA: Harv. Univ. Press

Williams W. 1984. Equality's riddle: pregnancy and the equal treatment/special treatment debate. *NY Univ. Rev. Law Soc. Change* 13: 325–80

Annu. Rev. Sociol. 2000. 26:667–92

PATHWAYS TO ADULTHOOD IN CHANGING SOCIETIES: Variability and Mechanisms in Life Course Perspective

Michael J. Shanahan

Department of Human Development & Family Studies and Population Research Institute, Pennsylvania State University, University Park, Pennsylvania 16802; e-mail: mxs54@psu.edu

Key Words   life course, adulthood, agency, social structure, demography, social stratification

■ **Abstract**   The transition to adulthood has become a thriving area of research in life course studies. This review is organized around two of the field's emerging themes. The first theme is the increasing variability in pathways to adult roles through historical time. The second theme is a heightened sensitivity to transition behaviors as developmental processes. Accounts of such processes typically examine the active efforts of young people to shape their biographies or the socially structured opportunities and limitations that define pathways into adulthood. By joining these concepts, I suggest new lines of inquiry that focus on the interplay between agency and social structures in the shaping of lives.

OVERVIEW

In their 1986 contribution to the *Annual Review of Sociology*, Hogan & Astone proposed a population-based, dynamic approach to the transition to adulthood. Accordingly, they emphasized the contextual and institutional factors that explain differences in the transition to adult roles across different societies, among social strata within a society, and through historical time. Research since then has consolidated and expanded this view considerably, focusing on markers of the transition to adulthood. These markers include leaving school, starting a full-time job, leaving the home of origin, getting married, and becoming a parent for the first time. Many investigations have emphasized central tendencies in these life course events (for example, the median age at first marriage). Research of the past two decades, however, has increasingly focused on the variability of these markers (George 1993, Rindfuss et al 1987), including their dispersion (for example, variation in age at first marriage), their variable sequencing, their degree of co-occurrence, and the duration of intervals among them.

0360-0572/00/0815-0667$14.00

This review explores two central themes. First, trends reveal significant changes in the transition to adulthood through historical time. Part one evaluates influential arguments that the modernization of societies has coincided with the standardization and individualization of the life course. Standardization appears in the increasing "compactness" in the ages of school completion, marriage, parenthood, and beginning one's career, whereas individualization is found in increasingly diverse sequences of these markers. In turn, these trends have been complicated by short-term economic fluctuations and discrete historical events and, within cohorts, by social inequalities such as gender, race, and socioeconomic status.

Greater diversity in the transition to adulthood has inspired research that explores the second theme, the widespread adoption of a developmental stance by sociologists as they link the experiences of youth and adulthood. The transition to adulthood is now viewed less as a discrete set of experiences that are temporally bounded in the life course and more as an integral part of a biography that reflects the early experiences of youth and also that shapes later life. Part two considers this developmental stance as it reflects both young people's active efforts to shape their biographies and the structured set of opportunities and limitations that define pathways into adulthood. In the concluding section of this essay, I identify several methodological innovations that are well suited to the study of the transition to adulthood.

HISTORICAL PATTERNS IN THE TRANSITION TO ADULTHOOD

The timing and sequencing of transition markers have changed through historical time, simultaneously reflecting long-term trends and short-term fluctuations between cohorts, as well as variability within cohorts (Hogan 1981). The modernization of societies is often considered the underlying process driving long-term trends that differentiate successive cohorts, but short-term economic changes and discrete historical events have complicated these trends. In turn, differences within cohorts reflect inequalities due to race, gender, and socioeconomic status.

Long-Term Patterns in Transition Markers: The Modernity Argument Evaluated

Paradoxically, many commentators argue that modernization has promoted both standardization and variability in the transition to adulthood.[1] Kohli (1986) argued

---

[1] "Modernization" has assumed many meanings since its early use in European sociological theory and subsequent dissemination across the American social sciences. Common to many conceptions, however, is a constellation of societal changes thought to mark a break with previous forms of social organization: rapid technological changes, the emergence of market economies, urbanization, industrialization, the decline of agricultural life, secularization, broad-based political participation, the use of currency, and the spread of science (e.g. Ross 1994, Singal 1998).

that the life course has become less determined by the family and locale (the individualization hypothesis) and at the same time more standardized by age (the age-grading or institutionalization hypothesis). According to this argument, individualization and standardization reflect the modernization of society, especially changes in labor markets (see also Beck 1992) and the increasing role of the state in people's lives (see also Mayer & Muller 1986). Empirical evidence suggests that the transition to adulthood has indeed both standardized and diversified, although these trends reflect many historical developments. It may be that the transition to adulthood has become especially diversified since the 1960s.

Standardization of the Life Course   According to Kohli (1986), the organization of public services, transfer payments, and employment opportunities by age renders the life course more orderly and calculable. Similarly, Buchmann (1989) maintained that the rationalization of the economy and polity have promoted institutionalization of the life course. The state increased the number of rights that an individual could claim on a universalistic, standardized basis through the twentieth century, but at the same time it restricted the individual's right to organize many aspects of life (for example, with respect to education and entry into and exit from the labor market).

Consistent with these arguments, several strands of evidence suggest that the transition to adulthood has standardized. Examining the prevalence of different female life course patterns (for example, spinster vs widowed mother) among cohorts of women born between 1830 and 1920, Uhlenberg (1969) observed a convergence on the "typical" female life course pattern, involving survival to age 20, marriage, having children, and surviving with husband until age 55. Among women born in 1830, ~21% experienced this "typical" pattern in contrast to ~57% of women born in 1920. He also observed a narrowing of the age range in which women typically married and had children. The primary factor promoting standardization of the life course was improvement in mortality rates brought about by the management of contagious and infectious diseases such as smallpox (see also Uhlenberg 1974).

Similarly, between 1880 and 1970, it took 80% of both men and women markedly less time to leave the household of origin, marry, and establish their own household among those who experienced these transitions (Modell et al 1976). Modell & Goodman (1990) likewise observed greater "compactness" among the transition markers between 1900 and 1960 in both the United States and Britain, reflecting the upward movement of the median age of school-leaving and the decline in the median age of marriage (see also Hogan 1981, Modell et al 1978, Stevens 1990, Winsborough 1979, 1980). Indeed, drawing on multivariate analyses, Hogan (1981) reported that a measure of modernity—reflecting the educational experiences of the population, life expectancy, infant and youth mortality rates, and percentage of youths in the labor market—is significantly associated with a compression of the transition markers for the cohorts born between 1907 and 1946 (for a review of additional supporting material, see Hagestad & Neugarten 1985).

Thus, the transition to adulthood has standardized in that the time it took most people to pass through a range of transition markers has constricted since the early nineteenth century. Theoreticians have emphasized the critical role of "modernity" in explaining this long-term pattern, but, more precisely, compression of the transition markers from about 1830 to 1920 primarily reflected improvements in health, whereas standardization since roughly 1905 has reflected the expansion of the educational system (Hogan 1981, National Center for Educational Statistics 1995). After World War II, the removal of the draft, the expansion of the economy, and the GI Bill operated in joint and complex ways to standardize transition behaviors (Stevens 1990).

Individualization of the Life Course   Many theorists also maintain that as people were freed from the traditional constraints of family and locale, they were able to exercise more agency in the construction of their biographies (e.g. Beck 1992, Giddens 1991). In fact, Graff (1995) maintained that an understanding of one's life course as a deliberate project was not common before the nineteenth century. Previously, the individual's life was powerfully shaped by the exigencies of family life, especially the illness or death of a parent or sibling (e.g. Hareven 1982). Consistent with these arguments, Modell and his colleagues (1976) observed that, between 1880 and 1970, the familial and nonfamilial transition markers increasingly overlapped, creating more diverse sequence patterns.

Hogan (1981) provided empirical evidence for variability in the sequencing of markers among cohorts born between 1907 and 1946. The percentage of men experiencing an "intermediate nonnormative" order of transition markers (beginning work before school completion, or marriage before beginning work but after school completion) increased from $\sim$20% in the cohorts born between 1907 and 1912 to $\sim$30% for men born in 1951. The prevalence of "extreme nonnormative" ordering (marriage before school completion) increased from <10% among cohorts born between 1907 and 1911 to >20% for cohorts born between 1924 and 1947. Modernity has a large negative effect on the prevalence of the normative pattern, but a large positive effect on the prevalence of the extreme non-normative pattern. That is, in times of greater educational attainment, lower infant mortality, greater longevity, and fewer youths in the adult labor market, men are more likely to make an extremely non-normative transition to adulthood. Thus the available evidence suggests a trend toward individualization of the life course as found in the increased variability in the sequencing and overlap of transitions.[2]

The New Individualization   Some commentators further argue that the process of individualization has become markedly different or acceleratedsince the late

---

[2]Stevens (1990) likewise observed greater overlap among the markers through historical time, although this may be limited to mixes of familial and nonfamilial transitions (e.g. workforce entry and marriage). His analysis also suggests, however, that the sequencing of transitions has remained unchanged (with some exceptions), in contrastto arguments about

1960s. According to Kohli, "the new thrust of individualization" occurs against the "background of a regulated labor market and . . . public social security systems" (Kohli 1986, p. 303). Within the framework of a highly predictable life course, people are able to improvise considerably in the planning of their lives.

Buchmann's (1989) argument is different, emphasizing that the highly standardized trajectories of school, work, and family have been "shattered" by several structural and cultural developments since the 1960s, leading to new levels and forms of individualization. Links between educational certification and occupational status have been weakened, the "half-life" of occupational training and expertise has decreased substantially, the family has reached new levels of instability, and cultural representations of love and work emphasize flexibility, choice, and impermanence.

The processes underlying this new individualization, and whether such a trend even exists, are subjects of controversy. The new individualization hypothesis is difficult to demonstrate by empirical study because it requires a systematic analysis of the timing and sequencing of adult transition markers based on an adequate time series both before and after the mid-1960s. Although no such study has been conducted, some evidence suggests that the transition to adulthood has indeed become more variable since the 1960s.

First, transition markers have "decompressed," yet continue to overlap. In their study of the compactness of transition markers, Modell & Goodman (1990) observed increasing compactness of the markers from 1900 to 1960, at which point spacing between them started to diverge. Yet overlap among some of the markers persisted, arguably representing heightened complexity. [Stevens (1990) also observed the decompression of markers, but this was limited largely to familial markers and began in the 1970s.]

Also, new pathways have emerged, and greater variability in the sequencing of markers is observed (Buchmann 1989). This basic impression has been supported by much research that documents loose couplings among marriage, parenthood, and home leaving (Goldscheider & Goldscheider 1993), as well as the increased likelihood of returning to higher education after leaving school, transferring from a community college to a university, and mixing employment with schooling and parenthood (Bingham & Giele 1998, Morris et al 1998). Modell's (1989) detailed analysis of courtship and marriage shows that the school-work-marriage sequence of earlier times became less prevalent between 1920 and 1975, as did the marriage-coitus sequence (see also Rindfuss 1991, Rindfuss & Parnell 1989). Activities constituting family formation become further complicated by cohabitation beginning in the 1980s (Bumpass & Sweet 1989, Bumpass et al 1991). These strands of evidence suggest that the life course may have experienced heightened individualization since the late 1960s, especially in the emergence of new pathways into adult roles.

---

increased individualization in the form of more variable sequences of transition markers. This disagreement may reflect methodological differences (e.g. Stevens examines pairs of markers, whereas Hogan examines sequences of three markers). Further research is needed to clarify this discrepancy in findings.

Short-Term Intercohort Trends: The Economy and Discrete Historical Events

Trends in the transition to adulthood are also differentiated by changing economic circumstances and historical events. Although many well-documented factors complicate long-term trends in specific transition markers (e.g. the sex ratio in an area influences the likelihood of marriage), contemporary research has emphasized economic conditions as a source of intercohort variations in the transition to adulthood with respect to first births, courting patterns and marriage, educational continuation, and entry into the labor market. Research on the timing of first births and the acquisition of a first job is illustrative.[3] Further, discrete historical events involving the mass mobilization of youth (most notably, war) often lead to very different transition patterns among successive cohorts.

Economic Change and the Timing of Markers   Unemployment, inflation, and economic reorganization in the form of sectoral shifts have exerted substantial period effects on the age of first birth, affecting all cohorts in the child-bearing years (Rindfuss et al 1988). For example, delays in parenthood have been observed since the 1960s; between 1966 and 1976, first births to women >30 years of age increased ~33%, but the number of women in that age group increased only 6%. Likewise Rindfuss and his colleagues (1996) showed substantial percentage increases in births among women >30 and percentage decreases among women <25, between 1973 and 1988. These trends are thought to reflect in part economic opportunities: women's work has shifted to career-oriented, white-collar jobs, especially the professions (Mare 1995), which are perceived to penalize workers for time spent out of the labor force and to foster preferences for nonfamilial responsibilities and rewards.

Patterns of delayed parenting among cohorts of the Great Depression and World War II vividly illustrate intercohort variability due to economic change (Rindfuss et al 1988). The unemployment rate during the Great Depression delayed first births among women aged 25 and 30, but not among women 35 years of age; it may be that women were less willing to delay childbearing past age 30 because they were uncertain how long hard times would last and were pressing biological realities. In the postwar period, however, the inflation rate uniformly delayed first births among women aged 25, 30, and 35. In contrast, first births occurred earlier for all women of childbearing age during the economic boom immediately after World War II, as well as during the war years themselves.

With respect to employment, the transition to a full-year job took longer for a cohort making the transition in 1980 than for a 1960 cohort (Morris et al 1998). This difference can be explained in part by a greater likelihood of "switching"

---

[3]For the timing of marriage, see Cooney & Hogan 1991, Lichter et al 1991, and Lichter et al 1992. For school completion, see for example Shanahan et al 1998 and Walters & O'Connell 1988.

from nonparticipation to participation in the labor force in the more recent group. Indeed, the number of switches was greater and the duration of years between the first and last switch was longer for the 1980 cohort. Morris and her colleagues speculated that this increased "career turbulence" is due in part to a shift from jobs in manufacturing and government to the retail and business sectors, which pay low wages and suffer high turnover. These authors noted, however, that changes in the industrial distribution cannot explain all of the differences between the two groups. Further changes within sectors, perhaps at the level of the firm, are also relevant.

In addition to documenting the central role of economic conditions in the transition to adulthood, these and similar studies offer several general lessons about economic influences. First, previous research tended to assess the economy in static, objective terms, to the neglect of dynamic, complex measures involving both objective (e.g. unemployment rate) and subjective indicators (e.g. perceived employment prospects among those looking for work). Yet, as Rindfuss and his colleagues (1988) noted in their study of first births, prospective mothers tended to evaluate their life chances and formulate plans according to their past experiences and to their projections of opportunity in the future. This intuitively appealing position suggests the importance of young adults' interpretations of their economic circumstances, past, present, and future.

Second, measures of the economy typically have emphasized the level of opportunity (e.g. the unemployment rate) to the neglect of how opportunity is distributed. Yet as Morris & Western (1999) argue, sociologists may have prematurely abandoned research on economic sectors and their social implications (see also Kerckhoff 1995; for an exception, see Schömann et al 1995). In short, the use of dynamic and complex measures may enhance the value of economic factors in explaining changes in the transition to adulthood.

Mass Mobilization and Knifing-Off Experiences   In addition to economic fluctuations, discrete historical events, especially wars, have altered the transition to adulthood. In World War II, military service often created a "social moratorium," a postponement of the acquisition of adult roles and responsibilities (Elder 1986, 1987). Indeed, younger entrants were significantly more likely than older entrants to enter the war before they acquired full-time jobs, married, or completed their education. Service in the military at an early age maximized the discontinuity between youth and adulthood, redirected the life course through delayed entry into family roles, and provided opportunities for educational and occupational advancement. In contrast, entry into the military at a late age often coincided with the disruption of nascent family life and careers, leading to, for example, a greater likelihood of divorce (Pavalko & Elder 1990).

The "knifing-off" experience of military service, separating youth and adulthood, was particularly beneficial for men from disadvantaged backgrounds (Elder & Hareven 1993, Xie 1992). The pronounced benefits of knifing-off experiences are illustrated in a study of the Glueck sample of juvenile delinquents (Sampson

& Laub 1996). The positive effect of being sent overseas on wages and economic status at age 32 was significantly greater among delinquents than among a non-delinquent control group. As Sampson & Laub observed, "overseas duty emerged as a crucial life experience because it facilitated the knifing off of past disadvantages (e.g. poverty or deviant peers) and stigmatization of the criminal justice system." Mass mobilization can prove deleterious, however, even during the same war (for the case of German veterans, see Mayer 1988, Mayer & Huinink 1990; for Japanese veterans, see Elder & Meguro 1987).

Social Stratification and Intracohort Variability

The general analytic model—positing long-term trends in the transition to adulthood marked by short-term economic fluctuations and discrete historical events—is further complicated by social inequalities within cohorts. Compared with early historical periods, many differences in the transition markers today are becoming less dramatic across subgroups of society, although differences remain by economic resources (e.g. Oppenheimer et al 1997, Oppenheimer & Lewin 1999), gender (Mare 1995, Spain & Bianchi 1996), and race (Farley 1996, Mare 1995, Tucker & Mitchell-Kernan 1996).

Several emerging research themes have been especially promising with respect to social inequalities in the life course. First, researchers now have a heightened sense of the spuriousness of many purported racial differences, which often reflect compositional differences such as family background. For example, Ahituv et al (1997) show that racial-ethnic differences in choices made about school and work during the transition to adulthood largely disappear when parental education and income, family structure, and aptitude test scores are controlled. Indeed, among youths who are comparable in these respects, black and Hispanic youth are more likely to prolong school and less likely to remain idle (that is, not in school or in the workplace) than white youths.

Second, however, compositional effects do not always account for racial and ethnic differences, and, in many instances, progress has been made in identifying possible mechanisms that underlie racial and ethnic differences in transition behaviors. This has been the case especially for black-white differences in the timing of marriage and first births. Childbirth before marriage is much more common among blacks than whites; in 1992, two thirds of all black births occurred outside wedlock, compared with one quarter of all white births (see Spain & Bianchi 1996). Many of these births are to teenage mothers (Cherlin 1992). Research now identifies a wide range of possible explanations for this pattern, including, for example, the lack of men who are economically attractive as marriage partners (Wilson 1996), and the lack of role models and opportunities that would otherwise encourage postponing intercourse and pregnancy (Brewster 1994).

Finally, although differences in the life course may reflect criteria such as income, gender, or race-ethnicity, it is probably unfavorable combinations of these factors that define groups that are markedly at risk. This is vividly demonstrated in the study by Oppenheimer and her colleagues (1997) of the economic attractiveness of men and the timing of their marriage. About 48% of both black and white males with 16 years or more of schooling had married within 4 years of finishing school. With lower levels of educational attainment, however, black-white differences began to emerge; among high school graduates, $\sim$20% of black males had married within 4 years of graduation, compared with 40% of white males. The differences became even more pronounced when difficulty of career progression was taken into account; among males who had less than a high school diploma and experienced difficulties starting their careers, $\sim$5% of blacks were married within 4 years of finishing school, in contrast to $\sim$25% of whites. Life course differences are greatest when inequality is viewed as a multidimensional phenomenon that encompasses combinations of race, gender, and economic resources.

MECHANISMS IN THE TRANSITION TO ADULTHOOD

Growing diversity in the transition to adulthood has coincided with one of the most significant advances in life course studies, the widespread adoption of a developmental stance by sociologists as they link the experiences of childhood, adolescence, and the phases of adulthood (Elder 1998). This fresh orientation reflects interest in how people formulate and pursue their life goals, but also how people are constrained and enabled by socially structured opportunities and limitations. The mechanisms considered in this section reflect these central elements, emphasizing social psychological and structural factors that promote variability in the transition to adulthood.

Agency and the Pursuit of Goals

As the duration, sequencing, and directionality of movement between age-graded statuses become more tenuous during the transition to adulthood, it may be that social psychological factors become more important in determining the life course (Mortimer 1994). An interesting set of these factors describes agency in the life course, defined as the active process of choosing of appropriate institutional involvements, organizational memberships, and interpersonal relationships. Life course agency has been examined in terms of planful competence and biographical orientations, although it also reflects social psychological constructs often not considered in a life course framework, including indicators of defense mechanisms and mental illness.

Agency and the Transition to Adulthood   According to Clausen (1991a), planful competence refers to the thoughtful, assertive, and self-controlled processes that underlie one's choices about institutional involvements and interpersonal relationships. Planful competence is especially well suited to life course research in two respects. First, although these traits can be found in approaches to competence and personality (e.g. conscientiousness), planful competence is uniquely concerned with the capacity to select social settings that best match an individual's goals, values, and strengths. That is, planful competence describes the self's ability to negotiate the life course as it represents a socially structured set of age-graded opportunities and limitations.

Second, Clausen (1991b, 1993) maintains that a planful orientation during mid-adolescence (about ages 14 and 15) is especially relevant to the life course because it promotes realistic decisions about the roles and relationships of adulthood. Self-reflexivity, confidence, and self-regulation during mid-adolescence lead to better choices during the transition to adulthood, choices that in turn have implications for later life. Drawing on extensive longitudinal archives from the Berkeley and Oakland samples at the Institute of Child Welfare, Clausen (1991a, 1991b, 1993) demonstrated that planful competence in senior high school (ages 15–18 years) had pervasive effects on functioning in later life, including marital stability, educational attainment for both males and females, occupational attainment and career stability for males, and life satisfaction in later adulthood (see also Clausen & Jones 1998).

Yet Clausen focused on planfulness as a personality construct to the neglect of how it is manifested in social settings. In fact, some evidence suggests that planfulness has little consequence for later life in times of restricted choice. For example, among men whose lives were disrupted by the Great Depression and World War II, planfulness had little effect on educational attainment, in contrast to cohorts of men whose lives were not similarly disrupted (Shanahan et al 1997). Likewise, the capacity to make choices has been less influential among youth of the former German Democratic Republic (East Germany), with its relatively high level of state control over the individual's biography, when compared with youth from the former Federal Republic of Germany (West Germany) (Silbereisen 1999).

Heinz and his colleagues (1998) propose a different approach to agency with their concept of the "biographical orientation." According to this perspective, agency in the life course refers to "entire planning-performance-outcomes sequences," especially as the individual's decisions bear on education, work, and family life. Drawing on interview data from German youth in diverse career paths, Heinz and his colleagues developed a typology of biographical action orientations, defined as stable modes of coping with occupational opportunities and constraints. For example, the "wage worker habitus mode" is a biographical orientation that regards extrinsic characteristics of work (e.g. job security) as most important, whereas the "company identification mode" emphasizes good interpersonal relationships at work. In contrast to Clausen's formulation of planful competence, these modes are linked to social structures, especially the worker's class background. For example, in Heinz's German sample, the "wage-worker habitus" mode is most common among working-class males who are training to become mechanics. These orientations help explain both how individuals choose occupations and how they adapt to the economic and social realities of their chosen work.

Although young people may have clear goals and plans during the transition to adulthood, the inability to carry through with these plans in everyday settings may seriously detract from one's agency in the life course. Thus, the manner in which people respond to challenges and stressors may account for differences in the transition to adulthood. Some defense mechanisms (that is, coping patterns) are immature and counterproductive (e.g. projection and denial), but others are mature and effective (e.g. humor and anticipation) (Vaillant 1993). Drawing on extensive longitudinal data from several studies, Vaillant observed that the maturity of one's coping responses to stressors—typically assessed between ages 20 and 47—was significantly and often strongly correlated with job success and marital stability at age 47 and life satisfaction at ages 60–65 (see also Snarey & Vaillant 1985).

An inability to self-regulate may also interfere with critical transition markers. Externalizing disorders (especially conduct disorders) significantly affect educational attainment. For example, people with a prior mental disorder have a 10% lower probability of college graduation compared with people with no prior history of disorder; the link between psychiatric problems and educational attainment is strongest among those with conduct disorder or substance abuse (Kessler et al 1995). Similarly, in a noteworthy longitudinal study Miech and his colleagues (1999) showed that the number of externalizing symptoms—reflecting conduct disorders, as well as attention deficit disorders—significantly curtails educational continuation. The relationship between symptom counts and educational continuation is potentially important given the substantial prevalence of externalizing symptoms in community samples. As Kessler and his colleagues observed, however, very little is known about how psychopathology interferes with entry into the labor market. The same may be said of less pathological indicators of the ability to function in social settings, such as self-regulation and sociability.

Social Structures and Variability in the Life Course

Social psychological considerations suggest that young people exhibit variability in the transition to adulthood because of individual differences in life course agency, but the social organization of opportunities for and constraints on them can also differentiate transition behaviors. Research has emphasized differences in the ways that school and work are connected, both cross-nationally and in the United States, as well as the variable nature of family experiences during childhood and adolescence.

Institutional Connections Between School and Work   Institutionalized connections between school and work have been conceptualized as networks of associations among educators, students, and prospective employers (for a review, see Rosenbaum et al 1990), as well as articulated links between positions in the educational system and labor market. Many studies have examined the articulated connections between positions in the educational systems and labor markets of Western countries (Heinz 1999), particularly the United States, Germany, and

Britain. Germany organizes the transition from school to work with a standardized vocational education and training system comprising a set of "clearly marked" institutionalized pathways between the educational and occupational systems (Heinz 1997). (Countries with a similarly structured system can be found, for example, in Switzerland, Austria, and Denmark.)

In contrast, many Western societies (including the United States, Canada, and Britain), and countries of Eastern Europe have systems with less structure: The majority of students have common educational experiences, educational certificates are not closely related to qualifications for specific occupations, and vocational training occurs in the workplace. Unstructured systems require each student to construct "one's own individualized amalgam of school and work" (Mortimer & Krueger 2000).

Cross-national studies indicate that the German system produces less variability in the transition to work than do the open systems of the United States and Britain. Among students with similar levels of education, there is more variability in job placement in the United States than in Germany (DiPrete & McManus 1996). Earnings for entrants into the labor market in the United States are also more variable across levels of education than in Germany. Heinz (1997) emphasizes the "equalizing" force of the German system with its provisions for students who do not receive tertiary education, noting that systems that "glorify" higher education with few provisions for the non-college bound result in more fragmented transitions into work and more variability among workers in job placements (see also Kerckhoff 1995, Marshall 1997).

Kerckhoff's (1993) model of diverging pathways is a longitudinally sensitive tool for further research in this area. The model's central insight is that the advantages or disadvantages of one's position in the educational and occupational systems will cumulate as individuals increasingly diverge in their educational and labor market attainments. He observes this pattern of increasing divergence through the early life course in a British sample, and a similar pattern is likely to be obtained in the United States. The analyses by DiPrete & McManus, as well as the work of Heinz and others, suggest that divergence after education may be less prominent in Germany than in the United States, because the former has strong training programs for those not electing higher education. In any event, cross-national studies drawing on Kerckhoff's (1993) orientation would be of great value in identifying the implications of various school-to-work systems for variability in educational and occupational careers.

Within the United States, one also observes substantial diversity in connections between school and work. Unlike youths in many Western countries, secondary students in the United States are heavily engaged in paid work, experiences that are typically disconnected from the school curriculum and not related to their future careers (National Research Council 1998). Paid work is common through high school, but young people differ markedly in their timing and levels of involvement in employment, as well as the quality of their work experiences, differences that have implications for the transition to adulthood. Students who work long hours are less likely to continue schooling after graduation from high school (Carr et al 1996, Ruhm 1997, Steel 1991), although paid employment is associated with a series of positive work-related consequences after high school, including getting a job, longer employment, and higher income (Mihalic & Elliott 1997, Ruhm 1995, Stern & Nakata 1989).

Drawing on a community study that is unique for its detailed work histories, Mortimer & Johnson (1998) noted that students differ considerably in the duration of paid work (i.e. number of months worked during the academic year) and its intensity (number of hours worked per week among those employed) through the high school years. Boys with a high-duration, low-intensity work pattern— employed a long time during high school but limited in their work hours—attend school more months each year during 2 of the 4 years after high school than all other boys. In contrast, boys with a high-duration, high-intensity pattern had the lowest level of schooling. As the authors note, ". . . high intensity work during high school is associated with indicators of an accelerated transition to adulthood—a more hasty withdrawal from the student role for boys, and more rapid incumbency of full-time employment for boys and girls."

Dynamic Accounts of Family Life: Variability Within Cohorts   Links between early experiences in the family and transition behaviors are now well established. Different family experiences, associated with variations in family structure and economic resources, often lead to different pathways into adulthood. Several conceptual distinctions have emerged to describe the diversity of family experiences through time, and together they represent a fundamental reorientation from viewing families as snapshots to viewing families as longitudinal complexities (Martinson & Wu 1992).

First, a common analytic strategy considers whether an adverse event (such as divorce or a poverty spell) has ever occurred in the life of a child. For example, Cherlin et al (1995) examined transition behaviors among British youths who lived with both parents at age 7. Young men or women between the ages of 7 and 16 who had experienced the divorce of their parents were more likely than youths who had not experienced the divorce of their parents to leave home because of friction, to cohabit before marriage, and to parent a child before marriage. Research likewise links divorce with socioeconomic attainment through adulthood and propensities to marry at a young age and to cohabit (Furstenberg & Teitler 1994, Goldscheider & Goldscheider 1993, McLanahan & Sandefur 1994, Thorton 1991).

Second, the persistence or duration of a specific family circumstance may be salient to transition behaviors. Numerous studies show that it is the duration of poverty—not poverty status at a single point in time—that is associated with poor psychosocial functioning through youth and with disadvantaged profiles during the transition to adulthood (e.g. Duncan & Brooks-Gunn 1997, Haveman et al 1991). On the other hand, net of economic resources, the stability of family structures may lead to positive outcomes, owing to a greater stability of roles, rights, and responsibilities within stable family structures. For example, results from Goldscheider

& Goldscheider's (1998) study of home-leaving suggests that nonparental adults contribute to the higher education of children when these unrelated adults are members of a stable living arrangement. Little research has investigated how the duration of time spent in living arrangements other than two-parent households shapes development. It may be, for example, that the transition into a stepfamily has negative effects on a range of outcomes among youths, but that youths from stepfamilies that remain together for an extended period do not differ from youths with both biological parents.

Third, a growing number of studies suggest that the number of changes in early family life may be associated with stresses in the family. For example, the number of times a child's household moves is significantly related to high school completion, a relationship that holds with extensive controls (Haveman et al 1991). Indeed, the number of moves, the number of parental separations, the number of remarriages, and the number of other changes in family structure are jointly significant in predicting high school completion. This finding is consistent with the "focal theory of change," which maintains that young people are better able to cope with significant life events serially rather than simultaneously (Coleman 1974; see also Simmons & Blyth 1987). Similarly, Aquilino (1996) reported that, among young people born to unmarried mothers, an increase in the number of family transitions experienced through youth decreases the likelihood of postsecondary education, but increases the likelihood of residential independence and the transition to work by age 18 (for additional examples, see Teachman et al 1996, Wu 1996).

Fourth, specific patterns of change may be worthy of investigation. That is, some changes in families may prove more salient than others to development. For categorical variables, this may involve changes from one state to another (e.g. specific sequences of household living arrangements). Hill and her colleagues (1999) showed that the sequence involving mother-only to two-parent and back to mother-only households by age 15 adversely affects years of school completed among sons and increases the risk of premarital birth among daughters, compared with those who spent their entire youth in a two-parent household. Other research shows that, compared with children growing up in intact families, children who experience the transition from intact to single-parent, stepparent, or other nonparental living arrangements have earlier residential independence, earlier marriage and cohabitation, and a lower probability of school completion (Aquilino 1991, 1996; Goldscheider & Goldscheider 1998; McLanahan & Bumpass 1988; McLanahan & Sandefur 1994; Michael & Tuma 1985). Not all family changes are alike in their capacity to influence development and subsequent transition behaviors, an observation that warrants both specific theories about family change and finely grained empirical analyses.

For variables that are not categorical, a trajectory approach can be used to depict change as a continuous, directional stream. For example, Wu (1996) assessed change in economic resources by way of the slope of income regressed on three measurement occasions. He found that change in parental income significantly increases the likelihood of premarital birth, controlling level of income and other family experiences. Similarly, Amato & Booth (1997) showed that change in parental income can have enduring effects on offspring in the young adult years; a decline in income in the family of origin is associated with less parental assistance to their married offspring, as well as lowered marital quality in the offspring's marriage.

Finally, some research suggests that the timing of experiences may render them more or less salient for development, although there are difficulties with this analytic strategy. As Allison & Furstenberg (1989) observed in the context of divorce, it is difficult to disentangle the age at which an event is experienced and the duration of time between the event and subsequent measurement of the outcome variable. That is, divorce by parents of older children may be identified as "more salient," although this may reflect the recency of a negative experience. Furthermore, developmental psychologists have offered differing schemes to identify sensitive age periods (e.g. Sroufe & Rutter 1984), but research has yet to examine this range of possibilities.

Nevertheless, research suggests that the timing of negative family experiences may be important. For example, Haveman and his colleagues (1991) examined how the number of residential moves, years that the mother worked, years in poverty, and years on welfare affect high school completion. They observed a heightened sensitivity to these factors from ages 12 to 15 years with respect to school completion, a finding open to the recency interpretation. On the other hand, some evidence suggests that both divorce and a lack of economic resources are most detrimental during early childhood (e.g. Alwin & Thorton 1984; Duncan & Brooks-Gunn 1997, especially Table 18.3; Krein 1986; Krein & Beller 1988).

Although studies that draw on these distinctions have enhanced our understanding of the connections between youth and the transition to adulthood, the relatively small number of studies that consider issues such as number of changes and sequence of changes do not lead to consistent results. In part, this may reflect methodological issues, including, for example, the failure to simultaneously consider family structure and income or to control possible endogenous factors, perhaps with sibling designs (e.g. Teachman et al 1997). In part, it reflects the preliminary nature of attempts to address these complexities. As the analyses by Hill and her colleagues (1999) suggest, it is combinations of timing and changes in family structure that matter, but these complexities matter differently for boys and girls and for various outcomes. They further noted that such findings call for theoretical developments that can direct the analyst's attention among the myriad of possibilities.

Thus far, researchers have identified a range of possible mechanisms by which these dynamic experiences shape adaptation through childhood, adolescence, and the transition to adulthood: a lack of stable role models, heightened family stresses, lowered levels of parental investment, weakened emotional bonds between parents and their children, lowered levels of social capital and social control, the inability to provide settings conducive to cognitive and psychosocial development, and a lack of hope in one's future. Yet inquiries into human lives must take the concept of adaptation seriously; how do changes in the family adversely affect children, but, as important, how do people counter these threats to their well being?

Most research shares an underlying assumption that the relationships of interest involve negative family circumstances and troubled developmental outcomes. Such an assumption deserves further scrutiny. In fact, there is surprisingly little consensus on the magnitude of the poverty and divorce effects for different outcomes and whether short-term developmental consequences persist into adulthood (Lichter et al 1999, Rein & Winship 1999). More generally, researchers have noted the small magnitude of relationships between putative stressors and distress (e.g. Shanahan & Mortimer 1996). This is well illustrated for poverty experiences by Mayer's (1997) systematic statistical analyses of several different nationally representative data sets. She concluded that family income during childhood is only modestly associated with a variety of negative outcomes in late adolescence (e.g. behavioral problems) and early adulthood (e.g. teen pregnancy, male unemployment, and so forth).

This form of variability—transition behaviors that do not reflect a challenging or disadvantaged experience of childhood or adolescence—requires more sociological investigations focused on resilience, a concept that has traditionally referenced positive outcomes in the face of adversity. Drawing on Coleman's (1988) work on social capital, Furstenberg & Hughes (1995) explained that networks of affiliations may protect people who are otherwise at risk for adverse outcomes such as failing to complete high school or to continue education beyond the secondary level. These social connections may include networks of parents within a community, the availability of community resources, and positive relationships with peers, teachers, and other potentially significant adults (e.g. Laub & Sampson 1993, Laub et al 1998). Despite adverse circumstances, many parents and nonparental adults nevertheless provide positive role models and nurturing relationships, as one finds, for example, among rural families contending with the farm crisis (Elder & Conger 2000) and among families of the inner city Furstenberg et al 1999.

The Dynamic Interplay Between Person and Context: Bounded Strategic Action

Young people are strategic in that they foster plans and pursue them, but they are also constrained by the limits that attend their position in the educational and occupational systems. Very few studies attempt to examine transition behaviors with this dualism in mind, although extant research suggests ways to conceptualize the problem.

A well-established research tradition raises the possibility of a cyclical or "reciprocal" relationship between social structures and purposive action (House & Mortimer 1990). For example, it may be that unemployment among young people leads to decrements in self-concept (including efficacy), psychological distress, and a lowering of expectations about work (Mortimer 1994); these processes in turn debilitate the job search and application process, creating a cycle between joblessness and lowered motivation to find work. This dynamic may apply to the quality of one's work and attempts at upward occupational mobility, as well as dating experiences in high school and one's active orientation toward mate selection and marriage.

A different perspective is offered by studies of educational tracking, which suggest that social structures foster orientations underlying selections into positions in the stratified educational system (the socialization process) and allocate individuals into these same positions (the allocative process) (Gamoran 1996). That is, the experiences that are associated with positions in the stratified school both foster active strivings toward and channel people into the same destinations.

Research also suggests, however, that an appreciable percentage of students have unrealistic expectations for the future (Agnew & Jones 1988); other students have plans that are congruent with their previous experiences, but they are nonetheless "blocked" from fulfilling them (Hanson 1994). These findings call for more detailed studies of how young people formulate their plans and expectations regarding future school, work, and family roles. Why are some people's plans and aspirations reasonable whereas those of others are not? Beyond this, do young people with similar plans adopt similar life course strategies? Or does strategic action directed to the same goal differ by socioeconomic status, race, or gender? And how do people react to setbacks at school, at work, and in family life? These types of questions bridge sociology, with their emphasis on situated action and the life course, and psychology, with their emphasis on goals, motivation, and coping strategies.

ANALYTIC STRATEGIES AND THE TRANSITION TO ADULTHOOD

Demographers have been prominent in the study of the transition to adulthood and, consequently, the knowledge base reflects their methods. Research in this area typically uses event-history models to examine the timing of and precursors to established transition markers such as school completion and the birth of a first child.

Perhaps a major limitation has been the almost exclusive reliance on these markers. First, in many cases, one marker is chosen as a critical indicator of adulthood, although researchers reasonably disagree on which marker is most appropriate. Second, the markers are often not discrete, clearly bounded occurrences, as the use of event history or logistic-regression models would suggest. For example, the transition to work, traditionally operationalized as one's entry into a full-time, civilian job after leaving full-time schooling, is now recognized as a complex process that commences during high school for most youth (Ahituv et al 1997, Mortimer et al 1999). Third, unlike typical demographic transitions (e.g. birth and death), many aspects of the transition to adulthood are reversible; for example, young people may experience a divorce and later remarry or leave the home of origin and later return. Fourth, as Marini's (1987) meticulous research shows, some of the markers are sensitive to how they are operationalized. She also noted that the predictors of a marker are contingent on the sequence in which the marker occurs. For example, marriages before and after the completion of school are likely to have different precursors.

In fact, the independence that all of these transitions connote is complex and multifaceted, suggesting the use of latent constructs. For example, drawing on latent transition analysis (Collins & Wugalter 1992), one can study the latent variable "transition to adulthood" as it reflects a sequence of stages, or "latent statuses." A model could be tested according to which the transition to adulthood reflects progression through the following three latent statuses: (*a*) finished school, (*b*) finished school and started a full-time job, and (*c*) finished school, started a full-time job, and married. This model can then be compared with alternative specifications (e.g. a non-normative order of markers or a sequence involving reversibility among the statuses). Such an approach can offer valuable descriptive information, including the proportion of young people in each latent status and the probabilities of transition from one status to another. Moreover, predictor variables can be incorporated into such a model, allowing one to examine the precursors of a latent status. In any event, given rapid methodological developments in the latent analysis of categorical variables (e.g. von Eye & Clogg 1996), researchers have new tools for viewing transition markers as observed indicators of a latent phenomenon.

A second modeling innovation involves Abbott's (1995) optimal-matching strategy, whereby the similarity of life histories can be evaluated. In the context of the transition to adulthood, one could classify cases by their degree of dissimilarity to Hogan's normative sequence of transition markers. Predictors and consequences of non-normative transition patterns could then be examined. This approach has the advantage of viewing the transition to adulthood as a sequence of events that, when viewed together, form a unity that may have distinct precursors and implications for later adulthood.

Both latent transition analysis and the optimal matching strategy identify patterns of transition markers into adulthood and their precursors, thus allowing researchers to examine how pathways into adulthood vary by race and ethnicity, gender, income, and other variables. Methods that draw on Boolean algebra could also be used to identify complex combinations of precursors to transition patterns. Ragin's (1987) Qualitative Comparative Method identifies sets of conditions that must be met before an outcome occurs (e.g. in the context of historical sociology, a revolution, or strike). Singer and his colleagues (1998) illustrated this basic approach in the context of life course studies, linking detailed life histories of women who had experienced depression with mental health categories in later life (e.g. resilient or depressed). This approach could also be used to interrelate complex patterns of experiences in childhood and adolescence with the transition to adulthood.

Beyond the use of objective markers, surprisingly little attention has been paid to the subjective understanding of adulthood as a self-attributed status. That is, respondents are sometimes asked to assign hypothetical people to various stages of the life course based on their student, marital, work, and similar status positions, but very few attempts have been made to assess whether people view themselves as adults (Settersten & Mayer 1997). Yet as Aronson's (1998) ethnographic work suggests, young people not uncommonly describe themselves as adults without having experienced many transition markers, whereas others have passed through most markers but do not consider themselves adult. More refined measures of self-perceived adult status would allow researchers to examine the connections between transition markers, life circumstances, and self-perceptions.

Finally, life course sociologists need to develop closer collaborations with scientists who are interested in biosocial processes, including behavioral geneticists and endocrinologists. Such collaborations will entail the collection of new forms of data (such as blood assays; for a useful example and discussion, see Booth & Dabbs 1993) and the use of research designs and statistical models that enable examination of the additive and interactive effects of genetic heritability and environment (Shanahan et al 2000).

With respect to behavioral genetics, sociologists have emphasized the central role of family experiences in shaping the transition to adulthood, and yet, as Udry (1995) cogently observed, studies of family influence are vulnerable to alternative explanations based on genetics. Consider relationships observed between early experiences in the family of origin and the timing of first births. It may be that early maturing mothers transmit a genetic predisposition toward early puberty and the same genes produce traits in the mother, which affect her parenting (Rowe 2000). Is early menses due to the home environment, including parenting, or the genotype, or, most likely, is it due to a complex network of context-genotype interactions? Furthermore, to the extent that context does matter for transition behaviors like parenthood and marriage, these behaviors reflect contextual experiences that are not shared by siblings (Plomin et al 1990, Reiss 1995), including interactions between genes and the environment. Indeed, it is likely that a review of this literature in a decade will have as one of its major themes the integration of life course and biosocial paradigms.

CONCLUDING REMARKS

The early life course has been fraught with uncertainty throughout the modern era (Graff 1995), although evidence suggests that we are now experiencing heightened levels of variability in the transition to adulthood across many Western societies. The ensuing sense of uncertainty is not unlike the reactions to the social changes that led to the emergence of sociology (Mazlish 1991). These reactions, sometimes celebratory but more often concerned, are once again a special invitation to sociologists to study the reciprocal relations between life histories and social organization.

The possibility that the transition to adulthood has become less predictable and more precarious requires further study at the level of both the society and the individual. When compared with whites, many racial and ethnic minorities—including some immigrant groups—are more likely to experience transition patterns that cast a long shadow over their adult lives, including diminished prospects for socioeconomic achievement and for a fulfilling family life. Yet these groups will constitute an even larger segment of the population in the future. Will they continue to have diminished prospects, and, if so, what are the implications for social order, productivity, and national identity?

Indeed, what steps can we take to maximize the life chances of all youth? Cross-national comparisons suggest more vocational guidance, more clearly marked connections between educational experiences and occupations, and more extensive educational programs for students who are not college bound (Kerckhoff 1995). A full answer to this question, however, requires two types of basic information. First, what are the transition experiences of young people based on race/ethnicity, gender, and socioeconomic status? Second, how is the transition to adulthood being experienced as a developmental process? How are goals for school, work, and family formulated, pursued, and modified? How do goal-directed behaviors interact with normative expectations and the social organization of schools and labor markets to define pathways into adulthood? By addressing these questions, sociologists can reveal how lives reflect the imprint of society, but also how society reflects lived experience.

ACKNOWLEDGMENTS

This review was prepared while the author was a Fellow at the Center for Advanced Study in the Behavioral Sciences. I am grateful for financial support provided by the William T. Grant Foundation (95167795), The Hewlett Foundation, and the NSF (SBR-9730265). I thank Glen H. Elder Jr., Dennis Hogan, Daniel Lichter, Jeylan Mortimer, and Frank Sulloway for helpful comments.

Visit the Annual Reviews home page at www.AnnualReviews.org

LITERATURE CITED

Abbott A. 1995. Sequence analysis: new methods for old ideas. *Annu. Rev. Sociol.* 21:93–113

Agnew R, Jones D. 1988. Adapting to deprivation: an examination of inflated educational expectations. *Soc. Psychol. Q.* 29:315–37

Ahituv A, Tienda M, Hotz VJ. 1997. *Transition from School to Work: Black, Hispanic, and White Men in the 1980s.* Chicago, IL: Popul. Res. Cent., Univ. Chicago

Allison PD, Furstenberg FF Jr. 1989. How mar-

ital dissolution affects children: variations by age and sex. *Dev. Psychol.* 25:540–49

Alwin D, Thorton A. 1984. Family origins and the schooling process: early versus late influence of parental characteristics. *Am. Sociol. Rev.* 49:784–802

Amato PR, Booth A. 1997. *A Generation at Risk.* Cambridge, MA: Harvard Univ. Press. 319 pp.

Aquilino WS. 1991. Family structure and home-leaving: a further specification of the relationship. *J. Marriage Fam.* 53:999–1010

Aquilino WS. 1996. The life course of children born to unmarried mothers: childhood living arrangements and young adult outcomes. *J. Marriage Fam.* 58:293–310

Aronson P. 1998. *Blurring Life Course Strategies: Women's Transition from Adolescence to Adulthood in the Contemporary Era.* Dep. Sociol., Indiana Univ., Bloomington

Beck U. 1992. *Risk Society: Towards a New Modernity.* Transl. M Ritter. London: Sage

Bingham RA, Giele JZ. 1998. *Poor and working class women's transitions to adulthood in the 1970s, 1980s, and 1990s.* Presented Ann. Meet. Am. Sociol. Assoc., San Francisco

Booth A, Dabbs JM. 1993. Testosterone and men's marriages. *Soc. Forces* 72:463–77

Brewster K. 1994. Race differences in sexual activity among adolescent women: the role of neighborhood characteristics. *Am. Sociol. Rev.* 59:408–24

Buchmann M. 1989. *The Script of Life in Modern Society: Entry into Adulthood in a Changing World.* Chicago: Univ. Chicago Press. 249 pp.

Bumpass LL, Sweet JA. 1989. National estimates of cohabitation. *Demography* 26:615–25

Bumpass LL, Sweet JA, Cherlin A. 1991. The role of cohabitation in declining rates of marriage. *J. Marriage Fam.* 53:913–27

Carr RV, Wright JD, Brody CJ. 1996. Effects of high school work experiences a decade later: evidence from the National Longitudinal Survey. *Sociol. Educ.* 69:66–81

Cherlin AJ. 1992. *Marriage, Divorce, and Remarriage.* Cambridge, MA: Harvard Univ. Press. 142 pp.

Cherlin AJ, Kiernan KE, Chase-Lansdale PL. 1995. Parental divorce in childhood and demographic outcomes in young adulthood. *Demography* 32:299–318

Clausen J. 1991a. Adolescent competence and the shaping of the life course. *Am. J. Sociol.* 96:805–42

Clausen J. 1991b. Adolescent competence and the life course, or why one social psychologist needed a concept of personality. *Soc. Psychol. Q.* 54:4–14

Clausen J. 1993. *American Lives: Looking Back at the Children of the Great Depression.* Berkeley, CA: Univ. Calif. Press. 592 pp.

Clausen J, Jones C. 1998. Predicting personality stability across the life span: the role of competence and work and family commitments. *J. Adult Dev.* 5:73–83

Coleman JC. 1974. *Relationships in Adolescence.* Boston/London: Routledge and Kegan Paul

Coleman JS. 1988. Social capital in the creation of human capital. *Am. J. Sociol.* 94:S95–S120

Collins LM, Wugalter SE. 1992. Latent class models for stage-sequential dynamic latent variables. *Multivar. Behav. Res.* 27:131–57

Cooney TM, Hogan DP. 1991. Marriage in an institutionalized life course: first marriage among American men in the twentieth century. *J. Marriage Fam.* 53:178–90

DiPrete TA, McManus PA. 1996. Education, earnings gain, and earnings loss in loosely and tightly structured labor markets: a comparison between the United States and Germany. In *Generating Social Stratification: Toward a New Research Agenda,* ed. AC Kerckhoff, pp. 201–21. Boulder, CO: Westview

Duncan GJ, Brooks-Gunn J. 1997. Income effects across the life-span: integration and interpretation. In *Consequences of Growing Up Poor,* ed. GJ Duncan, J Brooks-Gunn, pp. 596–610. New York: Russell Sage Found.

Elder GH Jr. 1986. Military times and turning points in men's lives. *Dev. Psychol.* 22:233–45

Elder GH Jr. 1987. War mobilization and the life course: a cohort of World War II veterans. *Soc. Forum* 2:449–72

Elder GH Jr. 1998. The life course and human development. In *Handbook of Child Psychology,* Vol. 1. *Theoretical Models of Human Development,* ed. RM Lerner, W Damon, pp. 939–91. New York: Wiley

Elder GH Jr, Conger RD. 2000. *Children of the*

Land: Adversity and Success in Rural America. Chicago: Univ. Chicago Press. In press

Elder GH Jr, Hareven TK. 1993. Rising above life's disadvantages: from the Great Depression to war. In *Children in Time and Place: Developmental and Historical Insights,* ed. GH Elder Jr, J Modell, RD Parke, pp. 42–72. New York: Cambridge Univ. Press

Elder GH Jr, Meguro Y. 1987. Wartime in men's lives: a comparative study of American and Japanese cohorts. *Int. J. Behav. Dev.* 10:439–66

Farley R. 1996. *The New American Reality.* New York: Russell Sage Found. 385 pp.

Furstenberg FF Jr, Cook TA, Eccks J, Elder GH Jr, Sameroff A. 1999. *Managing to Make It: Urban Families and Adolescent Success.* Chicago: Univ. Chicago Press. 305 pp.

Furstenberg FF Jr, Hughes ME. 1995. Social capital and successful development among at-risk youth. *J. Marriage Fam.* 57:580–92

Furstenberg FF Jr, Teitler JO. 1994. Reconsidering the effects of marital dissolution: What happens to children of divorce in early adulthood? *J. Fam. Issues* 15:173–90

Gamoran A. 1996. Educational stratification and individual careers. In *Generating Social Stratification: Toward a New Research Agenda,* ed. AC Kerckhoff, pp. 59–74. Boulder CO: Westview

George LK. 1993. Sociological perspectives on life transitions. *Annu. Rev. Sociol.* 19:353–73

Giddens A. 1991. *Modernity and Self-Identity: Self and Society in the Late Modern Age.* Stanford CA: Stanford Univ. Press. 256 pp.

Goldscheider FK, Goldscheider C. 1993. *Leaving Home Before Marriage: Ethnicity, Familism, and Generational Relationships.* Madison, WI: Univ. Wisc. Press. 242 pp.

Goldscheider FK, Goldscheider C. 1998. The effects of childhood family structure on leaving and returning home. *J. Marriage Fam.* 60:745–56

Graff HJ. 1995. *Conflicting Paths: Growing Up in America.* Cambridge MA: Harvard Univ. Press. 426 pp.

Hagestad GO, Neugarten BL. 1985. Age and the life course. In *Handbook of Aging and the Social Sciences,* ed. GL Maddox, GC Myers, JH Schulz, pp. 35–61. New York: van Nostrand Reinhold

Hanson S. 1994. Lost talent: unrealized educational aspirations and expectations among U.S. youth. *Sociol. Educ.* 71:175–98

Hareven TK. 1982. *Family Time and Industrial Time: The Relationship between the Family and Work in a New England Industrial Community.* New York: Cambridge Univ. Press. 474 pp.

Haveman R, Wolfe B, Spaulding J. 1991. Childhood events and circumstances influencing high school completion. *Demography* 28:133–57

Heinz WR. 1997. Youth education and work in Germany. In *Germany Today: Phoenix in Trouble?* ed. M Zimmer, pp. 229–48. Edmonton: Univ. Alberta Press

Heinz WR, ed. 1999. *From Education to Work: Cross-National Perspectives.* New York: Cambridge Univ. Press. 352 pp.

Heinz WR, Kelle U, Witzel A, Zinn J. 1998. Vocational training and career development in Germany: results from a longitudinal study. *Int. J. Behav. Dev.* 22:77–101

Hill MS, Yeung WJ, Duncan GJ. 1999. How have the changing structures of opportunities affected transitions to adulthood? In *Transitions to Adulthood in a Changing Economy,* ed. A Booth, C Crouter, M Shanahan. Westport, CT: Greenwood

Hogan DP. 1981. *Transitions and Social Change: The Early Lives of American Men.* New York: Academic. 232 pp.

Hogan DP, Astone NM. 1986. The transition to adulthood. *Annu. Rev. Sociol.* 12:109–30

House JS, Mortimer JT. 1990. Social structure and the individual: emerging themes and new directions. *Soc. Psychol. Q.* 53:525–35

Kerckhoff AC. 1993. *Diverging Pathways: Social Structure and Career Deflections.* New York/London: Cambridge Univ. Press. 254 pp.

Kerckhoff AC. 1995. Building conceptual and empirical bridges between studies of education and labor force careers. In *Generating Social Stratification: Toward a New Research Agenda*, ed. AC Kerckhoff, pp. 37–56. Boulder, CO: Westview

Kessler RC, Foster CL, Saunders W, Stang P. 1995. Social consequences of psychiatric disorders. I. Educational attainment. *Am. J. Psychiatr.* 152:1026–32

Kohli M. 1986. The world we forgot: a historical review of the life course. In *Later Life*, ed. VW Marshall, pp. 271–303. Beverly Hills, CA: Sage

Krein SF. 1986. Growing up in a single parent family: the effect on education and earnings on young men. *Fam. Relat.* 35:161–68

Krein SF, Beller AH. 1988. Educational attainment of children from single-parent families: differences by exposure gender and race. *Demography* 25:221–34

Laub JH, Nagin DS, Sampson RJ. 1998. Trajectories of change in criminal offending: good marriages and the desistance process. *Am. Sociol. Rev.* 63:225–38

Laub JH, Sampson RJ. 1993. Turning points in the life course: why change matters to the study of crime. *Criminology* 31:301–25

Lichter DT, LeClere FB, McLaughlin DK. 1991. Local marriage markets and the marital behavior of Black and White women. *Am. J. Sociol.* 96:843–67

Lichter DT, McLaughlin DK, Landry DJ. 1992. Race and the retreat from marriage: a shortage of marriageable men? *Am. Sociol. Rev.* 57:781–99

Lichter DT, Shanahan MJ, Gardner E. 1999. *Good citizens bad citizens? The long term consequences of poverty and family instability during childhood.* Presented at Popul. Assoc. Am., New York, NY

McLanahan S, Bumpass L. 1988. Intergenerational consequences of family disruption. *Am. J. Sociol.* 94:130–52

McLanahan S, Sandefur G. 1994. *Growing Up with a Single Parent: What Helps, What Hurts.* Cambridge MA: Harvard Univ. Press. 196 pp.

Mare RD. 1995. Changes in educational attainment and school enrollment. In *State of the Union: America in the 1990s*, Vol. 1: Economic Trends, ed. R Farley, pp. 155–213. New York: Russell Sage Found.

Marini MM. 1987. Measuring the process of role change during the transition to adulthood. *Soc. Sci. Res.* 16:1–38

Marshall R. 1997. School-to-work processes in the United States. In *Preparing Adolescents for the Twenty-First Century*, ed. R Takanishi, DA Hamburg, pp. 195–226. New York: Cambridge Univ. Press

Martinson BC, Wu LL. 1992. Parent histories: patterns of change in early life. *J. Fam. Issues* 13:351–77

Mayer KU. 1988. German survivors of World War II: the impact on the life course of the collective experience of birth cohorts. In *Social Structures and Human Lives*, ed. MW Riley, pp. 211–28. Newbury Park, CA: Sage

Mayer KU, Huinink J. 1990. Age period and cohort in the study of the life course: a comparison of the classical A-P-C analysis with event history analysis or a farewell to Lexis? In *Data Quality in Longitudinal Research*, ed. D Magnusson, L Bergman, pp. 211–32. New York: Cambridge Univ. Press. 230 pp.

Mayer KU, Muller W. 1986. The state and the structure of the life course. In *Human Development and the Life Course*, ed. AB Sorensen, FE Weinert, LR Sherrod, pp. 217–45. Hillsdale, NJ: Erlbaum

Mayer SE. 1997. *What Money Can't Buy: Family Income and Children's Life Chances.* Cambridge, MA: Harvard Univ. Press

Mazlish B. 1993. *A New Science: The Breakdown of Connections and the Birth of Sociology.* University Park, PA: Pa. State Univ. Press. 333 pp.

Michael RT, Tuma NB. 1985. Entry into marriage and parenthood by young men and women: the influence of family background. *Demography* 22:515–44.

Miech RA, Caspi A, Moffitt TE, Wright BE, Silva B. 1999. Low socioeconomic status and mental disorders: a longitudinal study of selection and causation during young adulthood. *Am. J. Sociol.* 104(4):1096–1131

Mihalic SW, Elliott D. 1997. Short- and long-term consequences of adolescent work. *Youth Soc.* 28:464–98

Modell J. 1989. *Into One's Own.* Berkeley, CA: Univ. Calif. Press

Modell J, Furstenberg FF, Hershberg T. 1976. Social change and transitions to adulthood in historical perspective. *J. Fam. Hist.* 1:7–32

Modell J, Furstenberg FF, Strong D. 1978. The timing of marriage in the transition to adulthood: continuity and change, 1860–1975. *Am. J. Sociol.* S84:120–50

Modell J, Goodman M. 1990. Historical perspectives. In *At the Threshold: The Developing Adolescent,* ed. SS Feldman, GR Elliott, pp. 93–122. Cambridge, MA: Harvard Univ. Press. 414 pp.

Morris M, Bernhardt A, Handcock M, Scott M. 1998. *The transition to work in the post-industrial labor market.* Presented at Ann. Meet. Am. Sociol. Assoc., San Francisco

Morris M, Western B. 1998. Inequality in earnings at the close of the 20th century. *Annu. Rev. Sociol.* 25:623–57

Mortimer JT. 1994. Individual differences as precursors of youth unemployment. In *Youth, Employment, and Society,* ed. AC Petersen, JT Mortimer, pp. 172–98. New York: Cambridge Univ. Press

Mortimer JT, Harley C, Aronson PJ. 1999. How do prior experiences in the workplace set the stage for the transition to adulthood? In *Transitions to Adulthood in a Changing Economy,* ed. A Booth, C Crouter, M Shanahan, pp. 131–59. Westport, CT: Greenwood

Mortimer JT, Johnson MK. 1998. New perspectives on adolescent work and the transition to adulthood. In *New Perspectives on Adolescent Risk Behaviors,* ed. R Jessor, pp. 425–96. New York: Cambridge Univ. Press

Mortimer JT, Krueger H. 2000. Transition from school to work in the United States and Germany: formal pathways matter. In *Handbook of the Sociology of Education,* ed. M. Hallinan. New York: Plenum

National Center for Educational Statistics. 1995. *Digest of Educational Statistics.* Washington, DC: US Govt. Print. Off.

National Research Council. 1998. *Protecting Youth at Work: Health, Safety, and Development of Working Children and Adolescents in the United States.* Washington, DC: Natl. Acad. Press

Oppenheimer VK, Kalmijn M, Lim N. 1997. Men's career development and marriage timing during a period of rising inequality. *Demography* 34:311–30

Oppenheimer VK, Lewin A. 1999. Career development and marriage formation in a period of rising inequality: Who is at risk? What are their prospects? In *Transitions to Adulthood in a Changing Economy,* ed. A Booth, C Crouter, M Shanahan. Westport, CT: Greenwood

Pavalko EK, Elder GH Jr, 1990. World War II and divorce: a life course perspective. *Am. J. Sociol.* 95:1213–34

Plomin R, DeFries JC, McClearn GE. 1990. *Behavioral Genetics: A Primer.* New York: Freeman. 455 pp

Ragin C. 1987. *The Comparative Method: Moving Beyond Qualitative and Quantitative Strategies.* Berkeley, CA: Univ. Calif. Press. 185 pp.

Rein M, Winship C. 1999. The dangers of "strong" causal reasoning in public policy. *Society* 36(5):38–46

Reiss D. 1995. Genetic influences on family systems: Implications for development. *J. Marriage Fam.* 57:543–60

Rindfuss R. 1991. The young adult years: diversity, structural change, and fertility. *Demography* 28:493–513

Rindfuss RR, Morgan SP, Offutt K. 1996. Education and the changing age pattern of American fertility. *Demography* 33:277–90

Rindfuss RR, Morgan SP, Swicegood G. 1988. *First Births in America.* Berkeley, CA: Univ. Calif. Press. 291 pp.

Rindfuss RR, Parnell AM. 1989. The varying connection between marital status and childbearing in the United States. *Popul. Dev. Rev.* 15:447–70

Rindfuss RR, Swicegood GG, Rosenfeld RA. 1987. Disorder in the life course: How common and does it matter? *Am. Sociol. Rev.* 52:785–801

Rosenbaum JE, Kariya T, Settersten R, Maier T. 1990. Market and network theories of the transition from high school to work: their application to industrialized societies. *Annu. Rev. Sociol.* 16:263–89

Ross D, ed. 1994. *Modernist Impulses in the Human Sciences, 1870–1930.* Baltimore, MD: Johns Hopkins Univ. Press. 379 pp.

Rowe DC. 2000. Environmental and genetic influences on pubertal development: evolutionary life history traits? In *Genetic Influences on Fertility and Sexuality*, ed. J Rogers, D Rowe. Boston: Kluwer. In press

Ruhm CJ. 1995. The extent and consequences of high school employment. *J. Labor Res.* 16:293–303

Ruhm CJ. 1997. Is high school employment consumption or investment? *J. Labor Econ.* 15:735–76

Sampson RJ, Laub JH. 1996. Socioeconomic achievement in the life course of disadvantaged men: military service as a turning point circa 1940–1965. *Am. Sociol. Rev.* 61:347–67

Schömann K, Blossfeld HP, Hannan MT. 1995. The segmentation of transitions from school to work in postwar Germany. *Comp. Soc. Res.* 15:103–27

Settersten RA Jr, Mayer KU. 1997. The measurement of age structuring and the life course. *Annu. Rev. Sociol.* 23:233–61

Shanahan MJ, Elder GH Jr, Miech RA. 1997. History and agency in men's lives: pathways to achievement in cohort perspective. *Sociol. Educ.* 70:54–67

Shanahan MJ, Miech RA, Elder GH Jr, 1998. Changing pathways to attainment in men's lives: historical patterns of school work and social class. *Soc. Forces* 77:231–56

Shanahan MJ, Mortimer JT. 1996. Understanding the positive consequences of psychosocial stressors. *Adv. Group Process.* 13:189–209

Shanahan MJ, Sulloway FJ, Hofer SM. 2000. Change and constancy in developmental contexts. *Int. J. Behav. Dev.* In press

Silbereisen RK. 1999. German unification and adolescents' developmental trajectories: continuities and discontinuities. In *Negotiating Adolescence in Times of Social Change*, ed. LJ Crockett, RK Silbereisen, pp. 104–22. New York: Cambridge Univ. Press

Simmons RG, Blyth DA. 1987. *Moving into Adolescence: The Impact of Pubertal Change and School Context.* Hawthorne, NY/Berlin: de Gruyter Aldine. 441 pp.

Singal DJ. 1998. Modernism. In *Companion to American Thought*, ed. RW Fox JT, Kloppenberg, pp. 462–64. Cambridge, MA: Blackwell

Singer B, Ryff CD, Carr D, Magee WJ. 1998. Linking life histories and mental health: a person-centered strategy. *Sociol. Methodol.* 28:1–51

Snarey JR, Vaillant GE. 1985. How lower- and working-class youth become middle-class adults: the association between ego defense mechanisms and upward mobility. *Child Dev.* 56:899–910

Spain DG, Bianchi SM. 1996. *Balancing Act: Motherhood, Marriage and Employment among American Women.* New York: Russell Sage Found. 240 pp.

Sroufe LA, Rutter M. 1984. The domain of developmental psychopathology. *Child Dev.* 55:17–29

Steel L. 1991. Early work experience among white and non-white youths: implications for subsequent enrollment and employment. *Youth Soc.* 22:419–47

Stern D, Nakata YF. 1989. Characteristics of high school students paid jobs and employment experience after graduation. In *Adolescence and Work: Influences of Social Structures, Labor Markets, and Culture*, ed. D Stern, D Eichorn, pp. 189–234. Hillsdale, NJ: Erlbaum

Stevens DA. 1990. New evidence on the timing of early life course transitions: the United States, 1900 to 1980. *J. Fam. Hist.* 15:163–78

Teachman JD, Paasch K, Carver K. 1996.

Social capital and dropping out of school early. *J. Marriage Fam.* 58:773–83

Teachman JD, Paasch K, Day RD, Carver KP. 1997. Poverty during adolescence and subsequent educational attainment. In *Consequences of Growing Up Poor*, ed. GJ Duncan, J Brooks-Gunn, pp. 382–418. New York: Russell Sage Found.

Thorton A, Axinn WG, Teachman JD. 1995. The influence of school enrollment and accumulation on cohabitation and marriage in early adulthood. *Am. Sociol. Rev.* 60:762–74

Tucker MB, Mitchell-Kernan C. 1995. Trends in African American family formation: a theoretical and statistical overview. In *The Decline in Marriage among African Americans*, ed. MB Tucker, C Mitchell-Kernan, pp. 3–26. New York: Russell Sage Found.

Udry RJ. 1995. Sociology and biology: What biology do sociologists need to know? *Soc. Forces* 73:1267–78

Uhlenberg P. 1969. A study of cohort life cycles: cohorts of native born Massachusetts women, 1830–1920. *Popul. Stud.* 23:407–20

Uhlenberg P. 1974. Cohort variations in family life cycle experiences of U.S. females.

J. Marriage Fam. 36:284–92

Vaillant GE. 1993. *The Wisdom of the Ego.* Cambridge, MA: Harvard Univ. Press

von Eye A, Clogg CC, eds. 1996. *Categorical Variables in Developmental Research: Methods of Analysis.* San Diego: Academic

Walters PB, O'Connell PJ. 1988. The family economy: work and educational participation in the United States, 1890 to 1940. *Am. J. Sociol.* 93:1116–52

Wilson WJ. 1996. *When Work Disappears: The World of the New Urban Poor.* New York: Knopf. 322 pp.

Winsborough HH. 1979. Changes in the transition to adulthood. In *Aging from Birth to Death: Interdisciplinary Perspectives*, ed. MW Riley. Boulder, CO: Westview

Winsborough HH. 1980. A demographic approach to the life cycle. In *Life Course: Integrative Theories and Exemplary Populations*, ed. KW Back. Boulder, Co: Westview

Wu LL. 1996. Effects of family instability income and income instability on the risk of premarital birth. *Am. Sociol. Rev.* 61:386–406

Xie Y. 1992. The socioeconomic status of young male veterans, 1964–1984. *Soc. Sci. Q.* 73:379–96

Annu. Rev. Sociol. 2000. 26:693–95

A SOCIOLOGY FOR THE SECOND GREAT TRANSFORMATION?

Michael Burawoy

Department of Sociology, University of California, Berkeley, California 94720;
e-mail: burawoy@violet.berkeley.edu

At the turn of the millennium, sociology faces theoretical disorientation. The issue is not what we don't know, but how to interpret what we do know. Nowhere is this more true than in the transformations that have overtaken the former Soviet Union and its satellites during the last decade of the century. The salient realities with which we have to grapple are twofold: first, the general failure to realize utopian hopes for rebuilding postsocialist societies, and second, the diversity between and within postsocialisms. The disintegration of the Soviet order has taken many routes, from reprimitivization in Russia to the firm embrace of modern capitalism in Central Europe. What has the sociological canon to say about these epochal changes? And how might the canon be reconstituted to accommodate them?

One hundred years ago Marxism enjoyed its Golden Age, flourishing alongside a socialism it inspired, a socialism that had expanded from its German epicenter to embrace most of Europe. Socialism was fast becoming the international movement Marx and Engels had hoped and anticipated—a hope dashed by World War I and its aftermath. The writings of Weber and Durkheim were born on this political terrain. Durkheim claimed that socialism, although he did not call it that, understood as equality of opportunity and social justice, was an immanent tendency of industrialism that would appear as we patiently built up civic associations, while Weber argued that socialism would only bring more bureaucracy. Taking stock of the century—the rise and fall of the Soviet Union, fascism and even social democracy—the anticipations of Durkheim and Weber have endured remarkably well. Marxism, on the other hand, which inspired so many of these changes both by emulation and by reaction, has had to continually reconstruct itself to keep up with the twentieth century.

If the classic sociology of Marx, Durkheim, and Weber was invented to interpret the first "great transformation" to the market economy, how should we reinvent sociology to take up the challenge of the second "great transformation"? Let us deal with each in turn. The transition from socialism to capitalism was not something either Marx and Engels or their successors ever seriously contemplated. But their historical analyses do offer clues and guidelines. Working with the model of

0360-0572/00/0815-0693$14.00

the transition from feudalism to capitalism, one might expect a struggle between a new bourgeoisie and an old nomenclatura class but, from what we know, it is hard to place that at the center of the transition, although the diversity of post-socialist formations might be interpreted as different accommodations of old and new classes. It is even harder to work with the model of the transition from capitalism to socialism, that is, to center the struggle between the working class and the nomenclatura, although this most definitely did play a role leading up to the Polish denouement (Solidarity) and the Russian exit (miners' strikes).

The alternative Marxist interpretation would be to consider the way state socialism fettered its forces of production, creating irresolvable contradictions. In this regard we could explain the divergence of state socialisms by the degree to which capitalism had already begun to incubate within state socialism. In this respect we might say Hungary was most advanced and Russia the most backward, leading to their radically different postsocialist trajectories. The molecular changes in Hungary's political and economic order during the last two decades of communism ensured that it was better prepared to enter the new era than Russia's more brittle communism. When the Soviet Union collapsed, there were none of the embryonic forms of capitalism around which a new order could crystallize. But even Hungary has belied the great expectations for the second great transformation.

A Durkheimian perspective might look upon the transformation as a "transition" from mechanical to organic solidarity, from a totalitarian order in which individuality was lost, in which, to use Hannah Arendt's phrase, individuals were bound together by the iron band of terror, to a civic order in which the division of labor becomes the basis of a new solidarity. Durkheimians might concern themselves with the development of those noncontractual elements of contract, that underlying consensus without which instability reigns. The collapse of Soviet institutions left little to replace them, creating institutional vacuum and anomie, whereas Hungary and Poland were better equipped for succession. Durkheimians might attend to the ways a new collective consciousness is being forged through the reinvention of tradition or through the enactment of national rituals. Equally, they could focus on the continuity of old values that might promote stability but at the cost of transformation. They might play up, for example, a Soviet-induced habitus of state dependence or hostility toward inequality as an impediment to entrepreneurialism. If the transition doesn't go as well as might be hoped, legacies of the old order can be blamed.

A Weberian approach to the second great transformation might conceptualize the past as a patrimonial order, in which the party state operated not so much as a modern bureaucracy but through particularistic and family-like ties. The collapse of the party state would be a condition for the rise of a modern rational legal capitalism but not its guarantee. Building capitalism on the ruins of state socialism is very different from building it from feudalism. The absence of an emergent bourgeoisie means, as Eyal, Szelényi, and Townsley argue, making capitalism without capitalists.[1] They ask whether other actors—a cultural bourgeoisie in

---

[1] Gil Eyal, Iván Szelényi, Eleanor Townsley, *Making Capitalism Without Capitalists* (London: Verso, 1998).

alliance with technocrats—can substitute for a class of independent entrepreneurs. Glancing over their shoulders to Russia, there they see capitalists but without the framework of capitalism. A Weberian sociology abandons the notion of socialism and focuses on the plurality of capitalisms.

Weberian sociology has always been ambivalent about the idea and inevitability of progress. The second great transformation confirms the skepticism. Some, such as Zygmunt Bauman, propose that the collapse of the Soviet Union signals the collapse of the enlightenment project, of the possibility of a rationally planned society. Others have argued that the second great transformation is a regression to previous orders, whether to merchant capitalism or even feudalism. In any event these perspectives refuse the celebratory visions that were packaged with the end of communism.

Consonant with this postmodern pessimism, one might think of postsocialist theory as analogous to postcolonial theory that attempts to grapple with the continued subordination of colonized people even after they have been blessed with nationalism, democracy, market, and all the other gifts of modernity. Struggles against colonialism at one level embrace the very premises of Western thought at another level—premises that founded their previous imprisonment. Postsocialist thinking could arrive at a similar conclusion—free markets, liberal democracies, and national independence are all chimera that bind new nations under Western hegemony.

Such postsocialist thought is even more pessimistic than postcolonial thought since it spells the demise not only of an old form of domination but also of the emancipatory visions that accompanied it. Postsocialist thought would be quintessentially postmodern, spelling the end of utopian visions as infeasible, unviable, and dangerous. Against this messianic pessimism we need not accumulate more facts that root us in an eternal present, but rather we need cultivate a critical imagination for feasible alternatives. Instead of empiricism we need new cognitive maps to help us see possibilities beyond the horizon. This is a time not for normal sociology, collecting more data, but for revolutionary sociology that reconfigures what we already know.

Visit the Annual Reviews home page at www.AnnualReviews.org

Annu. Rev. Sociol. 2000. 26:697–98

AGENDA FOR SOCIOLOGY AT THE START
OF THE TWENTY-FIRST CENTURY

Michael Hechter

Department of Sociology, University of Washington, Seattle, Washington 98195;
e-mail: Hechter@u.washington.edu

I have always taken the sociologist's principal task to be that of explaining variations in collective action, institutions, and formal organizations, among other social
outcomes. I seek to learn why revolutions occur in some places and times rather
than others, why certain societies have norms that foster development while the
norms of others inhibit it, why some firms succeed when others fail. This is quite a
different task from the explanation of cognition, perception, personality, and other
individual-level outcomes.

At first glance, explaining social outcomes would appear to be a straightforward
mandate, but any such impression is misleading. Ultimately, social outcomes result
from individuals' relations with one another and with aspects of their (nonsocial)
environment. Although the environment—think of natural disasters like earth-
quakes, hurricanes, and droughts—often exerts a strong influence on social outcomes, it is the realm of social interaction that causes the greatest difficulties.
While many of the necessary tools are now at hand for the analysis of *existing* social networks, institutions, and organizations, our capacity to predict their specific
forms ex ante is modest.

In part, social outcomes depend on the values, or motives, that lurk behind
our actions (they also depend on other subjective elements, such as beliefs and
attitudes toward risk). Among other things, the efficacy of the incentives that are
used to channel our behavior—by lovers, friends, advertisers, social movements,
employers, and states—depends wholly on people's values. These values vary
widely—both within the same society (some people seem more interested in at-
taining wealth, while others just as doggedly pursue status) and cross-culturally
(Americans now seem to be besotted by celebrity, whereas Evans-Pritchard tells
us that the Nuer valued cattle and cattle products above all else). It stands to reason
that the institutions and organizations that are devised by altruists will differ from
those that are created by egoists.

Yet our capacity to accurately assess these values is unimpressive. Responses to
survey questions about values often fail to predict a person's subsequent behavior.
Skeptics can always evade this methodological quandary simply by making assumptions about individual values. But this strategy is problematic as well. Aware

697

of these difficulties, many social scientists have tacitly conspired to ignore subjectivity in their analyses: The current popularity of structural theories in the social sciences is by no means confined to sociology.

Developing better instruments to measure individual values—and better theories to explain them—should help us determine the rightful place of subjectivity in social analysis, whatever place that may turn out to be. Lacking such measures, we can never know the causal importance of values for individual behavior compared with such objective factors as class, race, and gender. This question is far from merely academic; around it swirl long-standing controversies about what role, if any, culture plays in the perpetuation of poverty in this country and of underdevelopment in the world at large. We are condemned to repeat these debates ad infinitum unless valid and reliable measures of values can be found. This is a formidable task, however (for one recent attempt, see Hechter et al 1999).

Getting a better grip on individual values and other internal states would be an important contribution, but this information alone will not enable us to account for social outcomes. The institutions and organizations created by altruists may not be as resilient as those devised by egoists. The road to hell is paved with good intentions: At the end of the day, the factories built by that noble idealist Robert Owen failed, while automobile plants built by that wretched anti-Semite Henry Ford were a grand success. Much the same might be said of socialism's disappointing track record relative to capitalism's.

These lessons alert us to the fact that many social outcomes, indeed perhaps most of them, do not emerge from the action of multiple individuals in any simple fashion. Whereas elections are determined by the mere aggregation of individual actions, this is an atypical case. There is no rule of "one man, one vote" when it comes to the making of most social outcomes. Social interaction often leads to unintended consequences. Modern societies are repositories of great power disparities between individuals and between collective actors, like firms and trade unions, and these disparities affect social outcomes in a myriad of ways.

Although much is known about the effect of existing power disparities on a variety of outcomes—after all, this was a field first plowed by the likes of Marx and Weber—a powerful general theory of the *emergence* of social structures continues to elude us.

Visit the Annual Reviews home page at www.AnnualReviews.org

LITERATURE CITED

Hechter M, Ranger-Moore J, Jasso G, Horne C. 1999. Do values matter? An analysis of advance directives for medical treatment. *Eur. Sociol. Rev.* 15:405–30

Annu. Rev. Sociol. 2000. 26:699–701

WHAT I DON'T KNOW ABOUT MY FIELD BUT WISH I DID

Douglas S. Massey

Department of Sociology, University of Pennsylvania, Philadelphia, Pennsylvania 19104

As a young college student in the early 1970s, I was very indecisive. I had always been attracted to academia but, having come of age during the 1960s, I was determined to do something "relevant" with my life. Earning a decent living was the last thing on my mind. Like most of my contemporaries, I assumed that a good job with a high salary was a birthright. My duty was to find a higher calling.

The search for moral fulfillment brought me first to medicine, the most obvious of "relevant" professions. As a premed student I took a full load of courses in math, chemistry, biology, anatomy, and physics. But I really hated premed students, who were generally self-serving, competitive, and arrogant. Who wants to be like that? Although I had already completed a chemistry minor, I gave up the idea of helping people through medicine and turned decisively away from the natural sciences.

My search for relevance brought me next to the social sciences. I began in psychology, to which I was attracted by its elegant experimental designs, complex theoretical models, and rigorous statistical analyses. Although I eventually completed a psychology major and took most of the courses needed for a master's degree, running rats through mazes in a laboratory lost its allure and I once again began looking for something more "relevant."

My search led me then to anthropology. After an early fascination with physical anthropology and hominid evolution, I became intrigued by the concept of cultural relativism and eagerly read ethnography after ethnography of nonwestern cultures. Eventually, however, I suffered another crisis of faith. If all judgments were culturally relative, and all cultures were equally valid, then the possibility of knowing anything at all seemed to disappear before my eyes as a solipsism. I retreated back into the study of Spanish literature, where professors made no pretense of offering cumulative knowledge. At least I could indulge my love of the language by reading my way through the new genre of magical realism that was then taking Latin America by storm.

Suddenly I found myself in my fourth year of undergraduate studies having completed three majors and a chemistry minor, but still having no clear idea of who I was or what I wanted to do in life. At this moment, I stumbled upon demography, which to my mind combined the rigor of psychology with the relevance of

0360-0572/00/0815-0699$14.00

anthropology, while offering some hope of intellectual advance. I thus resolved to become a demographer, and toward that end began taking every sociology course I could find. Eventually I stayed on for two extra quarters to bone up on theory and methods, to steel myself for what I imagined to be my dim prospects for success in graduate school.

The rest, as they say, is history: I went on to finish a PhD in sociology at Princeton, where I was trained in classical demographic methods but actually worked in the heterodox fields (for Princeton) of migration and human ecology. This is a long-winded way of coming to what I don't know about my field but wish that I did. Although my various intellectual journeys have given me a relatively broad intellectual formation, I nonetheless find myself wishing I had a better grasp of human beings as biological organisms.

Indeed, I have come to the reluctant conclusion that sociologists have gone too far in privileging the social over the biological, a fact that haunts me now as I try to comprehend the signal event that has occurred in my own fields of migration and human ecology: the urbanization of the human population. The urban industrialism in the nineteenth century lulled sociologists into the false belief that society could be understood by studying social structures alone, without considering human beings as organisms with biological traits and predispositions. Although we don't like to admit it, we are primates who share 99% of our genetic endowment with chimpanzees.

Humans emerged from the savannahs of East Africa 7 million years ago. In adapting to this niche, we evolved as upright, tool-using hominids who survived through *collective* strategies implemented by small groups. Over the course of millions of years, the reptilian brain governing our instinctual and emotional responses was supplemented with a newer and thicker mass of cerebral cortex. The expansion of brain size enabled the perfection of collective strategies of survival involving language, culture, and technology. These innovations ultimately led to larger and more complex forms of social organization, but 99.9% of human experience has nonetheless transpired in the hunting and gathering state. Thus, the delicate balance between the rational and emotional brain, which largely defines us as human beings, *must be* oriented toward the needs of small group survival.

It was only about six thousand years ago that we settled down as a species and began farming, thus enabling the first semi-permanent human habitations. It was only about three thousand years ago that our technology advanced sufficiently to allow some of these settlements to become cities; and it was only in the last century that our capabilities matured to the point where a majority of us can now live in cities. In evolutionary terms, our experience in urban settings has occurred in the blink of an eye.

It is clear, however, that early in the next century the human population will finally and decisively urbanize. All demographic projections show that for the first time in history a majority of the world's human beings will soon live in cities, and increasingly in large ones at that. The social world to which we have adapted over millions of years will recede into memory and cease to exist. Small bands of hunters and gatherers, larger nomadic tribes, isolated rural villages, and small semi-independent towns—all will ultimately disappear. In the next century, the modal human experience will be one of intense concentrations of people, with all their vices and virtues.

A central question is how we, as a biological species adapted to life in small groups, will fare in this new environment. The beginning point in coming to terms with our situation must be the realization that we are indeed biological organisms. I and other sociologists thus need to understand better the fundamentals of human physiology and psychology at both the systemic and molecular levels. We need to educate ourselves in the exciting work now being done on brain functioning, cognition, the regulation of emotion, and the biological bases of behavior. We need to give up our historical resistence to the idea that social behavior has biological roots and accept the fact that we, as human beings, have inherited certain predispositions to thought and behavior that influence and constrain the social structures that we unconsciously evolve and rationally select. At this point, therefore, I really wish I knew more about human beings as biological rather than social organisms, and I have begun reading to catch up.

Visit the Annual Reviews home page at www.AnnualReviews.org

Annu. Rev. Sociol. 2000. 26:703–06

FAMILY, STATE, AND CHILD WELL-BEING

Sara McLanahan

Department of Sociology, Princeton University, Princeton, New Jersey 08544-2091;
e-mail: mclanaha@princeton.edu

INTRODUCTION

Sociologists have long recognized the importance of the family in social mobility and in the reproduction of poverty (Featherman & Hauser 1978, McLanahan & Sandefur 1994). More recently, they have begun to study the role of the state in these processes (Skocpol 1992, O'Connor et al 1999). Children depend on their parents to provide them with the resources they need to develop into healthy and successful adults. Parents, in turn, depend on their communities and on government to share the costs of raising children. Changes that undermine children's claims on parental resources or parents' claims on public resources are likely to have long-term negative consequences for society. As we enter the twenty-first century, two such changes are underway—an increase in nonmarital childbearing and a restructuring of the welfare state. Nonmarital childbearing, a trend that now affects one of three children born in the United States, undermines children's claims on fathers' resources (time and money). Welfare reform, which curtails welfare benefits and strengthens child support enforcement, undermines the claims of poor parents on public resources. These changes disproportionately affect families at the lower end of the income distribution, who have the highest rates of nonmarital childbearing and welfare receipt.[1]

In order to assess the full impact of these changes in the family and the state, sociologists need answers to several questions. First, they need to know more about the capabilities of the men and women who bear children outside marriage, especially the fathers. Second, they need a better understanding of the relationship between unwed parents and between parents and children. And third, they need to understand how welfare and child support policies affect parents' relationships and ultimately children's well-being.

---

[1] The two trends are interrelated, although analysts disagree about the direction of causality. Some view welfare as a response to poor labor market conditions and father absence, whereas others argue that welfare causes father absence (Murray 1984).

0360-0572/00/0815-0703$14.00

PARENTS' CAPABILITIES

Implicit in the notion that nonmarital childbearing represents a loss for children is the assumption that unwed fathers can afford to support their children and that children would be better off if their parents were married. This assumption is also implicit in recent welfare legislation that is attempting to shift more of the cost of poor children from taxpayers to parents. Some people dispute these assumptions on the grounds that unwed fathers have very low earnings' capacity, problems with drugs or alcohol abuse, and problems with domestic violence. (For reviews, see Garfinkel, McLanahan & Hanson 1998, Raphael & Tolman 1997).

At this point, we lack the information necessary to test these arguments. Although we know quite a bit about unwed mothers (Moore 1995), our knowledge of fathers is much more limited. In part, the problem is due to the fact that our surveys have paid much more attention to single mothers than to nonresident fathers (which include a large proportion of unwed fathers). In part it is due to the fact that many fathers are missing from these surveys (Garfinkel et al 1998).[2]

Thus, a major objective for sociologists in the next decade should be to develop a more detailed and more accurate description of the characteristics and capacities of the men who father children outside marriage.[3]

PARENTAL RELATIONSHIPS

Unmarried couples are a very heterogeneous group. At one extreme are couples who are living in marriage-like relationships. At the other extreme are couples whose only connection is a brief sexual encounter. In between are couples who live apart but have a romantic relationship, couples who are "just friends," and couples who never want to see one another again. In order to assess the costs of nonmarital childbearing, sociologists must go beyond these demographic profiles to gather information on parents' commitments, attitudes about the rights and obligations of unwed fathers, and ability to cooperate in raising their child. If parents are committed and able to cooperate, pressures to marry and coparent are likely to have positive effects on children. If their relationship is highly contentious, such pressures are likely to harm children.

The ethnographic literature provides some insight into the relationships between unwed parents, but the picture is inconsistent. Anderson (1989) tells a story

---

[2]Garfinkel and his colleagues (1998) estimate that as many as 4 million fathers are missing from the NSFH, which is arguably the best national data set for studying families and households. The problem exists in other data sets as well and is particularly serious for low-income fathers and unwed fathers (also see Rendall et al 1997, Sorensen 1995).

[3]Two new surveys promise to be a valuable resource for information on unwed fathers: the 1997 National Longitudinal Survey of Youth, which is following a sample of young men and women born between 1980 and 1987, and the Fragile Families and Child Wellbeing Study (McLanahan & Garfinkel 1999) which is following a cohort of children born between 1998 and 2000 to (mostly) unwed parents in 21 cities throughout the United States.

in which young, inner-city men exploit young women in order to fulfill their sexual needs. Other researchers argue that poor fathers are doing what they can to help (Stack 1974, Furstenberg et al 1992), and that mothers are redefining fatherhood in ways that de-emphasize the breadwinner role (Waller 1997). These perspectives are not necessarily incompatible with each other. Many unwed couples may start out with high hopes for a stable relationship, only to find that they (or their partners) cannot meet their expectations. Sociologists need to reconcile these different visions and understand how they evolve over time.

Welfare States and Children's Well-Being

Young unwed mothers have the longest stays on welfare of all single mothers (Bane & Ellwood 1994). The Personal Responsibility and Work Reconciliation Act (1996) is designed to reduce this dependence by forcing mothers into the labor force and by forcing unwed fathers to establish paternity and pay child support. On the one hand, these new laws are likely to strengthen children's claims on fathers' resources. On the other hand, they are likely to reduce the time that mothers spend with their children; and, in cases where fathers have been providing support "under the table," they are likely to reduce total family income. Reductions in time and money, in turn, should increase family stress, parental conflict, and harsh parenting.

Outcomes for children will depend on how states tailor their welfare programs. Welfare reform consists of 50 different programs, since states have considerable discretion in how they structure their new systems. Some states are offering carrots such as generous child care and health care benefits to encourage former welfare recipients to become self-sufficient. Other states are using sticks to discourage parents from applying for welfare. The variation in state policy provides sociologists with an excellent set of natural experiments for studying the effects of state policies on family formation and behavior.

Ultimately, sociologists are concerned with how parental capabilities, parental relationships, and welfare state policies affect children. Recent changes in family formation and welfare laws provide researchers with both a challenge and an opportunity. By focusing attention on how these changes affect our most vulnerable children, we stand to learn a great deal about the fundamental relationships between family, state, and social mobility.

Visit the Annual Reviews home page at www.AnnualReviews.org

LITERATURE CITED

Anderson E. 1989. Sex codes and family life among poor inner city youths. *Ann. Am. Acad. Polit. Soc. Sci.* 501:59–78

Bane MJ, Ellwood D. T. 1994. *Welfare Reali-ties: From Rhetoric to Reform.* Cambridge, MA: Harvard Univ. Press

Featherman D, Hauser R. 1978. *Opportunity and Change.* New York: Academic

Furstenberg FF, Sherwood K, Sullivan M. 1992. *Caring and Paying: What Fathers and Mothers Say About Child Support.* New York: Manpower Demonstration Res. Corp.

Garfinkel I, McLanahan S, Hanson T. 1998. A patchwork portrait of nonresident fathers. In *Fathers Under Fire: The Revolution in Child Support Reform.* New York: Russell Sage Found

McLanahan S, Sandefur G. 1994. *Growing Up With a Single Parent.* Cambridge, MA: Harvard Univ. Press

McLanahan S, Garfinkel I. 1999. The fragile families and child well-being study: questions, design, and a few preliminary results. Paper presented at the *Conf. on Non-marital Childbearing,* Inst. Res. Poverty, Madison, WI

Moore K. 1995. Births to unmarried mothers: United States, 1980–92. *Report to Congress on Out-of-Wedlock Childbearing.* Washington, DC: Dep. Health & Human Serv.

Murray C. 1984. *Losing Ground: American Social Policy 1950–1980.* New York: Basic

O'Connor J, Orloff A, Shaver S. 1999. *States, Markets, Families: Gender, Liberalism and Social Policy in Australia, Canada, Great Britain and the United States.* Cambridge, MA: Cambridge Univ. Press

Raphael J, Tolman RM. 1997. *Trapped by poverty and trapped by abuse: New evidence documenting the relationship between domestic violence and welfare. Executive Summary.* Chicago: Taylor Inst.

Rendall MS, Clarke L, Peters HE, Ranjit N, Verropoulou G. 1999. Incomplete reporting of male fertility in the United States and Britain: a research note. *Demography* 36(1):135–44

Scokpol T. 1992. *Protecting Soldiers and Mothers: The Political Origins of Social Policy in the United States.* Cambridge, MA: Belknap

Sorenson E. 1995. Noncustodial fathers: Can they afford to pay more child support? Unpublished manuscript. Washington, DC: Urban Inst.

Stack CB. 1974. *All Our Kin: Strategies for Survival in a Black Community.* New York: Harper & Row

Ventura SJ, Bachrach CA, Hill L, Kaye K, Holcomb P, Koff E. 1995. The demography of out-of-wedlock childbearing. *Report to Congress on Out-of-Wedlock Childbearing.* Washington, DC: Dep. Health Hum. Serv.

Waller M. 1997. *Redefining fatherhood: paternal involvement, masculinity, and responsibility in the "other America."* PhD Diss. Princeton Univ., Princeton, NJ.

Annu. Rev. Sociol. 2000. 26:707–09

GETTING IT RIGHT: SEX AND RACE INEQUALITY IN WORK ORGANIZATIONS

Barbara F. Reskin

Department of Sociology, Harvard University, Cambridge, Massachusetts 02138;
e-mail: reskin@wjh.harvard.edu

One of sociology's major accomplishments in the last quarter of the twentieth century was establishing that race and gender matter at work. We have been far less successful in explaining why workers' sex and race affect their employment outcomes, however, especially why jobs are segregated by sex and race, and why whites outearn people of color and men outearn women. When sex segregation first attracted attention, its high level of incidence led scholars to hypothesize *universal* explanatory processes: gender-role socialization, the domestic division of labor, patriarchal impulses by employers, male workers' responses to competitive threat. Because most readily available data were for workers, researchers concentrated on individual-level explanations. Despite a growing body of research on why the sexes aspired to, pursued, and abandoned more or less sex-typical occupations, and why race and sex were related to earnings, neither line of research has illuminated why race and sex inequality exists to varying degrees across work organizations.

A few researchers recognized that understanding on-the-job inequality required studying work organizations. From them we learned why some California establishments were more or less segregated in the 1960s and 1970s (although there wasn't a lot of variability to explain; Bielby & Baron 1984), and the factors that led California state agencies to become more or less integrated during the 1980s (Baron et al 1991). These and a handful of other studies have shown that levels of inequality in work organizations are affected by organizational demography, organizational leadership, the degree to which personnel practices are formalized, recruitment methods, external pressure, and the availability of slack resources. But we failed to grasp their most important message: Inequality at work does not just happen; it occurs through the acts and the failures to act by the people who run and work for organizations.

The first challenge for the twenty-first century in this area of sociology is to formulate empirically realistic accounts of how a range of jobs are filled in a cross-section of organizations. These accounts must be based on interviews with informants at multiple levels in the organization. Researchers must learn what if any organizational constraints determine how the opening came about, who specifies the necessary qualifications, and who can authorize exceptions? Who defines the applicant pool, whether anyone has an inside track, and if so, who, why, and with what result? What is the demographic composition of the pool? Of the decisionmakers? At what levels are relevant decisions made, and what are their consequences? Does the decision create expectations about future job-assignment decisions? Given the way that a position is filled, how likely is it that someone of an atypical race or sex could be appointed? Are there other ways the job in question could be filled and that other positions are filled that would alter these probabilities? In short, we need to identify the actors, how they define the situation, whose definitions prevail, and why.

Gaining access to organizations is feasible, especially if we don't view our object as catching discriminators in the act. Numerous work organizations open their doors to ethographers and survey researchers. Unfortunately, few of the latter have been interested in race and gender inequality. The reasons employers are more or less indifferent to workers' sex and race will be found in variability within and across establishments in personnel practices, organizational arrangements, and the actions of managers and workers, and we must design our studies to capture that variability. Getting it right will require multiple in-depth organizational case studies whose designs are sufficiently uniform to permit comparative analysis. The mandate for such a concerted effort must come from sociologists committed to understanding gender and racial inequality in work organizations. A research consortium may provide the most productive structure.

A second challenge is to close the gap between reality and our explanatory frameworks. Scholars theorize race and sex inequality in organizations primarily either in terms of active exclusionary processes such as discrimination or status closure or in terms of structural discrimination. The former assumes that segregation and other unequal outcomes stem from out-group antipathy or competitive threat. Social psychological research suggests an important alternative: in-group preference (Brewer & Brown 1998, Fiske 1998). Although opportunity hoarding (Tilly 1998) and status closure (Tomaskovic-Devey 1993) are consistent with in-group preference, conflict-based approaches may distort its etiology. The effect of acting on a preference for a subordinate from one's own group may equal that of indulging an aversion, but these are theoretically different phenomena, and the organizational practices that effectively reduce race and gender inequality stemming from the former almost certainly differ from those that minimize inequality resulting from the latter.

Turning to structural discrimination, although the idea that discrimination is built into organizational structures is sociologically attractive and although examples of structural discrimination exist (work schedules designed with in-group members in mind, requirements that predictably exclude certain groups), there is little contemporary evidence of structural discrimination. Moreover, the premise that much employment discrimination is structural implies greater indifference to race and sex by organizational personnel than social psychological research suggests (Heilman 1995) or employers acknowledge (Wilson 1996). The discretion many personnel decisions entail invites stereotyping, evaluation bias, and attribution error by decisionmakers, and these almost certainly maintain inequality. Rather than assuming structural discrimination, we need to assess its prevalence, forms, and loci. And we must investigate how organizational actors use structures to heighten or minimize the importance of race and sex.

Work settings vary in the extent that they disadvantage people of color and white women. Much of this variation reflects real organizational differences in the limiting or licensing of exclusionary and inclusionary behavior by owners, managers, and workers. Identifying the covariates of this variation within and across organizations is the *only* way to explain race and gender inequality at work (e.g., Nelson & Bridges 1999). Who gets what job is the product of the actions of individuals (who are motivated partly by the sex and race group to which they belong) and the organizational practices that to varying degrees constrain and are circumvented by individuals. Getting it right requires getting serious about the questions we pose and the ways we try to answer them.

Visit the Annual Reviews home page at www.AnnualReviews.org

LITERATURE CITED

Baron JN, Mittman BS, Newman AE. 1991. Targets of opportunity: organizational and environmental determinants of gender integration within the California Civil Service, 1979–1985. *Am. J. Sociol.* 96:1362–1401

Bielby WT, Baron JN. 1984. A woman's place is with other women. In *Sex Segregation in the Workplace: Trends, Explanations, Remedies*, ed. BF Reskin, pp. 27–55. Washington, DC: Natl. Acad. Press.

Brewer MB, Brown RJ. 1998. Intergroup relations. In *Handbook of Social Psychology*, ed. DT Gilbert, ST Fiske, and G Lindzey, 2:554–94. New York: McGraw-Hill 4th ed.

Fiske ST. 1998. Stereotyping, prejudice, and discrimination. In *Handbook of Social Psy-* *chology*, ed. DT Gilbert, ST Fiske, and G Lindzey, pp. 554–94. New York: McGraw-Hill. 4th ed.

Heilman ME. 1995. Sex stereotypes and their effects in the workplace: what we know and what we don't know. *J. Soc. Issues* 10:3–26

Nelson RL, Bridges WP. 1999. *Legalizing Gender Inequality.* New York: Cambridge Univ. Press

Tilly C. 1998. *Durable Inequality.* Berkeley: Univ. Calif. Press

Tomaskovic-Devey D. 1993. *Gender and Racial Inequality at Work.* Ithaca, NY: Cornell: ILR Press

Wilson WJ. 1996. *When Work Disappears. The World of the New Urban Poor.* New York: Knopf

Annu. Rev. Sociol. 2000. 26:711–14

WHITHER THE SOCIOLOGICAL STUDY OF CRIME?

Robert J. Sampson

*Department of Sociology, University of Chicago, 1126 E 59 Street, Chicago,
Illinois 60637; e-mail: rjsam@src.uchicago.edu*

The study of crime and deviance has always been one of the most theoretically
fertile areas in sociology. Fundamental questions on why individuals violate norms,
the origins of social order, official reactions to deviance, and macro-level sources
of violence—to name but a few—have attracted some of the best minds in the
discipline. The result is a rich lineage of sociologically oriented criminological
theory (e.g., control, subcultural, strain, differential association, labeling).

It is perhaps axiomatic, however, that fundamental questions yield equally fundamental challenges. Criminology is no exception, and indeed the facts on crime
continue to trouble extant theories. This is especially the case for theories that
have hitched their wagon to the dominant strains of accepted sociological wisdom.
Stratification *is* sociology to many, and in criminology it comes as no surprise that
deprivation theories privileging materialism and economic motives are perenni-
ally popular. Everybody believes that "poverty causes crime" it seems; in fact, I
have heard many a senior sociologist express frustration as to why criminologists
would waste time with theories outside the poverty paradigm. The reason we do,
as Jack Katz brilliantly demonstrated in *Seductions of Crime* (1988), is that the
facts demand it. Whether increases in crime during periods of economic growth,
epidemics of violence in wealthy countries such as the United States, the weak
correlation of social class with delinquency, or crime in the suites, materialist
theory is clearly insufficient. But it is not just deprivation-based theory that has
failed. Most criminological theory is static in logic and handicapped by a focus on
(allegedly) fixed explanatory categories, thereby failing to address the processes
and dynamics leading to criminal events. The most important thing about crime
that we do not know, in other words, concerns its causal *social processes*.

Within-Individual Variability

Consider first the question of individual variations in common-law crime. Criminologists typically address this question by studying why some individuals commit
crimes and others do not, leading to between-individual analysis and a bevy of well-
known correlates (race, gender, class, personality, family background, peers, and
so on). Although this research tradition is important, a different way of looking at
the world can be found in life-course criminology. Taking a developmental view,

0360-0572/00/0815-0711$14.00

longitudinal research has revealed an apparent paradox: although adult criminality is nearly always preceded by "antisocial behavior" in childhood, most antisocial children do not become criminals as adults. Despite aggregate stability, that is, there is far more heterogeneity in criminal behavior over time within individuals than individual-difference or structural-causation models allow. Change is near ubiquitous.

There is marked variability in adult outcomes even among serious and persistent juvenile delinquents. In my research with John Laub, for example, we found that none of the static variables measuring family background—such as poverty, parental criminality, and child supervision—predicted trajectories of adult offending among formerly incarcerated delinquents (Sampson & Laub 1993). Personality characteristics fared no better. Measures of childhood extroversion, egocentricity, aggressiveness, difficult temperament, and tantrums all failed to distinguish persistent offenders from desisters. Looking *forward* from childhood thus reveals the successes and failures, including troubled adolescents who desist. Apropos the paradox noted earlier, looking *back* over the careers of adult criminals suggests a picture of stability.

In short, background variables are surprisingly modest prognostic devices in the prospective explanation of trajectories of crime over the life course. Within-individual changes in criminality are not called forth from the distant past but are mediated by proximate and time-varying social processes grounded in life transitions, situational interactions, routine activities, and turning points. Theories limited to time-stable factors are thus incapable of unpacking the zigzagging and temporally variable patterns of offending. Studying variation within individuals over the full life course requires not only creative methodologies (e.g., the integration of life-history narratives with dynamic modeling), but also integrative theories that reconcile the social interactional and hence changing features of the self (a la Mead, Blumer, and Becker) with stable individual differences.

Community-Level Processes

Consider next the study of variations in rates of crime. Once again the logic in criminology is largely static—over the twentieth century we have been repeatedly confronted with structural correlates (attributes?) associated with crime-rate variation (e.g., poverty, racial composition, family disruption). By contrast, the social mechanisms hypothesized to account for the effects of neighborhood and community-level structural characteristics remain relatively unknown (Sampson et al 1999). Why, for instance, should concentrated poverty (a compositional attribute defined by the concentration of poor people) matter? If "neighborhood effects" on crime exist, presumably they are constituted from processes that involve collective aspects of community life (e.g., informal social control, spatial diffusion, subcultures). How do we theorize and measure neighborhood variations in social mechanisms and processes? What are their structural antecedents? Are neighborhood collective properties embedded in metropolitan-wide dynamics that transcend local boundaries and structural characteristics? Simply put, what social processes explain crime rates in modern communities?

Answering these questions has proven difficult. Differential selection of individuals into communities (compositional and selection effects), indirect community effects that work through family and peer mechanisms, measurement error, spatial interdependence, and simultaneity bias (e.g., does crime cause concentrated poverty?) represent serious challenges to drawing conclusions on the role of neighborhood and community contexts. Perhaps the biggest challenge is direct measurement of the processes hypothesized to generate crime. As interest in the social sciences turns increasingly to an integrated approach that emphasizes individual factors in social context, a potential mismatch has arisen in the quality of measures. Standing behind individual measurements are decades of psychometric research, producing measures that often have excellent statistical properties. Neighborhood-level research, on the other hand, is dominated by the study of poverty and other demographic characteristics drawn from census data or other government statistics that do not provide information on social mechanisms and collective processes. (Not to mention the reliance on official definitions and measures of crime.) Equally important, the methodology needed to evaluate neighborhood effects is in its infancy. What is needed is a concerted effort to enhance the science of ecological assessment ("ecometrics") by developing systematic procedures for directly measuring social mechanisms in community context, and by developing tools to improve the quality of community-level research (Raudenbush & Sampson 1999). I would argue that an important yet neglected ecometric strategy is systematic social observation (Sampson & Raudenbush 1999). The ultimate goal would be to understand processes of change in the community as a social system, along with the role of individual social actions in shaping collective properties.

In sum, I believe that social processes should be at the heart of sociological inquiry. The fact that criminology as well as many other specialty areas in sociology has become mired in static research is not just a methodological problem, for many a longitudinal study succumbs to between-individual or between-community explanations that reify fixed categories and stability. To get at the major unanswered questions in the study of crime thus requires a renewed focus on the unfolding of social action, process, and change within both individuals and communities. Such a focus is, of course, foundational to the sociological imagination–Chicago-School style.

Visit the Annual Reviews home page at www.AnnualReviews.org

LITERATURE CITED

Katz J. 1988. *Seductions of Crime: Moral and Sensual Attractions in Doing Evil.* New York: Basic

Raudenbush S, Sampson RJ. 1999. 'Ecometrics': toward a science of assessing ecological settings, with application to the systematic social observation of neighborhoods. *Sociol. Method.* 29:1–41

Sampson RJ, Laub JH. 1993. *Crime in the Making: Pathways and Turning Points Through Life.* Cambridge, MA: Harvard Univ. Press

Sampson RJ, Morenoff J, Earls F. 1999. Beyond social capital: spatial dynamics of collective efficacy for children. *Am. Sociol. Rev.* 64:633–60

Sampson RJ, Raudenbush S. 1999. Systematic social observation of public spaces: a new look at disorder in urban neighborhoods. *Am. J. Sociol.* 105:603–51

Annu. Rev. Sociol. 2000. 26:715–20

On Granularity

Emanuel Schegloff

Department of Sociology, University of California at Los Angeles, Los Angeles,
California 90095

From early in conversation-analytic inquiry and through to contemporary work, examination of how persons in a variety of interactional contexts refer to or formulate elements of their immediate environment or past experience has paid off, whether the domain in question is reference to persons (Sacks 1972a,b, 1992; Sacks & Schegloff 1979; Schegloff, 1996a) or to places (Schegloff 1972)—to mention only the most rewarding domains so far. Referring to persons in talk-in-interaction involves selection from among alternative resources, and this selection is a locus of interactional order, exploited to accomplish determinate actions.

For example, if a speaker figures that their interlocutor knows the referent (the one to be referred to) and knows that the speaker knows this, the normative reference practice is a "recognitional reference form," like first name or some descriptive phrase that taps how the speaker figures the interlocutor knows the referent. In talking in this manner, in choosing such a reference form, the speaker is "doing" something; this is a social action of a determinate type, with determinate consequences for the recipient's understanding and for the relationship between speaker and interlocutor(s). By contrast, saying "someone told me ... " conveys that the person referred to (by "someone") is *not* known to the recipient (or that their identity is being hidden), and this embodies a different action and stance. Referring to places and spaces constitutes a similar locus of order (Schegloff 1972). Can this order of finding and of inquiry be extended to the domain of actions or events?

One observation encountered early in an effort to do so is the bearing of "granularity" in this domain. In practices of formulating place, granularity showed up as an aspect of the range of potential answers to a question like "where are you,"— including such reference forms as "back in the States," "in California," "in L.A.," "in Topanga," "at home," "in the study," "at my desk," "at the computer," "on page 2," etc. The "degree of resolution" or order of place organization invoked by each term "zeroes in" or "pans out" from the target, and this feature is material to the action or other effect achieved by the selection of the term.

What form(s) does granularity take in the domain of actions or events? Here is a brief account—offered in both its explicative and exemplary capacities. The datum is taken from the start of a story told by Curt to Gary and Mike in the course of an automobile discussion at an backyard picnic in 1970s Ohio. After introducing the main human protagonist and his "companion," a classic, original, 1932 Oldsmobile, Curt segues into his account of the story's action this way:

```
1   Curt:   En he wz tellin us, we were kind'v admiring th'car=
2           =en 'e siz yah, I gotta get rid'v it though.
3           (0.5)
4   Curt:   I said why dihyou have  tih get rid'v it. 'n 'e sid well
5           I'm afraid my wife will get it. <er my ex wife.
6           (1.0)
```

For economy's sake, I focus on the first two lines and organize my observations in a simple listing of points.

1. Curt's first start of the account of the action begins with a frame for so-called indirect speech; "telling" marks that what follows is not a quote, and not a characterization of what was being done by the talk to be reported, but rather a paraphrase of its "content"—not exactly what "he" said or did, but what he conveyed by what he said—its topic or upshot.

2. As will become clear in a moment, line 2 is a return to this start of the account, after the start at line 1 has been abandoned. This second pass at reporting the talk is formatted differently. It is framed not as a report of the content or the upshot, but—by the use of a quotation marker ("he says")—as a direct quote of the talk being reported.

3. These two utterance parts—at lines 1 and 2—are two distinct practices for telling about the same event in the world, which embody two different levels of detail. One offers a rough characterization of "what was told," whatever the particulars of the way in which it was told. The other offers—here, *insists on*—just *how* it was told, exactly what was said.

4. The first pass at this bit of telling is abandoned after the frame for reporting what the protagonist said. What follows is designed to embody the telling of something that needs to be told "first" because it occurred first, i.e., before the utterance whose reporting has been abandoned. So:

   (*a*) what replaces the incipiently-reported utterance embodies an account for the abandoning of it; and

   (*b*) the appropriateness of the abandoning is that, to appreciate the import of the incipiently reported utterance, one must know its context—in response/relation to what it was said.

   (*c*) And this is more than a promissory note. When the second try at reporting the utterance is produced, it is begun and ended with components that mark its relationship to what has (and had) preceded. The "yah" marks an alignment—if only pro forma—with what has just been said, which underscores the orientation of the quoted speaker to the immediate sequential context into which the utterance is being delivered. And the "though" with which the utterance is reported to have ended registers a stance of contrast and irony to that context.

(*d*) So the grounds for abandoning the initial telling tack are embodied and displayed in what immediately follows it, which is not an *alternative* formulation but a reordering of the telling to have something else told first, with the second telling tack being designed in detail to be fitted to what has now been pre-positioned to it.

5. Note that what is interpolated between the two tacks of reporting itself represents a third order of detail in reporting on talk, "We were kind of admiring the car" neither quotes exactly what was ostensibly said nor does it deliver or report indirectly the "content" of what was said. Rather it characterizes or formulates *the action* being implemented by that talk ("admiring"), and subsumes not necessarily only one utterance, or even the utterances of a single speaker. Rather it glosses the contributions of several participants over a stretch of talking.

6. With these observations I mean to have registered differences in "granularity" between these three characterizations of what went on on some occasion.

   • "We were kind of admiring" groups together a batch of speakings as a single unit of activity—as a single reportable occurrence;

   • "he was telling us" groups together a set of actual productions—whether a string of sentences, or the particulars of a single utterance—as a single unit;

   • "'e siz yah, I gotta get rid'v it though" presents a single turn at talk in its contextual particularity, while glossing or disattending details of its production.[1]

Actually, this way of putting it is itself at odds with the constructional feature I mean to register—for each level of granularity has the effect precisely of constituting *its* formulation as the relevant structuring of events, without alluding to or conveying that it is a gloss for a subsumed order of events of which it is arguably composed.

Note then that shifting from "we were admiring . . . " to "and he says . . ."—from one level of granularity to another—is itself a practice for constituting in its course the telling being accomplished by the speaker in

---

[1] Note, for example, that the next bit of the telling is reported to have focused on the element of constraint—de-emphasized (though present) in the previously quoted utterance—"I gotta get rid'v it"—and highlighted by the stress on "have" in the reported response—"why dihyou have tih get rid'v it."

the conversation from which I have taken all of this. One might (for now merely) conjecture that "we were kind of admiring . . ." is a way of providing for the "backgroundness" of this component of the telling—especially in contrast with the preceding, aborted "en he was telling us . . ."; and that "en he says" marks a step into the core plot of the story itself and its approaching climax.[2]

7. So much for "granularity," and an initial gloss of the sorts of occurrences I mean to catch with it. Why is it important to understand better? What lines of inquiry does it provide for?

8. One is the access we may be able to exploit to the terms in which the world is observed, noticed, and experienced by members of a society in the range of settings in which they live their lives. Surely this is one central component of what "culture" is meant to encompass. In order to formulate the world and their experience of it across the range of orders of granularity, members need to have oriented to it, or have been prepared to notice and register it, across that range of granularities. In the formulated experience exhibited in talk-in-interaction, we gain access to at least some of the terms and orders of relevance that shape it—and not only in what persons choose overtly to talk about; perhaps there least of all. At the same time, we gain access to the ways in which experience, its retrieval in memory, and its shaping in discourse are designed by reference to context, co-participants, stance, the realization of action, and the trajectories of activity in which it is embedded.

9. A second line of inquiry opened up by an enhanced grasp of granularity concerns the terms by reference to which explorations of the organization of action need to be pressed. Another central component of culture is the inventory of actions that compose the warp and weft of moment-to-moment conduct and experience. It is clear that the conventional lexicon for referring to actions does not exhaust the actions that people can do. For example, in a recent paper (Schegloff 1996b), I described an action I had not known existed as a discrete "do-able"—"confirming an allusion" (i.e., confirming another's understanding of what one had conveyed inexplicitly,

---

[2]Calibrations and shifts of granularity are common and central features of accounts given of courses of action, and they are by no means limited to characterizations of talking. For example, later in this same story, we find the following recounting (in standardized orthography and punctuation) of what his ex-wife did that prompts getting rid of the car. "He said, 'well I drove it down to this car show, uh someplace in Ohio.' And uh, he got down in it, and the engine heated up and blew on the way back. Took it up, tore the damn thing apart, and found a rag stuffed in the radiator hose." Notice here the order of events captured by "drove it down to this car show" on the one hand (and all the "events" which compose it), and what happened after "the engine heated up and blew on the way back"—namely, "took it up, tore the damn thing apart and found a rag stuffed in the radiator hose," the last of these itself embodying a shift in granularity from the two which precede it–exemplifying again the relationship between "finer" granularity and climax of narrative trajectory.

and confirming at the same time that it had indeed been conveyed inexplicitly). Grasping it analytically and describing it showed that persons do actions at a level of granularity that has been minimally explored by social science, but that has been largely in the arena of literature and the other arts. It will surely remain in that arena, but it is also accessible to our inquiry—should even be foundational to it. Indeed, as the neurosciences develop in the new century/millenium, one interaction with the social world and its study will surely be in the neurobiological substrates of action. In order for this not to become a reductionist undertaking, it will be crucial to understand the social/cultural/interactional terms of the organization of action and the practices by which actions are produced—the most plausible intersection point with the neurological substrate. For this, a better grasp than we have now of granularity will be needed, for we will need to know at what levels of detail actions and practices are orderly and are oriented to in the production of the quotidien life of the society.

10. Finally, let me observe that my noticing all the particulars of the interactional fragment examined above, and my registering of these noticings in the preceding text, themselves embody a level of granularity—and one rarely informing sociological work, even of the so-called ethnographic or qualitative or "micro" sort. On the one hand, the introduction of this order of observation and the insistence on its relevance to sociology is grounded in the claim—amply supported by prior work—that interaction is co-constructed by its participants at this level of "detail" and finer yet, and that by the deployment of such resources for interaction, determinate social actions are differentially deployed, relationships constituted, etc. On the other hand, the level of granularity at which noticing is done matters not only for the social actors being studied, but for us as investigators as well; so too at what level the observed or noticed world is described. On the selection we make in these respects may depend whether we make a discovery or not, whether our account of it is adequate or not, whether it succeeds in convincing a skeptical audience or not, and the like. In other words, a concern with granularity is a reflexive one. It is, as Garfinkel used to put it (Garfinkel 1967), both a topic and a feature of inquiry. Knowing how granularity works matters then not just substantively, but methodologically.

I don't know if the workings of granularity is the single most important thing that I don't know, but knowing it better is surely among the most important things I look forward to.

ACKNOWLEDGMENTS

This document was first drafted during a year's Fellowship at the Center for Advanced Study in the Behavioral Sciences, and I am grateful to the Center for its support, as well as for financial support provided through the Center by the National

Science Foundation, Grant #SBR-9022192, and for financial support provided to me by a Fellowship from the John Simon Guggenheim Memorial Foundation.

Visit the Annual Reviews home page at www.AnnualReviews.org

LITERATURE CITED

Garfinkel H. 1967. *Studies in Ethnomethodology.* Englewood Cliffs, NJ: Prentice-Hall

Sacks H. 1972a. An initial investigation of the usability of conversational materials for doing sociology. In *Studies in Social Interaction,* ed. DN Sudnow, pp. 31–74. New York: Free Press

Sacks H. 1972b. On the analyzability of stories by children. In *Directions in Sociolinguistics: The Ethnography of Communication,* ed. JJ Gumperz, D Hymes, pp. 325–45. New York: Holt, Rinehart & Winston

Sacks H. 1992. *Lectures on Conversation.* 2 vol. ed. G Jefferson, with Introductions by EA Schegloff. Oxford: Blackwell

Sacks H, Schegloff EA. 1979. Two preferences in the organization of reference to persons and their interaction. In *Everyday Language: Studies in Ethnomethodology,* ed. G. Psathas, pp. 15–21. New York: Irvington

Schegloff EA. 1972. Notes on a conversational practice: formulating place. In *Studies in Social Interaction,* ed. DN Sudnow, pp. 75–119. New York: Free Press

Schegloff EA. 1996a. Some practices for referring to persons in talk-in-interaction: a partial sketch of a systematics. In *Studies in Anaphora,* ed. BA Fox, pp. 437–85. Amsterdam: John Benjamins

Schegloff EA. 1996b. Confirming allusions: toward an empirical account of action. *Am. J. Sociol.* 104(l):161–216

Annu. Rev. Sociol. 2000. 26:721–23

HOW DO RELATIONS STORE HISTORIES?

Charles Tilly

Department of Sociology, Columbia University, New York, NY 10027-7001

For most of us, alas, crucial moments in a lifetime of inquiry involve discoveries that we have been asking the wrong questions. Any effort to lay the burden of our ignorance on the next generation of researchers—which is, after all, the point of the present exercise—will therefore serve chiefly to make members of that generation feel superior. Visibly violating the interest of my future reputation, let me ask out loud a deeply bothersome question: how do relations store histories? How does interaction among social locations both constrain subsequent interactions and alter the relations involved?

My question concerns relations among social locations—not just persons but also jobs, organizations, communities, networks, and other such sites, just so long as they include some distinguishing properties and coordinating structure. It rests on the assumption that individuals as such do not constitute the bedrock of social life, but emerge from interaction as other social locations do.

The question has two parts. First, how does the history of a social relation impinge on subsequent activations of that relation? Second, how does interaction within a given relation transform that relation? Examples of relevant processes include changes in contentious repertoires, shifts in the content and form of conversation, alterations of rights or obligations, and moves of a pair between war and peace:

- In the case of contentious repertoires, relations between claimants and objects of claims (e.g. peasants and landlords, workers and bosses) mostly change incrementally, but as they do so claim-making strategies, mutual definitions, voiced grievances, and stories told about past relations all change as well. How and why does that happen? Exactly how, for example, did the political demonstration whose routines are now so familiar to militants and television viewers evolve from Western European petition marches and military displays of the late eighteenth century?

- In the case of conversation, people draw on previous interchanges with the same interlocutors, improvise within limits set by shared understandings, convey the character of their relationship through talk, yet transform the relationship as they do so. How and why does that happen? Precisely what processes, for example, go on as one friend solicits and gets effective advice on a risky choice from another friend, or as two competing groups of engineers within a firm work out a compromise proposal for presentation to management? In what ways do those processes depend on histories of the relationships in question?

- Rights and obligations consist of enforceable claims connecting social sites—individual or otherwise. Although participants in rights and obligations sometimes write contracts or constitutions, most of the time they create bit-by-bit redefinitions of the enforceable claims in question. How and why does that happen? Through what interactions and appeals to memory, for example, do companies of soldiers and their officers work out the limits on what each can demand of the other?

- War and peace name extreme positions on a continuum of relations between political units running from 1) outright mutual destruction by means of organized armed force to 2) coexistence without collective strife. No war between two powers precisely mimics its predecessor, yet the history of relations between the parties strongly constrains the current round of conflict. How and why does that happen? To what extent and how, for example, does accumulated knowledge of their relationship affect how leaders of Israel and Syria shift among open warfare, mutual harassment, proxy battles, and uneasy peace?

Bad answers beckon. The first bad answer, quite popular these days, declares that experience of interaction alters individual consciousness, either by changing means-end calculations or by adjusting the link between feeling and memory. The answer is bad because it begs the question: How do pairs or larger sets of actors actually create and change shared understandings in the form of recognizable claim-making performances, dialects, bodies of law, and diplomacy?

A second bad answer used to be much more popular, but has lost much of its appeal in recent decades. The answer: Society does it. The answer is doubly bad because it invokes a dubious agent and fails to state how or why that agent accomplishes its transformative work.

A third bad answer declares that culture, as the repository of collective experience, embeds histories in relations. The answer is even worse than the first two because it combines their defects. It begs the question of how culture—that is, shared understandings and their representations—changes as it invokes a dubious agent and fails to specify how that agent creates effects in social life.

Astonished by my ignorance, students of conversation, strong interaction, symbolic interaction, collective memory, and cultural evolution will no doubt claim that they have already provided superior accounts of how relations store histories. To them I reply in advance: show us. My own attempts to adapt accounts in those fields to contentious repertoires, rights, and war have so far yielded tantalizing suggestions, but no persuasive answers. Most of them incorporate one version or another of the three bad answers.

Good answers? If I really knew, I wouldn't be writing this essay. For the sake of stimulating argument, let me nevertheless identify two paths that seem worth exploring. We might call them *creative interaction* and *cultural ecology*.

Creative interaction appears most visibly in such activities as jazz and soccer. In these cases, participants work within rough agreements on procedures and outcomes, arbiters set limits on performances, individual dexterity, knowledge, and disciplined preparation generally yield superior play, yet the rigid equivalent of military drill destroys the enterprise. Both jazz and soccer, when well executed, proceed through improvised interaction, surprise, incessant error and error-correction, alternation between solo and ensemble action, and repeated responses to understandings shared by at least pairs of players. After the fact, participants and spectators create shared stories of what happened, and striking improvisations shape future performances. If we could explain how human beings bring off such improvisatory adventures, we could be well on our way to accounting for how relations store histories in contentious repertoires, conversation, rights and obligations, war and peace, and similar phenomena.

Cultural ecology? Social life consists of transactions among social sites, some of them occupied by individual persons, but most of them occupied by shifting aspects or clusters of persons. None of the sites, goes the reasoning, contains all the culture—all the shared understandings—on which transactions in its vicinity draw. But transactions among sites produce interdependence among extensively connected sites, deposit related cultural material in those sites, transform shared understandings in the process, and thus make large stores of culture available to any particular site through its connections with other sites. Relations store histories in this dispersed way.

Neither the creative interaction nor the cultural ecology path is necessarily inconsistent with the genetic, evolutionary, and neurophysiological accounts of human social life that will surely loom much larger in sociologists' thinking during the next few decades than they have during the twentieth century. In fact, if genetic, evolutionary, or neurophysiological theorists would take the storage of histories by relations seriously, they might supply the breakthrough that has so far eluded workaday sociologists.

Visit the Annual Reviews home page at www.AnnualReviews.org

SUBJECT INDEX

Savings rates, 71
Scandinavian states
  social democracy in,
    195–96, 204
SCF
  See Survey of Consumer
    Finances
School
  institutional connections
    with work, 677–79
School discipline, 409–11
School organizations,
  399–400
  assuming *loco parentis*
    authority, 409
  democratic processes in,
    397
School redefinition
  social capital and, 398
Schools and communities,
  395–418
  curriculum variation in,
    406–7
  inequality in resources,
    404–6
  neighborhood effects in,
    400–2
  prior conceptualizations of,
    397–98
  racial segregation and,
    402–4
  recent reformulations of,
    398–400
School-to-work transitions,
  407–9
Schultz-Firebaugh finding
  on between-nation income
    inequality, 334–35
Schumpeterian workfare
  state, 203–4
Scientific knowledge
  in environmentalism,
    574–77
Scripps Howard Polls, 44
Second great transformation
  sociology for, 693–95
Secularism

rising, 5
Securities and Exchange Act,
  299
Security
  financial, 64
Seductions of Crime, 711
Segregation
  See Race factors
Selection
  differential, 713
  marital, 6
Self defense
  plea of, 51
Self-absorption
  volunteerism reducing, 232
Self-employment
  defining, 357
Semiotics
  nature in capitalist
    production, 567
Serial monogamy, 117–18
Severity and leniency
  gender regimes of, 649–50
Sex ratio
  in crime rates, 92
  See also Gender inequality
Sexual "availability"
  during wartime, 107–9
Sexual behavior
  double standards for, 35
Sexual identities
  politics of, 116
  social bases of, 377–78
"Sexual revolution," 5
Sexual "scripting," 115
Sexualities
  essentialist views of, 109
  ethnic differences in,
    107–33
  intersections with
    nationalisms, 118–20
  social constructionist
    models of, 109, 114–18
Sherman Act, 535
Shifting standards, 27, 30
Short-term intercohort trends,
  672–74

Short-term work, 353–54
Single mothers, 3–4
  welfare policy work
    expectations for, 242–49
SIPP
  See Survey of Income and
    Program Participation
Skills
  perceptions of, 30
SMOs
  See Social movement
    organizations
Social action
  See Activism; Social
    movements
Social capital approach,
  401–2
  and school redefinition,
    398
Social cognition, 368–71
  processes, 370–71
  structures, 368–70
Social conflict
  new lines of, 206
  patterns of future, 519
Social constructionist models
  of ethnicity, 109–13,
    174–75
  of identity, 367–93
  of sexuality, 109
Social control, 231, 480
Social Darwinism, 174–75
Social disorganization theory,
  90
Social dominance theory,
  151–52
Social forces
  and the New Deal, 307–16
  See also Activism
Social Forces, 441
Social mobility, 74–76
Social movement
  organizations (SMOs),
    614–20, 627
Social movements
  audience effects in, 630
  framing processes and,

CUMULATIVE INDEXES

CONTRIBUTING AUTHORS, VOLUMES 1–26

CHAPTER TITLES, VOLUMES 1–26

Social Process

Institutions and Culture

Formal Organizations

Individual and Society

Demography

Urban and Rural Community Sociology

Policy

Historical Sociology

Sociology of World Regions

Bicentennial Articles

Special Supplement: Reflections on Sociology in the 21st Century